THE COMPLETE
HANS CHRISTIAN
ANDERSEN
FAIRY TALES

HANS CHRISTIAN ANDERSEN

The Complete
Hans Christian
Andersen
Fairy Tales

Edited by Lily Owens

Illustrated

Portland House

Used by permission of The Heritage Press, Norwalk, Connecticut, are the stories
from "The Gardener and the Noble Family" through "Godfather's Picture Book"
and from "Moving Day" to the end of the book
(with the exception of "What the Moon Saw").

The frontispiece, by Arthur Rackham, originally appeared in *Fairy Tales
by Hans Andersen*, published by George G. Harrap, Ltd.,
and has been printed here with permission.

This 1997 edition is published by Portland House,
a division of Random House Value Publishing, Inc.,
201 East 50th Street, New York, New York 10022

Printed and bound in the United States of America

ISBN 0-517-20148-8

8 7 6 5 4 3 2 1

CONTENTS

INTRODUCTION

UNLIKE the Brothers Grimm, who collected and recorded popular tales, Hans Christian Andersen wrote his own "folk" tales, using story elements and images culled, to be sure, from his childhood recollections. In his native Odense, Denmark, his parents, grandmother, and elderly townspeople, including the inmates of the lunatic asylum where his grandmother worked, regaled him with fairy tales and myths. He also borrowed themes from Danish history and foreign literature, but his stories and his fame reflect most his fertile imagination and ability to transform his own experiences into the stuff of legend.

Andersen meant to be remembered as an author of "serious" works, not these *smaating*, or trifles, as he called his fairy tales. But though he wrote plays, novels, poetry, travel books, and several autobiographies, most of these are almost unknown outside of Denmark. His fairy tales, however, are among the most-published works in all literary history.

Unlike typical fairy tales, many of Andersen's do not end happily. Though Andersen eventually won wide acclaim and a measure of material comfort from his writing, the hardships he suffered and witnessed along the way were incorporated, as was all else, into his tales.

Many of his fairy tales and stories are moralistic; others are strongly Christian. And yet he retained a mischievous sense that people's ethical standards are not always the highest and that this can be treated with humor as well as moral exhortation—as in "Little Claus and Big Claus."

Some of his tales, like "What One Can Invent," and "'The Will-O'-the-Wisp is in Town,' Says the Moor-Woman," express his feelings about writing and imagination. Others are futuristic: "The New Century's Goddess" and "In a Thousand Years."

One can see that Andersen was not a typical children's author and indeed, he bridled at the suggestion. In his own time, he often read his tales for the pleasure of adult friends. During a stay with the King and Queen of Denmark, he read the King a story most evenings, often repeating the King's favorites: "The Nightingale" and "The Swineherd." The poetry, the subtlety, and the humor of his stories commend them to people of any age.

Most of the stories in this book were translated in the nineteenth century by Mrs. H. B. Paull. We have chosen her translation wherever possible because we found it the most pleasurably readable. Mrs. Paull, however, did not translate all of Andersen's tales. Thus, a number of them have been collected from translations by H. Oskar Sommer, Jean Hersholt and several unknown translators.

We are pleased to have the works of six distinguished artists to illustrate this book. They include Alfred Walter Bayes (1832–1909); Henry Justice Ford (1860–1941), the popular illustrator of Andrew Lang's fairy book series; Arthur Rackham (1867–1939), whose delightful drawing needs no introduction; Hans Richter (1803–1884), a well-known German artist; and Hans Tegner (1853–1932), a Dane popular for his Andersen illustrations. Except for Richter and Tegner, the illustrators are all English.

Bayes', Ford's and Gaskin's illustrations may be identified by initials printed within the pictures' borders. Rackham's are signed with his last name. There is only one Richter illustration—for "The Little Match-Seller." Thus, by elimination, Tegner's illustrations may be recognized as those that are unsigned.

Even quite young readers are probably familiar with "The Ugly Duckling," "The Little Mermaid" and "Thumbelina," and are anxious to rediscover them. Do you know, as well, "The Snow Queen?" "Aunty Toothache?" "Anne Lisbeth?" With this collection of fairy tales and stories, these and many other unforgettable characters will find a permanent place in your memory.

LILY OWENS

THE FIR-TREE

FAR down in the forest, where the warm sun and the fresh air made a sweet resting-place, grew a pretty little fir-tree; and yet it was not happy, it wished so much to be tall like its companions — the pines and firs which grew around it. The sun shone, and the soft air fluttered its leaves, and the little peasant children passed by, prattling merrily, but the fir-tree heeded them not. Sometimes the children would bring a large basket of raspberries or strawberries, wreathed on a straw, and seat themselves near the fir-tree, and say, "Is it not a pretty little tree?" which made it feel more unhappy than before. And yet all this while the tree grew a notch or joint taller every year; for by the number of joints in the stem of a fir-tree we can discover its age. Still, as it grew, it complained, "Oh! how I wish I were as tall as the other trees, then I would spread out my branches on every side, and my top would over-look the wide world. I should have the birds building their nests on my boughs, and when the wind blew, I should bow with stately dignity like my tall companions." The tree was so discontented, that it took no pleasure in the warm sunshine, the birds, or the rosy clouds that floated over it morning and evening. Sometimes, in winter, when the snow lay white and glittering on the ground, a hare would come springing along, and jump right over the little tree; and then how mortified it would feel! Two winters passed, and when the third arrived, the tree had grown so tall that the hare was obliged to run round it. Yet it remained unsatisfied, and would exclaim, "Oh, if I could but keep on growing tall and old! There is nothing else worth caring for in the world!" In the autumn, as usual, the wood-cutters came and cut down several of the tallest trees, and the young fir-tree, which was now grown to its full height, shuddered as the noble trees fell to the earth with a crash. After the branches were lopped off, the trunks looked so slender and bare, that they could scarcely be recognized. Then they were placed upon wagons, and drawn by horses out of the forest. "Where were they going? What would become of them?" The young fir-tree wished very much to know; so in the spring, when the swallows and the storks came, it asked, "Do you know where those trees were taken? Did you meet them?"

The swallows knew nothing, but the stork, after a little reflection, nodded his head, and said, "Yes, I think I do. I met several new ships when I flew from Egypt, and they had fine masts that smelt like fir. I think these must have been the trees; I assure you they were stately, very stately."

1

"Oh, how I wish I were tall enough to go on the sea," said the fir-tree. "What is the sea, and what does it look like?"

"It would take too much time to explain," said the stork, flying quickly away.

"Rejoice in thy youth," said the sunbeam; "rejoice in thy fresh growth, and the young life that is in thee."

And the wind kissed the tree, and the dew watered it with tears; but the fir-tree regarded them not.

Christmas-time drew near, and many young trees were cut down, some even smaller and younger than the fir-tree who enjoyed neither rest nor peace with longing to leave its forest home. These young trees, which were chosen for their beauty, kept their branches, and were also laid on wagons and drawn by horses out of the forest.

"Where are they going?" asked the fir-tree. "They are not taller than I am: indeed, one is much less; and why are the branches not cut off? Where are they going?"

"We know, we know," sang the sparrows; "we have looked in at the windows of the houses in the town, and we know what is done with them. They are dressed up in the most splendid manner. We have seen them standing in the middle of a warm room, and adorned with all sorts of beautiful things, — honey cakes, gilded apples, playthings, and many hundreds of wax tapers."

"And then," asked the fir-tree, trembling through all its branches, "and then what happens?"

"We did not see any more," said the sparrows; "but this was enough for us."

"I wonder whether anything so brilliant will ever happen to me," thought the fir-tree. "It would be much better than crossing the sea. I long for it almost with pain. Oh! when will Christmas be here? I am now as tall and well grown as those which were taken away last year. Oh! that I were now laid on the wagon, or standing in the warm room, with all that brightness and splendor around me! Something better and more beautiful is to come after, or the trees would not be so decked out. Yes, what follows will be grander and more splendid. What can it be? I am weary with longing. I scarcely know how I feel."

"Rejoice with us," said the air and the sunlight. "Enjoy thine own bright life in the fresh air."

But the tree would not rejoice, though it grew taller every day; and, winter and summer, its dark-green foliage might be seen in the forest, while passers by would say, "What a beautiful tree!"

A short time before Christmas, the discontented fir-tree was the first to fall. As the axe cut through the stem, and divided the pith, the tree fell with a groan to the earth, conscious of pain and faintness, and forgetting all its anticipations of happiness, in sorrow at leaving its home in the forest. It knew that it should never again see its dear old companions, the trees, nor the little bushes and many-colored flowers that had grown by its side; perhaps not even the birds. Neither was the journey at all pleasant. The tree first recovered itself while being unpacked in the courtyard of a house, with several other trees; and it heard a man say, "We only want one, and this is the prettiest."

Then came two servants in grand livery, and carried the fir-tree into a large and beautiful apartment. On the walls hung pictures, and near the great stove stood great china vases, with lions on the lids. There were rocking-chairs, silken sofas, large tables, covered with pictures, books, and playthings, worth a great deal of money, — at least, the children said so. Then the fir-tree was placed in a large tub, full of sand; but green baize hung all around it, so that no one could see it was a tub, and it stood on a very handsome carpet. How the fir-tree trembled! "What was going to happen to him now?" Some young ladies came, and the servants helped them to adorn the tree. On one branch they hung little bags cut out of colored paper, and each bag was filled with sweetmeats; from other branches hung gilded apples and walnuts, as if they had grown there; and above, and all round, were hundreds of red, blue, and white tapers, which were fastened on the branches. Dolls, exactly like real babies, were placed under the green leaves, — the tree had never seen such things before, — and at the very top was fastened a glittering star, made of tinsel. Oh, it was very beautiful!

"This evening," they all exclaimed, "how bright it will be!" "Oh, that the evening were come," thought the tree, "and the tapers lighted! then I shall know what else is going to happen. Will the trees of the forest come to see me? I wonder if the sparrows will peep in at the windows as they fly? shall I grow faster here, and keep on all these ornaments summer and winter?" But guessing was of very little use; it made his bark ache, and this pain is as bad for a slender fir-tree, as headache is for us. At last the tapers were lighted, and then what a glistening blaze of light the tree presented! It trembled so with joy in all its branches, that one of the candles fell among the green leaves and burnt some of them. "Help! help!" exclaimed the young ladies, but there was no danger, for they quickly extinguished the fire. After this, the tree tried not to tremble at all, though the fire frightened him; he was so anxious not to hurt any of the beautiful ornaments, even while their brilliancy dazzled him. And now the folding doors were thrown open, and a troop of children rushed in as if they intended to upset the tree; they were followed more silently by their elders. For a moment the little ones stood silent with astonishment, and then they shouted for joy, till the room rang, and they danced merrily round the tree, while one present after another was taken from it.

"What are they doing? What will happen next?" thought the fir. At last the candles burnt down to the branches and were put out. Then the children received permission to plunder the tree.

Oh, how they rushed upon it, till the branches cracked, and had it not been fastened with the glistening star to the ceiling, it must have been thrown down. The children then danced about with their pretty toys, and no one noticed the tree, except the children's maid who came and peeped among the branches to see if an apple or a fig had been forgotten.

"A story, a story," cried the children, pulling a little fat man towards the tree.

"Now we shall be in the green shade," said the man, as he seated himself under it, "and the tree will have the pleasure of hearing also, but I shall only relate one story; what shall it be? Ivede-Avede, or Humpty Dumpty, who fell down stairs, but soon got up again, and at last married a princess."

"Ivede-Avede," cried some. "Humpty Dumpty," cried others, and there was a fine shouting and crying out. But the fir-tree remained quite still, and thought to himself, "Shall I have anything to do with all this?" but he had already amused them as much as they wished. Then the old man told them the story of Humpty Dumpty, how he fell down stairs, and was raised up again, and married a princess. And the children clapped their hands and cried, "Tell another, tell another," for they wanted to hear the story of "Ivede-Avede;" but they only had "Humpty Dumpty." After this the fir-tree became quite silent and thoughtful; never had the birds in the forest told such tales as "Humpty Dumpty," who fell down stairs, and yet married a princess.

"Ah! yes, so it happens in the world," thought the fir-tree; he believed it all, because it was related by such a nice man. "Ah! well," he thought, "who knows? perhaps I may fall down too, and marry a princess;" and he looked forward joyfully to the next evening, expecting to be again decked out with lights and playthings, gold and fruit. "To-morrow I will not tremble," thought he; "I will enjoy all my splendor, and I shall hear the story of Humpty Dumpty again, and perhaps Ivede-Avede." And the tree remained quiet and thoughtful all night. In the morning the servants and the housemaid came in. "Now," thought the fir, "all my splendor is going to begin again." But they dragged him out of the room and up stairs to the garret, and threw him on the floor, in a dark corner, where no daylight shone, and there they left him. "What does this mean?" thought the tree, "what am I to do here? I can hear nothing in a place like this," and he had time enough to think, for days and nights passed and no one came near him, and when at last somebody did come, it was only to put away large boxes in a corner. So the tree was completely hidden from sight as if it had never existed. "It is winter now," thought the tree, "the ground is hard and covered with snow, so that people cannot plant me. I shall be sheltered here, I dare say, until spring comes. How thoughtful and kind everybody is to me! Still I wish this place were not so dark, as well as lonely, with not even a little hare to look at. How pleasant it was out in the forest while the snow lay on the ground, when the hare would run by, yes, and jump over me too, although I did not like it then. Oh! it is terrible lonely here."

"Squeak, squeak," said a little mouse, creeping cautiously towards the tree; then came another; and they both sniffed at the fir-tree and crept between the branches.

"Oh, it is very cold," said the little mouse, "or else we should be so comfortable here, shouldn't we, you old fir-tree?"

"I am not old," said the fir-tree, "there are many who are older than I am."

"Where do you come from? and what do you know?" asked the mice, who were full of curiosity. "Have you seen the most beautiful places in the world, and can you tell us all about them? and have you been in the storeroom, where cheeses lie on the shelf, and hams hang from the ceiling? One can run about on tallow candles there, and go in thin and come out fat."

"I know nothing of that place," said the fir-tree, "but I know the wood where the sun shines and the birds sing." And then the tree told the little mice all about its youth. They had never heard such an account in their lives; and after they had listened to it attentively, they said, "What a number of things you have seen? you must have been very happy."

"Happy!" exclaimed the fir-tree, and then as he reflected upon what he had been telling them, he said, "Ah, yes! after all those were happy days." But when he went on and related all about Christmas-eve, and how he had been dressed up with cakes and lights, the mice said, "How happy you must have been, you old fir-tree."

"I am not old at all," replied the tree, "I only came from the forest this winter, I am now checked in my growth."

"What splendid stories you can relate," said the little mice. And the next night four other mice came with them to hear what the tree had to tell. The more he talked the more he remembered, and then he thought to himself, "Those were happy days, but they may come again. Humpty Dumpty fell down stairs, and yet he married the princess; perhaps I may marry a princess too." And the fir-tree thought of the pretty little birch-tree that grew in the forest, which was to him a real beautiful princess.

"Who is Humpty Dumpty?" asked the little mice. And then the tree related the whole story; he could remember every single word, and the little mice was so delighted with it, that they were ready to jump to the top of the tree. The next night a great many more mice made their appearance, and on Sunday two rats came with them; but they said, it was not a pretty story at all, and the little mice were very sorry, for it made them also think less of it.

"Do you know only one story?" asked the rats.

"Only one," replied the fir-tree; "I heard it on the happiest evening of my life; but I did not know I was so happy at the time."

"We think it is a very miserable story," said the rats. "Don't you know any story about bacon, or tallow in the storeroom."

"No," replied the tree.

"Many thanks to you then," replied the rats, and they marched off.

The little mice also kept away after this, and the tree sighed, and said, "It was very pleasant when the merry little mice sat round me and listened while I talked. Now that is all passed too. However, I shall consider myself happy when some one comes to take me out of this place." But would this ever happen? Yes; one morning people came to clear out the garret, the boxes were packed away, and the tree was pulled out of the corner, and thrown roughly on the garret floor; then the servant dragged it out upon the staircase where the daylight shone. "Now life is beginning again," said the tree, rejoicing in the sunshine and fresh air. Then it was carried down stairs and taken into the courtyard so quickly, that it forgot to think of itself, and could only look about, there was so much to be seen. The court was close to a garden, where everything looked blooming. Fresh and fragrant roses hung over the little palings. The linden-trees were in blossom; while the swallows flew here and there, crying, "Twit,twit, twit, my mate is coming,"—but it was not the fir-tree they meant. "Now I shall live," cried the tree, joyfully spreading out its branches; but alas! they were all withered and yellow, and it lay in a corner amongst weeds and nettles. The star of gold paper still stuck in the top of the tree and glittered in the sunshine. In the same courtyard two of the merry children were playing who had danced round the tree at Christmas, and had been so happy. The youngest saw the gilded star, and ran and pulled it off the tree. "Look what is sticking to the ugly old fir-tree," said the child, treading on the branches till they crackled under his boots. And the tree saw all the fresh bright flowers in the garden, and then looked at itself, and wished it had remained in the dark corner of the garret. It thought of its fresh youth in the forest, of the merry Christmas evening, and of the little mice who had listened to the story of "Humpty Dumpty." "Past! past!" said the old tree; "Oh, had I but enjoyed myself while I could have done so! but now it is too late." Then a lad came and chopped the tree into small pieces, till a large bundle lay in a heap on the ground. The pieces were placed in a fire under the copper, and they quickly blazed up brightly, while the tree sighed so deeply that each sigh was like a pistol-shot. Then the children, who were at play, came and seated themselves in front of the fire, and looked at it and cried, "Pop, pop." But at each "pop," which was a deep sigh, the tree was thinking of a summer day in the forest; and of Christmas evening, and of "Humpty Dumpty," the only story it had ever heard or knew how to relate, till at last it was consumed. The boys still played in the garden, and the youngest wore the golden star on his breast, with which the tree had been adorned during the happiest evening of its existence. Now all was past; the tree's life was past, and the story also, — for all stories must come to an end at last.

LITTLE TINY
OR THUMBELINA

THERE was once a woman who wished very much to have a little child, but she could not obtain her wish. At last she went to a fairy, and said, "I should so very much like to have a little child; can you tell me where I can find one?"

"Oh, that can be easily managed," said the fairy. "Here is a barleycorn of a different kind to those which grow in the farmer's fields, and which the chickens eat; put it into a flower-pot, and see what will happen."

"Thank you," said the woman, and she gave the fairy twelve shillings, which was the price of the barleycorn. Then she went home and planted it, and immediately there grew up a large handsome flower, something like a tulip in appearance, but with its leaves tightly closed as if it were still a bud. "It is a beautiful flower," said the woman, and she kissed the red and golden-colored leaves, and while she did so the flower opened, and she could see that it was a real tulip. Within the flower, upon the green velvet stamens, sat a very delicate and graceful little maiden. She was scarcely half as long as a thumb, and they gave her the name of "Thumbelina," or Tiny, because she was so small. A walnut-shell, elegantly polished, served her for a cradle; her bed was formed of blue violet-leaves, with a rose-leaf for a counterpane. Here she slept at night, but during the day she amused herself on a table, where the woman had placed a plateful of water. Round this plate were wreaths of flowers with their stems in the water, and upon it floated a large tulip-leaf, which served Tiny for a boat. Here the little maiden sat and rowed herself from side to side, with two oars made of white horse-hair. It really was a very pretty sight. Tiny could, also, sing so softly and sweetly that nothing like her singing had ever before been heard. One night, while she lay in her pretty bed, a large, ugly, wet toad crept through a broken pane of glass in the window, and leaped right upon the table where Tiny lay sleeping under her rose-leaf quilt. "What a pretty little wife this would make for my son," said the toad, and she took up the walnut-shell in which little Tiny lay asleep, and jumped through the window with it into the garden.

In the swampy margin of a broad stream in the garden lived the toad, with her son. He was uglier even than his mother, and when he saw the pretty little maiden in her elegant bed, he could only cry, "Croak, croak, croak."

"Don't speak so loud, or she will wake," said the toad, "and then she might run away, for she is as light as swan's down. We will place her on one of the water-lily leaves out in the stream; it will be like an island to her, she is so light and small, and then she cannot escape; and, while she is away, we will make haste and prepare the state-room under the marsh, in which you are to live when you are married."

Far out in the stream grew a number of water-lilies, with broad green leaves, which seemed to float on the top of the water. The largest of these leaves appeared farther off than the rest, and the old toad swam out to it with the walnut-shell, in which little Tiny lay still asleep. The tiny little creature woke very early in the morning, and began to cry bitterly when she found where she was, for she could see nothing but water on every side of the large green leaf, and no way of reaching the land. Meanwhile the old toad was very busy under the marsh, decking her room with rushes and wild yellow flowers, to make it look pretty for her new daughter-in-law. Then she swam out with her ugly son to the leaf on which she had placed poor little Tiny. She wanted to fetch the pretty bed, that she might put it in the bridal chamber to be ready for her. The old toad bowed low to her in the water, and said, "Here is my son, he will be your husband, and you will live happily in the marsh by the stream."

"Croak, croak, croak," was all her son could say for himself; so the toad took up the elegant little bed, and swam away with it, leaving Tiny all alone on the green leaf, where she sat and wept. She could not bear to think of living with the old toad, and having her ugly son for a husband. The little fishes, who swam about in the water beneath, had seen the toad, and heard what she said, so they lifted their heads above the water to look at the little maiden. As soon as they caught sight of her, they saw she was very pretty, and it made them very sorry to think that she must go and live with the ugly toads. "No, it must never be!" so they assembled together in the water, round the green stalk which held the leaf on which the little maiden stood, and gnawed it away at the root with their teeth. Then the leaf floated down the stream, carrying Tiny far away out of reach of land.

Tiny sailed past many towns, and the little birds in the bushes saw her, and sang, "What a lovely little creature;" so the leaf swam away with her farther and farther, till it brought her to other lands. A graceful little white butterfly constantly fluttered round her, and at last alighted on the leaf. Tiny pleased him, and she was glad of it, for now the toad could not possibly reach her, and the country through which she sailed was beautiful, and the sun shone upon the water, till it glittered like liquid gold. She took off her girdle and tied one end of it round the butterfly, and the other end of the ribbon she fastened to the leaf, which now glided on much faster than ever, taking little Tiny with it as she stood. Presently a large cockchafer flew by; the moment he caught sight of her, he seized her round her delicate waist with his claws, and flew with her into a tree. The green leaf floated away on the brook, and the butterfly flew with it, for he was fastened to it, and could not get away.

Oh, how frightened little Tiny felt when the cockchafer flew with her to the tree! But especially was she sorry for the beautiful white butterfly which she had fastened to the leaf, for if he could not free himself he would die of hunger. But the cockchafer did not trouble himself at all about the matter. He seated himself by her side on a large green leaf, gave her some honey from the flowers to eat, and told her she was very pretty, though not in the least like a cockchafer. After a time, all the cockchafers turned up their feelers, and said, "She has only two legs! how ugly that looks." "She has no feelers," said another. "Her waist is quite slim. Pooh! she is like a human being."

"Oh! she is ugly," said all the lady cockchafers, although Tiny was very pretty. Then the cockchafer who had run away with her, believed all the others when they said she was ugly, and would have nothing more to say to her, and told her she might go where she liked. Then he flew down with her from the tree, and placed her on a daisy, and she wept at the thought that she was so ugly that even the cockchafers would have nothing to say to her. And all the while she was really the loveliest creature that one could imagine, and as tender and delicate as a beautiful rose-leaf. During the whole summer poor little Tiny lived quite alone in the wide forest. She wove herself a bed with blades of grass, and hung it up under a broad leaf, to protect herself from the rain. She sucked the honey from the flowers for food, and drank the dew from their leaves every morning. So passed away the summer and the autumn, and then came the winter, — the long, cold winter. All the birds who had sung to her so sweetly were flown away, and the trees and the flowers had withered. The large clover leaf under the shelter of which she had lived, was now rolled together and shrivelled up, nothing remained but a yellow withered stalk. She felt dreadfully cold, for her clothes were torn, and she was herself so frail and delicate, that poor little Tiny was nearly frozen to death. It began to snow too; and the snow-flakes, as they fell upon her, were like a whole shovelful falling upon one of us, for we are tall, but she was only an inch high. Then she wrapped herself up in a dry leaf, but it cracked in the middle and could not keep her warm, and she shivered with cold. Near the wood in which she had been living lay a corn-field, but the corn had been cut a long time; nothing remained but the bare dry stubble standing up out of the frozen ground. It was to her like struggling through a large wood. Oh! how she shivered with the cold. She came at last to the door of a field-mouse, who had a little den under the corn-stubble. There dwelt the field-mouse in warmth and comfort, with a whole roomful of corn, a kitchen, and a beautiful dining room. Poor little Tiny stood before the door just like a little beggar-girl, and begged for a small piece of barley-corn, for she had been without a morsel to eat for two days.

"You poor little creature," said the field-mouse, who was really a good old field-mouse, "come into my warm room and dine with me." She was very pleased with Tiny, so she said, "You are quite welcome to stay with me all the winter, if you like; but you must keep my rooms clean and neat, and tell me stories, for I shall like to hear them very much." And Tiny did all the field-mouse asked her, and found herself very comfortable.

"We shall have a visitor soon," said the field-mouse one day; "my neighbor pays me a visit once a week. He is better off than I am; he has large rooms, and wears a beautiful black velvet coat. If you could only have him for a husband, you would be well provided for indeed. But he is blind, so you must tell him some of your prettiest stories."

But Tiny did not feel at all interested about this neighbor, for he was a mole. However, he came and paid his visit dressed in his black velvet coat.

"He is very rich and learned, and his house is twenty times larger than mine," said the field-mouse.

He was rich and learned, no doubt, but he always spoke slightingly of the sun and the pretty flowers, because he had never seen them. Tiny was obliged to sing to him, "Lady-bird, lady-bird, fly away home," and many other pretty songs. And the mole fell in love with her because she had such a sweet voice; but he said nothing yet, for he was very cautious. A short time before, the mole had dug a long passage under the earth, which led from the dwelling of the field-mouse to his own, and here she had permission to walk with Tiny whenever she liked. But he warned them not to be alarmed at the sight of a dead bird which lay in the passage. It was a perfect bird, with a beak and feathers, and could not have been dead long, and was lying just where the mole had made his passage. The mole took a piece of phosphorescent wood in his mouth, and it glittered like fire in the dark; then he went before them to light them through the long, dark passage. When they came to the spot where lay the dead bird, the mole pushed his broad nose through the ceiling, the earth gave way, so that there was a large hole, and the daylight shone into the passage. In the middle of the floor lay a dead swallow, his beautiful wings pulled close to his sides, his feet and his head drawn up under his feathers; the poor bird had evidently died of the cold. It made little Tiny very sad to see it, she did so love the little birds; all the summer they had sung and twittered for her so beautifully. But the mole pushed it aside with his crooked legs, and said, "He will sing no more now. How miserable it must be to be born a little bird! I am thankful that none of my children will ever be birds, for they can do nothing but cry, 'Tweet, tweet,' and always die of hunger in the winter."

"Yes, you may well say that, as a clever man!" exclaimed the field-mouse, "What is the use of his twittering, for when winter comes he must either starve or be frozen to death. Still birds are very high bred."

Tiny said nothing; but when the two others had turned their backs on the bird, she stooped down and stroked aside the soft feathers which covered the head, and kissed the closed eyelids. "Perhaps this was the one who sang to me so sweetly in the summer," she said; "and how much pleasure it gave me, you dear, pretty bird."

The mole now stopped up the hole through which the daylight shone, and then accompanied the lady home. But during the night Tiny could not sleep; so she got out of bed and wove a large, beautiful carpet of hay; then she carried it to the dead bird, and spread it over him; with some down from the flowers which she had found in the field-mouse's room. It was as soft as wool, and she spread some of it on each side of the bird, so that he might lie warmly in the cold earth. "Farewell, you pretty little bird," said she, "farewell; thank you for your delightful singing during the summer, when all the trees were green, and the warm sun shone upon us. Then she laid her head on the bird's breast, but she was alarmed immediately, for it seemed as if something inside the bird went "thump, thump." It was the bird's heart; he was not really dead, only benumbed with the cold, and the warmth had restored him to life. In autumn, all the swallows fly away into warm countries, but if one happens to linger, the cold seizes it, it becomes frozen, and falls down as if dead; it remains where it fell, and the cold snow covers it. Tiny trembled very much; she was quite frightened, for the bird was large, a great deal larger than her-self, — she was only an inch high. But she took courage, laid the wool more thickly over the poor swallow, and then took a leaf which she had used for her own counterpane, and laid it over the head of the poor bird. The next morning she again stole out to see him. He was alive but very weak; he could only open his eyes for a moment to look at Tiny, who stood by holding a piece of decayed wood in her hand, for she had no other lantern. "Thank you, pretty little maiden," said the sick swallow; "I have been so nicely warmed, that I shall soon regain my strength, and be able to fly about again in the warm sunshine."

"Oh," said she, "it is cold out of doors now; it snows and freezes. Stay in your warm bed; I will take care of you."

Then she brought the swallow some water in a flower-leaf, and after he had drank, he told her that he had wounded one of his wings in a thorn-bush, and could not fly as fast as the others, who were soon far away on their journey to warm countries. Then at last he had fallen to the earth, and could remember no more, nor how he came to be where she had found him. The whole winter the swallow remained underground, and Tiny nursed him with care and love. Neither the mole nor the field-mouse knew anything about it, for they did not like swallows. Very soon the spring time came, and the sun warmed the earth. Then the swallow bade farewell to Tiny, and she opened the hole in the ceiling which the mole had made. The sun shone in upon them so beautifully, that the swallow asked her if she would go with him; she could sit on his back, he said, and he would fly away with her into the green woods. But Tiny knew it would make the field-mouse very grieved if she left her in that manner, so she said, "No, I cannot."

"Farewell, then, farewell, you good, pretty little maiden," said the swallow; and he flew out into the sunshine.

Tiny looked after him, and the tears rose in her eyes. She was very fond of the poor swallow.

"Tweet, tweet," sang the bird, as he flew out into the green woods, and Tiny felt very sad. She was not allowed to go out into the warm sunshine. The corn which had been sown in the field over the house of the field-mouse had grown up high into the air, and formed a thick wood to Tiny, who was only an inch in height.

"You are going to be married, Tiny," said the field-mouse. "My neighbor has asked for you. What good fortune for a poor child like you. Now we will prepare your wedding clothes. They must be both woollen and linen. Nothing must be wanting when you are the mole's wife."

Tiny had to turn the spindle, and the field-mouse hired four spiders, who were to weave day and night. Every evening the mole visited her, and was continually speaking of the time when the summer would be over. Then he would keep his wedding-day with Tiny; but now the heat of the sun was so great that it burned the earth, and made it quite hard, like a stone. As soon, as the summer was over, the wedding should take place. But Tiny was not at all pleased; for she did not like the tiresome mole. Every morning when the sun rose, and every evening when it went down, she would creep out at the door, and as the wind blew aside the ears of corn, so that she could see the blue sky, she thought how beautiful and bright it seemed out there, and wished so much to see her dear swallow again. But he never returned; for by this time he had flown far away into the lovely green forest.

When autumn arrived, Tiny had her outfit quite ready; and the field-mouse said to her, "In four weeks the wedding must take place."

Then Tiny wept, and said she would not marry the disagreeable mole.

"Nonsense," replied the field-mouse. "Now don't be obstinate, or I shall bite you with my white teeth. He is a very handsome mole; the queen herself does not wear more beautiful velvets and furs. His kitchen and cellars are quite full. You ought to be very thankful for such good fortune."

So the wedding-day was fixed, on which the mole was to fetch Tiny away to live with him, deep under the earth, and never again to see the warm sun, because *he* did not like it. The poor child was very unhappy at the thought of saying farewell to the beautiful sun, and as the field-mouse had given her permission to stand at the door, she went to look at it once more.

"Farewell bright sun," she cried, stretching out her arm towards it; and then she walked a short distance from the house; for the corn had been cut, and only the dry stubble remained in the fields. "Farewell, farewell," she repeated, twining her arm round a little red flower that grew just by her side. "Greet the little swallow from me, if you should see him again."

"Tweet, tweet," sounded over her head suddenly. She looked up, and there was the swallow himself flying close by. As soon as he spied Tiny, he was delighted; and then she told him how unwilling she felt to marry the ugly mole, and to live always beneath the earth, and never to see the bright sun any more. And as she told him she wept.

"Cold winter is coming," said the swallow, "and I am going to fly away into warmer countries. Will you go with me? You can sit on my back, and fasten yourself on with your sash. Then we can fly away from the ugly mole and his gloomy rooms, — far away, over the mountains, into warmer countries, where the sun shines more brightly than here; where it is always summer, and the flowers bloom in greater beauty. Fly now with me, dear little Tiny; you saved my life when I lay frozen in that dark passage."

"Yes, I will go with you," said Tiny; and she seated herself on the bird's back, with her feet on his outstretched wings, and tied her girdle to one of his strongest feathers.

Then the swallow rose in the air, and flew over forest and over sea, high above the highest mountains, covered with eternal snow. Tiny would have been frozen in the cold air, but she crept under the bird's warm feathers, keeping her little head uncovered, so that she might admire the beautiful lands over which they passed. At length they reached the warm countries, where the sun shines brightly, and the sky seems so much higher above the earth. Here, on the hedges, and by the wayside, grew purple, green, and white grapes; lemons and oranges hung from trees in the woods; and the air was fragrant with myrtles and orange blossoms. Beautiful children ran along the country lanes, playing with large gay butterflies; and as the swallow flew farther and farther, every place appeared still more lovely.

At last they came to a blue lake, and by the side of it, shaded by trees of the deepest green, stood a palace of dazzling white marble, built in the olden times. Vines clustered round its lofty pillars, and at the top were many swallows' nests, and one of these was the home of the swallow who carried Tiny.

"This is my house," said the swallow; "but it would not do for you to live there—you would not be comfortable. You must choose for yourself one of those lovely flowers, and I will put you down upon it, and then you shall have everything that you can wish to make you happy."

"That will be delightful," she said, and clapped her little hands for joy.

A large marble pillar lay on the ground, which, in falling, had been broken into three pieces. Between these pieces grew the most beautiful large white flowers; so the swallow flew down with Tiny, and placed her on one of the broad leaves. But how surprised she was to see in the middle of the flower, a tiny little man, as white and transparent as if he had been made of crystal! He had a gold crown on his head, and delicate wings at his shoulders, and was not much larger than Tiny herself. He was the angel of the flower; for a tiny man and a tiny woman dwell in every flower; and this was the king of them all.

"Oh, how beautiful he is!" whispered Tiny to the swallow.

The little prince was at first quite frightened at the bird, who was like a giant, compared to such a delicate little creature as himself; but when he saw Tiny, he was delighted, and thought her the prettiest little maiden he had ever seen. He took the gold crown from his head, and placed it on hers, and asked her name, and if she would be his wife, and queen over all the flowers.

This certainly was a very different sort of husband to the son of a toad, or the mole, with his black velvet and fur; so she said, "Yes," to the handsome prince. Then all the flowers opened, and out of each came a little lady or a tiny lord, all so pretty it was quite a pleasure to look at them. Each of them brought Tiny a present; but the best gift was a pair of beautiful wings, which had belonged to a large white fly and they fastened them to Tiny's shoulders, so that she might fly from flower to flower. Then there was much rejoicing, and the little swallow, who sat above them, in his nest, was asked to sing a wedding song, which he did as well as he could; but in his heart he felt sad, for he was very fond of Tiny, and would have liked never to part from her again.

"You must not be called Tiny any more," said the spirit of the flowers to her. "It is an ugly name, and you are so very pretty. We will call you Maia."

"Farewell, farewell," said the swallow, with a heavy heart as he left the warm countries to fly back into Denmark. There he had a nest over the window of a house in which dwelt the writer of fairy tales. The swallow sang, "Tweet, tweet," and from his song came the whole story.

THE BRAVE TIN SOLDIER

THERE were once five-and-twenty tin soldiers, who were all brothers, for they had been made out of the same old tin spoon. They shouldered arms and looked straight before them, and wore a splendid uniform, red and blue. The first thing in the world they ever heard were the words, "Tin soldiers!" uttered by a little boy, who clapped his hands with delight when the lid of the box, in which they lay, was taken off. They were given him for a birthday present, and he stood at the table to set them up. The soldiers were all exactly alike, excepting one, who had only one leg; he had been left to the last, and then there was not enough of the melted tin to finish him, so they made him to stand firmly on one leg, and this caused him to be very remarkable.

The table on which the tin soldiers stood, was covered with other playthings, but the most attractive to the eye was a pretty little paper castle. Through the small windows the rooms could be seen. In front of the castle a number of little trees surrounded a piece of looking-glass, which was intended to represent a transparent lake. Swans, made of wax, swam on the lake, and were reflected in it. All this was very pretty, but the prettiest of all was a tiny little lady, who stood at the open door of the castle; she, also, was made of paper, and she wore a dress of clear muslin, with a narrow blue ribbon over her shoulders just like a scarf. In front of these was fixed a glittering tinsel rose, as large as her whole face. The little lady was a dancer, and she stretched out both her arms, and raised one of her legs so high, that the tin soldier could not see it at all, and he thought that she, like himself, had only one leg. "That is the wife for me," he thought; "but she is too grand, and lives in a castle, while I have only a box to live in, five-and-twenty of us altogether, that is no place for her. Still I must try and make her acquaintance." Then he laid himself at full length on the table behind a snuff-box that stood upon it, so that he could peep at the little delicate lady, who continued to stand on one leg without losing her balance. When evening came, the other tin soldiers were all placed in the box, and the people of the house went to bed. Then the playthings began to have their own games together, to pay visits, to have sham fights, and to give balls. The tin soldiers rattled in their box; they wanted to get out and join the amusements, but they could not open the lid. The nut-crackers played at leap-frog, and the pencil jumped about the table. There was such a noise that the canary woke up and began to talk, and in poetry too. Only the tin soldier and the dancer remained in their places. She stood on tiptoe, with her legs stretched out, as firmly as he did on his one leg. He never took his eyes from her for even a moment. The clock struck twelve, and, with a bounce, up sprang the lid of the snuff-box; but, instead of snuff, there jumped up a little black goblin; for the snuff-box was a toy puzzle.

"Tin soldier," said the goblin, "don't wish for what does not belong to you."

But the tin soldier pretended not to hear.

"Very well; wait till to-morrow, then," said the goblin.

When the children came in the next morning, they placed the tin soldier in the window. Now, whether it was the goblin who did it, or the draught, is not known, but the window flew open, and out fell the tin soldier, heels over head, from the third story, into the street beneath. It was a terrible fall; for he came head downwards, his helmet and his bayonet stuck in between the flag-stones, and his one leg up in the air. The servant maid and the little boy went down stairs directly to look for him; but he was nowhere to be seen, although once they nearly trod upon him. If he had called out, "Here I am," it would have been all right, but he was too proud to cry out for help while he wore a uniform.

Presently it began to rain, and the drops fell faster and faster, till there was a heavy shower. When it was over, two boys happened to pass by, and one of them said, "Look, there is a tin soldier. He ought to have a boat to sail in."

So they made a boat out of a newspaper, and placed the tin soldier in it, and sent him sailing down the gutter, while the two boys ran by the side of it, and clapped their hands. Good gracious, what large waves arose in that gutter! and how fast the stream rolled on! for the rain had been very heavy. The paper boat rocked up and down, and turned itself round sometimes so quickly that the tin soldier trembled; yet he remained firm; his countenance did not change; he looked straight before him, and shouldered his musket. Suddenly the boat shot under a bridge which formed a part of a drain, and then it was as dark as the tin soldier's box.

"Where am I going now?" thought he. "This is the black goblin's fault, I am sure. Ah, well, if the little lady were only here with me in the boat, I should not care for any darkness."

Suddenly there appeared a great water-rat, who lived in the drain.

"Have you a passport?" asked the rat, "give it to me at once." But the tin soldier remained silent and held his musket tighter than ever. The boat sailed on and the rat followed it. How he did gnash his teeth and cry out to the bits of wood and straw, "Stop him, stop him; he has not paid toll, and has not shown his pass." But the stream rushed on stronger and stronger. The tin soldier could already see daylight shining where the arch ended. Then he heard a roaring sound quite terrible enough to frighten the bravest man. At the end of the tunnel the drain fell into a large canal over a steep place, which made it as dangerous for him as a waterfall would be to us. He was too close to it to stop, so the boat rushed on, and the poor tin soldier could only hold himself as stiffly as possible, without moving an eyelid, to show that he was not afraid. The boat whirled round three or four times, and then filled with water to the very edge; nothing could save it from sinking. He now stood up to his neck in water, while deeper and deeper sank the boat, and the paper became soft and loose with the wet, till at last the water closed over the soldier's head. He thought of the elegant little dancer whom he should never see again, and the words of the song sounded in his ears —

> "Farewell, warrior! ever brave,
> Drifting onward to thy grave."

Then the paper boat fell to pieces, and the soldier sank into the water and immediately afterwards was swallowed up by a great fish. Oh how dark it was inside the fish! A great deal darker than in the tunnel, and narrower too, but the tin soldier continued firm, and lay at full length shouldering his musket. The fish swam to and fro, making the most wonderful movements, but at last he became quite still. After a while, a flash of lightning seemed to pass through him, and then the daylight approached, and a voice cried out, "I declare here is the tin soldier." The fish had been caught, taken to the market and sold to the cook, who took him into the kitchen and cut him open with a large knife. She picked up the soldier and held him by the waist between her finger and thumb, and carried him into the room. They were all anxious to see this wonderful soldier who had travelled about inside a fish; but he was not at all proud. They placed him on the table, and — how many curious things do happen in the world! — there he was in the very same room from the window of which he had fallen, there were the same children, the same playthings, standing on the table, and the pretty castle with the elegant little dancer at the door; she still balanced herself on one leg, and held up the other, so she was as firm as himself. It touched the tin soldier so much to see her that he almost wept tin tears, but he kept them back. He only looked at her and they both remained silent. Presently one of the little boys took up the tin soldier, and threw him into the stove. He had no reason for doing so, therefore it must have been the fault of the black goblin who lived in the snuff-box. The flames lighted up the tin soldier, as he stood, the heat was very terrible, but whether it proceeded from the real fire or from the fire of love he could not tell. Then he could see that the bright colors were faded from his uniform, but whether they had been washed off during his journey or from the effects of his sorrow, no one could say. He looked at the little lady, and she looked at him. He felt himself melting away, but he still remained firm with his gun on his shoulder. Suddenly the door of the room flew open and the draught of air caught up the little dancer, she fluttered like a sylph right into the stove by the side of the tin soldier, and was instantly in flames and was gone. The tin soldier melted down into a lump, and the next morning, when the maid servant took the ashes out of the stove, she found him in the shape of a little tin heart. But of the little dancer nothing remained but the tinsel rose, which was burnt black as a cinder.

THE UGLY DUCKLING

IT was lovely summer weather in the country, and the golden corn, the green oats, and the haystacks piled up in the meadows looked beautiful. The stork walking about on his long red legs chattered in the Egyptian language, which he had learnt from his mother. The corn-fields and meadows were surrounded by large forests, in the midst of which were deep pools. It was, indeed, delightful to walk about in the country. In a sunny spot stood a pleasant old farm-house close by a deep river, and from the house down to the water side grew great burdock leaves, so high, that under the tallest of them a little child could stand upright. The spot was as wild as the centre of a thick wood. In this snug retreat sat a duck on her nest, watching for her young brood to hatch; she was beginning to get tired of her task, for the little ones were a long time coming out of their shells, and she seldom had any visitors. The other ducks liked much better to swim about in the river than to climb the slippery banks, and sit under a burdock leaf, to have a gossip with her. At length one shell cracked, and then another, and from each egg came a living creature that lifted its head and cried, "Peep, peep." "Quack, quack," said the mother, and then they all quacked as well as they could, and looked about them on every side at the large green leaves. Their mother allowed them to look as much as they liked, because green is good for the eyes. "How large the world is," said the young ducks, when they found how much more room they now had than while they were inside the egg-shell. "Do you imagine this is the whole world?" asked the mother; "Wait till you have seen the garden; it stretches far beyond that to the parson's field, but I have never ventured to such a distance. Are you all out?" she continued, rising; "No, I declare, the largest egg lies there still. I wonder how long this is to last, I am quite tired of it;" and she seated herself again on the nest.

"Well, how are you getting on?" asked an old duck, who paid her a visit.

"One egg is not hatched yet," said the duck, "it will not break. But just look at all the others, are they not the prettiest little ducklings you ever saw? They are the image of their father, who is so unkind, he never comes to see me."

"Let me see the egg that will not break," said the duck; "I have no doubt it is a turkey's egg. I was persuaded to hatch some once, and after all my care and trouble with the young ones, they were afraid of the water. I quacked and clucked, but all to no purpose. I could not get them to venture in. Let me look at the egg. Yes, that is a turkey's egg; take my advice, leave it where it is and teach the other children to swim."

"I think I will sit on it a little while longer," said the duck; "as I have sat so long already, a few days will be nothing."

"Please yourself," said the old duck, and she went away.

At last the large egg broke, and a young one crept forth crying, "Peep, peep." It was very large and ugly. The duck stared at it and exclaimed, "It is very large and not at all like the others. I wonder if it really is a turkey. We shall soon find it out, however when we go to the water. It must go in, if I have to push it myself."

On the next day the weather was delightful, and the sun shone brightly on the green burdock leaves, so the mother duck took her young brood down to the water, and jumped in with a splash. "Quack, quack," cried she, and one after another the little ducklings jumped in. The water closed over their heads, but they came up again in an instant, and swam about quite prettily with their legs paddling under them as easily as possible, and the ugly duckling was also in the water swimming with them.

"Oh," said the mother, "that is not a turkey; how well he uses his legs, and how upright he holds himself! He is my own child, and he is not so very ugly after all if you look at him properly. Quack, quack! come with me now, I will take you into grand society, and introduce you to the farmyard, but you must keep close to me or you may be trodden upon; and, above all, beware of the cat."

When they reached the farmyard, there was a great disturbance, two families were fighting for an eel's head, which, after all, was carried off by the cat. "See, children, that is the way of the world," said the mother duck, whetting her beak, for she would have liked the eel's head herself. "Come, now, use your legs, and let me see how well you can behave. You must bow your heads prettily to that old duck yonder; she is the highest born of them all, and has Spanish blood, therefore, she is well off. Don't you see she has a red flag tied to her leg, which is something very grand, and a great honor for a duck; it shows that every one is anxious not to lose her, as she can be recognized both by man and beast. Come, now, don't turn your toes, a well-bred duckling spreads his feet wide apart, just like his father and mother, in this way; now bend your neck, and say 'quack.'"

The ducklings did as they were bid, but the other duck stared, and said, "Look, here comes another brood, as if there were not enough of us already! and what a queer looking object one of them is; we don't want him here," and then one flew out and bit him in the neck.

"Let him alone," said the mother; "he is not doing any harm."

"Yes, but he is so big and ugly," said the spiteful duck "and therefore he must be turned out."

"The others are very pretty children," said the old duck, with the rag on her leg, "all but that one; I wish his mother could improve him a little."

"That is impossible, your grace," replied the mother; "he is not pretty; but he has a very good disposition, and swims as well or even better than the others. I think he will grow up pretty, and perhaps be smaller; he has remained too long in the egg, and therefore his figure is not properly formed;" and then she stroked his neck and smoothed the feathers, saying, "It is a drake, and therefore not of so much consequence. I think he will grow up strong, and able to take care of himself."

"The other ducklings are graceful enough," said the old duck. "Now make yourself at home, and if you can find an eel's head, you can bring it to me."

And so they made themselves comfortable; but the poor duckling, who had crept out of his shell last of all, and looked so ugly, was bitten and pushed and made fun of, not only by the ducks, but by all the poultry. "He is too big," they all said, and the turkey cock, who had been born into the world with

THE UGLY DUCKLING

spurs, and fancied himself really an emperor, puffed himself out like a vessel in full sail, and flew at the duckling, and became quite red in the head with passion, so that the poor little thing did not know where to go, and was quite miserable because he was so ugly and laughed at by the whole farmyard. So it went on from day to day till it got worse and worse. The poor duckling was driven about by every one; even his brothers and sisters were unkind to him, and would say, "Ah, you ugly creature, I wish the cat would get you," and his mother said she wished he had never been born. The ducks pecked him, the chickens beat him, and the girl who fed the poultry kicked him with her feet. So at last he ran away, frightening the little birds in the hedge as he flew over the palings.

"They are afraid of me because I am ugly," he said. So he closed his eyes, and flew still farther, until he came out on a large moor, inhabited by wild ducks. Here he remained the whole night, feeling very tired and sorrowful.

In the morning, when the wild ducks rose in the air, they stared at their new comrade. "What sort of a duck are you?" they all said, coming round him.

He bowed to them, and was as polite as he could be, but he did not reply to their question. "You are exceedingly ugly," said the wild ducks, "but that will not matter if you do not want to marry one of our family."

Poor thing! he had no thoughts of marriage; all he wanted was permission to lie among the rushes, and drink some of the water on the moor. After he had been on the moor two days, there came two wild geese, or rather goslings, for they had not been out of the egg long, and were very saucy. "Listen, friend," said one of them to the duckling, "you are so ugly, that we like you very well. Will you go with us, and become a bird of passage? Not far from here is another moor, in which there are some pretty wild geese, all unmarried. It is a chance for you to get a wife; you may be lucky, ugly as you are."

"Pop, pop," sounded in the air, and the two wild geese fell dead among the rushes, and the water was tinged with blood. "Pop, pop," echoed far and wide in the distance, and whole flocks of wild geese rose up from the rushes. The sound continued from every direction, for the sportsmen surrounded the moor, and some were even seated on branches of trees, overlooking the rushes. The blue smoke from the guns rose like clouds over the dark trees, and as it floated away across the water, a number of sporting dogs bounded in among the rushes, which bent beneath them wherever they went. How they terrified the poor duckling! He turned away his head to hide it under his wing, and at the same moment a large terrible dog passed quite near him. His jaws were open, his tongue hung from his mouth, and his eyes glared fearfully. He thrust his nose close to the duckling, showing his sharp teeth, and then, "splash, splash," he went into the water without touching him, "Oh," sighed the duckling, "how thankful I am for being so ugly; even a dog will not bite me." And so he lay quite still, while the shot rattled through the rushes, and gun after gun was fired over him. It was late in the day before all became quiet, but even then the poor young thing did not dare to move. He waited quietly for several hours, and then, after looking carefully around him, hastened away from the moor as fast as he could. He ran over field and meadow till a storm arose, and he could hardly struggle against it. Towards evening, he reached a poor little cottage that seemed ready to fall, and only remained standing because it could not decide on which side to fall first. The storm continued so violent, that the duckling could go no farther; he sat down by the cottage, and then he noticed that the door was not quite closed in consequence of one of the hinges having given way. There was therefore a narrow opening near the bottom large enough for him to slip through, which he did very quietly, and got a shelter for the night. A woman, a tom cat, and a hen lived in this cottage. The tom cat, whom the mistress called, "My little son," was a great favorite; he could raise his back, and purr, and could even throw out sparks from his fur if it were stroked the wrong way. The hen had very short legs, so she was called "Chickie short legs." She laid good eggs, and her mistress loved her as if she had been her own child. In the morning, the strange visitor was discovered, and the tom cat began to purr, and the hen to cluck.

"What is that noise about?" said the old woman, looking round the room, but her sight was not very good; therefore, when she saw the duckling she thought it must be a fat duck, that had strayed from home. "Oh what a prize!" she exclaimed, "I hope it is not a drake, for then I shall have some duck's eggs. I must wait and see." So the duckling was allowed to remain on trial for three weeks, but there were no eggs. Now the tom cat was the master of the house, and the hen was mistress, and they always said, "We and the world," for they believed themselves to be half the world, and the better half too. The duckling thought that others might hold a different opinion on the subject, but the hen would not listen to such doubts. "Can you lay eggs?" she asked. "No." "Then have the goodness to hold your tongue." "Can you raise your back, or purr, or throw out sparks?" said the tom cat. "No." "Then you have no right to express an opinion when sensible people are speaking." So the duckling sat in a corner, feeling very low spirited, till the sunshine and the fresh air came into the room through the open door, and then he began to feel such a great longing for a swim on the water, that he could not help telling the hen.

"What an absurd idea," said the hen. "You have nothing else to do, therefore you have foolish fancies. If you could purr or lay eggs, they would pass away."

"But it is so delightful to swim about on the water," said the duckling, "and so refreshing to feel it close over your head, while you dive down to the bottom."

"Delightful, indeed!" said the hen, "why you must be crazy! Ask the cat, he is the cleverest animal I know, ask him how he would like to swim about on the water, or to dive under it, for I will not speak of my own opinion; ask our mistress, the old woman—there is no one in the world more clever than she is. Do you think she would like to swim, or to let the water close over her head?"

"You don't understand me," said the duckling.

"We don't understand you? Who can understand you, I wonder? Do you consider yourself more clever than the cat, or the old woman? I will say nothing of myself. Don't imagine such nonsense, child, and thank your good fortune that you have been received here. Are you not in a warm room, and in society from which you may learn something. But you are a chatterer, and your company is not very agreeable. Believe me, I speak only for your own good. I may tell you unpleasant truths, but that is a proof of my friendship. I advise you, therefore, to lay eggs, and learn to purr as quickly as possible."

"I believe I must go out into the world again," said the duckling.

"Yes, do," said the hen. So the duckling left the cottage, and soon found water on which it could swim and dive, but was avoided by all other animals, because of its ugly appearance. Autumn came, and the leaves in the forest turned to orange and gold. then, as winter approached, the wind caught them as they fell and whirled them in the cold air. The clouds, heavy with hail and snow-flakes, hung low in the sky, and the raven stood on the ferns crying, "Croak, croak." It made one shiver with cold to look at him. All this was very sad for the poor little duckling. One evening, just as the sun set amid radiant clouds, there came a large flock of beautiful birds out of the bushes. The duckling had never seen any like them before. They were swans, and they curved their graceful necks, while their soft plumage shown with dazzling whiteness. They uttered a singular cry, as they spread their glorious wings and flew away from those cold regions to warmer countries across the sea. As they mounted higher and higher in the air, the ugly little duckling felt quite a strange sensation as he watched them. He whirled himself in the water like a wheel, stretched out his neck towards them, and uttered a cry so strange that it frightened himself. Could he ever forget those beautiful, happy birds; and when at last they were out of his sight, he dived under the water, and rose again almost beside himself with excitement. He knew not the names of these birds, nor where they had flown, but he felt towards them as he had never felt for any other bird in the world. He was not envious of these beautiful creatures, but wished to be as lovely as they. Poor ugly creature, how gladly he would have lived even with the ducks had they only given him encouragement. The winter grew colder and colder; he was obliged to swim about on the water to keep it from freezing, but every night the space on which he swam became smaller and smaller. At length it froze so hard that the ice in the water crackled as he moved, and the duckling had to paddle with his legs as well as he could, to keep the space from closing up. He became exhausted at last, and lay still and helpless, frozen fast in the ice.

Early in the morning, a peasant, who was passing by, saw what had happened. He broke the ice in pieces with his wooden shoe, and carried the duckling home to his wife. The warmth revived the poor little creature; but when the children wanted to play with him, the duckling thought they would do him some harm; so he started up in terror, fluttered into the milk-pan, and splashed the milk about the room. Then the woman clapped her hands, which frightened him still more. He flew first into the butter-cask, then into the meal-tub, and out again. What a condition he was in! The woman screamed, and struck at him with the tongs; the children laughed and screamed, and tumbled over each other, in their efforts to catch him; but luckily he escaped. The door stood open; the poor creature could just manage to slip out among the bushes, and lie down quite exhausted in the newly fallen snow.

It would be very sad, were I to relate all the misery and privations which the poor little duckling endured during the hard winter; but when it had passed, he found himself lying one morning in a moor, amongst the rushes. He felt the warm sun shining, and heard the lark singing, and saw that all around was beautiful spring. Then the young bird felt that his wings were strong, as he flapped them against his sides, and rose high into the air. They bore him onwards, until he found himself in a large garden, before he well knew how it had happened. The apple-trees were in full blossom, and the fragrant elders bent their long green branches down to the stream which wound round a smooth lawn. Everything looked beautiful, in the freshness of early spring. From a thicket close by came three beautiful white swans, rustling their feathers, and swimming lightly over the smooth water. The duckling remembered the lovely birds, and felt more strangely unhappy than ever.

"I will fly to those royal birds," he exclaimed, "and they will kill me, because I am so ugly, and dare to approach them; but it does not matter: better be killed by them than pecked by the ducks, beaten by the hens, pushed about by the maiden who feeds the poultry, or starved with hunger in the winter."

Then he flew to the water, and swam towards the beautiful swans. The moment they espied the stranger, they rushed to meet him with outstretched wings.

"Kill me," said the poor bird; and he bent his head down to the surface of the water, and awaited death.

But what did he see in the clear stream below? His own image; no longer a dark, gray bird, ugly and disagreeable to look at, but a graceful and beautiful swan. To be born in a duck's nest, in a farmyard, is of no consequence to a bird, if it is hatched from a swan's egg. He now felt glad at having suffered sorrow and trouble, because it enabled him to enjoy so much better all the pleasure and happiness around him; for the great swans swam round the new-comer, and stroked his neck with their beaks, as a welcome.

Into the garden presently came some little children, and threw bread and cake into the water.

"See," cried the youngest, "there is a new one;" and the rest were delighted, and ran to their father and mother, dancing and clapping their hands, and shouting joyously, "There is another swan come; a new one has arrived."

Then they threw more bread and cake into the water, and said, "The new one is the most beautiful of all; he is so young and pretty." And the old swans bowed their heads before him.

Then he felt quite ashamed, and hid his head under his wing; for he did not know what to do, he was so happy, and yet not at all proud. He had been persecuted and despised for his ugliness, and now he heard them say he was the most beautiful of all the birds. Even the elder-tree bent down its bows into the water before him, and the sun shone warm and bright. Then he rustled his feathers, curved his slender neck, and cried joyfully, from the depths of his heart, "I never dreamed of such happiness as this, while I was an ugly duckling."

LITTLE IDA'S FLOWERS

"MY poor flowers are quite dead," said little Ida, "they were so pretty yesterday evening, and now all the leaves are hanging down quite withered. What do they do that for," she asked, of the student who sat on the sofa; she liked him very much, he could tell the most amusing stories, and cut out the prettiest pictures; hearts, and ladies dancing, castles with doors that opened, as well as flowers; he was a delightful student. "Why do the flowers look so faded to-day?" she asked again, and pointed to her nosegay, which was quite withered.

"Don't you know what is the matter with them?" said the student. "The flowers were at a ball last night, and therefore, it is no wonder they hang their heads."

"But flowers cannot dance?" cried little Ida.

"Yes indeed, they can," replied the student. "When it grows dark, and everybody is asleep, they jump about quite merrily. They have a ball almost every night."

"Can children go to these balls?"

"Yes," said the student, "little daisies and lilies of the valley."

"Where do the beautiful flowers dance?" asked little Ida.

"Have you not often seen the large castle outside the gates of the town, where the king lives in summer, and where the beautiful garden is full of flowers? And have you not fed the swans with bread when they swam towards you? Well, the flowers have capital balls there, believe me."

"I was in the garden out there yesterday with my mother," said Ida, "but all the leaves were off the trees, and there was not a single flower left. Where are they? I used to see so many in the summer."

"They are in the castle," replied the student. "You must know that as soon as the king and all the court are gone into the town, the flowers run out of the garden into the castle, and you should see how merry they are. The two most beautiful roses seat themselves on the throne, and are called the king and queen, then all the red cockscombs range themselves on each side, and bow, these are the lords-in-waiting. After that the pretty flowers come in, and there is a grand ball. The blue violets represent little naval cadets, and dance with hyacinths and crocuses which they call young ladies. The tulips and tiger-lilies are the old ladies who sit and watch the dancing, so that everything may be conducted with order and propriety."

"But," said little Ida, "is there no one there to hurt the flowers for dancing in the king's castle?"

"No one knows anything about it," said the student. "The old steward of the castle, who has to watch there at night, sometimes comes in; but he carries a great bunch of keys, and as soon as the flowers hear the keys rattle, they run and hide themselves behind the long curtains, and stand quite still, just peeping their heads out. Then the old steward says, 'I smell flowers here,' but he cannot see them."

"Oh how capital," said little Ida, clapping her hands. "Should I be able to see these flowers?"

"Yes," said the student, "mind you think of it the next time you go out, no doubt you will see them, if you peep through the window. I did so to-day, and I saw a long yellow lily lying stretched out on the the sofa. She was a court lady."

"Can the flowers from the Botanical Gardens go to these balls?" asked Ida. "It is such a distance!"

"Oh yes," said the student 'whenever they like, for they can fly. Have you not seen those beautiful red, white, and yellow butterflies, that look like flowers? They were flowers once. They have flown off their stalks into the air, and flap their leaves as if they were little wings to make them fly. Then, if they behave well, they obtain permission to fly about during the day, instead of being obliged to sit still on their stems at home, and so in time their leaves become real wings. It may be, however, that the flowers in the Botanical Gardens have never been to the king's palace, and, therefore, they know nothing of the merry doings at night, which take place there. I will tell you what to do, and the botanical professor, who lives close by here, will be so surprised. You know him very well, do you not? Well, next time you go into his garden, you must tell one of the flowers that there is going to be a grand ball at the castle, then that flower will tell all the others, and they will fly away to the castle as soon as possible. And when the professor walks into his garden, there will not be a single flower left. How he will wonder what has become of them!"

"But how can one flower tell another? Flowers cannot speak?"

"No, certainly not," replied the student; "but they can make signs. Have you not often seen that when the wind blows they nod at one another, and rustle all their green leaves?"

"Can the professor understand the signs?" asked Ida.

"Yes, to be sure he can. He went one morning into his garden, and saw a stinging nettle making signs with its leaves to a beautiful red carnation. It was saying, 'You are so pretty, I like you very much.' But the professor did not approve of such nonsense, so he clapped his hands on the nettle to stop it. Then the leaves, which are its fingers, stung him so sharply that he has never ventured to touch a nettle since."

"Oh how funny!" said Ida, and she laughed.

"How can anyone put such notions into a child's head?" said a tiresome lawyer, who had come to pay a visit, and sat on the sofa. He did not like the student, and would grumble when he saw him cutting out droll or amusing pictures. Sometimes it would be a man hanging on a gibbet and holding a heart in his hand as if he had been stealing hearts. Sometimes it was an old witch riding through the air on a broom and carrying her husband on her nose. But the lawyer did not like such jokes, and he would say as he had just said, "How can anyone put such nonsense into a child's head! what absurd fancies there are!"

But to little Ida, all these stories which the student told her about the flowers, seemed very droll, and she thought over them a great deal. The flowers did hang their heads, because they had been dancing all night, and were very tired, and most likely they were ill. Then she took them into the room where a number of toys lay on a pretty little table, and the whole of the table drawer besides was full of beautiful things. Her doll Sophy lay in the doll's bed asleep, and little Ida said to her, "You must really get up Sophy, and be content to lie in the drawer to-night; the poor flowers are ill, and they must lie in your bed, then perhaps they will get well again." So she took the doll out, who looked quite cross, and said not a single word, for she was angry at being turned out of her bed. Ida placed the flowers in the doll's bed, and drew the quilt over them. Then she told them to lie quite still and be good, while she made some tea for them, so that they might be quite well and able to get up the next morning. And she drew the curtains close round the little bed, so that the sun might not shine in their eyes. During the whole evening she could not help thinking of what the student had told her. And before she went to bed herself, she was obliged to peep behind the curtains into the garden where all her mother's beautiful flowers grew, hyacinths and tulips, and many others. Then she whispered to them quite softly, "I know you are going to a ball to-night." But the flowers appeared as if they did not understand, and not a leaf moved; still Ida felt quite sure she knew all about it. She lay awake a long time after she was in bed, thinking how pretty it must be to see all the beautiful flowers dancing in the king's garden. "I wonder if my flowers have really been there," she said to herself, and then she fell asleep. In the night she awoke; she had been dreaming of the flowers and of the student, as well as of the tiresome lawyer who found fault with him. It was quite still in Ida's bedroom; the night-lamp burnt on the table, and her father and mother were asleep. "I wonder if my flowers are still lying in Sophy's bed," she thought to herself; "how much I should like to know." She raised herself a little, and glanced at the door of the room where all her flowers and playthings lay; it was partly open, and as she listened, it seemed as if some one in the room was playing the piano, but softly and more prettily than she had ever before heard it. "Now all the flowers are certainly dancing in there," she thought, "oh how much I should like to see them," but she did not dare move for fear of disturbing her father and mother. "If they would only come in here," she thought; but they did not come, and the music continued to play so beautifully, and was so pretty, that she could resist no longer. She crept out of her little bed, went softly to the door and looked into the room. Oh what a splendid sight there was to be sure! There was no night-lamp burning, but the room appeared quite light, for the moon shone through the window upon the floor, and made it almost like day. All the hyacinths and tulips stood in two long rows down the room, not a single flower remained in the window, and the flower-pots were all empty. The flowers were dancing gracefully on the floor, making turns and holding each other by their long green leaves as they swung round. At the piano sat a large yellow lily which little Ida was sure she had seen in the summer, for she remembered the student saying she was very much like Miss Lina, one of Ida's friends. They all laughed at him then, but now it seemed to little Ida as if the tall, yellow flower was really like the young lady. She had just the same manners while playing, bending her long yellow face from side to side, and nodding in time to the beautiful music. Then she saw a large purple crocus jump into the middle of the table where the playthings stood, go up to the doll's bedstead and draw back the curtains; there lay the sick flowers, but they got up directly, and nodded to the others as a sign that they wished to dance with them. The old rough doll, with the broken mouth, stood up and bowed to the pretty flowers. They did not look ill at all now, but jumped about and were very merry, yet none of them noticed little Ida. Presently it seemed as if something fell from the table. Ida looked that way, and saw a slight carnival rod jumping down among the flowers as if it belonged to them; it was, however, very smooth and neat, and a little wax doll with a broad brimmed hat on her head, like the one worn by the lawyer, sat upon it. The carnival rod hopped about among the flowers on its three red stilted feet, and stamped quite loud when it danced the Mazurka; the flowers could not perform this dance, they were too light to stamp in that manner. All at once the wax doll which rode on the carnival rod seemed to grow larger and taller, and it turned round and said to the paper flowers, "How can you put such things in a child's head? they are all foolish fancies;" and then the doll was exactly like the lawyer with the broad brimmed hat, and looked as yellow and as cross as he did; but the paper dolls struck him on his thin legs, and he shrunk up again and became quite a little wax doll. This

LITTLE IDA'S FLOWERS

was very amusing, and Ida could not help laughing. The carnival rod went on dancing, and the lawyer was obliged to dance also. It was no use, he might make himself great and tall, or remain a little wax doll with a large black hat; still he must dance. Then at last the other flowers interceded for him, especially those who had lain in the doll's bed, and the carnival rod gave up his dancing. At the same moment a loud knocking was heard in the drawer, where Ida's doll Sophy lay with many other toys. Then the rough doll ran to the end of the table, laid himself flat down upon it, and began to pull the drawer out a little way.

Then Sophy raised himself, and looked round quite astonished, "There must be a ball here to-night," said Sophy. "Why did not somebody tell me?"

"Will you dance with me?" said the rough doll.

"You are the right sort to dance with, certainly," said she, turning her back upon him.

Then she seated herself on the edge of the drawer, and thought that perhaps one of the flowers would ask her to dance; but none of them came. Then she coughed, "Hem, hem, a-hem;" but for all that not one came. The shabby doll now danced quite alone, and not very badly, after all. As none of the flowers seemed to notice Sophy, she let herself down from the drawer to the floor, so as to make a very great noise. All the flowers came round her directly, and asked if she had hurt herself, especially those who had lain in her bed. But she was not hurt at all, and Ida's flowers thanked her for the use of the nice bed, and were very kind to her. They led her into the middle of the room, where the moon shone, and danced with her, while all the other flowers formed a circle round them. Then Sophy was very happy, and said they might keep her bed; she did not mind lying in the drawer at all. But the flowers thanked her very much, and said, —

"We cannot live long. To-morrow morning we shall be quite dead; and you must tell little Ida to bury us in the garden, near to the grave of the canary; then, in the summer we shall wake up and be more beautiful than ever."

"No, you must not die," said Sophy, as she kissed the flowers.

Then the door of the room opened, and a number of beautiful flowers danced in. Ida could not imagine where they could come from, unless they were the flowers from the king's garden. First came two lovely roses, with little golden crowns on their heads; these were the king and queen. Beautiful stocks and carnations followed, bowing to every one present. They had also music with them. Large poppies and peonies had pea-shells for instruments, and blew into them till they were quite red in the face. The bunches of blue hyacinths and the little white snowdrops jingled their bell-like flowers, as if they were real bells. Then came many more flowers: blue violets, purple heart's-ease, daisies, and lilies of the valley, and they all danced together, and kissed each other. It was very beautiful to behold.

At last the flowers wished each other good-night. Then little Ida crept back into her bed again, and dreamt of all she had seen. When she arose the next morning, she went quickly to the little table, to see if the flowers were still there. She drew aside the curtains of the little bed. There they all lay, but quite faded; much more so than the day before. Sophy was lying in the drawer where Ida had placed her; but she looked very sleepy.

"Do you remember what the flowers told you to say to me?" said little Ida. But Sophy looked quite stupid, and said not a single word.

"You are not kind at all," said Ida; "and yet they all danced with you."

Then she took a little paper box, on which were painted beautiful birds, and laid the dead flowers in it.

"This shall be your pretty coffin," she said; "and by and by, when my cousins come to visit me, they shall help me to bury you out in the garden; so that next summer you may grow up again more beautiful than ever."

Her cousins were two good-tempered boys, whose names were James and Adolphus. Their father had given them each a bow and arrow, and they had brought them to show Ida. She told them about the poor flowers which were dead; and as soon as they obtained permission, they went with her to bury them. The two boys walked first, with their crossbows on their shoulders, and little Ida followed, carrrying the pretty box containing the dead flowers. They dug a little grave in the garden. Ida kissed her flowers and then laid them, with the box, in the earth. James and Adolphus then fired their crossbows over the grave, as they had neither guns nor cannons.

THE STORKS

O n the last house in a little village the storks had built a nest, and the mother stork sat in it with her four young ones, who stretched out their necks and pointed their black beaks, which had not yet turned red like those of the parent birds. A little way off, on the edge of the roof, stood the father stork, quite upright and stiff; not liking to be quite idle, he drew up one leg, and stood on the other, so still that it seemed almost as if he were carved in wood. "It must look very grand," thought he, "for my wife to have a sentry guarding her nest. They do not know that I am her husband; they will think I have been commanded to stand here, which is quite aristocratic;" and so he continued standing on one leg.

In the street below were a number of children at play, and when they caught sight of the storks, one of the boldest amongst the boys began to sing a song about them, and very soon he was joined by the rest. These are the words of the song, but each only sang what he could remember of them in his own way.

> "Stork, stork, fly away,
> Stand not on one leg, I pray,
> See your wife is in her nest,
> With her little ones at rest.
> They will hang one,
> And fry another;
> They will shoot a third,
> And roast his brother."

"Just hear what those boys are singing," said the young storks; "they say we shall be hanged and roasted."

"Never mind what they say; you need not listen," said the mother. "They can do no harm."

But the boys went on singing and pointing at the storks, and mocking at them, excepting one of the boys whose name was Peter; he said it was a shame to make fun of animals, and would not join with them at all. The mother stork comforted her young ones, and told them not to mind. "See," she said, "How quiet your father stands, although he is only on one leg."

"But we are very much frightened," said the young storks, and they drew back their heads into the nests.

The next day when the children were playing together, and saw the storks, they sang the song again —

"They will hang one,
And roast another."

"Shall we be hanged and roasted?" asked the young storks.

"No, certainly not," said the mother. "I will teach you to fly, and when you have learnt, we will fly into the meadows, and pay a visit to the frogs, who will bow themselves to us in the water, and cry 'Croak, croak,' and then we shall eat them up; that will be fun."

"And what next?" asked the young storks.

"Then," replied the mother, "all the storks in the country will assemble together, and go through their autumn manœuvres, so that it is very important for every one to know how to fly properly. If they do not, the general will thrust them through with his beak, and kill them. Therefore you must take pains and learn, so as to be ready when the drilling begins."

"Then we may be killed after all, as the boys say; and hark! they are singing again."

"Listen to me, and not to them," said the mother stork. "After the great review is over, we shall fly away to warm countries far from hence, where there are mountains and forests. To Egypt, where we shall see three-cornered houses built of stone, with pointed tops that reach nearly to the clouds. They are called Pyramids, and are older than a stork could imagine; and in that country, there is a river that overflows its banks, and then goes back, leaving nothing but mire; there we can walk about, and eat frogs in abundance."

"Oh, o — h!" cried the young storks.

"Yes, it is a delightful place; there is nothing to do all day long but eat, and while we are so well off out there, in this country there will not be a single green leaf on the trees, and the weather will be so cold that the clouds will freeze, and fall on the earth in little white rags." The stork meant snow, but she could not explain it in any other way.

"Will the naughty boys freeze and fall in pieces?" asked the young storks.

"No, they will not freeze and fall into pieces," said the mother, "but they will be very cold, and be obliged to sit all day in a dark, gloomy room, while we shall be flying about in foreign lands, where there are blooming flowers and warm sunshine."

Time passed on, and the young storks grew so large that they could stand upright in the nest and look about them. The father brought them, every day, beautiful frogs, little snakes, and all kinds of stork-dainties that he could find. And then, how funny it was to see the tricks he would perform to amuse them. He would lay his head quite round over his tail, and clatter with his beak, as if it had been a rattle; and then he would tell them stories all about the marshes and fens.

"Come," said the mother one day, "Now you must learn to fly." And all the four young ones were obliged to come out on the top of the roof. Oh, how they tottered at first, and were obliged to balance themselves with their wings, or they would have fallen to the ground below.

"Look at me," said the mother, "you must hold your heads in this way, and place your feet so. Once, twice, once, twice — that is it. Now you will be able to take care of yourselves in the world."

Then she flew a little distance from them, and the young ones made a spring to follow her; but down they fell plump, for their bodies were still too heavy.

"I don't want to fly," said one of the young storks, creeping back into the nest. "I don't care about going to warm countries."

"Would you like to stay here and freeze when the winter comes?" said the mother, "or till the boys comes to hang you, or to roast you? — Well then, I'll call them."

"Oh no, no," said the young stork, jumping out on the roof with the others; and now they were all attentive, and by the third day could fly a little. Then they began to fancy they could soar, so they tried to do so, resting on their wings, but they soon found themselves falling, and had to flap their wings as quickly as possible. The boys came again in the street singing their song: —

"Stork, stork, fly away."

"Shall we fly down, and pick their eyes out?" asked the young storks.

"No; leave them alone," said the mother. "Listen to me; that is much more important. Now then. One-two-three. Now to the right. One-two-three. Now to the left, round the chimney. There now, that was very good. That last flap of the wings was so easy and graceful, that I shall give you permission to fly with me to-morrow to the marshes. There will be a number of very superior storks there with their families, and I expect you to show them that my children are the best brought up of any who may be present. You must strut about proudly — it will look well and make you respected."

"But may we not punish those naughty boys?" asked the young storks.

"No; let them scream away as much as they like. You can fly from them now up high amid the clouds, and will be in the land of the pyramids when they are freezing, and have not a green leaf on the trees or an apple to eat."

"We will revenge ourselves," whispered the young storks to each other, as they again joined the exercising.

Of all the boys in the street who sang the mocking song about the storks, not one was so determined to go on with it as he who first began it. Yet he was a little fellow not more than six years old. To the young storks he appeared at least a hundred, for he was so much bigger than their father and mother. To be sure, storks cannot be expected to know how old children and grown-up people are. So they determined to have their revenge on this boy, because he began the song first and would keep on with it. The young storks were very angry, and grew worse as they grew older; so at last their mother was obliged to promise that they should be revenged, but not until the day of their departure.

"We must see first, how you acquit yourselves at the grand review," said she. "If you get on badly there, the general will thrust his beak through you, and you will be killed, as the boys said, though not exactly in the same manner. So we must wait and see."

"You shall see," said the young birds, and then they took such pains and practised so well every day, that at last it was quite a pleasure to see them fly so lightly and prettily. As soon as the autumn arrived, all the storks began to assemble together before taking their departure for warm countries during the winter. Then the review commenced. They flew over forests and villages to show what they could do, for they had a long journey before them. The young storks performed their part so well that they received a mark of honor, with frogs and snakes as a present. These presents were the best part of the affair, for they could eat the frogs and snakes, which they very quickly did.

"Now let us have our revenge," they cried.

"Yes, certainly," cried the mother stork. "I have thought upon the best way to be revenged. I know the pond in which all the little children lie, waiting till the storks come to take them to their parents. The prettiest little babies lie there dreaming more sweetly than they will ever dream in the time to come. All parents are glad to have a little child, and children are so pleased with a little brother or sister. Now we will fly to the pond and fetch a little baby for each of the children who did not sing that naughty song to make game of the storks."

"But the naughty boy, who began the song first, what shall we do to him?" cried the young storks.

"There lies in the pond a little dead baby who has dreamed itself to death," said the mother. "We will take it to the naughty boy, and he will cry because we have brought him a little dead brother. But you have not forgotten the good boy who said it was a shame to laugh at animals: we will take him a little brother and sister too, because he was good. He is called Peter, and you shall all be called Peter in future."

So they all did what their mother had arranged, and from that day, even till now, all the storks have been called Peter.

THE MONEY-BOX

IN a nursery where a number of toys lay scattered about, a money-box stood on the top of a very high wardrobe. It was made of clay in the shape of a pig, and had been bought of the potter. In the back of the pig was a slit, and this slit had been enlarged with a knife, so that dollars, or crown pieces, might slip through; and, indeed there were two in the box, besides a number of pence. The money-pig was stuffed so full that it could no longer rattle, which is the highest state of perfection to which a money-pig can attain. There he stood upon the cupboard, high and lofty, looking down upon everything else in the room. He knew very well that he had enough inside him to buy up all the other toys, and this gave him a very good opinion of his own value. The rest thought of this fact also, although they did not express it, for there were so many other things to talk about. A large doll, still handsome, though rather old, for her neck had been mended, lay inside one of the drawers which was partly open. She called out to the others, "Let us have a game at being men and women, that is something worth playing at."

Upon this there was a great uproar; even the engravings, which hung in frames on the wall, turned round in their excitement, and showed that they had a wrong side to them, although they had not the least intention to expose themselves in this way, or to object to the game. It was late at night, but as the moon shone through the windows, they had light at a cheap rate. And as the game was now to begin, all were invited to take part in it, even the children's wagon, which certainly belonged to the coarser playthings. "Each has its own value," said the wagon; "we cannot all be noblemen; there must be some to do the work."

The money-pig was the only one who received a written invitation. He stood so high that they were afraid he would not accept a verbal message. But in his reply, he said, if he had to take a part, he must enjoy the sport from his own home; they were to arrange for him to do so; and so they did. The little toy theatre was therefore put up in such a way that the money-pig could look directly into it. Some wanted to begin with a comedy, and afterwards to have a tea party and a discussion for mental improvement, but they commenced with the latter first. The rocking-horse spoke of training and races; the wagon of railways and steam power, for these subjects belonged to each of their professions, and it was right they should talk of them. The clock talked politics—"tick, tick;" he professed to know what was the time of day, but there was a whisper that he did not go correctly. The bamboo cane stood by, looking stiff and proud: he was vain of his brass ferrule and silver top, and on the sofa lay two worked cushions, pretty but stupid. When the play at the little theatre began, the rest sat and looked on; they were requested to applaud and stamp, or crack, when they felt gratified with what they saw. But the riding-whip said he never cracked for old people, only for the young who were not yet married. "I crack for everybody," said the cracker.

"Yes, and a fine noise you make," thought the audience, as the play went on.

It was not worth much, but it was very well played, and all the characters turned their painted sides to the audience, for they were made only to be seen on one side. The acting was wonderful, excepting that sometimes they came out beyond the lamps, because the wires were a little too long. The doll, whose neck had been darned, was so excited that the place in her neck burst, and the money-pig declared he must do something for one of the players, as they had all pleased him so much. So he made up his mind to remember one of them in his will, as the one to be buried with him in the family vault, whenever that event should happen. They all enjoyed the comedy so much, that they gave up all thoughts of the tea party, and only carried out their idea of intellectual amusement, which they called playing at men and women; and there was nothing wrong about it, for it was only play. All the while, each one thought most of himself, or of what the money-pig could be thinking. His thoughts were on, as he supposed, a very distant time—of making his will, and of his burial, and of when it might all come to pass. Certainly sooner than he expected—for all at once down he came from the top of the press, fell on the ground, and was broken to pieces. Then the pennies hopped and danced about in the most amusing manner. The little ones twirled round like tops, and the large ones rolled away as far as they could, especially the one great silver crown piece who had often to go out into the world, and now he had his wish as well as all the rest of the money. The pieces of the money-pig were thrown into the dust-bin, and the next day there stood a new money-pig on the cupboard, but it had not a farthing in its inside yet, and therefore, like the old one, it could not rattle. This was the beginning with him, and we will make it the end of our story.

THE TOP AND BALL

A WHIPPING-TOP and a little ball lay together in a box, among other toys, and the top said to the ball, "Shall we be married, as we live in the same box?"

But the ball, which wore a dress of morocco leather, and thought as much of herself as any other young lady, would not even condescend to reply.

The next day came the little boy to whom the playthings belonged, and he painted the top red and yellow, and drove a brass-headed nail into the middle, so that while the top was spinning round it looked splendid.

"Look at me," said the top to the ball. "What do you say now? Shall we be engaged to each other? We should suit so well; you spring, and I dance. No one could be happier than we should be."

"Indeed! do you think so? Perhaps you do not know that my father and mother were morocco slippers, and that I have a Spanish cork in my body."

"Yes; but I am made of mahogany," said the top. "The major himself turned me. He has a turning lathe of his own, and it is a great amusement to him."

"Can I believe it?" asked the ball.

"May I never be whipped again," said the top, "if I am not telling you the truth."

"You certainly know how to speak for yourself very well," said the ball; "but I cannot accept your proposal. I am almost engaged to a swallow. Every time I fly up in the air, he puts his head out of the nest, and says, 'Will you?' and I have said, 'Yes,' to myself silently, and that is as good as being half engaged; but I will promise never to forget you."

"Much good that will be to me," said the top; and they spoke to each other no more.

Next day the ball was taken out by the boy. The top saw it flying high in the air, like a bird, till it would go quite out of sight. Each time it came back, as it touched the earth, it gave a higher leap than before, either because it longed to fly upwards, or from having a Spanish cork in its body. But the ninth time it rose in the air, it remained away, and did not return. The boy searched everywhere for it, but he searched in vain, for it could not be found; it was gone.

"I know very well where she is," sighed the top; "she is in the swallow's nest, and has married the swallow."

The more the top thought of this, the more he longed for the ball. His love increased the more, just because he could not get her; and that she should have been won by another, was the worst of all. The top still twirled about and hummed, but he continued to think of the ball; and the more he thought of her, the more beautiful she seemed to his fancy.

Thus several years passed by, and his love became quite old. The top, also, was no longer young; but there came a day when he looked handsomer than ever; for he was gilded all over. He was now a golden top, and whirled and danced about till he hummed quite loud, and was something worth looking at; but one day he leaped too high, and then he, also, was gone. They searched everywhere, even in the cellar, but he was nowhere to be found. Where could he be? He had jumped into the dust-bin, where all sorts of rubbish were lying: cabbage-stalks, dust, and rain-droppings that had fallen down from the gutter under the roof.

"Now I am in a nice place," said he; "my gilding will soon be washed off here. Oh dear, what a set of rabble I have got amongst!" And then he glanced at a curious round thing like an old apple, which lay near a long, leafless cabbage-stalk. It was, however, not an apple, but an old ball, which had lain for years in the gutter, and was soaked through with water.

"Thank goodness, here comes one of my own class, with whom I can talk," said the ball, examining the gilded top. "I am made of morocco," she said. "I was sewn together by a young lady, and I have a Spanish cork in my body; but no one would think it, to look at me now. I was once engaged to a swallow; but I fell in here from the gutter under the roof, and I have lain here more than five years, and have been thoroughly drenched. Believe me, it is a long time for a young maiden."

The top said nothing, but he thought of his old love; and the more she said, the more clear it became to him that this was the same ball.

The servant then came to clean out the dust-bin.

"Ah," she exclaimed, "here is a gilt top." So the top was brought again to notice and honor, but nothing more was heard of the little ball. He spoke not a word about his old love; for that soon died away. When the beloved object has lain for five years in a gutter, and has been drenched through, no one cares to know her again on meeting her in a dust-bin.

THE WILD SWANS

FAR away in the land to which the swallows fly when it is winter, dwelt a king who had eleven sons, and one daughter, named Eliza. The eleven brothers were princes, and each went to school with a star on his breast, and a sword by his side. They wrote with diamond pencils on gold slates, and learnt their lessons so quickly and read so easily that every one might know they were princes. Their sister Eliza sat on a little stool of plate-glass, and had a book full of pictures, which had cost as much as half a kingdom. Oh, these children were indeed happy, but it was not to remain so always. Their father, who was king of the country, married a very wicked queen, who did not love the poor children at all. They knew this from the very first day after the wedding. In the palace there were great festivities, and the children played at receiving company; but instead of having, as usual, all the cakes and apples that were left, she gave them some sand in a tea-cup, and told them to pretend it was cake. The week after, she sent little Eliza into the country to a peasant and his wife, and then she told the king so many untrue things about the young princes, that he gave himself no more trouble respecting them.

"Go out into the world and get your own living," said the queen. "Fly like great birds, who have no voice." But she could not make them ugly as she wished, for they were turned into eleven beautiful wild swans. Then, with a strange cry, they flew through the windows of the palace, over the park, to the forest beyond. It was early morning when they passed the peasant's cottage, where their sister Eliza lay asleep in her room. They hovered over the roof, twisted their long necks and flapped their wings, but no one heard them or saw them, so were at last obliged to fly away, high up in the clouds; and over the wide world they flew till they came to a thick, dark wood, which stretched far away to the seashore. Poor little Eliza was alone in her room playing with a green leaf, for she had no other playthings, and she pierced a hole through the leaf, and looked through it at the sun, and it was as if she saw her brothers' clear eyes, and when the warm sun shone on her cheeks, she thought of all the kisses they had given her. One day passed just like another; sometimes the winds rustled through the leaves of the rose-bush, and would whisper to the roses, "Who can be more beautiful than you!" But the roses would shake their heads, and say, "Eliza is." And when the old woman sat at the cottage door on Sunday, and read her hymn-book, the wind would flutter the leaves, and say to the book, "Who can be more pious than you?" and then the hymn-book would answer "Eliza." And the roses and the hymn-book told the real truth. At fifteen she returned home, but when the queen saw how beautiful she was, she became full of spite and hatred towards her. Willingly would she have turned her into a swan, like her brothers, but she did not dare to do so yet, because the king wished to see his daughter. Early one morning the queen went into the bath-room; it was built of marble, and had soft cushions, trimmed with the most beautiful tapestry. She took three toads with her, and kissed them, and said to one, "When Eliza comes to the bath, seat yourself upon her head, that she may become as stupid as you are." Then she said to another, "Place yourself on her forehead, that she may become as ugly as you are, and that her father may not know her." "Rest on her heart," she whispered to the third, "then she will have evil inclinations, and suffer in consequence." So she put the toads into the clear water, and they turned green immediately. She next called Eliza, and helped her to undress and get into the bath. As Eliza dipped her head under the water, one of the toads sat on her hair, a second on her forehead, and a third on her breast, but she did not seem to notice them, and when she rose out of the water, there were three red poppies floating upon it. Had not the creatures been venomous or been kissed by the witch, they would have been changed into red roses. At all events they became flowers, because they had rested on Eliza's head, and on her heart. She was too good and too innocent for witchcraft to have any power over her. When the wicked queen saw this, she rubbed her face with walnut-juice, so that she was quite brown; then she tangled her beautiful hair and smeared it with disgusting ointment, till it was quite impossible to recognize the beautiful Eliza.

When her father saw her, he was much shocked, and declared she was not his daughter. No one but the watch-dog and the swallows knew her; and they were only poor animals, and could say nothing. Then poor Eliza wept, and thought of her eleven brothers, who were all away. Sorrowfully, she stole away from the palace, and walked, the whole day, over fields and moors, till she came to the great forest. She knew not in what direction to go; but she was so

BUT one of them, the youngest remained behind, and the swan laid his head in her lap and she stroked his wings; and the whole day they remained together.

THE WILD SWANS

unhappy, and longed so for her brothers, who had been, like herself, driven out into the world, that she was determined to seek them. She had been but a short time in the wood when night came on, and she quite lost the path; so she laid herself down on the soft moss, offered up her evening prayer, and leaned her head against the stump of a tree. All nature was still, and the soft, mild air fanned her forehead. The light of hundreds of glow-worms shone amidst the grass and the moss, like green fire; and if she touched a twig with her hand, ever so lightly, the brilliant insects fell down around her, like shooting-stars.

All night long she dreamt of her brothers. She and they were children again, playing together. She saw them writing with their diamond pencils on golden slates, while she looked at the beautiful picture-book which had cost half a kingdom. They were not writing lines and letters, as they used to do; but descriptions of the noble deeds they had performed, and of all they had discovered and seen. In the picture-book, too, everything was living. The birds sang, and the people came out of the book, and spoke to Eliza and her brothers; but, as the leaves turned over, they darted back again to their places, that all might be in order.

When she awoke, the sun was high in the heavens; yet she could not see him, for the lofty trees spread their branches thickly over her head; but his beams were glancing through the leaves here and there, like a golden mist. There was a sweet fragrance from the fresh green verdure, and the birds almost perched upon her shoulders. She heard water rippling from a number of springs, all flowing in a lake with golden sands. Bushes grew thickly round the lake, and at one spot an opening had been made by a deer, through which Eliza went down to the water. The lake was so clear that, had not the wind rustled the branches of the trees and the bushes, so that they moved, they would have appeared as if painted in the depths of the lake; for every leaf was reflected in the water, whether it stood in the shade or the sunshine. As soon as Eliza saw her own face, she was quite terrified at finding it so brown and ugly; but when she wetted her little hand, and rubbed her eyes and forehead, the white skin gleamed forth once more; and, after she had undressed, and dipped herself in the fresh water, a more beautiful king's daughter could not be found in the wide world. As soon as she had dressed herself again, and braided her long hair, she went to the bubbling spring, and drank some water out of the hollow of her hand. Then she wandered far into the forest, not knowing whither she went. She thought of her brothers, and felt sure that God would not forsake her. It is God who makes the wild apples grow in the wood, to satisfy the hungry, and He now led her to one of these trees, which was so loaded with fruit, that the boughs bent beneath the weight. Here she held her noonday repast, placed props under the boughs, and then went into the gloomiest depths of the forest. It was so still that she could hear the sound of her own footsteps, as well as the rustling of every withered leaf which she crushed under her feet. Not a bird was to be seen, not a sunbeam could penetrate through the large, dark boughs of the trees. Their lofty trunks stood so close together, that, when she looked before her, it seemed as if she were enclosed within trellis-work. Such solitude she had never known before. The night was very dark. Not a single glow-worm glittered in the moss.

Sorrowfully she laid herself down to sleep; and, after a while, it seemed to her as if the branches of the trees parted over her head, and that the mild eyes of angels looked down upon her from heaven. When she awoke in the morning, she knew not whether she had dreamt this, or if it had really been so. Then she continued her wandering; but she had not gone many steps forward, when she met an old woman with berries in her basket, and she gave her a few to eat. Then Eliza asked her if she had not seen eleven princes riding through the forest.

"No," replied the old woman, "But I saw yesterday eleven swans, with gold crowns on their heads, swimming on the river close by." Then she led Eliza a little distance farther to a sloping bank, and at the foot of it wound a little river. The trees on its banks stretched their long leafy branches across the water towards each other, and where the growth prevented them from meeting naturally, the roots had torn themselves away from the ground, so that the branches might mingle their foliage as they hung over the water. Eliza bade the old woman farewell, and walked by the flowing river, till she reached the shore of the open sea. And there, before the young maiden's eyes, lay the glorious ocean, but not a sail appeared on its surface, not even a boat could be seen. How was she to go farther? She noticed how the countless pebbles on the sea-shore had been smoothed and rounded by the action of the water. Glass, iron, stones, everything that lay there mingled together, had taken its shape from the same power, and felt as smotth, or even smoother than her own delicate hand. "The water rolls on without weariness," she said, "till all that is hard becomes smooth; so will I be unwearied in my task. Thanks for your lessons, bright rolling waves; my heart tells me you will lead me to my dear brothers." On the foam-covered sea-weeds, lay eleven white swan feathers, which she gathered up and placed together. Drops of water lay upon them; whether they were dew-drops or tears no one could say. Lonely as it was on the sea-shore, she did not observe it, for the ever-moving sea showed more changes in a few hours than the most varying lake could produce during a whole year. If a black heavy cloud arose, it was as if the sea said, "I can look dark and angry too;" and then the wind blew, and the waves turned to white foam as they rolled. When the wind slept, and the clouds glowed with the red sunlight, then the sea looked like a rose leaf. But however quietly its white glassy surface rested, there was still a motion on the shore, as its waves rose and fell like the breast of a sleeping child. When the sun was about to set, Eliza saw eleven white swans with golden crowns on their heads, flying towards the land, one behind the other, like a long white ribbon. Then Eliza went down the slope from the shore, and hid herself behind the bushes. The swans alighted quite close to her and flapped their great white wings. As soon as the sun had disappeared under the water, the feathers of the swans fell off, and eleven beautiful princes, Eliza's brothers, stood near her. She uttered a loud cry, for, although they were very much changed, she knew them immediately. She sprang into their arms, and called them each by name. Then, how happy the princes were at meeting their little sister again, for they recognized her, although she had grown so tall and beautiful. They laughed, and they wept, and very soon understood how wickedly their mother had acted to them all. "We brothers," said the eldest, "fly about as wild swans, so long as the sun is in the sky; but as soon as it sinks behind the hills, we recover our human shape. Therefore must we always be near a resting place for our feet before sunset; for if we should be flying towards the clouds at the time we recovered our natural shape as men, we should sink deep into the sea. We do not dwell here, but in a land just as fair, that lies beyond the ocean, which we have to cross for a long distance; there is no island in our passage upon which we could pass the night; nothing but a little rock rising out of the sea, upon which we can scarcely stand with safety, even closely crowded together. If the sea is rough, the foam dashes over us, yet we thank God even for this rock; we have passed whole nights upon it, or we should never have reached our beloved fatherland, for our flight across the sea occupies two of the longest days in the year. We have permission to visit out home once in every year, and to remain eleven days, during which we fly across the forest to look once more at the palace where our father dwells, and where we were born, and at the church, where our mother lies buried. Here it seems as if the very trees and bushes were related to us. The wild horses leap over the plains as we have seen them in our childhood. The charcoal burners sing the old songs, to which we have danced as children. This is our fatherland, to which we are drawn by loving ties; and here we have found you, our dear little sister. Two days longer we can remain here, and then must we fly away to a beautiful land which is not our home; and how can we take you with us? We have neither ship nor boat."

"How can I break this spell?" said their sister. And then she talked about it nearly the whole night, only slumbering for a few hours. Eliza was awakened by the rustling of the swans' wings as they soared above. Her brothers were again changed to swans, and they flew in circles wider and wider, till they were far away; but one of them, the youngest swan, remained behind, and laid his head in his sister's lap, while she stroked his wings; and they remained together the whole day. Towards evening, the rest came back, and as the sun went down they resumed their natural forms. "To-morrow," said one, "we shall fly away, not to return again till a whole year has passed. But we cannot leave you here. Have you courage to go with us? My arm is strong enough to carry you through the wood; and will not all our wings be strong enough to fly with you over the sea?"

"Yes, take me with you," said Eliza. Then they spent the whole night in weaving a net with the pliant willow and rushes. It was very large and strong. Eliza laid herself down on the net, and when the sun rose, and her brothers again became wild swans, they took up the net with their beaks, and flew up to the clouds with their dear sister, who still slept. The sunbeams fell on her face, therefore one of the swans soared over her head, so that his broad wings might shade her. They were far from the land when Eliza woke. She thought she must still be dreaming, it seemed so strange to her to feel herself being carried so high in the air over the sea. By her side lay a branch full of beautiful ripe berries, and a bundle of sweet roots; the youngest of her brothers had gathered them for her, and placed them by her side. She smiled her thanks to him; she knew it was the same who had hovered over her to shade her with his wings. They were now so high, that a large ship beneath them looked like a white sea-gull skimming the waves. A great cloud floating behind them appeared like a vast mountain, and upon it Eliza saw her own shadow and those of the eleven swans, looking gigantic in size. Altogether it formed a more beautiful picture than she had ever seen; but as the sun rose higher, and the clouds were left behind, the shadowy picture vanished away. Onward the whole day they flew through the air like a winged arrow, yet more slowly than usual, for they had their sister to carry. The weather seemed inclined to be stormy, and Eliza watched the sinking sun with great anxiety, for the little rock in the ocean was not yet in sight. It appeared to her as if the swans were making great efforts with their wings. Alas! she was the cause of their not advancing more quickly. When the sun set, they would change to men, fall into the sea and be drowned. Then she offered a prayer from her inmost heart, but still no appearance of the rock. Dark clouds came nearer, the gusts of wind told of a coming storm, while from a thick, heavy mass of clouds the lightning burst forth flash after flash. The sun had reached the edge of the sea, when the swans darted down so swiftly, that Eliza's head trembled; she believed they were falling, but they again soared onward. Presently she caught sight of the rock just below them, and by this time the sun was half hidden by the waves. The rock did not appear larger than a seal's head thrust out of the water. They sunk so rapidly, that at the moment their feet touched the rock, it shone only like a star, and at last disappeared like the last spark in a piece of burnt paper. Then she saw her brothers standing closely round her with their arms linked together. There was but just room enough for them, and not the smallest space to spare. The sea dashed against the rock, and covered them with spray. The heavens were lighted up with continual flashes, and peal after peal of thunder rolled. But the sister and brothers sat holding each other's hands, and singing hymns, from which they gained hope and courage. In the early dawn the air became calm and still, and at sunrise the swans flew away from the rock with Eliza. The sea was still rough, and from their high position in the air, the white foam on the dark green waves looked like millions of swans swimming on the water. As the sun rose higher, Eliza saw before her, floating on the air, a range of mountains, with shining masses of ice on their summits. In the centre, rose a castle apparently a mile long, with rows of columns, rising one above another, while, around it, palm-trees waved and flowers bloomed as large as mill wheels. She asked if this was the land to which they were hastening. The swans shook their heads, for what she beheld were the beautiful ever-changing cloud palaces of the "Fata Morgana," into which no mortal can enter. Eliza was still gazing at the scene, when mountains, forests, and castles melted away, and twenty stately churches rose in their stead, with high towers and pointed gothic windows. Eliza even fancied she could hear the tones of the organ, but it was the music of the murmuring sea which she heard. As they drew nearer to the churches, they also changed into a fleet of ships, which seemed to be sailing beneath her; but as she looked again, she found it was only a sea mist gliding over the ocean. So there continued to pass before her eyes a constant change of scene, till at last she saw the real land to which they were bound, with its blue mountains, its cedar forests, and its cities and palaces. Long before the sun went down, she sat on a rock, in front of a large cave, on the floor of which the over-grown yet delicate green creeping plants looked like an embroidered carpet. "Now we shall expect to hear what you dream of to-night," said the youngest brother, as he showed his sister her bedroom.

"Heaven grant that I may dream how to save you," she replied. And this thought took such hold upon her mind that she prayed earnestly to God for help, and even in her sleep she continued to pray. Then it appeared to her as if she were flying high in the air, towards the cloudy palace of the "Fata Morgana," and a fairy came out to meet her, radiant and beautiful in ap-

pearance, and yet very much like the old woman who had given her berries in
the wood, and who had told her of the swans with golden crowns on their
heads. "Your brothers can be released," said she, "if you have only courage
and perseverance. True, water is softer than your own delicate hands, and yet
it polishes stones into shapes; it feels no pain as your fingers would feel, it has
no soul, and cannot suffer such agony and torment as you will have to endure. Do you see the stinging nettle which I hold in my hand? Quantities of
the same sort grow round the cave in which you sleep, but none will be of any
use to you unless they grow upon the graves in a churchyard. These you must
gather even while they burn blisters on your hands. Break them to pieces with
your hands and feet, and they will become flax, from which you must spin
and weave eleven coats with long sleeves; if these are then thrown over the
eleven swans, the spell will be broken. But remember, that from the moment
you commence your task until it is finished, even should it occupy years of
your life, you must not speak. The first word you utter will pierce through the
hearts of your brothers like a deadly dagger. Their lives hang upon your
tongue. Remember all I have told you." And as she finished speaking, she
touched her hand lightly with the nettle, and a pain, as of burning fire,
awoke Eliza.

It was broad daylight, and close by where she had been sleeping lay a nettle
like the one she had seen in her dream. She fell on her knees and offered her
thanks to God. Then she went forth from the cave to begin her work with her
delicate hands. She groped in amongst the ugly nettles, which burnt great
blisters on her hands and arms, but she determined to bear it gladly if she
could only release her dear brothers. So she bruised the nettles with her bare
feet and spun the flax. At sunset her brothers returned and were very much
frightened when they found her dumb. They believed it to be some new sorcery of their wicked step-mother. But when they saw her hands they understood what she was doing on their behalf, and the youngest brother wept,
and where his tears fell the pain ceased, and the burning blisters vanished.
She kept to her work all night, for she could not rest till she had released her
dear brothers. During the whole of the following day, while her brothers were
absent, she sat in solitude, but never before had the time flown so quickly.
One coat was already finished and she had begun the second, when she heard
the huntsman's horn, and was struck with fear. The sound came nearer and
nearer, she heard the dogs barking, and fled with terror into the cave. She
hastily bound together the nettles she had gathered into a bundle and sat
upon them. Immediately a great dog came bounding towards her out of the
ravine, and then another and another; they barked loudly, ran back, and
then came again. In a very few minutes all the huntsmen stood before the
cave, and the handsomest of them was the king of the country. He advanced
towards her, for he had never seen a more beautiful maiden.

"How did you come here, my sweet child?" he asked. But Eliza shook her
head. She dared not speak, at the cost of her brothers' lives. And she hid her
hands under her apron, so that the king might not see how she must be
suffering.

"Come with me," he said; "here you cannot remain. If you are as good as
you are beautiful, I will dress you in silk and velvet, I will place a golden
crown upon your head, and you shall dwell, and rule, and make your home
in my richest castle." And then he lifted her on his horse. She wept and wrung

her hands, but the king said, "I wish only for your happiness. A time will come when you will thank me for this." And then he galloped away over the mountains, holding her before him on this horse, and the hunters followed behind them. As the sun went down, they approached a fair royal city, with churches, and cupolas. On arriving at the castle the king led her into marble halls, where large fountains played, and where the walls and the ceilings were covered with rich paintings. But she had no eyes for all these glorious sights, she could only mourn and weep. Patiently she allowed the women to array her in royal robes, to weave pearls in her hair, and draw soft gloves over her blistered fingers. As she stood before them in all her rich dress, she looked so dazzlingly beautiful that the court bowed low in her presence. Then the king declared his intention of making her his bride, but the archbishop shook his head, and whispered that the fair young maiden was only a witch who had blinded the king's eyes and bewitched his heart. But the king would not listen to this; he ordered the music to sound, the daintiest dishes to be served, and the loveliest maidens to dance. Afterwards he led her through fragrant gardens and lofty halls, but not a smile appeared on her lips or sparkled in her eyes. She looked the very picture of grief. Then the king opened the door of a little chamber in which she was to sleep; it was adorned with rich green tapestry, and resembled the cave in which he had found her. On the floor lay the bundle of flax which she had spun from the nettles, and under the ceiling hung the coat she had made. These things had been brought away from the cave as curiosities by one of the huntsmen.

"Here you can dream yourself back again in the old home in the cave," said the king; "here is the work with which you employed yourself. It will amuse you now in the midst of all this splendor to think of that time."

When Eliza saw all these things which lay so near her heart, a smile played around her mouth, and the crimson blood rushed to her cheeks. She thought of her brothers, and their release made her so joyful that she kissed the king's hand. Then he pressed her to his heart. Very soon the joyous church bells announced the marriage feast, and that the beautiful dumb girl out of the wood was to be made the queen of the country. Then the archbishop whispered wicked words in the king's ear, but they did not sink into his heart. The marriage was still to take place, and the archbishop himself had to place the crown on the bride's head; in his wicked spite, he pressed the narrow circlet so tightly on her forehead that it caused her pain. But a heavier weight encircled her heart—sorrow for her brothers. She felt not bodily pain. Her mouth was closed; a single word would cost the lives of her brothers. But she loved the kind, handsome king, who did everything to make her happy more and more each day; she loved him with all her heart, and her eyes beamed with the love she dared not speak. Oh! if she had only been able to confide in him and tell him of her grief. But dumb she must remain till her task was finished. Therefore at night she crept away into her little chamber, which had been decked out to look like the cave, and quickly wove one coat after another. But when she began the seventh she found she had no more flax. She knew that the nettles she wanted to use grew in the churchyard, and that she must pluck them herself. How should she get out there? "Oh, what is the pain in my fingers to the torment which my heart endures?" said she. "I must venture, I shall not be denied help from heaven." Then with a trembling heart, as if she were about to perform a wicked deed, she crept into the garden in the broad moonlight, and passed through the narrow walks and the deserted streets, till she reached the churchyard. Then she saw on one of the broad tombstones a group of ghouls. These hideous creatures took off their rags, as if they intended to bathe, and then clawing open the fresh graves with their long, skinny fingers, pulled out the dead bodies and ate the flesh! Eliza had to pass close by them, and they fixed their wicked glances upon her, but she prayed silently, gathered the burning nettles, and carried them home with her to the castle. One person only had seen her, and that was the archbishop—he was awake while everybody was asleep. Now he thought his opinion was evidently correct. All was not right with the queen. She was a witch, and had bewitched the king and all the people. Secretly he told the king what he had seen and what he feared, and as the hard words came from his tongue, the carved images of the saints shook their heads as if they would say. "It is not so. Eliza is innocent."

But the archbishop interpreted it in another way; he believed that they witnessed against her, and were shaking their heads at her wickedness. Two large tears rolled down the king's cheeks, and he went home with doubt in his heart, and at night he pretended to sleep, but there came no real sleep to his eyes, for he saw Eliza get up every night and disappear in her own chamber. From day to day his brow became darker, and Eliza saw it and did not understand the reason, but it alarmed her and made her heart tremble for her brothers. Her hot tears glittered like pearls on the regal velvet and diamonds, while all who saw her were wishing they could be queens. In the mean time she had almost finished her task; only one coat of mail was wanting, but she had no flax left, and not a single nettle. Once more only, and for the last time, must she venture to the churchyard and pluck a few handfuls. She thought with terror of the solitary walk, and of the horrible ghouls, but her will was firm, as well as her trust in Providence. Eliza went, and the king and the archbishop followed her. They saw her vanish through the wicket gate into the churchyard, and when they came nearer they saw the ghouls sitting on the tombstone, as Eliza had seen them, and the king turned away his head, for he thought she was with them—she whose head had rested on his breast that very evening. "The people must condemn her," said he, and she was very quickly condemned by every one to suffer death by fire. Away from the gorgeous regal halls was she led to a dark, dreary cell, where the wind whistled through the iron bars. Instead of the velvet and silk dresses, they gave her the coats of mail which she had woven to cover her, and the bundle of nettles for a pillow; but nothing they could give her would have pleased her more. She continued her task with joy, and prayed for help, while the street-boys sang jeering songs about her, and not a soul comforted her with a kind word. Towards evening, she heard at the grating the flutter of a swan's wing, it was her youngest brother—he had found his sister, and she sobbed for joy, although she knew that very likely this would be the last night she would have to live. But still she could hope, for her task was almost finished, and her brothers were come. Then the archbishop arrived, to be with her during her last hours, as he had promised the king. But she shook her head, and begged him, by looks and gestures, not to stay; for in this night she knew she must finish her task, otherwise all her pain and tears and sleepless nights would have been suffered in vain. The archbishop withdrew, uttering bitter words against her; but poor Eliza knew that she was innocent, and diligently continued her work.

The little mice ran about the floor, they dragged the nettles to her feet, to help as well as they could; and the thrush sat outside the grating of the window, and sang to her the whole night long, as sweetly as possible, to keep up her spirits.

It was still twilight, and at least an hour before sunrise, when the eleven brothers stood at the castle gate, and demanded to be brought before the king. They were told it could not be, it was yet almost night, and as the king slept they dared not disturb him. They threatened, they entreated. Then the guard appeared, and even the king himself, inquiring what all the noise meant. At this moment the sun rose. The eleven brothers were seen no more, but eleven wild swans flew away over the castle.

And now all the people came streaming forth from the gates of the city, to see the witch burnt. An old horse drew the cart on which she sat. They had dressed her in a garment of coarse sackcloth. Her lovely hair hung loose on her shoulders, her cheeks were deadly pale, her lips moved silently, while her fingers still worked at the green flax. Even on the way to death, she would not give up her task. The ten coats of mail lay at her feet, she was working hard at the eleventh, while the mob jeered her and said, "See the witch, how she mutters! She has no hymn-book in her hand. She sits there with her ugly sorcery. Let us tear it in a thousand pieces."

And then they pressed towards her, and would have destroyed the coats of mail, but at the same moment eleven wild swans flew over her, and alighted on the cart. Then they flapped their large wings, and the crowd drew on one side in alarm.

"It is a sign from heaven that she is innocent," whispered many of them; but they ventured not to say it aloud.

As the executioner seized her by the hand, to lift her out of the cart, she hastily threw the eleven coats of mail over the swans, and they immediately became eleven handsome princes; but the youngest had a swan's wing, instead of an arm; for she had not been able to finish the last sleeve of the coat.

"Now I may speak," she exclaimed. "I am innocent."

Then the people, who saw what happened, bowed to her, as before a saint; but she sank lifeless in her brothers' arms, overcome with suspense, anguish, and pain.

"Yes, she is innocent," said the eldest brother; and then he related all that had taken place; and while he spoke there rose in the air a fragrance as from millions of roses. Every piece of faggot in the pile had taken root, and threw out branches, and appeared a thick hedge, large and high, covered with roses; while above all bloomed a white and shining flower, that glittered like a star. This flower the king plucked, and placed in Eliza's bosom, when she awoke from her swoon, with peace and happiness in her heart. And all the church bells rang of themselves, and the birds came in great troops. And a marriage procession returned to the castle, such as no king had ever before seen.

OLE-LUK-OIE, THE DREAM-GOD

THERE is nobody in the world who knows so many stories as Ole-Luk-Oie, or who can relate them so nicely. In the evening, while the children are seated at the table or in their little chairs, he comes up the stairs very softly, for he walks in his socks, then he opens the doors without the slightest noise, and throws a small quantity of very fine dust in their eyes, just enough to prevent them from keeping them open, and so they do not see him. Then he creeps behind them, and blows softly upon their necks, till their heads begin to droop. But Ole-Luk-Oie does not wish to hurt them, for he is very fond of children, and only wants them to be quiet that he may relate to them pretty stories, and they never are quiet until they are in bed and asleep. As soon as they are asleep, Ole-Luk-Oie seats himself upon the bed. He is nicely dressed; his coat is made of silken stuff; it is impossible to say of what color, for it changes from green to red, and from red to blue as he turns from side to side. Under each arm he carries an umbrella; one of them, with pictures on the inside, he spreads over the good children, and then they dream the most beautiful stories the whole night. But the other umbrella has no pictures, and this he holds over the naughty children so that they sleep heavily, and wake in the morning without having dreamed at all.

Now we shall hear how Ole-Luk-Oie came every night during a whole week to the little boy named Hjalmar, and what he told him. There were seven stories, as there are seven days in the week.

MONDAY

"Now pay attention," said Ole-Luk-Oie, in the evening, when Hjalmar was in bed, "and I will decorate the room."

Immediately all the flowers in the flower-pots became large trees, with long branches reaching to the ceiling, and stretching along the walls, so that the whole room was like a greenhouse. All the branches were loaded with flowers, each flower as beautiful and as fragrant as a rose; and, had any one tasted them, he would have found them sweeter even than jam. The fruit glittered like gold, and there were cakes so full of plums that they were nearly bursting. It was incomparably beautiful. At the same time sounded dismal moans from the table-drawer in which lay Hjalmar's school books.

"What can that be now?" said Ole-Luk-Oie, going to the table and pulling out the drawer.

It was a slate, in such distress because of a false number in the sum, that it had almost broken itself to pieces. The pencil pulled and tugged at its string as if it were a little dog that wanted to help, but could not.

And then came a moan from Hjalmar's copy-book. Oh, it was quite terrible to hear! On each leaf stood a row of capital letters, every one having a small letter by its side. This formed a copy; under these were other letters, which Hjalmar had written: they fancied they looked like the copy, but they were mistaken; for they were leaning on one side as if they intended to fall over the pencil-lines.

"See, this is the way you should hold yourselves," said the copy. "Look here, you should slope thus, with a graceful curve."

"Oh, we are very willing to do so, but we cannot," said Hjalmar's letters; "we are so wretchedly made."

"You must be scratched out, then," said Ole-Luk-Oie.

"Oh, no!" they cried, and then they stood up so gracefully it was quite a pleasure to look at them.

"Now we must give up our stories, and exercise these letters," said Ole-Luk-Oie; "One, two — one, two — " So he drilled them till they stood up gracefully, and looked as beautiful as a copy could look. But after Ole-Luk-Oie was gone, and Hjalmar looked at them in the morning, they were as wretched and as awkward as ever.

TUESDAY

As soon as Hjalmar was in bed, Ole-Luk-Oie touched, with his little magic wand, all the furniture in the room, which immediately began to chatter, and each article only talked of itself.

Over the chest of drawers hung a large picture in a gilt frame, representing a landscape, with fine old trees, flowers in the grass, and a broad stream, which flowed through the wood, past several castles, far out into the wild ocean. Ole-Luk-Oie touched the picture with his magic wand, and immediately the birds commenced singing, the branches of the trees rustled, and the clouds moved across the sky, casting their shadows on the landscape beneath them. Then Ole-Luk-Oie lifted little Hjalmar up to the frame, and placed his feet in the picture, just on the high grass, and there he stood with the sun shining down upon him through the branches of the trees. He ran to the water, and seated himself in a little boat which lay there, and which was painted red and white. The sails glittered like silver, and six swans, each with a golden circlet round its neck, and a bright blue star on its forehead, drew the boat past the green wood, where the trees talked of robbers and witches, and the flowers of beautiful little elves and fairies, whose histories the butterflies had related to them. Brilliant fish, with scales like silver and gold, swam after the boat, sometimes making a spring and splashing the water round them, while birds, red and blue, small and great, flew after him in two long lines. The gnats danced round them, and the cockchafers cried "Buz, buz." They all wanted to follow Hjalmar, and all had some story to tell him. It was a most pleasant sail. Sometimes the forests were thick and dark, sometimes like a beautiful garden, gay with sunshine and flowers; then he passed great palaces of glass and of marble, and on the balconies stood princesses, whose faces were those of little girls whom Hjalmar knew well, and had often played with. One of them held out her hand, in which was a heart made of sugar, more beautiful than any confectioner ever sold. As Hjalmar sailed by, he caught hold of one side of the sugar heart, and held it fast, and the princess held fast also, so that it broke in two pieces. Hjalmar had one piece, and the princess the other, but Hjalmar's was the largest. At each castle stood little princes acting as sentinels. They presented arms, and had golden swords, and made it rain plums and tin soldiers, so that they must have been real princes.

Hjalmar continued to sail, sometimes through woods, sometimes as it were through large halls, and then by large cities. At last he came to the town where his nurse lived, who had carried him in her arms when he was a very little boy, and had always been kind to him. She nodded and beckoned to him, and then sang the little verses she had herself composed and set to him, —

> "How oft my memory turns to thee,
>   My own Hjalmar, ever dear!
> When I could watch thy infant glee,
>   Or kiss away a pearly tear.
> 'Twas in my arms thy lisping tongue
>   First spoke the half-remembered word,
> While o'er thy tottering steps I hung,
>   My fond protection to afford.
> Farewell! I pray the Heavenly Power
> To keep thee till thy dying hour."

And all the birds sang the same tune, the flowers danced on their stems, and the old trees nodded as if Ole-Luk-Oie had been telling them stories as well.

WEDNESDAY

How the rain did pour down! Hjalmar could hear it in his sleep; and when Ole-Luk-Oie opened the window, the water flowed quite up to the window-sill. It had the appearance of a large lake outside, and a beautiful ship lay close to the house.

"Wilt thou sail with me to-night, little Hjalmar?" said Ole-Luk-Oie; "then we shall see foreign countries, and thou shalt return here in the morning."

All in a moment, there stood Hjalmar, in his best clothes, on the deck of the noble ship; and immediately the weather became fine. They sailed through the streets, round by the church, and on every side rolled the wide, great sea. They sailed till the land disappeared, and then they saw a flock of storks, who had left their own country, and were travelling to warmer climates. The storks flew one behind the other, and had already been a long, long time on the wing. One of them seemed so tired that his wings could scarcely carry him. He was the last of the row, and was soon left very far behind. At length he sunk lower and lower, with outstretched wings, flapping them in vain, till his feet touched the rigging of the ship, and he slided from the sails to the deck, and stood before them. Then a sailor-boy caught him, and put him in the hen-house, with the fowls, the ducks, and the turkeys, while the poor stork stood quite bewildered amongst them.

"Just look at that fellow," said the chickens.

Then the turkey-cock puffed himself out as large as he could, and inquired who he was; and the ducks waddled backwards, crying, "Quack, quack."

Then the stork told them all about warm Africa, of the pyramids, and of the ostrich, which, like a wild horse, runs across the desert. But the ducks did not understand what he said, and quacked amongst themselves, "We are all of the same opinion; namely, that he is stupid."

"Yes, to be sure, he is stupid," said the turkey-cock; and gobbled.

Then the stork remained quite silent, and thought of his home in Africa.

"Those are handsome thin legs of yours," said the turkey-cock. "What do they cost a yard?"

"Quack, quack, quack," grinned the ducks; but the stork pretended not to hear.

"You may as well laugh," said the turkey; "for that remark was rather witty, or perhaps it was above you. Ah, ah, is he not clever? He will be a great amusement to us while he remains here." And then he gobbled, and the ducks quacked, "Gobble, gobble; Quack, quack."

What a terrible uproar they made, while they were having such fun among themselves!

Then Hjalmar went to the hen-house; and, opening the door, called to the stork. Then he hopped out on the deck. He had rested himself now, and he looked happy, and seemed as if he nodded to Hjalmar, as if to thank him. Then he spread his wings, and flew away to warmer countries, while the hens clucked, the ducks quacked, and the turkey-cock turned quite scarlet in the head.

"To-morrow you shall be made into soup," said Hjalmar to the fowls; and then he awoke, and found himself lying in his little bed.

It was a wonderful journey which Ole-Luk-Oie had made him take this night.

THURSDAY

"What do you think I have got here?" said Ole-Luk-Oie, "Do not be frightened, and you shall see a little mouse." And then he held out his hand to him, in which lay a lovely little creature. "It has come to invite you to a wedding. Two little mice are going to enter into the marriage state tonight. They reside under the floor of your mother's store-room, and that must be a fine dwelling-place."

"But how can I get through the little mouse-hole in the floor?" asked Hjalmar.

"Leave me to manage that," said Ole-Luk-Oie. "I will soon make you small enough." And then he touched Hjalmar with his magic wand, whereupon he became less and less, until at last he was not longer than a little finger. "Now you can borrow the dress of the tin soldier. I think it will just fit you. It looks well to wear a uniform when you go into company."

"Yes, certainly," said Hjalmar; and in a moment he was dressed as neatly as the neatest of all tin soldiers.

"Will you be so good as to seat yourself in your mamma's thimble," said the little mouse, "that I may have the pleasure of drawing you to the wedding."

"Will you really take so much trouble, young lady?" said Hjalmar. And so in this way he rode to the mouse's wedding.

First they went under the floor, and then passed through a long passage, which was scarcely high enough to allow the thimble to drive under, and the whole passage was lit up with the phosphorescent light of rotten wood.

"Does it not smell delicious?" asked the mouse, as she drew him along. "The wall and the floor have been smeared with bacon-rind; nothing can be nicer."

Very soon they arrived at the bridal hall. On the right stood all the little lady-mice, whispering and giggling, as if they were making game of each other. To the left were the gentlemen-mice, stroking their whiskers with their fore-paws; and in the centre of the hall could be seen the bridal pair, standing side by side, in a hollow cheese-rind, and kissing each other, while all eyes were upon them; for they had already been betrothed, and were soon to be married. More and more friends kept arriving, till the mice were nearly treading each other to death; for the bridal pair now stood in the doorway, and none could pass in or out.

The room had been rubbed over with bacon-rind, like the passage, which was all the refreshment offered to the guests. But for dessert they produced a pea, on which a mouse belonging to the bridal pair had bitten the first letters of their names. This was something quite uncommon. All the mice said it was a very beautiful wedding, and that they had been very agreeably entertained.

After this, Hjalmar returned home. He had certainly been in grand society; but he had been obliged to creep under a room, and to make himself small enough to wear the uniform of a tin soldier.

FRIDAY

"It is incredible how many old people there are who would be glad to have me at night," said Ole-Luk-Oie, "especially those who have done something wrong. 'Good little Ole,' say they to me, 'we cannot close our eyes, and we lie awake the whole night and see all our evil deeds sitting on our beds like little imps, and sprinkling us with hot water. Will you come and drive them away, that we may have a good night's rest?' and then they sigh so deeply and say, 'We would gladly pay you for it. Good-night, Ole-Luk, the money lies on the window.' But I never do anything for gold." "What shall we do to-night?" asked Hjalmar. "I do not know whether you would care to go to another wedding," he replied, "although it is quite a different affair to the one we saw last night. Your sister's large doll, that is dressed like a man, and is called Herman, intends to marry the doll Bertha. It is also the dolls' birthday, and they will receive many presents."

"Yes, I know that already," said Hjalmar, "my sister always allows her dolls to keep their birthdays or to have a wedding when they require new clothes; that has happened already a hundred times, I am quite sure."

"Yes, so it may; but to-night is the hundred and first wedding, and when that has taken place it must be the last, therefore this is to be extremely beautiful. Only look."

Hjalmar looked at the table, and there stood the little card-board doll's-house, with lights in all the windows, and drawn up before it were the tin soldiers presenting arms. The bridal pair were seated on the floor, leaning against the leg of the table, looking very thoughtful, and with good reason. Then Ole-Luk-Oie dressed up in grandmother's black gown married them.

As soon as the ceremony was concluded, all the furniture in the room joined in singing a beautiful song, which had been composed by the lead pencil, and which went to the melody of a military tattoo.

> "What merry sounds are on the wind,
> As marriage rites together bind
> A quiet and a loving pair,
> Though formed of kid, yet smooth and fair!
> Hurrah! If they are deaf and blind,
> We'll sing, though weather prove unkind."

And now came the present; but the bridal pair had nothing to eat, for love was to be their food.

"Shall we go to a country house, or travel?" asked the bridegroom.

Then they consulted the swallow who had travelled so far, and the old hen in the yard, who had brought up five broods of chickens.

And the swallow talked to them of warm countries, where the grapes hang in large clusters on the vines, and the air is soft and mild, and about the mountains glowing with colors more beautiful than we can think of.

"But they have no red cabbage like we have," said the hen, "I was once in the country with my chickens for a whole summer, there was a large sand-pit, in which we could walk about and scratch as we liked. Then we got into a garden in which grew red cabbage; oh, how nice it was, I cannot think of anything more delicious."

"But one cabbage stalk is exactly like another," said the swallow; "and here we have often bad weather."

"Yes, but we are accustomed to it," said the hen.

"But it is so cold here, and freezes sometimes."

"Cold weather is good for cabbages," said the hen; "besides we do have it warm here sometimes. Four years ago, we had a summer that lasted more than five weeks, and it was so hot one could scarcely breathe. And then in this country we have no poisonous animals, and we are free from robbers. He must be wicked who does not consider our country the finest of all lands. He ought not to be allowed to live here." And then the hen wept very much and said, "I have also travelled. I once went twelve miles in a coop, and it was not pleasant travelling at all."

"The hen is a sensible woman," said the doll Bertha. "I don't care for travelling over mountains, just to go up and come down again. No, let us go to the sand-pit in front of the gate, and then take a walk in the cabbage garden."

And so they settled it.

SATURDAY

"Am I to hear any more stories?" asked little Hjalmar, as soon as Ole-Luk-Oie had sent him to sleep.

"We shall have no time this evening," said he, spreading out his prettiest umbrella over the child. "Look at these Chinese," and then the whole umbrella appeared like a large china bowl, with blue trees and pointed bridges, upon which stood little Chinamen nodding their heads. "We must make all the world beautiful for to-morrow morning," said Ole-Luk-Oie, "for it will be a holiday, it is Sunday. I must now go to the church steeple and see if the little sprites who live there have polished the bells, so that they may sound sweetly. Then I must go into the fields and see if the wind has blown the dust from the grass and the leaves, and the most difficult task of all which I have to do, is to take down all the stars and brighten them up. I have to number them first before I put them in my apron, and also to number the places from which I take them, so that they may go back into the right holes, or else they would not remain, and we should have a number of falling stars, for they would all tumble down one after the other."

"Hark ye! Mr. Luk-Oie," said an old portrait which hung on the wall of Hjalmar's bedroom. "Do you know me? I am Hjalmar's great-grandfather. I thank you for telling the boy stories, but you must not confuse his ideas. The stars cannot be taken down from the sky and polished; they are spheres like our earth, which is a good thing for them."

"Thank you, old great-grandfather," said Ole-Luk-Oie. "I thank you; you may be the head of the family, as no doubt you are, but I am older than you. I am an ancient heathen. The old Romans and Greeks named me the Dream-god. I have visited the noblest houses, and continue to do so; still I know how to conduct myself both to high and low, and now you may tell the stories yourself:" and so Ole-Luk-Oie walked off, taking his umbrellas with him.

"Well, well, one is never to give an opinion, I suppose," grumbled the portrait. And it woke Hjalmar.

SUNDAY

"Good evening," said Ole-Luk-Oie.

Hjalmar nodded, and then sprang out of bed, and turned his great-grandfather's portrait to the wall, so that it might not interrupt them as it had done yesterday. "Now," said he, "you must tell me some stories about five green peas that lived in one pod; or of the chickseed that courted the chickweed; or of the darning needle, who acted so proudly because she fancied herself an embroidery needle."

"You may have too much of a good thing," said Ole-Luk-Oie. "You know that I like best to show you something, so I will show you my brother. He is also called Ole-Luk-Oie but he never visits any one but once, and when he does come, he takes him away on his horse, and tells him stories as they ride along. He knows only two stories. One of these is so wonderfully beautiful, that no one in the world can imagine anything at all like it; but the other is just as ugly and frightful, so that it would be impossible to describe it." Then Ole-Luk-Oie lifted Hjalmar up to the window. "There now, you can see my brother, the other Ole-Luk-Oie; he is also called Death. You perceive he is not so bad as they represent him in picture books; there he is a skeleton, but now his coat is embroidered with silver, and he wears the splendid uniform of a hussar, and a mantle of black velvet flies behind him, over the horse. Look, how he gallops along." Hjalmar saw that as this Ole-Luk-Oie rode on, he lifted up old and young, and carried them away on his horse. Some he seated in front of him, and some behind, but always inquired first, "How stands the mark-book?"

"Good," they all answered.

"Yes, but let me see for myself," he replied; and they were obliged to give him the books. Then all those who had "Very good," or "Exceedingly good," came in front of the horse, and heard the beautiful story; while those who had "Middling," or "Tolerably good," in their books, were obliged to sit behind, and listen to the frightful tale. They trembled and cried, and wanted to jump down from the horse, but they could not get free, for they seemed fastened to the seat.

"Why, Death is a most splendid Luk-Oie," said Hjalmar. "I am not in the least afraid of him."

"You need have no fear of him," said Ole-Luk-Oie, "if you take care and keep a good conduct book."

"Now I call that very instructive," murmured the great-grandfather's portrait. "It is useful sometimes to express an opinion;" so he was quite satisfied.

These are some of the doings and sayings of Ole-Luk-Oie. I hope he may visit you himself this evening, and relate some more.

LITTLE TUK

YES, they called him Little Tuk, but it was not his real name; he had called himself so before he could speak plainly, and he meant it for Charles. It was all very well for those who knew him, but not for strangers.

Little Tuk was left at home to take care of his little sister, Gustava, who was much younger than himself, and he had to learn his lessons at the same time, and the two things could not very well be performed together. The poor boy sat there with his sister on his lap, and sung to her all the songs he knew, and now and then he looked into his geography lesson that lay open before him. By the next morning he had to learn by heart all the towns in Zealand, and all that could be described of them.

His mother came home at last, and took little Gustava in her arms. Then Tuk ran to the window, and read so eagerly that he nearly read his eyes out; for it had become darker and darker every minute, and his mother had no money to buy a light.

"There goes the old washerwoman up the lane," said the mother, as she looked out of the window; "the poor woman can hardly drag herself along, and now she had to drag a pail of water from the well. Be a good boy, Tuk, and run across and help the old woman, won't you?"

So Tuk ran across quickly, and helped her, but when he came back into the room it was quite dark, and there was not a word said about a light, so he was obliged to go to bed on his little truckle bedstead, and there he lay and thought of his geography lesson, and of Zealand, and of all the master had told him. He ought really to have read it over again, but he could not for want of light. So he put the geography book under his pillow, for he had heard that this was a great help towards learning a lesson, but not always to be depended upon. He still lay thinking and thinking, when all at once it seemed as if some one kissed him on his eyes and mouth. He slept and yet he did not sleep; and it appeared as if the old washerwoman looked at him with kind eyes and said, "It would be a great pity if you did not know your lesson to-morrow morning; you helped me, and now I will help you, and Providence will always keep those who help themselves;" and at the same time the book under Tuk's pillow began to move about. "Cluck, cluck, cluck," cried a hen as she crept towards him. "I am a hen from Kjöge,"* and then she told him how many inhabitants the town contained, and about a battle that had been fought there, which really was not worth speaking of.

"Crack, crack," down fell something. It was a wooden bird, the parrot which is used as a target as Prästöe.† He said there were as many inhabitants in that town as he had nails in his body. He was very proud, and said, "Thorwalsden lived close to me,‡ and here I am now, quite comfortable."

But now little Tuk was no longer in bed; all in a moment he found himself

---

*Kjöge, a little town on Kjöge Bay. Lifting up children by placing the hands on each side of their heads, is called "showing them Kjöge hens."

†Prästöe, a still smaller town.

‡About a hundred paces from Prästöe lies the estate of Nysöe, where Thorwalsden usually resided while in Denmark, and where he executed many memorable works.

on horseback. Gallop, gallop, away he went, seated in front of a richly-attired knight, with a waving plume, who held him on the saddle, and so they rode through the wood by the old town of Wordingburg, which was very large and busy. The king's castle was surrounded by lofty towers, and radiant light streamed from all the windows. Within there were songs and dancing; King Waldemar and the young gayly-dressed ladies of the court were dancing together. Morning dawned, and as the sun rose, the whole city and the king's castle sank suddenly down together. One tower after another fell, till at last only one remained standing on the hill where the castle had formerly been.*

The town now appeared small and poor, and the school-boys read in their books, which they carried under their arms, that it contained two thousand inhabitants; but this was a mere boast, for it did not contain so many.

And again little Tuk lay in his bed, scarcely knowing whether he was dreaming or not, for some one stood by him.

"Tuk! little Tuk!" said a voice. It was a very little person who spoke. He was dressed as a sailor, and looked small enough to be a middy, but he was not one. "I bring you many greetings from Corsör.† It is a rising town, full of life. It has steamships and mail-coaches. In times past they used to call it ugly, but that is no longer true. I lie on the sea-shore," said Corsör; "I have high-roads and pleasure-gardens; I have given birth to a poet who was witty and entertaining, which they are not all. I once wanted to fit out a ship to sail round the world, but I did not accomplish it, though most likely I might have done so. But I am fragrant with perfume, for close to my gates most lovely roses bloom."

Then before the eyes of little Tuk appeared a confusion of colors, red and green; but it cleared off, and he could distinguish a cliff close to the bay, the slopes of which were quite overgrown with verdure, and on its summit stood a fine old church with pointed towers. Springs of water flowed out of the cliff in thick waterspouts, so that there was a continual splashing. Close by sat an old king with a golden crown on his white head. This was King Hroar of the Springs‡ and near the springs stood the town of Roeskilde, as it is called. Then all the kings and queens of Denmark went up the ascent to the old church, hand in hand, with golden crowns on their heads, while the organ played and the fountains sent forth jets of water.

Little Tuk saw and heard it all. "Don't forget the names of these towns," said King Hroar.

All at once everything vanished; but where! It seemed to him like turning over the leaves of a book. And now there stood before him an old peasant woman, who had come from Soröe,§ where the grass grows in the market-

---

*Wordingburg under King Waldemar was a place of great importance; now it is a very insignificant town: only a lonely tower and the remains of a well show where the castle once stood.

† Corsör, on the Great Belt, used to be called the most tiresome town in Denmark before the establishment of steamers. Travellers had to wait for a favorable wind. The title of "tiresome" was ingeniously added to the Danish escutcheon by a witticism of Vaudeville Heibergs. The poet Baggesen was born here.

‡ Roeskilde (from Roesquelle, rose-spring, falsely called Rothschild), once the capital of Denmark. The town took its name from King Hroar, and from the numerous springs in the neighborhood. In its beautiful cathedral most of the kings and queens of Denmark are buried. In Roeskilde the Danish States used to assemble.

§ Soröe, a very quiet little town in a beautiful situation, surrounded by forests and lakes. Holberg, the Molière of Denmark, founded a noble academy here. The poets Hanck and Jugeman were professors here. Letztern lives there still.

place. She had a green linen apron thrown over her head and shoulders, and it was quite wet, as if it had been raining heavily. "Yes, that it has," said she, and then, just as she was going to tell him a great many pretty stories from Holberg's comedies, and about Waldemar and Absalom, she suddenly shrunk up together, and wagged her head as if she were a frog about to spring. "Croak," she cried; "it is always wet, and as quiet as death in Soröe." Then little Tuk saw she was changed into a frog. "Croak," and again she was an old woman. "One must dress according to the weather," said she. "It is wet, and my town is just like a bottle. By the cork we must go in, and by the cork we must come out again. In olden times I had beautiful fish, and now I have fresh, rosy-cheeked boys in the bottom of the bottle, and they learn wisdom, Hebrew and Greek."

"Croak." How it sounded like the cry of the frogs on the moor, or like the creaking of great boots when some one is marching, — always the same tone, so monotonous and wearing, that little Tuk at length fell fast asleep, and then the sound could not annoy him. But even in this sleep came a dream or something like it. His little sister Gustava, with her blue eyes, and fair curly hair, had grown up a beautiful maiden all at once, and without having wings she could fly. And they flew together over Zealand, over green forests and blue lakes.

"Hark, so you hear the cock crow, little Tuk. 'Cock-a-doodle-doo.' The fowls are flying out of Kjöge. You shall have a large farm-yard. You shall never suffer hunger or want. The bird of good omen shall be yours, and you shall become a rich and happy man; your house shall rise up like King Waldemar's towers, and shall be richly adorned with marble statues, like those at Prästöe. Understand me well; your name shall travel with fame round the world like the ship that was to sail from Corsör, and at Roeskilde, — Don't forget the names of the towns, as King Hroar said, — you shall speak well and clearly little Tuk, and when at last you lie in your grave you shall sleep peacefully, as —"

"As if I lay in Soröe," said little Tuk awaking. It was bright daylight, and he could not remember his dream, but that was not necessary, for we are not to know what will happen to us in the future. Then he sprang out of bed quickly, and read over his lesson in the book, and knew it all at once quite correctly. The old washerwoman put her head in at the door, and nodded to him quite kindly, and said, "Many thanks, you good child, for your help yesterday. I hope all your beautiful dreams will come true."

Little Tuk did not at all know what he had dreamt, but One above did.

THE SNOW QUEEN
IN SEVEN STORIES
STORY THE FIRST

WHICH describes a looking-glass and the broken fragments.

You must attend to the commencement of this story, for when we get to the end we shall know more than we do now about a very wicked hobgoblin; he was one of the very worst, for he was a real demon. One day, when he was in a merry mood, he made a looking-glass which had the power of making everything good or beautiful that was reflected in it almost shrink to nothing, while everything that was worthless and bad looked increased in size and worse than ever. The most lovely landscapes appeared like boiled spinach, and the people became hideous, and looked as if they stood on their heads and had no bodies. Their countenances were so distorted that no one could recognize them, and even one freckle on the face appeared to spread over the whole of the nose and mouth. The demon said this was very amusing. When a good or pious thought passed through the mind of any one it was misrepresented in the glass; and then how the demon laughed at his cunning invention. All who went to the demon's school — for he kept a school — talked everywhere of the wonders they had seen, and declared that people could now, for the first time, see what the world and mankind were really like. They carried the glass about everywhere, till at last there was not a land nor a people who had not been looked at through this distorted mirror. They wanted even to fly with it up to heaven to see the angels, but the higher they flew the more slippery the glass became, and they could scarcely hold it, till at last it slipped from their hands, fell to the earth, and was broken into millions of pieces. But now the looking-glass caused more unhappiness than ever, for some of the fragments were not so large as a grain of sand, and they flew about the world into every country. When one of these tiny atoms flew into a person's eye, it stuck there unknown to him, and from that moment he saw everything through a distorted medium, or could see only the worst side of what he looked at, for even the smallest fragment retained the same power which had belonged to the whole mirror. Some few persons even got a fragment of the looking-glass in their hearts, and this was very terrible, for their hearts became cold like a lump of ice. A few of the pieces were so large that they could be used as window-panes; it would have been a sad thing to look at our friends through them. Other pieces were made into spectacles; this was dreadful for those who wore them, for they could see nothing either rightly or justly. At all this the wicked demon laughed till his sides shook — it tickled him so to see the mischief he had done. There were still a number of these little fragments of glass floating about in the air, and now you shall hear what happened with one of them.

SECOND STORY
A LITTLE BOY AND A LITTLE GIRL

In a large town, full of houses and people, there is not room for everybody to have even a little garden, therefore they are obliged to be satisfied with a few flowers in flower-pots. In one of these large towns lived two poor children who had a garden something larger and better than a few flower-pots. They were not brother and sister, but they loved each other almost as much as if they had been. Their parents lived opposite to each other in two garrets, where the roofs of neighboring houses projected out towards each other and the water-pipe ran between them. In each house was a little window, so that any one could step across the gutter from one window to the other. The parents of these children had each a large wooden box in which they cultivated kitchen herbs for their own use, and a little rose-bush in each box, which grew splendidly. Now after a while the parents decided to place these two boxes across the waterpipe, so that they reached from one window to the other and looked like two banks of flowers. Sweet-peas drooped over the boxes, and the rose-bushes shot forth long branches, which were trained round the windows and clustered together almost like a triumphal arch of leaves and flowers. The boxes were very high, and the children knew they must not climb upon them, without permission, but they were often, however, allowed to step out together and sit upon their little stools under the rose-bushes, or play quietly. In winter all this pleasure came to an end, for the windows were sometimes quite frozen over. But then they would warm copper pennies on the stove, and hold the warm pennies against the frozen pane; there would be very soon a little round hole through which they could peep, and the soft bright eyes of the little boy and girl would beam through the hole at each window as they looked at each other. Their names were Kay and Gerda. In summer they could be together with one jump from the window, but in winter they had to go up and down the long staircase, and out through the snow before they could meet.

"See there are the white bees swarming," said Kay's old grandmother one day when it was snowing.

"Have they a queen bee?" asked the little boy, for he knew that the real bees had a queen.

"To be sure they have," said the grandmother. "She is flying there where the swarm is thickest. She is the largest of them all, and never remains on the earth, but flies up to the dark clouds. Often at midnight she flies through the streets of the town, and looks in at the windows, then the ice freezes on the panes into wonderful shapes, that look like flowers and castles."

"Yes, I have seen them," said both the children, and they knew it must be true.

"Can the Snow Queen come in here?" asked the little girl.

"Only let her come," said the boy, "I'll set her on the stove and then she'll melt."

Then the grandmother smoothed his hair and told him some more tales. One evening, when little Kay was at home, half undressed, he climbed on a chair by the window and peeped out through the little hole. A few flakes of snow were falling, and one of them, rather larger than the rest, alighted on the edge of one of the flower boxes. This snow-flake grew larger and larger, till at last it became the figure of a woman, dressed in garments of white gauze, which looked like millions of starry snow-flakes linked together. She was fair and beautiful, but made of ice—shining and glittering ice. Still she was alive and her eyes sparkled like bright stars, but there was neither peace nor rest in their glance. She nodded towards the window and waved her hand. The little boy was frightened and sprang from the chair; at the same moment it seemed as if a large bird flew by the window. On the following day there was a clear frost, and very soon came the spring. The sun shone; the young green leaves burst forth; the swallows built their nests; windows were opened, and the children sat once more in the garden on the roof, high above all the other rooms. How beautiful the roses blossomed this summer. The little girl had learnt a hymn in which roses were spoken of, and then she thought of their own roses, and she sang the hymn to the little boy, and he sang too: —

"Roses bloom and cease to be,
But we shall the Christ-child see."

Then the little ones held each other by the hand, and kissed the roses, and looked at the bright sunshine, and spoke to it as if the Christ-child were there. Those were splendid summer days. How beautiful and fresh it was out among the rose-bushes, which seemed as if they would never leave off blooming. One day Kay and Gerda sat looking at a book full of pictures of animals and birds, and then just as the clock in the church tower struck twelve, Kay said, "Oh, something has struck my heart!" and soon after, "There is something in my eye."

The little girl put her arm round his neck, and looked into his eye, but she could see nothing.

"I think it is gone," he said. But it was not gone; it was one of those bits of the looking-glass—that magic mirror, of which we have spoken—the ugly glass which made everything great and good appear small and ugly, while all that was wicked and bad became more visible, and every little fault could be plainly seen. Poor little Kay had also received a small grain in his heart, which very quickly turned to a lump of ice. He felt no more pain, but the glass was there still. "Why do you cry?" said he at last; "it makes you look ugly. There is nothing the matter with me now. Oh, see!" he cried suddenly, "that rose is worm-eaten, and this one is quite crooked. After all they are ugly roses, just like the box in which they stand," and then he kicked the boxes with his foot, and pulled off the two roses.

"Kay, what are you doing?" cried the little girl; and then, when he saw how frightened she was, he tore off another rose, and jumped through his own window away from little Gerda.

When she afterwards brought out the picture book, he said, "It was only fit for babies in long clothes," and when grandmother told any stories, he would interrupt her with "but;" or, when he could manage it, he would get behind her chair, put on a pair of spectacles, and imitate her very cleverly, to make people laugh. By-and-by he began to mimic the speech and gait of persons in the street. All that was peculiar or disagreeable in a person he would imitate directly, and people said, "That boy will be very clever; he has a remarkable genius." But it was the piece of glass in his eye, and the coldness in his heart, that made him act like this. He would even tease little Gerda, who loved him with all her heart. His games, too, were quite different; they were not so childish. One winter's day, when it snowed, he brought out a burning-glass, then he held out the tail of his blue coat, and let the snow-flakes fall upon it. "Look in this glass, Gerda," said he; and she saw how every flake of snow was magnified, and looked like a beautiful flower or a glittering star. "Is it not clever?" said Kay, "and much more interesting than looking at real flowers. There is not a single fault in it, and the snow-flakes are quite perfect till they begin to melt."

Soon after Kay made his appearance in large thick gloves, and with his sledge at his back. He called up stairs to Gerda, "I've got to leave to go into the great square, where the other boys play and ride." And away he went.

In the great square, the boldest among the boys would often tie their sledges to the country people's carts, and go with them a good way. This was capital. But while they were all amusing themselves, and Kay with them, a

THE SNOW QUEEN APPEARS TO LITTLE KAY

THE SNOW QUEEN

great sledge came by; it was painted white, and in it sat some one wrapped in a rough white fur, and wearing a white cap. The sledge drove twice round the square, and Kay fastened his own little sledge to it, so that when it went away, he followed with it. It went faster and faster right through the next street, and then the person who drove turned round and nodded pleasantly to Kay, just as if they were acquainted with each other, but whenever Kay wished to loosen his little sledge the driver nodded again, so Kay sat still, and they drove out through the town gate. Then the snow began to fall so heavily that the little boy could not see a hand's breadth before him, but still they drove on; then he suddenly loosened the cord so that the large sled might go on without him, but it was of no use, his little carriage held fast, and away they went like the wind. Then he called out loudly, but nobody heard him, while the snow beat upon him, and the sledge flew onwards. Every now and then it gave a jump as if it were going over hedges and ditches. The boy was frightened, and tried to say a prayer, but he could remember nothing but the multiplication table.

The snow-flakes became larger and larger, till they appeared like great white chickens. All at once they sprang on one side, the great sledge stopped, and the person who had driven it rose up. The fur and the cap, which were made entirely of snow, fell off, and he saw a lady, tall and white, it was the Snow Queen.

"We have driven well," said she, "but why do you tremble? here, creep into my warm fur." Then she seated him beside her in the sledge, and as she wrapped the fur round him he felt as if he were sinking into a snow drift.

"Are you still cold," she asked, as she kissed him on the forehead. The kiss was colder than ice; it went quite through to his heart, which was already almost a lump of ice; he felt as if he were going to die, but only for a moment; he soon seemed quite well again, and did not notice the cold around him.

"My sledge! don't forget my sledge," was his first thought, and then he looked and saw that it was bound fast to one of the white chickens, which flew behind him with the sledge at its back. The Snow Queeen kissed little Kay again, and by this time he had forgotten little Gerda, his grandmother, and all at home.

"Now you must have no more kisses," she said, "or I should kiss you to death."

Kay looked at her, and saw that she was so beautiful, he could not imagine a more lovely and intelligent face; she did not now seem to be made of ice, as when he had seen her through his window, and she had nodded to him. In his eyes she was perfect, and she did not feel at all afraid. He told her he could do mental arithmetic, as far as fractions, and that he knew the number of square miles and the number of inhabitants in the country. And she always smiled so that he thought he did not know enough yet, and she looked round the vast expanse as she flew higher and higher with him upon a black cloud, while the storm blew and howled as if it were singing old songs. They flew over woods and lakes, over sea and land; below them roared the wild wind; the wolves howled and the snow crackled; over them flew the black screaming crows, and above all shone the moon, clear and bright, — and so Kay passed through the long winter's night, and by day he slept at the feet of the Snow Queen.

THIRD STORY
THE FLOWER GARDEN OF THE WOMAN
WHO COULD CONJURE

But how fared little Gerda during Kay's absence? What had become of him, no one knew, nor could any one give the slightest information, excepting the boys, who said that he had tied his sledge to another very large one, which had driven through the street, and out at the town gate. Nobody knew where it went; many tears were shed for him, and little Gerda wept bitterly for a long time. She said she knew he must be dead; that he was drowned in the river which flowed close by the school. Oh, indeed those long winter days were very dreary. But at last spring came, with warm sunshine. "Kay is dead and gone," said little Gerda.

"I don't believe it," said the sunshine.

"He is dead and gone," she said to the sparrows.

"We don't believe it," they replied; and at last little Gerda began to doubt it herself. "I will put on my new red shoes," she said one morning, "those that Kay has never seen, and then I will go down to the river, and ask for him." It was quite early when she kissed her old grandmother, who was still asleep; then she put on her red shoes, and went quite alone out of the town gates toward the river. "Is it true that you have taken my little playmate away from me?" said she to the river. "I will give you my red shoes if you will give him back to me." And it seemed as if the waves nodded to her in a strange manner. Then she took off her red shoes, which she liked better than anything else, and threw them both into the river, but they fell near the bank, and the little waves carried them back to the land, just as if the river would not take from her what she loved best, because they could not give her back little Kay. But she thought the shoes had not been thrown out far enough. Then she crept into a boat that lay among the reeds, and threw the shoes again from the farther end of the boat into the water, but it was not fastened. And her movement sent it gliding away from the land. When she saw this she hastened to reach the end of the boat, but before she could so it was more than a yard from the bank, and drifting away faster than ever. Then little Gerda was very much frightened, and began to cry, but no one heard her except the sparrows, and they could not carry her to land, but they flew along by the shore, and sang, as if to comfort her, "Here we are! Here we are!" The boat floated with the stream; little Gerda sat quite still with only her stockings on her feet; the red shoes floated after her, but she could not reach them because the boat kept so much in advance. The banks on each side of the river were very pretty. There were beautiful flowers, old trees, sloping fields, in which cows and sheep were grazing, but not a man to be seen. Perhaps the river will carry me to little Kay, thought Gerda, and then she became more cheerful, and raised her head, and looked at the beautiful green banks; and so the boat sailed on for hours. At length she came to a large cherry orchard, in which stood a small red house with strange red and blue windows. It had also a thatched roof, and outside were two wooden soldiers, that presented arms to her as she sailed past. Gerda called out to them, for she thought they were alive, but of course they did not answer; and as the boat drifted nearer to the shore, she saw what they really were. Then Gerda called still louder, and there came a very old woman out of the house, leaning on a crutch. She wore a large hat to shade her from the sun, and on it were painted all sorts of pretty flowers. "You poor little child," said the old woman, "how did you manage to come all this distance into the wide world on such a rapid rolling stream?" And then the old woman walked in the water, seized the boat with her crutch, drew it to land, and lifted Gerda out. And Gerda was glad to feel herself on dry ground, although she was rather afraid of the strange old woman. "Come and tell me who you are," said she, "and how came you here."

Then Gerda told her everything, while the old woman shook her head, and said, "Hem-hem;" and when she had finished, Gerda asked if she had not seen little Kay, and the old woman told her he had not passed by that way, but he very likely would come. So she told Gerda not to be sorrowful, but to taste the cherries and look at the flowers; they were better than any picture-book, for each of them could tell a story. Then she took Gerda by the hand and led her into the little house, and the old woman closed the door. The windows were very high, and as the panes were red, blue, and yellow, the daylight shone through them in all sorts of singular colors. On the table stood beautiful cherries, and Gerda had permission to eat as many as she would. While she was eating them the old woman combed out her long flaxen ringlets with a golden comb, and the glossy curls hung down on each side of the little round pleasant face, which looked fresh and blooming as a rose. "I have long been wishing for a dear little maiden like you," said the old woman, "and now you must stay with me, and see how happily we shall live together." And while she went on combing little Gerda's hair, she thought less and less about her adopted brother Kay, for the old woman could conjure, although she was not a wicked witch; she conjured only a little for her own amusement, and now, because she wanted to keep Gerda. Therefore she went into the garden, and stretched out her crutch towards all the rose-trees, beautiful though they were; and they immediately sunk into the dark earth, so that no one could tell where they had once stood. The old woman was afraid that if little Gerda saw roses she would think of those at home, and then remember little Kay, and run away. Then she took Gerda into the flower-garden. How fragrant and beautiful it was! Every flower that could be thought of for every season of the year was here in full bloom; no picture-book could have more beautiful colors. Gerda jumped for joy, and played till the sun went down behind the tall cherry-trees; then she slept in an elegant bed with red silk pillows, embroidered with colored violets; and then she dreamed as pleasantly as a queen on her wedding day. The next day, and for many days after, Gerda played with the flowers in the warm sunshine. She knew every flower, and yet, although there were so many of them, it seemed as if one were missing, but which it was she could not tell. One day, however, as she sat looking at the old woman's hat with the painted flowers on it, she saw that the prettiest of them all was a rose. The old woman had forgotten to take it from her hat when she made all the roses sink into the earth. But it is difficult to keep the thoughts together in everything; one little mistake upsets all our arrangements.

"What, are there no roses here?" cried Gerda; and she ran out into the garden, and examined all the beds, and searched and searched. There was not one to be found. Then she sat down and wept, and her tears fell just on the place where one of the rose-trees had sunk down. The warm tears moistened the earth, and the rose-tree sprouted up at once, as blooming as when it had sunk; and Gerda embraced it and kissed the roses, and thought of the beautiful roses at home, and, with them, of little Kay.

"Oh, how I have been detained!" said the little maiden, "I wanted to seek for little Kay. Do you know where he is?" she asked the roses; "do you think he is dead?"

And the roses answered, "No, he is not dead. We have been in the ground where all the dead lie; but Kay is not there."

"Thank you," said little Gerda, and then she went to the other flowers, and looked into their little cups, and asked, "Do you know where little Kay is?" But each flower, as it stood in the sunshine, dreamed only of its own little fairy tale of history. Not one knew anything of Kay. Gerda heard many stories from the flowers, as she asked them one after another about him.

And what, said the tiger-lily? "Hark, do you hear the drum?—'tum, tum,'—there are only two notes always, 'tum, tum.' Listen to the women's song of mourning! Hear the cry of the priest! In her long red robe stands the Hindoo widow by the funeral pile. The flames rise around her as she places herself on the dead body of her husband; but the Hindoo woman is thinking of the living one in that circle; of him, her son, who lighted those flames. Those shining eyes trouble her heart more painfully than the flames which will soon consume her body to ashes. Can the fire of the heart be extinguished in the flames of the funeral pile?"

"I don't understand that at all," said little Gerda.

"That is my story," said the tiger-lily.

What, says the convolvulus? "Near yonder narrow road stands an old knight's castle; thick ivy creeps over the old ruined walls, leaf over leaf, even to the balcony, in which stands a beautiful maiden. She bends over the balustrades, and looks up the road. No rose on its stem is fresher than she; no apple-blossom, wafted by the wind, floats more lightly than she moves. Her rich silk rustles as she bends over and exclaims, 'Will he not come?' "

"Is it Kay you mean?" asked Gerda.

"I am only speaking of a story of my dream," replied the flower.

What, said the little snow-drop? "Between two trees a rope is hanging; there is a piece of board upon it; it is a swing. Two pretty little girls, in dresses white as snow, and with long green ribbons fluttering from their hats, are sitting upon it swinging. Their brother who is taller than they are, stands in the swing; he has one arm round the rope, to steady himself; in one hand he holds a little bowl, and in the other a clay pipe; he is blowing bubbles. As the swing goes on, the bubbles fly upward, reflecting the most beautiful varying colors. The last still hangs from the bowl of the pipe, and sways in the wind. On goes the swing; and then a little black dog comes running up. He is almost as light as the bubble, and he raises himself on his hind legs, and wants to be taken into the swing; but it does not stop, and the dog falls; then he barks and gets angry. The children stoop towards him, and the bubble bursts. A swinging plank, a light sparkling foam picture,—that is my story."

"It may be all very pretty what you are telling me," said little Gerda, "but you speak so mournfully, and you do not mention little Kay at all."

What do the hyacinths say? "There were three beautiful sisters, fair and delicate. The dress of one was red, of the second blue, and of the third pure white. Hand in hand they danced in the bright moonlight, by the calm lake; but they were human beings, not fairy elves. The sweet fragrance attracted them, and they disappeared in the wood; here the fragrance became stronger. Three coffins, in which lay the three beautiful maidens, glided from the thickest part of the forest across the lake. The fire-flies flew lightly over them, like little floating torches. Do the dancing maidens sleep, or are they dead? The scent of the flower says that they are corpses. The evening bell tolls their knell."

"You make me quite sorrowful," said little Gerda; "your perfume is so strong, you make me think of the dead maidens. Ah! is little Kay really dead then? The roses have been in the earth, and they say no."

"Cling, clang," tolled the hyacinth bells. "We are not tolling for little Kay; we do not know him. We sing our song, the only one we know."

Then Gerda went to the buttercups that were glittering amongst the bright green leaves.

"You are little bright suns," said Gerda; "tell me if you know where I can find my play-fellow."

And the buttercups sparkled gayly, and looked again at Gerda. What song could the buttercups sing? It was not about Kay.

"The bright warm sun shone on a little court, on the first warm day of spring. His bright beams rested on the white walls of the neighboring house; and close by bloomed the first yellow flower of the season, glittering like gold in the sun's warm ray. An old woman sat in her arm chair at the house door, and her granddaughter, a poor and pretty servant-maid came to see her for a short visit. When she kissed her grandmother there was gold everywhere: the gold of the heart in that holy kiss; it was a golden morning; there was gold in the beaming sunlight, gold in the leaves of the lowly flower, and on the lips of the maiden. There, that is my story," said the buttercup.

"My poor old grandmother!" sighed Gerda; "she is longing to see me, and grieving for me as she did for little Kay; but I shall soon go home now, and take little Kay with me. It is no use asking the flowers; they know only their own songs, and can give me no information."

And then she tucked up her little dress, that she might run faster, but the narcissus caught her by the leg as she was jumping over it; so she stopped and looked at the tall yellow flower, and said, "Perhaps you may know something."

Then she stooped down quite close to the flower, and listened; and what did he say?

"I can see myself, I can see myself," said the narcissus. "Oh, how sweet is my perfume! Up in a little room with a bow window, stands a little dancing girl, half undressed; she stands sometimes on one leg, and sometimes on both, and looks as if she would tread the whole world under her feet. She is nothing but a delusion. She is pouring water out of a tea-pot on a piece of stuff which she holds in her hand; it is her bodice. 'Cleanliness is a good thing,' she says. Her white dress hangs on a peg; it has also been washed in the tea-pot, and dried on the roof. She puts it on, and ties a saffron-colored handkerchief round her neck, which makes the dress look whiter. See how she stretches out her legs, as if she were showing off on a stem. I can see myself, I can see myself."

"What do I care for all that," said Gerda, "you need not tell me such stuff." And then she ran to the other end of the garden. The door was fastened, but she pressed against the rusty latch, and it gave way. The door sprang open, and little Gerda ran out with bare feet into the wide world. She looked back three times, but no one seemed to be following her. At last she could run no longer, so she sat down to rest on a great stone, and when she looked round she saw that the summer was over, and autumn very far advanced. She had known nothing of this in the beautiful garden, where the sun shone and the flowers grew all the year round.

"Oh, how I have wasted my time?" said little Gerda; "it is autumn. I must not rest any longer," and she rose up to go on. But her little feet were wounded and sore, and everything around her looked so cold and bleak. The long willow-leaves were quite yellow. The dew-drops fell like water, leaf after leaf dropped from the trees, the sloe-thorn alone still bore fruit, but the sloes were sour, and set the teeth on edge. Oh, how dark and weary the whole world appeared!

FOURTH STORY
THE PRINCE AND PRINCESS

Gerda was obliged to rest again, and just opposite the place where she sat, she saw a great crow come hopping across the snow toward her. He stood looking at her for some time, and then he wagged his head and said, "Caw, caw; good-day, good-day." He pronounced the words as plainly as he could, because he meant to be kind to the little girl; and then he asked her where she was going all alone in the wide world.

The word *alone* Gerda understood very well, and knew how much it expressed. So then she told the crow the whole story of her life and adventures, and asked him if he had seen little Kay.

The crow nodded his head very gravely, and said, "Perhaps I have—it may be."

"No! Do you think you have?" cried little Gerda, and she kissed the crow, and hugged him almost to death with joy.

"Gently, gently," said the crow. "I believe I know. I think it may be little Kay; but he has certainly forgotten you by this time for the princess."

"Does he live with a princess?" asked Gerda.

"Yes, listen," replied the crow, "but it is so difficult to speak your language. If you understand the crows' language* then I can explain it better. Do you?"

"No, I have never learnt it," said Gerda, but my grandmother understands it, and used to speak it to me. I wish I had learnt it."

"It does not matter," answered the crow; "I will explain as well as I can, although it will be very badly done;" and he told her what he had heard. "In this kingdom where we now are," said he, "there lives a princess, who is so wonderfully clever that she has read all the newspapers in the world, and forgotten them too, although she is so clever. A short time ago, as she was sit-

---

*Children have a kind of language, or gibberish, which is sometimes called "crows' language;" it is formed by adding letters or syllables to every word.

ting on her throne, which people say is not such an agreeable seat as is often supposed, she began to sing a song which commences in these words:

'Why should I not be married?'

'Why not indeed?' said she, and so she determined to marry if she could find a husband who knew what to say when he was spoken to, and not one who could only look grand, for that was so tiresome. Then she assembled all her court ladies together at the beat of the drum, and when they heard of her intentions they were very much pleased. 'We are so glad to hear it,' said they, 'we were talking about it ourselves the other day.' You may believe that every word I tell you is true," said the crow, "for I have a tame sweetheart who goes freely about the palace, and she told me all this."

Of course his sweetheart was a crow, for "birds of a feather flock together," and one crow always chooses another crow.

"Newspapers were published immediately, with a border of hearts, and the initials of the princess among them. They gave notice that every young man who was handsome was free to visit the castle and speak with the princess; and those who could reply loud enough to be heard when spoken to, were to make themselves quite at home at the palace; but the one who spoke best would be chosen as a husband for the princess. Yes, yes, you may believe me, it is all as true as I sit here," said the crow. "The people came in crowds. There was a great deal of crushing and running about, but no one succeeded either on the first or second day. They could all speak very well while they were outside in the streets, but when they entered the palace gates, and saw the guards in silver uniforms, and the footmen in their golden livery on the staircase, and the great halls lighted up, they became quite confused. And when they stood before the throne on which the princess sat, they could do nothing but repeat the last words she had said; and she had no particular wish to hear her own words over again. It was just as if they had all taken something to make them sleepy while they were in the palace, for they did not recover themselves nor speak till they got back again into the street. There was quite a long line of them reaching from the town-gate to the palace. I went myself to see them," said the crow. "They were hungry and thirsty, for at the palace they did not get even a glass of water. Some of the wisest had taken a few slices of bread and butter with them, but they did not share it with their neighbors; they thought if they went in to the princess looking hungry, there would be a better chance for themselves."

"But Kay! tell me about little Kay!" said Gerda, "was he amongst the crowd?"

"Stop a bit, we are just coming to him. It was on the third day, there came marching cheerfully along to the palace a little personage, without horses or carriage, his eyes sparkling like yours; he had beautiful long hair, but his clothes were very poor."

"That was Kay!" said Gerda joyfully. "Oh, then I have found him;" and she clapped her hands.

"He had a little knapsack on his back," added the crow.

"No, it must have been his sledge," said Gerda; "for he went away with it."

"It may have been so," said the crow; "I did not look at it very closely. But I know from my tame sweetheart that he passed through the palace gates, saw the guards in their silver uniform, and the servants in their liveries of gold on the stairs, but he was not in the least embarrassed. 'It must be very tiresome to stand on the stairs,' he said. 'I prefer to go in." The rooms were blazing with light. Councillors and ambassadors walked about with bare feet, carrying golden vessels; it was enough to make any one feel serious. His boots creaked loudly as he walked, and yet he was not at all uneasy."

"It must be Kay," said Gerda, "I know he had new boots on, I have heard them creak in grandmother's room."

"They really did creak," said the crow, "yet he went boldly up to the princess herself, who was sitting on a pearl as large as a spinning wheel, and all the ladies of the court were present with their maids, and all the cavaliers with their servants; and each of the maids had another maid to wait upon her, and the cavaliers' servants had their own servants, as well as a page each. They all stood in circles round the princess, and the nearer they stood to the door, the prouder they looked. The servants' pages, who always wore slippers, could hardly be looked at, they held themselves up so proudly by the door."

"It must be quite awful," said little Gerda, "but did Kay win the princess?"

"If I had not been a crow," said he, "I would have married her myself, although I am engaged. He spoke just as well as I do, when I speak the crows' language, so I heard from my tame sweetheart. He was quite free and agreeable and said he had not come to woo the princess, but to hear her wisdom; and he was as pleased with her as she was with him."

"Oh, certainly that was Kay," said Gerda, "he was so clever; he could work mental arithmetic and fractions. Oh, will you take me to the palace?"

"It is very easy to ask that," replied the crow, "but how are we to manage it? However, I will speak about it to my tame sweetheart, and ask her advice; for I must tell you it will be very difficult to gain permission for a little girl like you to enter the palace."

"Oh, yes; but I shall gain permission easily," said Gerda, "for when Kay hears that I am here, he will come out and fetch me in immediately."

"Wait for me here by the palings," said the crow, wagging his head as he flew away.

It was late in the evening before the crow returned. "Caw, caw," he said, she sends you greeting, and here is a little roll which she took from the kitchen for you; there is plenty of bread there, and she thinks you must be hungry. It is not possible for you to enter the palace by the front entrance. The guards in silver uniform and the servants in gold livery would not allow it. But do not cry, we will manage to get you in; my sweetheart knows a little back-staircase that leads to the sleeping apartments, and she knows where to find the key."

Then they went into the garden through the great avenue, where the leaves were falling one after another, and they could see the light in the palace being put out in the same manner. And the crow led little Gerda to the back door, which stood ajar. Oh! how little Gerda's heart beat with anxiety and longing; it was just as if she were going to do something wrong, and yet she only wanted to know where little Kay was. "It must be he," she thought, "with those clear eyes, and that long hair." She could fancy she saw him smiling at her, as he used to at home, when they sat among the roses. He would certainly be glad to see her, and to hear what a long distance she had come for his sake, and to know how sorry they had been at home because he did not come back. Oh what joy and yet fear she felt! They were now on the stairs, and in a small closet at the top a lamp was burning. In the middle of the floor stood the tame crow, turning her head from side to side, and gazing at Gerda, who curtseyed as her grandmother had taught her to do.

"My betrothed has spoken so very highly of you, my little lady," said the tame crow, "your life-history, *Vita*, as it may be called, is very touching. If you will take the lamp I will walk before you. We will go straight along this way, then we shall meet no one."

"It seems to me as if somebody were behind us," said Gerda, as something rushed by her like a shadow on the wall, and then horses with flying manes and thin legs, hunters, ladies and gentlemen on horseback, glided by her, like shadows on the wall.

"They are only dreams," said the crow, "they are coming to fetch the thoughts of the great people out hunting."

"All the better, for we shall be able to look at them in their beds more safely. I hope that when you rise to honor and favor, you will show a grateful heart."

"You may be quite sure of that," said the crow from the forest.

They now came into the first hall, the walls of which were hung with rose-colored satin, embroidered with artificial flowers. Here the dreams again flitted by them but so quickly that Gerda could not distinguish the royal persons. Each hall appeared more splendid than the last, it was enought to bewilder any one. At length they reached a bedroom. The ceiling was like a great palm-tree, with glass leaves of the most costly crystal, and over the centre of the floor two beds, each resembling a lily, hung from a stem of gold. One, in which the princess lay, was white, the other was red; and in this Gerda had to seek for little Kay. She pushed one of the red leaves aside, and saw a little brown neck. Oh, that must be Kay! She called his name out quite loud, and held the lamp over him. The dreams rushed back into the room on horseback. He woke, and turned his head round, it was not little Kay! The prince was only like him in the neck, still he was young and pretty. Then the princess peeped out of her white-lily bed, and asked what was the matter. Then little Gerda wept and told her story, and all that the crows had done to help her.

"You poor child," said the prince and princess; then they praised the crows, and said they were not angry for what they had done, but that it must not happen again, and this time they should be rewarded.

"Would you like to have your freedom?" asked the princess, "or would you prefer to be raised to the position of court crows, with all that is left in the kitchen for yourselves?"

Then both the crows bowed, and begged to have a fixed appointment, for they thought of their old age, and said it would be so comfortable to feel that they had provision for their old days, as they called it. And then the prince got out of his bed, and gave it up to Gerda, —he could do no more; and she lay down. She folded her little hands, and thought, "How good everyone is to me, men and animals too;" then she closed her eyes and fell into a sweet sleep. All the dreams came flying back again to her, and they looked like angels, and one of them drew a little sledge, on which sat Kay, and nodded to her. But all this was only a dream, and vanished as soon as she awoke.

The following day she was dressed from head to foot in silk and velvet, and they invited her to stay at the palace for a few days, and enjoy herself, but she only begged for a pair of boots, and a little carriage, and a horse to draw it, so that she might go into the wide world to seek for Kay. And she obtained, not only boots, but also a muff, and she was neatly dressed; and when she was ready to go, there, at the door, she found a coach made of pure gold, with the coat-of-arms of the prince and princess shining upon it like a star, and the coachman, footman, and outriders all wearing golden crowns on their heads. The prince and princess themselves helped her into the coach, and wished her success. The forest crow, who was now married, accompanied her for the first three miles; he sat by Gerda's side, as he could not bear riding backwards. The tame crow stood in the door-way flapping her wings. She could not go with them, because she had been suffering from headache ever since the new appointment, no doubt from eating too much. The coach was well stored with sweet cakes, and under the seat were fruit and gingerbread nuts. "Farewell, farewell," cried the prince and princess, and little Gerda wept, and the crow wept; and then, after a few miles, the crow also said "Farewell," and this was the saddest parting. However, he flew to a tree, and stood flapping his black wings as long as he could see the coach, which glittered in the bright sunshine.

FIFTH STORY
LITTLE ROBBER-GIRL

The coach drove on through a thick forest, where it lighted up the way like a torch, and dazzled the eyes of some robbers, who could not bear to let it pass them unmolested.

"It is gold! it is gold!" cried they, rushing forward, and seizing the horses. Then they struck the little jockeys, the coachman, and the footman dead, and pulled little Gerda out of the carriage.

"She is fat and pretty, and she has been fed with the kernels of nuts," said the old robber-woman, who had a long beard and eyebrows that hung over her eyes. "She is as good as a little lamb; how nice she will taste!" and as she said this, she drew forth a shining knife, that glittered horribly. "Oh!" screamed the old woman the same moment; for her own daughter, who held her back, had bitten her in the ear. She was a wild and naughty girl, and the mother called her an ugly thing, and had not time to kill Gerda.

"She shall play with me," said the little robber-girl; "she shall give me her muff and her pretty dress, and sleep with me in my bed." And then she bit her mother again, and made her spring in the air, and jump about; and all the robbers laughed, and said, "See how she is dancing with her young cub."

"I will have a ride in the coach," said the little robber-girl; and she would have her own way; for she was so self-willed and obstinate.

She and Gerda seated themselves in the coach, and drove away, over stumps and stones, into the depths of the forest. The little robber-girl was about the same size as Gerda, but stronger; she had broader shoulders and a darker skin; her eyes were quite black, and she had a mournful look. She clasped little Gerda round the waist, and said, —

"They shall not kill you as long as you don't make us vexed with you. I suppose you are a princess."

"No," said Gerda; and then she told her all her history, and how fond she was of little Kay.

The robber-girl looked earnestly at her, nodded her head slightly, and said, "They sha'nt kill you, even if I do get angry with you; for I will do it myself." And then she wiped Gerda's eyes, and stuck her own hands in the beautiful muff which was so soft and warm.

The coach stopped in the courtyard of a robber's castle, the walls of which were cracked from top to bottom. Ravens and crows flew in and out of the holes and crevices, while great bulldogs, either of which looked as if it could swallow a man, were jumping about; but they were not allowed to bark. In the large and smoky hall a bright fire was burning on the stone floor. There was no chimney; so the smoke went up to the ceiling, and found a way out for itself. Soup was boiling in a large cauldron, and hares and rabbits were roasting on the spit.

"You shall sleep with me and all my little animals to-night," said the robber-girl, after they had had something to eat and drink. So she took Gerda to a corner of the hall, where some straw and carpets were laid down. Above them, on laths and perches, were more than a hundred pigeons, who all seemed to be asleep, although they moved slightly when the two little girls came near them. "These all belong to me," said the robber-girl; and she seized the nearest to her, held it by the feet, and shook it till it flapped its wings. "Kiss it," cried she, flapping it in Gerda's face. "There sit the wood-pigeons," continued she, pointing to a number of laths and a cage which had been fixed into the walls, near one of the openings. "Both rascals would fly away directly, if they were not closely locked up. And here is my old sweetheart 'Ba;' and she dragged out a reindeer by the horn; he wore a bright copper ring round his neck, and was tied up. "We are obliged to hold him tight too, or else he would run away from us also. I tickle his neck every evening with my sharp knife, which frightens him very much." And then the robber-girl drew a long knife from a chink in the wall, and let it slide gently over the reindeer's neck. The poor animal began to kick, and the little robber-girl laughed, and pulled down Gerda into bed with her.

"Will you have that knife with you while you are asleep?" asked Gerda, looking at it in great fright.

"I always sleep with the knife by me," said the robber-girl. "No one knows what may happen. But now tell me again all about little Kay, and why you went out into the world."

Then Gerda repeated her story over again, while the wood-pigeons in the cage over her cooed, and the other pigeons slept. The little robber-girl put one arm across Gerda's neck, and held the knife in the other, and was soon fast asleep and snoring. But Gerda could not close her eys at all; she knew not whether she was to live or die. The robbers sat round the fire, singing and drinking, and the old woman stumbled about. It was a terrible sight for a little girl to witness.

Then the wood-pigeons said, "Coo, coo; we have seen little Kay. A white fowl carried his sledge, and he sat in the carriage of the Snow Queen, which drove through the wood while we were lying in our nest. She blew upon us, and all the young ones died excepting us two. Coo, coo."

"What are you saying up there?" cried Gerda. "Where was the Snow Queen going? Do you know anything about it?"

"She was most likely travelling to Lapland, where there is always snow and ice. Ask the reindeer that is fastened up there with a rope."

"Yes, there is always snow and ice," said the reindeer; "and it is a glorious place; you can leap and run about freely on the sparkling ice plains. The Snow Queen has her summer tent there, but her strong castle is at the North Pole, on an island called Spitzbergen."

"Oh, Kay, little Kay!" sighed Gerda.

"Lie still," said the robber-girl, "or I shall run my knife into your body."

In the morning Gerda told her all that the wood-pigeons had said; and the litte robber-girl looked quite serious, and nodded her head, and said, "That is all talk, that is all talk. Do you know where Lapland is?" she asked the reindeer.

"Who should know better than I do?" said the animal, while his eyes sparkled. "I was born and brought up there, and used to run about the snow-covered plains."

"Now listen," said the robber-girl; "all our men are gone away, — only mother is here, and here she will stay; but at noon she always drinks out of a great bottle, and afterwards sleeps for a little while; and then, I'll do something for you." Then she jumped out of bed, clasped her mother round the neck, and pulled her by the beard, crying, "My own little nanny goat, good morning." Then her mother filliped her nose till it was quite red; yet she did it all for love.

When the mother had drunk out of the bottle, and was gone to sleep, the little robber-maiden went to the reindeer, and said, "I should like very much to tickle your neck a few times more with my knife, for it makes you look so funny; but never mind, — I will untie your cord, and set you free, so that you may run away to Lapland; but you must make good use of your legs, and carry this little maiden to the castle of the Snow Queen, where her play-fellow is. You have heard what she told me, for she spoke loud enough, and you were listening.

Then the reindeer jumped for joy; and the little robber-girl lifted Gerda on his back, and had the forethought to tie her on, and even to give her her own little cushion to sit on.

"Here are your fur boots for you," said she; "for it will be very cold; but I must keep the muff; it is so pretty. However, you shall not be frozen for the want of it; here are my mother's large warm mittens; they will reach up to your elbows. Let me put them on. There, now your hands look just like my mother's."

But Gerda wept for joy.

"I don't like to see you fret," said the little robber-girl; "you ought to look quite happy now; and here are two loaves and a ham, so that you need not starve." These were fastened on the reindeer, and then the little robber-maiden opened the door, coaxed in all the great dogs, and then cut the string with which the reindeer was fastened, with her sharp knife, and said, "Now run, but mind you take good care of the little girl." And then Gerda stretched out her hand, with the great mitten on it, towards the little robber-girl, and said, "Farewell," and away flew the reindeer, over stumps and stones, through the great forest, over marshes and plains, as quickly as he could. The wolves howled, and the ravens screamed; while up in the sky quivered red lights like flames of fire. "There are my old northern lights," said the reindeer; "see how they flash." And he ran on day and night still faster and faster, but the loaves and the ham were all eaten by the time they reached Lapland.

SIXTH STORY
THE LAPLAND WOMAN AND
THE FINLAND WOMAN

They stopped at a little hut; it was very mean looking; the roof sloped nearly down to the ground, and the door was so low that the family had to creep in on their hands and knees, when they went in and out. There was no one at home but an old Lapland woman, who was cooking fish by the light of a train-oil lamp. The reindeer told her all about Gerda's story, after having first told his own, which seemed to him the most important, but Gerda was so pinched with the cold that she could not speak. "Oh, you poor things," said the Lapland woman, "you have a long way to go yet. You must travel more than a hundred miles farther, to Finland. The Snow Queen lives there now, and she burns Bengal lights every evening. I will write a few words on a dried stock-fish, for I have no paper, and you can take it from me to the Finland woman who lives there; she can give you better information than I can." So when Gerda was warmed, and had taken something to eat and drink, the woman wrote a few words on the dried fish, and told Gerda to take great care of it. Then she tied her again on the reindeer, and he set off at full speed. Flash, flash, went the beautiful blue northern lights in the air the whole night long. And at length they reached Finland, and knocked at the chimney of the Finland woman's hut, for it had no door above the ground. They crept in, but it was so terribly hot inside that that woman wore scarcely any clothes; she was small and very dirty looking. She loosened little Gerda's dress, and took off the fur boots and the mittens, or Gerda would have been unable to bear the heat; and then she placed a piece of ice on the reindeer's head, and read what was written on the dried fish. After she had read it three times, she knew it by heart, so she popped the fish into the soup saucepan, as she knew it was good to eat, and she never wasted anything. The reindeer told his own story first, and then little Gerda's, and the Finlander twinkled with her clever eyes, but she said nothing. "You are so clever," said the reindeer; "I know you can tie all the winds of the world with a piece of twine. If a sailor unties one knot, he has a fair wind; when he unties the second, it blows hard; but if the third and fourth are loosened, then comes a storm, which will root up whole forests. Cannot you give this little maiden something which will make her as strong as twelve men, to overcome the Snow Queen?"

"The power of twelve men!" said the Finland woman; "that would be of very little use." But she went to a shelf and took down and unrolled a large skin, on which were inscribed wonderful characters, and she read till the perspiration ran down from her forehead. But the reindeer begged so hard for little Gerda, and Gerda looked at the Finland woman with such beseeching tearful eyes, that her own eyes began to twinkle again; so she drew the reindeer into a corner, and whispered to him while she laid a fresh piece of ice on his head, "Little Kay is really with the Snow Queen, but he finds everything there so much to his taste and his liking, that he believes it is the finest place in the world; but this is because he has a piece of broken glass in his heart, and a

THE SNOW QUEEN

little piece of glass in his eye. These must be taken out, or he will never be a human being again, and the Snow Queen will retain her power over him."

"But can you not give little Gerda something to help her to conquer this power?"

"I can give her no greater power than she has already," said the woman; "don't you see how strong that is? How men and animals are obliged to serve her, and how well she has got through the world, barefooted as she is. She cannot receive any power from me greater than she now has, which consists in her own purity and innocence of heart. If she cannot herself obtain access to the Snow Queen, and remove the glass fragments from little Kay, we can do nothing to help her. Two miles from here the Snow Queen's garden begins; you can carry the little girl so far, and set her down by the large bush which stands in the snow, covered with red berries. Do not stay gossiping, but come back here as quickly as you can." Then the Finland woman lifted little Gerda upon the reindeer, and he ran away with her as quickly as he could.

"Oh, I have forgotten my boots and my mittens," cried little Gerda, as soon as she felt the cutting cold, but the reindeer dared not stop, so he ran on till he reached the bush with the red berries; here he set Gerda down, and he kissed her, and the great bright tears trickled over the animal's cheeks; then he left her and ran back as fast as he could.

There stood poor Gerda, without shoes, without gloves, in the midst of cold, dreary, ice-bound Finland. She ran forwards as quickly as she could, when a whole regiment of snow-flakes came round her; they did not, however, fall from the sky, which was quite clear and glittering with the northern lights. The snow-flakes ran along the ground, and the nearer they came to her, the larger they appeared. Gerda remembered how large and beautiful they looked through the burning-glass. But these were really larger, and much more terrible, for they were alive, and were the guards of the Snow Queen, and had the strangest shapes. Some were like great porcupines, others like twisted serpents with their heads stretching out, and some few were like little fat bears with their hair bristled; but all were dazzlingly white, and all were living snow-flakes. Then little Gerda repeated the Lord's Prayer, and the cold was so great that she could see her own breath come out of her mouth like steam as she uttered the words. The steam appeared to increase, as she continued her prayer, till it took the shape of little angels who grew larger the moment they touched the earth. They all wore helmets on their heads, and carried spears and shields. Their number continued to increase more and more; and by the time Gerda had finished her prayers, a whole legion stood round her. They thrust their spears into the terrible snow-flakes, so that they shivered into a hundred pieces, and little Gerda could go forward with courage and safety. The angels stroked her hands and feet, so that she felt the cold less, and she hastened on to the Snow Queen's castle.

But now we must see what Kay is doing. In truth he thought not of little Gerda, and never supposed she could be standing in the front of the palace.

SEVENTH STORY

OF THE PALACE OF THE SNOW QUEEN,
AND WHAT HAPPENED THERE AT LAST

The walls of the palace were formed of drifted snow, and the windows and doors of the cutting winds. There were more than a hundred rooms in it, all as if they had been formed with snow blown together. The largest of them extended for several miles; they were all lighted up by the vivid light of the aurora, and they were so large and empty, so icy cold and glittering! There were no amusements here, not even a little bear's ball, when the storm might have been the music, and the bears could have danced on their hind legs, and shown their good manners. There were no pleasant games of snap-dragon, or touch, or even a gossip over the tea-table, for the young-lady foxes. Empty, vast, and cold were the halls of the Snow Queen. The flickering flame of the northern lights could be plainly seen, whether they rose high or low in the heavens, from every part of the castle. In the midst of its empty, endless hall of snow was a frozen lake, broken on its surface into a thousand forms; each piece resembled another, from being in itself perfect as a work of art, and in the centre of this lake sat the Snow Queen, when she was at home. She called the lake "The Mirror of Reason," and said that it was the best, and indeed the only one in the world.

Little Kay was quite blue with cold, indeed almost black, but he did not feel it; for the Snow Queen had kissed away the icy shiverings, and his heart was already a lump of ice. He dragged some sharp, flat pieces of ice to and fro, and placed them together in all kinds of positions, as if he wished to make something out of them; just as we try to form various figures with little tablets of wood which we call "a Chinese puzzle." Kay's fingers were very artistic; it was the icy game of reason at which he played, and in his eyes the figures were very remarkable, and of the highest importance; this opinion was owing to the piece of glass still sticking in his eye. He composed many complete figures, forming different words, but there was one word he never could manage to form, although he wished it very much. It was the word "Eternity." The Snow Queen had said to him, "When you can find out this, you shall be your own master, and I will give you the whole world and a new pair of skates." But he could not accomplish it.

"Now I must hasten away to warmer countries," said the Snow Queen. "I will go and look into the black craters of the tops of the burning mountains, Etna and Vesuvius, as they are called, — I shall make them look white, which will be good for them, and for the lemons and the grapes." And away flew the Snow Queen, leaving little Kay quite alone in the great hall which was so many miles in length; so he sat and looked at his pieces of ice, and was thinking so deeply, and sat so still, that any one might have supposed he was frozen.

Just at this moment it happened that little Gerda came through the great door of the castle. Cutting winds were raging around her, but she offered up a prayer and the winds sank down as if they were going to sleep; and she went on till she came to the large empty hall, and caught sight of Kay; she knew him directly; she flew to him and threw her arms round his neck, and held him fast, while she exclaimed, "Kay, dear little Kay, I have found you at last."

But he sat quite still, stiff and cold.

Then little Gerda wept hot tears, which fell on his breast, and penetrated into his heart, and thawed the lump of ice, and washed away the little piece of glass which had stuck there. Then he looked at her, and she sang —

> "Roses bloom and cease to be,
> But we shall the Christ-child see."

Then Kay burst into tears, and he wept so that the splinter of glass swam out of his eye. Then he recognized Gerda, and said, joyfully, "Gerda, dear little Gerda, where have you been all this time, and where have I been?" And he looked all around him, and said, "How cold it is, and how large and empty it all looks," and he clung to Gerda, and she laughed and wept for joy. It was so pleasing to see them that the pieces of ice even danced about; and when they were tired and went to lie down, they formed themselves into the letters of the word which the Snow Queen had said he must find out before he could be his own master, and have the whole world and a pair of new skates. Then Gerda kissed his cheeks, and they became blooming; and she kissed his eyes, and they shone like her own; she kissed his hands and his feet, and then he became quite healthy and cheerful. The Snow Queen might come home now when she pleased, for there stood his certainty of freedom, in the word she wanted, written in shining letters of ice.

Then they took each other by the hand, and went forth from the great palace of ice. They spoke of the grandmother, and of the roses on the roof, and as they went on the winds were at rest, and the sun burst forth. When they arrived at the bush with red berries, there stood the reindeer waiting for them, and he had brought another young reindeer with him, whose udders were full, and the children drank her warm milk and kissed her on the mouth. Then they carried Kay and Gerda first to the Finland woman, where they warmed themselves thoroughly in the hot room, and she gave them directions about their journey home. Next they went to the Lapland woman, who had made some new clothes for them, and put their sleighs in order. Both the reindeer ran by their side, and followed them as far as the boundaries of the country, where the first green leaves were budding. And here they took leave of the two reindeer and the Lapland woman, and all said — Farewell. Then the birds began to twitter, and the forest too was full of green young leaves; and out of it came a beautiful horse, which Gerda remembered, for it was one which had drawn the golden coach. A young girl was riding upon it, with a shining red cap on her head, and pistols in her belt. It was the little robber-maiden, who had got tired of staying at home; she was going first to the north, and if that did not suit her, she meant to try some other part of the world. She knew Gerda directly, and Gerda remembered her: it was a joyful meeting.

"You are a fine fellow to go gadding about in this way," said she to little Kay, "I should like to know whether you deserve that any one should go to the end of the world to find you."

But Gerda patted her cheeks, and asked after the prince and princess.

"They are gone to foreign countries," said the robber-girl.

"And the crow?" asked Gerda.

"Oh, the crow is dead," she replied; "his tame sweetheart is now a widow, and wears a bit of black worsted round her leg. She mourns very pitifully, but it is all stuff. But now tell me how you managed to get him back."

Then Gerda and Kay told her all about it.

"Snip, snap, snare! it's all right at last," said the robber-girl.

Then she took both their hands, and promised that if ever she should pass through the town, she would call and pay them a visit. And then she rode away into the wide world. But Gerda and Kay went hand-in-hand towards home; and as they advanced, spring appeared more lovely with its green verdure and its beautiful flowers. Very soon they recognized the large town where they lived, and the tall steeples of the churches, in which the sweet bells were ringing a merry peal as they entered it, and found their way to their grandmother's door. They went upstairs into the little room, where all looked just as it used to do. The old clock was going "tick, tick," and the hands pointed to the time of day, but as they passed through the door into the room they perceived that they were both grown up, and become a man and woman. The roses out on the roof were in full bloom, and peeped in at the window; and there stood the little chairs, on which they had sat when children; and Kay and Gerda seated themselves each on their own chair, and held each other by the hand, while the cold empty grandeur of the Snow Queen's palace vanished from their memories like a painful dream. The grandmother sat in God's bright sunshine, and she read aloud from the Bible, "Except ye become as little children, ye shall in no wise enter into the kingdom of God." And Kay and Gerda looked into each other's eyes, and all at once understood the words of the old song,

> "Roses bloom and cease to be,
> But we shall the Christ-child see."

And they both sat there, grown up, yet children at heart; and it was summer, — warm, beautiful summer.

THE OLD HOUSE

A VERY old house stood once in a street with several that were quite new and clean. The date of its erection had been carved on one of the beams, and surrounded by scrolls formed of tulips and hop-tendrils; by this date it could be seen that the old house was nearly three hundred years old. Verses too were written over the windows in old-fashioned letters, and grotesque faces, curiously carved, grinned at you from under the cornices. One story projected a long way over the other, and under the roof ran a leaden gutter, with a dragon's head at the end. The rain was intended to pour out at the dragon's mouth, but it ran out of his body instead, for there was a hole in the gutter. The other houses in the street were new and well built, with large window panes and smooth walls. Any one could see they had nothing to do with the old house. Perhaps they thought, "How long will that heap of rubbish remain here to be a disgrace to the whole street. The parapet projects so far forward that no one can see out of our windows what is going on in that direction. The stairs are as broad as the staircase of a castle, and as steep as if they led to a church-tower. The iron railing looks like the gate of a cemetery, and there are brass knobs upon it. It is really too ridiculous."

Opposite to the old house were more nice new houses, which had just the same opinion as their neighbors.

At the window of one of them sat a little boy with fresh rosy cheeks, and clear sparkling eyes, who was very fond of the old house, in sunshine or in moonlight. He would sit and look at the wall from which the plaster had in some places fallen off, and fancy all sorts of scenes which had been in former times. How the street must have looked when the houses had all gable roofs, open staircases, and gutters with dragons at the spout. He could even see soldiers walking about with halberds. Certainly it was a very good house to look at for amusement.

An old man lived in it, who wore knee-breeches, a coat with large brass buttons, and a wig, which any one could see was a real wig. Every morning an old man came to clean the rooms, and to wait upon him, otherwise the old man in the knee-breeches would have been quite alone in the house. Sometimes he came to one of the windows and looked out; then the little boy nodded to him, and the old man nodded back again, till they became acquainted, and were friends, although they had never spoken to each other; but that was of no consequence.

The little boy one day heard his parents say, "The old man opposite is very well off, but is terribly lonely." The next Sunday morning the little boy wrapped something in a piece of paper and took it to the door of the old house, and said to the attendant who waited upon the old man, "Will you please give this from me to the gentleman who lives here; I have two tin soldiers, and this is one of them, and he shall have it, because I know he is terribly lonely."

And the old attendant nodded and looked very pleased, and then he carried the tin soldier into the house.

Afterwards he was sent over to ask the little boy if he would not like to pay a visit himself. His parents gave him permission, and so it was that he gained admission to the old house.

The brassy knobs on the railings shone more brightly than ever, as if they had been polished on account of his visit; and on the door were carved trumpeters standing in tulips, and it seemed as if they were blowing with all their might, their cheeks were so puffed out. "Tanta-ra-ra, the little boy is coming; Tanta-ra-ra, the little boy is coming."

Then the door opened. All round the hall hung old portraits of knights in armor, and ladies in silk gowns; and the armor rattled, and the silk dresses rustled. Then came a staircase which went up a long way, and then came down a little way and led to a balcony, which was in a very ruinous state. There were large holes and long cracks, out of which grew grass and leaves, indeed the whole balcony, the courtyard, and the walls were so overgrown with green that they looked like a garden. In the balcony stood flower-pots, on which were heads having asses' ears, but the flowers in them grew just as they pleased. In one pot pinks were growing all over the sides, at least the green leaves were shooting forth stalk and stem, and saying as plainly as they could speak, "The air has fanned me, the sun has kissed me, and I am promised a little flower for next Sunday — really for next Sunday."

Then they entered a room in which the walls were covered with leather, and the leather had golden flowers stamped upon it.

> "Gilding will fade in damp weather,
> To endure, there is nothing like leather,"

said the walls. Chairs handsomely carved, with elbows on each side, and with very high backs, stood in the room, and as they creaked they seemed to say, "Sit down. Oh dear, how I am creaking. I shall certainly have the gout like the old cupboard. Gout in my back, ugh."

And then the little boy entered the room where the old man sat.

"Thank you for the tin soldier my little friend," said the old man, "and thank you also for coming to see me."

"Thanks, thanks," or "Creak, creak," said all the furniture.

There was so much that the pieces of furniture stood in each other's way to get a sight of the little boy.

On the wall near the centre of the room hung the picture of a beautiful lady, young and gay, dressed in the fashion of the olden times, with powdered hair, and a full, stiff skirt. She said neither "thanks" nor "creak," but she looked down upon the little boy with her mild eyes; and then he said to the old man,

"Where did you get that picture?"

"From the shop opposite," he replied. "Many portraits hang there that none seem to trouble themselves about. The persons they represent have been dead and buried long since. But I knew this lady many years ago, and she has been dead nearly half a century."

Under a glass beneath the picture hung a nosegay of withered flowers, which were no doubt half a century old too, at least they appeared so.

And the pendulum of the old clock went to and fro, and the hands turned round; and as time passed on, everything in the room grew older, but no one seemed to notice it.

"They say at home," said the little boy, "that you are very lonely."

"Oh," replied the old man, "I have pleasant thoughts of all that has passed, recalled by memory; and now you are come to visit me, and that is very pleasant."

Then he took from the book-case, a book full of pictures representing long processions of wonderful coaches, such as are never seen at the present time. Soldiers like the knave of clubs, and citizens with waving banners. The tailors had a flag with a pair of scissors supported by two lions, and on the shoemakers' flag there were not boots, but an eagle with two heads, for the shoemakers must have everything arranged so that they can say, "This is a pair." What a picture-book it was; and then the old man went into another room to fetch apples and nuts. It was very pleasant, certainly, to be in that old house.

"I cannot endure it," said the tin soldier, who stood on a shelf, "it is so lonely and dull here. I have been accustomed to live in a family, and I cannot get used to this life. I cannot bear it. The whole day is long enough, but the evening is longer. It is not here like it was in your house opposite, when your father and mother talked so cheerfully together, while you and all the dear children made such a delightful noise. No, it is all lonely in the old man's house. Do you think he gets any kisses? Do you think he ever has friendly looks, or a Christmas tree? He will have nothing now but the grave. Oh, I cannot bear it."

"You must not look only on the sorrowful side," said the little boy; "I think everything in this house is beautiful, and all the old pleasant thoughts come back here to pay visits."

"Ah, but I never see any, and I don't know them," said the tin soldier, "and I cannot bear it."

"You must bear it," said the little boy. Then the old man came back with a pleasant face; and brought with him beautiful preserved fruits, as well as apples and nuts; and the little boy thought no more of the tin soldier. How happy and delighted the little boy was; and after he returned home, and while days and weeks passed, a great deal of nodding took place from one house to the other, and then the little boy went to pay another visit. The carved trumpeters blew "Tanta-ra-ra. There is the little boy. Tanta-ra-ra." The swords and armor on the old knight's pictures rattled. The silk dresses rustled, the leather repeated its rhyme, and the old chairs had the gout in their backs, and cried, "Creak;" it was all exactly like the first time; for in that house, one day and one hour were just like another. "I cannot bear it any longer," said the tin soldier; "I have wept tears of tin, it is so melancholy here. Let me go to the wars, and lose an arm or a leg, that would be some change; I cannot bear it. Now I know what it is to have visits from one's old recollections, and all they bring with them. I have had visits from mine, and you may believe me it is not altogether pleasant. I was very nearly jumping from the shelf. I saw you all in your house opposite, as if you were really present. It was Sunday morning, and you children stood round the table, singing the hymn that you sing every morning. You were standing quietly, with your hands folded, and your father and mother. You were standing quietly, with your hands folded, and your father and mother were looking just as serious, when the door opened, and your little sister Maria, who is not two years old, was brought into the room. You know she always dances when she hears music and singing of any sort; so she began to dance immediately, although she ought not to have done so, but she could not get into the right time because the tune was so slow; so she stood first on one leg and then on the other, and bent her head very low, but it would not suit the music. You all stood looking very grave, although it was very difficult to do so, but I laughed so to myself that I fell down from the table, and got a bruise, which is there still; I know it was not right to laugh. So all this, and everything else that I have seen, keeps running in my head, and these must be the old recollections that bring so many thoughts with them. Tell me whether you still sing on Sundays, and tell me about your little sister Maria, and how my old comrade is, the other tin soldier. Ah, really he must be very happy; I cannot endure this life."

"You are given away," said the little boy; "you must stay. Don't you see that?" Then the old man came in, with a box containing many curious things to show him. Rouge-pots, scent-boxes, and old cards, so large and so richly gilded, that none are ever seen like them in these days. And there were smaller boxes to look at, and the piano was opened, and inside the lid were painted landscapes. But when the old man played, the piano sounded quite out of tune. Then he looked at the picture he had bought at the broker's, and his eyes sparkled brightly as he nodded at it, and said, "Ah, she could sing that tune."

"I will go to the wars! I will go to the wars!" cried the tin soldier as loud as he could, and threw himself down on the floor. Where could he have fallen? The old man searched, and the little boy searched, but he was gone, and could not be found. "I shall find him again," said the old man, but he did not find him. The boards of the floor were open and full of holes. The tin soldier had fallen through a crack between the boards, and lay there now in an open grave. The day went by, and the little boy returned home; the week passed, and many more weeks. It was winter, and the windows were quite frozen, so the little boy was obliged to breathe on the panes, and rub a hole to peep through at the old house. Snow drifts were lying in all the scrolls and on the inscriptions, and the steps were covered with snow as if no one were at home. And indeed nobody was home, for the old man was dead. In the evening, a hearse stopped at the door, and the old man in his coffin was placed in it. He was to be taken to the country to be buried there in his own grave; so they carried him away; no one followed him, for all his friends were dead; and the little boy kissed his hand to the coffin as the hearse moved away with it. A few days after, there was an auction at the old house, and from his window the little boy saw the people carrying away the pictures of old knights and ladies, the flower-pots with the long ears, the old chairs, and the cup-boards. Some were taken one way, some another. *Her* portrait, which had been bought at the picture dealer's, went back again to his shop, and there it remained, for no one seemed to know her, or to care for the old picture. In the spring; they began to pull the house itself down; people called it complete rubbish. From the street could be seen the room in which the walls were covered with leather, ragged and torn, and the green in the balcony hung straggling over the beams; they pulled it down quickly, for it looked ready to fall, and at last it was cleared away altogether. "What a good riddance," said the neighbors' houses. Very shortly, a fine new house was built farther back from the road; it had lofty windows and smooth walls, but in front, on the spot where the old house really stood, a little garden was planted, and wild vines grew up over the neighboring walls; in front of the garden were large iron railings and a great gate, which looked very stately. People used to stop and peep through the railings. The sparrows assembled in dozens upon the wild vines, and chattered all together as loud as they could, but not about the old house; none of them could remember it, for many years had passed by, so many indeed, that the little boy was now a man, and a really good man too, and his parents were very proud of him. He was just married, and had come, with his young wife, to reside in the new house with the garden in front of it, and now he stood there by her side while she planted a field flower that she thought very pretty. She was planting it herself with her little hands, and pressing down the earth with her fingers. "Oh dear, what was that?" she exclaimed, as something pricked her. Out of the soft earth something was sticking up. It was—only think!—it was really the tin soldier, the very same which had been lost up in the old man's room, and had been hidden among old wood and rubbish for a long time, till it sunk into the earth, where it must have been for many years. And the young wife wiped the soldier, first with a green leaf, and then with her fine pocket-handkerchief, that smelt of such beautiful perfume. And the tin soldier felt as if he was recovering from a fainting fit. "Let me see him," said the young man, and then he smiled and shook his head, and said, "It can scarcely be the same, but it reminds me of something that happened to one of my tin soldiers when I was a little boy." And then he told his wife about the old house and the old man, and of the tin soldier which he had sent across, because he thought the old man was lonely; and he related the story so clearly that tears came into the eyes of the young wife for the old house and the old man. "It is very likely that this is really the same soldier," said she, "and I will take care of him, and always remember what you have told me; but some day you must show me the old man's grave."

"I don't know where it is," he replied; "no one knows. All his friends are dead; no one took care of him, and I was only a little boy."

"Oh, how dreadfully lonely he must have been," said she.

"Yes, terribly lonely," cried the tin soldier; "still it is delightful not to be forgotten."

"Delightful indeed," cried a voice quite near to them; no one but the tin soldier saw that it came from a rag of the leather which hung in tatters; it had lost all its gilding, and looked like wet earth, but it had an opinion, and it spoke it thus: —

> "Gilding will fade in damp weather,
> To endure, there is nothing like leather."

But the tin soldier did not believe any such thing.

THE HAPPY FAMILY

THE largest green leaf in this country is certainly the burdock-leaf. If you hold it in front of you, it is large enough for an apron; and if you hold it over your head, it is almost as good as an umbrella, it is so wonderfully large. A burdock never grows alone; where it grows, there are many more, and it is a splendid sight; and all this splendor is good for snails. The great white snails, which grand people in olden times used to have made into fricassees; and when they had eaten them, they would say, "O, what a delicious dish!" for these people really thought them good; and these snails lived on burdock-leaves, and for them the burdock was planted.

There was once an old estate where no one now lived to require snails; indeed, the owners had all died out, but the burdock still flourished; it grew over all the beds and walks of the garden—its growth had no check—till it became at last quite a forest of burdocks. Here and there stood an apple or a plum-tree; but for this, nobody would have thought the place had ever been a garden. It was burdock from one end to the other; and here lived the last two surviving snails. They knew not themselves how old they were; but they could remember the time when there were a great many more of them, and that they were descended from a family which came from foreign lands, and that the whole forest had been planted for them and theirs. They had never been away from the garden; but they knew that another place once existed in the world, called the Duke's Palace Castle, in which some of their relations had been boiled till they became black, and were then laid on a silver dish; but what was done afterwards they did not know. Besides, they could not imagine exactly how it felt to be boiled and placed on a silver dish; but no doubt it was something very fine and highly genteel. Neither the cockchafer, nor the toad, nor the earth-worm, whom they questioned about it, would give them the least information; for none of their relations had ever been cooked or served on a silver dish. The old white snails were the most aristocratic race in the world, — they knew that. The forest had been planted for them, and the nobleman's castle had been built entirely that they might be cooked and laid on silver dishes.

They lived quite retired and very happily; and as they had no children of their own, they had adopted a little common snail, which they brought up as their own child. The little one would not grow, for he was only a common snail; but the old people, particularly the mother-snail, declared that she could easily see how he grew; and when the father said he could not perceive it, she begged him to feel the little snail's shell, and he did so, and found that the mother was right.

One day it rained very fast. "Listen, what a drumming there is on the bur-dock-leaves; tum, tum, tum; tum, tum, tum," said the father-snail.

"There come the drops," said the mother; "they are trickling down the stalks. We shall have it very wet here presently. I am very glad we have such good houses, and that the little one has one of his own. There has been really more done for us than for any other creature; it is quite plain that we are the most noble people in the world. We have houses from our birth, and the bur-dock forest has been planted for us. I should very much like to know how far it extends, and what lies beyond it."

"There can be nothing better than we have here," said the father-snail; "I wish for nothing more."

"Yes, but I do," said the mother; "I should like to be taken to the palace, and boiled, and laid upon a silver dish, as was done to all our ancestors; and you may be sure it must be something very uncommon."

"The nobleman's castle, perhaps, has fallen to decay," said the snail-father, "or the burdock wood may have grown out. You need not be in a hurry; you are always so impatient, and the youngster is getting just the same. He has been three days creeping to the top of that stalk. I feel quite giddy when I look at him."

"You must not scold him," said the mother-snail; "he creeps so very carefully. He will be the joy of our home; and we old folks have nothing else to live for. But have you ever thought where we are to get a wife for him? Do you think that farther out in the wood there may be others of our race?"

"There may be black snails, no doubt," said the old snail; "black snails without houses; but they are so vulgar and conceited too. But we can give the ants a commission; they run here and there, as if they all had so much business to get through. They, most likely, will know of a wife for our youngster."

"I certainly know a most beautiful bride," said one of the ants; "but I fear it would not do, for she is a queen."

"That does not matter," said the old snail; "has she a house?"

"She has a palace," replied the ant, — "a most beautiful ant-palace with seven hundred passages."

"Thank-you," said the mother-snail; "but our boy shall not go to live in an ant-hill. If you know of nothing better, we will give the commission to the white gnats; they fly about in rain and sunshine; they know the burdock wood from one end to the other."

"We have a wife for him," said the gnats; "a hundred man-steps from here there is a little snail with a house, sitting on a gooseberry-bush; she is quite alone, and old enough to be married. It is only a hundred man-steps from here."

"Then let her come to him," said the old people. "He has the whole burdock forest; she has only a bush."

So they brought the little lady-snail. She took eight days to perform the journey; but that was just as it ought to be; for it showed her to be one of the right breeding. And then they had a wedding. Six glow-worms gave as much light as they could; but in other respects it was all very quiet; for the old snails could not bear festivities or a crowd. But a beautiful speech was made by the mother-snail. The father could not speak; he was too much overcome. Then they gave the whole burdock forest to the young snails as an inheritance, and repeated what they had so often said, that it was the finest place in the world, and that if they led upright and honorable lives, and their family increased, they and their children might some day be taken to the nobleman's palace, to be boiled black, and laid on a silver dish. And when they had finished speaking, the old couple crept into their houses, and came out no more; for they slept.

The young snail pair now ruled in the forest, and had a numerous progeny. But as the young ones were never boiled or laid in silver dishes, they concluded that the castle had fallen into decay, and that all the people in the world were dead; and as nobody contradicted them, they thought they must be right. And the rain fell upon the burdock-leaves, to play the drum for them, and the sun shone to paint colors on the burdock forest for them, and they were very happy; the whole family were entirely and perfectly happy.

THE ELF OF THE ROSE

IN the midst of a garden grew a rose-tree, in full blossom, and in the prettiest of all the roses lived an elf. He was such a little wee thing, that no human eye could see him. Behind each leaf of the rose he had a sleeping chamber. He was as well formed and as beautiful as a little child could be, and had wings that reached from his shoulders to his feet. Oh, what sweet fragrance there was in his chambers! and how clean and beautiful were the walls! for they were the blushing leaves of the rose.

During the whole day he enjoyed himself in the warm sunshine, flew from flower to flower, and danced on the wings of the flying butterflies. Then he took it into his head to measure how many steps he would have to go through the roads and cross-roads that are on the leaf of a linden-tree. What we call the veins on a leaf, he took for roads; ay, and very long roads they were for him; for before he had half finished his task, the sun went down: he had commenced his work too late. It became very cold, the dew fell, and the wind blew; so he thought the best thing he could do would be to return home. He hurried himself as much as he could; but he found the roses all closed up, and he could not get in; not a single rose stood open. The poor little elf was very much frightened. He had never before been out at night, but had always slumbered secretly behind the warm rose-leaves. Oh, this would certainly be his death. At the other end of the garden, he knew there was an arbor, overgrown with beautiful honey-suckles. The blossoms looked like large painted horns; and he thought to himself, he would go and sleep in one of these till the morning. He flew thither; but "hush!" two people were in the arbor, — a handsome young man and a beautiful lady. They sat side by side, and wished that they might never be obliged to part. They loved each other much more than the best child can love its father and mother.

"But we must part," said the young man; "your brother does not like our engagement, and therefore he sends me so far away on business, over mountains and seas. Farewell, my sweet bride; for so you are to me."

And then they kissed each other, and the girl wept, and gave him a rose; but before she did so, she pressed a kiss upon it so fervently that the flower opened. Then the little elf flew in, and leaned his head on the delicate, fragrant walls. Here he could plainly hear them say, "Farewell, farewell;" and he felt that the rose had been placed on the young man's breast. Oh, how his heart did beat! The little elf could not go to sleep, it thumped so loudly. The young man took it out as he walked through the dark wood alone, and kissed the flower so often and so violently, that the little elf was almost crushed. He could feel through the leaf how hot the lips of the young man were, and the rose had opened, as if from the heat of the noonday sun.

There came another man, who looked gloomy and wicked. He was the wicked brother of the beautiful maiden. He drew out a sharp knife, and while the other was kissing the rose, the wicked man stabbed him to death; then he cut off his head, and buried it with the body in the soft earth under the linden-tree.

"Now he is gone, and will soon be forgotten," thought the wicked brother; "he will never come back again. He was going on a long journey over mountains and seas; it is easy for a man to lose his life in such a journey. My sister will suppose he is dead; for he cannot come back, and she will not dare to question me about him."

Then he scattered the dry leaves over the light earth with his foot, and went home through the darkness; but he went not alone, as he thought, — the little elf accompanied him. He sat in a dry rolled-up linden-leaf, which had fallen from the tree on to the wicked man's head, as he was digging the grave. The hat was on the head now, which made it very dark, and the little elf shuddered with fright and indignation at the wicked deed.

It was the dawn of morning before the wicked man reached home; he took off his hat, and went into his sister's room. There lay the beautiful, blooming girl, dreaming of him whom she loved so, and who was now, she supposed, travelling far away over mountain and sea. Her wicked brother stopped over her, and laughed hideously, as fiends only can laugh. The dry leaf fell out of his hair upon the counterpane; but he did not notice it, and went to get a little sleep during the early morning hours. But the elf slipped out of the withered leaf, placed himself by the ear of the sleeping girl, and told her, as in a dream, of the horrid murder; described the place where her brother had slain her lover, and buried his body; and told her of the linden-tree, in full blossom, that stood close by.

"That you may not think this is only a dream that I have told you," he said, "you will find on your bed a withered leaf."

Then she awoke, and found it there. Oh, what bitter tears she shed! and she could not open her heart to any one for relief.

The window stood open the whole day, and the little elf could easily have reached the roses, or any of the flowers; but he could not find it in his heart to leave one so afflicted. In the window stood a bush bearing monthly roses. He seated himself in one of the flowers, and gazed on the poor girl. Her brother often came into the room, and would be quite cheerful, in spite of his base conduct; so she dare not say a word to him of her heart's grief.

As soon as night came on, she slipped out of the house, and went into the wood, to the spot where the linden-tree stood; and after removing the leaves from the earth, she turned it up, and there found him who had been murdered. Oh, how she wept and prayed that she also might die! Gladly would she have taken the body home with her; but that was impossible; so she took up the poor head with the closed eyes, kissed the cold lips, and shook the mould out of the beautiful hair.

"I will keep this," said she; and as soon as she had covered the body again with the earth and leaves, she took the head and a little sprig of jasmine that bloomed in the wood, near the spot where he was buried, and carried them home with her. As soon as she was in her room, she took the largest flower-pot she could find, and in this she placed the head of the dead man, covered it up with earth, and planted the twig of jasmine in it.

"Farewell, farewell," whispered the little elf. He could not any longer endure to witness all this agony of grief; he therefore flew away to his own rose in the garden. But the rose was faded; only a few dry leaves still clung to the green hedge behind it.

"Alas! how soon all that is good and beautiful passes away," sighed the elf.

After a while he found another rose, which became his home, for among its delicate fragrant leaves he could dwell in safety. Every morning he flew to the window of the poor girl, and always found her weeping by the flower pot. The bitter tears fell upon the jasmine twig, and each day, as she became paler and paler, the sprig appeared to grow greener and fresher. One shoot after another sprouted forth, and little white buds blossomed, which the poor girl fondly kissed. But her wicked brother scolded her, and asked her if she was going mad. He could not imagine why she was weeping over that flower-pot, and it annoyed him. He did not know whose closed eyes were there, nor what red lips were fading beneath the earth. And one day she sat and leaned her head against the flower-pot, and the little elf of the rose found her asleep. Then he seated himself by her ear, talked to her of that evening in the arbor, of the sweet perfume of the rose, and the loves of the elves. Sweetly she dreamed, and while she dreamt, her life passed away calmly and gently, and her spirit was with him whom she loved, in heaven. And the jasmine opened its large white bells, and spread forth its sweet fragrance; it had no other way of showing its grief for the dead. But the wicked brother considered the beautiful blooming plant as his own property, left to him by his sister, and he placed it in his sleeping room, close by his bed, for it was very lovely in appearance, and the fragrance sweet and delightful. The little elf of the rose followed it, and flew from flower to flower, telling each little spirit that dwelt in them the story of the murdered young man, whose head now formed part of the earth beneath them, and of the wicked brother and the poor sister. "We know it," said each little spirit in the flowers, "we know it, for have we not sprung from the eyes and lips of the murdered one. We know it, we know it," and the flowers nodded with their heads in a peculiar manner. The elf of the rose could not understand how they could rest so quietly in the matter, so he flew to the bees, who were gathering honey, and told them of the wicked brother. And the bees told it to their queen, who commanded that the next morning they should go and kill the murderer. But during the night, the first after the sister's death, while the brother was sleeping in his bed, close to where he had placed the fragrant jasmine, every flower cup opened, and invisibly the little spirits stole out, armed with poisonous spears. They placed themselves by the ear of the sleeper, told him dreadful dreams and then flew across his lips, and pricked his tongue with their poisoned spears. "Now have we revenged the dead," said they, and flew back into the white bells of the jasmine flowers. When the morning came, and as soon as the window was opened, the rose elf, with the queen bee, and the whole swarm of bees, rushed in to kill him. But he was already dead. People were standing round the bed, and saying that the scent of the jasmine had killed him. Then the elf of the rose understood the revenge of the flowers, and explained it to the queen bee, and she, with the whole swarm, buzzed about the flower-pot. The bees could not be driven away. Then a man took it up to remove it, and one of the bees stung him in the hand, so that he let the flower-pot fall, and it was broken to pieces. Then every one saw the whitened skull, and they knew the dead man in the bed was a murderer. And the queen bee hummed in the air, and sang of the revenge of the flowers, and of the elf of the rose, and said that behind the smallest leaf dwells *One,* who can discover evil deeds, and punish them also.

THE ANGEL

"WHENEVER a good child dies, an angel of God comes down from heaven, takes the dead child in his arms, spreads out his great white wings, and flies with him over all the places which the child had loved during his life. Then he gathers a large handful of flowers, which he carries up to the Almighty, that they may bloom more brightly in heaven than they do on earth. And the Almighty presses the flowers to His heart, but He kisses the flower that pleases Him best, and it receives a voice, and is able to join the song of the chorus of bliss."

These words were spoken by an angel of God, as he carried a dead child up to heaven, and the child listened as if in a dream. Then they passed over well-known spots, where the little one had often played, and through beautiful gardens full of lovely flowers.

"Which of these shall we take with us to heaven to be transplanted there?" asked the angel.

Close by grew a slender, beautiful, rose-bush, but some wicked hand had broken the stem, and the half-opened rosebuds hung faded and withered on the trailing branches.

"Poor rose-bush!" said the child, "let us take it with us to heaven, that it may bloom above in God's garden."

The angel took up the rose-bush; then he kissed the child, and the little one half opened his eyes. The angel gathered also some beautiful flowers, as well as a few humble buttercups and heart's-ease.

"Now we have flowers enough," said the child; but the angel only nodded, he did not fly upward to heaven.

It was night, and quite still in the great town. Here they remained, and the angel hovered over a small, narrow street, in which lay a large heap of straw, ashes, and sweepings from the houses of people who had removed. There lay fragments of plates, pieces of plaster, rags, old hats, and other rubbish not pleasant to see. Amidst all this confusion, the angel pointed to the pieces of a broken flower-pot, and to a lump of earth which had fallen out of it. The earth had been kept from falling to pieces by the roots of a withered field-flower, which had been thrown amongst the rubbish.

"We will take this with us," said the angel, "I will tell you why as we fly along."

And as they flew the angel related the history.

"Down in that narrow lane, in a low cellar, lived a poor sick boy; he had been afflicted from his childhood, and even in his best days he could just manage to walk up and down the room on crutches once or twice, but no more. During some days in summer, the sunbeams would lie on the floor of the cellar for about half an hour. In this spot the poor sick boy would sit warming himself in the sunshine, and watching the red blood through his delicate fingers as he held them before his face. Then he would say he had been out, yet he knew nothing of the green forest in its spring verdure, till a neighbor's son brought him a green bough from a beech-tree. This he would place over his head, and fancy that he was in the beech-wood while the sun shone, and the birds carolled gayly. One spring day the neighbor's boy brought him some field-flowers, and among them was one to which the root still adhered. This he carefully planted in a flower-pot, and placed in a window-seat near his bed. And the flower had been planted by a fortunate hand, for it grew, put forth fresh shoots, and blossomed every year. It became a splendid flower-garden to the sick boy, and his little treasure upon earth. He watered it, and cherished it, and took care it should have the benefit of every sunbeam that found its way into the cellar, from the earliest morning ray to the evening sunset. The flower entwined itself even in his dreams—for him it bloomed, for him spread its perfume. And it gladdened his eyes, and to the flower he turned, even in death, when the Lord called him. He has been one year with God. During that time the flower has stood in the window, withered and forgotten, till at length cast out among the sweepings into the street, on the day of the lodgers' removal. And this poor flower, withered and faded as it is, we have added to our nosegay, because it gave more real joy than the most beautiful flower in the garden of a queen."

"But how do you know all this?" asked the child whom the angel was carrying to heaven.

"I know it," said the angel, "because I myself was the poor sick boy who walked upon crutches, and I know my own flower well."

THE ANGEL

Then the child opened his eyes and looked into the glorious happy face of the angel, and at the same moment they found themselves in that heavenly home where all is happiness and joy. And God pressed the dead child to His heart, and wings were given him so that he could fly with the angel, hand in hand. Then the Almighty pressed all the flowers to His heart; but He kissed the withered field-flower, and it received a voice. Then it joined in the song of the angels, who surrounded the throne, some near, and others in a distant circle, but all equally happy. They all joined in the chorus of praise, both great and small,—the good, happy child, and the poor field-flower, that once lay withered and cast away on a heap of rubbish in a narrow, dark street.

THE STORY OF THE YEAR

IT was near the end of January, and a terrible fall of snow was pelting down, and whirling through the streets and lanes; the windows were plastered with snow on the outside, snow fell in masses from the roofs. Every one seemed in a great hurry; they ran, they flew, fell into each other's arms, holding fast for a moment as long as they could stand safely. Coaches and horses looked as if they had been frosted with sugar. The footmen stood with their backs against the carriages, so as to turn their faces from the wind. The foot passengers kept within the shelter of the carriages, which could only move slowly on in the deep snow. At last the storm abated, and a narrow path was swept clean in front of the houses; when two persons met in this path they stood still, for neither liked to take the first step on one side into the deep snow to let the other pass him. There they stood silent and motionless, till at last, as if by tacit consent, they each sacrificed a leg and buried it in the deep snow. Towards evening, the weather became calm. The sky, cleared from the snow, looked more lofty and transparent, while the stars shone with new brightness and purity. The frozen snow crackled under foot, and was quite firm enough to bear the sparrows, who hopped upon it in the morning dawn. They searched for food in the path which had been swept, but there was very little for them, and they were terribly cold. "Tweet, tweet," said one to another; "they call this a new year, but I think it is worse than the last. We might just as well have kept the old year; I'm quite unhappy, and I have a right to be so."

"Yes, you have; and yet the people ran about and fired off guns, to usher in the new year," said a little shivering sparrow. "They threw things against the doors, and were quite beside themselves with joy, because the old year had disappeared. I was glad too, for I expected we should have some warm days, but my hopes have come to nothing. It freezes harder than ever; I think mankind have made a mistake in reckoning time."

"That they have," said a third, an old sparrow with a white poll; "they have something they call a calendar; it's an invention of their own, and everything must be arranged according to it, but it won't do. When spring comes, then the year begins. It is the voice of nature, and I reckon by that."

"But when will spring come?" asked the others.

"It will come when the stork returns, but he is very uncertain, and here in the town no one knows anything about it. In the country they have more knowledge; shall we fly away there and wait? we shall be nearer to spring then, certainly."

"That may be all very well," said another sparrow, who had been hopping about for a long time, chirping, but not saying anything of consequence, "but I have found a few comforts here in town which, I'm afraid, I should miss out in the country. Here in this neighborhood, there lives a family of people who have been so sensible as to place three or four flower-pots against the wall in the court-yard, so that the openings are all turned inward, and the bottom of each points outward. In the latter a hole has been cut large enough for me to fly in and out. I and my husband have built a nest in one of these pots, and all our young ones, who have now flown away, were brought up there. The people who live there of course made the whole arrangement that they might have the pleasure of seeing us, or they would not have done it. It pleased them also to strew bread-crumbs for us, and so we have food, and may consider ourselves provided for. So I think my husband and I will stay where we are; although we are not very happy, but we shall stay."

"And we will fly into the country," said the others, "to see if spring is coming." And away they flew.

In the country it was really winter, a few degrees colder than in the town. The sharp winds blew over the snow-covered fields. The farmer, wrapped in warm clothing, sat in his sleigh, and beat his arms across his chest to keep off the cold. The whip lay on his lap. The horses ran till they smoked. The snow crackled, the sparrows hopped about in the wheel-ruts, and shivered, crying, "Tweet, tweet; when will spring come? It is very long in coming."

"Very long indeed," sounded over the field, from the nearest snow-covered hill. It might have been the echo which people heard, or perhaps the words of that wonderful old man, who sat high on a heap of snow, regardless of wind or weather. He was all in white; he had on a peasant's coarse white coat of frieze. He had long white hair, a pale face, and large clear blue eyes. "Who is that old man?" asked the sparrows.

"I know who he is," said an old raven, who sat on the fence, and was condescending enough to acknowledge that we are all equal in the sight of Heaven, even as little birds, and therefore he talked with the sparrows, and gave them the information they wanted. "I know who the old man is," he said. "It is Winter, the old man of last year; he is not dead yet, as the calendar says, but acts as guardian to little Prince Spring who is coming. Winter rules here still. Ugh! the cold makes you shiver, little ones, does it not?"

"There! Did I not tell you so?" said the smallest of the sparrows. "The calendar is only an invention of man, and is not arranged according to nature. They should leave these things to us; we are created so much more clever than they are."

One week passed, and then another. The forest looked dark, the hard-frozen lake lay like a sheet of lead. The mountains had disappeared, for over the land hung damp, icy mists. Large black crows flew about in silence; it was as if nature slept. At length a sunbeam glided over the lake, and it shone like burnished silver. But the snow on the fields and the hills did not glitter as before. The white form of Winter sat there still, with his unwandering gaze fixed on the south. He did not perceive that the snowy carpet seemed to sink as it were into the earth; that here and there a little green patch of grass appeared, and that these patches were covered with sparrows.

"Tee-wit, tee-wit; is spring coming at last?"

Spring! How the cry resounded over field and meadow, and through the dark-brown woods, where the fresh green moss still gleamed on the trunks of the trees, and from the south came the two first storks flying through the air, and on the back of each sat a lovely little child, a boy and a girl. They greeted the earth with a kiss, and wherever they placed their feet white flowers sprung up from beneath the snow. Hand in hand they approached the old ice-man, Winter, embraced him and clung to his breast; and as they did so, in a moment all three were enveloped in a thick, damp mist, dark and heavy, that closed over them like a veil. The wind arose with mighty rustling tone, and cleared away the mist. Then the sun shone out warmly. Winter had vanished away, and the beautiful children of Spring sat on the throne of the year.

"This is really a new year," cried all the sparrows, "now we shall get our rights, and have some return for what we suffered in winter."

Wherever the two children wandered, green buds burst forth on bush and tree, the grass grew higher, and the corn-fields became lovely in delicate green.

The little maiden strewed flowers in her path. She held her apron before her: it was full of flowers; it was as if they sprung into life there, for the more she scattered around her, the more flowers did her apron contain. Eagerly she showered snowy blossoms over apple and peach-trees, so that they stood in full beauty before even their green leaves had burst from the bud. Then the boy and the girl clapped their hands, and troops of birds came flying by, no one knew from whence, and they all twittered and chirped, singing "Spring has come!" How beautiful everything was! Many an old dame came forth from her door into the sunshine, and shuffled about with great delight, glancing at the golden flowers which glittered everywhere in the fields, as they used to do in her young days. The world grew young again to her, as she said, "It is a blessed time out here to-day." The forest already wore its dress of dark-green buds. The thyme blossomed in fresh fragrance. Primroses and anemones sprung forth, and violets bloomed in the shade, while every blade of grass was full of strength and sap. Who could resist sitting down on such a beautiful carpet? and then the young children of Spring seated themselves, holding each other's hands, and sang, and laughed, and grew. A gentle rain fell upon them from the sky, but they did not notice it, for the rain-drops were their own tears of joy. They kissed each other, and were betrothed; and in the same moment the buds of the trees unfolded, and when the sun rose, the forest was green. Hand in hand the two wandered beneath the fresh pendant canopy of foliage, while the sun's rays gleamed through the opening of the shade, in changing and varied colors. The delicate young leaves filled the air with refreshing odor. Merrily rippled the clear brooks and rivulets between the green, velvety rushes, and over the many-colored pebbles beneath. All nature spoke of abundance and plenty. The cuckoo sang, and the lark carolled, for it was now beautiful spring. The careful willows had, however, covered their blossoms with woolly gloves; and this carefulness is rather tedious. Days and weeks went by, and the heat increased. Warm air waved the corn as it grew golden in the sun. The white northern lily spread its large green leaves over the glossy mirror of the woodland lake, and the fishes sought the shadows beneath them. In a sheltered part of the wood, the sun shone upon the walls of a farm-house, brightening the blooming roses, and ripening the black juicy berries, which hung on the loaded cherry-trees, with his hot beams. Here sat the lovely wife of Summer, the same whom we have seen as a child and a bride; her eyes were fixed on dark gathering clouds, which in wavy outlines of black and indigo were piling themselves up like mountains, higher and higher. They came from every side, always increasing like a rising, rolling sea. Then they swooped towards the forest, where every sound had been silenced as if by magic, every breath hushed, every bird mute. All nature stood still in grave suspense. But in the lanes and the highways, passengers on foot or in carriages were hurrying to find a place of shelter. Then came a flash of light, as if the sun had rushed forth from the sky, flaming, burning, all-devouring, and darkness returned amid a rolling crash of thunder. The rain poured down in streams, — now there was darkness, then blinding light, — now thrilling silence, then deafening din. The young brown reeds on the moor waved to and fro in feathery billows; the forest boughs were hidden in a watery mist, and still light and darkness followed each other, still came the silence after the roar, while the corn and the blades of grass lay beaten down and swamped, so that it seemed impossible they could ever raise themselves again. But after a while the rain began to fall gently, the sun's rays pierced the clouds, and the water-drops glittered like pearls on leaf and stem. The birds sang, the fishes leaped up to the surface of the water, the gnats danced in the sunshine, and yonder, on a rock by the heaving salt sea, sat Summer himself, a strong man with sturdy limbs and long, dripping hair. Strengthened by the cool bath, he sat in the warm sunshine, while all around him renewed nature bloomed strong, luxuriant, and beautiful: it was summer, warm, lovely summer. Sweet and pleasant was the fragrance wafted from the clover-field, where the bees swarmed round the ruined tower, the bramble twined itself over the old altar, which, washed by the rain, glittered in the sunshine; and thither flew the queen bee with her swarm, and prepared wax and honey. But Summer and his bosom-wife saw it with different eyes, to them the altar-table was covered with the offerings of nature. The evening sky shone like gold, no church dome could ever gleam so brightly, and between the golden evening and the blushing morning there was moonlight. It was indeed summer. And days and weeks passed, the bright scythes of the reapers glittered in the corn-fields, the branches of the apple-trees bent low, heavy with the red and golden fruit. The hop, hanging in clusters, filled the air with sweet fragrance, and beneath the hazel-bushes, where the nuts hung in great bunches, rested a man and a woman — Summer and his grave consort.

"See," she exclaimed, "what wealth, what blessings surround us. Everything is home-like and good, and yet, I know not why, I long for rest and peace; I can scarcely express what I feel. They are already ploughing the fields again; more and more the people wish for gain. See, the storks are flocking together, and following the plough at a short distance. They are the birds from Egypt, who carried us through the air. Do you remember how we came as children to this land of the north; we brought with us flowers and bright sunshine, and green to the forests, but the wind has been rough with them, and they are now become dark and brown, like the trees of the south, but they do not, like them, bear golden fruit."

"Do you wish to see golden fruit?" said the man, "then rejoice," and he lifted his arm. The leaves of the forest put on colors of red and gold, and bright tints covered the woodlands. The rose-bushes gleamed with scarlet hips, and the branches of the elder-trees hung down with the weight of the full, dark berries. The wild chestnuts fell ripe from their dark, green shells, and in the forests the violets bloomed for the second time. But the queen of the year became more and more silent and pale.

"It blows cold," she said, "and night brings the damp mist; I long for the land of my childhood." Then she saw the storks fly away every one, and she stretched out her hands towards them. She looked at the empty nests; in one of them grew a long-stalked corn flower, in another the yellow mustard seed, as if the nest had been placed there only for its comfort and protection, and the sparrows were flying round them all.

"Tweet, where has the master of the nest gone?" cried one, "I suppose he could not bear it when the wind blew, and therefore he has left this country. I wish him a pleasant journey."

The forest leaves became more and more yellow, leaf after leaf fell, and the stormy winds of Autumn howled. The year was now far advanced, and upon the fallen, yellow leaves, lay the queen of the year, looking up with mild eyes at a gleaming star, and her husband stood by her. A gust of wind swept through the foliage, and the leaves fell in a shower. The summer queen was gone, but a butterfly, the last of the year, flew through the cold air. Damp fogs came, icy winds blew, and the long, dark nights of winter approached. The ruler of the year appeared with hair white as snow, but he knew it not; he thought snow-flakes falling from the sky covered his head, as they decked the green fields with a thin, white covering of snow. And then the church bells rang out for Christmas time.

"The bells are ringing for the new-born year," said the ruler, "soon will a new ruler and his bride be born, and I shall go to rest with my wife in yonder light-giving star."

In the fresh, green fir-wood, where the snow lay all around, stood the angel of Christmas, and consecrated the young trees that were to adorn his feast.

"May there be joy in the rooms, and under the green boughs," said the old ruler of the year. In a few weeks he had become a very old man, with hair as white as snow. "My resting-time draws near; the young pair of the year will soon claim my crown and sceptre."

"But the night is still thine," said the angel of Christmas, "for power, but not for rest. Let the snow lie warmly upon the tender seed. Learn to endure the thought that another is worshipped whilst thou art still lord. Learn to endure being forgotten while yet thou livest. The hour of thy freedom will come when Spring appears."

"And when will Spring come?" asked Winter.

"It will come when the stork returns."

And with white locks and snowy beard, cold, bent, and hoary, but strong as the wintry storm, and firm as the ice, old Winter sat on the snowdrift-covered hill, looking towards the south, where Winter had sat before, and gazed. The ice glittered, the snow crackled, the skaters skimmed over the polished surface of the lakes; ravens and crows formed a pleasing contrast to the white ground, and not a breath of wind stirred, and in the still air old Winter clenched his fists, and the ice lay fathoms deep between the lands. Then came the sparrows again out of the town, and asked, "Who is that old man?" The raven sat there still, or it might be his son, which is the same thing, and he said to them, —

"It is Winter, the old man of the former year; he is not dead, as the calendar says, but he is guardian to the spring, which is coming."

"When will Spring come?" asked the sparrows, "for we shall have better times then, and a better rule. The old times are worth nothing."

And in quiet thought old Winter looked at the leafless forest, where the graceful form and bends of each tree and branch could be seen; and while Winter slept, icy mists came from the clouds, and the ruler dreamt of his youthful days and of his manhood, and in the morning dawn the whole forest glittered with hoar frost, which the sun shook from the branches, — and this was the summer dream of Winter.

"When will Spring come?" asked the sparrows. "Spring!" Again the echo sounded from the hills on which the snow lay. The sunshine became warmer, the snow melted, and the birds twittered, "Spring is coming!" And high in the air flew the first stork, and the second followed; a lovely child sat on the back of each, and they sank down on the open field, kissed the earth, and kissed the quiet old man; and, as the mist from the mountain top, he vanished away and disappeared. And the story of the year was finished.

"This is all very fine, no doubt," said the sparrows, "and it is very beautiful, but it is not according to the calendar, therefore, it must be all wrong."

THE CONCEITED APPLE-BRANCH

IT was the month of May. The wind still blew cold; but from bush and tree, field and flower, came the welcome sound, "Spring is come." Wildflowers in profusion covered the hedges. Under the little apple-tree, Spring seemed busy, and told his tale from one of the branches which hung fresh and blooming, and covered with delicate pink blossoms that were just ready to open. The branch well knew how beautiful it was; this knowledge exists as much in the leaf as in the blood; I was therefore not surprised when a nobleman's carriage, in which sat the young countess, stopped in the road just by. She said that an apple-branch was a most lovely object, and an emblem of spring in its most charming aspect. Then the branch was broken off for her, and she held it in her delicate hand, and sheltered it with her silk parasol. Then they drove to the castle, in which were lofty halls and splendid drawing-rooms. Pure white curtains fluttered before the open windows, and beautiful flowers stood in shining, transparent vases; and in one of them, which looked as if it had been cut out of newly fallen snow, the apple-branch was placed, among some fresh, light twigs of beech. It was a charming sight. Then the branch became proud, which was very much like human nature.

People of every description entered the room, and, according to their position in society, so dared they to express their admiration. Some few said nothing, others expressed too much, and the apple-branch very soon got to understand that there was as much difference in the characters of human beings as in those of plants and flowers. Some are all for pomp and parade, others have a great deal to do to maintain their own importance, while the rest might be spared without much loss to society. So thought the apple-branch, as he stood before the open window, from which he could see out over gardens and fields, where there were flowers and plants enough for him to think and reflect upon; some rich and beautiful, some poor and humble indeed.

"Poor, despised herbs," said the apple-branch; "there is really a difference between them and such as I am. How unhappy they must be, if they can feel as those in my position do! There is a difference indeed, and so there ought to be, or we should all be equals."

And the apple-branch looked with a sort of pity upon them, especially on a certain little flower that is found in fields and in ditches. No one bound these flowers together in a nosegay; they were too common; they were even known to grow between the paving-stones, shooting up everywhere, like bad weeds; and they bore the very ugly name of "dog-flowers" or "dandelions."

"Poor, despised plants," said the apple-bough, "it is not your fault that you are so ugly, and that you have such an ugly name; but it is with plants as with men, —there must be a difference."

"A difference!" cried the sunbeam, as he kissed the blooming apple-branch, and then kissed the yellow dandelion out in the fields. All were brothers, and the sunbeam kissed them—the poor flowers as well as the rich.

The apple-bough had never thought of the boundless love of God, which extends over all the works of creation, over everything which lives, and moves, and has its being in Him; he had never thought of the good and beautiful which are so often hidden, but can never remain forgotten by Him, —not only among the lower creation, but also among men. The sunbeam, the ray of light, knew better.

"You do not see very far, nor very clearly," he said to the apple-branch. "Which is the despised plant you so specially pity?"

"The dandelion," he replied. "No one ever places it in a nosegay; it is often trodden under foot, there are so many of them; and when they run to seed, they have flowers like wool, which fly away in little pieces over the roads, and cling to the dresses of the people. They are only weeds; but of course there must be weeds. O, I am really very thankful that I was not made like one of these flowers."

There came presently across the fields a whole group of children, the youngest of whom was so small that it had to be carried by the others; and when he was seated on the grass, among the yellow flowers, he laughed aloud with joy, kicked out his little legs, rolled about, plucked the yellow flowers, and kissed them in childlike innocence. The elder children broke off the flowers with long stems, bent the stalks one round the other, to form links, and made first a chain for the neck, then one to go across the shoulders, and hang down to the waist, and at last a wreath to wear round the head, so that they looked quite splendid in their garlands of green stems and golden flowers. But the eldest among them gathered carefully the faded flowers, on the stem of which was grouped together the seed, in the form of a white feathery coronal. These loose, airy wool-flowers are very beautiful, and look like fine snowy feathers or down. The children held them to their mouths, and tried to blow away the whole coronal with one puff of the breath. They had been told by their grandmothers that who ever did so would be sure to have new clothes before the end of the year. The despised flower was by this raised to the position of a prophet or foreteller of events.

"Do you see," said the sunbeam, "do you see the beauty of these flowers? do you see their powers of giving pleasure?"

"Yes, to children," said the apple-bough.

By-and-by an old woman came into the field, and, with a blunt knife without a handle, began to dig round the roots of some of the dandelion-plants, and pull them up. With some of these she intended to make tea for herself; but the rest she was going to sell to the chemist, and obtain some money.

"But beauty is of higher value than all this," said the apple-tree branch; "only the chosen ones can be admitted into the realms of the beautiful. There is a difference between plants, just as there is a difference between men."

Then the sunbeam spoke of the boundless love of God, as seen in creation, and over all that lives, and of the equal distribution of His gifts, both in time and in eternity.

"That is your opinion," said the apple-bough.

Then some people came into the room, and, among them, the young countess, — the lady who had placed the apple-bough in the transparent vase, so pleasantly beneath the rays of the sunlight. She carried in her hand something that seemed like a flower. The object was hidden by two or three great leaves, which covered it like a shield, so that no draught or gust of wind could injure it, and it was carried more carefully than the apple-branch had ever been. Very cautiously the large leaves were removed, and there appeared the feathery seed-crown of the despised dandelion. This was what the lady had so carefully plucked, and carried home so safely covered, so that not one of the delicate feathery arrows of which its mist-like shape was so lightly formed, should flutter away. She now drew it forth quite uninjured, and wondered at its beautiful form, and airy lightness, and singular construction, so soon to be blown away by the wind.

"See," she exclaimed, "how wonderfully God has made this little flower. I will paint it with the apple-branch together. Every one admires the beauty of the apple-bough; but this humble flower has been endowed by Heaven with another kind of loveliness; and although they differ in appearance, both are the children of the realms of beauty."

Then the sunbeam kissed the lowly flower, and he kissed the blooming apple-branch, upon whose leaves appeared a rosy blush.

THE PEA BLOSSOM

THERE were once five peas in one shell, they were green, the shell was green, and so they believed that the whole world must be green also, which was a very natural conclusion. The shell grew, and the peas grew, they accommodated themselves to their position, and sat all in a row. The sun shone without and warmed the shell, and the rain made it clear and transparent; it was mild and agreeable in broad daylight, and dark at night, as it generally is; and the peas as they sat there grew bigger and bigger, and more thoughtful as they mused, for they felt there must be something else for them to do.

"Are we to sit here forever?" asked one; "shall we not become hard by sitting so long? It seems to me there must be something outside, and I feel sure of it."

And as weeks passed by, the peas became yellow, and the shell became yellow.

"All the world is turning yellow, I suppose," said they, — and perhaps they were right.

Suddenly they felt a pull at the shell; it was torn off, and held in human hands, then slipped into the pocket of a jacket in company with other full pods.

"Now we shall soon be opened," said one, — just what they all wanted.

"I should like to know which of us will travel furthest," said the smallest of the five; "we shall soon see now."

"What is to happen will happen," said the largest pea.

"Crack" went the shell as it burst, and the five peas rolled out into the bright sunshine. There they lay in a child's hand. A little boy was holding them tightly, and said they were fine peas for his pea-shooter. And immediately he put one in and shot it out.

"Now I am flying out into the wide world," said he; "catch me if you can;" and he was gone in a moment.

"I," said the second, "intend to fly straight to the sun, that is a shell that lets itself be seen, and it will suit me exactly;" and away he went.

"We will go to sleep wherever we find ourselves," said the two next, "we shall still be rolling onwards;" and they did certainly fall on the floor, and roll about before they got into the pea-shooter; but they were put in for all that. "We shall go farther than the others," said they.

"What is to happen will happen," exclaimed the last, as he was shot out of the pea-shooter; and as he spoke he flew up against an old board under a garret-window, and fell into a little crevice, which was almost filled up with moss and soft earth. The moss closed itself round him, and there he lay, a captive indeed, but not unnoticed by God.

"What is to happen will happen," said he to himself.

Within the little garret lived a poor woman, who went out to clean stoves, chop wood into small pieces and perform such-like hard work, for she was strong and industrious. Yet she remained always poor, and at home in the garret lay her only daughter, not quite grown up, and very delicate and weak. For a whole year she had kept her bed, and it seemed as if she could neither live nor die.

"She is going to her little sister," said the woman; "I had but the two children, and it was not an easy thing to support both of them; but the good God helped me in my work, and took one of them to Himself and provided for her. Now I would gladly keep the other that was left to me, but I suppose they are not to be separated, and my sick girl will very soon go to her sister above." But the sick girl still remained where she was, quietly and patiently she lay all the day long, while her mother was away from home at her work.

Spring came, and one morning early the sun shone brightly through the little window, and threw its rays over the floor of the room. Just as the mother was going to her work, the sick girl fixed her gaze on the lowest pane of the window—"Mother," she exclaimed, "what can that little green thing be that peeps in at the window? It is moving in the wind."

The mother stepped to the window and half opened it. "Oh!" she said, "there is actually a little pea which has taken root and is putting out its green leaves. How could it have got into this crack? Well now, here is a little garden for you to amuse yourself with." So the bed of the sick girl was drawn nearer to the window, that she might see the budding plant; and the mother went out to her work.

"Mother, I believe I shall get well," said the sick child in the evening, "the sun has shone in here so brightly and warmly to-day, and the little pea is thriving so well: I shall get on better, too, and go out into the warm sunshine again."

"God grant it!" said the mother, but she did not believe it would be so. But she propped up with the little stick the green plant which had given her child such pleasant hopes of life, so that it might not be broken by the winds; she tied the piece of string to the window-sill and to the upper part of the frame, so that the pea-tendrils might twine round it when it shot up. And it did shoot up, indeed it might almost be seen to grow from day to day.

"Now really here is a flower coming," said the old woman one morning, and now at last she began to encourage the hope that her sick daughter might really recover. She remembered that for some time the child had spoken more cheerfully, and during the last few days had raised herself in bed in the morning to look with sparkling eyes at her little garden which contained only a single pea-plant. A week after, the invalid sat up for the first time a whole hour, feeling quite happy by the open window in the warm sunshine, while outside grew the little plant, and on it a pink pea-blossom in full bloom. The little maiden bent down and gently kissed the delicate leaves. This day was to her like a festival.

"Our heavenly Father Himself has planted that pea, and made it grow and flourish, to bring joy to you and hope to me, my blessed child," said the happy mother, and she smiled at the flower, as if it had been an angel from God.

But what became of the other peas? Why the one who flew out into the wide world, and said, "Catch me if you can," fell into a gutter on the roof of a house, and ended his travels in the crop of a pigeon. The two lazy ones were carried quite as far, for they also were eaten by pigeons, so they were at least of some use; but the fourth, who wanted to reach the sun, fell into a sink and lay there in the dirty water for days and weeks, till he had swelled to a great size.

"I am getting beautifully fat," said the pea, "I expect I shall burst at last; no pea could do more that that, I think; I am the most remarkable of all the five which were in the shell." And the sink confirmed the opinion.

But the young maiden stood at the open garret window, with sparkling eyes and the rosy hue of health on her cheeks, she folded her thin hands over the pea-blossom, and thanked God for what He had done.

"I," said the sink, "shall stand up for *my* pea."

THE BEETLE WHO WENT
ON HIS TRAVELS

THERE was once an Emperor who had a horse shod with gold. He had a golden shoe on each foot, and why was this? He was a beautiful creature, with slender legs, bright, intelligent eyes, and a mane that hung down over his neck like a veil. He had carried his master through fire and smoke in the battle-field, with the bullets whistling round him; he had kicked and bitten, and taken part in the fight, when the enemy advanced; and, with his master on his back, he had dashed over the fallen foe, and saved the golden crown and the Emperor's life, which was of more value than the brightest gold. This is the reason of the Emperor's horse wearing golden shoes.

A beetle came creeping forth from the stable, where the farrier had been shoeing the horse. "Great ones, first, of course," said he, "and then the little ones; but size is not always a proof of greatness." He stretched out his thin leg as he spoke.

"And pray what do you want?" asked the farrier.

"Golden shoes," replied the beetle.

"Why, you must be out of your senses," cried the farrier. "Golden shoes for you, indeed!"

"Yes, certainly; golden shoes," replied the beetle. "Am I not just as good as that great creature yonder, who is waited upon and brushed, and has food and drink placed before him? And don't I belong to the royal stables?"

"But why does the horse have golden shoes?" asked the farrier; "of course you understand the reason?"

"Understand! Well, I understand that it is a personal slight to me," cried the beetle. "It is done to annoy me, so I intend to go out into the world and seek my fortune."

"Go along with you," said the farrier.

"You're a rude fellow," cried the beetle, as he walked out of the stable; and then he flew for a short distance, till he found himself in a beautiful flower-garden, all fragrant with roses and lavender. The lady-birds, with red and black shells on their backs, and delicate wings, were flying about, and one of them said, "Is it not sweet and lovely here? Oh, how beautiful everything is."

"I am accustomed to better things," said the beetle. "Do you call this beautiful? Why, there is not even a dung-heap." Then he went on, and under the shadow of a large haystack he found a caterpillar crawling along. "How beautiful this world is!" said the caterpillar. "The sun is so warm, I quite enjoy it. And soon I shall go to sleep, and die as they call it, but I shall wake up with beautiful wings to fly with, like a butterfly."

"How conceited you are!" exclaimed the beetle. "Fly about as a butterfly, indeed! what of that. I have come out of the Emperor's stable, and no one there, not even the Emperor's horse, who, in fact, wears my cast-off golden shoes, has any idea of flying, excepting myself. To have wings and fly! why, I can do that already;" and so saying, he spread his wings and flew away. "I don't want to be disgusted," he said to himself, "and yet I can't help it." Soon after, he fell down upon an extensive lawn, and for a time pretended to sleep, but at last fell asleep in earnest. Suddenly a heavy shower of rain came falling from the clouds. The beetle woke up with the noise and would have been glad to creep into the earth for shelter, but he could not. He was tumbled over and over with the rain, sometimes swimming on his stomach and sometimes on his back; and as for flying, that was out of the question. He began to doubt whether he should escape with his life, so he remained, quietly lying where he was. After a while the weather cleared up a little, and the beetle was able to rub the water from his eyes, and look about him. He saw something gleaming, and he managed to make his way up to it. It was linen which had been laid to bleach on the grass. He crept into a fold of the damp linen, which certainly was not so comfortable a place to lie in as the warm stable, but there was nothing better, so he remained lying there for a whole day and night, and the rain kept on all the time. Towards morning he crept out of his hiding-place, feeling in a very bad temper with the climate. Two frogs were sitting on the linen, and their bright eyes actually glistened with pleasure.

"Wonderful weather this," cried one of them, "and so refreshing. This linen holds the water together so beautifully, that my hind legs quiver as if I were going to swim."

"I should like to know," said another, "If the swallow who flies so far in her many journeys to foreign lands, ever met with a better climate than this. What delicious moisture! It is as pleasant as lying in a wet ditch. I am sure any one who does not enjoy this has no love for his fatherland."

"Have you ever been in the Emperor's stable?" asked the beetle. "There the moisture is warm and refreshing; that's the climate for me, but I could not take it with me on my travels. Is there not even a dunghill here in this garden, where a person of rank, like myself, could take up his abode and feel at home?" But the frogs either did not or would not understand him.

"I never ask a question twice," said the beetle, after he had asked this one three times, and received no answer. Then he went on a little farther and stumbled against a piece of broken crockery-ware, which certainly ought not to have been lying there. But as it was there, it formed a good shelter against wind and weather to several families of earwigs who dwelt in it. Their requirements were not many, they were very sociable, and full of affection for their children, so much so that each mother considered her own child the most beautiful and clever of them all.

"Our dear son has engaged himself," said one mother, "dear innocent boy; his greatest ambition is that he may one day creep into a clergyman's ear. That is a very artless and loveable wish; and being engaged will keep him steady. What happiness for a mother!"

"Our son," said another, "had scarcely crept out of the egg, when he was off on his travels. He is all life and spirits, I expect he will wear out his horns with running. How charming this is for a mother, is it not Mr. Beetle?" for she knew the stranger by his horny coat.

"You are both quite right," said he; so they begged him to walk in, that is to come as far as he could under the broken piece of earthenware.

"Now you shall also see my little earwigs," said a third and a fourth mother, "they are lovely little things, and highly amusing. They are never ill-behaved, except when they are uncomfortable in their inside, which unfortunately often happens at their age."

Thus each mother spoke of her baby, and their babies talked after their own fashion, and made use of the little nippers they have in their tails to nip the beard of the beetle.

"They are always busy about something, the little rogues," said the mother, beaming with maternal pride; but the beetle felt it a bore, and he therefore inquired the way to the nearest dung-heap.

"That is quite out in the great world, on the other side of the ditch," answered an earwig, "I hope none of my children will ever go so far, it would be the death of me."

"But I shall try to get so far," said the beetle, and he walked off without taking any formal leave, which is considered a polite thing to do.

When he arrived at the ditch, he met several friends, all them beetles; "We live here," they said, "and we are very comfortable. May we ask you to step down into this rich mud, you must be fatigued after your journey."

"Certainly," said the beetle, "I shall be most happy; I have been exposed to the rain, and have had to lie upon linen, and cleanliness is a thing that greatly exhausts me; I have also pains in one of my wings from standing in the draught under a piece of broken crockery. It is really quite refreshing to be with one's own kindred again."

"Perhaps you came from a dung-heap," observed the oldest of them.

"No, indeed, I came from a much grander place," replied the beetle; "I came from the emperor's stable, where I was born, with golden shoes on my feet. I am travelling on a secret embassy, but you must not ask me any questions, for I cannot betray my secret."

Then the beetle stepped down into the rich mud, where sat three young-lady beetles, who tittered, because they did not know what to say.

"None of them are engaged yet," said their mother, and the beetle maidens tittered again, this time quite in confusion.

"I have never seen greater beauties, even in the royal stables," exclaimed the beetle, who was now resting himself.

"Don't spoil my girls," said the mother; "and don't talk to them, pray, unless you have serious intentions."

But of course the beetle's intentions were serious, and after a while our friend was engaged. The mother gave them her blessing, and all the other beetles cried "hurrah."

Immediately after the betrothal came the marriage, for there was no reason to delay. The following day passed very pleasantly, and the next was tolerably comfortable; but on the third it became necessary for him to think of getting food for his wife, and, perhaps, for children.

"I have allowed myself to be taken in," said our beetle to himself, "and now there's nothing to be done but to take them in, in return."

No sooner said than done. Away he went, and stayed away all day and all night, and his wife remained behind a forsaken widow.

"Oh," said the other beetles, "this fellow that we have received into our family is nothing but a complete vagabond. He has gone away and left his wife a burden upon our hands."

"Well, she can be unmarried again, and remain here with my other daughters," said the mother. "Fie on the villain that forsook her!"

In the mean time the beetle, who had sailed across the ditch on a cabbage leaf, had been journeying on the other side. In the morning two persons came up to the ditch. When they saw him they took him up and turned him over and over, looking very learned all the time, especially one, who was a boy. "Allah sees the black beetle in the black stone, and the black rock. Is not that written in the Koran?" he asked.

Then he translated the beetle's name into Latin, and said a great deal upon the creature's nature and history. The second person, who was older and a scholar, proposed to carry the beetle home, as they wanted just such good specimens as this. Our beetle considered this speech a great insult, so he flew suddenly out of the speaker's hand. His wings were dry now, so they carried him to a great distance, till at last he reached a hothouse, where a sash of the glass roof was partly open, so he quietly slipped in and buried himself in the warm earth. "It is very comfortable here," he said to himself, and soon after fell asleep. Then he dreamed that the emperor's horse was dying, and had left him his golden shoes, and also promised that he should have two more. All this was very delightful, and when the beetle woke up he crept forth and looked around him. What a splendid place the hothouse was! At the back, large palm-trees were growing; and the sunlight made the leaves look quite glossy; and beneath them what a profusion of luxuriant green, and of flowers red like flame, yellow as amber, or white as new-fallen snow! "What a wonderful quantity of plants," cried the beetle; "how good they will taste when they are decayed! This is a capital store-room. There must certainly be some relations of mine living here; I will just see if I can find any one with whom I can associate. I'm proud, certainly; but I'm also proud of being so." Then he prowled about in the earth, and thought what a pleasant dream that was about the dying horse, and the golden shoes he had inherited. Suddenly a hand seized the beetle, and squeezed him, and turned him round and round. The gardener's little son and his playfellow had come into the hothouse, and, seeing the beetle, wanted to have some fun with him. First, he was wrapped in a vine-leaf, and put into a warm trousers' pocket. He twisted and turned about with all his might, but he got a good squeeze from the boy's hand, as a hint for him to keep quiet. Then the boy went quickly towards a lake that lay at the end of the garden. Here the beetle was put into an old broken wooden shoe, in which a little stick had been fastened upright for a mast, and to this mast the beetle was bound with a piece of worsted. Now he was a sailor, and had to sail away. The lake was not very large, but to the beetle it seemed an ocean, and he was so astonished at its size that he fell over on his back, and kicked out his legs. Then the little ship sailed away; sometimes the current of the water seized it, but whenever it went too far from the shore one of the boys turned up his trousers, and went in after it, and brought it back to land. But at last, just as it went merrily out again, the two boys were called, and so angrily, that they hastened to obey, and ran away as fast as they could from the pond, so that the little ship was left to its fate. It was carried away farther and farther from the shore, till it reached the open sea. This was a terrible prospect for the beetle, for he could not escape in consequence of being bound to the mast. Then a fly came and paid him a visit. "What beautiful weather," said the fly; "I shall rest here and sun myself. You must have a pleasant time of it."

"You speak without knowing the facts," replied the beetle; "don't you see that I am a prisoner?"

"Ah, but I'm not a prisoner," remarked the fly, and away he flew.

"Well, now I know the world," said the beetle to himself; "it's an abominable world; I'm the only respectable person in it. First, they refuse me my golden shoes; then I have to lie on damp linen, and to stand in a draught; and to crown all, they fasten a wife upon me. Then, when I have made a step forward in the world, and found out a comfortable position, just as I could wish it to be, one of these human boys comes and ties me up, and leaves me to the mercy of the wild waves, while the emperor's favorite horse goes prancing about proudly on his golden shoes. This vexes me more than anything. But it is useless to look for sympathy in this world. My career has been very interesting, but what's the use of that if nobody knows anything about it? The world does not deserve to be made acquainted with my adventures, for it ought to have given me golden shoes when the emperor's horse was shod, and I stretched out my feet to be shod, too. If I had received golden shoes I should have been an ornament to the stable; now I am lost to the stable and to the world. It is all over with me."

But all was not yet over. A boat, in which were a few young girls, came rowing up. "Look, yonder is an old wooden shoe sailing along," said one of the younger girls.

"And there's a poor little creature bound fast in it," said another.

The boat now came close to our beetle's ship, and the young girls fished it out of the water. One of them drew a small pair of scissors from her pocket, and cut the worsted without hurting the beetle, and when she stepped on shore she placed him on the grass. "There," she said, "creep away, or fly, if thou canst. It is a splendid thing to have thy liberty." Away flew the beetle, straight through the open window of a large building; there he sank down, tired and exhausted, exactly on the mane of the emperor's favorite horse, who was standing in his stable; and the beetle found himself at home again. For some time he clung to the mane, that he might recover himself. "Well," he said, "here I am, seated on the emperor's favorite horse, — sitting upon him as if I were the emperor himself. But what was it the farrier asked me? Ah, I remember now, — that's a good thought, — he asked me why the golden shoes were given to the horse. The answer is quite clear to me, now. They were given to the horse on *my* account." And this reflection put the beetle into a good temper. The sun's rays also came streaming into the stable, and shone upon him, and made the place lively and bright. "Travelling expands the mind very much," said the beetle. "The world is not so bad after all, if you know how to take things as they come."

THE BOTTLE NECK

CLOSE to the corner of a street, among other abodes of poverty, stood an exceedingly tall, narrow house, which had been so knocked about by time that it seemed out of joint in every direction. This house was inhabited by poor people, but the deepest poverty was apparent in the garret lodging in the gable. In front of the little window, an old bent bird-cage hung in the sunshine, which had not even a proper water-glass, but instead of it the broken neck of a bottle, turned upside down, and a cork stuck in to make it hold the water with which it was filled. An old maid stood at the window; she had hung chickweed over the cage, and the little linnet which it contained hopped from perch to perch and sang and twittered merrily.

"Yes, it's all very well for you to sing," said the bottle neck: that is, he did not really speak the words as we do, for the neck of a bottle cannot speak; but he thought them to himself in his own mind, just as people sometimes talk quietly to themselves.

"Yes, you may sing very well, you have all your limbs uninjured; you should feel what it is like to lose your body, and only have a neck and a mouth left, with a cork stuck in it, as I have: you wouldn't sing then, I know. After all, it is just as well that there are some who can be happy. I have no reason to sing, nor could I sing now if I were ever so happy; but when I was a whole bottle, and they rubbed me with a cork, didn't I sing then? I used to be called a complete lark. I remember when I went out to a picnic with the furrier's family, on the day his daughter was betrothed, — it seems as if it only happened yesterday. I have gone through a great deal in my time, when I come to recollect: I have been in the fire and in the water, I have been deep in the earth, and have mounted higher in the air than most other people, and now I am swinging here, outside a bird-cage, in the air and the sunshine. Oh, indeed, it would be worth while to hear my history; but I do not speak it aloud, for a good reason — because I cannot."

Then the bottle neck related his history, which was really rather remarkable; he, in fact, related it to himself, or, at least, thought it in his own mind. The little bird sang his own song merrily; in the street below there was driving and running to and fro, every one thought of his own affairs, or perhaps of nothing at all; but the bottle neck thought deeply. He thought of the blazing furnace in the factory, where he had been blown into life; he remembered how hot it felt when he was placed in the heated oven, the home from which he sprang, and that he had a strong inclination to leap out again directly; but after a while it became cooler, and he found himself very comfortable. He had been placed in a row, with a whole regiment of his brothers and sisters all brought out of the same furnace; some of them had certainly been blown into champagne bottles, and others into beer bottles, which made a little difference between them. In the world it often happens that a beer bottle may contain the most precious wine, and a champagne bottle be filled with blacking, but even in decay it may always be seen whether a man has been well born. Nobility remains noble, as a champagne bottle remains the same, even with blacking in its interior. When the bottles were packed our bottle was packed amongst them; it little expected then to finish its career as a bottle neck, or to be used as a water-glass to a bird's-cage, which is, after all, a place of honor, for it is to be of some use in the world. The bottle did not behold the light of day again, until it was unpacked with the rest in the wine merchant's cellar, and, for the first time, rinsed with water, which caused some very curious sensations. There it lay empty, and without a cork, and it had a peculiar feeling, as if it wanted something it knew not what. At last it was filled with rich and costly wine, a cork was placed in it, and sealed down. Then it was labelled "first quality," as if it had carried off the first prize at an examination; besides, the wine and the bottle were both good, and while we are young is the time for poetry. There were sounds of song within the bottle, of things it could not understand, of green sunny mountains, where the vines grow and where the merry vine-dressers laugh, sing, and are merry. "Ah, how beautiful is life." All these tones of joy and song in the bottle were like the working of a young poet's brain, who often knows not the meaning of the tones which are sounding within him. One morning the bottle found a purchaser in the furrier's apprentice, who was told to bring one of the best bottles of wine. It was placed in the provision basket with ham and cheese and sausages. The sweetest fresh butter and the finest bread were put into the basket by the furrier's daughter herself, for she packed it. She was young and pretty; her brown eyes laughed, and a smile lingered round her mouth as sweet as that in her eyes. She had delicate hands, beautifully white, and her neck was whiter still. It could easily be seen that she was a very lovely girl, and as yet she was not engaged. The provision basket lay in the lap of the young girl as the family drove out to the forest, and the neck of the bottle peeped out from between the folds of the white napkin. There was the red wax on the cork, and the bottle looked straight at the young girl's face, and also at the face of the young sailor who sat near her. He was a young friend, the son of a portrait painter. He had lately passed his examination with honor, as mate, and the next morning he was to sail in his ship to a distant coast. There had been a great deal of talk on this subject while the basket was being packed, and during this conversation the eyes and the mouth of the furrier's daughter did not wear a very joyful expression. The young people wandered away into the green wood, and talked together. What did they talk about? The bottle could not say, for he was in the provision basket. It remained there a long time; but when at last it was brought forth it appeared as if something pleasant had happened, for every one was laughing; the furrier's daughter laughed too, but she said very little, and her cheeks were like two roses. Then her father took the bottle and the cork-screw into his hands. What a strange sensation it was to have the cork drawn for the first time! The bottle could never after that forget the performance of that moment; indeed there was quite a convulsion within him as the cork flew out, and a gurgling sound as the wine was poured forth into the glasses.

"Long life to the betrothed," cried the papa, and every glass was emptied to the dregs, while the young sailor kissed his beautiful bride.

"Happiness and blessing to you both," said the old people—father and mother, and the young man filled the glasses again.

"Safe return, and a wedding this day next year," he cried; and when the glasses were empty he took the bottle, raised it on high, and said, "Thou hast been present here on the happiest day of my life; thou shalt never be used by others!" So saying, he hurled it high in the air.

The furrier's daughter thought she should never see it again, but she was mistaken. It fell among the rushes on the borders of a little woodland lake. The bottle neck remembered well how long it lay there unseen. "I gave them wine, and they gave me muddy water," he had said to himself, "but I suppose it was all well meant." He could no longer see the betrothed couple, nor the cheerful old people; but for a long time he could hear them rejoicing and singing. At length there came by two peasant boys, who peeped in among the reeds and spied out the bottle. Then they took it up and carried it home with them, so that once more it was provided for. At home in their wooden cottage these boys had an elder brother, a sailor, who was about to start on a long voyage. He had been there the day before to say farewell, and his mother was now very busy packing up various things for him to take with him on his voyage. In the evening his father was going to carry the parcel to

THE BOTTLE NECK

the town to see his son once more, and take him a farewell greeting from his mother. A small bottle had already been filled with herb tea, mixed with brandy, and wrapped in a parcel; but when the boys came in they brought with them a larger and stronger bottle, which they had found. This bottle would hold so much more than the little one, and they all said the brandy would be so good for complaints of the stomach, especially as it was mixed with medical herbs. The liquid which they now poured into the bottle was not like the red wine with which it had once been filled; these were bitter drops, but they are of great use sometimes — for the stomach. The new large bottle was to go, not the little one: so the bottle once more started on its travels. It was taken on board (for Peter Jensen was one of the crew) the very same ship in which the young mate was to sail. But the mate did not see the bottle: indeed, if he had he would not have known it, or supposed it was the one out of which they had drunk to the felicity of the betrothed and to the prospect of a marriage on his own happy return. Certainly the bottle no longer poured forth wine, but it contained something quite as good; and so it happened that whenever Peter Jensen brought it out, his messmates gave it the name of "the apothecary," for it contained the best medicine to cure the stomach, and he gave it out quite willingly as long as a drop remained. Those were happy days, and the bottle would sing when rubbed with a cork, and it was called a "great lark," "Peter Jensen's lark."

Long days and months rolled by, during which the bottle stood empty in a corner, when a storm arose — whether on the passage out or home it could not tell, for it had never been ashore. It was a terrible storm, great waves arose, darkly heaving and tossing the vessel to and fro. The main mast was split asunder, the ship sprang a leak, and the pumps became useless, while all around was black as night. At the last moment, when the ship was sinking, the young mate wrote on a piece of paper, "We are going down: God's will be done." Then he wrote the name of his betrothed, his own name, and that of the ship. Then he put the leaf in an empty bottle that happened to be at hand, corked it down tightly, and threw it into the foaming sea. He knew not that it was the very same bottle from which the goblet of joy and hope had once been filled for him, and now it was tossing on the waves with his last greeting, and a message from the dead. The ship sank, and the crew sank with her; but the bottle flew on like a bird, for it bore within it a loving letter from a loving heart. And as the sun rose and set, the bottle felt as at the time of its first existence, when in the heated glowing stove it had a longing to fly away. It outlived the storms and the calm, it struck against no rocks, was not devoured by sharks, but drifted on for more than a year, sometimes towards the north, sometimes towards the south, just as the current carried it. It was in all other ways its own master, but even of that one may get tired. The written leaf, the last farewell of the bridegroom to his bride, would only bring sorrow when once it reached her hands; but where were those hands, so soft and delicate, which had once spread the table-cloth on the fresh grass in the green wood, on the day of her betrothal? Ah, yes! where was the furrier's daughter? and where was the land which might lie nearest to her home?

The bottle knew not, it travelled onward and onward, and at last all this wandering about became wearisome; at all events it was not its usual occupation. But it had to travel, till at length it reached land — a foreign country. Not a word spoken in this country could the bottle understand; it was a language it had never before heard, and it is a great loss not to be able to understand a language. The bottle was fished out of the water, and examined on all sides. The little letter contained within it was discovered, taken out, and turned and twisted in every direction; but the people could not understand what was written upon it. They could be quite sure that the bottle had been thrown overboard from a vessel, and that something about it was written on this paper: but what was written? that was the question, — so the paper was put back into the bottle, and then both were put away in a large cupboard of one of the great houses of the town. Whenever any strangers arrived, the paper was taken out and turned over and over, so that the address, which was only written in pencil, became almost illegible, and at last no one could distinguish any letters on it at all. For a whole year the bottle remained standing in the cupboard, and then it was taken up to the loft, where it soon became covered with dust and cobwebs. Ah! how often then it thought of those better days—of the times when in the fresh, green wood, it had poured forth rich wine; or, while rocked by the swelling waves, it had carried in its bosom a secret, a letter, a last parting sigh. For full twenty years it stood in the loft, and it might have stayed there longer but that the house was going to be rebuilt. The bottle was discovered when the roof was taken off; they talked about it, but the bottle did not understand what they said—a language is not to be learnt by living in a loft, even for twenty years. "If I had been down stairs in the room," thought the bottle, "I might have learnt it." It was now washed and rinsed, which process was really quite necessary, and afterwards it looked clean and transparent, and felt young again in its old age; but the paper which it had carried so faithfully was destroyed in the washing. They filled the bottle with seeds, though it scarcely knew what had been placed in it. Then they corked it down tightly, and carefully wrapped it up. There not even the light of a torch or lantern could reach it, much less the brightness of the sun or moon. "And yet," thought the bottle, "men go on a journey that they may see as much as possible, and I can see nothing." However, it did something quite as important; it travelled to the place of its destination, and was unpacked.

"What trouble they have taken with that bottle over yonder!" said one, "and very likely it is broken after all." But the bottle was not broken, and, better still, it understood every word that was said: this language it had heard at the furnaces and at the wine merchant's; in the forest and on the ship, —it was the only good old language it could understand. It had returned home, and the language was as a welcome greeting. For very joy, it felt ready to jump out of people's hands, and scarcely noticed that its cork had been drawn, and its contents emptied out, till it found itself carried to a cellar, to be left there and forgotten. "There's no place like home, even if it's a cellar." It never occurred to him to think that he might lie there for years, he felt so comfortable. For many long years he remained in the cellar, till at last some people came to carry away the bottles, and ours amongst the number.

Out in the garden there was a great festival. Brilliant lamps hung in festoons from tree to tree; and paper lanterns, through which the light shone till they looked like transparent tulips. It was a beautiful evening, and the weather mild and clear. The stars twinkled; and the new moon, in the form of a crescent, was surrounded by the shadowy disc of the whole moon, and looked like a gray globe with a golden rim: it was a beautiful sight for those who had good eyes. The illumination extended even to the most retired of the garden walks, at least not so retired that any one need lose himself there. In the borders were placed bottles, each containing a light, and among them the bottle with which we are acquainted, and whose fate it was, one day, to be only a bottle neck, and to serve as a water-glass to a bird's-cage. Everything here appeared lovely to our bottle, for it was again in the green wood, amid joy and feasting; again it heard music and song, and the noise and murmur of a crowd, especially in that part of the garden where the lamps blazed, and the paper lanterns displayed their brilliant colors. It stood in a distant walk certainly, but a place pleasant for contemplation; and it carried a light; and was at once useful and ornamental. In such an hour it is easy to forget that one has spent twenty years in a loft, and a good thing it is to be able to do so. Close before the bottle passed a single pair, like the bridal pair—the mate and the furrier's daughter—who had so long ago wandered in the wood. It seemed to the bottle as if he were living that time over again. Not only the guests but other people were walking in the garden, who were allowed to witness the splendor and the festivities. Among the latter came an old maid, who seemed to be quite alone in the world. She was thinking, like the bottle, of the green wood, and of a young betrothed pair, who were closely connected with herself; she was thinking of that hour, the happiest of her life, in which she had taken part, when she had herself been one of that betrothed pair; such hours are never to be forgotten, let a maiden be as old as she may. But she did not recognize the bottle, neither did the bottle notice the old maid. And so we often pass each other in the world when we meet, as did these two, even while together in the same town.

The bottle was taken from the garden, and again sent to a wine merchant, where it was once more filled with wine, and sold to an aeronaut, who was to make an ascent in his balloon on the following Sunday. A great crowd assembled to witness the sight; military music had been engaged, and many other preparations made. The bottle saw it all from the basket in which he lay close to a live rabbit. The rabbit was quite excited because he knew that he was to be taken up, and let down again in a parachute. The bottle, however, knew nothing of the "up," or the "down;" he saw only that the balloon was swelling larger and larger till it could swell no more, and began to rise and be restless. Then the ropes which held it were cut through, and the aerial ship rose in the air with the aeronaut and the basket containing the bottle and the rabbit, while the music sounded and all the people shouted "Hurrah."

"This is a wonderful journey up into the air," thought the bottle; "it is a new way of sailing, and here, at least, there is no fear of striking against anything."

Thousands of people gazed at the balloon, and the old maid who was in the garden saw it also; for she stood at the open window of the garret, by which hung the cage containing the linnet, who then had no water-glass, but was obliged to be contented with an old cup. In the window-sill stood a myrtle in a pot, and this had been pushed a little on one side, that it might not fall out; for the old maid was leaning out of the window, that she might see. And she did see distinctly the aeronaut in the balloon, and how he let down the rabbit in the parachute, and then drank to the health of all the spectators in the wine from the bottle. After doing this, he hurled it high into the air. How little she thought that this was the very same bottle which her friend had thrown aloft in her honor, on that happy day of rejoicing, in the green wood, in her youthful days. The bottle had no time to think, when raised so suddenly; and before it was aware, it reached the highest point it had ever attained in its life. Steeples and roofs lay far, far beneath it, and the people looked as tiny as possible. Then it began to descend much more rapidly than the rabbit had done, made somersaults in the air, and felt itself quite young and unfettered, although it was half full of wine. But this did not last long. What a journey it was! All the people could see the bottle; for the sun shone upon it. The balloon was already far away, and very soon the bottle was far away also; for it fell upon a roof, and broke in pieces. But the pieces had got such an impetus in them, that they could not stop themselves. They went jumping and rolling about, till at last they fell into the court-yard, and were broken into still smaller pieces; only the neck of the bottle managed to keep whole, and it was broken off as clean as if it had been cut with a diamond.

"That would make a capital bird's glass," said one of the cellar-men; but none of them had either a bird or a cage, and it was not to be expected they would provide one just because they had found a bottle neck that could be used as a glass. But the old maid who lived in the garret had a bird, and it really might be useful to her; so the bottle neck was provided with a cork, and taken up to her; and, as it often happens in life, the part that had been uppermost was now turned downwards, and it was filled with fresh water. Then they hung it in the cage of the little bird, who sang and twittered more merrily than ever.

"Ah, you have good reason to sing," said the bottle neck, which was looked upon as something very remarkable, because it had been in a balloon; nothing further was known of its history. As it hung there in the bird's-cage, it could hear the noise and murmur of the people in the street below, as well as the conversation of the old maid in the room within. An old friend had just come to visit her, and they talked, not about the bottle neck, but of the myrtle in the window.

"No, you must not spend a dollar for your daughter's bridal bouquet," said the old maid; "you shall have a beautiful little bunch for a nosegay, full of blossoms. Do you see how splendidly the tree has grown? It has been raised from only a little sprig of myrtle that you gave me on the day after my betrothal, and from which I was to make my own bridal bouquet when a year had passed: but that day never came; the eyes were closed which were to have been my light and joy through life. In the depths of the sea my beloved sleeps sweetly; the myrtle has become an old tree, and I am a still older woman. Before the sprig you gave me faded, I took a spray, and planted it in the earth; and now, as you see, it has become a large tree, and a bunch of the blossoms shall at last appear at a wedding festival, in the bouquet of your daughter."

There were tears in the eyes of the old maid, as she spoke of the beloved of her youth, and of their betrothal in the wood. Many thoughts came into her mind; but the thought never came, that quite close to her, in that very window, was a remembrance of those olden times, — the neck of the bottle which had, as it were, shouted for joy when the cork flew out with a bang on the betrothal day. But the bottle neck did not recognize the old maid; he had not been listening to what she had related, perhaps because he was thinking so much about her.

THE LAST DREAM OF THE OLD OAK

IN the forest, high up on the steep shore, and not far from the open sea-coast, stood a very old oak-tree. It was just three hundred and sixty-five years old, but that long time was to the tree as the same number of days might be to us; we wake by day and sleep by night, and then we have our dreams. It is different with the tree; it is obliged to keep awake through three seasons of the year, and does not get any sleep till winter comes. Winter is its time for rest; its night after the long day of spring, summer, and autumn. On many a warm summer, the Ephemera, the flies that exist for only a day, had fluttered about the old oak, enjoyed life and felt happy and if, for a moment, one of the tiny creatures rested on one of his large fresh leaves, the tree would always say, "Poor little creature! your whole life consists only of a single day. How very short. It must be quite melancholy."

"Melancholy! what do you mean?" the little creature would always reply. "Everything around me is so wonderfully bright and warm, and beautiful, that it makes me joyous."

"But only for one day, and then it is all over."

"Over!" repeated the fly; "what is the meaning of all over? Are you all over too?"

"No; I shall very likely live for thousands of your days, and my day is whole seasons long; indeed it is so long that you could never reckon it out."

"No? then I don't understand you. You may have thousands of my days, but I have thousands of moments in which I can be merry and happy. Does all the beauty of the world cease when you die?"

"No," replied the tree; "it will certainly last much longer, — infinitely longer than I can even think of."

"Well, then," said the little fly, "we have the same time to live; only we reckon differently." And the little creature danced and floated in the air, rejoicing in her delicate wings of gauze and velvet, rejoicing in the balmy breezes, laden with the fragrance of clover-fields and wild roses, elder-blossoms and honeysuckle, from the garden hedges, wild thyme, primroses, and mint, and the scent of all these was so strong that the perfume almost intoxicated the little fly. The long and beautiful day had been so full of joy and sweet delights, that when the sun sank low it felt tired of all its happiness and enjoyment. Its wings could sustain it no longer, and gently and slowly it glided down upon the soft waving blades of grass, nodded its little head as well as it could nod, and slept peacefully and sweetly. The fly was dead.

"Poor little Ephemera!" said the oak; "what a terribly short life!" And so, on every summer day the dance was repeated, the same questions asked, and the same answers given. The same thing was continued through many generations of Ephemera; all of them felt equally merry and equally happy.

The oak remained awake through the morning of spring, the noon of summer, and the evening of autumn; its time of rest, its night drew nigh — winter was coming. Already the storms were singing, "Good-night, good-night." Here fell a leaf and there fell a leaf. "We will rock you and lull you. Go to sleep, go to sleep. We will sing you to sleep, and shake you to sleep, and it will do your old twigs good; they will even crackle with pleasure. Sleep sweetly, sleep sweetly, it is your three-hundred-and-sixty-fifth night. Correctly speaking, you are but a youngster in the world. Sleep sweetly, the clouds will drop snow upon you, which will be quite a cover-lid, warm and sheltering to your feet. Sweet sleep to you, and pleasant dreams." And there stood the oak, stripped of all its leaves, left to rest during the whole of a long winter, and to dream many dreams of events that had happened in its life, as in the dreams of men. The great tree had once been small; indeed, in its cradle it had been an acorn. According to human computation, it was now in the fourth century of its existence. It was the largest and best tree in the forest. Its summit towered above all the other trees, and could be seen far out at sea, so that it served as a landmark to the sailors. It had no idea how many eyes looked eagerly for it. In its topmost branches the wood-pigeon built her nest, and the cuckoo carried out his usual vocal performances, and his well-known notes echoed amid the boughs; and in autumn, when the leaves looked like beaten copper plates, the birds of passage would come and rest upon the branches before taking their flight across the sea. But now it was winter, the tree stood leafless, so that every one could see how crooked and bent were the branches that sprang forth from the trunk. Crows and rooks came by turns and sat on them, and talked of the hard times which were beginning, and how difficult it was in winter to obtain food.

It was just about holy Christmas time that the tree dreamed a dream. The tree had, doubtless, a kind of feeling that the festive time had arrived, and in his dream fancied he heard the bells ringing from all the churches round, and yet it seemed to him to be a beautiful summer's day, mild and warm. His mighty summits was crowned with spreading fresh green foliage; the sunbeams played among the leaves and branches, and the air was full of fragrance from herb and blossom; painted butterflies chased each other; the summer flies danced around him, as if the world had been created merely for them to dance and be merry in. All that had happened to the tree during every year of his life seemed to pass before him, as in a festive procession. He saw the knights of olden times and noble ladies ride by through the wood on their gallant steeds, with plumes waving in their hats, and falcons on their wrists. The hunting horn sounded, and the dogs barked. He saw hostile warriors, in colored dresses and glittering armor, with spear and halberd, pitching their tents, and anon striking them. The watchfires again blazed, and men sang and slept under the hospitable shelter of the tree. He saw lovers meet in quiet happiness near him in the moonshine, and carve the initials of their names in the grayish-green bark on his trunk. Once, but long years had intervened since then, guitars and Eolian harps had been hung on his boughs by merry travellers; now they seemed to hang there again, and he could hear their marvellous tones. The wood-pigeons cooed as if to explain the feelings of the tree, and the cuckoo called out to tell him how many summer days he had yet to live. Then it seemed as if new life was thrilling through every fibre of root and stem and leaf, rising even to the highest branches. The tree felt itself stretching and spreading out, while through the root beneath the earth ran the warm vigor of life. As he grew higher and still higher, with increased strength, his topmost boughs became broader and fuller; and in proportion to his growth, so was his self-satisfaction increased, and with it arose a joyous longing to grow higher and higher, to reach even to the warm, bright sun itself. Already had his topmost branches pierced the clouds, which floated beneath them like troops of birds of passage, or large white swans; every leaf seemed gifted with sight, as if it possessed eyes to see. The stars became visible in broad daylight, large and sparkling, like clear and gentle eyes. They recalled to the memory the well-known look in the eyes of a child, or in the eyes of lovers who had once met beneath the branches of the old oak. These were wonderful and happy moments for the old tree, full of peace and joy; and yet, amidst all this happiness, the tree felt a yearning, longing desire that all the other trees, bushes, herbs, and flowers beneath him, might be able also to rise higher, as he had done, and to see all this splendor, and experience the same happiness. The grand, majestic oak could not be quite happy in the midst of his enjoyment, while all the rest, both great and small, were not with him. And this feeling of yearning trembled through every branch, through every leaf, as warmly and fervently as if they had been the fibres of a human heart. The summit of the tree waved to and fro, and bent downwards as if in his silent longing he sought for something. Then there came to him the fragrance of thyme, followed by the more powerful scent of honeysuckle and violets; and he fancied he heard the note of the cuckoo. At length his longing was satisfied. Up through the clouds came the green summits of the forest trees, and beneath him, the oak saw them rising, and growing higher and higher. Bush and herb shot upward, and some even tore themselves up by the roots to rise more quickly. The birch-tree was the quickest of all. Like a lightning flash the slender stem shot upwards in a zigzag line, the branches spreading around it like green gauze and banners. Every native of the wood, even to the brown and feathery rushes, grew with the rest, while the birds ascended with the melody of song. On a blade of grass, that fluttered in the air like a long, green ribbon, sat a grasshopper, cleaning his wings with his legs. May beetles hummed, the bees murmured, the birds sang, each in his own way; the air was filled with the sounds of song and gladness.

"But where is the little blue flower that grows by the water?" asked the oak, "and the purple bell-flower, and the daisy?" You see the oak wanted to have them all with him.

"Here we are, we are here," sounded in voice and song.

"But the beautiful thyme of last summer, where is that? and the lilies-of-the-valley, which last year covered the earth with their bloom? and the wild apple-tree with its lovely blossoms, and all the glory of the wood, which has flourished year after year? even what may have but now sprouted forth could be with us here."

"We are here, we are here," sounded voices higher in the air, as if they had flown there beforehand.

"Why this is beautiful, too beautiful to be believed," said the oak in a joyful tone. "I have them all here, both great and small; not one has been forgotten. Can such happiness be imagined?" It seemed almost impossible.

"In heaven with the Eternal God, it can be imagined, and it is possible," sounded the reply through the air.

And the old tree, as it still grew upwards and onwards, felt that his roots were loosening themselves from the earth.

"It is right so, it is best," said the tree, "no fetters hold me now. I can fly up to the very highest point in light and glory. And all I love are with me, both small and great. All—all are here."

Such was the dream of the old oak: and while he dreamed, a mighty storm came rushing over land and sea, at the holy Christmas time. The sea rolled in great billows towards the shore. There was a cracking and crushing heard in the tree. The root was torn from the ground just at the moment when in his dream he fancied it was being loosened from the earth. He fell—his three hundred and sixty-five years were passed as the single day of the Ephemera. On the morning of Christmas-day, when the sun rose, the storm had ceased. From all the churches sounded the festive bells, and from every hearth, even of the smallest hut, rose the smoke into the blue sky, like the smoke from the festive thank-offerings on the Druids' altars. The sea gradually became calm, and on board a great ship that had withstood the tempest during the night, all the flags were displayed, as a token of joy and festivity. "The tree is down! The old oak,—our landmark on the coast!" exclaimed the sailors. "It must have fallen in the storm of last night. Who can replace it? Alas! no one." This was a funeral oration over the old tree; short, but well-meant. There it lay stretched on the snow-covered shore, and over it sounded the notes of a song from the ship—a song of Christmas joy, and of the redemption of the soul of man, and of eternal life through Christ's atoning blood.

> "Sing aloud on the happy morn,
> All is fulfilled, for Christ is born;
> With songs of joy let us loudly sing,
> 'Hallelujahs to Christ our King.' "

Thus sounded the old Christmas carol, and every one on board the ship felt his thoughts elevated, through the song and the prayer, even as the old tree had felt lifted up in its last, its beautiful dream on that Christmas morn.

THE PORTUGUESE DUCK

A DUCK once arrived from Portugal, but there were some who said she came from Spain, which is almost the same thing. At all events, she was called the "Portuguese," and she laid eggs, was killed, and cooked, and there was an end of her. But the ducklings which crept forth from the eggs were also called "Portuguese," and about that there may be some question. But of all the family one only remained in the duckyard, which may be called a farmyard, as the chickens were admitted, and the cock strutted about in a very hostile manner. "He annoys me with his loud crowing," said the Portuguese duck; "but, still, he's a handsome bird, there's no denying that, although he's not a drake. He ought to moderate his voice, like those little birds who are singing in the lime-trees over there in our neighbor's garden, but that is an art only acquired in polite society. How sweetly they sing there; it is quite a pleasure to listen to them! I call it Portuguese singing. If I had only such a little singing-bird, I'd be kind and good as a mother to him, for it's in my nature, in my Portuguese blood."

While she was speaking, one of the little singing-birds came tumbling head over heels from the roof into the yard. The cat was after him, but he had escaped from her with a broken wing, and so came tumbling into the yard.

"That's just like the cat, she's a villain," said the Portuguese duck. "I remember her ways when I had children of my own. How can such a creature be allowed to live, and wander about upon the roofs. I don't think they allow such things in Portugal." She pitied the little singing-bird, and so did all the other ducks who were not Portuguese.

"Poor little creature!" they said, one after another, as they came up. "We can't sing, certainly; but we have a sounding-board, or something of the kind, within us; we can feel that, though we don't talk about it."

"But I can talk," said the Portuguese duck; "and I'll do something for the little fellow; it's my duty;" and she stepped into the water-trough, and beat her wings upon the water so strongly that the bird was nearly drowned by a shower-bath; but the duck meant it kindly. "That is a good deed," she said; "I hope the others will take example by it."

"Tweet, tweet!" said the little bird, for one of his wings being broken, he found it difficult to shake himself; but he quite understood that the bath was meant kindly, and he said, "You are very kind-hearted, madam;" but he did not wish for a second bath.

"I have never thought about my heart," replied the Portuguese duck, "but I know that I love all my fellow-creatures, except the cat, and nobody can expect me to love her, for she ate up two of my ducklings. But pray make yourself at home; it is easy to make one's self comfortable. I am myself from a foreign country, as you may see by my feathery dress. My drake is a native of these parts; he's not of my race; but I am not proud on that account. If any one here can understand you, I may say positively I am that person."

"She's quite full of 'Portulak,' " said a little common duck, who was witty. All the common ducks considered the word "Portulak" a good joke, for it sounded like Portugal. They nudged each other, and said, "Quack! that was witty!"

Then the other ducks began to notice the little bird. "The Portuguese had certainly a great flow of language," they said to the little bird. "For our part we don't care to fill our beaks with such long words, but we sympathize with you quite as much. If we don't do anything else, we can walk about with you everywhere, and we think that is the best thing we can do."

"You have a lovely voice," said one of the eldest ducks; "it must be great satisfaction to you to be able to give so much pleasure as you do. I am certainly no judge of your singing so I keep my beak shut, which is better than talking nonsense, as others do."

"Don't plague him so, interposed the Portuguese duck; "he requires rest and nursing. My little singing-bird do you wish me to prepare another bath for you?"

"Oh, no! no! pray let me dry," implored the little bird.

"The water-cure is the only remedy for me, when I am not well," said the Portuguese. "Amusement, too, is very beneficial. The fowls from the neighborhood will soon be here to pay you a visit. There are two Cochin Chinese amongst them; they wear feathers on their legs, and are well educated. They have been brought from a great distance, and consequently I treat them with greater respect than I do the others."

Then the fowls arrived, and the cock was polite enough to-day to keep from being rude. "You are a real songster," he said, "you do as much with your little voice as it is possible to do; but there requires more noise and shrillness in any one who wishes it to be known who he is."

The two Chinese were quite enchanted with the appearance of the singing-bird. His feathers had been much ruffled by his bath, so that he seemed to them quite like a tiny Chinese fowl. "He's charming," they said to each other, and began a conversation with him in whispers, using the most aristocratic Chinese dialect: "We are of the same race as yourself," they said. "The ducks, even the Portuguese, are all aquatic birds, as you must have noticed. You do not know us yet, — very few know us, or give themselves the trouble to make our acquaintance, not even any of the fowls, though we are born to occupy a higher grade in society than most of them. But that does not disturb us, we quietly go on in our own way among the rest, whose ideas are certainly not ours; for we look at the bright side of things, and only speak what is good, although that is sometimes very difficult to find where none exists. Except ourselves and the cock there is not one in the yard who can be called talented or polite. It cannot even be said of the ducks, and we warn you, little bird, not to trust that one yonder, with the short tail feathers, for she is cunning; that curiously marked one, with the crooked stripes on her wings, is a mischief-maker, and never lets any one have the last word, though she is always in the wrong. That fat duck yonder speaks evil of every one, and that is against our principles. If we have nothing good to tell, we close our beaks. The Portuguese is the only one who has had any education, and with whom we can associate, but she is passionate, and talks too much about 'Portugal.' "

"I wonder what those two Chinese are whispering about," whispered one duck to another; "they are always doing it, and it annoys me. We never speak to them."

Now the drake came up, and he thought the little singing-bird was a sparrow. "Well, I don't understand the difference," he said; "it appears to me all the same. He's only a plaything, and if people will have playthings, why let them, I say."

"Don't take any notice of what he says," whispered the Portuguese; "he's very well in matters of business, and with him business is placed before everything. But now I shall lie down and have a little rest. It is a duty we owe to ourselves that we may be nice and fat when we come to be embalmed with sage and onions and apples." So she laid herself down in the sun and winked with one eye; she had a very comfortable place, and felt so comfortable that she fell asleep. The little singing-bird busied himself for some time with his broken wing, and at last he lay down, too, quite close to his protectress. The sun shone warm and bright, and he found out that it was a very good place. But the fowls of the neighborhood were all awake, and, to tell the truth, they had paid a visit to the duckyard, simply and solely to find food for themselves. The Chinese were the first to leave, and the other fowls soon followed them.

The witty little duck said of the Portuguese, that the old lady was getting quite a "doting ducky," All the other ducks laughed at this. "Doting ducky," they whispered. "Oh, that's too 'witty!' " And then they repeated the former joke about "Portulak," and declared it was most amusing. Then they all lay down to have a nap.

They had been lying asleep for some time, when suddenly something was thrown into the yard for them to eat. It came down with such a bang, that the whole company started up and clapped their wings. The Portuguese awoke too, and rushed over to the other side: in so doing she trod upon the little singing-bird.

"Tweet," he cried; "you trod very hard upon me, madam."

"Well, then, why do you lie in my way?" she retorted, "you must not be so touchy. I have nerves of my own, but I do not cry 'tweet.'"

"Don't be angry," said the little bird; "the 'tweet' slipped out of my beak unawares."

The Portuguese did not listen to him, but began eating as fast as she could, and made a good meal. When she had finished, she lay down again, and the little bird, who wished to be amiable, began to sing, —

> "Chirp and twitter,
>   The dew-drops glitter,
> In the hours of sunny spring,
>   I'll sing my best,
>   Till I go to rest,
> With my head behind my wing."

"Now I want rest after my dinner," said the Portuguese; "you must conform to the rules of the house while you are here. I want to sleep now."

The little bird was quite taken aback, for he meant it kindly. When madam awoke afterwards, there he stood before her with a little corn he had found, and laid it at her feet; but as she had not slept well, she was naturally in a bad temper. "Give that to a chicken," she said, "and don't be always standing in my way."

"Why are you angry with me?" replied the little singing-bird, "what have I done?"

"Done!" repeated the Portuguese duck, "your mode of expressing yourself is not very polite. I must call your attention to that fact."

"It was sunshine here yesterday," said the little bird, "but to-day it is cloudy and the air is close."

"You know very little about the weather, I fancy," she retorted, "the day is not over yet. Don't stand there, looking so stupid."

"But you are looking at me just as the wicked eyes looked when I fell into the yard yesterday."

"Impertinent creature!" exclaimed the Portuguese duck: "would you compare me with the cat—that beast of prey? There's not a drop of malicious blood in me. I've taken your part, and now I'll teach you better manners." So saying, she made a bite at the little singing-bird's head, and he fell dead on the ground. "Now whatever is the meaning of this?" "she said; "could he not bear even such a little peck as I gave him? Then certainly he was not made for this world. I've been like a mother to him, I know that, for I've a good heart."

Then the cock from the neighboring yard stuck his head in, and crowed with steam-engine power.

"You'll kill me with your crowing," she cried, "it's all your fault. He's lost his life, and I'm very near losing mine."

"There's not much of him lying there," observed the cock.

"Speak of him with respect," said the Portuguese duck, "for he had manners and education, and he could sing. He was affectionate and gentle, and that is as rare a quality in animals as in those who call themselves human beings."

Then all the ducks came crowding round the little dead bird. Ducks have strong passions, whether they feel envy or pity. There was nothing to envy here, so they all showed a great deal of pity, even the two Chinese. "We shall never have another singing-bird again amongst us; he was almost a Chinese," they whispered, and then they wept with such a noisy, clucking sound, that all the other fowls clucked too, but the ducks went about with redder eyes afterwards. "We have hearts of our own," they said, "nobody can deny that."

"Hearts!" repeated the Portuguese, "indeed you have, almost as tender as the ducks in Portugal."

"Let us think of getting something to satisfy our hunger," said the drake, "that's the most important business. If one of our toys is broken, why we have plenty more."

THE SNOW MAN

"IT is so delightfully cold," said the Snow Man, "that it makes my whole body crackle. This is just the kind of wind to blow life into one. How that great red thing up there is staring at me!" He meant the sun, who was just setting. "It shall not make me wink. I shall manage to keep the pieces."

He had two triangular pieces of tile in his head, instead of eyes; his mouth was made of an old broken rake, and was, of course, furnished with teeth. He had been brought into existence amidst the joyous shouts of boys, the jingling of sleigh-bells, and the slashing of whips. The sun went down, and the full moon rose, large, round, and clear, shining in the deep blue.

"There it comes again, from the other side," said the Snow Man, who supposed the sun was showing himself once more. "Ah, I have cured him of staring, though; now he may hang up there, and shine, that I may see myself. If I only knew how to manage to move away from this place, — I should so like to move. If I could, I would slide along yonder on the ice, as I have seen the boys do; but I don't understand how; I don't even know how to run."

"Away, away," barked the old yard-dog. He was quite hoarse, and could not pronounce "Bow wow" properly. He had once been an indoor dog, and lay by the fire, and he had been hoarse ever since. "The sun will make you run some day. I saw him, last winter, make your predecessor run, and his predecessor before him. Away, away, they all have to go."

"I don't understand you, comrade," said the Snow Man. "Is that thing up yonder to teach me to run? I saw it running itself a little while ago, and now it has come creeping up from the other side."

"You know nothing at all," replied the yard-dog; "but then, you've only lately been patched up. What you see yonder is the moon, and the one before it was the sun. It will come again to-morrow, and most likely teach you to run down into the ditch by the well; for I think the weather is going to change. I can feel such pricks and stabs in my left leg; I am sure there is going to be a change."

"I don't understand him," said the Snow Man to himself; "but I have a feeling that he is talking of something very disagreeable. The one who stared so just now, and whom he calls the sun, is not my friend; I can feel that too."

"Away, away," barked the yard-dog, and then he turned round three times, and crept into his kennel to sleep.

There was really a change in the weather. Towards morning, a thick fog covered the whole country round, and a keen wind arose, so that the cold seemed to freeze one's bones; but when the sun rose, the sight was splendid. Trees and bushes were covered with hoar frost, and looked like a forest of white coral; while on every twig glittered frozen dew-drops. The many delicate forms concealed in summer by luxuriant foliage, were now clearly defined, and looked like glittering lace-work. From every twig glistened a white radiance. The birch, waving in the wind, looked full of life, like trees in summer; and its appearance was wondrously beautiful. And where the sun shone, how everything glittered and sparkled, as if diamond dust had been strewn about; while the snowy carpet of the earth appeared as if covered with diamonds, from which countless lights gleamed, whiter than even the snow itself.

"This is really beautiful," said a young girl, who had come into the garden with a young man; and they both stood still near the Snow Man, and contemplated the glittering scene. "Summer cannot show a more beautiful sight," she exclaimed, while her eyes sparkled.

"And we can't have such a fellow as this in the summer time," replied the young man, pointing to the Snow Man; "he is capital."

The girl laughed, and nodded at the Snow Man, and then tripped away over the snow with her friend. The snow creaked and crackled beneath her feet, as if she had been treading on starch.

"Who are these two?" asked the Snow Man of the yard-dog. "You have been here longer than I have; do you know them?"

"Of course I know them," replied the yard-dog; "she has stroked my back many times, and he has given me a bone of meat. I never bite those two."

"But what are they?" asked the Snow Man.

"They are lovers," he replied; "they will go and live in the same kennel by-and-by, and gnaw at the same bone. Away, away!"

"Are they the same kind of beings as you and I?" asked the Snow Man.

"Well, they belong to the same master," retorted the yard-dog. "Certainly people who were only born yesterday know very little. I can see that in you. I have age and experience. I know every one here in the house, and I know there was once a time when I did not lie out here in the cold, fastened to a chain. Away, away!"

"The cold is delightful," said the Snow Man; "but do tell me tell me; only you must not clank your chain so; for it jars all through me when you do that."

"Away, away!" barked the yard-dog; "I'll tell you; they said I was a pretty little fellow once; then I used to lie in a velvet-covered chair, up at the master's house, and sit in the mistress's lap. They used to kiss my nose, and wipe my paws with an embroidered handkerchief, and I was called 'Ami, dear Ami, sweet Ami.' But after a while I grew too big for them, and they sent me away to the housekeeper's room; so I came to live on the lower story. You can look into the room from where you stand, and see where I was master once; for I was indeed master to the housekeeper. It was certainly a smaller room than those up stairs; but I was more comfortable; for I was not being continually taken hold of and pulled about by the children as I had

"The Sun will soon teach you to run" said the Yard-dog.

THE SNOW MAN

been. I received quite as good food, or even better. I had my own cushion, and there was a stove—it is the finest thing in the world at this season of the year. I used to go under the stove, and lie down quite beneath it. Ah, I still dream of that stove. Away, away!"

"Does a stove look beautiful?" asked the Snow Man, "is it at all like me?"

"It is just the reverse of you,' said the dog; "it's as black as a crow, and has a long neck and a brass knob; it eats firewood, so that fire spurts out of its mouth. We should keep on one side, or under it, to be comfortable. You can see it through the window, from where you stand."

Then the Snow Man looked, and saw a bright polished thing with a brazen knob, and fire gleaming from the lower part of it. The Snow Man felt quite a strange sensation come over him; it was very odd, he knew not what it meant, and he could not account for it. But there are people who are not men of snow, who understand what it is. "'And why did you leave her?" asked the Snow Man, for it seemed to him that the stove must be of the female sex. "How could you give up such a comfortable place?"

"I was obliged," replied the yard-dog. "They turned me out of doors, and chained me up here. I had bitten the youngest of my master's sons in the leg, because he kicked away the bone I was gnawing. 'Bone for bone,' I thought; but they were so angry, and from that time I have been fastened with a chain, and lost my bone. Don't you hear how hoarse I am. Away, away! I can't talk any more like other dogs. Away, away, that is the end of it all."

But the Snow Man was no longer listening. He was looking into the housekeeper's room on the lower storey; where the stove stood on its four iron legs, looking about the same size as the Snow Man himself. "What a strange crackling I feel within me," he said. "Shall I ever get in there? It is an innocent wish, and innocent wishes are sure to be fulfilled. I must go in there and lean against her, even if I have to break the window."

"You must never go in there," said the yard-dog, "for if you approach the stove, you'll melt away, away."

"I might as well go," said the Snow Man, "for I think I am breaking up as it is."

During the whole day the Snow Man stood looking in through the window, and in the twilight hour the room became still more inviting, for from the stove came a gentle glow, not like the sun or the moon; no, only the bright light which gleams from a stove when it has been well fed. When the door of the stove was opened, the flames darted out of its mouth; this is customary with all stoves. The light of the flames fell directly on the face and breast of the Snow Man with a ruddy gleam. "I can endure it no longer," said he; "how beautiful it looks when it stretches out its tongue?"

The night was long, but did not appear so to the Snow Man, who stood there enjoying his own reflections, and crackling with the cold. In the morning, the window-panes of the housekeeper's room were covered with ice. They were the most beautiful ice-flowers any Snow Man could desire, but they concealed the stove. These window-panes would not thaw, and he could see nothing of the stove, which he pictured to himself, as if it had been a lovely human being. The snow crackled and the wind whistled around him; it was just the kind of frosty weather a Snow Man might thoroughly enjoy. But he did not enjoy it; how, indeed, could he enjoy anything when he was "stove sick?"

"That is terrible disease for a Snow Man," said the yard-dog; "I have suffered from it myself, but I got over it. Away, away," he barked and then he added, "the weather is going to change." And the weather did change; it began to thaw. As the warmth increased, the Snow Man decreased. He said nothing and made no complaint, which is a sure sign. One morning he broke, and sunk down altogether; and, behold, where he had stood, something like a broomstick remained sticking up in the ground. It was the pole round which the boys had built him up. "Ah, now I understand why he had such a great longing for the stove," said the yard-dog. "Why, there's the shovel that is used for cleaning out the stove, fastened to the pole." The Snow Man had a stove scraper in his body; that was what moved him so. "But it's all over now. Away, away." And soon the winter passed. "Away, away," barked the hoarse yard-dog. But the girls in the house sang,

"Come from your fragrant home, green thyme;
Stretch your soft branches, willow-tree;
The months are bringing the sweet spring-time,
When the lark in the sky sings joyfully.
Come gentle sun, while the cuckoo sings,
And I'll mock his note in my wanderings."

And nobody thought any more of the Snow Man.

THE PEN AND THE INKSTAND

IN a poet's room, where his inkstand stood on the table, the remark was once made, "It is wonderful what can be brought out of an inkstand. What will come next? It is indeed wonderful."

"Yes, certainly," said the inkstand to the pen, and to the other articles that stood on the table; "that's what I always say. It is wonderful and extraordinary what a number of things come out of me. It's quite incredible, and I really don't know what is coming next when that man dips his pen into me. One drop out of me is enough for half a page of paper, and what cannot half a page contain? From me, all the works of a poet are produced; all those imaginary characters whom people fancy they have known or met. All the deep feeling, the humor, and the vivid pictures of nature. I myself don't understand how it is, for I am not acquainted with nature, but it is certainly in me. From me have gone forth to the world those wonderful descriptions of troops of charming maidens, and of brave knights on prancing steeds; of the halt and the blind, and I know not what more, for I assure you I never think of these things."

"There you are right," said the pen, "for you don't think at all; if you did, you would see that you can only provide the means. You give the fluid that I may place upon the paper what dwells in me, and what I wish to bring to light. It is the pen that writes: no man doubts that; and, indeed, most people understand as much about poetry as an old inkstand."

"You have had very little experience," replied the inkstand. "You have hardly been in service a week, and are already half worn out. Do you imagine you are a poet? You are only a servant, and before you came I had many like you, some of the goose family, and others of English manufacture. I know a quill pen as well as I know a steel one. I have had both sorts in my service, and I shall have many more when *he* comes—the man who performs the mechanical part—and writes down what he obtains from me. I should like to know what will be the next thing he gets out of me."

"Inkpot!" exclaimed the pen contemptuously.

Late in the evening the poet came home. He had been to a concert, and had been quite enchanted with the admirable performance of a famous violin player whom he had heard there. The performer had produced from his instrument a richness of tone that sometimes sounded like tinkling waterdrops or rolling pearls; sometimes like the birds twittering in chorus, and then rising and swelling in sound like the wind through the fir-trees. The poet felt as if his own heart were weeping, but in tones of melody like the sound of a woman's voice. It seemed not only the strings, but every part of the instrument from which these sounds were produced. It was a wonderful performance and a difficult piece, and yet the bow seemed to glide across the strings so easily that it was as if any one could do it who tried. Even the violin and the bow appeared to perform independently of their master who guided them; it was as if soul and spirit had been breathed into the instrument, so the audience forgot the performer in the beautiful sounds he produced. Not so the poet; he remembered him, and named him, and wrote down his thoughts on the subject. "How foolish it would be for the violin and the bow to boast of their performance, and yet we men often commit that folly. The poet, the artist, the man of science in his laboratory, the general,—we all do it; and yet we are only the instruments which the Almighty uses; to Him alone the honor is due. We have nothing of ourselves of which we should be proud." Yes, this is what the poet wrote down. He wrote it in the form of a parable, and called it "The Master and the Instruments."

"That is what you have got, madam," said the pen to the inkstand, when the two were alone again. "Did you hear him read aloud what I had written down?"

"Yes, what I gave you to write," retorted the inkstand. "That was a cut at you because of your conceit. To think that you could not understand that you were being quizzed. I gave you a cut from within me. Surely I must know my own satire."

"Ink-pitcher!" cried the pen.

"Writing-stick!" retorted the inkstand. And each of them felt satisfied that he had given a good answer. It is pleasing to be convinced that you have settled a matter by your reply; it is something to make you sleep well, and they both slept well upon it. But the poet did not sleep. Thoughts rose up within him like the tones of the violin, falling like pearls, or rushing like the strong wind through the forest. He understood his own heart in these thoughts; they were as a ray from the mind of the Great Master of all minds.

"To Him be all the honor."

THE BUTTERFLY

THERE was once a butterfly who wished for a bride, and, as may be supposed, he wanted to choose a very pretty one from among the flowers. He glanced, with a very critical eye, at all the flower-beds, and found that the flowers were seated quietly and demurely on their stalks, just as maidens should sit before they are engaged; but there was a great number of them, and it appeared as if his search would become very wearisome. The butterfly did not like to take too much trouble, so he flew off on a visit to the daisies. The French call this flower "Marguerite," and they say that the little daisy can prophesy. Lovers pluck off the leaves, and as they pluck each leaf, they ask a question about their lovers; thus: "Does he or she love me? — Ardently? Distractedly? Very much? A little? Not at all?" and so on. Every one speaks these words in his own language. The butterfly came also to Marguerite to inquire, but he did not pluck off her leaves; he pressed a kiss on each of them, for he thought there was always more to be done by kindness.

"Darling Marguerite daisy," he said to her, "you are the wisest woman of all the flowers. Pray tell me which of the flowers I shall choose for my wife. Which will be my bride? When I know, I will fly directly to her, and propose."

But Marguerite did not answer him; she was offended that he should call her a woman when she was only a girl; and there is a great difference. He asked her a second time, and then a third; but she remained dumb, and answered not a word. Then he would wait no longer, but flew away, to commence his wooing at once. It was in the early spring, when the crocus and the snowdrop were in full bloom.

"They are very pretty," thought the butterfly; "charming little lasses; but they are rather formal."

Then, as the young lads often do, he looked out for the elder girls. He next flew to the anemones; these were rather sour to his taste. The violet, a little too sentimental. The lime-blossoms, too small, and besides, there was such a large family of them. The apple-blossoms, though they looked like roses, bloomed to-day, but might fall off to-morrow, with the first wind that blew; and he thought that a marriage with one of them might last too short a time. The pea-blossom pleased him most of all; she was white and red, graceful and slender, and belonged to those domestic maidens who have a pretty appearance, and can yet be useful in the kitchen. He was just about to make her an offer, when, close by the maiden, he saw a pod, with a withered flower hanging at the end.

"Who is that?" he asked.

"That is my sister," replied the pea-blossom.

"Oh, indeed; and you will be like her some day," said he; and he flew away directly, for he felt quite shocked.

A honeysuckle hung forth from the hedge, in full bloom; but there were so many girls like her, with long faces and sallow complexions. No; he did not like her. But which one did he like?

Spring went by, and summer drew towards its close; autumn came; but he had not decided. The flowers now appeared in their most gorgeous robes, but all in vain; they had not the fresh, fragrant air of youth. For the heart asks for fragrance, even when it is no longer young; and there is very little of that to be found in the dahlias or the dry chrysanthemums; therefore the butterfly turned to the mint on the ground. You know, this plant has no blossom; but it is sweetness all over, — full of fragrance from head to foot, with the scent of a flower in every leaf.

"I will take her," said the butterfly; and he made her an offer. But the mint stood silent and stiff, as she listened to him. At last she said, —

"Friendship, if you please; nothing more. I am old, and you are old, but we may live for each other just the same; as to marrying — no; don't let us appear ridiculous at our age."

And so it happened that the butterfly got no wife at all. He had been too long choosing, which is always a bad plan. And the butterfly became what is called an old bachelor.

It was late in the autumn, with rainy and cloudy weather. The cold wind blew over the bowed backs of the willows, so that they creaked again. It was not the weather for flying about in summer clothes; but fortunately the butterfly was not out in it. He had got a shelter by chance. It was in a room heated by a stove, and as warm as summer. He could exist here, he said, well enough.

"But it is not enough merely to exist," said he, "I need freedom, sunshine, and a little flower for a companion."

Then he flew against the window-pane, and was seen and admired by those in the room, who caught him, and stuck him on a pin, in a box of curiosities. They could not do more for him.

"Now I am perched on a stalk, like the flowers," said the butterfly. "It is not very pleasant, certainly; I should imagine it is something like being married; for here I am stuck fast." And with this thought he consoled himself a little.

"That seems very poor consolation," said one of the plants in the room, that grew in a pot.

"Ah," thought the butterfly, "one can't very well trust these plants in pots; they have too much to do with mankind."

SOUP FROM A SAUSAGE SKEWER

"WE had such an excellent dinner yesterday," said an old mouse of the female sex to another who had not been present at the feast. "I sat number twenty-one below the mouse-king, which was not a bad place. Shall I tell you what we had? Everything was first rate. Mouldy bread, tallow candle, and sausage. And then, when we had finished that course, the same came on all over again; it was as good as two feasts. We were very sociable, and there was as much joking and fun as if we had been all of one family circle. Nothing was left but the sausage skewers, and this formed a subject of conversation, till at last it turned to the proverb, 'Soup from sausage skins;' or, as the people in the neighboring country call it, 'Soup from a sausage skewer.' Every one had heard the proverb, but no one had ever tasted the soup, much less prepared it. A capital toast was drunk to the inventor of the soup, and some one said he ought to be made a relieving officer to the poor. Was not that witty? Then the old mouse-king rose and promised that the young lady-mouse who should learn how best to prepare this much-admired and savory soup should be his queen, and a year and a day should be allowed for the purpose."

"That was not at all a bad proposal," said the other mouse; "but how is the soup made?"

"Ah, that is more than I can tell you. All the young lady mice were asking the same question. They wished very much to be queen, but they did not want to take the trouble of going out into the world to learn how to make soup, which was absolutely necessary to be done first. But it is not every one who would care to leave her family, or her happy corner by the fire-side at home, even to be made queen. It is not always easy to find bacon and cheese-rind in foreign lands every day, and it is not pleasant to have to endure hunger, and be perhaps, after all, eaten up alive by the cat."

Most probably some such thoughts as these discouraged the majority from going out into the world to collect the required information. Only four mice gave notice that they were ready to set out on the journey. They were young and lively, but poor. Each of them wished to visit one of the four divisions of the world, so that it might be seen which was the most favored by fortune. Every one took a sausage skewer as a traveller's staff, and to remind them of the object of their journey. They left home early in May, and none of them returned till the first of May in the following year, and then only three of them. Nothing was seen or heard of the fourth, although the day of decision was close at hand. "Ah, yes, there is always some trouble mixed up with the greatest pleasure," said the mouse-king; but he gave orders that all the mice within a circle of many miles should be invited at once. They were to assemble in the kitchen, and the three travelled mice were to stand in a row before them, while a sausage skewer, covered with crape, was to be stuck up instead of the missing mouse. No one dared to express an opinion until the king spoke, and desired one of them to go on with her story. And now we shall hear what she said.

WHAT THE FIRST LITTLE MOUSE SAW AND HEARD ON HER TRAVELS.

"When I first went out into the world," said the little mouse, "I fancied, as so many of my age do, that I already knew everything, but it was not so. It takes years to acquire great knowledge. I went at once to sea in a ship bound for the north. I had been told that the ship's cook must know how to prepare every dish at sea, and it is easy enough to do that with plenty of sides of bacon, and large tubs of salt meat and mouldy flour. There I found plenty of delicate food, but no opportunity for learning how to make soup from a sausage skewer. We sailed on for many days and nights; the ship rocked fearfully, and we did not escape without a wetting. As soon as we arrived at the port to which the ship was bound, I left it, and went on shore at a place far towards the north. It is a wonderful thing to leave your own little corner at home, to hide yourself in a ship where there are sure to be some nice snug corners for shelter, then suddenly to find yourself thousands of miles away in a foreign land. I saw large pathless forests of pine and birch trees, which smelt so strong that I sneezed and thought of sausage. There were great lakes also which looked as black as ink at a distance, but were quite clear when I came close to them. Large swans were floating upon them, and I thought at first they were only foam, they lay so still; but when I saw them walk and fly, I knew what they were directly. They belong to the goose species, one can see that by their walk. No one can attempt to disguise family descent. I kept with my own kind, and associated with the forest and field mice, who, however, knew very little, especially about what I wanted to know, and which had actually made me travel abroad. The idea that soup could be made from a sausage skewer was to them such an out-of-the-way, unlikely thought, that it was repeated from one to another through the whole forest. They declared that the problem would never be solved, that the thing was an impossibility. How little I thought that in this place, on the very first night, I should be initiated into the manner of its preparation.

"It was the height of summer, which the mice told me was the reason that the forest smelt so strong, and that the herbs were so fragrant, and the lakes with the white swimming swans so dark, and yet so clear. On the margin of the wood, near to three or four houses, a pole, as large as the mainmast of a ship, had been erected, and from the summit hung wreaths of flowers and fluttering ribbons; it was the Maypole. Lads and lasses danced round the pole, and tried to outdo the violins of the musicians with their singing. They were as merry as ever at sunset and in the moonlight, but I took no part in the merry-making. What has a little mouse to do with a Maypole dance? I sat in the soft moss, and held my sausage skewer tight. The moon threw its beams particularly on one spot where stood a tree covered with exceedingly fine moss. I may almost venture to say that it was as fine and soft as the fur of the mouse-king, but it was green, which is a color very agreeable to the eye. All at once I saw the most charming little people marching towards me. They did not reach higher than my knee; they looked like human beings, but were better proportioned, and they called themselves elves. Their clothes were very delicate and fine, for they were made of the leaves of flowers, trimmed with the wings of flies and gnats, which had not a bad effect. By their manner, it appeared as if they were seeking for something. I knew not what, till at last one of them espied me and came towards me, and the foremost pointed to my sausage skewer, and said, 'There, that is just what we want; see, it is pointed at the top; is it not capital?' and the longer he looked at my pilgrim's staff, the more delighted he became. 'I will lend it to you,' said I, 'but not to keep.'

" 'Oh no, we won't keep it!' they all cried; and then they seized the skewer, which I gave up to them, and danced with it to the spot where the delicate moss grew, and set it up in the middle of the green. They wanted a maypole, and the one they now had seemed cut out on purpose for them. Then they decorated it so beautifully that it was quite dazzling to look at. Little spiders spun golden threads around it, and then it was hung with fluttering veils and flags so delicately white that they glittered like snow in the moonshine. After that they took colors from the butterfly's wing, and sprinkled them over the white drapery which gleamed as if covered with flowers and diamonds, so that I could not recognize my sausage skewer at all. Such a maypole had never been seen in all the world as this. Then came a great company of real elves. Nothing could be finer than their clothes, and they invited me to be present at

SOUP FROM A SAUSAGE SKEWER

the feast; but I was to keep at a certain distance, because I was too large for them. Then commenced such music that it sounded like a thousand glass bells, and was so full and strong that I thought it must be the song of the swans. I fancied also that I heard the voices of the cuckoo ,and the black-bird, and it seemed at last as if the whole forest sent forth glorious melodies—the voices of children, the tinkling of bells, and the songs of the birds; and all this wonderful melody came from the elfin maypole. My sausage peg was a complete peal of bells. I could scarcely believe that so much could have been produced from it, till I remembered into what hands it had fallen. I was so much affected that I wept tears such as a little mouse can weep, but they were tears of joy. The night was far too short for me; there are no long nights there in summer, as we often have in this part of the world. When the morning dawned, and the gentle breeze rippled the glassy mirror of the forest lake, all the delicate veils and flags fluttered away into thin air; the waving garlands of the spider's web, the hanging bridges and galleries, or whatever else they may be called, vanished away as if they had never been. Six elves brought me back my sausage skewer, and at the same time asked me to make any request, which they would grant if in their power; so I begged them, if they could, to tell me how to make soup from a sausage skewer.

" 'How do we make it?' said the chief of the elves with a smile. 'Why you have just seen it; you scarcely knew your sausage skewer again, I am sure.'

"They think themselves very wise, thought I to myself. Then I told them all about it, and why I had travelled so far, and also what promise had been made at home to the one who should discover the method of preparing this soup. 'What use will it be,' I asked, 'to the mouse-king or to our whole mighty kingdom that I have seen all these beautiful things? I cannot shake the sausage peg and say, Look, here is the skewer, and now the soup will come. That would only produce a dish to be served when people were keeping a fast.'

"Then the elf dipped his finger into the cup of a violet, and said to me, 'Look here, I will anoint your pilgrim's staff, so that when you return to your own home and enter the king's castle, you have only to touch the king with your staff, and violets will spring forth and cover the whole of it, even in the coldest winter time; so I think I have given you really something to carry home, and a little more than something.' "

But before the little mouse explained what this something more was, she stretched her staff out to the king, and as it touched him the most beautiful bunch of violets sprang forth and filled the place with perfume. The smell was so powerful that the mouse-king ordered the mice who stood nearest the chimney to thrust their tails into the fire, that there might be a smell of burning, for the perfume of the violets was overpowering, and not the sort of scent that every one liked.

"But what was the something more of which you spoke just now?" asked the mouse-king.

"Why," answered the little mouse, "I think it is what they call 'effect;' " and thereupon she turned the staff round, and behold not a single flower was to be seen upon it! She now only held the naked skewer, and lifted it up as a conductor lifts his baton at a concert. "Violets, the elf told me," continued the mouse, "are for the sight, the smell, and the touch; so we have only now to produce the effect of hearing and tasting;" and then, as the little mouse beat

time with her staff, there came sounds of music, not such music as was heard
in the forest, at the elfin feast, but such as is often heard in the kitchen—the
sounds of boiling and roasting. It came quite suddenly, like wind rushing
through the chimneys, and seemed as if every pot and kettle were boiling
over. The fire-shovel clattered down on the brass fender; and then, quite as
suddenly, all was still,—nothing could be heard but the light, vapory song of
the tea-kettle, which was quite wonderful to hear, for no one could rightly
distinguish whether the kettle was just beginning to boil or going to stop. And
the little pot steamed, and the great pot simmered, but without any regard
for each; indeed there seemed no sense in the pots at all. And as the little
mouse waved her baton still more wildly, the pots foamed and threw up bubbles, and boiled over; while again the wind roared and whistled through the
chimney, and at last there was such a terrible hubbub, that the little mouse
let her stick fall.

"That is a strange sort of soup," said the mouse-king; "shall we not now
hear about the preparation?"

"That is all," answered the little mouse, with a bow.

"That all!" said the mouse-king; "then we shall be glad to hear what information the next may have to give us."

WHAT THE SECOND MOUSE HAD TO TELL

"I was born in the library, at a castle," said the second mouse. "Very few
members of our family ever had the good fortune to get into the dining-room,
much less the store-room. On my journey, and here to-day, are the only times
I have ever seen a kitchen. We were often obliged to suffer hunger in the
library, but then we gained a great deal of knowledge. The rumor reached us
of the royal prize offered to those who should be able to make soup from a
sausage skewer. Then my old grandmother sought out a manuscript which,
however, she could not read, but had heard it read, and in it was written,
'Those who are poets can make soup of sausage skewers.' She then asked me if
I was a poet. I felt myself quite innocent of any such pretensions. Then she
said I must go out and make myself a poet. I asked again what I should be
required to do, for it seemed to me quite as difficult as to find out how to
make soup of a sausage skewer. My grandmother had heard a great deal of
reading in her day, and she told me three principal qualifications were
necessary—understanding, imagination, and feeling. 'If you can manage to
acquire these three, you will be a poet, and the sausage-skewer soup will be
quite easy to you.'

"So I went forth into the world, and turned my steps towards the west, that
I might become a poet. Understanding is the most important matter in
everything. I knew that, for the two other qualifications are not thought
much of; so I went first to seek for understanding. Where was I to find it? 'Go
to the ant and learn wisdom,' said the great Jewish king. I knew that from
living in a library. So I went straight on till I came to the first great ant-hill,
and then I set myself to watch, that I might become wise. The ants are a very
respectable people, they are wisdom itself. All they do is like the working of a
sum in arithmetic, which comes right. 'To work and to lay eggs,' say they,
'and to provide for posterity, is to live out your time properly;' and that they
truly do. They are divided into the clean and the dirty ants, their rank is

pointed out by a number, and the ant-queen is number ONE; and her opinion is the only correct one on everything; she seems to have the whole wisdom of the world in her, which was just the important matter I wished to acquire. She said a great deal which was no doubt very clever; yet to me it sounded like nonsense. She said the ant-hill was the loftiest thing in the world, and yet close to the mound stood a tall tree, which no one could deny was loftier, much loftier, but no mention was made of the tree. One evening an ant lost herself on this tree; she had crept up the stem, not nearly to the top, but higher than any ant had ever ventured; and when at last she returned home she said that she had found something in her travels much higher than the ant-hill. The rest of the ants considered this an insult to the whole community; so she was condemned to wear a muzzle and to live in perpetual solitude. A short time afterwards another ant got on the tree, and made the same journey and the same discovery, but she spoke of it cautiously and indefinitely, and as she was one of the superior ants and very much respected, they believed her, and when she died they erected an eggshell as a monument to her memory, for they cultivated a great respect for science. I saw," said the little mouse, "that the ants were always running to and fro with her burdens on their backs. Once I saw one of them drop her load; she gave herself a great deal of trouble in trying to raise it again, but she could not succeed. Then two others came up and tried with all their strength to help her, till they nearly dropped their own burdens in doing so; then they were obliged to stop for a moment in their help, for every one must think of himself first. And the ant-queen remarked that their conduct that day showed that they possessed kind hearts and good understanding. 'These two qualities,' she continued, 'place us ants in the highest degree above all other reasonable beings. Understanding must therefore be seen among us in the most prominent manner, and my wisdom is greater than all.' And so saying she raised herself on her two hind legs, that no one else might be mistaken for her. I could not therefore make an error, so I ate her up. We are to go to the ants to learn wisdom, and I had got the queen.

"I now turned and went nearer to the lofty tree already mentioned, which was an oak. It had a tall trunk with a wide-spreading top, and was very old. I knew that a living being dwelt here, a dryad as she is called, who is born with the tree and dies with it. I had heard this in the library, and here was just such a tree, and in it an oak-maiden. She uttered a terrible scream when she caught sight of me so near to her; like many women, she was very much afraid of mice. And she had more real cause for fear than they have, for I might have gnawed through the tree on which her life depended. I spoke to her in a kind and friendly manner, and begged her to take courage. At last she took me up in her delicate hand, and then I told her what had brought me out into the world, and she promised me that perhaps on that very evening she should be able to obtain for me one of the two treasures for which I was seeking. She told me that Phantæsus was her very dear friend, that he was as beautiful as the god of love, that he remained often for many hours with her under the leafy boughs of the tree which then rustled and waved more than ever over them both. He called her his dryad, she said, and the tree his tree; for the grand old oak, with its gnarled trunk, was just to his taste. The root, spreading deep into the earth, the top rising high in the fresh air, knew the value of the drifted snow, the keen wind, and the warm sunshine, as it ought to be known. 'Yes,' continued the dryad, 'the birds sing up above in the branches, and talk to each other about the beautiful fields they have visited in foreign lands; and on one of the withered boughs a stork has built his nest, —it is beautifully arranged, and besides it is pleasant to hear a little about the land of the pyramids. All this pleases Phantæsus, but it is not enough for him; I am obliged to relate to him of my life in the woods; and to go back to my childhood, when I was little, and the tree so small and delicate that a stinging-nettle could overshadow it, and I have to tell everything that has happened since then till now that the tree is so large and strong. Sit you down now under the green bindwood and pay attention, when Phantæsus comes I will find an opportunity to lay hold of his wing and to pull out one of the little feathers. That feather you shall have; a better was never given to any poet, it will be quite enough for you.'

"And when Phantæsus came the feather was plucked, and," said the little mouse, "I seized and put it in water, and kept it there till it was quite soft. It was very heavy and indigestible, but I managed to nibble it up at last. It is not so easy to nibble one's self into a poet, there are so many things to get through. Now, however, I had two of them, understanding and imagination; and through these I knew that the third was to be found in the library. A great man has said and written that there are novels whose sole and only use appeared to be that they might relieve mankind of overflowing tears—a kind of sponge, in fact, for sucking up feelings and emotions. I remembered a few of these books, they had always appeared tempting to the appetite; they had been much read, and were so greasy, that they must have absorbed no end of emotions in themselves. I retraced my steps to the library, and literally devoured a whole novel, that is, properly speaking, the interior or soft part of it; the crust, or binding, I left. When I had digested not only this, but a second, I felt a stirring within me; then I ate a small piece of a third romance, and felt myself a poet. I said it to myself, and told others the same. I had head-ache and back-ache, and I cannot tell what aches besides. I thought over all the stories that may be said to be connected with sausage pegs, and all that has ever been written about skewers, and sticks, and staves, and splinters came to my thoughts; the ant-queen must have had a wonderfully clear understanding. I remembered the man who placed a white stick in his mouth by which he could make himself and the stick invisible. I thought of sticks as hobby-horses, staves of music or rhyme, of breaking a stick over a man's back, and heaven knows how many more phrases of the same sort relating to sticks, staves, and skewers. All my thoughts ran on skewers, sticks of wood, and staves; and as I am, at last, a poet, and I have worked terribly hard to make myself one, I can of course make poetry on anything. I shall therefore be able to wait upon you every day in the week with a poetical history of a skewer. And that is my soup."

"In that case," said the mouse-king, "we will hear what the third mouse has to say."

"Squeak, squeak," cried a little mouse at the kitchen door; it was the fourth, and not the third, of the four who were contending for the prize, one whom the rest supposed to be dead. She shot in like an arrow, and overturned the sausage peg that had been covered with crape. She had been running day and night. She had watched an opportunity to get into a goods train, and had travelled by the railway; and yet she had arrived almost too late. She pressed forward, looking very much ruffled. She had lost her sausage skewer, but not her voice; for she began to speak at once as if they only waited for her, and would hear her only, and as if nothing else in the world was of the least consequence. She spoke out so clearly and plainly, and she had come in so suddenly, that no one had time to stop her or to say a word while she was speaking. And now let us hear what she said.

WHAT THE FOURTH MOUSE, WHO SPOKE BEFORE THE THIRD, HAD TO TELL

"I started off at once to the largest town," said she, "but the name of it has escaped me. I have a very bad memory for names. I was carried from the railway, with some forfeited goods, to the jail, and on arriving I made my escape, and ran into the house of the turnkey. The turnkey was speaking of his prisoners, especially of one who had uttered thoughtless words. These words had given rise to other words, and at length they were written down and registered: 'The whole affair is like making soup of sausage skewers,' said he, 'but the soup may cost him his neck.'

"Now this raised in me an interest for the prisoner," continued the little mouse, "and I watched my opportunity, and slipped into his apartment, for there is a mouse-hole to be found behind every closed door. The prisoner looked pale; he had a great beard and large, sparkling eyes. There was a lamp burning, but the walls were so black that they only looked the blacker for it. The prisoner scratched pictures and verses with white chalk on the black walls, but I did not read the verses. I think he found his confinement wearisome, so that I was a welcome guest. He enticed me with bread-crumbs, with whistling, and with gentle words, and seemed so friendly towards me, that by degrees I gained confidence in him, and we became friends; he divided his bread and water with me, gave me cheese and sausage, and I really began to love him. Altogether, I must own that it was a very pleasant intimacy. He let me run about on his hand, and on his arm, and into his sleeve; and I even crept into his beard, and he called me his little friend. I forgot what I had come out into the world for; forgot my sausage skewer which I had laid in a crack in the floor—it is lying there still. I wished to stay with him always where I was, for I knew that if I went away the poor prisoner would have no one to be his friend, which is a sad thing. I stayed, but he did not. He spoke to me so mournfully for the last time, gave me double as much bread and cheese as usual, and kissed his hand to me. Then he went away, and never came back. I know nothing more of his history.

"The jailer took possession of me now. He said something about soup from a sausage skewer, but I could not trust him. He took me in his hand certainly, but it was to place me in a cage like a tread-mill. Oh how dreadful it was! I had to run round and round without getting any farther in advance, and only to make everybody laugh. The jailer's grand-daughter was a charming little thing. She had curly hair like the brightest gold, merry eyes, and such a smiling mouth.

" 'You poor little mouse,' said she, one day as she peeped into my cage, 'I will set you free.' She then drew forth the iron fastening, and I sprang out on the window-sill, and from thence to the roof. Free! free! that was all I could think of; not of the object of my journey. It grew dark, and as night was coming on I found a lodging in an old tower, where dwelt a watchman and an owl. I had no confidence in either of them, least of all in the owl, which is like a cat, and has a great failing, for she eats mice. One may however be mistaken sometimes; and so was I, for this was a respectable and well-educated old owl, who knew more than the watchman, and even as much as I did myself. The young owls made a great fuss about everything, but the only rough words she would say to them were, 'You had better go and make some soup from sausage skewers.' She was very indulgent and loving to her children. Her conduct gave me such confidence in her, that from the crack where I sat I called out 'squeak.' This confidence of mine pleased her so much that she assured me she would take me under her own protection, and that not a creature should do me harm. The fact was, she wickedly meant to keep me in reserve for her own eating in winter, when food would be scarce. Yet she was a very clever lady-owl; she explained to me that the watchman could only hoot with the horn that hung loose at his side; and then she said he is so terribly proud of it, that he imagines himself an owl in the tower; — wants to do great things, but only succeeds in small; all soup on a sausage skewer. Then I begged the owl to give me the recipe for this soup. 'Soup from a sausage skewer,' said she, 'is only a proverb amongst mankind, and may be understood in many ways. Each believes his own way the best, and after all, the proverb signifies nothing.' 'Nothing!' I exclaimed. I was quite struck. Truth is not always agreeable, but truth is above everything else, as the old owl said. I thought over all this, and saw quite plainly that if truth was really so far above everything else, it must be much more valuable than soup from a sausage skewer. So I hastened to get away, that I might be home in time, and bring what was highest and best, and above everything — namely, the truth. The mice are an enlightened people, and the mouse-king is above them all. He is therefore capable of making me queen for the sake of truth."

"Your truth is a falsehood," said the mouse who had not yet spoken; "I can prepare the soup, and I mean to do so."

HOW IT WAS PREPARED

"I did not travel," said the third mouse; "I stayed in this country: that was the right way. One gains nothing by travelling — everything can be acquired here quite as easily; so I stayed at home. I have not obtained what I know from supernatural beings. I have neither swallowed it, nor learnt it from conversing with owls. I have got it all from my reflections and thoughts. Will you now set the kettle on the fire — so? Now pour the water in — quite full — up to the brim; place it on the fire; make up a good blaze; keep it burning, that the water may boil; it must boil over and over. There, now I throw in the skewer. Will the mouse-king be pleased now to dip his tail into the boiling water, and stir it round with the tail. The longer the king stirs it, the stronger the soup will become. Nothing more is necessary, only to stir it."

"Can no one else do this?" asked the king.

"No," said the mouse; "only in the tail of the mouse-king is this power contained."

And the water boiled and bubbled, as the mouse-king stood close beside the kettle. It seemed rather a dangerous performance; but he turned round, and put out his tail, as mice do in a dairy, when they wish to skim the cream from a pan of milk with their tails and afterwards lick it off. But the mouse-king's tail had only just touched the hot steam, when he sprang away from the chimney in a great hurry, exclaiming, "Oh, certainly, by all means, you must be my queen; and we will let the soup question rest till our golden wedding, fifty years hence; so that the poor in my kingdom, who are then to have plenty of food, will have something to look forward to for a long time, with great joy."

And very soon the wedding took place. But many of the mice, as they were returning home, said that the soup could not be properly called "soup from a sausage skewer," but "soup from a mouse's tail." They acknowledged also that some of the stories were very well told; but that the whole could have been managed differently. "I should have told it so — and so — and so." These were the critics who are always so clever *afterwards*.

When this story was circulated all over the world, the opinions upon it were divided; but the story remained the same. And, after all, the best way in everything you undertake, great as well as small, is to expect no thanks for anything you may do, even when it refers to "soup from a sausage skewer."

THE LITTLE MERMAID

FAR out in the ocean, where the water is as blue as the prettiest cornflower, and as clear as crystal, it is very, very deep; so deep, indeed, that no cable could fathom it: many church steeples, piled one upon another, would not reach from the ground beneath to the surface of the water above. There dwell the Sea King and his subjects. We must not imagine that there is nothing at the bottom of the sea but bare yellow sand. No, indeed; the most singular flowers and plants grow there; the leaves and stems of which are so pliant, that the slightest agitation of the water causes them to stir as if they had life. Fishes, both large and small, glide between the branches, as birds fly among the trees here upon land. In the deepest spot of all, stands the castle of the Sea King. Its walls are built of coral, and the long, gothic windows are of the clearest amber. The roof is formed of shells, that open and close as the water flows over them. Their appearance is very beautiful, for in each lies a glittering pearl, which would be fit for the diadem of a queen.

The Sea King had been a widower for many years, and his aged mother kept house for him. She was a very wise woman, and exceedingly proud of her high birth; on that account she wore twelve oysters on her tail; while others, also of high rank, were only allowed to wear six. She was, however, deserving of very great praise, especially for her care of the little sea-princesses, her grand-daughters. They were six beautiful children; but the youngest was the prettiest of them all; her skin was as clear and delicate as a rose-leaf, and her eyes as blue as the deepest sea; but, like all the others, she had no feet, and her body ended in a fish's tail. All day long they played in the great halls of the castle, or among the living flowers that grew out of the walls. The large amber windows were open, and the fish swam in, just as the swallows fly into our houses when we open the windows, excepting that the fishes swam up to the princesses, ate out of their hands, and allowed themselves to be stroked. Outside the castle there was a beautiful garden, in which grew bright red and dark blue flowers, and blossoms like flames of fire; the fruit glittered like gold, and the leaves and stems waved to and fro continually. The earth itself was the finest sand, but blue as the flame of burning sulphur. Over everything lay a peculiar blue radiance, as if it were surrounded by the air from above, through which the blue sky shone, instead of the dark depths of the sea. In calm weather the sun could be seen, looking like a purple flower, with the light streaming from the calyx. Each of the young princesses had a little plot of ground in the garden, where she might dig and plant as she pleased. One arranged her flower-bed into the form of a whale; another thought it better to make hers like the figure of a little mermaid; but that of the youngest was round like the sun, and contained flowers as red as his rays at sunset. She was a strange child, quiet and thoughtful; and while her sisters would be delighted with the wonderful things which they obtained from the wrecks of vessels, she cared for nothing but her pretty red flowers, like the sun, excepting a beautiful marble statue. It was the representation of a handsome boy, carved out of pure white stone, which had fallen to the bottom of the sea from a wreck. She planted by the statue a rose-colored weeping willow. It grew splendidly, and very soon hung its fresh branches over the statue, almost down to the blue sands. The shadow had a violet tint, and waved to and fro like the branches; it seemed as if the crown of the tree and the root were at play, and trying to kiss each other. Nothing gave her so much pleasure as to hear about the world above the sea. She made her old grandmother tell her all she knew of the ships and of the towns, the people and the animals. To her it seemed most wonderful and beautiful to hear that the flowers of the land should have fragrance, and not those below the sea; that the trees of the forest should be green; and that the fishes among the trees could sing so sweetly, that it was quite a pleasure to hear them. Her grandmother called the little birds fishes, or she would not have understood her; for she had never seen birds.

"When you have reached your fifteenth year," said the grand-mother, "you will have permission to rise up out of the sea, to sit on the rocks in the moonlight, while the great ships are sailing by; and then you will see both forests and towns."

In the following year, one of the sisters would be fifteen: but as each was a year younger than the other, the youngest would have to wait five years before her turn came to rise up from the bottom of the ocean, and see the earth as we do. However, each promised to tell the others what she saw on her first visit, and what she thought the most beautiful; for their grandmother could not tell them enough; there were so many things on which they wanted information. None of them longed so much for her turn to come as the youngest, she who had the longest time to wait, and who was so quiet and thoughtful. Many nights she stood by the open window, looking up through the dark blue water, and watching the fish as they splashed about with their fins and tails. She could see the moon and stars shining faintly; but through the water they looked larger than they do to our eyes. When something like a black cloud passed between her and them, she knew that it was either a whale swimming over her head, or a ship full of human beings, who never imagined that a pretty little mermaid was standing beneath them, holding out her white hands towards the keel of their ship.

As soon as the eldest was fifteen, she was allowed to rise to the surface of the ocean. When she came back, she had hundreds of things to talk about; but the most beautiful, she said, was to lie in the moonlight, on a sandbank, in the quiet sea, near the coast, and to gaze on a large town nearby, where the lights were twinkling like hundreds of stars; to listen to the sounds of the music, the noise of carriages, and the voices of human beings, and then to hear the merry bells peal out from the church steeples; and because she could not go near to all those wonderful things, she longed for them more than ever. Oh, did not the youngest sister listen eagerly to all these descriptions? and afterwards, when she stood at the open window looking up through the dark blue water, she thought of the great city, with all its bustle and noise, and even fancied she could hear the sound of the church bells, down in the depths of the sea.

In another year the second sister received permission to rise to the surface of the water, and to swim about where she pleased. She rose just as the sun was setting, and this, she said, was the most beautiful sight of all. The whole sky looked like gold, while violet and rose-colored clouds, which she could not describe, floated over her; and, still more rapidly than the clouds, flew a large flock of wild swans towards the setting sun, looking like a long white veil across the sea. She also swam towards the sun; but it sunk into the waves, and the rosy tints faded from the clouds and from the sea.

The third sister's turn followed; she was the boldest of them all, and she swam up a broad river that emptied itself into the sea. On the banks she saw green hills covered with beautiful vines; palaces and castles peeped out from amid the proud trees of the forest; she heard the birds singing, and the rays of the sun were so powerful that she was obliged often to dive down under the water to cool her burning face. In a narrow creek she found a whole troop of little human children, quite naked, and sporting about in the water; she wanted to play with them, but they fled in a great fright; and then a little black animal came to the water; it was a dog, but she did not know that, for she had never before seen one. This animal barked at her so terribly that she became frightened, and rushed back to the open sea. But she said she should never forget the beautiful forest, the green hills, and the pretty little children who could swim in the water, although they had not fish's tails.

The fourth sister was more timid; she remained in the midst of the sea, but she said it was quite as beautiful there as nearer the land. She could see for so many miles around her, and the sky above looked like a bell of glass. She had seen the ships, but at such a great distance that they looked like sea-gulls. The dolphins sported in the waves, and the great whales spouted water from their nostrils till it seemed as if a hundred fountains were playing in every direction.

The fifth sister's birthday occurred in the winter; so when her turn came, she saw what the others had not seen the first time they went up. The sea looked quite green, and large icebergs were floating about, each like a pearl, she said, but larger and loftier than the churches built by men. They were of the most singular shapes, and glittered like diamonds. She had seated herself upon one of the largest, and let the wind play with her long hair, and she remarked that all the ships sailed by rapidly, and steered as far away as they could from the iceberg, as if they were afraid of it. Towards evening, as the sun went down, dark clouds covered the sky, the thunder rolled and the light-ning flashed, and the red light glowed on the icebergs as they rocked and tossed on the heaving sea. On all the ships the sails were reefed with fear and trembling, while she sat calmly on the floating iceberg, watching the blue lightning, as it darted its forked flashes into the sea.

When first the sisters had permission to rise to the surface, they were each delighted with the new and beautiful sights they saw; but now, as grown-up girls, they could go when they pleased, and they had become indifferent about it. They wished themselves back again in the water, and after a month had passed they said it was much more beautiful down below, and pleasanter to be at home. Yet often, in the evening hours, the five sisters would twine their arms round each other, and rise to the surface, in a row. They had more beautiful voices than any human being could have; and before the approach of a storm, and when they expected a ship would be lost, they swam before the vessel, and sang sweetly of the delights to be found in the depths of the sea, and begging the sailors not to fear if they sank to the bottom. But the sailors could not understand the song, they took it for the howling of the storm. And these things were never to be beautiful for them; for if the ship sank, the men were drowned, and their dead bodies alone reached the palace of the Sea King.

When the sisters rose, arm-in-arm, through the water in this way, their youngest sister would stand quite alone, looking after them, ready to cry, only that the mermaids have no tears, and therefore they suffer more. "Oh, were I but fifteen years old," said she: "I know that I shall love the world up there, and all the people who live in it."

At last she reached her fifteenth year. "Well, now, you are grown up," said the old dowager, her grandmother; "so you must let me adorn you like your other sisters;" and she placed a wreath of white lilies in her hair, and every flower leaf was half a pearl. Then the old lady ordered eight great oysters to attach themselves to the tail of the princess to show her high rank.

"But they hurt me so," said the little mermaid.

"Pride must suffer pain," replied the old lady. Oh, how gladly she would have shaken off all this grandeur, and laid aside the heavy wreath! The red flowers in her own garden would have suited her much better, but she could not help herself: so she said, "Farewell," and rose as lightly as a bubble to the surface of the water. The sun had just set as she raised her head above the waves; but the clouds were tinted with crimson and gold, and through the glimmering twilight beamed the evening star in all its beauty. The sea was calm, and the air mild and fresh. A large ship, with three masts, lay becalmed on the water, with only one sail set; for not a breeze stirred, and the sailors sat idle on deck or amongst the rigging. There was music and song on board; and, as darkness came on, a hundred colored lanterns were lighted, as if the flags of all nations waved in the air. The little mermaid swam close to the cabin windows; and now and then, as the waves lifted her up, she could look in through clear glass window-panes, and see a number of well-dressed people within. Among them was a young prince, the most beautiful of all, with large black eyes; he was sixteen years of age, and his birthday was being kept with much rejoicing. The sailors were dancing on deck, but when the prince came out of the cabin, more than a hundred rockets rose in the air, making it as bright as day. The little mermaid was so startled that she dived under water; and when she again stretched out her head, it appeared as if all the stars of heaven were falling around her, she had never seen such fireworks before. Great suns spurted fire about, splendid fireflies flew into the blue air, and everything was reflected in the clear, calm sea beneath. The ship itself was so brightly illuminated that all the people, and even the smallest rope, could be distinctly and plainly seen. And how handsome the young prince looked, as he pressed the hands of all present and smiled at them, while the music resounded through the clear night air.

It was very late; yet the little mermaid could not take her eyes from the ship, or from the beautiful prince. The colored lanterns had been extinguished, no more rockets rose in the air, and the cannon had ceased firing; but the sea became restless, and a moaning, grumbling sound could be heard beneath the waves: still the little mermaid remained by the cabin window, rocking up and down on the water, which enabled her to look in. After a while, the sails were quickly unfurled, and the noble ship continued her passage; but soon the waves rose higher, heavy clouds darkened the sky, and lightning appeared in the distance. A dreadful storm was approaching; once more the sails were reefed, and the great ship pursued her flying course over the raging sea. The waves rose mountains high, as if they would have overtopped the mast; but the ship dived like a swan between them, and then rose again on their lofty, foaming crests. To the little mermaid this appeared pleasant sport; not so to the sailors. At length the ship groaned and creaked; the thick planks gave way under the lashing of the sea as it broke over the deck; the mainmast snapped asunder like a reed; the ship lay over on her side; and the water rushed in. The little mermaid now perceived that the crew were in danger; even she herself was obliged to be careful to avoid the beams and planks of the wreck which lay scattered on the water. At one moment it was so pitch dark that she could not see a single object, but a flash of lightning revealed the whole scene; she could see every one who had been on board excepting the prince; when the ship parted, she had seen him sink into the deep waves, and she was glad, for she thought he would now be with her; and then she remembered that human beings could not live in the water, so that when he got down to her father's palace he would be quite dead. But he must not die. So she swam about among the beams and planks which strewed the surface of the sea, forgetting that they could crush her to pieces. Then she dived deeply under the dark waters, rising and falling with the waves, till at length she managed to reach the young prince, who was fast losing the power of swimming in that stormy sea. His limbs were failing him, his beautiful eyes were closed, and he would have died had not the little mermaid come to his assistance. She held his head above the water, and let the waves drift them where they would.

In the morning the storm had ceased; but of the ship not a single fragment could be seen. The sun rose up red and glowing from the water, and its beams brought back the hue of health to the prince's cheeks; but his eyes remained closed. The mermaid kissed his high, smooth forehead, and stroked back his wet hair; he seemed to her like the marble statue in her little garden, and she kissed him again, and wished that he might live. Presently they came in sight of land; she saw lofty blue mountains, on which the white snow rested as if a flock of swans were lying upon them. Near the coast were beautiful green forests, and close by stood a large building, whether a church or a convent she could not tell. Orange and citron trees grew in the garden, and before the door stood lofty palms. The sea here formed a little bay, in which the water was quite still, but very deep; so she swam with the handsome prince to the beach, which was covered with fine, white sand, and there she laid him in the warm sunshine, taking care to raise his head higher than his body. Then bells sounded in the large white building, and a number of young girls came into the garden. The little mermaid swam out farther from the shore and placed herself between some high rocks that rose out of the water; then she covered her head and neck with the foam of the sea so that her little face might not be seen, and watched to see what would become of the poor prince. She did not wait long before she saw a young girl approach the spot where he lay. She seemed frightened at first, but only for a moment; then she fetched a number of people, and the mermaid saw that the prince came to life again, and smiled upon those who stood round him. But to her he sent no smile; he knew not that she had saved him. This made her very unhappy, and when he was led away into the great building, she dived down sorrowfully into the water, and returned to her father's castle. She had always been silent and thoughtful, and now she was more so than ever. Her sisters asked her what she had seen during her first visit to the surface of the water; but she would tell them nothing. Many an evening and morning did she rise to the place where she had left the prince. She saw the fruits in the garden ripen till they were gathered, the snow on the tops of the mountains melt away; but she never saw the prince, and therefore she returned home, always more sorrowful than before. It was her only comfort to sit in her own little garden, and fling her arm round the beautiful marble statue which was like the prince; but she gave up tending her flowers, and they grew in wild confusion over the paths, twining their long leaves and stems round the branches of the trees, so that the whole place became dark and gloomy. At length she could bear it no longer, and told one of her sisters all about it. Then the others heard the secret, and very soon it became known to two mermaids whose intimate friend happened to know who the prince was. She had also seen the festival on board ship, and she told them where the prince came from, and where his palace stood.

"Come, little sister," said the other princesses; then they entwined their arms and rose up in a long row to the surface of the water, close by the spot where they knew the prince's palace stood. It was built of bright yellow shining stone, with long flights of marble steps, one of which reached quite down to the sea. Splendid gilded cupolas rose over the roof, and between the pillars that surrounded the whole building stood life-like statues of marble. Through the clear crystal of the lofty windows could be seen noble rooms, with costly silk curtains and hangings of tapestry; while the walls were covered with beautiful paintings which were a pleasure to look at. In the centre of the largest saloon a fountain threw its sparkling jets high up into the glass cupola of the ceiling, through which the sun shone down upon the water and upon the beautiful plants growing round the basin of the fountain. Now that she knew where he lived, she spent many an evening and many a night on the water near the palace. She would swim much nearer the shore than any of the others ventured to do; indeed once she went quite up the narrow channel under the marble balcony, which threw a broad shadow on the water. Here she would sit and watch the young prince, who thought himself quite alone in the bright moonlight. She saw him many times of an evening sailing in a pleasant boat, with music playing and flags waving. She peeped out from among the green rushes, and if the wind caught her long silvery-white veil, those who saw it believed it to be a swan, spreading out its wings. On many a night, too, when the fishermen, with their torches, were out at sea, she heard them relate so many good things about the doings of the young prince, that she was glad she had saved his life when he had been tossed about half-dead on the waves. And she remembered that his head had rested on her bosom, and how heartily she had kissed him; but he knew nothing of all this, and could not even dream of her. She grew more and more fond of human beings, and wished more and more to be able to wander about with those whose world seemed to be so much larger than her own. They could fly over the sea in ships, and mount the high hills which were far above the clouds; and the lands they possessed, their woods and their fields, stretched far away beyond the reach of her sight. There was so much that she wished to know, and her sisters were unable to answer all her questions. Then she applied to her old grandmother, who knew all about the upper world, which she very rightly called the lands above the sea.

"If human beings are not drowned," asked the little mermaid, "can they live forever? do they never die as we do here in the sea?"

"Yes," replied the old lady, "they must also die, and their term of life is even shorter than ours. We sometimes live to three hundred years, but when we cease to exist here we only become the foam on the surface of the water, and we have not even a grave down here of those we love. We have not immortal souls, we shall never live again; but, like the green sea-weed, when once it has been cut off, we can never flourish more. Human beings, on the contrary, have a soul which lives forever, lives after the body has been turned to dust. It rises up through the clear, pure air beyond the glittering stars. As we rise out of the water, and behold all the land of the earth, so do they rise to unknown and glorious regions which we shall never see."

"Why have not we an immortal soul?" asked the little mermaid mournfully; "I would give gladly all the hundreds of years that I have to live, to be a human being only for one day, and to have the hope of knowing the happiness of that glorious world above the stars."

"You must not think of that," said the old woman; "we feel ourselves to be much happier and much better off than human beings."

"So I shall die," said the little mermaid, "and as the foam of the sea I shall be driven about never again to hear the music of the waves, or to see the pretty flowers nor the red sun. Is there anything I can do to win an immortal soul?"

"No," said the old woman, "unless a man were to love you so much that you were more to him than his father or mother; and if all his thoughts and all his love were fixed upon you, and the priest placed his right hand in yours, and he promised to be true to you here and hereafter, then his soul would glide into your body and you would obtain a share in the future happiness of mankind. He would give a soul to you and retain his own as well; but this can never happen. Your fish's tail, which amongst us is considered so beautiful, is thought on earth to be quite ugly; they do not know any better, and they think it necessary to have two stout props, which they call legs, in order to be handsome."

Then the little mermaid sighed, and looked sorrowfully at her fish's tail. "Let us be happy," said the old lady, "and dart and spring about during the three hundred years that we have to live, which is really quite long enough; after that we can rest ourselves all the better. This evening we are going to have a court ball."

It is one of those splendid sights which we can never see on earth. The walls and the ceiling of the large ball-room were of thick, but transparent crystal. May hundreds of colossal shells, some of a deep red, others of a grass green, stood on each side in rows, with blue fire in them, which lighted up the whole saloon, and shone through the walls, so that the sea was also illuminated. Innumerable fishes, great and small, swam past the crystal walls; on some of them the scales glowed with a purple brilliancy, and on others they shone like silver and gold. Through the halls flowed a broad stream, and in it danced the mermen and the mermaids to the music of their own sweet singing. No one on earth has such a lovely voice as theirs. The little mermaid sang more sweetly than them all. The whole court applauded her with hands and tails; and for a moment her heart felt quite gay, for she knew she had the loveliest voice of any on earth or in the sea. But she soon thought again of the world above her, for she could not forget the charming prince, nor her sorrow that she had not an immortal soul like his; therefore she crept away silently out of her father's palace, and while everything within was gladness and song, she sat in her own little garden sorrowful and alone. Then she heard the bugle sounding through the water, and thought—"He is certainly sailing above, he on whom my wishes depend, and in whose hands I should like to place the happiness of my life. I will venture all for him, and to win an immortal soul, while my sisters are dancing in my father's palace, I will go to the sea witch, of whom I have always been so much afraid, but she can give me counsel and help."

And then the little mermaid went out from her garden, and took the road to the foaming whirlpools, behind which the sorceress lived. She had never been that way before: neither flowers nor grass grew there; nothing but bare, gray, sandy ground stretched out to the whirlpool, where the water, like foaming mill-wheels, whirled round everything that it seized, and cast it into the fathomless deep. Through the midst of these crushing whirlpools the little mermaid was obliged to pass, to reach the dominions of the sea witch; and also for a long distance the only road lay right across a quantity of warm, bubbling mire, called by the witch her turfmoor. Beyond this stood her house, in the centre of a strange forest, in which all the trees and flowers were polypi, half animals and half plants; they looked like serpents with a hundred heads growing out of the ground. The branches were long slimy arms, with fingers like flexible worms, moving limb after limb from the root to the top. All that could be reached in the sea they seized upon, and held fast, so that it never escaped from their clutches. The little mermaid was so alarmed at what she saw, that she stood still, and her heart beat with fear, and she was very nearly turning back; but she thought of the prince, and of the human soul for which she longed, and her courage returned. She fastened her long flowing hair round her head, so that the polypi might not seize hold of it. She laid her hands together across her bosom, and then she darted forward as a fish shoots through the water, between the supple arms and fingers of the ugly polypi, which were stretched out on each side of her. She saw that each held in its grasp something it had seized with its numerous little arms, as if they were iron bands. The white skeletons of human beings who had perished at sea, and had sunk down into the deep waters, skeletons of land animals, oars, rudders, and chests of ships were lying tightly grasped by their clinging arms; even a little mermaid, whom they had caught and strangled; and this seemed the most shocking of all to the little princess.

She now came to a space of marshy ground in the wood, where large, fat water-snakes were rolling in the mire, and showing their ugly, drab-colored bodies. In the midst of this spot stood a house, built with the bones of shipwrecked human beings. There sat the sea witch, allowing a toad to eat from her mouth, just as people sometimes feed a canary with a piece of sugar. She called the ugly water-snakes her little chickens, and allowed them to crawl all over her bosom.

"I know what you want," said the sea witch; "it is very stupid of you, but you shall have your way, and it will bring you to sorrow, my pretty princess. You want to get rid of your fish's tail, and to have two supports instead of it, like human beings on earth, so that the young prince may fall in love with you, and that you may have an immortal soul." And then the witch laughed so loud and disgustingly, that the toad and the snakes fell to the ground, and lay there wriggling about. "You are but just in time," said the witch; "for after sunrise to-morrow I should not be able to help you till the end of another year. I will prepare a draught for you, with which you must swim to land to-morrow before sunrise, and sit down on the shore and drink it. Your tail will then disappear, and shrink up into what mankind calls legs, and you will feel great pain, as if a sword were passing through you. But all who see you will say that you are the prettiest little human being they ever saw. You will still have the same floating gracefulness of movement, and no dancer will ever tread so lightly; but at every step you take it will feel as if you were treading upon sharp knives, and that the blood must flow. If you will bear all this, I will help you."

"Yes, I will," said the little princess in a trembling voice, as she thought of the prince and the immortal soul.

"But think again," said the witch; "for when once your shape has become like a human being, you can no more be a mermaid. You will never return through the water to your sisters, or to your father's palace again; and if you do not win the love of the prince, so that he is willing to forget his father and mother for your sake, and to love you with his whole soul, and allow the priest to join your hands that you may be man and wife, then you will never have an immortal soul. The first morning after he marries another your heart will break, and you will become foam on the crest of the waves."

"I will do it," said the little mermaid, and she became pale as death.

"But I must be paid also," said the witch, "and it is not a trifle that I ask. You have the sweetest voice of any who dwell here in the depths of the sea, and you believe that you will be able to charm the prince with it also, but this voice you must give to me; the best thing you possess will I have for the price of my draught. My own blood must be mixed with it, that it may be as sharp as a two-edged sword."

"But if you take away my voice," said the little mermaid, "what is left for me?"

"Your beautiful form, your graceful walk, and your expressive eyes; surely

THE LITTLE MERMAID

with these you can enchain a man's heart. Well, have you lost your courage? Put out your little tongue that I may cut it off as my payment; then you shall have the powerful draught."

"It shall be," said the little mermaid.

Then the witch placed her cauldron on the fire, to prepare the magic draught.

"Cleanliness is a good thing," said she, scouring the vessel with snakes, which she had tied together in a large knot; then she pricked herself in the breast, and let the black blood drop into it. The steam that rose formed itself into such horrible shapes that no one could look at them without fear. Every moment the witch threw something else into the vessel, and when it began to boil, the sound was like the weeping of a crocodile. When at last the magic draught was ready, it looked like the clearest water. "There it is for you," said the witch. Then she cut off the mermaid's tongue, so that she became dumb, and would never again speak or sing. "If the polypi should seize hold of you as you return through the wood," said the witch, "throw over them a few drops of the potion, and their fingers will be torn into a thousand pieces." But the little mermaid had no occasion to do this, for the polypi sprang back in terror when they caught sight of the glittering draught, which shone in her hand like a twinkling star.

So she passed quickly through the wood and the marsh, and between the rushing whirlpools. She saw that in her father's palace the torches in the ballroom were extinguished, and all within asleep; but she did not venture to go in to them, for now she was dumb and going to leave them forever, she felt as if her heart would break. She stole into the garden, took a flower from the flower-beds of each of her sisters, kissed her hand a thousand times towards the palace, and then rose up through the dark blue waters. The sun had not risen when she came in sight of the prince's palace, and approached the beautiful marble steps, but the moon shone clear and bright. Then the little mermaid drank the magic draught, and it seemed as if a two-edged sword went through her delicate body: she fell into a swoon, and lay like one dead. When the sun arose and shone over the sea, she recovered, and felt a sharp pain; but just before her stood the handsome young prince. He fixed his coal-black eyes upon her so earnestly that she cast down her own, and then became aware that her fish's tail was gone, and that she had as pretty a pair of white legs and tiny feet as any little maiden could have; but she had no clothes, so she wrapped herself in her long, thick hair. The prince asked her who she was, and where she came from, and she looked at him mildly and sorrowfully with her deep blue eyes; but she could not speak. Every step she took was as the witch had said it would be, she felt as if treading upon the points of needles or sharp knives; but she bore it willingly, and stepped as lightly by the prince's side as a soap-bubble, so that he and all who saw her wondered at her graceful-swaying movements. She was very soon arrayed in costly robes of silk and muslin, and was the most beautiful creature in the palace; but she was dumb, and could neither speak nor sing.

Beautiful female slaves, dressed in silk and gold, stepped forward and sang before the prince and his royal parents: one sang better than all the others, and the prince clapped his hands and smiled at her. This was great sorrow to the little mermaid; she knew how much more sweetly she herself could sing once, and she thought, "Oh if he could only know that! I have given away my voice forever, to be with him."

The slaves next performed some pretty fairy-like dances, to the sound of beautiful music. Then the little mermaid raised her lovely white arms, stood on the tips of her toes, and glided over the floor, and danced as no one yet had been able to dance. At each moment her beauty became more revealed, and her expressive eyes appealed more directly to the heart than the songs of the slaves. Every one was enchanted, especially the prince, who called her his little foundling; and she danced again quite readily, to please him, though each time her foot touched the floor it seemed as if she trod on sharp knives.

The prince said she should remain with him always, and she received permission to sleep at his door, on a velvet cushion. He had a page's dress made for her, that she might accompany him on horseback. They rode together through the sweet-scented woods, where the green boughs touched their shoulders, and the little birds sang among the fresh leaves. She climbed with the prince to the tops of high mountains; and although her tender feet bled so that even her steps were marked, she only laughed, and followed him till they could see the clouds beneath them looking like a flock of birds travelling to distant lands. While at the prince's palace, and when all the household were asleep, she would go and sit on the broad marble steps; for it eased her burning feet to bathe them in the cold sea-water; and then she thought of all those below in the deep.

Once during the night her sisters came up arm-in-arm, singing sorrowfully, as they floated on the water. She beckoned to them, and then they recognized her, and told her how she had grieved them. After that, they came to the same place every night; and once she saw in the distance her old grandmother, who had not been to the surface of the sea for many years, and the old Sea King, her father, with his crown on his head. They stretched out their hands towards her, but they did not venture so near the land as her sisters did.

As the days passed, she loved the prince more fondly, and he loved her as he would love a little child, but it never came into his head to make her his wife; yet, unless he married her, she could not receive an immortal soul; and, on the morning after his marriage with another, she would dissolve into the foam of the sea.

"Do you not love me the best of them all?" the eyes of the little mermaid seemed to say, when he took her in his arms, and kissed her fair forehead.

"Yes, you are dear to me," said the prince; "for you have the best heart, and you are the most devoted to me; you are like a young maiden whom I once saw, but whom I shall never meet again. I was in a ship that was wrecked, and the waves cast me ashore near a holy temple, where several young maidens performed the service. The youngest of them found me on the shore, and saved my life. I saw her but twice, and she is the only one in the world whom I could love; but you are like her, and you have almost driven her image out of my mind. She belongs to the holy temple, and my good fortune has sent you to me instead of her; and we will never part."

"Ah, he knows not that it was I who saved his life," thought the little mermaid. "I carried him over the sea to the wood where the temple stands: I sat beneath the foam, and watched till the human beings came to help him. I saw the pretty maiden that he loves better than he loves me;" and the mermaid sighed deeply, but she could not shed tears. "He says the maiden belongs to the holy temple, therefore she will never return to the world. They will meet no more: while I am by his side, and see him every day. I will take care of him, and love him, and give up my life for his sake."

Very soon it was said that the prince must marry, and that the beautiful daughter of a neighboring king would be his wife, for a fine ship was being fitted out. Although the prince gave out that he merely intended to pay a visit to the king, it was generally supposed that he really went to see his daughter. A great company were to go with him. The little mermaid smiled, and shook her head. She knew the prince's thoughts better than any of the others.

"I must travel," he had said to her; "I must see this beautiful princess; my parents desire it; but they will not oblige me to bring her home as my bride. I cannot love her; she is not like the beautiful maiden in the temple, whom you resemble. If I were forced to choose a bride, I would rather choose you, my dumb foundling, with those expressive eyes." And then he kissed her rosy mouth, played with her long waving hair, and laid his head on her heart, while she dreamed of human happiness and an immortal soul. "You are not afraid of the sea, my dumb child," said he, as they stood on the deck of the noble ship which was to carry them to the country of the neighboring king. And then he told her of storm and of calm, of strange fishes in the deep beneath them, and of what the divers had seen there; and she smiled at his descriptions, for she knew better than any one what wonders were at the bottom of the sea.

In the moonlight, when all on board were asleep, excepting the man at the helm, who was steering, she sat on the deck, gazing down through the clear water. She thought she could distinguish her father's castle, and upon it her aged grandmother, with the silver crown on her head, looking through the rushing tide at the keel of the vessel. Then her sisters came up on the waves, and gazed at her mournfully, wringing their white hands. She beckoned to them, and smiled, and wanted to tell them how happy and well off she was; but the cabin-boy approached, and when her sisters dived down he thought it was only the foam of the sea which he saw.

The next morning the ship sailed into the harbor of a beautiful town belonging to the king whom the prince was going to visit. The church bells were ringing, and from the high towers sounded a flourish of trumpets; and soldiers, with flying colors and glittering bayonets, lined the rocks through which they passed. Every day was a festival; balls and entertainments followed one another.

But the princess had not yet appeared. People said that she was being brought up and educated in a religious house, where she was learning every royal virtue. At last she came. Then the little mermaid, who was very anxious to see whether she was really beautiful, was obliged to acknowledge that she had never seen a more perfect vision of beauty. Her skin was delicately fair, and beneath her long dark eye-lashes her laughing blue eyes shone with truth and purity.

"It was you," said the prince, "who saved my life when I lay dead on the beach," and he folded his blushing bride in his arms. "Oh, I am too happy," said he to the little mermaid; "my fondest hopes are all fulfilled. You will rejoice at my happiness; for your devotion to me is great and sincere."

The little mermaid kissed his hand, and felt as if her heart were already broken. His wedding morning would bring death to her, and she would change into the foam of the sea. All the church bells rung, and the heralds rode about the town proclaiming the betrothal. Perfumed oil was burning in costly silver lamps on every altar. The priests waved the censers, while the bride and bridegroom joined their hands and received the blessing of the bishop. The little mermaid, dressed in silk and gold, held up the bride's train; but her ears heard nothing of the festive music, and her eyes saw not the holy ceremony; she thought of the night of death which was coming to her, and of all she had lost in the world. On the same evening the bride and bridegroom went on board ship; cannons were roaring, flags waving, and in the centre of the ship a costly tent of purple and gold had been erected. It contained elegant couches, for the reception of the bridal pair during the night. The ship, with swelling sails and a favorable wind, glided away smoothly and lightly over the calm sea. When it grew dark a number of colored lamps were lit, and the sailors danced merrily on the deck. The little mermaid could not help thinking of her first rising out of the sea, when she had seen similar festivities and joys; and she joined in the dance, poised herself in the air as a swallow when he pursues his prey, and all present cheered her with wonder. She had never danced so elegantly before. Her tender feet felt as if cut with sharp knives, but she cared not for it; a sharper pang had pierced through her heart. She knew this was the last evening she should ever see the prince, for whom she had forsaken her kindred and her home; she had given up her beautiful voice, and suffered unheard-of pain daily for him, while he knew nothing of it. This was the last evening that she would breathe the same air with him, or gaze on the starry sky and the deep sea; an eternal night, without a thought or a dream, awaited her: she had no soul and now she could never win one. All was joy and gayety on board ship till long after midnight; she laughed and danced with the rest, while the thoughts of death were in her heart. The prince kissed his beautiful bride, while she played with his raven hair, till they went arm-in-arm to rest in the splendid tent. Then all became still on board the ship; the helmsman, alone awake, stood at the helm. The little mermaid leaned her white arms on the edge of the vessel, and looked towards the east for the first blush of morning, for that first ray of dawn that would bring her death. She saw her sisters rising out of the flood: they were as pale as herself; but their long beautiful hair waved no more in the wind, and had been cut off.

"We have given our hair to the witch," said they, "to obtain help for you, that you may not die to-night. She has given us a knife: here it is, see it is very sharp. Before the sun risess you must plunge it into the heart of the prince; when the warm blood falls upon your feet they will grow together again, and form into a fish's tail, and you will be once more a mermaid, and return to us to live out your three hundred years before you die and change into the salt sea foam. Haste, then; he or you must die before sunrise. Our old grand-mother moans so for you, that her white hair is falling off from sorrow, as ours fell under the witch's scissors. Kill the prince and come back; hasten: do you not see the first red streaks in the sky? In a few minutes the sun will rise, and you must die." And then they sighed deeply and mournfully, and sank down beneath the waves.

The little mermaid drew back the crimson curtain of the tent, and beheld the fair bride with her head resting on the prince's breast. She bent down and kissed his fair brow, then looked at the sky on which the rosy dawn grew brighter and brighter; then she glanced at the sharp knife, and again fixed her eyes on the prince, who whispered the name of his bride in his dreams. *She* was in his thoughts, and the knife trembled in the hand of the little mermaid: then she flung it far away from her into the waves; the water turned red where it fell, and the drops that spurted up looked like blood. She cast one more lingering, half-fainting glance at the prince, and then threw herself from the ship into the sea, and thought her body was dissolving into foam. The sun rose above the waves, and his warm rays fell on the cold foam of the little mermaid, who did not feel as if she were dying. She saw the bright sun, and all around her floated hundreds of transparent beautiful beings; she could see through them the white sails of the ship, and the red clouds in the sky; their speech was melodious, but too ethereal to be heard by mortal ears, as they were also unseen by mortal eyes. The little mermaid perceived that she had a body like theirs, and that she continued to rise higher and higher out of the foam. "Where am I?" asked she, and her voice sounded ethereal, as the voice of those who were with her; no earthly music could imitate it.

"Among the daughters of the air," answered one of them. "A mermaid has not an immortal soul, nor can she obtain one unless she wins the love of a human being. On the power of another hangs her eternal destiny. But the daughters of the air, although they do not possess an immortal soul, can, by their good deeds, procure one for themselves. We fly to warm countries, and cool the sultry air that destroys mankind with the pestilence. We carry the perfume of the flowers to spread health and restoration. After we have striven for three hundred years to all the good in our power, we receive an immortal soul and take part in the happiness of mankind. You, poor little mermaid, have tried with your whole heart to do as we are doing; you have suffered and endured and raised yourself to the spirit-world by your good deeds; and now, by striving for three hundred years in the same way, you may obtain an immortal soul."

The little mermaid lifted her glorified eyes towards the sun, and felt them, for the first time, filling with tears. On the ship, in which she had left the prince, there were life and noise; she saw him and his beautiful bride searching for her; sorrowfully they gazed at the pearly foam, as if they knew she had thrown herself into the waves. Unseen she kissed the forehead of her bride, and fanned the prince, and then mounted with the other children of the air to a rosy cloud that floated through the æther.

"After three hundred years, thus shall we float into the kingdom of heaven," said she. "And we may even get there sooner," whispered one of her companions. "Unseen we can enter the houses of men, where there are children, and for every day on which we find a good child, who is the joy of his parents and deserves their love, our time of probation is shortened. The child does not know, when we fly through the room, that we smile with joy at his good conduct, for we can count one year less of our three hundred years. But when we see a naughty or a wicked child, we shed tears of sorrow, and for every tear a day is added to our time of trial!"

THE OLD STREET LAMP

Did you ever hear the story of the old street lamp? It is not remarkably interesting, but for once in a way you may as well listen to it. It was a most respectable old lamp, which had seen many, many years of service, and now was to retire with a pension. It was this evening at its post for the last time, giving light to the street. His feelings were something like those of an old dancer at the theatre, who is dancing for the last time, and knows that on the morrow she will be in her garret, alone and forgotten. The lamp had very great anxiety about the next day, for he knew that he had to appear for the first time at the town hall, to be inspected by the mayor and the council, who were to decide if he were fit for further service or not; — whether the lamp was good enough to be used to light the inhabitants of one of the suburbs, or in the country, at some factory; and if not, it would be sent at once to an iron foundry, to be melted down. In this latter case it might be turned into anything, and he wondered very much whether he would then be able to remember that he had once been a street lamp, and it troubled him exceedingly. Whatever might happen, one thing seemed certain, that he would be separated from the watchman and his wife, whose family he looked upon as his own. The lamp had first been hung up on that very evening that the watchman, then a robust young man, had entered upon the duties of his office. Ah, well, it was a very long time since one became a lamp and the other a watchman. His wife had a little pride in those days; she seldom condescended to glance at the lamp, excepting when she passed by in the evening, never in the daytime. But in later years, when all these, — the watchman, the wife, and the lamp — had grown old, she had attended to it, cleaned it, and supplied it with oil. The old people were thoroughly honest, they had never cheated the lamp of a single drop of the oil provided for it.

This was the lamp's last night in the street, and to-morrow he must go to the town-hall, — two very dark things to think of. No wonder he did not burn brightly. Many other thoughts also passed through his mind. How many persons he had lighted on their way, and how much he had seen; as much, very likely, as the mayor and corporation themselves! None of these thoughts were uttered aloud, however; for he was a good, honorable old lamp, who would not willingly do harm to any one, especially to those in authority. As many things were recalled to his mind, the light would flash up with sudden brightness; he had, at such moments, a conviction that he would be remembered. "There was a handsome young man once," thought he; "it is certainly a long while ago, but I remember he had a little note, written on pink paper with a gold edge; the writing was elegant, evidently a lady's hand: twice he read it through, and kissed it, and then looked up at me, with eyes that said quite plainly, 'I am the happiest of men!' Only he and I know what was written on this his first letter from his lady-love. Ah, yes, and there was another pair of eyes that I remember, — it is really wonderful how the thoughts jump from one thing to another! A funeral passed through the street; a young and beautiful woman lay on a bier, decked with garlands of flowers, and attended by torches, which quite overpowered my light. All along the street stood the people from the houses, in crowds, ready to join the procession. But when the torches had passed from before me, and I could look round, I saw one person alone, standing, leaning against my post, and weeping. Never shall I forget the sorrowful eyes that looked up at me." These and similar reflections occupied the old street lamp, on this the last time that his light would shine. The sentry, when he is relieved from his post, knows at least who will succeed him, and may whisper a few words to him, but the lamp did not know his successor, or he could have given him a few hints respecting rain, or mist, and could have informed him how far the moon's rays would rest on the pavement, and from which side the wind generally blew, and so on.

On the bridge over the canal stood three persons, who wished to recommend themselves to the lamp, for they thought he could give the office to whomsoever he chose. The first was a herring's head, which could emit light in the darkness. He remarked that it would be a great saving of oil if they placed him on the lamp-post. Number two was a piece of rotten wood, which also shines in the dark. He considered himself descended from an old stem, once the pride of the forest. The third was a glow-worm, and how he found his way there the lamp could not imagine, yet there he was, and could really give light as well as the others. But the rotten wood and the herring's head declared most solemnly, by all they held sacred, that the glow-worm only gave light at certain times, and must not be allowed to compete with themselves. The old lamp assured them that not one of them could give sufficient light to fill the position of a street lamp; but they would believe nothing he said. And when they discovered that he had not the power of naming his successor, they said they were very glad to hear it, for the lamp was too old and worn-out to make a proper choice.

At this moment the wind came rushing round the corner of the street, and through the air-holes of the old lamp. "What is this I hear?" said he; "that you are going away to-morrow? Is this evening the last time we shall meet? Then I must present you with a farewell gift. I will blow into your brain, so that in future you shall not only be able to remember all that you have seen or heard in the past, but your light within shall be so bright, that you shall be able to understand all that is said or done in your presence."

"Oh, that is really a very, very great gift," said the old lamp; "I thank you most heartily. I only hope I shall not be melted down."

"That is not likely to happen yet," said the wind; "and I will also blow a memory into you, so that should you receive other similar presents your old age will pass very pleasantly."

"That is if I am not melted down," said the lamp. "But should I in that case still retain my memory?"

"Do be reasonable, old lamp," said the wind, puffing away.

At this moment the moon burst forth from the clouds. "What will you give the old lamp?" asked the wind.

"I can give nothing," she replied; "I am on the wane, and no lamps have ever given me light while I have frequently shone upon them." And with these words the moon hid herself again behind the clouds, that she might be saved from further importunities. Just then a drop fell upon the lamp, from the roof of the house, but the drop explained that he was a gift from those gray clouds, and perhaps the best of all gifts. "I shall penetrate you so thoroughly," he said, "that you will have the power of becoming rusty, and, if you wish it, to crumble into dust in one night."

But this seemed to the lamp a very shabby present, and the wind thought so too. "Does no one give any more? Will no one give any more?" shouted the breath of the wind, as loud as it could. Then a bright falling star came down, leaving a broad, luminous streak behind it.

"What was that?" cried the herring's head. "Did not a star fall? I really believe it went into the lamp. Certainly, when such high-born personages try for the office, we may as well say 'Good-night,' and go home."

And so they did, all three, while the old lamp threw a wonderfully strong light all around him.

"This is a glorious gift," said he; "the bright stars have always been a joy to me, and have always shone more brilliantly than I ever could shine, though I have tried with my whole might; and now they have noticed me, a poor old lamp, and have sent me a gift that will enable me to see clearly everything that I remember, as if it still stood before me, and to be seen by all those who love me. And herein lies the truest pleasure, for joy which we cannot share with others is only half enjoyed."

"That sentiment does you honor," said the wind; "but for this purpose wax lights will be necessary. If these are not lighted in you, your particular faculties will not benefit others in the least. The stars have not thought of this; they suppose that you and every other light must be a wax taper: but I must go down now." So he laid himself to rest.

"Wax tapers, indeed!" said the lamp, "I have never yet had these, nor is it likely I ever shall. If I could only be sure of not being melted down!"

The next day. Well, perhaps we had better pass over the next day. The evening had come, and the lamp was resting in a grandfather's chair, and guess where! Why, at the old watchman's house. He had begged, as a favor, that the mayor and corporation would allow him to keep the street lamp, in consideration of his long and faithful service, as he had himself hung it up and lit it on the day he first commenced his duties, four-and-twenty years ago. He looked upon it almost as his own child; he had no children, so the lamp was given to him. There it lay in the great arm-chair near to the warm stove. It seemed almost as if it had grown larger, for it appeared quite to fill the chair. The old people sat at their supper, casting friendly glances at the old lamp, whom they would willingly have admitted to a place at the table. It is quite true that they dwelt in a cellar, two yards deep in the earth, and they had to cross a stone passage to get to their room, but within it was warm and comfortable and strips of list had been nailed round the door. The bed and the little window had curtains, and everything looked clean and neat. On the window seat stood two curious flower-pots which a sailor, named Christian, had brought over from the East or West Indies. They were of clay, and in the form of two elephants, with open backs; they were hollow and filled with earth, and through the open space flowers bloomed. In one grew some very fine chives or leeks; this was the kitchen garden. The other elephant, which contained a beautiful geranium, they called their flower garden. On the wall hung a large colored print, representing the congress of Vienna, and all the kings and emperors at once. A clock, with heavy weights, hung on the wall and went "tick, tick," steadily enough; yet it was always rather too fast, which, however, the old people said was better than being too slow. They were now eating their supper, while the old street lamp, as we have heard, lay in the grandfather's arm-chair near the stove. It seemed to the lamp as if the whole world had turned round; but after a while the old watchman looked at the lamp, and spoke of what they had both gone through together, — in rain and in fog; during the short bright nights of summer, or in the long winter nights, through the drifting snow-storms, when he longed to be at home in the cellar. Then the lamp felt it was all right again. He saw everything that had happened quite clearly, as if it were passing before him. Surely the wind had given him an excellent gift. The old people were very active and industrious, they were never idle for even a single hour. On Sunday afternoons they would bring out some books, generally a book of travels which they were very fond of. The old man would read aloud about Africa, with its great forests and the wild elephants, while his wife would listen attentively, stealing a glance now and then at the clay elephants, which served as flower-pots.

"I can almost imagine I am seeing it all," she said; and then how the lamp wished for a wax taper to be lighted in him, for then the old woman would have seen the smallest detail as clearly as he did himself. The lofty trees, with their thickly entwined branches, the naked negroes on horseback, and whole herds of elephants treading down bamboo thickets with their broad, heavy feet.

"What is the use of all my capabilities," sighed the old lamp, "when I cannot obtain any wax lights; they have only oil and tallow here, and these will not do." One day a great heap of wax-candle ends found their way into the cellar. The larger pieces were burnt, and the smaller ones the old woman kept for waxing her thread. So there were now candles enough, but it never occurred to any one to put a little piece in the lamp.

"Here I am now with my rare powers," thought the lamp, "I have faculties within me, but I cannot share them; they do not know that I could cover these white walls with beautiful tapestry, or change them into noble forests, or, indeed, to anything else they might wish for." The lamp, however, was always kept clean and shining in a corner where it attracted all eyes. Strangers looked upon it as lumber, but the old people did not care for that; they loved the lamp. One day—it was the watchman's birthday—the old woman approached the lamp, smiling to herself, and said, "I will have an illumination to-day in honor of my old man." And the lamp rattled in his metal frame, for he thought, "Now at last I shall have a light within me," but after all no wax light was placed in the lamp, but oil as usual. The lamp burned through the whole evening, and began to perceive too clearly that the gift of the stars would remain a hidden treasure all his life. Then he had a dream; for, to one with his faculties, dreaming was no difficulty. It appeared to him that the old people were dead, and that he had been taken to the iron foundry to be melted down. It caused him quite as much anxiety as on the day when he had been called upon to appear before the mayor and the council at the town-hall. But though he had been endowed with the power of falling into decay from rust when he pleased, he did not make use of it. He was therefore put into the melting-furnace and changed into as elegant an iron candlestick as you could wish to see, one intended to hold a wax taper. The candlestick was in the form of an angel holding a nosegay, in the centre of which the wax taper was to be placed. It was to stand on a green writing table, in a very pleasant room; many books were scattered about, and splendid paintings hung on the walls. The owner of the room was a poet, and a man of intellect; everything he thought or wrote was pictured around him. Nature showed herself to him sometimes in the dark forests, at others in cheerful meadows where the storks were strutting about, or on the deck of a ship sailing across the foaming sea with the clear, blue sky above, or at night the glittering stars. "What powers I possess!" said the lamp, awaking from his dream; "I could almost wish to be melted down; but no, that must not be while the old people live. They love me for myself alone, they keep me bright, and supply me with oil. I am as well off as the picture of the congress, in which they take so much pleasure." And from that time he felt at rest in himself, and not more so than such an honorable old lamp really deserved to be.

THE DARNING-NEEDLE

THERE was once a darning-needle who thought herself so fine that she fancied she must be fit for embroidery. "Hold me tight," she would say to the fingers, when they took her up, "don't let me fall; if you do I shall never be found again, I am so very fine."

"That is your opinion, is it?" said the fingers, as they seized her round the body.

"See, I am coming with a train," said the darning-needle, drawing a long thread after her; but there was no knot in the thread.

The fingers then placed the point of the needle against the cook's slipper. There was a crack in the upper leather, which had to be sewn together.

"What coarse work!" said the darning-needle, "I shall never get through. I shall break!—I am breaking!" and sure enough she broke. "Did I not say so?" said the darning-needle, "I know I am too fine for such work as that."

"This needle is quite useless for sewing now," said the fingers; but they still held it fast, and the cook dropped some sealing-wax on the needle, and fastened her handkerchief with it in front.

"So now I am a breast-pin," said the darning-needle; "I knew very well I should come to honor some day: merit is sure to rise;" and she laughed, quietly to herself, for of course no one ever saw a darning-needle laugh. And there she sat as proudly as if she were in a state coach, and looked all around her. "May I be allowed to ask if you are made of gold?" she inquired of her neighbor, a pin; "you have a very pretty appearance, and a curious head, although you are rather small. You must take pains to grow, for it is not every one who has sealing-wax dropped upon him;" and as she spoke, the darning-needle drew herself up so proudly that she fell out of the handkerchief right into the sink, which the cook was cleaning. "Now I am going on a journey," said the needle, as she floated away with the dirty water, "I do hope I shall not be lost." But she really was lost in a gutter. "I am too fine for this world," said the darning-needle, as she lay in the gutter; "but I know who I am, and that is always some comfort." So the darning-needle kept up her proud behavior, and did not lose her good humor. Then there floated over her all sorts of things,—chips and straws, and pieces of old newspaper. "See how they sail," said the darning-needle; "they do not know what is under them. I am here, and here I shall stick. See, there goes a chip, thinking of nothing in the world but himself—only a chip. There's a straw going by now; how he turns and twists about! Don't be thinking too much of yourself, or you may chance to run against a stone. There swims a piece of newspaper; what is written upon it has been forgotten long ago, and yet it gives itself airs. I sit here patiently and quietly. I know who I am, so I shall not move."

One day something lying close to the darning-needle glittered so splendidly that she thought it was a diamond; yet it was only a piece of broken bottle. The darning-needle spoke to it, because it sparkled, and represented herself as a breast-pin. "I suppose you are really a diamond?" she said.

"Why yes, something of the kind," he replied; and so each believed the other to be very valuable, and then they began to talk about the world, and the conceited people in it.

"I have been in a lady's work-box," said the darning-needle, "and this lady was the cook. She had on each hand five fingers, and anything so conceited as these five fingers I have never seen; and yet they were only employed to take me out of the box and to put me back again."

"Were they not high-born?"

"High-born!" said the darning-needle, "no indeed, but so haughty. They were five brothers, all born fingers; they kept very proudly together, though they were of different lengths. The one who stood first in the rank was named the thumb, he was short and thick, and had only one joint in his back, and could therefore make but one bow; but he said that if he were cut off from a man's hand, that man would be unfit for a soldier. Sweet-tooth, his neighbor, dipped himself into sweet or sour, pointed to the sun and moon, and formed the letters when the fingers wrote. Longman, the middle finger, looked over the heads of all the others. Gold-band, the next finger, wore a golden circle round his waist. And little Playman did nothing at all, and seemed proud of it. They were boasters, and boasters they will remain; and therefore I left them."

"And now we sit here and glitter," said the piece of broken bottle.

At the same moment more water streamed into the gutter, so that it overflowed, and the piece of bottle was carried away.

"So he is promoted," said the darning-needle, "while I remain here; I am too fine, but that is my pride, and what do I care?" And so she sat there in her pride, and had many such thoughts as these, — "I could almost fancy that I came from a sunbeam, I am so fine. It seems as if the sunbeams were always looking for me under the water. Ah! I am so fine that even my mother cannot find me. Had I still my old eye, which was broken off, I believe I should weep; but no, I would not do that, it is not genteel to cry."

One day a couple of street boys were paddling in the gutter, for they sometimes found old nails, farthings, and other treasures. It was dirty work, but they took great pleasure in it. "Hallo!" cried one, as he pricked himself with the darning-needle, "here's a fellow for you."

"I am not a fellow, I am a young lady," said the darning-needle; but no one heard her.

The sealing-wax had come off, and she was quite black; but black makes a person look slender, so she thought herself even finer than before.

"Here comes an egg-shell sailing along," said one of the boys; so they stuck the darning-needle into the egg-shell.

"White walls, and I am black myself," said the darning-needle, "that looks well; now I can be seen, but I hope I shall not be sea-sick, or I shall break again." She was not sea-sick, and she did not break. "It is a good thing against sea-sickness to have a steel stomach, and not to forget one's own importance. Now my sea-sickness has past: delicate people can bear a great deal."

Crack went the egg-shell, as a waggon passed over it. "Good heavens, how it crushes!" said the darning-needle. "I shall be sick now. I am breaking!" but she did not break, though the waggon went over her as she lay at full length; and there let her lie.

A ROSE FROM HOMER'S GRAVE

ALL the songs of the east speak of the love of the nightingale for the rose in the silent starlight night. The winged songster serenades the fragrant flowers.

Not far from Smyrna, where the merchant drives his loaded camels, proudly arching their long necks as they journey beneath the lofty pines over holy ground, I saw a hedge of roses. The turtle-dove flew among the branches of the tall trees, and as the sunbeams fell upon her wings, they glistened as if they were mother-of-pearl. On the rose-bush grew a flower, more beautiful than them all, and to her the nightingale sung of his woes; but the rose remained silent, not even a dewdrop lay like a tear of sympathy on her leaves. At last she bowed her head over a heap of stones, and said, "Here rests the greatest singer in the world; over his tomb will I spread my fragrance, and on it I will let my leaves fall when the storm scatters them. He who sung of Troy became earth, and from that earth I have sprung. I, a rose from the grave of Homer, am too lofty to bloom for a nightingale." Then the nightingale sung himself to death. A camel-driver came by, with his loaded camels and his black slaves; his little son found the dead bird, and buried the lovely songster in the grave of the great Homer, while the rose trembled in the wind.

The evening came, and the rose wrapped her leaves more closely round her, and dreamed: and this was her dream.

It was a fair sunshiny day; a crowd of strangers drew near who had undertaken a pilgrimage to the grave of Homer. Among the strangers was a minstrel from the north, the home of the clouds and the brilliant lights of the aurora borealis. He plucked the rose and placed it in a book, and carried it away into a distant part of the world, his fatherland. The rose faded with grief, and lay between the leaves of the book, which he opened in his own home, saying, "Here is a rose from the grave of Homer."

Then the flower awoke from her dream, and trembled in the wind. A drop of dew fell from the leaves upon the singer's grave. The sun rose, and the flower bloomed more beautiful than ever. The day was hot, and she was still in her own warm Asia. Then footsteps approached, strangers, such as the rose had seen in her dream, came by, and among them was a poet from the north; he plucked the rose, pressed a kiss upon her fresh mouth, and carried her away to the home of the clouds and the northern lights. Like a mummy, the flower now rests in his "Iliad," and, as in her dream, she hears him say, as he opens the book, "Here is a rose from the grave of Homer."

THE FLAX

THE flax was in full bloom; it had pretty little blue flowers as delicate as the wings of a moth, or even more so. The sun shone, and the showers watered it; and this was just as good for the flax as it is for little children to be washed and then kissed by their mother. They look much prettier for it, and so did the flax.

"People say that I look exceedingly well," said the flax, "and that I am so fine and long that I shall make a beautiful piece of linen. How fortunate I am; it makes me so happy, it is such a pleasant thing to know that something can be made of me. How the sunshine cheers me, and how sweet and refreshing is the rain; my happiness overpowers me, no one in the world can feel happier than I am."

"Ah, yes, no doubt," said the fern, "but you do not know the world yet as well as I do, for my sticks are knotty;" and then it sung quite mournfully —

> "Snip, snap, snurre,
> Basse lurre:
> The song is ended."

"No, it is not ended," said the flax. "To-morrow the sun will shine, or the rain descend. I feel that I am growing. I feel that I am in full blossom. I am the happiest of all creatures."

Well, one day some people came, who took hold of the flax, and pulled it up by the roots; this was painful; then it was laid in water as if they intended to drown it; and, after that, placed near a fire as if it were to be roasted; all this was very shocking. "We cannot expect to be happy always," said the flax; "by experiencing evil as well as good, we become wise." And certainly there was plenty of evil in store for the flax. It was steeped, and roasted, and broken, and combed; indeed, it scarcely knew what was done to it. At last it was put on the spinning wheel. "Whirr, whirr," went the wheel so quickly that the flax could not collect its thoughts. "Well, I have been very happy," he thought in the midst of his pain, "and must be contented with the past;" and contented he remained till he was put on the loom, and became a beautiful piece of white linen. All the flax, even to the last stalk, was used in making this one piece. "Well, this is quite wonderful; I could not have believed that I should be so favored by fortune. The fern was not wrong with its song of

> 'Snip, snap, snurre,
> Basse lurre.'

But the song is not ended yet, I am sure; it is only just beginning. How wonderful it is, that after all I have suffered, I am made something of at last; I am the luckiest person in the world — so strong and fine; and how white, and what a length! This is something different to being a mere plant and bearing flowers. Then I had no attention, nor any water unless it rained; now, I am watched and taken care of. Every morning the maid turns me over, and I have a shower-bath from the watering-pot every evening. Yes, and the clergyman's wife noticed me, and said I was the best piece of linen in the whole parish. I cannot be happier than I am now."

After some time, the linen was taken into the house, placed under the scissors, and cut and torn into pieces, and then pricked with needles. This certainly was not pleasant; but at last it was made into twelve garments of that kind which people do not like to name, and yet everybody should wear one. "See, now, then," said the flax; "I have become something of importance. This was my destiny; it is quite a blessing. Now I shall be of some use in the world, as everyone ought to be; it is the only way to be happy. I am now divided into twelve pieces, and yet we are all one and the same in the whole dozen. It is most extraordinary good fortune."

Years passed away, and at last the linen was so worn it could scarcely hold together. "It must end very soon," said the pieces to each other; "we would gladly have held together a little longer, but it is useless to expect impossibilities." And at length they fell into rags and tatters, and thought it was all over with them, for they were torn to shreds, and steeped in water, and made into a pulp, and dried, and they knew not what besides, till all at once they found themselves beautiful white paper. "Well, now, this is a surprise; a glorious surprise too," said the paper. "I am now finer than ever, and I shall be written upon, and who can tell what fine things I may have written upon me. This is wonderful luck!" And sure enough the most beautiful stories and poetry were written upon it, and only once was there a blot, which was very fortunate. Then people heard the stories and poetry read, and it made them wiser and better; for all that was written had a good and sensible meaning, and a great blessing was contained in the words on this paper.

"I never imagined anything like this," said the paper, "when I was only a little blue flower, growing in the fields. How could I fancy that I should ever be the means of bringing knowledge and joy to man? I cannot understand it myself, and yet it is really so. Heaven knows that I have done nothing myself, but what I was obliged to do with my weak powers for my own preservation; and yet I have been promoted from one joy and honor to another. Each time I think that the song is ended; and then something higher and better begins for me. I suppose now I shall be sent on my travels about the world, so that people may read me. It cannot be otherwise; indeed, it is more than probable; for I have more splendid thoughts written upon me, than I had pretty flowers in olden times. I am happier than ever."

But the paper did not go on its travels; it was sent to the printer, and all the words written upon it were set up in type, to make a book, or rather, many hundreds of books; for so many more persons could derive pleasure and profit from a printed book, than from the written paper; and if the paper had been sent around the world, it would have been worn out before it had got half through its journey.

"This is certainly the wisest plan," said the written paper; "I really did not think of that. I shall remain at home, and be held in honor, like some old grandfather, as I really am to all these new books. They will do some good. I could not have wandered about as they do. Yet he who wrote all this has looked at me, as every word flowed from his pen upon my surface. I am the most honored of all."

Then the paper was tied in a bundle with other papers, and thrown into a tub that stood in the washhouse.

"After work, it is well to rest," said the paper, "and a very good opportunity to collect one's thoughts. Now I am able, for the first time, to think of my real condition; and to know one's self is true progress. What will be done with me now, I wonder? No doubt I shall still go forward. I have always progressed hitherto, as I know quite well."

Now it happened one day that all the paper in the tub was taken out, and laid on the hearth to be burnt. People said it could not be sold at the shop, to wrap up butter and sugar, because it had been written upon. The children in the house stood round the stove; for they wanted to see the paper burn, because it flamed up so prettily, and afterwards, among the ashes, so many red sparks could be seen running one after the other, here and there, as quick as the wind. They called it seeing the children come out of school, and the last spark was the schoolmaster. They often thought the last spark had come; and one would cry, "There goes the schoolmaster;" but the next moment another spark would appear, shining so beautifully. How they would like to know where the sparks all went to! Perhaps we shall find out some day, but we don't know now.

The whole bundle of paper had been placed on the fire, and was soon alight. "Ugh," cried the paper, as it burst into a bright flame; "ugh." It was certainly not very pleasant to be burning; but when the whole was wrapped in flames, the flames mounted up into the air, higher than the flax had ever been able to raise its little blue flower, and they glistened as the white linen never could have glistened. All the written letters became quite red in a moment, and all the words and thoughts turned to fire.

"Now I am mounting straight up to the sun," said a voice in the flames; and it was as if a thousand voices echoed the words; and the flames darted up through the chimney, and went out at the top. Then a number of tiny beings, as many in number as the flowers on the flax had been, and invisible to mortal eyes, floated above them. They were even lighter and more delicate than the flowers from which they were born; and as the flames were extinguished, and nothing remained of the paper but black ashes, these little beings danced upon it; and whenever they touched it, bright red sparks appeared.

"The children are all out of school, and the schoolmaster was the last of all," said the children. It was good fun, and they sang over the dead ashes, —

> "Snip, snap, snurre,
> Basse lure:
> The song is ended."

But the little invisible beings said, "The song is never ended; the most beautiful is yet to come."

But the children could neither hear nor understand this, nor should they; for children must not know everything.

THE SHIRT-COLLAR

THERE was once a fine gentleman who possessed among other things a boot-jack and a hair-brush; but he had also the finest shirt-collar in the world, and of this collar we are about to hear a story. The collar had become so old that he began to think about getting married; and one day he happened to find himself in the same washing-tub as a garter. "Upon my word," said the shirt-collar, "I have never seen anything so slim and delicate, so neat and soft before. May I venture to ask your name?"

"I shall not tell you," replied the garter.

"Where do you reside when you are at home?" asked the shirt-collar. But the garter was naturally shy, and did not know how to answer such a question.

"I presume you are a girdle," said the shirt-collar, "a sort of under girdle. I see that you are useful, as well as ornamental, my little lady."

"You must not speak to me," said the garter; "I do not think I have given you any encouragement to do so."

"Oh, when any one is as beautiful as you are," said the shirt-collar, "is not that encouragement enough?"

"Get away; don't come so near me," said the garter, "you appear to me quite like a man."

"I am a fine gentleman certainly," said the shirt-collar, "I possess a boot-jack and a hair-brush." This was not true, for these things belonged to his master; but he was a boaster.

"Don't come so near me," said the garter; "I am not accustomed to it."

"Affectation!" said the shirt-collar.

Then they were taken out of the wash-tub, starched, and hung over a chair in the sunshine, and then laid on the ironing-board. And now came the glowing iron. "Mistress widow," said the shirt-collar, "little mistress widow, I feel quite warm. I am changing, I am losing all my creases. You are burning a hole in me. Ugh! I propose to you."

"You old rag," said the flat-iron, driving proudly over the collar, for she fancied herself a steam-engine, which rolls over the railway and draws carriages. "You old rag!" said she.

The edges of the shirt-collar were a little frayed, so the scissors were brought to cut them smooth. "Oh!" exclaimed the shirt-collar, "what a first-rate dancer you would make; you can stretch out your leg so well. I never saw anything so charming; I am sure no human being could do the same."

"I should think not," replied the scissors.

"You ought to be a countess," said the shirt collar; "but all I possess consists of a fine gentleman, a boot-jack, and a comb. I wish I had an estate for your sake."

"What! is he going to propose to me?" said the scissors, and she became so angry that she cut too sharply into the shirt collar, and it was obliged to be thrown by as useless.

"I shall be obliged to propose to the hair-brush," thought the shirt collar; so he remarked one day, "It is wonderful what beautiful hair you have, my little lady. Have you never thought of being engaged?"

"You might know I should think of it," answered the hair brush; "I am engaged to the boot-jack."

"Engaged!" cried the shirt collar, "now there is no one left to propose to;" and then he pretended to despise all love-making.

A long time passed, and the shirt collar was taken in a bag to the paper-mill. Here was a large company of rags, the fine ones lying by themselves, separated from the coarser, as it ought to be. They had all many things to relate, especially the shirt collar, who was a terrible boaster. "I have had an immense number of love affairs," said the shirt collar, "no one left me any peace. It is true I was a very fine gentleman; quite stuck up. I had a boot-jack and a brush that I never used. You should have seen me then, when I was turned down. I shall never forget my first love; she was a girdle, so charming, and fine, and soft, and she threw herself into a washing tub for my sake. There was a widow too, who was warmly in love with me, but I left her alone, and she became quite black. The next was a first-rate dancer; she gave me the wound from which I still suffer, she was so passionate. Even my own hair-brush was in love with me, and lost all her hair through neglected love. Yes, I have had great experience of this kind, but my greatest grief was for the garter — the girdle I meant to say — that jumped into the wash-tub. I have a great deal on my conscience, and it is really time I should be turned into white paper."

And the shirt collar came to this at last. All the rags were made into white paper, and the shirt collar became the very identical piece of paper which we now see, and on which this story is printed. It happened as a punishment to him, for having boasted so shockingly of things which were not true. And this is a warning to us, to be careful how we act, for we may some day find ourselves in the rag-bag, to be turned into white paper, on which our whole history may be written, even its most secret actions. And it would not be pleasant to have to run about the world in the form of a piece of paper, telling everything we have done, like the boasting shirt collar.

THE LITTLE MATCH-SELLER

It was terribly cold and nearly dark on the last evening of the old year, and the snow was falling fast. In the cold and the darkness, a poor little girl, with bare head and naked feet, roamed through the streets. It is true she had on a pair of slippers when she left home, but they were not of much use. They were very large, so large, indeed, that they had belonged to her mother, and the poor little creature had lost them in running across the street to avoid two carriages that were rolling along at a terrible rate. One of the slippers she could not find, and a boy seized upon the other and ran away with it, saying that he could use it as a cradle, when he had children of his own. So the little girl went on with her little naked feet, which were quite red and blue with the cold. In an old apron she carried a number of matches, and had a bundle of them in her hands. No one had bought anything of her the whole day, nor had any one given here even a penny. Shivering with cold and hunger, she crept along; poor little child, she looked the picture of misery. The snowflakes fell on her long, fair hair, which hung in curls on her shoulders, but she regarded them not.

Lights were shining from every window, and there was a savory smell of roast goose, for it was New-year's eve — yes, she remembered that. In a corner, between two houses, one of which projected beyond the other, she sank down and huddled herself together. She had drawn her little feet under her, but she could not keep off the cold; and she dared not go home, for she had sold no matches, and could not take home even a penny of money. Her father would certainly beat her; besides, it was almost as cold at home as here, for they had only the roof to cover them, through which the wind howled, although the largest holes had been stopped up with straw and rags. Her little hands were almost frozen with the cold. Ah! perhaps a burning match might be some good, if she could draw it from the bundle and strike it against the wall, just to warm her fingers. She drew one out — "scratch!" how it sputtered as it burnt! It gave a warm, bright light, like a little candle, as she held her hand over it. It was really a wonderful light. It seemed to the little girl that she

THE LITTLE MATCH-SELLER

was sitting by a large iron stove, with polished brass feet and a brass ornament. How the fire burned! and seemed so beautifully warm that the child stretched out her feet as if to warm them, when, lo! the flame of the match went out, the stove vanished, and she had only the remains of the half-burnt match in her hand.

She rubbed another match on the wall. It burst into a flame, and where its light fell upon the wall it became as transparent as a veil, and she could see into the room. The table was covered with a snowy white table-cloth, on which stood a splendid dinner service, and a steaming roast goose, stuffed with apples and dried plums. And what was still more wonderful, the goose jumped down from the dish and waddled across the floor, with a knife and fork in its breast, to the little girl. Then the match went out, and there remained nothing but the thick, damp, cold wall before her.

She lighted another match, and then she found herself sitting under a beautiful Christmas-tree. It was larger and more beautifully decorated than the one which she had seen through the glass door at the rich merchant's. Thousands of tapers were burning upon the green branches, and colored pictures, like those she had seen in the show-windows, looked down upon it all. The little one stretched out her hand towards them, and the match went out.

The Christmas lights rose higher and higher, till they looked to her like the stars in the sky. Then she saw a star fall, leaving behind it a bright streak of fire. "Some one is dying," thought the little girl, for her old grandmother, the only one who had ever loved her, and who was now dead, had told her that when a star falls, a soul was going up to God.

She again rubbed a match on the wall, and the light shone round her; in the brightness stood her old grandmother, clear and shining, yet mild and loving in her appearance. "Grandmother," cried the little one, "O take me with you; I know you will go away when the match burns out; you will vanish like the warm stove, the roast goose, and the large, glorious Christmas-tree." And she made haste to light the whole bundle of matches, for she wished to keep her grandmother there. And the matches glowed with a light that was brighter than the noon-day, and her grandmother had never appeared so large or so beautiful. She took the little girl in her arms, and they both flew upwards in brightness and joy far above the earth, where there was neither cold nor hunger nor pain, for they were with God.

In the dawn of morning there lay the poor little one, with pale cheeks and smiling mouth, leaning against the wall; she had been frozen to death on the last evening of the year; and the New-year's sun rose and shone upon a little corpse! The child still sat, in the stiffness of death, holding the matches in her hand, one bundle of which was burnt. "She tried to warm herself," said some. No one imagined what beautiful things she had seen, nor into what glory she had entered with her grandmother, on New-year's day.

THE BUCKWHEAT

VERY often, after a violent thunder-storm, a field of buckwheat appears blackened and singed, as if a flame of fire had passed over it. The country people say that this appearance is caused by lightning; but I will tell you what the sparrow says, and the sparrow heard it from an old willow-tree which grew near a field of buckwheat, and is there still. It is a large venerable tree, though a little crippled by age. The trunk has been split, and out of the crevice grass and brambles grow. The tree bends forward slightly, and the branches hang quite down to the ground just like green hair. Corn grows in the surrounding fields, not only rye and barley, but oats, — pretty oats that, when ripe, look like a number of little golden canary-birds sitting on a bough. The corn has a smiling look and the heaviest and richest ears bend their heads low as if in pious humility. Once there was also a field of buckwheat, and this field was exactly opposite to old willow-tree. The buckwheat did not bend like the other grain, but erected its head proudly and stiffly on the stem. "I am as valuable as any other corn," said he, "and I am much handsomer; my flowers are as beautiful as the bloom of the apple blossom, and it is a pleasure to look at us. Do you know of anything prettier than we are, you old willow-tree?"

And the willow-tree nodded his head, as if he would say, "Indeed I do."

But the buckwheat spread itself out with pride, and said, "Stupid tree; he is so old that grass grows out of his body."

There arose a very terrible storm. All the field-flowers folded their leaves together, or bowed their little heads, while the storm passed over them, but the buckwheat stood erect in its pride. "Bend your head as we do," said the flowers.

"I have no occasion to do so," replied the buckwheat.

"Bend your head as we do," cried the ears of corn; "the angel of the storm is coming; his wings spread from the sky above to the earth beneath. He will strike you down before you can cry for mercy."

"But I will not bend my head," said the buckwheat.

"Close your flowers and bend your leaves," said the old willow-tree. "Do not look at the lightning when the cloud bursts; even men cannot do that. In a flash of lightning heaven opens, and we can look in; but the sight will strike even human beings blind. What then must happen to us, who only grow out of the earth, and are so inferior to them, if we venture to do so?"

"Inferior, indeed!" said the buckwheat. "Now I intend to have a peep into heaven." Proudly and boldly he looked up, while the lightning flashed across the sky as if the whole world were in flames.

When the dreadful storm had passed, the flowers and the corn raised their drooping heads in the pure still air, refreshed by the rain, but the buckwheat lay like a weed in the field, burnt to blackness by the lightning. The branches of the old willow-tree rustled in the wind, and large water-drops fell from his green leaves as if the old willow were weeping. Then the sparrows asked why he was weeping, when all around him seemed so cheerful. "See," they said, how the sun shines, and the clouds float in the blue sky. Do you not smell the sweet perfume from flower and bush? Wherefore do you weep, old willow-tree?" Then the willow told them of the haughty pride of the buckwheat, and of the punishment which followed in consequence.

This is the story told me by the sparrows one evening when I begged them to relate some tale to me.

LITTLE CLAUS AND BIG CLAUS

IN a village there once lived two men who had the same name. They were both called Claus. One of them had four horses, but the other had only one; so to distinguish them, people called the owner of the four horses, "Great Claus," and he who had only one, "Little Claus." Now we shall hear what happened to them, for this is a true story.

Through the whole week, Little Claus was obliged to plough for Great Claus, and lend him his one horse; and once a week, on a Sunday, Great Claus lent him all his four horses. Then how Little Claus would smack his whip over all five horses, they were as good as his own on that one day. The sun shone brightly, and the church bells were ringing merrily as the people passed by, dressed in their best clothes, with their prayer-books under their arms. They were going to hear the clergyman preach. They looked at Little Claus ploughing with his five horses, and he was so proud that he smacked his whip, and said, "Gee-up, my five horses."

"You must not say that," said Big Claus; "for only one of them belongs to you." But Little Claus soon forgot what he ought to say, and when any one passed he would call out, "Gee-up, my five horses!"

"Now I must beg you not to say that again," said Big Claus; "for if you do, I shall hit your horse on the head, so that he will drop dead on the spot, and there will be an end of him."

"I promise you I will not say it any more," said the other; but as soon as people came by, nodding to him, and wishing him "Good day," he became so pleased, and thought how grand it looked to have five horses ploughing in his field, that he cried out again, "Gee-up, all my horses!"

"I'll gee-up your horses for you," said Big Claus; and seizing a hammer, he struck the one horse of Little Claus on the head, and he fell dead instantly.

"Oh, now I have no horse at all, said Little Claus, weeping. But after a while he took off the dead horse's skin, and hung the hide to dry in the wind. Then he put the dry skin into a bag, and, placing it over his shoulder, went out into the next town to sell the horse's skin. He had a very long way to go, and had to pass through a dark, gloomy forest. Presently a storm arose, and he lost his way, and before he discovered the right path, evening came on, and it was still a long way to the town, and too far to return home before night. Near the road stood a large farmhouse. The shutters outside the windows were closed, but lights shone through the crevices at the top. "I might get permission to stay here for the night," thought Little Claus; so he went up to the door and knocked. The farmer's wife opened the door; but when she heard what he wanted, she told him to go away, as her husband would not allow her to admit strangers. "Then I shall be obliged to lie out here," said Little Claus to himself, as the farmer's wife shut the door in his face. Near to the farmhouse stood a large haystack, and between it and the house was a small shed, with a thatched roof. "I can lie up there," said Little Claus, as he saw the roof; "it will make a famous bed, but I hope the stork will not fly down and bite my legs;" for on it stood a living stork, whose nest was in the roof. So Little Claus climbed to the roof of the shed, and while he turned himself to get comfortable, he discovered that the wooden shutters, which were closed, did not reach to the tops of the windows of the farmhouse, so that he could see into a room, in which a large table was laid out with wine, roast meat, and a splendid fish. The farmer's wife and the sexton were sitting at the table together; and she filled his glass, and helped him plenteously to fish, which appeared to be his favorite dish. "If I could only get some, too," thought Little Claus; and then, as he stretched his neck towards the window he spied a large, beautiful pie, — indeed they had a glorious feast before them.

At this moment he heard some one riding down the road, towards the farmhouse. It was the farmer returning home. He was a good man, but still he had a very strange prejudice, — he could not bear the sight of a sexton. If one appeared before him, he would put himself in a terrible rage. In consequence of this dislike, the sexton had gone to visit the farmer's wife during her husband's absence from home, and the good woman had placed before him the best she had in the house to eat. When she heard the farmer coming she was frightened, and begged the sexton to hide himself in a large empty chest that stood in the room. He did so, for he knew her husband could not endure the sight of a sexton. The woman then quickly put away the wine, and hid all the rest of the nice things in the oven; for if her husband had seen them he would have asked what they were brought out for.

"Oh, dear," sighed Little Claus from the top of the shed, as he saw all the good things disappear.

"Is any one up there?" asked the farmer, looking up and discovering Little Claus. "Why are you lying up there? Come down, and come into the house with me." So Little Claus came down and told the farmer how he had lost his way and begged for a night's lodging.

"All right," said the farmer; "but we must have something to eat first."

The woman received them both very kindly, laid the cloth on a large table, and placed before them a dish of porridge. The farmer was very hungry, and ate his porridge with a good appetite, but Little Claus could not help thinking of the nice roast meat, fish and pies, which he knew were in the oven. Under the table, at his feet, lay the sack containing the horse's skin, which he intended to sell at the next town. Now Little Claus did not relish the porridge at all, so he trod with his foot on the sack under the table, and the dry skin squeaked quite loud. "Hush!" said Little Claus to his sack, at the same time treading upon it again, till it squeaked louder than before.

"Hallo! what have you got in your sack!" asked the farmer.

"Oh, it is a conjuror," said Little Claus; "and he says we need not eat porridge, for he has conjured the oven full of roast meat, fish, and pie."

"Wonderful!" cried the farmer, starting up and opening the oven door; and there lay all the nice things hidden by the farmer's wife, but which he supposed had been conjured there by the wizard under the table. The woman dared not say anything; so she placed the things before them, and they both ate of the fish, the meat, and the pastry.

Then Little Claus trod again upon his sack, and it squeaked as before. "What does he say now?" asked the farmer.

"He says," replied Little Claus, "that there are three bottles of wine for us, standing in the corner, by the oven."

So the woman was obliged to bring out the wine also, which she had hidden, and the farmer drank it till he became quite merry. He would have liked such a conjuror as Little Claus carried in his sack. "Could he conjure up the evil one?" asked the farmer. "I should like to see him now, while I am so merry."

"Oh, yes!" replied Little Claus, "my conjuror can do anything I ask him, — can you not?" he asked, treading at the same time on the sack till it squeaked. "Do you hear? he answers 'Yes,' but he fears that we shall not like to look at him."

"Oh, I am not afraid. What will he be like?"

"Well, he is very much like a sexton."

"Ha!" said the farmer, "then he must be ugly. Do you know I canot endure the sight of a sexton. However, that doesn't matter, I shall know who it is; so I shall not mind. Now then, I have got up my courage, but don't let him come too near me."

"Stop, I must ask the conjuror," said Little Claus; so he trod on the bag, and stooped his ear down to listen.

"What does he say?"

"He says that you must go and open that large chest which stands in the corner, and you will see the evil one crouching down inside; but you must hold the lid firmly, that he may not slip out."

"Will you come and help me hold it?" said the farmer, going towards the chest in which his wife had hidden the sexton, who now lay inside, very much frightened. The farmer opened the lid a very little way, and peeped in.

"Oh," cried he, springing backwards, "I saw him, and he is exactly like our sexton. How dreadful it is!" So after that he was obliged to drink again, and they sat and drank till far into the night.

"You must sell your conjuror to me," said the farmer; "ask as much as you like, I will pay it; indeed I would give you directly a whole bushel of gold."

"No, indeed, I cannot," said Little Claus; "only think how much profit I could make out of this conjuror."

"But I should like to have him," said the farmer, still continuing his entreaties.

"Well," said Little Claus at length, "you have been so good as to give me a night's lodging, I will not refuse you; you shall have the conjuror for a bushel of money, but I will have quite full measure."

"So you shall," said the farmer; "but you must take away the chest as well. I would not have it in the house another hour; there is no knowing if *he* may not be still there."

So Little Claus gave the farmer the sack containing the dried horse's skin, and received in exchange a bushel of money—full measure. The farmer also gave him a wheelbarrow on which to carry away the chest and the gold.

"Farewell," said Little Claus, as he went off with his money and the great chest, in which the sexton lay still concealed. On one side of the forest was a broad, deep river, the water flowed so rapidly that very few were able to swim against the stream. A new bridge had lately been built across it, and in the middle of this bridge Little Claus stopped, and said, loud enough to be heard by the sexton, "Now what shall I do with this stupid chest; it is as heavy as if it were full of stones: I shall be tired if I roll it any farther, so I may as well throw it in the river; if it swims after me to my house, well and good, and if not, it will not much matter."

So he seized the chest in his hand and lifted it up a little, as if he were going to throw it into the water.

"No, leave it alone," cried the sexton from within the chest; "let me out first."

"Oh," exclaimed Little Claus, pretending to be frightened, "he is in there still, is he? I must throw him into the river, that he may be drowned."

"Oh, no; oh, no," cried the sexton; "I will give you a whole bushel full of money if you will let me go."

"Why, that is another matter," said Little Claus, opening the chest. The sexton crept out, pushed the empty chest into the water, and went to his house, then he measured out a whole bushel full of gold for Little Claus, who had already received one from the farmer, so that now he had a barrow full.

"I have been well paid for my horse," said he to himself when he reached home, entered his own room, and emptied all his money into a heap on the floor. "How vexed Great Claus will be when he finds out how rich I have become all through my one horse; but I shall not tell him exactly how it all happened." Then he sent a boy to Great Claus to borrow a bushel measure.

"What can he want it for?" thought Great Claus; so he smeared the bottom of the measure with tar, that some of whatever was put into it might stick there and remain. And so it happened; for when the measure returned, three new silver florins were sticking to it.

"What does this mean?" said Great Claus; so he ran off directly to Little Claus, and asked, "Where did you get so much money?"

"Oh, for my horse's skin, I sold it yesterday."

"It was certainly well paid for then," said Great Claus; and he ran home to his house, seized a hatchet, and knocked all his four horses on the head, flayed off their skins, and took them to the town to sell. "Skins, skins, who'll buy skins?" he cried, as he went through the streets. All the shoemakers and tanners came running, and asked how much he wanted for them.

"A bushel of money, for each," replied Great Claus.

"Are you mad?" they all cried; "do you think we have money to spend by the bushel?"

"Skins, skins," he cried again, "who'll buy skins?" but to all who inquired the price, his answer was, "a bushel of money."

"He is making fools of us," said they all; then the shoemakers took their straps, and the tanners their leather aprons, and began to beat Great Claus.

"Skins, skins!" they cried, mocking him; "yes, we'll mark your skin for you, till it is black and blue."

"Out of the town with him," said they. And Great Claus was obliged to run as fast as he could, he had never before been so thoroughly beaten.

"Ah," said he, as he came to his house; "Little Claus shall pay me for this; I will beat him to death."

Meanwhile the old grandmother of Little Claus died. She had been cross, unkind, and really spiteful to him; but he was very sorry, and took the dead woman and laid her in his warm bed to see if he could bring her to life again. There he determined that she should lie the whole night, while he seated himself in a chair in a corner of the room as he had often done before. During the night, as he sat there, the door opened, and in came Great Claus with a hatchet. He knew well where Little Claus's bed stood; so he went right up to it, and struck the old grandmother on the head, thinking it must be Little Claus.

"There," cried he, "now you cannot make a fool of me again;" and then he went home.

"That is a very wicked man," thought Little Claus; "he meant to kill me. It is a good thing for my old grandmother that she was already dead, or he would have taken her life." Then he dressed his old grandmother in her best clothes, borrowed a horse of his neighbor, and harnessed it to a cart. Then he placed the old woman on the back seat, so that she might not fall out as he drove, and rode away through the wood. By sunrise they reached a large inn, where Little Claus stopped and went to get something to eat. The landlord was a rich man, and a good man too; but as passionate as if he had been made of pepper and snuff.

"Good morning," said he to Little Claus; "you are come betimes to-day."

"Yes," said Little CLaus; "I am going to the town with my old grand-mother; she is sitting at the back of the wagon, but I cannot bring her into the room. Will you take her a glass of mead? but you must speak very loud, for she cannot hear well."

"Yes, certainly I will," replied the landlord; and, pouring out a glass of mead, he carried it out to the dead grandmother, who sat upright in the cart. "Here is a glass of mead from your grandson," said the landlord. The dead woman did not answer a word, but sat quite still. "Do you not hear?" cried the landlord as loud as he could; "here is a glass of mead from your grandson."

Again and again he bawled it out, but as she did not stir he flew into a passion, and threw the glass of mead in her face; it struck her on the nose, and she fell backwards out of the cart, for she was only seated there, not tied in.

"Hallo!" cried Little Claus, rushing out of the door, and seizing hold of the landlord by the throat; "you have killed my grandmother; see, here is a great hole in her forehead."

"Oh, how unfortunate," said the landlord, wringing his hands. "This all comes of my fiery temper. Dear Little Claus, I will give you a bushel of money; I will bury your grandmother as if she were my own; only keep silent, or else they will cut off my head, and that would be disagreeable."

So it happened that Little Claus received another bushel of money, and the landlord buried his old grandmother as if she had been his own. When Little Claus reached home again, he immediately sent a boy to Great Claus, requesting him to lend him a bushel measure. "How is this?" thought Great Claus; "did I not kill him? I must go and see for myself." So he went to Little Claus, and took the bushel measure with him. "How did you get all this money?" asked Great Claus, staring with wide open eyes at his neighbor's treasures.

"You killed my grandmother instead of me," said Little Claus; "so I have sold her for a bushel of money."

"That is a good price at all events," said Great Claus. So he went home, took a hatchet, and killed his old grandmother with one blow. Then he placed her on a cart, and drove into the town to the apothecary, and asked him if he would buy a dead body.

"Whose is it, and where did you get it?" asked the apothecary.

"It is my grandmother," he replied; "I killed her with a blow, that I might get a bushel of money for her."

"Heaven preserve us!" cried the apothecary, "you are out of your mind. Don't say such things, or you will lose your head." And then he talked to him seriously about the wicked deed he had done, and told him that such a wicked

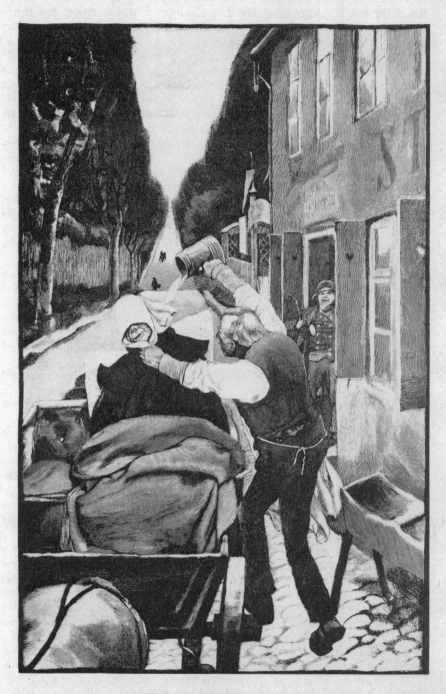

LITTLE CLAUS AND BIG CLAUS

man would surely be punished. Great Claus got so frightened that he rushed out of the surgery, jumped into the cart, whipped up his horses, and drove home quickly. The apothecary and all the people thought him mad, and let him drive where he liked.

"You shall pay for this," said Great Claus, as soon as he got into the highroad, "that you shall, Little Claus." So as soon as he reached home he took the largest sack he could find and went over to Little Claus. "You have played me another trick," said he. "First, I killed all my horses, and then my old grandmother, and it is all your fault; but you shall not make a fool of me any more." So he laid hold of Little Claus round the body, and pushed him into the sack, which he took on his shoulders, saying, "Now I'm going to drown you in the river."

He had a long way to go before he reached the river, and Little Claus was not a very light weight to carry. The road led by the church, and as they passed he could hear the organ playing and the people singing beautifully. Great Claus put down the sack close to the church-door, and thought he might as well go in and hear a psalm before he went any farther. Little Claus could not possibly get out of the sack, and all the people were in church; so in he went.

"Oh dear, oh dear," sighed Little Claus in the sack, as he turned and twisted about; but he found he could not loosen the string with which it was tied. Presently an old cattle driver, with snowy hair, passed by, carrying a large staff in his hand, with which he drove a large herd of cows and oxen before him. They stumbled against the sack in which lay Little Claus, and turned it over. "Oh dear," sighed Little Claus, "I am very young, yet I am soon going to heaven."

"And I, poor fellow," said the drover, "I who am so old already, cannot get there."

"Open the sack," creid Little Claus; "creep into it instead of me, and you will soon be there."

"With all my heart," replied the drover, opening the sack, from which sprung Little Claus as quickly as possible. "Will you take care of my cattle?" said the old man, as he crept into the bag.

"Yes," said Little Claus, and he tied up the sack, and then walked off with all the cows and oxen.

When Great Claus came out of church, he took up the sack, and placed it on his shoulders. It appeared to have become lighter, for the old drover was not half so heavy as Little Claus.

"How light he seems now," said he. "Ah, it is because I have been to a church." So he walked on to the river, which was deep and broad, and threw the sack containing the old drover into the water, believing it to be Little Claus. "There you may lie!" he exclaimed; "you will play me no more tricks now." Then he turned to go home, but when he came to a place where two roads crossed, there was Little Claus driving the cattle. "How is this?" said Great Claus. "Did I not drown you just now?"

"Yes," said Little Claus; "you threw me into the river about half an hour ago."

"But wherever did you get all these fine beasts?" asked Great Claus.

"These beasts are sea-cattle," replied Little Claus. "I'll tell you the whole story, and thank you for drowning me; I am above you now, I am really very rich. I was frightened, to be sure, while I lay tied up in the sack, and the wind whistled in my ears when you threw me into the river from the bridge, and I sank to the bottom immediately; but I did not hurt myself, for I fell upon beautifully soft grass which grows down there; and in a moment, the sack opened, and the sweetest little maiden came towards me. She had snow-white robes, and a wreath of green leaves on her wet hair. She took me by the hand, and said, 'So you are come, Little Claus, and here are some cattle for you to begin with. About a mile farther on the road, there is another herd for you.' Then I saw that the river formed a great highway for the people who live in the sea. They were walking and driving here and there from the sea to the land at the spot where the river terminates. The bed of the river was covered with the loveliest flowers and sweet fresh grass. The fish swam past me as rapidly as the birds do here in the air. How handsome all the people were, and what fine cattle were grazing on the hills and in the valleys!"

"But why did you come up again," said Great Claus, "if it was all so beautiful down there? I should not have done so?"

"Well," said Little Claus, "it was good policy on my part; you heard me say just now that I was told by the sea-maiden to go a mile farther on the road, and I should find a whole herd of cattle. By the road she meant the river, for she could not travel any other way; but I knew the winding of the river, and how it bends, sometimes to the right and sometimes to the left, and it seemed a long way, so I chose a shorter one; and, by coming up to the land, and then driving across the fields back again to the river, I shall save half a mile, and get all my cattle more quickly."

"What a lucky fellow you are!" exclaimed Great Claus. "Do you think I should get any sea-cattle if I went down to the bottom of the river?"

"Yes, I think so," said Little Claus; "but I cannot carry you there in a sack, you are too heavy. However if you will go there first, and then creep into a sack, I will throw you in with the greatest pleasure."

"Thank you," said Great Claus; "but remember, if I do not get any sea-cattle down there I shall come up again and give you a good thrashing."

"No, now, don't be too fierce about it!" said Little Claus, as they walked on towards the river. When they approached it, the cattle, who were very thirsty, saw the stream, and ran down to drink.

"See what a hurry they are in," said Little Claus, "they are longing to get down again,"

"Come, help me, make haste," said Great Claus; "or you'll get beaten." So he crept into a large sack, which had been lying across the back of one of the oxen.

"Put in a stone," said Great Claus, "or I may not sink."

"Oh, there's not much fear of that," he replied; still he put a large stone into the bag, and then tied it tightly, and gave it a push.

"Plump!" In went Great Claus, and immediately sank to the bottom of the river.

"I'm afraid he will not find any cattle," said Little Claus, and then he drove his own beasts homewards.

THE TRAVELLING COMPANION

POOR John was very sad; for his father was so ill, he had no hope of his recovery. John sat alone with the sick man in the little room, and the lamp had nearly burnt out; for it was late in the night.

"You have been a good son, John," said the sick father, "and God will help you on in the world." He looked at him, as he spoke, with mild, earnest eyes, drew a deep sigh, and died; yet it appeared as if he still slept.

John wept bitterly. He had no one in the wide world now; neither father, mother, brother, nor sister. Poor John! he knelt down by the bed, kissed his dead father's hand, and wept many, many bitter tears. But at last his eyes closed, and he fell asleep with his head resting against the hard bedpost. Then he dreamed a strange dream; he thought he saw the sun shining upon him, and his father alive and well, and even heard him laughing as he used to do when he was very happy. A beautiful girl, with a golden crown on her head, and long, shining hair, gave him her hand; and his father said, "See what a bride you have won. She is the loveliest maiden on the whole earth." Then he awoke, and all the beautiful things vanished before his eyes, his father lay dead on the bed, and he was all alone. Poor John!

During the following week the dead man was buried. The son walked behind the coffin which contained his father, whom he so dearly loved, and would never again behold. He heard the earth fall on the coffin-lid, and watched it till only a corner remained in sight, and at last that also disappeared. He felt as if his heart would break with its weight of sorrow, till those who stood round the grave sang a psalm, and the sweet, holy tones brought tears into his eyes, which relieved him. The sun shone brightly down on the green trees, as if it would say, "You must not be so sorrowful, John. Do you see the beautiful blue sky above you? Your father is up there, and he prays to the loving Father of all, that you may do well in the future."

"I will always be good," said John, "and then I shall go to be with my father in heaven. What joy it will be when we see each other again! How much I shall have to relate to him, and how many things he will be able to explain to me of the delights of heaven, and teach me as he once did on earth. Oh, what joy it will be!"

He pictured it all so plainly to himself, that he smiled even while the tears ran down his cheeks.

The little birds in the chestnut-trees twittered, "Tweet, tweet;" they were so happy, although they had seen the funeral; but they seemed as if they knew that the dead man was now in heaven, and that he had wings much larger and more beautiful than their own; and he was happy now, because he had been good here on earth, and they were glad of it. John saw them fly away out of the green trees into the wide world, and he longed to fly with them; but first he cut out a large wooden cross, to place on his father's grave; and when he brought it there in the evening, he found the grave decked out with gravel and flowers. Strangers had done this; they who had known the good old father who was now dead, and who had loved him very much.

Early the next morning, John packed up his little bundle of clothes, and placed all his money, which consisted of fifty dollars and a few shillings, in his girdle; with this he determined to try his fortune in the world. But first he went into the churchyard; and, by his father's grave, he offered up a prayer, and said, "Farewell."

As he passed through the fields, all the flowers looked fresh and beautiful in the warm sunshine, and nodded in the wind, as if they wished to say, "Welcome to the green wood, where all is fresh and bright."

Then John turned to have one more look at the old church, in which he had been christened in his infancy, and where his father had taken him every Sunday to hear the service and join in singing the psalms. As he looked at the old tower, he espied the ringer standing at one of the narrow openings, with his little pointed red cap on his head, and shading his eyes from the sun with his bent arm. John nodded farewell to him, and the little ringer waved his red cap, laid his hand on his heart, and kissed his hand to him a great many times, to show that he felt kindly towards him, and wished him a prosperous journey.

John continued his journey, and thought of all the wonderful things he should see in the large, beautiful world, till he found himself farther away from home than ever he had been before. He did not even know the names of the places he passed through, and could scarcely understand the language of the people he met, for he was far away, in a strange land. The first night he slept on a haystack, out in the fields, for there was no other bed for him; but it seemed to him so nice and comfortable that even a king need not wish for a better. The field, the brook, the haystack, with the blue sky above, formed a beautiful sleeping-room. The green grass, with the little red and white flowers, was the carpet; the elder-bushes and the hedges of wild roses looked like garlands on the walls; and for a bath he could have the clear, fresh water of the brook; while the rushes bowed their heads to him, to wish him good morning and good evening. The moon, like a large lamp, hung high up in the blue ceiling, and he had no fear of its setting fire to his curtains. John slept here quite safely all night; and when he awoke, the sun was up, and all the little birds were singing round him, "Good morning, good morning. Are you not up yet?"

It was Sunday, and the bells were ringing for church. As the people went in, John followed them; he heard God's word, joined in singing the psalms, and listened to the preacher. It seemed to him just as if he were in his own church, where he had been christened, and had sung the psalms with his father. Out in the churchyard were several graves, and on some of them the grass had grown very high. John thought of his father's grave, which he knew at last would look like these, as he was not there to weed and attend to it. Then he set to work, pulled up the high grass, raised the wooden crosses which had fallen down, and replaced the wreaths which had been blown away from their places by the wind, thinking all the time, "Perhaps some one is doing the same for my father's grave, as I am not there to do it."

Outside the church door stood an old beggar, leaning on his crutch. John have him his silver shillings, and then he continued his journey, feeling lighter and happier than ever. Towards evening, the weather became very stormy, and he hastened on as quickly as he could, to get shelter; but it was quite dark by the time he reached a little lonely church which stood on a hill. "I will go in here," he said, "and sit down in a corner; for I am quite tired, and want rest."

So he went in, and seated himself; then he folded his hands, and offered up his evening prayer, and was soon fast asleep and dreaming, while the thunder rolled and the lightning flashed without. When he awoke, it was still night; but the storm had ceased, and the moon shone in upon him through the windows. Then he saw an open coffin standing in the centre of the church, which contained a dead man, waiting for burial. John was not at all timid; he had a good conscience, and he knew also that the dead can never injure any one. It is living wicked men who do harm to others. Two such wicked persons stood now by the dead man, who had been brought to the church to be buried. Their evil intentions were to throw the poor dead body outside the church door, and not leave him to rest in his coffin.

"Why do you do this?" asked John, when he saw what they were going to do; "it is very wicked. Leave him to rest in peace, in Christ's name."

"Nonsense," replied the two dreadful men. "He has cheated us; he owed us money which he could not pay, and now he is dead we shall not get a penny; so we mean to have our revenge, and let him lie like a dog outside the church door."

"I have only fifty dollars," said John, "it is all I possess in the world, but I will give it to you if you will promise me faithfully to leave the dead man in peace. I shall be able to get on without the money; I have strong and healthy limbs, and God will always help me."

"Why, of course," said the horrid men, "if you will pay his debt we will both promise not to touch him. You may depend upon that;" and then they took the money he offered them, laughed at him for his good nature, and went their way.

Then he laid the dead body back in the coffin, folded the hands, and took leave of it; and went away contentedly through the great forest. All around him he could see the prettiest little elves dancing in the moonlight, which shone through the trees. They were not disturbed by his appearance, for they knew he was good and harmless among men. They are wicked people only who can never obtain a glimpse of fairies. Some of them were not taller than the breadth of a finger, and they wore golden combs in their long, yellow hair. They were rocking themselves two together on the large dew-drops with which the leaves and the high grass were sprinkled. Sometimes the dew-drops would roll away, and then they fell down between the stems of the long grass, and caused a great deal of laughing and noise among the other little people. It was quite charming to watch them at play. Then they sang songs, and John remembered that he had learnt those pretty songs when he was a little boy. Large speckled spiders, with silver crowns on their heads, were employed to spin suspension bridges and palaces from one hedge to another, and when the tiny drops fell upon them, they glittered in the moonlight like shining glass. This continued till sunrise. Then the little elves crept into the flower-buds, and the wind seized the bridges and palaces, and fluttered them in the air like cobwebs.

As John left the wood, a strong man's voice called after him, "Hallo, comrade, where are you travelling?"

"Into the wide world," he replied; "I am only a poor lad, I have neither father nor mother, but God will help me."

"I am going into the wide world also," replied the stranger; "shall we keep each other company?"

"With all my heart," he said, and so they went on together. Soon they began to like each other very much, for they were both good; but John found out that the stranger was much more clever than himself. He had travelled all over the world, and could describe almost everything. The sun was high in the heavens when they seated themselves under a large tree to eat their breakfast, and at the same moment an old woman came towards them. She was very old and almost bent double. She leaned upon a stick and carried on her back a bundle of firewood, which she had collected in the forest; her apron was tied round it, and John saw three great stems of fern and some willow twigs peeping out. Just as she came close up to them, her foot slipped and she fell to the ground screaming loudly; poor old woman, she had broken her leg! John proposed directly that they should carry the old woman home to her cottage; but the stranger opened his knapsack and took out a box, in which he said he had a salve that would quickly make her leg well and strong again, so that she would be able to walk home herself, as if her leg had never been broken. And all that he would ask in return was the three fern stems which she carried in her apron.

"That is rather too high a price," said the old woman, nodding her head quite strangely. She did not seem at all inclined to part with the fern stems. However, it was not very agreeable to lie there with a broken leg, so she gave them to him; and such was the power of the ointment, that no sooner had he rubbed her leg with it than the old mother rose up and walked even better than she had done before. But then this wonderful ointment could not be bought at a chemist's.

"What can you want with those three fern rods?" asked John of his fellow-traveller.

"Oh, they will make capital brooms," said he; "and I like them because I have strange whims sometimes." Then they walked on together for a long distance.

"How dark the sky is becoming," said John; "and look at those thick, heavy clouds."

"Those are not clouds," replied his fellow-traveller; "they are mountains—large lofty mountains—on the tops of which we should be above the clouds, in the pure, free air. Believe me, it is delightful to ascend so high, to-morrow we shall be there." But the mountains were not so near as they appeared; they had to travel a whole day before they reached them, and pass through black forests and piles of rock as large as a town. The journey had been so fatiguing that John and his fellow-traveller stopped to rest at a road-side inn, so that they might gain strength for their journey on the morrow. In the large public room of the inn a great many persons were assembled to see a comedy performed by dolls. The showman had just erected his little theatre, and the people were sitting round the room to witness the performance. Right in front, in the very best place, sat a stout butcher, with a great bull-dog by his side who seemed very much inclined to bite. He sat staring with all his eyes, and so indeed did every one else in the room. And then the play began. It was a pretty piece, with a king and a queen in it, who sat on a beautiful throne, and had gold crowns on their heads. The trains to their dresses were very long, according to the fashion; while the prettiest of wooden dolls, with glass eyes and large mustaches, stood at the doors, and opened and shut them, that the fresh air might come into the room. It was a very pleasant play, not at all mournful; but just as the queen stood up and walked across the stage, the great bull-dog, who should have been held back by his master, made a spring forward, and caught the queen in the teeth by the slender wrist, so that it snapped in two. This was a very dreadful disaster. The poor man, who was exhibiting the dolls, was much annoyed, and quite sad about his queen; she was the prettiest doll he had, and the bull-dog had broken her head and shoulders off. But after all the people were gone away, the stranger, who came with John, said that he could soon set her to rights. And then he brought out his box and rubbed the doll with some of the salve with which he had cured the old woman when she broke her leg. As soon as this was done the doll's back became quite right again; her head and shoulders were fixed on, and she could even move her limbs herself: there was now no occasion to pull the wires, for the doll acted just like a living creature, excepting that she could not speak. The man to whom the show belonged was quite delighted at having a doll who could dance of herself without being pulled by the wires; none of the other dolls could do this.

During the night, when all the people at the inn were gone to bed, some one was heard to sigh so deeply and painfully, and the sighing continued for so long a time, that every one got up to see what could be the matter. The showman went at once to his little theatre and found that it proceeded from the dolls, who all lay on the floor sighing piteously, and staring with their glass eyes; they all wanted to be rubbed with the ointment, so that, like the queen, they might be able to move of themselves. The queen threw herself on her knees, took off her beautiful crown, and, holding it in her hand, cried, "Take this from me, but do rub my husband and his courtiers."

The poor man who owned the theatre could scarcely refrain from weeping; he was so sorry that he could not help them. Then he immediately spoke to John's comrade, and promised him all the money he might receive at the next evening's performance, if he would only rub the ointment on four or five of his dolls. But the fellow-traveller said he did not require anything in return, excepting the sword which the showman wore by his side. As soon as he received the sword he anointed six of the dolls with the ointment, and they were able immediately to dance so gracefully that all the living girls in the room could not help joining in the dance. The coachman danced with the cook, and the waiters with the chambermaids, and all the strangers joined; even the tongs and the fire-shovel made an attempt, but they fell down after the first jump. So after all it was a very merry night. The next morning John and his companion left the inn to continue their journey through the great pine-forests and over the high mountains. They arrived at last at such a great height that towns and villages lay beneath them, and the church steeples looked like little specks between the green trees. They could see for miles round, far away to places they had never visited, and John saw more of the beautiful world than he had ever known before. The sun shone brightly in the blue firmament above, and through the clear mountain air came the sound of the huntsman's horn, and the soft, sweet notes brought tears into his eyes, and he could not help exclaiming, "How good and loving God is to give us all this beauty and loveliness in the world to make us happy!"

His fellow-traveller stood by with folded hands, gazing on the dark wood and the towns bathed in the warm sunshine. At this moment there sounded over their heads sweet music. They looked up, and discovered a large white swan hovering in the air, and singing as never bird sang before. But the song soon became weaker and weaker, the bird's head drooped, and he sunk slowly down, and lay dead at their feet.

"It is a beautiful bird," said the traveller, "and these large white wings are worth a great deal of money. I will take them with me. You see now that a sword will be very useful."

So he cut off the wings of the dead swan with one blow, and carried them away with him.

They now continued their journey over the mountains for many miles, till they at length reached a large city, containing hundreds of towers, that shone in the sunshine like silver. In the midst of the city stood a splendid marble palace, roofed with pure red gold, in which dwelt the king. John and his companion would not go into the town immediately; so they stopped at an inn outside the town, to change their clothes; for they wished to appear respectable as they walked through the streets. The landlord told them that the king was a very good man, who never injured any one: but as to his daughter, "Heaven defend us!"

She was indeed a wicked princess. She possessed beauty enough — nobody could be more elegant or prettier than she was; but what of that? for she was a wicked witch; and in consequence of her conduct many noble young princes had lost their lives. Any one was at liberty to make her an offer; were he a prince or a beggar, it mattered not to her. She would ask him to guess three things which she had just thought of, and if he succeed, he was to marry her, and be king over all the land when her father died; but if he could not guess these three things, then she ordered him to be hanged or to have his head cut off. The old king, her father, was very much grieved at her conduct, but he could not prevent her from being so wicked, because he once said he would have nothing more to do with her lovers; she might do as she pleased. Each prince who came and tried the three guesses, so that he might marry the princess, had been unable to find them out, and had been hanged or beheaded. They had all been warned in time, and might have left her alone, if they would. The old king became at last so distressed at all these dreadful circumstances, that for a whole day every year he and his soldiers knelt and prayed that the princess might become good; but she continued as wicked as ever. The old women who drank brandy would color it quite black before they drank it, to show how they mourned; and what more could they do?

"What a horrible princess!" said John; "she ought to be well flogged. If I were the old king, I would have her punished in some way."

Just then they heard the people outside shouting, "Hurrah!" and, looking out, they saw the princess passing by; and she was really so beautiful that everybody forgot her wickedness, and shouted "Hurrah!" Twelve lovely maidens in white silk dresses, holding golden tulips in their hands, rode by her side on coal-black horses. The princess herself had a snow-white steed, decked with diamonds and rubies. Her dress was of cloth of gold, and the whip she held in her hand looked like a sunbeam. The golden crown on her head glittered like the stars of heaven, and her mantle was formed of thousands of butterflies' wings sewn together. Yet she herself was more beautiful than all.

When John saw her, his face became as red as a drop of blood, and he could scarcely utter a word. The princess looked exactly like the beautiful lady with the golden crown, of whom he had dreamed on the night his father died. She appeared to him so lovely that he could not help loving her.

"It could not be true," he thought, "that she was really a wicked witch, who ordered people to be hanged or beheaded, if they could not guess her thoughts. Every one has permission to go and ask her hand, even the poorest beggar. I shall pay a visit to the palace," he said; "I must go, for I cannot help myself."

Then they all advised him not to attempt it; for he would be sure to share the same fate as the rest. His fellow-traveller also tried to persuade him against it; but John seemed quite sure of success. He brushed his shoes and his coat, washed his face and his hands, combed his soft flaxen hair, and then went out alone into the town, and walked to the palace.

"Come in," said the king, as John knocked at the door. John opened it, and the old king, in a dressing gown and embroidered slippers, came towards him. He had the crown on his head, carried his sceptre in one hand, and the orb in the other. "Wait a bit," said he, and he placed the orb under his arm, so that he could offer the other hand to John; but when he found that John was another suitor, he began to weep so violently, that both the sceptre and the orb fell to the floor, and he was obliged to wipe his eyes with his dressing gown. Poor old king! "Let her alone," he said; "you will fare as badly as all the others. Come, I will show you." Then he led him out into the princess's pleasure gardens, and there he saw a frightful sight. On every tree hung three or four king's sons who had wooed the princess, but had not been able to guess the riddles she gave them. Their skeletons rattled in every breeze, so that the terrified birds never dared to venture into the garden. All the flowers were supported by human bones instead of sticks, and human skulls in the flower-pots grinned horribly. It was really a doleful garden for a princess. "Do you see all this?" said the old king; "your fate will be the same as those who are here, therefore do not attempt it. You really make me very unhappy, — I take these things to heart so very much."

John kissed the good old king's hand, and said he was sure it would be all right, for he was quite enchanted with the beautiful princess. Then the princess herself came riding into the palace yard with all her ladies, and he wished her "Good morning." She looked wonderfully fair and lovely when she offered her hand to John, and he loved her more than ever. How could she be a wicked witch, as all the people asserted? He accompanied her into the hall, and the little pages offered them gingerbread nuts and sweetmeats, but the old king was so unhappy he could eat nothing, and besides, gingerbread nuts were too hard for him. It was decided that John should come to the palace the next day, when the judges and the whole of the counsellors would be present, to try if he could guess the first riddle. If he succeeded, he would have to come a second time; but if not, he would lose his life, — and no one had ever been able to guess even one. However, John was not at all anxious about the result of his trial; on the contrary, he was very merry. He thought only of the beautiful princess, and believed that in some way he should have help, but how he knew not, and did not like to think about it; so he danced along the high-road as he went back to the inn, where he had left his fellow-traveller waiting for him. John could not refrain from telling him how gracious the princess had been, and how beautiful she looked. He longed for the next day so much, that he might go to the palace and try his luck at guessing the riddles. But his comrade shook his head, and looked very mournful. "I do so wish you to do well," said he; "we might have continued together much longer, and now I am likely to lose you; you poor dear John! I could shed

THE TRAVELLING COMPANION

tears, but I will not make you unhappy on the last night we may be together. We will be merry, really merry this evening; to-morrow, after you are gone, I shall be able to weep undisturbed."

It was very quickly known among the inhabitants of the town that another suitor had arrived for the princess, and there was great sorrow in consequence. The theatre remained closed, the women who sold sweetmeats tied crape round the sugar-sticks, and the king and the priests were on their knees in the church. There was a great lamentation, for no one expected John to succeed better than those who had been suitors before.

In the evening John's comrade prepared a large bowl of punch, and said, "Now let us be merry, and drink to the health of the princess." But after drinking two glasses, John became so sleepy, that he could not possibly keep his eyes open, and fell fast asleep. Then his fellow-traveller lifted him gently out of his chair, and laid him on the bed; and as soon as it was quite dark, he took the two large wings which he had cut from the dead swan, and tied them firmly to his own shoulders. Then he put into his pocket the largest of the three rods which he had obtained from the old woman who had fallen and broken her leg. After this he opened the window, and flew away over the town, straight towards the palace, and seated himself in a corner, under the window which looked into the bedroom of the princess.

The town was perfectly still when the clocks struck a quarter to twelve. Presently the window opened, and the princess, who had large black wings to her shoulders, and a long white mantle, flew away over the city towards a high mountain. The fellow-traveller, who had made himself invisible, so that she could not possibly see him, flew after her through the air, and whipped the princess with his rod, so that the blood came whenever he struck her. Ah, it was a strange flight through the air! The wind caught her mantle, so that it spread out on all sides, like the large sail of a ship, and the moon shone through it. "How it hails, to be sure!" said the princess, at each blow she received from the rod; and it served her right to be whipped.

At last she reached the side of the mountain, and knocked. The mountain opened with a noise like the roll of thunder, and the princess went in. The traveller followed her; no one could see him, as he had made himself invisible. They went through a long, wide passage. A thousand gleaming spiders ran here and there on the walls, causing them to glitter as if they were illuminated with fire. They next entered a large hall built of silver and gold. Large red and blue flowers shone on the walls, looking like sunflowers in size, but no one could dare to pluck them, for the stems were hideous poisonous snakes, and the flowers were flames of fire, darting out of their jaws. Shining glow-worms covered the ceiling, and sky-blue bats flapped their transparent wings. Altogether the place had a frightful appearance. In the middle of the floor stood a throne supported by four skeleton horses, whose harness had been made by fiery-red spiders. The throne itself was made of milk-white glass, and the cushions were little black mice, each biting the other's tail. Over it hung a canopy of rose-colored spider's webs, spotted with the prettiest little green flies, which sparkled like precious stones. On the throne sat an old magician with a crown on his ugly head, and a sceptre in his hand. He kissed the princess on the forehead, seated her by his side on the splendid throne, and then the music commenced. Great black grasshoppers played the mouth organ, and the owl struck herself on the body instead of a drum. It was altogether a ridiculous concert. Little black goblins with false lights in their caps danced about the hall; but no one could see the traveller, and he had placed himself just behind the throne where he could see and hear everything. The courtiers who came in afterwards looked noble and grand; but any one with common sense could see what they really were, only broomsticks, with cabbages for heads. The magician had given them life, and dressed them in embroidered robes. It answered very well, as they were only wanted for show. After there had been a little dancing, the princess told the magician that she had a new suitor, and asked him what she could think of for the suitor to guess when he came to the castle the next morning.

"Listen to what I say," said the magician, "you must choose something very easy, he is less likely to guess it then. Think of one of your shoes, he will never imagine it is that. Then cut his head off; and mind you do not forget to bring his eyes with you to-morrow night, that I may eat them."

The princess curtsied low, and said she would not forget the eyes.

The magician then opened the mountain and she flew home again, but the traveller followed and flogged her so much with the rod, that she sighed quite deeply about the heavy hail-storm, and made as much haste as she could to get back to her bedroom through the window. The traveller then returned to the inn where John still slept, took off his wings and laid down on the bed, for he was very tired. Early in the morning John awoke, and when his fellow-traveller got up, he said that he had a very wonderful dream about the princess and her shoe, he therefore advised John to ask her if she had not thought of her shoe. Of course the traveller knew this from what the magician in the mountain had said.

"I may as well say that as anything," said John. "Perhaps your dream may come true; still I will say farewell, for if I guess wrong I shall never see you again."

Then they embraced each other, and John went into the town and walked to the palace. The great hall was full of people, and the judges sat in arm-chairs, with eider-down cushions to rest their heads upon, because they had so much to think of. The old king stood near, wiping his eyes with his white pocket-handkerchief. When the princess entered, she looked even more beautiful than she had appeared the day before, and greeted every one present most gracefully; but to John she gave her hand, and said, "Good morning to you."

Now came the time for John to guess what she was thinking of; and oh, how kindly she looked at him as she spoke. But when he uttered the single word shoe, she turned as pale as a ghost; all her wisdom could not help her, for he had guessed rightly. Oh, how pleased the old king was! It was quite amusing to see how he capered about. All the people clapped their hands, both on his account and John's, who had guessed rightly the first time. His fellow-traveller was glad also, when he heard how successful John had been. But John folded his hands, and thanked God, who, he felt quite sure, would help him again; and he knew he had to guess twice more. The evening passed pleasantly like the one preceding. While John slept, his companion flew behind the princess to the mountain, and flogged her even harder than before; this time he had taken two rods with him. No one saw him go in with her, and he heard all that was said. The princess this time was to think of a glove, and he told John as if he had again heard it in a dream. The next day, therefore, he was able to guess correctly the second time, and it caused great rejoicing at the palace. The whole court jumped about as they had seen the king do the day before, but the princess lay on the sofa, and would not say a single word. All now depended upon John. If he only guessed rightly the third time, he would marry the princess, and reign over the kingdom after the death of the old king; but if he failed, he would lose his life, and the magician would have his beautiful blue eyes. That evening John said his prayers and went to bed very early, and soon fell asleep calmly. But his companion tied on his wings to his shoulders, took three rods, and, with his sword at his side, flew to the palace. It was a very dark night, and so stormy that the tiles flew from the roofs of the houses, and the trees in the garden upon which the skeletons hung bent themselves like reeds before the wind. The lightning flashed, and the thunder rolled in one long-continued peal all night. The window of the castle opened, and the princess flew out. She was pale as death, but she laughed at the storm as if it were not bad enough. Her white mantle fluttered in the wind like a large sail, and the traveller flogged her with the three rods till the blood trickled down, and at last she could scarcely fly; she contrived, however, to reach the mountain. "What a hail-storm!" she said, as she entered; "I have never been out in such weather as this."

"Yes, there may be too much of a good thing sometimes," said the magician.

Then the princess told him that John had guessed rightly the second time, and if he succeeded the next morning, he would win, and she could never come to the mountain again, or practice magic as she had done, and therefore she was quite unhappy. "I will find out something for you to think of which he will never guess, unless he is a greater conjuror than myself. But now let us be merry."

Then he took the princess by both hands, and they danced with all the little goblins and Jack-o'-lanterns in the room. The red spiders sprang here and there on the walls quite as merrily, and the flowers of fire appeared as if they were throwing out sparks. The owl beat the drum, the crickets whistled and the grasshoppers played the mouth-organ. It was a very ridiculous ball. After they had danced enough, the princess was obliged to go home, for fear she should be missed at the palace. The magician offered to go with her, that they might be company to each other on the way. Then they flew away through the bad weather, and the traveller followed them, and broke his three rods across their shoulders. The magician had never been out in such a hail-storm as this. Just by the palace the magician stopped to wish the princess farewell, and to whisper in her ear, "To-morrow think of my head."

But the traveller heard it, and just as the princess slipped through the window into her bedroom, and the magician turned round to fly back to the mountain, he seized him by the long black beard, and with his sabre cut off the wicked conjuror's head just behind the shoulders, so that he could not even see who it was. He threw the body into the sea to the fishes, and after dipping the head into the water, he tied it up in a silk handkerchief, took it with him to the inn, and then went to bed. The next morning he gave John the handkerchief, and told him not to untie it till the princess asked him what she was thinking of. There were so many people in the great hall of the palace that they stood as thick as radishes tied together in a bundle. The council sat in their arm-chairs with the white cushions. The old king wore new robes, and the golden crown and sceptre had been polished up so that he looked quite smart. But the princess was very pale, and wore a black dress as if she were going to a funeral.

"What have I thought of?" asked the princess, of John. He immediately untied the handkerchief, and was himself quite frightened when he saw the head of the ugly magician. Every one shuddered, for it was terrible to look at; but the princess sat like a statue, and could not utter a single word. At length she rose and gave John her hand, for he had guessed rightly.

She looked at no one, but sighed deeply, and said, "You are my master now; this evening our marriage must take place."

"I am very pleased to hear it," said the old king. "It is just what I wish."

Then all the people shouted "Hurrah." The band played music in the streets, the bells rang, and the cake-women took the black crape off the sugar-sticks. There was universal joy. Three oxen, stuffed with ducks and chickens, were roasted whole in the market-place, where every one might help himself to a slice. The fountains spouted forth the most delicious wine, and whoever bought a penny loaf at the baker's received six large buns, full of raisins, as a present. In the evening the whole town was illuminated. The soldiers fired off cannons, and the boys let off crackers. There was eating and drinking, dancing and jumping everywhere. In the palace, the high-born gentlemen and beautiful ladies danced with each other, and they could be heard at a great distance singing the following song: —

> "Here are maidens, young and fair,
> Dancing in the summer air;
> Like two spinning-wheels at play,
> Pretty maidens dance away —
> Dance the spring and summer through
> Till the sole falls from your shoe."

But the princess was still a witch, and she could not love John. His fellow-traveller had thought of that, so he gave John three feathers out of the swan's wings, and a little bottle with a few drops in it. He told him to place a large bath full of water by the princess's bed, and put the feathers and the drops into it. Then, at the moment she was about to get into bed, he must give her a little push, so that she might fall into the water, and then dip her three times. This would destroy the power of the magician, and she would love him very much. John did all that his companion told him to do. The princess shrieked aloud when he dipped her under the water the first time, and struggled under his hands in the form of a great black swan with fiery eyes. As she rose the second time from the water, the swan had become white, with a black ring round its neck. John allowed the water to close once more over the bird, and at the same time it changed into a most beautiful princess. She was more lovely even than before, and thanked him, while her eyes sparkled with tears, for having broken the spell of the magician. The next day, the king came with the whole court to offer their congratulations, and stayed till quite late. Last of all came the travelling companion; he had his staff in his hand and his knapsack on his back. John kissed him many times and told him he must not go, he must remain with him, for he was the cause of all his good fortune. But the traveller shook his head, and said gently and kindly, "No: my time is up now; I have only paid my debt to you. Do you remember the dead man whom the bad people wished to throw out of his coffin? You gave all you possessed that he might rest in his grave; I am that man." As he said this, he vanished.

The wedding festivities lasted a whole month. John and his princess loved each other dearly, and the old king lived to see many a happy day, when he took their little children on his knees and let them play with his sceptre. And John became king over the whole country.

THE GOLOSHES OF FORTUNE
A BEGINNING

In a house in Copenhagen, not far from the king's new market, a very large party had assembled, the host and his family expecting, no doubt, to receive invitations in return. One half of the company were already seated at the card-tables, the other half seemed to be waiting the result of their hostess's question, "Well, how shall we amuse ourselves?"

Conversation followed, which, after a while, began to prove very entertaining. Among other subjects, it turned upon the events of the middle ages, which some persons maintained were more full of interest than our own times. Counsellor Knapp defended this opinion so warmly that the lady of the house immediately went over to his side, and both exclaimed against Oersted's Essays on Ancient and Modern Times, in which the preference is given to our own. The counsellor considered the times of the Danish king, Hans,* as the noblest and happiest.

The conversation on this topic was only interrupted for a moment by the arrival of a newspaper, which did not, however, contain much worth reading, and while it is still going on we will pay a visit to the ante-room, in which cloaks, sticks, and goloshes were carefully placed. Here sat two maidens, one young, and the other old, as if they had come and were waiting to accompany their mistresses home; but on looking at them more closely, it could easily be seen that they were no common servants. Their shapes were too graceful, their complexions too delicate, and the cut of their dresses much too elegant. They were two fairies. The younger was not Fortune herself, but the chambermaid of one of Fortune's attendants, who carries about her more trifling gifts. The elder one, who was named Care, looked rather gloomy; she always goes about to perform her own business in person; for then she knows it is properly done. They were telling each other where they had been during the day. The messenger of Fortune had only transacted a few unimportant matters; for instance, she had preserved a new bonnet from a shower of rain, and obtained for an honest man a bow from a titled nobody, and so on; but she had something extraordinary to relate, after all.

"I must tell you," said she, "that to-day is my birthday; and in honor of it I have been intrusted with a pair of goloshes, to introduce amongst mankind.

*He died in 1513. He married Christine, daughter of the Electoral Prince Ernest of Saxony.

These goloshes have the property of making every one who puts them on imagine himself in any place he wishes, or that he exists at any period. Every wish is fulfilled at the moment it is expressed, so that for once mankind have the chance of being happy."

"No," replied Care; "you may depend upon it that whoever puts on those goloshes will be very unhappy, and bless the moment in which he can get rid of them."

"What are you thinking of?" replied the other. "Now see; I will place them by the door; some one will take them instead of his own, and he will be the happy man."

This was the end of their conversation.

WHAT HAPPENED TO THE COUNSELLOR

IT was late when Counsellor Knapp, lost in thought about the times of King Hans, desired to return home; and fate so ordered it that he put on the goloshes of Fortune instead of his own, and walked out into the East Street. Through the magic power of the goloshes, he was at once carried back three hundred years, to the times of King Hans, for which he had been longing when he put them on. Therefore he immediately set his foot into the mud and mire of the street, which in those days possessed no pavement.

"Why, this is horrible; how dreadfully dirty it is!" said the counsellor; and the whole pavement has vanished, and the lamps are all out."

The moon had not yet risen high enough to penetrate the thick foggy air, and all the objects around him were confused together in the darkness. At the nearest corner, a lamp hung before a picture of the Madonna; but the light it gave was almost useless, for he only perceived it when he came quite close and his eyes fell on the painted figures of the Mother and Child.

"That is most likely a museum of art," thought he, "and they have forgotten to take down the sign."

Two men, in the dress of olden times, passed by him.

"What odd figures!" thought he; "they must be returning from some masquerade."

Suddenly he heard the sound of a drum and fifes, and then a blazing light from torches shone upon him. The counsellor stared with astonishment as he beheld a most strange procession pass before him. First came a whole troop of drummers, beating their drums very cleverly; they were followed by life-guards, with longbows and crossbows. The principal person in the procession was a clerical-looking gentleman. The astonished counsellor asked what it all meant, and who the gentleman might be.

"That is the bishop of Zealand."

"Good gracious!" he exclaimed; "what in the world has happened to the bishop? what can he be thinking about?" Then he shook his head and said, "It cannot possibly be the bishop himself."

While musing on this strange affair, and without looking to the right or left, he walked on through East Street and over Highbridge Place. The bridge, which he supposed led to Palace Square, was nowhere to be found; but instead, he saw a bank and some shallow water, and two people, who sat in a boat.

"Does the gentleman wish to be ferried over the Holm?" asked one.

"To the Holm!" exclaimed the counsellor, not knowing in what age he was now existing; "I want to go to Christian's Haven, in Little Turf Street." The men stared at him. "Pray tell me where the bridge is!" said he. "It is shameful that the lamps are not lighted here, and it is as muddy as if one were walking in a marsh." But the more he talked with the boatmen the less they could understand each other.

"I don't understand your outlandish talk," he cried at last, angrily turning his back upon them. He could not, however, find the bridge nor any railings.

"What a scandalous condition this place is in," said he; never, certainly, had he found his own times so miserable as on this evening. "I think it will be better for me to take a coach; but where are they?" There was not one to be seen! "I shall be obliged to go back to the king's new market," said he, "where there are plenty of carriages standing, or I shall never reach Christian's Haven." Then he went towards East Street, and had nearly passed through it, when the moon burst forth from a cloud.

"Dear me, what have they been erecting here?" he cried, as he caught sight of the East gate, which in olden times used to stand at the end of East Street. However, he found an opening through which he passed, and came out upon where he expected to find the new market. Nothing was to be seen but an open meadow, surrounded by a few bushes, through which ran a broad canal or stream. A few miserable-looking wooden booths, for the accommodation of Dutch watermen, stood on the opposite shore.

"Either I behold a *fata morgana,* or I must be tipsy," groaned the counsellor. "What can it be? What is the matter with me?" He turned back in the full conviction that he must be ill. In walking through the street this time, he examined the houses more closely; he found that most of them were built of lath and plaster, and many had only a thatched roof.

"I am certainly all wrong," said he, with a sigh; and yet I only drank one glass of punch. But I cannot bear even that, and it was very foolish to give us punch and hot salmon; I shall speak about it to our hostess, the agent's lady. Suppose I were to go back now and say how ill I feel, I fear it would look so ridiculous, and it is not very likely that I should find any one up." Then he looked for the house, but it was not in existence.

"This is really frightful; I cannot even recognize East Street. Not a shop to be seen; nothing but old, wretched, tumble-down houses, just as if I were at Roeskilde or Ringstedt. Oh, I really must be ill! It is no use to stand upon ceremony. But where in the world is the agent's house. There *is* a house, but it is not his; and people still up in it, I can hear. Oh dear! I certainly am very queer." As he reached the half-open door, he saw a light and went in. It was a tavern of the olden times, and seemed a kind of beershop. The room had the appearance of a Dutch interior. A number of people, consisting of seamen, Copenhagen citizens, and a few scholars, sat in deep conversation over their mugs, and took very little notice of the new comer.

"Pardon me," said the counsellor, addressing the landlady, "I do not feel quite well, and I should be much obliged if you will send for a fly to take me to Christian's Haven." The woman stared at him and shook her head. Then she spoke to him in German. The counsellor supposed from this that she did not understand Danish; he therefore repeated his request in German. This, as well as his singular dress, convinced the woman that he was a foreigner. She

THE GOLOSHES OF FORTUNE

soon understood, however, that he did not find himself quite well, and therefore brought him a mug of water. It had something of the taste of sea-water, certainly, although it had been drawn from the well outside. Then the counsellor leaned his head on his hand, drew a deep breath, and pondered over all the strange things that had happened to him.

"Is that to-day's number of the *Day?*"* he asked, quite mechanically, as he saw the woman putting by a large piece of paper. She did not understand what he meant, but she handed him the sheet; it was a woodcut, representing a meteor, which had appeared in the town of Cologne.

"That is very old," said the counsellor, becoming quite cheerful at the sight of this antique drawing. "Where did you get this singular sheet? It is very interesting, although the whole affair is a fable. Meteors are easily explained in these days; they are northern lights, which are often seen, and are no doubt caused by electricity."

Those who sat near him, and heard what he said, looked at him in great astonishment, and one of them rose, took off his hat respectfully, and said in a very serious manner, "You must certainly be a very learned man, monsieur."

"Oh no," replied the counsellor; "I can only discourse on topics which every one should understand."

"*Modestia* is a beautiful virtue," said the man. "Moreover, I must add to your speech *mihi secus videtur;* yet in this case I would suspend my *judicium.*"

"May I ask to whom I have the pleasure of speaking?"

"I am a Bachelor of Divinity," said the man. This answer satisfied the counsellor. The title agreed with the dress.

"This is surely," thought he, "an old village schoolmaster, a perfect original, such as one meets with sometimes even in Jutland."

"This is not certainly a *locus docendi,*" began the man; "still I must beg you to continue the conversation. You must be well read in ancient lore."

"Oh yes," replied the counsellor; "I am very fond of reading useful old books, and modern ones as well, with the exception of every-day stories, of which we really have more than enough.

"Every-day stories?" asked the bachelor.

"Yes, I mean the new novels that we have at the present day."

"Oh," replied the man, with a smile; "and yet they are very witty, and are much read at Court. The king likes especially the romance of Messeurs Iffven and Gaudian, which describes King Arthur and his knights of the round table. He has joked about it with the gentlemen of his Court."

"Well, I have certainly not read that," replied the counsellor. "I suppose it is quite new, and published by Heiberg."

"No," answered the man, "it is not by Heiberg; Godfred von Gehman brought it out."

"Oh, is he the publisher? That is a very old name," said the counsellor; "was it not the name of the first publisher in Denmark?"

"Yes; and he is our first printer and publisher now," replied the scholar.

So far all had passed off very well; but now one of the citizens began to speak of a terrible pestilence which had been raging a few years before, meaning the plague of 1484. The counsellor thought he referred to the

_____
*An evening paper in Copenhagen.

cholera, and they could discuss this without finding out the mistake. The war in 1490 was spoken of as quite recent. The English pirates had taken some ships in the Channel in 1801, and the counsellor, supposing they referred to these, agreed with them in finding fault with the English. The rest of the talk, however, was not so agreeable; every moment one contradicted the other. The good bachelor appeared very ignorant, for the simplest remark of the counsellor seemed to him either too bold or too fantastic. They stared at each other, and when it became worse the bachelor spoke in Latin, in the hope of being better understood; but it was all useless.

"How are you now?" asked the landlady, pulling the counsellor's sleeve.

Then his recollection returned to him. In the course of conversation he had forgotten all that had happened previously.

"Goodness me! where am I?" said he. It bewildered him as he thought of it.

"We will have some claret, or mead, or Bremen beer," said one of the guests; "will you drink with us?"

Two maids came in. One of them had a cap on her head of two colors.* They poured out the wine, bowed their heads, and withdrew.

The counsellor felt a cold shiver run all over him. "What is this? what does it mean?" said he; but he was obliged to drink with them, for they over-powered the good man with their politeness. He became at last desperate; and when one of them said he was tipsy, he did not doubt the man's word in the least—only begged them to get a droschky; and then they thought he was speaking the Muscovite language. Never before had he been in such rough and vulgar company. "One might believe that the country was going back to heathenism," he observed. "This is the most terrible moment of my life."

Just then it came into his mind that he would stoop under the table, and so creep to the door. He tried it; but before he reached the entry, the rest discovered what he was about, and seized him by the feet, when, luckily for him, off came the goloshes, and with them vanished the whole enchantment. The counsellor now saw quite plainly a lamp, and a large building behind it; everything looked familiar and beautiful. He was in East Street, as it now appears; he lay with his legs turned towards a porch, and just by him sat the watchman asleep.

"Is it possible that I have been lying here in the street dreaming?" said he. "Yes, this is East Street; how beautifully bright and gay it looks! It is quite shocking that one glass of punch should have upset me like this."

Two minutes afterwards he sat in a droschky, which was to drive him to Christian's Haven. He thought of all the terror and anxiety which he had undergone, and felt thankful from his heart for the reality and comfort of modern times, which, with all their errors, were far better than those in which he so lately found himself.

THE WATCHMAN'S ADVENTURES

"Well, I declare, there lies a pair of goloshes," said the watchman. "No doubt, they belong to the lieutenant who lives up stairs. They are lying just by his door." Gladly would the honest man have rung, and given them in, for a light was still burning, but he did not wish to disturb the other people in the

---

*In the time of King Hans, chambermaids were obliged to wear caps of two colors.

house; so he let them lie. "These things must keep the feet very warm," said he; "they are of such nice soft leather." Then he tried them on, and they fitted his feet exactly. "Now," said he, "how droll things are in this world! There's that man can lie down in his warm bed, but he does not do so. There he goes pacing up and down the room. He ought to be a happy man. He has neither wife nor children, and he goes out into company every evening. Oh, I wish I were he; then I should be a happy man."

As he uttered this wish, the goloshes which he had put on took effect, and the watchman at once became the lieutenant. There he stood in his room, holding a little piece of pink paper between his fingers, on which was a poem, — a poem written by the lieutenant himself. Who has not had, for once in his life, a moment of poetic inspiration? and at such a moment, if the thoughts are written down, they flow in poetry. The following verses were written on the pink paper: —

"OH WERE I RICH!

"Oh were I rich! How oft, in youth's bright hour,
    When youthful pleasures banish every care,
I longed for riches but to gain a power,
    The sword and plume and uniform to wear!
The riches and the honor came for me;
    Yet still my greatest wealth was poverty:
        Ah, help and pity me!

"Once in my youthful hours, when gay and free,
    A maiden loved me; and her gentle kiss,
Rich in its tender love and purity,
    Taught me, alas! too much of earthly bliss.
Dear child! She only thought of youthful glee;
    She loved no wealth, but fairy tales and me.
        Thou knowest: ah, pity me!

"Oh were I rich! again is all my prayer:
    That child is now a woman, fair and free,
As good and beautiful as angels are.
    Oh, were I rich in lovers' poetry,
To tell my fairy tale, love's richest lore!
    But no; I must be silent — I am poor.
        Ah, wilt thou pity me?

"Oh were I rich in truth and peace below,
    I need not then my poverty bewail.
To thee I dedicate these lines of woe;
    Wilt thou not understand the mournful tale?
A leaf on which my sorrows I relate —
    Dark story of a darker night of fate.
        Ah, bless and pity me!"

"Well, yes; people write poems when they are in love, but a wise man will not print them. A lieutenant in love, and poor. This is a triangle, or more properly speaking, the half of the broken die of fortune." The lieutenant felt this very keenly, and therefore leaned his head against the window-frame, and sighed deeply. "The poor watchman in the street," said he, "is far happier than I am. He knows not what I call poverty. He has a home, a wife and children, who weep at his sorrow and rejoice at his joy. Oh, how much happier I should be could I change my being and position with him, and pass through life with his humble expectations and hopes! Yes, he is indeed happier than I am."

At this moment the watchman again became a watchman; for having, through the goloshes of Fortune, passed into the existence of the lieutenant, and found himself less contented than he expected, he had preferred his former condition, and wished himself again a watchman. "That was an ugly dream," said he, "but droll enough. It seemed to me as if I were the lieutenant up yonder, but there was no happiness for me. I missed my wife and the little ones, who are always ready to smother me with kisses." He sat down again and nodded, but he could not get the dream out of his thoughts, and he still had the goloshes on his feet. A falling star gleamed across the sky. "There goes one!" cried he. "However, there are quite enough left; I should very much like to examine these a little nearer, especially the moon, for that could not slip away under one's hands. The student, for whom my wife washes, says that when we die we shall fly from one star to another. If that were true, it would be very delightful, but I don't believe it. I wish I could make a little spring up there now; I would willingly let my body lie here on the steps."

There are certain things in the world which should be uttered very cautiously; doubly so when the speaker has on his feet the goloshes of Fortune. Now we shall hear what happened to the watchman.

Nearly every one is acquainted with the great power of steam; we have proved it by the rapidity with which we can travel, both on a railroad or in a steamship across the sea. But this speed is like the movements of the sloth, or the crawling march of the snail, when compared to the swiftness with which light travels; light flies nineteen million times faster than the fleetest racehorse, and electricity is more rapid still. Death is an electric shock which we receive in our hearts, and on the wings of electricity the liberated soul flies away swiftly, the light from the sun travels to our earth ninety-five millions of miles in eight minutes and a few seconds; but on the wings of electricity, the mind requires only a second to accomplish the same distance. The space between the heavenly bodies is, to thought, no farther than the distance which we may have to walk from one friend's house to another in the same town; yet this electric shock obliges us to use our bodies here below, unless, like the watchman, we have on the goloshes of Fortune.

In a very few seconds the watchman had travelled more than two hundred thousand miles to the moon, which is formed of a lighter material than our earth, and may be said to be as soft as new fallen snow. He found himself on one of the circular range of mountains which we see represented in Dr. Mädler's large map of the moon. The interior had the appearance of a large hollow, bowl-shaped, with a depth about half a mile from the brim. Within this hollow stood a large town; we may form some idea of its appearance by pouring the white of an egg into a glass of water. The materials of which it was built seemed just as soft, and pictured forth cloudy turrets and sail-like terraces, quite transparent, and floating in the thin air. Our earth hung over his head like a great dark red ball. Presently he discovered a number of beings, which might certainly be called men, but were very different to ourselves. A more fantastical imagination than Herschel's must have discovered these. Had they been placed in groups, and painted, it might have been said, "What beautiful foliage!" They had also a language of their own. No one could have expected the soul of the watchman to understand it, and yet he did understand it, for our souls have much greater capabilities then we are inclined to believe. Do we not, in our dreams, show a wonderful dramatic talent? each of our acquaintance appears to us then in his own character, and with his own voice; no man could thus imitate them in his waking hours. How clearly, too, we are reminded of persons whom we have not seen for many years; they start up suddenly to the mind's eye with all their peculiarities as living realities. In fact, this memory of the soul is a fearful thing; every sin, every sinful thought it can bring back, and we may well ask how we are to give account of "every idle word" that may have been whispered in the heart or uttered with the lips. The spirit of the watchman therefore understood very well the language of the inhabitants of the moon. They were disputing about our earth, and doubted whether it could be inhabited. The atmosphere, they asserted, must be too dense for any inhabitants of the moon to exist there. They maintained that the moon alone was inhabited, and was really the heavenly body in which the old world people lived. They likewise talked politics.

But now we will descend to East Street, and see what happened to the watchman's body. He sat lifeless on the steps. His staff had fallen out of his hand, and his eyes stared at the moon, about which his honest soul was wandering.

"What is it o'clock, watchman?" inquired a passenger. But there was no answer from the watchman.

The man then pulled his nose gently, which caused him to lose his balance. The body fell forward, and lay at full length on the ground as one dead.

All his comrades were very much frightened, for he seemed quite dead; still they allowed him to remain after they had given notice of what had happened; and at dawn the body was carried to the hospital. We might imagine it to be no jesting matter if the soul of the man should chance to return to him, for most probably it would seek for the body in East Street without being able to find it. We might fancy the soul inquiring of the police, or at the address office, or among the missing parcels, and then at length finding it at the hospital. But we may comfort ourselves by the certainty that the soul, when acting upon its own impulses, is wiser than we are; it is the body that makes it stupid.

As we have said, the watchman's body had been taken to the hospital, and here it was placed in a room to be washed. Naturally, the first thing done here was to take off the goloshes, upon which the soul was instantly obliged to return, and it took the direct road to the body at once, and in a few seconds the man's life returned to him. He declared, when he quite recovered himself, that this had been the most dreadful night he had ever passed; not for a hundred pounds would he go through such feelings again. However, it was all over now.

The same day he was allowed to leave, but the goloshes remained at the hospital.

THE EVENTFUL MOMENT — A MOST UNUSUAL JOURNEY

Every inhabitant of Copenhagen knows what the entrance to Frederick's Hospital is like; but as most probably a few of those who read this little tale may not reside in Copenhagen, we will give a short description of it.

The hospital is separated from the street by an iron railing, in which the bars stand so wide apart that, it is said, some very slim patients have squeezed through, and gone to pay little visits in the town. The most difficult part of the body to get through was the head; and in this case, as it often happens in the world, the small heads were the most fortunate. This will serve as sufficient introduction to our tale. One of the young volunteers, of whom, physically speaking, it might be said that he had a great head, was on guard that evening at the hospital. The rain was pouring down, yet, in spite of these two obstacles, he wanted to go out just for a quarter of an hour; it was not worth while, he thought, to make a confidant of the porter, as he could easily slip through the iron railings. There lay the goloshes, which the watchman had forgotten. It never occurred to him that these could be goloshes of Fortune. They would be very serviceable to him in this rainy weather, so he drew them on. Now came the question whether he could squeeze through the palings; he certainly had never tried, so he stood looking at them. "I wish to goodness my head was through," said he, and instantly, though it was so thick and large, it slipped through quite easily. The goloshes answered that purpose very well, but his body had to follow, and this was impossible. "I am too fat," he said; "I thought my head would be the worst, but I cannot get my body through, that is certain." Then he tried to pull his head back again, but without success; he could move his neck about easily enough, and that was all. His first feeling was one of anger, and then his spirits sank below zero. The goloshes of Fortune had placed him in this terrible position, and unfortunately it never occurred to him to wish himself free. No, instead of wishing he kept twisting about, yet did not stir from the spot. The rain poured, and not a creature could be seen in the street. The porter's bell he was unable to reach, and however was he to get loose! He foresaw that he should have to stay there till morning, and then they must send for a smith to file away the iron bars, and that would be a work of time. All the charity children would just be going to school: and all the sailors who inhabited that quarter of the town would be there to see him standing in the pillory. What a crowd there would be. "Ha," he cried, "the blood is rushing to my head, and I shall go mad. I believe I am crazy already; oh, I wish I were free, then all these sensations would pass off." This is just what he ought to have said at first. The moment he had expressed the thought his head was free. He started back, quite bewildered with the fright which the goloshes of Fortune had caused him. But we must not suppose it was all over; no, indeed, there was worse to come yet. The night passed, and the whole of the following day; but no one sent for the goloshes. In the evening a declamatory performance was to take place at the amateur theatre in a distant street. The house was crowded; among the audience was the young volunteer from the hospital, who seemed to have quite forgotten his adventures of the previous evening. He had on the goloshes; they had not been sent for, and as the streets were still very dirty, they were of great service to him. A new poem, entitled "My Aunt's Spectacles," was being recited. It described these spectacles as possessing a wonderful power; if any one put them on in a large assembly the people appeared like cards, and the future events of ensuing years could be easily foretold by them. The idea struck him that he should very much like to have such a pair of spectacles; for, if used rightly, they would perhaps enable him to see into the hearts of people, which he thought would be more interesting than to know what was going to happen next year; for future events would be sure to show themselves, but the hearts of people never. "I can fancy what I should see in the whole row of ladies and gentlemen on the first seat, if I could only look into their hearts; that lady, I imagine, keeps a store for things of all descriptions; how my eyes would wander about in that collection; with many ladies I should no doubt find a large millinery establishment. There is another that is perhaps empty, and would be all the better for cleaning out. There may be some well stored with good articles. Ah, yes," he sighed, "I know one, in which everything is solid, but a servant is there already, and that is the only thing against it. I dare say from many I should hear the words, 'Please to walk in.' I only wish I could slip into the hearts like a little tiny thought." This was the word of command for the goloshes. The volunteer shrunk up together, and commenced a most unusual journey through the hearts of the spectators in the first row. The first heart he entered was that of a lady, but he thought he must have got into one of the rooms of an orthopedic institution where plaster casts of deformed limbs were hanging on the walls, with this difference, that the casts in the institution are formed when the patient enters, but here they were formed and preserved after the good people had left. These were casts of the bodily and mental deformities of the lady's female friends carefully preserved. Quickly he passed into another heart, which had the appearance of a spacious, holy church, with the white dove of innocence fluttering over the altar. Gladly would he have fallen on his knees in such a sacred place; but he was carried on to another heart, still, however, listening to the tones of the organ, and feeling himself that he had become another and a better man. The next heart was also a sanctuary, which he felt almost unworthy to enter; it represented a mean garret, in which lay a sick mother; but the warm sunshine streamed through the window, lovely roses bloomed in a little flowerbox on the roof, two blue birds sang of childlike joys, and the sick mother prayed for a blessing on her daughter. Next he crept on his hands and knees through an overfilled butcher's shop; there was meat, nothing but meat, wherever he stepped; this was the heart of a rich, respectable man, whose name is doubtless in the directory. Then he entered the heart of this man's wife; it was an old, tumble-down pigeon-house; the husband's portrait served as a weather-cock; it was connected with all the doors, which opened and shut just as the husband's decision turned. The next heart was a complete cabinet of mirrors, such as can be seen in the Castle of Rosenberg. But these mirrors magnified in an astonishing degree; in the middle of the floor sat, like the Grand Lama, the insignificant *I* of the owner, astonished at the contemplation of his own features. At his next visit he fancied he must have got into a narrow needle-case, full of sharp needles: "Oh," thought he, "this must be the heart of an old maid;" but such was not the fact; it belonged to a young officer, who wore several orders, and was said to be a man of intellect and heart.

The poor volunteer came out of the last heart in the row quite bewildered. He could not collect his thoughts, and imagined his foolish fancies had carried him away. "Good gracious!" he sighed, "I must have a tendency to softening of the brain, and here it is so exceedingly hot that the blood is rushing to my head." And then suddenly recurred to him the strange event of the evening before, when his head had been fixed between the iron railings in front of the hospital. "That is the cause of it all!" he exclaimed, "I must do something in time. A Russian bath would be a very good thing to begin with. I wish I were lying on one of the highest shelves." Sure enough, there he lay on an upper shelf of a vapor bath, still in his evening costume, with his boots and goloshes on, and the hot drops from the ceiling falling on his face. "Ho!" he cried, jumping down and rushing towards the plunging bath. The attendant stopped him with a loud cry, when he saw a man with all his clothes on. The volunteer had, however, presence of mind enough to whisper, "It is for a wager;" but the first thing he did, when he reached his own room, was to put a large blister on his neck, and another on his back, that his crazy fit might be cured. The next morning his back was very sore, which was all he gained by the goloshes of Fortune.

THE CLERK'S TRANSFORMATION

The watchman, whom we of course have not forgotten, thought, after a while, of the goloshes which he had found and taken to the hospital; so he went and fetched them. But neither the lieutenant nor any one in the street could recognize them as their own, so he gave them up to the police. "They look exactly like my own goloshes," said one of the clerks, examining the unknown articles, as they stood by the side of his own. "It would require even more than the eye of a shoemaker to know one pair from the other."

"Master clerk," said a servant who entered with some papers. The clerk turned and spoke to the man; but when he had done with him, he turned to look at the goloshes again, and now he was in greater doubt than ever as to whether the pair on the right or on the left belonged to him. "Those that are wet must be mine," thought he; but he thought wrong, it was just the reverse. The goloshes of Fortune were the wet pair; and, besides, why should not a clerk in a police office be wrong sometimes? So he drew them on, thrust his papers into his pocket, placed a few manuscripts under his arm, which he had to take with him, and to make abstracts from at home. Then, as it was Sunday morning and the weather very fine, he said to himself, "A walk to Fredericksburg will do me good:" so away he went.

There could not be a quieter or more steady young man than this clerk. We will not grudge him this little walk, it was just the thing to do him good after sitting so much. He went on at first like a mere automaton, without thought or wish; therefore the goloshes had no opportunity to display their magic power. In the avenue he met with an acquaintance, one of our young poets, who told him that he intended to start on the following day on a summer excursion. "Are you really going away so soon?" asked the clerk. "What a free, happy man you are. You can roam about where you will, while such as we are tied by the foot."

"But it is fastened to the bread-tree," replied the poet. "You need have no anxiety for the morrow; and when you are old there is a pension for you."

"Ah, yes; but you have the best of it," said the clerk; "it must be so delightful to sit and write poetry. The whole world makes itself agreeable to you, and then you are your own master. You should try how you would like to listen to all the trivial things in a court of justice." The poet shook his head, so also did the clerk; each retained his own opinion, and so they parted. "They are strange people, these poets," thought the clerk. "I should like to try what it is to have a poetic taste, and to become a poet myself. I am sure I should not write such mournful verses as they do. This is a splendid spring day for a poet, the air is so remarkably clear, the clouds are so beautiful, and the green grass has such a sweet smell. For many years I have not felt as I do at this moment."

We perceive, by these remarks, that he had already become a poet. By most poets what he had said would be considered common-place, or as the Germans call it, "insipid." It is a foolish fancy to look upon poets as different to other men. There are many who are more the poets of nature than those who are professed poets. The difference is this, the poet's intellectual memory is better; he seizes upon an idea or a sentiment, until he can embody it, clearly and plainly in words, which the others cannot do. But the transition from a character of every-day life to one of a more gifted nature is a great transition; and so the clerk became aware of the change after a time. "What a delightful perfume," said he; "it reminds me of the violets at Aunt Lora's. Ah, that was when I was a little boy. Dear me, how long it seems since I thought of those days! She was a good old maiden lady! she lived yonder, behind the Exchange. She always had a sprig or a few blossoms in water, let the winter be ever so severe. I could smell the violets, even while I was placing warm penny pieces against the frozen panes to make peep-holes, and a pretty view it was on which I peeped. Out in the river lay the ships, icebound, and forsaken by their crews; a screaming crow represented the only living creature on board. But when the breezes of spring came, everything started into life. Amidst shouting and cheers the ships were tarred and rigged, and then they sailed to foreign lands.

"I remain here, and always shall remain, sitting at my post at the police of-fice, and letting others take passports to distant lands. Yes, this is my fate," and he sighed deeply. Suddenly he paused. "Good gracious, what has come over me? I never felt before as I do now; it must be the air of spring. It is over-powering, and yet it is delightful."

He felt in his pockets for some of his papers. "These will give me something else to think of," said he. Casting his eyes on the first page of one, he read, " 'Mistress Sigbirth; an original Tragedy, in Five Acts.' What is this?—in my own handwriting, too! Have I written this tragedy?" He read again, " 'The In-trigue on the Promenade; or, the Fast-Day. A Vaudeville.' However did I get all this? Some one must have put them into my pocket. And here is a letter!" It was from the manager of a theatre; the pieces were rejected, not at all in polite terms.

"Hem, hem!" said he, sitting down on a bench; his thoughts were very elastic, and his heart softened strangely. Involuntarily he seized one of the nearest flowers; it was a little, simple daisy. All that botanists can say in many lectures was explained in a moment by this little flower. It spoke of the glory of its birth; it told of the strength of the sunlight, which had caused its delicate leaves to expand, and given to it such sweet perfume. The struggles of life which arouse sensations in the bosom have their type in the tiny flowers. Air and light are the lovers of the flowers, but light is the favored one; towards light it turns, and only when light vanishes does it fold its leaves together, and sleep in the embraces of the air.

"It is light that adorns me," said the flower.

"But the air gives you the breath of life," whispered the poet.

Just by him stood a boy, splashing with his stick in a marshy ditch. The water-drops spurted up among the green twigs, and the clerk thought of the millions of animalculæ which were thrown into the air with every drop of water, at a height which must be the same to them as it would be to us if we were hurled beyond the clouds. As the clerk thought of all these things, and became conscious of the great change in his own feelings, he smiled, and said to himself, "I must be asleep and dreaming; and yet, if so, how wonderful for a dream to be so natural and real, and to know at the same time too that it is but a dream. I hope I shall be able to remember it all when I wake tomorrow. My sensations seem most unaccountable. I have a clear perception of everything as if I were wide awake. I am quite sure if I recollect all this tomorrow, it will appear utterly ridiculous and absurd. I have had this happen to me before. It is with the clever or wonderful things we say or hear in dreams, as with the gold which comes from under the earth, it is rich and beautiful when we possess it, but when seen in a true light it is but as stones and withered leaves."

"Ah!" he sighed mournfully, as he gazed at the birds singing merrily, or hopping from branch to branch, "they are much better off than I. Flying is a glorious power. Happy is he who is born with wings. Yes, if I could change myself into anything I would be a little lark." At the same moment his coat-tails and sleeves grew together and formed wings, his clothes changed to feathers, and his goloshes to claws. He felt what was taking place, and laughed to himself. "Well, now it is evident I must be dreaming; but I never had such a wild dream as this." And then he flew up into the green boughs and sang, but there was no poetry in the song, for his poetic nature had left him. The goloshes, like all persons who wish to do a thing thoroughly, could only attend to one thing at a time. He wished to be a poet, and he became one. Then he wanted to be a little bird, and in this change he lost the characteristics of the former one. "Well," thought he, "this is charming; by day I sit in a police-office, amongst the dryest law papers, and at night I can dream that I am a lark, flying about in the gardens of Fredericksburg. Really a complete comedy could be written about it." Then he flew down into the grass, turned his head about in every direction, and tapped his beak on the bending blades of grass, which, in proportion to his size, seemed to him as long as the palm-leaves in northern Africa.

In another moment all was darkness around him. It seemed as if something immense had been thrown over him. A sailor boy had flung his large cap over the bird, and a hand came underneath and caught the clerk by the back and wings so roughly, that he squeaked, and then cried out in his alarm, "You impudent rascal, I am a clerk in the police-office!" but it only sounded to the boy like "tweet, tweet;" so he tapped the bird on the beak, and walked away with him. In the avenue he met two school-boys, who appeared to belong to a better class of society, but whose inferior abilities kept them in the lowest class at school. These boys bought the bird for eightpence, and so the clerk returned to Copenhagen. "It is well for me that I am dreaming," he thought; "otherwise I should become really angry. First I was a poet, and now I am a lark. It must have been the poetic nature that changed me into this little creature. It is a miserable story indeed, especially now I have fallen into the hands of boys. I wonder what will be the end of it." The boys carried him into a very elegant room, where a stout, pleasant-looking lady received them, but she was not at all gratified to find that they had brought a lark — a common field-bird as she called it. However, she allowed them for one day to place the bird in an empty cage that hung near the window. "It will please Polly perhaps," she said, laughing at a large gray parrot, who was swinging himself proudly on a ring in a handsome brass cage. "It is Polly's birthday," she added in a simpering tone, "and the little field-bird has come to offer his congratulations."

Polly did not answer a single word, he continued to swing proudly to and fro; but a beautiful canary, who had been brought from his own warm, fragrant fatherland, the summer previous, began to sing as loud as he could.

"You screamer!" said the lady, throwing a white handkerchief over the cage.

"Tweet, tweet," sighed he, "what a dreadful snowstorm!" and then he became silent.

The clerk, or as the lady called him the field-bird, was placed in a little cage close to the canary, and not far from the parrot. The only human speech which Polly could utter, and which she sometimes chattered forth most comically, was "Now let us be men." All besides was a scream, quite as unintelligible as the warbling of the canary-bird, excepting to the clerk, who being now a bird, could understand his comrades very well.

"I flew beneath green palm-trees, and amidst the blooming almond-trees," sang the canary. "I flew with my brothers and sisters over beautiful flowers, and across the clear, bright sea, which reflected the waving foliage in its glittering depths; and I have seen many gay parrots, who could relate long and delightful stories."

"They were wild birds," answered the parrot, "and totally uneducated. Now let us be men. Why do you not laugh? If the lady and her visitors can laugh at this, surely you can. It is a great failing not to be able to appreciate what is amusing. Now let us be men."

"Do you remember," said the canary, "the pretty maidens who used to dance in the tents that were spread out beneath the sweet blossoms? Do you remember the delicious fruit and the cooling juice from the wild herbs?"

"Oh, yes," said the parrot; "but here I am much better off. I am well fed, and treated politely. I know that I have a clever head; and what more do I want? Let us be men now. You have a soul for poetry. I have deep knowledge and wit. You have genius, but no discretion. You raise your naturally high notes so much, that you get covered over. They never serve me so. Oh, no; I cost them something more than you. I keep them in order with my beak, and fling my wit about me. Now let us be men."

"O my warm, blooming fatherland," sang the canary bird, "I will sing of thy dark-green trees and thy quiet streams, where the bending branches kiss the clear, smooth water. I will sing of the joy of my brothers and sisters, as their shining plumage flits among the dark leaves of the plants which grow wild by the springs."

"Do leave off those dismal strains," said the parrot; "sing something to make us laugh; laughter is the sign of the highest order of intellect. Can a dog or a horse laugh? No, they can cry; but to man alone is the power of laughter given. Ha! ha! ha!" laughed Polly, and repeated his witty saying, "Now let us be men."

"You little gray Danish bird," said the canary, "you also have become a prisoner. It is certainly cold in your forests, but still there is liberty there. Fly out! they have forgotten to close the cage, and the window is open at the top. Fly, fly!"

Instinctively, the clerk obeyed, and left the cage; at the same moment the half-opened door leading into the next room creaked on its hinges, and, stealthily, with green fiery eyes, the cat crept in and chased the lark round the room. The canary-bird fluttered in his cage, and the parrot flapped his wings and cried, "Let us be men;" the poor clerk, in the most deadly terror, flew through the window, over the houses, and through the streets, till at length he was obliged to seek a resting-place. A house opposite to him had a look of home. A window stood open; he flew in, and perched upon the table. It was his own room. "Let us be men now," said he, involuntarily imitating the parrot; and at the same moment he became a clerk again, only that he was sitting on the table. "Heaven preserve us!" said he; "How did I get up here and fall asleep in this way? It was an uneasy dream too that I had. The whole affair appears most absurd."

THE BEST THING THE GOLOSHES DID

Early on the following morning, while the clerk was still in bed, his neighbor, a young divinity student, who lodged on the same storey, knocked at his door, and then walked in. "Lend me your goloshes," said he; "it is so wet in the garden, but the sun is shining brightly. I should like to go out there and smoke my pipe." He put on the goloshes, and was soon in the garden, which contained only one plum-tree and one apple-tree; yet, in a town, even a small garden like this is a great advantage.

The student wandered up and down the path; it was just six o'clock, and he could hear the sound of the post-horn in the street. "Oh, to travel, to travel!" cried he; "there is no greater happiness in the world: it is the height of my ambition. This restless feeling would be stilled, if I could take a journey far away from this country. I should like to see beautiful Switzerland, to travel through Italy, and,"——It was well for him that the goloshes acted immediately, otherwise he might have been carried too far for himself as well as for us. In a moment he found himself in Switzerland, closely packed with eight others in the diligence. His head ached, his back was stiff, and the blood had ceased to circulate, so that his feet were swelled and pinched by his boots. He wavered in a condition between sleeping and waking. In his right-hand pocket he had a letter of credit; in his left-hand pocket was his passport; and a few louis d'ors were sewn into a little leather bag which he carried in his breast-pocket. Whenever he dozed, he dreamed that he had lost one or another of these possessions; then he would awake with a start, and the first movements of his hand formed a triangle from his right-hand pocket to his breast, and from his breast to his left-hand pocket, to feel whether they were all safe. Umbrellas, sticks, and hats swung in the net before him, and almost obstructed the prospect, which was really very imposing; and as he glanced at it, his memory recalled the words of one poet at least, who has sung of Switzerland, and whose poems have not yet been printed: —

"How lovely to my wondering eyes
Mont Blanc's fair summits gently rise;
'Tis sweet to breathe the mountain air, —
If you have gold enough to spare."

Grand, dark, and gloomy appeared the landscape around him. The pine-forests looked like little groups of moss on high rocks, whose summits were lost in clouds of mist. Presently it began to snow, and the wind blew keen and cold. "Ah," he sighed, "if I were only on the other side of the Alps now, it would be summer, and I should be able to get money on my letter of credit. The anxiety I feel on this matter prevents me from enjoying myself in Switzerland. Oh, I wish I was on the other side of the Alps."

And there, in a moment, he found himself, far away in the midst of Italy, between Florence and Rome, where the lake Thrasymene glittered in the evening sunlight like a sheet of molten gold between the dark blue mountains. There, where Hannibal defeated Flaminius, the grape vines clung to each other with the friendly grasp of their green tendril fingers; while, by the wayside, lovely half-naked children were watching a herd of coal-black swine under the blossoms of fragrant laurel. Could we rightly describe this picturesque scene, our readers would exclaim, "Delightful Italy!"

But neither the student nor either of his travelling companions felt the least inclination to think of it in this way. Poisonous flies and gnats flew into the coach by thousands. In vain they drove them away with a myrtle branch, the flies stung them notwithstanding. There was not a man in the coach whose face was not swollen and disfigured with the stings. The poor horses looked wretched; the flies settled on their backs in swarms, and they were only relieved when the coachmen got down and drove the creatures off.

As the sun set, an icy coldness filled all nature, not however of long duration. It produced the feeling which we experience when we enter a vault at a funeral, on a summer's day; while the hills and the clouds put on that singular green hue which we often notice in old paintings, and look upon as unnatural until we have ourselves seen nature's coloring in the south. It was a glorious spectacle; but the stomachs of the travellers were empty, their bodies exhausted with fatigue, and all the longings of their heart turned towards a resting-place for the night; but where to find one they knew not. All the eyes were too eagerly seeking for this resting-place, to notice the beauties of nature.

The road passed through a grove of olive-trees; it reminded the student of the willow-trees at home. Here stood a lonely inn, and close by it a number of crippled beggars had placed themselves; the brightest among them looked, to quote the words of Marryat, "like the eldest son of Famine who had just come of age." The others were either blind, or had withered legs, which obliged them to creep about on their hands and knees, or they had shrivelled arms and hands without fingers. It was indeed poverty arrayed in rags. *"Eccellenza, miserabili!"* they exclaimed, stretching forth their diseased limbs. The hostess received the travellers with bare feet, untidy hair, and a dirty blouse. The doors were fastened together with string; the floors of the rooms were of brick, broken in many places; bats flew about under the roof; and as to the odor within—

"Let us have supper laid in the stable," said one of the travellers; "then we shall know what we are breathing."

The windows were opened to let in a little fresh air, but quicker than air came in the withered arms and the continual whining sounds, *"Miserabili, eccellenza.* On the walls were inscriptions, half of them against *"la bella Italia."*

The supper made its appearance at last. It consisted of watery soup, seasoned with pepper and rancid oil. This last delicacy played a principal part in the salad. Musty eggs and roasted cocks'-combs were the best dishes on the table; even the wine had a strange taste, it was certainly a mixture. At night, all the boxes were placed against the doors, and one of the travellers watched while the others slept. The student's turn came to watch. How close the air felt in that room; the heat overpowered him. The gnats were buzzing about and stinging, while the *miserabili*, outside, moaned in their dreams.

"Travelling would be all very well," said the student of divinity to himself, "if we had no bodies, or if the body could rest while the soul if flying. Wherever I go I feel a want which oppresses my heart, for something better presents itself at the moment; yes, something better, which shall be the best of all; but where is that to be found? In fact, I know in my heart very well what I want. I wish to attain the greatest of all happiness."

No sooner were the words spoken than he was at home. Long white curtains shaded the windows of his room, and in the middle of the floor stood a black coffin, in which he now lay in the still sleep of death; his wish was fulfilled, his body was at rest, and his spirit travelling.

"Esteem no man happy until he is in his grave," were the words of Solon. Here was a strong fresh proof of their truth. Every corpse is a sphinx of immortality. The sphinx in this sarcophagus might unveil its own mystery in the words which the living had himself written two days before—

> "Stern death, thy chilling silence waketh dread;
>   Yet in thy darkest hour there may be light.
> Earth's garden reaper! from the grave's cold bed
>   The soul on Jacob's ladder takes her flight.

> Man's greatest sorrows often are a part
>   Of hidden griefs, concealed from human eyes,
> Which press far heavier on the lonely heart
>   Than now the earth that on his coffin lies."

Two figures were moving about the room; we know them both. One was the fairy named Care, the other the messenger of Fortune. They bent over the dead.

"Look!" said Care; "what happiness have your goloshes brought to mankind?"

"They have at least brought lasting happiness to him who slumbers here," she said.

"Not so," said Care, "he went away of himself, he was not summoned. His mental powers were not strong enough to discern the treasures which he had been destined to discover. I will do him a favor now." And she drew the goloshes from his feet.

The sleep of death was ended, and the recovered man raised himself. Care vanished, and with her the goloshes; doubtless she looked upon them as her own property.

THE FLYING TRUNK

THERE was once a merchant who was so rich that he could have paved the whole street with gold, and would even then have had enough for a small alley. But he did not do so; he knew the value of money better than to use it in this way. So clever was he, that every shilling he put out brought him a crown; and so he continued till he died. His son inherited his wealth, and he lived a merry life with it; he went to a masquerade every night, made kites out of five pound notes, and threw pieces of gold into the sea instead of stones, making ducks and drakes of them. In this manner he soon lost all his money. At last he had nothing left but a pair of slippers, an old dressing-gown, and four shillings. And now all his friends deserted him, they could not walk with him in the streets; but one of them, who was very good-natured, sent him an old trunk with this message, "Pack up!" "Yes," he said, "it is all very well to say 'pack up,' " but he had nothing left to pack up, therefore he seated himself in the trunk. It was a very wonderful trunk; no sooner did any one press on the lock than the trunk could fly. He shut the lid and pressed the lock, when away flew the trunk up the chimney with the merchant's son in it, right up into the clouds. Whenever the bottom of the trunk cracked, he was in a great fright, for if the trunk fell to pieces he would have made a tremendous somerset over the trees. However, he got safely in his trunk to the land of Turkey. He hid the trunk in the wood under some dry leaves, and then went into the town: he could so this very well, for the Turks always go about dressed in dressing-gowns and slippers, as he was himself. He happened to meet a nurse with a little child. "I say, you Turkish nurse," cried he, "what castle is that near the town, with the windows placed so high?"

"The king's daughter lives there," she replied; "it has been prophesied that she will be very unhappy about a lover, and therefore no one is allowed to visit her, unless the king and queen are present."

"Thank you," said the merchant's son. So he went back to the wood, seated himself in his trunk, flew up to the roof of the castle, and crept through the window into the princess's room. She lay on the sofa asleep, and she was so beautiful that the merchant's son could not help kissing her. Then she awoke, and was very much frightened; but he told her he was a Turkish angel, who had come down through the air to see her, which pleased her very much. He sat down by her side and talked to her: he said her eyes were like beautiful dark lakes, in which the thoughts swam about like little mermaids, and he told her that her forehead was a snowy mountain, which contained splendid halls full of pictures. And then he related to her about the stork who brings the beautiful children from the rivers. These were delightful stories; and when he asked the princess if she would marry him, she consented immediately.

"But you must come on Saturday," she said; "for then the king and queen will take tea with me. They will be very proud when they find that I am going to marry a Turkish angel; but you must think of some very pretty stories to tell them, for my parents like to hear stories better than anything. My mother prefers one that is deep and moral; but my father likes something funny, to make him laugh."

"Very well," he replied; "I shall bring you no other marriage portion than a

HE TOLD HER STORIES ABOUT HER EYES

THE FLYING TRUNK

story," and so they parted. But the princess gave him a sword which was studded with gold coins, and these he could use.

Then he flew away to the town and bought a new dressing-gown, and afterwards returned to the wood, where he composed a story, so as to be ready for Saturday, which was no easy matter. It was ready however by Saturday, when he went to see the princess. The king, and queen, and the whole court, were at tea with the princess; and he was received with great politeness.

"Will you tell us a story?" said the queen, — "one that is instructive and full of deep learning."

"Yes, but with something in it to laugh at," said the king.

"Certainly," he replied, and commenced at once, asking them to listen attentively. "There was once a bundle of matches that were exceedingly proud of their high descent. Their genealogical tree, that is, a large pine-tree from which they had been cut, was at one time a large, old tree in the wood. The matches now lay between a tinder-box and an old iron saucepan, and were talking about their youthful days. 'Ah! then we grew on the green boughs, and were as green as they; every morning and evening we were fed with diamond drops of dew. Whenever the sun shone, we felt his warm rays, and the little birds would relate stories to us as they sung. We knew that we were rich, for the other trees only wore their green dress in summer, but our family were able to array themselves in green, summer and winter. But the wood-cutter came, like a great revolution, and our family fell under the axe. The head of the house obtained a situation as mainmast in a very fine ship, and can sail round the world when he will. The other branches of the family were taken to different places, and our office now is to kindle a light for common people. This is how such high-born people as we came to be in a kitchen.'

" 'Mine has been a very different fate,' said the iron pot, which stood by the matches; 'from my first entrance into the world I have been used to cooking and scouring. I am the first in this house, when anything solid or useful is required. My only pleasure is to be made clean and shining after dinner, and to sit in my place and have a little sensible conversation with my neighbors. All of us, excepting the water-bucket, which is sometimes taken into the courtyard, live here together within these four walls. We get our news from the market-basket, but he sometimes tells us very unpleasant things about the people and the government. Yes, and one day an old pot was so alarmed, that he fell down and was broken to pieces. He was a liberal, I can tell you.'

" 'You are talking too much,' said the tinder-box, and the steel struck against the flint till some sparks flew out, crying, 'We want a merry evening, don't we?'

" 'Yes, of course,' said the matches, 'let us talk about those who are the highest born.'

" 'No, I don't like to be always talking of what we are,' remarked the saucepan; 'let us think of some other amusement; I will begin. We will tell something that has happened to ourselves; that will be very easy, and interesting as well. On the Baltic Sea, near the Danish shore' ——

" 'What a pretty commencement!' said the plates; 'we shall all like that story, I am sure.'

" 'Yes; well in my youth, I lived in a quiet family, where the furniture was polished, the floors scoured, and clean curtains put up every fortnight.'

THE PRINCESS WAITED ALL DAY ON THE ROOF.

THE FLYING TRUNK

" 'What an interesting way you have of relating a story,' said the carpet-broom; 'it is easy to perceive that you have been a great deal in women's society, there is something so pure runs through what you say.'

" 'That is quite true,' said the water-bucket; and he made a spring with joy, and splashed some water on the floor.

" Then the saucepan went on with his story, and the end was as good as the beginning.

" The plates rattled with pleasure, and the carpet-broom brought some green parsley out of the dust-hole and crowned the saucepan, for he knew it would vex the others; and he thought, 'If I crown him to-day he will crown me to-morrow.'

" 'Now, let us have a dance,' said the fire-tongs; and then how they danced and stuck up one leg in the air. The chair-cushion in the corner burst with laughter when she saw it.

" 'Shall I be crowned now?' asked the fire-tongs; so the broom found another wreath for the tongs.

" 'They were only common people after all,' thought the matches. The tea-urn was now asked to sing, but she said she had a cold, and could not sing without boiling heat. They all thought this was affectation, and because she did not wish to sing excepting in the parlor, when on the table with the grand people.

"In the window sat an old quill-pen, with which the maid generally wrote. There was nothing remarkable about the pen, excepting that it had been dipped too deeply in the ink, but it was proud of that.

" 'If the tea-urn won't sing,' said the pen, 'she can leave it alone; there is a nightingale in a cage who can sing; she has not been taught much, certainly, but we need not say anything this evening about that.'

" 'I think it highly improper,' said the tea-kettle, who was kitchen singer, and half-brother to the tea-urn, 'that a rich foreign bird should be listened to here. Is it patriotic? Let the market-basket decide what is right.'

" 'I certainly am vexed,' said the basket; 'inwardly vexed, more than any one can imagine. Are we spending the evening properly? Would it not be more sensible to put the house in order? If each were in his own place I would lead a game; this would be quite another thing.'

" 'Let us act a play,' said they all. At the same moment the door opened, and the maid came in. Then not one stirred; they all remained quite still; yet, at the same time, there was not a single pot amongst them who had not a high opinion of himself, and of what he could do if he chose.

" 'Yes, if we had chosen,' they each thought, 'we might have spent a very pleasant evening.'

"The maid took the matches and lighted them; dear me, how they sputtered and blazed up!

" 'Now then,' they thought, 'every one will see that we are the first. How we shine; what a light we give!' Even while they spoke their light went out."

"What a capital story," said the queen, "I feel as if I were really in the kitchen, and could see the matches; yes, you shall marry our daughter."

"Certainly," said the king, "thou shalt have our daughter." The king said *thou* to him because he was going to be one of the family. The wedding-day was fixed, and, on the evening before, the whole city was illuminated. Cakes and sweetmeats were thrown among the people. The street boys stood on tiptoe and shouted "hurrah," and whistled between their fingers; altogether it was a very splendid affair.

"I will give them another treat," said the merchant's son. So he went and bought rockets and crackers, and all sorts of fire-works that could be thought of; packed them in his trunk, and flew up with it into the air. What a whizzing and popping they made as they went off! The Turks, when they saw such a sight in the air, jumped so high that their slippers flew about their ears. It was easy to believe after this that the princess was really going to marry a Turkish angel.

As soon as the merchant's son had come down in his flying trunk to the wood after the fireworks, he thought, "I will go back into the town now, and hear what they think of the entertainment." It was very natural that he should wish to know. And what strange things people did say, to be sure! every one whom he questioned had a different tale to tell, though they all thought it very beautiful.

"I saw the Turkish angel myself," said one; "he had eyes like glittering stars, and a head like foaming water."

"He flew in a mantle of fire," cried another, "and lovely little cherubs peeped out from the folds."

He heard many more fine things about himself, and that the next day he was to be married. After this he went back to the forest to rest himself in his trunk. It had disappeared! A spark from the fireworks which remained had set it on fire; it was burnt to ashes! So the merchant's son could not fly any more, nor go to meet his bride. She stood all day on the roof waiting for him, and most likely she is waiting there still; while he wanders through the world telling fairy tales, but none of them so amusing as the one he related about the matches.

THE RACES

A PRIZE, or rather two prizes, a great one and a small one, had been awarded for the greatest swiftness in running, — not in a single race, but for the whole year.

"I obtained the first prize," said the hare. "Justice must still be carried out, even when one has relations and good friends among the prize committee; but that the snail should have received the second prize, I consider almost an insult to myself."

"No," said the fence-rail, who had been a witness at the distribution of prizes; "there should be some consideration for industry and perseverance. I have heard many respectable people say so, and I can quite understand it. The snail certainly took half a year to get over the threshold of the door; but he injured himself, and broke his collar-bone by the haste he made. He gave himself up entirely to the race, and ran with his house on his back, which was all, of course, very praiseworthy; and therefore he obtained the second prize."

"I think I ought to have had some consideration too," said the swallow. "I should imagine no one can be swifter in soaring and flight than I am; and how far I have been! far, far away."

"Yes, that is your misfortune," said the fence-rail; "you are so fickle, so unsettled; you must always be travelling about into foreign lands when the cold commences here. You have no love of fatherland in you. There can be no consideration for you."

"But now, if I have been lying the whole winter in the moor," said the swallow, "and suppose I slept the whole time, would that be taken into account?"

"Bring a certificate from the old moor-hen," said he, "that you have slept away half your time in fatherland; then you will be treated with some consideration."

"I deserved the first prize, and not the second," said the snail. "I know so much, at least, that the hare only ran from cowardice, and because he thought there was danger in delay. I, on the other hand, made running the business of my life, and have become a cripple in the service. If any one had a first prize, it ought to have been myself. But I do not understand chattering and boasting; on the contrary, I despise it." And the snail spat at them with contempt.

"I am able to affirm with word of oath, that each prize — at least, those for which I voted — was given with just and proper consideration," said the old boundary post in the wood, who was a member of the committee of judges. "I always act with due order, consideration, and calculation. Seven times have I already had the honor to be present at the distribution of the prizes, and to vote; but to-day is the first time I have been able to carry out my will. I always reckon the first prize by going through the alphabet from the beginning, and the second by going through from the end. Be so kind as to give me your attention, and I will explain to you how I reckon from the beginning. The eighth letter from A is H, and there we have H for hare; therefore I awarded to the hare the first prize. The eighth letter from the end of the alphabet is S, and therefore the snail received the second prize. Next year, the letter I will have its turn for the first prize, and the letter R for the second."

"I should really have voted for myself," said the mule, "if I had not been one of the judges on the committee. Not only the rapidity with which advance is made, but every other quality should have due consideration; as, for instance, how much weight a candidate is able to draw; but I have not brought this quality forward now, nor the sagacity of the hare in his flight, nor the cunning with which he suddenly springs aside and doubles, to lead people on a false track, thinking he has concealed himself. No; there is something else on which more stress should be laid, and which ought not be left unnoticed. I mean that which mankind call the beautiful. It is on the beautiful that I particularly fix my eyes. I observed the well-grown ears of the hare; it is a pleasure to me to observe how long they are. It seemed as if I saw myself again in the days of my childhood; and so I voted for the hare."

"Buz," said the fly; "there, I'm not going to make a long speech; but I wish to say something about hares. I have really overtaken more than one hare, when I have been seated on the engine in front of a railway train. I often do so. One can then so easily judge of one's own swiftness. Not long ago, I crushed the hind legs of a young hare. He had been running a long time before the engine; he had no idea that *I* was travelling there. At last he had to stop in his career, and the engine ran over his hind legs, and crushed them; for *I* set upon it. I left him lying there, and rode on farther. I call that conquering him; but I do not want the prize."

"It really seems to me," thought the wild rose, though she did not express her opinion aloud—it is not in her nature to do so,—though it would have been quite as well if she had; "it certainly seems to me that the sunbeam ought to have had the honor of receiving the first prize. The sunbeam flies in a few minutes along the immeasurable path from the sun to us. It arrives in such strength, that all nature awakes to loveliness and beauty; we roses blush and exhale fragrance in its presence. Our worshipful judges don't appear to have noticed this at all. Were I the sunbeam, I would give each one of them a sun stroke; but that would only make them mad, and they are mad enough already. I only hope," continued the rose, "that peace may reign in the wood. It is glorious to bloom, to be fragrant, and to live; to live in story and in song. The sunbeam will outlive us all."

"What is the first prize?" asked the earthworm, who had overslept the time, and only now came up.

"It contains a free admission to a cabbage-garden," replied the mule. "I proposed that as one of the prizes. The hare most decidedly must have it; and I, as an active and thoughtful member of the committee, took especial care that the prize should be one of advantage to him; so now he is provided for. The snail can now sit on the fence, and lick up moss and sunshine. He has also been appointed one of the first judges of swiftness in racing. It is worth much to know that *one* of the members is a man of talent in the thing men call a 'committee.' I must say I expect much in the future; we have already made such a good beginning."

THE METAL PIG

IN the city of Florence, not far from the *Piazza del Granduca*, runs a little street called *Porta Rosa*. In this street, just in front of the market-place where vegetables are sold, stands a pig, made of brass and curiously formed. The bright color has been changed by age to dark green; but clear, fresh water pours from the snout, which shines as if it had been polished, and so indeed it has, for hundreds of poor people and children seize it in their hands as they place their mouths close to the mouth of the animal, to drink. It is quite a picture to see a half-naked boy clasping the well-formed creature by the head, as he presses his rosy lips against its jaws. Every one who visits Florence can very quickly find the place; he has only to ask the first beggar he meets for the Metal Pig, and he will be told where it is.

It was late on a winter evening; the mountains were covered with snow, but the moon shone brightly, and moonlight in Italy is like a dull winter's day in the north; indeed it is better, for clear air seems to raise us above the earth, while in the north a cold, gray, leaden sky appears to press us down to earth, even as the cold damp earth shall one day press on us in the grave. In the garden of the grand duke's palace, under the roof of one of the wings, where a thousand roses bloom in winter, a little ragged boy had been sitting the whole day long; a boy, who might serve as a type of Italy, lovely and smiling, and yet still suffering. He was hungry and thirsty, yet no one gave him anything; and when it became dark, and they were about to close the gardens, the porter turned him out. He stood a long time musing on the bridge which crosses the

Arno, and looking at the glittering stars, reflected in the water which flowed between him and the elegant marble bridge *Della Trinità*. He then walked away towards the Metal Pig, half knelt down, clasped it with his arms, and then put his mouth to the shining snout and drank deep draughts of the fresh water. Close by, lay a few salad-leaves and two chestnuts, which were to serve for his supper. No one was in the street but himself; it belonged only to him, so he boldly seated himself on the pig's back, leaned forward so that his curly head could rest on the head of the animal, and, before he was aware, he fell asleep.

It was midnight. The Metal Pig raised himself gently, and the boy heard him say quite distinctly, "Hold tight, little boy, for I am going to run;" and away he started for a most wonderful ride. First, they arrived at the *Piazza del Granduca,* and the metal horse which bears the duke's statue, neighed aloud. The painted coats-of-arms on the old council-house shone like transparent pictures, and Michael Angelo's David tossed his sling; it was as if everything had life. The metallic groups of figures, among which were Perseus and the Rape of the Sabines, looked like living persons, and cries of terror sounded from them all across the noble square. By the *Palazzo degli Uffizi*, in the arcade, where the nobility assemble for the carnival, the Metal Pig stopped. "Hold fast," said the animal; "hold fast, for I am going up stairs."

The little boy said not a word; he was half pleased and half afraid. They entered a long gallery, where the boy had been before. The walls were resplendent with paintings; here stood statues and busts, all in a clear light as if it were day. But the grandest appeared when the door of a side room opened; the little boy could remember what beautiful things he had seen there, but to-night everything shone in its brightest colors. Here stood the figure of a beautiful woman, as beautifully sculptured as possible by one of the great masters. Her graceful limbs appeared to move; dolphins sprang at her feet, and immortality shone from her eyes. The world called her the *Venus de' Medici.* By her side were statues, in which the spirit of life breathed in stone; figures of men, one of whom whetted his sword, and was named the Grinder; wrestling gladiators formed another group, the sword had been sharpened for them, and they strove for the goddess of beauty. The boy was dazzled by so much glitter; for the walls were gleaming with bright colors, all appeared living reality.

As they passed from hall to hall, beauty everywhere showed itself; and as the Metal Pig went step by step from one picture to the other, the little boy could see it all plainly. One glory eclipsed another; yet there was one picture that fixed itself on the little boy's memory, more especially because of the happy children it represented, for these the little boy had seen in daylight. Many pass this picture by with indifference, and yet it contains a treasure of poetic feeling; it represents Christ descending into Hades. They are not the lost whom the spectator sees, but the heathen of olden times. The Florentine, Angiolo Bronzino, painted this picture; most beautiful is the expression on the face of the two children, who appear to have full confidence that they shall reach heaven at last. They are embracing each other, and one little one stretches out his hand towards another who stands below him, and points to himself, as if he were saying, "I am going to heaven." The older people stand as if uncertain, yet hopeful, and they bow in humble adoration to the Lord Jesus. On this picture the boy's eyes rested longer than on any other: the

Metal Pig stood still before it. A low sigh was heard. Did it come from the picture or from the animal? The boy raised his hands towards the smiling children, and then the Pig ran off with him through the open vestibule.

"Thank you, thank you, you beautiful animal," said the little boy, caressing the Metal Pig as it ran down the steps.

"Thanks to yourself also," replied the Metal Pig; "I have helped you and you have helped me, for it is only when I have an innocent child on my back that I receive the power to run. Yes; as you see, I can even venture under the rays of the lamp, in front of the picture of the Madonna, but I may not enter the church; still from without, and while you are upon my back, I may look in through the open door. Do not get down yet, for if you do, then I shall be lifeless, as you have seen me in the *Porta Rosa.*"

"I will stay with you, my dear creature," said the little boy. So then they went on at a rapid pace through the streets of Florence, till they came to the square before the church of *Santa Croce.* The folding-doors flew open, and light streamed from the altar through the church into the deserted square. A wonderful blaze of light streamed from one of the monuments in the left-side aisle, and a thousand moving stars seemed to form a glory round it; even the coat-of-arms on the tomb-stone shone, and a red ladder on a blue field gleamed like fire. It was the grave of Galileo. The monument is unadorned, but the red ladder is an emblem of art, signifying that the way to glory leads up a shining ladder, on which the prophets of mind rise to heaven, like Elias of old. In the right aisle of the church every statue on the richly carved sarcophagi seemed endowed with life. Here stood Michael Angel; there Dante, with the laurel wreath round his brow; Alfieri and Machiavelli; for here side by side rest the great men—the pride of Italy.* The church itself is very beautiful, even more beautiful than the marble cathedral at Florence, though not so large. It seemed as if the carved vestments stirred, and as if the marble figures they covered raised their heads higher, to gaze upon the brightly colored glowing altar where the white-robed boys swung the golden censers, amid music and song, while the strong fragrance of incense filled the church, and streamed forth into the square. The boy stretched forth his hands towards the light, and at the same moment the Metal Pig started again so rapidly that he was obliged to cling tightly to him. The wind whistled in his ears, he heard the church door creak on its hinges as it closed, and it seemed to him as if he had lost his senses—then a cold shudder passed over him, and he awoke.

It was morning; the Metal Pig stood in its old place on the *Porta Rosa,* and the boy found he had slipped nearly off its back. Fear and trembling came upon him as he thought of his mother; she had sent him out the day before to get some money, he had not done so, and now he was hungry and thirsty. Once more he clasped the neck of his metal horse, kissed its nose, and nodded farewell to it. Then he wandered away into one of the narrowest streets, where there was scarcely room for a loaded donkey to pass. A great iron-

*Opposite to the grave of Galileo is the tomb of Michael Angelo. His bust stands upon it, with three figures, representing sculpture, painting, and architecture. Close by is a monument to Dante, whose body is buried at Ravenna. On this monument Italy is represented pointing to the colossal statue of Dante, while poetry weeps over his loss. A few steps farther is Alfieri's monument, which is adorned with laurel, the lyre, and dramatic masks: Italy weeps over the grave. Machiavelli is the last in the list of these celebrated men.

bound door stood ajar; he passed through, and climbed up a brick staircase, with dirty walls and a rope for a balustrade, till he came to an open gallery hung with rags. From here a flight of steps led down to a court, where from a well water was drawn up by iron rollers to the different stories of the house, and where the water-buckets hung side by side. Sometimes the roller and the bucket danced in the air, splashing the water all over the court. Another broken-down staircase led from the gallery, and two Russian sailors running down it almost upset the poor boy. They were coming from their nightly carousal. A woman not very young, with an unpleasant face and a quantity of black hair, followed them. "What have you brought home?" she asked, when she saw the boy.

"Don't be angry," he pleaded; "I received nothing, I have nothing at all;" and he seized his mother's dress and would have kissed it. Then they went into a little room. I need not describe it, but only say that there stood in it an earthen pot with handles, made for holding fire, which in Italy is called a *marito*. This pot she took in her lap, warmed her fingers, and pushed the boy with her elbow.

"Certainly you must have some money," she said. The boy began to cry, and then she struck him with her foot till he cried out louder.

"Will you be quiet? or I'll break your screaming head;" and she swung about the fire-pot which she held in her hand, while the boy crouched to the earth and screamed.

Then a neighbor came in, and she had also a *marito* under her arm. "Felicita," she said, "what are you doing to the child?"

"The child is mine," she answered; "I can murder him if I like, and you too, Giannina." And then she swung about the fire-pot. The other woman lifted up hers to defend herself, and the two pots clashed together so violently that they were dashed to pieces, and fire and ashes flew about the room. The boy rushed out at the sight, sped across the courtyard, and fled from the house. The poor child ran till he was quite out of breath; at last he stopped at the church, the doors of which were opened to him the night before, and went in. Here everything was bright, and the boy knelt down by the first tomb on his right, the grave of Michael Angelo, and sobbed as if his heart would break. People came and went, mass was performed, but no one noticed the boy, excepting an elderly citizen, who stood still and looked at him for a moment, and then went away like the rest. Hunger and thirst overpowered the child, and he became quite faint and ill. At last he crept into a corner behind the marble monuments, and went to sleep. Towards evening he was awakened by a pull at his sleeve; he started up, and the same old citizen stood before him.

"Are you ill? where do you live? have you been here all day?" were some of the questions asked by the old man. After hearing his answers, the old man took him home to a small house close by, in a back street. They entered a glovemaker's shop, where a woman sat sewing busily. A little white poodle, so closely shaven that his pink skin could plainly be seen, frisked about the room, and gambolled upon the boy.

"Innocent souls are soon intimate," said the woman, as she caressed both the boy and the dog. These good people gave the child food and drink, and said he should stay with them all night, and that the next day the old man, who was called Giuseppe, would go and speak to his mother. A little homely bed was prepared for him, but to him who had so often slept on the hard stones it was a royal couch, and he slept sweetly and dreamed of the splendid pictures and of the Metal Pig. Giuseppe went out the next morning, and the poor child was not glad to see him go, for he knew that the old man was gone to his mother, and that, perhaps, he would have to go back. He wept at the thought, and then he played with the little, lively dog, and kissed it, while the old woman looked kindly at him to encourage him. And what news did Giuseppe bring back? At first the boy could not hear, for he talked a great deal to his wife, and she nodded and stroked the boy's cheek.

Then she said, "He is a good lad, he shall stay with us, he may become a clever glovemaker, like you. Look what delicate fingers he has got; Madonna intended him for a glovemaker." So the boy stayed with them, and the woman herself taught him to sew; and he ate well, and slept well, and became very merry. But at last he began to tease Bellissima, as the little dog was called. This made the woman angry, and she scolded him and threatened him, which made him very unhappy, and he went and sat in his own room full of sad thoughts. This chamber looked upon the street, in which hung skins to dry, and there were thick iron bars across his window. That night he lay awake, thinking of the Metal Pig; indeed, it was always in his thoughts. Suddenly he fancied he heard feet outside going pit-a-pat. He sprung out of bed and went to the window. Could it be the Metal Pig? But there was nothing to be seen; whatever he had heard had passed already. Next morning, their neighbor, the artist, passed by, carrrying a paint-box and a large roll of canvas.

"Help the gentleman to carry his box of colors," said the woman to the boy; and he obeyed instantly, took the box, and followed the painter. They walked on till they reached the picture gallery, and mounted the same staircase up which he had ridden that night on the Metal Pig. He remembered all the statues and pictures, the beautiful marble Venus, and again he looked at the Madonna with the Saviour and St. John. They stopped before the picture by Bronzino, in which Christ is represented as standing in the lower world, with the children smiling before Him, in the sweet expectation of entering heaven; and the poor boy smiled, too, for here was his heaven.

"You may go home now," said the painter, while the boy stood watching him, till he had set up his easel.

"May I see you paint?" asked the boy; "may I see you put the picture on this white canvas?"

"I am not going to paint yet," replied the artist; then he brought out a piece of chalk. His hand moved quickly, and his eye measured the great picture; and though nothing appeared but a faint line, the figure of the Saviour was as clearly visible as in the colored picture.

"Why don't you go?" said the painter. Then the boy wandered home silently, and seated himself on the table, and learned to sew gloves. But all day long his thoughts were in the picture gallery; and so he pricked his fingers and was awkward. But he did not tease Bellissima. When evening came, and the house door stood open, he slipped out. It was a bright, beautiful, starlight evening, but rather cold. Away he went through the already-deserted streets, and soon came to the Metal Pig; he stooped down and kissed its shining nose, and then seated himself on its back.

"You happy creature," he said; "how I have longed for you! we must take a ride to-night."

But the Metal Pig lay motionless, while the fresh stream gushed forth from its mouth. The little boy still sat astride on its back, when he felt something pulling at his clothes. He looked down, and there was Bellissima, little smooth-shaven Bellissima, barking as if she would have said, "Here I am too; why are you sitting there?"

A fiery dragon could not have frightened the little boy so much as did the little dog in this place. "Bellissima in the street, and not dressed!" as the old lady called it; "what would be the end of this?"

The dog never went out in winter, unless she was attired in a little lambskin coat which had been made for her; it was fastened round the little dog's neck and body with red ribbons, and was decorated with rosettes and little bells. The dog looked almost like a little kid when she was allowed to go out in winter, and trot after her mistress. And now here she was in the cold, and not dressed. Oh, how would it end? All his fancies were quickly put to flight; yet he kissed the Metal Pig once more, and then took Bellissima in his arms. The poor little thing trembled so with cold, that the boy ran homeward as fast as he could.

"What are you running away with there?" asked two of the police whom he met, and at whom the dog barked. "Where have you stolen that pretty dog?" they asked; and they took it away from him.

"Oh, I have not stolen it; do give it to me back again," cried the boy, despairingly.

"If you have not stolen it, you may say at home that they can send to the watch-house for the dog." Then they told him where the watch-house was, and went away with Bellissima.

Here was a dreadful trouble. The boy did not know whether he had better jump into the Arno, or go home and confess everything. They would certainly kill him, he thought.

"Well, I would gladly be killed," he reasoned; "for then I shall die, and go to heaven:" and so he went home, almost hoping for death.

The door was locked, and he could not reach the knocker. No one was in the street; so he took up a stone, and with it made a tremendous noise at the door.

"Who is there?" asked somebody from within.

"It is I," said he. "Bellissima is gone. Open the door, and then kill me."

Then indeed there was a great panic. Madame was so very fond of Bellissima. She immediately looked at the wall where the dog's dress usually hung; and there was the little lambskin.

"Bellissima in the watch-house!" she cried. "You bad boy! how did you entice her out? Poor little delicate thing, with those rough policemen! and she'll be frozen with cold."

Giuseppe went off at once, while his wife lamented, and the boy wept. Several of the neighbors came in, and amongst them the painter. He took the boy between his knees, and questioned him; and, in broken sentences, he soon heard the whole story, and also about the Metal Pig, and the wonderful ride to the picture-gallery, which was certainly rather incomprehensible. The painter, however, consoled the little fellow, and tried to soften the lady's anger; but she would not be pacified till her husband returned with Bellissima, who had been with the police. Then there was great rejoicing, and the painter caressed the boy, and gave him a number of pictures. Oh, what beautiful pictures these were!—figures with funny heads; and, above all, the

Metal Pig was there too. Oh, nothing could be more delightful. By means of a few strokes, it was made to appear on the paper; and even the house that stood behind it had been sketched in. Oh, if he could only draw and paint! He who could do this could conjure all the world before him. The first leisure moment during the next day, the boy got a pencil, and on the back of one of the other drawings he attempted to copy the drawing of the Metal Pig, and he succeeded. Certainly it was rather crooked, rather up and down, one leg thick, and another thin; still it was like the copy, and he was overjoyed at what he had done. The pencil would not go quite as it ought, — he had found that out; but the next day he tried again. A second pig was drawn by the side of the first, and this looked a hundred times better; and the third attempt was so good, that everybody might know what it was meant to represent.

And now the glovemaking went on but slowly. The orders given by the shops in the town were not finished quickly; for the Metal Pig had taught the boy that all objects may be drawn upon paper; and Florence is a picture-book in itself for any one who chooses to turn over its pages. On the *Piazza dell Trinita* stands a slender pillar, and upon it is the goddess of Justice, blind-folded, with her scales in her hand. She was soon represented on paper, and it was the glovemaker's boy who placed her there. His collection of pictures increased; but as yet they were only copies of lifeless objects, when one day Bellissima came gambolling before him: "Stand still," cried he, "and I will draw you beautifully, to put amongst my collection."

But Bellissima would not stand still, so she must be bound fast in one position. He tied her head and tail; but she barked and jumped, and so pulled and tightened the string, that she was nearly strangled; and just then her mistress walked in.

"You wicked boy! the poor little creature!" was all she could utter.

She pushed the boy from her, thrust him away with her foot, called him a most ungrateful, good-for-nothing, wicked boy, and forbade him to enter the house again. Then she wept, and kissed her litle half-strangled Bellissima. At this moment the painter entered the room.

*　　*　　*　　*　　*　　*　　*

In the year 1834 there was an exhibition in the Academy of Arts at Florence. Two pictures, placed side by side, attracted a large number of spectators. The smaller of the two represented a little boy sitting at a table, drawing; before him was a little white poodle, curiously shaven; but as the animal would not stand still, it had been fastened with a string to its head and tail, to keep it in one position. The truthfulness and life in this picture interested every one. The painter was said to be a young Florentine, who had been found in the streets, when a child, by an old glovemaker, who had brought him up. The boy had taught himself to draw: it was also said that a young artist, now famous, had discovered talent in the child just as he was about to be sent away for having tied up madame's favorite little dog, and using it as a model. The glovemaker's boy had also become a great painter, as the picture proved; but the larger picture by its side was a still greater proof of his talent. It represented a handsome boy, clothed in rags, lying asleep, and leaning against the Metal Pig in the street of the *Porta Rosa*. All the spectators knew the spot well. The child's arms were round the neck of the Pig, and he was in a deep sleep. The lamp before the picture of the Madonna threw a strong, effective light on the pale, delicate face of the child. It was a beautiful picture. A large gilt frame surrounded it, and on one corner of the frame a laurel wreath had been hung; but a black band, twined unseen among the green leaves, and a streamer of crape, hung down from it; for within the last few days the young artist had —— died.

THE SHEPHERDESS AND THE SHEEP

HAVE you ever seen an old wooden cupboard quite black with age, and or-namented with carved foliage and curious figures? Well, just such a cupboard stood in a parlor, and had been left to the family as a legacy by the great-grandmother. It was covered from top to bottom with carved roses and tulips; the most curious scrolls were drawn upon it, and out of them peeped little stags' heads, with antlers. In the middle of the cupboard door was the carved figure of a man most ridiculous to look at. He grinned at you, for no one could call it laughing. He had goat's legs, little horns on his head, and a long beard; the children in the room always called him, "Major general-field-sergeant-commander Billy-goat's-legs." It was certainly a very difficult name to pronounce, and there are very few who ever receive such a title, but then it seemed wonderful how he came to be carved at all; yet there he was, always looking at the table under the looking-glass, where stood a very pretty little shepherdess made of china. Her shoes were gilt, and her dress had a red rose or an ornament. She wore a hat, and carried a crook, that were both gilded, and looked very bright and pretty. Close by her side stood a little chimney-sweep, as black as coal, and also made of china. He was, however, quite as clean and neat as any other china figure; he only represented a black chim-ney-sweep, and the china workers might just as well have made him a prince, had they felt inclined to do so. He stood holding his ladder quite handily, and his face was as fair and rosy as a girl's; indeed, that was rather a mistake, it should have had some black marks on it. He and the shepherdess had been placed close together, side by side; and, being so placed, they became engaged to each other, for they were very well suited, being both made of the same sort of china, and being equally fragile. Close to them stood another figure, three times as large as they were, and also made of china. He was an old Chinaman, who could nod his head, and used to pretend that he was the grandfather of the shepherdess, although he could not prove it. He however assumed authority over her, and therefore when "Major-general-field-ser-geant-commander Billy-goat's-legs" asked for the little shepherdess to be his wife, he nodded his head to show that he consented. "You will have a husband," said the old Chinaman to her, "who I really believe is made of mahogany. He will make you a lady of Major-general-field-sergeant-commander Billy-goat's-legs. He has the whole cupboard full of silver plate, which he keeps locked up in secret drawers."

"I won't go into the dark cupboard," said the little shepherdess. "I have heard that he has eleven china wives there already."

"Then you shall be the twelfth," said the old Chinaman. "To-night as soon as you hear a rattling in the old cupboard, you shall be married, as true as I am a Chinaman;" and then he nodded his head and fell asleep.

Then the little shepherdess cried, and looked at her sweetheart, the china chimney-sweep. "I must entreat you," said she, "to go out with me into the wide world, for we cannot stay here."

"I will do whatever you wish," said the little chimney-sweep; "let us go immediately: I think I shall be able to maintain you with my profession."

"If we were but safely down from the table!" said she; "I shall not be happy till we are really out in the world."

Then he comforted her, and showed her how to place her little foot on the carved edge and gilt-leaf ornaments of the table. He brought his little ladder to help her, and so they contrived to reach the floor. But when they looked at the old cupboard, they saw it was all in an uproar. The carved stags pushed out their heads, raised their antlers, and twisted their necks. The major-general sprung up in the air; and cried out to the old Chinaman, "They are running away! they are running away!" The two were rather frightened at this, so they jumped into the drawer of the window-seat. Here were three or four packs of cards not quite complete, and a doll's theatre, which had been built up very neatly. A comedy was being performed in it, and all the queens of diamonds, clubs, and hearts, and spades, sat in the first row fanning themselves with tulips, and behind them stood all the knaves, showing that they had heads above and below as playing cards generally have. The play was about two lovers, who were not allowed to marry, and the shepherdess wept because it was so like her own story. "I cannot bear it," said she, "I must get out of the drawer;" but when they reached the floor, and cast their eyes on the table, there was the old Chinaman awake and shaking his whole body, till all at once down he came on the floor, "plump." "The old Chinaman is coming," cried the little shepherdess in a fright, and down she fell on one knee.

"I have thought of something," said the chimney-sweep; "let us get into the great pot-pourri jar which stands in the corner; there we can lie on rose-leaves and lavender, and throw salt in his eyes if he comes near us."

"No, that will never do," said she, "because I know that the Chinaman and the pot-pourri jar were lovers once, and there always remains behind a feeling of good-will between those who have been so intimate as that. No, there is nothing left for us but to go out into the wide world."

"Have you really courage enough to go out into the wide world with me?" said the chimney-sweep; "have you thought how large it is, and that we can never come back here again?"

"Yes, I have," she replied.

When the chimney-sweep saw that she was quite firm, he said, "My way is through the stove and up the chimney. Have you courage to creep with me through the fire-box, and the iron pipe? When we get to the chimney I shall know how to manage very well. We shall soon climb too high for any one to reach us, and we shall come through a hole in the top out into the wide world." So he led her to the door of the stove.

"It looks very dark," said she; still she went in with him through the stove and through the pipe, where it was as dark as pitch.

"Now we are in the chimney," said he; "and look, there is a beautiful star shining above it." It was a real star shining down upon them as if it would show them the way. So they clambered, and crept on, and a frightful steep place it was; but the chimney-sweep helped her and supported her, till they got higher and higher. He showed her the best places on which to set her little china foot, so at last they reached the top of the chimney, and sat themselves down, for they were very tired, as may be supposed. The sky, with all its stars, was over their heads, and below were the roofs of the town. They could see for a very long distance out into the wide world, and the poor little shepherdess leaned her head on her chimney-sweep's shoulder, and wept till she washed the gilt off her sash; the world was so different to what she expected. "This is too much," she said; "I cannot bear it, the world is too large. Oh, I wish I were safe back on the table again, under the looking glass; I shall never be happy till I am safe back again. Now I have followed you out into the wide world, you will take me back, if you love me."

Then the chimney-sweep tried to reason with her, and spoke of the old Chinaman, and of the Major-general-field-sergeant-commander Billy-goat's-legs; but she sobbed so bitterly, and kissed her little chimney-sweep till he was obliged to do all she asked, foolish as it was. And so, with a great deal of trouble, they climbed down the chimney, and then crept through the pipe and stove, which were certainly not very pleasant places. Then they stood in the dark fire-box, and listened behind the door, to hear what was going on in the room. As it was all quiet, they peeped out. Alas! there lay the old Chinaman on the floor; he had fallen down from the table as he attempted to run after them, and was broken into three pieces; his back had separated entirely, and his head had rolled into a corner of the room. The major-general stood in his old place, and appeared lost in thought.

"This is terrible," said the little shepherdess. "My poor old grandfather is broken to pieces, and it is our fault. I shall never live after this;" and she wrung her little hands.

"He can be riveted," said the chimney-sweep; "he can be riveted. Do not be so hasty. If they cement his back, and put a good rivet in it, he will he as good as new, and be able to say as many disagreeable things to us as ever."

"Do you think so?" said she; and then they climbed up to the table, and stood in their old places.

"As we have done no good," said the chimney-sweep, "we might as well have remained here, instead of taking so much trouble."

"I wish grandfather was riveted," said the shepherdess. "Will it cost much, I wonder?"

And she had her wish. The family had the Chinaman's back mended, and a strong rivet put through his neck; he looked as good as new, but he could no longer nod his head.

"You have become proud since your fall broke you to pieces," said Major-general-field-sergeant-commander Billy-goat's-legs. "You have no reason to give yourself such airs. Am I to have her or not?"

The chimney-sweep and the little shepherdess looked piteously at the old Chinaman, for they were afraid he might nod; but he was not able: besides, it was so tiresome to be always telling strangers he had a rivet in the back of his neck.

And so the little china people remained together, and were glad of the grandfather's rivet, and continued to love each other till they were broken to pieces.

THE NIGHTINGALE

IN China, you know, the emperor is a Chinese, and all those about him are Chinamen also. The story I am going to tell you happened a great many years ago, so it is well to hear it now before it is forgotten. The emperor's palace was the most beautiful in the world. It was built entirely of porcelain, and very costly, but so delicate and brittle that whoever touched it was obliged to be careful. In the garden could be seen the most singular flowers, with pretty silver bells tied to them, which tinkled so that every one who passed could not help noticing the flowers. Indeed, everything in the emperor's garden was remarkable, and it extended so far that the gardener himself did not know where it ended. Those who travelled beyond its limits knew that there was a noble forest, with lofty trees, sloping down to the deep blue sea, and the great ships sailed under the shadow of its branches. In one of these trees lived a nightingale, who sang so beautifully that even the poor fishermen, who had so many other things to do, would stop and listen. Sometimes, when they went at night to spread their nets, they would hear her sing, and say, "Oh, is not that beautiful?" But when they returned to their fishing, they forgot the bird until the next night. Then they would hear it again, and exclaim "Oh, how beautiful is the nightingale's song!"

Travellers from every country in the world came to the city of the emperor, which they admired very much, as well as the palace and gardens; but when they heard the nightingale, they all declared it to be the best of all. And the travellers, on their return home, related what they had seen; and learned men wrote books, containing descriptions of the town, the palace, and the gardens; but they did not forget the nightingale, which was really the greatest wonder. And those who could write poetry composed beautiful verses about the nightingale, who lived in a forest near the deep sea. The books travelled all over the world, and some of them came into the hands of the emperor; and he sat in his golden chair, and, as he read, he nodded his approval every moment, for it pleased him to find such a beautiful description of his city, his palace, and his gardens. But when he came to the words, "the nightingale is the most beautiful of all," he exclaimed, "What is this? I know nothing of any nightingale. Is there such a bird in my empire? and even in my garden? I have never heard of it. Something, it appears, may be learnt from books."

Then he called one of his lords-in-waiting, who was so high-bred, that when any in an inferior rank to himself spoke to him, or asked him a question, he would answer, "Pooh," which means nothing.

"There is a very wonderful bird mentioned here, called a nightingale," said the emperor; "they say it is the best thing in my large kingdom. Why have I not been told of it?"

"I have never heard the name," replied the cavalier; "she has not been presented at court."

"It is my pleasure that she shall appear this evening." said the emperor; "the whole world knows what I possess better than I do myself."

"I have never heard of her," said the cavalier; "yet I will endeavor to find her."

But where was the nightingale to be found? The nobleman went up stairs and down, through halls and passages; yet none of those whom he met had heard of the bird. So he returned to the emperor, and said that it must be a fable, invented by those who had written the book. "Your imperial majesty," said he, "cannot believe everything contained in books; sometimes they are only fiction, or what is called the black art."

"But the book in which I have read this account," said the emperor, "was sent to me by the great and mighty emperor of Japan, and therefore it cannot contain a falsehood. I will hear the nightingale, she must be here this evening; she has my highest favor; and if she does not come, the whole court shall be trampled upon after supper is ended."

"Tsing-pe!" cried the lord-in-waiting, and again he ran up and down stairs, through all the halls and corridors; and half the court ran with him, for they did not like the idea of being trampled upon. There was a great inquiry about this wonderful nightingale, whom all the world knew, but who was unknown to the court.

At last they met with a poor little girl in the kitchen, who said, "Oh, yes, I know the nightingale quite well; indeed, she can sing. Every evening I have permission to take home to my poor sick mother the scraps from the table; she lives down by the sea-shore, and as I come back I feel tired, and I sit down in the wood to rest, and listen to the nightingale's song. Then the tears come into my eyes, and it is just as if my mother kissed me."

"Little maiden," said the lord-in-waiting, "I will obtain for you constant employment in the kitchen, and you shall have permission to see the emperor dine, if you will lead us to the nightingale; for she is invited for this evening to the palace." So she went into the wood where the nightingale sang, and half the court followed her. As they went along, a cow began lowing.

"Oh," said a young courtier, "now we have found her; what wonderful power for such a small creature; I have certainly heard it before."

"No, that is only a cow lowing," said the little girl; "we are a long way from the place yet."

Then some frogs began to croak in the marsh.

"Beautiful," said the young courtier again. "Now I hear it, tinkling like little church bells."

"No, those are frogs," said the little maiden; "but I think we shall soon hear her now:" and presently the nightingale began to sing.

"Hark, hark! there she is," said the girl, "and there she sits," she added, pointing to a little gray bird who was perched on a bough.

"Is it possible?" said the lord-in-waiting, "I never imagined it would be a little, plain, simple thing like that. She has certainly changed color at seeing so many grand people around her."

"Little nightingale," cried the girl, raising her voice, "our most gracious emperor wishes you to sing before him."

"With the greatest pleasure," said the nightingale, and began to sing most delightfully.

"It sounds like tiny glass bells," said the lord-in-waiting, "and see how her little throat works. It is surprising that we have never heard this before; she will be a great success at court."

"Shall I sing once more before the emperor?" asked the nightingale, who thought he was present.

"My excellent little nightingale," said the courtier, "I have the great

THE NIGHTINGALE

pleasure of inviting you to a court festival this evening, where you will gain imperial favor by your charming song."

"My song sounds best in the green wood," said the bird; but still she came willingly when she heard the emperor's wish.

The palace was elegantly decorated for the occasion. The walls and floors of porcelain glittered in the light of a thousand lamps. Beautiful flowers, round which little bells were tied, stood in the corridors: what with the running to and fro and the draught, these bells tinkled so loudly that no one could speak to be heard. In the centre of the great hall, a golden perch had been fixed for the nightingale to sit on. The whole court was present, and the little kitchen-maid had received permission to stand by the door. She was not installed as a real court cook. All were in full dress, and every eye was turned to the little gray bird when the emperor nodded to her to begin. The nightingale sang so sweetly that the tears came into the emperor's eyes, and then rolled down his cheeks, as her song became still more touching and went to every one's heart. The emperor was so delighted that he declared the nightingale should have his gold slipper to wear round her neck, but she declined the honor with thanks: she had been sufficiently rewarded already. "I have seen tears in an emperor's eyes," she said, "that is my richest reward. An emperor's tears have wonderful power, and are quite sufficient honor for me;" and then she sang again more enchantingly than ever.

"That singing is a lovely gift;" said the ladies of the court to each other; and then they took water in their mouths to make them utter the gurgling sounds of the nightingale when they spoke to any one, so thay they might fancy themselves nightingales. And the footmen and chambermaids also expressed their satisfaction, which is saying a great deal, for they are very difficult to please. In fact the nightingale's visit was most successful. She was now to remain at court, to have her own cage, with liberty to go out twice a day, and once during the night. Twelve servants were appointed to attend her on these occasions, who each held her by a silken string fastened to her leg. There was certainly not much pleasure in this kind of flying.

The whole city spoke of the wonderful bird, and when two people met, one said "nightin," and the other said "gale," and they understood what was meant, for nothing else was talked of. Eleven peddlers' children were named after her, but not of them could sing a note.

One day the emperor received a large packet on which was written "The Nightingale." "Here is no doubt a new book about our celebrated bird," said the emperor. But instead of a book, it was a work of art contained in a casket, an artificial nightingale made to look like a living one, and covered all over with diamonds, rubies, and sapphires. As soon as the artificial bird was wound up, it could sing like the real one, and could move its tail up and down, which sparkled with silver and gold. Round its neck hung a piece of ribbon, on which was written "The Emperor of China's nightingale is poor compared with that of the Emperor of Japan's."

"This is very beautiful," exclaimed all who saw it, and he who had brought the artificial bird received the title of "Imperial nightingale-bringer-in-chief."

"Now they must sing together," said the court, "and what a duet it will be." But they did not get on well, for the real nightingale sang in its own natural way, but the artificial bird sang only waltzes.

"That is not a fault," said the music-master, "it is quite perfect to my taste," so then it had to sing alone, and was as successful as the real bird; besides, it was so much prettier to look at, for it sparkled like bracelets and breast-pins. Three and thirty times did it sing the same tunes without being tired; the people would gladly have heard it again, but the emperor said the living nightingale ought to sing something. But where was she? No one had noticed her when she flew out at the open window, back to her own green woods.

"What strange conduct," said the emperor, when her flight had been discovered; and all the courtiers blamed her, and said she was a very ungrateful creature.

"But we have the best bird after all," said one, and then they would have the bird sing again, although it was the thirty-fourth time they had listened to the same piece, and even then they had not learnt it, for it was rather difficult. But the music-master praised the bird in the highest degree, and even asserted that it was better than a real nightingale, not only in its dress and the beautiful diamonds, but also in its musical power. "For you must perceive, my chief lord and emperor, that with a real nightingale we can never tell what is going to be sung, but with this bird everything is settled. It can be opened and explained, so that people may understand how the waltzes are formed, and why one note follows upon another."

"This is exactly what we think," they all replied, and then the music-master received permission to exhibit the bird to the people on the following Sunday, and the emperor commanded that they should be present to hear it sing. When they heard it they were like people intoxicated; however it must have been with drinking tea, which is quite a Chinese custom. They all said "Oh!" and held up their forefingers and nodded, but a poor fisherman, who had heard the real nightingale, said, "it sounds prettily enough, and the melodies are all alike; yet there seems something wanting, I cannot exactly tell what."

And after this the real nightingale was banished from the empire, and the artificial bird placed on a silk cushion close to the emperor's bed. The presents of gold and precious stones which had been received with it were round the bird, and it was now advanced to the title of "Little Imperial Toilet Singer," and to the rank of No. 1 on the left hand; for the emperor considered the left side, on which the heart lies, as the most noble, and the heart of an emperor is in the same place as that of other people.

The music-master wrote a work, in twenty-five volumes, about the artificial bird, which was very learned and very long, and full of the most difficult Chinese words; yet all the people said they had read it, and understood it, for fear of being thought stupid and having their bodies trampled upon.

So a year passed, and the emperor, the court, and all the other Chinese knew every little turn in the artificial bird's song; and for that same reason it pleased them better. They could sing with the bird, which they often did. The street-boys sang, "Zi-zi-zi, cluck, cluck, cluck," and the emperor himself could sing it also. It was really most amusing.

One evening, when the artificial bird was singing its best, and the emperor lay in bed listening to it, something inside the bird sounded "whizz." Then a spring cracked. "Whir-r-r-r" went all the wheels, running round, and then the music stopped. The emperor immediately sprang out of bed, and called for his physician; but what could he do? Then they sent for a watchmaker; and, after a great deal of talking and examination, the bird was put into something like order; but he said that it must be used very carefully, as the barrels were worn, and it would be impossible to put in new ones without injuring the music. Now there was great sorrow, as the bird could only be allowed to play once a year; and even that was dangerous for the works inside it. Then the music-master made a little speech, full of hard words, and declared that the bird was as good as ever; and, of course no one contradicted him.

Five years passed, and then a real grief came upon the land. The Chinese really were fond of their emperor, and he now lay so ill that he was not expected to live. Already a new emperor had been chosen and the people who stood in the street asked the lord-in-waiting how the old emperor was; but he only said, "Pooh!" and shook his head.

Cold and pale lay the emperor in his royal bed; the whole court thought he was dead, and every one ran away to pay homage to his successor. The chamberlains went out to have a talk on the matter, and the ladies'-maids invited company to take coffee. Cloth had been laid down on the halls and passages, so that not a footstep should be heard, and all was silent and still. But the emperor was not yet dead, although he lay white and stiff on his gorgeous bed, with the long velvet curtains and heavy gold tassels. A window stood open, and the moon shone in upon the emperor and the artificial bird. The poor emperor, finding he could scarcely breathe with a strange weight on his chest, opened his eyes, and saw Death sitting there. He had put on the emperor's golden crown, and held in one hand his sword of state, and in the other his beautiful banner. All around the bed, and peeping through the long velvet curtains, were a number of strange heads, some very ugly, and others lovely and gentle-looking. These were the emperor's good and bad deeds, which stared him in the face now Death sat at his heart.

"Do you remember this?" "Do you recollect that?" they asked one after another, thus bringing to his remembrance circumstances that made the perspiration stand on his brow.

"I know nothing about it," said the emperor. "Music! music!" he cried; "the large Chinese drum! that I may not hear what they say." But they still went on, and Death nodded like a Chinaman to all they said. "Music! music!" shouted the emperor. "You little precious golden bird, sing, pray sing! I have given you gold and costly presents; I have even hung my golden slipper round your neck. Sing! sing!" But the bird remained silent. There was no one to wind it up, and therefore it could not sing a note.

Death continued to stare at the emperor with his cold, hollow eyes, and the room was fearfully still. Suddenly there came through the open window the sound of sweet music. Outside, on the bough of a tree, sat the living nightingale. She had heard of the emperor's illness, and was therefore come to sing to him of hope and trust. And as she sung, the shadows grew paler and paler; the blood in the emperor's veins flowed more rapidly, and gave life to his weak limbs; and even Death himself listened, and said, "Go on, little nightingale, go on."

"Then will you give me the beautiful golden sword and that rich banner? and will you give me the emperor's crown?" said the bird.

So Death gave up each of these treasures for a song; and the nightingale continued her singing. She sung of the quiet churchyard, where the white roses grow, where the elder-tree wafts its perfume on the breeze, and the fresh, sweet grass is moistened by the mourners' tears. Then Death longed to go and see his garden, and floated out through the window in the form of a cold, white mist.

"Thanks, thanks, you heavenly little bird. I know you well. I banished you from my kingdom once, and yet you have charmed away the evil faces from my bed, and banished Death from my heart, with your sweet song. How can I reward you?"

"You have already rewarded me," said the nightingale. "I shall never forget that I drew tears from your eyes the first time I sang to you. These are the jewels that rejoice a singer's heart. But now sleep, and grow strong and well again. I will sing to you again."

And as she sung, the emperor fell into a sweet sleep; and how mild and refreshing that slumber was! When he awoke, strengthened and restored, the sun shone brightly through the window; but not one of his servants had returned—they all believed he was dead; only the nightingale still sat beside him, and sang.

"You must always remain with me," said the emperor. "You shall sing only when it pleases you; and I will break the artificial bird into a thousand pieces."

"No; do not do that," replied the nightingale; "the bird did very well as long as it could. Keep it here still. I cannot live in the palace, and build my nest; but let me come when I like. I will sit on a bough outside your window, in the evening, and sing to you, so that you may be happy, and have thoughts full of joy. I will sing to you of those who are happy, and those who suffer; of the good and the evil, who are hidden around you. The little singing bird flies far from you and your court to the home of the fisherman and the peasant's cot. I love your heart better than your crown; and yet something holy lingers round that also. I will come, I will sing to you; but you must promise me one thing."

"Everything," said the emperor, who, having dressed himself in his imperial robes, stood with the hand that held the heavy golden sword pressed to his heart.

"I only ask one thing," she replied; "let no one know that you have a little bird who tells you everything. It will be best to conceal it." So saying, the nightingale flew away.

The servants now came in to look after the dead emperor; when, lo! there he stood, and, to their astonishment, said, "Good morning."

SHE WAS GOOD FOR NOTHING

THE mayor stood at the open window. He looked smart, for his shirt-frill, in which he had stuck a breast-pin, and his ruffles, were very fine. He had shaved his chin uncommonly smooth, although he had cut himself slightly, and had stuck a piece of newspaper over the place. "Hark 'ee, youngster!" cried he.

The boy to whom he spoke was no other than the son of a poor washerwoman, who was just going past the house. He stopped, and respectfully took off his cap. The peak of this cap was broken in the middle, so that he could easily roll it up and put it in his pocket. He stood before the mayor in his poor but clean and well-mended clothes, with heavy wooden shoes on his feet, looking as humble as if it had been the king himself.

"You are a good and civil boy," said the mayor. "I suppose your mother is busy washing the clothes down by the river, and you are going to carry that thing to her that you have in your pocket. It is very bad for your mother. How much have you got in it?"

"Only half a quartern," stammered the boy in a frightened voice.

"And she has had just as much this morning already?"

"No, it was yesterday," replied the boy.

"Two halves make a whole," said the mayor. "She's good for nothing. What a sad thing it is with these people. Tell your mother she ought to be ashamed of herself. Don't you become a drunkard, but I expect you will though. Poor child! there, go now."

The boy went on his way with his cap in his hand, while the wind fluttered his golden hair till the locks stood up straight. He turned round the corner of the street into the little lane that led to the river, where his mother stood in the water by her washing bench, beating the linen with a heavy wooden bar. The floodgates at the mill had been drawn up, and as the water rolled rapidly on, the sheets were dragged along by the stream, and nearly overturned the bench, so that the washerwoman was obliged to lean against it to keep it steady. "I have been very nearly carried away," she said; "it is a good thing that you are come, for I want something to strengthen me. It is cold in the water, and I have stood here six hours. Have you brought anything for me?"

The boy drew the bottle from his pocket, and the mother put it to her lips, and drank a little.

"Ah, how much good that does, and how it warms me," she said; "it is as good as a hot meal, and not so dear. Drink a little, my boy; you look quite pale; you are shivering in your thin clothes, and autumn has really come. Oh, how cold the water is! I hope I shall not be ill. But no, I must not be afraid of that. Give me a little more, and you may have a sip too, but only a sip; you must not get used to it, my poor, dear child." She stepped up to the bridge on which the boy stood as she spoke, and came on shore. The water dripped from the straw mat which she had bound round her body, and from her gown. "I work hard and suffer pain with my poor hands," said she, "but I do it willingly, that I may be able to bring you up honestly and truthfully, my dear boy."

At the same moment, a woman, rather older than herself, came towards them. She was a miserable-looking object, lame of one leg, and with a large false curl hanging down over one of her eyes, which was blind. This curl was intended to conceal the blind eye, but it made the defect only more visible. She was a friend of the laundress, and was called, among the neighbors, "Lame Martha, with the curl." "Oh, you poor thing; how you do work, standing there in the water!" she exclaimed. "You really do need something to give you a little warmth, and yet spiteful people cry out about the few drops you take." And then Martha repeated to the laundress, in a very few minutes, all that the mayor had said to her boy, which she had overheard; and she felt very angry that any man could speak, as he had done, of a mother to her own child, about the few drops she had taken; and she was still more angry because, on that very day, the mayor was going to have a dinner-party, at which there would be wine, strong, rich wine, drunk by the bottle. "Many will take more than they ought, but they don't call that drinking! *They* are all right, you are good for nothing indeed!" cried Martha indignantly.

"And so he spoke to you in that way, did he, my child?" said the washer-woman, and her lips trembled as she spoke. "He says you have a mother who is good for nothing. Well, perhaps he is right, but he should not have said it to my child. How much has happened to me from that house!"

"Yes," said Martha; "I remember you were in service there, and lived in the house when the mayor's parents were alive; how many years ago that is. Bushels of salt have been eaten since then, and people may well be thirsty," and Martha smiled. "The mayor's great dinner-party to-day ought to have been put off, but the news came too late. The footman told me the dinner was already cooked, when a letter came to say that the mayor's younger brother in Copenhagen is dead."

"Dead!" cried the laundress, turning pale as death.

"Yes, certainly," replied Martha; "but why do you take it so much to heart? I suppose you knew him years ago, when you were in service there?"

"Is he dead?" she exclaimed. "Oh, he was such a kind, good-hearted man, there are not many like him," and the tears rolled down her cheeks as she spoke. Then she cried, "Oh, dear me; I feel quite ill: everything is going round me, I cannot bear it. Is the bottle empty?" and she leaned against the plank.

"Dear me, you are ill indeed," said the other woman. "Come, cheer up; perhaps it will pass off. No, indeed, I see you are really ill; the best thing for me to do is to lead you home."

"But my washing yonder?"

"I will take care of that. Come, give me your arm. The boy can stay here and take care of the linen, and I'll come back and finish the washing; it is but a trifle."

The limbs of the laundress shook under her, and she said, "I have stood too long in the cold water, and I have had nothing to eat the whole day since the morning. O kind Heaven, help me to get home; I am in a burning fever. Oh, my poor child," and she burst into tears. And he, poor boy, wept also, as he sat alone by the river, near to and watching the damp linen.

The two women walked very slowly. The laundress slipped and tottered through the lane, and round the corner, into the street where the mayor lived; and just as she reached the front of his house, she sank down upon the pavement. Many persons came round her, and Lame Martha ran into the house for help. The mayor and his guests came to the window.

"Oh, it is the laundress," said he; "she has had a little drop too much. She is good for nothing. It is a sad thing for her pretty little son. I like the boy very well; but the mother is good for nothing."

After a while the laundress recovered herself, and they led her to her poor dwelling, and put her to bed. Kind Martha warmed a mug of beer for her, with butter and sugar—she considered this the best medicine—and then hastened to the river, washed and rinsed, badly enough, to be sure, but she did her best. Then she drew the linen ashore, wet as it was, and laid it in a basket. Before evening, she was sitting in the poor little room with the laundress. The mayor's cook had given her some roasted potatoes and a beautiful piece of fat for the sick woman. Martha and the boy enjoyed these good things very much; but the sick woman could only say that the smell was very nourishing, she thought. By-and-by the boy was put to bed, in the same bed as the one in which his mother lay; but he slept at her feet, covered with an old quilt made of blue and white patchwork. The laundress felt a little better by this time. The warm beer had strengthened her, and the smell of the good food had been pleasant to her.

"Many thanks, you good soul," she said to Martha. "Now the boy is asleep, I will tell you all. He is soon asleep. How gentle and sweet he looks as he lies there with his eyes closed! He does not know how his mother has suffered; and Heaven grant he never may know it. I was in service at the counsellor's, the father of the mayor, and it happened that the youngest of his sons, the student, came home. I was a young wild girl then, but honest; that I can declare in the sight of Heaven. The student was merry and gay, brave and affectionate; every drop of blood in him was good and honorable; a better man never lived on earth. He was the son of the house, and I was only a maid; but he loved me truly and honorably, and he told his mother of it. She was to him as an angel upon earth; she was so wise and loving. He went to travel, and before he started he placed a gold ring on my finger; and as soon as he was out of the house, my mistress sent for me. Gently and earnestly she drew me to her, and spake as if an angel were speaking. She showed me clearly, in spirit and in truth, the difference there was between him and me. 'He is pleased now,' she said, 'with your pretty face; but good looks do not last long. You have not been educated like he has. You are not equals in mind and rank, and therein lies the misfortune. I esteem the poor,' she added. 'In the sight of God, they may occupy a higher place than many of the rich; but here upon earth we must beware of entering upon a false track, lest we are overturned in our plans, like a carriage that travels by a dangerous road. I know a worthy man, an artisan, who wishes to marry you. I mean Eric, the glovemaker. He is a widower, without children, and in a good position. Will you think it over?' Every word she said pierced my heart like a knife; but I knew she was right, and the thought pressed heavily upon me. I kissed her hand, and wept bitter tears, and I wept still more when I went to my room, and threw myself on the bed. I passed through a dreadful night; God knows what I suffered, and how I struggled. The following Sunday I went to the house of God to pray for light to direct my path. It seemed like a providence that as I stepped out of church Eric came towards me; and then there remained not a doubt in my mind. We were suited to each other in rank and circumstances. He was, even then, a man of good means. I went up to him, and took his hand, and said, 'Do you still feel the same for me?' 'Yes; ever and always,' said he. 'Will you, then, marry a maiden who honors and esteems you, although she cannot offer you her love? but that may come.' 'Yes, it will come,' said he; and we joined our hands together, and I went home to my mistress. The gold ring which her son had given me I wore next to my heart. I could not place it on my finger during the daytime, but only in the evening, when I went to bed. I kissed the ring till my lips almost bled, and then I gave it to my mistress, and told her that the banns were to be put up for me and the glovemaker the following week. Then my mistress threw her arms round me, and kissed me. She did not say that I was 'good for nothing;" very likely I was better then than I am now; but the misfortunes of this world were unknown to me then. At Michaelmas we were married, and for the first year everything went well with us. We had a journeyman and an apprentice, and you were our servant, Martha."

"Ah, yes, and you were a dear, good mistress," said Martha, "I shall never forget how kind you and your husband were to me."

"Yes, those were happy years when you were with us, although we had no children at first. The student I never met again. Yet I saw him once, although he did not see me. He came to his mother's funeral. I saw him, looking pale as death, and deeply troubled, standing at her grave; for she was his mother. Sometime after, when his father died, he was in foreign lands, and did not come home. I know that he never married, I believe he became a lawyer. He had forgotten me, and even had we met he would not have known me, for I have lost all my good looks, and perhaps that is all for the best." And then she spoke of the dark days of trial, when misfortune had fallen upon them.

"We had five hundred dollars," she said, "and there was a house in the street to be sold for two hundred, so we thought it would be worth our while to pull it down and build a new one in its place; so it was bought. The builder and carpenter made an estimate that the new house would cost ten hundred and twenty dollars to build. Eric had credit, so he borrowed the money in the chief town. But the captain, who was bringing it to him, was shipwrecked, and the money lost. Just about this time, my dear sweet boy, who lies sleeping there, was born, and my husband was attacked with a severe lingering illness. For three quarters of a year I was obliged to dress and undress him. We were backward in our payments, we borrowed more money, and all that we had was lost and sold, and then my husband died. Since then I have worked, toiled, and striven for the sake of the child. I have scrubbed and washed both coarse and fine linen, but I have not been able to make myself better off; and it was God's will. In His own time He will take me to Himself, but I know He will never forsake my boy." Then she fell asleep. In the morning she felt much refreshed, and strong enough, as she thought, to go on with her work. But as soon as she stepped into the cold water, a sudden faintness seized her; she clutched at the air convulsively with her hand, took one step forward, and fell. Her head rested on dry land, but her feet were in the water; her wooden shoes, which were only tied on by a wisp of straw, were carried away by the stream, and thus she was found by Martha when she came to bring her some coffee.

In the meantime a messenger had been sent to her house by the mayor, to say that she must come to him immediately, as he had something to tell her. It was too late; a surgeon had been sent for to open a vein in her arm, but the poor woman was dead.

"She has drunk herself to death," said the cruel mayor. In the letter, containing the news of his brother's death, it was stated that he had left in his will a legacy of six hundred dollars to the glovemaker's widow, who had been his mother's maid, to be paid with discretion, in large or small sums to the widow or her child.

"There was something between my brother and her, I remember," said the mayor; "it is a good thing that she is out of the way, for now the boy will have the whole. I will place him with honest people to bring him up, that he may become a respectable working man." And the blessing of God rested upon these words. The mayor sent for the boy to come to him, and promised to take care of him, but most cruelly added that it was a good thing that his mother was dead, for "she was good for nothing." They carried her to the churchyard, the churchyard in which the poor were buried. Martha strewed sand on the grave and planted a rose-tree upon it, and the boy stood by her side.

"Oh, my poor mother!" he cried, while the tears rolled down his cheeks. "Is it true what they say, that she was good for nothing?"

"No, indeed, it is not true," replied the old servant, raising her eyes to heaven; "she was worth a great deal; I knew it years ago, and since the last night of her life I am more certain of it than ever. I say she was a good and worthy woman, and God, who is in heaven, knows I am speaking the truth, though the world may say, even now she was good for nothing."

THE GOBLIN AND THE HUCKSTER

THERE was once a regular student, who lived in a garret, and had no possessions. And there was also a regular huckster, to whom the house belonged, and who occupied the ground floor. A goblin lived with the huckster, because at Christmas he always had a large dish full of jam, with a great piece of butter in the middle. The huckster could afford this; and therefore the goblin remained with the huckster, which was very cunning of him.

One evening the student came into the shop through the back door to buy candles and cheese for himself; he had no one to send, and therefore he came himself; he obtained what he wished, and then the huckster and his wife nodded good evening to him, and she was a woman who could do more than merely nod, for she had usually plenty to say for herself. The student nodded in return as he turned to leave, then suddenly stopped, and began reading the piece of paper in which the cheese was wrapped. It was a leaf torn out of an old book, a book that ought not to have been torn up, for it was full of poetry.

"Yonder lies some more of the same sort," said the huckster: " I gave an old woman a few coffee berries for it; you shall have the rest for sixpence, if you will."

"Indeed I will," said the student; "give me the book instead of the cheese; I can eat my bread and butter without cheese. It would be a sin to tear up a book like this. You are a clever man; and a practical man; but you understand no more about poetry than that cask yonder."

This was a very rude speech, especially against the cask; but the huckster and the student both laughed, for it was only said in fun. But the goblin felt very angry that any man should venture to say such things to a huckster who was a householder and sold the best butter. As soon as it was night, and the shop closed, and every one in bed except the student, the goblin stepped softly into the bedroom where the huckster's wife slept, and took away her tongue, which of course, she did not then want. Whatever object in the room he placed his tongue upon immediately received voice and speech, and was able to express its thoughts and feelings as readily as the lady herself could do. It could only be used by one object at a time, which was a good thing, as a number speaking at once would have caused great confusion. The goblin laid the tongue upon the cask, in which lay a quantity of old newspapers.

What the GOBLIN saw in the Student's room

THE GOBLIN AND THE HUCKSTER

"Is it really true," he asked, "that you do not know what poetry is?"

"Of course I know," replied the cask: "poetry is something that always stand in the corner of a newspaper, and is sometimes cut out; and I may venture to affirm that I have more of it in me than the student has, and I am only a poor tub of the huckster's."

Then the goblin placed the tongue on the coffee mill; and how it did go to be sure! Then he put it on the butter tub and the cash box, and they all expressed the same opinion as the waste-paper tub; and a majority must always be respected.

"Now I shall go and tell the student," said the goblin; and with these words he went quietly up the back stairs to the garrret where the student lived. He had a candle burning still, and the goblin peeped through the keyhole and saw that he was reading in the torn book, which he had brought out of the shop. But how light the room was! From the book shot forth a ray of light which grew broad and full, like the stem of a tree, from which bright rays spread upward and over the student's head. Each leaf was fresh, and each flower was like a beautiful female head; some with dark and sparkling eyes, and others with eyes that were wonderfully blue and clear. The fruit gleamed like stars, and the room was filled with sounds of beautiful music. The little goblin had never imagined, much less seen or heard of, any sight so glorious as this. He stood still on tiptoe, peeping in, till the light went out in the garret. The student no doubt had blown out his candle and gone to bed; but the little goblin remained standing there nevertheless, and listening to the music which still sounded on, soft and beautiful, a sweet cradle-song for the student, who had lain down to rest.

"This is a wonderful place," said the goblin; "I never expected such a thing. I should like to stay here with the student;" and the little man thought it over, for he was a sensible little spirit. At last he sighed, "but the student has no jam!" So he went down stairs again into the huckster's shop, and it was a good thing he got back when he did, for the cask had almost worn out the lady's tongue; he had given a description of all that he contained on one side, and was just about to turn himself over to the other side to describe what was there, when the goblin entered and restored the tongue to the lady. But from that time forward, the whole shop, from the cash box down to the pinewood logs, formed their opinions from that of the cask; and they all had such confidence in him, and treated him with so much respect, that when the huckster read the criticisms on theatricals and art of an evening, they fancied it must all come from the cask.

But after what he had seen, the goblin could no longer sit and listen quietly to the wisdom and understanding down stairs; so, as soon as the evening light glimmered in the garret, he took courage, for it seemed to him as if the rays of light were strong cables, drawing him up, and obliging him to go and peep through the keyhole; and, while there, a feeling of vastness came over him such as we experience by the ever-moving sea, when the storm breaks forth; and it brought tears into his eyes. He did not himself know why he wept, yet a kind of pleasant feeling mingled with his tears. "How wonderfully glorious it would be to sit with the student under such a tree;" but that was out of the question, he must be content to look through the keyhole, and be thankful for even that.

There he stood on the old landing, with the autumn wind blowing down upon him through the trap-door. It was very cold; but the little creature did not really feel it, till the light in the garret went out, and the tones of music died away. Then how he shivered, and crept down stairs again to his warm corner, where it felt home-like and comfortable. And when Christmas came again, and brought the dish of jam and the great lump of butter, he liked the huckster best of all.

Soon after, in the middle of the night, the goblin was awoke by a terrible noise and knocking against the window shutters and the house doors, and by the sound of the watchman's horn; for a great fire had broken out, and the whole street appeared full of flames. Was it in their house, or a neighbor's? No one could tell, for terror had seized upon all. The huckster's wife was so bewildered that she took her gold ear-rings out of her ears and put them in her pocket, that she might save something at least. The huckster ran to get his business papers, and the servant resolved to save her blue silk mantle, which she had managed to buy. Each wished to keep the best things they had. The goblin had the same wish; for, with one spring, he was up stairs and in the student's room, whom he found standing by the open window, and looking quite calmly at the fire, which was raging at the house of a neighbor opposite. The goblin caught up the wonderful book which lay on the table, and popped it into his red cap, which he held tightly with both hands. The greatest treasure in the house was saved; and he ran away with it to the roof, and seated himself on the chimney. The flames of the burning house opposite illuminated him as he sat, both hands pressed tightly over his cap, in which the treasure lay; and then he found out what feelings really reigned in his heart, and knew exactly which way they tended. And yet, when the fire was extinguished, and the goblin again began to reflect, he hesitated, and said at last, "I must divide myself between the two; I cannot quite give up the huckster, because of the jam."

And this is a representation of human nature. We are like the goblin; we all go to visit the huckster "because of the jam."

WHAT THE OLD MAN DOES IS ALWAYS RIGHT

I WILL tell you a story that was told me when I was a little boy. Every time I thought of this story, it seemed to me more and more charming; for it is with stories as it is with many people — they become better as they grow older.

I have no doubt that you have been in the country, and seen a very old farmhouse, with a thatched roof, and mosses and small plants growing wild upon it. There is a stork's nest on the ridge of the gable, for we cannot do without the stork. The walls of the house are sloping, and the windows are low, and only one of the latter is made to open. The baking-oven sticks out of the wall like a great knob. An elder-tree hangs over the palings; and beneath its branches, at the foot of the paling, is a pool of water, in which a few ducks are disporting themselves. There is a yard-dog too, who barks at all comers. Just such a farmhouse as this stood in a country lane; and in it dwelt an old couple, a peasant and his wife. Small as their possessions were, they had one article they could not do without, and that was a horse, which contrived to live upon the grass which it found by the side of the high road. The old peasant rode into the town upon this horse, and his neighbors often borrowed it of him, and paid for the loan of it by rendering some service to the old couple. After a time they thought it would be as well to sell the horse, or exchange it for something which might be more useful to them. But what might this *something* be?

"You'll know best, old man," said the wife. "It is fair-day to-day; so ride into town, and get rid of the horse for money, or make a good exchange; whichever you do will be right to me, so ride to the fair."

And she fastened his neckerchief for him; for she could do that better than he could, and she could also tie it very prettily in a double bow. She also smoothed his hat round and round with the palm of her hand, and gave him a kiss. Then he rode away upon the horse that was to be sold or bartered for something else. Yes, the old man knew what he was about. The sun shone with great heat, and not a cloud was to be seen in the sky. The road was very dusty; for a number of people, all going to the fair, were driving, riding, or walking upon it. There was no shelter anywhere from the hot sunshine. Among the rest a man came trudging along, and driving a cow to the fair. The cow was as beautiful a creature as any cow could be.

"She gives good milk, I am certain," said the peasant to himself. "That would be a very good exchange: the cow for the horse. Hallo there! you with the cow," he said. "I tell you what; I dare say a horse is of more value than a cow; but I don't care for that, — a cow will be more useful to me; so, if you like, we'll exchange."

"To be sure I will," said the man.

Accordingly the exchange was made; and as the matter was settled, the peasant might have turned back; for he had done the business he came to do. But, having made up his mind to go to the fair, he determined to do so, if only to have a look at it; so on he went to the town with his cow. Leading the animal, he strode on sturdily, and, after a short time, overtook a man who was driving a sheep. It was a good fat sheep, with a fine fleece on its back.

"I should like to have that fellow," said the peasant to himself. "There is plenty of grass for him by our palings, and in the winter we could keep him in the room with us. Perhaps it would be more profitable to have a sheep than a cow. Shall I exchange?"

The man with the sheep was quite ready, and the bargain was quickly made. And then our peasant continued his way on the high-road with his sheep. Soon after this, he overtook another man, who had come into the road from a field, and was carrying a large goose under his arm.

"What a heavy creature you have there!" said the peasant; "it has plenty of feathers and plenty of fat, and would look well tied to a string, or paddling in the water at our place. That would be very useful to my old woman; she could make all sorts of profits out of it. How often she has said, 'If now we only had a goose!' Now here is an opportunity, and, if possible, I will get it for her. Shall we exchange? I will give you my sheep for your goose, and thanks into the bargain."

The other had not the least objection, and accordingly the exchange was made, and our peasant became possessor of the goose. By this time he had arrived very near the town. The crowd on the high road had been gradually increasing, and there was quite a rush of men and cattle. The cattle walked on the path and by the palings, and at the turnpike-gate they even walked

WHAT THE OLD MAN DOES IS ALWAYS RIGHT

into the toll-keeper's potato-field, where one fowl was strutting about with a string tied to its leg, for fear it should take fright at the crowd, and run away and get lost. The tail-feathers of the fowl were very short, and it winked with both its eyes, and looked very cunning, as it said "Cluck, cluck." What were the thoughts of the fowl as it said this I cannot tell you; but directly our good man saw it, he thought, "Why that's the finest fowl I ever saw in my life; it's finer than our parson's brood hen, upon my word. I should like to have that fowl. Fowls can always pick up a few grains that lie about, and almost keep themselves. I think it would be a good exchange if I could get it for my goose. Shall we exchange?" he asked the toll-keeper.

"Exchange," repeated the man; "well, it would not be a bad thing."

And so they made an exchange, — the toll-keeper at the turnpike-gate kept the goose, and the peasant carried off the fowl. Now he had really done a great deal of business on his way to the fair, and he was hot and tired. He wanted something to eat, and a glass of ale to refresh himself; so he turned his steps to an inn. He was just about to enter when the ostler came out, and they met at the door. The ostler was carrying a sack. "What have you in that sack?" asked the peasant.

"Rotten apples," answered the ostler; "a whole sackful of them. They will do to feed the pigs with."

"Why that will be terrible waste," he replied; "I should like to take them home to my old woman. Last year the old apple-tree by the grass-plot only bore one apple, and we kept it in the cupboard till it was quite withered and rotten. It was always property, my old woman said; and here she would see a great deal of property — a whole sackful; I should like to show them to her."

"What will you give me for the sackful?" asked the ostler.

"What will I give? Well, I will give you my fowl in exchange."

So he gave up the fowl, and received the apples, which he carried into the inn parlor. He leaned the sack carefully against the stove, and then went to the table. But the stove was hot, and he had not thought of that. Many guests were present — horse dealers, cattle drovers, and two Englishmen. The Englishmen were so rich that their pockets quite bulged out and seemed ready to burst; and they could bet too, as you shall hear. "Hiss — s — s, hiss — s — s." What could that be by the stove? The apples were beginning to roast. "What is that?" asked one.

"Why, do you know" — said our peasant. And then he told them the whole story of the horse, which he had exchanged for a cow, and all the rest of it, down to the apples.

"Well, your old woman will give it you well when you get home," said one of the Englishmen. "Won't there be a noise?"

"What! Give me what?" said the peasant. "Why, she will kiss me, and say, 'what the old man does is always right.'"

"Let us lay a wager on it," said the Englishmen. "We'll wager you a ton of coined gold, a hundred pounds to the hundred-weight."

"No; a bushel will be enough," replied the peasant. "I can only set a bushel of apples against it, and I'll throw myself and my old woman into the bargain; that will pile up the measure, I fancy."

"Done! taken!" and so the bet was made.

Then the landlord's coach came to the door, and the two Englishmen and the peasant got in, and away they drove, and soon arrived and stopped at the peasant's hut. "Good evening, old woman." "Good evening, old man." "I've made the exchange."

"Ah, well, you understand what you're about," said the woman. Then she embraced him, and paid no attention to the strangers, nor did she notice the sack.

"I got a cow in exchange for the horse."

"Thank Heaven," said she. "Now we shall have plenty of milk, and butter, and cheese on the table. That was a capital exchange."

"Yes, but I changed the cow for a sheep."

"Ah, better still!" cried the wife. "You always think of everything; we have just enough pasture for a sheep. Ewe's milk and cheese, woollen jackets and stockings! The cow could not give all these, and her hair only falls off. How you think of everything!"

"But I changed away the sheep for a goose."

"Then we shall have roast goost to eat this year. You dear old man, you are always thinking of something to please me. This is delightful. We can let the goose walk about with a string tied to her leg, so she will be fatter still before we roast her."

"But I gave away the goose for a fowl."

"A fowl! Well, that was a good exchange," replied the woman. "The fowl will lay eggs and hatch them, and we shall have chickens; we shall soon have a poultry-yard. Oh, this is just what I was wishing for.

"Yes, but I exchanged the fowl for a sack of shrivelled apples."

"What! I really must give you a kiss for that!" exclaimed the wife. "My dear, good husband, now I'll tell you something. Do you know, almost as soon as you left me this morning, I began to think of what I could give you nice for supper this evening, and then I thought of fried eggs and bacon, with sweet herbs; I had eggs and bacon, but I wanted the herbs; so I went over to the schoolmaster's: I knew they had plenty of herbs, but the schoolmistress is very mean, although she can smile so sweetly. I begged her to lend me a handful of herbs. 'Lend!' she exclaimed, 'I have nothing to lend; nothing at all grows in our garden, not even a shrivelled apple; I could not even lend you a shrivelled apple, my dear woman. But now I can lend her ten, or a whole sackful, which I'm very glad of; it makes me laugh to think about it;" and then she gave him a hearty kiss.

"Well, I like all this," said both the Englishmen; "always going down the hill, and yet always merry; it's worth the money to see it." So they paid a hundred-weight of gold to the peasant, who, whatever he did, was not scolded but kissed.

Yes, it always pays best when the wife sees and maintains that her husband knows best, and whatever he does is right.

That is a story which I heard when I was a child; and now you have heard it too, and know that "What the old man does is always right."

THE STORY OF A MOTHER

A MOTHER sat by her little child; she was very sad, for she feared it would die. It was quite pale, and its little eyes were closed, and sometimes it drew a heavy deep breath, almost like a sigh; and then the mother gazed more sadly than ever on the poor little creature. Some one knocked at the door, and a poor old man walked in. He was wrapped in something that looked like a great horse-cloth; and he required it truly to keep him warm, for it was cold winter; the country everywhere lay covered with snow and ice, and the wind blew so sharply that it cut one's face. The little child had dozed off to sleep for a moment, and the mother, seeing that the old man shivered with the cold, rose and placed a small mug of beer on the stove to warm for him. The old man sat and rocked the cradle; and the mother seated herself on a chair near him, and looked at her sick child who still breathed heavily, and took hold of its little hand.

"You think I shall keep him, do you not?" she said. "Our all-merciful God will surely not take him away from me."

The old man, who was indeed Death himself, nodded his head in a peculiar manner, which might have signified either Yes, or No; and the mother cast down her eyes, while the tears rolled down her cheeks. Then her head became heavy, for she had not closed her eyes for three days and nights, and she slept, but only for a moment. Shivering with cold, she started up and looked round the room. The old man was gone, and her child—it was gone too!—the old man had taken it with him. In the corner of the room the old clock began to strike; "whirr" went the chains, the heavy weight sank to the ground, and the clock stopped; and the poor mother rushed out of the house calling for her child. Out in the snow sat a woman in long black garments, and she said to the mother, "Death has been with you in your room. I saw him hastening away with your little child; he strides faster than the wind, and never brings back what he has taken away."

"Only tell me which way he has gone," said the mother; "tell me the way, I will find him."

"I know the way," said the woman in the black garments; "but before I tell you, you must sing to me all the songs that you have sung to your child; I love these songs, I have heard them before. I am Night, and I saw your tears flow as you sang."

"I will sing them all to you," said the mother; "but do not detain me now. I must overtake him, and find my child."

But Night sat silent and still. Then the mother wept and sang, and wrung her hands. And there were many songs, and yet even more tears; till at length Night said, "Go to the right, into the dark forest of fir-trees; for I saw Death take that road with your little child."

Within the wood the mother came to cross roads, and she knew not which to take. Just by stood a thorn-bush; it had neither leaf nor flower, for it was the cold winter time, and icicles hung on the branches. "Have you not seen Death go by, with my little child?" she asked.

"Yes," replied the thorn-bush; "but I will not tell you which way he has taken until you have warmed me in your bosom. I am freezing to death here, and turning to ice."

THE STORY OF A MOTHER

Then she pressed the bramble to her bosom quite close, so that it might be thawed, and the thorns pierced her flesh, and great drops of blood flowed; but the bramble shot forth fresh green leaves, and they became flowers on the cold winter's night, so warm is the heart of a sorrowing mother. Then the bramble-bush told her the path she must take. She came at length to a great lake, on which there was neither ship nor boat to be seen. The lake was not frozen sufficiently for her to pass over on the ice, nor was it open enough for her to wade through; and yet she must cross it, if she wished to find her child. Then she laid herself down to drink up the water of the lake, which was of course impossible for any human being to do; but the bereaved mother thought that perhaps a miracle might take place to help her. "You will never succeed in this," said the lake; let us make an agreement together which will be better. I love to collect pearls, and your eyes are the purest I have ever seen. If you will weep those eyes away in tears into my waters, then I will take you to the large hothouse where Death dwells and rears flowers and trees, every one of which is a human life."

"Oh, what would I not give to reach my child!" said the weeping mother; and as she still continued to weep, her eyes fell into the depths of the lake, and became two costly pearls.

Then the lake lifted her up, and wafted her across to the opposite shore as if she were on a swing, where stood a wonderful building many miles in length. No one could tell whether it was a mountain covered with forests and full of caves, or whether it had been built. But the poor mother could not see, for she had wept her eyes into the lake. "Where shall I find Death, who went away with my little child?" she asked.

"He has not arrived here yet," said an old gray-haired woman, who was walking about, and watering Death's hothouse. "How have your found your way here? and who helped you?"

"God has helped me," she replied. "He is merciful; will you not be merciful too? Where shall I find my little child?"

"I did not know the child," said the old woman; "and you are blind. Many flowers and trees have faded to-night, and Death will soon come to transplant them. You know already that every human being has a life-tree or a life-flower, just as may be ordained for him. They look like other plants; but they have hearts that beat. Children's hearts also beat: from that you may perhaps be able to recognize your child. But what will you give me, if I tell you what more you will have to do?

"I have nothing to give," said the afflicted mother; "but I would go to the ends of the earth for you."

"I can give you nothing to do for me there," said the old woman; "but you can give me your long black hair. You know yourself that it is beautiful, and it pleases me. You can take my white hair in exchange, which will be something in return."

"Do you ask nothing more than that?" said she. "I will give it to you with pleasure."

And she gave up her beautiful hair, and received in return the white locks of the old woman. Then they went into Death's vast hothouse, where flowers and trees grew together in wonderful profusion. Blooming hyacinths, under glass bells, and peonies, like strong trees. There grew water-plants, some quite fresh, and others looking sickly, which had water-snakes twining round them, and black crabs clinging to their stems. There stood noble palm-trees, oaks, and plantains, and beneath them bloomed thyme and parsley. Each tree and flower had a name; each represented a human life, and belonged to men still living, some in China, others in Greenland, and in all parts of the world. Some large trees had been planted in little pots, so that they were cramped for room, and seemed about to burst the pot to pieces; while many weak little flowers were growing in rich soil, with moss all around them, carefully tended and cared for. The sorrowing mother bent over the little plants, and heard the human heart beating in each, and recognized the beatings of her child's heart among millions of others.

"That is it," she cried, stretching out her hand towards a little crocus-flower which hung down its sickly head.

"Do not touch the flower," exclaimed the old woman; "but place yourself here; and when Death comes—I expect him every minute—do not let him pull up that plant, but threaten him that if he does you will serve the other flowers in the same manner. This will make him afraid; for he must account to God for each of them. None can be uprooted, unless he receives permission to do so."

There rushed through the hothouse a chill of icy coldness, and the blind mother felt that Death had arrived.

"How did you find your way hither?" asked he; "how could you come here faster than I have?"

"I am a mother," she answered.

And Death stretched out his hand towards the delicate little flower; but she held her hands tightly round it, and held it fast at the same time, with the most anxious care, lest she should touch one of the leaves. Then Death breathed upon her hands, and she felt his breath colder than the icy wind, and her hands sank down powerless.

"You cannot prevail against me," said Death.

"But a God of mercy can," said she.

"I only do His will," replied Death. "I am his gardener. I take all His flowers and trees, and transplant them into the gardens of Paradise in an unknown land. How they flourish there, and what that garden resembles, I may not tell you."

"Give me back my child," said the mother, weeping and imploring; and she seized two beautiful flowers in her hands, and cried to Death, "I will tear up all your flowers, for I am in despair."

"Do not touch them," said Death. "You say you are unhappy; and would you make another mother as unhappy as yourself?"

"Another mother!" cried the poor woman, setting the flowers free from her hands.

"There are your eyes," said Death. "I fished them up out of the lake for you. They were shining brightly; but I knew not they were yours. Take them back—they are clearer now than before—and then look into the deep well which is close by here. I will tell you the names of the two flowers which you wished to pull up; and you will see the whole future of the human beings they represent, and what you were about to frustrate and destroy."

Then she looked into the well; and it was a glorious sight to behold how one of them became a blessing to the world, and how much happiness and joy it spread around. But she saw that the life of the other was full of care and poverty, misery and woe.

"Both are the will of God," said Death.

"Which is the unhappy flower, and which is the blessed one?" she said.

"That I may not tell you," said Death; "but thus far you may learn, that one of the two flowers represents your own child. It was the fate of your child that you saw, — the future of your own child."

Then the mother screamed aloud with terror, "Which of them belongs to my child? Tell me that. Deliver the unhappy child. Release it from so much misery. Rather take it away. Take it to the kingdom of God. Forget my tears and my entreaties; forget all that I have said or done."

"I do not understand you," said Death. "Will you have your child back? or shall I carry him away to a place that you do not know?"

Then the mother wrung her hands, fell on her knees, and prayed to God, "Grant not my prayers, when they are contrary to Thy will, which at all times must be the best. Oh, hear them not;" and her head sank on her bosom.

Then Death carried away her child to the unknown land.

IB AND LITTLE CHRISTINA

IN the forest that extends from the banks of the Gudenau, in North Jutland, a long way into the country, and not far from the clear stream, rises a great ridge of land, which stretches through the wood like a wall. Westward of this ridge, and not far from the river, stands a farmhouse, surrounded by such poor land that the sandy soil shows itself between the scanty ears of rye and wheat which grow in it. Some years have passed since the people who lived here cultivated these fields; they kept three sheep, a pig, and two oxen; in fact they maintained themselves very well, they had quite enough to live upon, as people generally have who are content with their lot. They even could have afforded to keep two horses, but it was a saying among the farmers in those parts, "The horse eats himself up;" that is to say, he eats as much as he earns. Jeppe Jans cultivated his fields in summer, and in the winter he made wooden shoes. He also had an assistant, a lad who understood as well as he himself did how to make wooden shoes strong, but light, and in the fashion. They carved shoes and spoons, which paid well; therefore no one could justly call Jeppe Jans and his family poor people. Little Ib, a boy of seven years old and the only child, would sit by, watching the workmen, or cutting a stick, and sometimes his finger instead of the stick. But one day Ib succeeded so well in his carving that he made two pieces of wood look really like two little wooden shoes, and he determined to give them as a present to Little Christina.

"And who was Little Christina?" She was the boatman's daughter, graceful and delicate as the child of a gentleman; had she been dressed differently, no one would have believed that she lived in a hut on the neighboring heath with her father. He was a widower, and earned his living by carrying firewood in his large boat from the forest to the eel-pond and eel-weir, on the estate of Silkborg, and sometimes even to the distant town of Randers. There was no one under whose care he could leave Little Christina; so she was almost always with him in his boat, or playing in the wood among the blossoming heath,or picking the ripe wild berries. Sometimes, when her father had to go as far as the town, he would take Little Christina, who was a year younger than Ib, across the heath to the cottage of Jeppe Jans, and leave her there. Ib and Christina agreed together in everything; they divided their bread and berries when they were hungry; they were partners in digging their little gardens; they ran, and crept, and played about everywhere. Once they wandered a long way into the forest, and even ventured together to climb the high ridge. Another time they found a few snipes' eggs in the wood, which was a great event. Ib had never been on the heath where Christina's father lived, nor on the river; but at last came an opportunity. Christina's father invited him to go for a sail in his boat; and the evening before, he accompanied the boatman across the heath to his house. The next morning early, the two children were placed on the top of a high pile of firewood in the boat, and sat eating bread and wild strawberries, while Christina's father and his man drove the boat forward with poles. They floated on swiftly, for the tide was in their favor, passing over lakes, formed by the stream in its course; sometimes they seemed quite enclosed by reeds and water-plants, yet there was always room for them to pass out, although the old trees overhung the water and the old oaks stretched out their bare branches, as if they had turned up their sleeves and wished to show their knotty, naked arms. Old alder-trees, whose roots were loosened from the banks, clung with their fibres to the bottom of the stream, and the tops of the branches above the water looked like little woody islands. The water-lilies waved themselves to and fro on the river, everything made the excursion beautiful, and at last they came to the great eel-weir, where the water rushed through the flood-gates; and the children thought this a beautiful sight. In those days there was no factory nor any town house, nothing but the great farm, with its scanty-bearing fields, in which could be seen a few herd of cattle, and one or two farm laborers. The rushing of the water through the sluices, and the scream of the wild ducks, were almost the only signs of active life at Silkborg. After the firewood had been unloaded, Christina's father bought a whole bundle of eels and a sucking-pig, which were all placed in a basket in the stern of the boat. Then they returned again up the stream; and as the wind was favorable, two sails were hoisted, which carried the boat on as well as if two horses had been harnessed to it. As they sailed on, they came by chance to the place where the boatman's assistant lived, at a little distance from the bank of the river. The boat was moored; and the two men, after desiring the children to sit still, both went on shore. they obeyed this order for a very short time, and then forgot it altogether. First they peeped into the basket containing the eels and the sucking-pig; then they must needs pull out the pig and take it in their hands, and feel it, and touch it; and as they both wanted to hold it at the same time, the consequence was that they let it fall into the water, and the pig sailed away with the stream.

Here was a terrible disaster. Ib jumped ashore, and ran a little distance from the boat.

"Oh, take me with you," cried Christina; and she sprang after him. In a few minutes they found themselves deep in a thicket, and could no longer see the boat or the shore. They ran on a little farther, and then Christina fell down, and began to cry.

Ib helped her up, and said, "Never mind; follow me. Yonder is the house." But the house was not yonder; and they wandered still farther, over the dry rustling leaves of the last year, and treading on fallen branches that crackled under their little feet; then they heard a loud, piercing cry, and they stood still to listen. Presently the scream of an eagle sounded through the wood; it was an ugly cry, and it frightened the children; but before them, in the thickest part of the forest, grew the most beautiful blackberries, in wonderful quantities. They looked so inviting that the children could not help stopping; and they remained there so long eating, that their mouths and cheeks became quite black with the juice.

Presently they heard the frightful scream again, and Christina said, "We shall get into trouble about that pig."

"Oh, never mind," said Ib; "we will go home to my father's house. It is here in the wood." So they went on, but the road led them out of the way; no house could be seen, it grew dark, and the children were afraid. The solemn stillness that reigned around them was now and then broken by the shrill cries of the great horned owl and other birds that they knew nothing of. At last they both lost themselves in the thicket; Christina began to cry, and then Ib cried too; and, after weeping and lamenting for some time, they stretched themselves down on the dry leaves and fell asleep.

The sun was high in the heavens when the two children woke. They felt cold; but not far from their resting-place, on a hill, the sun was shining through the trees. They thought if they went there they should be warm, and Ib fancied he should be able to see his father's house from such a high spot. But they were far away from home now, in quite another part of the forest. They clambered to the top of the rising ground, and found themselves on the edge of a declivity, which sloped down to a clear transparent lake. Great quantities of fish could be seen through the clear water, sparkling in the sun's rays; they were quite surprised when they came so suddenly upon such an unexpected sight.

Close to where they stood grew a hazel-bush, covered with beautiful nuts. They soon gathered some, cracked them, and ate the fine young kernels, which were only just ripe. But there was another surprise and fright in store for them. Out of the thicket stepped a tall old woman, her face quite brown, and her hair of a deep shining black; the whites of her eyes glittered like a Moor's; on her back she carried a bundle, and in her hand a knotted stick. She was a gypsy. The children did not at first understand what she said. She drew out of her pocket three large nuts, in which she told them were hidden the most beautiful and lovely things in the world, for they were wishing nuts. Ib looked at her, and as she spoke so kindly, he took courage, and asked her if she would give him the nuts; and the woman gave them to him, and then gathered some more from the bushes for herself, quite a pocket full. Ib and Christina looked at the wishing nuts with wide open eyes.

"Is there in this nut a carriage, with a pair of horses?" asked Ib.

"Yes, there is a golden carriage, with two golden horses," replied the woman.

"Then give me that nut," said Christina; so Ib gave it to her, and the strange woman tied up the nut for her in her handkerchief.

Ib held up another nut. "Is there, in this nut, a pretty little neckerchief like the one Christina has on her neck?" asked Ib.

"There are ten neckerchiefs in it," she replied, "as well as beautiful dresses, stockings, and a hat and veil."

"Then I will have that one also," said Christina; "and it is a pretty one too." And then Ib gave her the second nut.

IB AND LITTLE CHRISTINA

The third was a little black thing. "You may keep that one," said Christina; "it is quite as pretty."

"What is in it?" asked Ib.

"The best of all things for you," replied the gypsy. So Ib held the nut very tight.

Then the woman promised to lead the children to the right path, that they might find their way home: and they went forward certainly in quite another direction to the one they meant to take; therefore no one ought to speak against the woman, and say that she wanted to steal the children. In the wild wood-path they met a forester who knew Ib, and, by his help, Ib and Christina reached home, where they found every one had been very anxious about them. They were pardoned and forgiven, although they really had both done wrong, and deserved to get into trouble; first, because they had let the sucking-pig fall into the water; and, secondly, because they had run away. Christina was taken back to her father's house on the heath, and Ib remained in the farm-house on the borders of the wood, near the great land ridge.

The first thing Ib did that evening was to take out of his pocket the little black nut, in which the best thing of all was said to be enclosed. He laid it carefully between the door and the door-post, and then shut the door so that the nut cracked directly. But there was not much kernel to be seen; it was what we should call hollow or worm-eaten, and looked as if it had been filled with tobacco or rich black earth. "It is just what I expected!" exclaimed Ib. "How should there be room in a little nut like this for the best thing of all? Christina will find her two nuts just the same; there will be neither fine clothes or a golden carriage in them."

Winter came; and the new year, and indeed many years passed away; until Ib was old enough to be confirmed, and, therefore, he went during a whole winter to the clergyman of the nearest village to be prepared.

One day, about this time, the boatman paid a visit to Ib's parents, and told them that Christina was going to service, and that she had been remarkably fortunate in obtaining a good place, with most respectable people. "Only think," he said, "She is going to the rich innkeeper's, at the hotel in Herning, many miles west from here. She is to assist the landlady in the housekeeping; and, if afterwards she behaves well and remains to be confirmed, the people will treat her as their own daughter."

So Ib and Christina took leave of each other. People already called them "the betrothed," and at parting the girl showed Ib the two nuts, which she had taken care of ever since the time that they lost themselves in the wood; and she told him also that the little wooden shoes he once carved for her when he was a boy, and gave her as a present, had been carefully kept in a drawer ever since. And so they parted.

After Ib's confirmation, he remained at home with his mother, for he had become a clever shoemaker, and in summer managed the farm for her quite alone. His father had been dead some time, and his mother kept no farm servants. Sometimes, but very seldom, he heard of Christina, through a postillion or eel-seller who was passing. But she was well off with the rich innkeeper; and after being confirmed she wrote a letter to her father, in which was a kind message to Ib and his mother. In this letter, she mentioned that her master and mistress had made her a present of a beautiful new dress, and some nice under-clothes. This was, of course, pleasant news.

One day, in the following spring, there came a knock at the door of the house where Ib's old mother lived; and when they opened it, lo and behold, in stepped the boatman and Christina. She had come to pay them a visit, and to spend the day. A carriage had to come from the Herning hotel to the next village, and she had taken the opportunity to see her friends once more. She looked as elegant as a real lady, and wore a pretty dress, beautifully made on purpose for her. There she stood, in full dress, while Ib wore only his working clothes. He could not utter a word; he could only seize her hand and hold it fast in his own, but he felt too happy and glad to open his lips. Christina, however, was quite at her ease; she talked and talked, and kissed him in the most friendly manner. Even afterwards, when they were left alone, and she asked, "Did you know me again, Ib?" he still stood holding her hand, and said at last, "You are become quite a grand lady, Christina, and I am only a rough working man; but I have often thought of you and of old times." Then they wandered up the great ridge, and looked across the stream to the heath, where the little hills were covered with the flowering broom. Ib said nothing; but before the time came for them to part, it became quite clear to him that Christina must be his wife: had they not even in childhood been called the betrothed? To him it seemed as if they were really engaged to each other, although not a word had been spoken on the subject. They had only a few more hours to remain together, for Christina was obliged to return that evening to the neighboring village, to be ready for the carriage which was to start the next morning early for Herning. Ib and her father accompanied her to the village. It was a fine moonlight evening; and when they arrived, Ib stood holding Christina's hand in his, as if he could not let her go. His eyes brightened, and the words he uttered came with hesitation from his lips, but from the deepest recesses of his heart: "Christina, if you have not become too grand, and if you can be contented to live in my mother's house as my wife, we will be married some day. But we can wait for a while."

"Oh yes," she replied; "let us wait a little longer, Ib. I can trust you, for I believe that I do love you. But let me think it over." Then he kissed her lips; and so they parted.

On the way home, Ib told the boatman that he and Christina were as good as engaged to each other; and the boatman found out that he had always expected it would be so, and went home with Ib that evening, and remained the night in the farmhouse; but nothing further was said of the engagement. During the next year, two letters passed between Ib and Christina. They were signed, "Faithful till death;" but at the end of that time, one day the boatman came over to see Ib, with a kind greeting from Christina. He had something else to say, which made him hesitate in a strange manner. At last it came out that Christina, who had grown a very pretty girl, was more lucky than ever. She was courted and admired by every one; but her master's son, who had been home on a visit, was so much pleased with Christina that he wished to marry her. He had a very good situation in an office at Copenhagen, and as she had also taken a liking for him, his parents were not unwilling to consent. But Christina, in her heart, often thought of Ib, and knew how much he thought of her; so she felt inclined to refuse this good fortune, added the boatman. At first Ib said not a word, but he became as white as the wall, and shook his head gently, and then he spoke, — "Christina must not refuse this good fortune."

"Then will you write a few words to her?" said the boatman.

Ib sat down to write, but he could not get on at all. The words were not what he wished to say, so he tore up the page. The following morning, however, a letter lay ready to be sent to Christina, and the following is what he wrote: —

"The letter written by you to your father I have read, and see from it that you are prosperous in everything, and that still better fortune is in store for you. Ask your own heart, Christina, and think over carefully what awaits you if you take me for your husband, for I possess very little in the world. Do not think of me or of my position; think only of your own welfare. You are bound to me by no promises; and if in your heart you have given me one, I release you from it. May every blessing and happiness be poured out upon you, Christina. Heaven will give me the heart's consolation.

Ever your sincere friend, IB."

This letter was sent, and Christina received it in due time. In the course of the following November, her banns were published in the church on the heath, and also in Copenhagen, where the bridegroom lived. She was taken to Copenhagen under the protection of her future mother-in-law, because the bridegroom could not spare time from his numerous occupations for a journey so far into Jutland. On the journey, Christina met her father at one of the villages through which they passed, and here he took leave of her. Very little was said about the matter to Ib, and he did not refer to it; his mother, however, noticed that he had grown very silent and pensive. Thinking as he did of old times, no wonder the three nuts came into his mind which the gypsy woman had given him when a child, and of the two which he had given to Christina. These wishing nuts, after all, had proved true fortune-tellers. One had contained a gilded carriage and noble horses, and the other beautiful clothes; all of these Christina would now have in her new home at Copenhagen. Her part had come true. And for him the nut had contained only black earth. The gypsy woman had said it was the best for him. Perhaps it was, and this also would be fulfilled. He understood the gypsy woman's meaning now. The black earth—the dark grave—was the best thing for him now.

Again years passed away; not many, but they seemed long years to Ib. The old innkeeper and his wife died one after the other; and the whole of their property, many thousand dollars, was inherited by their son. Christina could have the golden carriage now, and plenty of fine clothes. During the two long years which followed, no letter came from Christina to her father; and when at last her father received one from her, it did not speak of prosperity or happiness. Poor Christina! Neither she nor her husband understood how to economize or save, and the riches brought no blessing with them, because they had not asked for it.

Years passed; and for many summers the heath was covered with bloom; in winter the snow rested upon it, and the rough winds blew across the ridge under which stood Ib's sheltered home. One spring day the sun shone brightly, and he was guiding the plough across his field. The ploughshare struck against something which he fancied was a firestone, and then he saw glittering in the earth a splinter of shining metal which the plough had cut from something which gleamed brightly in the furrow. He searched, and found a large golden armlet of superior workmanship, and it was evident that the plough had disturbed a Hun's grave. He searched further, and found more valuable treasures, which Ib showed to the clergyman, who explained their value to him. Then he went to the magistrate, who informed the president of the museum of the discovery, and advised Ib to take the treasures himself to the president.

"You have found in the earth the best thing you could find," said the magistrate.

"The best thing," thought Ib; "the very best thing for me, — and found in the earth! Well, if it really is so, then the gypsy woman was right in her prophecy."

So Ib went in the ferry-boat from Aarhus to Copenhagen. To him who had only sailed once or twice on the river near his own home, this seemed like a voyage on the ocean; and at length he arrived at Copenhagen. The value of the gold he had found was paid to him; it was a large sum — six hundred dollars. Then Ib of the heath went out, and wandered about in the great city.

On the evening before the day he had settled to return with the captain of the passage-boat, Ib lost himself in the streets, and took quite a different turning to the one he wished to follow. He wandered on till he found himself in a poor street of the suburb called Christian's Haven. Not a creature could be seen. At last a very little girl came out of one of the wretched-looking houses, and Ib asked her to tell him the way to the street he wanted; she looked up timidly at him, and began to cry bitterly. He asked her what was the matter; but what she said he could not understand. So he went along the street with her; and as they passed under a lamp, the light fell on the little girl's face. A strange sensation came over Ib, as he caught sight of it. The living, breathing embodiment of Little Christina stood before him, just as he remembered her in the days of her childhood. He followed the child to the wretched house, and ascended the narrow, crazy staircase which led to a little garret in the roof. The air in the room was heavy and stifling, no light was burning, and from one corner came sounds of moaning and sighing. It was the mother of the child who lay there on a miserable bed. With the help of a match, Ib struck a light, and approached her.

"Can I be of any service to you?" he asked. "This little girl brought me up here; but I am a stranger in this city. Are there no neighbors or any one whom I can call?"

Then he raised the head of the sick woman, and smoothed her pillow. He started as he did so. It was Christina of the heath! No one had mentioned her name to Ib for years; it would have disturbed his peace of mind, especially as the reports respecting her were not good. The wealth which her husband had inherited from his parents had made him proud and arrogant. He had given up his certain appointment, and travelled for six months in foreign lands, and, on his return, had lived in great style, and got into terrible debt. For a time he had trembled on the high pedestal on which he had placed himself, till at last he toppled over, and ruin came. His numerous merry companions, and the visitors at his table, said it served him right, for he had kept house like a madman. One morning his corpse was found in the canal. The cold hand of death had already touched the heart of Christina. Her youngest child, looked for in the midst of prosperity, had sunk into the grave when only a few weeks old; and at last Christina herself became sick unto death, and lay, forsaken and dying, in a miserable room, amid poverty she might have borne in her younger days, but which was now more painful to her from the luxuries to which she had lately been accustomed. It was her eldest child, also a Little Christina, whom Ib had followed to her home, where she suffered hunger and poverty with her mother.

"It makes me unhappy to think that I shall die, and leave this poor child," sighed she. "Oh, what will become of her?" She could say no more.

Then Ib brought out another match, and lighted a piece of candle which he found in the room, and it threw a glimmering light over the wretched dwelling. Ib looked at the little girl, and thought of Christina in her young days. For her sake, could he not love this child, who was a stranger to him? As he thus reflected, the dying woman opened her eyes, and gazed at him. Did she recognize him? He never knew; for not another word escaped her lips.

    *   *   *   *   *   *   *

In the forest by the river Gudenau, not far from the heath, and beneath the ridge of land, stood the little farm, newly painted and whitewashed. The air was heavy and dark; there were no blossoms on the heath; the autumn winds whirled the yellow leaves towards the boatman's hut, in which strangers dwelt; but the little farm stood safely sheltered beneath the tall trees and the high ridge. The turf blazed brightly on the hearth, and within was sunlight, the sparkling light from the sunny eyes of a child; the birdlike tones from the rosy lips ringing like the song of a lark in spring. All was life and joy. Little Christina sat on Ib's knee. Ib was to her both father and mother; her own parents had vanished from her memory, as a dream-picture vanishes alike from childhood and age. Ib's house was well and prettily furnished; for he was a prosperous man now, while the mother of the little girl rested in the churchyard at Copenhagen, where she had died in poverty. Ib had money now — money which had come to him out of the black earth; and he had Christina for his own, after all.

UNDER THE WILLOW-TREE

THE region round the little town of Kjöge is very bleak and cold. The town lies on the sea shore, which is always beautiful; but here it might be more beautiful than it is, for on every side the fields are flat, and it is a long way to the forest. But when persons reside in a place and get used to it, they can always find something beautiful in it, — something for which they long, even in the most charming spot in the world which is not home. It must be owned that there are in the outskirts of the town some humble gardens on the banks of a little stream that runs on towards the sea, and in summer these gardens look very pretty. Such indeed was the opinion of two little children, whose parents were neighbors, and who played in these gardens, and forced their way from one garden to the other through the gooseberry-bushes that divided them. In one of the gardens grew an elder-tree, and in the other an old willow, under which the children were very fond of playing. They had permission to do so, although the tree stood close by the stream, and they might easily have fallen into the water; but the eye of God watches over the little ones, otherwise they would never be safe. At the same time, these children were very careful not to go too near the water; indeed, the boy was so afraid of it, that in the summer, while the other children were splashing about in the sea, nothing could entice him to join them. They jeered and laughed at him, and he was obliged to bear it all as patiently as he could. Once the neighbor's little girl, Joanna, dreamed that she was sailing in a boat, and the boy—Knud was his name—waded out in the water to join her, and the water came up to his neck, and at last closed over his head, and in a moment he had disappeared. When little Knud heard this dream, it seemed as if he could not bear the mocking and jeering again; how could he dare to go into the water now, after Joanna's dream! He never would do it, for this dream always satisfied him. The parents of these children, who were poor, often sat together while Knud and Joanna played in the gardens or in the road. Along this road a row of willow-trees had been planted to separate it from a ditch on one side of it. They were not very handsome trees, for the tops had been cut off; however, they were intended for use, and not for show. The old willow-tree in the garden was much handsomer, and therefore the children were very fond of sitting under it. The town had a large market-place; and at the fair-time there would be whole rows, like streets, of tents and booths containing silks and ribbons, and toys and cakes, and everything that could be wished for. There were crowds of people, and sometimes the weather would be rainy, and splash with moisture the woollen jackets of the peasants; but it did not destroy the beautiful fragrance of the honey-cakes and gingerbread with which one booth was filled; and the best of it was, that the man who sold these cakes always lodged during the fair-time with little Knud's parents. So every now and then he had a present of gingerbread, and of course Joanna always had a share. And, more delightful still, the gingerbread seller knew all sorts of things to tell and could even relate stories about his own gingerbread. So one evening he told them a story that made such a deep impression on the children that they never forgot it; and therefore I think we may as well hear it too, for it is not very long.

"Once upon a time," said he, "there lay on my counter two gingerbread cakes, one in the shape of a man wearing a hat, the other of a maiden without a bonnet. Their faces were on the side that was uppermost, for on the other side they looked very different. Most people have a best side to their characters, which they take care to show to the world. On the left, just where the heart is, the gingerbread man had an almond stuck in to represent it, but the maiden was honey cake all over. They were placed on the counter as samples, and after lying there a long time they at last fell in love with each other; but neither of them spoke of it to the other, as they should have done if they expected anything to follow. 'He is a man, he ought to speak the first word,' thought the gingerbread maiden; but she felt quite happy—she was sure that her love was returned. But his thoughts were far more ambitious, as the thoughts of a man often are. He dreamed that he was a real street boy, that he possessed four real pennies, and that he had bought the gingerbread lady, and ate her up. And so they lay on the counter for days and weeks, till they grew hard and dry; but the thoughts of the maiden became ever more tender and womanly. 'Ah well, it is enough for me that I have been able to live on the same counter with him,' said she one day; when suddenly, 'crack,' and she broke in two. 'Ah,' said the gingerbread man to himself, 'if she had only known of my love, she would have kept together a little longer.' And here they both are, and that is their history," said the cake man. "You think the history of their lives and their silent love, which never came to anything, very remarkable; and there they are for you." So saying, he gave Joanna the gingerbread man, who was still quite whole—and to Knud the broken maiden; but the children had been so much impressed by the story, that they had not the heart to eat the lovers up.

The next day they went into the churchyard, and took the two cake figures with them, and sat down under the church wall, which was covered with luxuriant ivy in summer and winter, and looked as if hung with rich tapestry. They stuck up the two gingerbread figures in the sunshine among the green leaves, and then told the story, and all about the silent love which came to nothing, to a group of children. They called it, "love," because the story was so lovely, and the other children had the same opinion. But when they turned to look at the gingerbread pair, the broken maiden was gone! A great boy, out of wickedness, had eaten her up. At first the children cried about it; but afterwards, thinking very probably that the poor lover ought not to be left alone in the world, they ate him up too: but they never forgot the story.

The two children still continued to play together by the elder-tree, and under the willow; and the little maiden sang beautiful songs, with a voice that was as clear as a bell. Knud, on the contrary, had not a note of music in him, but knew the words of the songs, and that of course is something. The people of Kjöge, and even the rich wife of the man who kept the fancy shop, would stand and listen while Joanna was singing, and say, "She has really a very sweet voice."

Those were happy days; but they could not last forever. The neighbors were separated, the mother of the little girl was dead, and her father had thoughts of marrying again and of residing in the capital, where he had been promised a very lucrative appointment as messenger. The neighbors parted with tears, the children wept sadly; but their parents promised that they should write to each other at least once a year.

After this, Knud was bound apprentice to a shoemaker; he was growing a great boy, and could not be allowed to run wild any longer. Besides, he was going to be confirmed. Ah, how happy he would have been on that festal day in Copenhagen with little Joanna; but he still remained at Kjöge, and had never seen the great city, though the town is not five miles from it. But far across the bay, when the sky was clear, the towers of Copenhagen could be seen; and on the day of his confirmation he saw distinctly the golden cross on the principal church glittering in the sun. How often his thoughts were with Joanna! but did she think of him? Yes. About Christmas came a letter from her father to Knud's parents, which stated that they were going on very well in Copenhagen, and mentioning particularly that Joanna's beautiful voice was likely to bring her a brilliant fortune in the future. She was engaged to sing at a concert, and she had already earned money by singing, out of which she sent her dear neighbors at Kjöge a whole dollar, for them to make merry on Christmas eve, and they were to drink her health. She had herself added this in a postscript, and in the same postscript she wrote, "Kind regards to Knud."

The good neighbors wept, although the news was so pleasant; but they wept tears of joy. Knud's thoughts had been daily with Joanna, and now he knew that she also had thought of him; and the nearer the time came for his apprenticeship to end, the clearer did it appear to him that he loved Joanna,

UNDER THE WILLOW-TREE

and that she must be his wife; and a smile came on his lips at the thought, and at one time he drew the thread so fast as he worked, and pressed his foot so hard against the knee strap, that he ran the awl into his finger; but what did he care for that? He was determined not to play the dumb lover as both the gingerbread cakes had done; the story was a good lesson to him.

At length he become a journeyman; and then, for the first time, he prepared for a journey to Copenhagen, with his knapsack packed and ready. A master was expecting him there, and he thought of Joanna, and how glad she would be to see him. She was now seventeen, and he nineteen years old. He wanted to buy a gold ring for her in Kjöge, but then he recollected how far more beautiful such things would be in Copenhagen. So he took leave of his parents, and on a rainy day, late in the autumn, wandered forth on foot from the town of his birth. The leaves were falling from the trees; and, by the time he arrived at his new master's in the great metropolis, he was wet through. On the following Sunday he intended to pay his first visit to Joanna's father. When the day came, the new journeyman's clothes were brought out, and a new hat, which he had brought in Kjöge. The hat became him very well, for hitherto he had only worn a cap. He found the house that he sought easily, but had to mount so many stairs that he became quite giddy; it surprised him to find how people lived over one another in this dreadful town.

On entering a room in which everything denoted prosperity, Joanna's father received him very kindly. The new wife was a stranger to him, but she shook hands with him, and offered him coffee.

"Joanna will be very glad to see you," said her father. "You have grown quite a nice young man, you shall see her presently; she is a good child, and is the joy of my heart, and, please God, she will continue to be so; she has her own room now, and pays us rent for it." And the father knocked quite politely at a door, as if he were a stranger, and then they both went in. How pretty everything was in that room! a more beautiful apartment could not be found in the whole town of Kjöge; the queen herself could scarcely be better accommodated. There were carpets, and rugs, and window curtains hanging to the ground. Pictures and flowers were scattered about. There was a velvet chair, and a looking-glass against the wall, into which a person might be in danger of stepping, for it was as large as a door. All this Knud saw at a glance, and yet, in truth, he saw nothing but Joanna. She was quite grown up, and very different from what Knud had fancied her, and a great deal more beautiful. In all Kjöge there was not a girl like her; and how graceful she looked, although her glance at first was odd, and not familiar; but for a moment only, then she rushed towards him as if she would have kissed him; she did not, however, although she was very near it. Yes, she really was joyful at seeing the friend of her childhood once more, and the tears even stood in her eyes. Then she asked so many questions about Knud's parents, and everything, even to the elder-tree and the willow, which she called "elder-mother and willow-father," as if they had been human beings; and so, indeed, they might be, quite as much as the gingerbread cakes. Then she talked about them, and the story of their silent love, and how they lay on the counter together and split in two; and then she laughed heartily; but the blood rushed into Knud's cheeks, and his heart beat quickly. Joanna was not proud at all; he noticed that through her he was invited by her parents to remain the whole evening with them, and she poured out the tea and gave him a cup herself;

and afterwards she took a book and read aloud to them, and it seemed to Knud as if the story was all about himself and his love, for it agreed so well with his own thoughts. And then she sang a simple song, which, through her singing, became a true story, and as if she poured forth the feelings of her own heart.

"Oh," he thought, "she knows I am fond of her." The tears he could not restrain rolled down his cheeks, and he was unable to utter a single word; it seemed as if he had been struck dumb.

When he left, she pressed his hand, and said, "You have a kind heart, Knud: remain always as you are now." What an evening of happiness this had been; to sleep after it was impossible, and Knud did not sleep.

At parting, Joanna's father had said, "Now, you won't quite forget us; you must not let the whole winter go by without paying us another visit;" so that Knud felt himself free to go again the following Sunday evening, and so he did. But every evening after working hours—and they worked by candle-light then—he walked out into the town, and through the street in which Joanna lived, to look up at her window. It was almost always lighted up; and one evening he saw the shadow of her face quite plainly on the window blind; that was a glorious evening for him. His master's wife did not like his always going out in the evening, idling, wasting time, as she called it, and she shook her head.

But his master only smiled, and said, "He is a young man, my dear, you know."

"On Sunday I shall see her," said Knud to himself, "and I will tell her that I love her with my whole heart and soul, and that she must be my little wife. I know I am now only a poor journeyman shoemaker, but I will work and strive, and become a master in time. Yes, I will speak to her; nothing comes from silent love. I learnt that from the gingerbread-cake story."

Sunday came, but when Knud arrived, they were all unfortunately invited out to spend the evening, and were obliged to tell him so.

Joanna pressed his hand, and said, "Have you ever been to the theatre? you must go once; I sing there on Wednesday, and if you have time on that day, I will send you a ticket; my father knows where your master lives." How kind this was of her! And on Wednesday, about noon, Knud received a sealed packet with no address, but the ticket was inside; and in the evening Knud went, for the first time in his life, to a theatre. And what did he see? He saw Joanna, and how beautiful and charming she looked! He certainly saw her being married to a stranger, but that was all in the play, and only a pretence; Knud well knew that. She could never have the heart, he thought, to send him a ticket to go and see it, if it had been real. So he looked on, and when all the people applauded and clapped their hands, he shouted "hurrah." He could see that even the king smiled at Joanna, and seemed delighted with her singing. How small Knud felt; but then he loved her so dearly, and thought she loved him, and the man must speak the first word, as the gingerbread maiden had thought. Ah, how much there was for him in that childish story. As soon as Sunday arrived, he went again, and felt as if he were about to enter on holy ground. Joanna was alone to welcome him, nothing could be more fortunate.

"I am so glad you are come," she said. "I was thinking of sending my father for you, but I had a presentiment that you would be here this evening. The fact is, I wanted to tell you that I am going to France. I shall start on Friday. It is necessary for me to go there, if I wish to become a first-rate performer."

Poor Knud! it seemed to him as if the whole room was whirling round with him. His courage failed, and he felt as if his heart would burst. He kept down the tears, but it was easy to see how sorrowful he was.

"You honest, faithful soul," she exclaimed; and the words loosened Knud's tongue, and he told her how truly he had loved her, and that she must be his wife; and as he said this, he saw Joanna change color, and turn pale. She let his hand fall, and said, earnestly and mournfully, "Knud, do not make yourself and me unhappy. I will always be a good sister to you, one in whom you can trust; but I can never be anything more." And she drew her white hand over his burning forehead, and said, "God gives strength to bear a great deal, if we only strive ourselves to endure."

At this moment her stepmother came into the room, and Joanna said quickly, "Knud is so unhappy, because I am going away;" and it appeared as if they had only been talking of her journey. "Come, be a man," she added, placing her hand on his shoulder; "you are still a child, and you must be good and reasonable, as you were when we were both children, and played together under the willow-tree."

Knud listened, but he felt as if the world had slid out of its course. His thoughts were like a loose thread fluttering to and fro in the wind. He stayed, although he could not tell whether she had asked him to do so. But she was kind and gentle to him; she poured out his tea, and sang to him; but the song had not the old tone in it, although it was wonderfully beautiful, and made his heart feel ready to burst. And then he rose to go. He did not offer his hand, but she seized it, and said —

"Will you not shake hands with your sister at parting, my old playfellow?" and she smiled through the tears that were rolling down her cheeks. Again she repeated the word "brother," which was a great consolation certainly; and thus they parted.

She sailed to France, and Knud wandered about the muddy streets of Copenhagen. The other journeymen in the shop asked him why he looked so gloomy, and wanted him to go and amuse himself with them, as he was still a young man. So he went with them to a dancing-room. He saw many handsome girls there, but none like Joanna; and here, where he thought to forget her, she was more life-like before his mind than ever. "God gives us strength to bear much, if we try to do our best," she had said; and as he thought of this, a devout feeling came into his mind, and he folded his hands. Then, as the violins played and the girls danced round the room, he started; for it seemed to him as if he were in a place where he ought not to have brought Joanna, for she was here with him in his heart; and so he went out at once. As he went through the streets at a quick pace, he passed the house where she used to live; it was all dark, empty, and lonely. But the world went on its course, and Knud was obliged to go on too.

Winter came; the water was frozen, and everything seemed buried in a cold grave. But when spring returned, and the first steamer prepared to sail, Knud was seized with a longing to wander forth into the world, but not to France. So he packed his knapsack, and travelled through Germany, going from town to town, but finding neither rest or peace. It was not till he arrived at the glorious old town of Nuremberg that he gained the mastery over himself, and rested his weary feet; and here he remained.

Nuremberg is a wonderful old city, and looks as if it had been cut out of an old picture-book. The streets seem to have arranged themselves according to their own fancy, and as if the houses objected to stand in rows or rank and file. Gables, with little towers, ornamented columns, and statues, can be seen even to the city gate; and from the singular-shaped roofs, waterspouts, formed like dragons, or long lean dogs, extend far across to the middle of the street. Here, in the market-place, stood Knud, with his knapsack on his back, close to one of the old fountains which are so beautifully adorned with figures, scriptural and historical, and which spring up between the sparkling jets of water. A pretty servant-maid was just filling her pails, and she gave Knud a refreshing draught; she had a handful of roses, and she gave him one, which appeared to him like a good omen for the future. From a neighboring church came the sounds of music, and the familiar tones reminded him of the organ at home at Kjöge; so he passed into the great cathedral. The sunshine streamed through the painted glass windows, and between two lofty slender pillars. His thoughts became prayerful, and calm peace rested on his soul. He next sought and found a good master in Nuremberg, with whom he stayed and learnt the German language.

The old moat round the town had been converted into a number of little kitchen gardens; but the high walls, with their heavy-looking towers, are still standing. Inside these walls the ropemaker twisted his ropes along a walk built like a gallery, and in the cracks and crevices of the walls elderbushes grow and stretch their green boughs over the small houses which stand below. In one of these houses lived the master for whom Knud worked; and over the little garret window where he sat, the elder-tree waved its branches. Here he dwelt through one summer and winter, but when spring came again, he could endure it no longer. The elder was in blossom, and its fragrance was so home-like, that he fancied himself back again in the gardens of Kjöge. So Knud left his master, and went to work for another who lived farther in the town, where no elder grew. His workshop was quite close to one of the old stone bridges, near to a water-mill, round which the roaring stream rushed and foamed always, yet restrained by the neighboring houses, whose old, decayed balconies hung over, and seemed ready to fall into the water. Here grew no elder; here was not even a flower-pot, with its little green plant; but just opposite the workshop stood a great willow-tree, which seemed to hold fast to the house for fear of being carried away by the water. It stretched its branches over the stream just as those of the willow-tree in the garden at Kjöge had spread over the river. Yes, he had indeed gone from elder-mother to willow-father. There was a something about the tree here, especially in the moonlight nights, that went direct to his heart; yet it was not in reality the moonlight, but the old tree itself. However, he could not endure it: and why? Ask the willow, ask the blossoming elder! At all events, he bade farewell to Nuremberg and journeyed onwards. He never spoke of Joanna to any one; his sorrow was hidden in his heart. The old childish story of the two cakes had a deep meaning for him. He understood now why the gingerbread man had a bitter almond in his left side; his was the feeling of bitterness, and Joanna, so mild and friendly, was represented by the honeycake maiden. As he thought upon all this, the strap of his knapsack pressed across his chest so that he could hardly breathe; he loosened it, but gained no relief. He saw but half the world around him; the other half he carried with him in his inward thoughts; and this is the condition in which he left Nuremberg. Not till he caught sight of the lofty mountains did the world appear more free to him; his thoughts were attracted to outer objects, and tears came into his eyes. The Alps appeared to him like the wings of earth folded together; unfolded, they would display the variegated pictures of dark woods, foaming waters, spreading clouds, and masses of snow. "At the last day," thought he, "the earth will unfold its great wings, and soar upwards to the skies, there to burst like a soap-bubble in the radiant glance of the Deity. Oh," sighed he, "that the last day were come!"

Silently he wandered on through the country of the Alps, which seemed to him like a fruit garden, covered with soft turf. From the wooden balconies of the houses the young lacemakers nodded as he passed. The summits of the mountains glowed in the red evening sunset, and the green lakes beneath the dark trees reflected the glow. Then he thought of the sea coast by the bay Kjöge, with a longing in his heart that was, however, without pain. There, where the Rhine rolls onward like a great billow, and dissolves itself into snowflakes, where glistening clouds are ever changing as if here was the place of their creation, while the rainbow flutters about them like a many-colored ribbon, there did Knud think of the water-mill at Kjöge, with its rushing, foaming waters. Gladly would he have remained in the quiet Rhenish town, but there were too many elders and willow-trees.

So he travelled onwards, over a grand, lofty chain of mountains, over rugged, rocky precipices, and along roads that hung on the mountain's side like a swallow's nest. The waters foamed in the depths below him. The clouds lay beneath him. He wandered on, treading upon Alpine roses, thistles, and snow, with the summer sun shining upon him, till at length he bid farewell to the lands of the north. Then he passed on under the shade of blooming chest-nut-trees, through vineyards, and fields of Indian corn, till conscious that the mountains were as a wall between him and his early recollections; and he wished it to be so.

Before him lay a large and splendid city, called Milan, and here he found a German master who engaged him as a workman. The master and his wife, in whose workshop he was employed, were an old, pious couple; and the two old people became quite fond of the quiet journeyman, who spoke but little, but worked more, and led a pious, Christian life; and even to himself it seemed as if God had removed the heavy burden from his heart. His greatest pleasure was to climb, now and then, to the roof of the noble church, which was built of white marble. The pointed towers, the decorated and open cloisters, the stately columns, the white statues which smiled upon him from every corner and porch and arch, — all, even the church itself, seemed to him to have been formed from the snow of his native land. Above him was the blue sky; below him, the city and the wide-spreading plains of Lombardy; and towards the north, the lofty mountains, covered with perpetual snow. And then he thought of the church of Kjöge, with its red, ivy-clad walls, but he had no longing to go there; here, beyond the mountains, he would die and be buried.

Three years had passed away since he left his home; one year of that time he had dwelt at Milan.

One day his master took him into the town; not to the circus in which riders performed, but to the opera, a large building, itself a sight well worth seeing. The seven tiers of boxes, which reached from the ground to a dizzy height, near the ceiling, were hung with rich, silken curtains; and in them were seated elegantly-dressed ladies, with bouquets of flowers in their hands. The gentlemen were also in full dress, and many of them wore decorations of gold and silver. The place was so brilliantly lighted that it seemed like sunshine, and glorious music rolled through the building. Everything looked more beautiful than in the theatre at Copenhagen, but then Joanna had been there, and—could it be? Yes—it was like magic,—she was here also: for, when the curtain rose, there stood Joanna, dressed in silk and gold, and with a golden crown upon her head. She sang, he thought, as only an angel could sing; and then she stepped forward to the front and smiled, as only Joanna could smile, and looked directly at Knud. Poor Knud! he seized his master's hand, and cried out loud, "Joanna," but no one heard him, excepting his master, for the music sounded above everything.

"Yes, yes, it is Joanna," said his master; and he drew forth a printed bill, and pointed to her name, which was there in full. Then it was not a dream. All the audience applauded her, and threw wreaths of flowers at her; and every time she went away they called for her again, so that she was always coming and going. In the street the people crowded round her carriage, and drew it away themselves without the horses. Knud was in the foremost row, and shouted as joyously as the rest; and when the carriage stopped before a brilliantly lighted house, Knud placed himself close to the door of her carriage. It flew open, and she stepped out; the light fell upon her dear face, and he could see that she smiled as she thanked them, and appeared quite overcome. Knud looked straight in her face, and she looked at him, but she did not recognize him. A man, with a glittering star on his breast, gave her his arm, and people said the two were engaged to be married. Then Knud went home and packed up his knapsack; he felt he must return to the home of his childhood, to the elder-tree and the willow. "Ah, under that willow-tree!" A man may live a whole life in one single hour.

The old couple begged him to remain, but words were useless. In vain they reminded him that winter was coming, and that the snow had already fallen on the mountains. He said he could easily follow the track of the closely-moving carriages, for which a path must be kept clear, and with nothing but his knapsack on his back, and leaning on his stick, he could step along briskly. So he turned his steps to the mountains, ascended one side and descended the other, still going northward till his strength began to fail, and not a house or village could be seen. The stars shone in the sky above him, and down in the valley lights glittered like stars, as if another sky were beneath him; but his head was dizzy and his feet stumbled, and he felt ill. The lights in the valley grew brighter and brighter, and more numerous, and he could see them moving to and fro, and then he understood that there must be a village in the distance; so he exerted his failing strength to reach it, and at length obtained shelter in a humble lodging. He remained there that night and the whole of the following day, for his body required rest and refreshment, and in the valley there was rain and a thaw. But early in the morning of the third day, a man came with an organ and played one of the melodies of home; and after that Knud could remain there no longer, so he started again on his journey toward the north. He travelled for many days with hasty steps, as if he were trying to reach home before all whom he remembered should die; but he spoke to no one of this longing. No one would have believed or understood this sorrow of his heart, the deepest that can be felt by human nature. Such grief is not for the world; it is not entertaining even to friends, and poor Knud had no friends; he was a stranger, wandering through strange lands to his home in the north.

He was walking one evening through the public roads, the country around him was flatter, with fields and meadows, the air had a frosty feeling. A willow-tree grew by the roadside, everything reminded him of home. He felt very tired; so he sat down under the tree, and very soon began to nod, then his eyes closed in sleep. Yet still he seemed conscious that the willow-tree was stretching its branches over him; in his dreaming state the tree appeared like a strong, old man — the "willow-father" himself, who had taken his tired son up in his arms to carry him back to the land of home, to the garden of his childhood, on the bleak open shores of Kjöge. And then he dreamed that it was really the willow-tree itself from Kjöge, which had travelled out in the world to seek him, and now had found him and carried him back into the little garden on the banks of the streamlet; and there stood Joanna, in all her splendor, with the golden crown on her head, as he had last seen her, to welcome him back. And then there appeared before him two remarkable shapes, which looked much more like human beings than when he had seen them in his childhood; they were changed, but he remembered that they were the two gingerbread cakes, the man and the woman, who had shown their best sides to the world and looked so good.

"We thank you," they said to Knud, "for you have loosened our tongues; we have learnt from you that thoughts should be spoken freely, or nothing will come of them; and now something has come of our thoughts, for we are engaged to be married." Then they walked away, hand-in-hand, through the streets of Kjöge, looking very respectable on the best side, which they were quite right to show. They turned their steps to the church, and Knud and Joanna followed them, also walking hand-in-hand; there stood the church, as of old, with its red walls, on which the green ivy grew.

The great church door flew open wide, and as they walked up the broad aisle, soft tones of music sounded from the organ. "Our master first," said the gingerbread pair, making room for Knud and Joanna. As they knelt at the altar, Joanna bent her head over him, and cold, icy tears fell on his face from her eyes. They were indeed tears of ice, for her heart was melting towards him through his strong love, and as her tears fell on his burning cheeks he awoke. He was still sitting under the willow-tree in a strange land, on a cold winter evening, with snow and hail falling from the clouds, and beating upon his face.

"That was the most delightful hour of my life," said he, "although it was only a dream. Oh, let me dream again." Then he closed his eyes once more, and slept and dreamed.

Towards morning there was a great fall of snow; the wind drifted it over him, but he still slept on. The villagers came forth to go to church; by the roadside they found a workman seated, but he was dead! frozen to death under a willow-tree.

THE SHEPHERD'S STORY OF THE BOND
OF FRIENDSHIP

THE little dwelling in which we lived was of clay, but the door-posts were columns of fluted marble, found near the spot on which it stood. The roof sloped nearly to the ground. It was at this time dark, brown, and ugly, but had originally been formed of blooming olive and laurel branches, brought from beyond the mountains. The house was situated in a narrow gorge, whose rocky walls rose to a perpendicular height, naked and black, while round their summits clouds often hung, looking like white living figures. Not a singing bird was ever heard there, neither did men dance to the sound of the pipe. The spot was one sacred to olden times; even its name recalled a memory of the days when it was called "Delphi." Then the summits of the dark, sacred mountains were covered with snow, and the highest, mount Parnassus, glowed longest in the red evening light. The brook which rolled from it near our house, was also sacred. How well I can remember every spot in that deep, sacred solitude! A fire had been kindled in the midst of the hut, and while the hot ashes lay there red and glowing, the bread was baked in them. At times the snow would be piled so high around our hut as almost to hide it, and then my mother appeared most cheerful. She would hold my head between her hands, and sing the songs she never sang at other times, for the Turks, our masters, would not allow it. She sang, —

"On the summit of mount Olympus, in a forest of dwarf firs, lay an old stag. His eyes were heavy with tears, and glittering with colors like dewdrops; and there came by a roebuck, and said, 'What ailest thee, that thou weepest blue and red tears?' And the stag answered, 'The Turk has come to our city; he has wild dogs for the chase, a goodly pack.' 'I will drive them away across the islands!' cried the young roebuck; 'I will drive them away across the islands into the deep sea.' But before evening the roebuck was slain, and before night the hunted stag was dead."

And when my mother sang thus, her eyes would become moist; and on the long eyelashes were tears, but she concealed them and watched the black bread baking in the ashes. Then I would clench my fist, and cry, "We will kill these Turks!" But she repeated the words of the song, "I will drive them across the islands to the deep sea; but before evening came the roebuck was slain, and before the night the hunted stag was dead."

We had been lonely in our hut for several days and nights when my father came home. I knew he would bring me some shells from the gulf of Lepanto, or perhaps a knife with a shining blade. This time he brought, under his sheep-skin cloak, a little child, a little half-naked girl. She was wrapped in a fur; but when this was taken off, and she lay in my mother's lap, three silver coins were found fastened in her dark hair; they were all her possessions. My father told us that the child's parents had been killed by the Turks, and he talked so much about them that I dreamed of Turks all night. He himself had been wounded, and my mother bound up his arm. It was a deep wound, and the thick sheep-skin cloak was stiff with congealed blood. The little maiden was to be my sister. How pretty and bright she looked: even my mother's eyes were not more gentle than hers. Anastasia, as she was called, was to be my sister, because her father had been united to mine by an old custom, which we still follow. They had sworn brotherhood in their youth, and the most beautiful and virtuous maiden in the neighborhood was chosen to perform the act of consecration upon this bond of friendship. So now this little girl was my sister. She sat in my lap, and I brought her flowers, and feathers from the birds of the mountain. We drank together of the waters of Parnassus, and dwelt for many years beneath the laurel roof of the hut, while, winter after winter, my mother sang her song of the stag who shed red tears. But as yet I did not understand that the sorrows of my own countrymen were mirrored in those tears.

One day there came to our hut Franks, men from a far country, whose dress was different to ours. They had tents and beds with them, carried by horses; and they were accompanied by more than twenty Turks, all armed with swords and muskets. These Franks were friends of the Pacha, and had letters from him, commanding an escort for them. They only came to see our mountain, to ascend Parnassus amid the snow and clouds, and to look at the strange black rocks which raised their steep sides near our hut. They could not find room in the hut, nor endure the smoke that rolled along the ceiling till it found its way out at the low door; so they pitched their tents on a small space outside our dwelling. Roasted lambs and birds were brought forth, and strong, sweet wine, of which the Turks are forbidden to partake.

When they departed, I accompanied them for some distance, carrying my little sister Anastasia, wrapped in a goat-skin, on my back. One of the Frankish gentlemen made me stand in front of a rock, and drew us both as we stood there, so that we looked like one creature. I did not think of it then, but Anastasia and I were really one. She was always sitting on my lap, or riding in the goat-skin on my back; and in my dreams she always appeared to me.

Two nights after this, other men, armed with knives and muskets, came into our tent. They were Albanians, brave men, my mother told me. They only stayed a short time. My sister Anastasia sat on the knee of one of them; and when they were gone, she had not three, but two silver coins in her hair — one had disappeared. They wrapped tobacco in strips of paper, and smoked it; and I remember they were uncertain as to the road they ought to take. But they were obliged to go at last, and my father went with them. Soon after, we heard the sound of firing. The noise continued, and presently soldiers rushed into out hut, and took my mother and myself and Anastasia prisoners. They declared that we had entertained robbers, and that my father had acted as their guide, and therefore we must now go with them. The corpses of the robbers, and my father's corpse, were brought into the hut. I saw my poor dead father, and cried till I fell asleep. When I awoke, I found myself in a prison; but the room was not worse than our own in the hut. They gave me onions and musty wine from a tarred cask; but we were not accustomed to much better fare at home. How long we were kept in prison, I do not know; but many days and nights passed by. We were set free about Easter-time. I carried Anastasia on my back, and we walked very slowly; for my mother was very weak, and it is a long way to the sea, to the Gulf of Lepanto.

On our arrival, we entered a church, in which there were beautiful pictures in golden frames. They were pictures of angels, fair and bright; and yet our little Anastasia looked equally beautiful, as it seemed to me. In the centre of the floor stood a coffin filled with roses. My mother told me it was the Lord Jesus Christ who was represented by these roses. Then the priest announced, "Christ is risen," and all the people greeted each other. Each one carried a burning taper in his hand, and one was given to me, as well as to little Anastasia. The music sounded, and the people left the church hand-in-hand, with joy and gladness. Outside, the women were roasting the paschal lamb. We were invited to partake; and as I sat by the fire, a boy, older than myself, put his arms round my neck, and kissed me, and said, "Christ is risen." And thus it was that for the first time I met Aphtanides.

My mother could make fishermen's nets, for which there was a great demand here in the bay; and we lived a long time by the side of the sea, the beautiful sea, that had a taste like tears, and in its colors reminded me of the stag that wept red tears; for sometimes its waters were red, and sometimes green or blue. Aphtanides knew how to manage our boat, and I often sat in it, with my little Anastasia, while it glided on through the water, swift as a bird flying through the air. Then, when the sun set, how beautifully, deeply blue, would be the tint on the mountains, one rising above the other in the far distance, and the summit of mount Parnassus rising above them all like a glorious crown. Its top glittered in the evening rays like molten gold, and it seemed as if the light came from within it; for long after the sun had sunk beneath the horizon, the mountain-top would glow in the clear, blue sky. The white aquatic birds skimmed the surface of the water in their flight, and all was calm and still as amid the black rocks at Delphi. I lay on my back in the boat, Anastasia leaned against me, while the stars above us glittered more brightly than the lamps in our church. They were the same stars, and in the same position over me as when I used to sit in front of our hut at Delphi, and I had almost begun to fancy I was still there, when suddenly there was a splash in the water—Anastasia had fallen in; but in a moment Aphtanides has sprung in after her, and was now holding her up to me. We dried her clothes as well as we were able, and remained on the water till they were dry; for we did not wish it to be known what a fright we had had, nor the danger which our little adopted sister had incurred, in whose life Aphtanides had now a part.

The summer came, and the burning heat of the sun tinted the leaves of the trees with lines of gold. I thought of our cool mountain-home, and the fresh water that flowed near it; my mother, too, longed for it, and one evening we wandered towards home. How peaceful and silent it was as we walked on through the thick, wild thyme, still fragrant, though the sun had scorched the leaves. Not a single herdsman did we meet, not a solitary hut did we pass; everything appeared lonely and deserted—only a shooting star showed that in the heavens there was yet life. I know not whether the clear, blue atmosphere gleamed with its own light, or if the radiance came from the stars; but we could distinguish quite plainly the outline of the mountains. My mother lighted a fire, and roasted some roots she had brought with her, and I and my little sister slept among the bushes, without fear of the ugly smidraki,* from whose throat issues fire, or of the wolf and the jackal; for my mother sat by us, and I considered her presence sufficient protection.

We reached our old home; but the cottage was in ruins, and we had to build a new one. With the aid of some neighbors, chiefly women, the walls were in a few days erected, and very soon covered with a roof of olive-branches. My mother obtained a living by making bottle-cases of bark and

*According to a superstition among the Greeks, this is a monster produced from the unopened entrails of slaughtered sheep, which have been thrown away in the fields.

skins, and I kept the sheep belonging to the priests, who were sometimes peasants,* while I had for my playfellows Anastasia and the turtles.

Once our beloved Aphtanides paid us a visit. He said he had been longing to see us so much; and he remained with us two whole happy days. A month afterwards he came again to wish us good-bye, and brought with him a large fish for my mother. He told us he was going in a ship to Corfu and Patras, and could relate a great many stories, not only about the fishermen who lived near the gulf of Lepanto, but also of kings and heroes who had once possessed Greece, just as the Turks possess it now.

I have seen a bud on a rose-bush gradually, in the course of a few weeks, unfold its leaves till it became a rose in all its beauty; and, before I was aware of it, I beheld it blooming in rosy loveliness. The same thing had happened to Anastasia. Unnoticed by me, she had gradually become a beautiful maiden, and I was now also a stout, strong youth. The wolf-skins that covered the bed in which my mother and Anastasia slept, had been taken from wolves which I had myself shot.

Years had gone by when, one evening, Aphtanides came in. He had grown tall and slender as a reed, with strong limbs, and a dark, brown skin. He kissed us all, and had so much to tell of what he had seen of the great ocean, of the fortifications at Malta, and of the marvellous sepulchres of Egypt, that I looked up to him with a kind of veneration. His stories were as strange as the legends of the priests of olden times.

"How much you know!" I exclaimed, "and what wonders you can relate?"

"I think what you once told me, the finest of all," he replied; "you told me of a thing that has never been out of my thoughts — of the good old custom of 'the bond of friendship,' — a custom I should like to follow. Brother, let you and I go to church, as your father and Anastasia's father once did. Your sister Anastasia is the most beautiful and most innocent of maidens, and she shall consecrate the deed. No people have such grand old customs as we Greeks."

Anastasia blushed like a young rose, and my mother kissed Aphtanides.

At about two miles from our cottage, where the earth on the hill is sheltered by a few scattered trees, stood the little church, with a silver lamp hanging before the altar. I put on my best clothes, and the white tunic fell in graceful folds over my hips. The red jacket fitted tight and close, the tassel on my Fez cap was of silver, and in my girdle glittered a knife and my pistols. Aphtanides was clad in the blue dress worn by the Greek sailors; on his breast hung a silver medal with the figure of the Virgin Mary, and his scarf was as costly as those worn by rich lords. Every one could see that we were about to perform a solemn ceremony. When we entered the little, unpretending church, the evening sunlight streamed through the open door on the burning lamp, and glittered on the golden picture frames. We knelt down together on the altar steps, and Anastasia drew near and stood beside us. A long, white garment fell in graceful folds over her delicate form, and on her white neck and bosom hung a chain entwined with old and new coins, forming a kind of collar. Her black hair was fastened into a knot, and confined by a headdress formed of gold and silver coins which had been found in an ancient temple.

---

*A peasant who can read is often made a priest; he is addressed as "Most holy sir," and the other peasants kiss the ground on which he has stepped.

No Greek girl had more beautiful ornaments than these. Her countenance glowed, and her eyes were like two stars. We all three offered a silent prayer, and then she said to us, "Will you be friends in life and in death?"

"Yes," we replied.

"Will you each remember to say, whatever may happen, 'My brother is a part of myself; his secret is my secret, my happiness is his; self-sacrifice, patience, everything belongs to me as they do to him?' "

And we again answered, "Yes." Then she joined out hands and kissed us on the forehead, and we again prayed silently. After this a priest came through a door near the altar, and blessed us all three. Then a song was sung by other holy men behind the altar-screen, and the bond of eternal friendship was confirmed. When we arose, I saw my mother standing by the church door, weeping.

How cheerful everything seemed now in our little cottage by the Delphian springs! On the evening before his departure, Aphtanides sat thoughtfully beside me on the slopes of the mountain. His arm was flung around me, and mine was round his neck. We spoke of the sorrows of Greece, and of the men of the country who could be trusted. Every thought of our souls lay clear before us. Presently I seized his hand: "Aphtanides," I exclaimed, "there is one thing still that you must know, — one thing that till now has been a secret between myself and Heaven. My whole soul is filled with love, — with a love stronger than the love I bear to my mother and to thee."

"And whom do you love?" asked Aphtanides. And his face and neck grew red as fire.

"I love Anastasia," I replied.

Then his hand trembled in mine, and he became pale as a corpse. I saw it, I understood the cause, and I believe my hand trembled too. I bent towards him, I kissed his forehead, and whispered, "I have never spoken of this to her, and perhaps she does not love me. Brother, think of this; I have seen her daily, she has grown up beside me, and has become a part of my soul."

"And she *shall* be thine," he exclaimed; "thine! I may not wrong thee, nor will I do so. I also love her, but tomorrow I depart. In a year we will see each other again, but then you will be married; shall it not be so? I have a little gold of my own, it shall be yours. You must and shall take it."

We wandered silently homeward across the mountains. It was late in the evening when we reached my mother's door. Anastasia held the lamp as we entered; my mother was not there. She looked at Aphtanides with a sweet but mournful expression on her face. "To-morrow you are going to leave us," she said. "I am very sorry."

"Sorry!" he exclaimed, and his voice was troubled with a grief as deep as my own. I could not speak; but he seized her hand and said, "Our brother yonder loves you, and is he not dear to you? His very silence now proves his affection."

Anastasia trembled, and burst into tears. Then I saw no one, thought of none, but her. I threw my arms round her, and pressed my lips to hers. As she flung her arms round my neck, the lamp fell to the ground, and we were in darkness, dark as the heart of poor Aphtanides.

Before daybreak he rose, kissed us all, and said "Farewell," and went away. He had given all his money to my mother for us. Anastasia was betrothed to me, and in a few days afterwards she became my wife.

THE JEWISH MAIDEN

IN a charity school, among the children, sat a little Jewish girl. She was a good, intelligent child, and very quick at her lessons; but the Scripture-lesson class she was not allowed to join, for this was a Christian school. During the hour of this lesson, the Jewish girl was allowed to learn her geography, or to work her sum for the next day; and when her geography lesson was perfect, the book remained open before her, but she read not another word, for she sat silently listening to the words of the Christian teacher. He soon became aware that the little one was paying more attention to what he said than most of the other children. "Read your book, Sarah," he said to her gently.

But again and again he saw her dark, beaming eyes fixed upon him; and once, when he asked her a question, she could answer him even better than the other children. She had not only heard, but understood his words, and pondered them in her heart. Her father, a poor but honest man, had placed his daughter at the school on the conditions that she should not be instructed in the Christian faith. But it might have caused confusion, or raised discontent in the minds of the other children if she had been sent out of the room, so she remained; and now it was evident this could not go on. The teacher went to her father, and advised him to remove his daughter from the school, or to allow her to become a Christian. "I cannot any longer be an idle spectator of those beaming eyes, which express such a deep and earnest longing for the words of the gospel," said he.

Then the father burst into tears. "I know very little of the law of my fathers," said he; "but Sarah's mother was firm in her belief as a daughter of Israel, and I vowed to her on her deathbed that our child should never be baptized. I must keep my vow: it is to me even as a covenant with God Himself." And so the little Jewish girl left the Christian school.

Years rolled by. In one of the smallest provincial towns, in a humble household, lived a poor maiden of the Jewish faith, as a servant. Her hair was black as ebony, her eye dark as night, yet full of light and brilliancy so peculiar to the daughters of the east. It was Sarah. The expression in the face of the grown-up maiden was still the same as when, a child, she sat on the schoolroom form listening with thoughtful eyes to the words of the Christian teacher. Every Sunday there sounded forth from a church close by the tones of an organ and the singing of the congregation. The Jewish girl heard them in the house where, industrious and faithful in all things, she performed her household duties. "Thou shalt keep the Sabbath holy," said the voice of the law in her heart; but her Sabbath was a working day among the Christians, which was a great trouble to her. And then as the thought arose in her mind, "Does God reckon by days and hours?" her conscience felt satisfied on this question, and she found it a comfort to her, that on the Christian Sabbath she could have an hour for her own prayers undisturbed. The music and singing of the congregation sounded in her ears while at work in her kitchen, till the place itself became sacred to her. Then she would read in the Old Testament, that treasure and comfort to her people, and it was indeed the only Scriptures she could read. Faithfully in her inmost thoughts had she kept the words of her father to her teacher when she left the school, and the vow he had made

THE JEWISH MAIDEN

to her dying mother that she should never receive Christian baptism. The New Testament must remain to her a sealed book, and yet she knew a great deal of its teaching, and the sound of the gospel truths still lingered among the recollections of her childhood.

One evening she was sitting in a corner of the dining-room, while her master read aloud. It was not the gospel he read, but an old story-book; therefore she might stay and listen to him. The story related that a Hungarian knight, who had been taken prisoner by a Turkish pasha, was most cruelly treated by him. He caused him to be yoked with his oxen to the plough, and driven with blows from the whip till the blood flowed, and he almost sunk with exhaustion and pain. The faithful wife of the knight at home gave up all her jewels, mortgaged her castle and land, and his friends raised large sums to make up the ransom demanded for his release, which was most enormously high. It was collected at last, and the knight released from slavery and misery. Sick and exhausted, he reached home.

Ere long came another summons to a struggle with the foes of Christianity. The still living knight heard the sound; he could endure no more, he had neither peace nor rest. He caused himself to be lifted on his war-horse; the color came into his cheeks, and his strength returned to him again as he went forth to battle and to victory. The very same pasha who had yoked him to the plough, became his prisoner, and was dragged to a dungeon in the castle. But an hour had scarcely passed, when the knight stood before the captive pasha, and inquired, "What do you suppose awaiteth thee?"

"I know," replied the pasha; "retribution."

"Yes, the retribution of a Christian," replied the knight. "The teaching of Christ, the Teacher, commands us to forgive our enemies, to love our neighbors; for God is love. Depart in peace: return to thy home. I give thee back to thy loved ones. But in future be mild and humane to all who are in trouble."

Then the prisoner burst into tears, and exclaimed, "Oh how could I imagine such mercy and forgiveness! I expected pain and torment. It seemed to me so sure that I took poison, which I secretly carried about me; and in a few hours its effects will destroy me. I must die! Nothing can save me! But before I die, explain to me the teaching which is so full of love and mercy, so great and God-like. Oh, that I may hear his teaching, and die a Christian!" And his prayer was granted.

This was the legend which the master read out of the old story-book. Every one in the house who was present listened, and shared the pleasure; but Sarah, the Jewish girl, sitting so still in a corner, felt her heart burn with excitement. Great tears came into her shining dark eyes; and with the same gentle piety with which she had once listened to the gospel while sitting on the form at school, she felt its grandeur now, and the tears rolled down her cheeks. Then the last words of her dying mother rose before her, "Let not my child become a Christian;" and with them sounded in her heart the words of the law, "Honor thy father and thy mother."

"I am not admitted among the Christians," she said; "they mock me as a Jewish girl; the neighbors' boys did so last Sunday when I stood looking in through the open church door at the candles burning on the altar, and listening to the singing. Ever since I sat on the school-bench I have felt the power of Christianity; a power which, like a sunbeam, streams into my heart, however closely I may close my eyes against it. But I will not grieve thee, my mother, in thy grave. I will not be unfaithful to my father's vow. I will not read the Bible of the Christian. I have the God of my fathers, and in Him I will trust."

And again years passed by. Sarah's master died, and his widow found herself in such reduced circumstances that she wished to dismiss her servant maid; but Sarah refused to leave the house, and she became a true support in time of trouble, and kept the household together by working till late at night, with her busy hands, to earn their daily bread. Not a relative came forward to assist them, and the widow was confined to a sick bed for months and grew weaker from day to day. Sarah worked hard, but contrived to spare time to amuse her and watch by the sick bed. She was gentle and pious, an angel of blessing in that house of poverty.

"My Bible lies on the table younder," said the sick woman one day to Sarah. "Read me something from it; the night appears so long, and my spirit thirsts to hear the word of God."

And Sarah bowed her head. She took the book, and folded her hand over the Bible of the Christians, and at last opened it, and read to the sick woman. Tears stood in her eyes as she read, and they shone with brightness, for in her heart it was light.

"Mother," she murmured, "thy child may not receive Christian baptism, nor be admitted into the congregation of Christian people. Thou hast so willed it, and I will respect thy command. We are therefore still united here on earth; but in the next world there will be a higher union, even with God Himself, who leads and guides His people till death. He came down from heaven to earth to suffer for us, that we should bring forth the fruits of repentance. I understand it now. I know not how I learnt this truth, unless it is through the name of Christ." Yet she trembled as she pronounced the holy name. She struggled against these convictions of the truth of Christianity for some days, till one evening while watching her mistress she was suddenly taken very ill; her limbs tottered under her, and she sank fainting by the bedside of the sick woman.

"Poor Sarah," said the neighbors; "she is overcome with hard work and night watching." And then they carried her to the hospital for the sick poor. There she died; and they bore her to her resting-place in the earth, but not to the churchyard of the Christians. There was no place for the Jewish girl; but they dug a grave for her outside the wall. And God's sun, which shines upon the graves of the churchyard of the Christians, also throws its beams on the grave of the Jewish maiden beyond the wall. And when the psalms of the Christians sound across the churchyard, their echo reaches her lonely resting-place; and she who sleeps there will be counted worthy at the resurrection, through the name of Christ the Lord, who said to His disciples, "John baptized you with water, but I will baptize you with the Holy Ghost."

THE OLD BACHELOR'S NIGHTCAP

THERE is a street in Copenhagen with a very strange name. It is called "Hysken" street. Where the name came from, and what it means is very uncertain. It is said to be German, but that is unjust to the Germans, for it would then be called "Hauschen," not "Hysken." "Hauschen," means a little house; and for many years it consisted only of a few small houses, which were scarcely larger than the wooden booths we see in the market-places at fair time. They were perhaps a little higher, and had windows; but the panes consisted of horn or bladder-skins, for glass was then too dear to have glazed windows in every house. This was a long time ago, so long indeed that our grandfathers, and even great-grandfathers, would speak of those days as "olden times;" indeed, many centuries have passed since then.

The rich merchants in Bremen and Lubeck, who carried on trade in Copenhagen, did not reside in the town themselves, but sent their clerks, who dwelt in the wooden booths in the Hauschen street, and sold beer and spices. The German beer was very good, and there were many sorts—from Bremen, Prussia, and Brunswick—and quantities of all sorts of spices, saffron, aniseed, ginger, and especially pepper; indeed, pepper was almost the chief article sold here; so it happened at last that the German clerks in Denmark got their nickname of "pepper gentry." It had been made a condition with these clerks that they should not marry; so that those who lived to be old had to take care of themselves, to attend to their own comforts, and even to light their own fires, when they had any to light. Many of them were very aged; lonely old boys, with strange thoughts and eccentric habits. From this, all unmarried men, who have attained a certain age, are called, in Denmark, "pepper gentry;" and this must be remembered by all those who wish to understand the story. These "pepper gentlemen," or, as they are called in England, "old bachelors," are often made a butt of ridicule; they are told to put on their nightcaps, draw them over their eyes, and go to sleep. The boys in Denmark make a song of it, thus:—

> "Poor old bachelor, cut your wood,
>   Such a nightcap was never seen;
>   Who would think it was ever clean?
> Go to sleep, it will do you good."

So they sing about the "pepper gentleman;" so do they make sport of the poor old bachelor and his nightcap, and all because they really know nothing of either. It is a cap that no one need wish for, or laugh at. And why not? Well, we shall hear in the story.

In olden times, Hauschen Street was not paved, and passengers would stumble out of one hole into another, as they generally do in unfrequented highways; and the steet was so narrow, and the booths leaning against each other were so close together, that in the summer time a sail would be stretched across the street from one booth to another opposite. At these times the odor of the pepper, saffron, and ginger became more powerful than ever. Behind the counter, as a rule, there were no young men. The clerks were almost all old boys; but they did not dress as we are accustomed to see old men represented, wearing wigs, nightcaps, and knee-breeches, and with coat and waistcoat buttoned up to the chin. We have seen the portraits of our great-grandfathers dressed in this way; but the "pepper gentlemen" had no money to spare to have their portraits taken, though one of them would have made a very interesting picture for us now, if taken as he appeared standing behind his counter, or going to church, or on holidays. On these occasions, they wore high-crowned, broad-brimmed hats, and sometimes a younger clerk would stick a feather in his. The woollen shirt was concealed by a broad, linen collar; the close jacket was buttoned up to the chin, and the cloak hung loosely over it; the trousers were tucked into the broad, tipped shoes, for the clerks wore no stockings. They generally stuck a table-knife and spoon in their girdles, as well as a larger knife, as a protection to themselves; and such a weapon was often very necessary.

After this fashion was Anthony dressed on holidays and festivals, excepting that, instead of a high-crowned hat, he wore a kind of bonnet, and under it a knitted cap, a regular nightcap, to which he was so accustomed that it was always on his head; he had two, nightcaps I mean, not heads. Anthony was one of the oldest of the clerks, and just the subject for a painter. He was as thin as a lath, wrinkled round the mouth and eyes, had long, bony fingers, bushy, gray eyebrows, and over his left eye hung a thick tuft of hair, which did not look handsome, but made his appearance very remarkable. People knew that he came from Bremen; it was not exactly his home, although his master resided there. His ancestors were from Thuringia, and had lived in the town of Eisenach, close by Wartburg. Old Anthony seldom spoke of this place, but he thought of it all the more.

The old clerks of Hauschen Street very seldom met together; each one remained in his own booth, which was closed early enough in the evening, and then it looked dark and dismal out in the street. Only a faint glimmer of light struggled through the horn panes in the little window on the roof, while within sat the old clerk, generally on his bed, singing his evening hymn in a low voice; or he would be moving about in his booth till late in the night, busily employed in many things. It certainly was not a very lively existence. To be a stranger in a strange land is a bitter lot; no one notices you unless you happen to stand in their way. Often, when it was dark night outside, with rain or snow falling, the place looked quite deserted and gloomy. There were no lamps in the street, excepting a very small one, which hung at one end of the street, before a picture of the Virgin, which had been painted on the wall. The dashing of the water against the bulwarks of a neighboring castle could plainly be heard. Such evenings are long and dreary, unless people can find something to do; and so Anthony found it. There were not always things to be packed or unpacked, nor paper bags to be made, nor the scales to be polished. So Anthony invented employment; he mended his clothes and patched his boots, and when he at last went to bed, his nightcap, which he had worn from habit, still remained on his head; he had only to pull it down a little farther over his forehead. Very soon, however, it would be pushed up again to see if the light was properly put out; he would touch it, press the wick together, and at last pull his nightcap over his eyes and lie down again on the other side. But often there would arise in his mind a doubt as to whether every coal had been quite put out in the little fire-pan in the shop below. If even a tiny spark had remained it might set fire to something, and cause great damage. Then he would rise from his bed, creep down the ladder—for it could scarcely be called a flight of stairs—and when he reached the fire-pan not a spark could be seen; so he had just to go back again to bed. But often, when he had got half way back, he would fancy the iron shutters of the door were not properly fastened, and his thin legs would carry him down again. And when at last he crept into bed, he would be so cold that his teeth chattered in his head. He would draw the coverlet closer round him, pull his nightcap over his eyes, and try to turn his thoughts from trade, and from the labors of the day, to olden times. But this was scarcely an agreeable entertainment; for thoughts of olden memories raise the curtains from the past, and sometimes pierce the heart with painful recollections till the agony brings tears to the waking eyes. And so it was with Anthony; often the scalding tears, like pearly drops, would fall from his eyes to the coverlet and roll on the floor with a sound as if one of his heartstrings had broken. Sometimes, with a lurid flame, memory would light up a picture of life which had never faded from his heart. If he dried his eyes with his nightcap, then the tear and the picture would be crushed; but the source of the tears remained and welled up again in his heart. The pictures did not follow one another in order, as the circumstances they represented had occurred; very often the most painful would come together, and when those came which were most full of joy, they had always the deepest shadow thrown upon them.

The beech woods of Denmark are acknowledged by every one to be very beautiful, but more beautiful still in the eyes of old Anthony were the beech woods in the neighborhood of Wartburg. More grand and venerable to him seemed the old oaks around the proud baronial castle, where the creeping plants hung over the stony summits of the rocks; sweeter was the perfume there of the apple-blossom than in all the land of Denmark. How vividly were represented to him, in a glittering tear that rolled down his cheek, two children at play—a boy and a girl. The boy had rosy cheeks, golden ringlets, and clear, blue eyes; he was the son of Anthony, a rich merchant; it was himself. The little girl had brown eyes and black hair, and was clever and courageous; she was the mayor's daughter, Molly. The children were playing with an apple; they shook the apple, and heard the pips rattling in it. Then they cut it in two, and each of them took half. They also divided the pips and ate all but one, which the little girl proposed should be placed in the ground.

"You will see what will come out," she said; "something you don't expect. A whole apple-tree will come out, but not directly." Then they got a flower-pot, filled it with earth, and were soon both very busy and eager about it. The boy made a hole in the earth with his finger, and the little girl placed the pip in the hole, and then they both covered it over with earth.

"Now you must not take it out to-morrow to see if it has taken root," said Molly; "no one ever should do that. I did so with my flowers, but only twice; I wanted to see if they were growing. I didn't know any better then, and the flowers all died."

Little Anthony kept the flower-pot, and every morning during the whole winter he looked at it, but there was nothing to be seen but black earth. At last, however, the spring came, and the sun shone warm again, and then two little green leaves sprouted forth in the pot.

"They are Molly and me," said the boy. "How wonderful they are, and so beautiful!"

Very soon a third leaf made its appearance.

"Who does that stand for?" thought he, and then came another and another. Day after day, and week after week, till the plant became quite a tree. And all this about the two children was mirrored to old Anthony in a single tear, which could soon be wiped away and disappear, but might come again from its source in the heart of the old man.

In the neighborhood of Eisenach stretches a ridge of stony mountains, one of which has a rounded outline, and shows itself above the rest without tree, bush, or grass on its barren summits. It is called the "Venus Mountain," and the story goes that the "Lady Venus," one of the heathen goddesses, keeps house there. She is also called "Lady Halle," as every child round Eisenach well knows. She it was who enticed the noble knight, Tannhauser, the minstrel, from the circle of singers at Wartburg into her mountain.

Little Molly and Anthony often stood by this mountain, and one day Molly said, "Do you dare to knock and say, 'Lady Halle, Lady Halle, open the door: Tannhauser is here!' " But Anthony did not dare. Molly, however, did, though she only said the words, "Lady Halle, Lady Halle," loudly and distinctly; the rest she muttered so much under her breath that Anthony felt certain she had really said nothing; and yet she looked quite bold and saucy, just as she did sometimes when she was in the garden with a number of other little girls; they would all stand round him together, and want to kiss him, because he did not like to be kissed, and pushed them away. Then Molly was the only one who dared to resist him. "*I* may kiss him," she would say proudly, as she threw her arms round his neck; she was vain of her power over Anthony, for he would submit quietly and think nothing of it. Molly was very charming, but rather bold; and how she did tease!

They said Lady Halle was beautiful, but her beauty was that of a tempting fiend. Saint Elizabeth, the tutelar saint of the land, the pious princess of Thuringia, whose good deeds have been immortalized in so many places through stories and legends, had greater beauty and more real grace. Her picture hung in the chapel, surrounded by silver lamps; but it did not in the least resemble Molly.

The apple-tree, which the two children had planted, grew year after year, till it became so large that it had to be transplanted into the garden, where the dew fell and the sun shone warmly. And there it increased in strength so much as to be able to withstand the cold of winter; and after passing through the severe weather, it seemed to put forth its blossoms in spring for very joy that the cold season had gone. In autumn it produced two apples, one for Molly and one for Anthony; it could not well do less. The tree after this grew very rapidly, and Molly grew with the tree. She was as fresh as an apple-blossom, but Anthony was not to behold this flower for long. All things change; Molly's father left his old home, and Molly went with him far away. In our time, it would be only a journey of a few hours, but then it took more than a day and a night to travel so far eastward from Eisenbach to a town still called Weimar, on the borders of Thuringia. And Molly and Anthony both wept, but these tears all flowed together into one tear which had the rosy shimmer of joy. Molly had told him that she loved him — loved him more than all the splendors of Weimar.

One, two, three years went by, and during the whole time he received only two letters. One came by the carrier, and the other a traveller brought. The way was very long and difficult, with many turnings and windings through towns and villages. How often had Anthony and Molly heard the story of Tristan and Isolda, and Anthony had thought the story applied to him, although Tristan means born in sorrow, which Anthony certainly was not; nor was it likely he would ever say of Molly as Tristan said of Isolda, "She has forgotten me." But in truth, Isolda had not forgotten him, her faithful friend; and when both were laid in their graves, one on each side of the church, the linden-trees that grew by each grave spread over the roof, and, bending towards each other, mingled their blossoms together. Anthony thought it a very beautiful but mournful story; yet he never feared anything so sad would happen to him and Molly, as he passed the spot, whistling the air of a song, composed by the minstrel Walter, called the "Willow bird," beginning—

"Under the linden-trees,
Out on the heath."

One stanza pleased him exceedingly—

"Through the forest, and in the vale,
Sweetly warbles the nightingale."

This song was often in his mouth, and he sung or whistled it on a moonlight night, when he rode on horseback along the deep, hollow way, on his road to Weimar, to visit Molly. He wished to arrive unexpectedly, and so indeed he did. He was received with a hearty welcome, and introduced to plenty of grand and pleasant company, where overflowing winecups were passed about. A pretty room and a good bed were provided for him, and yet his reception was not what he had expected and dreamed it would be. He could not comprehend his own feelings nor the feelings of others; but it is easily understood how a person can be admitted into a house or a family without becoming one of them. We converse in company with those we meet, as we converse with our fellow-travellers in a stage-coach, on a journey; we know nothing of them, and perhaps all the while we are incommoding one another, and each is wishing himself or his neighbor away. Something of this kind Anthony felt when Molly talked to him of old times.

"I am a straightforward girl," she said, "and I will tell you myself how it is. There have been great changes since we were children together; everything is different, both inwardly and outwardly. We cannot control our wills, nor the feelings of our hearts, by the force of custom. Anthony, I would not, for the world, make an enemy of you when I am far away. Believe me, I entertain for you the kindest wishes in my heart; but to feel for you what I now know can be felt for another man, can never be. You must try and reconcile yourself to this. Farewell, Anthony."

Anthony also said, "Farewell." Not a tear came into his eye; he felt he was no longer Molly's friend. Hot iron and cold iron alike take the skin from our lips, and we feel the same sensation if we kiss either; and Anthony's kiss was now the kiss of hatred, as it had once been the kiss of love. Within four-and-twenty hours Anthony was back again to Eisenach, though the horse that he rode was entirely ruined.

"What matters it?" said he; "I am ruined also. I will destroy everything that can remind me of her, or of Lady Halle, or Lady Venus, the heathen woman. I will break down the apple-tree, and tear it up by the roots; never more shall it blossom or bear fruit."

The apple-tree was not broken down; for Anthony himself was struck with a fever, which caused him to break down, and confined him to his bed. But something occurred to raise him up again. What was it? A medicine was offered to him, which he was obliged to take: a bitter remedy, at which the sick body and the oppressed spirit alike shuddered. Anthony's father lost all his property, and, from being known as one of the richest merchants, he became very poor. Dark days, heavy trials, with poverty at the door, came rolling into the house upon them like the waves of the sea. Sorrow and suffering deprived Anthony's father of his strength, so that he had something else to think of besides nursing his love-sorrows and his anger against Molly. He had to take his father's place, to give orders, to act with energy, to help, and, at last, to go out into the world and earn his bread. Anthony went to Bremen, and there he learnt what poverty and hard living really were. These things often harden the character, but sometimes soften the heart, even too much.

How different the world, and the people in it, appeared to Anthony now, to what he had thought in his childhood! What to him were the minstrel's songs? An echo of the past, sounds long vanished. At times he would think in this way; yet again and again the songs would sound in his soul, and his heart become gentle and pious.

"God's will is the best," he would then say. "It was well that I was not allowed to keep my power over Molly's heart, and that she did not remain true to me. How I should have felt it now, when fortune has deserted me! She left me before she knew of the change in my circumstances, or had a thought of what was before me. That is a merciful providence for me. All has happened for the best. She could not help it, and yet I have been so bitter, and in such enmity against her."

Years passed by: Anthony's father died, and strangers lived in the old house. He had seen it once again since then. His rich master sent him journeys on business, and on one occasion his way led him to his native town of Eisenach. The old Wartburg castle stood unchanged on the rock where the monk and the nun were hewn out of the stone. The great oaks formed an outline to the scene which he so well remembered in his childhood. The Venus mountain stood out gray and bare, overshadowing the valley beneath. He would have been glad to call out "Lady Halle, Lady Halle, unlock the mountain. I would fain remain here always in my native soil." That was a sinful thought, and he offered a prayer to drive it away. Then a little bird in the thicket sang out clearly, and old Anthony thought of the minstrel's song. How much came back to his remembrance as he looked through the tears once more on his native town! The old house was still standing as in olden times, but the garden had been greatly altered; a pathway led through a portion of the ground, and outside the garden, and beyond the path, stood the old apple-tree, which he had not broken down, although he talked of doing so in his trouble. The sun still threw its rays upon the tree, and the refreshing dew fell upon it as of old; and it was so overloaded with fruit that the branches bent towards the earth with the weight. "That flourishes still," said he, as he gazed. One of the branches of the tree had, however, been broken: mischievous hands must have done this in passing, for the tree now stood in a public thoroughfare. "The blossoms are often plucked," said Anthony; "the fruit is stolen and the branches broken without a thankful thought of their profusion and beauty. It might be said of a tree, as it has been said of some men — it was not predicted at his cradle that he should come to this. How brightly began the history of this tree, and what is it now? Forsaken and forgotten, in a garden by a hedge in a field, and close to a public road. There it stands, unsheltered, plundered, and broken. It certainly has not yet withered; but in the course of years the number of blossoms from time to time will grow less, and at last it was cease altogether to bear fruit; and then its history will be over."

Such were Anthony's thoughts as he stood under the tree, and during many a long night as he lay in his lonely chamber in the wooden house in Hauschen Street, Copenhagen, in the foreign land to which the rich merchant of Bremen, his employer, had sent him on condition that he should never marry. "Marry! ha, ha!" and he laughed bitterly to himself at the thought.

Winter one year set in early, and it was freezing hard. Without, a snow-storm made every one remain at home who could do so. Thus it happened that Anthony's neighbors, who lived opposite to him, did not notice that his house remained unopened for two days, and that he had not showed himself during that time, for who would go out in such weather unless he were obliged to do so. They were gray, gloomy days, and in the house whose windows were not glass, twilight and dark nights reigned in turns. During these two days old Anthony had not left his bed, he had not the strength to do so. The bitter weather had for some time affected his limbs. There lay the old bachelor, forsaken by all, and unable to help himself. He could scarcely reach the water jug that he had placed by his bed, and the last drop was gone. It was not fever, nor sickness, but old age, that had laid him low. In the little corner, where his bed lay, he was over-shadowed as it were by perpetual night. A little spider, which he could however not see, busily and cheerfully spun its web above him, so that there should be a kind of little banner waving over the old man, when his eyes closed. The time passed slowly and painfully. He had no tears to shed, and he felt no pain; no thought of Molly came into his mind. He felt as if the world was now nothing to him, as if he were lying beyond it, with no one to think of him. Now and then he felt slight sensations of hunger and thirst; but no one came to him, no one tended him. He thought of all those who had once suffered from starvation, of Saint Elizabeth, who once wandered on the earth, the saint of his home and his childhood, the noble Duchess of Thuringia, that highly esteemed lady who visited the poorest villages, bringing hope and relief to the sick inmates. The recollection of her pious deeds was as light to the soul of poor Anthony. He thought of her as she went about speaking words of comfort, binding up the wounds of the afflicted and feeding the hungry, although often blamed for it by her stern husband. He remembered a story told of her, that on one occasion, when she was carrying a basket full of wine and provisions, her husband, who had watched her footsteps, stepped forward and asked her angrily what she carried in her basket, whereupon, with fear and trembling, she answered, "Roses, which I have plucked from the garden." Then he tore away the cloth which covered the basket, and what could equal the surprise of the pious woman, to find that by a miracle, everything in her basket—the wine, the bread—had all been changed into roses.

In this way the memory of the kind lady dwelt in the calm mind of Anthony. She was as a living reality in his little dwelling in the Danish land. He uncovered his face that he might look into her gentle eyes, while everything around him changed from its look of poverty and want, to a bright rose tint. The fragrance of roses spread through the room, mingled with the sweet smell of apples. He saw the branches of an apple-tree spreading above him. It was the tree which he and Molly had planted together. The fragrant leaves of the tree fell upon him and cooled his burning brow; upon his parched lips they seemed like refreshing bread and wine; and as they rested on his breast, a peaceful calm stole over him, and he felt inclined to sleep. "I shall sleep now," he whispered to himself. "Sleep will do me good. In the morning I shall be upon my feet again, strong and well. Glorious! wonderful! That apple-tree, planted in love, now appears before me in heavenly beauty." And he slept.

The following day, the third day during which his house had been closed, the snow-storm ceased. Then his opposite neighbor stepped over to the house in which old Anthony lived, for he had not yet showed himself. There he lay stretched on his bed, dead, with his old nightcap tightly clasped in his two hands. The nightcap, however, was not placed on his head in his coffin; he had a clean white one on then. Where now were the tears he had shed? What had become of those wonderful pearls? They were in the nightcap still. Such tears as these cannot be washed out, even when the nightcap is forgotten. The old thoughts and dreams of a bachelor's nightcap still remain. Never wish for such a nightcap. It would make your forehead hot, cause your pulse to beat with agitation, and conjure up dreams which would appear realities.

The first who wore old Anthony's cap felt the truth of this, though it was half a century afterwards. That man was the mayor himself, who had already made a comfortable home for his wife and eleven children, by his industry. The moment he put the cap on he dreamed of unfortunate love, of bankruptcy, and of dark days. "Hallo! how the nightcap burns!" he exclaimed, as he tore it from his head. Then a pearl rolled out, and then another, and another, and they glittered and sounded as they fell. "What can this be? Is it paralysis, or something dazzling my eyes?" They were the tears which old Anthony had shed half a century before.

To every one who afterwards put this cap on his head, came visions and dreams which agitated him not a little. His own history was changed into that of Anthony till it became quite a story, and many stories might be made by others, so we will leave them to relate their own. We have told the first; and our last word is, don't wish for a "bachelor's nightcap."

THE PUPPET-SHOW MAN

On board a steamer I once met an elderly man, with such a merry face that, if it was really an index of his mind, he must have been the happiest fellow in creation; and indeed he considered himself so, for I heard it from his own mouth. He was a Dane, the owner of a travelling theatre. He had all his company with him in a large box, for he was the proprietor of a puppet-show. His inborn cheerfulness, he said, had been tested by a member of the Polytechnic Institution, and the experiment had made him completely happy. I did not at first understand all this, but afterwards he explained the whole story to me; and here it is: —

"I was giving a representation," he said, "in the hall of the posting-house in the little town of Slagelse; there was a splendid audience, entirely juvenile excepting two respectable matrons. All at once, a person in black, of student-like appearance, entered the room, and sat down; he laughed aloud at the telling points, and applauded quite at the proper time. This was a very unusual spectator for me, and I felt anxious to know who he was. I heard that he was a member of the Polytechnic Institution in Copenhagen, who had been sent out to lecture to the people in the provinces. Punctually at eight o'clock my performance closed, for children must go early to bed, and a manager must also consult the convenience of the public.

"At nine o'clock the lecturer commenced his lecture and his experiments, and then I formed a part of his audience. It was wonderful both to hear and to see. The greater part of it was beyond my comprehension, but it led me to think that if we men can acquire so much, we must surely be intended to last longer than the little span which extends only to the time when we are hidden away under the earth. His experiments were quite miracles on a small scale, and yet the explanations flowed as naturally as water from his lips. At the time of Moses and the prophets, such a man would have been placed among the sages of the land; in the middle ages they would have burnt him at the stake.

"All night long I could not sleep; and the next evening when I gave another performance and the lecturer was present, I was in one of my best moods.

"I once heard of an actor, who, when he had to act the part of a lover, always thought of one particular lady in the audience; he only played for her, and forgot all the rest of the house, and now the Polytechnic lecturer was my *she,* my only auditor, for whom alone I played.

"When the performance was over, and the puppets removed behind the curtain, the Polytechnic lecturer invited me into his room to take a glass of wine. He talked of my comedies, and I of his science, and I believe we were both equally pleased. But I had the best of it, for there was much in what he did that he could not always explain to me. For instance, why a piece of iron which is rubbed on a cylinder, should become magnetic. How does this happen? The magnetic sparks come to it, —but how? It is the same with people in the world; they are rubbed about on this spherical globe till the electric spark comes upon them, and then we have a Napoleon, or a Luther, or some one of the kind.

" 'The whole world is but a series of miracles,' said the lecturer, 'but we are so accustomed to them that we call them everyday matters.' And he went on explaining things to me till my skull seemed lifted from my brain, and I declared that were I not such an old fellow, I would at once become a member of the Polytechnic Institution, that I might learn to look at the bright side of everything, although I was one of the happiest of men.

" 'One of the happiest!' said the lecturer, as if the idea pleased him; 'are you really happy?'

" 'Yes,' I replied; 'for I am welcomed in every town, when I arrive with my company; but I certainly have one wish which sometimes weighs upon my cheerful temper like a mountain of lead. I should like to become the manager of a real theatre, and the director of a real troupe of men and women.'

" 'I understand,' he said; 'you would like to have life breathed into your puppets, so that they might be living actors, and you their director. And would you then be quite happy?'

"I said I believed so. But he did not; and we talked it over in all manner of ways, yet could not agree on the subject. However, the wine was excellent, and we clanked our glasses together as we drank. There must have been

THE PUPPET-SHOW MAN

magic in it, or I should most certainly become tipsy; but that did not happen, for my mind seemed quite clear; and, indeed, a kind of sunshine filled the room, and beamed from the eyes of the Polytechnic lecturer. It made me think of the old stories when the gods, in their immortal youth, wandered upon this earth, and paid visits to mankind. I said so to him, and he smiled; and I could have sworn that he was one of these ancient deities in disguise, or, at all events, that he belonged to the race of the gods. The result seemed to prove I was right in my suspicions; for it was arranged that my highest wish should be granted, that my puppets were to be gifted with life, and that I was to be the manager of a real company. We drank to my success, and clanked our glasses. Then he packed all my dolls into the box, and fastened it on my back, and I felt as if I were spinning round in a circle, and presently found myself lying on the floor. I remember that quite well. And then the whole company sprang from the box. The spirit had come upon us all; the puppets had become distinguished actors—at least, so they said themselves—and I was their director.

"When all was ready for the first representation, the whole company requested permission to speak to me before appearing in public. The dancing lady said the house could not be supported unless she stood on one leg; for she was a great genius, and begged to be treated as such. The lady who acted the part of the queen expected to be treated as a queen off the stage, as well as on it, or else she said she should get out of practice. The man whose duty it was to deliver a letter gave himself as many airs as he who took the part of first lover in the piece; he declared that the inferior parts were as important as the great ones, and deserving equal consideration, as parts of an artistic whole. The hero of the piece would only play in a part containing points likely to bring down the applause of the house. The 'prima donna' would only act when the lights were red, for she declared that a blue light did not suit her complexion. It was like a company of flies in a bottle, and I was in the bottle with them; for I was their director. My breath was taken away, my head whirled, and I was as miserable as a man could be. It was quite a novel, strange set of beings among whom I now found myself. I only wished I had them all in my box again, and that I had never been their director. So I told them roundly that, after all, they were nothing but puppets; and then they killed me. After a while I found myself lying on my bed in my room; but how I got there, or how I got away at all from the Polytechnic professor, he may perhaps know, I don't. The moon shone upon the floor, the box lay open, and the dolls were all scattered about in great confusion; but I was not idle. I jumped off the bed, and into the box they all had to go, some on their heads, some on their feet. Then I shut down the lid, and seated myself upon the box. 'Now you'll have to stay,' said I, 'and I shall be cautious how I wish you flesh and blood again.'

"I felt quite light, my cheerfulness had returned, and I was the happiest of mortals. The Polytechnic professor had fully cured me. I was as happy as a king, and went to sleep on the box. Next morning—correctly speaking, it was noon, for I slept remarkably late that day—I found myself still sitting there, in happy consciousness that my former wish had been a foolish one. I inquired for the Polytechnic professor; but he had disappeared like the Greek and Roman gods; from that time I have been the happiest man in the world. I am a happy director; for none of my company ever grumble, nor the public either, for I always make them merry. I can arrange my pieces just as I please.

I choose out of every comedy what I like best, and no one is offended. Plays that are neglected now-a-days by the great public were ran after thirty years ago, and listened to till the tears ran down the cheeks of the audience. These are the pieces I bring forward. I place them before the little ones, who cry over them as papa and mamma used to cry thirty years ago. But I make them shorter, for the youngsters don't like long speeches; and if they have anything mournful, they like it to be over quickly."

ANNE LISBETH

ANNE LISBETH was a beautiful young woman, with a red and white complexion, glittering white teeth, and clear soft eyes; and her footstep was light in the dance, but her mind was lighter still. She had a little child, not at all pretty; so he was put out to be nursed by a laborer's wife, and his mother went to the count's castle. She sat in splendid rooms, richly decorated with silk and velvet; not a breath of air was allowed to blow upon her, and no one was allowed to speak to her harshly, for she was nurse to the count's child. He was fair and delicate as a prince, and beautiful as an angel; and how she loved this child! Her own boy was provided for by being at the laborer's where the mouth watered more frequently than the pot boiled, and where in general no one was at home to take care of the child. Then he would cry, but what nobody knows nobody cares for; so he would cry till he was tired, and then fall asleep; and while we are asleep we can feel neither hunger nor thirst. Ah, yes; sleep is a capital invention.

As years went on, Anne Lisbeth's child grew apace like weeds, although they said his growth had been stunted. He had become quite a member of the family in which he dwelt; they received money to keep him, so that his mother got rid of him altogether. She had become quite a lady; she had a comfortable home of her own in the town; and out of doors, when she went for a walk, she wore a bonnet; but she never walked out to see the laborer: that was too far from the town, and, indeed, she had nothing to go for, the boy now belonged to these laboring people. He had food, and he could also do something towards earning his living; he took care of Mary's red cow, for he knew how to tend cattle and make himself useful.

The great dog by the yard gate of a nobleman's mansion sits proudly on the top of his kennel when the sun shines, and barks at every one that passes; but if it rains, he creeps into his house, and there he is warm and dry. Anne Lisbeth's boy also sat in the sunshine on the top of the fence, cutting out a little toy. If it was spring-time, he knew of three strawberry-plants in blossom, which would certainly bear fruit. This was his most hopeful thought, though it often came to nothing. And he had to sit out in the rain in the worst weather, and get wet to the skin, and let the cold wind dry the clothes on his back afterwards. If he went near the farmyard belonging to the count, he was pushed and knocked about, for the men and the maids said he was so horrible ugly; but he was used to all this, for nobody loved him. This was how the world treated Anne Lisbeth's boy, and how could it be otherwise. It was his fate to be beloved by no one. Hitherto he had been a land crab; the land at last cast him adrift. He went to sea in a wretched vessel, and sat at the helm, while the skipper sat over the grog-can. He was dirty and ugly, half-frozen and half-starved; he always looked as if he never had enough to eat, which was really the case.

Late in the autumn, when the weather was rough, windy, and wet, and the cold penetrated through the thickest clothing, especially at sea, a wretched boat went out to sea with only two men on board, or, more correctly, a man and a half, for it was the skipper and his boy. There had only been a kind of twilight all day, and it soon grew quite dark, and so bitterly cold, that the skipper took a dram to warm him. The bottle was old, and the glass too. It was perfect in the upper part, but the foot was broken off, and it had therefore been fixed upon a little carved block of wood, painted blue. A dram is a great comfort, and two are better still, thought the skipper, while the boy sat at the helm, which he held fast in his hard seamed hands. He was ugly, and his hair was matted, and he looked crippled and stunted; they called him the field-laborer's boy, though in the church register he was entered as Anne Lisbeth's son. The wind cut through the rigging, and the boat cut through the sea. The sails, filled by the wind, swelled out and carried them along in wild career. It was wet and rough above and below, and might still be worse. Hold! what is that? What has struck the boat? Was it a waterspout, or a heavy sea rolling suddenly upon them?

"Heaven help us!" cried the boy at the helm, as the boat heeled over and lay on its beam ends. It had struck on a rock, which rose from the depths of the sea, and sank at once, like an old shoe in a puddle. "It sank at once with mouse and man," as the saying is. There might have been mice on board, but only one man and a half, the skipper and the laborer's boy. No one saw it but the skimming sea-gulls and the fishes beneath the water; and even they did not see it properly, for they darted back with terror as the boat filled with water and sank. There it lay, scarcely a fathom below the surface, and those two were provided for, buried, and forgotten. The glass with the foot of blue wood was the only thing that did not sink, for the wood floated and the glass drifted away to be cast upon the shore and broken; where and when, is indeed of no consequence. It had served its purpose, and it had been loved, which Anne Lisbeth's boy had not been. But in heaven no soul will be able to say, "Never loved."

Anne Lisbeth had now lived in the town many years; she was called "Madame," and felt dignified in consequence; she remembered the old, noble days, in which she had driven in the carriage, and had associated with countess and baroness. Her beautiful, noble child had been a dear angel, and possessed the kindest heart; he had loved her so much, and she had loved him in return; they had kissed and loved each other, and the boy had been her joy, her second life. Now he was fourteen years of age, tall, handsome, and clever. She had not seen him since she carried him in her arms; neither had she been for years to the count's palace; it was quite a journey thither from the town.

"I must make one effort to go," said Anne Lisbeth, "to see my darling, the count's sweet child, and press him to my heart. Certainly he must long to see me, too, the young count; no doubt he thinks of me and loves me, as in those days when he would fling his angel-arms round my neck, and lisp 'Anne Liz.' It was music to my ears. Yes, I must make an effort to see him again." She drove across the country in a grazier's cart, and then got out, and continued her journey on foot, and thus reached the count's castle. It was as great and magnificent as it had always been, and the garden looked the same as ever; all the servants were strangers to her, not one of them knew Anne Lisbeth, nor of what consequence she had once been there; but she felt sure the countess would soon let them know it, and her darling boy, too: how she longed to see him!

Now that Anne Lisbeth was at her journey's end, she was kept waiting a long time; and for those who wait, time passes slowly. But before the great people went in to dinner, she was called in and spoken to very graciously. She was to go in again after dinner, and then she would see her sweet boy once more. How tall, and slender, and thin he had grown; but the eyes and the sweet angel mouth were still beautiful. He looked at her, but he did not speak, he certainly did not know who she was. He turned round and was going away, but she seized his hand and pressed it to her lips.

"Well, well," he said; and with that he walked out of the room. He who filled her every thought! he whom she loved best, and who was her whole earthly pride!

Anne Lisbeth went forth from the castle into the public road, feeling mournful and sad; he whom she had nursed day and night, and even now carried about in her dreams, had been cold and strange, and had not a word or thought respecting her. A great black raven darted down in front of her on the high road, and croaked dismally.

"Ah," said she, "what bird of ill omen art thou?" Presently she passed the laborer's hut; his wife stood at the door, and the two women spoke to each other.

"You look well," said the woman; "you're fat and plump; you are well off."

"Oh yes," answered Anne Lisbeth.

"The boat went down with them," continued the woman; "Hans the skipper and the boy were both drowned; so there's an end of them. I always thought the boy would be able to help me with a few dollars. He'll never cost you anything more, Anne Lisbeth."

"So they were drowned," repeated Anne Lisbeth; but she said no more, and the subject was dropped. She felt very low-spirited, because her count-child had shown no inclination to speak to her who loved him so well, and who had travelled so far to see him. The journey had cost money too, and she had derived no great pleasure from it. Still she said not a word of all this; she could not relieve her heart by telling the laborer's wife, lest the latter should think she did not enjoy her former position at the castle. Then the raven flew over her, screaming again as he flew.

"The black wretch!" said Anne Lisbeth, "he will end by frightening me to-day." She had brought coffee and chicory with her, for she thought it would be a charity to the poor woman to give them to her to boil a cup of coffee, and then she would take a cup herself.

The woman prepared the coffee, and in the meantime Anne Lisbeth seated her in a chair and fell asleep. Then she dreamed of something which she had never dreamed before; singularly enough she dreamed of her own child, who had wept and hungered in the laborer's hut, and had been knocked about in heat and in cold, and who was now lying in the depths of the sea, in a spot only known by God. She fancied she was still sitting in the hut, where the woman was busy preparing the coffee, for she could smell the coffee-berries roasting. But suddenly it seemed to her that there stood on the threshold a beautiful young form, as beautiful as the count's child, and this apparition said to her, "The world is passing away; hold fast to me, for you are my mother after all; you have an angel in heaven, hold me fast;" and the child-angel stretched out his hand and seized her. Then there was a terrible crash, as of a world crumbling to pieces, and the angel-child was rising from the earth, and holding her by the sleeve so tightly that she felt herself lifted from the ground; but, on the other hand, something heavy hung to her feet and dragged her down, and it seemed as if hundreds of women were clinging to her, and crying, "If thou art to be saved, we must be saved too. Hold fast, hold fast." And then they all hung on her, but there were too many; and as they clung the sleeve was torn, and Anne Lisbeth fell down in horror, and awoke. Indeed she was on the point of falling over in reality with the chair on which she sat; but she was so startled and alarmed that she could not remember what she had dreamed, only that it was something very dreadful.

They drank their coffee and had a chat together, and then Anne Lisbeth went away towards the little town where she was to meet the carrier, who was to drive her back to her own home. But when she came to him she found that he would not be ready to start till the evening of the next day. Then she began to think of the expense, and what the distance would be to walk. She remembered that the route by the sea-shore was two miles shorter than by the high road; and as the weather was clear, and there would be moonlight, she determined to make her way on foot, and to start at once, that she might reach home the next day.

The sun had set, and the evening bells sounded through the air from the tower of the village church, but to her it was not the bells, but the cry of the frogs in the marshes. Then they ceased, and all around became still; not a bird could be heard, they were all at rest, even the owl had not left her hiding place; deep silence reigned on the margin of the wood by the sea-shore. As Anne Lisbeth walked on she could hear her own footsteps in the sands; even the waves of the sea were at rest, and all in the deep waters had sunk into silence. There was quiet among the dead and the living in the deep sea. Anne Lisbeth walked on, thinking of nothing at all, as people say, or rather her thoughts wandered, but not away from her, for thought is never absent from us, it only slumbers. Many thoughts that have lain dormant are roused at the proper time, and begin to stir in the mind and the heart, and seem even to come upon us from above. It is written, that a good deed bears a blessing for its fruit; and it is also written, that the wages of sin is death. Much has been said and much written which we pass over or know nothing of. A light arises within us, and then forgotten things make themselves remembered; and thus it was with Anne Lisbeth. The germ of every vice and every virtue lies in our heart, in yours and in mine; they lie like little grains of seed, till a ray of sunshine, or the touch of an evil hand, or you turn the corner to the right or to the left, and the decision is made. The little seed is stirred, it swells and shoots up, and pours its sap into your blood, directing your course either for good or evil. Troublesome thoughts often exist in the mind, fermenting there, which are not realized by us while the senses are as it were slumbering; but still they are there. Anne Lisbeth walked on thus with her senses half asleep, but the thoughts were fermenting within her.

From one Shrove Tuesday to another, much may occur to weigh down the heart; it is the reckoning of a whole year; much may be forgotten, sins against heaven in word and thought, sins against our neighbor, and against our own conscience. We are scarcely aware of their existence; and Anne Lisbeth did not think of any of her errors. *She* had committed no crime against the law of the land; she was an honorable person, in a good position—that she knew.

She continued her walk along by the margin of the sea. What was it she saw lying there? An old hat; a man's hat. Now when might that have been washed overboard? She drew nearer, she stopped to look at the hat; "Ha! what was lying yonder?" She shuddered; yet it was nothing save a heap of grass and tangled seaweed flung across a long stone, but it looked like a corpse. Only tangled grass, and yet she was frightened at it. As she turned to walk away, much came into her mind that she had heard in her childhood: old superstitions of spectres by the sea-shore; of the ghosts of drowned but unburied people, whose corpses had been washed up on the desolate beach. The body, she knew, could do no harm to any one, but the spirit could pursue the lonely wanderer, attach itself to him, and demand to be carried to the churchyard, that it might rest in consecrated ground. "Hold fast! hold fast!" the spectre would cry; and as Anne Lisbeth murmured these words to herself, the whole of her dream was suddenly recalled to her memory, when the mother had clung to her, and uttered these words, when, amid the crashing of worlds, her sleeve had been torn, and she had slipped from the grasp of her child, who wanted to hold her up in that terrible hour. Her child, her own child, which she had never loved, lay now buried in the sea, and might rise up, like a spectre, from the waters, and cry, "Hold fast; carry me to consecrated ground!"

As these thoughts passed through her mind, fear gave speed to her feet, so that she walked faster and faster. Fear came upon her as if a cold, clammy hand had been laid upon her heart, so that she almost fainted. As she looked across the sea, all there grew darker; a heavy mist came rolling onwards, and clung to bush and tree, distorting them into fantastic shapes. She turned and glanced at the moon, which had risen behind her. It looked like a pale, rayless surface, and a deadly weight seemed to hang upon her limbs. "Hold," thought she; and then she turned round a second time to look at the moon. A white face appeared quite close to her, with a mist hanging like a garment from its shoulders. "Stop! carry me to consecrated earth," sounded in her ears, in strange, hollow tones. The sound did not come from frogs or ravens; she saw no sign of such creatures. "A grave! dig me a grave!" was repeated quite loud. Yes, it was indeed the spectre of her child. The child that lay beneath the ocean, and whose spirit could have no rest until it was carried to the churchyard, and until a grave had been dug for it in consecrated ground. She would go there at once, and there she would dig. She turned in the direction of the church, and the weight on her heart seemed to grow lighter, and even to vanish altogether; but when she turned to go home by the shortest way, it returned. "Stop! stop!" and the words came quite clear, though they were like the croak of a frog, or the wail of a bird. "A grave! dig me a grave!"

The mist was cold and damp, her hands and face were moist and clammy with horror, a heavy weight again seized her and clung to her, her mind became clear for thoughts that had never before been there.

In these northern regions, a beech-wood often buds in a single night and appears in the morning sunlight in its full glory of youthful green. So, in a single instant, can the consciousness of the sin that has been committed in thoughts, words, and actions of our past life, be unfolded to us. When once the conscience is awakened, it springs up in the heart spontaneously, and God awakens the conscience when we least expect it. Then we can find no excuse for ourselves; the deed is there and bears witness against us. The thoughts seem to become words, and to sound far out into the world. We are horrified at the thought of what we have carried within us, and at the consciousness that we have not overcome the evil which has its origin in thoughtlessness and pride. The heart conceals within itself the vices as well as the virtues, and they grow in the shallowest ground. Anne Lisbeth now experienced in thought what we have clothed in words. She was overpowered by them, and sank down and crept along for some distance on the ground. "A grave! dig me a grave!" sounded again in her ears, and she would have gladly buried herself, if in the grave she could have found forgetfulness of her actions.

It was the first hour of her awakening, full of anguish and horror. Superstition made her alternately shudder with cold or burn with the heat of fever. Many things, of which she had feared even to speak, came into her mind. Silently, as the cloud-shadows in the moonshine, a spectral apparition flitted by her; she had heard of it before. Close by her galloped four snorting steeds, with fire flashing from their eyes and nostrils. They dragged a burning coach, and within it sat the wicked lord of the manor, who had ruled there a hundred years before. The legend says that every night, at twelve o'clock, he drove into his castleyard and out again. He was not as pale as dead men are, but black as a coal. He nodded, and pointed to Anne Lisbeth, crying out, "Hold fast! hold fast! and then you may ride again in a nobleman's carriage, and forget your child."

She gathered herself up, and hastened to the churchyard; but black crosses and black ravens danced before her eyes, and she could not distinguish one from the other. The ravens croaked as the raven had done which she saw in the daytime, but now she understood what they said. "I am the raven-mother; I am the raven-mother," each raven croaked, and Anne Lisbeth felt that the name also applied to her; and she fancied she should be transformed into a black bird, and have to cry as they cried, if she did not dig the grave. And she threw herself upon the earth, and with her hands dug a grave in the hard ground, so that the blood ran from her fingers. "A grave! dig me a grave!" still sounded in her ears; she was fearful that the cock might crow, and the first red streak appear in the east, before she had finished her work; and then she would be lost. And the cock crowed, and the day dawned in the east, and the grave was only half dug. An icy hand passed over her head and face, and down towards her heart. "Only half a grave," a voice wailed, and fled away. Yes, it fled away over the sea; it was the ocean spectre; and, exhausted and overpowered, Anne Lisbeth sunk to the ground, and her senses left her.

It was a bright day when she came to herself, and two men were raising her up; but she was not lying in the churchyard, but on the sea-shore, where she had dug a deep hole in the sand, and cut her hand with a piece of broken glass, whose sharp stem was stuck in a little block of painted wood. Anne Lisbeth was in a fever. Conscience had roused the memories of superstitions, and had so acted upon her mind, that she fancied she had only half a soul, and that her child had taken the other half down into the sea. Never would she be able to cling to the mercy of Heaven till she had recovered this other half which was now held fast in the deep water.

ANNE LISBETH

Anne Lisbeth returned to her home, but she was no longer the woman she had been. Her thoughts were like a confused, tangled skein; only one thread, only one thought was clear to her, namely that she must carry the spectre of the sea-shore to the churchyard, and dig a grave for him there; that by so doing she might win back her soul. Many a night she was missed from her home, and was always found on the sea-shore waiting for the spectre.

In this way a whole year passed; and then one night she vanished again, and was not to be found. The whole of the next day was spent in a useless search after her.

Towards evening, when the clerk entered the church to toll the vesper bell, he saw by the altar Anne Lisbeth, who had spent the whole day there. Her powers of body were almost exhausted, but her eyes flashed brightly, and on her cheeks was a rosy flush. The last rays of the setting sun shone upon her, and gleamed over the altar upon the shining clasps of the Bible, which lay open at the words of the prophet Joel, "Rend your hearts and not your garments, and turn unto the Lord."

"That was just a chance," people said; but do things happen by chance? In the face of Anne Lisbeth, lighted up by the evening sun, could be seen peace and rest. She said she was happy now, for she had conquered. The spectre of the shore, her own child, had come to her the night before, and had said to her, "Thou hast dug me only half a grave: but thou hast now, for a year and a day, buried me altogether in thy heart, and it is there a mother can best hide her child!" And then he gave her back her lost soul, and brought her into the church. "Now I am in the house of God," she said, "and in that house we are happy."

When the sun set, Anne Lisbeth's soul had risen to that region where there is no more pain; and Anne Lisbeth's troubles were at an end.

BEAUTY OF FORM AND BEAUTY OF MIND

THERE was once a sculptor, named Alfred, who having won the large gold medal and obtained a travelling scholarship, went to Italy, and then came back to his native land. He was young at that time — indeed, he is young still, although he is ten years older than he was then. On his return, he went to visit one of the little towns in the island of Zealand. The whole town knew who the stranger was; and one of the richest men in the place gave a party in his honor, and all who were of any consequence, or who possessed some property, were invited. It was quite an event, and all the town knew of it, so that it was not necessary to announce it by beat of drum. Apprentice-boys, children of the poor, and even the poor people thenselves, stood before the house, watching the lighted windows; and the watchman might easily fancy he was giving a party also, there were so many people in the streets. There was quite an air of festivity about it, and the house was full of it; for Mr. Alfred, the sculptor, was there. He talked and told anecdotes, and every one listened to him with pleasure, not unmingled with awe; but none felt so much respect for him as did the elderly widow of a naval officer. She seemed, so far as Mr. Alfred was concerned, to be like a piece of fresh blotting-paper that absorbed all he said and asked for more. She was very appreciative, and incredibly ignorant—a kind of female Gaspar Hauser.

"I should like to see Rome," she said; "it must be a lovely city, or so many foreigners would not be constantly arriving there. Now, do give me a description of Rome. How does the city look when you enter in at the gate?"

"I cannot very well describe it," said the sculptor; "but you enter on a large open space, in the centre of which stands an obelisk, which is a thousand years old."

"An organist!" exclaimed the lady, who had never heard the word 'obelisk.'

Several of the guests could scarcely forbear laughing, and the sculptor would have had some difficulty in keeping his countenance, but the smile on his lips faded away; for he caught sight of a pair of dark-blue eyes close by the side of the inquisitive lady. They belonged to her daughter; and surely no one who had such a daughter could be silly. The mother was like a fountain of questions; and the daughter, who listened but never spoke, might have passed for the beautiful maid of the fountain. How charming she was! She was a study for the sculptor to contemplate, but not to converse with; for she did not speak, or, at least, very seldom.

"Has the pope a great family?" inquired the lady.

The young man answered considerately, as if the question had been a different one, "No; he does not come from a great family."

"That is not what I asked," persisted the widow; "I mean, has he a wife and children?"

"The pope is not allowed to marry," replied the gentleman.

"I don't like that," was the lady's remark.

She certainly might have asked more sensible questions; but if she had not been allowed to say just what she liked, would her daughter have been there, leaning so gracefully on her shoulder, and looking straight before her, with a smile that was almost mournful on her face?

Mr. Alfred again spoke of Italy, and of the glorious colors in Italian scenery; the purple hills, the deep blue of the Mediterranean, the azure of southern skies, whose brightness and glory could only be surpassed in the north by the deep-blue eyes of a maiden; and he said this with a peculiar intonation; but she who should have understood his meaning looked quite unconscious of it, which also was charming.

"Beautiful Italy!" sighed some of the guests.

"Oh, to travel there!" exclaimed others.

"Charming! Charming!" echoed from every voice.

"I may perhaps win a hundred thousand dollars in the lottery," said the naval officer's widow; "and if I do, we will travel—I and my daughter; and you, Mr. Alfred, must be our guide. We can all three travel together, with one or two more of our good friends." And she nodded in such a friendly way at the company, that each imagined himself to be the favored person who was to accompany them to Italy. "Yes, we must go," she continued; "but not to those parts where there are robbers. We will keep to Rome. In the public roads one is always safe."

The daughter sighed very gently; and how much there may be in a sigh, or attributed to it! The young man attributed a great deal of meaning to this sigh. Those deep-blue eyes, which had been lit up this evening in honor of him, must conceal treasures, treasures of heart and mind, richer than all the glories of Rome; and so when he left the party that night, he had lost it completely to the young lady. The house of the naval officer's widow was the one most constantly visited by Mr. Alfred, the sculptor. It was soon understood that his visits were not intended for that lady, though they were the persons who kept up the conversation. He came for the sake of the daughter. They called her Kæla. Her name was really Karen Malena, and these two names had been contracted into the one name Kæla. She was really beautiful; but some said she was rather dull, and slept late of a morning.

"She has been accustomed to that," her mother said. "She is a beauty, and they are always easily tired. She does sleep rather late; but that makes her eyes so clear."

What power seemed to lie in the depths of those dark eyes! The young man felt the truth of the proverb, "Still waters run deep:" and his heart had sunk into their depths. He often talked of his adventures, and the mamma was as simple and eager in her questions as on the first evening they met. It was a pleasure to hear Alfred describe anything. He showed them colored plates of Naples, and spoke of excursions to Mount Vesuvius, and the eruptions of fire from it. The naval officer's widow had never heard of them before.

"Good heavens!" she exclaimed. "So that is a burning mountain; but is it not very dangerous to the people who live near it?"

"Whole cities have been destroyed," he replied; "for instance, Herculaneum and Pompeii."

"Oh, the poor people! And you saw all that with your own eyes?"

"No; I did not see any of the eruptions which are represented in those pictures; but I will show you a sketch of my own, which represents an eruption I once saw."

He placed a pencil sketch on the table; and mamma, who had been overpowered with the appearance of the colored plates, threw a glance at the pale drawing and cried in astonishment, "What, did you see it throw up white fire?"

For a moment, Alfred's respect for Kæla's mamma underwent a sudden shock, and lessened considerably; but, dazzled by the light which surrounded Kæla, he soon found it quite natural that the old lady should have no eye for color. After all, it was of very little consequence; for Kæla's mamma had the best of all possessions; namely, Kæla herself.

Alfred and Kæla were betrothed, which was a very natural result; and the betrothal was announced in the newspaper of the little town. Mama purchased thirty copies of the paper, that she might cut out the paragraph and send it to friends and acquaintances. The betrothed pair were very happy, and the mother was happy too. She said it seemed like connecting herself with Thorwalsden.

"You are a true successor of Thorwalsden," she said to Alfred; and it seemed to him as if, in this instance, mamma had said a clever thing. Kæla was silent; but her eyes shone, her lips smiled, every movement was graceful, — in fact, she was beautiful; that cannot be repeated too often. Alfred decided to take a bust of Kæla as well as of her mother. They sat to him accordingly, and saw how he moulded and formed the soft clay with his fingers.

"I suppose it is only on our acount that you perform this common-place work yourself, instead of leaving it to your servant to do all that sticking together."

"It is really necessary that I should mould the clay myself," he replied.

"Ah, yes, you are always so polite," said mamma, with a smile; and Kæla silently pressed his hand, all soiled as it was with the clay.

Then he unfolded to them both the beauties of Nature, in all her works; he pointed out to them how, in the scale of creation, inanimate matter was inferior to animate nature; the plant above the mineral, the animal above the plant, and man above them all. He strove to show them how the beauty of the mind could be displayed in the outward form, and that it was the sculptor's task to seize upon that beauty of expression, and produce it in his works. Kæla stood silent, but nodded in approbation of what he said, while mamma-in-law made the following confession: —

"It is difficult to follow you; but I go hobbling along after you with my thoughts, though what you say makes my head whirl round and round. Still I contrive to lay hold on some of it."

Kæla's beauty had a firm hold on Alfred; it filled his soul, and held a mastery over him. Beauty beamed from Kæla's every feature, glittered in her eyes, lurked in the corners of her mouth, and pervaded every movement of her agile fingers. Alfred, the sculptor, saw this. He spoke only to her, thought only of her, and the two became one; and so it may be said she spoke much, for he was always talking to her; and he and she were one. Such was the betrothal, and then came the wedding, with bride's-maids and wedding presents, all duly mentioned in the wedding speech. Mamma-in-law had set up Thorwalsden's bust at the end of the table, attired in a dressing-gown; it was her fancy that he should be a guest. Songs were sung, and cheers given; for it was a gay wedding, and they were a handsome pair. "Pygmalion loved his Galatea," said one of the songs.

"Ah, that is some of your mythologies," said mamma-in-law.

Next day the youthful pair started for Copenhagen, where they were to live; mamma-in-law accompanied them, to attend to the "coarse work," as she always called the domestic arrangements. Kæla looked like a doll in a doll's house, for everything was bright and new, and so fine. There they sat, all three; and as for Alfred, a proverb may describe his position — he looked like a swan amongst the geese. The magic of form had enchanted him; he had looked at the casket without caring to inquire what it contained, and that omission often brings the greatest unhappiness into married life. The casket may be injured, the gilding may fall off, and then the purchaser regrets his bargain.

In a large party it is very disagreeable to find a button giving way, with no studs at hand to fall back upon; but it is worse still in a large company to be conscious that your wife and mother-in-law are talking nonsense, and that you cannot depend upon yourself to produce a little ready wit to carry off the stupidity of the whole affair.

The young married pair often sat together hand in hand; he would talk, but she could only now and then let fall a word in the same melodious voice, the same bell-like tones. It was a mental relief when Sophy, one of her friends, came to pay them a visit. Sophy was not pretty. She was, however, quite free from any physical deformity, although Kæla used to say she was a little crooked; but no eye, save an intimate acquaintance, would have noticed it. She was a very sensible girl, yet it never occurred to her that she might be a dangerous person in such a house. Her appearance created a new atmosphere in the doll's house, and air was really required, they all owned that. They felt the want of a change of air, and consequently the young couple and their mother travelled to Italy.

"Thank heaven we are at home again within our own four walls," said mamma-in-law and daughter both, on their return after a year's absence.

"There is no real pleasure in travelling," said mamma; "to tell the truth, it's very wearisome; I beg pardon for saying so. I was soon very tired of it, although I had my children with me; and, besides, it's very expensive work travelling, very expensive. And all those galleries one is expected to see, and the quantity of things you are obliged to run after! It must be done, for very shame; you are sure to be asked when you come back if you have seen everything, and will most likely be told that you've omitted to see what was best worth seeing of all. I got tired at last of those endless Madonnas; I began to think I was turning into a Madonna myself."

"And then the living, mamma," said Kæla.

"Yes, indeed," she replied, "no such a thing as a respectable meat soup—their cookery is miserable stuff."

The journey had also tired Kæla; but she was always fatigued, that was the worst of it. So they sent for Sophy, and she was taken into the house to reside with them, and her presence there was a great advantage. Mamma-in-law acknowledged that Sophy was not only a clever housewife, but well-informed and accomplished, though that could hardly be expected in a person of her limited means. She was also a generous-hearted, faithful girl; she showed that thoroughly while Kæla lay sick, fading away. When the casket is everything, the casket should be strong, or else all is over. And all was over with the casket, for Kæla died.

"She was beautiful," said her mother; "she was quite different from the beauties they call 'antiques,' for they are so damaged. A beauty ought to be perfect, and Kæla was a perfect beauty."

Alfred wept, and mamma wept, and they both wore mourning. The black dress suited mamma very well, and she wore mourning the longest. She had also to experience another grief in seeing Alfred marry again, marry Sophy, who was nothing at all to look at. "He's gone to the very extreme," said mamma-in-law; "he has gone from the most beautiful to the ugliest, and he has forgotten his first wife. Men have no constancy. My husband was a very different man,—but then he died before me."

" 'Pygmalion loved his Galatea,' was in the song they sung at my first wedding," said Alfred; "I once fell in love with a beautiful statue, which awoke to life in my arms; but the kindred soul, which is a gift from heaven, the angel who can feel and sympathize with and elevate us, I have not found and won till now. You came, Sophy, not in the glory of outward beauty, though you are even fairer than is necessary. The chief thing still remains. You came to teach the sculptor that his work is but dust and clay only, an outward form made of a material that decays, and that what we should seek to obtain is the ethereal essence of mind and spirit. Poor Kæla! our life was but as a meeting by the way-side; in yonder world, where we shall know each other from a union of mind, we shall be but mere acquaintances."

"That was not a loving speech," said Sophy, "nor spoken like a Christian. In a future state, where there is neither marrying nor giving in marriage, but where, as you say, souls are attracted to each other by sympathy; there everything beautiful develops itself, and is raised to a higher state of existence: her soul will acquire such completeness that it may harmonize with yours, even more than mine, and you will then once more utter your first rapturous exclamation of your love, 'Beautiful, most beautiful!' "

THE PHILOSOPHER'S STONE

FAR away towards the east, in India, which seemed in those days the world's end, stood the Tree of the Sun; a noble tree, such as we have never seen, and perhaps never may see.

The summit of this tree spread itself for miles like an entire forest, each of its smaller branches forming a complete tree. Palms, beech-trees, pines, plane-trees, and various other kinds, which are found in all parts of the world, were here like small branches, shooting forth from the great tree; while the larger boughs, with their knots and curves, formed valleys and hills, clothed with velvety green and covered with flowers. Everywhere it was like a blooming meadow or a lovely garden. Here were birds from all quarters of the world assembled together; birds from the primeval forests of America, from the rose gardens of Damascus, and from the deserts of Africa, in which the elephant and the lion may boast of being the only rulers. Birds from the Polar regions came flying here, and of course the stork and the swallow were not absent. But the birds were not the only living creatures. There were stags, squirrels, antelopes, and hundreds of other beautiful and light-footed animals here found a home.

The summit of the tree was a wide-spreading garden, and in the midst of it, where the green boughs formed a kind of hill, stood a castle of crystal, with a view from it towards every quarter of heaven. Each tower was erected in the form of a lily, and within the stem was a winding staircase, through which one could ascend to the top and step out upon the leaves as upon balconies. The calyx of the flower itself formed a most beautiful, glittering, circular hall, above which no other roof arose than the blue firmament and the sun and stars.

Just as much splendor, but of another kind, appeared below, in the wide halls of the castle. Here, on the walls, were reflected pictures of the world, which represented numerous and varied scenes of everything that took place daily, so that it was useless to read the newspapers, and indeed there were none to be obtained in this spot. All was to be seen in living pictures by those who wished it, but all would have been too much for even the wisest man, and this man dwelt here. His name is very difficult; you would not be able to pronounce it, so it may be omitted. He knew everything that a man on earth can know or imagine. Every invention already in existence or yet to be, was known to him, and much more; still everything on earth has a limit. The wise king Solomon was not half so wise as this man. He could govern the powers of nature and held sway over potent spirits; even Death itself was obliged to give him every morning a list of those who were to die during the day. And King Solomon himself had to die at last, and this fact it was which so often occupied the thoughts of this great man in the castle on the Tree of the Sun. He knew that he also, however high he might tower above other men in wisdom, must one day die. He knew that his children would fade away like the leaves of the forest and become dust. He saw the human race wither and fall like leaves from the tree; he saw new men come to fill their places, but the leaves that fell off never sprouted forth again; they crumbled to dust or were absorbed into other plants.

"What happens to man," asked the wise man of himself, "when touched by the angel of death? What can death be? The body decays, and the soul. Yes; what is the soul, and whither does it go?"

"To eternal life," says the comforting voice of religion.

"But what is this change? Where and how shall we exist?"

"Above; in heaven," answers the pious man; "it is there we hope to go."

"Above!" repeated the wise man, fixing his eyes upon the moon and stars above him. He saw that to this earthly sphere *above* and *below* were constantly changing places, and that the position varied according to the spot on which a man found himself. He knew, also, that even if he ascended to the top of the highest mountain which rears its lofty summit on this earth, the air, which to us seems clear and transparent, would there be dark and cloudy; the sun would have a coppery glow and send forth no rays, and our earth would lie beneath him wrapped in an orange-colored mist. How narrow are the limits which confine the bodily sight, and how little can be seen by the eye of the soul. How little do the wisest among us know of that which is so important to us all.

In the most secret chamber of the castle lay the greatest treasure on earth—the Book of Truth. The wise man had read it through page after page. Every man may read in this book, but only in fragments. To many eyes the characters seem so mixed in confusion that the words cannot be distinguished. On certain pages the writing often appears so pale or so blurred that the page becomes a blank. The wiser a man becomes, the more he will read, and those who are wisest read most.

The wise man knew how to unite the sunlight and the moonlight with the light of reason and the hidden powers of nature; and through this stronger light, many things in the pages were made clear to him. But in the portion of the book entitled "Life after Death" not a single point could he see distinctly. This pained him. Should he never be able here on earth to obtain a light by which everything written in the Book of Truth should become clear to him? Like the wise King Solomon, he understood the language of animals, and could interpret their talk into song; but that made him none the wiser. He found out the nature of plants and metals, and their power in curing diseases and arresting death, but none to destroy death itself. In all created things within his reach he sought the light that should shine upon the certainty of an eternal life, but he found it not. The Book of Truth lay open before him, but its pages were to him as blank paper. Christianity placed before him in the Bible a promise of eternal life, but he wanted to read it in *his* book, in which nothing on the subject appeared to be written.

He had five children; four sons, educated as the children of such a wise father should be, and a daughter, fair, gentle, and intelligent, but she was blind; yet this deprivation appeared as nothing to her; her father and brothers were outward eyes to her, and a vivid imagination made everything clear to her mental sight. The sons had never gone farther from the castle than the branches of the trees extended, and the sister had scarcely ever left home. They were happy children in that home of their childhood, the beautiful and fragrant Tree of the Sun. Like all children, they loved to hear stories related to them, and their father told them many things which other children would not have understood; but these were as clever as most grown-up people are among us. He explained to them what they saw in the pictures of life on the castle walls — the doings of man, and the progress of events in all the lands of the earth; and the sons often expressed a wish that they could be present, and take a part in these great deeds. Then their father told them that in the world there was nothing but toil and difficulty; that it was not quite what it appeared to them, as they looked upon it in their beautiful home. He spoke to them of the true, the beautiful, and the good, and told them that these three held together in the world, and by that union they became crystallized into a precious jewel, clearer than a diamond of the first water — a jewel, whose splendor had a value even in the sight of God, in whose brightness all things are dim. This jewel was called the philosopher's stone. He told them that, by searching, man could attain to a knowledge of the existence of God, and that it was in the power of every man to discover the certainty that such a jewel as the philosopher's stone really existed. This information would have been beyond the perception of other children; but these children understood, and others will learn to comprehend its meaning after a time. They questioned their father about the true, the beautiful, and the good, and he explained it to them in many ways. He told them that God, when He made man out of the dust of the earth, touched His work five times, leaving five intense feelings, which we call the five senses. Through these, the true, the beautiful, and the good are seen, understood, and perceived, and through these they are valued, protected, and encouraged. Five senses have been given mentally and corporeally, inwardly and outwardly, to body and soul.

The children thought deeply on all these things, and meditated upon them day and night. Then the eldest of the brothers dreamt a splendid dream. Strange to say, not only the second brother but also the third and fourth brothers all dreamt exactly the same thing; namely, that each went out into the world to find the philosopher's stone. Each dreamt that he found it, and that, as he rode back on his swift horse, in the morning dawn, over the velvety green meadows, to his home in the castle of his father, that the stone gleamed from his forehead like a beaming light; and threw such a bright radiance upon the pages of the Book of Truth that every word was illuminated which spoke of the life beyond the grave. But the sister had no dream of going out into the wide world; it never entered her mind. Her world was her father's house.

"I shall ride forth into the wide world," said the eldest brother. "I must try what life is like there, as I mix with men. I will practise only the good and true; with these I will protect the beautiful. Much shall be changed for the better while I am there."

Now these thoughts were great and daring, as our thoughts generally are at home, before we have gone out into the world, and encountered its storms and tempests, its thorns and its thistles. In him, and in all his brothers, the five senses were highly cultivated, inwardly and outwardly; but each of them had one sense which in keenness and development surpassed the other four. In the case of the eldest, this pre-eminent sense was *sight,* which he hoped would be of special service. He had eyes for all times and all people; eyes that could discover in the depths of the earth hidden treasures, and look into the hearts of men, as through a pane of glass; he could read more than is often seen on the cheek that blushes or grows pale, in the eye that droops or smiles. Stags and antelopes accompanied him to the western boundary of his home, and there he found the wild swans. These he followed, and found himself far away in the north, far from the land of his father, which extended eastward to the ends of the earth. How he opened his eyes with astonishment! How many things were to be seen here! and so different to the mere representation of pictures such as those in his father's house. At first he nearly lost his eyes in astonishment at the rubbish and mockery brought forward to represent the beautiful; but he kept his eyes, and soon found full employment for them. He wished to go thoroughly and honestly to work in his endeavor to understand the true, the beautiful, and the good. But how were they represented in the world? He observed that the wreath which rightly belonged to the beautiful was often given the hideous; that the good was often passed by unnoticed, while mediocrity was applauded, when it should have been hissed. People look at the dress, not at the wearer; thought more of a name than of doing their duty; and trusted more to reputation than to real service. It was everywhere the same.

"I see I must make a regular attack on these things," said he; and he accordingly did not spare them. But while looking for the truth, came the evil one, the father of lies, to intercept him. Gladly would the fiend have plucked out the eyes of this *Seer,* but that would have been a too straightforward path for him; he works more cunningly. He allowed the young man to seek for, and discover, the beautiful and the good; but while he was contemplating them, the evil spirit blew one mote after another into each of his eyes; and such a proceeding would injure the strongest sight. Then he blew upon the motes, and they became beams, so that the clearness of his sight was gone, and the *Seer* was like a blind man in the world, and had no longer any faith in it. He had lost his good opinion of the world, as well as of himself; and when a man gives up the world, and himself too, it is all over with him.

"All over," said the wild swan, who flew across the sea to the east.

"All over," twittered the swallows, who were also flying eastward towards the Tree of the Sun. It was no good news which they carried home.

"I think the *Seer* has been badly served," said the second brother, "but the *Hearer* may be more successful."

This one possessed the sense of *hearing* to a very high degree: so acute was this sense, that it was said he could hear the grass grow. He took a fond leave of all at home, and rode away, provided with good abilities and good intentions. The swallows escorted him, and he followed the swans till he found himself out in the world, and far away from home. But he soon discovered that one may have too much of a good thing. His hearing was too fine. He not only heard the grass grow, but could hear every man's heart beat, whether in sorrow or in joy. The whole world was to him like a clockmaker's great workshop, in which all the clocks were going "tick, tick," and all the turret clocks striking "ding, dong." It was unbearable. For a long time his ears endured it, but at last all the noise and tumult became too much for one man to bear.

There were rascally boys of sixty years old—for years do not alone make a man—who raised a tumult, which might have made the *Hearer* laugh, but for the applause which followed, echoing through every street and house, and was even heard in country roads. Falsehood thrust itself forward and played the hypocrite; the bells on the fool's cap jingled, and declared they were church-bells, and the noise became so bad for the *Hearer* that he thrust his fingers into his ears. Still, he could hear false notes and bad singing, gossip and idle words, scandal and slander, groaning and moaning, without and within. "Heaven help us!" He thrust his fingers farther and farther into his ears, till at last the drums burst. And now he could hear nothing more of the true, the beautiful, and the good; for his hearing was to have been the means by which he hoped to acquire his knowledge. He became silent and suspicious, and at last trusted no one, not even himself, and no longer hoping to find and bring home the costly jewel, he gave it up, and gave himself up too, which was worse than all.

The birds in their flight towards the east, carried the tidings, and the news reached the castle in the Tree of the Sun.

"*I* will try now," said the third brother; "I have a keen *nose*." Now that was not a very elegant expression, but it was his way, and we must take him as he was. He had a cheerful temper, and was, besides, a real poet; he could make many things appear poetical, by the way in which he spoke of them, and ideas struck him long before they occurred to the minds of others. "I can smell," he would say; and he attributed to the sense of smelling, which he possessed in a high degree, a great power in the region of the beautiful. "I can smell," he would say, "and many places are fragrant or beautiful according to the taste of the frequenters. One man feels at home in the atmosphere of the tavern, among the flaring tallow candles, and when the smell of spirits mingles with the fumes of bad tobacco. Another prefers sitting amidst the overpowering scent of jasmine, or perfuming himself with scented olive oil. This man seeks the fresh sea breeze, while that one climbs the lofty mountain-top, to look down upon the busy life in miniature beneath him."

As he spoke in this way, it seemed as if he had already been out in the world, as if he had already known and associated with man. But this experience was intuitive—it was the poetry within him, a gift from Heaven bestowed on him in his cradle. He bade farewell to his parental roof in the Tree of the Sun, and departed on foot, from the pleasant scenes that surrounded his home. Arrived at its confines, he mounted on the back of an ostrich, which runs faster than a horse, and afterwards, when he fell in with the wild swans, he swung himself on the strongest of them, for he loved change, and away he flew over the sea to distant lands, where there were great forests, deep lakes, lofty mountains, and proud cities. Wherever he came it seemed as if sunshine travelled with him across the fields, for every flower, every bush, exhaled a renewed fragrance, as if conscious that a friend and protector was near; one who understood them, and knew their value. The stunted rose-bush shot forth twigs, unfolded its leaves, and bore the most beautiful roses; every one could see it, and even the black, slimy wood-snail noticed its beauty. "I will give my seal to the flower," said the snail, "I have trailed my slime upon it, I can do no more."

"Thus it always fares with the beautiful in this world," said the poet. And he made a song upon it, and sung it after his own fashion, but nobody listened. Then he gave a drummer twopence and a peacock's feather, and composed a song for the drum, and the drummer beat it through the streets of the town, and when the people heard it they said, "That is a capital tune." The poet wrote many songs about the true, the beautiful, and the good. His songs were listened to in the tavern, where the tallow candles flared, in the fresh clover field, in the forest, and on the high-seas; and it appeared as if this brother was to be more fortunate than the other two.

But the evil spirit was angry at this, so he set to work with soot and incense, which he can mix so artfully as to confuse an angel, and how much more easily a poor poet. The evil one knew how to manage such people. He so completely surrounded the poet with incense that the man lost his head, forgot his mission and his home, and at last lost himself and vanished in smoke.

But when the little birds heard of it, they mourned, and for three days they sang not one song. The black wood-snail became blacker still; not for grief, but for envy. "They should have offered me incense," he said, "for it was I who gave him the idea of the most famous of his songs—the drum song of 'The Way of the World;' and it was I who spat at the rose; I can bring a witness to that fact."

But no tidings of all this reached the poet's home in India. The birds had all been silent for three days, and when the time of mourning was over, so deep had been their grief, that they had forgotten for whom they wept. Such is the way of the world.

"Now I must go out into the world, and disappear like the rest," said the fourth brother. He was as good-tempered as the third, but no poet, though he could be witty.

The two eldest had filled the castle with joyfulness, and now the last brightness was going away. Sight and hearing have always been considered two of the chief senses among men, and those which they wish to keep bright; the other senses are looked upon as of less importance.

But the younger son had a different opinion; he had cultivated his taste in every way, and taste is very powerful. It rules over what goes into the mouth, as well as over all which is presented to the mind; and, consequently, this brother took upon himself to *taste* everything stored up in bottles or jars; this he called the rough part of his work. Every man's mind was to him as a vessel in which something was concocting; every land a kind of mental kitchen. "There are no delicacies here," he said; so he wished to go out into the world to find something delicate to suit his taste. "Perhaps fortune may be more favorable to me than it was to my brothers. I shall start on my travels, but what conveyance shall I choose? Are air balloons invented yet?" he asked of his father, who knew of all inventions that had been made, or would be made.

Air balloons had not then been invented, nor steam-ships, nor railways.

"Good," said he; "then I shall choose an air balloon; my father knows how they are to be made and guided. Nobody has invented one yet, and the people will believe that it is an aerial phantom. When I have done with the balloon I shall burn it, and for this purpose, you must give me a few pieces of another invention, which will come next; I mean a few chemical matches."

He obtained what he wanted, and flew away. The birds accompanied him farther than they had the other brothers. They were curious to know how this flight would end. Many more of them came swooping down; they thought it must be some new bird, and he soon had a goodly company of followers.

BEAUTY OF FORM AND BEAUTY OF MIND

They came in clouds till the air became darkened with birds as it was with the cloud of locusts over the land of Egypt.

And now he was out in the wide world. The balloon descended over one of the greatest cities, and the aëronaut took up his station at the highest point, on the church steeple. The balloon rose again into the air, which it ought not to have done; what became of it is not known, neither is it of any consequence, for balloons had not then been invented.

There he sat on the church steeple. The birds no longer hovered over him; they had got tired of him, and he was tired of them. All the chimneys in the town were smoking.

"There are altars erected to my honor," said the wind, who wished to say something agreeable to him as he sat there boldly looking down upon the people in the street. There was one stepping along, proud of his purse; another, of the key he carried behind him, though he had nothing to lock up; another took a pride in his moth-eaten coat; and another, in his mortified body. "Vanity, all vanity!" he exclaimed. "I must go down there by-and-by, and touch and taste; but I shall sit here a little while longer, for the wind blows pleasantly at my back. I shall remain here as long as the wind blows, and enjoy a little rest. It is comfortable to sleep late in the morning when one had a great deal to do," said the sluggard; "so I shall stop here as long as the wind blows, for it pleases me."

And there he stayed. But as he was sitting on the weather-cock of the steeple, which kept turning round and round with him, he was under the false impression that the same wind still blew, and that he could stay where he was without expense.

But in India, in the castle on the Tree of the Sun, all was solitary and still, since the brothers had gone away one after the other.

"Nothing goes well with them," said the father; "they will never bring the glittering jewel home, it is not made for me; they are all dead and gone." Then he bent down over the Book of Truth, and gazed on the page on which he should have read of the life after death, but for him there was nothing to be read or learned upon it.

His blind daughter was his consolation and joy; she clung to him with sincere affection, and for the sake of his happiness and peace she wished the costly jewel could be found and brought home.

With longing tenderness she thought of her brothers. Where were they? Where did they live? How she wished she might dream of them; but it was strange that not even in dreams could she be brought near to them. But at last one night she dreamt that she heard the voices of her brothers calling to her from the distant world, and she could not refrain herself, but went out to them, and yet it seemed in her dream that she still remained in her father's house. She did not *see* her brothers, but she *felt* as it were a fire burning in her hand, which, however, did not hurt her, for it was the jewel she was bringing to her father. When she awoke she thought for a moment that she still held the stone, but she only grasped the knob of her distaff.

During the long evenings she had spun constantly, and round the distaff were woven threads finer than the web of a spider; human eyes could never have distinguished these threads when separated from each other. But she had wetted them with her tears, and the twist was as strong as a cable. She rose with the impression that her dream must be a reality, and her resolution was taken.

It was still night, and her father slept; she pressed a kiss upon his hand, and then took her distaff and fastened the end of the thread to her father's house. But for this, blind as she was, she would never have found her way home again; to this thread she must hold fast, and trust not to others or even to herself. From the Tree of the Sun she broke four leaves; which she gave up to the wind and the weather, that they might be carried to her brothers as letters and a greeting, in case she did not meet them in the wide world. Poor blind child, what would become of her in those distant regions? But she had the invisible thread, to which she could hold fast; and she possessed a gift which all the others lacked. This was a determination to throw herself entirely into whatever she undertook, and it made her feel as if she had eyes even at the tips of her fingers, and could hear down into her very heart. Quietly she went forth into the noisy, bustling, wonderful world, and wherever she went the skies grew bright, and she felt the warm sunbeam, and a rainbow above in the blue heavens seemed to span the dark world. She heard the song of the birds, and smelt the scent of the orange groves and apple orchards so strongly that she seemed to taste it. Soft tones and charming songs reached her ear, as well as harsh sounds and rough words—thoughts and opinions in strange contradiction to each other. Into the deepest recesses of her heart penetrated the echoes of human thoughts and feelings. Now she heard the following words sadly sung, —

> "Life is a shadow that flits away
>   In a night of darkness and woe."

But then would follow brighter thoughts:

> "Life has the rose's sweet perfume
>   With sunshine, light, and joy."

And if one stanza sounded painfully—

> "Each mortal thinks of himself alone,
>   Is a truth, alas, too clearly known;"

Then, on the other hand, came the answer—

> "Love, like a mighty flowing stream,
>   Fills every heart with its radiant gleam."

She heard, indeed, such words as these—

> "In the pretty turmoil here below,
>   All is a vain and paltry show.

Then came also words of comfort—

> "Great and good are the actions done
>   By many whose worth is never known."

And if sometimes the mocking strain reached her —

> "Why not join in the jesting cry
> That contemns all gifts from the throne on high?"

In the blind girl's heart a stronger voice repeated —

> "To trust in thyself and God is best,
> In His holy will forever to rest."

But the evil spirit could not see this and remain contented. He has more cleverness than ten thousand men, and he found means to compass his end. He betook himself to the marsh, and collected a few little bubbles of stagnant water. Then he uttered over them the echoes of lying words that they might become strong. He mixed up together songs of praise with lying epitaphs, as many as he could find, boiled them in tears shed by envy; put upon them rouge, which he had scraped from faded cheeks, and from these he produced a maiden, in form and appearance like the blind girl, the angel of completeness, as men called her. The evil one's plot was successful. The world knew not which was the true, and indeed how should the world know?

> "To trust in thyself and God is best,
> In his Holy will forever to rest."

So sung the blind girl in full faith. She had entrusted the four green leaves from the Tree of the Sun to the winds, as letters of greeting to her brothers, and she had full confidence that the leaves would reach them. She fully believed that the jewel which outshines all the glories of the world would yet be found, and that upon the forehead of humanity it would glitter even in the castle of her father. "Even in my father's house," she repeated. "Yes, the place in which this jewel is to be found is earth, and I shall bring more than the promise of it with me. I feel it glow and swell more and more in my closed hand. Every grain of truth which the keen wind carried up and whirled towards me I caught and treasured. I allowed it to be penetrated with the fragrance of the beautiful, of which there is so much in the world, even for the blind. I took the beatings of a heart engaged in a good action, and added them to my treasure. All that I can bring is but dust; still, it is a part of the jewel we seek, and there is plenty, my hand is quite full of it."

She soon found herself again at home; carried thither in a flight of thought, never having loosened her hold of the invisible thread fastened to her father's house. As she stretched out her hand to her father, the powers of evil dashed with the fury of a hurricane over the Tree of the Sun; a blast of wind rushed through the open doors, and into the sanctuary, where lay the Book of Truth.

"It will be blown to dust by the wind," said the father, as he seized the open hand she held towards him.

"No," she replied, with quiet confidence, "it is indestructible. I feel its beam warming my very soul."

Then her father observed that a dazzling flame gleamed from the white page on which the shining dust had passed from her hand. It was there to prove the certainty of eternal life, and on the book glowed one shining word, and only one, the word BELIEVE. And soon the four brothers were again with the father and daughter. When the green leaf from home fell on the bosom of each, a longing had seized them to return. They had arrived, accompanied by the birds of passage, the stag, the antelope, and all the creatures of the forest who wished to take part in their joy.

We have often seen, when a sunbeam burst through a crack in the door into a dusty room, how a whirling column of dust seems to circle round. But this was not poor, insignificant, common dust, which the blind girl had brought; even the rainbow's colors are dim when compared with the beauty which shone from the page on which it had fallen. The beaming word BELIEVE, from every grain of truth, had the brightness of the beautiful and the good, more bright than the mighty pillar of flame that led Moses and the children of Israel to the land of Canaan, and from the word BELIEVE arose the bridge of hope, reaching even to the unmeasurable Love in the realms of the infinite.

"IN THE UTTERMOST PARTS OF THE SEA"

SOME years ago, large ships were sent towards the north pole, to explore the distant coasts, and to try how far men could penetrate into those unknown regions. For more than a year one of these ships had been pushing its way northward, amid snow and ice, and the sailors had endured many hardships; till at length winter set in, and the sun entirely disappeared; for many weeks there would be constant night. All around, as far as the eye could reach, nothing could be seen but fields of ice, in which the ship remained stuck fast. The snow lay piled up in great heaps, and of these the sailors made huts, in the form of bee-hives, some of them as large and spacious as one of the "Huns' graves," and others only containing room enough to hold three or four men. It was not quite dark; the northern lights shot forth red and blue flames, like continuous fireworks, and the snow glittered, and reflected back the light, so that the night here was one long twilight. When the moon was brightest, the natives came in crowds to see the sailors. They had a very singular appearance in their rough, hairy dresses of fur, and riding in sledges over the ice. They brought with them furs and skins in great abundance, so that the snow-houses were soon provided with warm carpets, and the furs also served for the sailors to wrap themselves in, when they slept under the roofs of snow, while outside it was freezing with a cold far more severe than in the winter with us. In our country it was still autumn, though late in the season; and they thought of that in their distant exile, and often pictured to themselves the yellow leaves on the trees at home. Their watches pointed to the hours of evening, and time to go to sleep, although in these regions it was now always night.

In one of the huts, two of the men laid themselves down to rest. The younger of these men had brought with him from home his best, his dearest treasure—a Bible, which his grandmother had given him on his departure. Every night the sacred volume rested under his head, and he had known from his childhood what was written in it. Every day he read in the book, and while stretched on his cold couch, the holy words he had learnt would come into his mind: "If I take the wings of the morning, and fly to the uttermost parts of the sea, even there Thou art with me, and Thy right hand shall uphold me;" and under the influence of that faith which these holy words inspired, sleep came upon him, and dreams, which are the manifestations of God to the spirit. The soul lives and acts, while the body is at rest. He felt this life in him, and it was as if he heard the sound of dear, well-known melodies, as if the breezes of summer floated around him; and over his couch shone a ray of brightness, as if it were shining through the covering of his snow-roof. He lifted his head, and saw that the bright gleaming was not the reflection of the glittering snow, but the dazzling brightness of the pinions of a mighty angel, into whose beaming face he was gazing. As from the cup of a lily, the angel rose from amidst the leaves of the Bible; and, stretching out his arm, the walls of the hut sunk down, as though they had been formed of a light, airy veil of mist, and the green hills and meadows of home, with its ruddy woods, lay spread around him in the quiet sunshine of a lovely autumn day. The nest of the stork was empty, but ripe fruit still hung on the wild apple-tree, although the leaves had fallen. The red hips gleamed on the hedges, and the starling which hung in the green cage outside the window of the peasant's hut, which was his home, whistled the tune which he had taught him. His grandmother hung green birds'-food around the cage, as he, her grandson, had been accustomed to do. The daughter of the village blacksmith, who was young and fair, stood at the well, drawing water. She nodded to the grandmother, and the old woman nodded to her, and pointed to a letter which had come from a long way off. That very morning the letter had arrived from the cold regions of the north; there, where the absent one was sweetly sleeping under the protecting hand of God. They laughed and wept over the letter; and he, far away, amid ice and snow, under the shadow of the angel's wings, wept and smiled with them in spirit; for he saw and heard it all in his dream. From the letter they read aloud the words of Holy Writ: "In the uttermost parts of the sea, Thy right hand shall uphold me." And as the angel spread his wings like a veil over the sleeper, there was the sound of beautiful music and a hymn. Then the vision fled. It was dark again in the snow-hut: but the Bible still rested beneath his head, and faith and hope dwelt in his heart. God was with him, and he carried home in his heart, even "in the uttermost parts of the sea."

THE MARSH KING'S DAUGHTER

THE storks relate to their little ones a great many stories, and they are all about moors and reed banks, and suited to their age and capacity. The youngest of them are quite satisfied with "kribble, krabble," or such nonsense, and think it very grand; but the elder ones want something with a deeper meaning, or at least something about their own family.

We are only acquainted with one of the two longest and oldest stories which the storks relate — it is about Moses, who was exposed by his mother on the banks of the Nile, and was found by the king's daughter, who gave him a good education, and he afterwards became a great man; but where he was buried is still unknown.

Every one knows this story, but not the second; very likely because it is quite an inland story. It has been repeated from mouth to mouth, from one stork-mamma to another, for thousands of years; and each has told it better than the last; and now *we* mean to tell it better than all.

The first stork pair who related it lived at the time it happened, and had their summer residence on the rafters of the Viking's* house, which stood near the wild moorlands of Wendsyssell; that is, to speak more correctly, the great moorheath, high up in the north of Jutland, by the Skjagen peak. This wilderness is still an immense wild heath of marshy ground, about which we can read in the "Official Directory." It is said that in olden times the place was a lake, the ground of which had heaved up from beneath, and now the moorland extends for miles in every direction, and is surrounded by damp meadows, trembling, undulating swamps, and marshy ground covered with turf, on which grow bilberry bushes and stunted trees. Mists are almost always hovering over this region, which, seventy years ago, was overrun with wolves. It may well be called the Wild Moor; and one can easily imagine, with such a wild expanse of marsh and lake, how lonely and dreary it must have been a thousand years ago. Many things may be noticed now that existed then. The reeds grow to the same height, and bear the same kind of long, purple-brown leaves, with their feathery tips. There still stands the birch, with its white bark and its delicate, loosely hanging leaves; and with regard to the living beings who frequented this spot, the fly still wears a gauzy dress of the same cut, and the favorite colors of the stork are white, with black and red for stockings. The people, certainly, in those days, wore very different dresses to those they now wear, but if any of them, be he huntsman or squire, master or servant, ventured on the wavering, undulating, marshy ground of the moor, they met with the same fate a thousand years ago as they would now. The wanderer sank, and went down to the Marsh King, as he is named, who rules in the great moorland empire beneath. They also called him "Gunkel King," but we like the name of "Marsh King" better, and we will give him that name as the storks do. Very little is known of the Marsh King's rule, but that, perhaps, is a good thing.

In the neighborhood of the moorlands, and not far from the great arm of the North Sea and the Cattegat which is called the Lumfjorden, lay the castle of the Viking, with its water-tight stone cellars, its tower, and its three projecting storeys. On the ridge of the roof the stork had built his nest, and there the stork-mamma sat on her eggs and felt sure her hatching would come to something.

One evening, stork-papa stayed out rather late, and when he came home he seemed quite busy, bustling, and important. "I have something very dreadful to tell you," said he to the stork-mamma.

"Keep it to yourself then," she replied. "Remember that I am hatching eggs; it may agitate me, and will affect them."

"You must know it at once," said he. "The daughter of our host in Egypt has arrived here. She has ventured to take this journey, and now she is lost."

"She who sprung from the race of the fairies, is it?" cried the mother stork. "Oh, tell me all about it; you know I cannot bear to be kept waiting at a time when I am hatching eggs."

*Sea Kings, or pirates of the north.

"Well, you see, mother," he replied, "she believed what the doctors said, and what I have heard you state also, that the moor-flowers which grow about here would heal her sick father; and she has flown to the north in swan's plumage, in company with some other swan-princesses, who come to these parts every year to renew their youth. She came, and where is she now!"

"You enter into particulars too much," said the mamma stork, "and the eggs may take cold; I cannot bear such suspense as this."

"Well," said he, "I have kept watch; and this evening I went among the rushes where I thought the marshy ground would bear me, and while I was there three swans came. Somehting in their manner of flying seemed to say to me, 'Look carefully now; there is one not all swan, only swan's feathers.' You know, mother, you have the same intuitive feeling that I have; you know whether a thing is right or not immediately."

"Yes, of course," said she; "but tell me about the princess; I am tired of hearing about the swan's feathers."

"Well, you know that in the middle of the moor there is something like a lake," said the stork-papa. "You can see the edge of it if you raise yourself a little. Just there, by the reeds and the green banks, lay the trunk of an elder-tree; upon this the three swans stood flapping their wings, and looking about them; one of them threw off her plumage, and I immediately recognized her as one of the princesses of our home in Egypt. There she sat, without any covering but her long, black hair. I heard her tell the two others to take great care of the swan's plumage, while she dipped down into the water to pluck the flowers which she fancied she saw there. The others nodded, and picked up the feather dress, and took possession of it. I wonder what will become of it? thought I, and she most likely asked herself the same question. If so, she received an answer, a very practical one; for the two swans rose up and flew away with her swan's plumage. 'Dive down now!' they cried; 'thou shalt never more fly in the swan's plumage, thou shalt never again see Egypt; here, on the moor, thou wilt remain.' So saying, they tore the swan's plumage into a thousand pieces, the feathers drifted about like a snow-shower, and then the two deceitful princesses flew away."

"Why, that is terrible," said the stork-mamma; "I feel as if I could hardly bear to hear any more, but you must tell me what happened next."

"The princess wept and lamented aloud; her tears moistened the elder stump, which was really not an elder stump but the Marsh King himself, he who in marshy ground lives and rules. I saw myself how the stump of the tree turned round, and was a tree no more, while long, clammy branches like arms, were extended from it. Then the poor child was terribly frightened, and started up to run away. She hastened to cross the green, slimy ground; but it will not bear any weight, much less hers. She quickly sank, and the elder stump dived immediately after her; in fact, it was he who drew her down. Great black bubbles rose up out of the moor-slime, and with these every trace of the two vanished. And now the princess is buried in the wild marsh, she will never now carry flowers to Egypt to cure her father. It would have broken your heart, mother, had you seen it."

"You ought not to have told me," said she, "at such a time as this; the eggs might suffer. But I think the princess will soon find help; some one will rise up to help her. Ah! if it had been you or I, or one of our people, it would have been all over with us."

THE MARSH KING'S DAUGHTER

"I mean to go every day," said he, "to see if anything comes to pass;" and so he did.

A long time went by, but at last he saw a green stalk shooting up out of the deep, marshy ground. As it reached the surface of the marsh, a leaf spread out, and unfolded itself broader and broader, and close to it came forth a bud.

One morning, when the stork-papa was flying over the stem, he saw that the power of the sun's rays had caused the bud to open, and in the cup of the flower lay a charming child — a little maiden, looking as if she had just come out of a bath. The little one was so like the Egyptian princess, that the stork, at the first moment, thought it must be the princess herself; but after a little reflection he decided that it was much more likely to be the daughter of the princess and the Marsh King; and this explained also her being placed in the cup of a water-lily. "But she cannot be left to lie here," thought the stork, "and in my nest there are already so many. But stay, I have thought of something: the wife of the Viking has no children, and how often she has wished for a little one. People always say the stork brings the little ones; I will do so in earnest this time. I shall fly with the child to the Viking's wife; what rejoicing there will be!"

And then the stork lifted the little girl out of the flower-cup, flew to the castle, picked a hole with his beak in the bladder-covered window, and laid the beautiful child in the bosom of the Viking's wife. Then he flew back quickly to the stork-mamma and told her what he had seen and done; and the little storks listened to it all, for they were then quite old enough to do so. "So you see," he continued, "that the princess is not dead, for she must have sent her little one up here; and now I have found a home for her."

"Ah, I said it would be so from the first," replied the stork-mamma; "but now think a little of your own family. Our travelling time draws near, and I sometimes feel a little irritation already under the wings. The cuckoos and the nightingale are already gone, and I heard the quails say they should go too as soon as the wind was favorable. Our youngsters will go through all the manœuvres at the review very well, or I am much mistaken in them."

The Viking's wife was above measure delighted when she awoke the next morning and found the beautiful little child lying in her bosom. She kissed it and caressed it; but it cried terribly, and struck out with its arms and legs, and did not seem to be pleased at all. At last it cried itself to sleep; and as it lay there so still and quiet, it was a most beautiful sight to see. The Viking's wife was so delighted, that body and soul were full of joy. Her heart felt so light within her, that it seemed as if her husband and his soldiers, who were absent, must come home as suddenly and unexpectedly as the little child had done. She and her whole household therefore busied themselves in preparing everything for the reception of her lord. The long, colored tapestry, on which she and her maidens had worked pictures of their idols, Odin, Thor, and Friga, was hung up. The slaves polished the old shields that served as ornaments; cushions were placed on the seats, and dry wood laid on the fireplaces in the centre of the hall, so that the flames might be fanned up at a moment's notice. The Viking's wife herself assisted in the work, so that at night she felt very tired, and quickly fell into a sound sleep. When she awoke, just before morning, she was terribly alarmed to find that the infant had vanished. She sprang from her couch, lighted a pine-chip, and searched all round the room, when, at last, in that part of the bed where her feet had been, lay, not the child, but a great, ugly frog. She was quite disgusted at this sight, and seized a heavy stick to kill the frog; but the creature looked at her with such strange, mournful eyes, that she was unable to strike the blow. Once more she searched round the room; then she started at hearing the frog utter a low, painful croak. She sprang from the couch and opened the window hastily; at the same moment the sun rose, and threw its beams through the window, till it rested on the couch where the great frog lay. Suddenly it appeared as if the frog's broad mouth contracted, and became small and red. The limbs moved and stretched out and extended themselves till they took a beautiful shape; and behold there was the pretty child lying before her, and the ugly frog was gone. "How is this?" she cried, "have I had a wicked dream? Is it not my own lovely cherub that lies there." Then she kissed it and fondled it; but the child struggled and fought, and bit as if she had been a little wild cat.

The Viking did not return on that day, nor the next; he was, however, on the way home; but the wind, so favorable to the storks, was against him; for it blew towards the south. A wind in favor of one is often against another.

After two or three days had passed, it became clear to the Viking's wife how matters stood with the child; it was under the influence of a powerful sorcerer. By day it was charming in appearance as an angel of light, but with a temper wicked and wild; while at night, in the form of an ugly frog, it was quiet and mournful, with eyes full of sorrow. Here were two natures, changing inwardly and outwardly with the absence and return of sunlight. And so it happened that by day the child, with the actual form of its mother, possessed the fierce disposition of its father; at night, on the contrary, its outward appearance plainly showed its descent on the father's side, while inwardly it had the heart and mind of its mother. Who would be able to loosen this wicked charm which the sorcerer had worked upon it? The wife of the Viking lived in constant pain and sorrow about it. Her heart clung to the little creature, but she could not explain to her husband the circumstances in which it was placed. He was expected to return shortly; and were she to tell him, he would very likely, as was the custom at that time, expose the poor child in the public highway, and let any one take it away who would. The good wife of the Viking could not let that happen, and she therefore resolved that the Viking should never see the child excepting by daylight.

One morning there sounded a rushing of storks' wings over the roof. More than a hundred pair of storks had rested there during the night, to recover themselves after their excursion; and now they soared aloft, and prepared for the journey southward.

"All the husbands are here, and ready!" they cried; "wives and children also!"

"How light we are!" screamed the young storks in chorus. "Something pleasant seems creeping over us, even down to our toes, as if we were full of live frogs. Ah, how delightful it is to travel into foreign lands!"

"Hold yourselves properly in the line with us," cried papa and mamma. "Do not use your beaks so much; it tries the lungs." And then the storks flew away.

About the same time sounded the clang of the warriors' trumpets across the heath. The Viking had landed with his men. They were returning home, richly laden with spoil from the Gallic coast, where the people, as did also the inhabitants of Britain, often cried in alarm, "Deliver us from the wild northmen."

Life and noisy pleasure came with them into the castle of the Viking on the moorland. A great cask of mead was drawn into the hall, piles of wood blazed, cattle were slain and served up, that they might feast in reality. The priest who offered the sacrifice sprinkled the devoted parishioners with the warm blood; the fire crackled, and the smoke rolled along beneath the roof; the soot fell upon them from the beams; but they were used to all these things. Guests were invited, and received handsome presents. All wrongs and un-faithfulness were forgotten. They drank deeply, and threw in each other's faces the bones that were left, which was looked upon as a sign of good feeling amongst them. A bard, who was a kind of musician as well as warrior, and who had been with the Viking in his expedition, and knew what to sing about, gave them one of his best songs, in which they heard all their warlike deeds praised, and every wonderful action brought forward with honor. Every verse ended with this refrain, —

> "Gold and possessions will flee away,
> Friends and foes must die one day;
> Every man on earth must die,
> But a famous name will never die."

And with that they beat upon their shields, and hammered upon the table with knives and bones, in a most outrageous manner.

The Viking's wife sat upon a raised cross seat in the open hall. She wore a silk dress, golden bracelets, and large amber beads. She was in costly attire, and the bard named her in his song, and spoke of the rich treasure of gold which she had brought to her husband. Her husband had already seen the wonderfully beautiful child in the daytime, and was delighted with her beauty; even her wild ways pleased him. He said the little maiden would grow up to be a heroine, with the strong will and determination of a man. She would never wink her eyes, even if, in joke, an expert hand should attempt to cut off her eye-brows with a sharp sword.

The full cask of mead soon became empty, and a fresh one was brought in; for these were people who liked plenty to eat and drink. The old proverb, which every one knows, says that "the cattle know when to leave their pasture, but a foolish man knows not the measure of his own appetite." Yes, they all knew this; but men may know what is right, and yet often do wrong. They also knew "that even the welcome guest becomes wearisome when he sits too long in the house." But there they remained; for pork and mead are good things. And so at the Viking's house they stayed, and enjoyed themselves; and at night the bondmen slept in the ashes, and dipped their fingers in the fat, and licked them. Oh, it was a delightful time!

Once more in the same year the Viking went forth, though the storms of autumn had already commenced to roar. He went with his warriors to the coast of Britain; he said that it was but an excursion of pleasure across the water, so his wife remained at home with the little girl. After a while, it is quite certain the foster-mother began to love the poor frog, with its gentle eyes and its deep sighs, even better than the little beauty who bit and fought with all around her.

The heavy, damp mists of autumn, which destroy the leaves of the wood, had already fallen upon forest and heath. Feathers of plucked birds, as they call the snow, flew about in thick showers, and winter was coming. The sparrows took possession of the stork's nest, and conversed about the absent owners in their own fashion; and they, the stork pair and all their young ones, where were they staying now? The storks might have been found in the land of Egypt, where the sun's rays shone forth bright and warm, as it does here at midsummer. Tamarinds and acacias were in full bloom all over the country, the crescent of Mahomet glittered brightly from the cupolas of the mosques, and on the slender pinnacles sat many of the storks, resting after their long journey. Swarms of them took divided possession of the nests — nests which lay close to each other between the venerable columns, and crowded the arches of temples in forgotten cities. The date and the palm lifted themselves as a screen or as a sun-shade over them. The gray pyramids looked like broken shadows in the clear air and the far-off desert, where the ostrich wheels his rapid flight, and the lion, with his subtle eyes, gazes at the marble sphinx which lies half buried in sand. The waters of the Nile had retreated, and the whole bed of the river was covered with frogs, which was a most acceptable prospect for the stork families. The young storks thought their eyes deceived them, everything around appeared so beautiful.

"It is always like this here, and this is how we live in our warm country," said the stork-mamma; and the thought made the young ones almost beside themselves with pleasure.

"Is there anything more to see?" they asked; "are we going farther into the country?"

"There is nothing further for us to see," answered the stork-mamma. "Beyond this delightful region there are immense forests, where the branches of the trees entwine round each other, while prickly, creeping plants cover the paths, and only an elephant could force a passage for himself with his great feet. The snakes are too large, and the lizards too lively for us to catch. Then there is the desert; it you went there, your eyes would soon be full of sand with the lightest breeze, and if it should blow great guns, you would most likely find yourself in a sand-drift. Here is the best place for you, where there are frogs and locusts; here I shall remain, and so must you." And so they stayed.

The parents sat in the nest on the slender minaret, and rested, yet still were busily employed in cleaning and smoothing their feathers, and in sharpening their beaks against their red stockings; then they would stretch out their necks, salute each other, and gravely raise their heads with the high-polished forehead, and soft, smooth feathers, while their brown eyes shone with intelligence. The female young ones strutted about amid the moist rushes, glancing at the other young storks and making acquaintances, and swallowing a frog at every third step, or tossing a little snake about with their beaks, in a way they considered very becoming, and besides it tasted very good. The young male storks soon began to quarrel; they struck at each other with their wings, and pecked with their beaks till the blood came. And in this manner many of the young ladies and gentlemen were betrothed to each other: it was, of course, what they wanted, and indeed what they lived for. Then they returned to a nest, and there the quarrelling began afresh; for in hot countries people are almost all violent and passionate. But for all that it was pleasant, especially for the old people, who watched them with great joy: all that their young ones did suited them. Every day here there was sunshine, plenty to eat, and nothing to think of but pleasure. But in the rich castle of their Egyptian host, as they called him, pleasure was not to be found. The rich and mighty lord of the castle lay on his couch, in the midst of the great hall, with its many colored walls looking like the centre of a great tulip; but he was stiff and powerless in all his limbs, and lay stretched out like a mummy. His family and servants stood round him; he was not dead, although he could scarcely be said to live. The healing moor-flower from the north, which was to have been found and brought to him by her who loved him so well, had not arrived. His young and beautiful daughter who, in swan's plumage, had flown over land and seas to the distant north, had never returned. She is dead, so the two swan-maidens had said when they came home; and they made up quite a story about her, and this is what they told, —

"We three flew away together through the air," said they: "a hunter caught sight of us, and shot at us with an arrow. The arrow struck our young friend and sister, and slowly singing her farewell song she sank down, a dying swan, into the forest lake. On the shores of the lake, under a spreading birch-tree, we laid her in the cold earth. We had our revenge; we bound fire under the wings of a swallow, who had a nest on the thatched roof of the huntsman. The house took fire, and burst into flames; the hunter was burnt with the house, and the light was reflected over the sea as far as the spreading birch, beneath which we laid her sleeping dust. She will never return to the land of Egypt." And then they both wept. And stork-papa, who heard the story, snapped with his beak so that it might be heard a long way off.

'Deceit and lies!" cried he; "I should like to run my beak deep into their chests."

"And perhaps break it off," said the mamma stork, "then what a sight you would be. Think first of yourself, and then of your family; all others are nothing to us."

"Yes, I know," said the stork-papa; "but to-morrow I can easily place myself on the edge of the open cupola, when the learned and wise men assemble to consult on the state of the sick man; perhaps they may come a little nearer to the truth." And the learned and wise men assembled together, and talked a great deal on every point; but the stork could make no sense out of anything they said; neither were there any good results from their consultations, either for the sick man, or for his daughter in the marshy heath. When we listen to what people say in this world, we shall hear a great deal; but it is an advantage to know what has been said and done before, when we listen to a conversation. The stork did, and we know at least as much as he, the stork.

"Love is a life-giver. The highest love produces the highest life. Only through love can the sick man be cured." This had been said by many, and even the learned men acknowledged that it was a wise saying.

"What a beautiful thought!" exclaimed the papa stork immediately.

"I don't quite understand it," said the mamma stork, when her husband repeated it; "however, it is not my fault, but the fault of the thought; whatever it may be, I have something else to think of."

Now the learned men had spoken also of love between this one and that one; of the difference of the love which we have for our neighbor, to the love that exists between parents and children; of the love of the plant for the light, and how the germ springs forth when the sunbeam kisses the ground. All these things were so elaborately and learnedly explained, that it was im-

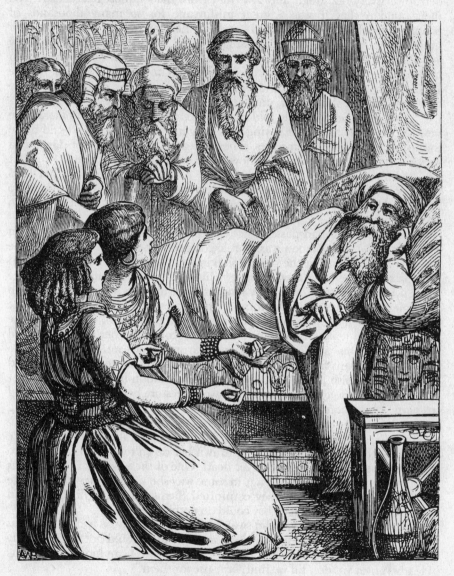

THE MARSH KING'S DAUGHTER

possible for stork-papa to follow it, much less to talk about it. His thoughts on the subject quite weighed him down; he stood the whole of the following day on one leg, with half-shut eyes, thinking deeply. So much learning was quite a heavy weight for him to carry. One thing, however, the papa stork could understand. Every one, high and low, had from their inmost hearts expressed their opinion that it was a great misfortune for so many thousands of people—the whole country indeed—to have this man so sick, with no hopes of his recovery. And what joy and blessing it would spread around if he could by any means be cured! But where bloomed the flower that could bring him health? They had searched for it everywhere; in learned writings, in the shining stars, in the weather and wind. Inquiries had been made in every by-way that could be thought of, until at last the wise and learned men has asserted, as we have been already told, that "love, the life-giver, could alone give new life to a father;" and in saying this, they had overdone it, and said more than they understood themselves. They repeated it, and wrote it down as a recipe, "Love is a life-giver." But how could such a recipe be prepared—that was a difficulty they could not overcome. At last it was decided that help could only come from the princess herself, whose whole soul was wrapped up in her father, especially as a plan had been adopted by her to enable her to obtain a remedy.

More than a year had passed since the princess had set out at night, when the light of the young moon was soon lost beneath the horizon. She had gone to the marble sphinx in the desert, shaking the sand from her sandals, and then passed through the long passage, which leads to the centre of one of the great pyramids, where the mighty kings of antiquity, surrounded with pomp and splendor, lie veiled in the form of mummies. She had been told by the wise men, that if she laid her head on the breast of one of them, from the head she would learn where to find life and recovery for her father. She had performed all this, and in a dream had learnt that she must bring home to her father the lotus flower, which grows in the deep sea, near the moors and heath in the Danish land. The very place and situation had been pointed out to her, and she was told that the flower would restore her father to health and strength. And, therefore, she had gone forth from the land of Egypt, flying over to the open marsh and the wild moor in the plumage of a swan.

The papa and mamma storks knew all this, and we also know it now. We know, too, that the Marsh King has drawn her down to himself, and that to the loved ones at home she is forever dead. One of the wisest of them said, as the stork-mamma also said, "That in some way she would, after all, manage to succeed;" and so at last they comforted themselves with this hope, and would wait patiently; in fact, they could do nothing better.

"I should like to get away the swan's feathers from those two treacherous princesses," said the papa stork; "then, at least, they would not be able to fly over again to the wild moor, and do more wickedness. I can hide the two suits of feathers over yonder, till we find some use for them."

"But were will you put them?" asked the mamma stork.

"In our nest on the moor. I and the young ones will carry them by turns during our flight across; and as we return, should they prove too heavy for us, we shall be sure to find plenty of places on the way in which we can conceal them till our next journey. Certainly one suit of swan's feathers would be enough for the princess, but two are always better. In those northern countries no one can have too many travelling wrappers."

"No one will thank you for it," said stork-mamma; "but you are master; and, excepting at breeding time, I have nothing to say."

In the Viking's castle on the wild moor, to which the storks directed their flight in the following spring, the little maiden still remained. They had named her Helga, which was rather too soft a name for a child with a temper like hers, although her form was still beautiful. Every month this temper showed itself in sharper outlines; and in the course of years, while the storks still made the same journeys in autumn to the hill, and in spring to the moors, the child grew to be almost a woman, and before any one seemed aware of it, she was a wonderfully beautiful maiden of sixteen. The casket was splendid, but the contents were worthless. She was, indeed, wild and savage even in those hard, uncultivated times. It was a pleasure to her to splash about with her white hands in the warm blood of the horse which had been slain for sacrifice. In one of her wild moods she bit off the head of the black cock, which the priest was about to slay for the sacrifice. To her foster-father she said one day, "If thine enemy were to pull down thine house about thy ears, and thou shouldest be sleeping in unconscious security, I would not wake thee; even if I had the power I would never do it, for my ears still tingle with the blow that thou gavest me years ago. I have never forgotten it." But the Viking treated her words as a joke; he was, like every one else, bewitched with her beauty, and knew nothing of the change in the form and temper of Helga at night. Without a saddle, she would sit on a horse as if she were a part of it, while it rushed along at full speed; nor would she spring from its back, even when it quarrelled with other horses and bit them. She would often leap from the high shore into the sea with all her clothes on, and swim to meet the Viking, when his boat was steering home towards the shore. She once cut off a long lock of her beautiful hair, and twisted it into a string for her bow. "If a thing is to be done well," said she, "I must do it myself."

The Viking's wife was, for the time in which she lived, a woman of strong character and will; but, compared to her daughter, she was a gentle, timid woman, and she knew that a wicked sorcerer had the terrible child in his power. It was sometimes as if Helga acted from sheer wickedness; for often when her mother stood on the threshold of the door, or stepped into the yard, she would seat herself on the brink of the well, wave her arms and legs in the air, and suddenly fall right in. Here she was able, from her frog nature, to dip and dive about in the water of the deep well, until at last she would climb forth like a cat, and come back into the hall dripping with water, so that the green leaves that were strewed on the floor were whirled round, and carried away by the streams that flowed from her.

But there was one time of the day which placed a check upon Helga. It was the evening twilight; when this hour arrived she became quiet and thoughtful, and allowed herself to be advised and led; then also a secret feeling seemed to draw her towards her mother. And as usual, when the sun set, and the transformation took place, both in body and mind, inwards and outwards, she would remain quiet and mournful, with her form shrunk together in the shape of a frog. Her body was much larger than those animals ever are, and on this account it was much more hideous in appearance; for she looked like a wretched dwarf, with a frog's head, and webbed fingers. Her eyes had a most piteous expression; she was without a voice, excepting a hollow, croaking sound, like the smothered sobs of a dreaming child.

Then the Viking's wife took her on her lap, and forgot the ugly form, as she looked into the mournful eyes, and often said, "I could wish that thou wouldst always remain my dumb frog child, for thou art too terrible when thou art clothed in a form of beauty." And the Viking woman wrote Runic characters against sorcery and spells of sickness, and threw them over the wretched child; but they did no good.

"One can scarcely believe that she was ever small enough to lie in the cup of the water-lily," said the papa stork; "and now she is grown up, and the image of her Egyptian mother, especially about the eyes. Ah, we shall never see her again; perhaps she has not discovered how to help herself, as you and the wise men said she would. Year after year have I flown across and across the moor, but there was no sign of her being still alive. Yes, and I may as well tell you that you that each year, when I arrived a few days before you to repair the nest, and put everything in its place, I have spent a whole night flying here and there over the marshy lake, as if I had been an owl or a bat, but all to no purpose. The two suits of swan's plumage, which I and the young ones dragged over here from the land of the Nile, are of no use; trouble enough it was to us to bring them here in three journeys, and now they are lying at the bottom of the nest; and if a fire should happen to break out, and the wooden house be burnt down, they would be destroyed."

"And our good nest would be destroyed, too," said the mamma stork; "but you think less of that than of your plumage stuff and your moor-princess. Go and stay with her in the marsh if you like. You are a bad father to your own children, as I have told you already, when I hatched my first brood. I only hope neither we nor our children may have an arrow sent through our wings, owing to that wild girl. Helga does not know in the least what she is about. We have lived in this house longer than she has, she should think of that, and we have never forgotten our duty. We have paid every year our toll of a feather, an egg, and a young one, as it is only right we should do. You don't suppose I can wander about the court-yard, or go everywhere as I used to do in old times. I can do it in Egypt, where I can be a companion of the people, without forgetting myself. But here I cannot go and peep into the pots and kettles as I do there. No, I can only sit up here and feel angry with that girl, the little wretch; and I am angry with you, too; you should have left her lying in the water lily, then no one would have known anything about her."

"You are far better than your conversation," said the papa stork; "I know you better than you know yourself." And with that he gave a hop, and flapped his wings twice, proudly; then he stretched his neck and flew, or rather soared away, without moving his outspread wings. He went on for some distance, and then he gave a great flap with his wings and flew on his course at a rapid rate, his head and neck bending proudly before him, while the sun's rays fell on his glossy plumage.

"He is the handsomest of them all," said the mamma stork, as she watched him; "but I won't tell him so."

Early in the autumn, the Viking again returned home laden with spoil, and bringing prisoners with him. Among them was a young Christian priest, one of those who contemned the gods of the north. Often lately there had been, both in hall and chamber, a talk of the new faith which was spreading far and wide in the south, and which, through the means of the holy Ansgarius, had already reached as far as Hedeby on the Schlei. Even Helga had heard of this belief in the teachings of One who was named Christ, and who for the love of mankind, and for their redemption, had given up His life. But to her all this had, as it were, gone in one ear and out the other. It seemed that she only understood the meaning of the word "love," when in the form of a miserable frog she crouched together in the corner of the sleeping chamber; but the Viking's wife had listened to the wonderful story, and had felt herself strangely moved by it.

On their return, after this voyage, the men spoke of the beautiful temples built of polished stone, which had been raised for the public worship of this holy love. Some vessels, curiously formed of massive gold, had been brought home among the booty. There was a peculiar fragrance about them all, for they were incense vessels, which had been swung before the altars in the temples by the Christian priests. In the deep stony cellars of the castle, the young Christian priest was immured, and his hands and feet tied together with strips of bark. The Viking's wife considered him as beautiful as Baldur, and his distress raised her pity; but Helga said he ought to have ropes fastened to his heels, and be tied to the tails of wild animals.

"I would let the dogs loose after him" she said; "over the moor and across the heath. Hurrah! that would be a spectacle for the gods, and better still to follow in its course."

But the Viking would not allow him to die such a death as that, especially as he was the disowned and despiser of the high gods. In a few days, he had decided to have him offered as a sacrifice on the blood-stone in the grove. For the first time, a man was to be sacrificed here. Helga begged to be allowed to sprinkle the assembled people with the blood of the priest. She sharpened her glittering knife; and when one of the great, savage dogs, who were running about the Viking's castle in great numbers, sprang towards her, she thrust the knife into his side, merely, as she said, to prove its sharpness.

The Viking's wife looked at the wild, badly disposed girl, with great sorrow; and when night came on, and her daughter's beautiful form and disposition were changed, she spoke in eloquent words to Helga of the sorrow and deep grief that was in her heart. The ugly frog, in its monstrous shape, stood before her, and raised its brown mournful eyes to her face, listening to her words, and seeming to understand them with the intelligence of a human being.

"Never once to my lord and husband has a word passed my lips of what I have to suffer through you; my heart is full of grief about you," said the Viking's wife. "The love of a mother is greater and more powerful than I ever imagined. But love never entered thy heart; it is cold and clammy, like the plants on the moor."

Then the miserable form trembled; it was as if these words had touched an invisible bond between body and soul, for great tears stood in the eyes.

"A bitter time will come for thee at last," continued the Viking's wife; "and it will be terrible for me too. It had been better for thee if thou hadst been left on the high-road, with the cold night wind to lull thee to sleep." And the Viking's wife shed bitter tears, and went away in anger and sorrow, passing under the partition of furs, which hung loose over the beam and divided the hall.

The shrivelled frog still sat in the corner alone. Deep silence reigned around. At intervals, a half-stifled sigh was heard from its inmost soul; it was the soul of Helga. It seemed in pain, as if a new life were arising in her heart.

Then she took a step forward and listened; then stepped again forward, and seized with her clumsy hands the heavy bar which was laid across the door. Gently, and with much trouble, she pushed back the bar, as silently lifted the latch, and then took up the glimmering lamp which stood in the ante-chamber of the hall. It seemed as if a stronger will than her own gave her strength. She removed the iron bolt from the closed cellar-door, and slipped in to the prisoner. He was slumbering. She touched him with her cold, moist hand, and as he awoke and caught sight of the hideous form, he shuddered as if he beheld a wicked apparition. She drew her knife, cut through the bonds which confined his hands and feet, and beckoned to him to follow her. He uttered some holy names and made the sign of the cross, while the form remained motionless by his side.

"Who art thou?" he asked, "whose outward appearance is that of an animal, while thou willingly performest acts of mercy?"

The frog-figure beckoned to him to follow her, and led him through a long gallery concealed by hanging drapery to the stables, and then pointed to a horse. He mounted upon it, and she sprang up also before him, and held tightly by the animal's mane. The prisoner understood her, and they rode on at a rapid trot, by a road which he would never have found by himself, across the open heath. He forgot her ugly form, and only thought how the mercy and loving-kindness of the Almighty was acting through this hideous apparition. As he offered pious prayers and sang holy songs of praise, she trembled. Was it the effect of prayer and praise that caused this? or, was she shuddering in the cold morning air at the thought of approaching twilight? What were her feelings? She raised herself up, and wanted to stop the horse and spring off, but the Christian priest held her back with all his might, and then sang a pious song, as if this could loosen the wicked charm that had changed her into the semblance of a frog.

And the horse galloped on more wildly than before. The sky painted itself red, the first sunbeam pierced through the clouds, and in the clear flood of sunlight the frog became changed. It was Helga again, young and beautiful, but with a wicked demoniac spirit. He held now a beautiful young woman in his arms, and he was horrified at the sight. He stopped the horse, and sprang from its back. He imagined that some new sorcery was at work. But Helga also leaped from the horse and stood on the ground. The child's short garment reached only to her knee. She snatched the sharp knife from her girdle, and rushed like lightning at the astonished priest. "Let me get at thee!" she cried; "let me get at thee, that I may plunge this knife into thy body. Thou art pale as ashes, thou beardless slave." She pressed in upon him. They struggled with each other in heavy combat, but it was as if an invisible power had been given to the Christian in the struggle. He held her fast, and the old oak under which they stood seemed to help him, for the loosened roots on the ground became entangled in the maiden's feet, and held them fast. Close by rose a bubbling spring, and he sprinkled Helga's face and neck with the water, commanded the unclean spirit to come forth, and pronounced upon her a Christian blessing. But the water of faith has no power unless the well-spring of faith flows within. And yet even here its power was shown; something more than the mere strength of a man opposed itself, through his means, against the evil which struggled within her. His holy action seemed to overpower her. She dropped her arms, glanced at him with pale cheeks and

THE MARSH KING'S DAUGHTER

looks of amazement. He appeared to her a mighty magician skilled in secret arts; his language was the darkest magic to her, and the movements of his hands in the air were as the secret signs of a magician's wand. She would not have blinked had he waved over her head a sharp knife or a glittering axe; but she shrunk from him as he signed her with the sign of the cross on her forehead and breast, and sat before him like a tame bird, with her head bowed down. Then he spoke to her, in gentle words, of the deed of love she had performed for him during the night, when she had come to him in the form of an ugly frog, to loosen his bonds, and to lead him forth to life and light; and he told her that she was bound in closer fetters than he had been, and that she could recover also life and light by his means. He would take her to Hedeby* to St. Ansgarius, and there, in that Christian town, the spell of the sorcerer would be removed. But he would not let her sit before him on the horse, though of her own free will she wished to do so. "Thou must sit behind me, not before me," said he. "Thy magic beauty has a magic power which comes from an evil origin, and I fear it; still I am sure to overcome through my faith in Christ." Then he knelt down, and prayed with pious fervor. It was as if the quiet woodland were a holy church consecrated by his worship. The birds sang as if they were also of this new congregation; and the fragrance of the wild flowers was as the ambrosial perfume of incense; while, above all, sounded the words of Scripture, "A light to them that sit in darkness and in the shadow of death, to guide their feet into the way of peace." And he spoke these words with the deep longing of his whole nature.

Meanwhile, the horse that had carried them in wild career stood quietly by, plucking at the tall bramble-bushes, till the ripe young berries fell down upon Helga's hands, as if inviting her to eat. Patiently she allowed herself to be lifted on the horse, and sat there like a somnambulist — as one who walked in his sleep. The Christian bound two branches together with bark, in the form of a cross, and held it on high as they rode through the forest. The way gradually grew thicker of brushwood, as they rode along, till at last it became a trackless wilderness. Bushes of the wild sloe here and there blocked up the path, so that they had to ride over them. The bubbling spring formed not a stream, but a marsh, round which also they were obliged to guide the horse; still there were strength and refreshment in the cool forest breeze, and no trifling power in the gentle words spoken in faith and Christian love by the young priest, whose inmost heart yearned to lead this poor lost one into the way of light and life. It is said that rain-drops can make a hollow in the hardest stone, and the waves of the sea can smooth and round the rough edges of the rocks; so did the dew of mercy fall upon Helga, softening what was hard, and smoothing what was rough in her character. These effects did not yet appear; she was not herself aware of them; neither does the seed in the lap of earth know, when the refreshing dew and the warm sunbeams fall upon it, that it contains within itself power by which it will flourish and bloom. The song of the mother sinks into the heart of the child, and the little one prattles the words after her, without understanding their meaning; but after a time the thoughts expand, and what has been heard in childhood seems to the mind clear and bright. So now the "Word," which is all-powerful to create, was working in the heart of Helga.

*Now the town of Sleswig.

They rode forth from the thick forest, crossed the heath, and again entered a pathless wood. Here, towards evening, they met with robbers.

"Where hast thou stolen that beauteous maiden?" cried the robbers, seizing the horse by the bridle, and dragging the two riders from its back.

The priest had nothing to defend himself with, but the knife he had taken from Helga, and with this he struck out right and left. One of the robbers raised his axe against him; but the young priest sprang on one side, and avoided the blow, which fell with great force on the horse's neck, so that the blood gushed forth, and the animal sunk to the ground. Then Helga seemed suddenly to awake from her long, deep reverie; she threw herself hastily upon the dying animal. The priest placed himself before her, to defend and shelter her; but one of the robbers swung his iron axe against the Christian's head with such force that it was dashed to pieces, the blood and brains were scattered about, and he fell dead upon the ground. Then the robbers seized beautiful Helga by her white arms and slender waist; but at that moment the sun went down, and as its last ray disappeared, she was changed into the form of a frog. A greenish white mouth spread half over her face; her arms became thin and slimy; while broad hands, with webbed fingers, spread themselves out like fans. Then the robbers, in terror, let her go, and she stood among them, a hideous monster; and as is the nature of frogs to do, she hopped up as high as her own size, and disappeared in the thicket. Then the robbers knew that this must be the work of an evil spirit or some secret sorcery, and, in a terrible fright, they ran hastily from the spot.

The full moon had already risen, and was shining in all her radiant splendor over the earth, when from the thicket, in the form of a frog, crept poor Helga. She stood still by the corpse of the Christian priest, and the carcase of the dead horse. She looked at them with eyes that seemed to weep, and from the frog's head came forth a croaking sound, as when a child bursts into tears. She threw herself first upon one, and then upon the other; brought water in her hand, which, from being webbed, was large and hollow, and poured it over them; but they were dead, and dead they would remain. She understood that at last. Soon wild animals would come and tear their dead bodies; but no, that must not happen. Then she dug up the earth, as deep as she was able, that she might prepare a grave for them. She had nothing but a branch of a tree and her two hands, between the fingers of which the webbed skin stretched, and they were torn by the work, while the blood ran down her hands. She saw at last that her work would be useless, more than she could accomplish; so she fetched more water, and washed the face of the dead, and then covered it with fresh green leaves; she also brought large boughs and spread over him, and scattered dried leaves between the branches. Then she brought the heaviest stones that she could carry, and laid them over the dead body, filling up the crevices with moss, till she thought she had fenced in his resting-place strongly enough. The difficult task had employed her the whole night; and as the sun broke forth, there stood the beautiful Helga in all her loveliness, with her bleeding hands, and, for the first time, with tears on her maiden cheeks. It was, in this transformation, as if two natures were striving together within her; her whole frame trembled, and she looked around her as if she had just awoke from a painful dream. She leaned for support against the trunk of a slender tree, and at last climbed to the topmost branches, like a cat, and seated herself firmly upon them. She remained there the whole day, sitting alone, like a frightened squirrel, in the silent solitude of the wood, where the rest and stillness is as the calm of death.

Butterflies fluttered around her, and close by were several ant-hills, each with its hundreds of busy little creatures moving quickly to and fro. In the air, danced myriads of gnats, swarm upon swarm, troops of buzzing flies, lady-birds, dragon-flies with golden wings, and other little winged creatures. The worm crawled forth from the moist ground, and the moles crept out; but, ex-cepting these, all around had the stillness of death: but when people say this, they do not quite understand themselves what they mean. None noticed Helga but a flock of magpies, which flew chattering round the top of the tree on which she sat. These birds hopped close to her on the branches with bold curiosity. A glance from her eyes was a signal to frighten them away, and they were not clever enough to find out who she was; indeed she hardly knew her-self.

When the sun was near setting, and the evening's twilight about to com-mence, the approaching transformation aroused her to fresh exertion. She let herself down gently from the tree, and, as the last sunbeam vanished, she stood again in the wrinkled form of a frog, with the torn, webbed skin on her hands, but her eyes now gleamed with more radiant beauty than they had ever possessed in her most beautiful form of loveliness; they were now pure, mild maidenly eyes that shone forth in the face of a frog. They showed the existence of deep feeling and a human heart, and the beauteous eyes over-flowed with tears, weeping precious drops that lightened the heart.

On the raised mound which she had made as a grave for the dead priest, she found the cross made of the branches of a tree, the last work of him who now lay dead and cold beneath it. A sudden thought came to Helga, and she lifted up the cross and planted it upon the grave, between the stones that covered him and the dead horse. The sad recollection brought the tears to her eyes, and in this gentle spirit she traced the same sign in the sand round the grave; and as she formed, with both her hands, the sign of the cross, the web skin fell from them like a torn glove. She washed her hands in the water of the spring, and gazed with astonishment at their delicate whiteness. Again she made the holy sign in the air, between herself and the dead man; her lips trembled, her tongue moved, and the name which she in her ride through the forest had so often heard spoken, rose to her lips, and she uttered the words, "Jesus Christ." Then the frog skin fell from her; she was once more a lovely maiden. Her head bent wearily, her tired limbs required rest, and then she slept.

Her sleep, however, was short. Towards midnight, she awoke; before her stood the dead horse, prancing and full of life, which shone forth from his eyes and from his wounded neck. Close by his side appeared the murdered Christian priest, more beautiful than Baldur, as the Viking's wife had said; but now he came as if in a flame of fire. Such gravity, such stern justice, such a piercing glance shone from his large, gentle eyes, that it seemed to penetrate into every corner of her heart. Beautiful Helga trembled at the look, and her memory returned with a power as if it had been the day of judgment. Every good deed that had been done for her, every loving word that had been said, were vividly before her mind. She understood now that love had kept her here during the day of her trial; while the creature formed of dust and clay, soul and spirit, had wrestled and struggled with evil. She acknowledged that she had only followed the impulses of an evil disposition, that she had done nothing to cure herself; everything had been given her, and all had happened as it were by the ordination of Providence. She bowed herself humbly, confessed her great imperfections in the sight of Him who can read every fault of the heart, and then the priest spoke. "Daughter of the moorland, thou hast come from the swamp and the marshy earth, but from this thou shalt arise. The sunlight shining into thy inmost soul proves the origin from which thou hast really sprung, and has restored the body to its natural form. I am come to thee from the land of the dead, and thou also must pass through the valley to reach the holy mountains where mercy and perfection dwell. I cannot lead thee to Hedeby that thou mayst receive Christian baptism, for first thou must remove the thick veil with which the waters of the moorland are shrouded, and bring forth from its depths the living author of thy being and thy life. Till this is done, thou canst not receive consecration."

Then he lifted her on the horse and gave her a golden censer, similar to those she had already seen at the Viking's house. A sweet perfume arose from it, while the open wound in the forehead of the slain priest, shone with the rays of a diamond. He took the cross from the grave, and held it aloft, and now they rode through the air over the rustling trees, over the hills where warriors lay buried each by his dead war-horse; and the brazen monumental figures rose up and galloped forth, and stationed themselves on the summits of the hills. The golden crescent on their foreheads, fastened with golden knots, glittered in the moonlight, and their mantles floated in the wind. The dragon, that guards buried treasure, lifted his head and gazed after them. The goblins and the satyrs peeped out from beneath the hills, and flitted to and fro in the fields, waving blue, red, and green torches, like the glowing sparks in burning paper. Over woodland and heath, flood and fen, they flew on, till they reached the wild moor, over which they hovered in broad circles. The Christian priest held the cross aloft, and it glittered like gold, while from his lips sounded pious prayers. Beautiful Helga's voice joined with his in the hymns he sung, as a child joins in her mother's song. She swung the censer, and a wonderful fragrance of incense arose from it; so powerful, that the reeds and rushes of the moor burst forth into blossom. Each germ came forth from the deep ground: all that had life raised itself. Blooming water-lilies spread themselves forth like a carpet of wrought flowers, and upon them lay a slumbering woman, young and beautiful. Helga fancied that it was her own image she saw reflected in the still water. But it was her mother she beheld, the wife of the Marsh King, the princess from the land of the Nile.

The dead Christian priest desired that the sleeping woman should be lifted on the horse, but the horse sank beneath the load, as if he had been a funeral pall fluttering in the wind. But the sign of the cross made the airy phantom strong, and then the three rode away from the marsh to firm ground.

At the same moment the cock crew in the Viking's castle, and the dream figures dissolved and floated away in the air, but mother and daughter stood opposite to each other.

"Am I looking at my own image in the deep water?" said the mother.

"Is it myself that I see represented on a white shield?" cried the daughter.

Then they came nearer to each other in a fond embrace. The mother's heart beat quickly, and she understood the quickened pulses. "My child!" she exclaimed, "the flower of my heart—my lotus flower of the deep water!" and she embraced her child again and wept, and the tears were as a baptism of new life and love for Helga. "In swan's plumage I came here," said the mother, "and here I threw off my feather dress. Then I sank down through the wavering ground, deep into the marsh beneath, which closed like a wall around me; I found myself after a while in fresher water; still a power drew me down deeper and deeper. I felt the weight of sleep upon my eyelids. Then I slept, and dreams hovered round me. It seemed to me as if I were again in the pyramids of Egypt, and yet the waving elder trunk that had frightened me on the moor stood ever before me. I observed the clefts and wrinkles in the stem; they shone forth in strange colors, and took the form of hieroglyphics. It was the mummy case on which I gazed. At last it burst, and forth stepped the thousand years' old king, the mummy form, black as pitch, black as the shining wood-snail, or the slimy mud of the swamp. Whether it was really the mummy or the Marsh King I know not. He seized me in his arms, and I felt as if I must die. When I recovered myself, I found in my bosom a little bird, flapping its wings, twittering and fluttering. The bird flew away from my bosom, upwards towards the dark, heavy canopy above me, but a long, green band kept it fastened to me. I heard and understood the tenor of its longings. Freedom! sunlight! to my father! Then I thought of my father, and the sunny land of my birth, my life, and my love. Then I loosened the band, and let the bird fly away to its home—to a father. Since that hour I have ceased to dream; my sleep has been long and heavy, till in this very hour, harmony and fragrance awoke me, and set me free."

The green band which fastened the wings of the bird to the mother's heart, where did it flutter now? whither had it been wafted? The stork only had seen it. The band was the green stalk, the cup of the flower the cradle in which lay the child, that now in blooming beauty had been folded to the mother's heart.

And while the two were resting in each other's arms, the old stork flew round and round them in narrowing circles, till at length he flew away swiftly to his nest, and fetched away the two suits of swan's feathers, which he had preserved there for many years. Then he returned to the mother and daughter, and threw the swan's plumage over them; the feathers immediately closed around them, and they rose up from the earth in the form of two white swans.

"And now we can converse with pleasure," said the stork-papa; "we can understand one another, although the beaks of birds are so different in shape. It is very fortunate that you came to-night. To-morrow we should have been gone. The mother, myself and the little ones, we're about to fly to the south. Look at me now: I am an old friend from the Nile, and a mother's heart contains more than her beak. She always said that the princess would know how to help herself. I and the young ones carried the swan's feathers over here, and I am glad of it now, and how lucky it is that I am here still. When the day dawns we shall start with a great company of other storks. We'll fly first, and you can follow in our track, so that you cannot miss your way. I and the young ones will have an eye upon you."

"And the lotus-flower which I was to take with me," said the Egyptian princess, "is flying here by my side, clothed in swan's feathers. The flower of my heart will travel with me; and so the riddle is solved. Now for home! now for home!"

THE MARSH KING'S DAUGHTER

But Helga said she could not leave the Danish land without once more seeing her foster-mother, the loving wife of the Viking. Each pleasing recollection, each kind word, every tear from the heart which her foster-mother had wept for her, rose in her mind, and at that moment she felt as if she loved this mother the best.

"Yes, we must go to the Viking's castle," said the stork; "mother and the young ones are waiting for me there. How they will open their eyes and flap their wings! My wife, you see, does not say much; she is short and abrupt in her manner; but she means well, for all that. I will flap my wings at once, that they may hear us coming." Then stork-papa flapped his wings in first-rate style, and he and the swans flew away to the Viking's castle.

In the castle, every one was in a deep sleep. It had been late in the evening before the Viking's wife retired to rest. She was anxious about Helga, who, three days before, had vanished with the Christian priest. Helga must have helped him in his flight, for it was her horse that was missed from the stable; but by what power had all this been accomplished? The Viking's wife thought of it with wonder, thought on the miracles which they said could be performed by those who believed in the Christian faith, and followed its teachings. These passing thoughts formed themselves into a vivid dream, and it seemed to her that she was still lying awake on her couch, while without darkness reigned. A storm arose; she heard the lake dashing and rolling from east and west, like the waves of the North Sea or the Cattegat. The monstrous snake which, it is said, surrounds the earth in the depths of the ocean, was trembling in spasmodic convulsions. The night of the fall of the gods was come, "Ragnorock," as the heathens call the judgment-day, when everything shall pass away, even the high gods themselves. The war trumpet sounded; riding upon the rainbow, came the gods, clad in steel, to fight their last battle on the last battle-field. Before them flew the winged vampires, and the dead warriors closed up the train. The whole firmament was ablaze with the northern lights, and yet the darkness triumphed. It was a terrible hour. And, close to the terrified woman, Helga seemed to be seated on the floor, in the hideous form of a frog, yet trembling, and clinging to her foster-mother, who took her on her lap, and lovingly caressed her, hideous and frog-like as she was. The air was filled with the clashing of arms and the hissing of arrows, as if a storm of hail was descending upon the earth. It seemed to her the hour when earth and sky would burst asunder, and all things be swallowed up in Saturn's fiery lake; but she knew that a new heaven and a new earth would arise, and that corn-fields would wave where now the lake rolled over desolate sands, and the ineffable God reign. Then she saw rising from the region of the dead, Baldur the gentle, the loving, and as the Viking's wife gazed upon him, she recognized his countenance. It was the captive Christian priest. "White Christian!" she exclaimed aloud, and with the words, she pressed a kiss on the forehead of the hideous frog-child. Then the frog-skin fell off, and Helga stood before her in all her beauty, more lovely and gentle-looking, and with eyes beaming with love. She kissed the hands of her foster-mother, blessed her for all her fostering love and care during the days of her trial and misery, for the thoughts she had suggested and awoke in her heart, and for naming the Name which she now repeated. Then beautiful Helga rose as a mighty swan, and spread her wings with the rushing sound of troops of birds of passage flying through the air.

Then the Viking's wife awoke, but she still heard the rushing sound without. She knew it was the time for the storks to depart, and that it must be their wings which she heard. She felt she should like to see them once more, and bid them farewell. She rose from her couch, stepped out on the threshold, and beheld, on the ridge of the roof, a party of storks ranged side by side. Troops of the birds were flying in circles over the castle and the highest trees; but just before her, as she stood on the threshold and close to the well where Helga had so often sat and alarmed her with her wildness, now stood two swans, gazing at her with intelligent eyes. Then she remembered her dream, which still appeared to her as a reality. She thought of Helga in the form of a swan. She thought of a Christian priest, and suddenly a wonderful joy arose in her heart. The swans flapped their wings and arched their necks as if to offer her a greeting, and the Viking's wife spread out her arms towards them, as if she accepted it, and smiled through her tears. She was roused from deep thought by a rustling of wings and snapping of beaks; all the storks arose, and started on their journey towards the south.

"We will not wait for the swans," said the mamma stork; "if they want to go with us, let them come now; we can't sit here till the plovers start. It is a fine thing after all to travel in families, not like the finches and the partridges. There the male and the female birds fly in separate flocks, which, to speak candidly, I consider very unbecoming."

"What are those swans flapping their wings for?"

"Well, every one flies in his own fashion," said the papa stork. "The swans fly in an oblique line; the cranes, in the form of a triangle; and the plovers, in a curved line like a snake."

"Don't talk about snakes while we are flying up here," said stork-mamma. "It puts ideas into the children's heads that can not be realized."

"Are those the high mountains I have heard spoken of?" asked Helga, in the swan's plumage.

"They are storm-clouds driving along beneath us," replied her mother.

"What are yonder white clouds that rise so high?" again inquired Helga.

"Those are mountains covered with perpetual snows, that you see yonder," said her mother. And then they flew across the Alps towards the blue Mediterranean.

"Africa's land! Egyptia's strand!" sang the daughter of the Nile, in her swan's plumage, as from the upper air she caught sight of her native land, a narrow, golden, wavy strip on the shores of the Nile; the other birds espied it also and hastened their flight.

"I can smell the Nile mud and the wet frogs," said the stork-mamma, "and I begin to feel quite hungry. Yes, now you shall taste something nice, and you will see the marabout bird, and the ibis, and the crane. They all belong to our family, but they are not nearly so handsome as we are. They give themselves great airs, especially the ibis. The Egyptians have spoilt him. They make a mummy of him, and stuff him with spices. I would rather be stuffed with live frogs, and so would you, and so you shall. Better have something in your inside while you are alive, than to be made a parade of after you are dead. That is my opinion, and I am always right."

"The storks are come," was said in the great house on the banks of the Nile, where the lord lay in the hall on his downy cushions, covered with a leopard skin, scarcely alive, yet not dead, waiting and hoping for the lotus-flower from the deep moorland in the far north. Relatives and servants were standing by his couch, when the two beautiful swans who had come with the storks flew into the hall. They threw off their soft white plumage, and two lovely female forms approached the pale, sick old man, and threw back their long hair, and when Helga bent over her grandfather, redness came back to his cheeks, his eyes brightened, and life returned to his benumbed limbs. The old man rose up with health and energy renewed; daughter and grandchild welcomed him as joyfully as if with a morning greeting after a long and troubled dream.

Joy reigned through the whole house, as well as in the stork's nest; although there the chief cause was really the good food, especially the quantities of frogs, which seemed to spring out of the ground in swarms.

Then the learned men hastened to note down, in flying characters, the story of the two princesses, and spoke of the arrival of the health-giving flower as a mighty event, which had been a blessing to the house and the land. Meanwhile, the stork-papa told the story to his family in his own way; but not till they had eaten and were satisfied; otherwise they would have had something else to do than to listen to stories.

"Well," said the stork-mamma, when she had heard it, "you will be made something of at last; I suppose they can do nothing less."

"What could I be made?" said stork-papa; "what have I done? — just nothing."

"You have done more than all the rest," she replied. "But for you and the youngsters the two young princesses would never have seen Egypt again, and the recovery of the old man would not have been effected. You will become something. They must certainly give you a doctor's hood, and our young ones will inherit it, and their children after them, and so on. You already look like an Egyptian doctor, at least in my eyes."

"I cannot quite remember the words I heard when I listened on the roof," said stork-papa, while relating the story to his family; "all I know is, that what the wise men said was so complicated and so learned, that they received not only rank, but presents; even the head cook at the great house was honored with a mark of distinction, most likely for the soup."

"And what did you receive?" said the stork-mamma. "They certainly ought not to forget the most important person in the affair, as you really are. The learned men have done nothing at all but use their tongues. Surely they will not overlook you."

Late in the night, while the gentle sleep of peace rested on the now happy house, there was still one watcher. It was not stork-papa, who, although he stood on guard on one leg, could sleep soundly. Helga alone was awake. She leaned over the balcony, gazing at the sparkling stars that shone clearer and brighter in the pure air than they had done in the north, and yet they were the same stars. She thought of the Viking's wife in the wild moorland, of the gentle eyes of her foster-moster, and of the tears she had shed over the poor frog-child that now lived in splendor and starry beauty by the waters of the Nile, with air balmy and sweet as spring. She thought of the love that dwelt in the breast of the heathen woman, love that had been shown to a wretched creature, hateful as a human being, and hideous when in the form of an animal. She looked at the glittering stars, and thought of the radiance that had shone forth on the forehead of the dead man, as she had fled with him over the woodland and moor. Tones were awakened in her memory; words which she had heard him speak as they rode onward, when she was carried, wondering and trembling, through the air; words from the great Fountain of love, the highest love that embraces all the human race. What had not been won and achieved by this love?

Day and night beautiful Helga was absorbed in the contemplation of the great amount of her happiness, and lost herself in the contemplation, like a child who turns hurriedly from the giver to examine the beautiful gifts. She was over-powered with her good fortune, which seemed always increasing, and therefore what might it become in the future? Had she not been brought by a wonderful miracle to all this joy and happiness? And in these thoughts she indulged, until at last she thought no more of the Giver. It was the over-abundance of youthful spirits unfolding its wings for a daring flight. Her eyes sparkled with energy, when suddenly arose a loud noise in the court below, and the daring thought vanished. She looked down, and saw two large ostriches running round quickly in narrow circles; she had never seen these creatures before, — great, coarse, clumsy-looking birds with curious wings that looked as if they had been clipped, and the birds themselves had the appearance of having been roughly used. She inquired about them, and for the first time heard the legend which the Egyptians relate respecting the ostrich.

Once, say they, the ostriches were a beautiful and glorious race of birds, with large, strong wings. One evening the other large birds of the forest said to the ostrich, "Brother, shall we fly to the river to-morrow morning to drink, *God willing?*" and the ostrich answered, "I will."

With the break of day, therefore, they commenced their flight; first rising high in the air, towards the sun, which is the eye of God; still higher and higher the ostrich flew, far above the other birds, proudly approaching the light, trusting in its own strength, and thinking not of the Giver, or saying, *"if God will."* When suddenly the avenging angel drew back the veil from the flaming ocean of sunlight, and in a moment the wings of the proud bird were scorched and shrivelled, and they sunk miserably to the earth. Since that time the ostrich and his race have never been able to rise in the air; they can only fly terror-stricken along the ground, or run round and round in narrow circles. It is a warning to mankind, that in all our thoughts and schemes, and in every action we undertake, we should say, *"if God will."*

Then Helga bowed her head thoughtfully and seriously, and looked at the circling ostrich, as with timid fear and simple pleasure it glanced at its own great shadow on the sunlit walls. And the story of the ostrich sunk deeply into the heart and mind of Helga: a life of happiness, both in the present and in the future, seemed secure for her, and what was yet to come might be the best of all, *God willing.*

Early in the spring, when the storks were again about to journey northward, beautiful Helga took off her golden bracelets, scratched her name on them, and beckoned to the stork-father. He came to her, and she placed the golden circlet round his neck, and begged him to deliver it safely to the Viking's wife, so that she might know that her foster-daughter still lived, was happy, and had not forgotten her.

"It is rather heavy to carry," thought stork-papa, when he had it on his neck; "but gold and honor are not to be flung into the street. The stork brings good fortune — they'll be obliged to acknowledge that at last."

"You lay gold, and I lay eggs," said stork-mamma; "with you it is only once in a way, I lay eggs every year But no one appreciates what we do; I call it very mortifying."

"But then we have a consciousness of our own worth, mother," replied stork-papa.

"What good will that do you?" retorted stork-mamma; "it will neither bring you a fair wind, nor a good meal."

"The little nightingale, who is singing yonder in the tamarind grove, will soon be going north, too." Helga said she had often heard her singing on the wild moor, so she determined to send a message by her. While flying in the swan's plumage she had learnt the bird language; she had often conversed with the stork and the swallow, and she knew that the nightingale would understand. So she begged the nightingale to fly to the beechwood, on the peninsula of Jutland, where a mound of stone and twigs had been raised to form the grave, and she begged the nightingale to persuade all the other little birds to build their nests round the place, so that evermore should resound over that grave music and song. And the nightingale flew away, and time flew away also.

In the autumn, an eagle, standing upon a pyramid, saw a stately train of richly laden camels, and men attired in armor on foaming Arabian steeds, whose glossy skins shone like silver, their nostrils were pink, and their thick, flowing manes hung almost to their slender legs. A royal prince of Arabia, handsome as a prince should be, and accompanied by distinguished guests, was on his way to the stately house, on the roof of which the storks' empty nests might be seen. They were away now in the far north, but expected to return very soon. And, indeed, they returned on a day that was rich in joy and gladness.

A marriage was being celebrated, in which the beautiful Helga, glittering in silk and jewels, was the bride, and the bridegroom the young Arab prince. Bride and bridegroom sat at the upper end of the table, between the bride's mother and grandfather. But her gaze was not on the bridegroom, with his manly, sunburnt face, round which curled a black beard, and whose dark fiery eyes were fixed upon her; but away from him, at a twinkling star, that shone down upon her from the sky. Then was heard the sound of rushing wings beating the air. The storks were coming home; and the old stork pair, although tired with the journey and requiring rest, did not fail to fly down at once to the balustrades of the verandah, for they knew already what feast was being celebrated. They had heard of it on the borders of the land, and also that Helga had caused their figures to be represented on the walls, for they belonged to her history.

"I call that very sensible and pretty," said stork-papa.

"Yes, but it is very little," said mamma stork; "they could not possibly have done less."

But, when Helga saw them, she rose and went out into the verandah to stroke the backs of the storks. The old stork pair bowed their heads, and curved their necks, and even the youngest among the young ones felt honored by this reception.

Helga continued to gaze upon the glittering star, which seemed to glow brighter and purer in its light; then between herself and the star floated a form, purer than the air, and visible through it. It floated quite near to her, and she saw that it was the dead Christian priest, who also was coming to her wedding feast—coming from the heavenly kingdom.

"The glory and brightness, yonder, outshines all that is known on earth," said he.

Then Helga the fair prayed more gently, and more earnestly, than she had ever prayed in her life before, that she might be permitted to gaze, if only for a single moment, at the glory and brightness of the heavenly kingdom. Then she felt herself lifted up, as it were, above the earth, through a sea of sound and thought; not only around her, but within her, was there light and song, such as words cannot express.

"Now we must return;" he said; "you will be missed."

"Only one more look," she begged; "but one short moment more."

"We must return to earth; the guests will have all departed. Only one more look!—the last!"

Then Helga stood again in the verandah. But the marriage lamps in the festive hall had been all extinguished, and the torches outside had vanished. The storks were gone; not a guest could be seen; no bridegroom—all in those few short moments seemed to have died. Then a great dread fell upon her. She stepped from the verandah through the empty hall into the next chamber, where slept strange warriors. She opened a side door, which once led into her own apartment, but now, as she passed through, she found herself suddenly in a garden which she had never before seen here, the sky blushed red, it was the dawn of morning. Three minutes only in heaven, and a whole night on earth had passed away! Then she saw the storks, and called to them in their own language.

Then stork-papa turned his head towards here, listened to her words, and drew near. "You speak our language," said he, "what do you wish? Why do you appear,—you—a strange woman?"

"It is I—it is Helga! Dost thou not know me? Three minutes ago we were speaking together yonder in the verandah."

"That is a mistake," said the stork, "you must have dreamed all this."

"No, no," she exclaimed. Then she reminded him of the Viking's castle, of the great lake, and of the journey across the ocean.

Then stork-papa winked his eyes, and said, "Why that's an old story which happened in the time of my grandfather. There certainly was a princess of that kind here in Egypt once, who came from the Danish land, but she vanished on the evening of her wedding day, many hundred years ago, and never came back. You may read about it yourself yonder, on a monument in the garden. There you will find swans and storks sculptured, and on the top is a figure of the princess Helga, in marble."

And so it was; Helga understood it all now, and sank on her knees. The sun burst forth in all its glory, and, as in olden times, the form of the frog vanished in his beams, and the beautiful farm stood forth in all its loveliness; so now, bathed in light, rose a beautiful form, purer, clearer than air—a ray of brightness—from the Source of light Himself. The body crumbled into dust, and a faded lotus-flower lay on the spot on which Helga had stood.

"Now that is a new ending to the story," said stork-papa; "I really never expected it would end in this way, but it seems a very good ending."

"And what will the young ones say to it, I wonder?" said stork-mamma.

"Ah, that is a very important question," replied the stork.

THE CHILD IN THE GRAVE

IT was a very sad day, and every heart in the house felt the deepest grief; for the youngest child, a boy of four years old, the joy and hope of his parents, was dead. Two daughters, the elder of whom was going to be confirmed, still remained: they were both good, charming girls; but the lost child always seems the dearest; and when it is youngest, and a son, it makes the trial still more heavy. The sisters mourned as young hearts can mourn, and were especially grieved at the sight of their parents' sorrow. The father's heart was bowed down, but the mother sunk completely under the deep grief. Day and night she had attended to the sick child, nursing and carrying it in her bosom, as a part of herself. She could not realize the fact that the child was dead, and must be laid in a coffin to rest in the ground. She thought God *could not* take her darling little one from her; and when it did happen notwithstanding her hopes and her belief, and there could be no more doubt on the subject, she said in her feverish agony, "God does not know it. He has hard-hearted ministering spirits on earth, who do according to their own will, and heed not a mother's prayers." Thus in her great grief she fell away from her faith in God, and dark thoughts arose in her mind respecting death and a future state. She tried to believe that man was but dust, and that with his life all existence ended. But these doubts were no support to her, nothing on which she could rest, and she sunk into the fathomless depths of despair. In her darkest hours she ceased to weep, and thought not of the young daughters who were still left to her. The tears of her husband fell on her forehead, but she took no notice of him; her thoughts were with her dead child; her whole existence seemed wrapped up in the remembrances of the little one and of every innocent word it had uttered.

The day of the little child's funeral came. For nights previously the mother had not slept, but in the morning twilight of this day she sunk from weariness into a deep sleep; in the mean time the coffin was carried into a distant room, and there nailed down, that she might not hear the blows of the hammer. When she awoke, and wanted to see her child, the husband, with tears, said, "We have closed the coffin; it was necessary to do so."

"When God is so hard to me, how can I expect men to be better?" she said with groans and tears.

The coffin was carried to the grave, and the disconsolate mother sat with her young daughters. She looked at them, but she saw them not; for her thoughts were far away from the domestic hearth. She gave herself up to her grief, and it tossed her to and fro, as the sea tosses a ship without compass or rudder. So the day of the funeral passed away, and similar days followed, of dark, wearisome pain. With tearful eyes and mournful glances, the sorrowing daughters and the afflicted husband looked upon her who would not hear their words of comfort; and, indeed, what comforting words could they speak, when they were themselves so full of grief? It seemed as if she would never again know sleep, and yet it would have been her best friend, one who would have strengthened her body and poured peace into her soul. They at last persuaded her to lie down, and then she would lie as still as if she slept.

One night, when her husband listened, as he often did, to her breathing, he quite believed that she had at length found rest and relief in sleep. He folded his arms and prayed, and soon sunk himself into healthful sleep; therefore he did not notice that his wife arose, threw on her clothes, and glided silently from the house, to go where her thoughts constantly lingered — to the grave of her child. She passed through the garden, to a path across a field that led to the churchyard. No one saw her as she walked, nor did she see any one; for her eyes were fixed upon the one object of her wanderings. It was a lovely starlight night in the beginning of September, and the air was mild and still. She entered the churchyard, and stood by the little grave, which looked like a large nosegay of fragrant flowers. She sat down, and bent her head low over the grave, as if she could see her child through the earth that covered him — her little boy, whose smile was so vividly before her, and the gentle expression of whose eyes, even on his sick-bed, she could not forget. How full of meaning that glance had been, as she leaned over him, holding in hers the pale hand which he had no longer strength to raise! As she had sat by his little cot, so now she sat by his grave; and here she could weep freely, and her tears fell upon it.

"Thou wouldst gladly go down and be with thy child," said a voice quite close to her, — a voice that sounded so deep and clear, that it went to her heart.

She looked up, and by her side stood a man wrapped in a black cloak, with a hood closely drawn over his face; but her keen glance could distinguish the face under the hood. It was stern, yet awakened confidence, and the eyes beamed with youthful radiance.

"Down to my child," she repeated; and tones of despair and entreaty sounded in the words.

"Darest thou to follow me?" asked the form. "I am Death."

She bowed her head in token of assent. Then suddenly it appeared as if all the stars were shining with the radiance of the full moon on the many-colored flowers that decked the grave. The earth that covered it was drawn back like a floating drapery. She sunk down, and the spectre covered her with a black cloak; night closed around her, the night of death. She sank deeper than the spade of the sexton could penetrate, till the churchyard became a roof above her. Then the cloak was removed, and she found herself in a large hall, of wide-spreading dimensions, in which there was a subdued light, like twilight, reigning, and in a moment her child appeared before her, smiling, and more beautiful than ever; with a silent cry she pressed him to her heart. A glorious strain of music sounded — now distant, now near. Never had she listened to such tones as these; they came from beyond a large dark curtain which separated the regions of death from the land of eternity.

"My sweet, darling mother," she heard the child say. It was the well-known, beloved voice; and kiss followed kiss, in boundless delight. Then the child pointed to the dark curtain. "There is nothing so beautiful on earth as it is here. Mother, do you not see them all? Oh, it is happiness indeed."

But the mother saw nothing of what the child pointed out, only the dark curtain. She looked with earthly eyes, and could not see as the child saw, — he whom God has called to be with Himself. She could hear the sounds of music, but she heard not the words, *the Word* in which she was to trust.

"I can fly now, mother," said the child; "I can fly with other happy children into the presence of the Almighty. I would fain fly away now; but if you weep for me as you are weeping now, you may never see me again. And yet I would go so gladly. May I not fly away? And you will come to me soon, will you not, dear mother?"

"Oh, stay, stay!" implored the mother; "only one moment more; only once more, that I may look upon thee, and kiss thee, and press thee to my heart."

Then she kissed and fondled her child. Suddenly her name was called from above; what could it mean? her name uttered in a plaintive voice.

"Hearest thou?" said the child. "It is my father who calls thee." And in a few moments deep sighs were heard, as of children weeping. "They are my sisters," said the child. "Mother, surely you have not forgotten them."

And then she remembered those she left behind, and a great terror came over her. She looked around her at the dark night. Dim forms flitted by. She seemed to recognize some of them, as they floated through the regions of death towards the dark curtain, where they vanished. Would her husband and her daughters flit past? No; their sighs and lamentations still sounded from above; and she had nearly forgotten them, for the sake of him who was dead.

"Mother, now the bells of heaven are ringing," said the child; "mother, the sun is going to rise."

An overpowering light streamed in upon her, the child had vanished, and she was being borne upwards. All around her became cold; she lifted her head, and saw that she was lying in the churchyard, on the grave of her child. The Lord, in a dream, had been a guide to her feet and a light to her spirit. She bowed her knees, and prayed for forgiveness. She had wished to keep back a soul from its immortal flight; she had forgotten her duties towards the living who were left her. And when she had offered this prayer, her heart felt lighter. The sun burst forth, over her head a little bird carolled his song, and the church-bells sounded for the early service. Everything around her seemed holy, and her heart was chastened. She acknowledged the goodness of God, she acknowledged the duties she had to perform, and eagerly she returned home. She bent over her husband, who still slept; her warm, devoted kiss awakened him, and words of heartfelt love fell from the lips of both. Now she was gentle and strong as a wife can be; and from her lips came the words of faith: "Whatever he doeth is right and best."

Then her husband asked, "From whence hast thou all at once derived such strength and comforting faith?"

And as she kissed him and her children, she said, "It came from God, through my child in the grave."

THE ELFIN HILL

A FEW large lizards were running nimbly about in the clefts of an old tree; they could understand one another very well, for they spoke the lizard language.

"What a buzzing and a rumbling there is in the elfin hill," said one of the lizards; "I have not been able to close my eyes for two nights on account of the noise; I might just as well have had the toothache, for that always keeps me awake."

"There is something going on within there," said the other lizard; "they propped up the top of the hill with four red posts, till cock-crow this morning, so that it is thoroughly aired, and the elfin girls have learnt new dances; there is something."

"I spoke about it to an earth-worm of my acquaintance," said a third lizard; "the earth-worm had just come from the elfin hill, where he has been groping about in the earth day and night. He has heard a great deal; although he cannot see, poor miserable creature, yet he understands very well how to wriggle and lurk about. They expect friends in the elfin hill, grand company, too; but who they are the earth-worm would not say, or, perhaps, he really did not know. All the will-o'-the-wisps are ordered to be there to hold a torch dance, as it is called. The silver and gold which is plentiful in the hill will be polished and placed out in the moonlight."

"Who can the strangers be?" asked the lizards; "what can the matter be? Hark, what a buzzing and humming there is!"

Just at this moment the elfin hill opened, and an old elfin maiden, hollow behind,* came tripping out; she was the old elf king's housekeeper, and a distant relative of the family; therefore she wore an amber heart on the middle of her forehead. Her feet moved very fast, "trip, trip;" good gracious, how she could trip right down to the sea to the night-raven.†

"You are invited to the elf hill for this evening," said she; "but will you do me a great favor and undertake the invitations? you ought to do something, for you have no housekeeping to attend to as I have. We are going to have some very grand people, conjurors, who have always something to say; and therefore the old elf king wishes to make a great display."

"Who is to be invited?" asked the raven.

"All the world may come to the great ball, even human beings, if they can only talk in their sleep, or do something after our fashion. But for the feast the company must be carefully selected; we can only admit persons of high rank; I have had a dispute myself with the elf king, as he thought we could not admit ghosts. The merman and his daughter must be invited first, although it may not be agreeable to them to remain so long on dry land, but they shall have a wet stone to sit on, or perhaps something better; so I think they will not refuse this time. We must have all the old demons of the first class, with tails, and the hobgoblins and imps; and then I think we ought not to leave out the death-horse,‡ or the grave-pig, or even the church dwarf, although they do belong to the clergy, and are not reckoned among our people; but that is merely their office, they are nearly related to us, and visit us very frequently."

"Croak," said the night-raven as he flew away with the invitations.

The elfin maidens were already dancing on the elf hill, and they danced in shawls woven from moonshine and mist, which look very pretty to those who like such things. The large hall within the elf hill was splendidly decorated;

*There is a superstition respecting these elfin maidens, that they are only to be looked at in front, and are therefore made hollow, like the inside of a mask.

†In former times, when a ghost appeared, the priest condemned it to enter the earth; when this was done, a stake was driven into the spot to which it had been banished. At midnight a cry was heard, "Let me out!" The stake was then pulled out, and the ex-communicated spirit flew away, in the form of a raven, with a hole in its left wing. This ghost-like bird was called the night-raven.

‡It is a popular superstition in Denmark that a living horse, or a living pig, has been buried under every church that is built. The ghost of the dead horse is supposed to limp upon three legs every night to some house, in which any one was going to die. The ghost of the pig was called a grave-pig.

the floor had been washed with moonshine, and the walls had been rubbed with magic ointment, so that they glowed like tulip-leaves in the light. In the kitchen were frogs roasting on the spit, and dishes preparing of snail skins, with children's fingers in them, salad of mushroom seed, hemlock, noses and marrow of mice, beer from the marsh woman's brewery, and sparkling salt-petre wine from the grave cellars. These were all substantial food. Rusty nails and church-window glass formed the dessert. The old elf king had his gold crown polished up with powdered slate-pencil; it was like that used by the first form, and very difficult for an elf king to obtain. In the bedrooms, curtains were hung up and fastened with the slime of snails; there was, indeed, a buzzing and humming everywhere.

"Now we must fumigate the place with burnt horse-hair and pig's bristles, and then I think I shall have done my part," said the elf man-servant.

"Father, dear," said the youngest daughter, "may I now hear who our high-born visitors are?"

"Well, I suppose I must tell you now," he replied; "two of my daughters must prepare themselves to be married, for the marriages certainly will take place. The old goblin from Norway, who lives in the ancient Dovre mountains, and who possesses many castles built of rock and freestone, besides a gold mine, which is better than all, so it is thought, is coming with his two sons, who are both seeking a wife. The old goblin is a true-hearted, honest, old Norwegian graybeard; cheerful and straightforward. I knew him formerly, when we used to drink together to our good fellowship: he came here once to fetch his wife, she is dead now. She was the daughter of the king of the chalk-hills at Moen. They say he took his wife from chalk; I shall be delighted to see him again. It is said that the boys are ill-bred, forward lads, but perhaps that is not quite correct, and they will become better as they grow older. Let me see that you know how to teach them good manners."

"And when are they coming?" asked the daughter.

"That depends upon wind and weather," said the elf king; "they travel economically. They will come when there is the chance of a ship. I wanted them to come over to Sweden, but the old man was not inclined to take my advice. He does not go forward with the times, and that I do not like."

Two will-o'-the-wisps came jumping in, one quicker than the other, so of course, one arrived first. "They are coming! they are coming!" he cried.

"Give me my crown," said the elf king, "and let me stand in the moon-shine."

The daughters drew on their shawls and bowed down to the ground. There stood the old goblin from the Dovre mountains, with his crown of hardened ice and polished fir-cones. Besides this, he wore a bear-skin, and great, warm boots, while his sons went with their throats bare and wore no braces, for they were strong men.

"Is that a hill?" said the youngest of the boys, pointing to the elf hill, "we should call it a hole in Norway."

"Boys," said the old man, "a hole goes in, and a hill stands out; have you no eyes in your heads?"

Another thing they wondered at was, that they were able without trouble to understand the language.

"Take care," said the old man, "or people will think you have not been well brought up."

Then they entered the elfin hill, where the select and grand company were assembled, and so quickly had they appeared that they seemed to have been blown together. But for each guest the neatest and pleasantest arrangement had been made. The sea folks sat at table in great water-tubs, and they said it was just like being at home. All behaved themselves properly excepting the two young northern goblins; they put their legs on the table and thought they were all right.

"Feet off the table-cloth!" said the old goblin. They obeyed, but not immediately. Then they tickled the ladies who waited at table, with the fir-cones, which they carried in their pockets. They took off their boots, that they might be more at ease, and gave them to the ladies to hold. But their father, the old goblin, was very different; he talked pleasantly about the stately Norwegian rocks, and told fine tales of the waterfalls which dashed over them with a clattering noise like thunder or the sound of an organ, spreading their white foam on every side. He told of the salmon that leaps in the rushing waters, while the water-god plays on his golden harp. He spoke of the bright winter nights, when the sledge bells are ringing, and the boys run with burning torches across the smooth ice, which is so transparent that they can see the fishes dart forward beneath their feet. He described everything so clearly, that those who listened could see it all; they could see the saw-mills going, the men-servants and the maidens singing songs, and dancing a rattling dance, — when all at once the old goblin gave the old elfin maiden a kiss, such a tremendous kiss, and yet they were almost strangers to each other.

Then the elfin girls had to dance, first in the usual way, and then with stamping feet, which they performed very well; then followed the artistic and solo dance. Dear me, how they did throw their legs about! No one could tell where the dance begun, or where it ended, nor indeed which were legs and which were arms, for they were all flying about together, like the shavings in a saw-pit! And then they spun round so quickly that the death-horse and the grave-pig became sick and giddy, and were obliged to leave the table.

"Stop!" cried the old goblin, " is that the only house-keeping they can perform? Can they do anything more than dance and throw about their legs, and make a whirlwind?"

"You shall soon see what they can do," said the elf king. And then he called his youngest daughter to him. She was slender and fair as moonlight, and the most graceful of all the sisters. She took a white chip in her mouth, and vanished instantly; this was her accomplishment. But the old goblin said he should not like his wife to have such an accomplishment, and thought his boys would have the same objection. Another daughter could make a figure like herself follow her, as if she had a shadow, which none of the goblin folk ever had. The third was of quite a different sort; she had learnt in the brew-house of the moor witch how to lard elfin puddings with glow-worms.

"She will make a good housewife," said the old goblin, and then saluted her with his eyes instead of drinking her health; for he did not drink much.

Now came the fourth daughter, with a large harp to play upon; and when she struck the first chord, every one lifted up the left leg (for the goblins are left-legged), and at the second chord they found they must all do just what she wanted.

"That is a dangerous woman," said the old goblin; and the two sons walked out of the hill; they had had enough of it. "And what can the next daughter do?" asked the old goblin.

"I have learnt everything that is Norwegian," said she; "and I will never marry, unless I can go to Norway."

Then her youngest sister whispered to the old goblin, "That is only because she has heard, in a Norwegian song, that when the world shall decay, the cliffs of Norway will remain standing like monuments; and she wants to get there, that she may be safe; for she is so afraid of sinking."

"Ho! ho!" said the old goblin, "is that what she means? Well, what can the seventh and last do?"

"The sixth comes before the seventh," said the elf king, for he could reckon; but the sixth would not come forward.

"I can only tell people the truth," said she. "No one cares for me, nor troubles himself about me; and I have enough to do to sew my grave clothes."

So the seventh and last came; and what could she do? Why, she could tell stories, as many as you liked, on any subject.

"Here are my five fingers," said the old goblin; "now tell me a story for each of them."

So she took him by the wrist, and he laughed till he nearly choked; and when she came to the fourth finger, there was a gold ring on it, as if it knew there was to be a betrothal. Then the old goblin said, "Hold fast what you have: this hand is yours; for I will have you for a wife myself."

Then the elfin girl said that the stories about the ring-finger and little Peter Playman had not yet been told.

"We will hear them in the winter," said the old goblin, "and also about the fir and the birch-trees, and the ghost stories, and of the tingling frost. You shall tell your tales, for no one over there can do it so well; and we will sit in the stone rooms, where the pine logs are burning, and drink mead out of the golden drinking-horn of the old Norwegian kings. The water-god has given me two; and when we sit there, Nix comes to pay us a visit, and will sing you all the songs of the mountain shepherdesses. How merry we shall be! The salmon will be leaping in the waterfalls, and dashing against the stone walls, but he will not be able to come in. It is indeed very pleasant to live in old Norway. But where are the lads?"

Where indeed were they? Why, running about the fields, and blowing out the will-o'-the-wisps, who so good-naturedly came and brought their torches.

"What tricks have you been playing?" said the old goblin. "I have taken a mother for you, and now you may take one of your aunts."

But the youngsters said they would rather make a speech and drink to their good fellowship; they had no wish to marry. Then they made speeches and drank toasts, and tipped their glasses, to show that they were empty. Then they took off their coats, and lay down on the table to sleep; for they made themselves quite at home. But the old goblin danced about the room with his young bride, and exchanged boots with her, which is more fashionable than exchanging rings.

"The cock is crowing," said the old elfin maiden who acted as housekeeper; "now we must close the shutters, that the sun may not scorch us."

Then the hill closed up. But the lizards continued to run up and down the riven tree; and one said to the other, "Oh, how much I was pleased with the old goblin!"

"The boys pleased me better," said the earth-worm. But then the poor miserable creature could not see.

THE MARSH KING'S DAUGHTER

THE GARDEN OF PARADISE

THERE was once a king's son who had a larger and more beautiful collection of books than any one else in the world, and full of splendid copper-plate engravings. He could read and obtain information respecting every people of every land; but not a word could he find to explain the situation of the garden of paradise, and this was just what he most wished to know. His grandmother had told him when he was quite a little boy, just old enough to go to school, that each flower in the garden of paradise was a sweet cake, that the pistils were full of rich wine, that on one flower history was written, on another geography or tables; so those who wished to learn their lessons had only to eat some of the cakes, and the more they ate, the more history, geography, or tables they knew. He believed it all then; but as he grew older, and learnt more and more, he became wise enough to understand that the splendor of the garden of paradise must be very different to all this. "Oh, why did Eve pluck the fruit from the tree of knowledge? why did Adam eat the forbidden fruit?" thought the king's son: "if I had been there it would never have happened, and there would have been no sin in the world." The garden of paradise occupied all his thoughts till he reached his seventeenth year.

One day he was walking alone in the wood, which was his greatest pleasure, when evening came on. The clouds gathered, and the rain poured down as if the sky had been a waterspout; and it was as dark as the bottom of a well at midnight; sometimes he slipped over the smooth grass, or fell over stones that projected out of the rocky ground. Every thing was dripping with moisture, and the poor prince had not a dry thread about him. He was obliged at last to climb over great blocks of stone, with water spurting from the thick moss. He began to feel quite faint, when he heard a most singular rushing noise, and saw before him a large cave, from which came a blaze of light. In the middle of the cave an immense fire was burning, and a noble stag, with its branching horns, was placed on a spit between the trunks of two pine-trees. It was turning slowly before the fire, and an elderly woman, as large and strong as if she had been a man in disguise, sat by, throwing one piece of wood after another into the flames.

"Come in," she said to the prince; "sit down by the fire and dry yourself."

"There is a great draught here," said the prince, as he seated himself on the ground.

"It will be worse when my sons come home," replied the woman; "you are now in the cavern of the Winds, and my sons are the four Winds of heaven: can you understand that?"

"Where are your sons?" asked the prince.

"It is difficult to answer stupid questions," said the woman. "My sons have plenty of business on hand; they are playing at shuttlecock with the clouds up yonder in the king's hall," and she pointed upwards.

"Oh, indeed," said the prince; "but you speak more roughly and harshly and are not so gentle as the women I am used to."

"Yes, that is because they have nothing else to do; but I am obliged to be harsh, to keep my boys in order, and I can do it, although they are so head-strong. Do you see those four sacks hanging on the wall? Well, they are just as much afraid of those sacks, as you used to be of the rat behind the looking-glass. I can bend the boys together, and put them in the sacks without any resistance on their parts, I can tell you. There they stay, and dare not attempt to come out until I allow them to do so. And here comes one of them."

It was the North Wind who came in, bringing with him a cold, piercing blast; large hailstones rattled on the floor, and snowflakes were scattered around in all directions. He wore a bearskin dress and cloak. His sealskin cap was drawn over his ears, long icicles hung from his beard, and one hailstone after another rolled from the collar of his jacket.

"Don't go too near the fire," said the prince, "or your hands and face will be frost-bitten."

"Frost-bitten!" said the North Wind, with a loud laugh; "why frost is my greatest delight. What sort of a little snip are you, and how did you find your way to the cavern of the Winds?"

"He is my guest," said the old woman, "and if you are not satisfied with that explanation you can go into the sack. Do you understand me?"

That settled the matter. So the North Wind began to relate his adventures, whence he came, and where he had been for a whole month. "I come from the polar seas," he said; "I have been on the Bear's Island with the Russian walrus-hunters. I sat and slept at the helm of their ship, as they sailed away from North Cape. Sometimes when I woke, the storm-birds would fly about my legs. They are curious birds; they give one flap with their wings, and then on their outstretched pinions soar far away."

"Don't make such a long story of it," said the mother of the winds; "what sort of a place is Bear's Island?"

"A very beautiful place, with a floor for dancing as smooth and flat as a plate. Half-melted snow, partly covered with moss, sharp stones, and skeletons of walruses and polar-bears, lie all about, their gigantic limbs in a state of green decay. It would seem as if the sun never shone there. I glew gently, to clear away the mist, and then I saw a little hut, which had been built from the wood of a wreck, and was covered with the skins of the walrus, the fleshy side outwards; it looked green and red, and on the roof sat a growling bear. Then I went to the sea shore, to look after birds' nests, and saw the unfledged nestlings opening their mouths and screaming for food. I blew into the thousand little throats, and quickly stopped their screaming. Farther on were the walruses with pig's heads, and teeth a yard long, rolling about like great worms."

"You relate your adventures very well, my son," said the mother, "it makes my mouth water to hear you."

"After that," continued the North Wind, "the hunting commenced. The harpoon was flung into the breast of the walrus, so that a smoking stream of blood spurted forth like a fountain, and besprinkled the ice. Then I thought of my own game; I began to blow, and set my own ships, the great icebergs sailing, so that they might crush the boats. Oh, how the sailors howled and cried out! but I howled louder than they. They were obliged to unload their cargo, and throw their chests and the dead walruses on the ice. Then I sprinkled snow over them, and left them in their crushed boats to drift southward, and to taste salt water. They will never return to Bear's Island."

"So you have done mischief," said the mother of the Winds.

"I shall leave others to tell the good I have done," he replied. "But here comes my brother from the West; I like him best of all, for he has the smell of the sea about him, and brings in a cold, fresh air as he enters."

"Is that the little Zephyr?" asked the prince.

"Yes, it is the little Zephyr," said the old woman; "but he is not little now. In years gone by he was a beautiful boy; now that is all past."

He came in, looking like a wild man, and he wore a slouched hat to protect his head from injury. In his hand he carried a club, cut from a mahogany tree in the American forests, not a trifle to carry.

"Whence do you come?" asked the mother.

"I come from the wilds of the forests, where the thorny brambles form thick hedges between the trees; where the water-snake lies in the wet grass, and mankind seem to be unknown."

"What were you doing there?"

"I looked into the deep river, and saw it rushing down from the rocks. The water drops mounted to the clouds and glittered in the rainbow. I saw the wild buffalo swimming in the river, but the strong tide carried him away amidst a flock of wild ducks, which flew into the air as the waters dashed onwards, leaving the buffalo to be hurled over the waterfall. This pleased me; so I raised a storm, which rooted up old trees, and sent them floating down the river."

"And what else have you done?" asked the old woman.

"I have rushed wildly across the savannahs; I have stroked the wild horses, and shaken the cocoa-nuts from the trees. Yes, I have many stories to relate; but I need not tell everything I know. You know it all very well, don't you, old lady?" And he kissed his mother so roughly, that she nearly fell backwards. Oh, he was, indeed, a wild fellow.

Now in came the South Wind, with a turban and a flowing Bedouin cloak.

"How cold it is here!" said he, throwing more wood on the fire. "It is easy to feel that the North Wind has arrived here before me."

"Why it is hot enough here to roast a bear," said the North Wind.

"You are a bear yourself," said the other.

"Do you want to be put in the sack, both of you?" said the old woman. "Sit down, now, on that stone, yonder, and tell me where you have been."

"In Africa, mother. I went out with the Hottentots, who were lion-hunting in the Kaffir land, where the plains are covered with grass the color of a green olive; and here I ran races with the ostrich, but I soon outstripped him in swiftness. At last I came to the desert, in which lie the golden sands, looking like the bottom of the sea. Here I met a caravan, and the travellers had just killed their last camel, to obtain water; there was very little for them, and they continued their painful journey beneath the burning sun, and over the hot sands, which stretched before them a vast, boundless desert. Then I rolled myself in the loose sand, and whirled it in burning columns over their heads. The dromedarys stood still in terror, while the merchants drew their caftans over their heads, and threw themselves on the ground before me, as they do before Allah, their god. Then I buried them beneath a pyramid of sand, which covers them all. When I blow that away on my next visit, the sun will bleach their bones, and travellers will see that others have been there before them; otherwise, in such a wild desert, they might not believe it possible."

"So you have done nothing but evil," said the mother. "Into the sack with you;" and, before he was aware, she had seized the South Wind round the body, and popped him into the bag. He rolled about on the floor, till she sat herself upon him to keep him still.

"These boys of yours are very lively," said the prince.

"Yes," she replied, "but I know how to correct them, when necessary; and here comes the fourth." In came the East Wind, dressed like a Chinese.

"Oh, you come from that quarter, do you?" said she; "I thought you had been to the garden of paradise."

"I am going there to-morrow," he replied; "I have not been there for a hundred years. I have just come from China, where I danced round the porcelain tower till all the bells jingled again. In the streets an official flogging was taking place, and bamboo canes were being broken on the shoulders of men of every high position, from the first to the ninth grade. They cried, 'Many thanks, my fatherly benefactor;' but I am sure the words did not come from their hearts, so I rang the bells till they sounded, 'ding, ding-dong.' "

"You are a wild boy," said the old woman; "it is well for you that you are going to-morrow to the garden of paradise; you always get improved in your education there. Drink deeply from the fountain of wisdom while you are there, and bring home a bottleful for me."

"That I will," said the East Wind; "but why have you put my brother South in a bag? Let him out; for I want him to tell me about the phœnix-bird. The princess always wants to hear of this bird when I pay her my visit every hundred years. If you will open the sack, sweetest mother, I will give you two pocketfuls of tea, green and fresh as when I gathered it from the spot where it grew."

"Well, for the sake of the tea, and because you are my own boy, I will open the bag."

She did so, and the South Wind crept out, looking quite cast down, because the prince had seen his disgrace.

"There is a palm-leaf for the princess," he said. "The old phœnix, the only one in the world, gave it to me himself. He has scratched on it with his beak the whole of his history during the hundred years he has lived. She can there read how the old phœnix set fire to his own nest, and sat upon it while it was burning, like a Hindoo widow. The dry twigs around the nest crackled and smoked till the flames burst forth and consumed the phœnix to ashes. Amidst the fire lay an egg, red hot, which presently burst with a loud report, and out flew a young bird. He is the only phœnix in the world, and the king over all the other birds. He has bitten a hole in the leaf which I give you, and that is his greeting to the princess."

"Now let us have something to eat," said the mother of the Winds. So they all sat down to feast on the roasted stag; and as the prince sat by the side of the East Wind, they soon became good friends.

"Pray tell me," said the prince, "who is that princess of whom you have been talking! and where lies the garden of paradise?"

"Ho! ho!" said the East Wind, "would you like to go there? Well, you can fly off with me to-morrow; but I must tell you one thing—no human being has been there since the time of Adam and Eve. I suppose you have read of them in your Bible."

"Of course I have," said the prince.

"Well," continued the East Wind, "when they were driven out of the garden of paradise, it sunk into the earth; but it retained its warm sunshine, its balmy air, and all its splendor. The fairy queen lives there, in the island of happiness, where death never comes, and all is beautiful. I can manage to take you there to-morrow, if you will sit on my back. But now don't talk any more, for I want to go to sleep;" and then they all slept.

When the prince awoke in the early morning, he was not a little surprised at finding himself high up above the clouds. He was seated on the back of the East Wind, who held him faithfully; and they were so high in the air that woods and fields, rivers and lakes, as they lay beneath them, looked like a painted map.

"Good morning," said the East Wind. "You might have slept on a while; for there is very little to see in the flat country over which we are passing unless you like to count the churches; they look like spots of chalk on a green board." The green board was the name he gave to the green fields and meadows.

"It was very rude of me not to say good-bye to your mother and your brothers," said the prince.

"They will excuse you, as you were asleep," said the East Wind; and then they flew on faster than ever.

The leaves and branches of the trees rustled as they passed. When they flew over seas and lakes, the waves rose higher, and the large ships dipped into the water like diving swans. As darkness came on, towards evening, the great towns looked charming; lights were sparkling, now seen now hidden, just as the sparks go out one after another on a piece of burnt paper. The prince clapped his hands with pleasure; but the East Wind advised him not to express his admiration in that manner, or he might fall down, and find himself hanging on a church steeple. The eagle in the dark forests flies swiftly; but faster than he flew the East Wind. The Cossack, on his small horse, rides lightly o'er the plains; but lighter still passed the prince on the winds of the wind.

"There are the Himalayas, the highest mountains in Asia," said the East Wind. "We shall soon reach the garden of paradise now."

Then, they turned southward, and the air became fragrant with the perfume of spices and flowers. Here figs and pomegranates grew wild, and the vines were covered with clusters of blue and purple grapes. Here they both descended to the earth, and stretched themselves on the soft grass, while the flowers bowed to the breath of the wind as if to welcome it. "Are we now in the garden of paradise?" asked the prince.

"No, indeed," replied the East Wind; "but we shall be there very soon. Do you see that wall of rocks, and the cavern beneath it, over which the grape vines hang like a green curtain? Through that cavern we must pass. Wrap your cloak round you; for while the sun scorches you here, a few steps farther it will be icy cold. The bird flying past the entrance to the cavern feels as if one wing were in the region of summer, and the other in the depths of winter."

"So this then is the way to the garden of paradise?" asked the prince, as they entered the cavern. It was indeed cold; but the cold soon passed, for the East Wind spread his wings, and they gleamed like the brightest fire. As they passed on through this wonderful cave, the prince could see great blocks of stone, from which water trickled, hanging over their heads in fantastic shapes. Sometimes it was so narrow that they had to creep on their hands and knees, while at other times it was lofty and wide, like the free air. It had the appearance of a chapel for the dead, with petrified organs and silent pipes. "We seem to be passing through the valley of death to the garden of paradise," said the prince.

But the East Wind answered not a word, only pointed forwards to a lovely blue light which gleamed in the distance. The blocks of stone assumed a misty appearance, till at last they looked like white clouds in moonlight. The air was fresh and balmy, like a breeze from the mountains perfumed with flowers from a valley of roses. A river, clear as the air itself, sparkled at their feet, while in its clear depths could be seen gold and silver fish sporting in the bright water, and purple eels emitting sparks of fire at every moment, while the broad leaves of the water-lilies, that floated on its surface, flickered with all the colors of the rainbow. The flower in its color of flame seemed to receive its nourishment from the water, as a lamp is sustained by oil. A marble bridge, of such exquisite workmanship that it appeared as if formed of lace and pearls, led to the island of happiness, in which bloomed the garden of paradise. The East Wind took the prince in his arms, and carried him over, while the flowers and the leaves sang the sweet songs of his childhood in tones so full and soft that no human voice could venture to imitate. Within the garden grew large trees, full of sap; but whether they were palm-trees or gigantic water-plants, the prince knew not. The climbing plants hung in garlands of green and gold, like the illuminations on the margins of old missals or twined among the initial letters. Birds, flowers, and festoons appeared intermingled in seeming confusion. Close by, on the grass, stood a group of peacocks, with radiant tails outspread to the sun. The prince touched them, and found, to his surprise, that they were not really birds, but the leaves of the burdock tree, which shone with the colors of a peacock's tail. The lion and the tiger, gentle and tame, were springing about like playful cats among the green bushes, whose perfume was like the fragrant blossom of the olive. The plumage of the wood-pigeon glistened like pearls as it struck the lion's mane with its wings; while the antelope, usually so shy, stood near, nodding its head as if it wished to join in the frolic. The fairy of paradise next made her appearance. Her raiment shone like the sun, and her serene countenance beamed with happiness like that of a mother rejoicing over her child. She was young and beautiful, and a train of lovely maidens followed her, each wearing a bright star in her hair. The East Wind gave her the palm-leaf, on which was written the history of the phœnix; and her eyes sparkled with joy. She then took the prince by the hand, and led him into her palace, the walls of which were richly colored, like a tulip-leaf when it is turned to the sun. The roof had the appearance of an inverted flower, and the colors grew deeper and brighter to the gazer. The prince walked to a window, and saw what appeared to be the tree of knowledge of good and evil, with Adam and Eve standing by, and the serpent near them. "I thought they were banished from paradise," he said.

The princess smiled, and told him that time had engraved each event on a window-pane in the form of a picture; but, unlike other pictures, all that it represented lived and moved, — the leaves rustled, and the persons went and came, as in a looking-glass. He looked through another pane, and saw the ladder in Jacob's dream, on which the angels were ascending and descending with outspread wings. All that had ever happened in the world here lived and moved on the panes of glass, in pictures such as time alone could produce. The fairy now led the prince into a large, lofty room with transparent walls, through which the light shone. Here were portraits, each one appearing more beautiful than the other—millions of happy beings, whose laughter and song mingled in one sweet melody: some of these were in such an elevated position that they appeared smaller than the smallest rosebud, or like pencil dots on paper. In the centre of the hall stood a tree, with drooping branches, from which hung golden apples, both great and small, looking like oranges amid the green leaves. It was the tree of knowledge of good and evil, from which Adam and Eve had plucked and eaten the forbidden fruit, and from each leaf trickled a bright red dewdrop, as if the tree were weeping tears of blood for their sin. "Let us now take the boat," said the fairy: "a sail on the cool waters will refresh us. But we shall not move from the spot, although the boat may rock on the swelling water; the countries of the world will glide before us, but we shall remain still."

It was indeed wonderful to behold. First came the lofty Alps, snow-clad, and covered with clouds and dark pines. The horn resounded, and the shepherds sang merrily in the valleys. The banana-trees bent their drooping branches over the boat, black swans floated on the water, and singular animals and flowers appeared on the distant shore. *New Holland,* the fifth division of the world, now glided by, with mountains in the background, looking blue in the distance. They heard the song of the priests, and saw the wild dance of the savage to the sound of the drums and trumpets of bone; the pyramids of Egypt rising to the clouds; columns and sphinxes, overthrown and buried in the sand, followed in their turn; while the northern lights flashed out over the extinguished volcanoes of the north, in fireworks none could imitate.

The prince was delighted, and yet he saw hundreds of other wonderful things more than can be described. "Can I stay here forever?" asked he.

"That depends upon yourself," replied the fairy. "If you do not, like Adam, long for what is forbidden, you can remain here always."

"I should not touch the fruit on the tree of knowledge," said the prince; "there is abundance of fruit equally beautiful."

"Examine your own heart," said the princess, "and if you do not feel sure of its strength, return with the East Wind who brought you. He is about to fly back, and will not return here for a hundred years. The time will not seem to you more than a hundred hours, yet even that is a long time for temptation and resistance. Every evening, when I leave you, I shall be obliged to say, 'Come with me,' and to beckon to you with my hand. But you must not listen, nor move from your place to follow me; for with every step you will find your power to resist weaker. If once you attempted to follow me, you would soon find yourself in the hall, where grows the tree of knowledge, for I sleep beneath its perfumed branches. If you stooped over me, I should be forced to smile. If you then kissed my lips, the garden of paradise would sink into the earth, and to you it would be lost. A keen wind from the desert would howl around you; cold rain fall on your head, and sorrow and woe be your future lot."

"I will remain," said the prince.

So the East Wind kissed him on the forehead, and said, "Be firm; then shall we meet again when a hundred years have passed. Farewell, farewell." Then the East Wind spread his broad pinions, which shone like the lightning in harvest, or as the northern lights in a cold winter.

"Farewell, farewell," echoed the trees and the flowers.

Storks and pelicans flew after him in feathery bands, to accompany him to the boundaries of the garden.

"Now we will commence dancing," said the fairy; and when it is nearly over at sunset, while I am dancing with you, I shall make a sign, and ask you to follow me: but do not obey. I shall be obliged to repeat the same thing for a hundred years; and each time, when the trial is past, if you resist, you will gain strength, till resistance becomes easy, and at last the temptation will be quite overcome. This evening, as it will be the first time, I have warned you."

After this the fairy led him into a large hall, filled with transparent lilies. The yellow stamina of each flower formed a tiny golden harp, from which came forth strains of music like the mingled tones of flute and lyre. Beautiful maidens, slender and graceful in form, and robed in transparent gauze, floated through the dance, and sang of the happy life in the garden of paradise, where death never entered, and where all would bloom forever in immortal youth. As the sun went down, the whole heavens became crimson and gold, and tinted the lilies with the hue of roses. Then the beautiful maidens offered to the prince sparkling wine; and when he had drank, he felt happiness greater than he had ever known before. Presently the background of the hall opened and the tree of knowledge appeared, surrounded by a halo of glory that almost blinded him. Voices, soft and lovely as his mother's sounded in his ears, as if she were singing to him, "My child, my beloved child." Then the fairy beckoned to him, and said in sweet accents, "Come with me, come with me." Forgetting his promise, forgetting it even on the very first evening, he rushed towards her, while she continued to beckon to him and to smile. The fragrance around him overpowered his senses, the music from the harps sounded more entrancing, while around the tree appeared millions of smiling faces, nodding and singing. "Man should know everything; man is the lord of the earth." The tree of knowledge no longer wept tears of blood, for the dewdrops shone like glittering stars.

"Come, come," continued that thrilling voice, and the prince followed the call. At every step his cheeks glowed, and the blood rushed wildly through his veins. "I must follow," he cried; "it is not a sin, it cannot be, to follow beauty and joy. I only want to see her sleep, and nothing will happen unless I kiss her, and that I will not do, for I have strength to resist, and a determined will."

The fairy threw off her dazzling attire, bent back the boughs, and in another moment was hidden among them.

"I have not sinned yet," said the prince, "and I will not;" and then he pushed aside the boughs to follow the princess. She was lying already asleep, beautiful as only a fairy in the garden of paradise could be. She smiled as he bent over her, and he saw tears trembling out of her beautiful eyelashes. "Do you weep for me?" he whispered. "Oh weep not, thou loveliest of women. Now do I begin to understand the happiness of paradise; I feel it to my inmost soul, in every thought. A new life is born within me. One moment of such happiness is worth an eternity of darkness and woe." He stooped and kissed the tears from her eyes, and touched her lips with his.

A clap of thunder, loud and awful, resounded through the trembling air. All around him fell into ruin. The lovely fairy, the beautiful garden, sunk deeper and deeper. The prince saw it sinking down in the dark night till it shone only like a star in the distance beneath him. Then he felt a coldness, like death, creeping over him; his eyes closed, and he became insensible.

When he recovered, a chilling rain was beating upon him, and a sharp wind blew on his head. "Alas! what have I done?" he sighed; "I have sinned like Adam, and the garden of paradise has sunk into the earth." He opened his eyes, and saw the star in the distance, but it was the morning star in heaven which glitterd in the darkness.

Presently he stood up and found himself in the depths of the forest, close to the cavern of the Winds, and the mother of the Winds sat by his side. She looked angry, and raised her arm in the air as she spoke. "The very first evening!" she said. "Well, I expected it! If you were my son, you should go into the sack."

"And there he will have to go at last," said a strong old man, with large black wings, and a scythe in his hand, whose name was Death. "He shall be laid in his coffin, but not yet. I will allow him to wander about the world for a while, to atone for his sin, and to give him time to become better. But I shall return when he least expects me. I shall lay him in a black coffin, place it on my head, and fly away with it beyond the stars. There also blooms a garden of paradise, and if he is good and pious he will be admitted; but if his thoughts are bad, and his heart is full of sin, he will sink with his coffin deeper than the garden of paradise has sunk. Once in every thousand years I shall go and fetch him, when he will either be condemned to sink still deeper, or be raised to a happier life in the world beyond the stars."

THE TINDER-BOX

A SOLDIER came marching along the high road: "Left, right — left, right." He had his knapsack on his back, and a sword at his side; he had been to the wars, and was now returning home.

As he walked on, he met a very frightful-looking old witch in the road. Her under-lip hung quite down on her breast, and she stopped and said, "Good evening, soldier; you have a very fine sword, and a large knapsack, and you are a real soldier; so you shall have as much money as ever you like."

"Thank you, old witch," said the soldier.

"Do you see that large tree," said the witch, pointing to a tree which stood beside them. "Well, it is quite hollow inside, and you must climb to the top, when you will see a hole, through which you can let yourself down into the tree to a great depth. I will tie a rope round your body, so that I can pull you up again when you call out to me."

"But what am I to do, down there in the tree?" asked the soldier.

"Get money," she replied; "for you must know that when you reach the ground under the tree, you will find yourself in a large hall, lighted up by three hundred lamps; you will then see three doors, which can be easily opened, for the keys are in all the locks. On entering the first of the chambers, to which these doors lead, you will see a large chest, standing in the middle of the floor, and upon it a dog seated, with a pair of eyes as large as teacups. But you need not be at all afraid of him; I will give you my blue checked apron,

THE TINDER-BOX

which you must spread upon the floor, and then boldly seize hold of the dog, and place him upon it. You can then open the chest, and take from it as many pence as you please, they are only copper pence; but if you would rather have silver money, you must go into the second chamber. Here you will find another dog, with eyes as big as mill-wheels; but do not let that trouble you. Place him upon my apron, and then take what money you please. If, however, you like gold best, enter the third chamber, where there is another chest full of it. The dog who sits on this chest is very dreadful; his eyes are as big as a tower, but do not mind him. If he also is placed upon my apron, he cannot hurt you, and you may take from the chest what gold you will."

"This is not a bad story," said the soldier; "but what am I to give you, you old witch? for, of course, you do not mean to tell me all this for nothing."

"No," said the witch; "but I do not ask for a single penny. Only promise to bring me an old tinder-box, which my grandmother left behind the last time she went down there."

"Very well; I promise. Now tie the rope round my body."

"Here it is," replied the witch; "and here is my blue checked apron."

As soon as the rope was tied, the soldier climbed up the tree, and let himself down through the hollow to the ground beneath; and here he found, as the witch had told him, a large hall, in which many hundred lamps were all burning. Then he opened the first door. "Ah!" there sat the dog, with the eyes as large as teacups, staring at him.

"You're a pretty fellow," said the soldier, seizing him, and placing him on the witch's apron, while he filled his pockets from the chest with as many pieces as they would hold. Then he closed the lid, seated the dog upon it again, and walked into another chamber, And, sure enough, there sat the dog with eyes as big as mill-wheels.

"You had better not look at me in that way," said the soldier; "you will make your eyes water;" and then he seated him also upon the apron, and opened the chest. But when he saw what a quantity of silver money it contained, he very quickly threw away all the coppers he had taken, and filled his pockets and his knapsack with nothing but silver.

Then he went into the third room, and there the dog was really hideous; his eyes were, truly, as big as towers, and they turned round and round in his head like wheels.

"Good morning," said the soldier, touching his cap, for he had never seen such a dog in his life. But after looking at him more closely, he thought he had been civil enough, so he placed him on the floor, and opened the chest. Good gracious, what a quantity of gold there was! enough to buy all the sugar-sticks of the sweet-stuff women; all the tin soldiers, whips, and rocking-horses in the world, or even the whole town itself. There was, indeed, an immense quantity. So the soldier now threw away all the silver money he had taken, and filled his pockets and his knapsack with gold instead; and not only his pockets and his knapsack, but even his cap and boots, so that he could scarcely walk.

He was really rich now; so he replaced the dog on the chest, closed the door, and called up through the tree, "Now pull me out, you old witch."

"Have you got the tinder-box?" asked the witch.

"No; I declare I quite forgot it." So he went back and fetched the tinder-box, and then the witch drew him up out of the tree, and he stood again in the high road, with his pockets, his knapsack, his cap, and his boots full of gold.

"What are you going to do with the tinder-box?" asked the soldier.

"That is nothing to you," replied the witch; "you have the money, now give me the tinder-box."

"I tell you what," said the soldier, "if you don't tell me what you are going to do with it, I will draw my sword and cut off your head."

"No," said the witch.

The soldier immediately cut off her head, and there she lay on the ground. Then he tied up all his money in her apron, and slung it on his back like a bundle, put the tinderbox in his pocket, and walked off to the nearest town. It was a very nice town, and he put up at the best inn, and ordered a dinner of all his favorite dishes, for now he was rich and had plenty of money.

The servant, who cleaned his boots, thought they certainly were a shabby pair to be worn by such a rich gentleman, for he had not yet bought any new ones. The next day, however, he procured some good clothes and proper boots, so that our soldier soon became known as a fine gentleman, and the people visited him, and told him all the wonders that were to be seen in the town, and of the king's beautiful daughter, the princess.

"Where can I see her?" asked the soldier.

"She is not to be seen at all," they said; "she lives in a large copper castle, surrounded by walls and towers. No one but the king himself can pass in or out, for there has been a prophecy that she will marry a common soldier, and the king cannot bear to think of such a marriage."

"I should like very much to see her," thought the soldier; but he could not obtain permission to do so. However, he passed a very pleasant time; went to the theatre, drove in the king's garden, and gave a great deal of money to the poor, which was very good of him; he remembered what it had been in olden times to be without a shilling. Now he was rich, had fine clothes, and many friends, who all declared he was a fine fellow and a real gentleman, and all this gratified him exceedingly. But his money would not last forever; and as he spent and gave away a great deal daily, and received none, he found himself at last with only two shillings left. So he was obliged to leave his elegant rooms, and live in a little garret under the roof, where he had to clean his own boots, and even mend them with a large needle. None of his friends came to see him, there were too many stairs to mount up. One dark evening, he had not even a penny to buy a candle; then all at once he remembered that there was a piece of candle stuck in the tinder-box, which he had brought from the old tree, into which the witch had helped him.

He found the tinder-box, but no sooner had he struck a few sparks from the flint and steel, than the door flew open and the dog with eyes as big as teacups, whom he had seen while down in the tree, stood before him, and said, "What orders, master?"

"Hallo," said the soldier; "well this is a pleasant tinderbox, if it brings me all I wish for."

"Bring me some money," said he to the dog.

He was gone in a moment, and presently returned, carrying a large bag of coppers in his month. The soldier very soon discovered after this the value of the tinder-box. If he struck the flint once, the dog who sat on the chest of copper money made his appearance; if twice, the dog came from the chest of silver; and if three times, the dog with eyes like towers, who watched over the gold. The soldier had now plenty of money; he returned to his elegant rooms, and reappeared in his fine clothes, so that his friends knew him again directly, and made as much of him as before.

After a while he began to think it was very strange that no one could get a look at the princess. "Every one says she is very beautiful," thought he to himself; "but what is the use of that if she is to be shut up in a copper castle surrounded by so many towers. Can I by any means get to see her. Stop! where is my tinder-box?" Then he struck a light, and in a moment the dog, with eyes as big as teacups, stood before him.

"It is midnight," said the soldier, "yet I should very much like to see the princess, if only for a moment."

The dog disappeared instantly, and before the soldier could even look round, he returned with the princess. She was lying on the dog's back asleep, and looked so lovely, that every one who saw her would know she was a real princess. The soldier could not help kissing her, true soldier as he was. Then the dog ran back with the princess; but in the morning, while at breakfast with the king and queen, she told them what a singular dream she had had during the night, of a dog and a soldier, that she had ridden on the dog's back, and been kissed by the soldier.

"That is a very pretty story, indeed," said the queen. So the next night one of the old ladies of the court was set to watch by the princess's bed, to discover whether it really was a dream, or what else it might be.

The soldier longed very much to see the princess once more, so he sent for the dog again in the night to fetch her, and to run with her as fast as ever he could. But the old lady put on water boots, and ran after him as quickly as he did, and found that he carried the princess into a large house. She thought it would help her to remember the place if she made a large cross on the door with a piece of chalk. Then she went home to bed, and the dog presently returned with the princess. But when he saw that a cross had been made on the door of the house, where the soldier lived, he took another piece of chalk and made crosses on all the doors in the town, so that the lady-in-waiting might not be able to find out the right door.

Early the next morning the king and queen accompanied the lady and all the officers of the household, to see where the princess had been.

"Here it is," said the king, when they came to the first door with a cross on it.

"No, my dear husband, it must be that one," said the queen, pointing to a second door having a cross also.

"And here is one, and there is another!" they all exclaimed; for there were crosses on all the doors in every direction.

So they felt it would be useless to search any farther. But the queen was a very clever woman; she could do a great deal more than merely ride in a carriage. She took her large gold scissors, cut a piece of silk into squares, and made a neat little bag. This bag she filled with buckwheat flour, and tied it round the princess's neck; and then she cut a small hole in the bag, so that the flour might be scattered on the ground as the princess went along. During the night, the dog came again and carried the princess on his back, and ran with her to the soldier, who loved her very much, and wished that he had been a prince, so that he might have her for a wife. The dog did not observe how the flour ran out of the bag all the way from the castle wall to the soldier's house, and even up to the window, where he had climbed with the princess. Therefore in the morning the king and queen found out where their daughter had been, and the soldier was taken up and put in prison. Oh, how dark and disagreeable it was as he sat there, and the people said to him, "To-morrow you will be hanged." It was not very pleasant news, and besides, he had left the tinder-box at the inn. In the morning he could see through the iron grating of the little window how the people were hastening out of the town to see him hanged; he heard the drums beating, and saw the soldiers marching. Every one ran out to look at them, and a shoemaker's boy, with a leather apron and slippers on, galloped by so fast, that one of his slippers flew off and struck against the wall where the soldier sat looking through the iron grating. "Hallo, you shoemaker's boy, you need not be in such a hurry," cried the soldier to him. "There will be nothing to see till I come; but if you will run to the house where I have been living, and bring me my tinder-box, you shall have four shillings, but you must put your best foot foremost."

The shoemaker's boy liked the idea of getting the four shillings, so he ran very fast and fetched the tinder-box, and gave it to the soldier. And now we shall see what happened. Outside the town a large gibbet had been erected, round which stood the soldiers and several thousands of people. The king and the queen sat on splendid thrones opposite to the judges and the whole council. The soldier already stood on the ladder; but as they were about to place the rope around his neck, he said that an innocent request was often granted to a poor criminal before he suffered death. He wished very much to smoke a pipe, as it would be the last pipe he should ever smoke in the world. The king could not refuse this request, so the soldier took his tinder-box, and struck fire, once, twice, thrice, — and there in a moment stood all the dogs; — the one with eyes as big as teacups, the one with eyes as large as mill-wheels, and the third, whose eyes were like towers. "Help me now, that I may not be hanged," cried the soldier.

And the dogs fell upon the judges and all the councillors; seized one by the legs, and another by the nose, and tossed them many feet high in the air, so that they fell down and were dashed to pieces.

"I will not be touched," said the king. But the largest dog seized him, as well as the queen, and threw them after the others. Then the soldiers and all the people were afraid, and cried, "Good soldier, you shall be our king, and you shall marry the beautiful princess."

So they placed the soldier in the king's carriage, and the three dogs ran on in front and cried "Hurrah!" and the little boys whistled through their fingers, and the soldiers presented arms. The princess came out of the copper castle, and became queen, which was very pleasing to her. The wedding festivities lasted a whole week, and the dogs sat at the table, and stared with all their eyes.

THE SHADOW

IN very hot climates, where the heat of the sun has great power, people are usually as brown as mahogany; and in the hottest countries they are negroes, with black skins. A learned man once travelled into one of these warm climates, from the cold regions of the north, and thought he would roam about as he did at home; but he soon had to change his opinion. He found that, like all sensible people, he must remain in the house during the whole day, with every window and door closed, so that it looked as if all in the house were asleep or absent. The houses of the narrow street in which he lived were so lofty that the sun shone upon them from morning till evening, and it became quite unbearable. This learned man from the cold regions was young as well as clever; but it seemed to him as if he were sitting in an oven, and he became quite exhausted and weak, and grew so thin that his shadow shrivelled up, and became much smaller than it had been at home. The sun took away even what was left of it, and he saw nothing of it till the evening, after sunset. It was really a pleasure, as soon as the lights were brought into the room, to see the shadow stretch itself against the wall, even to the ceiling, so tall was it; and it really wanted a good stretch to recover its strength. The learned man would sometimes go out into the balcony to stretch himself also; and as soon as the stars came forth in the clear, beautiful sky, he felt revived. People at this hour began to make their appearance in all the balconies in the street; for in warm climates every window has a balcony, in which they can breathe the fresh evening air, which is very necessary, even to those who are used to a heat that makes them as brown as mahogany; so that the street presented a very lively appearance. Here were shoemakers, and tailors, and all sorts of people sitting. In the street beneath, they brought out tables and chairs, lighted candles by hundreds, talked and sang, and were very merry. There were people walking, carriages driving, and mules trotting along, with their bells on the harness, "tingle, tingle," as they went. Then the dead were carried to the grave with the sound of solemn music, and the tolling of the church bells. It was indeed a scene of varied life in the street. One house only, which was just opposite to the one in which the foreign learned man lived, formed a contrast to all this, for it was quite still; and yet somebody dwelt there, for flowers stood in the balcony, blooming beautifully in the hot sun; and this could not have been unless they had been watered carefully. Therefore some one must be in the house to do this. The doors leading to the balcony were half opened in the evening; and although in the front room all was dark, music could be heard from the interior of the house. The foreign learned man considered this music very delightful; but perhaps he fancied it; for everything in these warm countries pleased him, excepting the heat of the sun. The foreign landlord said he did not know who had taken the opposite house—nobody was to be seen there; and as to the music, he thought it seemed very tedious, to him most uncommonly so.

"It is just as if some one was practising a piece that he could not manage; it is always the same piece. He thinks, I suppose, that he will be able to manage it at last; but I do not think so, however long he may play it."

Once the foreigner woke in the night. He slept with the door open which led to the balcony; the wind had raised the curtain before it, and there appeared a wonderful brightness over all in the balcony of the opposite house. The flowers seemed like flames of the most gorgeous colors, and among the flowers stood a beautiful slender maiden. It was to him as if light streamed from her, and dazzled his eyes; but then he had only just opened them, as he awoke from his sleep. With one spring he was out of bed, and crept softly behind the curtain. But she was gone — the brightness had disappeared; the flowers no longer appeared like flames, although still as beautiful as ever. The door stood ajar, and from an inner room sounded music so sweet and so lovely, that it produced the most enchanting thoughts, and acted on the senses with magic power. Who could live there? Where was the real entrance? for, both in the street and in the lane at the side, the whole ground floor was a continuation of shops; and people could not always be passing through them.

One evening the foreigner sat in the balcony. A light was burning in his own room, just behind him. It was quite natural, therefore, that his shadow should fall on the wall of the opposite house; so that, as he sat amongst the flowers on his balcony, when he moved, his shadow moved also.

"I think my shadow is the only living thing to be seen opposite," said the learned man; "see how pleasantly it sits among the flowers. The door is only ajar; the shadow ought to be clever enough to step in and look about him, and then to come back and tell me what he has seen. You could make yourself useful in this way," said he, jokingly; "be so good as to step in now, will you?" and then he nodded to the shadow, and the shadow nodded in return. "Now go, but don't stay away altogether."

Then the foreigner stood up, and the shadow on the opposite balcony stood up also; the foreigner turned round, the shadow turned; and if any one had observed, they might have seen it go straight into the half-opened door of the opposite balcony, as the learned man re-entered his own room, and let the curtain fall. The next morning he went out to take his coffee and read the newspapers.

"How is this?" he exclaimed, as he stood in the sunshine. "I have lost my shadow. So it really did go away yesterday evening, and it has not returned. This is very annoying."

And it certainly did vex him, not so much because the shadow was gone, but because he knew there was a story of a man without a shadow. All the people at home, in his country, knew this story; and when he returned, and related his own adventures, they would say it was only an imitation; and he had no desire for such things to be said of him. So he decided not to speak of it at all, which was a very sensible determination.

In the evening he went out again on his balcony, taking care to place the light behind him; for he knew that a shadow always wants his master for a screen; but he could not entice him out. He made himself little, and he made himself tall; but there was no shadow, and no shadow came. He said, "Hem, a-hem;" but it was all useless. That was very vexatious; but in warm countries everything grows very quickly; and, after a week had passed, he saw, to his great joy, that a new shadow was growing from his feet, when he walked in the sunshine; so that the root must have remained. After three weeks, he had quite a respectable shadow, which, during his return journey to northern lands, continued to grow, and became at last so large that he might very well have spared half of it. When this learned man arrived at home, he wrote books about the true, the good, and the beautiful, which are to be found in this world; and so days and years passed — many, many years.

One evening, as he sat in his study, a very gentle tap was heard at the door. "Come in," said he; but no one came. He opened the door, and there stood before him a man so remarkably thin that he felt seriously troubled at his appearance. He was, however, very well dressed, and looked like a gentleman. "To whom have I the honor of speaking?" said he.

"Ah, I hoped you would recognize me," said the elegant stranger; "I have gained so much that I have a body of flesh, and clothes to wear. You never expected to see me in such a condition. Do you not recognize your old shadow? Ah, you never expected that I should return to you again. All has been prosperous with me since I was with you last; I have become rich in every way, and, were I inclined to purchase my freedom from service, I could easily do so." And as he spoke he rattled between his fingers a number of costly trinkets which hung to a thick gold watch-chain he wore round his neck. Diamond rings sparkled on his fingers, and it was all real.

"I cannot recover from my astonishment," said the learned man. "What does all this mean?"

"Something rather unusual," said the shadow; "but you are yourself an uncommon man, and you know very well that I have followed in your footsteps ever since your childhood. As soon as you found that I have travelled enough to be trusted alone, I went my own way, and I am now in the most brilliant circumstances. But I felt a kind of longing to see you once more before you die, and I wanted to see this place again, for there is always a clinging to the land of one's birth. I know that you have now another shadow; do I owe you anything? If so, have the goodness to say what it is."

"No! Is it really you?" said the learned man. "Well, this is most remarkable; I never supposed it possible that a man's old shadow could become a human being."

"Just tell me what I owe you," said the shadow, "for I do not like to be in debt to any man."

"How can you talk in that manner?" said the learned man. "What question of debt can there be between us? You are as free as any one. I rejoice exceedingly to hear of your good fortune. Sit down, old friend, and tell me a little of how it happened, and what you saw in the house opposite to me while we were in those hot climates."

"Yes, I will tell you all about it," said the shadow, sitting down; "but then you must promise me never to tell in this city, wherever you may meet me, that I have been your shadow. I am thinking of being married, for I have more than sufficient to support a family."

"Make yourself quite easy," said the learned man; "I will tell no one who you really are. Here is my hand, — I promise, and a word is sufficient between man and man."

"Between man and a shadow," said the shadow; for he could not help saying so.

It was really most remarkable how very much he had become a man in appearance. He was dressed in a suit of the very finest black cloth, polished boots, and an opera crush hat, which could be folded together so that nothing could be seen but the crown and the rim, besides the trinkets, the gold chain, and the diamond rings already spoken of. The shadow was, in fact, very well dressed, and this made a man of him. "Now I will relate to you what you wish to know," said the shadow, placing his foot with the polished leather boot as firmly as possible on the arm of the new shadow of the learned man, which lay at his feet like a poodle dog. This was done, it might be from pride, or perhaps that the new shadow might cling to him, but the prostrate shadow remained quite quiet and at rest, in order that it might listen, for it wanted to know how a shadow could be sent away by its master, and become a man itself. "Do you know," said the shadow, "that in the house opposite to you lived the most glorious creature in the world? It was poetry. I remained there three weeks, and it was more like three thousand years, for I read all that has ever been written in poetry or prose; and I may say, in truth, that I saw and learnt everything."

"Poetry!" exclaimed the learned man. "Yes, she lives as a hermit in great cities. Poetry! Well, I saw her once for a very short moment, while sleep weighed down my eyelids. She flashed upon me from the balcony like the radiant aurora borealis, surrounded with flowers like flames of fire. Tell me, you were on the balcony that evening; you went through the door, and what did you see?"

"I found myself in an ante-room," said the shadow. "You still sat opposite to me, looking into the room. There was no light, or at least it seemed in partial darkness, for the door of a whole suite of rooms stood open, and they were brilliantly lighted. The blaze of light would have killed me, had I approached too near the maiden myself; but I was cautious, and took time, which is what every one ought to do."

"And what didst thou see?" asked the learned man.

"I saw everything, as you shall hear. But — it really is not pride on my part, as a free man and possessing the knowledge that I do, besides my position, not to speak of my wealth — I wish you would say *you* to me instead of *thou.*"

"I beg your pardon," said the learned man; "it is an old habit, which it is difficult to break. You are quite right; I will try to think of it. But now tell me everything that you saw."

"Everything," said the shadow; "for I saw and know everything."

"What was the appearance of the inner rooms?" asked the scholar. "Was it there like a cool grove, or like a holy temple? Were the chambers like a starry sky seen from the top of a high mountain?"

"It was all that you describe," said the shadow; "but I did not go quite in — I remained in the twilight of the ante-room — but I was in a very good position, — I could see and hear all that was going on in the court of poetry."

"But what did you see? Did the gods of ancient times pass through the rooms? Did old heroes fight their battles over again? Were there lovely children at play, who related their dreams?"

"I tell you I have been there, and therefore you may be sure that I saw everything that was to be seen. If you had gone there, you would not have remained a human being, whereas I became one; and at the same moment I became aware of my inner being, my inborn affinity to the nature of poetry. It is true I did not think much about it while I was with you, but you will remember that I was always much larger at sunrise and sunset, and in the moonlight even more visible than yourself, but I did not then understand my inner existence. In the ante-room it was revealed to me. I became a man; I came out in full maturity. But you had left the warm countries. As a man, I felt ashamed to go about without boots or clothes, and that exterior finish by which man is known. So I went my own way; I can tell you, for you will not put it in a book. I hid myself under the cloak of a cake woman, but she little thought who she concealed. It was not till evening that I ventured out. I ran about the streets in the moonlight. I drew myself up to my full height upon the walls, which tickled my back very pleasantly. I ran here and there, looked through the highest windows into the rooms, and over the roofs. I looked in, and saw what nobody else could see, or indeed ought to see; in fact, it is a bad world, and I would not care to be a man, but that men are of some importance. I saw the most miserable things going on between husbands and wives, parents and children, — sweet, incomparable children. I have seen what no human being has the power of knowing, although they would all be very glad to know — the evil conduct of their neighbors. Had I written a newspaper, how eagerly it would have been read! Instead of which, I wrote directly to the persons themselves, and great alarm arose in all the town I visited. They had so much fear of me, and yet how dearly they loved me. The professor made me a professor. The tailor gave me new clothes; I am well provided for in that way. The overseer of the mint struck coins for me. The women declared that I was handsome, and so I became the man you now see me. And now I must say adieu. Here is my card. I live on the sunny side of the street, and always stay at home in rainy weather." And the shadow departed.

"This is all very remarkable," said the learned man.

Years passed, days and years went by, and the shadow came again. "How are you going on now?" he asked.

"Ah!" said the learned man; "I am writing about the true, the beautiful, and the good; but no one cares to hear anything about it. I am quite in despair, for I take it to heart very much."

"That is what I never do," said the shadow; "I am growing quite fat and stout, which every one ought to be. You do not understand the world; you will make yourself ill about it; you ought to travel; I am going on a journey in the summer, will you go with me? I should like a travelling companion; will you travel with me as my shadow? It would give me great pleasure, and I will pay all expenses."

"Are you going to travel far?" asked the learned man.

"That is a matter of opinion," replied the shadow. "At all events, a journey will do you good, and if you will be my shadow, then all your journey shall be paid."

"It appears to me very absurd," said the learned man.

"But it is the way of the world," replied the shadow, "and always will be." Then he went away.

Everything went wrong with the learned man. Sorrow and trouble pursued him, and what he said about the good, the beautiful, and the true, was of as much value to most people as a nutmeg would be to a cow. At length he fell ill. "You really look like a shadow," people said to him, and then a cold shudder would pass over him, for he had his own thoughts on the subject.

"You really ought to go to some watering-place," said the shadow on his next visit. "There is no other chance for you. I will take you with me, for the sake of old acquaintance. I will pay the expenses of your journey, and you shall write a description of it to amuse us by the way. I should like to go to a watering-place; my beard does not grow as it ought, which is from weakness, and I must have a beard. Now do be sensible and accept my proposal; we shall travel as intimate friends."

And at last they started together. The shadow was master now, and the master became the shadow. They drove together, and rode and walked in company with each other, side by side, or one in front and the other behind, according to the position of the sun. The shadow always knew when to take the place of honor, but the learned man took no notice of it, for he had a good heart, and was exceedingly mild and friendly.

One day the master said to the shadow, "We have grown up together from our childhood, and now that we have become travelling companions, shall we not drink to our good fellowship, and say *thee* and *thou* to each other?"

"What you say is very straightforward and kindly meant," said the shadow, who was now really master. "I will be equally kind and straightforward. You are a learned man, and know how wonderful human nature is. There are some men who cannot endure the smell of brown paper; it makes them ill. Others will feel a shuddering sensation to their very marrow, if a nail is scratched on a pane of glass. I myself have a similar kind of feeling when I hear any one say *thou* to me. I feel crushed by it, as I used to feel in my former position with you. You will perceive that this is a matter of feeling, not pride. I cannot allow you to say *thou* to me; I will gladly say it to you, and therefore your wish will be half fulfilled." Then the shadow addressed his former master as *thou*.

"It is going rather too far," said the latter, "that I am to say *you* when I speak to him, and he is to say *thou* to me." However, he was obliged to submit.

They arrived at length at the baths, where there were many strangers, and among them a beautiful princess, whose real disease consisted in being too sharp-sighted, which made every one very uneasy. She saw at once that the new comer was very different to every one else. "They say he is here to make his beard grow," she thought; "but I know the real cause, he is unable to cast a shadow." Then she became very curious on the matter, and one day, while on the promenade, she entered into conversation with the strange gentleman. Being a princess, she was not obliged to stand upon much ceremony, so she said to him without hesitation, "Your illness consists in not being able to cast a shadow."

"Your royal highness must be on the high road to recovery from your illness," said he. "I know your complaint arose from being too sharp-sighted, and in this case it has entirely failed. I happen to have a most unusual shadow. Have you not seen a person who is always at my side? Persons often give their servants finer cloth for their liveries than for their own clothes, and so I have dressed out my shadow like a man; nay, you may observe that I have even given him a shadow of his own; it is rather expensive, but I like to have things about me that are peculiar."

"How is this?" thought the princess; "am I really cured? This must be the best watering-place in existence. Water in our times has certainly wonderful power. But I will not leave this place yet, just as it begins to be amusing. This foreign prince — for he must be a prince — pleases me above all things. I only hope his beard won't grow, or he will leave at once."

In the evening, the princess and the shadow danced together in the large assembly rooms. She was light, but he was lighter still; she had never seen such a dancer before. She told him from what country she had come, and found he knew it and had been there, but not while she was at home. He had looked into the windows of her father's palace, both the upper and the lower windows; he had seen many things, and could therefore answer the princess, and make allusions which quite astonished her. She thought he must be the cleverest man in all the world, and felt the greatest respect for his knowledge. When she danced with him again she fell in love with him, which the shadow quickly discovered, for she had with her eyes looked him through and through. They danced once more, and she was nearly telling him, but she had some discretion; she thought of her country, her kingdom, and the number of people over whom she would one day have to rule. "He is a clever man," she thought to herself, "which is a good thing, and he dances admirably, which is also good. But has he well-grounded knowledge? that is an important question, and I must try him." Then she asked him a most difficult question, she herself could not have answered it, and the shadow made a most unaccountable grimace.

"You cannot answer that," said the princess.

"I learnt something about it in my childhood," he replied; "and believe that even my very shadow, standing over there by the door, could answer it."

"Your shadow," said the princess; "indeed that would be very remarkable."

"I do not say so positively," observed the shadow; "but I am inclined to believe that he can do so. He has followed me for so many years, and has heard so much from me, that I think it is very likely. But your royal highness must allow me to observe, that he is very proud of being considered a man, and to put him in a good humor, so that he may answer correctly, he must be treated as a man."

"I shall be very pleased to do so," said the princess. So she walked up to the learned man, who stood in the doorway, and spoke to him of the sun, and the moon, of the green forests, and of people near home and far off; and the learned man conversed with her pleasantly and sensibly.

"What a wonderful man he must be, to have such a clever shadow!" thought she. "If I were to choose him it would be a real blessing to my country and my subjects, and I will do it." So the princess and the shadow were soon engaged to each other, but no one was to be told a word about it, till she returned to her kingdom.

"No one *shall* know," said the shadow; "not even my own shadow;" and he had very particular reasons for saying so.

After a time, the princess returned to the land over which she reigned, and the shadow accompanied her.

"Listen my friend," said the shadow to the learned man; "now that I am as fortunate and as powerful as any man can be, I will do something unusually good for you. You shall live in my palace, drive with me in the royal carriage, and have a hundred thousand dollars a year; but you must allow every one to call you a shadow, and never venture to say that you have been a man. And once a year, when I sit in my balcony in the sunshine, you must lie at my feet as becomes a shadow to do; for I must tell you I am going to marry the princess, and our wedding will take place this evening."

"Now, really, this is too ridiculous," said the learned man. "I cannot, and will not, submit to such folly. It would be cheating the whole country, and the princess also. I will disclose everything, and say that I am the man, and that you are only a shadow dressed up in men's clothes."

"No one would believe you," said the shadow; "be reasonable, now, or I will call the guards."

"I will go straight to the princess," said the learned man.

"But I shall be there first," replied the shadow, "and you will be sent to prison." And so it turned out, for the guards readily obeyed him, as they knew he was going to marry the king's daughter.

"You tremble," said the princess, when the shadow appeared before her. "Has anything happened? You must not be ill to-day, for this evening our wedding will take place."

"I have gone through the most terrible affair that could possibly happen," said the shadow; "only imagine, my shadow has gone mad; I suppose such a poor, shallow brain, could not bear much; he fancies that he has become a real man, and that I am his shadow."

"How very terrible," cried the princess; "is he locked up?"

"Oh yes, certainly; for I fear he will never recover."

"Poor shadow!" said the princess; "it is very unfortunate for him; it would really be a good deed to free him from his frail existence; and, indeed, when I think how often people take the part of the lower class against the higher, in these days, it would be policy to put him out of the way quietly."

"It is certainly rather hard upon him, for he was a faithful servant," said the shadow; and he pretended to sigh.

"Yours is a noble character," said the princess, and bowed herself before him.

In the evening the whole town was illuminated, and cannons fired "boom," and the soldiers presented arms. It was indeed a grand wedding. The princess and the shadow stepped out on the balcony to show themselves, and to receive one cheer more. But the learned man heard nothing of all these festivities, for he had already been executed.

THE MAIL-COACH PASSENGERS

IT was bitterly cold, the sky glittered with stars, and not a breeze stirred. "Bump"—an old pot was thrown at a neighbor's door; and "bang, bang," went the guns; for they were greeting the New Year. It was New Year's Eve, and the church clock was striking twelve. "Tan-ta-ra-ra, tan-ta-ra-ra," sounded the horn, and the mail-coach came lumbering up. The clumsy vehicle stopped at the gate of the town; all the places had been taken, for there were twelve passengers in the coach.

"Hurrah! hurrah!" cried the people in the town; for in every house the New Year was being welcomed; and as the clock struck, they stood up, the full glasses in their hands, to drink success to the new comer. "A happy New Year," was the cry; "a pretty wife, plenty of money, and no sorrow or care."

The wish passed round, and the glasses clashed together till they rang again; while before the town-gate the mail coach stopped with the twelve strange passengers. And who were these strangers? Each of them had his passport and his luggage with him; they even brought presents for me, and for you, and for all the people in the town. "Who were they? what did they want? and what did they bring with them?"

"Good-morning," they cried to the sentry at the town-gate.

"Good-morning," replied the sentry; for the clock had struck twelve. "Your name and profession?" asked the sentry of the one who alighted first from the carriage.

"See for yourself in the passport," he replied. "I am myself;" and a famous fellow he looked, arrayed in bear-skin and fur boots. "I am the man on whom many persons fix their hopes. Come to me to-morrow, and I'll give you a New Year's present. I throw shillings and pence among the people; I give balls, no less than thirty-one; indeed, that is the highest number I can spare for balls. My ships are often frozen in, but in my offices it is warm and comfortable. My name is JANUARY. I'm a merchant, and I generally bring my accounts with me."

Then the second alighted. He seemed a merry fellow. He was a director of a theatre, a manager of masked balls, and a leader of all the amusements we can imagine. His luggage consisted of a great cask.

"We'll dance the bung out of the cask at carnival time," said he; "I'll prepare a merry tune for you and for myself too. Unfortunately I have not long to live—the shortest time, in fact, of my whole family—only twenty-eight days. Sometimes they pop me in a day extra; but I trouble myself very little about that. Hurrah!"

"You must not shout so," said the sentry.

"Certainly I *may* shout," retorted the man; "I'm Prince Carnival, travelling under the name of FEBRUARY."

The third now got out. He looked a personification of fasting; but he carried his nose very high, for he was related to the "forty (k)nights," and was a weather prophet. But that is not a very lucrative office, and therefore he praised fasting. In his button-hole he carried a little bunch of violets, but they were very small.

"MARCH, March," the fourth called after him, slapping him on the shoulder, "don't you smell something? Make haste into the guard room; they're drinking punch there; that's your favorite drink. I can smell it out here already. Forward, Master *March.*" But it was not true; the speaker only wanted to remind him of his name, and to make an APRIL *fool* of him; for with that fun the fourth generally began his career. He looked very jovial, did little work, and had the more holidays. "If the world were only a little more settled," said he: "but sometimes I'm obliged to be in a good humor, and sometimes a bad one, according to circumstances; now rain, now sunshine. I'm kind of a house agent,* also a manager of funerals. I can laugh or cry, according to circumstances. I have my summer wardrobe in this box here, but it would be very foolish to put it on now. Here I am. On Sundays I go out walking in shoes and white silk stockings, and a muff."

After him, a lady stepped out of the coach. She called herself Miss MAY. She wore a summer dress and overshoes; her dress was a light green, and she

---

*It is the custom in Denmark to change houses in April, generally on one particular day of the month, which is therefore called "moving or flitting day." April is here, therefore, called a "house agent," as well as the manager of funerals, as the changeable weather in this month is considered very unhealthy.

THE MAIL-COACH PASSENGERS

wore anemones in her hair. She was so scented with wild-thyme, that it made the sentry sneeze.

"Your health, and God bless you," was her salutation to him.

How pretty she was! and such a singer! not a theatre singer, nor a ballad singer; no, but a singer of the woods; for she wandered through the gay green forest, and had a concert there for her own amusement.

"Now comes the young lady," said those in the carriage; and out stepped a young dame, delicate, proud, and pretty. It was Mistress JUNE, in whose service people become lazy and fond of sleeping for hours. She gives a feast on the longest day of the year, that there may be time for her guests to partake of the numerous dishes at her table. Indeed, she keeps her own carriage; but still she travelled by the mail, with the rest, because she wished to show that she was not high-minded. But she was not without a protector; her younger brother, JULY, was with her. He was a plump young fellow, clad in summer garments and wearing a straw hat. He had but very little luggage with him, because it was so cumbersome in the great heat; he had, however, swimming-trousers with him, which are nothing to carry. Then came the mother herself, in crinoline, Madame AUGUST, a wholesale dealer in fruit, proprietress of a large number of fish ponds and a land cultivator. She was fat and heated, yet she could use her hands well, and would herself carry out beer to the laborers in the field. "In the sweat of the face shalt thou eat bread," said she; "it is written in the Bible." After work, came the recreations, dancing and playing in the greenwood, and the "harvest homes." She was a thorough housewife.

After her a man came out of the coach, who is a painter; he is the great master of colors, and is named SEPTEMBER. The forest, on his arrival, had to change its colors when he wished it; and how beautiful are the colors he chooses! The woods glow with hues of red and gold and brown. This great master painter could whistle like a blackbird. He was quick in his work, and soon entwined the tendrils of the hop plant around his beer jug. This was an ornament to the jug, and he has a great love for ornament. There he stood with his color pot in his hand, and that was the whole of his luggage. A landowner followed, who in the month for sowing seed attended to the ploughing and was fond of field sports. Squire OCTOBER brought his dog and his gun with him, and had nuts in his game bag. "Crack, crack." He had a great deal of luggage, even an English plough. He spoke of farming, but what he said could scarcely be heard for the coughing and gasping of his neighbor. It was NOVEMBER, who coughed violently as he got out. He had a cold, which caused him to use his pocket-handkerchief continually; and yet he said he was obliged to accompany servant girls to their new places, and initiate them into their winter service. He said he thought his cold would never leave him when he went out woodcutting, for he was a master sawyer, and had to supply wood to the whole parish. He spent his evenings preparing wooden soles for skates, for he knew, he said, that in a few weeks these shoes would be wanted for the amusement of skating. At length the last passenger made her appearance, — old Mother DECEMBER, with her fire-stool. The dame was very old, but her eyes glistened like two stars. She carried on her arm a flower-pot, in which a little fir-tree was growing. "This tree I shall guard and cherish," she said, "that it may grow large by Christmas Eve, and reach from the ground to the ceiling, to be covered and adorned with flaming candles, golden apples, and little figures. The fire-stool will be as warm as a stove, and I shall then bring a story book out of my pocket, and read aloud till all the children in the room are quite quiet. Then the little figures on the tree will become lively, and the little waxen angel at the top spread out his wings of gold-leaf, and fly down from his green perch. He will kiss every one in the room, great and small; yes, even the poor children who stand in the passage, or out in the street singing a carol about the 'Star of Bethlehem.' "

"Well, now the coach may drive away," said the sentry; "we have the whole twelve. Let the horses be put up."

"First, let all the twelve come to me," said the captain on duty, "one after another. The passports I will keep here. Each of them is available for one month; when that has passed, I shall write the behavior of each on his passport. Mr. JANUARY, have the goodness to come here." And Mr. January stepped forward.

When a year has passed, I think I shall be able to tell you what the twelve passengers have brought to you, to me, and to all of us. Now I do not know, and probably even they don't know themselves, for we live in strange times.

GRANDMOTHER

GRANDMOTHER is very old, her face is wrinkled, and her hair is quite white; but her eyes are like two stars, and they have a mild, gentle expression in them when they look at you, which does you good. She wears a dress of heavy, rich silk, with large flowers worked on it; and it rustles when she moves. And then she can tell the most wonderful stories. Grandmother knows a great deal, for she was alive before father and mother — that's quite certain. She has a hymn-book with large silver clasps, in which she often reads; and in the book, between the leaves, lies a rose, quite flat and dry; it is not so pretty as the roses which are standing in the glass, and yet she smiles at it most pleasantly, and tears even come into her eyes. "I wonder why grandmother looks at the withered flower in the old book that way? Do you know?" Why, when grandmother's tears fall upon the rose, and she is looking at it, the rose revives, and fills the room with its fragrance; the walls vanish as in a mist, and all around her is the glorious green wood, where in summer the sunlight streams through thick foliage; and grandmother, why she is young again, a charming maiden, fresh as a rose, with round, rosy cheeks, fair, bright ringlets, and a figure pretty and graceful; but the eyes, those mild, saintly eyes, are the same, — they have been left to grandmother. At her side sits a young man, tall and strong; he gives her a rose and she smiles. Grandmother cannot smile like that now. Yes, she is smiling at the memory of that day, and many thoughts and recollections of the past; but the handsome young man is gone, and the rose has withered in the old book, and grandmother is sitting there, again an old woman, looking down upon the withered rose in the book.

Grandmother is dead now. She had been sitting in her arm-chair, telling us a long, beautiful tale; and when it was finished, she said she was tired, and leaned her head back to sleep awhile. We could hear her gentle breathing as she slept; gradually it became quieter and calmer, and on her countenance beamed happiness and peace. It was as if lighted up with a ray of sunshine. She smiled once more, and then people said she was dead. She was laid in a black coffin, looking mild and beautiful in the white folds of the shrouded linen, though her eyes were closed; but every wrinkle had vanished, her hair looked white and silvery, and around her mouth lingered a sweet smile. We did not feel at all afraid to look at the corpse of her who had been such a dear, good grandmother. The hymn-book, in which the rose still lay, was placed under her head, for so she had wished it; and then they buried grandmother.

On the grave, close by the churchyard wall, they planted a rose-tree; it was soon full of roses, and the nightingale sat among the flowers, and sang over the grave. From the organ in the church sounded the music and the words of the beautiful psalms, which were written in the old book under the head of the dead one.

The moon shone down upon the grave, but the dead was not there; every child could go safely, even at night, and pluck a rose from the tree by the churchyard wall. The dead know more than we do who are living. They know what a terror would come upon us if such a strange thing were to happen, as the appearance of a dead person among us. They are better off than we are; the dead return no more. The earth has been heaped on the coffin, and it is earth only that lies within it. The leaves of the hymn-book are dust; and the rose, with all its recollections, has crumbled to dust also. But over the grave fresh roses bloom, the nightingale sings, and the organ sounds; and there still lives a remembrance of old grandmother, with the loving, gentle eyes that always looked young. *Eyes can never die.* Ours will once again behold dear grandmother, young and beautiful as when, for the first time, she kissed the fresh, red rose, that is now dust in the grave.

THE LAST PEARL

WE are in a rich, happy house, where the master, the servants, the friends of the family are full of joy and felicity. For on this day a son and heir has been born, and mother and child are doing well. The lamp in the bedchamber had been partly shaded, and the windows were covered with heavy curtains of some costly silken material. The carpet was thick and soft, like a covering of moss. Everything invited to slumber, everything had a charming look of repose; and so the nurse had discovered, for she slept; and well she might sleep, while everything around her told of happiness and blessing. The guardian angel of the house leaned against the head of the bed; while over the child was spread, as it were, a net of shining stars, and each star was a pearl of happiness. All the good stars of life had brought their gifts to the newly born; here sparkled health, wealth, fortune, and love; in short, there seemed to be everything for which man could wish on earth.

"Everything has been bestowed here," said the guardian angel.

"No, not everything," said a voice near him — the voice of the good angel of the child; "one fairy has not yet brought her gift, but she will, even if years should elapse, she will bring her gift; it is the last pearl that is wanting."

"Wanting!" cried the guardian angel; "nothing must be wanting here; and if it is so, let us fetch it; let us seek the powerful fairy; let us go to her."

"She will come, she will come some day unsought!"

"Her pearl must not be missing; it must be there, that the crown, when worn, may be complete. Where is she to be found? Where does she dwell?" said the guardian angel. "Tell me, and I will procure the pearl."

"Will you do that?" replied the good angel of the child. "Then I will lead you to her directly, wherever she may be. She has no abiding place; she rules in the palace of the emperor, sometimes she enters the peasant's humble cot; she passes no one without leaving a trace of her presence. She brings her gift with her, whether it is a world or a bauble. To this child she must come. You think that to wait for this time would be long and useless. Well, then, let us go for this pearl — the only one lacking amidst all this wealth."

Then hand-in-hand they floated away to the spot where the fairy was now lingering. It was in a large house with dark windows and empty rooms, in which a peculiar stillness reigned. A whole row of windows stood open, so that the rude wind could enter at its pleasure, and the long white curtains waved to and fro in the current of air. In the centre of one of the rooms stood an open coffin, in which lay the body of a woman, still in the bloom of youth and very beautiful. Fresh roses were scattered over her. The delicate folded hands and the noble face glorified in death by the solemn, earnest look, which spoke of an entrance into a better world, were alone visible. Around the coffin stood the husband and children, a whole troop, the youngest in the father's arms. They were come to take a last farewell look of their mother. The husband kissed her hand, which now lay like a withered leaf, but which a short time before had been diligently employed in deeds of love for them all. Tears of sorrow rolled down their cheeks, and fell in heavy drops on the floor, but not a word was spoken. The silence which reigned here expressed a world of grief. With silent steps, still sobbing, they left the room. A burning light remained in the room, and a long, red wick rose far above the flame, which fluttered in the draught of air. Strange men came in and placed the lid of the coffin over the dead, and drove the nails firmly in; while the blows of the hammer resounded through the house, and echoed in the hearts that were bleeding.

"Whither art thou leading me?" asked the guardian angel. "Here dwells no fairy whose pearl could be counted amongst the best gifts of life."

"Yes, she is here; here in this sacred hour," replied the angel, pointing to a corner of the room; and there, — where in her life-time, the mother had taken her seat amidst flowers and pictures: in that spot, where she, like the blessed fairy of the house, had welcomed husband, children, and friends, and, like a sunbeam, had spread joy and cheerfulness around her, the centre and heart of them all, — there, in that very spot, sat a strange woman, clothed in long, flowing garments, and occupying the place of the dead wife and mother. It was the fairy, and her name was "Sorrow." A hot tear rolled into her lap, and formed itself into a pearl, glowing with all the colors of the rainbow. The angel seized it: the, pearl glittered like a star with seven-fold radiance. The pearl of Sorrow, the last, which must not be wanting, increases the lustre, and explains the meaning of all the other pearls.

"Do you see the shimmer of the rainbow, which unites earth to heaven?" So has there been a bridge built between this world and the next. Through the night of the grave we gaze upwards beyond the stars to the end of all things. Then we glance at the pearl of Sorrow, in which are concealed the wings which shall carry us away to eternal happiness.

SOMETHING

"I MEAN to be somebody, and do something useful in the world," said the eldest of five brothers. "I don't care how humble my position is, so that I can only do some good, which will be something. I intend to be a brickmaker; bricks are always wanted, and I shall be really doing something."

"Your 'something' is not enough for me," said the second brother; "what you talk of doing is nothing at all, it is journeyman's work, or might even be done by a machine. No! I should prefer to be a builder at once, there is something real in that. A man gains a position, he becomes a citizen, has his own sign, his own house of call for his workmen: so I shall be a builder. If all goes well, in time I shall become a master, and have my own journeymen, and my wife will be treated as a master's wife. This is what *I* call something."

"I call it all nothing," said the third; "not in reality any position. There are many in a town far above a master builder in position. You may be an upright man, but even as a master you will only be ranked among common men. I know better what to do than that. I will be an architect, which will place me among those who possess riches and intellect, and who speculate in art. I shall certainly have to rise by my own endeavors from a bricklayer's laborer, or as a carpenter's apprentice—a lad wearing a paper cap, although I now wear a silk hat. I shall have to fetch beer and spirits for the journeymen, and they will call me 'thou,' which will be an insult. I shall endure it, however, for I shall look upon it all as a mere representation, a masquerade, a mummery, which to-morrow, that is, when I myself as a journeyman, shall have served my time, will vanish, and I shall go my way, and all that has passed will be nothing to me. Then I shall enter the academy, and get instructed in drawing, and be called an architect. I may even attain to rank, and have something placed before or after my name, and I shall build as others have done before me. By this there will be always 'something' to make me remembered, and is not that worth living for?"

"Not in my opinion," said the fourth; "I will never follow the lead of others, and only imitate what they have done. I will be a genius, and become greater than all of you together. I will create a new style of building, and introduce a plan for erecting houses suitable to the climate, with material easily obtained in the country, and thus suit national feeling and the developments of the age, besides building a storey for my own genius."

"But supposing the climate and the material are not good for much," said the fifth brother, "that would be very unfortunate for you, and have an influence over your experiments. Nationality may assert itself until it becomes affectation, and the developments of a century may run wild, as youth often does. I see clearly that none of you will ever really be anything worth notice, however you may now fancy it. But do as you like, I shall not imitate you. I mean to keep clear of all these things, and criticize what you do. In every action something imperfect may be discovered, something not right, which I shall make it my business to find out and expose; that will be something, I fancy." And he kept his word, and became a critic.

People said of this fifth brother, "There is something very precise about him; he has a good head-piece, but he does nothing." And on that very account they thought he must be something.

Now, you see, this is a little history which will never end; as long as the world exists, there will always be men like these five brothers. And what became of them? Were they each nothing or something? You shall hear; it is quite a history.

The eldest brother, he who fabricated bricks, soon discovered that each brick, when finished, brought him in a small coin, if only a copper one; and many copper pieces, if placed one upon another, can be changed into a shining shilling; and at whatever door a person knocks, who has a number of these in his hands, whether it be the baker's, the butcher's, or the tailor's, the door flies open, and he can get all he wants. So you see the value of bricks. Some of the bricks, however, crumbled to pieces, or were broken, but the elder brother found a use for even these.

On the high bank of earth, which formed a dyke on the sea-coast, a poor woman named Margaret wished to build herself a house, so all the imperfect bricks were given to her, and a few whole ones with them; for the eldest brother was a kind-hearted man, although he never achieved anything higher than making bricks. The poor woman built herself a little house—it was small and narrow, and the window was quite crooked, the door too low, and the straw roof might have been better thatched. But still it was a shelter, and from within you could look far over the sea, which dashed wildly against the sea-wall on which the little house was built. The salt waves sprinkled their white foam over it, but it stood firm, and remained long after he who had given the bricks to build it was dead and buried.

The second brother of course knew better how to build than poor Margaret, for he served an apprenticeship to learn it. When his time was up, he packed up his knapsack, and went on his travels, singing the journeyman's song, —

> "While young, I can wander without a care,
> And build new houses everywhere;
> Fair and bright are my dreams of home,
> Always thought of wherever I roam.
>
> Hurrah for a workman's life of glee!
> There's a loved one at home who thinks of me;
> Home and friends I can ne'er forget,
> And I mean to be a master yet."

And that is what he did. On his return home, he became a master builder, —built one house after another in the town, till they formed quite a street, which, when finished, became really an ornament to the town. These houses built a house for him in return, which was to be his own. But how can houses build a house? If the houses were asked, they could not answer; but the people would understand, and say, "Certainly the street built his house for him." It was not very large, and the floor was of lime; but when he danced with his bride on the lime-covered floor, it was to him white and shining, and from every stone in the wall flowers seemed to spring forth and decorate the room as with the richest tapestry. It was really a pretty house, and in it were a happy pair. The flag of the corporation fluttered before it, and the journeymen and apprentices shouted "Hurrah." He had gained his position, he had made himself something, and at last he died, which was "something" too.

Now we come to the architect, the third brother, who had been first a carpenter's apprentice, had worn a cap, and served as an errand boy, but afterwards went to the academy, and risen to be an architect, a high and noble gentleman. Ah yes, the houses of the new street, which the brother who was a master builder erected, may have built his house for him, but the street received its name from the architect, and the handsomest house in the street became his property. That was something, and he was "something," for he had a list of titles before and after his name. His children were called "well-born," and when he died, his widow was treated as a lady of position, and that was "something." His name remained always written at the corner of the street, and lived in every one's mouth as its name. Yes, this also was "something."

And what about the genius of the family—the fourth brother—who wanted to invent something new and original? He tried to build a lofty storey himself, but it fell to pieces, and he fell with it and broke his neck. However, he had a splendid funeral, with the city flags and music in the procession; flowers were strewn on the pavement, and three orations were spoken over his grave, each one longer than the other. He would have liked this very much during his life, as well as the poems about him in the papers, for he liked nothing so well as to be talked of. A monument was also erected over his grave. It was only another storey over him, but that was "something," Now he was dead, like the three other brothers.

The youngest—the critic—outlived them all, which was quite right for him. It gave him the opportunity of having the last word, which to him was of great importance. People always said he had a good head-piece. At last his hour came, and he died, and arrived at the gates of heaven. Souls always enter these gates in pairs; so he found himself standing and waiting for admission with another; and who should it be but old dame Margaret, from the house on the dyke! "It is evidently for the sake of contrast that I and this wretched soul should arrive here exactly at the same time," said the critic. "Pray who are you, my good woman?" said he; "do you want to get in here too?"

And the old woman curtsied as well as she could; she thought it must be St. Peter himself who spoke to her. "I am a poor old woman," she said, "without my family. I am old Margaret, that lived in the house on the dyke."

"Well, and what have you done—what great deed have you performed down below?"

"I have done nothing at all in the world that could give me a claim to have these doors open for me," she said. "It would be only through mercy that I can be allowed to slip in through the gate."

"In what manner did you leave the world?" he asked, just for the sake of saying something; for it made him feel very weary to stand there and wait.

"How I left the world?" she replied; "why, I can scarcely tell you. During the last years of my life I was sick and miserable, and I was unable to bear creeping out of bed suddenly into the frost and cold. Last winter was a hard winter, but I have got over it all now. There were a few mild days, as your honor, no doubt, knows. The ice lay thickly on the lake, as far one could see. The people came from the town, and walked upon it, and they say there were dancing and skating upon it, I believe, and a great feasting. The sound of beautiful music came into my poor little room where I lay. Towards evening, when the moon rose beautifully, though not yet in her full splendor, I glanced from my bed over the wide sea; and there, just where the sea and sky met, rose a curious white cloud. I lay looking at the cloud till I observed a little black spot in the middle of it, which gradually grew larger and larger, and then I knew what it meant—I am old and experienced; and although this token is not often seen, I knew it, and a shuddering seized me. Twice in my life had I seen this same thing, and I knew that there would be an awful storm, with a spring tide, which would overwhelm the poor people who were now out on the ice, drinking, dancing, and making merry. Young and old, the whole city, were there; who was to warn them, if no one noticed the sign, or knew what it meant as I did? I was so alarmed, that I felt more strength and life than I had done for some time. I got out of bed, and reached the window; I could not crawl any farther from weakness and exhaustion; but I managed to open the window. I saw the people outside running and jumping about on the ice; I saw the beautiful flags waving in the wind; I heard the boys shouting, 'Hurrah!' and the lads and lasses singing, and everything full of merriment and joy. But there was the white cloud with the black spot hanging over them. I cried out as loudly as I could, but no one heard me; I was too far off from the people. Soon would the storm burst, the ice break, and all who were on it be irretrievably lost. They could not hear me, and to go to them was quite out of my power. Oh, if I could only get them safe on land! Then came the thought, as if from heaven, that I would rather set fire to my bed, and let the house be burnt down, than that so many people should perish miserably. I got a light, and in a few moments the red flames leaped up as a beacon to them. I escaped fortunately as far as the threshold of the door; but there I fell down and remained: I could go no farther. The flames rushed out towards me, flickered on the window, and rose high above the roof. The people on the ice became aware of the fire, and ran as fast as possible to help a poor sick woman, who, as they thought, was being burnt to death. There was not one who did not run. I heard them coming, and I also at the same time was conscious of a rush of air and a sound like the roar of heavy artillery. The spring flood was lifting the ice covering, which brake into a thousand pieces. But the people had reached the sea-wall, where the sparks were flying round. I had saved them all; but I suppose I could not survive the cold and fright; so I came up here to the gates of paradise. I am told they are open to poor creatures such as I am, and I have now no house left on earth; but I do not think that will give me a claim to be admitted here."

Then the gates were opened, and an angel led the old woman in. She had dropped one little straw out of her straw bed, when she set it on fire to save the lives of so many. It had been changed into the purest gold—into gold that constantly grew and expanded into flowers and fruit of immortal beauty.

"See," said the angel, pointing to the wonderful straw, "this is what the poor woman has brought. What dost thou bring? I know thou hast accomplished nothing, not even made a single brick. Even if thou couldst return, and at least produce so much, very likely, when made, the brick would be useless, unless done with a good will, which is always something. But thou canst not return to earth, and I can do nothing for thee."

Then the poor soul, the old mother who had lived in the house on the dyke, pleaded for him. She said, "His brother made all the stone and bricks, and sent them to me to build my poor little dwelling, which was a great deal to do for a poor woman like me. Could not all these bricks and pieces be as a wall of stone to prevail for him? It is an act of mercy; he is wanting it now; and here is the very fountain of mercy."

"Then," said the angel, "thy brother, he who has been looked upon as the meanest of you all, he whose honest deeds to thee appeared so humble, — it is he who has sent you this heavenly gift. Thou shalt not be turned away. Thou shalt have permission to stand without the gate and reflect, and repent of thy life on earth; but thou shalt not be admitted here until thou hast performed one good deed of repentance, which will indeed for thee be *something*."

"I could have expressed that better," thought the critic; but he did not say it aloud, which for him was SOMETHING, after all.

A CHEERFUL TEMPER

FROM my father I received the best inheritance, namely a "good temper." "And who was my father?" That has nothing to do with the good temper; but I will say he was lively, good-looking round, and fat; he was both in appearance and character a complete contradiction to his profession. "And pray what was his profession and his standing in respectable society?" Well, perhaps, if in the beginning of a book these were written and printed, many, when they read it, would lay the book down and say, "It seems to me a very miserable title, I don't like things of this sort." And yet my father was not a skin-dresser nor an executioner; on the contrary, his employment placed him at the head of the grandest people of the town, and it was his place by right. He had to precede the bishop, and even the princes of the blood; he always went first, — he was a hearse driver! There, now, the truth is out. And I will own, that when people saw my father perched up in front of the omnibus of death, dressed in his long, wide, black cloak, and his black-edged, three-cornered hat on his head, and then glanced at his round, jocund face, round as the sun, they could not think much of sorrow or the grave. That face said, "It is nothing, it will all end better than people think." So I have inherited from him, not only my good temper, but a habit of going often to the churchyard, which is good, when done in a proper humor; and then also I take in the *Intelligencer,* just as he used to do.

I am not very young, I have neither wife nor children, nor a library, but, as I said, I read the *Intelligencer,* which is enough for me; it is to me a delightful paper, and so it was to my father. It is of great use, for it contains all that a man requires to know; the names of the preachers at the church, and the new books which are published; where houses, servants, clothes, and provisions may be obtained. And then what a number of subscriptions to charities, and what innocent verses! Persons seeking interviews and engagements, all so plainly and naturally stated. Certainly, a man who takes in the *Intelligencer* may live merrily and be buried contentedly, and by the end of his life will have such a capital stock of paper that he can lie on a soft bed of it, unless he prefers wood shavings for his resting-place. The newspaper and the churchyard were always exciting objects to me. My walks to the latter were like bathing-places to my good humor. Every one can read the newspaper for himself; but come with me to the churchyard while the sun shines and the trees are green, and let us wander among the graves. Each of them is like a closed book, with the back uppermost, on which we can read the title of what the book contains, but nothing more. I had a great deal of information from my father, and I have noticed a great deal myself. I keep it in my diary, in which I write for my own use and pleasure a history of all who lie here, and a few more beside.

Now we are in the churchyard. Here, behind the white iron railings, once a rose-tree grew; it is gone now, but a little bit of evergreen, from a neighboring grave, stretches out its green tendrils, and makes some appearance; there rests a very unhappy man, and yet while he lived he might be said to occupy a very good position. He had enough to live upon, and something to spare; but owing to his refined tastes the least thing in the world annoyed him. If he went to a theatre of an evening, instead of enjoying himself he would be quite annoyed if the machinist had put too strong a light into one side of the moon, or if the representations of the sky hung *over* the scenes when they ought to have hung *behind* them; or if a palm-tree was introduced into a scene representing the Zoological Gardens of Berlin, or a cactus in a view of Tyrol, or a beech-tree in the north of Norway. As if these things were of any consequence! Why did he not leave them alone? Who would trouble themselves about such trifles? especially at a comedy, where every one is expected to be amused. Then sometimes the public applauded too much, or too little, to please him. "They are like wet wood," he would say, looking round to see what sort of people were present, "this evening; nothing fires them." Then he would vex and fret himself because they did not laugh at the right time, or because they laughed in the wrong places; and so he fretted and worried himself till at last the unhappy man fretted himself into the grave.

Here rests a happy man, that is to say, a man of high birth and position, which was very lucky for him, otherwise he would have been scarcely worth notice. It is beautiful to observe how wisely nature orders these things. He walked about in a coat embroidered all over, and in the drawing-rooms of society looked just like one of those rich pearl-embroidered bell-pulls, which are only made for show; and behind them always hangs a good thick cord for use. This man also had a stout, useful substitute behind him, who did duty for him, and performed all his dirty work. And there are still, even now, these serviceable cords behind other embroidered bell-ropes. It is all so wisely arranged, that a man may well be in a good humor.

Here rests, — ah, it makes one feel mournful to think of him! — but here rests a man who, during sixty-seven years, was never remembered to have said a good thing; he lived only in the hope of having a good idea. At last he felt convinced, in his own mind, that he really had one, and was so delighted that he positively died of joy at the thought of having at last caught an idea. Nobody got anything by it; indeed, no one even heard what the good thing was. Now I can imagine that this same idea may prevent him from resting quietly in his grave; for suppose that to produce a good effect, it is necessary to bring out his new idea at breakfast, and that he can only make his appearance on earth at midnight, as ghosts are believed generally to do; why then this good idea would not suit the hour, and the man would have to carry it down again with him into the grave — that must be a troubled grave.

The woman who lies here was so remarkably stingy, that during her life she would get up in the night and mew, that her neighbors might think she kept a cat. What a miser she was!

Here rests a young lady, of a good family, who would always make her voice heard in society, and when she sang "Mi manca la voce,"* it was the only true thing she ever said in her life.

Here lies a maiden of another description. She was engaged to be married, —but her story is one of every-day life; we will leave her to rest in the grave.

Here rests a widow, who, with music in her tongue, carried gall in her heart. She used to go round among the families near, and search out their faults, upon which she preyed with all the envy and malice of her nature. This is a family grave. The members of this family held so firmly together in their opinions, that they would believe in no other. If the newspapers, or even the whole world, said of a certain subject, "It is so-and-so;" and a little schoolboy declared he had learned quite differently, they would take his assertion as the only true one, because he belonged to the family. And it is well known that if the yard-cock belonging to this family happened to crow at midnight, they would declare it was morning, although the watchman and all the clocks in the town were proclaiming the hour of twelve at night.

The great poet Goethe concludes his Faust with the words, "may be continued;" so might our wanderings in the churchyard be continued. I come here often, and if any of my friends, or those who are not my friends, are too much for me, I go out and choose a plot of ground in which to bury him or her. Then I bury them, as it were; there they lie, dead and powerless, till they come back new and better characters. Their lives and their deeds, looked at after my own fashion, I write down in my diary, as every one ought to do. Then, if any of our friends act absurdly, no one need to be vexed about it. Let them bury the offenders out of sight, and keep their good temper. They can also read the *Intelligencer*, which is a paper written by the people, with their hands guided. When the time comes for the history of my life, to be bound by the grave, then they will write upon it as my epitaph—

"The man with a cheerful temper."

And this is my story.

THE STORY OF THE WIND

"Near the shores of the great Belt, which is one of the straits that connect the Cattegat with the Baltic, stands an old mansion with thick red walls. I know every stone of it," says the Wind. "I saw it when it was part of the castle of Marck Stig on the promontory. But the castle was obliged to be pulled down, and the stone was used again for the walls of a new mansion on another spot—the baronial residence of Borreby, which still stands near the coast. I knew them well, those noble lords and ladies, the successive generations that dwelt there; and now I'm going to tell you of Waldemar Daa and

*"I want a voice," or, "I have no voice."

his daughters. How proud was his bearing, for he was of royal blood, and could boast of more noble deeds than merely hunting the stag and emptying the wine-cup. His rule was despotic: 'It shall be,' he was accustomed to say. His wife, in garments embroidered with gold, stepped proudly over the polished marble floors. The tapestries were gorgeous, and the furniture of costly and artistic taste. She had brought gold and plate with her into the house. The cellars were full of wine. Black, fiery horses, neighed in the stables. There was a look of wealth about the house of Borreby at that time. They had three children, daughters, fair and delicate maidens — Ida, Joanna, and Anna Dorothea; I have never forgotten their names. They were a rich, noble family, born in affluence and nurtured in luxury.

"Whir-r-r, whir-r-r!" roared the Wind, and went on, "I did not see in this house, as in other great houses, the high-born lady sitting among her women, turning the spinning-wheel. She could sweep the sounding chords of the guitar, and sing to the music, not always Danish melodies, but the songs of a strange land. It was 'Live and let live,' here. Stranger guests came from far and near, music sounded, goblets clashed, and I," said the Wind, "was not able to drown the noise. Ostentation, pride, splendor, and display ruled, but not the fear of the Lord.

"It was on the evening of the first day of May," the Wind continued, "I came from the west, and had seen the ships overpowered with the waves, when all on board persisted or were cast shipwrecked on the coast of Jutland. I had hurried across the heath and over Jutland's wood-girt eastern coast, and over the island of Funen, and then I drove across the great belt, sighing and moaning. At length I lay down to rest on the shores of Zeeland, near to the great house of Borreby, where the splendid forest of oaks still flourished. The young men of the neighborhood were collecting branches and brushwood under the oak-trees. The largest and dryest they could find they carried into the village, and piled them up in a heap and set them on fire. Then the men and maidens danced, and sung in a circle round the blazing pile. I lay quite quiet," said the Wind, "but I silently touched a branch which had been brought by one of the handsomest of the young men, and the wood blazed up brightly, blazed brighter than all the rest. Then he was chosen as the chief, and received the name of the Shepherd; and might choose his lamb from among the maidens. There was greater mirth and rejoicing than I had ever heard in the halls of the rich baronial house. Then the noble lady drove by towards the baron's mansion with her three daughters, in a gilded carriage drawn by six horses. The daughters were young and beautiful — three charming blossoms — a rose, a lily, and a white hyacinth. The mother was a proud tulip, and never acknowledged the salutations of any of the men or maidens who paused in their sport to do her honor. The gracious lady seemed like a flower that was rather stiff in the stalk. Rose, lily, and hyacinth — yes, I saw them all three. Whose little lambs will they one day become? thought I; their shepherd will be a gallant knight, perhaps a prince. The carriage rolled on, and the peasants resumed their dancing. They drove about the summer through all the villages near. But one night, when I rose again, the high-born lady lay down to rise again no more; that thing came to her which comes to us all, in which there is nothing new. Waldemar Daa remained for a time silent and thoughtful. 'The loftiest tree may be bowed without being broken,' said a voice within him. His daughters wept; all the people in the mansion wiped their eyes, but Lady Daa had driven away, and I drove away too," said the Wind. "Whir-r-r, whir-r-r-!

"I returned again; I often returned and passed over the island of Funen and the shores of the Belt. Then I rested by Borreby, near the glorious wood, where the heron made his nest, the haunt of the wood-pigeons, the blue-birds, and the black stork. It was yet spring, some were sitting on their eggs, others had already hatched their young broods; but how they fluttered about and cried out when the axe sounded through the forest, blow upon blow! The trees of the forest were doomed. Waldemar Daa wanted to build a noble ship, a man-of-war, a three-decker, which the king would be sure to buy; and these, the trees of the wood, the landmark of the seamen, the refuge of the birds, must be felled. The hawk started up and flew away, for its nest was destroyed; the heron and all the birds of the forest became homeless, and flew about in fear and anger. I could well understand how they felt. Crows and ravens croaked, as if in scorn, while the trees were cracking and falling around them. Far in the interior of the wood, where a noisy swarm of laborers were working, stood Waldemar Daa and his three daughters, and all were laughing at the wild cries of the birds, excepting one, the youngest, Anna Dorothea, who felt grieved to the heart; and when they made preparations to fell a tree that was almost dead, and on whose naked branches the black stork had built her nest, she saw the poor little things stretching out their necks, and she begged for mercy for them, with the tears in her eyes. So the tree with the black stork's nest was left standing; the tree itself, however, was not worth much to speak of. Then there was a great deal of hewing and sawing, and at last the three-decker was built. The builder was a man of low origin, but possessing great pride; his eyes and forehead spoke of large intellect, and Waldemar Daa was fond of listening to him, and so was Waldemar's daughter Ida, the eldest, now about fifteen years old; and while he was building the ship for the father, he was building for himself a castle in the air, in which he and Ida were to live when they were married. This might have happened, indeed, if there had been a real castle, with stone walls, ramparts, and a moat. But in spite of his clever head, the builder was still but a poor, inferior bird; and how can a sparrow expect to be admitted into the society of peacocks?

"I passed on in my course," said the Wind, "and he passed away also. He was not allowed to remain, and little Ida got over it, because she was obliged to do so. Proud, black horses, worth looking at, were neighing in the stable. And they were locked up; for the admiral, who had been sent by the king to inspect the new ship, and make arrangements for its purchase, was loud in admiration of these beautiful horses. I heard it all," said the Wind, "for I accompanied the gentlemen through the open door of the stable, and strewed stalks of straw, like bars of gold, at their feet. Waldemar Daa wanted gold, and the admiral wished for the proud black horses; therefore he praised them so much. But the hint was not taken, and consequently the ship was not bought. It remained on the shore covered with boards, — a Noah's ark that never got to the water — Whir-r-r-r — and that was a pity.

"In the winter, when the fields were covered with snow, and the water filled with large blocks of ice which I had blown up to the coast," continued the Wind, "great flocks of crows and ravens, dark and black as they usually are, came and alighted on the lonely, deserted ship. Then they croaked in harsh

THE STORY OF THE WIND

accents of the forest that now existed no more, of the many pretty birds' nests destroyed and the little ones left without a home; and all for the sake of that great bit of lumber, that proud ship, that never sailed forth. I made the snowflakes whirl till the snow lay like a great lake round the ship, and drifted over it. I let it hear my voice, that it might know what the storm has to say. Certainly I did my part towards teaching it seamanship.

"That winter passed away, and another winter and summer both passed, as they are still passing away, even as I pass away. The snow drifts onwards, the apple-blossoms are scattered, the leaves fall, — everything passes away, and men are passing away too. But the great man's daughters are still young, and little Ida is a rose as fair to look upon as on the day when the shipbuilder first saw her. I often tumbled her long, brown hair, while she stood in the garden by the apple-tree, musing, and not heeding how I strewed the blossoms on her hair, and dishevelled it; or sometimes, while she stood gazing at the red sun and the golden sky through the opening branches of the dark, thick foliage of the garden trees. Her sister Joanna was bright and slender as a lily; she had a tall and lofty carriage and figure, though, like her mother, rather stiff in back. She was very fond of walking through the great hall, where hung the portraits of her ancestors. The women were represented in dresses of velvet and silk, with tiny little hats, embroidered with pearls, on their braided hair. They were all handsome women. The gentlemen appeared clad in steel, or in rich cloaks lined with squirrel's fur; they wore little ruffs, and swords at their sides. Where would Joanna's place be on that wall some day? and how would *he* look, — her noble lord and husband? This is what she thought of, and often spoke of in a low voice to herself. I heard it as I swept into the long hall, and turned round to come out again. Anna Dorothea, the pale hyacinth, a child of fourteen, was quiet and thoughtful; her large, deep, blue eyes had a dreamy look, but a childlike smile still played round her mouth. I was not able to blow it away, neither did I wish to do so. We have met in the garden, in the hollow lane, in the field and meadow, where she gathered herbs and flowers which she knew would be useful to her father in preparing the drugs and mixtures he was always concocting. Waldemar Daa was arrogant and proud, but he was also a learned man, and knew a great deal. It was no secret, and many opinions were expressed on what he did. In his fireplace there was a fire, even in summer time. He would lock himself in his room, and for days the fire would be kept burning; but he did not talk much of what he was doing. The secret powers of nature are generally discovered in solitude, and did he not soon expect to find out the art of making the greatest of all good things — the art of making gold? So he fondly hoped; therefore the chimney smoked and the fire crackled so constantly. Yes, I was there too," said the Wind. " 'Leave it alone,' I sang down the chimney; 'leave it alone, it will all end in smoke, air, coals, and ashes, and you will burn your fingers.' But Waldemar Daa did not leave it alone, and all he possessed vanished like smoke blown by me. The splendid black horses, where are they? What became of the cows in the field, the old gold and silver vessels in cupboards and chests, and even the house and home itself? It was easy to melt all these away in the gold-making crucible, and yet obtain no gold. And so it was. Empty are the barns and store-rooms, the cellars and cupboards; the servants decreased in number, and the mice multiplied. First one window became broken, and then another, so that I could get in at other places besides the door. 'Where the chimney smokes, the meal is being cooked,' says the proverb; but here a chimney smoked that devoured all the meals for the sake of gold. I blew round the courtyard," said the Wind, "like a watchman blowing his horn, but no watchman was there. I twirled the weather-cock round on the summit of the tower, and it creaked like the snoring of a warder, but no warder was there; nothing but mice and rats. Poverty laid the table-cloth; poverty sat in the wardrobe and in the larder. The door fell off its hinges, cracks and fissures made their appearance everywhere; so that I could go in and out at pleasure, and that is how I know all about it. Amid smoke and ashes, sorrow, and sleepless nights, the hair and beard of the master of the house turned gray, and deep furrows showed themselves around his temples; his skin turned pale and yellow, while his eyes still looked eagerly for gold, the longed-for gold, and the result of his labor was debt instead of gain. I blew the smoke and ashes into his face and beard; I moaned through the broken window-panes, and the yawning clefts in the walls; I blew into the chests and drawers belonging to his daughters, wherein lay the clothes that had become faded and threadbare, from being worn over and over again. Such a song had not been sung at the children's cradle as I sung now. The lordly life had changed to a life of penury. I was the only one who rejoiced aloud in that castle," said the Wind. "At last I snowed them up, and they say snow keeps people warm. It was good for them, for they had no wood, and the forest, from which they might have obtained it, had been cut down. The frost was very bitter, and I rushed through loop-holes and passages, over gables and roofs with keen and cutting swiftness. The three high-born daughters were lying in bed because of the cold, and their father crouching beneath his leather coverlet. Nothing to eat, nothing to burn, no fire on the hearth! Here was a life for high-born people! 'Give it up, give it up!' But my Lord Daa would not do that. 'After winter, spring will come,' he said, 'after want, good times. We must not lose patience, we must learn to wait. Now my horses and lands are all mortgaged, it is indeed high time; but gold will come at last — at Easter.'

"I heard him as he thus spoke; he was looking at a spider's web, and he continued, 'Thou cunning little weaver, thou dost teach me perseverance. Let any one tear thy web, and thou wilt begin again and repair it. Let it be entirely destroyed, thou wilt resolutely begin to make another till it is completed. So ought we to do, if we wish to succeed at last.'

"It was the morning of Easter-day. The bells sounded from the neighboring church, and the sun seemed to rejoice in the sky. The master of the castle had watched through the night, in feverish excitement, and had been melting and cooling, distilling and mixing. I heard him sighing like a soul in despair; I heard him praying, and I noticed how he held his breath. The lamp burnt out, but he did not observe it. I blew up the fire in the coals on the hearth, and it threw a red glow on his ghastly white face, lighting it up with a glare, while his sunken eyes looked out wildly from their cavernous depths, and appeared to grow larger and more prominent, as if they would burst from their sockets. 'Look at the alchymic glass,' he cried; 'something glows in the crucible, pure and heavy.' He lifted it with a trembling hand, and exclaimed in a voice of agitation, 'Gold! gold!' He was quite giddy, I could have blown him down," said the Wind; "but I only fanned the glowing coals, and accompanied him through the door to the room where his daughter sat shivering. His coat was powdered with ashes, and there were ashes in his beard and in his tangled hair. He stood erect, and held high in the air the brittle glass that contained his costly treasure. 'Found! found! Gold! gold!' he shouted, again holding the glass aloft, that it might flash in the sunshine; but his hand trembled, and the alchymic glass fell from it, clattering to the ground, and brake in a thousand pieces. The last bubble of his happiness had burst, with a whiz and a whir, and I rushed away from the gold-maker's house.

"Late in the autumn, when the days were short, and the mist sprinkled cold drops on the berries and the leafless branches, I came back in fresh spirits, rushed through the air, swept the sky clear, and snapped off the dry twigs, which is certainly no great labor to do, yet it must be done. There was another kind of sweeping taking place at Waldemar Daa's, in the castle of Borreby. His enemy, Owe Ramel, of Basnas, was there, with the mortgage of the house and everything it contained, in his pocket. I rattled the broken windows, beat against the old rotten doors, and whistled through cracks and crevices, so that Mr. Owe Ramel did not much like to remain there. Ida and Anna Dorothea wept bitterly, Joanna stood, pale and proud, biting her lips till the blood came; but what could that avail? Owe Ramel offered Waldemar Daa permission to remain in the house till the end of his life. No one thanked him for the offer, and I saw the ruined old gentleman lift his head, and throw it back more proudly than ever. Then I rushed against the house and the old lime-trees with such force, that one of the thickest branches, a decayed one, was broken off, and the branch fell at the entrance, and remained there. It might have been used as a broom, if any one had wanted to sweep the place out, and a grand sweeping-out there really was; I thought it would be so. It was hard for any one to preserve composure on such a day; but these people had strong wills, as unbending as their hard fortune. There was nothing they could call their own, excepting the clothes they wore. Yes, there was one thing more, an alchymist's glass, a new one, which had been lately bought, and filled with what could be gathered from the ground of the treasure which had promised so much but failed in keeping its promise. Waldemar Daa hid the glass in his bosom, and, taking his stick in his hand, the once rich gentleman passed with his daughters out of the house of Borreby. I blew coldly upon his flustered cheeks, I stroked his gray beard and his long white hair, and I sang as well as I was able, 'Whir-r-r, whir-r-r. Gone away! Gone away!' Ida walked on one side of the old man, and Anna Dorothea on the other; Joanna turned round, as they left the entrance. Why? Fortune would not turn because she turned. She looked at the stone in the walls which had once formed part of the castle of Marck Stig, and perhaps she thought of his daughters and of the old song, —

> "The eldest and youngest, hand-in-hand,
> Went forth alone to a distant land."

These were only two; here there were three, and their father with them also. They walked along the high-road, where once they had driven in their splendid carriage; they went forth with their father as beggars. They wandered across an open field to a mud hut, which they rented for a dollar and a half a year, a new home, with bare walls and empty cupboards. Crows and magpies fluttered about them, and cried, as if in contempt, 'Caw, caw, turned out of our nest — caw, caw,' as they had done in the wood at Borreby, when the trees were felled. Daa and his daughters could not help hearing it, so I blew about their ears to drown the noise; what use was it that they should listen? So they went to live in the mud hut in the open field, and I wandered away, over moor and meadow, through bare bushes and leafless forests, to the open sea, to the broad shores in other lands, 'Whir-r-r, whir-r-r! Away, away!' year after year."

And what became of Waldemar Daa and his daughters? Listen; the Wind will tell us:

"The last I saw of them was the pale hyacinth, Anna Dorothea. She was old and bent then; for fifty years had passed and she had outlived them all. She could relate the history. Yonder, on the heath, near the town of Wiborg, in Jutland, stood the fine new house of the canon. It was built of red brick, with projecting gables. It was inhabited, for the smoke curled up thickly from the chimneys. The canon's gentle lady and her beautiful daughters sat in the bay-window, and looked over the hawthorn hedge of the garden towards the brown heath. What were they looking at? Their glances fell upon a stork's nest, which was built upon an old tumbledown hut. The roof, as far as one existed at all, was covered with moss and lichen. The stork's nest covered the greater part of it, and that alone was in a good condition; for it was kept in order by the stork himself. That is a house to be looked at, and not to be touched," said the Wind. "For the sake of the stork's nest it had been allowed to remain, although it is a blot on the landscape. They did not like to drive the stork away; therefore the old shed was left standing, and the poor woman who dwelt in it allowed to stay. She had the Egyptian bird to thank for that; or was it perchance her reward for having once interceded for the preservation of the nest of its black brother in the forest of Borreby? At that time she, the poor woman, was a young child, a white hyacinth in a rich garden. She remembered that time well; for it was Anna Dorothea.

" 'O-h, o-h,' she sighed; for people can sigh like the moaning of the wind among the reeds and rushes. 'O-h, o-h,' she would say, 'no bell sounded at thy burial, Waldemar Daa. The poor school-boys did not even sing a psalm when the former lor of Borreby was laid in the earth to rest. O-h, everything has an end, even misery. Sister Ida became the wife of a peasant; that was the hardest trial which befell our father, that the husband of his own daughter should be a miserable serf, whom his owner could place for punishment on the wooden horse. I suppose he is under the ground now; and Ida — alas! alas! it is not ended yet; miserable that I am! Kind Heaven, grant me that I may die.'

"That was Anna Dorothea's prayer in the wretched hut that was left standing for the sake of the stork. I took pity on the proudest of the sisters," said the Wind. "Her courage was like that of a man; and in man's clothes she served as a sailor on board ship. She was of few words, and of a dark countenance; but she did not know how to climb, so I blew her overboard before any one found out that she was a woman; and, in my opinion, that was well done," said the Wind.

On such another Easter morning as that on which Waldemar Daa imagined he had discovered the art of making gold, I heard the tones of a psalm under the stork's nest, and within the crumbling walls. It was Anna

Dorothea's last song. There was no window in the hut, only a hole in the wall; and the sun rose like a globe of burnished gold, and looked through. With what splendor he filled that dismal dwelling! Her eyes were glazing, and her heart breaking; but so it would have been, even had the sun not shone that morning on Anna Dorothea. The stork's nest had secured her a home till her death. I sung over her grave; I sung at her father's grave. I know where it lies, and where her grave is too, but nobody else knows it.

"New times now; all is changed. The old high-road is lost amid cultivated fields; the new one now winds along over covered graves; and soon the railway will come, with its train of carriages, and rush over graves where lie those whose very names are forgoten. All passed away, passed away!

"This is the story of Waldemar Daa and his daughters. Tell it better, any of you, if you know how," said the Wind; and he rushed away, and was gone.

THE ICE MAIDEN

I. LITTLE RUDY

WE will pay a visit to Switzerland, and wander through that country of mountains, whose steep and rocky sides are overgrown with forest trees. Let us climb to the dazzling snow-fields at their summits, and descend again to the green meadows beneath, through which rivers and brooks rush along as if they could not quickly enough reach the sea and vanish. Fiercely shines the sun over those deep valleys, as well as upon the heavy masses of snow which lie on the mountains.

During the year these accumulations thaw or fall in the rolling avalance, or are piled up in shining glaciers. Two of these glaciers lie in the broad, rocky cliffs, between the Schreckhorn and the Wetterhorn, near the little town of Grindelwald. They are wonderful to behold, and therefore in the summer time strangers come here from all parts of the world to see them. They cross snow-covered mountains, and travel through the deep valleys, or ascend for hours, higher and still higher, the valleys appearing to sink lower and lower as they proceed, and become as small as if seen from an air balloon. Over the lofty summits of these mountains the clouds often hang like a dark veil; while beneath in the valley, where many brown, wooden houses are scattered about, the bright rays of the sun may be shining upon a little brilliant patch of green, making it appear almost transparent. The waters foam and dash along in the valleys beneath; the streams from above trickle and murmur as they fall down the rocky mountain's side, looking like glittering silver bands.

On both sides of the mountain-path stand these little wooden houses; and, as within, there are many children and many mouths to feed, each house has its own little potato garden. These children rush out in swarms, and surround travellers, whether on foot or in carriages. They are all clever at making a bargain. They offer for sale the sweetest little toy-houses, models of the mountain cottages in Switzerland. Whether it be rain or sunshine, these crowds of children are always to be seen with their wares.

About twenty years ago, there might be seen occasionally, standing at a short distance from the other children, a little boy, who was also anxious to sell his curious wares. He had an earnest, expressive countenance, and held the box containing his carved toys tightly with both hands, as if unwilling to part with it. His earnest look, and being also a very little boy, made him noticed by the strangers; so that he often sold the most, without knowing why. An hour's walk farther up the ascent lived his grandfather, who cut and carved the pretty little toy-houses; and in the old man's room stood a large press, full of all sorts of carved things — nut-crackers, knives and forks, boxes with beautifully carved foliage, leaping chamois. It contained everything that could delight the eyes of a child. But the boy, who was named Rudy, looked with still greater pleasure and longing at some old fire-arms which hung upon the rafters, under the ceiling of the room. His grandfather promised him that he should have them some day, but that he must first grow big and strong, and learn how to use them. Small as he was, the goats were placed in his care, and a good goat-keeper should also be a good climber, and such Rudy was; he sometimes, indeed, climbed higher than the goats, for he was fond of seeking for birds'-nests at the top of high trees; he was bold and daring, but was seldom seen to smile, excepting when he stood by the roaring cataract, or heard the descending roll of the avalanche. He never played with the other children, and was not seen with them, unless his grandfather sent him down to sell his curious workmanship. Rudy did not much like trade; he loved to climb the mountains, or to sit by his grandfather and listen to his tales of olden times, or of the people in Meyringen, the place of his birth.

"In the early ages of the world," said the old man, "these people could not be found in Switzerland. They are a colony from the north, where their ancestors still dwell, and are called Swedes."

This was something for Rudy to know, but he learnt more from other sources, particularly from the domestic animals who belonged to the house. One was a large dog, called Ajola, which had belonged to his father; and the other was a tom-cat. This cat stood very high in Rudy's favor, for he had taught him to climb.

"Come out on the roof with me," said the cat; and Rudy quite understood him, for the language of fowls, ducks, cats, and dogs, is as easily understood by a young child as his own native tongue. But it must be at the age when grandfather's stick becomes a neighing horse, with head, legs, and tail. Some children retain these ideas later than others, and they are considered backwards and childish for their age. People say so; but is it so?

"Come out on the roof with me, little Rudy," was the first thing he heard the cat say, and Rudy understood him. "What people say about falling down is all nonsense," continued the cat; "you will not fall, unless you are afraid. Come, now, set one foot here and another there, and feel your way with your fore-feet. Keep your eyes wide open, and move softly, and if you come to a hole jump over it, and cling fast as I do." And this was just what Rudy did. He was often on the sloping roof with the cat, or on the tops of high trees. But, more frequently, higher still on the ridges of the rocks where puss never came.

"Higher, higher!" cried the trees and the bushes, "see to what height we have grown, and how fast we hold, even to the narrow edges of the rocks."

Rudy often reached the top of the mountain before the sunrise, and there inhaled his morning draught of the fresh, invigorating mountain air, — God's

own gift, which men call the sweet fragrance of plant and herb on the moun-
tain-side, and the mint and wild thyme in the valleys. The overhanging
clouds absorb all heaviness from the air, and the winds convey them away
over the pine-tree summits. The spirit of fragrance, light and fresh, remained
behind, and this was Rudy's morning draught. The sunbeams—those
blessing-bringing daughters of the sun—kissed his cheeks. Vertigo might be
lurking on the watch, but he dared not approach him. The swallows, who
had not less than seven nests in his grandfather's house, flew up to him and his
goats, singing, "We and you, you and we." They brought him greetings from
his grandfather's house, even from two hens, the only birds of the household;
but Rudy was not intimate with them.

Although so young and such a little fellow, Rudy had travelled a great
deal. He was born in the canton of Valais, and brought to his grandfather
over the mountains. He had walked to Staubbach—a little town that seems to
flutter in the air like a silver veil—from the glittering, snow-clad mountain
Jungfrau. He had also been to the great glaciers; but this is connected with a
sad story, for here his mother met her death, and his grandfather used to say
that all Rudy's childish merriment was lost from that time. His mother had
written in a letter, that before he was a year old he had laughed more than he
cried; but after his fall into the snow-covered crevasse, his disposition had
completely changed. The grandfather seldom spoke of this, but the fact was
generally known. Rudy's father had been a postilion, and the large dog which
now lived in his grandfather's cottage had always followed him on his journeys
over the Simplon to the lake of Geneva. Rudy's relations, on his father's side,
lived in the canton of Valais, in the valley of the Rhone. His uncle was a
chamois hunter, and a well-known guide. Rudy was only a year old when his
father died, and his mother was anxious to return with her child to her own
relations, who lived in the Bernese Oberland. Her father dwelt at a few hours'
distance from Grindelwald; he was a carver in wood, and gained so much by
it that he had plenty to live upon. She set out homewards in the month of
June, carrying her infant in her arms, and, accompanied by two chamois
hunters, crossed the Gemmi on her way to Grindelwald. They had already
left more than half the journey behind them. They had crossed high ridges,
and traversed snow-fields; they could even see her native valley, with its
familiar wooden cottages. They had only one more glacier to climb. Some
newly fallen snow concealed a cleft which, though it did not extend to the
foaming waters in the depths beneath, was still much deeper than the height
of a man. The young woman, with the child in her arms, slipped upon it,
sank in, and disappeared. Not a shriek, not a groan was heard; nothing but
the whining of a little child. More than an hour elapsed before her two companions could obtain from the nearest house ropes and poles to assist in
raising them; and it was with much exertion that they at last succeeded in
raising from the crevasse what appeared to be two dead bodies. Every means
was used to restore them to life. With the child they were successful, but not
with the mother; so the old grandfather received his daughter's little son into
his house an orphan, —a little boy who laughed more than he cried; but it
seemed as if laughter had left him in the cold ice-world into which he had
fallen, where, as the Swiss peasants say, the souls of the lost are confined till
the judgment-day.

The glaciers appear as if a rushing stream had been frozen in its course, and pressed into blocks of green crystal, which, balanced one upon another, form a wondrous palace of crystal for the Ice Maiden — the queen of the glaciers. It is she whose mighty power can crush the traveller to death, and arrest the flowing river in its course. She is also a child of the air, and with the swiftness of the chamois she can reach the snow-covered mountain tops, where the boldest mountaineer has to cut footsteps in the ice to ascend. She will sail on a frail pine-twig over the raging torrents beneath, and spring lightly from one iceberg to another, with her long, snow-white hair flowing around her, and her dark-green robe glittering like the waters of the deep Swiss lakes. "Mine is the power to seize and crush," she cried. "Once a beautiful boy was stolen from me by man, — a boy whom I had kissed, but had not kissed to death. He is again among mankind, and tends the goats on the mountains. He is always climbing higher and higher, far away from all others, but not from me. He is mine; I will send for him." And she gave Vertigo the commission.

It was summer, and the Ice Maiden was melting amidst the green verdure, when Vertigo swung himself up and down. Vertigo has many brothers, quite a troop of them, and the Ice Maiden chose the strongest among them. They exercise their power in different ways, and everywhere. Some sit on the banisters of steep stairs, others on the outer rails of lofty towers, or spring like squirrels along the ridges of the mountains. Others tread the air as a swimmer treads the water, and lure their victims here and there till they fall into the deep abyss. Vertigo and the Ice Maiden clutch at human beings, as the polypus seizes upon all that comes within its reach. And now Vertigo was to seize Rudy.

"Seize him, indeed," cried Vertigo; "I cannot do it. That monster of a cat has taught him her tricks. That child of the human race has a power within him which keeps me at a distance; I cannot possibly reach the boy when he hangs from the branches of trees, over the precipice; or I would gladly tickle his feet, and send him heels over head through the air; but I cannot accomplish it."

"We must accomplish it," said the Ice Maiden; "either you or I must; and I will — I will!"

"No, no!" sounded through the air, like an echo on the mountain church bells chime. It was an answer in song, in the melting tones of a chorus from others of nature's spirits — good and loving spirits, the daughters of the sunbeam. They who place themselves in a circle every evening on the mountain peaks; there they spread out their rose-colored wings, which, as the sun sinks, become more flaming red, until the lofty Alps seem to burn with fire. Men call this the Alpine glow. After the sun has set, they disappear within the white snow on the mountain-tops, and slumber there till sunrise, when they again come forth. They have great love for flowers, for butterflies, and for mankind; and from among the latter they had chosen little Rudy. "You shall not catch him; you shall not seize him!" they sang.

"Greater and stronger than he have I seized!" said the Ice Maiden.

Then the daughters of the sun sang a song of the traveller, whose cloak had been carried away by the wind. "The wind took the covering, but not the man; it could even seize upon him, but not hold him fast. The children of strength are more powerful, more ethereal, even than we are. They can rise higher than our parent, the sun. They have the magic words that rule the wind and the waves, and compel them to serve and obey; and they can, at last, cast off the heavy, oppressive weight of mortality, and soar upwards." Thus sweetly sounded the bell-like tones of the chorus.

And each morning the sun's rays shone through the one little window of the grandfather's house upon the quiet child. The daughters of the sunbeam kissed him; they wished to thaw, and melt, and obliterate the ice kiss which the queenly maiden of the glaciers had given him as he lay in the lap of his dead mother, in the deep crevasse of ice from which he had been so wonderfully rescued.

II. THE JOURNEY TO THE NEW HOME

Rudy was just eight years old, when his uncle, who lived on the other side of the mountain, wished to have the boy, as he thought he might obtain a better education with him, and learn something more. His grandfather thought the same, so he consented to let him go. Rudy had many to say farewell to, as well as his grandfather. First, there was Ajola, the old dog.

"Your father was the postilion, and I was the postilion's dog," said Ajola. "We have often travelled the same journey together; I knew all the dogs and men on this side of the mountain. It is not my habit to talk much; but now that we have so little time to converse together, I will say something more than usual. I will relate to you a story, which I have reflected upon for a long time. I do not understand it, and very likely you will not, but that is of no consequence. I have, however, learnt from it that in this world things are not equally divided, neither for dogs nor for men. All are not born to lie on the lap and to drink milk: I have never been petted in this way, but I have seen a little dog seated in the place of a gentleman or lady, and travelling inside a post-chaise. The lady, who was his mistress, or of whom he was master, carried a bottle of milk, of which the little dog now and then drank; she also offered him pieces of sugar to crunch. He sniffed at them proudly, but would not eat one, so she ate them herself. I was running along the dirty road by the side of the carriage as hungry as a dog could be, chewing the cud of my own thoughts, which were rather in confusion. But many other things seemed in confusion also. *Why* was not I lying on a lap and travelling in a coach? I could not tell; yet I knew I could not alter my own condition, either by barking or growling."

This was Ajola's farewell speech, and Rudy threw his arms round the dog's neck and kissed his cold nose. Then he took the cat in his arms, but he struggled to get free.

"You are getting too strong for me," he said; "but I will not use my claws against *you*. Clamber away over the mountains; it was I who taught you to climb. Do not fancy you are going to fall, and you will be quite safe." Then the cat jumped down and ran away; he did not wish Rudy to see that there were tears in his eyes.

The hens were hopping about the floor; one of them had no tail; a traveller, who fancied himself a sportsman, had shot off her tail, he had mistaken her for a bird of prey.

"Rudy is going away over the mountains," said one of the hens.

"He is always in such a hurry," said the other; "and I don't like taking leave," so they both hopped out.

But the goats said farewell; they bleated and wanted to go with him, they were so very sorry.

Just at this time two clever guides were going to cross the mountains to the other side of the Gemmi, and Rudy was to go with them on foot. It was a long walk for such a little boy, but he had plenty of strength and invincible courage. The swallows flew with him a little way, singing, "We and you — you and we." The way led across the rushing Lutschine, which falls in numerous streams from the dark clefts of the Grindelwald glaciers. Trunks of fallen trees and blocks of stone form bridges over these streams. After passing a forest of alders, they began to ascend, passing by some blocks of ice that had loosened themselves from the side of the mountain and lay across their path; they had to step over these ice-blocks or walk round them. Rudy crept here and ran there, his eyes sparkling with joy, and he stepped so firmly with his iron-tipped mountain shoe, that he left a mark behind him wherever he placed his foot.

The earth was black where the mountain torrents or the melted ice had poured upon it, but the bluish green, glassy ice sparkled and glittered. They had to go round little pools, like lakes, enclosed between large masses of ice; and, while thus wandering out of their path, they came near an immense stone, which lay balanced on the edge of an icy peak. The stone lost its balance just as they reached it, and rolled over into the abyss beneath, while the noise of its fall was echoed back from every hollow cliff of the glaciers.

They were always going upwards. The glaciers seemed to spread above them like a continued chain of masses of ice, piled up in wild confusion between bare and rugged rocks. Rudy thought for a moment of what had been told him, that he and his mother had once lain buried in one of these cold, heart-chilling fissures; but he soon banished such thoughts, and looked upon the story as fabulous, like many other stories which had been told him. Once or twice, when the men thought the way was rather difficult for such a little boy, they held out their hands to assist him; but he would not accept their assistance, for he stood on the slippery ice as firmly as if he had been a chamois. They came at length to rocky ground; sometimes stepping upon moss-covered stones, sometimes passing beneath stunted fir-trees, and again through green meadows. The landscape was always changing, but ever above them towered the lofty snow-clad mountains, whose names not only Rudy but every other child knew — "The Jungfrau," "The Monk and the Eiger."

Rudy had never been so far away before; he had never trodden on the wide-spreading ocean of snow that lay here with its immovable billows, from which the wind blows off the snowflake now and then, as it cuts the foam from the waves of the sea. The glaciers stand here so close together it might almost be said they are hand-in-hand; and each is a crystal palace for the Ice Maiden, whose power and will it is to seize and imprison the unwary traveller.

The sun shone warmly, and the snow sparkled as if covered with glittering diamonds. Numerous insects, especially butterflies and bees, lay dead in heaps on the snow. They had ventured too high, or the wind had carried them here and left them to die of cold.

Around the Wetterhorn hung a feathery cloud, like a woolbag, and a threatening cloud too, for as it sunk lower it increased in size, and concealed within was a "föhn,"* fearful in its violence should it break loose. This journey, with its varied incidents, — the wild paths, the night passed on the mountain, the steep rocky precipices, the hollow clefts, in which the rustling waters from time immemorial had worn away passages for themselves through blocks of stone, — all these were firmly impressed on Rudy's memory.

In a forsaken stone building, which stood just beyond the seas of snow, they one night took shelter. Here they found some charcoal and pine branches, so that they soon made a fire. They arranged couches to lie on as well as they could, and then the men seated themselves by the fire, took out their pipes, and began to smoke. They also prepared a warm, spiced drink, of which they partook and Rudy was not forgotten — he had his share. Then they began to talk of those mysterious beings with which the land of the Alps abounds; the hosts of apparitions which come in the night, and carry off the sleepers through the air, to the wonderful floating town of Venice; of the wild herdsman, who drives the black sheep across the meadows. These flocks are never seen, yet the tinkle of their little bells has often been heard, as well as their unearthly bleating. Rudy listened eagerly, but without fear, for he knew not what fear meant; and while he listened, he fancied he could hear the roaring of the spectral herd. It seemed to come nearer and roar louder, till the men heard it also and listened in silence, till, at length, they told Rudy that he must not dare to sleep. It was a "föhn," that violent storm-wind which rushes from the mountain to the valley beneath, and in its fury snaps asunder the trunks of large trees as if they were but slender reeds, and carries the wooden houses from one side of a river to the other as easily as we could move the pieces on a chess-board. After an hour had passed, they told Rudy that it was all over, and he might go to sleep; and, fatigued with his long walk, he readily slept at the word of command.

Very early the following morning they again set out. The sun on this day lighted up for Rudy new mountains, new glaciers, and new snow-fields. They had entered the Canton Valais, and found themselves on the ridge of the hills which can be seen from Grindelwald; but he was still far from his new home. They pointed out to him other clefts, other meadows, other woods and rocky paths, and other houses. Strange men made their appearance before him, and what men! They were misshapen, wretched-looking creatures, with yellow complexions; and on their necks were dark, ugly lumps of flesh, hanging down like bags. They were called cretins. They dragged themselves along painfully, and stared at the strangers with vacant eyes. The women looked more dreadful than the men. Poor Rudy! were these the sort of people he should see at his new home?

III. THE UNCLE

Rudy arrived at last at his uncle's house, and was thankful to find the people like those he had been accustomed to see. There was only one cretin amongst them, a poor idiot boy, one of those unfortunate beings who, in their neglected conditions, go from house to house, and are received and taken care of in different families, for a month or two at a time.

Poor Saperli had just arrived at his uncle's house when Rudy came. The uncle was an experienced hunter; he also followed the trade of a cooper; his

---

*A moist wind from the south, which rises on the Swiss mountains and lakes, and foretells a storm.

wife was a lively little person, with a face like a bird, eyes like those of an eagle, and a long, hairy throat. Everything was new to Rudy—the fashion of the dress, the manners, the employments, and even the language; but the latter his childish ear would soon learn. He saw also that there was more wealth here, when compared with his former home at his grandfather's. The rooms were larger, the walls were adorned with the horns of the chamois, and brightly polished guns. Over the door hung a painting of the Virgin Mary, fresh alpine roses and a burning lamp stood near it. Rudy's uncle was, as we have said, one of the most noted chamois hunters in the whole district, and also one of the best guides. Rudy soon became the pet of the house; but there was another pet, an old hound, blind and lazy, who would never more follow the hunt, well as he had once done so. But his former good qualities were not forgotten, and therefore the animal was kept in the family and treated with every indulgence. Rudy stroked the old hound, but he did not like strangers, and Rudy was as yet a stranger; he did not, however, long remain so, he soon endeared himself to every heart, and became like one of the family.

"We are not very badly off, here in the canton Valais," said his uncle one day; "we have the chamois, they do not die so fast as the wild goats, and it is certainly much better here now than in former times. How highly the old times have been spoken of, but ours is better. The bag has been opened, and a current of air now blows through our once confined valley. Something better always makes its appearance when old, worn-out things fail."

When his uncle became communicative, he would relate stories of his youthful days, and farther back still of the warlike times in which his father had lived. Valais was then, as he expressed it, only a closed-up bag, quite full of sick people, miserable cretins; but the French soldiers came, and they were capital doctors, they soon killed the disease and the sick people, too. The French people knew how to fight in more ways than one, and the girls knew how to conquer too; and when he said this the uncle nodded at his wife, who was a French woman by birth, and laughed. The French could also do battle on the stones. "It was they who cut a road out of the solid rock over the Simplon—such a road, that I need only say to a child of three years old, 'Go down to Italy, you have only to keep in the high road,' and the child will soon arrive in Italy, if he followed my directions."

Then the uncle sang a French song, and cried, "Hurrah! long live Napoleon Buonaparte." This was the first time Rudy had ever heard of France, or of Lyons, that great city on the Rhone where his uncle had once lived. His uncle said that Rudy, in a very few years, would become a clever hunter, he had quite a talent for it; he taught the boy to hold a gun properly, and to load and fire it. In the hunting season he took him to the hills, and made him drink the warm blood of the chamois, which is said to prevent the hunter from becoming giddy; he taught him to know the time when, from the different mountains, the avalanche is likely to fall, namely, at noontide or in the evening, from the effects of the sun's rays; he made him observe the movements of the chamois when he gave a leap, so that he might fall firmly and lightly on his feet. He told him that when on the fissures of the rocks he could find no place for his feet, he must support himself on his elbows, and cling with his legs, and even lean firmly with his back, for this could be done when necessary. He told him also that the chamois are very cunning, they place lookers-out on the watch; but the hunter must be more cunning than they are, and find them out by the scent.

One day, when Rudy went out hunting with his uncle, he hung a coat and hat on an alpine staff, and the chamois mistook it for a man, as they generally do. The mountain path was narrow here; indeed it was scarcely a path at all, only a kind of shelf, close to the yawning abyss. The snow that lay upon it was partially thawed, and the stones crumbled beneath the feet. Every fragment of stone broken off struck the sides of the rock in its fall, till it rolled into the depths beneath, and sunk to rest. Upon this shelf Rudy's uncle laid himself down, and crept forward. At about a hundred paces behind him stood Rudy, upon the highest point of the rock, watching a great vulture hovering in the air; with a single stroke of his wing the bird might easily cast the creeping hunter into the abyss beneath, and make him his prey. Rudy's uncle had eyes for nothing but the chamois, who, with its young kid, had just appeared round the edge of the rock. So Rudy kept his eyes fixed on the bird, he knew well what the great creature wanted; therefore he stood in readiness to discharge his gun at the proper moment. Suddenly the chamois made a spring, and his uncle fired and struck the animal with the deadly bullet; while the young kid rushed away, as if for a long life he had been accustomed to danger and practised flight. The large bird, alarmed at the report of the gun, wheeled off in another direction, and Rudy's uncle was saved from danger, of which he knew nothing till he was told of it by the boy.

While they were both in pleasant mood, wending their way homewards, and the uncle whistling the tune of a song he had learnt in his young days, they suddenly heard a peculiar sound which seemed to come from the top of the mountain. They looked up, and saw above them, on the over-hanging rock, the snow-covering heave and lift itself as a piece of linen stretched on the ground to dry raises itself when the wind creeps under it. Smooth as polished marble slabs, the waves of snow cracked and loosened themselves, and then suddenly, with the rumbling noise of distant thunder, fell like a foaming cataract into the abyss. An avalanche had fallen, not upon Rudy and his uncle, but very near them. Alas, a great deal too near!

"Hold fast, Rudy!" cried his uncle; "hold fast, with all your might."

Then Rudy clung with his arms to the trunk of the nearest tree, while his uncle climbed above him, and held fast by the branches. The avalanche rolled past them at some distance; but the gust of wind that followed, like the storm-wings of the avalanche, snapped asunder the trees and bushes over which it swept, as if they had been but dry rushes, and threw them about in every direction. The tree to which Rudy clung was thus overthrown, and Rudy dashed to the ground. The higher branches were snapped off, and carried away to a great distance; and among these shattered branches lay Rudy's uncle, with his skull fractured. When they found him, his hand was still warm; but it would have been impossible to recognize his face. Rudy stood by, pale and trembling; it was the first shock of his life, the first time he had ever felt fear. Late in the evening he returned home with the fatal news, — to that home which was now to be so full of sorrow. His uncle's wife uttered not a word, nor shed a tear, till the corpse was brought in; then her agony burst forth. The poor cretin crept away to his bed, and nothing was seen of him during the whole of the following day. Towards evening, however, he came to Rudy, and said, "Will you write a letter for me? Saperli cannot write; Saperli can only take the letters to the post."

"A letter for you!" said Rudy; "who do you wish to write to?"

"To the Lord Christ," he replied.

"What do you mean?" asked Rudy.

Then the poor idiot, as the cretin was often called, looked at Rudy with a most touching expression in his eyes, clasped his hands, and said, solemnly and devoutly, "Saperli wants to send a letter to Jesus Christ, to pray Him to let Saperli die, and not the master of the house here."

Rudy pressed his hand, and replied, "A letter would not reach Him up above; it would not give him back whom we have lost."

It was not, however, easy for Rudy to convince Saperli of the impossibility of doing what he wished.

"Now you must work for us," said his foster-mother; and Rudy very soon became the entire support of the house.

IV. BABETTE

Who was the best marksman in the canton Valais? The chamois knew well. "Save yourselves from Rudy," they might well say. And who is the handsomest marksman? "Oh, it is Rudy," said the maidens; but *they* did not say, "Save yourselves from Rudy." Neither did anxious mothers say so; for he bowed to them as pleasantly as to the young girls. He was so brave and cheerful. His cheeks were brown, his teeth white, and his eyes dark and sparkling. He was now a handsome young man of twenty years. The most icy water could not deter him from swimming; he could twist and turn like a fish. None could climb like he, and he clung as firmly to the edges of the rocks as a limpet. He had strong muscular power, as could be seen when he leapt from rock to rock. He had learnt this first from the cat, and more lately from the chamois. Rudy was considered the best guide over the mountains; every one had great confidence in him. He might have made a great deal of money as guide. His uncle had also taught him the trade of a cooper; but he had no inclination for either; his delight was in chamois-hunting, which also brought him plenty of money. Rudy would be a very good match, as people said, if he would not look above his own station. He was also such a famous partner in dancing, that the girls often dreamt about him, and one and another thought of him even when awake.

"He kissed me in the dance," said Annette, the schoolmaster's daughter, to her dearest friend; but she ought not to have told this, even to her dearest friend. It is not easy to keep such secrets; they are like sand in a sieve; they slip out. It was therefore soon known that Rudy, so brave and so good as he was, had kissed some one while dancing, and yet he had never kissed her who was dearest to him.

"Ah, ah," said an old hunter, "he has kissed Annette, has he? he has begun with A, and I suppose he will kiss through the whole alphabet."

But a kiss in the dance was all the busy tongues could accuse him of. He certainly had kissed Annette, but she was not the flower of his heart.

Down in the valley, near Bex, among the great walnut-trees, by the side of a little rushing mountain-stream, lived a rich miller. His dwelling-house was a large building, three storeys high, with little turrets. The roof was covered with chips, bound together with tin plates, that glittered in sunshine and in the moonlight. The largest of the turrets had a weather-cock, representing an apple pierced by a glittering arrow, in memory of William Tell. The mill was a neat and well-ordered place, that allowed itself to be sketched and written about; but the miller's daughter did not permit any to sketch or write about her. So, at least, Rudy would have said, for her image was pictured in his heart; her eyes shone in it so brightly, that quite a flame had been kindled there; and, like all other fires, it had burst forth so suddenly, that the miller's daughter, the beautiful Babette, was quite unaware of it. Rudy had never spoken a word to her on the subject. The miller was rich, and, on that account, Babette stood very high, and was rather difficult to aspire to. But said Rudy to himself, "Nothing is too high for a man to reach: he must climb with confidence in himself, and he will not fail." He had learnt this lesson in his youthful home.

It happened once that Rudy had some business to settle at Bex. It was a long journey at that time, for the railway had not been opened. From the glaciers of the Rhone, at the foot of the Simplon, between its ever-changing mountain summits, stretches the valley of the canton Valais. Through it runs the noble river of the Rhone, which often overflows its banks, covering fields and highways, and destroying everything in its course. Near the towns of Sion and St. Maurice, the valley takes a turn, and bends like an elbow, and behind St. Maurice becomes so narrow that there is only space enough for the bed of the river and a narrow carriage-road. An old tower stands here, as if it were guardian to the canton Valais, which ends at this point; and from it we can look across the stone bridge to the toll-house on the other side, where the canton Vaud commences. Not far from this spot stands the town of Bex, and at every step can be seen an increase of fruitfulness and verdure. It is like entering a grove of chestnut and walnut-trees. Here and there the cypress and pomegranate blossoms peep forth; and it is almost as warm as an Italian climate. Rudy arrived at Bex, and soon finished the business which had brought him there, and then walked about the town; but not even the miller's boy could be seen, nor any one belonging to the mill, not to mention Babette. This did not please him at all. Evening came on. The air was filled with the perfume of the wild thyme and the blossoms of the lime-trees, and the green woods on the mountains seemed to be covered with a shining veil, blue as the sky. Over everything reigned a stillness, not of sleep or of death, but as if Nature were holding her breath, that her image might be photographed on the blue vault of heaven. Here and there, amidst the trees of the silent valley, stood poles which supported the wires of the electric telegraph. Against one of these poles leaned an object so motionless that it might have been mistaken for the trunk of a tree; but it was Rudy, standing there as still as at that moment was everything around him. He was not asleep, neither was he dead; but just as the various events in the world—matters of momentous importance to individuals—were flying through the telegraph wires, without the quiver of a wire or the slightest tone, so, through the mind of Rudy, thoughts of overwhelming importance were passing, without an outward sign of emotion. The happiness of his future life depended upon the decision of his present reflections. His eyes were fixed on one spot in the distance—a light that twinkled through the foliage from the parlor of the miller's house, where Babette dwelt. Rudy stood so still, that it might have been supposed he was watching for a chamois; but he was in reality like a chamois, who will stand for a moment, looking as if it were chiselled out of the rock, and then, if only a stone rolled by, would suddenly bound forward with a spring, far away from the hunter. And so with Rudy: a sudden roll of his thoughts roused him from his stillness, and made him bound forward with determination to act.

"Never despair!" cried he. "A visit to the mill, to say good evening to the miller, and good evening to little Babette, can do no harm. No one ever fails who has confidence in himself. If I am to be Babette's husband, I must see her some time or other."

Then Rudy laughed joyously, and took courage to go to the mill. He knew what he wanted; he wanted to marry Babette. The clear water of the river rolled over its yellow bed, and willows and lime-trees were reflected in it, as Rudy stepped along the path to the miller's house. But, as the children sing—

> "There was no one at home in the house,
> Only a kitten at play."

The cat standing on the steps put up its back and cried "mew." But Rudy had no inclination for this sort of conversation; he passed on, and knocked at the door. No one heard him, no one opened the door. "Mew," said the cat again; and had Rudy been still a child, he would have understood this language, and known that the cat wished to tell him there was no one at home. So he was obliged to go to the mill and make inquiries, and there he heard that the miller had gone on a journey to Interlachen, and taken Babette with him, to the great shooting festival, which began that morning, and would continue for eight days, and that people from all the German settlements would be there.

Poor Rudy! we may well say. It was not a fortunate day for his visit to Bex. He had just to return the way he came, through St. Maurice and Sion, to his home in the valley. But he did not despair. When the sun rose the next morning, his good spirits had returned; indeed he had never really lost them. "Babette is at Interlachen," said Rudy to himself, "many days' journey from here. It is certainly a long way for any one who takes the high-road, but not so far if he takes a short cut across the mountain, and that just suits a chamois-hunter. I have been that way before, for it leads to the home of my childhood, where, as a little boy, I lived with my grandfather. And there are shooting matches at Interlachen. I will go, and try to stand first in the match. Babette will be there, and I shall be able to make her acquaintance."

Carrying his light knapsack, which contained his Sunday clothes, on his back, and with his musket and his game-bag over his shoulder, Rudy started to take the shortest way across the mountain. Still it was a great distance. The shooting matches were to commence on that day, and to continue for a whole week. He had been told also that the miller and Babette would remain that time with some relatives at Interlachen. So over the Gemmi Rudy climbed bravely, and determined to descend the side of the Grindelwald. Bright and joyous were his feelings as he stepped lightly onwards, inhaling the invigorating mountain air. The valley sunk as he ascended, the circle of the horizon expanded. One snow-capped peak after another rose before him, till the whole of the glittering Alpine range became visible. Rudy knew each ice-clad peak, and he continued his course towards the Schreckhorn, with its white powdered stone finger raised high in the air. At length he had crossed the highest ridges, and before him lay the green pasture lands sloping down towards the valley, which was once his home. The buoyancy of the air made his heart light. Hill and valley were blooming in luxuriant beauty, and his thoughts were youthful dreams, in which old age or death were out of the question. Life, power, and enjoyment were in the future, and he felt free and light as a bird. And the swallows flew round him, as in the days of his childhood, singing "We and you—you and we." All was overflowing with joy. Beneath him lay the meadows, covered with velvety green, with the murmuring river flowing through them, and dotted here and there were small wooden houses. He could see the edges of the glaciers, loking like green glass against the soiled snow, and the deep chasms beneath the loftiest glacier. The church bells were ringing, as if to welcome him to his home with their sweet tones. His heart beat quickly, and for a moment he seemed to have foregotten Babette, so full were his thoughts of old recollections. He was, in imagination, once more wandering on the road where, when a little boy, he, with other children, came to sell their curiously carved toy houses. Yonder, behind the fir-trees, still stood his grandfather's house, his mother's father, but strangers dwelt in it now. Children came running to him, as he had once done, and wished to sell their wares. One of them offered him an Alpine rose. Rudy took the rose as a good omen, and thought of Babette. He quickly crossed the bridge where the two rivers flow into each other. Here he found a walk overshadowed with large walnut-trees, and their thick foliage formed a pleasant shade. Very soon he perceived in the distance, waving flags, on which glittered a white cross on a red ground—the standard of the Danes as well as of the Swiss—and before him lay Interlachen.

"It is really a splendid town, like none other that I have ever seen," said Rudy to himself. It was indeed a Swiss town in its holiday dress. Not like the many other towns, crowded with heavy stone houses, stiff and foreign looking. No; here it seemed as if the wooden houses on the hills had run into the valley, and placed themselves in rows and ranks by the side of the clear river, which rushes like an arrow in its course. The streets were rather irregular, it is true, but still this added to their picturesque appearance. There was one street which Rudy thought the prettiest of them all; it had been built since he had visited the town when a little boy. It seemed to him as if all the neatest and most curiously carved toy houses which his grandfather once kept in the large cupboard at home, had been brought out and placed in this spot, and that they had increased in size since then, as the old chestnut trees had done. The houses were called hotels; the woodwork on the windows and balconies was curiously carved. The roofs were gayly painted, and before each house was a flower garden, which separated it from the macadamized high-road. These houses all stood on the same side of the road, so that the fresh, green meadows, in which were cows grazing, with bells on their necks, were not hidden. The sound of these bells is often heard amidst Alpine scenery. These meadows were encircled by lofty hills, which receded a little in the centre, so that the most beautifully formed of Swiss mountains—the snow-crowned Jungfrau—could be distinctly seen glittering in the distance. A number of elegantly dressed gentlemen and ladies from foreign lands, and crowds of country people from the neighboring cantons, were assembled in the town. Each marksman wore the number of hits he had made twisted in a garland round his hat. Here were music and singing of all descriptions: hand-organs, trumpets, shouting, and noise. The houses and bridges were adorned with verses and inscriptions. Flags and banners were waving. Shot after shot was fired, which was the best music to Rudy's ears. And amidst all this excitement he quite forgot Babette, on whose account only he had come. The shooters were thronging round the target, and Rudy was soon amongst them. But when he took his turn to fire, he proved himself the best shot, for he always struck the bull's-eye.

"Who may that young stranger be?" was the inquiry on all sides. "He speaks French as it is spoken in the Swiss cantons."

"And makes himself understood very well when he speaks German," said some.

"He lived here, when a child, with his grandfather, in a house on the road to Grindelwald," remarked one of the sportsmen.

And full of life was this young stranger; his eyes sparkled, his glance was steady, and his arm sure, therefore he always hit the mark. Good fortune gives courage, and Rudy was always courageous. He soon had a circle of friends gathered round him. Every one noticed him, and did him homage. Babette had quite vanished from his thoughts, when he was struck on the shoulder by a heavy hand, and a deep voice said to him in French, "You are from the canton Valais."

Rudy turned round, and beheld a man with a ruddy, pleasant face, and a stout figure. It was the rich miller from Bex. His broad, portly person, hid the slender, lovely Babette; but she came forward and glanced at him with her bright, dark eyes. The rich miller was very much flattered at the thought that the young man, who was acknowledged to be the best shot, and was so praised by every one, should be from his own canton. Now was Rudy really fortunate: he had travelled all this way to this place, and those he had forgotten were now come to seek him. When country people go far from home, they often meet with those they know, and improve their acquaintance. Rudy, by his shooting, had gained the first place in the shooting-match, just as the miller at home at Bex stood first, because of his money and his mill. So the two men shook hands, which they had never done before. Babette, too, held out her hand to Rudy frankly, and he pressed it in his, and looked at her so earnestly, that she blushed deeply. The miller talked of the long journey they had travelled, and of the many towns they had seen. It was his opinion that he had really made as great a journey as if he had travelled in a steamship, a railway carriage, or a post-chaise.

"I came by a much shorter way," said Rudy; "I came over the mountains. There is no road so high that a man may not venture upon it."

"Ah, yes; and break your neck," said the miller; "and you look like one who will break his neck some day, you are so daring."

"Oh, nothing ever happens to a man if he has confidence in himself," replied Rudy.

The miller's relations at Interlachen, with whom the miller and Babette were staying, invited Rudy to visit them, when they found he came from the same canton as the miller. It was a most pleasant visit. Good fortune seemed to follow him, as it does those who think and act for themselves, and who remember the proverb, "Nuts are given to us, but they are not cracked for us." And Rudy was treated by the miller's relations almost like one of the family, and glasses of wine were poured out to drink to the welfare of the best shooter. Babette clinked glasses with Rudy, and he returned thanks for the toast. In the evening they all took a delightful walk under the walnut-trees, in front of the stately hotels; there were so many people, and such crowding, that Rudy was obliged to offer his arm to Babette. Then he told her how happy it made him to meet people from the canton Vaud, — for Vaud and Valais were neighboring cantons. He spoke of this pleasure so heartily that Babette could not resist giving his arm a slight squeeze; and so they walked on together, and talked and chatted like old acquaintances. Rudy felt inclined to laugh sometimes at the absurd dress and walk of the foreign ladies; but Babette did not wish to make fun of them, for she knew there must be some good, excellent people amongst them; she, herself, had a godmother, who was a high-born English lady. Eighteen years before, when Babette was christened, this lady was staying at Bex, and she stood godmother for her, and gave her the valuable brooch she now wore in her bosom.

Her godmother had twice written to her, and this year she was expected to visit Interlachen with her two daughters; "but they are old-maids," added Babette, who was only eighteen: "they are nearly thirty." Her sweet little mouth was never still a moment, and all that she said sounded in Rudy's ears as matters of the greatest importance, and at last he told her what he was longing to tell. How often he had been at Bex, how well he knew the mill, and how often he had seen Babette, when most likely she had not noticed him; and lastly, that full of many thoughts which he could not tell her, he had been to the mill on the evening when she and her father has started on their long journey, but not too far for him to find a way to overtake them. He told her all this, and a great deal more; he told her how much he could endure for her; and that it was to see *her,* and not the shooting-match, which had brought him to Interlachen. Babette became quite silent after hearing all this; it was almost too much, and it troubled her.

And while they thus wandered on, the sun sunk behind the lofty mountains. The Jungfrau stood out in brightness and splendor, as a back-ground to the green woods of the surrounding hills. Every one stood still to look at the beautiful sight, Rudy and Babette among them.

"Nothing can be more beautiful than this," said Babette.

"Nothing!" replied Rudy, looking at Babette.

"To-morrow I must return home," remarked Rudy a few minutes afterwards.

"Come and visit us at Bex," whispered Babette; "my father will be pleased to see you."

V. ON THE WAY HOME

Oh, what a number of things Rudy had to carry over the mountains, when he set out to return home! He had three silver cups, two handsome pistols, and a silver coffee-pot. This latter would be useful when he began housekeeping. But all these were not the heaviest weight he had to bear; something mightier and more important he carried with him in his heart, over the high mountains, as he journeyed homeward.

The weather was dismally dark, and inclined to rain; the clouds hung low, like a mourning veil on the tops of the mountains, and shrouded their glittering peaks. In the woods could be heard the sound of the axe and the heavy fall of the trunks of the trees, as they rolled down the slopes of the mountains. When seen from the heights, the trunks of these trees looked like slender stems; but on a nearer inspection they were found to be large and strong enough for the masts of a ship. The river murmured monotonously, the wind whistled, and the clouds sailed along hurriedly.

Suddenly there appeared, close by Rudy's side, a young maiden; he had not noticed her till she came quite near to him. She was also going to ascend the mountain. The maiden's eyes shone with an unearthly power, which obliged you to look into them; they were strange eyes, — clear, deep, and unfathomable.

"Hast thou a lover?" asked Rudy; all his thoughts were naturally on love just then.

"I have none," answered the maiden, with a laugh; it was as if she had not spoken the truth.

"Do not let us go such a long way round," said she. "We must keep to the left; it is much shorter."

"Ah, yes," he replied; "and fall into some crevasse. Do you pretend to be a guide, and not know the road better than that?"

"I know every step of the way," said she; "and my thoughts are collected, while yours are down in the valley yonder. We should think of the Ice Maiden while we are up here; men say she is not kind to their race."

"I fear her not," said Rudy. "She could not keep me when I was a child; I will not give myself up to her now I am a man."

Darkness came on, the rain fell, and then it began to snow, and the whiteness dazzled the eyes.

"Give me your hand," said the maiden; "I will help you to mount." And he felt the touch of her icy fingers.

"*You* help me," cried Rudy; "I do not yet require a woman to help me to climb." And he stepped quickly forwards away from her.

The drifting snow-shower fell like a veil between them, the wind whistled, and behind him he could hear the maiden laughing and singing, and the sound was most strange to hear.

"It certainly must be a spectre or a servant of the Ice Maiden," thought Rudy, who had heard such things talked about when he was a little boy, and had stayed all night on the mountain with the guides.

The snow fell thicker than ever, the clouds lay beneath him; he looked back, there was no one to be seen, but he heard sounds of mocking laughter, which were not those of a human voice.

When Rudy at length reached the highest part of the mountain, where the path led down to the valley of the Rhone, the snow had ceased, and in the clear heavens he saw two bright stars twinkling. They reminded him of Babette and of himself, and of his future happiness, and his heart glowed at the thought.

VI. THE VISIT TO THE MILL

"What beautiful things you have brought home!" said his old fostermother; and her strange-looking eagle-eyes sparkled, while she wriggled and twisted her skinny neck more quickly and strangely than ever. "You have brought good luck with you, Rudy. I must give you a kiss, my dear boy."

Rudy allowed himself to be kissed; but it could be seen by his countenance that he only endured the infliction as a homely duty.

"How handsome you are, Rudy!" said the old woman.

"Don't flatter," said Rudy, with a laugh; but still he was pleased.

"I must say once more," said the old woman, "that you are very lucky."

"Well, in that I believe you are right," said he, as he thought of Babette. Never had he felt such a longing for that deep valley as he now had. "They must have returned home by this time," said he to himself; "it is already two days over the time which they fixed upon. I must go to Bex."

So Rudy set out to go to Bex; and when he arrived there, he found the miller and his daughter at home. They received him kindly, and brought him many greetings from their friends at Interlachen. Babette did not say much. She seemed to have become quite silent; but her eyes spoke, and that was quite enough for Rudy. The miller had generally a great deal to talk about, and seemed to expect that every one should listen to his jokes, and laugh at them; for was not he the rich miller? But now he was more inclined to hear Rudy's adventures while hunting and travelling, and to listen to his descriptions of the difficulties the chamois-hunter has to overcome on the mountain-tops, or of the dangerous snow-drifts which the wind and weather cause to cling to the edges of the rocks, or to lie in the form of a frail bridge over the abyss beneath. The eyes of the brave Rudy sparkled as he described the life of a hunter, or spoke of the cunning of the chamois and their wonderful leaps; also of the powerful föhn and the rolling avalanche. He noticed that the more he described, the more interested the miller became, especially when he spoke of the fierce vulture and of the royal eagle. Not far from Bex, in the canton Valais, was an eagle's nest, more curiously built under a high, over-hanging rock. In this nest was a young eagle; but who would venture to take it? A young Englishman had offered Rudy a whole handful of gold, if he would bring him the young eagle alive.

"There is a limit to everything," was Rudy's reply. "The eagle could not be taken; it would be folly to attempt it."

The wine was passed round freely, and the conversation kept up pleasantly; but the evening seemed too short for Rudy, although it was midnight when he left the miller's house, after this his first visit.

While the lights in the windows of the miller's house still twinkled through the green foliage, out through the open skylight came the parlor-cat on to the roof, and along the water-pipe walked the kitchen-cat to meet her.

"What is the news at the mill?" asked the parlor-cat. "Here in the house there is secret love-making going on, which the father knows nothing about. Rudy and Babette have been treading on each other's paws, under the table, all the evening. They trod on my tail twice, but I did not mew; that would have attracted notice."

"Well, I should have mewed," said the kitchen-cat.

"What might suit the kitchen would not suit the parlor," said the other. "I am quite curious to know what the miller will say when he finds out this engagement."

Yes, indeed; what would the miller say? Rudy himself was anxious to know that; but to wait till the miller heard of it from others was out of the question. Therefore, not many days after this visit, he was riding in the omnibus that runs between the two cantons, Valais and Vaud. These cantons are separated by the Rhone, over which is a bridge that unites them. Rudy, as usual, had plenty of courage, and indulged in pleasant thoughts of the favorable answer he should receive that evening. And when the omnibus returned, Rudy was again seated in it, going homewards; and at the same time the parlor-cat at the miller's house ran out quickly, crying, —

"Here, you from the kitchen, what do you think? The miller knows all now. Everything has come to a delightful end. Rudy came here this evening, and he and Babette had much whispering and secret conversation together. They stood in the path near the miller's room. I lay at their feet; but they had no eyes or thoughts for me.

" 'I will go to your father at once,' said he; 'it is the most honorable way.'

" 'Shall I go with you?' asked Babette; 'it will give you courage.'

" 'I have plenty of courage,' said Rudy; 'but if you are with me, he must be friendly, whether he says Yes or No.'

"So they turned to go in, and Rudy trod heavily on my tail; he certainly is very clumsy. I mewed; but neither he nor Babette had any ears for me. They opened the door, and entered together. I was before them, and jumped on the back of a chair. I hardly know what Rudy said; but the miller flew into a rage, and threatened to kick him out of the house. He told him he might go to the mountains, and look after the chamois, but not after our little Babette."

"And what did they say? Did they speak?" asked the kitchen-cat.

"What did they say! why, all that people generally do say when they go a-wooing—'I love her, and she loves me; and when there is milk in the can for one, there is milk in the can for two.'

" 'But she is so far above you,' said the miller; 'she has heaps of gold, as you know. You should not attempt to reach her.'

" 'There is nothing so high that a man cannot reach, if he will,' answered Rudy; for he is a brave youth.

" 'Yet you could not reach the young eagle,' said the miller, laughing. 'Babette is higher than the eagle's nest.'

" 'I will have them both,' said Rudy.

" 'Very well; I will give her to you when you bring me the young eaglet alive,' said the miller; and he laughed till the tears stood in his eyes. 'But now I thank you for this visit, Rudy; and if you come to-morrow, you will find nobody at home. Good-bye, Rudy.'

"Babette also wished him farewell; but her voice sounded as mournful as the mew of a little kitten that has lost its mother.

" 'A promise is a promise between man and man,' said Rudy. 'Do not weep, Babette; I shall bring the young eagle.'

" 'You will break your neck, I hope,' said the miller, 'and we shall be relieved from your company.'

"I call that kicking him out of the house," said the parlor-cat. "And now Rudy is gone, and Babette sits and weeps, while the miller sings German songs that he learnt on his journey; but I do not trouble myself on the matter, —it would be of no use."

"Yet, for all that, it is a very strange affair," said the kitchen-cat.

VII. THE EAGLE'S NEST

From the mountain-path came a joyous sound of some person whistling, and it betokened good humor and undaunted courage. It was Rudy, going to meet his friend Vesinaud. "You must come and help," said he. "I want to carry off the young eaglet from the top of the rock. We will take young Ragli with us."

"Had you not better first try to take down the moon? That would be quite as easy a task," said Vesinaud. "You seem to be in good spirits."

"Yes, indeed I am. I am thinking of my wedding. But to be serious, I will tell you all about it, and how I am situated."

Then he explained to Vesinaud and Ragli what he wished to do, and why.

"You are a daring fellow," said they; "but it is no use; you will break your neck."

"No one falls, unless he is afraid," said Rudy.

So at midnight they set out, carrying with them poles, ladders, and ropes. The road lay amidst brushwood and underwood, over rolling stones, always upwards higher and higher in the dark night. Waters roared beneath them, or fell in cascades from above. Humid clouds were driving through the air as the hunters reached the precipitous ledge of the rock. It was even darker here, for the sides of the rocks almost met, and the light penetrated only through a small opening at the top. At a little distance from the edge could be heard the sound of the roaring, foaming waters in the yawning abyss beneath them. The three seated themselves on a stone, to await in stillness the dawn of day, when the parent eagle would fly out, as it would be necessary to shoot the old bird before they could think of gaining possession of the young one. Rudy sat motionless, as if he had been part of the stone on which he sat. He held his gun ready to fire, with his eyes fixed steadily on the highest point of the cliff, where the eagle's nest lay concealed beneath the overhanging rock.

The three hunters had a long time to wait. At last they heard a rustling, whirring sound above them, and a large hovering object darkened the air. Two guns were ready to aim at the dark body of the eagle as it rose from the nest. Then a shot was fired; for an instant the bird fluttered its wide-spreading wings, and seemed as if it would fill up the whole of the chasm, and drag down the hunters in its fall. But it was not so; the eagle sunk gradually into the abyss beneath, and the branches of trees and bushes were broken by its weight. Then the hunters roused themselves: three of the longest ladders were brought and bound together; the topmost ring of these ladders would just reach the edge of the rock which hung over the abyss, but no farther. The point beneath which the eagle's nest lay sheltered was much higher, and the sides of the rock were as smooth as a wall. After consulting together, they determined to bind together two more ladders, and to hoist them over the cavity, and so form a communication with the three beneath them, by binding the upper ones to the lower. With great difficulty they contrived to drag the two ladders over the rock, and there they hung for some moments, swaying over the abyss; but no sooner had they fastened them together, than Rudy placed his foot on the lowest step.

It was a bitterly cold morning; clouds of mist were rising from beneath, and Rudy stood on the lower step of the ladder as a fly rests on a piece of swinging straw, which a bird may have dropped from the edge of the nest it was building on some tall factory chimney; but the fly could fly away if the straw were shaken, Rudy could only break his neck. The wind whistled around him, and beneath him the waters of the abyss, swelled by the thawing of the glaciers, those palaces of the Ice Maiden, foamed and roared in their rapid course. When Rudy began to ascend, the ladder trembled like the web of the spider, when it draws out the long, delicate threads; but as soon as he reached the fourth of the ladders, which had been bound together, he felt more confidence, — he knew that they had been fastened securely by skilful hands. The fifth ladder, that appeared to reach the nest, was supported by the sides of the rock, yet it swung to and fro, and flapped about like a slender reed, and as if it had been bound by fishing lines. It seemed a most dangerous undertaking to ascend it, but Rudy knew how to climb; he had learnt that from the cat, and he had no fear. He did not observe Vertigo, who stood in the air behind him, trying to lay hold of him with his outstretched polypous arms.

When at length he stood on the topmost step of the ladder, he found that he was still some distance below the nest, and not even able to see into it. Only by using his hands and climbing could he possibly reach it. He tried the strength of the stunted trees, and the thick underwood upon which the nest rested, and of which it was formed, and finding they would support his weight, he grasped them firmly, and swung himself up from the ladder till his head and breast were above the nest, and then what an overpowering stench came from it, for in it lay the putrid remains of lambs, chamois, and birds. Vertigo, although he could not reach him, blew the poisonous vapor in his face, to make him giddy and faint; and beneath, in the dark, yawning deep, on the rushing waters, sat the Ice Maiden, with her long, pale, green hair falling around her, and her death-like eyes fixed upon him, like the two barrels of a gun. "I have thee now," she cried.

In a corner of the eagle's nest sat the young eaglet, a large and powerful bird, though still unable to fly. Rudy fixed his eyes upon it, held on by one hand with all his strength, and with the other threw a noose round the young eagle. The string slipped to its legs. Rudy tightened it, and thus secured the bird alive. Then flinging the sling over his shoulder, so that the creature hung a good way down behind him, he prepared to descend with the help of a ' rope, and his foot soon touched safely the highest step of the ladder. Then Rudy, remembering his early lesson in climbing, "Hold fast, and do not fear," descended carefully down the ladders, and at last stood safely on the ground with the young living eaglet, where he was received with loud shouts of joy and congratulations.

VIII. WHAT FRESH NEWS THE PARLOR-CAT HAD TO TELL

"There is what you asked for," said Rudy, as he entered the miller's house at Bex, and placed on the floor a large basket. He removed the lid as he spoke, and a pair of yellow eyes, encircled by a black ring, stared forth with a wild, fiery glance, that seemed ready to burn and destroy all that came in its way. Its short, strong beak was open, ready to bite, and on its red throat were short feathers, like stubble.

"The young eaglet!" cried the miller.

Babette screamed, and started back, while her eyes wandered from Rudy to the bird in astonishment.

"You are not to be discouraged by difficulties, I see," said the miller.

"And you will keep your word," replied Rudy. "Each has his own characteristic, whether it is honor or courage."

"But how is it you did not break your neck?" asked the miller.

"Because I held fast," answered Rudy; "and I mean to hold fast to Babette."

"You must get her first," said the miller, laughing; and Babette thought this a very good sign.

"We must take the bird out of the basket," said she. "It is getting into a rage; how its eyes glare. How did you manage to conquer it?"

Then Rudy had to describe his adventure, and the miller's eyes opened wide as he listened.

"With your courage and your good fortune you might win three wives," said the miller.

"Oh, thank you," cried Rudy.

"But you have not won Babette yet," said the miller, slapping the young Alpine hunter on the shoulder playfully.

"Have you heard the fresh news at the mill?" asked the parlor-cat of the kitchen-cat. "Rudy has brought us the young eagle, and he is to take Babette in exchange. They kissed each other in the presence of the old man, which is as good as an engagement. He was quite civil about it; drew in his claws, and took his afternoon nap, so that the two were left to sit and wag their tails as much as they pleased. They have so much to talk about that it will not be finished till Christmas." Neither was it finished till Christmas.

The wind whirled the faded, fallen leaves; the snow drifted in the valleys, as well as upon the mountains, and the Ice Maiden sat in the stately palace which, in winter time, she generally occupied. The perpendicular rocks were covered with slippery ice, and where in summer the stream from the rocks had left a watery veil, icicles large and heavy hung from the trees, while the snow-powdered fir-trees were decorated with fantastic garlands of crystal. The Ice Maiden rode on the howling wind across the deep valleys, the country, as far as Bex, was covered with a carpet of snow, so that the Ice Maiden could follow Rudy, and see him, when he visited the mill; and while in the room at the miller's house, where he was accustomed to spend so much of his time with Babette. The wedding was to take place in the following summer, and they heard enough of it, for so many of their friends spoke of the matter.

Then came sunshine to the mill. The beautiful Alpine roses bloomed, and joyous, laughing Babette, was like the early spring, which makes all the birds sing of summer time and bridal days.

"How those two do sit and chatter together," said the parlor-cat; "I have had enough of their mewing."

IX. THE ICE MAIDEN

The walnut and chestnut trees, which extend from the bridge of St. Maurice, by the river Rhone, to the shores of the lake of Geneva, were already covered with the delicate green garlands of early spring, just bursting into bloom, while the Rhone rushed wildly from its source among the green glaciers which form the ice palace of the Ice Maiden. She sometimes allows herself to be carried by the keen wind to the lofty snow-fields, where she stretches herself in the sunshine on the soft snowy-cushions. From thence she throws her far-seeing glance into the deep valley beneath, where human beings are busily moving about like ants on a stone in the sun. "Spirits of strength, as the children of the sun call you," cried the Ice Maiden, "ye are but worms! Let but a snow-ball roll, and you and your houses and your towns are crushed and swept away." And she raised her proud head, and looked around her with eyes that flashed death from their glance. From the valley came a rumbling sound; men were busily at work blasting the rocks to form tunnels, and laying down roads for the railway. "They are playing at work underground, like moles," said she. "They are digging passages beneath the earth, and the noise is like the reports of cannons. I shall throw down my palaces, for the clamor is louder than the roar of thunder." Then there ascended from the valley a thick vapor, which waved itself in the air like a fluttering veil. It rose, as a plume of feathers, from a steam engine, to which, on the lately-opened railway, a string of carriages was linked, carriage to carriage, looking like a winding serpent. The train shot past with the speed of an arrow. "They play at being masters down there, those spirits of strength!" exclaimed the Ice Maiden; "but the powers of nature are still the rulers." And she laughed and sang till her voice sounded through the valley, and people said it was the rolling of an avalanche. But the children of the sun sang in louder strains in praise of the mind of man, which can span the sea as with a yoke, can level mountains, and fill up valleys. It is the power of thought which gives man the mastery over nature.

Just at this moment there came across the snow-field, where the Ice Maiden sat, a party of travellers. They had bound themselves fast to each other, so that they looked like one large body on the slippery plains of ice encircling the deep abyss.

"Worms!" exclaimed the Ice Maiden. "You, the lords of the powers of nature!" And she turned away and looked maliciously at the deep valley where the railway train was rushing by. "There they sit, these thoughts!" she exclaimed. "There they sit in their power over nature's strength. I see them all. One sits proudly apart, like a king; others sit together in a group; yonder, half of them are asleep; and when the steam dragon stops, they will get out and go their way. The *thoughts* go forth into the world," and she laughed.

"There goes another avalanche," said those in the valley beneath.

"It will not reach us," said two who sat together behind the steam dragon. "Two hearts and one beat," as people say. They were Rudy and Babette, and the miller was with them. "I am like the luggage," said he; "I am here as a necessary appendage."

"There sit those two," said the Ice Maiden. "Many a chamois have I crushed. Millions of Alpine roses have I snapped and broken off; not a root have I spared. I know them all, and their thoughts, those spirits of strength!" and again she laughed.

"There rolls another avalanche," said those in the valley.

X. THE GODMOTHER

At Montreux, one of the towns which encircle the northeast part of the lake of Geneva, lived Babette's godmother, the noble English lady, with her daughters and a young relative. They had only lately arrived, yet the miller had paid them a visit, and informed them of Babette's engagement to Rudy. The whole story of their meeting at Interlachen, and his brave adventure with the eaglet, were related to them, and they were all very much interested, and as pleased about Rudy and Babette as the miller himself. The three were invited to come to Montreux; it was but right for Babette to become acquainted with her godmother, who wished to see her very much. A steam-boat started from the town of Villeneuve, at one end of the lake of Geneva, and arrived at Bernex, a little town beyond Montreux, in about half an hour. And in this boat, the miller, with his daughter and Rudy, set out to vist her godmother. They passed the coast which has been so celebrated in song. Here, under the walnut-trees, by the deep blue lake, sat Byron, and wrote his melodious verses about the prisoner confined in the gloomy castle of Chillon. Here, where Clarens, with its weeping-willows, is reflected in the clear water, wandered Rousseau, dreaming of Heloise. The river Rhone glides gently by beneath the lofty snow-capped hills of Savoy, and not far from its mouth lies a little island in the lake, so small that, seen from the shore, it looks like a ship. The surface of the island is rocky; and about a hundred years ago, a lady caused the ground to be covered with earth, in which three acacia-trees were planted, and the whole enclosed with stone walls. The acacia-trees now overshadow every part of the island. Babette was enchanted with the spot; it seemed to her the most beautiful object in the whole voyage, and she thought how much she should like to land there. But the steam-ship passed it by, and did not stop till it reached Bernex. The little party walked slowly from this place to Montreux, passing the sun-lit walls with which the vineyards of the little mountain town of Montreux are surrounded, and peasants' houses, overshadowed by fig-trees, with gardens in which grow the laurel and the cypress.

Halfway up the hill stood the boarding-house in which Babette's godmother resided. She was received most cordially; her godmother was a very friendly woman, with a round, smiling countenance. When a child, her head must have resembled one of Raphael's cherubs; it was still an angelic face, with its white locks of silvery hair. The daughters were tall, elegant, slender maidens.

The young cousin, whom they had brought with them, was dressed in white from head to foot; he had golden hair and golden whiskers, large enough to be divided amongst three gentlemen; and he began immediately to pay the greatest attention to Babette.

Richly bound books, note-paper, and drawings, lay on the large table. The balcony window stood open, and from it could be seen the beautiful wide extended lake, the water so clear and still, that the mountains of Savoy, with their villages, woods, and snow-crowned peaks, were clearly reflected in it.

Rudy, who was usually so lively and brave, did not in the least feel himself at home; he acted as if he were walking on peas, over a slippery floor. How long and wearisome the time appeared; it was like being in a treadmill. And then they went out for a walk, which was very slow and tedious. Two steps forward and one backwards had Rudy to take to keep pace with the others. They walked down to Chillon, and went over the old castle on the rocky island. They saw the implements of torture, the deadly dungeons, the rusty fetters in the rocky walls, the stone benches for those condemned to death, the trap-doors through which the unhappy creatures were hurled upon iron spikes, and impaled alive. They called looking at all these a pleasure. It certainly was the right place to visit. Byron's poetry had made it celebrated in the world. Rudy could only feel that it was a place of execution. He leaned against the stone framework of the window, and gazed down into the deep, blue water, and over to the little island with the three acacias, and wished himself there, away and free from the whole chattering party. But Babette was most unusually lively and good-tempered.

"I have been so amused," she said.

The cousin had found her quite perfect.

"He is a perfect fop," said Rudy; and this was the first time Rudy had said anything that did not please Babette.

The Englishman had made her a present of a little book, in remembrance of their visit to Chillon. It was Byron's poem, "The Prisoner of Chillon," translated into French, so that Babette could read it.

"The book may be very good," said Rudy; "but that finely combed fellow who gave it to you is not worth much."

"He looks something like a flour-sack without any flour," said the miller, laughing at his own wit. Rudy laughed, too, for so had he appeared to him.

XI. THE COUSIN

When Rudy went a few days after to pay a visit to the mill, he found the young Englishman there. Babette was just thinking of preparing some trout to set before him. She understood well how to garnish the dish with parsley, and make it look quite tempting. Rudy thought all this quite unnecessary. What did the Englishman want there? What was he about? Why should he be entertained, and waited upon by Babette? Rudy was jealous, and that made Babette happy. It amused her to discover all the feelings of his heart; the strong points and weak ones. Love was to her as yet only a pastime, and she played with Rudy's whole heart. At the same time it must be acknowledged that her fortune, her whole life, her inmost thoughts, her best and most noble feelings in this world were all for him. Still the more gloomy he looked, the more her eyes laughed. She could almost have kissed the fair Englishman, with the golden whiskers, if by so doing she could have put Rudy in a rage, and made him run out of the house. That would have proved how much he loved her. All this was not right in Babette, but she was only nineteen years of age, and she did not reflect on what she did, neither did she think that her conduct would appear to the young Englishman as light, and not even becoming the modest and much-loved daughter of the miller.

The mill at Bex stood in the highway, which passed under the snow-clad mountains, and not far from a rapid mountain-stream, whose waters seemed to have been lashed into a foam like soap-suds. This stream, however, did not pass near enough to the mill, and therefore the mill-wheel was turned by a smaller stream which tumbled down the rocks on the opposite side, where it was opposed by a stone mill-dam, and obtained greater strength and speed, till it fell into a large basin, and from thence through a channel to the mill-wheel. This channel sometimes overflowed, and made the path so slippery that any one passing that way might easily fall in, and be carried towards the mill wheel with frightful rapidity. Such a catastrophe nearly happened to the young Englishman. He had dressed himself in white clothes, like a miller's man, and was climbing the path to the miller's house, but he had never been taught to climb, and therefore slipped, and nearly went in head-foremost. He managed, however, to scramble out with wet sleeves and bespattered trousers. Still, wet and splashed with mud, he contrived to reach Babette's window, to which he had been guided by the light that shone from it. Here he climbed the old linden-tree that stood near it, and began to imitate the voice of an owl, the only bird he could venture to mimic. Babette heard the noise, and glanced through the thin window curtain; but when she saw the man in white, and guessed who he was, her little heart beat with terror as well as anger. She quickly put out the light, felt if the fastening of the window was secure, and then left him to howl as long as he liked. How dreadful it would be, thought Babette, if Rudy were here in the house. But Rudy was not in the house. No, it was much worse, he was outside, standing just under the linden-tree. He was speaking loud, angry words. He could fight, and there might be murder! Babette opened the window in alarm, and called Rudy's name; she told him to go away, she did not wish him to remain there.

"You do not wish me to stay," cried he; "then this is an appointment you expected—this good friend whom you prefer to me. Shame on you, Babette!"

"You are detestable!" exclaimed Babette, bursting into tears. "Go away. I hate you."

"I have not deserved this," said Rudy, as he turned away, his cheeks burning, and his heart like fire.

Babette threw herself on the bed, and wept bitterly. "So much as I loved thee, Rudy, and yet thou canst think ill of me."

Thus her anger broke forth it; it relieved her, however: otherwise she would have been more deeply grieved; but now she could sleep soundly, as youth only can sleep.

XII. EVIL POWERS

Rudy left Bex, and took his way home along the mountain-path. The air was fresh, but cold; for here amidst the deep snow, the Ice Maiden reigned. He was so high up that the large trees beneath him, with their thick foliage, appeared like garden plants, and the pines and bushes even less. The Alpine roses grew near the snow, which lay in detached stripes, and looked like linen laid out to bleach. A blue gentian grew in his path, and he crushed it with the butt end of his gun. A little higher up, he espied two chamois. Rudy's eyes glistened, and his thoughts flew at once in a different direction; but he was not near enough to take a sure aim. He ascended still higher, to a spot where a few rough blades of grass grew between the blocks of stone and the chamois passed quietly on over the snow-fields. Rudy walked hurriedly, while the clouds of mist gathered round him. Suddenly he found himself on the brink of a precipitous rock. The rain was falling in torrents. He felt a burning thirst, his head was hot, and his limbs trembled with cold. He seized his hunting-flask, but it was empty; he had not thought of filling it before ascending the mountain. He had never been ill in his life, nor ever experienced such sensations as those he now felt. He was so tired that he could scarcely resist lying down at his full length to sleep, although the ground was flooded with the rain. Yet when he tried to rouse himself a little, every object around him danced and trembled before his eyes.

Suddenly he observed in the doorway of a hut newly built under the rock, a young maiden. He did not remember having seen this hut before, yet there it stood; and he thought, at first, that the young maiden was Annette, the schoolmaster's daughter, whom he had once kissed in the dance. The maiden was not Annette; yet it seemed as if he had seen her somewhere before, perhaps near Grindelwald, on the evening of his return home from Interlachen, after the shooting-match.

"How did you come here?" he asked.

"I am at home," she replied; "I am watching my flocks."

"Your flocks!" he exclaimed; "where do they find pasture? There is nothing here but snow and rocks."

"Much you know of what grows here," she replied, laughing. "not far beneath us there is beautiful pasture-land. My goats go there. I tend them carefully; I never miss one. What is once mine remains mine."

"You are bold," said Rudy.

"And so are you," she answered.

"Have you any milk in the house?" he asked; "if so, give me some to drink; my thirst is intolerable."

"I have something better than milk," she replied, "which I will give you. Some travellers who were here yesterday with their guide left behind them a half a flask of wine, such as you have never tasted. They will not come back to fetch it, I know, and I shall not drink it; so you shall have it."

Then the maiden went to fetch the wine, poured some into a wooden cup, and offered it to Rudy.

"How good it is!" said he; "I have never before tasted such warm, invigorating wine." And his eyes sparkled with new life; a glow diffused itself over his frame; it seemed as if every sorrow, every oppression were banished from his mind, and a fresh, free nature were stirring within him. "You are surely Annette, the schoolmaster's daughter," cried he; "will you give me a kiss?"

"Yes, if you will give me that beautiful ring which you wear on your finger."

"My betrothal ring?" he replied.

"Yes, just so," said the maiden, as she poured out some more wine, and held it to his lips. Again he drank, and a living joy streamed through every vein.

"The whole world is mine, why therefore should I grieve?" thought he. "Everything is created for our enjoyment and happiness. The stream of life is a stream of happiness; let us flow on with it to joy and felicity."

Rudy gazed on the young maiden; it was Annette, and yet it was not Annette; still less did he suppose it was the spectral phantom, whom he had met near Grindelwald. The maiden up here on the mountain was fresh as the new fallen snow, blooming as an Alpine rose, and as nimble-footed as a young kid. Still, she was one of Adam's race, like Rudy. He flung his arms round the beautiful being, and gazed into her wonderfully clear eyes, — only for a moment; but in that moment words cannot express the effect of his gaze. Was it the spirit of life or of death that overpowered him? Was he rising higher, or sinking lower and lower into the deep, deadly abyss? He knew not; but the walls of ice shone like blue-green glass; innumerable clefts yawned around him, and the water-drops tinkled like the chiming of church bells, and shone clearly as pearls in the light of a pale-blue flame. The Ice Maiden, for she it was, kissed him, and her kiss sent a chill as of ice through his whole frame. A cry of agony escaped from him; he struggled to get free, and tottered from her. For a moment all was dark before his eyes, but when he opened them again it was light, and the Alpine maiden had vanished. The powers of evil had played their game; the sheltering hut was no more to be seen. The water trickled down the naked sides of the rocks, and snow lay thickly all around. Rudy shivered with cold; he was wet through to the skin; and his ring was gone, — the betrothal ring that Babette had given him. His gun lay near him in the snow; he took it up and tried to discharge it, but it missed fire. Heavy clouds lay on the mountain clefts, like firm masses of snow. Upon one of these Vertigo sat, lurking after his powerless prey, and from beneath came a sound as if a piece of rock had fallen from the cleft, and was crushing everything that stood in its way or opposed its course.

But, at the miller's, Babette sat alone and wept. Rudy had not been to see her for six days. He who was in the wrong, and who ought to ask her forgiveness; for did she not love him with her whole heart?

XIII. AT THE MILL

"What strange creatures human beings are," said the parlor-cat to the kitchen-cat; "Babette and Rudy have fallen out with each other. She sits and cries, and he thinks no more about her."

"That does not please me to hear," said the kitchen-cat.

"Nor me either," replied the parlor-cat; "but I do not take it to heart. Babette may fall in love with the red whiskers, if she likes, but he has not been here since he tried to get on the roof."

The powers of evil carry on their game both around us and within us. Rudy knew this, and thought a great deal about it. What was it that had happened to him on the mountain? Was it really a ghostly apparition, or a fever dream? Rudy knew nothing of fever, or any other ailment. But, while he judged Babette, he began to examine his own conduct. He had allowed wild thoughts to chase each other in his heart, and a fierce tornado to break loose. Could he confess to Babette, indeed, every thought which in the hour of temptation might have led him to wrong doing? He had lost her ring, and that very loss had won him back to her. Could she expect him to confess? He felt as if his heart would break while he thought of it, and while so many memories lingered on his mind. He saw her again, as she once stood before him, a laughing, spirited child; many loving words, which she had spoken to him out of the fulness of her love, came like a ray of sunshine into his heart, and soon it was all sunshine as he thought of Babette. But she must also confess she was wrong; that she should do.

He went to the mill — he went to confession. It began with a kiss, and ended with Rudy being considered the offender. It was such a great fault to doubt Babette's truth — it was most abominable of him. Such mistrust, such violence, would cause them both great unhappiness. This certainly was very true, she knew that; and therefore Babette preached him a little sermon, with which she was herself much amused, and during the preaching of which she looked quite lovely. She acknowledged, however, that on one point Rudy was right. Her godmother's nephew was a fop: she intended to burn the book which he had given her, so that not the slightest thing should remain to remind her of him.

"Well, that quarrel is all over," said the kitchen-cat. "Rudy is come back, and they are friends again, which they say is the greatest of all pleasures."

"I heard the rats say one night," said the kitchen-cat, "that the greatest pleasure in the world was to eat tallow candles and to feast on rancid bacon. Which are we to believe, the rats or the lovers?"

"Neither of them," said the parlor-cat; "it is always the safest plan to believe nothing you hear."

The greatest happiness was coming for Rudy and Babette. The happy day, as it is called, that is, their wedding-day, was near at hand. They were not to be married at the church at Bex, nor at the miller's house; Babette's god-mother wished the nuptials to be solemnized at Montreux, in the pretty little church in that town. The miller was very anxious that this arrangement should be agreed to. He alone knew what the newly-married couple would receive from Babette's godmother, and he knew also that it was a wedding present well worth a concession. The day was fixed, and they were to travel as far as Villeneuve the evening before, to be in time for the steamer which sailed in the morning for Montreux, and the godmother's daughters were to dress and adorn the bride.

"Here in this house there ought to be a wedding-day kept," said the parlor-cat, "or else I would not give a mew for the whole affair."

"There is going to be great feasting," replied the kitchen-cat. "Ducks and pigeons have been killed, and a whole roebuck hangs on the wall. It makes me lick my lips when I think of it."

"To-morrow morning they will begin the journey."

Yes, to-morrow! And this evening, for the last time, Rudy and Babette sat in the miller's house as an engaged couple. Outside, the Alps glowed in the evening sunset, the evening bells chimed, and the children of the sunbeam sang, "Whatever happens is best."

XIV. NIGHT VISIONS

The sun had gone down, and the clouds lay low on the valley of the Rhone. The wind blew from the south across the mountains; it was an African wind, a wind which scattered the clouds for a moment, and then suddenly fell. The broken clouds hung in fantastic forms upon the wood-covered hills by the rapid Rhone. They assumed the shapes of antediluvian animals, of eagles hovering in the air, of frogs leaping over a marsh, and then sunk down upon the rushing stream and appeared to sail upon it, although floating in the air. An uprooted fir-tree was being carried away by the current, and marking out its path by eddying circles on the water. Vertigo and his sisters were dancing upon it, and raising these circles on the foaming river. The moon lighted up the snow on the mountain-tops, shone on the dark woods, and on the drifting clouds those fantastic forms which at night might be taken for spirits of the powers of nature. The mountain-dweller saw them through the panes of his little window. They sailed in hosts before the Ice Maiden as she came out of her palace of ice. Then she seated herself on the trunk of the fir-tree as on a broken skiff, and the water from the glaciers carried her down the river to the open lake.

"The wedding guests are coming," sounded from air and sea. These were the sights and sounds without; within there were visions, for Babette had a wonderful dream. She dreamt that she had been married to Rudy for many years, and that, one day when he was out chamois hunting, and she alone in their dwelling at home, the young Englishman with the golden whiskers sat with her. His eyes were quite eloquent, and his words possessed a magic power; he offered her his hand, and she was obliged to follow him. They went out of the house and stepped downwards, always downwards, and it seemed to Babette as if she had a weight on her heart which continually grew heavier. She felt she was committing a sin against Rudy, a sin against God. Suddenly she found herself forsaken, her clothes torn by the thorns, and her hair gray; she looked upwards in her agony, and there, on the edge of the rock, she espied Rudy. She stretched out her arms to him, but she did not venture to call him or to pray; and had she called him, it would have been useless, for it was not Rudy, only his hunting coat and hat hanging on an alpenstock, as the hunters sometimes arrange them to deceive the chamois. "Oh!" she exclaimed in her agony; "oh, that I had died on the happiest day of my life, my wedding-day. O my God, it would have been a mercy and a blessing had Rudy travelled far away from me, and I had never known him. None know what will happen in the future." And then, in ungodly despair, she cast herself down into the deep rocky gulf. The spell was broken; a cry of terror escaped her, and she awoke.

The dream was over; it had vanished. But she knew she had dreamt something frightful about the young Englishman, yet months had passed since she had seen him or even thought of him. Was he still at Montreux, and should she meet him there on her wedding day? A slight shadow passed over her pretty mouth as she thought of this, and she knit her brows; but the smile soon returned to her lip, and joy sparkled in her eyes, for this was the morning of the day on which she and Rudy were to be married, and the sun was shining brightly. Rudy was already in the parlor when she entered it, and they very soon started for Villeneuve. Both of them were overflowing with happiness, and the miller was in the best of tempers, laughing and merry; he was a good, honest soul, and a kind father.

"Now we are masters of the house," said the parlor-cat.

XV. THE CONCLUSION

It was early in the afternoon, and just at dinner-time, when the three joyous travellers reached Villeneuve. After dinner, the miller placed himself in the arm-chair, smoked his pipe, and had a little nap. The bridal pair went arm-in-arm out through the town and along the high road, at the foot of the wood-covered rocks, and by the deep, blue lake.

The gray walls, and the heavy clumsy-looking towers of the gloomy castle of Chillon, were reflected in the clear flood. The little island, on which grew the three acacias, lay at a short distance, looking like a bouquet rising from the lake. "How delightful it must be to live there," said Babette, who again felt the greatest wish to visit the island; and an opportunity offered to gratify her wish at once, for on the shore lay a boat, and the rope by which it was moored could be very easily loosened. They saw no one near, so they took possession of it without asking permission of any one, and Rudy could row very well. The oars divided the pliant water like the fins of a fish — that water which, with all its yielding softness, is so strong to bear and to carry, so mild and smiling when at rest, and yet so terrible in its destroying power. A white streak of foam followed in the wake of the boat, which, in a few minutes, carried them both to the little island, where they went on shore; but there was only just room enough for two to dance. Rudy swung Babette round two or three times; and then, hand-in-hand, they sat down on a little bench under the drooping acacia-tree, and looked into each other's eyes, while everything around them glowed in the rays of the setting sun.

The fir-tree forests on the mountains were covered with a purple hue like the heather bloom; and where the woods terminated, and the rocks became prominent, they looked almost transparent in the rich crimson glow of the evening sky. The surface of the lake was like a bed of pink rose-leaves.

As the evening advanced, the shadows fell upon the snow-capped mountains of Savoy painting them in colors of deep blue, while their topmost peaks glowed like red lava; and for a moment this light was reflected on the cultivated parts of the mountains, making them appear as if newly risen from the lap of earth, and giving to the snow-crested peak of the Dent du Midi the appearance of the full moon as it rises above the horizon.

Rudy and Babette felt that they had never seen the Alpine glow in such perfection before. "How very beautiful it is, and what happiness to be here!" exclaimed Babette.

"Earth has nothing more to bestow upon me," said Rudy; "an evening like this is worth a whole life. Often have I realized my good fortune, but never more than in this moment. I feel that if my existence were to end now, I should still have lived a happy life. What a glorious world this is; one day ends, and another begins even more beautiful than the last. How infinitely good God is, Babette!"

"I have such complete happiness in my heart," said she.

"Earth has no more to bestow," answered Rudy. And then came the sound of the evening bells, borne upon the breeze over the mountains of Switzerland and Savoy, while still, in the golden splendor of the west, stood the dark blue mountains of Jura.

"God grant you all that is brightest and best!" exclaimed Babette.

"He will," said Rudy. "He will to-morrow. To-morrow you will be wholly mine, my own sweet wife."

"The boat!" cried Babette, suddenly. The boat in which they were to return had broken loose, and was floating away from the island.

"I will fetch it back," said Rudy; throwing off his coat and boots, he sprang into the lake, and swam with strong efforts towards it.

The dark-blue water, from the glaciers of the mountains, was icy cold and very deep. Rudy gave but one glance into the water beneath; but in that one glance he saw a gold ring rolling, glittering, and sparkling before him. His engaged ring came into his mind; but this was larger, and spread into a glittering circle, in which appeared a clear glacier. Deep chasms yawned around it, the water-drops glittered as if lighted with blue flame, and tinkled like the chiming of church bells. In one moment he saw what would require many words to describe. Young hunters, and young maidens—men and women who had sunk in the deep chasms of the glaciers—stood before him here in lifelike forms, with eyes open and smiles on their lips; and far beneath them could be heard the chiming of the church bells of buried villages, where the villagers knelt beneath the vaulted arches of churches in which ice-blocks formed the organ pipes, and the mountain stream the music.

On the clear, transparent ground sat the Ice Maiden. She raised herself towards Rudy, and kissed his feet; and instantly a cold, deathly chill, like an electric shock, passed through his limbs. Ice or fire! It was impossible to tell, the shock was so instantaneous.

"Mine! mine!" sounded around him, and within him; "I kissed thee when thou wert a little child. I once kissed thee on the mouth, and now I have kissed thee from heel to toe; thou art wholly mine." And then he disappeared in the clear, blue water.

All was still. The church bells were silent; the last tone floated away with the last red glimmer on the evening clouds. "Thou art mine," sounded from the depths below; but from the heights above, from the eternal world, also sounded the words, "Thou art mine!" Happy was he thus to pass from life to life, from earth to heaven. A chord was loosened, and tones of sorrow burst forth. The icy kiss of death had overcome the perishable body; it was but the prelude before life's real drama could begin, the discord which was quickly lost in harmony. Do you think this a sad story? Poor Babette! for her it was unspeakable anguish.

The boat drifted farther and farther away. No one on the opposite shore knew that the betrothed pair had gone over to the little island. The clouds sunk as the evening drew on, and it became dark. Alone, in despair, she waited and trembled. The weather became fearful; flash after flash lighted up the mountains of Jura, Savoy, and Switzerland, while peals of thunder, that lasted for many minutes, rolled over her head. The lightning was so vivid that every single vine stem could be seen for a moment as distinctly as in the sunlight at noon-day; and then all was veiled in darkness. It flashed across the lake in winding, zigzag lines, lighting it up on all sides; while the echoes of the thunder grew louder and stronger. On land, the boats were all carefully drawn up on the beach, every living thing sought shelter, and at length the rain poured down in torrents.

"Where can Rudy and Babette be in this awful weather?" said the miller.

Poor Babette sat with her hands clasped, and her head bowed down, dumb with grief; she had ceased to weep and cry for help.

"In the deep water!" she said to herself; "far down he lies, as if beneath a glacier."

Deep in her heart rested the memory of what Rudy had told her of the death of his mother, and of his own recovery, even after he had been taken up as dead from the cleft in the glacier.

"Ah," she thought, "the Ice Maiden has him at last."

Suddenly there came a flash of lightning, as dazzling as the rays of the sun on the white snow. The lake rose for a moment like a shining glacier; and before Babette stood the pallid, glittering, majestic form of the Ice Maiden, and at her feet lay Rudy's corpse.

"Mine!" she cried, and again all was darkness around the heaving water.

"How cruel," murmured Babette; "why should he die just as the day of happiness drew near? Merciful God, enlighten my understanding, shed light upon my heart; for I cannot comprehend the arrangements of Thy providence, even while I bow to the decree of Thy almighty wisdom and power." And God did enlighten her heart.

A sudden flash of thought, like a ray of mercy, recalled her dream of the preceding night; all was vividly represented before her. She remembered the words and wishes she had then expressed, that what was best for her and for Rudy she might piously submit to.

"Woe is me," she said; "was the germ of sin really in my heart? was my dream a glimpse into the course of my future life, whose thread must be violently broken to rescue me from sin? Oh, miserable creature that I am!"

Thus she sat lamenting in the dark night, while through the deep stillness the last words of Rudy seemed to ring in her ears. "This earth has nothing more to bestow." Words, uttered in the fulness of joy, were again heard amid the depths of sorrow.

Years have passed since this sad event happened. The shores of the peaceful lake still smile in beauty. The vines are full of luscious grapes. Steamboats, with waving flags, pass swiftly by. Pleasure-boats, with their swelling sails, skim lightly over the watery mirror, like white butterflies. The railway is opened beyond Chillon, and goes far into the deep valley of the Rhone. At every station strangers alight with red-bound guide-books in their hands, in which they read of every place worth seeing. They visit Chillon, and observe on the lake the little island with the three acacias, and then read in their guide-book the story of the bridal pair who, in the year 1856, rowed over to it. They read that the two were missing till the next morning, when some people on the shore heard the despairing cries of the bride, and went to her assistance, and by her were told of the bridegroom's fate.

But the guide-book does not speak of Babette's quiet life afterwards with her father, not at the mill—strangers dwell there now—but in a pretty house in a row near the station. On many an evening she sits at her window, and looks out over the chestnut-trees to the snow-capped mountains on which Rudy once roamed. She looks at the Alpine glow in the evening sky, which is caused by the children of the sun retiring to rest on the mountain-tops; and again they breathe their song of the traveller whom the whirlwind could deprive of his cloak but not of his life. There is a rosy tint on the mountain snow, and there are rosy gleams in each heart in which dwells the thought, "God permits nothing to happen, which is not the best for us." But this is not often revealed to all, as it was revealed to Babette in her wonderful dream.

THE OLD CHURCH BELL

(WRITTEN FOR THE SCHILLER ALBUM)

IN the country of Wurtemburg, in Germany, where the acacias grow by the public road, where the apple-trees and the pear-trees in autumn bend to the earth with the weight of the precious fruit, lies the little town of Marbach. As is often the case with many of these towns, it is charmingly situated on the banks of the river Neckar, which rushes rapidly by, passing villages, old knights' castles, and green vineyards, till its waters mingle with those of the stately Rhine. It was late in the autumn; the vine-leaves still hung upon the branches of the vines, but they were already tinted with red and gold; heavy showers fell on the surrounding country, and the cold autumn wind blew sharp and strong. It was not at all pleasant weather for the poor. The days grew shorter and more gloomy, and, dark as it was out of doors in the open air, it was still darker within the small, old-fashioned houses of the village. The gable end of one of these houses faced the street, and with its small, narrow windows, presented a very mean appearance. The family who dwelt in it were also very poor and humble, but they treasured the fear of God in their innermost hearts. And now He was about to send them a child. It was the hour of the mother's sorrow, when there pealed forth from the church tower the sound of festive bells. In that solemn hour the sweet and joyous chiming filled the hearts of those in the humble dwelling with thankfulness and trust; and when, amidst these joyous sounds, a little son was born to them, the words of prayer and praise arose from their overflowing hearts, and their happiness seemed to ring out over town and country in the liquid tones of the church bells' chime. The little one, with its bright eyes and golden hair, had been welcomed joyously on that dark November day. Its parents kissed it lovingly, and the father wrote these words in the Bible, "On the tenth of November, 1759, God sent us a son." And a short time after, when the child had been baptized, the names he had received were added, "John Christopher Frederick."

And what became of the little lad? — the poor boy of the humble town of Marbach? Ah, indeed, there was no one who thought or supposed, not even the old church bell which had been the first to sound and chime for him, that he would be the first to sing the beautiful song of "The Bell." The boy grew apace, and the world advanced with him.

While he was yet a child, his parents removed from Marbach, and went to reside in another town; but their dearest friends remained behind at Marbach, and therefore sometimes the mother and her son would start on a fine day to pay a visit to the little town. The boy was at this time about six years old, and already knew a great many stories out of the Bible, and several religious psalms. While seated in the evening on his little cane-chair, he had often heard his father read from Gellert's fables, and sometimes from Klopstock's grand poem, "The Messiah." He and his sister, two years older than himself, had often wept scalding tears over the story of Him who suffered death on the cross for us all.

On his first visit to Marbach, the town appeared to have changed but very little, and it was not far enough away to be forgotten. The house, with its pointed gable, narrow windows, overhanging walls and stories, projecting one beyond another, looked just the same as in former times. But in the churchyard there were several new graves; and there also, in the grass, close by the wall, stood the old church bell! It had been taken down from its high position, in consequence of a crack in the metal which prevented it from ever chiming again, and a new bell now occupied its place. The mother and son were walking in the churchyard when they discovered the old bell, and they stood still to look at it. Then the mother reminded her little boy of what a useful bell this had been for many hundred years. It had chimed for weddings and for christenings; it had tolled for funerals, and to give the alarm in case of fire. With every event in the life of man the bell had made its voice heard. His mother also told him how the chiming of that old bell had once filled her heart with joy and confidence, and that in the midst of the sweet tones her child had been given to her. And the boy gazed on the large, old bell with the deepest interest. He bowed his head over it and kissed it, old, thrown away, and cracked as it was, and standing there amidst the grass and nettles. The boy never forgot what his mother told him, and the tones of the old bell reverberated in his heart till he reached manhood. In such sweet remembrance was the old bell cherished by the boy, who grew up in poverty to be tall and slender, with a freckled complexion and hair almost red; but his eyes were clear and blue as the deep sea, and what was his career to be? His career was to be good, and his future life enviable. We find him taking high honors at the military school in the division commanded by the member of a family high in position, and this was an honor, that is to say, good luck. He wore gaiters, stiff collars, and powdered hair, and by this he was recognized; and, indeed, he might be known by the word of command—"March! halt! front!"

The old church bell had long been quite forgotten, and no one imagined it would ever again be sent to the melting furnace to make it as it was before. No one could possibly have foretold this. Equally impossible would it have been to believe that the tones of the old bell still echoed in the heart of the boy from Marbach; or that one day they would ring out loud enough and strong enough to be heard all over the world. They had already been heard in the narrow space behind the school-wall, even above the deafening sounds of "March! halt! front!" They had chimed so loudly in the heart of the youngster, that he had sung them to his companions, and their tones resounded to the very borders of the country. He was not a free scholar in the military school, neither was he provided with clothes or food. But he had his number, and his own peg; for everything here was ordered like clockwork, which we all know is of the greatest utility—people get on so much better together when their position and duties are understood. It is by pressure that a jewel is stamped. The pressure of regularity and discipline here stamped the jewel, which in the future the world so well knew.

In the chief town of the province a great festival was being celebrated. The light streamed forth from thousands of lamps, and the rockets shot upwards towards the sky, filling the air with showers of colored fiery sparks. A record of this bright display will live in the memory of man, for through it the pupil in the military school was in tears and sorrow. He had dared to attempt to reach foreign territories unnoticed, and must therefore give up fatherland, mother, his dearest friends, all, or sink down into the stream of common life. The old church bell had still some comfort; it stood in the shelter of the church wall in Marbach, once so elevated, now quite forgotten. The wind roared around it, and could have readily related the story of its origin and of its sweet chimes, and the wind could also tell of him to whom he had brought fresh air when, in the woods of a neighboring country, he had sunk down exhausted with fatigue, with no other worldly possessions than hope for the future, and a written leaf from "Fiesco." The wind could have told that his only protector was an artist, who, by reading each leaf to him, made it plain; and that they amused themselves by playing at nine-pins together. The wind could also describe the pale fugitive, who, for weeks and months, lay in a wretched little road-side inn, where the landlord got drunk and raved, and where the merry-makers had it all their own way. And he, the pale fugitive, sang of the ideal.

For many heavy days and dark nights the heart must suffer to enable it to endure trial and temptation; yet, amidst it all, would the minstrel sing. Dark days and cold nights also passed over the old bell, and it noticed them not; but the bell in the man's heart felt it to be a gloomy time. What would become of this young man, and what would become of the old bell?

The old bell was, after a time, carried away to a greater distance than any one, even the warder in the bell tower, ever imagined; and the bell in the breast of the young man was heard in countries where his feet had never wandered. The tones went forth over the wide ocean to every part of the round world.

We will now follow the career of the old bell. It was, as we have said, carried far away from Marbach and sold as old copper; then sent to Bavaria to be melted down in a furnace. And then what happened?

In the royal city of Bavaria, many years after the bell had been removed from the tower and melted down, some metal was required for a monument in honor of one of the most celebrated characters which a German people or a German land could produce. And now we see how wonderfully things are ordered. Strange things sometimes happen in this world.

In Denmark, in one of those green islands where the foliage of the beech-woods rustles in the wind, and where many Huns' graves may be seen, was another poor boy born. He wore wooden shoes, and when his father worked in a ship-yard, the boy, wrapped up in an old worn-out shawl, carried his dinner to him every day. This poor child was now the pride of his country; for the sculptured marble, the work of his hands, had astonished the world.* To him was offered the honor of forming from the clay, a model of the figure of him whose name, "John Christopher Frederick," had been written by his father in the Bible. The bust was cast in bronze, and part of the metal used for this purpose was the old church bell, whose tones had died away from the memory of those at home and elsewhere. The metal, glowing with heat, flowed into the mould, and formed the head and bust of the statue which was unveiled in the square in front of the old castle. The statue represented in living, breathing reality, the form of him who was born in poverty, the boy from Marbach, the pupil of the military school, the fugitive who struggled against poverty and oppression, from the outer world; Germany's great and immortal poet, who sung of Switzerland's deliverer, William Tell, and of the heaven-inspired Maid of Orleans.

It was a beautiful sunny day; flags were waving from tower and roof in royal Stuttgart, and the church bells were ringing a joyous peal. One bell was silent; but it was illuminated by the bright sunshine which streamed from the head and bust of the renowned figure, of which it formed a part. On this day, just one hundred years had passed since the day on which the chiming of the old church bell at Marbach had filled the mother's heart with trust and joy—the day on which her child was born in poverty, and in a humble home; the same who, in after-years, became rich, became the noble woman-hearted poet, a blessing to the world—the glorious, the sublime, the immortal bard, John Christoper Frederick Schiller!

HOLGER DANSKE

IN Denmark there stands an old castle named Kronenburg, close by the Sound of Elsinore, where large ships, both English, Russian, and Prussian, pass by hundreds every day. And they salute the old castle with cannons,

---

*The Danish sculptor Thorwaldsen.

"Boom, boom," which is as if they said, "Good-day." And the cannons of the old castle answer "Boom," which means "Many thanks." In winter no ships sail by, for the whole Sound is covered with ice as far as the Swedish coast, and has quite the appearance of a high-road. The Danish and the Swedish flags wave, and Danes and Swedes say, "Good-day," and "Thank you" to each other, not with cannons, but with a friendly shake of the hand; and they exchange white bread and biscuits with each other, because foreign articles taste the best.

But the most beautiful sight of all is the old castle of Kronenburg, where Holger Danske sits in the deep, dark cellar, into which no one goes. He is clad in iron and steel, and rests his head on his strong arm; his long beard hangs down upon the marble table, into which it has become firmly rooted; he sleeps and dreams, but in his dreams he sees everything that happens in Denmark. On each Christmas-eve an angel comes to him and tells him that all he has dreamed is true, and that he may go to sleep again in peace, as Denmark is not yet in any real danger; but should danger ever come, then Holger Danske will rouse himself, and the table will burst asunder as he draws out his beard. Then he will come forth in his strength, and strike a blow that shall sound in all the countries of the world.

An old grandfather sat and told his little grandson all this about Holger Danske, and the boy knew that what his grandfather told him must be true. As the old man related this story, he was carving an image in wood to represent Holger Danske, to be fastened to the prow of a ship; for the old grandfather was a carver in wood, that is, one who carved figures for the heads of ships, according to the names given to them. And now he had carved Holger Danske, who stood there erect and proud, with his long beard, holding in one hand his broad battle-axe, while with the other he leaned on the Danish arms. The old grandfather told the little boy a great deal about Danish men and women who had distinguished themselves in olden times, so that he fancied he knew as much even as Holger Danske himself, who, after all, could only dream; and when the little fellow went to bed, he thought so much about it that he actually pressed his chin against the counterpane, and imagined that he had a long beard which had become rooted to it. But the old grandfather remained sitting at his work and carving away at the last part of it, which was the Danish arms. And when he had finished he looked at the whole figure, and thought of all he had heard and read, and what he had that evening related to his little grandson. Then he nodded his head, wiped his spectacles and put them on, and said, "Ah, yes; Holger Danske will not appear in my lifetime, but the boy who is in bed there may very likely live to see him when the event really comes to pass." And the old grandfather nodded again; and the more he looked at Holger Danske, the more satisfied he felt that he had carved a good image of him. It seemed to glow with the color of life; the armor glittered like iron and steel. The hearts in the Danish arms grew more and more red; while the lions, with gold crowns on their heads, were leaping up.* "That is the most beautiful coat of arms in the world," said the old man. "The lions represent strength; and the hearts, gentleness and love." And as he gazed on the uppermost lion, he thought of King Canute, who chained great England to Denmark's throne; and he looked at

*The Danish arms consists of three lions between nine hearts.

the second lion, and thought of Waldemar, who untied Denmark and conquered the Vandals. The third lion reminded him of Margaret, who united Denmark, Sweden, and Norway. But when he gazed at the red hearts, their colors glowed more deeply, even as flames, and his memory followed each in turn. The first led him to a dark, narrow prison, in which sat a prisoner, a beautiful woman, daughter of Christian the Fourth, Eleanor Ulfeld,† and the flame became a rose on her bosom, and its blossoms were not more pure than the heart of this noblest and best of all Danish women. "Ah, yes; that is indeed a noble heart in the Danish arms," said the grandfather. and his spirit followed the second flame, which carried him out to sea,‡ where cannons roared and the ships lay shrouded in smoke, and the flaming heart attached itself to the breast of Hvitfeldt in the form of the ribbon of an order, as he blew himself and his ship into the air in order to save the fleet. And the third flame led him to Greenland's wretched huts, where the preacher, Hans Egede,§ ruled with love in every word and action. The flame was as a star on his breast, and added another heart to the Danish arms. And as the old grandfather's spirit followed the next hovering flame, he knew whither it would lead him. In a peasant woman's humble room stood Frederick the Sixth,** writing his name with chalk on the beam. The flame trembled on his breast and in his heart, and it was in the peasant's room that his heart became one for the Danish arms. The old grandfather wiped his eyes, for he had known King Frederick, with his silvery locks and his honest blue eyes, and had lived for him, and he folded his hands and remained for some time silent. Then his daughter came to him and said it was getting late, that he ought to rest for a while, and that the supper was on the table.

"What you have been carving is very beautiful, grandfather," said she. "Holger Danske and the old coat of arms; it seems to me as if I have seen the face somewhere."

"No, that is impossible," replied the old grandfather; "but *I* have seen it, and I have tried to carve it in wood, as I have retained it in my memory. It was a long time ago, while the English fleet lay in the roads, on the second of April,†† when we showed that we were true, ancient Danes. I was on board the *Denmark,* in Steene Bille's squadron; I had a man by my side whom even the cannon balls seemed to fear. He sung old songs in a merry voice, and fired

---

†This highly-gifted princess was the wife of Corfitz Ulfeld; he was accused of high treason, and Eleanor, whose only fault was the truest love to her unhappy husband, was compelled to remain for twenty-two years in a miserable dungeon, till the death of her persecutor, Queen Sophia Amelia.

‡In the naval battle, which took place in Kjöge Bay in 1710, between the Danes and the Swedes, Hvitfeldt's ship, the *Danebrog,* took fire. To save the town of Kjöge, and the Danish fleet which were being driven by the wind towards his burning ship, he blew up his vessel, with himself and his whole crew.

§Hans Egede went to Greenland in 1721, and worked there for fifteen long years amid incredible privations and difficulties. He not only spread the Christian religion, but was himself the pattern of a noble Christian.

**Once, while on a journey to the western coast of Jutland, the king came to the cottage of an old woman. As he was leaving, she ran after him, and asked him to write his name on a beam as a remembrance of his visit. The king turned back and complied with her request. Through his whole life he interested himself for the peasantry, and on that account it was that the Danish peasants begged to be allowed to carry the coffin to the royal vault at Roeskilde, four Danish miles from Copenhagen.

††On the second of April, 1801, occurred the sanguinary naval engagement between the Danes and the English, under Sir Hyde Parker and Nelson.

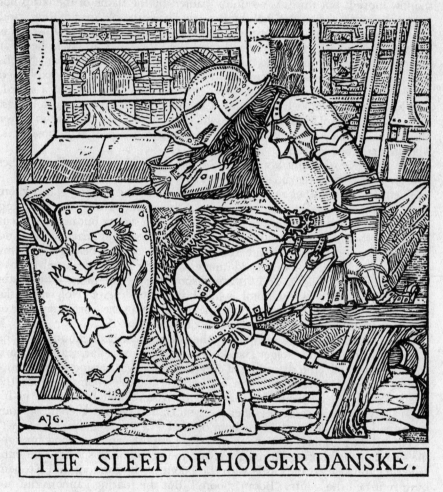

THE SLEEP OF HOLGER DANSKE.

HOLGER DANSKE

and fought as if he were something more than a man. I still remember his face, but from whence he came, or whither he went, I know not; no one knows. I have often thought it might have been Holger Danske himself, who had swam down to us from Kronenburg to help us in the hour of danger. That was my idea, and there stands his likeness."

The wooden figure threw a gigantic shadow on the wall, and even on part of the ceiling; it seemed as if the real Holger Danske stood behind it, for the shadow moved; but this was no doubt caused by the flame of the lamp not burning steadily. Then the daughter-in-law kissed the old grandfather, and led him to a large arm-chair by the table; and she, and her husband, who was the son of the old man and the father of the little boy who lay in bed, sat down to supper with him. And the old grandfather talked of the Danish lions and the Danish hearts, emblems of strength and gentleness, and explained quite clearly that there is another strength than that which lies in a sword, and he pointed to a shelf where lay a number of old books, and amongst them a collection of Holberg's plays, which are much read and are so clever and amusing that it is easy to fancy we have known the people of those days, who are described in them.

"He knew how to fight also," said the old man; "for he lashed the follies and prejudices of people during his whole life."

Then the grandfather nodded to a place above the looking-glass, where hung an almanac, with a representation of the Round Tower* upon it, and said "Tycho Brahe was another of those who used a sword, but not one to cut into the flesh and bone, but to make the way of the stars of heaven clear, and plain to be understood. And then *he* whose father belonged to my calling, —yes, he, the son of the old image-carver, he whom we ourselves have seen, with his silvery locks and his broad shoulders, whose name is known in all lands; —yes, he was a sculptor, while I am only a carver. Holger Danske can appear in marble, so that people in all countries of the world may hear of the strength of Denmark. Now let us drink the health of Bertel."†

But the little boy in bed saw plainly the old castle of Kronenburg, and the Sound of Elsinore, and Holger Danske, far down in the cellar, with his beard rooted to the table, and dreaming of everything that was passing above him.

And Holger Danske did dream of the little humble room in which the image-carver sat; he heard all that had been said, and he nodded in his dream, saying, "Ah, yes, remember me, you Danish people, keep me in your memory, I will come to you in the hour of need."

The bright morning light shone over Kronenburg, and the wind brought the sound of the hunting-horn across from the neighboring shores. The ships sailed by and saluted the castle with the boom of the cannon, and Kronenburg returned the salute, "Boom, boom." But the roaring cannons did not awake Holger Danske, for they meant only "Good morning," and "Thank you." They must fire in another fashion before he awakes; but wake he will, for there is energy yet in Holger Danske.

*The Astronomical Observatory at Copenhagen.
†Bertel Thorwaldsen.

THE SUNBEAM AND THE CAPTIVE

IT is autumn. We stand on the ramparts, and look out over the sea. We look at the numerous ships, and at the Swedish coast on the opposite side of the sound, rising far above the surface of the waters which mirror the glow of the evening sky. Behind us the wood is sharply defined; mighty trees surround us, and the yellow leaves flutter down from the branches. Below, at the foot of the wall, stands a gloomy looking building enclosed in palisades. The space between is dark and narrow, but still more dismal must it be behind the iron gratings in the wall which cover the narrow loopholes or windows, for in these dungeons the most depraved of the criminals are confined. A ray of the setting sun shoots into the bare cells of one of the captives, for God's sun shines upon the evil and the good. The hardened criminal casts an impatient look at the bright ray. Then a little bird flies towards the grating, for birds twitter to the just as well as to the unjust. He only cries, "Tweet, tweet," and then perches himself near the grating, flutters his wings, pecks a feather from one of them, puffs himself out, and sets his feathers on end round his breast and throat. The bad, chained man looks at him, and a more gentle expression comes into his hard face. In his breast there rises a thought which he himself cannot rightly analyze, but the thought has some connection with the sunbeam, with the bird, and with the scent of violets, which grow luxuriantly in spring at the foot of the wall. Then there comes the sound of the hunter's horn, merry and full. The little bird starts, and flies away, the sunbeam gradually vanishes, and again there is darkness in the room and in the heart of that bad man. Still the sun has shone into that heart, and the twittering of the bird has touched it.

Sound on, ye glorious strains of the hunter's horn; continue your stirring tones, for the evening is mild, and the surface of the sea, heaving slowly and calmly, is smooth as a mirror.

CHILDREN'S PRATTLE

AT a rich merchant's house there was a children's party, and the children of rich and great people were there. The merchant was a learned man, for his father had sent him to college, and he had passed his examination. His father had been at first only a cattle dealer, but always honest and industrious, so that he had made money, and his son, the merchant, had managed to increase his store. Clever as he was, he had also a heart; but there was less said of his heart than of his money. All descriptions of people visited at the merchant's house, well born, as well as intellectual, and some who possessed neither of these recommendations.

Now it was a children's party, and there was children's prattle, which always is spoken freely from the heart. Among them was a beautiful little girl, who was terribly proud; but this had been taught her by the servants, and not by her parents, who were far too sensible people.

Her father was groom of the Chambers, which is a high office at court, and she knew it. "I am a child of the court," she said; now she might just as well have been a child of the cellar, for no one can help his birth; and then she told the other children that she was well-born, and said that no one who was not well-born could rise in the world. It was no use to read and be industrious, for if a person was not well-born, he could never achieve anything. "And those whose names end with 'sen,' " said she, "can never be anything at all. We must put our arms akimbo, and make the elbow quite pointed, so as to keep these 'sen' people at a great distance." And then she stuck out her pretty little arms, and made the elbows quite pointed, to show how it was to be done; and her little arms were very pretty, for she was a sweet-looking child.

But the little daughter of the merchant became very angry at this speech, for her father's name was Petersen, and she knew that the name ended in "sen," and therefore she said as proudly as she could, "But my papa can buy a hundred dollars' worth of bonbons, and give them away to children. Can your papa do that?"

"Yes; and my papa," said the little daughter of the editor of a paper, "my papa can put your papa and everybody's papa into the newspaper. All sorts of people are afraid of him, my mamma says, for he can do as he likes with the paper." And the little maiden looked exceedingly proud, as if she had been a real princess, who may be expected to look proud.

But outside the door, which stood ajar, was a poor boy, peeping through the crack of the door. He was of such a lowly station that he had not been allowed even to enter the room. He had been turning the spit for the cook, and she had given him permission to stand behind the door and peep in at the well-dressed children, who were having such a merry time within; and for him that was a great deal. "Oh, if I could be one of them," thought he, and then he heard what was said about names, which was quite enough to make him more unhappy. His parents at home had not even a penny to spare to buy a newspaper, much less could they write in one; and worse than all, his father's name, and of course his own, ended in "sen," and therefore he could never turn out well, which was a very sad thought. But after all, he had been born into the world, and the station of life had been chosen for him, therefore he must be content.

And this is what happened on that evening.

*   *   *   *   *   *

Many years passed, and most of the children became grown-up persons.

There stood a splendid house in the town, filled with all kinds of beautiful and valuable objects. Everybody wished to see it, and people even came in form the country round to be permitted to view the treasures it contained.

Which of the children whose prattle we have described, could call this house his own? One would suppose it very easy to guess. No, no; it is not so very easy. The house belonged to the poor little boy who had stood on that night behind the door. He had really become something great, although his name ended in "sen," — for it was Thorwaldsen.

And the three other children — the children of good birth, of money, and of intellectual pride, — well, they were respected and honored in the world, for they had been well provided for by birth and position, and they had no cause to reproach themselves with what they had thought and spoken on that evening long ago, for, after all, it was mere *"children's prattle."*

THE SILVER SHILLING

THERE was once a shilling, which came forth from the mint springing and shouting, "Hurrah! now I am going out into the wide world." And truly it did go out into the wide world. The children held it with warm hands, the miser with a cold and convulsive grasp, and the old people turned it about, goodness knows how many times, while the young people soon allowed it to roll away from them. The shilling was made of silver, it contained very little copper, and considered itself quite out in the world when it had been circulated for a year in the country in which it had been coined. One day, it really did go out into the world, for it belonged to a gentleman who was about to travel in foreign lands. This gentleman was not aware that the shilling lay at the bottom of his purse when he started, till he one day found it between his fingers. "Why," cried he, "here is a shilling from home; well, it must go on its travels with me now!" and the shilling jumped and rattled for joy, when it was put back again into the purse.

Here it lay among a number of foreign companions, who were always coming and going, one taking the place of another, but the shilling from home was always put back, and had to remain in the purse, which was certainly a mark of distinction. Many weeks passed, during which the shilling had travelled a long distance in the purse, without in the least knowing where he was. He had found out that the other coins were French and Italian; and one coin said they were in this town, and another said they were in that, but the shilling was unable to make out or imagine what they meant. A man certainly cannot see much of the world if he is tied up in a bag, and this was really the shilling's fate. But one day, as he was lying in the purse, he noticed that it was not quite closed, and so he slipped near to the opening to have a little peep into society. He certainly had not the least idea of what would follow, but he was curious, and curiosity often brings its own punishment. In his eagerness, he came so near the edge of the purse that he slipped out into the pocket of the trousers; and when, in the evening, the purse was taken out, the shilling was left behind in the corner to which it had fallen. As the clothes were being carried into the hall, the shilling fell out on the floor, unheard and unnoticed by any one. The next morning the clothes were taken back to the room, the gentleman put them on, and started on his journey again; but the shilling remained behind on the floor. After a time it was found, and being considered a good coin, was placed with three other coins. "Ah," thought the shilling, "this is pleasant; I shall now see the world, become acquainted with other people, and learn other customs."

"Do you call that a shilling?" said some one the next moment. "That is not a genuine coin of the country, — it is false; it is good for nothing."

Now begins the story as it was afterwards related by the shilling himself. "'False! good for nothing!' said he. That remark went through and through me like a dagger. I knew that I had a true ring, and that mine was a genuine stamp. These people must at all events be wrong, or they could not mean me. But yes, I was the one they called 'false, and good for nothing.'

"'Then I must pay it away in the dark,' said the man who had received me. So I was to be got rid of in the darkness, and be again insulted in broad daylight.

" 'False! good for nothing!' Oh, I must contrive to get lost, thought I. And I trembled between the fingers of the people every time they tried to pass me off slyly as a coin of the country. Ah! unhappy shilling that I was! Of what use were my silver, my stamp, and my real value here, where all these qualities were worthless. In the eyes of the world, a man is valued just according to the opinion formed of him. It must be a shocking thing to have a guilty conscience, and to be sneaking about on account of wicked deeds. As for me, innocent as I was, I could not help shuddering before their eyes whenever they brought me out, for I knew I should be thrown back again up the table as a false pretender. At length I was paid away to a poor old woman, who received me as wages for a hard day's work. But she could not again get rid of me; no one would take me. I was to the woman a most unlucky shilling. 'I am positively obliged to pass this shilling to somebody,' said she; 'I cannot, with the best intentions, lay by a bad shilling. The rich baker shall have it, — he can bear the loss better than I can. But, after all, it is not a right thing to do.'

" 'Ah!' sighed I to myself, 'am I also to be a burden on the conscience of this poor woman? Am I then in my old days so completely changed?' The woman offered me to the rich baker, but he knew the current money too well, and as soon as he received me he threw me almost in the woman's face. She could get no bread for me, and I felt quite grieved to the heart that I should be cause of so much trouble to another, and be treated as a cast-off coin. I who, in my young days, felt so joyful in the certainty of my own value, and knew so well that I bore a genuine stamp. I was as sorrowful now as a poor shilling can be when nobody will have him. The woman took me home again with her, and looking at me very earnestly, she said, 'No, I will not try to deceive any one with thee again. I will bore a hole through thee, that everyone may know that thou art a false and worthless thing; and yet, why should I do that? Very likely thou art a lucky shilling. A thought has just struck me that it is so, and I believe it. Yes, I will make a hole in the shilling,' said she, 'and run a string through it, and then give it to my neighbor's little one to hang round her neck, as a lucky shilling.' So she drilled a hole through me.

"It is really not at all pleasant to have a hole bored through one, but we can submit to a great deal when it is done with a good intention. A string was drawn through the hole, and I became a kind of medal. They hung me round the neck of a little child, and the child laughed at me and kissed me, and I rested for one whole night on the warm, innocent breast of a child.

"In the morning the child's mother took me between her fingers, and had certain thoughts about me, which I very soon found out. First, she looked for a pair of scissors, and cut the string.

" 'Lucky shilling!' said she, 'certainly this is what I mean to try.' Then she laid me in vinegar till I became quite green, and after that she filled up the hole with cement, rubbed me a little to brighten me up, and went out in the twilight hour to the lottery collector, to buy herself a ticket, with a shilling that should bring luck. How everything seemed to cause me trouble. The lottery collector pressed me so hard that I thought I should crack. I had been called false, I had been thrown away, — that I knew; and there were many shillings and coins with inscriptions and stamps of all kinds lying about. I well knew how proud they were, so I avoided them from very shame. With the collector were several men who seemed to have a great deal to do, so I fell unnoticed into a chest, among several other coins.

THE SILVER SHILLING

"Whether the lottery ticket gained a prize, I know not; but this I know, that in a very few days after, I was recognized as a bad shilling, and laid aside. Everything that happened seemed always to add to my sorrow. Even if a man has a good character, it is of no use for him to deny what is said of him, for he is not considered an impartial judge of himself.

"A year passed, and in this way I had been changed from hand to hand; always abused, always looked at with displeasure, and trusted by no one; but I trusted in myself, and had no confidence in the world. Yes, that was a very dark time.

"At length one day I was passed to a traveller, a foreigner, the very same who had brought me away from home; and he was simple and true-hearted enough to take me for current coin. But would he also attempt to pass me? and should I again hear the outcry, 'False! good-for-nothing!' The traveller examined me attentively, 'I took thee for good coin,' said he; then suddenly a smile spread all over his face. I have never seen such a smile on any other face as on his. 'Now this is singular,' said he, 'it is a coin from my own country; a good, true, shilling from home. Some one has bored a hole through it, and people have no doubt called it false. How curious that it should come into my hands. I will take it home with me to my own house.'

"Joy thrilled through me when I heard this. I had been once more called a good, honest shilling, and I was to go back to my own home, where each and all would recognize me, and know that I was made of good silver, and bore a true, genuine stamp. I should have been glad in my joy to throw out sparks of fire, but it has never at any time been my nature to sparkle. Steel can do so, but not silver. I was wrapped up in fine, white paper, that I might not mix with the other coins and be lost; and on special occasions, when people from my own country happened to be present, I was brought forward and spoken of very kindly. They said I was very interesting, and it was really quite worth while to notice that those who are interesting have often not a single word to say for themselves.

"At length I reached home. All my cares were at an end. Joy again overwhelmed me; for was I not good silver, and had I not a genuine stamp? I had no more insults or disappointments to endure; although, indeed, there was a hole through me, as if I were false; but suspicions are nothing when a man is really true, and every one should persevere in acting honestly, for all will be made right in time. That is my firm belief," said the shilling.

THE OLD GRAVE-STONE

In a house, with a large courtyard, in a provincial town, at that time of the year in which people say the evenings are growing longer, a family circle were gathered together at their old home. A lamp burned on the table, although the weather was mild and warm, and the long curtains hung down before the open windows, and without the moon shone brightly in the dark-blue sky.

But they were not talking of the moon, but of a large, old stone that lay below in the courtyard not very far from the kitchen door. The maids often laid the clean copper saucepans and kitchen vessels on this stone, that they

THE OLD GRAVE-STONE

might dry in the sun, and the children were fond of playing on it. It was, in fact, an old grave-stone.

"Yes," said the master of the house, "I believe the stone came from the graveyard of the old church of the convent which was pulled down, and the pulpit, the monuments, and the grave-stones sold. My father bought the latter; most of them were cut in two and used for paving-stones, but that one stone was preserved whole, and laid in the courtyard."

"Any one can see that it is a grave-stone," said the eldest of the children; "the representation of an hour-glass and part of the figure of an angel can still be traced, but the inscription beneath is quite worn out, excepting the name 'Preben,' and a large 'S' close by it, and a little farther down the name of 'Martha' can be easily read. But nothing more, and even that cannot be seen unless it has been raining, or when we have washed the stone."

"Dear me! how singular. Why that must be the grave-stone of Preben Schwane and his wife."

The old man who said this looked old enough to be the grandfather of all present in the room

"Yes," he continued, "these people were among the last who were buried in the churchyard of the old convent. They were a very worthy old couple, I can remember them well in the days of my boyhood. Every one knew them, and they were esteemed by all. They were the oldest residents in the town, and people said they possessed a ton of gold, yet they were always very plainly dressed, in the coarsest stuff, but with linen of the purest whiteness. Preben and Martha were a fine old couple, and when they both sat on the bench, at the top of the steep stone steps, in front of their house, with the branches of the linden-tree waving above them, and nodded in a gentle, friendly way to passers by, it really made one feel quite happy. They were very good to the poor; they fed them and clothed them, and in their benevolence there was judgment as well as true Christianity. The old woman died first; that day is still quite vividly before my eyes. I was a little boy, and had accompanied my father to the old man's house. Martha had fallen into the sleep of death just as we arrived there. The corpse lay in a bedroom, near to the one in which we sat, and the old man was in great distress, and weeping like a child. He spoke to my father, and to a few neighbors who were there, of how lonely he should feel now she was gone, and how good and true she, his dead wife, had been during the number of years that they had passed through life together, and how they had become acquainted, and learnt to love each other. I was, as I have said, a boy, and only stood by and listened to what the others said; but it filled me with a strange emotion to listen to the old man, and to watch how the color rose in his cheeks as he spoke of the days of their courtship, of how beautiful she was, and how many little tricks he had been guilty of, that he might meet her. And then he talked of his wedding-day; and his eyes brightened, and he seemed to be carried back, by his words, to that joyful time. And yet there she was, lying in the next room, dead — an old woman, and he was an old man, speaking of the days of hope, long passed away. Ah, well, so it is; then I was but a child, and now I am old, as old as Preben Schwane then was. Time passes away, and all things changed. I can remember quite well the day on which she was buried, and how Old Preben walked close behind the coffin.

"A few years before this time the old couple had had their grave-stone prepared, with an inscription and their names, but not the date. In the evening the stone was taken to the churchyard, and laid on the grave. A year later it was taken up, that Old Preben might be laid by the side of his wife. They did not leave behind them wealth, they left behind them far less than people had believed they possessed; what there was went to families distantly related to them, of whom, till then, no one had ever heard. The old house, with its balcony of wickerwork, and the bench at the top of the high steps, under the lime-tree, was considered, by the road-inspectors, too old and rotten to be left standing. Afterwards, when the same fate befell the convent church, and the graveyard was destroyed, the grave-stone of Preben and Martha, like everything else, was sold to whoever would buy it. And so it happened that this stone was not cut in two as many others had been, but now lies in the courtyard below, a scouring block for the maids, and a playground for the children. The paved street now passes over the resting place of Old Preben and his wife; no one thinks of them any more now."

And the old man who had spoken of all this shook his head mournfully, and said, "Forgotten! Ah, yes, everything will be forgotten!" And then the conversation turned on other matters.

But the youngest child in the room, a boy, with large, earnest eyes, mounted upon a chair behind the window curtains, and looked out into the yard, where the moon was pouring a flood of light on the old grave-stone, — the stone that had always appeared to him so dull and flat, but which lay there now like a great leaf out of a book of history. All that the boy had heard of Old Preben and his wife seemed clearly defined on the stone, and as he gazed on it, and glanced at the clear, bright moon shining in the pure air, it was as if the light of God's countenance beamed over His beautiful world.

"Forgotten! Everything will be forgotten!" still echoed through the room, and in the same moment an invisible spirit whispered to the heart of the boy, "Preserve carefully the seed that has been entrusted to thee, that it may grow and thrive. Guard it well. Through thee, my child, shall the obliterated inscription on the old, weather-beaten grave-stone go forth to future generations in clear, golden characters. The old pair shall again wander through the streets arm-in-arm, or sit with their fresh, healthy cheeks on the bench under the lime-tree, and smile and nod at rich and poor. The seed of this hour shall ripen in the course of years into a beautiful poem. The beautiful and the good are never forgotten, they live always in story or in song."

THE LOVELIEST ROSE IN THE WORLD

THERE lived once a great queen, in whose garden were found at all seasons the most splendid flowers, and from every land in the world. She specially loved roses, and therefore she possessed the most beautiful varieties of this flower, from the wild hedge-rose, with its apple-scented leaves, to the splendid Provence rose. They grew near the shelter of the walls, wound themselves round columns and window-frames, crept along passages and over the ceilings of the halls. They were of every fragrance and color.

But care and sorrow dwelt within these halls; the queen lay upon a sick bed, and the doctors declared that she must die. "There is still one thing that could save her," said one of the wisest among them. "Bring her the loveliest rose in the world; one which exhibits the purest and brightest love, and if it is brought to her before her eyes close, she will not die."

Then from all parts came those who brought roses that bloomed in every garden, but they were not the right sort. The flower must be one from the garden of love; but which of the roses there showed forth the highest and purest love? The poets sang of this rose, the loveliest in the world, and each named one which he considered worthy of that title; and intelligence of what was required was sent far and wide to every heart that beat with love; to every class, age, and condition.

"No one has yet named the flower," said the wise man. "No one has pointed out the spot where it blooms in all its splendor. It is not a rose from the coffin of Romeo and Juliet, or from the grave of Walburg, though these roses will live in everlasting song. It is not one of the roses which sprouted forth from the blood-stained fame of Winkelreid. The blood which flows from the breast of a hero who dies for his country is sacred, and his memory is sweet, and no rose can be redder than the blood which flows from his veins. Neither is it the magic flower of Science, to obtain which wondrous flower a man devotes many an hour of his fresh young life in sleepless nights, in a lonely chamber."

"I know where it blooms," said a happy mother, who came with her lovely child to the bedside of the queen. "I know where the loveliest rose in the world is. It is seen on the blooming cheeks of my sweet child, when it expresses the pure and holy love of infancy; when refreshed by sleep it opens its eyes, and smiles upon me with childlike affection."

"This is a lovely rose," said the wise man; "but there is one still more lovely."

"Yes, one far more lovely," said one of the women. "I have seen it, and a loftier and purer rose does not bloom. But it was white, like the leaves of a blush-rose. I saw it on the cheeks of the queen. She had taken off her golden crown, and through the long, dreary night, she carried her sick child in her arms. She wept over it, kissed it, and prayed for it as only a mother can pray in that hour of her anguish."

"Holy and wonderful in its might is the white rose of grief, but it is not the one we seek."

"No; the loveliest rose in the world I saw at the Lord's table," said the good old bishop. "I saw it shine as if an angel's face had appeared. A young maiden knelt at the altar, and renewed the vows made at her baptism; and there were white roses and red roses on the blushing cheeks of that young girl. She looked up to heaven with all the purity and love of her young spirit, in all the expression of the highest and purest love."

"May she be blessed!" said the wise man: "but no one has yet named the loveliest rose in the world."

Then there came into the room a child — the queen's little son. Tears stood in his eyes, and glistened on his cheeks; he carried a great book and the binding was of velvet, with silver clasps. "Mother," cried the little boy; "only hear what I have read." And the child seated himself by the bedside, and read from the book of Him who suffered death on the cross to save all men, even

THE LOVELIEST ROSE IN THE WORLD

those who are yet unborn. He read, "Greater love hath no man than this," and as he read a roseate hue spread over the cheeks of the queen, and her eyes became so enlightened and clear, that she saw from the leaves of the book a lovely rose spring forth, a type of Him who shed His blood on the cross.

"I see it," she said. "He who beholds this, the loveliest rose on earth, shall never die."

A LEAF FROM HEAVEN

HIGH up in the clear, pure air flew an angel, with a flower plucked from the garden of heaven. As he was kissing the flower a very little leaf fell from it and sunk down into the soft earth in the middle of a wood. It immediately took root, sprouted, and sent out shoots among the other plants.

"What a ridiculous little shoot!" said one. "No one will recognize it; not even the thistle nor the stinging-nettle."

"It must be a kind of garden plant," said another; and so they sneered and despised the plant as a thing from a garden.

"Where are you coming?" said the tall thistles whose leaves were all armed with thorns. "It is stupid nonsense to allow yourself to shoot out in this way; we are not here to support you."

Winter came, and the plant was covered with snow, but the snow glittered over it as if it had sunshine beneath as well as above.

When spring came, the plant appeared in full bloom: a more beautiful object than any other plant in the forest. And now the professor of botany presented himself, one who could explain his knowledge in black and white. He examined and tested the plant, but it did not belong to his system of botany, nor could he possibly find out to what class it did belong. "It must be some degenerate species," said he; "I do not know it, and it is not mentioned in any system."

"Not known in any system!" repeated the thistles and the nettles.

The large trees which grew round it saw the plant and heard the remarks, but they said not a word either good or bad, which is the wisest plan for those who are ignorant.

There passed through the forest a poor innocent girl; her heart was pure, and her understanding increased by her faith. Her chief inheritance had been an old Bible, which she read and valued. From its pages she heard the voice of God speaking to her, and telling her to remember what was said of Joseph's brethren when persons wished to injure her. "They imagined evil in their hearts, but God turned it to good." If we suffer wrongfully, if we are misunderstood or despised, we must think of Him who was pure and holy, and who prayed for those who nailed Him to the cross, "Father forgive them, for they know not what they do."

The girl stood still before the wonderful plant, for the green leaves exhaled a sweet and refreshing fragrance, and the flowers glittered and sparkled in the sunshine like colored flames, and the harmony of sweet sounds lingered round them as if each concealed within itself a deep fount of melody, which thousands of years could not exhaust. With pious gratitude the girl looked

A LEAF FROM HEAVEN

upon this glorious work of God, and bent down over one of the branches, that she might examine the flower and inhale the sweet perfume. Then a light broke in on her mind, and her heart expanded. Gladly would she have plucked a flower, but she could not overcome her reluctance to break one off. She knew it would so soon fade; so she took only a single green leaf, carried it home, and laid it in her Bible, where it remained ever green, fresh, and unfading. Between the pages of the Bible it still lay when, a few weeks afterwards, that Bible was laid under the young girl's head in her coffin. A holy calm rested on her face, as if the earthly remains bore the impress of the truth that she now stood in the presence of God.

In the forest the wonderful plant still continued to bloom till it grew and became almost a tree, and all the birds of passage bowed themselves before it.

"That plant is a foreigner, no doubt," said the thistles and the burdocks. "We can never conduct ourselves like that in this country." And the black forest snails actually spat at the flower.

Then came the swineherd; he was collecting thistles and shrubs to burn them for the ashes. He pulled up the wonderful plant, roots and all, and placed it in his bundle. "This will be as useful as any," he said; so the plant was carried away.

Not long after, the king of the country suffered from the deepest melancholy. He was diligent and industrious, but employment did him no good. They read deep and learned books to him, and then the lightest and most trifling that could be found, but all to no purpose. Then they applied for advice to one of the wise men of the world, and he sent them a message to say that there was one remedy which would relieve and cure him, and that it was a plant of heavenly origin which grew in the forest in the king's own dominions. The messenger described the flower so that is appearance could not be mistaken.

Then said the swineherd, "I am afraid I carried this plant away from the forest in my bundle, and it has been burnt to ashes long ago. But I did not know any better."

"You did not know any better! Ignorance upon ignorance indeed!"

The poor swineherd took these words to heart, for they were addressed to him; he knew not that there were others who were equally ignorant. Not even a leaf of the plant could be found. There was one, but it lay in the coffin of the dead; no one knew anything about it.

Then the king, in his melancholy, wandered out to the spot in the wood. "Here is where the plant stood," he said; "it is a sacred place." Then he ordered that the place should be surrounded with a golden railing, and a sentry stationed near it.

The botanical professor wrote a long treatise about the heavenly plant, and for this he was loaded with gold, which improved the position of himself and his family.

And this part is really the most pleasant part of the story. For the plant had disappeared, and the king remained as melancholy and sad as ever, but the sentry said he had always been so.

THE GIRL WHO TROD ON THE LOAF

THERE was once a girl who trod on a loaf to avoid soiling her shoes, and the misfortunes that happened to her in consequence are well known. Her name was Ingé; she was a poor child, but proud and presuming, and with a bad and cruel disposition. When quite a little child she would delight in catching flies, and tearing off their wings, so as to make creeping things of them. When older, she would take cockchafers and beetles, and stick pins through them. Then she pushed a green leaf, or a little scrap of paper towards their feet, and when the poor creatures would seize it and hold it fast, and turn over and over in their struggles to get free from the pin, she would say, "The cockchafer is reading; see how he turns over the leaf." She grew worse instead of better with years, and, unfortunately, she was pretty, which caused her to be excused, when she should have been sharply reproved.

"Your headstrong will requires severity to conquer it," her mother often said to her. "As a little child you used to trample on my apron, but one day I fear you will trample on my heart." And, alas! this fear was realized.

Ingé was taken to the house of some rich people, who lived at a distance, and who treated her as their own child, and dressed her so fine that her pride and arrogance increased.

When she had been there about a year, her patroness said to her, "You ought to go, for once, and see your parents, Ingé."

So Ingé started to go and visit her parents; but she only wanted to show herself in her native place, that the people might see how fine she was. She reached the entrance of the village, and saw the young laboring men and maidens standing together chatting, and her own mother amongst them. Ingé's mother was sitting on a stone to rest, with a fagot of sticks lying before her, which she had picked up in the wood. Then Ingé turned back; she who was so finely dressed she felt ashamed of her mother, a poorly clad woman, who picked up wood in the forest. She did not turn back out of pity for her mother's poverty, but from pride.

Another half-year went by, and her mistress said, "you ought to go home again, and visit your parents, Ingé, and I will give you a large wheaten loaf to take to them, they will be glad to see you, I am sure."

So Ingé put on her best clothes, and her new shoes, drew her dress up around her, and set out, stepping very carefully, that she might be clean and neat about the feet, and there was nothing wrong in doing so. But when she came to the place where the footpath led across the moor, she found small pools of water, and a great deal of mud, so she threw the loaf into the mud, and trod upon it, that she might pass without wetting her feet. But as she stood with one foot on the loaf and the other lifted up to step forward, the loaf began to sink under her, lower and lower, till she disappeared altogether, and only a few bubbles on the surface of the muddy pool remained to show where she had sunk. And this is the story.

But where did Ingé go? She sank into the ground, and went down to the Marsh Woman, who is always brewing there.

The Marsh Woman is related to the elf maidens, who are well-known, for songs are sung and pictures painted about them. But of the Marsh Woman nothing is known, excepting that when a mist arises from the meadows, in summer time, it is because she is brewing beneath them. To the Marsh Woman's brewery Ingé sunk down to a place which no one can endure for long. A heap of mud is a palace compared with the Marsh Woman's brewery; and as Ingé fell she shuddered in every limb, and soon became cold and stiff as marble. Her foot was still fastened to the loaf, which bowed her down as a golden ear of corn bends the stem.

An evil spirit soon took possession of Ingé, and carried her to a still worse place, in which she saw crowds of unhappy people, waiting in a state of agony for the gates of mercy to be opened to them, and in every heart was a miserable and eternal feeling of unrest. It would take too much time to describe the various tortures these people suffered, but Ingé's punishment consisted in standing there as a statue, with her foot fastened to the loaf. She could move her eyes about, and see all the misery around her, but she could not turn her head; and when she saw the people looking at her she thought they were admiring her pretty face and fine clothes, for she was still vain and proud. But she had forgotten how soiled her clothes had become while in the Marsh Woman's brewery, and that they were covered with mud; a snake had also fastened itself in her hair, and hung down her back, while from each fold in her dress a geat toad peeped out and croaked like an asthmatic poodle. Worse than all was the terrible hunger that tormented her, and she could not stoop to break off a piece of the loaf on which she stood. No; her back was too stiff, and her whole body like a pillar of stone. And then came creeping over her face and eyes flies without wings; she winked and blinked, but they could not fly away, for their wings had been pulled off; this, added to the hunger she felt, was horrible torture.

"If this lasts much longer," she said, "I shall not be able to bear it." But it did last, and she had to bear it, without being able to help herself.

A tear, followed by many scalding tears, fell upon her head, and rolled over her face and neck, down to the loaf on which she stood. Who could be weeping for Ingé? She had a mother in the world still, and the tears of sorrow which a mother sheds for her child will always find their way to the child's heart, but they often increase the torment instead of being a relief. And Ingé could hear all that was said about her in the world she had left, and every one seemed cruel to her. The sin she had committed in treading on the loaf was known on earth, for she had been seen by the cowherd from the hill, when she was crossing the marsh and had disappeared.

When her mother wept and exclaimed, "Ah, Ingé! what grief thou hast caused thy mother" she would say, "Oh that I had never been born! My mother's tears are useless now."

And then the words of the kind people who had adopted her came to her ears, when they said, "Ingé was a sinful girl, who did not value the gifts of God, but trampled them under her feet."

"Ah," thought Ingé, "they should have punished me, and driven all my naughty tempers out of me."

A song was made about "The girl who trod on a loaf to keep her shoes from being soiled," and this song was sung everywhere. The story of her sin was also told to the little children, and they called her "wicked Ingé," and said she was so naughty that she ought to be punished. Ingé heard all this, and her heart became hardened and full of bitterness.

But one day, while hunger and grief were gnawing in her hollow frame, she heard a little, innocent child, while listening to the tale of the vain, haughty Ingé, burst into tears and exclaim, "But will she never come up again?"

And she heard the reply, "No, she will never come up again."

"But if she were to say she was sorry, and ask pardon, and promise never to do so again?" asked the little one.

"Yes, then she might come; but she will not beg pardon," was the answer.

"Oh, I wish she would!" said the child, who was quite unhappy about it. "I should be so glad. I would give up my doll and all my playthings, if she could only come here again. Poor Ingé! it is so dreadful for her."

These pitying words penetrated to Ingé's inmost heart, and seemed to do her good. It was the first time any one had said, "Poor Ingé!" without saying something about her faults. A little innocent child was weeping, and praying for mercy for her. It made her feel quite strange, and she would gladly have wept herself, and it added to her torment to find she could not do so. And while she thus suffered in a place where nothing changed, years passed away on earth, and she heard her name less frequently mentioned. But one day a sigh reached her ear, and the words, "Ingé! Ingé! what a grief thou hast been to me! I said it would be so." It was the last sigh of her dying mother.

After this, Ingé heard her kind mistress say, "Ah, poor Ingé! shall I ever see thee again? Perhaps I may, for we know not what may happen in the future." But Ingé knew right well that her mistress would never come to that dreadful place.

Time-passed—a long bitter time—then Ingé heard her name pronounced once more, and saw what seemed two bright stars shining above her. They were two gentle eyes closing on earth. Many years had passed since the little girl had lamented and wept about "poor Ingé." That child was now an old woman, whom God was taking to Himself. In the last hour of existence the events of a whole life often appear before us; and this hour the old woman remembered how, when a child, she had shed tears over the story of Ingé, and she prayed for her now. As the eyes of the old woman closed to earth, the eyes of the soul opened upon the hidden things of eternity, and then she, in whose last thoughts Ingé had been so vividly present, saw how deeply the poor girl had sunk. She burst into tears at the sight, and in heaven, as she had done when a little child on earth, she wept and prayed for poor Ingé. Her tears and her prayers echoed through the dark void that surrounded the tormented captive soul, and the unexpected mercy was obtained for it through an angel's tears. As in thought Ingé seemed to act over again every sin she had committed on earth, she trembled, and tears she had never yet been able to weep rushed to her eyes. It seemed impossible that the gates of mercy could ever be opened to her; but while she acknowledged this in deep penitence, a beam of radiant light shot suddenly into the depths upon her. More powerful than the sunbeam that dissolves the man of snow which the children have raised, more quickly than the snowflake melts and becomes a drop of water on the warm lips of a child, was the stony form of Ingé changed, and as a little bird she soared, with the speed of lightning, upward to the world of mortals. A bird that felt timid and shy to all things around it, that seemed to shrink with shame from meeting any living creature, and hurriedly sought to conceal itself in a dark corner of an old ruined wall; there it sat cowering and unable to utter a sound, for it was voiceless. Yet how quickly the little bird discovered the beauty of everything around it. The sweet, fresh air; the soft radiance of the moon, as its light spread over the earth; the fragrance which exhaled from bush and tree, made it feel happy as it sat there clothed in its fresh, bright plumage. All creation seemed to speak of beneficence and love. The bird wanted to give utterance to thoughts that stirred in his breast, as the cuckoo and the nightingale in the spring, but it could not. Yet in heaven can be heard the song of praise, even from a worm; and the notes trembling in the breast of the bird were as audible to Heaven even as the psalms of David before they had fashioned themselves into words and song.

Christmas-time drew near, and a peasant who dwelt close by the old wall stuck up a pole with some ears of corn fastened to the top, that the birds of heaven might have feast, and rejoice in the happy, blessed time. And on Christmas morning the sun arose and shone upon the ears of corn, which were quickly surrounded by a number of twittering birds. Then, from a hole in the wall, gushed forth in song the swelling thoughts of the bird as he issued from his hiding place to perform his first good deed on earth, — and in heaven it was well known who that bird was.

The winter was very hard; the ponds were covered with ice, and there was very little food for either the beasts of the field or the birds of the air. Our little bird flew away into the public roads, and found here and there, in the ruts of the sledges, a grain of corn, and at the halting places some crumbs. Of these he ate only a few, but he called around him the other birds and the hungry sparrows, that they too might have food. He flew into the towns, and looked about, and wherever a kind hand had strewed bread on the window-sill for the birds, he only ate a single crumb himself, and gave all the rest to the rest of the other birds. In the course of the winter the bird had in this way collected many crumbs and given them to other birds, till they equalled the weight of the loaf on which Ingé had trod to keep her shoes clean; and when the last bread-crumb had been found and given, the gray wings of the bird became white, and spread themselves out for flight.

"See, yonder is a sea-gull!" cried the children, when they saw the white bird, as it dived into the sea, and rose again into the clear sunlight, white and glittering. But no one could tell whither it went then although some declared it flew straight to the sun.

THE EMPEROR'S NEW SUIT

MANY, many years ago lived an emperor, who thought so much of new clothes that he spent all his money in order to obtain them; his only ambition was to be always well dressed. He did not care for his soldiers, and the theatre did not amuse him; the only thing, in fact, he thought anything of was to drive out and show a new suit of clothes. He had a coat for every hour of the day; and as one would say of a king "He is in his cabinet," so one could say of him, "The emperor is in his dressing-room."

The great city where he resided was very gay; every day many strangers from all parts of the globe arrived. One day two swindlers came to this city; they made people believe that they were weavers, and declared they could manufacture the finest cloth to be imagined. Their colours and patterns, they said, were not only exceptionally beautiful, but the clothes made of their material possessed the wonderful quality of being invisible to any man who was unfit for his office or unpardonably stupid.

"That must be wonderful cloth," thought the emperor. "If I were to be dressed in a suit made of this cloth I should be able to find out which men in my empire were unfit for their places, and I could distinguish the clever from the stupid. I must have this cloth woven for me without delay." And he gave a large sum of money to the swindlers, in advance, that they should set to work without any loss of time. They set up two looms, and pretended to be very hard at work, but they did nothing whatever on the looms. They asked for the finest silk and the most precious gold-cloth; all they got they did away with, and worked at the empty looms till late at night.

"I should very much like to know how they are getting on with the cloth," thought the emperor. But he felt rather uneasy when he remembered that he who was not fit for his office could not see it. Personally, he was of opinion that he had nothing to fear, yet he thought it advisable to send somebody else first to see how matters stood. Everybody in the town knew what a remarkable quality the stuff possessed, and all were anxious to see how bad or stupid their neighbours were.

"I shall send my honest old minister to the weavers," thought the emperor. "He can judge best how the stuff looks, for he is intelligent, and nobody understands his office better than he."

The good old minister went into the room where the swindlers sat before the empty looms. "Heaven preserve us!" he thought, and opened his eyes wide, "I cannot see anything at all," but he did not say so. Both swindlers requested him to come near, and asked him if he did not admire the exquisite pattern and the beautiful colours, pointing to the empty looms. The poor old minister tried his very best, but he could see nothing, for there was nothing to be seen. "Oh dear," he thought, "can I be so stupid? I should never have thought so, and nobody must know it! Is it possible that I am not fit for my office? No, no, I cannot say that I was unable to see the cloth."

"Now, have you got nothing to say?" said one of the swindlers, while he pretended to be busily weaving.

"Oh, it is very pretty, exceedingly beautiful," replied the old minister looking through his glasses. "What a beautiful pattern, what brilliant colours! I shall tell the emperor that I like the cloth very much."

"We are pleased to hear that," said the two weavers, and described to him the colours and explained the curious pattern. The old minister listened attentively, that he might relate to the emperor what they said; and so he did.

Now the swindlers asked for more money, silk and gold-cloth, which they required for weaving. They kept everything for themselves, and not a thread came near the loom, but they continued, as hitherto, to work at the empty looms.

Soon afterwards the emperor sent another honest courtier to the weavers to see how they were getting on, and if the cloth was nearly finished. Like the old minister, he looked and looked but could see nothing, as there was nothing to be seen.

"Is it not a beautiful piece of cloth?" asked the two swindlers, showing and explaining the magnificent pattern, which, however, did not exist.

"I am not stupid," said the man. "It is therefore my good appointment for which I am not fit. It is very strange, but I must not let any one know it;" and he praised the cloth, which he did not see, and expressed his joy at the beautiful colours and the fine pattern. "It is very excellent," he said to the emperor.

Everybody in the whole town talked about the precious cloth. At last the emperor wished to see it himself, while it was still on the loom. With a number of courtiers, including the two who had already been there, he went to the two clever swindlers, who now worked as hard as they could, but without using any thread.

"Is it not magnificent?" said the two old statesmen who had been there before. "Your Majesty must admire the colours and the pattern." And then they pointed to the empty looms, for they imagined the others could see the cloth.

"What is this?" thought the emperor, "I do not see anything at all. That is terrible! Am I stupid? Am I unfit to be emperor? That would indeed be the most dreadful thing that could happen to me."

"Really," he said, turning to the weavers, "your cloth has our most gracious approval;" and nodding contentedly he looked at the empty loom, for he did not like to say that he saw nothing. All his attendants, who were with him, looked and looked, and although they could not see anything more than the others, they said, like the emperor, "It is very beautiful." And all advised him to wear the new magnificent clothes at a great procession which was soon to take place. "It is magnificent, beautiful, excellent," one heard them say; everybody seemed to be delighted, and the emperor appointed the two swindlers "Imperial Court weavers."

The whole night previous to the day on which the procession was to take place, the swindlers pretended to work, and burned more than sixteen candles. People should see that they were busy to finish the emperor's new suit. They pretended to take the cloth from the loom, and worked about in the air with big scissors, and sewed with needles without thread, and said at last: "The emperor's new suit is ready now."

The emperor and all his barons then came to the hall; the swindlers held their arms up as if they held something in their hands and said: "These are the trousers!" "This is the coat!" and "Here is the cloak!" and so on. "They are all as light as a cobweb, and one must feel as if one had nothing at all upon the body; but that is just the beauty of them."

"Indeed!" said all the courtiers; but they could not see anything, for there was nothing to be seen.

"Does it please your Majesty now to graciously undress," said the swindlers, "that we may assist your Majesty in putting on the new suit before the large looking-glass?"

The emperor undressed, and the swindlers pretended to put the new suit upon him, one piece after another; and the emperor looked at himself in the glass from every side.

"How well they look! How well they fit!" said all. "What a beautiful pattern! What fine colours! That is a magnificent suit of clothes!"

The master of the ceremonies announced that the bearers of the canopy, which was to be carried in the procession, were ready.

"I am ready," said the emperor. "Does not my suit fit me marvellously?" Then he turned once more to the looking-glass, that people should think he admired his garments.

The chamberlains, who were to carry the train, stretched their hands to the ground as if they lifted up a train, and pretended to hold something in their hands; they did not like people to know that they could not see anything.

The emperor marched in the procession under the beautiful canopy, and all who saw him in the street and out of the windows exclaimed: "Indeed, the emperor's new suit is incomparable! What a long train he has! How well it fits him!" Nobody wished to let others know he saw nothing, for then he would have been unfit for his office or too stupid. Never emperor's clothes were more admired.

"But he has nothing on at all," said a little child at last. "Good heavens! listen to the voice of an innocent child," said the father, and one whispered to the other what the child had said. "But he has nothing on at all," cried at last the whole people. That made a deep impression upon the emperor, for it seemed to him that they were right; but he thought to himself, "Now I must bear up to the end." And the chamberlains walked with still greater dignity, as if they carried the train which did not exist.

THE DAISY

Now listen! In the country, close by the high road, stood a farmhouse; perhaps you have passed by and seen it yourself. There was a little flower garden with painted wooden palings in front of it; close by was a ditch, on its fresh green bank grew a little daisy; the sun shone as warmly and brightly upon it as on the magnificent garden flowers, and therefore it thrived well. One morning it had quite opened, and its little snow-white petals stood round the yellow centre, like the rays of the sun. It did not mind that nobody saw it in the grass, and that it was a poor despised flower; on the contrary, it was quite happy, and turned towards the sun, looking upward and listening to the song of the lark high up in the air.

The little daisy was as happy as if the day had been a great holiday, but it was only Monday. All the children were at school, and while they were sitting on the forms and learning their lessons, it sat on its thin green stalk and learnt from the sun and from its surroundings how kind God is, and it rejoiced that the song of the little lark expressed so sweetly and distinctly its own feelings. With a sort of reverence the daisy looked up to the bird that could fly and sing, but it did not feel envious. "I can see and hear," it thought; "the sun shines upon me, and the forest kisses me. How rich I am!"

In the garden close by grew many large and magnificent flowers, and, strange to say, the less fragrance they had the haughtier and prouder they were. The peonies puffed themselves up in order to be larger than the roses, but size is not everything! The tulips had the finest colours, and they knew it well, too, for they were standing bolt upright like candles, that one might see them the better. In their pride they did not see the little daisy, which looked over to them and thought, "How rich and beautiful they are! I am sure the pretty bird will fly down and call upon them. Thank God, that I stand so near and can at least see all the splendour." And while the daisy was still thinking, the lark came flying down, crying "Tweet," but not to the peonies and tulips—no, into the grass to the poor daisy. Its joy was so great that it did not know what to think. The little bird hopped round it and sang, "How beautifully soft the grass is, and what a lovely little flower with its golden heart and silver dress is growing here." The yellow centre in the daisy did indeed look like gold, while the little petals shone as brightly as silver.

How happy the daisy was! No one has the least idea. The bird kissed it with its beak, sang to it, and then rose again up to the blue sky. It was certainly more than a quarter of an hour before the daisy recovered its senses. Half ashamed, yet glad at heart, it looked over to the other flowers in the garden; surely they had witnessed its pleasure and the honour that had been done to it; they understood its joy. But the tulips stood more stiffly than ever, their faces were pointed and red, because they were vexed. The peonies were sulky; it was well that they could not speak, otherwise they would have given the daisy a good lecture. The little flower could very well see that they were ill at ease, and pitied them sincerely.

Shortly after this a girl came into the garden, with a large sharp knife. She went to the tulips and began cutting them off, one after another. "Ugh!" sighed the daisy, "that is terrible; now they are done for."

The girl carried the tulips away. The daisy was glad that it was outside, and only a small flower — it felt very grateful. At sunset it folded its petals, and fell asleep, and dreamt all night of the sun and the little bird.

On the following morning, when the flower once more stretched forth its tender petals, like little arms, towards the air and light, the daisy recognised the bird's voice, but what it sang sounded so sad. Indeed the poor bird had good reason to be sad, for it had been caught and put into a cage close by the open window. It sang of the happy days when it could merrily fly about, of fresh green corn in the fields, and of the time when it could soar almost up to the clouds. The poor lark was most unhappy as a prisoner in a cage. The little daisy would have liked so much to help it, but what could be done? Indeed, that was very difficult for such a small flower to find out. It entirely forgot how beautiful everything around it was, how warmly the sun was shining, and how splendidly white its own petals were. It could only think of the poor captive bird, for which it could do nothing. Then two little boys came out of the garden; one of them had a large sharp knife, like that with which the girl had cut the tulips. They came straight towards the little daisy, which could not understand what they wanted.

"Here is a fine piece of turf for the lark," said one of the boys, and began to cut out a square round the daisy, so that it remained in the centre of the grass.

"Pluck the flower off," said the other boy, and the daisy trembled for fear, for to be pulled off meant death to it; and it wished so much to live, as it was to go with the square of turf into the poor captive lark's cage.

"No, let it stay," said the other boy, "it looks so pretty."

And so it stayed, and was brought into the lark's cage. The poor bird was lamenting its lost liberty, and beating its wings against the wires; and the little daisy could not speak or utter a consoling word, much as it would have liked to do so. So the forenoon passed.

"I have no water," said the captive lark, "they have all gone out, and forgotten to give me anything to drink. My throat is dry and burning. I feel as if I had fire and ice within me, and the air is so oppressive. Alas! I must die, and part with the warm sunshine, the fresh green meadows, and all the beauty that God has created." And it thrust its beak into the piece of grass, to refresh itself a little. Then it noticed the little daisy, and nodded to it, and kissed it with its beak and said: "You must also fade in here, poor little flower. You and the piece of grass are all they have given me in exchange for the whole world, which I enjoyed outside. Each little blade of grass shall be a green tree for me, each of your white petals a fragrant flower. Alas! you only remind me of what I have lost."

"I wish I could console the poor lark," thought the daisy. It could not move one of its leaves, but the fragrance of its delicate petals streamed forth, and was much stronger than such flowers usually have: the bird noticed it, although it was dying with thirst, and in its pain tore up the green blades of grass, but did not touch the flower.

The evening came, and nobody appeared to bring the poor bird a drop of water; it opened its beautiful wings, and fluttered about in its anguish; a faint and mournful "Tweet, tweet," was all it could utter, then it bent its little head towards the flower, and its heart broke for want and longing. The flower could not, as on the previous evening, fold up its petals and sleep; it dropped sorrowfully. The boys only came the next morning; when they saw the dead bird, they began to cry bitterly, dug a nice grave for it, and adorned it with flowers. The bird's body was placed in a pretty red box; they wished to bury it with royal honours. While it was alive and sang they forgot it, and let it suffer want in the cage; now, they cried over it and covered it with flowers. The piece of turf, with the little daisy in it, was thrown out on the dusty highway. Nobody thought of the flower which had felt so much for the bird and had so greatly desired to comfort it.

THE SWINEHERD

ONCE upon a time lived a poor prince; his kingdom was very small, but it was large enough to enable him to marry, and marry he would. It was rather bold of him that he went and asked the emperor's daughter: "Will you marry me?" but he ventured to do so, for his name was known far and wide, and there were hundreds of princesses who would have gladly accepted him, but would she do so? Now we shall see.

On the grave of the prince's father grew a rose-tree, the most beautiful of its kind. It bloomed only once in five years, and then it had only one single rose upon it, but what a rose! It had such a sweet scent that one instantly forgot all sorrow and grief when one smelt it. He had also a nightingale, which could sing as if every sweet melody was in its throat. This rose and the nightingale he wished to give to the princess; and therefore both were put into big silver cases and sent to her.

The emperor ordered them to be carried into the great hall where the princess was just playing "Visitors are coming" with her ladies-in-waiting; when she saw the large cases with the presents therein, she clapped her hands for joy.

"I wish it were a little pussy cat," she said. But then the rose-tree with the beautiful rose was unpacked.

"Oh, how nicely it is made," exclaimed the ladies.

"It is more than nice," said the emperor, "it is charming."

The princess touched it and nearly began to cry.

"For shame, pa," she said, "it is not artificial, it is natural!"

"For shame, it is natural" repeated all her ladies.

"Let us first see what the other case contains before we are angry," said the emperor; then the nightingale was taken out, and it sang so beautifully that no one could possibly say anything unkind about it.

"*Superbe, charmant,*" said the ladies of the court, for they all prattled French, one worse than the other.

"How much the bird reminds me of the musical box of the late lamented empress," said an old courtier, "it has exactly the same tone, the same execution."

"You are right," said the emperor, and began to cry like a little child.

"I hope it is not natural," said the princess.

"Yes, certainly it is natural," replied those who had brought the presents.

"Then let it fly," said the princess, and refused to see the prince.

But the prince was not discouraged. He painted his face, put on common clothes, pulled his cap over his forehead, and came back.

"Good day, emperor," he said, "could you not give me some employment at the court?"

"There are so many," replied the emperor, "who apply for places, "that for the present I have no vacancy, but I will remember you. But wait a moment; it just comes into my mind, I require somebody to look after my pigs, for I have a great many."

Thus the prince was appointed imperial swineherd, and as such he lived in a wretchedly small room near the pigsty; there he worked all day long, and when it was night he had made a pretty little pot. There were little bells round the rim, and when the water began to boil in it, the bells began to play the old tune:

> "A jolly old sow once lived in a sty,
> Three little piggies had she," &c.

But what was more wonderful was that, when one put a finger into the steam rising from the pot, one could at once smell what meals they were preparing on every fire in the whole town. That was indeed much more remarkable than the rose. When the princess with her ladies passed by and heard the tune, she stopped and looked quite pleased, for she also could play it—in fact, it was the only tune she could play, and she played it with one finger.

"That is the tune I know," she exclaimed. "He must be a well-educated swineherd. Go and ask him how much the instrument is."

One of the ladies had to go and ask; but she put on pattens.

"What will you take for your pot?" asked the lady.

"I will have ten kisses from the princess," said the swineherd.

"God forbid," said the lady.

"Well, I cannot sell it for less," replied the swineherd.

"What did he say?" said the princess.

"I really cannot tell you," replied the lady.

"You can whisper it into my ear."

THE SWINEHERD

"It is very naughty," said the princess, and walked off.

But when she had gone a little distance, the bells rang again so sweetly:

> "A jolly old sow once lived in a sty,
> Three little piggies had she," &c.

"Ask him," said the princess, "if he will be satisfied with ten kisses from one of my ladies."

"No, thank you," said the swineherd: "ten kisses from the princess, or I keep my pot."

"That is tiresome,"said the princess. "But you must stand before me, so that nobody can see it."

The ladies placed themselves in front of her and spread out their dresses, and she gave the swineherd ten kisses and received the pot.

That was a pleasure! Day and night the water in the pot was boiling; there was not a single fire in the whole town of which they did not know what was preparing on it, the chamberlain's as well as the shoemaker's. The ladies danced and clapped their hands for joy.

"We know who will eat soup and pancakes; we know who will eat porridge and cutlets; oh, how interesting!"

"Very interesting, indeed," said the mistress of the household. "But you must not betray me, for I am the emperor's daughter."

"Of course not," they all said.

The swineherd—that is to say, the prince—but they did not know otherwise than that he was a real swineherd—did not waste a single day without doing something; he made a rattle, which, when turned quickly round, played all the waltzes, galops, and polkas known since the creation of the world.

"But that is *superbe*," said the princess passing by. "I have never heard a more beautiful composition. Go down and ask him what the instrument costs; but I shall not kiss him again."

"He will have a hundred kisses from the princess," said the lady, who had gone down to ask him.

"I believe he is mad," said the princess, and walked off, but soon she stopped. "One must encourage art," she said. "I am the emperor's daughter! Tell him I will give him ten kisses, as I did the other day; the remainder one of my ladies can give him."

"But we do not like to kiss him" said the ladies.

"That is nonsense," said the princess; "if I can kiss him, you can also do it. Remember that I give you food and employment." And the lady had to go down once more.

"A hundred kisses from the princess," said the swineherd, "or everybody keeps his own."

"Place yourselves before me," said the princess then. They did as they were bidden, and the princess kissed him.

"I wonder what that crowd near the pigsty means!" said the emperor, who had just come out on his balcony. He rubbed his eyes and put his spectacles on.

"The ladies of the court are up to some mischief, I think. I shall have to go down and see." He pulled up his shoes, for they were down at the heels, and he was very quick about it. When he had come down into the courtyard he walked quite softly, and the ladies were so busily engaged in counting the kisses, that all should be fair, that they did not notice the emperor. He raised himself on tiptoe.

"What does this mean?" he said, when he saw that his daughter was kissing the swineherd, and then hit their heads with his shoe just as the swineherd received the sixty-eighth kiss.

"Go out of my sight," said the emperor, for he was very angry; and both the princess and the swineherd were banished from the empire. There she stood and cried, the swineherd scolded her, and the rain came down in torrents.

"Alas, unfortunate creature that I am!" said the princess, "I wish I had accepted the prince. Oh, how wretched I am!"

The swineherd went behind a tree, wiped his face, threw off his poor attire and stepped forth in his princely garments; he looked so beautiful that the princess could not help bowing to him.

"I have now learnt to despise you," he said. "You refused an honest prince; you did not appreciate the rose and the nightingale; but you did not mind kissing a swineherd for his toys; you have no one but yourself to blame!"

And then he returned into his kingdom and left her behind. She could now sing at her leisure:

"A jolly old sow once lived in a sty,
Three little piggies has she," &c.

THE SAUCY BOY

ONCE upon a time there was an old poet, one of those right good old poets.

One evening, as he was sitting at home, there was a terrible storm going on outside; the rain was pouring down, but the old poet sat comfortably in his chimney-corner, where the fire was burning and the apples were roasting.

"There will not be a dry thread left on the poor people who are out in this weather," he said.

"Oh, open the door! I am so cold and wet through," called a little child outside. It was crying and knocking at the door, whilst the rain was pouring down and the wind was rattling all the windows.

"Poor creature!" said the poet, and got up and opened the door. Before him stood a little boy; he was naked, and the water flowed from his long fair locks. He was shivering with cold; if he had not been let in, he would certainly have perished in the storm.

"Poor little thing!" said the poet, and took him by the hand. "Come to me; I will soon warm you. You shall have some wine and an apple, for you are such a pretty boy."

And he was, too. His eyes sparkled like two bright stars, and although the water flowed down from his fair locks, they still curled quite beautifully.

He looked like a little angel, but was pale with cold, and trembling all over. In his hand he held a splendid bow, but it had been entirely spoilt by the rain, and the colours of the pretty arrows had run into one another by getting wet.

The old man sat down by the fire, and taking the little boy on his knee, wrung the water out of his locks and warmed his hands in his own.

He then made him some hot spiced wine, which quickly revived him; so that with reddening cheeks, he sprang upon the floor and danced around the old man.

"You are a merry boy," said the latter. "What is your name?"

"My name is Cupid," he answered. "Don't you know me? There lies my bow. I shoot with that, you know. Look, the weather is getting fine again — the moon is shining."

"But your bow is spoilt," said the old poet.

"That would be unfortunate," said the little boy, taking it up and looking at it. "Oh, it's quite dry and isn't damaged at all. The string is quite tight; I'll try it." So, drawing it back, he took an arrow, aimed, and shot the good old poet right in the heart. "Do you see now that my bow was not spoilt?" he said, and, loudly laughing, ran away. What a naughty boy to shoot the old poet like that, who had taken him into his warm room, had been so good to him, and had given him the nicest wine and the best apple!

The good old man lay upon the floor crying; he was really shot in the heart. "Oh!" he cried, "what a naughty boy this Cupid is! I shall tell all the good children about this, so that they take care never to play with him, lest he hurt them."

And all good children, both girls and boys, whom he told about this, were on their guard against wicked Cupid; but he deceives them all the same, for he is very deep. When the students come out of class, he walks beside them with a book under his arm, and wearing a black coat. They cannot recognize him. And then, if they take him by the arm, believing him to be a student too, he sticks an arrow into their chest. And when the girls go to church to be confirmed, he is amongst them too. In fact, he is always after people. He sits in the large chandelier in the theatre and blazes away, so that people think it is a lamp; but they soon find out their mistake. He walks about in the castle garden and on the promenades. Yes, once he shot your father and your mother in the heart too. Just ask them, and you will hear what they say. Oh! he is a bad boy, this Cupid, and you must never have anything to do with him, for he is after every one. Just think, he even shot an arrow at old grandmother; but that was a long time ago. The wound has long been healed, but such things are never forgotten.

Now you know what a bad boy this wicked Cupid is.

THE PRINCESS AND THE PEA

ONCE upon a time there was a prince who wanted to marry a princess; but she would have to be a real princess. He travelled all over the world to find one, but nowhere could he get what he wanted. There were princesses enough, but it was difficult to find out whether they were real ones. There was always something about them that was not as it should be. So he came home again and was sad, for he would have liked very much to have a real princess.

One evening a terrible storm came on; there was thunder and lightning,

THE PRINCESS AND THE PEA

and the rain poured down in torrents. Suddenly a knocking was heard at the city gate, and the old king went to open it.

It was a princess standing out there in front of the gate. But, good gracious! what a sight the rain and the wind had made her look. The water ran down from her hair and clothes; it ran down into the toes of her shoes and out again at the heels. And yet she said that she was a real princess.

"Well, we'll soon find that out," thought the old queen. But she said nothing, went into the bed-room, took all the bedding off the bedstead, and laid a pea on the bottom; then she took twenty mattresses and laid them on the pea, and then twenty eider-down beds on top of the mattresses.

On this the princess had to lie all night. In the morning she was asked how she had slept.

"Oh, very badly!" said she. "I have scarcely closed my eyes all night. Heaven only knows what was in the bed, but I was lying on something hard, so that I am black and blue all over my body. It's horrible!"

Now they knew that she was a real princess because she had felt the pea right through the twenty mattresses and the twenty eider-down beds.

Nobody but a real princess could be as sensitive as that.

So the prince took her for his wife, for now he knew that he had a real princess; and the pea was put in the museum, where it may still be seen, if no one has stolen it.

There, that is a true story.

THE RED SHOES

ONCE upon a time there was little girl, pretty and dainty. But in summer-time she was obliged to go barefooted because she was poor, and in winter she had to wear large wooden shoes, so that her little instep grew quite red.

In the middle of the village lived an old shoemaker's wife; she sat down and made, as well as she could, a pair of little shoes out of some old pieces of red cloth. They were clumsy, but she meant well, for they were intended for the little girl, whose name was Karen.

Karen received the shoes and wore them for the first time on the day of her mother's funeral. They were certainly not suitable for mourning; but she had no others, and so she put her bare feet into them and walked behind the humble coffin.

Just then a large old carriage came by, and in it sat an old lady; she looked at the little girl, and taking pity on her, said to the clergyman, "Look here, if you will give me the little girl, I will take care of her."

Karen believed that this was all on account of the red shoes, but the old lady thought them hideous, and so they were burnt. Karen herself was dressed very neatly and cleanly; she was taught to read and to sew, and people said that she was pretty. But the mirror told her, "You are more than pretty—you are beautiful."

One day the Queen was travelling through that part of the country, and had her little daughter, who was a princess, with her. All the people, amongst them Karen too, streamed towards the castle, where the little princess, in fine white clothes, stood before the window and allowed herself to be stared at. She wore neither a train nor a golden crown, but beautiful red morocco shoes; they were indeed much finer than those which the shoemaker's wife had sewn for little Karen. There is really nothing in the world that can be compared to red shoes!

Karen was now old enough to be confirmed; she received some new clothes, and she was also to have some new shoes. The rich shoemaker in the town took the measure of her little foot in his own room, in which there stood great glass cases full of pretty shoes and white slippers. It all looked very lovely, but the old lady could not see very well, and therefore did not get much pleasure out of it. Amongst the shoes stood a pair of red ones, like those which the princess had worn. How beautiful they were! and the shoemaker said that they had been made for a count's daughter, but that they had not fitted her.

"I suppose they are of shiny leather?" asked the old lady. "They shine so."

"Yes, they do shine," said Karen. They fitted her, and were bought. But the old lady knew nothing of their being red, for she would never have allowed Karen to be confirmed in red shoes, as she was now to be.

Everybody looked at her feet, and the whole of the way from the church door to the choir it seemed to her as if even the ancient figures on the monuments, in their stiff collars and long black robes, had their eyes fixed on her red shoes. It was only of these that she thought when the clergyman laid his hand upon her head and spoke of the holy baptism, of the covenant with God, and told her that she was now to be a grown-up Christian. The organ pealed forth solemnly, and the sweet children's voices mingled with that of their old leader; but Karen thought only of her red shoes. In the afternoon the old lady heard from everybody that Karen had worn red shoes. She said that it was a shocking thing to do, that it was very improper, and that Karen was always to go to church in future in black shoes, even if they were old.

On the following Sunday there was Communion. Karen looked first at the black shoes, then at the red ones—looked at the red ones again, and put them on.

The sun was shining gloriously, so Karen and the old lady went along the footpath through the corn, where it was rather dusty.

At the church door stood an old crippled soldier leaning on a crutch; he had a wonderfully long beard, more red than white, and he bowed down to the ground and asked the old lady whether he might wipe her shoes. Then Karen put out her little foot too. "Dear me, what pretty dancing-shoes!" said the soldier. "Sit fast, when you dance," said he, addressing the shoes, and slapping the soles with his hand.

The old lady gave the soldier some money and then went with Karen into the church.

And all the peole inside looked at Karen's red shoes, and all the figures gazed at them; when Karen knelt before the altar and put the golden goblet to her mouth, she thought only of the red shoes. It seemed to her as though they were swimming about in the goblet, and she forgot to sing the psalm, forgot to say the "Lord's Prayer."

Now every one came out of church, and the old lady stepped into her carriage. But just as Karen was lifting up her foot to get in too, the old soldier said: "Dear me, what pretty dancing shoes!" and Karen could not help it, she was obliged to dance a few steps; and when she had once begun, her legs continued to dance. It seemed as if the shoes had got power over them. She danced round the church corner, for she could not stop; the coachman had to run after her and seize her. He lifted her into the carriage, but her feet continued to dance, so that she kicked the good old lady violently. At last they took off her shoes, and her legs were at rest.

At home the shoes were put into the cupboard, but Karen could not help looking at them.

Now the old lady fell ill, and it was said that she would not rise from her bed again. She had to be nursed and waited upon, and this was no one's duty more than Karen's. But there was a grand ball in the town, and Karen was invited. She looked at the red shoes, saying to herself that there was no sin in doing that; she put the red shoes on, thinking there was no harm in that either; and then she went to the ball; and commenced to dance.

But when she wanted to go to the right, the shoes danced to the left, and when she wanted to dance up the room, the shoes danced down the room, down the stairs through the street, and out through the gates of the town. She danced, and was obliged to dance, far out into the dark wood. Suddenly something shone up among the trees, and she believed it was the moon, for it was a face. But it was the old soldier with the red beard; he sat there nodding his head and said: "Dear me, what pretty dancing shoes!"

She was frightened, and wanted to throw the red shoes away; but they stuck fast. She tore off her stockings, but the shoes had grown fast to her feet. She danced and was obliged to go on dancing over field and meadow, in rain and sunshine, by night and by day—but by night it was most horrible.

She danced out into the open churchyard; but the dead there did not dance. They had something better to do than that. She wanted to sit down on the pauper's grave where the bitter fern grows; but for her there was neither peace nor rest. And as she danced past the open church door she saw an angel there in long white robes, with wings reaching from his shoulders down to the earth; his face was stern and grave, and in his hand he held a broad shining sword.

"Dance you shall," said he, "dance in your red shoes till you are pale and cold, till your skin shrivels up and you are a skeleton! Dance you shall, from door to door, and where proud and wicked children live you shall knock, so that they may hear you and fear you! Dance you shall, dance——!"

"Mercy!" cried Karen. But she did not hear what the angel answered, for the shoes carried her through the gate into the fields, along highways and byways, and unceasingly she had to dance.

One morning she danced past a door that she knew well; they were singing a psalm inside, and a coffin was being carried out covered with flowers. Then she knew that she was forsaken by every one and damned by the angel of God.

She danced, and was obliged to go on dancing through the dark night. The shoes bore her away over thorns and stumps till she was all torn and bleeding; she danced away over the heath to a lonely little house. Here, she knew, lived the executioner; and she tapped with her finger at the window and said:

"Come out, come out! I cannot come in, for I must dance."

And the executioner said: "I don't suppose you know who I am. I strike off the heads of the wicked, and I notice that my axe is tingling to do so."

"Don't cut off my head!" said Karen, "for then I could not repent of my sin. But cut off my feet with the red shoes."

And then she confessed all her sin, and the executioner struck off her feet with the red shoes; but the shoes danced away with the little feet across the field into the deep forest.

And he carved her a pair of wooden feet and some crutches, and taught her a psalm which is always sung by sinners; she kissed the hand that guided the axe, and went away over the heath.

"Now, I have suffered enough for the red shoes," she said; "I will go to church, so that people can see me." And she went quickly up to the church-door; but when she came there, the red shoes were dancing before her, and she was frightened, and turned back.

During the whole week she was sad and wept many bitter tears, but when Sunday came again she said: "Now I have suffered and striven enough. I believe I am quite as good as many of those who sit in church and give themselves airs." And so she went boldly on; but she had not got farther than the churchyard gate when she saw the red shoes dancing along before her. Then she became terrified, and turned back and repented right heartily of her sin.

She went to the parsonage, and begged that she might be taken into service there. She would be industrious, she said, and do everything that she could; she did not mind about the wages as long as she had a roof over her, and was with good people. The pastor's wife had pity on her, and took her into service. And she was industrious and thoughtful. She sat quiet and listened when the pastor read aloud from the Bible in the evening. All the children liked her very much, but when they spoke about dress and grandeur and beauty she would shake her head.

On the following Sunday they all went to church, and she was asked whether she wished to go too; but, with tears in her eyes, she looked sadly at her crutches. And then the others went to hear God's Word, but she went alone into her little room; this was only large enough to hold the bed and a chair. Here she sat down with her hymn-book, and as she was reading it with a pious mind, the wind carried the notes of the organ over to her from the church, and in tears she lifted up her face and said: "O God! help me!"

Then the sun shone so brightly, and right before her stood an angel of God in white robes; it was the same one whom she had seen that night at the church-door. He no longer carried the sharp sword, but a beautiful green branch, full of roses; with this he touched the ceiling, which rose up very high, and where he had touched it there shone a golden star. He touched the walls, which opened wide apart, and she saw the organ which was pealing forth; she saw the pictures of the old pastors and their wives, and the congregation sitting in the polished chairs and singing from their hymn-books. The church itself had come to the poor girl in her narrow room, or the room had gone to the church. She sat in the pew with the rest of the pastor's household, and when they had finished the hymn and looked up, they nodded and said, "It was right of you to come, Karen."

"It was mercy," said she.

The organ played and the children's voices in the choir sounded soft and lovely. The bright warm sushine streamed through the window into the pew where Karen sat, and her heart became so filled with it, so filled with peace and joy, that it broke. Her soul flew on the sunbeams to Heaven, and no one was there who asked after the *Red Shoes*.

THE LITTLE ELDER-TREE MOTHER

THERE was once a little boy who had caught cold; he had gone out and got wet feet. Nobody had the least idea how it had happened; the weather was quite dry. His mother undressed him, put him to bed, and ordered the teapot to be brought in, that she might make him a good cup of tea from the elder-tree blossoms, which is so warming. At the same time, the kind-hearted old man who lived by himself in the upper storey of the house came in; he led a lonely life, for he had no wife and children; but he loved the children of others very much, and he could tell so many fairy tales and stories, that it was a pleasure to hear him.

"Now, drink your tea," said the mother; "perhaps you will hear a story."

"Yes, if I only knew a fresh one," said the old man, and nodded smilingly. "But how did the little fellow get his wet feet?" he then asked.

"That," replied the mother, "nobody can understand."

"Will you tell me a story?" asked the boy.

"Yes, if you can tell me as nearly as possible how deep is the gutter in the little street where you go to school."

"Just half as high as my top-boots," replied the boy; "but then I must stand in the deepest holes."

"There, now we know where you got your wet feet," said the old man. "I ought to tell you a story, but the worst of it is, I do not know any more."

"You can make one up," said the little boy. "Mother says you can tell a fairy tale about anything you look at or touch."

"That is all very well, but such tales or stories are worth nothing! No, the right ones come by themselves and knock at my forehead saying: 'Here I am.'"

"Will not one knock soon?" asked the boy; and the mother smiled while she put elder-tree blossoms into the teapot and poured boiling water over them. "Pray, tell me a story."

"Yes, if stories came by themselves; they are so proud, they only come when they please.—But wait," he said suddenly, "there is one. Look at the teapot; there is a story in it now."

And the little boy looked at the teapot; the lid rose up gradually, the elder-tree blossoms sprang forth one by one, fresh and white; long boughs came forth; even out of the spout they grew up in all directions, and formed a bush—nay, a large elder tree, which stretched its branches up to the bed and pushed the curtains aside; and there were so many blossoms and such a sweet fragrance! In the midst of the tree sat a kindly-looking old woman with a strange dress; it was as green as the leaves, and trimmed with large white blossoms, so that it was difficult to say whether it was real cloth, or the leaves and blossoms of the elder-tree.

"What is this woman's name?" asked the little boy.

"Well, the Romans and Greeks used to call her a Dryad," said the old man; "but we do not understand that. Out in the sailors' quarter they give her a better name; there she is called elder-tree mother. Now, you must attentively listen to her and look at the beautiful elder-tree.

"Just such a large tree, covered with flowers, stands out there; it grew in the corner of an humble little yard; under this tree sat two old people one af-

THE LITTLE ELDER-TREE MOTHER

ternoon in the beautiful sunshine. He was an old, old sailor, and she his old wife; they had already great-grandchildren, and were soon to celebrate their golden wedding, but they could not remember the date, and the elder-tree mother was sitting in the tree and looked as pleased as this one here. 'I know very well when the golden wedding is to take place,' she said; but they did not hear it—they were talking of bygone days.

" 'Well, do you remember?' said the old sailor, 'when we were quite small and used to run about and play—it was in the very same yard where we now are—we used to put little branches into the ground and make a garden.'

" 'Yes,' said the old woman, 'I remember it very well; we used to water the branches, and one of them, an elder-tree branch, took root, and grew and became the large tree under which we are now sitting as old people.'

" 'Certainly, you are right,' he said; 'and in yonder corner stood a large water-tub; there I used to sail my boat, which I had cut out myself—it sailed so well; but soon I had to sail somewhere else.'

" 'But first we went to school to learn something,' she said, 'and then we were confirmed; we both wept on that day, but in the afternoon we went out hand in hand, and ascended the high round tower and looked out into the wide world right over Copenhagen and the sea; then we walked to Fredericksburg, where the king and the queen were sailing about in their magnificent boat on the canals.'

" 'But soon I had to sail about somewhere else, and for many years I was travelling about far away from home.'

" 'And I often cried about you, for I was afraid lest you were drowned and lying at the bottom of the sea. Many a time I got up in the night and looked if the weathercock had turned; it turned often, but you did not return. I remember one day distinctly: the rain was pouring down in torrents; the dust-man had come to the house where I was in service; I went down with the dust-bin and stood for a moment in the doorway, and looked at the dreadful weather. Then the postman gave me a letter; it was from you. Heavens! how that letter had travelled about. I tore it open and read it; I cried and laughed at the same time, and was so happy! Therein was written that you were staying in the hot countries, where the coffee grows. These must be marvellous countries. You said a great deal about them, and I read all while the rain was pouring down and I was standing there with the dust-bin. Then suddenly some one put his arm round my waist——'

" 'Yes, and you gave him a hearty smack on the cheek,' said the old man.

" 'I did not know that it was you—you had come as quickly as your letter; and you looked so handsome, and so you do still. You had a large yellow silk handkerchief in your pocket and a shining hat on. You looked so well, and the weather in the street was horrible!'

" 'Then we married,' he said. 'Do you remember how we got our first boy, and then Mary, Niels, Peter, John, and Christian?'

" 'Oh yes; and now they have all grown up, and have become useful members of society, whom everybody cares for.'

" 'And their children have had children again,' said the old sailor. 'Yes, these are children's children, and they are strong and healthy. If I am not mistaken, our wedding took place at this season of the year.'

" 'Yes, to-day is your golden wedding-day,' said the little elder-tree mother, stretching her head down between the two old people, who thought that she was their neighbour who was nodding to them; they looked at each other and clasped hands. Soon afterwards the children and grandchildren came, for they knew very well that it was the golden wedding-day; they had already wished them joy and happiness in the morning, but the old people had forgotten it, although they remembered things so well that had passed many, many years ago. The elder-tree smelt strongly, and the setting sun illuminated the faces of the two old people, so that they looked quite rosy; the youngest of the grandchildren danced round them, and cried merrily that there would be a feast in the evening, for they were to have hot potatoes; and the elder mother nodded in the tree and cried 'Hooray' with the others."

"But that was no fairy tale," said the little boy who had listened to it.

"You will presently understand it," said the old man who told the story. "Let us ask little elder-tree mother about it."

"That was no fairy tale," said the little elder-tree mother; "but now it comes! Real life furnishes us with subjects for the msot wonderful fairy tales; for otherwise my beautiful elder-bush could not have grown forth out of the teapot."

And then she took the little boy out of bed and placed him on her bosom; the elder branches, full of blossoms, closed over them; it was as if they sat in a thick leafy bower which flew with them through the air; it was beautiful beyond all description. The little elder-tree mother had suddenly become a charming young girl, but her dress was still of the same green material, covered with white blossoms, as the elder-tree mother had worn; she had a real elder blossom on her bosom, and a wreath of the same flowers was wound round her curly golden hair; her eyes were so large and so blue that it was wonderful to look at them. She and the boy kissed each other, and then they were of the same age and felt the same joys. They walked hand in hand out of the bower, and now stood at home in a beautiful flower garden. Near the green lawn the father's walking-stick was tied to a post. There was life in this stick for the little ones, for as soon as they seated themselves upon it the polished knob turned into a neighing horse's head, a long black mane was fluttering in the wind, and four strong slender legs grew out. The animal was fiery and spirited; they galloped round the lawn. "Hooray! now we shall ride far away, many miles!" said the boy; "we shall ride to the nobleman's estate where we were last year." And they rode round the lawn again, and the little girl, who, as we know, was no other than the little elder-tree mother, continually cried, "Now we are in the country! Do you see the farmhouse there, with the large baking stove, which projects like a gigantic egg out of the wall into the road? The elder-tree spreads its branches over it, and the cock struts about and scratches for the hens. Look how proud he is! Now we are near the church; it stands on a high hill, under the spreading oak trees; one of them is half dead! Now we are at the smithy, where the fire roars and the half-naked men beat with their hammers so that the sparks fly far and wide. Let's be off to the beautiful farm!" And they passed by everything the little girl, who was sitting behind on the stick, described, and the boy saw it, and yet they only went round the lawn. Then they played in a side-walk, and marked out a little garden on the ground; she took elder-blossoms out of her hair and planted them, and they grew exactly like those the old people planted when they were children, as we have heard before. They walked about hand in hand, just as the old couple had done when they were little, but they did not go to the round tower nor to the Fredericksburg garden. No; the little girl seized the boy round the waist, and then they flew far into the country. It was spring and it became summer, it was autumn and it became winter, and thousands of pictures reflected themselves in the boy's eyes and heart, and the little girl always sang again, "You will never forget that!" And during their whole flight the elder-tree smelt so sweetly; he noticed the roses and the fresh beeches, but the elder-tree smelt much stronger, for the flowers were fixed on the little girl's bosom, against which the boy often rested his head during the flight.

"It is beautiful here in spring," said the little girl, and they were again in the green beechwood, where the thyme breathed forth sweet fragrance at their feet, and the pink anemones looked lovely in the green moss. "Oh! that it were always spring in the fragrant beechwood!"

"Here it is splendid in summer!" she said, and they passed by old castles of the age of chivalry. The high walls and indented battlements were reflected in the water of the ditches, on which swans were swimming and peering into the old shady avenues. The corn waved in the field like a yellow sea. Red and yellow flowers grew in the ditches, wild hops and convolvuli in full bloom in the hedges. In the evening the moon rose, large and round, and the hayricks in the meadows smelt sweetly. "One can never forget it!"

"Here it is beautiful in autumn!" said the little girl, and the atmosphere seemed twice as high and blue, while the wood shone with crimson, green, and gold. The hounds were running off, flocks of wild fowl flew screaming over the barrows, while the bramble bushes twined round the old stones. The dark-blue sea was covered with white-sailed ships, and in the barns sat old women, girls, and children picking hops into a large tub; the young ones sang songs, and the old people told fairy tales about goblins and sorcerers. It could not be more pleasant anywhere.

"Here it's agreeable in winter!" said the little girl, and all the trees were covered with hoar-frost, so that they looked like white coral. The snow creaked under one's feet, as if one had new boots on. One shooting star after another traversed the sky. In the room the Christmas tree was lit, and there were song and merriment. In the peasant's cottage the violin sounded, and games were played for apple quarters; even the poorest child said, "It is beautiful in winter!"

And indeed it was beautiful! And the little girl showed everything to the boy, and the elder-tree continued to breathe forth sweet perfume, while the red flag with the white cross was streaming in the wind; it was the flag under which the old sailor had served. The boy became a youth; he was to go out into the wide world, far away to the countries where the coffee grows. But at parting the little girl took an elder-blossom from her breast and gave it to him as a keepsake. He placed it in his prayer-book, and when he opened it in distant lands it was always at the place where the flower of remembrance was lying; and the more he looked at it the fresher it became, so that he could almost smell the fragrance of the woods at home. He distinctly saw the little girl, with her bright blue eyes, peeping out from behind the petals, and heard her whispering, "Here it is beautiful in spring, in summer, in autumn, and in winter," and hundreds of pictures passed through his mind.

Thus many years rolled by. He had now become an old man, and was sitting, with his old wife, under an elder-tree in full bloom. They held each other by the hand exactly as the great-grandfather and the great-grandmother had done outside, and, like them, they talked about bygone days and of their golden wedding. The little girl with the blue eyes and elder-blossoms in her hair was sitting high up in the tree, and nodded to them, saying, "To-day is the golden wedding!" And then she took two flowers out of her wreath and kissed them. They glittered at first like silver, then like gold, and when she placed them on the heads of the old people each flower became a golden crown. There they both sat like a king and queen under the sweet-smelling tree, which looked exactly like an elder-tree, and he told his wife the story of the elder-tree mother as it had been told him when he was a little boy. They were both of opinion that the story contained many points like their own, and these similarities they liked best.

"Yes, so it is," said the little girl in the tree. "Some call me Little Elder-tree Mother; others a Dryad; but my real name is 'Remembrance.' It is I who sit in the tree which grows and grows. I can remember things and tell stories! But let's see if you have still got your flower."

And the old man opened his prayer-book; the elder-blossom was still in it, and as fresh as if it had only just been put in. Remembrance nodded, and the two old people, with the golden crowns on their heads, sat in the glowing evening sun. They closed their eyes and — and —

Well, now the story is ended! The little boy in bed did not know whether he had dreamt it or heard it told; the teapot stood on the table, but no elder-tree was growing out of it, and the old man who had told the story was on the point of leaving the room, and he did go out.

"How beautiful it was!" said the little boy. "Mother, I have been to warm countries!"

"I believe you," said the mother; "if one takes two cups of hot elder-tea it is quite natural that one gets into warm countries!" And she covered him up well, so that he might not take cold. "You have slept soundly while I was arguing with the old man whether it was a story or a fairy tale!"

"And what has become of the little elder-tree mother?" asked the boy.

"She is in the teapot," said the mother; "and there she may remain."

THE NEIGHBOURING FAMILIES

ONE would have thought that something important was going on in the duck-pond, but it was nothing after all. All the ducks lying quietly on the water or standing on their heads in it — for they could do that — at once swam to the sides; the traces of their feet were seen in the wet earth, and their cackling was heard far and wide. The water, which a few moments before had been as clear and smooth as a mirror, became very troubled. Before, every tree, every neighbouring bush, the old farmhouse with the holes in the roof and the swallows' nest, and especially the great rose-bush full of flowers, had been reflected in it. The rose-bush covered the wall and hung out over the water, in which everything was seen as if in a picture, except that it all stood on its head; but when the water was troubled everything got mixed up, and the picture was gone. Two feathers which the fluttering ducks had lost floated up and down; suddenly they took a rush as if the wind were coming, but as it did not come they had to lie still, and the water once more became quiet and smooth. The roses were again reflected; they were very beautiful, but they did not know it, for no one had told them. The sun shone among the delicate leaves; everything breathed forth the loveliest fragrance, and all felt as we do when we are filled with joy at the thought of our happiness.

"How beautiful existence is!" said each rose. "The only thing that I wish for is to be able to kiss the sun, because it is so warm and bright. I should also like to kiss those roses down in the water, which are so much like us, and the pretty little birds down in the nest. There are some up above too; they put out their heads and pipe softly; they have no feathers like their father and mother. We have good neighbours, both below and above. How beautiful existence is!"

The young ones above and below—those below were really only shadows in the water—were sparrows; their parents were sparrows too, and had taken possession of the empty swallows' nest of last year, and now lived in it as if it were their own property.

"Are those the duck's children swimming here?" asked the young sparrows when they saw the feathers on the water.

"If you must ask questions, ask sensible ones," said their mother. "Don't you see that they are feathers, such as I wear and you will wear too? But ours are finer. Still, I should like to have them up in the nest, for they keep one warm. I am very curious to know what the ducks were so startled about; not about us, certainly, although I did say 'peep' to you pretty loudly. The thick-headed roses ought to know why, but they know nothing at all; they only look at themselves and smell. I am heartily tired of such neighbours."

"Listen to the dear little birds up there," said the roses; "they begin to want to sing too, but are not able to manage it yet. But it will soon come. What a pleasure that must be! It is fine to have such cheerful neighbours."

Suddenly two horses came galloping up to be watered. A peasant boy rode on one, and he had taken off all his clothes except his large broad black hat. The boy whistled like a bird, and rode into the pond where it was deepest, and as he passed the rose-bush he plucked a rose and stuck it in his hat. Now he looked dressed, and rode on. The other roses looked after their sister, and asked each other, "Where can she be going to?" But none of them knew.

"I should like to go out into the world for once," said one; "but here at home among our green leaves it is beautiful too. The whole day long the sun shines bright and warm, and in the night the sky shines more beautifully still; we can see that through all the little holes in it."

They meant the stars, but they knew no better.

"We make it lively about the house," said the sparrow-mother; "and people say that a swallows' nest brings luck; so they are glad of us. But such neighbours as ours! A rose-bush on the wall like that causes damp. I daresay it will be taken away; then we shall, perhaps, have some corn growing here. The roses are good for nothing but to be looked at and to be smelt, or at most to be stuck in a hat. Every year, as I have been told by my mother, they fall off. The farmer's wife preserves them and strews salt among them; then they get a French name which I neither can pronounce nor care to, and are put into the fire to make a nice smell. You see, that's their life; they exist only for the eye and the nose. Now you know."

In the evening, when the gnats were playing about in the warm air and in the red clouds, the nightingale came and sang to the roses that the beautiful was like sunshine to the world, and that the beautiful lived for ever. The roses thought that the nightingale was singing about itself, and that one might easily have believed; they had no idea that the song was about them. But they were very pleased with it, and wondered whether all the little sparrows could become nightingales.

"I understand the song of that bird very well," said the young sparrows. "There was only one word that was not clear to me. What does 'the beautiful' mean?"

"Nothing at all," answered their mother; "that's only something external. Up at the Hall, where the pigeons have their own house, and corn and peas are strewn before them every day—I have dined with them myself, and that you shall do in time, too; for tell me what company you keep and I'll tell you who you are—up at the Hall they have two birds with green necks and a crest upon their heads; they can spread out their tails like a great wheel, and these are so bright with various colours that it makes one's eyes ache. These birds are called peacocks, and that is 'the beautiful.' If they were only plucked a little they would look no better than the rest of us. I would have plucked them already if they had not been so big."

"I'll pluck them," piped the young sparrow, who had no feathers yet.

In the farmhouse lived a young married couple; they loved each other dearly, were industrious and active, and everything in their home looked very nice. On Sundays the young wife came down early, plucked a handful of the most beautiful roses, and put them into a glass of water, which she placed upon the cupboard.

"Now I see that it is Sunday," said the husband, kissing his little wife. They sat down, read their hymn-book, and held each other by the hand, while the sun shone down upon the fresh roses and upon them.

"This sight is really too tedious," said the sparrow-mother, who could see into the room from her nest; and she flew away.

The same thing happened on the following Sunday, for every Sunday fresh roses were put into the glass; but the rose-bush bloomed as beautifully as ever. The young sparrows now had feathers, and wanted very much to fly with their mother; but she would not allow it, and so they had to stay at home. In one of her flights, however it may have happened, she was caught, before she was aware of it, in a horse-hair net which some boys had attached to a tree. The horse-hair was drawn tightly round her leg—as tightly as if the latter were to be cut off; she was in great pain and terror. The boys came running up and seized her, and in no gentle way either.

"It's only a sparrow," they said; they did not, however, let her go, but took her home with them, and every time she cried they hit her on the beak.

In the farmhouse was an old man who understood making soap into cakes and balls, both for shaving and washing. He was a merry old man, always wandering about. On seeing the sparrow which the boys had brought, and which they said they did not want, he asked, "Shall we make it look very pretty?"

At these words an icy shudder ran through the sparrow-mother.

Out of his box, in which were the most beautiful colours, the old man took a quantity of shining leaf-gold, while the boys had to go and fetch some white of egg, with which the sparrow was to be smeared all over; the gold was stuck on to this, and the sparrow-mother was now gilded all over. But she, trembling in every limb, did not think of the adornment. Then the soap-man tore off a small piece from the red lining of his old jacket, and cutting it so as to make it look like a cock's comb, he stuck it to the bird's head.

"Now you will see the gold-jacket fly," said the old man, letting the sparrow go, which flew away in deadly fear, with the sun shining upon her. How she glittered! All the sparrows, and even a crow—and an old boy he was too—were startled at the sight; but still they flew after her to learn what kind of strange bird she was.

Driven by fear and horror, she flew homeward; she was almost sinking fainting to the earth, while the flock of pursuing birds increased, some even attempting to peck at her.

"Look at her! Look at her!" they all cried.

"Look at her! Look at her!" cried her little ones, as she approached the nest. "That is certainly a young peacock, for it glitters in all colours; it makes one's eyes ache, as mother told us. Peep! that's 'the beautiful'." And then they pecked at the bird with their little beaks so that it was impossible for her to get into the nest; she was so exhausted that she couldn't even say "Peep!" much less "I am your own mother!" The other birds, too, now fell upon the sparrow and plucked off feather after feather until she fell bleeding into the rose-bush.

"Poor creature!" said all the roses; "only be still, and we will hide you. Lean your little head against us."

The sparrow spread out her wings once more, then drew them closely to her, and lay dead near the neighbouring family, the beautiful fresh roses.

"Peep!" sounded from the nest. "Where can mother be so long? It's more than I can understand. It cannot be a trick of hers, and mean that we are now to take care of ourselves. She has left us the house as an inheritance; but to which of us is it to belong when we have families of our own?"

"Yes, it won't do for you to stay with me when I increase my household with a wife and children,'" said the smallest.

"I daresay I shall have more wives and children than you," said the second.

"But I am the eldest!" exclaimed the third. Then they all got excited; they hit out with their wings, pecked with their beaks, and flop! one after another was thrown out of the nest. There they lay with their anger, holding their heads on one side and blinking the eye that was turned upwards. That was their way of looking foolish.

They could fly a little; by practice they learned to improve, and at last they agreed upon a sign by which to recognise each other if they should meet in the world later on. It was to be one "Peep!" and three scratches on the ground with the left foot.

The young one who had remained behind in the nest made himself as broad as he could, for he was the proprietor. But this greatness did not last long. In the night the red flames burst through the window and seized the roof; the dry straw blazed up high, and the whole house, together with the young sparrow, was burned. The two others, who wanted to marry, thus saved their lives by a stroke of luck.

When the sun rose again and everything looked as refreshed as if it had had a quiet sleep, there only remained of the farmhouse a few black charred beams leaning against the chimney, which was now its own master. Thick smoke still rose from the ruins, but the rose-bush stood yonder, fresh, blooming, and untouched, every flower and every twig being reflected in the clear water.

"How beautifully the roses bloom before the ruined house," exclaimed a passer-by. "A pleasanter picture cannot be imagined. I must have that." And the man took out of his portfolio a little book with white leaves: he was a painter, and with his pencil he drew the smoking house, the charred beams and the overhanging chimney, which bent more and more; in the foreground he put the large, blooming rose-bush, which presented a charming view. For its sake alone the whole picture had been drawn.

Later in the day the two sparrows who had been born there came by. "Where is the house?" they asked. "Where is the nest? Peep! All is burned and our strong brother too. That's what he has now for keeping the nest. The roses got off very well; there they still stand with their red cheeks. They certainly do not mourn at their neighbours' misfortunes. I don't want to talk to them, and it looks miserable here — that's my opinion." And away they went.

On a beautiful sunny autumn day — one could almost have believed it was still the middle of summer — there hopped about in the dry clean-swept courtyard before the principal entrance of the Hall a number of black, white, and gaily-coloured pigeons, all shining in the sunlight. The pigeon-mothers said to their young ones: "Stand in groups, stand in groups! for that looks much better."

"What kind of creatures are those little grey ones that run about behind us?" asked an old pigeon, with red and green in her eyes. "Little grey ones! Little grey ones!" she cried.

"They are sparrows, and good creatures. We have always had the reputation of being pious, so we will allow them to pick up the corn with us; they don't interrupt our talk, and they scrape so prettily when they bow."

Indeed they were continually making three foot-scrapings with the left foot and also said "Peep!" By this means they recognised each other, for they were the sparrows from the nest on the burned house.

"Here is excellent fare!" said the sparrow. The pigeons strutted round one another, puffed out their chests mightily, and had their own private views and opinions.

"Do you see that pouter pigeon?" said one to the other. "Do you see how she swallows the peas? She eats too many, and the best ones too. Curoo! Curoo! How she lifts her crest, the ugly, spiteful creature! Curoo! Curoo!" And the eyes of all sparkled with malice. "Stand in groups! Stand in groups! Little grey ones, little grey ones! Curoo, curoo, curoo!"

So their chatter ran on, and so it will run on for thousands of years. The sparrows ate lustily; they listened attentively, and even stood in the ranks with the others, but it did not suit them at all. They were full, and so they left the pigeons, exchanging opinions about them, slipped in under the garden palings, and when they found the door leading into the house open, one of them, who was more than full, and therefore felt brave, hopped on to the threshold. "Peep!" said he; "I may venture that."

"Peep!" said the other; "so may I, and something more too!" and he hopped into the room. No one was there; the third sparrow, seeing this, flew still farther into the room, exclaiming, "All or nothing! It is a curious man's nest all the same; and what have they put up here? What is it?"

Close to the sparrows the roses were blooming; they were reflected in the water, and the charred beams leaned against the overhanging chimney. "Do tell me what this is. How comes this in a room at the Hall?" And all three sparrows wanted to fly over the roses and the chimney, but flew against a flat wall. It was all a picture, a great splendid picture, which the artist had painted from a sketch.

"Peep!" said the sparrows, "it's nothing. It only looks like something. Peep! that is 'the beautiful.' Do you understand it? I don't."

And they flew away, for some people came into the room.

Days and years went by. The pigeons had often cooed, not to say growled—the spiteful creatures; the sparrows had been frozen in winter and had lived merrily in summer: they were all betrothed, or married, or whatever you like to call it. They had little ones, and of course each one thought his own the handsomest and cleverest; one flew this way, another that, and when they met they recognised each other by their "Peep!" and the three scrapes with the left foot. The eldest had remained an old maid and had no nest nor young ones. It was her pet idea to see a great city, so she flew to Copenhagen.

There was a large house painted in many gay colours standing close to the castle and the canal, upon which latter were to be seen many ships laden with apples and pottery. The windows of the house were broader at the bottom than at the top, and when the sparrows looked through them, every room appeared to them like a tulip with the brightest colours and shades. But in the middle of the tulip stood white men, made of marble; a few were of plaster; still, looked at with sparrows' eyes, that comes to the same thing. Up on the roof stood a metal chariot drawn by metal horses, and the goddess of Victory, also of metal, was driving. It was *Thorwaldsen's Museum.*

"How it shines! how it shines!" said the maiden sparrow. "I suppose that is 'the beautiful.' Peep! But here it is larger than a peacock." She still remembered what in her childhood's days her mother had looked upon as the greatest among the beautiful. She flew down into the courtyard: there everything was extremely fine. Palms and branches were painted on the walls, and in the middle of the court stood a great blooming rose-tree spreading out its fresh boughs, covered with roses, over a grave. Thither flew the maiden sparrow, for she saw several of her own kind there. A "peep" and three foot-scrapings—in this way she had often greeted throughout the year, and no one here had responded, for those who are once parted do not meet every day; and so this greeting had become a habit with her. But to-day two old sparrows and a young one answered with a "peep" and the thrice-repeated scrape with the left foot.

"Ah! Good-day! good-day!" They were two old ones from the nest and a little one of the family. "Do we meet here? It's a grand place, but there's not much to eat. This is 'the beautiful.' Peep!"

Many people came out of the side rooms where the beautiful marble statues stood and approached the grave where lay the great master who had created these works of art. All stood with enraptured faces round Thorwaldsen's grave, and a few picked up the fallen rose-leaves and preserved them. They had come from afar: one from mighty England, others from Germany and France. The fairest of the ladies plucked one of the roses and hid it in her bosom. Then the sparrows thought that the roses reigned here, and that the house had been built for their sake. That appeared to them to be really too much, but since all the people showed their love for the roses, they did not wish to be behindhand. "Peep!" they said, sweeping the ground with their tails, and blinking with one eye at the roses, they had not looked at them long before they were convinced that they were their old neighbours. And so they really were. The painter who had drawn the rose-bush near the ruined house, had afterwards obtained permission to dig it up, and had given it to the architect, for finer roses had never been seen. The architect had planted it upon Thorwaldsen's grave, where it bloomed as an emblem of 'the beautiful' and yielded fragrant red rose-leaves to be carried as mementoes to distant lands.

"Have you obtained an appointment here in the city?" asked the sparrows. The roses nodded; they recognized their grey neighbours and were pleased to see them again. "How glorious it is to live and to bloom, to see old friends again, and happy faces every day. It is as if every day were a festival." "Peep!" said the sparrows. "Yes, they are really our old neighbours; we remember their origin near the pond. Peep! how they have got on. Yes, some succeed while they are asleep. Ah! there's a faded leaf; I can see that quite plainly." And they pecked at it till it fell off. But the tree stood there fresher and greener than ever; the roses bloomed in the sunshine on Thorwaldsen's grave and became associated with his immortal name.

THE WICKED PRINCE

THERE lived once upon a time a wicked prince whose heart and mind were set upon conquering all the countries of the world, and on frightening the people; he devastated their countries with fire and sword, and his soldiers trod down the crops in the fields and destroyed the peasants' huts by fire, so that the flames licked the green leaves off the branches, and the fruit hung dried up on the singed black trees. Many a poor mother fled, her naked baby in her arms, behind the still smoking walls of her cottage; but also there the soldiers followed her, and when they found her, she served as new nourishment to their diabolical enjoyments; demons could not possibly have done worse things than these soldiers! The prince was of opinion that all this was right, and that it was only the natural course which things ought to take. His power increased day by day, his name was feared by all, and fortune favoured his deeds.

He brought enormous wealth home from the conquered towns, and gradually accumulated in his residence riches which could nowhere be equalled. He erected magnificent palaces, churches, and halls, and all who saw these splendid buildings and great treasures exclaimed admiringly: "What a mighty prince!" But they did not know what endless misery he had brought upon other countries, nor did they hear the sighs and lamentations which rose up from the *débris* of the destroyed cities.

The prince often looked with delight upon his gold and his magnificent edifices, and thought, like the crowd: "What a mighty prince! But I must have more — much more. No power on earth must equal mine, far less exceed it."

He made war with all his neighbours, and defeated them. The conquered kings were chained up with golden fetters to his chariot when he drove through the streets of his city. These kings had to kneel at his and his courtiers' feet when they sat at table, and live on the morsels which they left. At last the prince had his own statue erected on the public places and fixed on the royal palaces; nay, he even wished it to be placed in the churches, on the altars, but in this the priests opposed him, saying: "Prince, you are mighty indeed, but God's power is much greater than yours; we dare not obey your orders."

"Well," said the prince. "Then I will conquer God too." And in his haughtiness and foolish presumption he ordered a magnificent ship to be constructed, with which he could sail through the air; it was gorgeously fitted out and of many colours; like the tail of a peacock, it was covered with thousands of eyes, but each eye was the barrel of a gun. The prince sat in the centre of the ship, and had only to touch a spring in order to make thousands of bullets fly out in all directions, while the guns were at once loaded again. Hundreds of eagles were attached to this ship, and it rose with the swiftness of an arrow up towards the sun. The earth was soon left far below, and looked, with its mountains and woods, like a cornfield where the plough had made furrows which separated green meadows; soon it looked only like a map with indistinct lines upon it; and at last it entirely disappeared in mist and clouds. Higher and higher rose the eagles up into the air; then God sent one of his numberless angels against the ship. The wicked prince showered thousands of bullets upon him, but they rebounded from his shining wings and fell down like ordinary hailstones. One drop of blood, one single drop, came out of the white feathers of the angel's wings and fell upon the ship in which the prince sat, burnt into it, and weighed upon it like thousands of hundredweights, dragging it rapidly down to the earth again; the strong wings of the eagles gave way, the wind roared round the prince's head, and the clouds around — were they formed by the smoke rising up from the burnt cities? — took strange shapes, like crabs many, many miles long, which stretched their claws out after him, and rose up like enormous rocks, from which rolling masses dashed down, and became fire-spitting dragons.

The prince was lying half-dead in his ship, when it sank at last with a terrible shock into the branches of a large tree in the wood.

"I will conquer God!" said the prince. "I have sworn it: my will must be done!"

And he spent seven years in the construction of wonderful ships to sail through the air, and had darts cast from the hardest steel to break the walls of heaven with. He gathered warriors from all countries, so many that when they were placed side by side they covered the space of several miles. They entered the ships and the prince was approaching his own, when God sent a swarm of gnats — one swarm of little gnats. They buzzed round the prince and stung his face and hands; angrily he drew his sword and brandished it, but he only touched the air and did not hit the gnats. Then he ordered his servants to bring costly coverings and wrap him in them, that the gnats might no longer be able to reach him. The servants carried out his orders, but one single gnat had placed itself inside one of the coverings, crept into the prince's ear and stung him. The place burnt like fire, and the poison entered into his blood. Mad with pain, he tore off the coverings and his clothes too, flinging them far away, and danced about before the eyes of his ferocious soldiers, who now mocked at him, the mad prince, who wished to make war with God, and was overcome by a single little gnat.

THE BELL

In the narrow streets of a large town people often heard in the evening, when the sun was setting, and his last rays gave a golden tint to the chimney-pots, a strange noise which resembled the sound of a church bell; it only lasted an instant, for it was lost in the continual roar of traffic and hum of voices which rose from the town. "The evening bell is ringing," people used to say; "the sun is setting!" Those who walked outside the town, where the houses were less crowded and interspersed by gardens and little fields, saw the evening sky much better, and heard the sound of the bell much more clearly. It seemed as though the sound came from a church, deep in the calm, fragrant wood, and thither people looked with devout feelings.

A considerable time elapsed: one said to the other, "I really wonder if there is a church out in the wood. The bell has indeed a strange sweet sound! Shall we go there and see what the cause of it is?" The rich drove, the poor walked, but the way seemed to them extraordinarily long, and when they arrived at a number of willow trees on the border of the wood they sat down, looked up into the great branches and thought they were now really in the wood. A confectioner from the town also came out and put up a stall there; then came another confectioner who hung a bell over his stall, which was covered with pitch to protect it from the rain, but the clapper was wanting.

When people came home they used to say that it had been very romantic, and that really means something else than merely taking tea. Three persons declared that they had gone as far as the end of the wood; they had always heard the strange sound, but there it seemed to them as if it came from the town. One of them wrote verses about the bell, and said that it was like the voice of a mother speaking to an intelligent and beloved child; no tune, he said, was sweeter than the sound of the bell.

The emperor of the country heard of it, and declared that he who would really find out where the sound came from should receive the title of "Bellringer to the World," even if there was no bell at all.

Now many went out into the wood for the sake of this splendid berth; but only one of them came back with some sort of explanation. None of them had gone far enough, nor had he, and yet he said that the sound of the bell came from a large owl in a hollow tree. It was a wisdom owl, which continually knocked its head against the tree, but he was unable to say with certainty whether its head or the hollow trunk of the tree was the cause of the noise.

He was appointed "Bellringer to the World," and wrote every year a short dissertation on the owl, but by this means people did not become any wiser than they had been before.

It was just confirmation-day. The clergyman had delivered a beautiful and touching sermon, the candidates were deeply moved by it; it was indeed a very important day for them; they were all at once transformed from mere children to grown-up people; the childish soul was to fly over, as it were, into a more reasonable being.

The sun shone most brightly; and the sound of the great unknown bell was heard more distinctly than ever. They had a mind to go thither, all except three. One of them wished to go home and try on her ball dress, for this very dress and the ball were the cause of her being confirmed this time, otherwise she would not have been allowed to go. The second, a poor boy, had borrowed a coat and a pair of boots from the son of his landlord to be confirmed in, and he had to return them at a certain time. The third said that he never went into strange places if his parents were not with him; he had always been a good child, and wished to remain so, even after being confirmed, and they ought not to tease him for this; they, however, did it all the same. These three, therefore, did not go; the others went on. The sun was shining, the birds were singing, and the confirmed children sang too, holding each other by the hand, for they had no position yet, and they were all equal in the eyes of God. Two of the smallest soon became tired and returned to the town; two little girls sat down and made garlands of flowers, they, therefore, did not go on. When the others arrived at the willow trees, where the confectioner had put up his stall, they said: "Now we are out here; the bell does not in reality exist — it is only something that people imagine!"

Then suddenly the sound of the bell was heard so beautifully and solemnly from the wood that four or five made up their minds to go still further on. The wood was very thickly grown. It was difficult to advance: wood lilies and anemones grew almost too high; flowering convolvuli and brambles were hanging like garlands from tree to tree; while the nightingales were singing and the sunbeams played. That was very beautiful! But the way was unfit for the girls; they would have torn their dresses. Large rocks, covered with moss of various hues, were lying about; the fresh spring water rippled forth with a peculiar sound. "I don't think that can be the bell," said one of the confirmed children, and then he lay down and listened. "We must try to find out if it is!" And there he remained, and let the others walk on.

They came to a hut built of the bark of trees and branches; a large crab-apple tree spread its branches over it, as if it intended to pour all its fruit on the roof, upon which roses were blooming; the long boughs covered the gable, where a little bell was hanging. Was this the one they had heard? All agreed that it must be so, except one who said that the bell was too small and too thin to be heard at such a distance, and that it had quite a different sound to that which had so touched men's hearts.

He who spoke was a king's son, and therefore the others said that such a one always wishes to be cleverer than other people.

Therefore they let him go alone; and as he walked on, the solitude of the wood produced a feeling of reverence in his breast; but still he heard the little bell about which the others rejoiced, and sometimes, when the wind blew in that direction, he could hear the sounds from the confectioner's stall, where the others were singing at tea. But the deep sounds of the bell were much stronger; soon it seemed to him as if an organ played an accompaniment — the sound came from the left, from the side where the heart is. Now something rustled among the bushes, and a little boy stood before the king's son, in wooden shoes and such a short jacket that the sleeves did not reach to his wrists. They knew each other: the boy was the one who had not been able to go with them because he had to take the coat and boots back to his landlord's son. That he had done, and had started again in his wooden shoes and old clothes, for the sound of the bell was too enticing — he felt he must go on.

"We might go together," said the king's son. But the poor boy with the wooden shoes was quite ashamed; he pulled at the short sleeves of his jacket, and said that he was afraid he could not walk so fast; besides, he was of opinion that the bell ought to be sought at the right, for there was all that was grand and magnificent.

"Then we shall not meet," said the king's son, nodding to the poor boy, who went into the deepest part of the wood, where the thorns tore his shabby clothes and scratched his hands, face, and feet until they bled. The king's son also received several good scratches, but the sun was shining on his way, and it is he whom we will now follow, for he was a quick fellow. "I will and must find the bell," he said, "if I have to go to the end of the world."

Ugly monkeys sat high in the branches and clenched their teeth. "Shall we beat him?" they said. "Shall we thrash him? He is a king's son!"

But he walked on undaunted, deeper and deeper into the wood, where the most wonderful flowers were growing; there were standing white star lilies with blood-red stamens, sky-blue tulips shining when the wind moved them; apple-trees covered with apples like large glittering soap bubbles: only think how resplendent these trees were in the sunshine! All around were beautiful green meadows, where hart and hind played in the grass. There grew magnificent oaks and beech-trees; and if the bark was split of any of them, long blades of grass grew out of the clefts; there were also large smooth lakes in the wood, on which the swans were swimming about and flapping their wings. The king's son often stood still and listened; sometimes he thought that the sound of the bell rose up to him out of one of these deep lakes, but soon he found that this was a mistake, and that the bell was ringing still farther in the wood. Then the sun set, the clouds were as red as fire; it became quiet in the wood; he sank down on his knees, sang an evening hymn and said: "I shall never find what I am looking for! Now the sun is setting, and the night, the dark night, is approaching. Yet I may perhaps see the round sun once more before he disappears beneath the horizon. I will climb up these rocks, they are as high as the highest trees!" And then, taking hold of the creepers and roots, he climbed up on the wet stones, where water-snakes were wriggling and the toads, as it were, barked at him: he reached the top before the sun, seen from such a height, had quite set. "Oh, what a splendour!" The sea, the great majestic sea, which was rolling its long waves against the shore, stretched out before him, and the sun was standing like a large bright altar and there where sea and heaven met — all melted together in the most glowing colours; the wood was singing, and his heart too. The whole of nature was one large holy church, in which the trees and hovering clouds formed the pillars, the flowers and grass the woven velvet carpet, and heaven itself was the great cupola; up there the flame colour vanished as soon as the sun disappeared, but millions of stars were lighted; diamond lamps were shining, and the king's son stretched his arms out towards heaven, towards the sea, and towards the wood. Then suddenly the poor boy with the short-sleeved jacket and the wooden shoes appeared; he had arrived just as quickly on the road he had chosen. And they ran towards each other and took one another's hand, in the great cathedral of nature and poesy, and above them sounded the invisible holy bell; happy spirits surrounded them, singing hallelujahs and rejoicing.

"THERE IS NO DOUBT ABOUT IT"

"THAT was a terrible affair!" said a hen, and in a quarter of the town, too, where it had not taken place. "That was a terrible affair in a hen-roost. I cannot sleep alone to-night. It is s a good thing that many of us sit on the roost together." And then she told a story that made the feathers on the other hens bristle up, and the cock's comb fall. There was no doubt about it.

But we will begin at the beginning, and that is to be found in a hen-roost in another part of the town. The sun was setting, and the fowls were flying on to their roost; one hen, with white feathers and short legs, used to lay her eggs according to the regulations, and was, as a hen, respectable in every way. As she was flying upon the roost, she plucked herself with her beak, and a little feather came out.

"There it goes," she said; "the more I pluck, the more beautiful do I get." She said this merrily, for she was the best of the hens, and, moreover, as had been said, very respectable. With that she went to sleep.

It was dark all around, and hen sat close to hen, but the one who sat nearest to her merry neighbour did not sleep. She had heard and yet not heard, as we are often obliged to do in this world, in order to live at peace; but she could not keep it from her neighbour on the other side any longer. "Did you hear what was said? I mention no names, but there is a hen here who intends to pluck herself in order to look well. If I were a cock, I should despise her."

Just over the fowls sat the owl, with father owl and the little owls. The family has sharp ears, and they all heard every word that their neighbour had said. They rolled their eyes, and mother owl, beating her wings, said: "Don't listen to her! But I suppose you heard what was said? I heard it with my own ears, and one has to hear a great deal before they fall off. There is one among the fowls who has so far forgotten what is becoming to a hen that she plucks out all her feathers and lets the cock see it."

"*Prenez garde aux enfants!*" said father owl; "children should not hear such things."

"But I must tell our neighbour owl about it; she is such an estimable owl to talk to." And with that she flew away.

"Too-whoo! Too-whoo!" they both hooted into the neighbour's dove-cot to the doves inside. "Have you heard? Have you heard? Too-whoo! There is a hen who has plucked out all her feathers for the sake of the cock; she will freeze to death, if she is not frozen already. Too-whoo!"

"Where? where?" cooed the doves.

"In the neighbour's yard. I have as good as seen it myself. It is almost unbecoming to tell the story, but there is no doubt about it."

"Believe every word of what we tell you," said the doves, and cooed down into their poultry-yard. "There is a hen—nay, some say that there are two—who have plucked out all their feathers, in order not to look like the others, and to attract the attention of the cock. It is a dangerous game, for one can easily catch cold and die from fever, and both of these are dead already."

"Wake up! wake up!" crowed the cock, and flew upon his board. Sleep was still in his eyes, but yet he crowed out: "Three hens have died of their un-

"THERE IS NO DOUBT ABOUT IT."

fortunate love for a cock. They had plucked out all their feathers. It is a horrible story: I will not keep it to myself, but let it go farther."

"Let it go farther," shrieked the bats, and the hens clucked and the cocks crowed, "Let it go farther! Let it go farther!" In this way the story travelled from poultry-yard to poultry-yard, and at last came back to the place from which it had really started.

"Five hens," it now ran, "have plucked out all their feathers to show which of them had grown leanest for love of the cock, and then they all pecked at each other till the blood ran down and they fell down dead, to the derision and shame of their family, and to the great loss of their owner."

The hen who had lost the loose little feather naturally did not recognise her own story, and being a respectable hen, said: "I despise those fowls; but there are more of that kind. Such things ought not to be concealed, and I will do my best to get the story into the papers, so that it becomes known throughout the land; the hens have richly deserved it, and their family too."

It got into the papers, it was printed; and there is no doubt about it, one little feather may easily grow into five hens.

A STORY

IN the garden all the apple-trees were in blossom. They had hastened to bring forth flowers before they got green leaves, and in the yard all the ducklings walked up and down, and the cat too: it basked in the sun and licked the sunshine from its own paws. And when one looked at the fields, how beautifully the corn stood and how green it shone, without comparison! and there was a twittering and a fluttering of all the little birds, as if the day were a great festival; and so it was, for it was Sunday. All the bells were ringing, and all the people went to church, looking cheerful, and dressed in their best clothes. There was a look of cheerfulness on everything. The day was so warm and beautiful that one might well have said: "God's kindness to us men is beyond all limits." But inside the church the pastor stood in the pulpit, and spoke very loudly and angrily. He said that all men were wicked, and God would punish them for their sins, and that the wicked, when they died, would be cast into hell, to burn for ever and ever. He spoke very excitedly, saying that their evil propensities would not be destroyed, nor would the fire be extinguished, and they should never find rest. That was terrible to hear, and he said it in such a tone of conviction; he described hell to them as a miserable hole where all the refuse of the world gathers. There was no air beside the hot burning sulphur flame, and there was no ground under their feet; they, the wicked ones, sank deeper and deeper, while eternal silence surrounded them! It was dreadful to hear all that, for the preacher spoke from his heart, and all the people in the church were terrified. Meanwhile, the birds sang merrily outside, and the sun was shining so beautifully warm, it seemed as though every little flower said: "God, Thy kindness towards us all is without limits." Indeed, outside it was not at all like the pastor's sermon.

The same evening, upon going to bed, the pastor noticed his wife sitting there quiet and pensive.

"What is the matter with you?" he asked her.

"Well, the matter with me is," she said, "that I cannot collect my thoughts, and am unable to grasp the meaning of what you said to-day in church — that there are so many wicked people, and that they should burn eternally. Alas! eternally — how long! I am only a woman and a sinner before God, but I should not have the heart to let even the worst sinner burn for ever, and how could our Lord to do so, who is so infinitely good, and who knows how the wickedness comes from without and within? No, I am unable to imagine that, although you say so."

It was autumn; the trees dropped their leaves, the earnest and severe pastor sat at the bedside of a dying person. A pious, faithful soul closed her eyes for ever; she was the pastor's wife.

. . . "If any one shall find rest in the grave and mercy before our Lord you shall certainly do so," said the pastor. He folded her hands and read a psalm over the dead woman.

She was buried; two large tears rolled over the cheeks of the earnest man, and in the parsonage it was empty and still, for its sun had set for ever. She had gone home.

It was night. A cold wind swept over the pastor's head; he opened his eyes, and it seemed to him as if the moon was shining into his room. It was not so, however; there was a being standing before his bed, and looking like the ghost of his deceased wife. She fixed her eyes upon him with such a kind and sad expression, just as if she wished to say something to him. The pastor raised himself in bed and stretched his arms towards her, saying, "Not even you can find eternal rest! You suffer, you best and most pious woman?"

The dead woman nodded her head as if to say "Yes," and put her hand on her breast.

"And can I not obtain rest in the grave for you?"

"Yes," was the answer.

"And how?"

"Give me one hair — only one single hair — from the head of the sinner for whom the fire shall never be extinguished, of the sinner whom God will condemn to eternal punishment in hell."

"Yes, one ought to be able to redeem you so easily, you pure, pious woman," he said.

"Follow me," said the dead woman. "It is thus granted to us. By my side you will be able to fly wherever your thoughts wish to go. Invisible to men, we shall penetrate into their most secret chambers; but with sure hand you must find out him who is destined to eternal torture, and before the cock crows he must be found!" As quickly as if carried by the winged thoughts they were in the great city, and from the walls the names of the deadly sins shone in flaming letters: pride, avarice, drunkenness, wantonness — in short, the whole seven-coloured bow of sin.

"Yes, therein, as I believed, as I knew it," said the pastor, "are living those who are abandoned to the eternal fire." And they were standing before the magnificently illuminated gate; the broad steps were adorned with carpets and flowers, and dance music was sounding through the festive halls. A footman dressed in silk and velvet stood with a large silver-mounted rod near the entrance.

"Our ball can compare favourably with the king's," he said, and turned with contempt towards the gazing crowd in the street. What he thought was sufficiently expressed in his features and movements: "Miserable beggars, who are looking in, you are nothing in comparison to me."

"Pride," said the dead woman; "do you see him?"

"The footman?" asked the pastor. "He is but a poor fool, and not doomed to be tortured eternally by fire!"

"Only a fool!" It sounded through the whole house of pride: they were all fools there.

Then they flew within the four naked walls of the miser. Lean as a skeleton, trembling with cold and hunger, the old man was clinging with all his thoughts to his money. They saw him jump up feverishly from his miserable couch and take a loose stone out of the wall; there lay gold coins in an old stocking. They saw him anxiously feeling over an old ragged coat in which pieces of gold were sewn, and his clammy fingers trembled.

"He is ill! That is madness — a joyless madness — besieged by fear and dreadful dreams!"

They quickly went away and came before the beds of the criminals; these unfortunate people slept side by side, in long rows. Like a ferocious animal, one of them rose out of his sleep and uttered a horrible cry, and gave his comrade a violent dig in the ribs with his pointed elbow, and this one turned round in his sleep:

"Be quiet, monster — sleep! This happens every night!"

"Every night!" repeated the other. "Yes, every night he comes and tortures me! In my violence I have done this and that. I was born with an evil mind, which has brought me hither for the second time; but if I have done wrong I suffer punishment for it. One thing, however, I have not yet confessed. When I came out a little while ago, and passed by the yard of my former master, evil thoughts rose within me when I remembered this and that. I struck a match a little bit on the wall; probably it came a little too close to the thatched roof. All burnt down — a great heat rose, such as sometimes overcomes me. I myself helped to rescue cattle and things, nothing alive burnt, except a flight of pigeons, which flew into the fire, and the yard dog, of which I had not thought; one could hear him howl out of the fire, and this howling I still hear when I wish to sleep; and when I have fallen asleep, the great rough dog comes and places himself upon me, and howls, presses, and tortures me. Now listen to what I tell you! You can snore; you are snoring the whole night, and I hardly a quarter of an hour!" And the blood rose to the head of the excited criminal; he threw himself upon his comrade, and beat him with his clenced fist in the face.

"Wicked Matz has become mad again!" they said amongst themselves. The other criminals seized him, wrestled with him, and bent him double, so that his head rested between his knees, and they tied him, so that the blood almost came out of his eyes and out of all his pores.

"You are killing the unfortunate man," said the pastor, and as he stretched out his hand to protect him who already suffered too much, the scene changed. They flew through rich halls and wretched hovels; wantonness and envy, all the deadly sins, passed before them. An angel of justice read their crimes and their defence; the latter was not a brilliant one, but it was read before God, Who reads the heart, Who knows everything, the wickedness that comes from within and from without, Who is mercy and love personified. The pastor's hand trembled; he dared not stretch it out, he did not venture to pull a hair out of the sinner's head. And tears gushed from his eyes like a stream of mercy and love, the cooling waters of which extinguished the eternal fire of hell.

Just then the cock crowed.

"Father of all mercy, grant Thou to her the peace that I was unable to procure for her!"

"I have it now!" said the dead woman. "It was your hard words, your despair of mankind, your gloomy belief in God and His creation, which drove me to you. Learn to know mankind! Even in the wicked one lives a part of God — and this extinguishes and conquers the flame of hell!"

The pastor felt a kiss on his lips; a gleam of light surrounded him — God's bright sun shone into the room, and his wife, alive, sweet and full of love, awoke him from a dream which God had sent him!

EVERYTHING IN THE RIGHT PLACE

IT is more than a hundred years ago! At the border of the wood, near a large lake, stood the old mansion: deep ditches surrounded it on every side, in which reeds and bulrushes grew. Close by the drawbridge, near the gate, there was an old willow-tree, which bent over the reeds.

From the narrow pass came the sound of bugles and the trampling of horses' feet; therefore a little girl who was watching the geese hastened to drive them away from the bridge, before the whole hunting party came galloping up; they came, however, so quickly, that the girl, in order to avoid being run over, placed herself on one of the high corner-stones of the bridge. She was still half a child and very delicately built; she had bright blue eyes, and a gentle, sweet expression. But such things the baron did not notice; while he was riding past the little goose-girl, he reversed his hunting crop, and in rough play gave her such a push with it that she fell backward into the ditch.

"Everything in the right place!" he cried. "Into the ditch with you."

Then he burst out laughing, for that he called fun; the others joined in — the whole party shouted and cried, while the hounds barked.

While the poor girl was falling she happily caught one of the branches of the willow-tree, by the help of which she held herself over the water, and as soon as the baron with his company and the dogs had disappeared through the gate, the girl endeavoured to scramble up, but the branch broke off, and she would have fallen backward among the rushes, had not a strong hand from above seized her at this moment. It was the hand of a pedlar; he had witnessed what had happened from a short distance, and now hastened to assist her.

"Everything in the right place," he said, imitating the noble baron, and pulling the little maid up to the dry ground. He wished to put the branch back in the place it had been broken off, but it is not possible to put "everything in the right place;" therefore he stuck the branch into the soft ground.

"Grow and thrive if you can, and produce a good flute for them yonder at the mansion," he said; it would have given him great pleasure to see the noble baron and his companions well thrashed. Then he entered the castle — but not the banqueting hall; he was too humble for that. No; he went to the servants' hall. The men-servants and maids looked over his stock of articles and bargained with him; loud crying and screaming were heard from the master's table above: they called it singing — indeed, they did their best. Laughter and the howls of dogs were heard through the open windows: there they were feasting and revelling; wine and strong old ale were foaming in the glasses and jugs; the favourite dogs ate with their masters; now and then the squires kissed one of these animals, after having wiped its mouth first with the tablecloth. They ordered the pedlar to come up, but only to make fun of him. The wine had got into their heads, and reason had left them. They poured beer into a stocking that he could drink with them, but quick. That's what they called fun, and it made them laugh. Then meadows, peasants, and farmyards were staked on one card and lost.

"Everything in the right place!" the pedlar said when he had at last safely got out of Sodon and Gomorrah, as he called it. "The open high road is my right place; up there I did not feel at ease."

The little maid, who was still watching the geese, nodded kindly to him as he passed through the gate.

Days and weeks passed, and it was seen that the broken willow-branch which the peddlar had stuck into the ground near the ditch remained fresh and green — nay, it even put forth fresh twigs; the little goose-girl saw that the branch had taken root, and was very pleased; the tree, so she said, was now her tree. While the tree was advancing, everything else at the castle was going backward, through feasting and gambling, for these are two rollers upon which nobody stands safely. Less than six years afterwards the baron passed out of his castle-gate a poor beggar, while the baronial seat had been bought by a rich tradesman. He was the very pedlar they had made fun of and poured beer into a stocking for him to drink; but honesty and industry bring one forward, and now the pedlar was the possessor of the baronial estate. From that time forward no card-playing was permitted there.

"That's a bad pastime," he said; "when the devil saw the Bible for the first time he wanted to produce a caricature in opposition to it, and invented card-playing."

The new proprietor of the estate took a wife, and whom did he take? — The little goose-girl, who had always remained good and kind, and who looked as beautiful in her new clothes as if she had been a lady of high birth. And how did all this come about? That would be too long a tale to tell in our busy time, but it really happened, and the most important events have yet to be told.

It was pleasant and cheerful to live in the old place now: the mother superintended the household, and the father looked after things out-of-doors, and they were indeed very prosperous.

Where honesty leads the way, prosperity is sure to follow. The old mansion was repaired and painted, the ditches were cleaned and fruit-trees planted; all was homely and pleasant, and the floors were as white and shining as a pasteboard. In the long winter evenings the mistress and her maids sat at the spinning-wheel in the large hall; every Sunday the counsellor—this title the pedlar had obtained, although only in his old days—read aloud a portion from the Bible. The children (for they had children) all received the best education, but they were not all equally clever, as is the case in all families.

In the meantime the willow-tree near the drawbridge had grown up into a splendid tree, and stood there, free, and was never clipped. "It is our genealogical tree," said the old people to their children, "and therefore it must be honoured."

A hundred years had elapsed. It was in our own days; the lake had been transformed into marsh land; the whole baronial seat had, as it were, disappeared. A pool of water near some ruined walls was the only remainder of the deep ditches; and here stood a magnificent old tree with overhanging branches—that was the genealogical tree. Here it stood, and showed how beautiful a willow can look if one does not interfere with it. The trunk, it is true, was cleft in the middle from the root to the crown; the storms had bent it a little, but it still stood there, and out of every crevice and cleft, in which wind and weather had carried mould, blades of grass and flowers sprang forth. Especially above, where the large boughs parted, there was quite a hanging garden, in which wild raspberries and hart's-tongue ferns throve, and even a little mistletoe had taken root, and grew gracefully in the old willow branches, which were reflected in the dark water beneath when the wind blew the chickweed into the corner of the pool. A footpath which led across the fields passed close by the old tree. High up, on the woody hillside, stood the new mansion. It had a splendid view, and was large and magnificent; its window panes were so clear that one might have thought there were none there at all. The large flight of steps which led to the entrance looked like a bower covered with roses and broad-leaved plants. The lawn was as green as if each blade of grass was cleaned separately morning and evening. Inside, in the hall, valuable oil paintings were hanging on the walls. Here stood chairs and sofas covered with silk and velvet, which could be easily rolled about on castors; there were tables with polished marble tops, and books bound in morocco with gilt edges. Indeed, well-to-do and distinguished people lived here; it was the dwelling of the baron and his family. Each article was in keeping with its surroundings. "Everything in the right place" was the motto according to which they also acted here, and therefore all the paintings which had once been the honour and glory of the old mansion were now hung up in the passage which led to the servants' rooms. It was all old lumber, especially two portraits—one representing a man in a scarlet coat with a wig, and the other a lady with powdered and curled hair holding a rose in her hand, each of them being surrounded by a large wreath of willow branches. Both portraits had many holes in them, because the baron's sons used the two old people as targets for their crossbows. They represented the counsellor and his wife, from whom the whole family descended. "But they did not properly belong to our family," said one of the boys; "he was a pedlar and she kept the geese. They were not like papa and mamma." The portraits were old lumber, and "everything in its right place." That was why the great-grandparents had been hung up in the passage leading to the servants' rooms.

The son of the village pastor was tutor at the mansion. One day he went for a walk across the fields with his young pupils and their elder sister, who had lately been confirmed. They walked along the road which passed by the old willow-tree, and while they were on the road she picked a bunch of field-flowers. "Everything in the right place," and indeed the bunch looked very beautiful. At the same time she listened to all that was said, and she very much liked to hear the pastor's son speak about the elements and of the great men and women in history. She had a healthy mind, noble in thought and deed, and with a heart full of love for everything that God had created. They stopped at the old willow-tree, as the youngest of the baron's sons wished very much to have a flute from it, such as had been cut for him from other willow-trees; the pastor's son broke a branch off. "Oh, pray do not do it!" said the young lady; but it was already done. "That is our famous old tree. I love it very much. They often laugh at me at home about it, but that does not matter. There is a story attached to this tree." And now she told him all that we already know about the tree—the old mansion, the pedlar and the goose-girl who had met there for the first time, and had become the ancestors of the noble family to which the young lady belonged.

"They did not like to be knighted, the good old people," she said; "their motto was 'everything in the right place,' and it would not be right, they thought, to purchase a title for money. My grandfather, the first baron, was their son. They say he was a very learned man, a great favourite with the princes and princesses, and was invited to all court festivities. The others at home love him best; but, I do not know why, there seemed to me to be something about the old couple that attracts my heart! How homely, how patriarchal, it must have been in the old mansion, where the mistress sat at the spinning-wheel with her maids, while her husband read aloud out of the Bible!"

"They must have been excellent, sensible people," said the pastor's son. And with this the conversation turned naturally to noblemen and commoners; from the manner in which the tutor spoke about the significance of being noble, it seemed almost as if he did not belong to a commoner's family.

"It is good fortune to be of a family who have distinguished themselves, and to possess as it were a spur in oneself to advance to all that is good. It is a splendid thing to belong to a noble family, whose name serves as a card of admission to the highest circles. Nobility is a distinction; it is a gold coin that bears the stamp of its own value. It is the fallacy of the time, and many poets express it, to say that all that is noble is bad and stupid, and that, on the contrary, the lower one goes among the poor, the more brilliant virtues one finds. I do not share this opinion, for it is wrong. In the upper classes one sees many touchingly beautiful traits; my own mother has told me of such, and I could mention several. One day she was visiting a nobleman's house in town; my grandmother, I believe, had been the lady's nurse when she was a child. My mother and the nobleman were alone in the room, when he suddenly noticed an old woman on crutches come limping into the courtyard; she came every Sunday to carry a gift away with her.

" 'There is the poor old woman,' said the nobleman; 'it is so difficult for her to walk.'

"My mother had hardly understood what he said before he disappeared from the room, and went downstairs, in order to save her the troublesome walk for the gift she came to fetch. Of course this is only a little incident, but it has its good sound like the poor widow's two mites in the Bible, the sound which echoes in the depth of every human heart; and this is what the poet ought to show and point out—more especially in our own time he ought to

EVERYTHING IN THE RIGHT PLACE

sing of this; it does good, it mitigates and reconciles! But when a man, simply because he is of noble birth and possesses a genealogy, stands on his hind legs and neighs in the street like an Arabian horse, and says when a commoner has been in a room: 'Some people from the street have been here,' there nobility is decaying; it has become a mask of the kind that Thespis created, and it is amusing when such a person is exposed in satire."

Such was the tutor's speech; it was a little long, but while he delivered it he had finished cutting the flute.

There was a large party at the mansion; many guests from the neighbourhood and from the capital had arrived. There were ladies with tasteful and with tasteless dresses; the big hall was quite crowded with people. The clergymen stood humbly together in a corner, and looked as if they were preparing for a funeral, but it was a festival — only the amusement had not yet begun. A great concert was to take place, and that is why the baron's young son had brought his willow flute with him; but he could not make it sound, nor could his father, and therefore the flute was good for nothing.

There was music and songs of the kind which delight most those that perform them; otherwise quite charming!

"Are you an artist?" said a cavalier, the son of his father; "you play on the flute, you have made it yourself; it is genius that rules — the place of honour is due to you."

"Certainly not! I only advance with the time, and that of course one can't help."

"I hope you will delight us all with the little instrument — will you not?" Thus saying he handed to the tutor the flute which had been cut from the willow tree by the pool; and then announced in a loud voice that the tutor wished to perform a solo on the flute. They wished to tease him — that was evident, and therefore the tutor declined to play, although he could do so very well. They urged and requested him, however, so long, that at last he took up the flute and placed it to his lips.

That was a marvellous flute! Its sound was as thrilling as the whistle of a steam engine; in fact it was much stronger, for it sounded and was heard in the yard, in the garden, in the wood, and many miles round in the country; at the same time a storm rose and roared; "Everything in the right place." And with this the baron, as if carried by the wind, flew out of the hall straight into the shepherd's cottage, and the shepherd flew — not into the hall, thither he could not come — but into the servants' hall, among the smart footmen who were striding about in silk stockings; these haughty menials looked horror-struck that such a person ventured to sit at table with them. But in the hall the baron's daughter flew to the place of honour at the end of the table — she was worthy to sit there; the pastor's son had the seat next to her; the two sat there as if they were a bridal pair. An old Count, belonging to one of the oldest families of the country, remained untouched in his place of honour; the flute was just, and it is one's duty to be so. The sharp-tongued cavalier who had caused the flute to be played, and who was the child of his parents, flew headlong into the fowl-house, but not he alone.

The flute was heard at the distance of a mile, and strange events took place. A rich banker's family, who were driving in a coach and four, were blown out of it, and could not even find room behind it with their footmen. Two rich farmers who had in our days shot up higher than their own corn-fields, were flung into the ditch; it was a dangerous flute. Fortunately it burst at the first sound, and that was a good thing, for then it was put back into its owner's pocket—"its right place."

The next day, nobody spoke a word about what had taken place; thus originated the phrase, "to pocket the flute." Everything was again in its usual order, except that the two old pictures of the peddlar and the goose-girl were hanging in the banqueting-hall. There they were on the wall as if blown up there; and as a real expert said that they were painted by a master's hand, they remained there and were restored. "Everything in the right place," and to this it will come. Eternity is long, much longer indeed than this story.

THE DUMB BOOK

IN the high-road which led through a wood stood a solitary farm-house; the road, in fact, ran right through its yard. The sun was shining and all the windows were open; within the house people were very busy. In the yard, in an arbour formed by lilac bushes in full bloom, stood an open coffin; thither they had carried a dead man, who was to be buried that very afternoon. Nobody shed a tear over him; his face was covered over with a white cloth, under his head they had placed a large thick book, the leaves of which consisted of folded sheets of blotting-paper, and withered flowers lay between them; it was the herbarium which he had gathered in various places and was to be buried with him, according to his own wish. Every one of the flowers in it was connected with some chapter of his life.

"Who is the dead man?" we asked.

"The old student," was the reply. "They say that he was once an energetic young man, that he studied the dead languages, and sang and even composed many songs; then something had happened to him, and in consequence of this he gave himself up to drink, body and mind. When at last he had ruined his health, they brought him into the country, where someone paid for his board and residence. He was gentle as a child as long as the sullen mood did not come over him; but when it came he was fierce, became as strong as a giant, and ran about in the wood like a chased deer. But when we succeeded in bringing him home, and prevailed upon him to open the book with the dried-up plants in it, he would sometimes sit for a whole day looking at this or that plant, while frequently the tears rolled over his cheeks. God knows what was in his mind; but he requested us to put the book into his coffin, and now he lies there. In a little while the lid will be placed upon the coffin, and he will have sweet rest in the grave!"

The cloth which covered his face was lifted up; the dead man's face expressed peace—a sunbeam fell upon it. A swallow flew with the swiftness of an arrow into the arbour, turning in its flight, and twittered over the dead man's head.

What a strange feeling it is—surely we all know it—to look through old letters of our young days; a different life rises up out of the past, as it were, with all its hopes and sorrows. How many of the people with whom in those days we used to be on intimate terms appear to us as if dead, and yet they are still alive—only we have not thought of them for such a long time, whom we imagined we should retain in our memories for ever, and share every joy and sorrow with them.

The withered oak leaf in the book here recalled the friend, the schoolfellow, who was to be his friend for life. He fixed the leaf to the student's cap in the green wood, when they vowed eternal friendship. Where does he dwell now? The leaf is kept, but the friendship does no longer exist. Here is a foreign hothouse plant, too tender for the gardens of the North. It is almost as if its leaves still smelt sweet! She gave it to him out of her own garden—a nobleman's daughter.

Here is a water-lily that he had plucked himself, and watered with salt tears—a lily of sweet water. And here is a nettle: what may its leaves tell us? What might he have thought when he plucked and kept it? Here is a little snowdrop out of the solitary wood; here is an evergreen from the flower-pot at the tavern; and here is a simple blade of grass.

The lilac bends its fresh fragrant flowers over the dead man's head; the swallow passes again—"twit, twit;" now the men come with hammer and nails, the lid is placed over the dead man, while his head rests on the dumb book—so long cherished, now closed for ever!

TWO BROTHERS

ON one of the Danish islands, where old Thingstones, the seats of justice of our forefathers, still stand in the cornfields, and huge trees rise in the forests of beech, there lies a little town whose low houses are covered with red tiles. In one of these houses strange things were brewing over the glowing coals on the open hearth; there was a boiling going on in glasses, and a mixing and distilling, while herbs were being cut up and pounded in mortars. An elderly man looked after it all.

"One must only do the right thing," he said; "yes, the right—the correct thing. One must find out the truth concerning every created particle, and keep to that."

In the room with the good housewife sat her two sons; they were still small, but had great thoughts. Their mother, too, had always spoken to them of right and justice, and exhorted them to keep to the truth, which she said was the countenance of the Lord in this world.

The elder of the boys looked roguish and enterprising. He took a delight in reading of the forces of nature, of the sun and the moon; no fairy tale pleased him so much. Oh, how beautiful it must be, he thought, to go on voyages of discovery, or to find out how to imitate the wings of birds and then to be able to fly! Yes, to find that out was the right thing. Father was right, and mother was right—truth holds the world together.

The younger brother was quieter, and buried himself entirely in his books. When he read about Jacob dressing himself in sheep-skins to personify Esau, and so to usurp his brother's birthright, he would clench his little fist in anger against the deceiver; when he read of tyrants and of the injustice and wickedness of the world, tears would come into his eyes, and he was quite filled with the thought of the justice and truth which must and would triumph.

THE DUMB BOOK

One evening he was lying in bed, but the curtains were not yet drawn close, and the light streamed in upon him; he had taken his book into bed with him, for he wanted to finish reading the story of Solon. His thoughts lifted and carried him away a wonderful distance; it seemed to him as if the bed had become a ship flying along under full sail. Was he dreaming, or what was happening? It glided over the rolling waves and across the ocean of time, and to him came the voice of Solon; spoken in a strange tongue, yet intelligible to him, he heard the Danish motto: "By law the land is ruled."

The genius of the human race stood in the humble room, bent down over the bed and imprinted a kiss on the boy's forehead: "Be thou strong in fame and strong in the battle of life! With truth in thy heart fly toward the land of truth!"

The elder brother was not yet in bed; he was standing at the window looking out at the mist which rose from the meadows. They were not elves dancing out there, as their old nurse had told him; he knew better—they were vapours which were warmer than the air, and that is why they rose. A shooting star lit up the sky, and the boy's thoughts passed in a second from the vapours of the earth up to the shining meteor. The stars gleamed in the heavens, and it seemed as if long golden threads hung down from them to the earth.

"Fly with me," sang a voice, which the boy heard in his heart. And the mighty genius of mankind, swifter than a bird and than an arrow—swifter than anything of earthly origin—carried him out into space, where the heavenly bodies are bound together by the rays that pass from star to star. Our earth revolved in the thin air, and the cities upon it seemed to lie close to each other. Through the spheres echoed the words:

"What is near, what is far, when thou art lifted by the mighty genius of mind?"

And again the boy stood by the window, gazing out, whilst his younger brother lay in bed. Their mother called them by their names: "Anders Sandoe" and "Hans Christian."

Denmark and the whole world knows them—the two brothers Oersted.

THE SNAIL AND THE ROSE-TREE

ROUND about the garden ran a hedge of hazel-bushes; beyond the hedge were fields and meadows with cows and sheep; but in the middle of the garden stood a Rose-tree in bloom, under which sat a Snail, whose shell contained a great deal—that is, himself.

"Only wait till my time comes," he said; "I shall do more than grow roses, bear nuts, or give milk, like the hazel-bush, the cows and the sheep."

"I expect a great deal from you," said the rose-tree. "May I ask when it will appear?"

"I take my time," said the snail. "You're always in such a hurry. That does not excite expectation."

The following year the snail lay in almost the same spot, in the sunshine under the rose-tree, which was again budding and bearing roses as fresh and beautiful as ever. The snail crept half out of his shell, stretched out his horns, and drew them in again.

"Everything is just as it was last year! No progress at all; the rose-tree sticks to its roses and gets no farther."

The summer and the autumn passed; the rose-tree bore roses and buds till the snow fell and the weather became raw and wet; then it bent down its head, and the snail crept into the ground.

A new year began; the roses made their appearance, and the snail made his too.

"You are an old rose-tree now," said the snail. "You must make haste and die. You have given the world all that you had in you; whether it was of much importance is a question that I have not had time to think about. But this much is clear and plain, that you have not done the least for your inner development, or you would have produced something else. Have you anything to say in defence? You will now soon be nothing but a stick. Do you understand what I say?"

"You frighten me," said the rose-tree. "I have never thought of that."

"No, you have never taken the trouble to think at all. Have you ever given yourself an account why you bloomed, and how your blooming comes about — why just in that way and in no other?"

"No," said the rose-tree. "I bloom in gladness, because I cannot do otherwise. The sun shone and warmed me, and the air refreshed me; I drank the clear dew and the invigorating rain. I breathed and I lived! Out of the earth there arose a power within me, whilst from above I also received strength; I felt an ever-renewed and ever-increasing happiness, and therefore I was obliged to go on blooming. That was my life; I could not do otherwise."

"You have led a very easy life," remarked the snail.

"Certainly. Everything was given me," said the rose-tree. "But still more was given to you. Yours is one of those deep-thinking natures, one of those highly gifted minds that astonishes the world."

"I have not the slightest intention of doing so," said the snail. "The world is nothing to me. What have I to do with the world? I have enough to do with myself, and enough in myself."

"But must we not all here on earth give up our best parts to others, and offer as much as lies in our power? It is true, I have only given roses. But you — you who are so richly endowed — what have you given to the world? What will you give it?"

"What have I given? What am I going to give? I spit at it; it's good for nothing, and does not concern me. For my part, you may go on bearing roses; you cannot do anything else. Let the hazel bush bear nuts, and the cows and sheep give milk; they have each their public. I have mine in myself. I retire within myself and there I stop. The world is nothing to me."

With this the snail withdrew into his house and blocked up the entrance.

"That's very sad," said the rose tree. "I cannot creep into myself, however much I might wish to do so; I have to go on bearing roses. Then they drop their leaves, which are blown away by the wind. But I once saw how a rose was laid in the mistress's hymn-book, and how one of my roses found a place in the bosom of a young beautiful girl, and how another was kissed by the lips of a child in the glad joy of life. That did me good; it was a real blessing. Those are my recollections, my life."

And the rose tree went on blooming in innocence, while the snail lay idling in his house—the world was nothing to him.

Years passed by.

The snail had turned to earth in the earth, and the rose tree too. Even the souvenir rose in the hymn-book was faded; but in the garden there were other rose trees and other snails. The latter crept into their houses and spat at the world, for it did not concern them.

Shall we read the story all over again? It will be just the same.

THE FARM-YARD COCK AND THE WEATHER-COCK

THERE were two cocks—one on the dung-hill, the other on the roof. They were both arrogant, but which of the two rendered most service? Tell us your opinion—we'll keep to ours just the same though.

The poultry yard was divided by some planks from another yard in which there was a dung-hill, and on the dung-hill lay and grew a large cucumber which was conscious of being a hot-bed plant.

"One is born to that," said the cucumber to itself. "Not all can be born cucumbers; there must be other things, too. The hens, the ducks, and all the animals in the next yard are creatures too. Now I have a great opinion of the yard cock on the plank; he is certainly of much more importance than the weather-cock who is placed so high and can't even creak, much less crow. The latter has neither hens nor chicks, and only thinks of himself and perspires verdigris. No, the yard cock is really a cock! His step is a dance! His crowing is music, and wherever he goes one knows what a trumpeter is like! If he would only come in here! Even if he ate me up stump, stalk, and all, and I had to dissolve in his body, it would be a happy death," said the cucumber.

In the night there was a terrible storm. The hens, chicks, and even the cock sought shelter; the wind tore down the planks between the two yards with a crash; the tiles came tumbling down, but the weather-cock sat firm. He did not even turn round, for he could not; and yet he was young and freshly cast, but prudent and sedate. He had been born old, and did not at all resemble the birds flying in the air—the sparrows, and the swallows; no, he despised them, these mean little piping birds, these common whistlers. He admitted that the pigeons, large and white and shining like mother-o'-pearl, looked like a kind of weather-cock; but they were fat and stupid, and all their thoughts and endeavours were directed to filling themselves with food, and besides, they were tiresome things to converse with . The birds of passage had also paid the weather-cock a visit and told him of foreign countries, of airy caravans and robber stories that made one's hair stand on end. All this was new and interesting; that is, for the first time, but afterwards, as the weather-cock found out, they repeated themselves and always told the same stories, and that's very tedious, and there was no one with whom one could associate, for one and all were stale and small-minded.

"The world is no good!" he said. "Everything in it is so stupid."

The weather-cock was puffed up, and that quality would have made him interesting in the eyes of the cucumber if it had known it, but it had eyes only for the yard cock, who was now in the yard with it.

The wind had blown the planks, but the storm was over.

"What do you think of that crowing?" said the yard cock to the hens and chickens. "It was a little rough — it wanted elegance."

And the hens and chickens came up on the dung-hill, and the cock strutted about like a lord.

"Garden plant!" he said to the cucumber, and in that one word his deep learning showed itself, and it forgot that he was pecking at her and eating it up. "A happy death!"

The hens and the chickens came, for where one runs the others run too; they clucked, and chirped, and looked at the cock, and were proud that he was of their kind.

"Cock-a-doodle-doo!" he crowed, "the chickens will grow up into great hens at once, if I cry it out in the poultry-yard of the world!"

And hens and chicks clucked and chirped, and the cock announced a great piece of news.

"A cock can lay an egg! And do you know what's in that egg? A basilisk. No one can stand the sight of such a thing; people know that, and now you know it too — you know what is in me, and what a champion of all cocks I am!"

With that the yard cock flapped his wings, made his comb swell up, and crowed again; and they all shuddered, the hens and the little chicks — but they were very proud that one of their number was such a champion of all cocks. They clucked and chirped till the weather-cock heard; he heard it; but he did not stir.

"Everything is very stupid," the weather-cock said to himself. "The yard cock lays no eggs, and I am too lazy to do so; if I liked, I could lay a wind-egg. But the world is not worth even a wind-egg. Everything is so stupid! I don't want to sit here any longer."

With that the weather-cock broke off; but he did not kill the yard cock, although the hens said that had been his intention. And what is the moral? "Better to crow than to be puffed up and break off!"

"DELAYING IS NOT FORGETTING"

THERE was an old mansion surrounded by a marshy ditch with a drawbridge which was but seldom let down: — not all guests are good people. Under the roof were loopholes to shoot through, and to pour down boiling water or even molten lead on the enemy, should he approach. Inside the house the rooms were very high and had ceilings of beams, and that was very useful considering the great deal of smoke which rose up from the chimney fire where the large, damp logs of wood smouldered. On the walls hung pictures of knights in armour and proud ladies in gorgeous dresses; the most stately of all walked about alive. She was called Meta Mogens; she was the mistress of the house, to her belonged the castle.

Towards the evening robbers came; they killed three of her people and also the yard-dog, and attached Mrs. Meta to the kennel by the chain, while they themselves made good cheer in the hall and drank the wine and the good ale out of her cellar. Mrs. Meta was now on the chain, she could not even bark.

But lo! the servant of one of the robbers secretly approached her; they must not see it, otherwise they would have killed him.

"Mrs Meta Mogens," said the fellow, "do you still remember how my father, when your husband was still alive, had to ride on the wooden horse? You prayed for him, but it was no good, he was to ride until his limbs were paralysed; but you stole down to him, as I steal now to you, you yourself put little stones under each of his feet that he might have support, nobody saw it, or they pretended not to see it, for you were then the young gracious mistress. My father has told me this, and I have not forgotten it! Now I will free you, Mrs. Meta Mogens!"

Then they pulled the horses out of the stable and rode off in rain and wind to obtain the assistance of friends.

"Thus the small service done to the old man was richly rewarded!" said Meta Mogens.

"Delaying is not forgetting," said the fellow.

The robbers were hanged.

There was an old mansion, it is still there; it did not belong to Mrs. Meta Mogens, it belonged to another old noble family.

We are now in the present time. The sun is shining on the gilt knob of the tower, little wooded islands lie like bouquets on the water, and wild swans are swimming round them. In the garden grow roses; the mistress of the house is herself the finest rose petal, she beams with joy, the joy of good deeds: however, not done in the wide world, but in her heart, and what is preserved there is not forgotten. Delaying is not forgetting!

Now she goes from the mansion to a little peasant hut in the field. Therein lives a poor paralysed girl; the window of her little room looks northward, the sun does not enter here. The girl can only see a small piece of field which is surrounded by a high fence. But to-day the sun shines here—the warm, beautiful sun of God is within the little room; it comes from the south through the new window, where formerly the wall was.

The paralysed girl sits in the warm sunshine and can see the wood and the lake; the world had become so large, so beautiful, and only through a single word from the kind mistress of the mansion.

"The word was so easy, the deed so small," she said, "the joy it afforded me was infinitely great and sweet!"

And therefore she does many a good deed, thinks of all in the humble cottages and in the rich mansions, where there are also afflicted ones. It is concealed and hidden, but God does not forget it. Delayed is not forgotten!

An old house stood there; it was in the large town with its busy traffic. There are rooms and halls in it, but we do not enter them, we remain in the kitchen, where it is warm and light, clean and tidy; the copper utensils are shining, the table as if polished with beeswax; the sink looks like a freshly scoured meatboard. All this a single servant has done, and yet she has time to spare as if she wished to go to church; she wears a bow on her cap, a black bow, that signifies mourning. But she has no one to mourn, neither father nor mother, neither relations nor sweetheart. She is a poor girl. One day she was engaged to a poor fellow; they loved each other dearly.

One day he came to her and said:

"We both have nothing! The rich widow over the way in the basement has made advances to me; she will make me rich, but you are in my heart; what do you advise me to do?"

"I advise you to do what you think will turn out to your happiness," said the girl. "Be kind and good to her, but remember this; from the hour we part we shall never see each other again."

Years passed; then one day she met the old friend and sweetheart in the street; he looked ill and miserable, and she could not help asking him, "How are you?"

"Rich and prospering in every respect," he said; "the woman is brave and good, but you are in my heart. I have fought the battle, it will soon be ended; we shall not see each other again now until we meet before God!"

A week has passed; this morning his death was in the newspaper, that is the reason of the girl's mourning! Her old sweetheart is dead and has left a wife and three step-children, as the paper says; it sounds as if there is a crack, but the metal is pure.

The black bow signifies mourning, the girl's face points to the same in a still higher degree; it is preserved in the heart and will never be forgotten. Delaying is not forgetting!

These are three stories you see, three leaves on the same stalk. Do you wish for some more trefoil leaves? In the little heartbook are many more of them. Delaying is not forgetting!

A STORY FROM THE SAND-HILLS

THIS story is from the sand-dunes or sand-hills of Jutland, but it does not begin there in the North, but far away in the South, in Spain. The wide sea is the highroad from nation to nation; journey in thought; then, to sunny Spain. It is warm and beautiful there; the fiery pomegranate flowers peep from among dark laurels; a cool refreshing breeze from the mountains blows over the orange gardens, over the Moorish halls with their golden cupolas and coloured walls. Children go through the streets in procession with candles and waving banners, and the sky, lofty and clear with its glittering stars, rises above them. Sounds of singing and castanets can be heard, and youths and maidens dance upon the flowering acacia trees, while even the beggar sits upon a block of marble, refreshing himself with a juicy melon, and dreamily enjoying life. It all seems like a beautiful dream.

Here dwelt a newly married couple who completely gave themselves up to the charm of life; indeed they possessed every good thing they could desire—health and happiness, riches and honour.

"We are as happy as human beings can be," said the young couple from the depths of their hearts. They had indeed only one step higher to mount on the ladder of happiness—they hoped that God would give them a child, a son like them in form and spirit. The happy little one was to be welcomed with rejoicing, to be cared for with love and tenderness, and enjoy every advantage of wealth and luxury that a rich and influential family can give. So the days went by like a joyous festival.

"Life is a gracious gift from God, almost too great a gift for us to appreciate!" said the young wife. "Yet they say that fulness of joy for ever and ever can only be found in the future life. I cannot realise it!"

"The thought arises, perhaps, from the arrogance of men," said the husband. "It seems a great pride to believe that we shall live for ever, that we shall be as gods! Were not these the words of the serpent, the father of lies?"

"Surely you do not doubt the existence of a future life?" exclaimed the young wife. It seemed as if one of the first shadows passed over her sunny thoughts.

"Faith realises it, and the priests tell us so," replied her husband; "but amid all my happiness I feel that it is arrogant to demand a continuation of it—another life after this. Has not so much been given us in this world that we ought to be, we *must* be, contented with it?"

"Yes, it has been given to us," said the young wife, "but this life is nothing more than one long scene of trial and hardship to many thousands. How many have been cast into this world only to endure poverty, shame, illness, and misfortune? If there were no future life, everything here would be too unequally divided, and God would not be the personification of justice."

"The beggar there," said her husband, "has joys of his own which seem to him great, and cause him as much pleasure as a king would find in the magnificence of his palace. And then do you not think that the beast of burden, which suffers blows and hunger, and works itself to death, suffers just as much from its miserable fate? The dumb creature might demand a future life also, and declare the law unjust that excludes it from the advantages of the higher creation."

"Christ said: 'In my father's house are many mansions,' " she answered. "Heaven is as boundless as the love of our Creator; the dumb animal is also His creature, and I firmly believe that no life will be lost, but each will receive as much happiness as he can enjoy, which will be sufficient for him."

"This world is sufficient for me," said the husband, throwing his arm round his beautiful, sweet-tempered wife. He sat by her side on the open balcony, smoking a cigarette in the cool air, which was loaded with the sweet scent of carnations and orange blossoms. Sounds of music and the clatter of castanets came from the road beneath, the stars shone above then, and two eyes full of affection—those of his wife—looked upon him with the expression of undying love. "Such a moment," he said, "makes it worth while to be born, to die, and to be annihilated!" He smiled—the young wife raised her hand in gentle reproof, and the shadow passed away from her mind, and they were happy—quite happy.

Everything seemed to work together for their good. They advanced in honour, in prosperity, and in happiness. A change came certainly, but it was only a change of place and not of circumstances.

The young man was sent by his Sovereign as ambassador to the Russian Court. This was an office of high dignity, but his birth and his acquirements entitled him to the honour. He possessed a large fortune, and his wife had brought him wealth equal to his own, for she was the daughter of a rich and respected merchant. One of this merchant's largest and finest ships was to be sent that year to Stockholm, and it was arranged that the dear young couple, the daughter and the son-in-law, should travel in it to St. Petersburg. All the arrangements on board were princely and silk and luxury on every side.

A STORY FROM THE SAND-HILLS

In an old war song, called "The King of England's Son," it says:

> "Farewell, he said, and sailed away.
> And many recollect that day.
> The ropes were of silk, the anchor of gold,
> And everywhere riches and wealth untold."

These words would aptly describe the vessel from Spain, for here was the same luxury, and the same parting thought naturally arose:

> "God grant that we once more may meet
> In sweet unclouded peace and joy."

There was a favourable wind blowing as they left the Spanish coast, and it would be but a short journey, for they hoped to reach their destination in a few weeks; but when they came out upon the wide ocean the wind dropped, the sea became smooth and shining, and the stars shone brightly. Many festive evenings were spent on board. At last the travellers began to wish for wind, for a favourable breeze; but their wish was useless—not a breath of air stirred, or if it did arise it was contrary. Weeks passed by in this way, two whole months, and then at length a fair wind blew from the south-west. The ship sailed on the high seas between Scotland and Jutland; then the wind increased, just as it did in the old song of "The King of England's Son."

> " 'Mid storm and wind, and pelting hail,
> Their efforts were of no avail.
> The golden anchor forth they threw;
> Towards Denmark the west wind blew."

This all happened a long time ago; King Christian VII, who sat on the Danish throne, was still a young man. Much has happened since then, much has altered or been changed. Sea and moorland have been turned into green meadows, stretches of heather have become arable land, and in the shelter of the peasant's cottages, apple-trees and rose-bushes grow, though they certainly require much care, as the sharp west wind blows upon them. In West Jutland one may go back in thought to old times, farther back than the days when Christian VII ruled. The purple heather still extends for miles, with its barrows and aerial spectacles, intersected with sandy uneven roads, just as it did then; towards the west, where broad streams run into the bays, are marshes and meadows encircled by lofty, sandy hills, which, like a chain of Alps, raise their pointed summits near the sea; they are only broken by high ridges of clay, from which the sea, year by year, bites out great mouthfuls, so that the overhanging banks fall down as if by the shock of an earthquake. Thus it is there today and thus it was long ago, when the happy pair were sailing in the beautiful ship.

It was a Sunday, towards the end of September; the sun was shining, and the chiming of the church bells in the Bay of Nissum was carried along by the breeze like a chain of sounds. The churches there are almost entirely built of hewn blocks of stone, each like a piece of rock. The North Sea might foam over them and they would not be disturbed. Nearly all of them are without steeples, and the bells are hung outside between two beams. The service was over, and the congregation passed out into the churchyard, where not a tree or bush was to be seen; no flowers were planted there, and they had not placed a single wreath upon any of the graves. It is just the same now. Rough mounds show where the dead have been buried, and rank grass, tossed by the wind, grows thickly over the whole churchyard; here and there a grave has a sort of monument, a block of half-decayed wood, rudely cut in the shape of a coffin; the blocks are brought from the forest of West Jutland, but the forest is the sea itself, and the inhabitants find beams, and planks, and fragments which the waves have cast upon the beach. One of these blocks had been placed by loving hands on a child's grave, and one of the women who had come out of the church walked up to it; she stood there, her eyes resting on the weather-beaten memorial, and a few moments afterwards her husband joined her. They were both silent, but he took her hand, and they walked together across the purple heath, over moor and meadow towards the sand-hills. For a long time they went on without speaking.

"It was a good sermon to-day," the man said at last. "If we had not God to trust in, we should have nothing."

"Yes," replied the woman, "He sends joy and sorrow, and He has a right to send them. To-morrow our little son would have been five years old if we had been permitted to keep him."

"It is no use fretting, wife," said the man. "The boy is well provided for. He is where we hope and pray to go to."

They said nothing more, but went out towards their houses among the sand-hills. All at once, in front of one of the houses where the sea grass did not keep the sand down with its twining roots, what seemed to be a column of smoke rose up. A gust of wind rushed between the hills, hurling the particles of sand high into the air; another gust, and the strings of fish hung up to dry flapped and beat violently against the walls of the cottage; then everything was quiet once more, and the sun shone with renewed heat.

The man and his wife went into the cottage. They had soon taken off their Sunday clothes and come out again, hurrying over the dunes which stood there like great waves of sand suddenly arrested in their course, while the sandweeds and dune grass with its bluish stalks spread a changing colour over them. A few neighbours also came out, and helped each other to draw the boats higher up on the beach. The wind now blew more keenly, it was chilly and cold, and when they went back over the sand-hills, sand and little sharp stones blew into their faces. The waves rose high, crested with white foam, and the wind cut off their crests, scattering the foam far and wide.

Evening came; there was a swelling roar in the air, a wailing or moaning like the voices of despairing spirits, that sounded above the thunder of the waves. The fisherman's little cottage was on the very margin, and the sand rattled against the window panes; every now and then a violent gust of wind shook the house to its foundation. It was dark, but about midnight the moon would rise. Later on the air became clearer, but the storm swept over the perturbed sea with undiminished fury; the fisher folks had long since gone to bed, but in such weather there was no chance of closing an eye. Presently there was a tapping at the window; the door was opened, and a voice said:

"There's a large ship stranded on the farthest reef."

In a moment the fisher people sprung from their beds and hastily dressed themselves. The moon had risen, and it was light enough to make the surrounding objects visible to those who could open their eyes in the blinding clouds of sand; the violence of the wind was terrible, and it was only possible to pass among the sand-hills if one crept forward between the gusts; the salt spray flew up from the sea like down, and the ocean foamed like a roaring cataract towards the beach. Only a practised eye could discern the vessel out in the offing; she was a fine brig, and the waves now lifted her over the reef, three or four cables' length out of the usual channel. She drove towards the shore, struck on the second reef, and remained fixed.

It was impossible to render assistance; the sea rushed in upon the vessel, making a clean breach over her. Those on shore thought they heard cries for help from those on board, and could plainly distinguish the busy but useless efforts made by the stranded sailors. Now a wave came rolling onward. It fell with enormous force on the bowsprit, tearing it from the vessel, and the stern was lifted high above the water. Two people were seen to embrace and plunge together into the sea, and the next moment one of the largest waves that rolled towards the sand-hills threw a body on the beach. It was a woman; the sailors said that she was quite dead, but the women thought they saw signs of life in her, so the stranger was carried across the sand-hills to the fisherman's cottage. How beautiful and fair she was! She must be a great lady, they said.

They laid her upon the humble bed; there was not a yard of linen on it, only a woollen coverlet to keep the occupant warm.

Life returned to her, but she was delirious, and knew nothing of what had happened or where she was; and it was better so, for everything she loved and valued lay buried in the sea. The same thing happened to her ship as to the one spoken of in the song about "The King of England's Son."

> "Alas! how terrible to see
> The gallant bark sink rapidly."

Fragments of the wreck and pieces of wood were washed ashore; they were all that remained of the vessel. The wind still blew violently on the coast.

For a few moments the strange lady seemed to rest; but she awoke in pain, and uttered cries of anguish and fear. She opened her wonderfully beautiful eyes, and spoke a few words, but nobody understood her. — And lo! as a reward for the sorrow and suffering she had undergone, she held in her arms a new-born babe. The child that was to have rested upon a magnificent couch, draped with silken curtains, in a luxurious home; it was to have been welcomed with joy to a life rich in all the good things of this world; and now Heaven had ordained that it should be born in this humble retreat, that it should not even receive a kiss from its mother, for when the fisherman's wife laid the child upon the mother's bosom, it rested on a heart that beat no more — she was dead.

The child that was to have been reared amid wealth and luxury was cast into the world, washed by the sea among the sand-hills to share the fate and hardships of the poor.

Here we are reminded again of the song about "The King of England's Son," for in it mention is made of the custom prevalent at the time, when knights and squires plundered those who had been saved from shipwreck. The ship had stranded some distance south of Nissum Bay, and the cruel, inhuman days, when, as we have just said, the inhabitants of Jutland treated the shipwrecked people so crudely were past, long ago. Affectionate sympathy and self-sacrifice for the unfortunate existed then, just as it does in our own time in many a bright example. The dying mother and the unfortunate child would have found kindness and help wherever they had been cast by the winds, but nowhere would it have been more sincere than in the cottage of the poor fisherman's wife, who had stood, only the day before, beside her child's grave, who would have been five years old that day if God had spared it to her.

No one knew who the dead stranger was, they could not even form a conjecture; the fragments of wreckage gave no clue to the matter.

No tidings reached Spain of the fate of the daughter and son-in-law. They did not arrive at their destination, and violent storms had raged during the past weeks. At last the verdict was given: "Foundered at sea—all lost." But in the fisherman's cottage among the sand-hills near Hunsby, there lived a little scion of the rich Spanish family.

Where Heaven sends food for two, a third can manage to find a meal, and in the depth of the sea there is many a dish of fish for the hungry.

They called the boy Jürgen.

"It must certainly be a Jewish child, its skin is so dark," the people said.

"It might be an Italian or a Spaniard," remarked the clergyman.

But to the fisherman's wife these nations seemed all the same, and she consoled herself with the thought that the child was baptized as a Christian.

The boy throve; the noble blood in his veins was warm, and he became strong on his homely fare. He grew apace in the humble cottage, and the Danish dialect spoken by the West Jutes became his language. The pomegranate seed from Spain became a hardy plant on the coast of West Jutland. Thus may circumstances alter the course of a man's life! To this home he clung with deep-rooted affection; he was to experience cold and hunger, and the misfortunes and hardships that surround the poor; but he also tasted of their joys.

Childhood has bright days for every one, and the memory of them shines through the whole after-life. The boy had many sources of pleasure and enjoyment; the coast for miles and miles was full of playthings, for it was a mosaic of pebbles, some red as coral or yellow as amber, and others again white and rounded like birds' eggs and smoothed and prepared by the sea. Even the bleached fishes' skeletons, the water plants dried by the wind, and seaweed, white and shining long linen-like bands waving between the stones—all these seemed made to give pleasure and occupation for the boy's thoughts, and he had an intelligent mind; many great talents lay dormant in him. How readily he remembered stories and songs that he heard, and how dexterous he was with his fingers! With stones and mussel-shells he could put together pictures and ships with which one could decorate the room; and he could make wonderful things from a stick, his foster-mother said, although he was still so young and little. He had a sweet voice, and every melody seemed to flow naturally from his lips. And in his heart were hidden chords, which might have sounded far out into the world if he had been placed anywhere else than in the fisherman's hut by the North Sea.

One day another ship was wrecked on the coast, and among other things a chest filled with valuable flower bulbs was washed ashore. Some were put into saucepans and cooked, for they were thought to be fit to eat, and others lay and shrivelled in the sand—they did not accomplish their purpose, or unfold their magnificent colours. Would Jürgen fare better? The flower bulbs had soon played their part, but he had years of apprenticeship before him. Neither he nor his friends noticed in what a monotonous, uniform way one day followed another, for there was always plenty to do and see. The ocean itself was a great lesson-book, and it unfolded a new leaf each day of calm or storm—the crested wave or the smooth surface.

The visits to the church were festive occasions, but among the fisherman's house one was especially looked forward to; this was, in fact, the visit of the brother of Jürgen's foster-mother, the eel-breeder from Fjaltring, near Bovbjerg. He came twice a year in a cart, painted red with blue and white tulips upon it, and full of eels; it was covered and locked like a box, two dun oxen drew it, and Jürgen was allowed to guide them.

The eel-breeder was a witty fellow, a merry guest, and brought a measure of brandy with him. They all received a small glassful or a cupful if there were not enough glasses; even Jürgen had about a thimbleful, that he might digest the fat eel, as the eel-breeder said; he always told one story over and over again, and if his hearers laughed he would immediately repeat it to them. Jürgen while still a boy, and also when he was older, used phrases from the eel-breeder's story on various occasions, so it will be as well for us to listen to it. It runs thus:

"The eels went into the bay, and the young ones begged leave to go a little farther out. 'Don't go too far,' said their mother; 'the ugly eel-spearer might come and snap you all up.' But they went too far, and of eight daughters only three came back to the mother, and these wept and said, 'We only went a little way out, and the ugly eel-spearer came immediatly and stabbed five of our sisters to death.' 'They'll come back again,' said the mother eel. 'Oh, no,' exclaimed the daughters, 'for he skinned them, cut them in two, and fried them.' 'Oh, they'll come back again,' the mother eel persisted. 'No,' replied the daughters, 'for he ate them up.' 'They'll come back again,' repeated the mother eel. 'But he drank brandy after them,' said the daughters. 'Ah, then they'll never come back,' said the mother, and she burst out crying, 'it's the brandy that buries the eels.' "

"And therefore," said the eel-breeder in conclusion, "it is always the proper thing to drink brandy after eating eels."

This story was the tinsel thread, the most humorous recollection of Jürgen's life. He also wanted to go a little way farther out and up the bay—that is to say, out into the world in a ship—but his mother said, like the eel-breeder, "There are so many bad people—eel-spearers!" He wished to go a little way past the sand-hills, out into the dunes, and at last he did: four happy days, the brightest of his childhood, fell to his lot, and the whole beauty and splendour of Jutland, all the happiness and sunshine of his home, were concentrated in these. He went to a festival, but it was a burial feast.

A rich relation of the fisherman's family had died; the farm was situated far eastward in the country and a little towards the north. Jürgen's foster-parents went there, and he also went with them from the dunes, over heath and moor, where the Skjærumaa takes its course through green meadows and contains many eels; mother eels live there with their daughters, who are caught and eaten up by wicked people. But do not men sometimes act quite as cruelly towards their own fellow-men? Was not the knight Sir Bugge murdered by wicked people? And though he was well spoken of, did he not also wish to kill the architect who built the castle for him, with its thick walls and tower, at the point where the Skjærumaa falls into the bay? Jürgen and his parents now stood there; the wall and the ramparts still remained, and red crumbling fragments lay scattered around. Here it was that Sir Bugge, after the architect had left him, said to one of his men, "Go after him and say, 'Master, the tower shakes.' If he turns round, kill him and take away the money I paid him, but if he does not turn round let him go in peace." The man did as he was told; the architect did not turn round, but called back "The tower does not shake in the least, but one day a man will come from the west in a blue cloak — he will cause it to shake!" And so indeed it happened a hundred years later, for the North Sea broke in and cast down the tower; but Predbjörn Gyldenstjerne, the man who then possessed the castle, built a new castle higher up at the end of the meadow, and that one is standing to this day, and is called Nörre-Vosborg.

Jürgen and his foster parents went past this castle. They had told him its story during the long winter evenings, and now he saw the stately edifice, with its double moat, and trees and bushes; the wall, covered with ferns, rose within the moat, but the lofty lime-trees were the most beautiful of all; they grew up to the highest windows, and the air was full of their sweet fragrance. In a north-west corner of the garden stood a great bush full of blossom, like winter snow amid the summer's green; it was a juniper bush, the first that Jürgen had ever seen in bloom. He never forgot it, nor the lime-trees; the child's soul treasured up these memories of beauty and fragrance to gladden the old man.

From Nörre-Vosborg, where the juniper blossomed, the journey became more pleasant, for they met some other people who were also going to the funeral and were riding in waggons. Our travellers had to sit all together on a little box at the back of the waggon, but even this, they thought, was better than walking. So they continued their journey across the rugged heath. The oxen which drew the waggon stopped every now and then, where a patch of fresh grass appeared amid the heather. The sun shone with considerable heat, and it was wonderful to behold how in the far distance something like smoke seemed to be rising; yet this smoke was clearer than the air; it was transparent, and looked like rays of light rolling and dancing afar over the heath.

"That is Lokeman driving his sheep," said some one.

And this was enough to excite Jürgen's imagination. He felt as if they were now about to enter fairyland, though everything was still real. How quiet it was! The heath stretched far and wide around them like a beautiful carpet. The heather was in blossom, and the juniper-bushes and fresh oak saplings rose like bouquets from the earth. An inviting place for a frolic, if it had not been for the number of poisonous adders of which the travellers spoke; they also mentioned that the place had formerly been infested with wolves, and that the district was still called Wolfsborg for this reason. The old man who was driving the oxen told them that in the lifetime of his father the horses had many a hard battle with the wild beasts that were now exterminated. One morning, when he himself had gone out to bring in the horses, he found one of them standing with its forefeet on a wolf it had killed, but the savage animal had torn and lacerated the brave horse's legs.

The journey over the heath and the deep sand was only too quickly at an end. They stopped before the house of mourning, where they found plenty of guests within and without. Waggon after waggon stood side by side, while the horses and oxen had been turned out to graze on the scanty pasture. Great sand-hills like those at home by the North Sea rose behind the house and extended far and wide. How had they come here, so many miles inland? They were as large and high as those on the coast, and the wind had carrried them there; there was also a legend attached to them.

Psalms were sung, and a few of the old people shed tears; with this exception, the guests were cheerful enough, it seemed to Jürgen, and there was plenty to eat and drink. There were eels of the fattest, requiring brandy to bury them, as the eel-breeder said; and certainly they did not forget to carry out his maxim here.

Jürgen went in and out the house; and on the third day he felt as much at home as he did in the fisherman's cottage among the sand-hills, where he had passed his early days. Here on the heath were riches unknown to him until now; for flowers, blackberries, and bilberries were to be found in profusion, so large and sweet that when they were crushed beneath the tread of passers-by the heather was stained with their red juice. Here was a barrow and yonder another. Then columns of smoke rose into the still air; it was a heath fire, they told him — how brightly it blazed in the dark evening!

The fourth day came, and the funeral festivities were at an end; they were to go back from the land-dunes to the sand-dunes.

"Ours are better," said the old fisherman, Jürgen's foster-father; "these have no strength."

And they spoke of the way in which the sand-dunes had come inland, and it seemed very easy to understand. This is how they explained it:

A dead body had been found on the coast, and the peasants buried it in the churchyard. From that time the sand began to fly about and the sea broke in with violence. A wise man in the district advised them to open the grave and see if the buried man was not lying sucking his thumb, for if so he must be a sailor, and the sea would not rest until it had got him back. The grave was opened, and he really was found with his thumb in his mouth. So they laid him upon a cart, and harnessed two oxen to it; and the oxen ran off with the sailor over heath and moor to the ocean, as if they had been stung by an adder. Then the sand ceased to fly inland, but the hills that had been piled up still remained.

All this Jürgen listened to and treasured up in his memory of the happiest days of his childhood — the days of the burial feast.

How delightful it was to see fresh places and to mix with strangers! And he was to go still farther, for he was not yet fourteen years old when he went out in a ship to see the world. He encountered bad weather, heavy seas, unkindness, and hard men — such were his experiences, for he became ship-boy. Cold nights, bad living, and blows had to be endured; then he felt his noble Spanish blood boil within him, and bitter, angry, words rose to his lips, but he gulped them down; it was better, although he felt as the eel must feel when it is skinned, cut up, and put into the frying-pan.

"I shall get over it," said a voice within him.

He saw the Spanish coast, the native land of his parents. He even saw the town where they had lived in joy and prosperity, but he knew nothing of his home or his relations, and his relations knew just as little about him.

The poor ship boy was not permitted to land, but on the last day of their stay he managed to get ashore. There were several purchases to be made, and he was sent to carry them on board.

Jürgen stood there in his shabby clothes which looked as if they had been washed in the ditch and dried in the chimney; he, who had always dwelt among the sand-hills, now saw a great city for the first time. How lofty the houses seemed, and what a number of people there were in the streets! some pushing this way, some that—a perfect maelstrom of citizens and peasants, monks and soldiers—the jingling of bells on the trappings of asses and mules, the chiming of church bells, calling, shouting, hammering and knocking—all going on at once. Every trade was located in the basement of the houses or in the side thoroughfares; and the sun shone with such heat, and the air was so close, that one seemed to be in an oven full of beetles, cockchafers, bees and flies, all humming and buzzing together. Jürgen scarcely knew where he was or which way he went. Then he saw just in front of him the great doorway of a cathedral; the lights were gleaming in the dark aisles, and the fragrance of incense was wafted towards him. Even the poorest beggar ventured up the steps into the sanctuary. Jürgen followed the sailor he was with into the church, and stood in the sacred edifice. Coloured pictures gleamed from their golden background, and on the altar stood the figure of the Virgin with the child Jesus, surrounded by lights and flowers; priests in festive robes were chanting, and choir boys in dazzling attire swung silver censers. What splendour and magnificence he saw there! It streamed in upon his soul and overpowered him: the church and the faith of his parents surrounded him, and touched a chord in his heart that caused his eyes to overflow with tears.

They went from the church to the market-place. Here a quantity of provisions were given him to carry. The way to the harbour was long; and weary and overcome with various emotions, he rested for a few moments before a splendid house, with marble pillars, statues, and broad steps. Here he rested his burden against the wall. Then a porter in livery came out, lifted up a silver-headed cane, and drove him away—him, the grandson of that house. But no one knew that, and he just as little as any one. Then he went on board again, and once more encountered rough words and blows, much work and little sleep—such was his experience of life. They say it is good to suffer in one's young days, if age brings something to make up for it.

His period of service on board the ship came to an end, and the vessel lay once more at Ringkjöbing in Jutland. He came ashore, and went home to the sand-dunes near Hunsby; but his foster-mother had died during his absence.

A hard winter followed this summer. Snow-storms swept over land and sea, and there was difficulty in getting from one place to another. How unequally things are distributed in this world! Here there was bitter cold and snow-storms, while in Spain there was burning sunshine and oppressive heat. Yet, when a clear frosty day came, and Jürgen saw the swans flying in numbers from the sea towards the land, across to Nörre-Vosborg, it seemed to him that people could breathe more freely here; the summer also in this part of the world was splendid. In imagination he saw the heath blossom and become purple with rich juicy berries, and the elder-bushes and lime-trees at Nörre-Vosborg in flower. He made up his mind to go there again.

Spring came, and the fishing began. Jürgen was now an active helper in this, for he had grown during the last year, and was quick at work. He was full of life, and knew how to swim, to tread water, and to turn over and tumble in the strong tide. They often warned him to beware of the sharks, which seize the best swimmer, draw him down, and devour him; but such was not to be Jürgen's fate.

At a neighbour's house in the dunes there was a boy named Martin, with whom Jürgen was on very friendly terms, and they both took service in the same ship to Norway, and also went together to Holland. They never had a quarrel, but a person can be easily excited to quarrel when he is naturally hot-tempered, for he often shows it in many ways; and this is just what Jürgen did one day when they fell out about the merest trifle. They were sitting behind the cabin door, eating from a delft plate, which they had placed between them. Jürgen held his pocket-knife in his hand and raised it towards Martin, and at the same time became ashy pale, and his eyes had an ugly look. Martin only said, "Ah! ah! you are one of that sort, are you? Fond of using the knife!"

The words were scarcely spoken, when Jürgen's hand sank down. He did not answer a syllable, but went on eating, and afterwards returned to his work. When they were resting again he walked up to Martin and said:

"Hit me in the face! I deserve it. But sometimes I feel as if I had a pot in me that boils over."

"There, let the thing rest," replied Martin.

And after that they were almost better friends than ever; when afterwards they returned to the dunes and began telling their adventures, this was told among the rest. Martin said that Jürgen was certainly passionate, but a good fellow after all.

They were both young and healthy, well-grown and strong; but Jurgen was the cleverer of the two.

In Norway the peasants go into the mountains and take the cattle there to find pasture. On the west coast of Jutland huts have been erected among the sand-hills; they are built of pieces of wreck, and thatched with turf and heather; there are sleeping places round the walls, and here the fishermen live and sleep during the early spring. Every fisherman has a female helper, or manager as she is called, who baits his hooks, prepares warm beer for him when he comes ashore, and gets the dinner cooked and ready for him by the time he comes back to the hut tired and hungry. Besides this the managers bring up the fish from the boats, cut them open, prepare them, and have generally a great deal to do.

Jürgen, his father, and several other fishermen and their managers inhabited the same hut; Martin lived in the next one.

One of the girls, whose name was Else, had known Jürgen from childhood; they were glad to see each other, and were of the same opinion on many points, but in appearance they were entirely opposite; for he was dark, and she was pale, and fair, and had flaxen hair, and eyes as blue as the sea in sunshine.

As they were walking together one day, Jürgen held her hand very firmly in his, and she said to him:

"Jürgen, I have something I want to say to you; let me be your manager, for you are like a brother to me; but Martin, whose housekeeper I am—he is my lover—but you need not tell this to the others."

It seemed to Jürgen as if the loose sand was giving way under his feet. He did not speak a word, but nodded his head, and that meant "yes." It was all that was necessary; but he suddenly felt in his heart that he hated Martin, and the more he thought the more he felt convinced that Martin had stolen away from him the only being he ever loved, and that this was Else: he had never thought of Else in this way before, but now it all became plain to him.

When the sea is rather rough, and the fishermen are coming home in their great boats, it is wonderful to see how they cross the reefs. One of them stands upright in the bow of the boat, and the others watch him sitting with the oars in their hands. Outside the reef it looks as if the boat was not approaching land but going back to sea; then the man who is standing up gives them the signal that the great wave is coming which is to float them across the reef. The boat is lifted high into the air, so that the keel is seen from the shore; the next moment nothing can be seen, mast, keel, and people are all hidden — it seems as though the sea had devoured them; but in a few moments they emerge like a great sea animal climbing up the waves, and the oars move as if the creature had legs. The second and third reef are passed in the same manner; then the fishermen jump into the water and push the boat towards the shore — every wave helps them — and at length they have it drawn up, beyond the reach of the breakers.

A wrong order given in front of the reef — the slightest hesitation — and the boat would be lost,

"Then it would be all over with me and Martin too!"

This thought passed through Jürgen's mind one day while they were out at sea, where his foster-father had been taken suddenly ill. The fever had seized him. They were only a few oars' strokes from the reef, and Jürgen sprang from his seat and stood up in the bow.

"Father — let me come!" he said, and he glanced at Martin and across the waves; every oar bent with the exertions of the rowers as the great wave came towards them, and he saw his father's pale face, and dared not obey the evil impulse that had shot through his brain. The boat came safely across the reef to land; but the evil thought remained in his heart, and roused up every little fibre of bitterness which he remembered between himself and Martin since they had known each other. But he could not weave the fibres together, nor did he endeavour to do so. He felt that Martin had robbed him, and this was enough to make him hate his former friend. Several of the fishermen saw this, but Martin did not — he remained as obliging and talkative as ever, in fact he talked rather too much.

Jürgen's foster-father took to his bed, and it became his death-bed, for he died a week afterwards; and now Jürgen was heir to the little house behind the sand-hills. It was small, certainly, but still it was something, and Martin had nothing of the kind.

"You will not go to sea again, Jürgen, I suppose," observed one of the old fishermen. "You will always stay with us now."

But this was not Jürgen's intention; he wanted to see something of the world. The eel-breeder of Fjaltring had an uncle at Old Skjagen, who was a fisherman, but also a prosperous merchant with ships upon the sea; he was said to be a good old man, and it would not be a bad thing to enter his service. Old Skjagen lies in the extreme north of Jutland, as far away from the Hunsby dunes as one can travel in that country; and this is just what pleased Jürgen, for he did not want to remain till the wedding of Martin and Else, which would take place in a week or two.

The old fisherman said it was foolish to go away, for now that Jürgen had a home Else would very likely be inclined to take him instead of Martin.

Jürgen gave such a vague answer that it was not easy to make out what he meant—the old man brought Else to him, and she said:

"You have a home now; you ought to think of that."

And Jürgen thought of many things.

The sea has heavy waves, but there are heavier waves in the human heart. Many thoughts, strong and weak, rushed through Jürgen's brain, and he said to Else:

"If Martin had a house like mine, which of us would you rather have?"

"But Martin has no house and cannot get one."

"Suppose he had one?"

"Well, then I would certainly take Martin, for that is what my heart tells me; but one cannot live upon love."

Jürgen turned these things over in his mind all night. Something was working within him, he hardly knew what it was, but it was even stronger than his love for Else; and so he went to Martin's, and what he said and did there was well considered. He let the house to Martin on most liberal terms, saying that he wished to go to sea again, because he loved it. And Else kissed him when she heard of it, for she loved Martin best.

Jürgen proposed to start early in the morning, and on the evening before his departure, when it was already getting rather late, he felt a wish to visit Martin once more. He started, and among the dunes met the old fisherman, who was angry at his leaving the place. The old man made jokes about Martin, and declared there must be some magic about that fellow, of whom the girls were so fond.

Jürgen did not pay any attention to his remarks, but said good-bye to the old man and went on towards the house where Martin dwelt. He heard loud talking inside; Martin was not alone, and this made Jürgen waver in his determination, for he did not wish to see Else again. On second thoughts, he decided that it was better not to hear any more thanks from Martin, and so he turned back.

On the following morning, before the sun rose, he fastened his knapsack on his back, took his wooden provision box in his hand, and went away among the sand-hills towards the coast path. This way was more pleasant than the heavy sand road, and besides it was shorter; and he intended to go first to Fjaltring, near Bovbjerg, where the eel-breeder lived, to whom he had promised a visit.

The sea lay before him, clear and blue, and the mussel shells and pebbles, the playthings of his childhood, crunched over his feet. While he thus walked on his nose suddenly began to bleed; it was a trifling occurrence, but trifles sometimes are of great importance. A few large drops of blood fell upon one of his sleeves. He wiped them off and stopped the bleeding, and it seemed to him as if this had cleared and lightened his brain. The sea-cale bloomed here and there in the sand as he passed. He broke off a spray and stuck it in his hat; he determined to be merry and light-hearted, for he was going out into the wide world—"a little way out, beyond the bay," as the young eels had said. "Beware of bad people who will catch you, and skin you, and put you in the frying-pan!" he repeated in his mind, and smiled, for he thought he should find his way through the world—good courage is a strong weapon!

The sun was high in the heavens when he approached the narrow entrance to Nissum Bay. He looked back and saw a couple of horsemen galloping a long distance behind hin, and there were other people with them. But this did not concern him.

The ferry-boat was on the opposite side of the bay. Jürgen called to the ferry-man, and the latter came over with his boat. Jürgen stepped in; but before he had got half-way across, the men whom he had seen riding so hastily, came up, hailed the ferry-man, and commanded him to return in the name of the law. Jürgen did not understand the reason of this, but he thought it would be best to turn back, and therefore he himself took an oar and returned. As soon as the boat touched the shore, the men sprang on board, and before he was aware of it, they had bound his hands with a rope.

"This wicked deed will cost you your life," they said. "It is a good thing we have caught you."

He was accused of nothing less than murder. Martin had been found dead, with his throat cut. One of the fishermen, late on the previous evening, had met Jürgen going towards Martin's house; this was not the first time Jürgen had raised his knife against Martin, so they felt sure that he was the murderer. The prison was in a town at a great distance, and the wind was contrary for going there by sea; but it would not take half an hour to get across the bay, and another quarter of an hour would bring them to Nörre-Vosborg, the great castle with ramparts and moat. One of Jürgen's captors was a fisherman, a brother of the keeper of the castle, and he said it might be managed that Jürgen should be placed for the present in the dungeon at Vosborg, where Long Martha the gipsy had been shut up till her execution. They paid no attention to Jürgen's defence; the few drops of blood on his shirt-sleeve bore heavy witness against him. But he was conscious of his innocence, and as there was no chance of clearing himself at present he submitted to his fate.

The party landed just at the place where Sir Bugge's castle had stood, and where Jürgen had walked with his foster-parents after the burial feast, during the four happiest days of his childhood. He was led by the well-known path, over the meadow to Vosborg; once more the elders were in bloom and the lofty lime-trees gave forth sweet fragrance, and it seemed as if it were but yesterday that he had last seen the spot. In each of the two wings of the castle there was a staircase which led to a place below the entrance, from whence there is access to a low, vaulted cellar. In this dungeon Long Martha had been imprisoned, and from here she was led away to the scaffold. She had eaten the hearts of five children, and had imagined that if she could obtain two more she would be able to fly and make herself invisible. In the middle of the roof of the cellar there was a little narrow air-hole, but no window. The flowering lime trees could not breathe refreshing fragrance into that abode, where everything was dark and mouldy. There was only a rough bench in the cell; but a good conscience is a soft pillow, and therefore Jürgen could sleep well.

The thick oaken door was locked, and secured on the outside by an iron bar; but the goblin of superstition can creep through a keyhole into a baron's castle just as easily as it can into a fisherman's cottage, and why should he not creep in here, where Jürgen sat thinking of Long Martha and her wicked deeds? Her last thoughts on the night before her execution had filled this place, and the magic that tradition asserted to have been practised here, in

Sir Svanwedel's time, came into Jürgen's mind, and made him shudder; but a sunbeam, a refreshing thought from without, penetrated his heart even here—it was the remembrance of the flowering elder and the sweet smelling lime-trees.

He was not left there long. They took him away to the town of Ringkjöbing, where he was imprisoned with equal severity.

Those times were not like ours. The common people were treated harshly; and it was just after the days when farms were converted into knights' estates, when coachmen and servants were often made magistrates, and had power to sentence a poor man, for a small offence, to lose his property and to corporeal punishment. Judges of this kind were still to be found; and in Jutland, so far from the capital, and from the enlightened, well-meaning, head of the Government, the law was still very loosely administered sometimes—the smallest grievance Jürgen could expect was that his case should be delayed.

His dwelling was cold and comfortless; and how long would he be obliged to bear all this? It seemed his fate to suffer misfortune and sorrow innocently. He now had plenty of time to reflect on the difference of fortune on earth, and to wonder why this fate had been allotted to him; yet he felt sure that all would be made clear in the next life, the existence that awaits us when this life is over. His faith had grown strong in the poor fisherman's cottage; the light which had never shone into his father's mind, in all the richness and sunshine of Spain, was sent to him to be his comfort in poverty and distress, a sign of that mercy of God which never fails.

The spring storms began to blow. The rolling and moaning of the North Sea could be heard for miles inland when the wind was blowing, and then it sounded like the rushing of a thousand waggons over a hard road with a mine underneath. Jürgen heard these sounds in his prison, and it was a relief to him. No music could have touched his heart as did these sounds of the sea—the rolling sea, the boundless sea, on which a man can be borne across the world before the wind, carrying his own house with him wherever he goes, just as the snail carries its home even into a strange country.

He listened eagerly to its deep murmur and then the thought arose—"Free! free! How happy to be free, even barefooted and in ragged clothes!" Sometimes, when such thoughts crossed his mind, the fiery nature rose within him, and he beat the wall with his clenched fists.

Weeks, months, a whole year had gone by, when Niels the thief, called also a horse-dealer, was arrested; and now better times came, and it was seen that Jürgen had been wrongly accused.

On the afternoon before Jürgen's departure from home, and before the murder, Niels the thief, had met Martin at a beer-house in the neighbourhood of Ringkjöbing. A few glasses were drank, not enough to cloud the brain, but enough to loosen Martin's tongue. He began to boast and to say that he had obtained a house and intended to marry, and when Niels asked him where he was going to get the money, he slapped his pocket proudly and said:

"The money is here, where it ought to be."

This boast cost him his life; for when he went home Niels followed him, and cut his throat, intending to rob the murdered man of the gold, which did not exist.

All this was circumstantially explained; but it is enough for us to know that

Jürgen was set free. But what compensation did he get for having been imprisoned a whole year, and shut out from all communication with his fellow creatures? They told him he was fortunate in being proved innocent, and that he might go. The burgomaster gave him two dollars for travelling expenses, and many citizens offered him provisions and beer—there were still good people; they were not all hard and pitiless. But the best thing of all was that the merchant Brönne, of Skjagen, into whose service Jürgen had proposed entering the year before, was just at that time on business in the town of Ringkjöbing. Brönne heard the whole story; he was kind-hearted, and understood what Jürgen must have felt and suffered. Therefore he made up his mind to make it up to the poor lad, and convince him that there were still kind folks in the world.

So Jürgen went forth from prison as if to paradise, to find freedom, affection, and trust. He was to travel this path now, for no goblet of life is all bitterness; no good man would pour out such a draught for his fellow-man, and how should He do it, Who is love personified?

"Let everything be buried and forgotten," said Brönne, the merchant. "Let us draw a thick line through last year: we will even burn the almanack. In two days we will start for dear, friendly, peaceful Skjagen. People call it an out-of-the-way corner; but it is a good warm chimney-corner, and its windows open towards every part of the world."

What a journey that was: It was like taking fresh breath out of the cold dungeon air into the warm sunshine. The heather bloomed in pride and beauty, and the shepherd-boy sat on a barrow and blew his pipe, which he had carved for himself out of a sheep bone. Fata Morgana, the beautiful aerial phenomenon of the wilderness, appeared with hanging gardens and waving forests, and the wonderful cloud called "Lokeman driving his sheep" also was seen.

Up towards Skjagen they went, through the land of the Wendels, whence the men with long beards (the Longobardi or Lombards) had emigrated in the reign of King Snio, when all the children and old people were to have been killed, till the noble Dame Gambaruk proposed that the young people should emigrate. Jürgen knew all this, he had some little knowledge; and although he did not know the land of the Lombards beyond the lofty Alps, he had an idea that it must be there, for in his boyhood he had been in the south, in Spain. He thought of the plenteousness of the southern fruit, of the red pomegranate flowers, of the humming, buzzing, and toiling in the great beehive of a city he had seen; but home is the best place after all, and Jürgen's home was Denmark.

At last they arrived at "Vendilskaga," as Skjagen is called in old Norwegian and Icelandic writings. At that time Old Skjagen, with the eastern and western town, extended for miles, with sand hills and arable land as far as the lighthouse near "Grenen." Then, as now, the houses were strewn among the wind-raised sand-hills—a wilderness in which the wind sports with the sand, and where the voice of the sea-gull and wild swan strikes harshly on the ear.

In the south-west, a mile from "Grenen," lies Old Skjagen; merchant Brönne dwelt here, and this was also to be Jürgen's home for the future. The dwelling-house was tarred, and all the small out-buildings had been put together from pieces of wreck. There was no fence, for indeed there was nothing to fence in except the long rows of fishes which were hung upon lines, one above the other, to dry in the wind. The entire coast was strewn with spoiled herrings, for there were so many of these fish that a net was scarcely thrown into the sea before it was filled. They were caught by carloads, and many of them were either thrown back into the sea or left to lie on the beach.

The old man's wife and daughter and his servants also came to meet him with great rejoicing. There was a great squeezing of hands, and talking and questioning. And the daughter, what a sweet face and bright eyes she had!

The inside of the house was comfortable and roomy. Fritters, that a king would have looked upon as a dainty dish, were placed on the table, and there was wine from the Skjagen vineyard — that is, the sea; for there the grapes come ashore ready pressed and prepared in barrels and in bottles.

When the mother and daughter heard who Jürgen was, and how innocently he had suffered, they looked at him in a still more friendly way; and pretty Clara's eyes had a look of especial interest as she listened to his story. Jürgen found a happy home in Old Skjagen. It did his heart good, for it had been sorely tried. He had drunk the bitter goblet of love which softens or hardens the heart, according to circumstances. Jurgen's heart was still soft — it was young, and therefore it was a good thing that Miss Clara was going in three weeks' time to Christiansand in Norway, in her father's ship, to visit an aunt and to stay there the whole winter.

On the Sunday before she went away they all went to church, to the Holy Communion. The church was large and handsome, and had been built centuries before by Scotchmen and Dutchmen; it stood some little way out of the town. It was rather ruinous certainly, and the road to it was heavy, through deep sand, but the people gladly surmounted these difficulties to get to the house of God, to sing psalms and to hear the sermon. The sand had heaped itself up round the walls of the church, but the graves were kept free from it.

It was the largest church north of the Limfjorden. The Virgin Mary, with a golden crown on her head and the child Jesus in her arms, stood lifelike on the altar; the holy Apostles had been carved in the choir, and on the walls there were portraits of the old burgomasters and councillors of Skjagen; the pulpit was of carved work. The sun shone brightly into the church, and its radiance fell on the polished brass chandelier and on the little ship that hung from the vaulted roof.

Jürgen felt overcome by a holy, childlike feeling, like that which possessed him, when, as a boy, he stood in the splendid Spanish cathedral. But here the feeling was different, for he felt conscious of being one of the congregation.

After the sermon followed Holy Communion. He partook of the bread and wine, and it so happened that he knelt by the side of Miss Clara; but his thoughts were so fixed upon heaven and the Holy Sacrament that he did not notice his neighbour until he rose from his knees, and then he saw tears rolling down her cheeks.

She left Skjagen and went to Norway two days later. He remained behind, and made himself useful on the farm and at the fishery. He went out fishing, and in those days fish were more plentiful and larger than they are now. The shoals of the mackerel glittered in the dark nights, and indicated where they were swimming; the gurnards snarled, and the crabs gave forth pitiful yells when they were chased, for fish are not so mute as people say.

Every Sunday Jürgen went to church; and when his eyes rested on the picture of the Virgin Mary over the altar as he sat there, they often glided away to the spot where they had knelt side by side.

THE GARDENER AND THE NOBLE FAMILY

Autumn came, and brought rain and snow with it; the water rose up right into the town of Skjagen, the sand could not suck it all in, one had to wade through it or go by boat. The storms threw vessel after vessel on the fatal reefs; there were snow-storms and sand-storms; the sand flew up to the houses, blocking the entrances, so that people had to creep up through the chimneys; that was nothing at all remarkable here. It was pleasant and cheerful indoors, where peat fuel and fragments of wood from the wrecks blazed and crackled upon the hearth. Merchant Brönne read aloud, from an old chronicle, about Prince Hamlet of Denmark, who had come over from England, landed near Bovbjerg, and fought a battle; close by Ramme was his grave, only a few miles from the place where the eel-breeder lived; hundreds of barrow rose there from the heath, forming as it were an enormous churchyard. Merchant Brönne had himself been at Hamlet's grave; they spoke about old times, and about their neighbours, the English and the Scotch, and Jürgen sang the air of "The King of England's Son," and of his splendid ship and its outfit.

> "In the hour of peril when most men fear,
> He clasped the bride that he held so dear,
> And proved himself the son of a King;
> Of his courage and valour let us sing."

This verse Jürgen sang with so much feeling that his eyes beamed, and they were black and sparkling since his infancy.

There was wealth, comfort, and happiness even among the domestic animals, for they were all well cared for, and well kept. The kitchen looked bright with its copper and tin utensils, and white plates, and from the rafters hung hams, beef, and winter stores in plenty. This can still be seen in many rich farms on the west coast of Jutland: plenty to eat and drink, clean, prettily decorated rooms, active minds, cheerful tempers, and hospitality can be found there, as in an Arab's tent.

Jürgen had never spent such a happy time since the famous burial feast, and yet Miss Clara was absent, except in the thoughts and memory of all.

In April a ship was to start for Norway, and Jürgen was to sail in it. He was full of life and spirits, and looked so sturdy and well that Dame Brönne said it did her good to see him.

"And it does one good to look at you also, old wife," said the merchant. "Jürgen has brought fresh life into our winter evenings, and into you too, mother. You look younger than ever this year, and seem well and cheerful. But then you were once the prettiest girl in Viborg, and that is saying a great deal, for I have always found the Viborg girls the prettiest of any."

Jürgen said nothing, but he thought of a certain maiden of Skjagen, whom he was soon to visit. The ship set sail for Christiansand in Norway, and as the wind was favourable it soon arrived there.

One morning merchant Brönne went out to the lighthouse, which stands a little way out of Old Skjagen, not far from "Grenen." The light was out, and the sun was already high in the heavens, when he mounted the tower. The sand-banks extend a whole mile from the shore, beneath the water, outside these banks; many ships could be seen that day, and with the aid of his telescope the old man thought he descried his own ship, the *Karen Brönne*.

Yes! certainly, there she was, sailing homewards with Clara and Jürgen on board.

Clara sat on deck, and saw the sand-hills gradually appearing in the distance; the church and lighthouse looked like a heron and a swan rising from the blue waters. If the wind held good they might reach home in about an hour. So near they were to home and all its joys—so near to death and all its terrors! A plank in the ship gave way, and the water rushed in; the crew flew to the pumps, and did their best to stop the leak. A signal of distress was hoisted, but they were still fully a mile from the shore. Some fishing boats were in sight, but they were too far off to be of any use. The wind blew towards the land, the tide was in their favour, but it was all useless; the ship could not be saved.

Jürgen threw his right arm round Clara, and pressed her to him. With what a look she gazed up into his face, as with a prayer to God for help he breasted the waves, which rushed over the sinking ship! She uttered a cry, but she felt safe and certain that he would not leave her to sink. And in this hour of terror and danger Jürgen felt as the king's son did, as told in the old song:

> "In the hour of peril when most men fear,
> He clasped the bride that he held so dear."

How glad he felt that he was a good swimmer! He worked his way onward with his feet and one arm, while he held the young girl up firmly with the other. He rested on the waves, he trod the water—in fact, did everything he could think of, in order not to fatigue himself, and to reserve strength enough to reach land. He heard Clara sigh, and felt her shudder convulsively, and he pressed her more closely to him. Now and then a wave rolled over them, the current lifted them; the water, although deep, was so clear that for a moment he imagined he saw the shoals of mackerel glittering, or Leviathan himself ready to swallow them. Now the clouds cast a shadow over the water, then again came the playing sunbeams; flocks of loudly screaming birds passed over him, and the plump and lazy wild ducks which allow themselves to be drifted by the waves rose up terrified at the sight of the swimmer. He began to feel his strength decreasing, but he was only a few cable lengths' distance from the shore, and help was coming, for a boat was approaching him. At this moment he distinctly saw a white staring figure under the water—a wave lifted him up, and he came nearer to the figure—he felt a violent shock, and everything became dark around him.

On the sand reef lay the wreck of a ship, which was covered with water at high tide; the white figure head rested against the anchor, the sharp iron edge of which rose just above the surface. Jürgen had come in contact with this; the tide had driven him against it with great force. He sank down stunned with the blow, but the next wave lifted him and the young girl up again. Some fishermen, coming with a boat, seized them and dragged them into it. The blood streamed down over Jürgen's face; he seemed dead, but still held the young girl so tightly that they were obliged to take her from him by force. She was pale and lifeless; they laid her in the boat, and rowed as quickly as possible to the shore. They tried every means to restore Clara to life, but it was all of no avail. Jürgen had been swimming for some distance with a corpse in his arms, and had exhausted his strength for one who was dead.

Jürgen still breathed, so the fishermen carried him to the nearest house upon the sand-hills, where a smith and general dealer lived who knew something of surgery, and bound up Jürgen's wounds in a temporary way until a surgeon could be obtained from the nearest town the next day. The injured man's brain was affected, and in his delirium he uttered wild cries; but on the third day he lay quiet and weak upon his bed; his life seemed to hang by a thread, and the physician said it would be better for him if this thread broke. "Let us pray that God may take him," he said, "for he will never be the same man again."

But life did not depart from him—the thread would not break, but the thread of memory was severed; the thread of his mind had been cut through, and what was still more grievous, a body remained—a living healthy body that wandered about like a troubled spirit.

Jürgen remained in merchant Brönne's house. "He was hurt while endeavouring to save our child," said the old man, "and now he is our son." People called Jürgen insane, but that was not exactly the correct term. He was like an instrument in which the strings are loose and will give no sound; only occasionally they regained their power for a few minutes, and then they sounded as they used to do. He would sing snatches of songs or old melodies, pictures of the past would rise before him, and then disappear in the mist, as it were, but as a general rule he sat staring into vacancy, without a thought. We may conjecture that he did not suffer, but his dark eyes lost their brightness, and looked like clouded glass.

"Poor mad Jürgen," said the people. And this was the end of a life whose infancy was to have been surrounded with wealth and splendour had his parents lived! All his great mental abilities had been lost, nothing but hardship, sorrow, and disappointment had been his fate. He was like a rare plant, torn from its native soil, and tossed upon the beach to wither there. And was this one of God's creatures, fashioned in His own likeness, to have no better fate? Was he to be only the plaything of fortune? No! the all-loving Creator would certainly repay him in the life to come for what he had suffered and lost here. "The Lord is good to all; and His mercy is over all His works." The pious old wife of the merchant repeated these words from the Psalms of David in patience and hope, and the prayer of her heart was that Jürgen might soon be called away to enter into eternal life.

In the churchyard where the walls were surrounded with sand Clara lay buried. Jürgen did not seem to know this; it did not enter his mind, which could only retain fragments of the past. Every Sunday he went to church with the old people, and sat there silently, staring vacantly before him. One day, when the Psalms were being sung, he sighed deeply, and his eyes became bright; they were fixed upon a place near the altar where he had knelt with his friend who was dead. He murmured her name, and became deadly pale, and tears rolled down his cheeks. They led him out of church; he told those standing round him that he was well, and had never been ill; he, who had been so grievously afflicted, the outcast, thrown upon the world, could not remember his sufferings. The Lord our Creator is wise and full of loving kindness—who can doubt it?

In Spain, where balmy breezes blow over the Moorish cupolas and gently stir the orange and myrtle groves, where singing and the sound of the castanets are always heard, the richest merchant in the place, a childless old man, sat in a luxurious house, while children marched in procession through the streets with waving flags and lighted tapers. If he had been able to press his children to his heart, his daughter, or her child, that had, perhaps never seen the light of day, far less the kingdom of heaven, how much of his wealth would he not have given! "Poor child!" Yes, poor child—a child still, yet more than thirty years old, for Jürgen had arrived at this age in Old Skjagen.

The shifting sands had covered the graves in the courtyard, quite up to the church walls, but still, the dead must be buried among their relatives and the dear ones who had gone before them. Merchant Brönne and his wife now rested with their children under the white sand.

It was in the spring—the season of storms. The sand from the dunes was whirled up in clouds; the sea was rough, and flocks of birds flew like clouds in the storm, screaming across the sand-hills. Shipwreck followed upon shipwreck on the reefs between Old Skagen and the Hunsby dunes.

One evening Jürgen sat in his room alone: all at once his mind seemed to become clearer, and a restless feeling came over him, such as had often, in his younger days, driven him out to wander over the sand-hills or on the heath. "Home, home!" he cried. No one heard him. He went out and walked towards the dunes. Sand and stones blew into his face, and whirled round him; he went in the direction of the church. The sand was banked up the walls, half covering the windows, but it had been cleared away in front of the door, and the entrance was free and easy to open, so Jürgen went into the church.

The storm raged over the town of Skjagen; there had not been such a terrible tempest within the memory of the inhabitants, nor such a rough sea. But Jürgen was in the temple of God, and while the darkness of night reigned outside, a light arose in his soul that was never to depart from it; the heavy weight that pressed on his brain burst asunder. He fancied he heard the organ, but it was only the storm and the moaning of the sea. He sat down on one of the seats, and lo! the candles were lighted one by one, and there was brightness and grandeur such as he had only seen in the Spanish cathedral. The portraits of the old citizens became alive, stepped down from the walls against which they had hung for centuries, and took seats near the church door. The gates flew open, and all the dead people from the churchyard came in, and filled the church, while beautiful music sounded. Then the melody of the psalm burst forth, like the sound of the waters, and Jürgen saw that his foster parents from the Hunsby dunes were there, also old merchant Brönne with his wife and their daughter Clara, who gave him her hand. They both went up to the altar where they had knelt before, and the priest joined their hands and united them for life. Then music was heard again; it was wonderfully sweet, like a child's voice, full of joy and expectation, swelling to the powerful tones of a full organ, sometimes soft and sweet, then like the sounds of a tempest, delightful and elevating to hear, yet strong enough to burst the stone tombs of the dead. Then the little ship that hung from the roof of the choir was let down and looked wonderfully large and beautiful with its silken sails and rigging:

"The ropes were of silk, the anchor of gold,
     And everywhere riches and pomp untold,"

as the old song says.

The young couple went on board, accompanied by the whole congregation, for there was room and enjoyment for them all. Then the walls and arches of the church were covered with flowering junipers and lime trees breathing forth fragrance; the branches waved, creating a pleasant coolness; they bent and parted, and the ship sailed between them through the air and over the sea. Every candle in the church became a star, and the wind sang a hymn in which they all joined. "Through love to glory, no life is lost, the future is full of blessings and happiness. Hallelujah!" These were the last words Jürgen uttered in this world, for the thread that bound his immortal soul was severed, and nothing but the dead body lay in the dark church, while the storm raged outside, covering it with loose sand.

The next day was Sunday, and the congregation and their pastor went to the church. The road had always been heavy, but now it was almost unfit for use, and when they at last arrived at the church, a great heap of sand lay piled up in front of them. The whole church was completely buried in sand. The clergyman offered a short prayer, and said that God had closed the door of His house here, and that the congregation must go and build a new one for Him somewhere else. So they sung a hymn in the open air, and went home again.

Jürgen could not be found anywhere in the town of Skjagen, nor on the dunes, though they searched for him everywhere. They came to the conclusion that one of the great waves, which had rolled far up on the beach, had carried him away; but his body lay buried in a great sepulchre—the church itself. The Lord had thrown down a covering for his grave during the storm, and the heavy mound of sand lies upon it to this day. The drifting sand had covered the vaulted roof of the church, the arched cloisters, and the stone aisles. The white thorn and the dog rose now blossom above the place where the church lies buried, but the spire, like an enormous monument over a grave, can be seen for miles round. No king has a more splendid memorial. Nothing disturbs the peaceful sleep of the dead. I was the first to hear this story, for the storm sung it to me among the sand-hills.

THE GARDENER AND THE NOBLE FAMILY

ABOUT four miles from the city stood an old manor house with thick walls, towers, and pointed gables. Here lived, but only in the summer season, a rich and noble family. Of all the different estates they owned, this was the best and the most beautiful; on the outside it looked as if it had just been cast in a foundry, and the inside was made for comfort and ease. The family coat of arms was carved in stone over the gate; beautiful roses climbed about the arms and the balconies; the courtyard was covered with grass; there were red thorn and white thorn, and many rare flowers, even outside the greenhouse.

The owner of the house also had a very skillful gardener. It was a pleasure to see the flower garden, the orchard, and the vegetable garden. A part of the manor's original old garden was still there, consisting of a few box-tree hedges cut so that they formed crowns and pyramids. Behind these stood two old, mighty trees, almost always without leaves, and one might easily think that a storm or a waterspout had scattered great lumps of dirt on their branches, but each lump was a bird's nest. Here, from time immemorial, a screaming swarm of crows and rooks had built their nests; it was a regular bird town, and the birds were the owners, the manor's oldest family. — the real lordship! The people below meant nothing to them; they tolerated these crawling creatures, even if every now and then they shot with their guns, making the birds' backbones shiver, so that every bird flew up in fear and cried, "Rak! Rak!"

The gardener often spoke to the noble family about cutting down the old trees; they did not look well, and by taking them away they might also get rid of the shrieking birds, which then would probably look for another place. But the family did not want to give up either the trees or the swarm of birds; that was something the manor could not lose, something from the olden times, which should never be forgotten.

"Why, those trees are the birds' heritage by this time, so let them keep them, my good Larsen!" Larsen was the gardener's name, but that is of very little consequence to this story.

"Haven't you space enough to work in, little Larsen? Have you not the flower garden, the greenhouse, the orchard, and the vegetable garden?"

Yes, those he had, and he cared for them; he kept them in order and cultivated them with affection and ability, and that the noble family knew; but they did not conceal from him that they often saw flowers and tasted fruits in other people's homes that surpassed what they had in their garden, and that made the gardener sad, for he always wished to do his best and really did his best. He was goodhearted and a good and faithful worker.

One day the noble family sent for him and told him, very kindly, that the day before, at some distinguished friend's home, they had eaten apples and pears that were so juicy and so well flavored that they and all the other guests had expressed their admiration. It was doubtful if the fruits were native, but they ought to be imported and grown here, provided the climate would permit it. It was known that they had been bought from the finest fruit dealer in the city, and it was decided that the gardener was to go there and find out where these apples and pears came from and then order some slips for grafting. The gardener knew the fruit dealer well, because he was the very person to whom he sold the superfluous fruit that grew in the manor garden.

And the gardener went to town and asked the dealer where he got those highly praised apples and pears. "Why, they are from your own garden," said the fruit dealer, and showed him both the apples and pears, which he recognized immediately.

How happy the gardener felt! He hurried back to the family and told them that both the apples and the pears were from their own garden. That they couldn't believe! "That's not possible, Larsen! Can you get a written guarantee to that effect from the fruit dealer?"

Yes, that he could, and written guarantee he brought.

"That certainly is remarkable!" said the noble family.

Now every day great dishes filled with wonderful apples and pears from their own garden were set on the table. Bushels and barrels of these fruits were sent to friends in the city and outside the city; yes, even to foreign lands. This afforded great pleasure; yet the family added that the last two summers had, of course, been remarkably good for tree fruits and these had done very well all over the country.

Some time passed. The family were dinner guests at court. The next day they sent for the gardener. At the royal table they had eaten melons, very juicy and wonderfully flavored, from their majesties' greenhouse.

"You must go to the court gardener, my good Larsen, and let him give you some seeds of those precious melons."

"But the court gardener got his melon seeds from us!" said the gardener, very pleased.

"Then that man knows how to bring the fruit to a higher perfection!" answered the family. "Each melon was splendid."

"Well, then, I really can feel proud!" said the gardener. "I must tell your lordship that the court gardener had had bad luck with his melons this year, and when he saw how beautiful ours looked, and then tasted them, he ordered three of them for the castle."

"Larsen, don't try to tell us that those were melons from our garden."

"I really believe so," said the gardener.

And he went to the court gardener, from whom he got a written guarantee to the effect that the melons on the royal table were from the manor. This was really a big surprise to the family, and they did not keep the story to themselves; the written guarantee was displayed, and melon seeds were sent far and wide, as grafting slips had been earlier.

These slips, the family learned, had taken and begun to bear fruit of an excellent kind. This was named after the family manor, and the name became known in English, German, and French. This, no one had expected. "Let's hope the gardener won't get big ideas about himself," said the family.

But he took it in a different way; he would strive now to be known as one of the best gardeners in the country and to produce something superior out of all sorts of garden stuff every year. And that he did. But often he was told that the very first fruits he brought out, the apples and the pears, were, after all, the best, that all later variations were very inferior to these. The melons were very good, to be sure, though, of course, they belonged to another species; his strawberries might be called delicious, but no better than those grown by other gardeners, and when one year his radishes did not turn out very well, they spoke only of the unsuccessful radishes and not about all the other fine products he had developed.

It almost seemed as if the family felt a relief in saying, "It didn't go well this year, little Larsen!" Yes, they seemed quite happy when they said, "It didn't go well this year!"

Twice a week the gardener brought fresh flowers up to their drawing room, always arranged with such taste and artistry that the colors seemed to appear even brighter.

"You have good taste, Larsen," said the noble family, "but that is a gift from our Lord, not from yourself!"

One day the gardener brought a large crystal bowl; in it floated a water-lily leaf upon which was laid a beautiful blue flower as big as a sunflower.

"The lotus of Hindustan!" exclaimed the family.

They had never seen a lotus flower before. In the daytime it was placed in the sunlight and in the evening under artificial light. Everyone who saw it found it remarkably beautiful and unusual; yes, even the most highborn young lady in the country, the wise and kindhearted Princess, said so. The family considered it an honor to present her with the flower, and the Princess took it with her to the castle. Then they went down to their garden to pick another flower of the same kind, but none was to be found. So they sent for the gardener and asked him where he got the blue lotus flower.

"We have been looking for it in vain," they said. "We have been in the greenhouses and round about the flower garden!"

"Oh, no, it's not there," said the gardener. "It is only a common flower from the vegetable garden; but, look, isn't it beautiful! It looks like a blue cactus, and yet it is only the flower of the artichoke!"

"You should have told us that immediately!" said the noble family. "Naturally, we supposed it was a rare, foreign flower. You have ridiculed us to the young Princess! She saw the flower in our house and thought it was beautiful; she didn't know the flower, although she knows her botany well, but then, of course, that science has nothing to do with kitchen herbs. How could you do it, Larsen! To place such a flower in our drawing room is enough to make us ridiculous!"

And the gorgeous blue flower from the vegetable garden was taken out of the drawing room, where it didn't belong; yes, and the noble family apologized to the Princess and told her that the flower was only a kitchen herb that the Gardener had had the idea of exhibiting, and that he had been severely reprimanded for it.

"That was a shame, and very unfair," said the Princess. "He has really opened our eyes to a magnificent flower we otherwise would have paid no attention to; he has shown us beauty where we didn't expect to find it. As long as the artichoke is in bloom, our court gardener shall daily bring one of them up to my private room!"

And this was done.

The noble family told the gardener that he could again bring them a fresh artichoke flower.

"It is really beautiful!" they said. "Highly remarkable!" And the gardener was praised.

"Larsen likes that," said the noble family. "He is like a spoiled child."

In the autumn there was a terrific storm. During the night it increased so violently that many of the large trees in the outskirts of the wood were torn up by the roots, and to the great grief of the noble family—yes, they called it grief—but to the gardener's delight, the two big trees with all the birds' nests blew down. Through the storm one could hear the screaming of the crows and the rooks as they beat their wings against the manor windows.

"Now, of course, you are happy, Larsen!" said the noble family. "The storm has felled the trees, and the birds have gone off into the forest. There is nothing from olden times left to see here; every sign and reference has disappered; it makes us very sad!"

The gardener said nothing, but he thought of what he had long had in his mind, how he could make use of that wonderful, sunny spot, now at his disposal; it could become the pride of the garden and the joy of the family.

The large trees, in falling, had crushed the very old box-tree hedges with all their fancy trimmings. Here he put in a multitude of plants, native plants from the fields and the woods. What no other gardener had ever thought of planting in a manor garden, he planted, giving each its appropriate soil, and sunlight or shadow, according to what the individual plant required. He gave them loving care, and everything grew magnificently.

The juniper tree from the heaths of Jutland rose in shape and color like the Italian cypress; the shiny, thorny Christ's-thorn, ever green, in the cold of winter and the sun of summer, was beautiful to behold. In the foreground grew ferns of various species; some of them looked as if they were children of the palm tree, others as if they were parents of the pretty plant we call Venus's-hair. Here stood the neglected burdock, so pretty in its freshness that it can be outstanding in a bouquet. The burdock stood in a dry place, but further down, in the moist soil, grew the coltsfoot, also a neglected plant and yet very picturesque with its enormous leaf and its tall stem. Six-feet tall, with flower after flower, like an enormous, many-armed candelabra, rose the mullein, just a mere field plant. Here grew the woodruff, the primrose, and the lily of the valley, the wild calla and the fine three-leaved wood sorrel. It was all wonderful to see.

In the front, in rows, grew very tiny pear trees from French soil, fastened to steel wires; by getting plenty of sun and good care they soon bore fruit as large and juicy as in their own country. In place of the two old leafless trees was set a tall flagpole from which Dannebrog—the flag of Denmark—proudly flew; and close by stood another pole, around which the hop tendril twisted and wound its fragrant flower cones in the summer and at harvesttime, but on which in the winter, according to an old custom, oat sheaves were hung, so that the birds could have a good meal during the happy Christmastime.

"Our good Larsen is getting sentimental in his old age," said the family, "but he is true and faithful to us!"

At New Year's, one of the city's illustrated papers published a picture of the old manor; it showed the flagpole and the oat sheaves for the birds at the happy Christmastime, and the paper commented that it was a beautiful thought to uphold and honor this old custom, so appropriate to the old manor.

"Anything that Larsen does," said the noble family, "they beat the drum for. He is a lucky man. We should almost be proud to have him!"

But they were not a bit proud of it; they knew they were the masters of the manor, and they could dismiss Larsen, but that they wouldn't do. They were good people, and there are many good people of their kind in the world—and that is fortunate for all the Larsens.

Yes, that is the story of the gardener and the noble family. Now you may think about it!

THE TALISMAN

A PRINCE and a Princess were still celebrating their honeymoon. They were extremely happy; only one thought disturbed them, and that was how to retain their present happiness. For that reason they wished to own a talisman with which to protect themselves against any unhappiness in their marriage.

Now, they had often been told about a man who lived out in the forest, acclaimed by everybody for his wisdom and known for his good advice in every need and difficulty. So the Prince and Princess called upon him and told him about their heart's desire. After the wise man had listened to them he said,

"Travel through every country in the world, and wherever you meet a completely happily married couple, ask them for a small piece of the linen they wear close to the body, and when you receive this, you must always carry it with you. That is a sure remedy!"

The Prince and the Princess rode forth, and on their way they soon heard of a knight and his wife who were said to be living the most happily married life. They went to the knight's castle and asked him and his wife if their marriage was truly as happy as was rumored.

"Yes, of course," was the answer, "with the one exception that we have no children!"

Here then the talisman was not to be found, and the Prince and Princess continued their journey in search of the completely happily married couple.

As they traveled on, they came to a country where they heard of an honest citizen who lived in perfect unity and happiness with his wife. So to him they went, and asked if he really was as happily married as people said.

"Yes, I am," answered the man. "My wife and I live in perfect harmony; if only we didn't have so many children, for they give us a lot of worries and sorrows!"

So neither with him was the talisman to be found, and the Prince and the Princess continued their journey through the country, always inquiring about happily married couples; but none presented themselves.

One day, as they rode along fields and meadows, they noticed a shepherd close by the road, cheerfully playing his flute. Just then a woman carrying a child in her arm, and holding a little boy by the hand, walked towards him. As soon as the shepherd saw her, he greeted her and took the little child, whom he kissed and caressed. The shepherd's dog ran to the boy, licked his little hand, and barked and jumped with joy. In the meantime the woman arranged a meal she had brought along, and then said, "Father, come and eat now!" The man sat down and took of the food, but the first bite he gave to the little boy, and the second he divided between the boy and the dog. All this was observed by the Prince and the Princess, who walked closer, and spoke to them, saying, "You must be a truly happily married couple."

"Yes, that we are," said the man. "God be praised; no prince or princess could be happier than we are!"

"Now listen then," said the Prince. "Do us a favor, and you shall never regret it. Give us a small piece of the linen garment you wear close to your body!"

As he spoke, the shepherd and his wife looked strangely at each other, and finally he said, "God knows we would be only too happy to give you not only a small piece, but the whole shirt, or undergarment, if we only had them, but we own not as much as a rag!"

So the Prince and the Princess journeyed on, their mission unaccomplished. Finally, their unsuccessful roaming discouraged them, and they decided to return home. As they passed the wise man's hut, they stopped by, related all their travel experiences, and reproached him for giving them such poor advice.

At that the wise man smiled and said, "Has your trip really been all in vain? Are you not returning richer in knowledge?"

"Yes," answered the Prince, "I have gained *this* knowledge, that contentment is a rare gift on this earth."

"And I have learned," said the Princess, "that to be contented, one needs nothing more than simply—to be contented!"

Whereupon the Prince took the Princess' hand; they looked at each other with an expression of deepest love. And the wise man blessed them and said, "In your own hearts you have found the true talisman! Guard it carefully, and the evil spirt of discontentment shall never in all eternity have any power over you!"

ON JUDGMENT DAY

THE most solemn of all the days of our life is the day we die. It is judgment day, the great sacred day of transfiguration. Have you really seriously given a fleeting thought to that grave and mighty last hour we shall spend on earth?

There was once a man, a stanch upholder of truth, as he was called, to whom the word of his God was law, a zealous servant of his zealous God. With a stern but heavenly look, the Angel of Death stood at his bedside.

"The hour has come; you shall follow me!" said Death, and touched the man's feet with ice-cold fingers, and his feet became like ice. Then Death touched his forehead, and lastly his heart, and when it burst, the soul was free to follow the Angel of Death.

But during those brief seconds while the icy touch shivered through feet and head and heart, there passed through the mind of the dying man, like great ocean waves, the recollection of all he had wrought and felt throughout his life. So does one terrified glance into a whirlpool reveal in thought as swift as lightning the whole unfathomable depth of it; so with one fleeting glance at the countless stars of heaven can one conceive the infinite multitude of worlds and spheres in the great universe.

In such a moment the terrified sinner shrinks into himself and has nothing to cling to, and he feels himself shrinking further into infinite emptiness. And at such times the devout soul bows its head to the Almighty and yields itself up to Him in childlike trust, praying, "Thy will be done with me!"

But this dying man had not the mind of a child, nor was he a terrified sinner; his thoughts were of self-praise. He knew that he had abided by religious traditions. Millions, he knew, would have to face judgment. But he believed most confidently that his path would lead straight heavenward, and that mercy, promised to all men, would open the gates to him.

And the soul followed the Angel of Death, casting only one wistful glance back at the bed where, in its white shroud, lay the lifeless image of clay, still bearing the print of the soul's individuality.

Now they hovered through the air, now glided along the ground. Were they passing through a vast, decorated hall, or perchance a forest? It was hard to tell. Nature appeared formally set out for show, as in the stately, artificial, old French gardens, and through its strange, carefully arranged scenes there passed many men and women, all clad as if for a masquerade.

"Such is human life!" spoke the Angel of Death.

It seemed as if the figures tried to disguise themselves; those who flaunted the glories of velvet and gold were not always the noblest and the richest, neither were all those who wore the garb of poverty the most wretched and vulgar. A strange masquerade indeed! And most strange of all was to see how each one carefully concealed under his clothing something he would not have the others discover. Each was determined to learn his neighbor's secret, and they tore at one another until here and there the heads of different animals were bared. One was that of a grinning ape, another the head of a goat, still others a clammy snake and a feeble fish.

In all was some token of the animal which is fast rooted in human nature, and which here was struggling and jumping to burst forth. And however closely a person might hold his garment over it to hide it, the others would never rest until they had torn aside the veil, and all kept crying out, "Look here! See! It is he! It is she!" and everyone mockingly laid bare his fellow's shame.

"Then what was the animal in me?" inquired the soul.

The Angel of Death silently pointed to a haughty form around whose head spread a bright glory of rays, with shining colors, but in whose heart could be seen lurking, half hidden, the feet of a peacock.

The spreading glory above was merely the speckled tail of the peacock.

As they passed on, huge birds shrieked horribly at them from the boughs of trees. In voices harsh but clear, intelligible, and human, they cried. "You who walk with Death, do you remember me?" All the evil thoughts and lusts that had lurked within the man from birth to death now called after him in forbidding tones, "Do you remember me?"

For a moment the soul shuddered, for it recognized the voices; it could not deny knowledge of the evil thoughts and desires that were now rising as witnesses against it.

"In our flesh, in our evil nature, nothing good lives!" said the soul. "But, at least with me, thoughts never turned into action; the world has not seen their evil fruit!"

The soul rushed on to escape the ugly screams, but the huge black birds swept in circles, screaming out their vicious words louder and louder, as though they wished to be heard to the ends of the world. The soul fled like a hunted stag, and at every step stumbled against sharp flint stones, painfully cutting his feet on them. "How came these sharp stones here? They seem like mere withered leaves lying on the ground."

"Each stone is some careless word you have spoken, which wounded your neighbor's heart far more deeply than these sharp flints that now hurt your feet."

"I never thought of that!" cried the soul.

"Judge not, that ye be not judged!" rang through the air.

In a moment the soul recovered from its self-abasement. "We have all sinned. But I have kept the Law and the Gospel. I have done what I could do; I am not like the others."

And then they stood at the gates of heaven itself, and the Angel who guarded the entrance asked, "Who are you? Tell me your faith, and show it to me in your works."

"I have faithfully kept all the Commandments," replied the soul proudly. "I have humbled myself in the eyes of the world. I have hated and persecuted evil and those who practice it, and I would do so still, with fire and sword, had I yet the power."

"Then you are a follower of Mohammed?" said the Angel.

"I? Never!"

" 'He who strikes with the sword shall perish by the sword,' thus spoke the Son. His religion you do not have. Are you then perchance one of the children of Israel, who with Moses said: 'An eye for an eye, and a tooth for a tooth?' "

"I am a Christian."

"I see it neither in your faith nor in your actions! The teaching of Christ is forgiveness, love, and mercy!"

"Mercy!" The echo of this rang through infinite space, the gates of heaven opened, and the soul hovered toward the realms of eternal bliss.

But the flood of light that streamed forth from within was so dazzling, so penetrating, that the soul shrank back as from a double-edged sword. And the sound of music was so soft and touching that no mortal tongue could describe it. The soul trembled and prostrated itself lower and lower, and the celestial light cut through it until it felt, as it had never felt before, the weight of its own pride and cruelty and sin.

"Whatever good I have done in the world, I did because I could not do otherwise; but the evil that I did—that was of myself!"

And more and more the soul was dazzled and overwhelmed by the pure light of heaven; it seemed falling into a bottomless abyss—the abyss of its own nakedness and unworthiness. Shrunk into itself, humbled, cast out, unfit for the Kingdom of Heaven, trembling at the thought of the just and holy God, hardly dared it to gasp, "Mercy!"

And the Angel of Mercy came to him—the mercy he had not expected; and in the infinite space of heaven, God's everlasting love filled the soul.

"Holy, loving, glorious forever shalt thou be, O erring human spirit!" sang the chorus of angels. And as this soul did, so shall we all, on our last day on earth, humbly tremble in the glorious sight of the Kingdom of Heaven. But the infinite love and mercy of our Heavenly Father will carry us through other spheres, so that, purified and strengthened, we may ascend into God's eternal light.

THIS FABLE IS INTENDED FOR YOU

WISE men of ancient times ingeniously discovered how to tell people the truth without being blunt to their faces. You see, they held a magic mirror before the people, in which all sorts of animals and various wondrous things appeared, producing amusing as well as instructive pictures. They called these fables, and whatever wise or foolish deeds the animals performed, the people were to imagine themselves in their places and thereby think, "This fable is intended for you!" In this way no one's feelings were hurt. Let us give you an example.

There were two high mountains, and at the top of each stood a castle. In the valley below ran a hungry dog, sniffing along the ground as if in search of mice or quail. Suddenly a trumpet sounded from one of the castles, to announce that mealtime was approaching. The dog immediately started running up the mountain, hoping to get his share; but when he was halfway up, the trumpeter ceased blowing, and a trumpet from the other castle commenced. "Up here," thought the dog, "they will have finished eating before I arrive, but over there they are just getting ready to eat." So he ran down, and up the other mountain. But now the first trumpet started again, while the second stopped. The dog ran down again, and up again; and this he continued until both trumpets stopped blowing, and the meals were over in both castles.

Now guess what the wise men of ancient times would have said about this fable, and who the fool could be who runs himself ragged without gaining anything, either here or there?

THE TEAPOT

THERE was a proud Teapot, proud of being made of porcelain, proud of its long spout and its broad handle. It had something in front of it and behind it; the spout was in front, and the handle behind, and that was what it talked about. But it didn't mention its lid, for it was cracked and it was riveted and full of defects, and we don't talk about our defects—other people do that. The cups, the cream pitcher, the sugar bowl—in fact, the whole tea service—thought much more about the defects in the lid and talked more about it than about the sound handle and the distinguished spout. The Teapot knew this.

"I know them," it told itself. "And I also know my imperfections, and I realise that in that very knowledge is my humility and my modesty. We all have many defects, but then we also have virtues. The cups have a handle, the sugar bowl has a lid, but of course I have both, and one thing more, one thing they can never have; I have a spout, and that makes me the queen of the tea table. The sugar bowl and the cream pitcher are permitted to be serving maids of delicacies, but I am the one who gives forth, the adviser. I spread blessings abroad among thirsty mankind. Inside of me the Chinese leaves give flavor to boiling, tasteless water."

This was the way the Teapot talked in its fresh young life. It stood on the table that was prepared for tea and it was lifted up by the most delicate hand. But that most delicate hand was very awkward. The Teapot was dropped; the spout broke off, and the handle broke off; the lid is not worth talking about; enough has been said about that. The Teapot lay in a faint on the floor, while the boiling water ran out of it. It was a great shock it got, but the worst thing of all was that the others laughed at it—and not at the awkward hand.

"I'll never be able to forget that!" said the Teapot, when later on it talked to itself about its past life. "They called me an invalid, and stood me in a corner, and the next day gave me to a woman who was begging for food. I fell into poverty, and was speechless both outside and inside, but as I stood there my better life began. One is one thing and then becomes quite another. They put earth in me, and for a Teapot that's the same as being buried, but in that earth they planted a flower bulb. Who put it there and gave it to me, I don't know; but it was planted there, a substitution for the Chinese leaves and the boiling water, the broken handle and spout. And the bulb lay in the earth, inside of me, and it became my heart, my living heart, a thing I never had before. There was life in me; there were power and might; my pulse beat. The bulb put out sprouts; thoughts and feeling sprang up and burst forth into flower. I saw it, I bore it, and I forgot myself in its beauty. It is a blessing to forget oneself in others!

"It didn't thank me, it didn't even think of me—everybody admired it and praised it. It made me very happy; how much more happy it must have made it!

"One day I heard them say it deserved a better pot. They broke me in two—that really hurt—and the flower was put into a better pot; then they threw me out into the yard, where I lie as an old potsherd. But I have my memory; *that* I can never lose!"

THE GOBLIN AND THE WOMAN

You know the Goblin, but do you know the Woman—the Gardener's wife? She was very well read and knew poems by heart; yes, and she could write them, too, easily, except that the rhymes—"clinchings," as she called them—gave her a little trouble. She had the gift of writing and the gift of speech; she could very well have been a parson or at least a parson's wife.

"The earth is beautiful in her Sunday gown," she said, and this thought she had expanded and set down in poetic form, with "clinchings," making a poem that was so long and lovely.

The Assistant Schoolmaster, Mr. Kisserup (not that his name matters at all), was her nephew, and on a visit to the Gardener's he heard the poem. It did her good, he said, a lot of good. "You have soul, Madam," he said.

"Stuff and nonsense!" said the Gardener. "Don't be putting such ideas in her head! Soul! A wife should be a body, a good, plain, decent body, and watch the pot, to keep the porridge from burning."

"I can take the burnt taste out of the porridge with a bit of charcoal," said the Woman. "And I can take the burnt taste out of you with a little kiss. You pretend you don't think of anything but cabbage and potatoes, but you love the flowers, too." Then she kissed him. "Flowers are the soul!"

"Mind your pot!" he said, as he went off to the garden. That was his pot, and he minded it.

But as the Assistant Schoolmaster stayed on, talking to the woman. Her lovely words, "Earth is beautiful," he made a whole sermon of, which was his habit.

"Earth is beautiful, and it shall be subject unto you! was said, and we became lords of the earth. One person rules with the mind, one with the body; one comes into the world like an exclamation mark of astonishment, another like a dash that denotes faltering thought, so that we pause and ask, why is he here? One man becomes a bishop, another just a poor assistant schoolmaster, but everything is for the best. Earth is beautiful and always in her Sunday gown. That was a thought-provoking poem, Madam, full of feeling and geography!"

"You have soul, Mr. Kisserup," said the Woman, "a great deal of soul, I assure you. After talking with you, one clearly understands oneself."

And so they talked on, equally well and beautifully. But out in the kitchen somebody else was talking, and that was the Goblin, the little gray-dressed Goblin with the red cap—you know the fellow. The Goblin was sitting in the kitchen, acting as pot watcher. He was talking, but nobody heard him except the big black Pussycat—"Cream Thief," the Woman called him.

The Goblin was mad at her because he had learned she didn't believe in his existence. Of course, she had never seen him, but with all her reading she ought to have realized he *did* exist and have paid him a little attention. On Christmas Eve she never thought of setting out so much as a spoonful of porridge for him, though all his ancestors had received that, and even from women who had no learning at all. Their porridge used to be so swimming with cream and butter that it made the Cat's mouth water to hear about it.

"She calls me just a notion!" said the Goblin. "And that's more than I can understand. In fact, she simply denies me! I've listened to her saying so before, and again just now in there, where she's driveling to that boy whipper, that Assistant Schoolmaster. I say with Pop, 'Mind the pot!' That she doesn't do, so now I'm going to make it boil over!"

And the Goblin blew on the fire till it burned and blazed up. "Surre-rurre-rup!" And the pot boiled over.

"And now I'm going to pick holes in Pop's socks," said the Goblin. "I'll unravel a large piece, both in toe and heel, so she'll have something to darn; that is, if she is not too busy writing poetry. Madam Poetess, please darn Pop's stocking!"

The Cat sneezed; he had caught a cold, thought he always wore a fur coat.

"I've opened the door to the larder," said the Goblin. "There's boiled cream in there as thick as paste. If you won't have a lick *I* will."

"If I'm going to get all the blame and the whipping for it, anyway," said the Cat, "I'll lick my share of the cream."

"First a lick, then a kick!" said the Goblin. "But now I'm off to the Assistant Schoolmaster's room, where I'll hang his suspenders on the mirror, put his socks into the water pitcher, and make him think the punch was too strong and has his brain in a whirl. Last night I sat on the woodpile by the kennel. I have a lot of fun teasing the watchdog; I let my legs dangle in front of him. The dog couldn't reach them, no matter how hard he jumped; that made him mad; he barked and barked, and I dangled and dangled; we made a lot of noise! The Assistant Schoolmaster woke up and jumped out of bed three times, but he couldn't see *me*, though he was wearing his spectacles. He always sleeps with his spectacles on."

"Say *mew* when you hear the Woman coming," said the Cat. "I'm a little deaf. I don't feel well today."

"You have the licking sickness," said the Goblin. "Lick away; lick your sickness away. But be sure to wipe your whiskers, so the cream won't show on it. I'm off to do a little eavesdropping."

So the Goblin stood behind the door, and the door stood ajar. There was nobody in the parlor except the Woman and the Assistant Schoolmaster. They were discussing things which, as the Assistant Schoolmaster so nobly observed, ought to rank in every household above pots and pans—the Gifts of the Soul.

"Mr. Kisserup," said the Woman, "since we are discussing this subject, I'll show you something along that line which I've never yet shown to a living soul—least of all a man. They're my smaller poems; however, some of them are rather long. I have called them 'Clinchings by a *Danneqvinde*.'[1] You see, I am very fond of old Danish words!"

"Yes, we should hold onto them," said the Assistant Schoolmaster. "We should root the German out of our language."

"That I am doing, too!" said the Woman. "You'll never hear me speak of *Kleiner* or *Butterteig;* no, I call them fatty cakes and paste leaves."

Then she took a writing book, in a light green cover, with two blotches of ink on it, from her drawer.

"There is much in this book that is serious," she said. "My mind tends toward the melancholy. Here is my 'The Sign in the Night,' 'My Evening Red,' and 'When I Got Klemmensen'—my husband; that one you may skip over, though it has thought and feeling. 'The Housewife's Duties' is the best one—sorrowful, like all the rest; that's my best style. Only one piece is comical; it contains some lively thoughts—one must indulge in them occasionally—thoughts about—now, you mustn't laugh at me—thoughts about being a poetess! Up to now it has been a secret between me and my drawer; now you know it, too, Mr. Kisserup. I love poetry; it haunts me; it jeers, advises, and commands. That's what I mean by my title, 'The Little Goblin.' You know the old peasants' superstitions about the Goblin who is always playing tricks in the house. I myself am the house, and my poetical feelings are the Goblin, the spirit that possesses me. I have written about his power and strength in 'The Little Goblin'; but you must promise with your hands and lips never to give away my secret, either to my husband or to anyone else. Read it loud, so that I can tell if you understand the meaning."

And the Assistant Schoolmaster read, and the Woman listened, and so did the little Goblin. He was eavesdropping, you'll remember, and he came just in time to hear the title 'The Little Goblin.'

"That's about me!" he said. "What could she have been writing about me? Oh, I'll pinch her! I'll chip her eggs, and pinch her chickens, and chase the fat off her fatted calf! Just watch me do it!"

And then he listened with pursed lips and long ears; but when he heard of the Goblin's power and glory, and his rule over the woman (she meant poetry, you know, but the Goblin took the name literally), the little fellow began grinning more and more. His eyes brightened with delight; then the corners of his mouth set sternly in lines of dignity; he drew himself up on his toes a whole inch higher than usual; he was greatly pleased with what was written about the Little Goblin.

"I've done her wrong! The Woman has soul and fine breeding! How I have done her wrong! She has put me into her 'Clinchings,' and they'll be printed and read. Now I won't allow the Cat to drink her cream; I'll do that myself! One drinks less than two, so that'll be a saving; and *that* I shall do, and pay honor and respect to the Woman!"

"He's a man all right, that Goblin," said the old Cat. "Just one sweet *mew* from the *Woman,* a mew about himself, and he immediately changes his mind! She is a sly one, the Woman!"

But the Woman wasn't sly; it was just that the Goblin was a man.

If you can't understand this story, ask somebody to explain it to you; but don't ask the Goblin or the Woman, either.

---

[1] Lady of probity.

WHICH WAS THE HAPPIEST?

"Such lovely roses!" said the sunshine. "And each bud will soon burst in bloom and be equally beautiful. These are my children. It is I who have kissed them to life."

"They are my children," said the Dew. "It is I who have nourished them with my tears."

"I should think I am their mother," the Rose Bush said. "You and Sunshine are only their godmothers, who have made them presents in keeping with your means and your good will."

"My lovely Rose Children!" they exclaimed, all three. They wished each flower to have the greatest happiness. But only one could be the happiest, and one must be the least happy. But which of them?

"I'll find out," said the Wind. "I roam far and wide. I find my way into the tiniest crevices. I know everything, inside and out."

Each rose in bloom heard his words, and each growing bud understood them.

Just then a sad devoted mother, in deep mourning, walked through the garden. She picked one of the roses; it was only half-blown but fresh and full. To her it seemed the loveliest of them all, and she took it to her quiet, silent room, where only a few days past her cheerful and lively young daughter had merrily tripped to and fro. Now she lay in the black coffin, as lifeless as a sleeping marble figure. The mother kissed her departed daughter. Then she kissed the half-blown rose, and laid it on the young girl's breast, as if by its freshness, and by the fond kiss of a mother, her beloved child's heart might again begin to beat.

The rose seemed to expand. Every petal trembled with joy. "What a lovely way has been set for me to go," it said. "Like a human child, I am given a mother's kiss and her blessing as I go to the blessed land unknown, dreaming upon the breast of Death's pale angel.

"Surely I am the happiest of all my sisters."

In the garden where the Rose Bush grew, walked an old woman whose business it was to weed the flower beds. She also looked at the beautiful bush, with especial interest in the largest full-blown rose. One more fall of dew, one more warm day, and its petals would shatter. When the old woman saw this she said that the rose had lived long enough for beauty, and that now she intended to put it to practical use. Then she picked it, wrapped it in old newspaper, and took it home, where she put it with other faded roses and those blue boys they call lavender, in a potpouri, embalmed in salt. Mind you, embalmed — an honor granted only to roses and kings.

"I will be the most highly honored," the rose declared, as the old weed puller took her. "I am the happiest one, for I am to be embalmed."

Then two young men came strolling through the garden. One was a painter; the other was a poet. Each plucked a rose most fair to see. The painter put upon a canvas a likeness of the rose in bloom, a picture so perfect and so lovely that the rose itself supposed it must be looking into a mirror.

"In this way," said the painter, "it shall live on, for generations upon generations, while countless other roses fade and die."

"Ah!" said the rose, "after all, it is I who have been most highly favored. I had the best luck of all."

But the poet looked at his rose, and wrote a poem about it to express the mystery of love. Yes, his book was a complete picture of love. It was a piece of immortal verse.

"This book has made me immortal," the rose said. "I am the most fortunate one."

In the midst of these splendid roses was one whom the others hid almost completely. By accident, and perhaps by good fortune, it had a slight defect. It sat slightly askew on its stem, and the leaves on one side of it did not match those on the other. Moreover, in the very heart of the flower grew a crippled leaf, small and green.

Such things happen, even to roses.

"Poor child," said the Wind, and kissed its cheek. The rose took this kiss for one of welcome and tribute. It had a feeling that it was made differently from the other roses, and that the green leaf growing in the heart of it was a mark of distinction. A butterfly fluttered down and kissed its petals. It was a suitor, but the rose let him fly away. Then a tremendously big grasshopper came, seated himself on a rose near-by, and rubbed his shins. Strangely enough, among grasshoppers this is a token of affection.

The rose on which he perched did not understand it that way, but the one with the green crippled leaf did, for the big grasshopper looked at her with eyes that clearly meant, "I love you so much I could eat you." Surely this is as far as love can go, when one becomes part of another. But the rose was not taken in, and flatly refused to become one with this jumping fop. Then, in the starlit night a nightingale sang.

"He is singing just for me," said the rose with the blemish, or with the mark of distinction as she considered it. "Why am I so honored, above all my sisters? Why was I given this peculiarity—which makes me the luckiest one?"

Next to appear in the garden were two gentlemen, smoking their cigars. They spoke about roses and about tobacco. Roses, they say, are not supposed to stand tobacco smoke; it fades them and turns them green. This was to be tested, but the gentlemen would not take it upon themselves to try it out on the more perfect roses.

They tried it on the one with the defect.

"Ah ha! a new honor," the rose said. "I am lucky indeed—the luckiest of all.'" And she turned green with conceit and tobacco smoke.

One rose, little more than a bud but perhaps the loveliest one on the bush, was chosen by the gardener for the place of honor in an artistically tied bouquet. It was taken to the proud young heir of the household, and rode beside him in his coach. Among other fragrant flowers and beautiful green leaves it sat in all its glory, sharing in the splendor of the festivities. Gentlemen and ladies, superbly dressed, sat there in the light of a thousand lamps as the music played. The theater was so brilliantly illuminated that it seemed a sea of light. Through it swept a storm of applause as a young dancer came upon the stage. One bouquet after another showered down, in a rain of flowers at her feet.

There fell the bouquet in which the lovely rose was set like a precious stone. The happiness it felt was complete, beyond any description. It felt all the honor and splendor around it, and as it touched the floor it fell to dancing too. The rose jumped for joy. It bounded across the stage at such a rate that it broke from its stem. The flower never came into the hands of the dancer. It rolled rapidly into the wings, where a stage hand picked it up. He saw how lovely and fragrant the rose was, but it had no stem. He pocketed it, and when he got home he put it in a wine glass filled with water. There the flower lay throughout the night, and early next morning it was placed beside his grandmother. Feeble and old, she sat in her easy chair and gazed at the lovely stemless rose that delighted her with its fragrance.

"You did not come to the fine table of a lady of fashion," she said.

"You came to a poor old woman. But to me you are like a whole rosebush. How lovely you are." Happy as a child, she gazed at the flower, and perhaps recalled the days of her own blooming youth that now had faded away.

"The window pane was cracked," said the Wind. "I got in without any trouble. I saw the old woman's eyes as bright as youth itself, and I saw the stemless but beautiful rose in the wine glass. Oh, it was the happiest of them all! I knew it! I could tell!"

Every rose on that bush in the garden had its own story. Each rose was convinced that it was the happiest one, and it is faith that makes us happy. But the last rose knew indeed that it was the happiest.

"I have outlasted them all," it said. "I am the last rose, the only one left, my mother's most cherished child!"

"And I am the mother of them all," the Rose Bush said.

"No, *I* am," said the sunshine.

"And *I*," said the Dew.

"Each had a share in it," the Wind at last decided, "and each shall have a part of it." And then the Wind swept its leaves out over the hedge where the dew had fallen, and where the sun was shining.

"I have my share too," said the Wind. "I have the story of all the roses, and I shall spread it throughout the wide world. Tell me then, which was the happiest of them all? Yes, that you must tell, for I have said enough."

PEITER, PETER, AND PEER

IT is unbelievable all that children know nowadays; one can scarcely say what they don't know. They no longer believe the old story that the stork brought them to father and mother out of the well or the millpond when they were little, and yet it is really true.

But how did the little ones get down into the millpond or the well? Ah, not everyone knows that, but there are some who do. Have you ever gazed at the sky on a clear, starry night and watched the many shooting stars? It is as if the stars fall from and disappear into nowhere. Even the most learned persons can't explain what they don't know themselves; but one can explain this when he knows it. It is like a little Christmas-tree candle that falls from heaven and is blown out. It is a soul spark from our Lord that flies toward the earth, and when it reaches our thick, heavy air, it loses its brilliancy, becoming something that our eyes cannot see, something much finer than air itself; it is a little child from heaven, a little angel, but without wings, for it is to become a human child.

Softly it glides through the air, and the wind carries it into a flower, which may be an orchid, a dandelion, a rose, or a cowslip, and there it lies and rests itself. And so light and airy is it that a fly can carry it off, as, of course, a bee can, when they alternately come to seek the sweetness of the flower. If the little air child lies in their way, they do not brush it aside. That they wouldn't have the heart to do! They take it and lay it under the leaf of a water lily in the sunshine, and from there it crawls and creeps into the water, where it sleeps and grows until it is large enough for the stork to see and bring to a human family that has been longing for a sweet little child. But whether it becomes sweet or not depends on whether it has drunk pure clean water or has swallowed mud and duckweed the wrong way; that makes one so filthy!

The stork, always without preference, takes the first one he sees. One goes to kind and loving parents in a fine home; another comes to unpleasant people in such misery that it would have been much better for it to have remained in the millpond.

The little ones can never remember afterward what they dreamed while they were lying under the water-lily leaf, listening to the frogs in the evening singing, "Coax! Coax! Coax!" In human language that means, "Now you go to sleep and dream!" Nor can they remember the flower where they first lay, nor how it smelled; and yet there is always something inside them, even when they are grown people, which makes them say, "I like this flower the best." That's because it is the one in which they were placed when they were air children.

The stork lives to be a very old bird, and he always has interest in the little ones he has brought and watches how they get along in the world and how they behave themselves. Of course, he can't do much for them or change anything in their lives, for he has his own family to look after, but at least he never lets them get out of his thoughts.

I know a very worthy, honest old stork who has had a great deal of experience, and has brought many little ones out of the water, and knows their stories—in which there is always a little mud and duckweed from the millpond. I begged him to tell me the story of one of them, and he said I should have three instead of one, and all from the Pietersens' house.

The Pietersens were an extremely nice family; the father was one of the thirty-two members of the town council, and that was an honor; he was completely wrapped up in his work with the thirty-two councilmen. When the stork brought a little fellow to this home he was named Peiter; the next year the stork brought another, and they named him Peter, and when the third one came they called him Peer—for all three names—Peiter, Peter, and Peer—are parts of the name Pietersen. So there was three brothers here—three shooting stars—and each had been cradled in a flower, then laid under the water-lily leaf in the millpond, and brought from there by the stork to the Pietersen family, whose house is on the corner, as you surely know.

They grew in body and mind, and wanted to become something more than the thirty-two councilmen were. Peiter had decided he wanted to be a robber; he had just seen the play *Fra Diavolo*, and that had convinced him that a robber's life was the most delightful in the world. Peter wanted to be a trash collector. And Peer, who was such a sweet and good boy, round and plump, whose only fault was biting his nails, wanted to be "Papa." That was what each of them said he was going to be in life, whenever anybody asked them about it.

Then they went to school. One was at the head of the class, and one at the foot, and one in the middle, but in spite of that they could be equally good and clever, and they were, said their very clearsighted parents. The three went to children's parties; they smoked when nobody was watching. They gained knowledge and made acquaintances.

From the time he was quite small, Peiter was quarrelsome, just the way a robber ought to be. He was a very naughty boy, but his mother said that came from worms — naughty children always have worms — or from mud in the stomach. And one day his mother's new silk dress suffered from his obstinacy and naughtiness.

"Don't push the tea table, my good little lamb," she had said. "You might tip over the cream pitcher, and then I'd get spots on my new silk dress."

And so the "good little lamb" firmly took up the cream pitcher and firmly poured all the cream right into Mamma's lap. Mamma couldn't help saying, "Oh, lamb, lamb, that was careless of you, lamb!" But she had to admit that the child had a will of his own. A will means character, and that's very promising to a mother.

He might, of course, have become a robber, but he didn't, in the actual sense of the word; he only came to look like one, with his slouch hat, bare throat, and long, lank hair. He was supposed to be an artist, but he only got as far as the clothes. He looked like a hollyhock, and all the people he made drawings of looked like hollyhocks, so lanky were they. He was very fond of hollyhocks, and the stork said he had lain in that flower when he was an air child.

Peter must have lain in a buttercup. He looked buttery around the corners of his mouth, and his skin was so yellow that one would think that if his cheek were cut, butter would ooze out. He should have been a butter dealer, and could have been his own signboard; but on the inside he was a trash collector with a rattle. He was the musician of the Pietersen family — "musical enough for all of them," the neighbors said. He composed seventeen new polkas in one week, and then put them all together and made an opera out of them, with a trumpet and rattle accompaniment. Ugh! How delightful that was!

Peer was white and red, small and quite ordinary; he had lain in a daisy. He never hit back when the other boys beat him up; he said he was the most sensible, and the most sensible always gives way first.

He was a collector, first of slate pencils, and later of letter seals. Then he got a little cabinet of curiosities of natural history, in which were the skeleton of a stickleback, three blind baby rats preserved in alcohol, and a stuffed mole. Peer had a keen appreciation of science and an eye for the beauties of nature, and that was a comfort to his parents and to him, too. He preferred wandering in the woods to going to school, preferred nature to education.

Both his brothers were engaged to be married, but he could think of nothing but completing his collection of water-bird eggs. He knew much more about animals than he did about human beings; he even thought we could never reach the heights of the animals in the feeling we consider the loftiest of all — love. He saw that when the female nightingale was setting on the nest, Papa Nightingale would perch on a branch close by and sing to his little wife all night, "Kluk-kluk! Zi-Zi! Lo-lo-li!" Peer knew he could never do that or even think of doing such a thing. When Mamma Stork had her babies in the nest, Father Stork stood guard on the edge of the roof all night, on one leg. Peer couldn't have stood that way for an hour!

Then one day when he examined a spider's web, and saw what was in it, he gave up completely any idea of marriage. Mr. Spider weaves his web for catching thoughtless flies, old and young, fat and lean; he lives only to weave and to support his family. But Madam Spider lives only for him. Out of sheer love she eats him up; she eats his heart, his head, his stomach, until only his long thin legs are left in the web where he used to sit, anxious for the welfare of his family. Now that's the real truth, right out of the natural-history book! When Peer saw all this he grew very thoughtful; to be so dearly loved by a wife that she eats one up out of violent love? No! No human being could love like that, and would it be desirable, anyway?

Peer resolved never to marry, or even to give or take a kiss, for that might seem the first step toward marriage. But he did receive a kiss, anyway, the same kiss we all get someday, the great kiss of Death. When we have lived long enough, Death is given the order, "kiss him away," and so away the human goes. A ray of sunshine comes straight from our Lord, so bright that it almost blinds one. Then the soul that came from heaven as a shooting star goes back like a shooting star, but this time not to sleep in a flower or dream beneath the leaf of the water lily; it has more important things than that to do. It enters the great land of eternity; but what that is like and what it looks like there, no one can say. No one has looked into it, not even the stork, though he sees far and knows much.

The stork knew nothing more of Peer, whereas he could have told me lots more about Peiter and Peter. But I had heard enough of them, and I suppose you have, too, so I thanked him and bade him good-bye for this time. But now he demands three frogs and a little snake as payment for this simple little story—you see, he takes his pay in food. Will you pay him? I can't; I have neither frogs nor snakes.

THE CANDLES

THERE was once a big wax candle who had the highest opinion of his merits.

"I," he said, "am made of the purest wax, cast in the best mold. I burn more brilliantly than any other candle, and I outlast them all. I belong in the high chandelier or the silver candlestick."

"What a delightful life you must lead," the tallow candle admitted. "I am only tallow. Just a tallow dip. But it's a comfort to think how much better off I am than the taper. He's only dipped twice, while I am dipped eight times to make a thick and respectable candle of me. I'm satisfied. To be sure it would be better to be born of wax than of tallow, and a lucky thing to be shaped in a mold, but one isn't asked how he wants to be born. Your place is in the big rooms with glass chandeliers. Mine is in the kitchen. But the kitchen is a good place too. All the food in the house comes from there."

"There are more important things in the world than food," the wax candle boasted. "There's the glitter of good society in which I shine. Why, I and all my family are invited to a ball that's being given here this very evening."

No sooner had he said this than all the wax candles were sent for. But the tallow candle was not left behind. The mistress of the house took it in her own hand and carried it to the kitchen, where a poor boy waited with his basket full of potatoes and a few apples that she had given him.

"And here's a candle for you too, my little friend," she told him. "Your mother can use it to work by when she sits up late at night."

The lady's small daughter stood close beside her mother, and when she heard the magic words "late at night," she forgot to be shy. "I'm going to stay up late tonight too!" she exclaimed. "We are to have a ball this evening, and I'm to wear my big red ribbon." No candle ever could shine like the eyes of a child.

"Happiness is a blessed thing to see," the tallow candle thought to himself. "I mustn't forget how it looks, for I certainly shan't see it again." They put him in the basket and closed the lid. Away the boy went with it.

"Where can he be taking me?" the candle wondered. "I may have to live with poor people who don't even own a brass candlestick, while the wax candle sits in silver and beams at all the best people. How fine it must be to shine in good company. But this is what I get for being tallow, not wax."

And the candle did come to live with poor people. They were a widow and her three children, who had a low-ceilinged room across the way from the well-to-do house.

"God bless our neighbor for all that she gave us," the widow said. "This good candle will burn far into the night."

She struck a match to it.

"Fut, fie," he sputtered. "What a vile smelling match she lights me with. Would anyone offer such a kitchen match to the wax candle, in the well-to-do house across the way?"

There the candles were lighted too. They made the street bright as carriages came rumbling with guests dressed in their best for the ball. The music struck up.

"Now the ball's beginning." The tallow candle burned brighter as he remembered the happy little girl whose face was more shining than the light of all those wax candles. "I'll never see anything like that again."

The smallest of the poor children reached up, for she was very small, and put her arms around the necks of her brother and sister. What she had to tell them was so important that it had to be whispered. "Tonight we're going to have—just think of it—warm potatoes, this very night."

Her face beamed with happiness and the candle beamed right back at her. He saw happiness again, and a gladness as great as when the little girl in the well-to-do house said, "We're having a ball this evening, and I'm to wear my big red ribbon."

"Is it such a treat to get warm potatoes?" the candle wondered. "Little children must manage to be happy here too." He wept tallow tears of joy, and more than that a candle cannot do.

The table was spread and the potatoes were eaten. How good they tasted! It was a real feast. There was an apple for everyone, and the smallest child said grace:

> "Now thanks, dear Lord, I give to Thee
> That Thou again hast filled me. Amen."

"And didn't I say it nicely?" the little girl asked.

"Don't say such things," her mother told her. "Just thank the good Lord for filling you up."

The children went to bed, were kissed good night, and fell fast asleep. Their mother sat up late and sewed to make a living for them and for herself. From the well-to-do house came light and music. But the stars overhead shone on all the houses, rich or poor, with the same light, clear and kind.

"This has been a wonderful evening," the tallow candle told himself. "Can the wax candle have had any better time of it in his silver candlestick? I'd like to know that before I'm burned out."

He remembered the two happy children, one face lighted up by the wax candle, the other shining in the tallow candle's light. One was happy as the other. Yes, that is the whole story!

THE MOST INCREDIBLE THING

WHOSOEVER could do the most incredible thing was to have the King's daughter and half of his kingdom.

The young men, yes, and the old ones too, bent their heads, their muscles, and their hearts upon winning. To do what they thought was the most incredible thing, two ate themselves to death, and one died of overdrinking. Even the boys in the street practiced spitting on their own backs, which they supposed was the most incredible thing anyone could do.

On a certain day there was to be an exhibition of things most incredible and everyone showed his best work. Judges were appointed, ranging from children of three to old men of ninety. It was a grand exposition of things out of the ordinary, but everybody promptly agreed that most incredible of all was a great hall clock — an extraordinary contraption, outside and in.

When the clock struck, out came lifelike figures to tell the hour. There were twelve separate performances of these moving figures, with speaking and singing. People said that nothing so incredible had ever before been seen.

The clock struck *one,* and there stood Moses on the mountain, writing in the tablets of the law the first great commandment: "There is only one true God." The clock struck *two,* and there were Adam and Eve, just as they first met in the Garden of Eden. Were ever two people so lucky! They didn't own so much as a clothes-closet, and they didn't need one. At the stroke of *three* the three Holy Kings appeared. One was as black as a coal, but he couldn't help that. The sun had blackened him. These kings brought incense and precious gifts. When the stroke of *four* sounded, the seasons advanced in their order. Spring carried a budding bough of beech, on which a cuckoo sang. Summer had for her sign a grasshopper on a ripening ear of wheat. Autumn had only an empty stork's nest, for the birds had flown away. Winter's tame crow perched on the corner of the stove, and told old tales of bygone days. At *five* o'clock there was a procession of the five senses. Sight was represented by a man who made spectacles. Hearing was a noisy coppersmith. Smell was a flower girl with violets for sale. Taste came dressed as a cook. Feeling was a mourner, with crape down to his heels. As the clock struck *six,* there sat a gambler, throwing dice for the highest cast of all, and they fell with the sixes up. Then came the *seven* days of the week, or they might be the seven deadly sins. People could not be sure which they were, for they were not easy to distinguish. Next came a choir of monks, to sing the *eight* o'clock evensong. At the stroke of *nine,* the nine muses appeared. One was an astronomer, one kept the books of history, and the others were connected with the theater. *Ten* o'clock struck, and Moses came forth again, this time with the tables in which were written all ten of God's commandments. When the clock struck again, boys and girls danced out. They played and sang this song:

> "All the way to heaven
> The clock struck eleven."

And *eleven* it struck. Then came the stroke of twelve. Out marched the night watchman, wearing his cap and carrying his morning star—which is a truncheon tipped with spikes. He sang the old watch song:

> " 'Twas at the midnight hour
> Our Saviour He was born—"

and as he sang the roses about him unfolded into the heads of angels, with rainbow-tinted wings.

It was good to hear. It was charming to see. The whole thing was a work of extraordinary craftsmanship, and everyone agreed that it was the most incredible thing. The artist who had made it was young, generous, and sincere, a true friend, and a great help to his poor father and mother. He was altogether worthy of the Princess and of half the kingdom.

On the day that they were to proclaim who had won, the whole town was bedecked and be-draped. The Princess sat on her throne. It had been newly stuffed with horsehair for the occasion, but it was still far from comfortable or pleasant. The judges winked knowingly at the man they had chosen, who stood there so happy and proud. His fortune was made, for had he not done the most incredible thing!

"No!" a tall, bony, powerful fellow bawled out. "Leave it to me, I am the man to do the most incredible thing," and then he swung his ax at the craftsman's clock. *Crack, crash, smash!* There lay the whole thing. Here rolled the wheels, and there flew the hairsprings. It was wrecked and ruined. "I did that," said the lout. "My work beat his, and bowled you over, all in one stroke. I have done the most incredible thing."

"To destroy such a work of art!" said the judges. "Why it's the most incredible thing we've ever seen." And the people said so too. So he was awarded the Princess and half the kingdom, because a law is a law, even if it happens to be a most incredible one.

They blew trumpets from the ramparts and the city towers, and they announced, "The wedding will now take place." The Princess was not especially happy about it, but she looked pretty and she wore her most expensive clothes. The church was at its best by candle-light, late in the evening. The ladies of the court sang in processions, and escorted the bride. The lords sung, and accompanied the groom. From the way he strutted and swaggered along, you'd think that nothing could ever bowl him over.

Then the singing stopped. It was so still that you could have heard a pin fall in the street. But it was not quiet for long. *Crash! crash!* the great church doors flew open, and *boom! boom!* all the works of the clock came marching down the church aisle and halted between the bride and the groom.

Dead men cannot walk the earth. That's true, but a work of art does not die. Its shape may be shattered, but the spirit of art cannot be broken. The spirit of art jested, and *that* was no joke.

To all appearances it stood there as if it were whole, and had never been wrecked. The clock struck one hour right after another, from one to twelve, and all the figures poured forth. First Moses came, shining as if bright flames issued from his forehead. He cast the heavy stone tablets of the law at the bridegroom's feet, and tied them to the church floor. "I cannot lift them again," said Moses, "for you have broken my arms. Stand where you are!"

Then came Adam and Eve, the three Wise Men of the East, and the four Seasons. Each told him the disagreeable truth. "Shame on you!" But he was not ashamed.

All the figures of all the hours marched out of the clock, and they grew wondrous big. There was scarcely room for the living people. And at the stroke of twelve out strode the watchman, with his cap and his many-spiked morning star. There was a strange commotion. The watchman went straight to the bridegroom, and smote him on the forehead with his morning star.

"Lie where you are," said the watchman. "A blow for a blow. We have taken our vengeance and the master's too, so now we will vanish."

And vanish they did, every cogwheel and figure. But the candles of the church flared up like flowers of fire, and the gilded stars under the roof cast down long clear shafts of light, and the organ sounded though no man had touched it. The people all said that they had lived to see the most incredible thing.

"Now," the Princess commanded, "summon the right man, the craftsman who made the work of art. He shall be my husband and my lord."

He stood beside her in the church. All the people were in his train. Everyone was happy for him, everyone blessed him, and there was no one who was envious. And that was the most incredible thing.

VÄNÖ AND GLÄNÖ

NEAR the coast of Zealand, off Holsteinborg Castle, there once lay two wooded islands, Vänö and Glänö, on which were villages, churches, and farms. The islands were quite close to the coast and quite close to each other; now there is but one of these tracts remaining.

One night a fierce tempest broke loose. The ocean rose higher than ever before within man's memory. The storm increased; it was like doomsday weather, and it sounded as if the earth were splitting. The church bells began to swing and rang without the help of man.

That night Vänö vanished into the ocean depths; it was as if the island had never existed. But afterward on many a summer night, when the still, clear water was at low tide, and the fisherman was out on his boat to catch eel by the light of a torch, he could, on looking sharply, see Vänö, with its white church tower and high church wall, deep down below. He would recall the saying, "Vänö is waiting to take Glänö," as he saw the island, and he could hear the church bells ringing down there, but in that he was mistaken, for the sound came from the many wild swans which frequently rested on the water there, and whose clucking and complaining sounded like far-away church bells.

There was a time when there were still many old people on Glänö who well remembered that stormy night, and that they, when little, had ridden between the two islands at ebb tide, as we nowadays ride from the coast of Zealand over to Glänö, the water reaching up only to the middle of the wheels.

"Vänö is waiting to take Glänö," it was said, and this saying was accepted as a certainty. Many little boys and girls would lie in bed on stormy nights and think, "Tonight the hour will come when Vänö calls for Glänö." In fear, they said the Lord's Prayer, fell asleep, had sweet dreams—and the following morning Glänö was still there, with its woods and cornfields, its friendly farmhouses and hop gardens; the bird sang and the deer sprang; the gopher couldn't smell sea water, however far he could dig.

And still Glänö's days were numbered; we could not say just how many there were, but they were numbered, and one beautiful morning the island would no longer exist.

You were perhaps down there at the beach on a day prior to this and saw the wild swans resting on the water between Zealand and Glänö, while a sailboat in full sail glided by the wooded shore, and perhaps you, too, rode across at low tide, with the horses trampling in the water as it splashed over the wagon wheels.

You went away from there, perhaps traveled out into the wide world, and after a few years you have returned. You see the same woods, now surrounding a large, green meadow, where fragrant hay is stacked in front of pretty farmhouses. Where are you? Holsteinborg, with its golden tower spires, is still there, but not close to the bay; it now lies farther up in the country. You walk through the woods, across the field, down toward the beach. Where is Glänö? You don't see the little wooded island before you; you see only the open water. Has Vänö finally taken Glänö, as it so long was expected to? On what stormy night did this happen, and when did an earthquake move old Holsteinborg so far inland?

There was no stormy night; it all happened on clear, sunny days. Human skill built a dam to hold back the ocean; human skill dried up the water and bound Glänö to the mainland. The bay has become a meadow with luxuriant grass; Glänö has become part of Zealand. And the old castle stands where it always stood. It was not Vänö that took Glänö; it was Zealand that, through mechanical skill, gained many new acres of land.

This is the truth; you can find it in the records. Glänö Island is no more.

GREAT-GRANDFATHER

GREAT-GRANDFATHER was so lovable, wise and good. All of us looked up to Great-Grandfather. As far back as I can remember, he was really called "Father's Father," and "Mother's Father" as well, but when my Brother Frederick's little son came along he was promoted, and got the title of "Great-Grandfather." He could not expect to go any higher than that.

He was very proud of us all, but he did not appear to be fond of our times. "Old times were the good times," he used to say. "Quiet and genuine they were. In these days there's too much hurrying and turning everything upside down. The young folk lay down the law, and even speak about the Kings as if they are their equals. Any ne'er-do-well can sop a rag in dirty water and wring it out over the head of an honorable man."

Great-Grandfather would get angry and red in the face when he talked of such things, but soon he would smile his kindly, sympathetic smile, and say, "Oh, well! I may be a bit wrong. I belong to the old days, and I can't quite get a foothold in the new. May God guide us and show us the right way to go."

When Great-Grandfather got started on the old days, it seemed to me as if they came back. I would imagine myself riding along in a gilded coach, with footmen in fine livery. I saw the guilds move their signs and march in procession with their banners aloft, preceded by music. And I attended the merry Christmas festivities, where people in fancy dress played games of forfeit.

True enough, in the old days dreadfully cruel and horrible things used to be done. There was torture, rack and wheel, and bloodshed, but even those horrible things had an excitement about them that fascinated me. But I also thought of many pleasant things. I used to imagine how things were when the Danish nobility freed the peasants, and when the Danish Crown Prince abolished slave trading. It was marvelous to hear Great-Grandfather talk of all these things, and to hear him tell of the days of his youth. But I think the times even earlier than that were the very best times of all — so mighty and glorious.

"They were barbarous times," Brother Frederick said. "Thank Heaven we are well rid of them." He used to say this right out to Great-Grandfather. This was most improper, I know, but just the same I always had great respect for Frederick. He was my oldest brother, and he used to say he was old enough to be my father — but then he was always saying the oddest things. He had graduated with the highest honors, and was so quick and clever in his work at Father's office that Father meant to make him a partner before long. Of us all, he was the one with whom Great-Grandfather talked most, but they always began to argue, for they did not get along well together. They did not understand each other, those two, and the family said they never would, but even as young as I was, I soon felt that they were indispensable to each other. Great-Grandfather would listen with the brightest look in his eyes while Frederick spoke of or read aloud about scientific progress, and new discoveries in the laws of nature, and about all the other marvels of our times.

"The human race gets cleverer, but it doesn't get better," Great-Grandfather would say. "People invent the most terrible and harmful weapons with which to kill and injure each other."

"Then the war will be over that much sooner," Frederick would tell him.

"No need now for us to wait seven years for the blessings of peace. The world is full-blooded, and it needs to be bled now and then. That is a necessity."

One day Frederick told him of something that actually happened in a small country and in our own times. The mayor's clock—the large one on the town hall—kept time for the whole town and for everyone who lived there. The clock did not run very well, but that didn't matter nor did it keep anyone from looking to it for the time. But by and by railroads were built in that country, and in all countries railroads run by the clock. One must therefore be sure of the time, and know it exactly, or there will be collisions. At the railroad station they had a clock that was absolutely reliable, and exactly in accord with the sun. But as the mayor's was not, everyone went by the railroad clock.

I laughed, and thought the story a funny one, but Great-Grandfather did not laugh. He became very serious.

"There is a profound meaning in what you have told me," he declared, "and I understood the thought that prompted you to tell me the story. There's a moral in the clockwork. It reminds me of another clock—my parents' simple, old-fashioned Bornholm clock, with lead weights. It measured out the time of their lives and of my childhood. Perhaps it didn't run any too well, but it ran just the same. We would look at the hour hand and believe in it, with never a thought about the works inside. In those days the machinery of government was like that old clock. Everybody believed in it and only looked at the hour hand. Now government machinery is like a clock in a glass case, so that one can look directly into the works and see the wheel turning and whizzing around. Sometimes we become quite frightened over this spring or that wheel, and then I wonder how it is possible for all these complicated parts to tell the right time. I have lost my childish belief in the rightness of the old clock. That is the weakness of this age."

Great-Grandfather would talk on until he became quite angry. He and Frederick could not agree, yet they could not bear to be separated—"just like old times and new." Both of them felt this—and so did our whole family—when Frederick was to set out on his journey to far-away America. It was on business for the Company, so the journey had to be made. To Great-Grandfather, it was a sad parting, and it seemed a long, long journey—all the way across a great ocean, and to the other side of the globe.

"You shall get a letter from me every fortnight," Frederick promised. "And faster than any letter can go, you shall hear from me by telegraph. The days will be like hours, and the hours like minutes."

By telegraph we received Frederick's greeting to us from England, just as he boarded the steamship. Sooner than any letter could reach us, even though the swift sailing clouds had been our postman, came greetings from America, where Frederick had landed only a few hours before.

"What a glorious and divine inspiration has been granted our age," said Great-Grandfather. "It is a true blessing to the human race."

"And it was in our country," I said, "that the natural principle underlying the telegraph was first understood and stated. Frederick told me so."

"Yes," Great-Grandfather said, and he kissed me. "Yes, and I once looked into the kindly eyes that were the first to see and understand this marvelous law of nature—his were the eyes of a child, like yours—and I have shaken his hand." Then he kissed me again.

More than a month had gone by, when a letter came from Frederick with the news that he was engaged to a beautiful and lovable young lady. He was sure that everyone in our family would be delighted with her, and he sent us her photograph. We looked at it first with our bare eyes, and then with a magnifying glass, for the advantage of photographs is not only that they stand close inspection through the strongest glass, but that then you see the full likeness even better. No painter has ever been able to do that, even in the greatest of the ages past.

"If only this discovery had been made earlier, then we could have seen the world's greatest and most illustrious men, face to face. How gentle and good this young girl looks," Great-Grandfather said, and stared through the glass.

"Now I know her face, and I shall recognize her the moment she comes in the door."

But that very nearly failed to happen. Fortunately, at home we did not hear of the danger until it had passed.

After a safe and pleasant trip, the young couple reached England. From there, they were to come by steamship to Copenhagen. When they came in sight of the Danish coast—the white sand dunes along the western shore of Jutland—a heavy sea arose and dashed the ship against the shore. The enormous waves threatened to break the grounded ship to pieces.

No lifeboat could reach them. Night fell, but out of the darkness burst a brightly flashing rocket from the shore. It shot far out over the grounded ship, and brought a line to those on board. Once this connection between ship and shore was made fast, a rescue buoy was carefully drawn through the rough, tumultuous sea, to the shore. In it was a lovely young woman, safe and sound, and marvelously happy when she and her young husband again stood together on the shore. Every soul on board was saved before the break of day.

Here in Copenhagen we were sound asleep, dreaming neither of grief nor of danger. When we were gathered at the breakfast table, we heard a rumor that an English steamship had been wrecked on the west coast. We grew heartsick with anxiety, but within an hour we received a telegram from those who were dear to us. Frederick and his young bride were saved—they would soon be with us.

Everyone cried, and I cried too. Great-Grandfather cried and clasped his hands. I am sure he gave thanks for the age in which we live, for that very day he gave two hundred dollars toward raising a monument to Hans Christian Oersted.[1] When Frederick came home with his bride, and heard of it, he said, "That was right, Great-Grandfather. Now let me read to you what Oersted wrote, a great many years ago, about the old times and the new."

THE GREAT SEA SERPENT

THERE was a little sea fish of good family, the name of which I don't remember; that the more learned will have to tell you. This little fish had eighteen hundred brothers and sisters, all the same age; they didn't know their father or mother, so they had to care for themselves and swim about on

---

[1] Hans Christian Örsted (1777–1851), physicist and philosopher, discoverer of electromagnetism.

their own, but that was a lot of fun. They had plenty of water to drink—the entire ocean. They didn't think about their food; that was sure to come their way. Each did as he pleased; each would have his own story, but then none of them thought about that.

The sun shone down into the water, making it light and clear. It was a world full of the strangest creatures, some of them enormously big, with great, horrible mouths that could swallow all the eighteen hundred brothers and sisters, but none of them thought about that, either, for none of them had ever been swallowed.

The little ones swam together, close to one another, as the herring and the mackerel swim. As they were swimming along at their best and thinking of nothing in particular, there sank from above, down into the midst of them, with a terrifying noise, a long, heavy thing which seemed to have no end to it; further and further it stretched out, and every one of the small fish that it struck was crushed or got a crack from which he couldn't recover. All the fishes, the small and the big as well, were thrown into a panic. That heavy, horrible thing sank deeper and deeper and grew longer and longer, extending for miles—through the entire ocean. Fishes and snails, everything that swims, everything that creeps or is driven by the currents, saw this fearful thing, this enormous unknown sea eel that all of a sudden had come from above.

What kind of thing was it? Yes, we know! It was the great telegraph cable that people were laying between Europe and America.

There were great fear and commotion among all the rightful inhabitants of the ocean where the cable was laid. The flying fish shot up above the surface as high as he could, and the blowfish sped off like a gunshot across the water, for it can do that; other fishes went to the bottom of the ocean with such haste that they reached it long before the telegraph cable was seen down there, and they scared both the codfish and the flounder, who lived peacefully at the bottom of the ocean and ate their neighbors. A couple of the starfish were so frightened that they turned their stomachs inside out, but in spite of that they lived, for they can do that. Many of the lobsters and crabs got out of their fine shells and had to leave their legs behind.

In all this fright and confusion, the eighteen hundred brothers and sisters had all become separated, never again to know or even meet each other, excepting ten of them who had remained at the same place; and after these had held themselves still for a couple of hours, they recovered from their first fright and began to be curious. They looked about; they looked up and they looked down, and there in the deep they thought they saw the frightful thing that had scared them, scared everyone, big and little. There it lay along the bottom of the ocean, extending as far as they could see; it was quite thin, but then they didn't know how thick it could make itself or how strong it was. It lay very quiet, but that, they thought, could be a trick.

"Let it lie where it is! It doesn't concern us," said the most cautious of the little fish.

But the very smallest one of them insisted on gaining some knowledge as to what that thing might be. It had come down from above, so above one could best find out about it.

And so they swam up to the surface, where there was calm weather. There they met a dolphin, which is a sort of jumping jack, an ocean rover, that can turn somersaults in the water. As these have eyes to see with, he must have seen what had happened and should know all about it. They inquired, but the dolphin had only been thinking of himself and his somersaults, had seen nothing, and didn't know what to answer, so he kept quiet and looked proud.

Thereupon they turned to the seal who had just ducked down; he was more polite, although seals eat small fishes, for today he had had his fill. He knew a little more than the dolphin.

"Many a night I have rested on a wet rock and looked far inland, miles away from here; there live some sneaky creatures who, in their language, are called people; they plot against us, but often we slip away from them, which I know how to do, and that is what the sea eel has done, too. He has been in their power, up there on the earth, for a long, long time, and from there they carried him off on a ship, to bring him across the ocean to a distant land. I saw what trouble they had, but they could manage him, because he had become weak on the earth. They laid him down in coils and circles; I heard how he 'ringled' and 'rangled' when they put him down, but still he got away from them. They held on to him with all their might; many hands held fast, but still he slipped away from them and reached the bottom; there he lies now, for a while at least, I think."

"He is rather thin!" said all the little fish.

"They have starved him," said the seal, "but he will soon be himself again, fat and big around. I suppose he is the great sea serpent that people are so afraid of and talk so much about. I had never seen him before and never believed he existed, but now I do; I'm sure he's the sea serpent!" And with that the seal dove down.

"How much he knew! How much he talked!" said all the little fish. "We have never been so enlightened before! If only it isn't all a lie!"

"We could swim down and investigate," said the smallest fish. "On the way, we can hear what others think about it."

"We're not going to move a fin to find out anything more!" said the others, and swam away.

"But I'm going to," said the smallest, and plunged down into deep water.

But the little fish was a considerable distance from the place where "that long sunken thing" lay. He looked and searched in a direction down in the deep water. Never before had he imagined the world to be so big. The herring swam in great masses, each school of them shining like a mighty boat of silver; the mackerel also swam together and looked even more magnificent. There were fishes of all shapes and with markings in all colors. Jellyfish, like half-transparent flowers, simply lay back and let the currents carry them along. Great plants grew up from the bottom of the ocean, as did fathom-high grass and palm-shaped trees, every leaf beset with shining shellfish.

At last the little fish saw a long, dark streak way down and swam toward it; but it was neither fish nor cable; it was the gunwale of a large sunken vessel, the upper and lower decks of which had broken in two by the force of the ocean. The little fish swam inside, where the many people who had perished with the sinking of the ship had since been washed away, except for two—a young woman lay stretched out with a little child in her arms. The water rocked them to and fro, and they seemed to be asleep. The little fish became quite frightened, for he didn't know that they never again could awaken. Seaweed hung like cultivated foliage over the rail above the fair forms of mother and child. It was so quiet there, so lonely. The little fish hurried away

THE GREAT SEA SERPENT

as fast as he could, out to where the water was clearer and there were fishes to see. He hadn't gone far when he met a young and terribly large whale.

"Don't swallow me!" said the little fish. "I'm so small that I'm not even a tiny bite, and it's a great pleasure for me to live!"

"What do you want way down here, where your kind never comes?" asked the whale.

So the little fish told of the strange long eel, or whatever that thing was, which had sunk and scared even the most courageous of ocean creatures.

"Ho, ho!" said the whale, and drew in such a lot of water that he had to make an enormous waterspout when he came to the surface for a breath. "Ho, ho!" he said, "so that was the thing that tickled my back when I turned around! I thought it was a ship's mast that I could use for a back-scratcher! However, it wasn't in this location; no, that thing is much farther out. I'll investigate it, though; I have nothing else to do."

And so he swam forth, the little fish following, but not too close, for there would be a powerful stream where the big whale shot through the water.

They met a shark and an old sawfish. These two had also heard of the strange sea eel that was so long and thin; they hadn't seen it, but they wanted to.

Then a catfish appeared. "I'm coming with you!" he said, and took the same course. "If the great sea serpent isn't thicker than a cable, then I'll bite it in two with one bite!" And he opened his mouth and showed his six rows of teeth. "I can bite dents in a ship's anchor, so I can easily bite through that stem!"

"There it is!" said the big whale. "I can see it!" He thought he saw better than the others. "See how it rises, see how it sways, bends, and curves!"

However, this was not the sea serpent, but an exceptionally large eel, who was many yards long, and came closer.

"I've seen him before," said the sawfish. "He's never made much fuss in the ocean here or frightened any big fishes."

And so they talked to him about the new eel and asked if he wanted to join them on their voyage of discovery.

"If that eel is longer than I," said the sea eel, "then something unfortunate will happen."

"That it will!" said the others. "There are enough of us not to have to tolerate it." And then they hurried along.

But now, directly in their way, there appeared a strange monster, bigger than them all. It looked like a floating island that could not hold itself up. It was a very old whale. His head was overgrown with seaweed, his back beset with barnacles and so many oysters and mussels that his black skin was entirely covered with white spots.

"Come along, old fellow," they said. "A new fish has come that we will not tolerate!"

"I'd rather lie where I am," said the old whale. "Leave me in peace. Let me lie. Oh, my, oh, my! I suffer from a dreadful sickness. The only relief I have is when I go up to the surface and get my back above it; then the big, nice birds come and pick at me, and that feels so good, as long as they don't drive their beaks in too far; often they go right into my blubber. Just see for yourself! There is a complete skeleton of a bird stuck in my back. That bird stuck his claws in too deep and couldn't get loose when I went down to the bottom.

Now the little fishes have eaten him. Just see how he looks, and how I look! I have a sickness!"

"That's just imagination!" said the other whale. "I am never sick. No fish is sick!"

"I beg your pardon!" said the old whale. "The eel has a skin disease, the carp has smallpox, and all of us have intestinal worms!"

"Nonsense!" said the shark, and didn't care to hear more; nor did the others; they had something else to do.

Finally, they came to the place where the telegraph cable lay. It had a very long resting place indeed at the bottom of the ocean, from Europe to America, over sandbanks and sea mud, rocky formations and sea-plant wilderness, and yes, entire forests of coral. The currents down there change, and whirlpools twist around; fishes crowd each other and swim in flocks greater than the countless multitudes of birds that people see when birds of passage are in flight. There are a commotion, a splashing, a humming, and a rushing; a little of that rushing still remains to haunt the big, empty conch shells when we hold them to our ears.

Yes, now they came to the place.

"There lies the animal!" said the big fishes, and the little one said so, too.

They saw the cable, its beginning and end beyond their horizon. Sponges, polyps, and seaweed swayed from the ground, rising and falling over the cable, so that now it was hidden and then visible again. Sea porcupines, snails and worms moved over it. Gigantic spiders, with whole fringes of vermin on them, crawled along the cable. Dark-blue "sea sausages," or whatever the creatures are called that eat with their entire bodies, lay beside it and smelled this new animal that had come down to lie at the bottom of the ocean. Flounders and codfish turned about in the water, in order to hear what was said from all sides. The starfish, who could hold himself down in the mud and keep his eyes outside, lay and stared to see what would come of all this confusion. The telegraph cable lay motionless. But life and thought were in it; human thoughts went through it.

"That thing is cunning," said the whale. "It's able to hit me in the stomach, and that's my weak point!"

"Let's feel our way," said a polyp. "I have long arms; I have limber fingers. I have touched it. Now I'll feel it a little more firmly." And then he stretched his longest and most flexible arms down to the cable and around it. "It has no scales!" said the polyp. "It has no skin! I don't believe it will ever bear young ones!"

The sea eel laid down alongside the telegraph cable and stretched himself as far as he could. "That thing is longer than I am!" he said. "But it isn't length that counts; one must have skin, stomach, and flexibility!"

The whale—that is, the young, strong whale—dove down deeper than he ever had been. "Are you a fish or a plant?" he asked the cable. "Or are you only some piece of work from above that can't thrive down here among us?"

But the telegraph cable didn't answer; it had no means of contacting anyone at such a location. Thoughts were going through it, people's thoughts, which in a single second were heard from land to land, many hundreds of miles apart.

"Will you answer, or do you want to be broken?" asked the fierce shark, and all the other big fishes asked the same. "Will you answer, or do you want to be broken?"

The cable didn't move, but it had its own private thoughts, which it had a right to have, considering that it was filled with others' thoughts. "Let them break me; then I'll be hauled up and put in order again—that has happened to others of my kind who were in shallower waters." And so it didn't answer; it had something else to do; it telegraphed and thereby did its just duty at the bottom of the sea.

Up above, the sun was going down, as people say. It blazed like the reddest fire, and all the clouds in the heavens glowed with a fiery hue, each more magnificent than the other.

"Now we're getting the red lighting," said the polyps, "and we may be able to see the thing better, if necessary."

"At it! At it!" shouted the shark, showing all his teeth.

"At it! At it!" said the swordfish, and the whale, and the sea eel. They rushed forward, the shark leading, but just as he was about to bite the cable, the swordfish, out of pure anxiety, ran his saw right into the back of the shark; that was a great mistake, and the shark had not strength left to bite. Everything became muddled in the mud. Big fishes, little fishes, "sea sausages," and snails ran into one another, ate each other—clashed and gnashed. The cable lay still and attended to its own business, as one should do.

The dark night brooded above; but in the ocean the millions and millions of small living creatures lighted it. Crawfish, not even as big as a pinhead, gave out light. It is quite wondrous, but now that's the way it is.

The ocean creatures looked at the telegraph cable. "What is that thing, and what isn't it?" Yes, that was the question.

Presently an old sea cow appeared. People call these mermaids or mermen. This one was a she, and had a tail and two short arms to splash with; she wore seaweed and parasites over her breasts and head, and she was proud of this.

"Are you seeking knowledge and wisdom?" she said. "I am the only one who can give you this; but in return I demand that you guarantee safe pasturage on the bottom of the ocean for me and mine. I am a fish like you are, but I am also a crawling animal, through practice. I am the wisest in the ocean; I know about everything that moves down here and about all that goes on up above. That thing you are pondering over is from above, and whatever falls down from up there is dead, or will be dead, and powerless; let it lie there for what it is. It's only a man-made invention."

"I believe there is more to it than that!" said the little fish.

"Hold your tongue, mackerel!" said the big sea cow.

"Stickleback!" said the others, and that was even more insulting.

And the sea cow explained further to them that this alarming thing, which, as a matter of fact, hadn't uttered a single sound, was in its entirety nothing more than some new device from the dry land, and she delivered a little lecture about people's deceitfulness. 'They want to catch us," she said; "that's all they live for. They stretch out nets for us, and come with bait on hooks to tempt us. That thing there is some sort of big string that they think we are going to bite. They are so stupid! But we are not! Don't touch that junk; in time it will unravel and all turn to dust and mud. Everything that comes from up there cracks and breaks—is good for nothing!"

"Good for nothing!" said the other ocean creatures, and held onto the sea cow's opinion, so as to have an opinion.

The little fish, however, had his own thoughts. "Perhaps that enormously

long, thin serpent is the most wonderful fish in the ocean. I have a feeling
it is."

"The most wonderful," say we humans, too, and we say it with knowledge
and assurance.

The great sea serpent has long been the theme of song and story. It was
conceived and born by man's ingenuity and laid on the bottom of the ocean,
stretching from the eastern to the western lands, and carrying messages as
swiftly as light flashes from the sun to our earth. It grows, grows in power and
length, grows year after year, through all oceans, around the world; it is
beneath the stormy seas and the glass-clear waters, where the skipper, as if
sailing through transparent air, looks down and sees crowds of fishes resembling many-colored fireworks.

Deepest down of all lies the outstretched serpent, a blessed Midgard[1] snake,
which bites its own tail as it encircles the earth. Fishes and other sea creatures
clash with it; they do not understand that thing from above. People's thoughts
rush noiselessly, in all languages, through the serpent of science, for both
good and evil; the most wondrous of the ocean's wonders is our time's—

GREAT SEA SERPENT

THE LITTLE GREEN ONES

A ROSE tree drooped in the window. Not so long ago it was green and
blooming, but now it looked sickly—something was wrong with it. A
regiment of invaders were eating it up; and, by the way, it was a very decent
and respectable regiment, dressed in green uniforms. I spoke to one of the invaders; he was only three days old but already a grandfather. Do you know
what he said? Well, what he said is all true—he spoke of himself and the rest
of the invaders. Listen!

"We're the strangest regiment of creatures in the world! Our young ones are
born in the summertime, for the weather is pleasant then. We're engaged and
have the wedding at once. When it gets cold we lay our eggs, and the little
ones are snug and warm. The ant, that wisest of creatures (we have a great
deal of respect for him!), studies us and appreciates us. He doesn't eat us up
all at once; instead, he takes our eggs and lays them out on the ground floor
of his and his family's anthill—stores layer after layer of them, all labeled and
numbered, side by side, so that every day a new one may creep out of the egg.
Then he keeps us in a stable, pinches our hind legs, and milks us, and then we
die. It is really a great pleasure. The ants have the prettiest name for us—'little milch cow!'

"All creatures who have the common sense that the ant has call us that; it's
only humans who don't, and that is an insult great enough to embitter all our
lives. Couldn't you write us a protest against it? Couldn't you put these people
in their right place? They look at us so stupidly, look at us with jealous eyes,
just because we eat rose leaves, while they eat everything that's created,

---

[1]The middle space between heaven and hell, where human beings dwell.

everything that is green or grows. Oh, they give us the most despicable, the most distasteful name; I won't even repeat it! Ugh! It turns my stomach; no, I won't repeat it—at least not when I'm wearing my uniform, and I am always wearing my uniform!

"I was born on a rose leaf. My whole regiment and I live off the rose tree; but then it lives again in us, who are of a higher order of beings. Humans detest us! They come and kill us with soapsuds. That's a horrible drink! I seem to smell it even now; it's dreadful to be washed when you're born not to be washed. Man, you who look at us with your stupid soapsud eyes, consider what our place in nature is; consider our artistic way of laying eggs and breeding children! We have been blessed to accomplish and multiply! We are born on the roses and we die in the roses—our whole life is a lovely poem. Don't call us by that name which you yourself think most despicable and ugly—that name I can't bear to speak or to repeat! Instead, call us the ants' milch cows, the rose-tree regiment, the little green ones!"

And I, the man, stood looking at the tree and at the little green ones—whose name I'll not mention, for I shouldn't like to hurt the feelings of a citizen of the rose tree, a large family with eggs and youngsters. And the soapsuds I was going to wash them in, for I had come with soap and water and evil intentions—I'll blow it to foam and use if for soap bubbles instead. Look at the splendor! Perhaps there's a fairy tale in each. And the bubble grows so large with radiant colors, looking as if there were a silvery pearl lying inside it!

The bubble swayed, and drifted to the door, and burst; but the door swung wide open, and there was Mother Fairy Tale herself! Yes, now she will tell you better than I can about—I won't say the name—the little green ones.

"Tree lice!" said Mother Fairy Tale. "You should call things by their right names; if you do not always dare to do so, you should at least be able to do it in a fairy tale!"

THE FLEA AND THE PROFESSOR

THERE was an aëronaut, and things went badly with him. His balloon burst, hurled him out, and went all to pieces. Just two minutes before, the aëronaut had sent his boy down by parachute—wasn't the boy lucky! He wasn't hurt, and he knew enough to be an aëronaut himself, but he had no balloon and no means of getting one.

Live he must, so he took to sleight-of-hand tricks, and to throwing his voice, which is called ventriloquism. He was young and good-looking. When he grew a mustache and wore his best clothes, he might well have been mistaken for the son of a nobleman. Ladies found him handsome and one young lady was so taken by his charm and dexterity that she eloped with him to foreign lands. There he called himself "The Professor"—he could scarcely do less.

He continually thought about how to get himself a balloon and sail through the air with his little wife. But they still lacked the means to do so.

"That will come yet," he said.

"Oh, if only it would," said she.

"We are still young people," he said, "and I'm a Professor."

"Crumbs are also bread!"

She helped him all she could, and sat at the door to sell tickets for his entertainments. In the wintertime this was a chilly sort of pleasure. She also helped him with one of his acts. He would put her into a table drawer—a large table drawer—and she would creep into the back drawer. From in front she was not to be seen, and as far as the audience was concerned she was invisible. But one evening, when he pulled out the drawer she was invisible to him too. She was not in the front drawer, not in the back one, and not in the whole house. She was nowhere to be seen or heard, and that was her contribution to the entertainment.

She never came back. She was tired of it all, and he became tired of it too. He lost his good humor and could not laugh or make jokes, so people stopped coming to see him. His earnings fell off and his clothes wore out, until at last, all that he had was a large flea, an heirloom from his wife; that's why he liked it so well. He trained the flea and taught it to perform—to present arms, and to fire off a cannon. Of course it was a very small cannon.

The Professor was proud of the flea, and the flea was proud of himself. He had learned a thing or two, and had human blood in him. He had been to the largest cities. Princes and Princesses has seen him and given him high praise, which was printed in the newspapers and on the billposters. He knew he was a famous flea who could support a Professor, yes, a whole household.

Proud he was and famous he was. Yet when he and the Professor traveled they went by fourth-class railway carriages, which took them along just as quickly as those of the first-class. They made a secret pledge to each other that they would never separate. Neither of them would marry. The flea would remain a bachelor and the Professor a widower. That made them even.

"Where one has the best luck," said the Professor, "one ought not go back a second time." He was a student of human nature, which is a science in itself. At length he had traveled through all countries except the savage ones, and to those he decided to go. There they eat Christian men. The Professor knew this, but then he was not much of a Christian, and the flea was not much of a man, so he thought they might venture successfully into the wilds, and make a lot of money.

They traveled by steamship and they travelled by sailboat. The flea performed his trick along the way in exchange for free passage, and thus they came to the country of savages. Here a little Princess ruled the land. She was only eight years old, but she ruled just the same. She had taken away the power from her papa and mamma, for she had a will of her own and was uncommonly beautiful, and uncommonly rude.

As soon as the flea presented arms and fired off his cannon, she took such a fancy to him that she cried, "Him or nobody!" She fell madly in love with the flea, and she was already a madcap in all other respects.

"My sweet, level-headed little child—" her papa said, "if only there were some way to make a man of him."

"Leave that to me, old fellow," said she, which was no way for a little princess to talk to her papa, but then she was a savage. She set the flea on her fair hand:

"Now you are a man, ruling with me, but you must do what I want you to do, or I shall kill you and eat the Professor."

The Professor had a large room to live in, with walls made of sugar cane. He could have licked them, but he didn't care for sweets. He had a hammock to sleep in, and that reminded him of being in a balloon, where he had always wanted to be. He thought of this continually.

The flea lived with the Princess. He sat upon her delicate hand or on her fair neck. She had taken a hair from her head and made the Professor fasten it to the flea's leg, and kept it tied to the big red coral pendant which hung from the tip of her ear. What a delightful time the Princess did have, and the flea too, she thought.

The Professor was not so delighted. He was a traveler, who liked to ride from town to town, and to read in the newspapers about how persevering and ingenious he had been to teach the flea tricks of human behavior. Day in and day out he lay lazily in his hammock. He ate good food: fresh birds' eggs, elephant eyes, and fried giraffe legs. Cannibals do not live entirely on human flesh. No, that is a special delicacy!

"Shoulder of child with pepper sauce," said the Princess's mamma, "is the most delicate."

The Professor was bored with it all, and preferred to leave this savage land, but his flea he must take with him, for it was his wonder and his bread and butter. How could be catch it? How could he get hold of it? This was not an easy thing to do. He racked his wits, and at last he declared:

"Now I have it! Papa of the Princess, give me something to do. Let me teach your people to present themselves before Your Royal Highness. This is what is known as culture in the great and powerful nations of the earth."

"Can I learn to do that too?" the Princess's papa asked.

"It's not quite proper," the Professor told him, "but I shall teach your Savage Papaship to fire off a cannon. It goes off with a bang. One sits high in the air, and then off it goes or down you come."

"Let me bang it off," the Princess's papa begged. But in all the land there was no cannon, except the one the flea had brought with him — and that was so tiny.

"I shall cast a bigger one," said the Professor. "Just give me the means to do so. I must have fine silk cloth, a needle and thread, and rope and cordage, besides stomach drops for the balloon. Stomach drops blow a person up so easily and give one the heaves. They are what make the report in the cannon's stomach."

"By all means." The Princess's papa gave him everything that he asked. The whole court, and all the populace gathered together to see the casting of the big cannon. The Professor did not call them until he had the balloon all ready to be filled and to go up. The flea sat there upon the Princess's hand, and looked on as the balloon was filled. It swelled out and became so violent that they could scarcely hold it down.

"I must take it up in the air to cool it off," said the Professor who took his seat in the basket that hung underneath.

"But — I cannot steer it alone, I must have a trained companion along to help me. There is no one here who can do that except the flea."

"I am not at all willing to permit it," said the Princess, but she held out her hand and gave the flea to the Professor, who placed it on his wrist.

"Let go the lines and ropes!" he shouted. "Now the balloon is going up." They thought he said "the cannon." So the balloon went higher and higher, up above the clouds and far away from that savage land.

The little Princess, her family, and all of her subjects sat and waited. They are waiting there still, and if you don't believe this, just you take a journey to the country of savages. Every child there is talking about the Professor and the flea, whom they expect back as soon as the cannon cools off.

But they won't be back. They are at home here with us. They are in their native land. They traveled by rail, first-class, not fourth. For they have a great success, an enormous balloon. Nobody asks them how they got their balloon, or where it came from. They are wealthy folk now—oh, most respectable folk—the flea and the Professor.

THE DAYS OF THE WEEK

THE days of the week once wanted to be free to get together and have a party. But each of the seven days was so occupied, the year around, that they had no time to spare. They wanted a whole extra day; but then they had that every four years, the intercalary day[1] that comes in February for the purpose of keeping order in chronology.

On the intercalary day they would get together for a party, and, as February is the month of carnivals, they would come in costumes of each one's taste and choice; they would eat well, drink well, make speeches, and be complimentary and disagreeable to one another in unrestrained comradeship. While the vikings of olden times used to throw their gnawed-off bones at each other's heads during mealtime, the days of the week intended to throw jokes and sarcastic witticisms such as might be in keeping with the innocent carnival spirit.

So when it was intercalary day, they assembled.

Sunday, foreman of the days of the week, appeared in a black silk cloak; pious people thought he was dressed for church in a minister's gown, but the worldly minded saw that he was attired in a domino for merriment and that the flashing carnation he wore in his buttonhole was a little red theater lantern on which it said, "All sold out; see now that you enjoy yourselves!"

Monday, a young fellow related to Sunday, and very fond of pleasures, came next. He left his workshop, he said, whenever he heard the music of the parade of the guard.

"I must go out and listen to Offenbach's music; it doesn't go to my head or to my heart; it tickles my leg muscles; I must dance, have a few drinks, get a black eye, sleep it off, and then the next day go to work. I am the new part of the week!"

Tuesday is Tyr's[2] day, the day of strength.

"Yes, that I am," said Tuesday. "I take a firm grip on my work; I fasten Mercury's wings onto the merchant's boots, see that the wheels in the factory are oiled and turning, that the tailor sits at his table, and that the street paver is by his paving stones; each attends to his business, for I keep my eye on all. Accordingly, I am here in a police uniform and call myself Tuesday, a well-used day! If this is a bad joke, then you others try to think of a better one!"

---

[1] February 29, leap-year day.
[2] God of war and of the sky.

"Then I come," said Wednesday. "I'm in the middle of the week. The Germans call me Herr Mittwoch.[3] I stand like a journeyman in a store and like a flower in the midst of the other esteemed days of the week! If we all march up in order, then I have three days before me and three days behind; they are like an honor guard, so I should think that I am the most prominent day in the week!"

Thursday appeared dressed as a coppersmith, with a hammer and copper kettle, as a symbol of his noble descent.

"I am the highest birth," he said, "paganish, godlike! In the Northern countries I am named after Thor, and in the Southern countries after Jupiter, who both knew how to thunder and lighten, and that has remained in the family!"

And then he beat his copper kettle, thereby proving his high birth.

Friday was dressed as a young girl, and called herself Freia, also Venus for a change, depending upon the language of the country in which she appeared. She was of a quiet, cheerful character, she said, but today she felt gay and free, for this was intercalary day, which, according to an old custom, gives a woman the right to dare propose to a man and not have to wait for him to propose to her.

Saturday appeared as an old housekeeper with a broom and other cleaning articles. Her favorite dish was beer soup, though at this festive occasion she did not request that it be served for everyone, only that she get it, and she got it.

And so the days of the week had their party.

Here they are in print, all seven of them, ready for use as tableaux at family parties. There you can make them as funny as you wish; we give them here as a joke on February, the only month with an extra day.

THE COMET

Now there came a comet with its shiny nucleus and its menacing tail. People from the great castles and people from the poor huts gazed at it. So did the man who went his solitary way across the pathless heath. Everyone had his own thoughts. "Come and look at the omen from heaven. Come out and see this marvelous sight," they cried, and everyone hastened to look.

But a little boy and his mother still stayed inside their room. The tallow candle was burning and the mother thought she saw a bit of wood-shaving in the light. The tallow formed a jagged edge around the candle, and then it curled. The mother believed these were signs that her son would soon die. The wood-shaving was circling towards him. This was an old superstition, but she believed it. The little boy lived many more years on earth. Indeed he lived to see the comet return, sixty years later.

The boy did not see the wood-shaving in the candle-light, and his thoughts were not about the comet which then, for the first time in his life, shone brightly in the sky. He sat quietly with an earthenware bowl before him. The bowl was filled with soapy water, into which he dipped the head of a clay

[3]Mr. Midweek.

pipe. Then he put the pipe stem in his mouth, and blew soap bubbles, large and small. They quivered and spun in beautiful colors. They changed from yellow to red, and from red to purple or blue, and then they turned bright green, like leaves when the sun shines through them.

The boy's mother said, "May God grant you many more years on earth—as many years as the bubbles you are blowing."

"So many, so many!" he cried. "I can never blow all the soapy water into bubbles. There goes one year, there goes another one; see how they fly!" he exclaimed, as bubbles came loose from his pipe and floated away. A few of them blew into his eye, where they burned, and smarted, and made his tears flow. In every bubble he saw a picture of the future, glimmering and glistening.

"This is the time to look at the comet," cried their neighbors. "Come outdoors. Don't sit in your room."

The mother took her boy by the hand. He had to put aside his clay pipe, and stop playing with the soap bubbles, because there was a comet to see.

The boy saw the bright ball of fire, with its shining tail. Some said it was three yards long, while others insisted it was several million yards long—such a difference.

Most of the people who said these things were dead and buried when the comet came again. But the little boy, toward whom the wood-shaving had circled, and of whom his mother thought, "He will soon die," still lived on, though he had grown old and his hair was white. "White hairs are the flowers of age," the saying goes, and he had many such flowers. He was now an old schoolmaster. The school children thought him very wise and learned, because he knew history, and geography, and all there is to be known about the heavens and the stars.

"Everything comes again," he said. "If you will pay attention to people and events, you will learn that they always come back. There may be a hundred years between, or many hundreds of years, but once again we shall see the same character, in another coat and in another country." And the schoolmaster then told them about William Tell, who was forced to shoot an apple from his son's head, but before he shot the arrow he hid another one in his shirt, to shoot into the heart of the wicked Gessler. This happened in Switzerland. But many years before, the same thing happened in Denmark to Palnatoke. He too was forced to shoot an apple from his son's head, and he too hid an arrow in his shirt to avenge the cruelty. And more than a thousand years before that, the same story was written in Egypt. It happened before and will happen again, just as sure as the comet returns. "Off it flies into space, and is gone for years, but still it comes back." He spoke of the comet that was expected, the same comet he had seen as a boy.

The schoolmaster knew what went on in the skies, and he thought much about it too, but he did not neglect history and geography. His garden was laid out in the shape of a map of Denmark. In it grew herbs and flowers which flourished in different parts of the land.

"Fetch me peas," he said, and they went to the garden bed that represented Laaland. "Fetch me buckwheat," he said, and they fetched it from Langeland. Lovely blue gentian was planted in Skagen, and the shining Christthorn in Silkeborg. Towns and cities were marked with small statues. Here was the dragon and St. Knud, who stood for Odense. Absalon with the bishop's staff stood for Sorö. The little boat with oars marked the site of Aarhus. In the schoolmaster's garden you could learn the geography of Denmark, but first you had to be instructed by him and that was a pleasure.

Now that the comet was expected again, he told about it, and he told what people had said in the old days when it last was seen. They had said that a comet year was a good year for wine, and that water could be mixed with this wine without being detected. Therefore the wine merchants thought well of a comet year.

For fourteen days and fourteen nights the sky was clouded over. They could not see the comet, and yet it was there. The old schoolmaster sat in his little chamber next to the schoolroom. The old Bornholm clock of his grandfather's time stood in the corner, though its heavy lead weights moved neither up nor down, nor did its pendulum ever swing. The little cuckoo, that used to come out to call the passing hours, had long ago stopped doing his duty. The clock neither struck nor ticked. The clock was decidedly out of order.

But the old clavichord at which he sat had been made in his parents' time, and it still had a tune or two left in it. The strings could still play. Tremulous though they were, they could play for him the melodies of a whole lifetime. As the old man heard them, he remembered many things, both pleasant and sad, that had happened in the long years which had gone by since he was a little boy and saw the comet. Now that the comet had come again, he remembered what his mother had said about the wood-shaving circling toward him. He remembered the fine soap bubbles he had blown, one for every year of his life he had said as he looked at them glistening and gleaming in wonderful colors. He saw in them all his pleasures and sorrow—everything, both the good and the bad. He saw the child at his play, and the youth with his fancies. His whole life, iridescent and bright, floated before his eyes. And in that splendor he saw his future too, in bubbles of time to come.

First the old man heard from the strings of the clavichord the melodies of times past, and saw the bubbles of years gone by, colored with memories. He heard his grandmother's knitting song:

> "Surely no Amazon
> The first stockings knit."

And then the strings played the songs his old nurse used to sing for him:

> "There were so many dangers
> In this world to pass through
> For people who were young
> And only little knew."

Now the melodies of his first ball were playing, for the minuet and molinasky—soft melancholy tunes that brought tears to the old man's eyes. A roaring war-march, then a psalm, then happy tunes. The years whirled past as if they were those bubbles he blew when he was a little boy.

His eyes were turned towards the window. A cloud billowed across the sky, and as it passed he saw the comet with its shining nucleus and its shining, misty veil. It seemed to him as though it were only yesterday evening when he had last seen that comet, yet a whole busy lifetime lay between that evening and this. Then he was a child, looking through bubbles into the future; now those bright bubbles were all behind him. Once more he had a child's outlook and a child's faith. His eyes sparkled, and his hands struck the keys. There was the sound of a breaking string.

"Come out and see," cried the neighbors. "The comet is here, and the sky is clear. Come out and look!"

The old schoolmaster did not answer. He had gone where he could see more clearly. His soul was on a journey far greater than the comet's, and the realm to which it went was far more spacious than that in which the comet moved.

Again the comet was seen from the high castle, and from the lowly hut. The crowd in the street gazed up at it, and so did the man who went his solitary way across the pathless heath. But the schoolmaster's soul was seen by God, and by those dear ones who had gone before him, and whom he longed to see.

WHAT THE WHOLE FAMILY SAID

WHAT did the whole family say? Well listen first to what little Marie said.

It was little Marie's birthday, the most wonderful of all days, she imagined. All her little boy friends and girl friends came to play with her, and she wore her prettiest dress, the one Grandmother, who was now with God, had sewn for her before she went up into the bright, beautiful heaven. The table in little Marie's room was loaded with presents; there was the prettiest little kitchen, with everything that belongs to a kitchen, and a doll that could close its eyes and say "Ouch!" when you pinched its stomach; yes, and there was also a picture book, with the most wonderful stories, to be read when one could read! But to have many birthdays was more wonderful than all the stories in the book.

"Yes, it's wonderful to be alive," said little Marie. And her godfather added that it was the most beautiful of all fairy tales.

In the next room were both her brothers; they were big boys, one of them nine years old, the other eleven. They thought it was wonderful to be alive, too; that is, to live in their own way, not to be a baby like Marie, but to be real smart schoolboys, to get A's on their report cards, to have friendly fights with their comrades, to go skating in the winter and bicycling in the summer, to read about the days of knighthood, with its castles, its drawbridges, and its dungeons, and to hear about new discoveries in Central Africa. On the latter subject, however, one of the boys felt very sad in that he feared everything might be discovered before he grew up, and then there would be no adventure left for him. But Godfather said, "Life itself is the most wonderful adventure, and you have a part in it yourself."

These children lived on the first floor of the house; in the flat above them lived another branch of the family, also with children, but these all had long since been shaken from their mother's apron strings, so big were they; one son was seventeen, and another twenty, but the third one was very old, said little Marie; he was twenty-five, and engaged to be married. They were all very well off, had nice parents, good clothes, and were well educated, and they knew what they wanted. "Look forward," they said. "Away with all the old fences! Let's have an open view into the wide world! That's the greatest thing we know of! Godfather is right—life is the most wonderful fairy tale!"

Father and Mother, both older people—naturally, they would have to be older than the children—said, with smiling lips and smiling eyes and hearts, "How young these young people are! Things usually don't happen in this world just as they expect them to, yet life goes on. Life is a strange and wonderful adventure."

On the next floor—a little closer to heaven, as we say when people live in an attic—lived Godfather. He was old, and yet so young in mind, always in good humor, and he certainly could tell stories, many and long ones. He had traveled the world over, and his room was filled with pretty tokens from every country. Pictures were hung from ceiling to floor, and some of the windowpanes were of red or yellow glass; if one looked through them, the whole world lay in sunshine, however gray the weather might be outside. Green plants grew in a large glass case, and in an enclosure therein swam goldfish; they looked at one as if they knew many things they didn't care to talk about. There was always a sweet fragrance of flowers, even in the wintertime. And then a great fire blazed in the fireplace; it was such a pleasure to sit and look at it and hear how it crackled and spat.

"It refreshes old memories to me," said Godfather. And to little Marie there seemed to appear many pictures in the fire.

But in the big bookcase close by stood real books; one of these Godfather often read, and this he called the Book of Books; it was the Bible. In it was pictured the history of the world and the history of all mankind, of the creation, the flood, the kings, and the King of Kings.

"All that has happened and all that will happen is written in this book," said Godfather; "so infinitely much in one single book! Just think of it! Yes, everything that a human being has to pray for is entered there, and said in a few words in the prayer 'Our Father'! It is the drop of mercy! It is the pearl of comfort from God. It is laid as a gift on the baby's cradle, laid on the child's heart. Little child, keep it safely; don't ever lose it, however big you may grow, and you will never be left alone on life's changeful way; it will shine within you and you will never be lost!"

Godfather's eyes radiated joy. Once, in his youth, they had wept, "and this was also good," he said. "That was a time of trial, when everything looked dark and gray. Now I have sunshine within me and around me. The older one grows, the clearer one sees, in both prosperity and misfortune, that our Lord always is with us and that life is the most beautiful of all fairy tales, and this He alone can give us—and so it will be into eternity."

"Yes, it is wonderful to be alive!" said little Marie.

So said also the small and the big boys, as well as Father and Mother and the whole family—but first of all, Godfather, who had had so much experience and was the oldest of them all. He knew all stories, all the fairy tales. And it was right from the bottom of his heart that he said, "Life is the most wonderful fairy tale of all!"

LUCK MAY LIE IN A PIN
A STORY TOLD FOR MY YOUNG AMERICAN FRIENDS

I'LL tell you a story about luck. All of us know what it is to be lucky. Some know good luck day in, day out; others only now and then in their lucky seasons; and there are some people who know it only once in a lifetime. But luck comes at some time or other to us all.

Now I needn't tell you what everyone knows, that it's God who puts little children in their mother's lap; maybe in a nobleman's castle, maybe in a workingman's home, or maybe in the open field where the cold wind blows. What you may not know, though it's just as true, is that when God leaves the child he always leaves it a lucky piece. He doesn't put this where the child is born, but tucks it away in some odd corner of the earth where we least expect it. Yes, you can rest assured that it always turns up, sooner or later, and that is nice to know.

This lucky piece may turn out to be an apple. That was the case with one man, a scholar called Newton. The apple fell into his lap, and his luck came with it. If you don't know the story, get someone to tell it to you. I've a different story to tell, about a pear.

Once there was a man born poor, bred poor, and married without a penny. By the way, he was a turner by trade, but as he made nothing except umbrella handles and umbrella rings, he earned only enough money to live from hand to mouth.

"I'll never find my luck," he used to say.

Now this is a Gospel true story. It really happened. I could name the man's country and his town, but that isn't important. Wild service berries, with their red, sour fruit, grew around his house and garden as if they were the richest ornament. However, in the garden was also a pear tree. It had never borne fruit, yet the man's luck lay hidden in the tree, in the shape of a pear not yet to be seen.

One night the wind blew in a terrible gale. In the next town men said that the great mail coach was lifted from one side of the road to the other as easily as a rag, so it was not to be wondered at that a large branch was torn from the pear tree. The branch was brought into the workshop and, just as a joke, the turner made from it wooden pears, big, little, and middle-sized.

"For once my tree has borne pears," he smiled, and gave them to his children for playthings.

Among the necessities of life are umbrellas, especially in lands where it rains a lot. But the turner's family had only one umbrella between them. When the wind blew hard, their umbrella would blow inside out. Sometimes it would break, and luckily the man knew how to mend it. However, with the button and loop that held the umbrella closed, things went from bad to worse. The button would always fly off just as they thought they had the umbrella neatly folded.

One day it popped off, and the turner hunted for it everywhere. In a crack of the floor he came across one of the smallest pears he had given his children for a toy.

"If I can't find the button," he said, "I'll make this do." He fitted a string through it, and the little pear buttoned up the umbrella to perfection. It was the best umbrella fastener that ever was seen.

The next time the turner sent umbrella handles and umbrella rings to the city, he added several of the small wooden pears. They were fitted to a few new umbrellas, and put with a thousand others on a ship bound for America. Americans catch on very quickly. They saw that the little pears held better than the other umbrella buttons, and the merchant gave orders that all the umbrellas sent to him henceforth should be fastened with little wooden pears.

There was work for you—thousands of pears to be made for all the umbrellas that went to America. The turner turned them out wholesale, until the whole pear tree was used up making little wooden pears. They brought pennies that grew into dollars. There was no end to the money he made.

"My luck was in that pear tree all along," the man said. Soon he had a great factory with plenty of workmen to help him. Now that he always had time for a joke he would say, "Good luck may lie in a pin."

And I who tell this story say so too, for it's a true proverb in Denmark that if you put a white pin in your mouth you'll be invisible. But it must be the right sort of pin, a lucky piece from God's own hand. I have one of them, and whenever I come to America, that new world so far away and yet so near me, I'll always carry that pin. Already my words have gone there. The ocean rolls toward America, and the wind blows that way. Any day I can be where my stories are read, and perhaps see the glittering of ringing gold—the gold that is best of all, which shines in children's eyes, or rings from their lips and the lips of their grown-ups. I am in all my friends' homes, even though they don't see me. I have the white pin in my mouth.

And luck may lie in a pin.

SUNSHINE STORIES

"I'LL tell you a story," said the Wind. "Kindly remember," said the Rain, "that it's my turn to talk. You've been howling around the corner at the top of your voice quite long enough."

"Is that the thanks I get for all of the favors I've done you?" the Wind blustered. "Many an umbrella I've turned inside out, or even blown to tatters, when people tried to avoid you."

"Be silent! It is I who shall speak," said the Sunshine, who spoke with such brilliance and warmth that the weary Wind fell flat on his back, and the Rain shook him and tried to rouse him, crying: "We won't stand for it. This Madam Sunshine is forever interrupting us. Don't let us listen to her. What she says is not worth hearing."

And the Sunshine began: "A beautiful swan flew over the rolling, tossing waves of the ocean. Each of its feathers shone like gold. One feather drifted down above a great merchant ship that sailed the sea with all its canvas spread. The feather came to rest upon the curly hair of a young overseer who looked after the goods aboard the ship—supercargo they called him. The bird of fortune's feather touched his forehead, became a quill pen in his hand, and brought him such luck that he soon became a merchant, a man of wealth, a man so rich that he could wear spurs of gold and change a golden dish into a nobleman's shield. I know—I have shone on it," said the Sunshine.

"The swan flew far away, over a green meadow where a little shepherd boy, not more than seven years old, lay in the shade of an old tree, the only tree in that meadow. As the swan flew past it, she brushed one leaf from the tree. This leaf fell into the boy's hands, where it turned into three leaves, ten leaves—yes, it turned into all the leaves of a book. In this book he read of the many wonderful things that are in nature, about his native language, about faith, and about knowledge. Before he went to sleep he laid the book under his pillow to keep from forgetting what he had learned during the day. The wonderful book led him first to school, and then far into the fields of learning. I have seen his name where they carve the names of great scholars," the Sunshine said.

"The swan flew over the forest, where it was lonely and quiet. She came to rest on a deep blue lake, where the water lilies grow, where wild apple trees flourish along the shore, and where the cuckoo and wild pigeon make their nests.

"A poor woman was in the forest, gathering fallen branches. She carried them on her back, and held a baby in her arms. She saw the golden swan, that bird of fortune, rise from the rush-covered shore. What was this glittering thing the swan had left? It was a golden egg, still warm. She put it in her bosom, and the warmth stayed in it. Truly there was life in that egg. Yes, she heard a tapping inside the shell, but it was so faint that she mistook it for the sound of her own heartbeat.

"When she came home to her own poor cottage, she took the egg out to look at it. 'Tick,' it said, 'tick', as if it had been a costly gold watch. But it was no watch. It was an egg, just about to hatch. The shell cracked open, and a dear little baby swan looked out. It was fully feathered, all in gold, and around its neck were four gold rings. As the poor woman had four boys—three at home and the baby she had carried in her arms—she knew that one of the rings was meant for each of her sons. As soon as she realized this, the little golden bird flew away. She kissed all of the rings, and she made each son kiss one of them, touch it against his heart, and wear it on his finger. I saw all this," said the Sunshine, "And I saw what came of it.

"As one of the boys played in the bed of a stream, he picked up a handful of clay. He turned it, and twisted it, and he shaped it in his fingers until he had made a statue of Jason. Like Jason, the young sculptor had found the golden fleece he sought.

"The second boy ran across the meadow, where there were flowers of every hue. He gathered a handful, and squeezed them so tightly that the colored juices wet his ring and splashed in his eye. They stuck to his fingers and colored his thoughts. The days went by, and the years went past, until people in the big city came to speak of him as 'the great painter.'

"The third boy clenched his ring in his teeth so tightly that it echoed the song that lay deep in his heart. The things he thought and the things he felt were turned to music. They rose like singing swans, and like swans they plunged down as deep as the depths of the sea, 'the deep Sea of Thoughts.' He became a great musician, a great composer of whom every land has the right to say: 'He belongs to me.'

"The fourth boy—the baby—was an outcast. They said he had the pip, and that like a sick little chicken he should be dosed with butter and pepper. They gave him pepper enough with his butter, but I gave him warmth and the kiss of the sun," said the Sunshine. "He got ten kisses for one that the other children received. He was a poet, who met with a blow and a kiss, all his life long. But he had something that no one could take from him. He had the ring of fame from the golden swan of fortune. There were golden wings to his thoughts. Up they flew and away they went, like golden butterflies, which are the symbol of things immortal."

"What an extremely long story," said the Will.

"And so awfully dull," the Rain agreed. "Fan me, if you please, so I may revive a little."

The Wind blew again, and the Sunshine said: "The swan of fortune flew over the deep gulf, where fishermen spread their nets. The poorest of the fishermen thought of getting married, and marry he did. And to him the swan brought a lump of amber. Amber had the power to draw things to it, and it drew the hearts to the fisherman's home. Amber makes the most wonderful incense, and there came a fragrant air as from a church, like a balmy breeze from God's nature. So the fisherman and his bride were happy and thankful in their quiet home. They were content with what little they had, and their life became a complete sunshine story."

"I think," said the Wind, "that these stories should stop. The Sunshine has talked long enough, and I am very bored."

"So am I," said the Rain

And what do we others who *knew* this story say?

We say: "Now it's out."

THE RAGS

OUTSIDE the paper mill, masses of rags lay piled in high stacks; they had been gathered from far and wide. Every rag had a tale to tell, and told it, too; but we can't listen to all of them. Some of the rags were native; others came from foreign countries.

Now here lay a Danish rag beside a rag from Norway; one was decidedly Danish, the other decidedly Norse, and that was the amusing part about the two, as any good Dane or Norwegian could tell you. They could understand each other well enough, though the two languages were as different, according to the Norwegian, as French and Hebrew. "We go to the hills for our language, and there get it pure and first hand, while the Dane cooks up some sort of a suckling-sweet lingo!"

So the rags talked — and a rag is a rag in every land the world over; they are considered of no value except in the rag heap.

"I am Norse!" said the Norwegian. "And when I've said I'm Norse I guess I've said enough. I'm firm of fiber, like the ancient granite rocks of old Norway. The land up there has a constitution, like the free United States. It makes my fibers tingle to thing what I am and to sound out my thoughts in words of granite!"

"But we have literature," said the Danish rag. "Do you understand what that is?"

"Understand?" repeated the Norwegian. "Lowland creature! Shall I give him a shove uphill and show him a northern light, rag that he is? When the sun of Norway has thawed the ice, then Danish fruit barges come up to us with butter and cheese—an eatable cargo, I grant you—but by way of ballast they bring Danish literature, too! We don't need the stuff. You don't need stale beer where fresh springs spout, and up there is a natural well that has never been tapped or been made known to Europeans by the cackling of newspapers, jobbers, and traveling authors in foreign countries. I speak freely from the bottom of my lungs, and the Dane must get used to a free voice. And so he will someday, when as a fellow Scandinavian he wants to cling to our proud mountain country, the summit of the world!"

"Now a Danish rag could never talk like that—never!" said the Dane. "It's not in our nature. I know myself, and all the other rags are like me. We're too good-natured, too unassuming; we think too little of ourselves. Not that we gain much by our modesty, but I like it; I think it's quite charming. Incidentally, I'm perfectly aware of my own good values, I assure you, but I don't talk about them; nobody can ever accuse me of that. I'm soft and easy going; bear everything patiently, envy nobody, and speak good of everybody—though there isn't much good to be said of most other people, but that's their business. I can afford to smile at them; I know I'm so gifted."

"Don't speak to me in that lowland, pasteboard language—it makes me sick!" said the Norwegian, as he caught a puff of wind and fluttered away from his own heap to another.

They both became paper; and, as it turned out, the Norwegian rag became a sheet on which a Norwegian wrote a love letter to a Danish girl, while the Danish rag became the manuscript for a Danish poem praising Norway's beauty and strength.

So something good may come even of rags when they have once come out of the rag heap and the change has been made into truth and beauty; they keep up understanding relations between us, and in that there is a blessing.

That is the story. It's rather amusing and offends no one—but the rags.

DANCE, DANCE, DOLL OF MINE!

"YES, this is a song for very small children!" declared Aunt Malle. "As much as I should like to, I cannot follow this 'Dance, Dance, Doll of Mine!' "

But little Amalie could; she was only three years old, played with dolls, and brought them up to be just as wise as Aunt Malle.

There was a student who came to the house to help her brothers with their lessons, and he frequently spoke to little Amalie and her dolls; he spoke differently from anyone else, and the little girl found him very amusing, although Aunt Malle said he didn't know how to converse with children—their little heads couldn't possibly grasp that silly talk. But little Amalie did. Yes, the student even taught her the whole song, "Dance, Dance, Doll of Mine!" and she sang it to her three dolls; two were new, one a girl doll and the other a boy doll, but the third doll was old; her name was Lise-moér. She also heard the song, and was even in it.

Dance, dance, doll of mine!
Girl doll's dress is very fine.
Boy doll is a dandy, too;
He wears gloves and hat and shoe;
White pants, blue coat, him adorn;
On his toe he has a corn.
He is fine and she is fine.
Dance, dance, doll of mine!

Old doll's name is Lise-moér;
She is from the year before;
Hair is new; it's made of flax,
Forehead polished up with wax.
Young again, not old and done.
Come along, my cherished one,
Let us dance a fast gavotte;
To watch it is worth a lot.

Dance, dance, doll of mine!
Watch your steps and get in line;
One foot forward; watch your feet.
Dancing makes you slender, sweet.
Bow and twist and turn around;
That will make you hale and sound.
What a sight it is to see!
You are doing fine, all three.

And the dolls understood the song; little Amalie understood it, and so did the student, but then he had written it himself and said it was excellent. Only Aunt Malle didn't understand it; she had passed over the fence of youth. "Silly song!" she said.

But not little Amalie! She sings it. It is from her that we know it.

AUNTY TOOTHACHE

WHERE did we get this story? Would you like to know?

We got it from the basket that the wastepaper is thrown into.

Many a good and rare book has been taken to the delicatessen store and the grocer's, not to be read, but to be used as wrapping paper for starch and coffee, beans, for salted herring, butter, and cheese. Used writing paper has also been found suitable.

Frequently one throws into the wastepaper basket what ought not to go there.

I know a grocer's assistant, the son of a delicatessen store owner. He has worked his way up from serving in the cellar to serving in the front shop; he is a well-read person, his reading consisting of the printed and written material matter to be found on the paper used for wrapping. He has an interesting collection, consisting of several important official documents from the wastepaper baskets of busy and absent-minded officials, a few confidential letters from one lady friend to another—reports of scandal which were not to go further, not to be mentioned by a soul. He is a living salvage institution for more than a little of our literature, and his collection covers a wide field; he has the run of his parents' shop and that of his present master and has there saved many a book, or leaves of a book, well worth reading twice.

He has shown me his collection of printed and written matter from the wastepaper basket, the most valued items of which have come from the delicatessen store. A couple of leaves from a large composition book lay among the collection; the unusually clear and neat handwriting attracted my attention at once.

"This was written by the student," he said, "the student who lived opposite here and died about a month ago. He suffered terribly from toothache, as one can see. It is quite amusing to read. This is only a small part of what he wrote; there was a whole book and more besides. My parents gave the student's landlady half a pound of green soap for it. This is what I have been able to save of it."

I borrowed it, I read it, and now I tell it.

The title was:

AUNTY TOOTHACHE.

I

Aunty gave me sweets when I was little. My teeth could stand it then; it didn't hurt them. Now I am older, am a student, and still she goes on spoiling me with sweets. She says I am a poet.

I have something of the poet in me, but not enough. Often when I go walking along the city streets, it seems to me as if I am walking in a big library; the houses are the bookshelves; and every floor is a shelf with books. There stands a story of everyday life; next to it is a good old comedy, and there are works of all scientific branches, bad literature and good reading. I can dream and philosophize among all this literature.

There is something of the poet in me, but not enough. No doubt many people have just as much of it in them as I, though they do not carry a sign or a necktie with the word "Poet" on it. They and I have been given a divine gift, a blessing great enough to satisfy oneself, but altogether too little to be portioned out again to others. It comes like a ray of sunlight and fills one soul's and thoughts; it comes like the fragrance of a flower, like a melody that one knows and yet cannot remember from where.

The other evening I sat in my room and felt an urge to read, but I had no book, no paper. Just then a leaf, fresh and green, fell from the lime tree, and the breeze carried it in through the window to me. I examined the many veins in it; a little insect was crawling across them, as if it were making a thorough study of the leaf. This made me think of man's wisdom; we also crawl about on a leaf; our knowledge is limited to that only, and yet we unhesitatingly deliver a lecture on the whole big tree—the root, the trunk, and the crown—the great tree comprised of God, the world, and immortality—and of all this we know only a little leaf!

AUNTY TOOTHACHE

As I was sitting there, I received a visit from Aunty Mille. I showed her the leaf with the insect and told her of my thoughts in connection with these. And her eyes lit up.

"You are a poet!" she said. "Perhaps the greatest we have. If I should live to see this, I would go to my grave gladly. Ever since the brewer Rasmussen's funeral you have amazed me with your powerful imagination."

So said Aunty Mille, and she then kissed me.

Who was Aunty Mille, and who was Rasmussen the brewer?

II

We children always called our mother's aunt "Aunty"; we had no other name for her.

She gave us jam and sweets, although they were very injurious to our teeth; but the dear children were her weakness, she said. It was cruel to deny them a few sweets, when they were so fond of them. And that's why we loved Aunty so much.

She was an old maid; as far back as I can remember, she was always old. Her age never seemed to change.

In earlier years she had suffered a great deal from toothache, and she always spoke about it; and so it happened that her friend, the brewer Rasmussen, who was a great wit, called her Aunty Toothache.

He had retired from the brewing business some years before and was then living on the interest of his money. He frequently visited Aunty; he was older than she. He had no teeth at all—only a few black stumps. When a child, he had eaten too much sugar, he told us children, and that's how he came to look as he did.

Aunty could surely never have eaten sugar in her childhood. For she had the most beautiful white teeth. She took great care of them, and she did not sleep with them at night!—said Rasmussen the brewer. We children knew that this was said in malice, but Aunty said he did not mean anything by it.

One morning, at the breakfast table, she told us of a terrible dream she had had during the night, in which one of her teeth had fallen out.

"That means," she said, "that I shall lose a true friend!"

"Was it a false tooth?" asked the brewer with a chuckle. "If so, it can only mean that you will lose a false friend!"

"You are an insolent old man!" said Aunty, angrier than I had seen her before or ever have since.

She later told us that her old friend had only been teasing her; he was the finest man on earth, and when he died he would become one of God's little angels in heaven.

I thought a good deal of this transformation, and wondered if I would be able to recognize him in this new character.

When Aunty and he had been young, he had proposed to her. She had settled down to think it over, had thought too long, and had become an old maid, but always remained his true friend.

And then Brewer Rasmussen died. He was taken to his grave in the most expensive hearse and was followed by a great number of folks, including people with orders and in uniform.

Aunty stood dressed in mourning by the window, together with all of us children, except our little brother, whom the stork had brought a week before. When the hearse and the procession had passed and the street was empty, Aunty wanted to go away from the window, but I did not want to; I was waiting for the angel, Rasmussen the brewer; surely he had by now become one of God's bewinged little children and would appear.

"Aunty," I said, "don't you think that he will come now? Or that when the stork again brings us a little brother, he'll then bring us the angel Rasmussen?"

Aunty was quite overwhelmed by my imagination, and said, "That child will become a great poet!" And this she kept repeating all the time I went to school, and even after my confirmation and, yes, still does now that I am a student.

She was, and is, to me the most sympathetic of friends, both in my poetical troubles and dental troubles, for I have attacks of both.

"Just write down all your thoughts," she said, "and put them in the table drawer! That's what Jean Paul did; he became a great poet, though I don't admire him; he does not excite one. You must be exciting! Yes, you will be exciting!"

The night after she said this, I lay awake, full of longings and anguish, with anxiety and fond hopes to become the great poet that Aunty saw and perceived in me; I went through all the pains of a poet! But there is an even greater pain — toothache — and it was grinding and crushing me; I became a writhing worm, with a bag of herbs and a mustard plaster.

"I know all about it," said Aunty. There was a sorrowful smile on her lips, and her white teeth glistened.

But I must begin a new chapter in my own and my aunt's story.

III

I had moved to a new flat and had been living there a month. I was telling Aunty about it.

"I live with a quiet family; they pay no attention to me, even if I ring three times. Besides, it is a noisy house, full of sounds and disturbances caused by the weather, the wind, and the people. I live just above the street gate; every carriage that drives out or in makes the pictures on the walls move about. The gate bangs and shakes the house as if there were an earthquake. If I am in bed, the shocks go right through all my limbs, but that is said to be strengthening to the nerves. If the wind blows, and it is always blowing in this country, the long window hooks outside swing to and fro, and strike against the wall. The bell on the gate to the neighbor's yard rings with every gust of wind.

"The people who live in the house come home at all hours, from late in the evening until far into the night; the lodger just above me, who in the daytime gives lessons on the trombone, comes home the latest and does not go to bed before he has taken a little midnight promenade with heavy steps and in iron-heeled shoes.

"There are no double windows. There is a broken pane in my room, over which the landlady has pasted some paper, but the wind blows through the crack despite that and produces a sound similar to that of a buzzing wasp. It is like the sort of music that makes one go to sleep. If at last I fall asleep, I am soon awakened by the crowing of the cocks. From the cellarman's hencoop the cocks and hens announce that it will soon be morning. The small ponies, which have no stable, but are tied up in the storeroom under the staircase, kick againt the door and the paneling as they move about.

"The day dawns. The porter, who lives with his family in the attic, comes thundering down the stairs; his wooden shoes clatter; the gate bangs and the house shakes. And when all this is over, the lodger above begins to occupy himself with gymnastic exercises; he lifts a heavy iron ball in each hand, but he is not able to hold onto them, and they are continually falling on the floor, while at the same time the young folks in the house, who are going to school, come screaming with all their might. I go to the window and open it to get some fresh air, and it is most refreshing — when I can get it, and when the young woman in the back building is not washing gloves in soapsuds, by which she earns her livelihood. Otherwise it is a pleasant house, and I live with a quiet family!"

This was the report I gave Aunty about my flat, though it was livelier at the time, for the spoken word has a fresher sound than the written.

"You are a poet!" cried Aunty. "Just write down all you have said, and you will be as good as Dickens! Indeed, to me, you are much more intersting. You paint when you speak. You describe your house so that one can see it. It makes one shudder. Go on with your poetry. Put some living beings into it — people, charming people, especially unhappy ones."

I wrote down my description of the house as it stands, with all its sounds, its noises, but included only myself. There was no plot in it. That came later.

IV

It was during wintertime, late at night, after theater hours; it was terrible weather; a snowstorm raged so that one could hardly move along.

Aunty had gone to the theater, and I went there to take her home; it was difficult for one to get anywhere, to say nothing of helping another. All the hiring carriages were engaged. Aunty lived in a distant section of the town, while my dwelling was close to the theater. Had this not been the case, we would have had to take refuge in a sentry box for a while.

We trudged along in the deep snow while the snowflakes whirled around us. I had to lift her, hold onto her, and push her along. Only twice did we fall, but we fell on the soft snow.

We reached my gate, where we shook some of the snow from ourselves. On the stairs, too, we shook some off, and yet there was still enough almost to cover the floor of the anteroom.

We took off our overcoats and boots and what other clothes might be removed. The landlady lent Aunty dry stockings and a nightcap; this she would need, said the landlady, and added that it would be impossible for my aunt to get home that night, which was true. Then she asked Aunty to make use of her parlor, where she would prepare a bed for her on the sofa, in front of the door that led into my room and that was always kept locked. And so she stayed.

The fire burned in my stove, the tea urn was placed on the table, and the little room became cozy, if not as cozy as Aunty's own room, where in the wintertime there are heavy curtains before the door, heavy curtains before the windows, and double carpets on the floor, with three layers of thick paper underneath. One sits there as if in a well-corked bottle, full of warm air; still, as I have said, it was also cozy at my place, while outside the wind was whistling.

Aunty talked and reminisced; she recalled the days of her youth; the brewer came back; many old memories were revived.

She could remember the time I got my first tooth, and the family's delight over it. My first tooth! The tooth of innocence, shining like a little drop of milk — the milk tooth!

When one had come, several more came, a whole rank of them, side by side, appearing both above and below — the finest of children's teeth, though these were only the "vanguard," not the real teeth, which have to last one's whole lifetime.

Then those also appeared, and the wisdom teeth as well, the flank men of each rank, born in pain and great tribulation.

They disappear, too, sometimes every one of them; they disappear before their time of service is up, and when the very last one goes, that is far from a happy day; it is a day for mourning. And so then one considers himself old, even if he feels young.

Such thoughts and talk are not pleasant. Yet we came to talk about all this; we went back to the days of my childhood and talked and talked. It was twelve o'clock before Aunty went to rest in the room near by.

"Good night, my sweet child," she called. "I shall now sleep as if I were in my own bed."

And she slept peacefully; but otherwise there was no peace either in the house or outside. The storm rattled the windows, struck the long, dangling iron hooks against the house, and rang the neighbor's back-yard bell. The lodger upstairs had come home. He was still taking his little nightly tour up and down the room; he then kicked off his boots and went to bed and to sleep; but he snores so that anyone with good ears can hear him through the ceiling.

I found no rest, no peace. The weather did not rest, either; it was lively. The wind howled and sang in its own way; my teeth also began to be lively, and they hummed and sang in their way. An awful toothache was coming on.

There was a draft from the window. The moon shone in upon the floor; the light came and went as the clouds came and went in the stormy weather. There was a restless change of light and shadow, but at last the shadow on the floor began to take shape. I stared at the moving form and felt an icy-cold wind against my face.

On the floor sat a figure, thin and long, like something a child would draw with a pencil on a slate, something supposed to look like a person, a single thin line forming the body, another two lines the arms, each leg being but a single line, and the head having a polygonal shape.

The figure soon became more distinct; it had a very thin, very fine sort of cloth draped around it, clearly showing that the figure was that of a female.

I heard a buzzing sound. Was it she or the wind which was buzzing like a hornet through the crack in the pane?

No, it was she, Madam Toothache herself! Her terrible highness, Satania Infernalis! God deliver and preserve us from her!

"It is good to be here!" she buzzed. "These are nice quarters — mossy ground, fenny ground! Gnats have been buzzing around here, with poison in their stings; and now I am here with such a sting. It must be sharpened on human teeth. Those belonging to the fellow in bed here shine so brightly. They have defied sweet and sour things, heat and cold, nutshells and plum stones; but I shall shake them, make them quake, feed their roots with drafty winds, and give them cold feet!"

That was a frightening speech! She was a terrible visitor!

"So you are a poet!" she said. "Well, I'll make you well versed in all the poetry of toothache! I'll thrust iron and steel into your body! I'll seize all the fibers of your nerves!"

I then felt as if a red-hot awl were being driven into my jawbone; I writhed and twisted.

"A splendid set of teeth," she said, "just like an organ to play upon! We shall have a grand concert, with jew's-harps, kettledrums, and trumpets, piccolo-flute, and a trombone in the wisdom tooth! Grand poet, grand music!"

And then she started to play; she looked terrible, even if one did not see more of her than her hand, the shadowy, gray, ice-cold hand, with the long, thin, pointed fingers; each of them was an instrument of torture; the thumb and the forefinger were the pincers and wrench; the middle finger ended in a pointed awl; the ring finger was a drill, and the little finger squirted gnat's poison.

"I am going to teach you meter!" she said. "A great poet must have a great toothache, a little poet a little toothache!"

"Oh, let me be a little poet!" I begged. "Let me be nothing at all! And I am not a poet; I have only fits of poetry, like fits of toothache. Go away, go away!"

"Will you acknowledge, then, that I am mightier than poetry, philosophy, mathematics, and all the music?" she said. "Mightier than all those notions that are painted on canvas or carved in marble? I am older than every one of them. I was born close to the garden of paradise, just outside, where the wind blew and the wet toadstools grew. It was I who made Eve wear clothes in the cold weather, and Adam also. Believe me, there was power in the first toothache!"

"I believe it all," I said. "But go away, go away!"

"Yes, if you will give up being a poet, never put verse on paper, slate, or any sort of writing material, then I will let you off; but I'll come again if you write poetry!"

"I swear!" I said; "only let me never see or feel you any more!"

"See me you shall, but in a more substantial shape, in a shape more dear to you than I am now. You shall see me as Aunty Mille, and I shall say, 'Write poetry, my sweet boy! You are a great poet, perhaps the greatest we have!' But if you believe me, and begin to write poetry, then I will set music to your verses, and play them on your mouth harp. You sweet child! Remember me when you see Aunt Mille!"

Then she disappeared.

At our parting I received a thrust through my jawbone like that of a red-hot awl; but it soon subsided, and then I felt as if I were gliding along the smooth water; I saw the white water lilies, with their large green leaves, bending and sinking down under me; they withered and dissolved, and I sank, too, and dissolved into peace and rest.

"To die, and melt away like snow!" resounded in the water; "to evaporate into air, to drift away like clouds!"

Great, glowing names and inscriptions on waving banners of victory, the letters patent of immortality, written on the wing of an ephemera, shone down to me through the water.

The sleep was deep, a sleep now without dreams. I did not hear the whistling wind, the banging gate, the ringing of the neighbor's gate bell, or the lodger's strenuous gymnastics.

What happiness!

Then came a gust of wind so strong that the locked door to Aunty's room burst open. Aunty jumped up, put on her shoes, got dressed, and came into my room. I was sleeping like one of God's angels, she said, and she had not the heart to awaken me.

I later awoke by myself and opened my eyes. I had completely forgotten that Aunty was in the house, but I soon remembered it and then remembered my toothache vision. Dream and reality were blended.

"I suppose you did not write anything last night after we said good night?" she said. "I wish you had; you are my poet and shall always be!"

It seemed to me that she smiled rather slyly. I did not know if it was the kindly Aunty Mille, who loved me, or the terrible one to whom I had made the promise the night before.

"Have you written any poetry, sweet child?"

"No, no!" I shouted. "You are Aunty Mille, aren't you?"

"Who else?" she said. And it *was* Aunty Mille.

She kissed me, got into a carriage, and drove home.

I wrote down what is written here. It is not in verse, and it will never be printed.

Yes, here ended the manuscript.

My young friend, the grocer's assistant, could not find the missing sheets; they had gone out into the world like the papers around the salted herring, the butter, and the green soap; they had fulfilled their destiny!

The brewer is dead; Aunty is dead; the student is dead, he whose sparks of genius went into the basket. This is the end of the story—the story of Aunty Toothache.

THE CRIPPLE

THERE was an old manor house where a young, splendid family lived. They had riches and many blessings; they liked to enjoy themselves, and yet they did a lot of good. They wanted to make everybody happy, as happy as they themselves were.

On Christmas Eve a beautifully decorated Christmas tree stood in the large old hall, where fire burned in the fireplaces and fir branches were hung around the old paintings. Here gathered the family and their guests; here they sang and danced.

The Christmas festivities had already been well under way earlier in the evening in the servants' quarters. Here also stood a large fire tree, with lighted red and white candles, small Danish flags, swans and fishing nets cut out of colored paper and filled with candies and other sweets. The poor children from the parish had been invited, and each had its mother along. The mothers didn't pay much attention to the Christmas tree, but looked rather at the Christmas table, where there lay woolen and linen cloths, for dresses and trousers. Yes, the mothers and the older children looked at this; only the smallest children stretched out their hands toward the candles, the tinsel, and the flags. This whole gathering had come early in the afternoon; they had been served Christmas porridge and roasted goose with red cabbage. Then when the Christmas tree had been looked over and the gifts distributed, each got a small glass of punch and apple-filled *aebleskiver*.[1]

When they returned to their own humble rooms, they talked about the "good living," by which they meant the good food they had had, and the presents were again thoroughly inspected.

Now, among these folks were Garden-Kirsten and Garden-Ole. They were married, and earned their lodging and their daily bread by weeding and digging in the manor house garden. At every Christmas party they received a goodly share of the gifts, but then they had five children, and all five of them were clothed by the wealthy family.

"Our masters are generous people," they said. "But then they can afford it, and they get pleasure out of it."

"The four children received some good clothing to wear," said Garden-Ole, "but why is there nothing here for the Cripple? They always used to think of him, too, even if he wasn't at the party."

It was the eldest of the children they called the Cripple, although his name was Hans. When little, he had been the most able and the liveliest child, but all of a sudden he had become "loose in the legs," as they called it. He could neither walk nor stand, and now he had been lying in bed for nearly five years.

"Yes, I got something for him, too," said the mother. "But it's nothing much; it is only a book for him to read!"

"That won't make him fat!" said the father.

But Hans was happy for it. He was a very bright boy who enjoyed reading, but who also used his time for working, doing as much as he, who always had to lie bedridden, could, to be of some benefit. He was useful with his hands, knitted woolen stockings, and, yes, even whole bedcovers. The lady at the manor house had praised him and bought them. It was a book of fairy tales Hans had received; in it there was much to read and much to think about.

"It is of no use here in this house," said the parents, "but let him read, for it passes the time, and he can't always be knitting stockings."

Spring came; green leaves and flowers began to sprout, and the weeds, too, as one may call the nettles, even if the psalm speaks so nicely about them:

> If every king, with power and might,
> Marched forth in stately row,
> They could not make the smallest leaf
> Upon a nettle grow.

---

[1] Danish apple batter cakes each fried in the form of a ball.

There was much to do in the manor house garden, not only for the gardener and his apprentices, but also for Garden-Kirsten and Garden-Ole.

"It's a lot of hard work," they said. "No sooner have we raked the walks, and made them look nice, than they are stepped on again. There is such a run of visitors at the manor house. How much it must cost! But the owners are rich people!"

"Things are strangely divided," said Ole. "We are our Lord's children, says the pastor. Why such a difference, then?"

"That comes from the fall·of man!" said Kirsten.

In the evening they talked about it again, while Cripple-Hans was reading his book of fairy tales. Hard times, work, and toil had made the parents not only hard in the hands but also hard in their judgment and opinion.

They couldn't understand, and consequently couldn't explain, the matter clearly, and as they talked they became more peevish and angry.

"Some people are prosperous and happy; others live in poverty. Why should we suffer because of our first parents' curiosity and disobedience! We would not have behaved as those two did!"

"Yes, we would!" said Cripple-Hans all of a sudden. "It is all here in this book!"

"What's in the book?" asked the parents.

And Hans read for them the old fairy tale about the woodcutter and his wife. They, too, argued about Adam's and Eve's curiosity, which was the cause of their misfortune also. The king of the country then came by. "Follow me home," he said, "and you shall be as well off as I, with a seven-course dinner and a course for display. That course is in a closed tureen, and you must not touch it, for if you do, your days of leisure are over!" "What can there be in the tureen?" said the wife. "That's none of our business," said the husband. "Well, I'm not inquisitive," said the woman, "but I would like to know why we don't dare lift the lid; it must be something delicious!" "I only hope there is nothing mechanical about it," said the man, "such as a pistol shot, which goes off and awakens the whole house!" "Oh, my!" said the woman, and she didn't touch the tureen. But during the night she dreamed that the lid lifted itself, and from the tureen came an odor of the most wonderful punch, such as is served at weddings and funerals. In it lay a large silver coin bearing the following inscription, "If you drink of this punch, you will become the two richest people in the world, and all other people will become beggars!" Just then the woman awoke and told her husband about her dream. "You think too much about that thing," he said. "We could lift it gently," said the woman. "Gently," said the man. And the woman lifted the lid very, very gently. Then two small, sprightly mice sprang out and disappeared into a mousehole. "Good night," said the king. "Now you can go home and lie in your own bed. Don't blame Adam and Eve any more; you two have been just as inquisitive and ungrateful!"

"Where has that story in the book come from?" said Garden-Ole. "It sounds as if it were meant for us. It is something to think about."

The next day they went to work again, and they were roasted by the sun and soaked to the skin by the rain. Within them were grumbling thoughts as they pondered over the story.

The evening was still light at home after they had eaten their milk porridge.

"Read the story about the woodcutter to us again," said Garden-Ole.

"But there are so many other beautiful stories in this book," said Hans, "so many you don't know."

"Yes, but those I don't care about!" said Garden-Ole. "I want to hear the one I know!"

And he and his wife heard it again.

More than one evening they returned to that story.

"It doesn't quite make everything clear to me," said Garden-Ole. "It's the same with people as it is with sweet milk when it sours; some becomes fine cheese, and the other only the thin, watery whey; so it is with people; some are lucky in everything they do, live high all their lives, and know no sorrow or want."

This Cripple-Hans heard. His legs were weak, but his mind was bright. He read for them from his book of fairy tales, read about "The Man Without Sorrow and Want." Yes, where could he be found, for found he must be! The king lay on his sickbed and could not be cured unless he wore the shirt that had belonged to, and been worn on the body of, a man who could truthfully say that he had never known sorrow or want. A command was sent to every country in the world, to all castles and manors, to all prosperous and happy people. But upon thorough questioning, every one of them was found to have known sorrow and want. "I haven't!" said the swineherd, who sat laughing and singing on the edge of the ditch. "I'm the happiest person!" "Then give us your shirt," said the messengers. "You will be paid for it with half of a kingdom." But he had no shirt at all, and yet he called himself the happiest person!

"He was a fine fellow!" shouted Garden-Ole, and he and his wife laughed as they hadn't laughed for years.

Then the schoolmaster came by.

"How pleased you are!" he said. "That is unusual in this house. Have you won a prize in the lottery?"

"No, it isn't that sort of pleasure," said Garden-Ole. "It is because Hans has been reading to us from his book of fairy tales; he read about 'The Man Without Sorrow and Want,' and that fellow had no shirt. Your eyes get moist when you hear such things, and from a printed book, at that! Everyone has a load to carry; one is not alone in that. That, at least, is a comfort!"

"Where did you get that book?" asked the schoolmaster.

"Our Hans got it at Christmastime over a year ago. The manor house family gave it to him. They know he likes reading and, of course, that he is a cripple. At the time, we would rather have seen him get two linen shirts. But that book is unusual; it can almost answer one's thoughts."

The schoolmaster took the book and opened it.

"Let's have the same story again," said Garden-Ole. "I don't quite get it yet. And then he must also read the one about the woodcutter."

These two stories were enough for Ole. They were like two sunbeams pouring into that humble room, into the oppressed thoughts that had made them cross and grumbly. Hans had read the whole book, read it many times. The fairy tales carried him out into the world, where he, of course, could not go because his legs would not carry him. The schoolmaster sat beside his bed; they talked together, and both of them enjoyed it.

From that day on, the schoolmaster visited Hans often when his parents were at work, and every time he came it was a great treat for the boy. How attentively he listened to what the old man told him—about the size of the world and about its many countries, and that the sun was nearly half a million times larger than the earth and so far away that a cannon ball in its course would take twenty-five years to travel from the sun to the earth, while the light beams could reach the earth in eight minutes. Of course, every studious schoolboy knew all that, but to Hans this was all new, and even more wonderful than what he had read in the book of fairy tales.

Two or three times a year the schoolmaster dined with the manor house family, and on one of these occasions he told of how important the book of fairy tales was in the poor house, how alone two stories in it had been the means of spiritual awakening and blessing, that the sickly, clever little boy had, through his reading, brought meditation and joy into the house. When the schoolmaster departed from the manor house, the lady pressed two shiny silver dollars in his hand for little Hans.

"Father and Mother must have them," said the boy, when the schoolmaster brought him the money.

And Garden-Ole and Garden-Kirsten both said, "Cripple-Hans, after all, is also a profit and a blessing to us!"

A couple of days later, when the parents were away at work at the manor house, the owners' carriage stopped outside; it was the kindhearted lady who came, happy that the Christmas gift had afforded so much comfort and pleasure to the boy and his parents. She brought fine bread, fruit, and a bottle of sweet sirup, but what was still more wonderful, she brought him, in a gilded cage, a little blackbird which whistled quite charmingly. The bird cage was placed on the old cabinet close by the boy's bed; there he could see and hear the bird; yes, and people way out on the highway could hear it sing.

Garden-Ole and Garden-Kirsten didn't return home until after the lady had driven away. Even though they saw how happy Hans was, they thought there would only be trouble with the present he had received.

"Rich people don't think very clearly," they said. "Now we have that to look after. Cripple-Hans can't do it. In the end, the cat will get it!"

Eight days went by, and still another eight days. During that time the cat was often in the room without frightening the bird, to say nothing of not harming it.

Then one day a great event occurred. It was in the afternoon, while the parents and the other children were at work, and Hans was quite alone. He had the book of fairy tales in his hand and was reading about the fisherman's wife who got her wishes fulfilled; she wished to be king, and that she became; she wished to be emperor, and that, too, she became; but then she wished to be the good Lord—and thereupon she again sat in the muddy ditch she had come from.

Now that story had nothing whatsoever to do with the bird or the cat, but it happened to be the story he was reading when this occurrence took place; he always remembered that afterward.

The cage stood on the cabinet, and the cat stood on the floor and stared, with its yellow-green eyes, at the bird. There was something in the cat's look that seemed to say, "How beautiful you are! I'd like to eat you!" That Hans understood; he could read it in the cat's face.

"Get away, cat!" he shouted. "You get out of this room!"

It looked as if the cat were getting ready to leap. Hans couldn't reach it and had nothing to throw at it but his greatest treasure, the book of fairy tales. This he threw, but the cover was loose and flew to one side, while the book itself, with all its leaves, flew to the other side. The cat slowly stepped backward in the room and looked at Hans as if to say, "Don't get yourself mixed up in this matter, little Hans! I can walk and I can jump. You can do neither."

Hans was greatly worried and kept his eyes on the cat, while the bird also became uneasy. There wasn't a person he could call; it seemed as if the cat knew that, and it prepared itself to jump again. Hans shook his bedcover at it — he could, remember, use his hands — but the cat paid no attention to the bedcover. And after Hans had thrown it without avail, the cat leaped up onto the chair and onto the sill; there it was closer to the bird.

Hans could feel his own warm blood rushing through his body, but that he didn't think of; he thought only about the cat and the bird. The boy could not get out of bed without help; nor, of course, could he stand on his legs, much less walk. It was as if his heart turned inside him when he saw the cat leap straight from the window onto the cabinet and push the cage so that it overturned. The bird fluttered about bewilderedly in the cage.

Hans screamed; a great shock went through him. And without thinking about it, he sprang out of bed, moved toward the cabinet, chased the cat down, and got hold of the cage, where the bird was flying about in great fear. Holding the cage in his hand, he ran out of the door, onto the road. Then tears streamed from his eyes, and joyously he shouted. "I can walk! I can walk!" He had recovered the use of his limbs. Such a thing can happen, and it had indeed happened to Hans.

The schoolmaster lived near by, and to him he ran on his bare feet, clad only in his shirt and jacket, and with the bird in the cage.

"I can walk!" he shouted. "Oh, Lord, my God!" And he cried out of sheer joy.

And there was joy in the house of Garden-Ole and Garden-Kirsten. "We shall never live to see a happier day," said both of them.

Hans was called to the manor house. He had not walked that road for many years. The trees and the nut bushes, which he knew so well, seemed to nod to him and say, "Good day, Hans! Welcome back out here!" The sun shone on his face and right into his heart.

The owners of the manor house, that young, blessed couple, let him sit with them, and looked as happy as if he were one of their own family. But the happiest of the two was the lady, for she had given him the book of fairy tales and the little songbird. The bird was now dead, having died of fright; but it had been the means of getting his health back. And the book had brought the awakening to him and his parents; he still had it, and he wanted to keep it and read it, no matter how old he became. Now he also could be of help to his family. He wanted to learn a trade; most of all he wanted to be a bookbinder, "because," he said, "then I can get all the new books to read!"

Later in the afternoon the lady called both his parents up to her. She and her husband had talked about Hans — he was a fine and clever boy, with a keen appreciation of reading and a capacity for learning. Our Lord always rewards the good.

That evening the parents were really happy when they returned home from the major house, especially Kirsten.

But the following week she cried, for then little Hans went away. He was dressed in good, new clothes. He was a good boy, but now he must travel far away across the sea, go to school, and learn Latin. And many years would pass before they would see him again.

The book of fairy tales he did not take with him, because his parents wanted to keep that in remembrance. And the father often read from it, but only the two stories, for those he understood.

And they had letters from Hans, each one happier than the last. He lived with nice people, in good circumstances. But best of all, he liked to go to school; there was so much to learn and to know. He only wished to live to be a hundred years old, and eventually to become a schoolmaster.

"If we could only live to see it!" said the parents, and held each other's hands.

"Just think of what has happened to Hans!" said Ole. "Our Lord thinks also of the poor man's child! And to think that this should have happened to the Cripple! Isn't it as if Hans might have read it for us from the book of fairy tales!"

THE GATE KEY

EVERY key has a history, and there are many kinds of keys—a chamberlain's key, a watch key, Saint Peter's key. We could tell you about all the keys; but now we will only tell about the Councilor's gate key.

It had come into being at a locksmith's, but it might well have believed it had been made by a blacksmith, the way the man had worked on it with hammer and file. It was too large for one's trouser pocket, so it had to be put into the overcoat pocket. There it often lay in utter darkness; yet it had its own special hanging place on the wall, beside a childhood silhouette of the Councilor, in which he looked like a dumpling dressed in a frilled shirt.

It is said that every human being acquires in his character and conduct something from the astrological sign under which he has been born, such as the Bull, the Virgin, or Scorpion, as they are called in the almanacs. The Councilor's wife never mentioned the names of any of these; she said that her husband was born under the sign of the "Wheelbarrow," for he always had to be pushed on. His father had pushed him into an office; his mother had pushed him into matrimony; and his wife had pushed him on to become a councilor; the latter fact, however, she did not mention, being a good, sensible sort of woman who kept quiet in the right place and spoke and pushed in the right place.

He was now along in years—"well proportioned," as he said himself—a well-read man, good-natured, and "key wise" as well, which is something we shall better understand later. He was always in a good humor, loved all mankind, and liked to talk to everybody. If he went into the city, it was difficult to get him home again when his wife was not with him to push him along. He simply had to talk to every acquaintance he met; he had a lot of acquaintances, and this often made him late for dinner. Mrs. Councilor would sit at the window and watch for him. "Here he comes," she would say to the maid; "put the pot on the fire. Now he has stopped to speak to somebody, so take the pot off, or the food will be cooked too much. Now he is finally coming, so put the pot on again!"

But then he wouldn't come, after all. He would stand right under the windows of the house and nod up to her, and if an acquaintance happened to come by then, he could not keep from saying a few words to him; if while he was talking to this one, another one came by, he would take hold of the first by the buttonhole, clasp the other's hand, and shout to a third who wanted to pass by.

This was a heavy trial for the patience of the Councilor's wife. "Councilor! Councilor!" she would shout. "Yes, indeed, that man was born under the sign of the 'Wheelbarrow'; he won't move unless he is being pushed."

He was very fond of visiting bookshops and looking at books and periodicals. He would give his bookseller a small amount of money for the privilege of reading the new books at home, which meant he had permission to cut the leaves of the books along the side but not across the top, for then they could not be sold as new. He was a living newspaper, but a harmless one, and knew everything about engagements, weddings, and funerals, book talk and town talk. Yes, and he even gave out mysterious hints regarding matters no one else knew anything about. This mysterious information came from the gate key.

The Councilor and his wife had lived in their own house since young and newly married, and they'd had that very same gate key since then; but in those days they hadn't yet come to know of its unusual powers, and not until much later had they learned of these.

It was at the time of King Frederick VI. Copenhagen had no gas then; it had only train-oil lamps; it had no Tivoli Gardens, no Casino Theater, no streetcars, and no railways. It had very few public amusements, compared with what it now has. On Sundays one would go for a walk, out beyond the city gates, to the Assistants' Churchyard, read the inscriptions on the graves, sit down in the grass, eat from one's food basket, and drink a glass of schnapps; or one would go to Frederiksberg, where in front of the palace military music was played; and many people would go to see the royal family rowing about in the small, narrow canals of the park, with the old King himself steering the boat, and he and the Queen greeting everyone, without distinction of rank. Well-to-do families from the city would come to this place and drink their afternoon tea. They could get hot water at a small farmhouse in the field outside the park, but they had to bring their own tea service along.

One sunny Sunday afternoon the Councillor and his wife went out to the park, the servant girl walking in front with the tea service, a basket of food, and a "sip of Spendrup's Liqueur."

"Bring the gate key," Mrs. Councilor had said, "so we can get in by ourselves when we return; you know, they lock the gate here at nightfall, and the bell cord was broken this morning! It will be late before we get home! After we've been in Frederiksberg Park, we are going to the Casorti's theater at Vesterbro to see the pantomime, *Harlequin, Chief of the Thrashers.* You see them come down in a cloud; it costs two kroner a person."

And so they went ot Frederiksberg, heard the music, saw the royal barges with their waving banners, saw the old King and the white swans. After drinking some very good tea, they hurried away; yet they did not arrive at the theater on time.

The rope-dance act was finished, the dance on stilts was finished, and the pantomime had started; as always, they were too late, and that was the Councilor's fault; every moment on the road, he had stopped to speak to an acquaintance. Within the theater he also found several good friends, and when the performance was over, he and his wife were obliged to accompany a family home at Vesterbro, to enjoy a glass of punch; they would stop for only ten minutes. But this was extended to a whole hour. They talked and talked. Especially entertaining was a Swedish baron, or, perhaps, he was German, for the Councilor hadn't quite caught which—but, on the other hand, the trick with the key that the baron taught him he caught and always remembered. This trick was extraordinarily interesting! He could get the key to answer everything that one asked it, even questions pertaining to the most secret matters. The Councilor's gate key was particularly suitable for performing this trick; its bit was heavy, and this part had to hang downward. The baron let the handle of the key rest on the forefinger of his right hand. There it hung loosely and lightly, and every pulsebeat in his finger could put it into motion and make it swing; and if this failed to happen, the baron understood how unnoticeably to make it turn as he wished. Every turn denoted a letter of the alphabet, and as many letters as desired, from A on through the alphabet, could be indicated by the key. When the first letter of a word was revealed, the key would turn to the opposite side; then the next letter would be sought, and in that manner one got whole words, sentences, and answers to questions. It was all a fake, but at any rate provided amusement; this was the Councilor's first thought, but he did not retain it; he became very engrossed in the key.

"Husband! Husband!" cried Mrs. Councilor. "The Westgate closes at twelve o'clock! We won't get through; we have only a quarter of an hour in which to hurry there."

They had to hurry indeed; several persons who were going into the city soon got ahead of them. They finally approached the outside guardhouse as the clock was striking twelve and the gates were being slammed shut. A number of people were locked out, and among these were the Councilor and his wife, with their servant girl, tea service, and empty food basket. Some stood there greatly frightened, while others were very annoyed, each reacting in his own manner. What could be done? Fortunately, an ordinance had been passed of late that one of the city gates, the Northgate, should not be locked at night, and there pedestrians were allowed to slip through the guardhouse into the city.

The road to the Northgate was by no means short, but the weather was fine, the sky bright with starlight and shooting stars; the frogs were croaking in the ditches and ponds. The party began singing and sang one song after another, but the Councilor did not sing; nor did he look up at the stars or even look at his own feet. He then fell down at the edge of the ditch, the full length of his body alongside it. One might have thought that he had had too much to drink; but it was not the punch, it was the key, that had gone to his head, and kept on turning there. They finally reached the Northgate guardhouse, slipped across the bridge and into the city.

"Now I am happy again," said the Councilor's wife. "Here's our gate."

"But where is the gate key," said the Councilor. It was neither in the back pocket nor in the side pocket.

"Good gracious!" cried the Councilor's wife. "Haven't you got the key? You must have lost it after letting the Baron use it for the key trick. How will we get in now? You know the bell cord was broken this morning, and the watchman doesn't have a key to our home. We are in a hopeless situation!"

The servant girl began to cry. The Councilor was the only one who showed presence of mind.

"We must break in a windowpane at the grocer's downstairs!" he said, "get him up, and then we can get into the building."

He broke one pane; he broke two. "Petersen!" he shouted, as he put the handle of his umbrella in through the windowpanes. Whereupon the grocer's daughter began to scream loudly. The grocer threw open the door of his shop and shouted, "Watchman!" And before he had a chance to see and recognize the Councilor's family and let them in, the watchman blew his whistle, and in the next street another watchman answered and whistled. People appeared in the windows. "Where is the fire? Where is the cause of all the excitement?" they asked, and were still asking such questions even after the Councilor was in his room. There he removed his overcoat—and in it lay the gate key, not in the pocket, but inside the lining; it had slipped through a hole that should not have been in the pocket.

From that night on, the gate key held a unique and great importance, not only when it was taken out in the evening, but also when remaining at home, for in either case the Councilor would show how clever he was by making the key answer questions. He would think of the most likely answer and then pretend to let the key give it. Finally, he himself came to believe in the power of the key.

That was not so of the Pharmacist, however, a young man closely related to the Councilor's wife. The Pharmacist had a good head, a critical mind; he had, as a mere schoolboy, sent in critical articles on books and the theater, but without his signature, which is always important. He was what one calls a *bel esprit,* but he by no means believed in spirits, and, least of all, key spirits.

"Yes, I believe, I believe," he said, "blessed Mr. Councilor, I believe in gate keys and all key spirits as firmly as I believe in that new science which is beginning to become known—the table dance and the spirits in old and new furniture. Have you heard about that? I have! I have doubted—you know I am a skeptic—but I have been converted by reading, in a quite reliable foreign paper, a dreadful story. Councilor, can you imagine! I will give you the story as I read it. Two clever children had seen their parents raise the spirits in a large dining-room table. The little ones were alone, and decided they would try, in the same manner, to rub life into an old chest of drawers. Life came, for a spirit was awakened; but it did not tolerate the commands of mere children; it arose, and the chest of drawers creaked; it then shot out the drawers, and with its wooden legs put each of the children in a separate drawer. The chest of drawers then ran off with them, out the open door, down the stairs, into the street, and over to canal, where it jumped out into water and drowned both the children. Their little bodies were given Christian burial, but the chest of drawers was taken to the town hall, tried for murder, and burned alive in the market place! I have read this," said the Pharmacist, "in a foreign paper; it is not something I have invented myself. This is the truth, and may the key take me if it isn't! I swear to it — on my oath!"

The Councilor found that such talk was all too much like a coarse joke. The two could never speak agreeably about the key. The Pharmacist was key ignorant.

The Councilor made progress in his key knowledge; the key was his diversion and channel of wisdom.

One evening, as the Councilor was getting ready to go to bed, and was half undressed, there was a knock on the front door. It was the shopkeeper from downstairs who was calling at this late hour; he, too, was half undressed, but he had suddenly had a thought, he said, which he was afraid he would not be able to retain through the night.

"It is my daughter Lotte-Lene I must talk about. She is a beautiful girl, and has been confirmed, and now I would like to see her well provided for."

"But I am not as yet a widower!" said the Councilor, and chuckled, "and I have no son to offer her."

"You must understand me, Councilor," said the man from downstairs. "She can play the piano, and she can sing; you must be able to hear her upstairs. You have no idea of all the things that little girl is able to do; she can talk and entertain people. She is made for the stage, and that is a good course for pretty girls of good families to take; they may even have an opportunity to marry a count, though neither I nor Lotte-Lene are thinking of that. She can indeed sing and play the piano, so the other day I took her up to the singing school. She sang; but she doesn't have a beer bass, as I call it in women, nor does she shriek those very high canary-bird notes which they now demand in singers, and so they advised her strongly against pursuing that career. Well, I thought, if she can't become a singer, she can always become an actress; that only requires the ability to speak. Today I talked about it to the Instructor, as they call him. 'Is she well read?' he asked. 'No,' I said, 'not at all.' 'But it is necessary for an actress to be well read!' said he. She still has time for that, was my opinion; and then I went home. She can go to a rental library and read what is to be had there, I thought.

"But then tonight, while I was undressing, it occurred to me — why rent books when one can borrow them? The Councilor has plenty of books; let her read them; there is enough reading here for her, and it could be hers, gratis!"

"Lotte-Lene is a nice girl," said the Councilor, "a beautiful girl! She shall have books to read. But has she what one calls grit and spirit — aptitude — genius? And, what is equally important, has she luck with her?"

"She has twice won in the lottery," said the grocer from downstaris. "Once she won a clothes cabinet, and another time six pairs of bed sheets; that I call luck, and that she has!"

"I shall ask the key," said the Councilor. And he placed the key on his right forefinger, and on the grocer's right forefinger as well, and then the key swung and gave out letter after letter.

The key said, "Victory and luck!" And so Lotte-Lene's future was decided.

The Councilor at once gave her two books to read, *Dyveke* and Knigge's *Social Intercourse*.

That night marked the beginning of a closer acquaintance between Lotte-Lene and the Councilor and his wife. She would come upstairs to the couple, and the Councilor found her to be a sensible girl; she believed in him and the key. The Councilor's wife saw something childish and innocent in the frankness with which she would at every moment show her great ignorance. The couple was fond of her, he in his way and she in hers, and Lotte-Lene was fond of them.

"It smells so lovely upstairs," Lotte-Lene would say. There was an odor, a fragrance, an apple fragrance, in the hallway, where the Councilor's wife had put away a whole barrel of gray-stone apples. There was also an incense odor of roses and lavender throughout all the rooms. "There is something refined in that!" Lotte-Lene would say.

Then, too, her eyes were pleased by the many flowers the Councilor's wife always had. Even in the middle of winter, lilacs and cherry-tree slips bloomed here. The leafless twigs were cut off and put into water and in the warm room soon bore leaves and flowers.

"One would have thought that all life was gone from these naked branches, but see how they rise from the dead. It has never occurred to me before," said Lotte-Lene, "how wonderful nature is!"

And the Councilor let her look at his "key book," in which were written strange things the key had said—even about the half of an apple cake that had disappeared from the cupboard on the very evening that the servant girl had had her sweetheart there for a visit. The Councilor had asked his key, "Who has eaten the apple cake, the cat or the sweetheart?" and the key had replied, "The sweetheart." The Councilor had already thought so before asking the key; and the servant girl had confessed, "That cursed key knows everything!"

"Yes, isn't it strange!" said the Councilor. "That key, that key! And about Lotte-Lene it has said, 'Victory and luck.' That we shall see! I swear to it."

"That's wonderful" said Lotte-Lene.

The Councilor's wife was not so confident, but she did not express her doubts when her husband was within hearing distance. She later told Lotte-Lene in confidence that the Councilor, when a young man, had been quite taken with the theater. Had someone pushed him a little in that direction, he surely would have become an actor; his family, however, had pushed him in the opposite direction. But, he had still aspired to the stage, and to further that ambition he had written a play.

"This is a great secret that I am entrusting you with, little Lotte-Lene. The play was not bad; it was accepted at the Royal Theater, and then hissed out, and no one has since heard of it, for which I am glad. I am his wife and know him. Now you want such a career, too. I wish you all that is good, but I don't think that things will work out as predicted; I don't believe in the gate key."

Lotte-Lene believed in it, and in that belief she was united with the Councilor. Within their hearts they had a mutual understanding, in all honor and chastity.

The girl had many qualifications that the Councilor's wife valued. Lotte-Lene knew how to make starch from potatoes, make silk gloves from old silk stockings, and recover her silk dancing shoes, although she could afford to buy all her clothes new. She had, as the grocer said, pennies in the table drawer and credit notes in her money safe. She would make just the wife for the Pharmacist, thought the Councilor's wife, but she did not say so, and of course didn't permit the key to say anything about it. The Pharmacist was going to settle down soon and have his own pharmacy in one of the nearest and largest provincial towns.

Lotte-Lene was continually reading *Dyveke* and Knigge's *Social Intercourse.* She kept the two books for two years, and by the end of that time she had learned one, *Dyveke,* by heart—all the parts, although she wished to play only one, that of Dyveke; she did not, however, want to appear at first in the capital, where there is so much envy, and where they would not have her, anyway. She wanted to start her artistic career, as the Councilor called it, in one of the country's large provincial towns. Now that, strangely enough, turned out to be the same place where the youthful Pharmacist had settled down as the youngest of the town's pharmacists.

The great, long-awaited night came on which Lotte-Lene was to make her debut and have "victory and luck," as the key had said.. The Councilor was not there, for he lay in his bed, and his wife was nursing him; he had to have warm napkins and camomile tea; the napkins about his body and the tea in his body.

While the couple was absent from the *Dyveke* performance, the Pharmacist was there, and wrote a letter about it to his relative, the Councilor's wife.

"Dyveke's ruff was the best thing about it," he wrote. "If I had had the Councilor's gate key in my pocket, I would have pulled it out and used it as a whistle; she deserved it, and the key deserved it, because of its nasty lie about her 'victory and luck.' "

The Councilor read the letter. It was all spitefulness, he said, key hatred, aimed at that innocent girl. And as soon as he was out of bed and was himself again, he sent a short but poisonous note to the Pharmacist, who in turn replied as if he had seen only jest and good humor in the whole epistle. He thanked him for this and for any future contribution to the revelation of the incomparable worth and significance of keys; next he confided to the Councilor that, apart from his activities as an apothecary, he was writing a great key novel in which all the characters were keys and keys alone. A gate key naturally was the central character and—patterned after the Councilor's gate key—was gifted with prophetic vision and second sight; around this all the other keys had to revolve—the old chamberlain's key, experienced in the splendor and festivity of the court; the watch key, small, refined, and distinguished, but worth only a few pennies at the ironmonger's; the key to the church pew, which counted itself among the clergy, and which, from remaining one night in its keyhole in the church, could see ghosts; the larder key, the wine-cellar key, and the coal-cellar key all appeared, and bowed before, and turned around, the gate key. The sunbeams brightened it into silver, and the wind, that spirit of the earth, entered its body and made it whistle!

It was the key of all keys; it was the Councilor's gate key. It was now the key of the heavenly gate itself; it was the papal key; it was infallible!

"Wickedness!" said the Councilor. "Great wickedness!"

He and the Pharmacist never saw each other again—except once, and that was at the funeral of the Councilor's wife.

She was the first to die. There were sorrow and an emptiness in the house.

Even the slips of cherry which had thrown out fresh roots and flowers seemed to mourn and fade away; they stood forgotten, for she was not there to tend them.

The Councilor and the Pharmacist walked behind her coffin, side by side, as the two nearest relations of the departed. This was not the time, nor were they in the mood, for quarreling. Lotte-Lene tied the mourning crape around the Councilor's hat. She was living in the house again, having long since returned without victory and luck in her career. Yet that still might come; Lotte-Lene had a future before her; the key had said so, and the Councilor had said so.

She went up to him. They talked about the departed and they wept, for Lotte-Lene was tenderhearted; but when they talked about the art, Lotte-Lene felt strong. "Life in the theater is charming," she said, "but there is so much nonsense and envy! I would rather go my own way. Myself first, then art!"

Knigge had told the truth in his chapter about actors; that she was aware of; the key had not told the truth, but she never spoke of this to the Councilor; she was fond of him. Besides, the gate key was his comfort and relief during the whole year of mourning. He gave it questions, and it gave him answers.

And when the year had passed, and he and Lotte-Lene were sitting together one inspiring evening, he asked the key, "Will I marry, and whom will I marry?" No one pushed him, but he pushed the key, and it answered, "Lotte-Lene!"

So it was said, and Lotte-Lene became Mrs. Councilor.

"Victory and luck!"

And these words had been said before — by the gate key.

WHAT OLD JOHANNE TOLD

THE wind whistles in the old willow tree. It is as if one were hearing a song; the wind sings it; the tree tells it. If you do not understand it, then ask old Johanne in the poorhouse; she knows about it; she was born here in the parish.

Many years ago, when the King's Highway still lay along here, the tree was already large and conspicuous. It stood, as it still stands, in front of the tailor's whitewashed timber house, close to the ditch, which then was so large that the cattle could be watered there, and where in the summertime the little peasant boys used to run about naked and paddle in the water. Underneath the tree stood a stone milepost cut from a big rock; now it is overturned, and a bramblebush grows over it.

The new King's Highway was built on the other side of the rich farmer's manor house; the old one became a field path; the ditch became a puddle overgrown with duckweed; if a frog tumbled down into it, the greenery was parted, and one saw the black water; all around it grew, and still grow, "muskedonnere," buckbean, and yellow iris.

The tailor's house was old and crooked; the roof was a hotbed for moss and houseleek. The dovecot had collapsed, and starlings built their nests there. The swallows hung nest after nest on the house gable and all along beneath the roof; it was just as if luck itself lived there.

And once it had; now, however, this was a lonely and silent place. Here in solitude lived weak-willed "Poor Rasmus," as they called him. He had been born here; he had played here, had leaped across meadow and over hedge, had splashed, as a child, in the ditch, and had climbed up the old tree. The tree would raise its big branches with pride and beauty, just as it raises them yet, but storms had already bent the trunk a little, and time had given it a crack. Wind and weather have since lodged earth in the crack, and there grow grass and greenery; yes, and even a little serviceberry has planted itself there.

When in spring the swallows came, they flew about the tree and the roof and plastered and patched their old nests, while Poor Rasmus let his nest stand or fall as it liked. His motto was, "What good will it do?" — and it had been his father's, too.

He stayed in his home. The swallows flew away, but they always came back, the faithful creatures! The starling flew away, but it returned, too, and whistled its song again. Once Rasmus had known how, but now he neither whistled nor sang.

The wind whistled in the old willow tree then, just as it now whistles; indeed, it is as if one were hearing a song; the wind sings it; the tree tells it. And if you do not understand it, then ask old Johanne in the poorhouse; she knows about it; she knows about everything of old; she is like a book of chronicles, with inscriptions and old recollections.

At the time the house was new and good, the country tailor, Ivar Ölse, and his wife, Maren, moved into it — industrious, honest folk, both of them. Old Johanne was then a child; she was the daughter of a wooden-shoemaker — one of the poorest in the parish. Many a good sandwich did she receive from Maren, who was in no want of food. The lady of the manor house liked Maren, who was always laughing and happy and never downhearted. She used her tongue a good deal, but her hands also. She could sew as fast as she could use her mouth, and, moreover, she cared for her house and children; there were nearly a dozen children — eleven altogether; the twelfth never made its appearance.

"Poor people always have a nest full of youngsters," growled the master of the manor house. "If one could drown them like kittens, and keep only one or two of the strongest, it would be less of a misfortune!"

"God have mercy!" said the tailor's wife. "Children are a blessing from God; they are such a delight in the house. Every child is one more Lord's prayer. If times are bad, and one has many mouths to feed, why, then a man works all the harder and finds out ways and means honestly; our Lord fails not when we do not fail."

The lady of the manor house agreed with her; she nodded kindly and patted Maren's cheeks; she had often done so; yes, and had kissed her as well, but that had been when the lady was a little child and Maren her nursemaid. The two were fond of each other, and this feeling did not wane.

Each year at Christmastime winter provisions would arrive at the tailor's house from the manor house — a barrel of meal, a pig, two geese, a tub of butter, cheese, and apples. That was indeed an asset to the larder. Ivar Ölse looked quite pleased, too, but soon came out with his old motto, "What good will it do?"

The house was clean and tidy, with curtains in the windows, and flowers as well, both carnations and balsams. A sampler hung in a picture frame, and close by hung a love letter in rhyme, which Maren Ölse herself had written; she knew how to put rhymes together. She was almost a little proud of the family name Ölse; it was the only word in the Danish language that rhymed with *pölse* [sausage] "At least that's an advantage to have over other people," she said, and laughed. She always kept her good humor, and never said, like her husband, "What good will it do?" Her motto was, "Depend on yourself and on our Lord." So she did, and that kept them all together. The children thrived, grew out over the nest, went out into the world, and prospered well.

Rasmus was the smallest; he was such a pretty child that one of the great portrait painters in the capital had borrowed him to paint from, and in the picture he was as naked as when he had come into this world. That picture was now hanging in the King's palace. The lady of the manor house saw it, and recognized little Rasmus, though he had no clothes on.

But now came hard times. The tailor had rheumatism in both hands, on which great lumps appeared. No doctor could help him, not even the wise Stine, who herself did some "doctoring."

"One must not be downhearted,' said Maren. "It never helps to hang the head. Now that we no longer have father's two hands to help us, I must try to use mine all the faster. Little Rasmus, too, can use the needle." He was already sitting on the sewing table, whistling and singing. He was a happy boy. "But he should not sit there the whole day long," said the mother; "that would be a shame for the child. He should play and jump about, too."

The shoemaker's Johanne was his favorite playmate. Her folks were still poorer than Rasmus'. She was not pretty. She went about barefooted, and her clothes hung in rags, for she had no one to mend them, and to do it herself did not occur to her—she was a child, and as happy as a bird in our Lord's sunshine.

By the stone milepost, under the large willow tree, Rasmus and Johanne played. He had ambitious thoughts; he would one day become a fine tailor and live in the city, where there were master tailors who had ten workmen at the table; this he had heard from his father. There he would be an apprentice, and there he would become a master tailor, and then Johanne could come to visit him; and if by that time she knew how to cook, she could prepare the meals for all of them and have a large apartment of her own. Johanne dared not expect that, but Rasmus believed it could happen. They sat beneath the old tree, and the wind whistled in the branches and leaves; it seemed as if the wind were singing and the tree talking.

In the autumn every single leaf fell off; rain dripped from the bare branches. "They will be green again," said Mother Ölse.

"What good will it do?" said her husband. "New year, new worries about our livelihood."

"The larder is full," said the wife. "We can thank our good lady for that. I am healthy and have plenty of strength. It is sinful for us to complain."

The master and lady of the manor house remained there in the country over Christmas, but the week after the new year, they were to go to the city, where they would spend the winter in festivity and amusement. They would even go to a reception and ball given by the King himself. The lady had brought two rich dresses from France; they were of such material, of such fashion, and so well sewn that the tailor's Maren had never seen such magnificence. She asked the lady if she might come up to the house with her husband, so that he could see the dresses as well. Such things had surely never been seen by a country tailor, she said. He saw them and had not a word to say until he returned home, and what he did say was only what he always said, "What good will it do?" And this time he spoke the truth.

The master and lady of the manor house went to the city, and the balls and merrymaking began. But amid all the splendor the old gentleman died, and the lady then, after all, did not wear her grand dresses. She was so sorrowful and was dressed from head to toe in heavy black mourning. Not so much as a white tucker was to be seen. All the servants were in black; even the state coach was covered with fine black cloth.

It was an icy-cold night; the snow glistened and the stars twinkled. The heavy hearse brought the body from the city to the country church, where it was to be laid in the family vault. The steward and the parish bailiff were waiting on horseback, with torches, in front of the cemetery gate. The church was lighted up, and the pastor stood in the open church door to receive the body. The coffin was carried up into the chancel; the whole congregation followed. The pastor spoke, and a psalm was sung. The lady was present in the church; she had been driven there in the black-draped state coach, which was black inside as well as outside; such a carriage had never before been seen in the parish.

Throughout the winter, people talked about this impressive display of grief; it was indeed a "nobleman's funeral."

"One could well see how important the man was," said the village folk. "He was nobly born and he was nobly buried."

"What good will it do him?" said the tailor. "Now he has neither life nor goods. At least we have one of these."

"Don't speak such words!" said Maren. "He has everlasting life in the kingdom of heaven."

"Who told you that, Maren?" said the tailor. "A dead man is good manure, but this man was too highborn to even do the soil any good; he must lie in a church vault."

"Don't speak so impiously!" said Maren. "I tell you again he has everlasting life!"

"Who told you that, Maren?" repeated the tailor. And Maren threw her apron over little Rasmus; he must not hear that kind of talk. She carried him off into the peathouse and wept.

"The words you heard over there, little Rasmus, were not your father's; it was the evil one who was passing through the room and took your father's voice. Say your Lord's Prayer. We'll both say it." She folded the child's hands. "Now I am happy again," she said. "Have faith in yourself and in our Lord."

The year of mourning came to an end. The widow lady dressed in half mourning, but she had whole happiness in her heart. It was rumored that she had a suitor and was already thinking of marriage. Maren knew something about it, and the pastor knew a little more.

On Palm Sunday, after the sermon, the banns of marriage for the widow lady and her betrothed were to be published. He was a wood carver or a sculptor; just what the name of his profession was, people did not know; at that time not many had heard of Thorvaldsen and his art. The future master of the manor was not a nobleman, but still he was a very stately man. His was one profession that people did not understand, they said; he cut out images, was clever in his work and young and handsome. "What good will it do?" said Tailor Ölse.

On Palm Sunday the banns were read from the pulpit; then followed a psalm and Communion. The tailor, his wife, and little Rasmus were in church; the parents received Communion, while Rasmus sat in the pew, for he was not yet confirmed. Of late there had been a shortage of clothes in the tailor's house; the old ones had been turned, and turned again, stitched and patched. Now they were all three dressed in new clothes, but of black material — as at a funeral. They were dressed in the drapery from the funeral coach. The man had a jacket and trousers of it; Maren, a high-necked dress, and Rasmus, a whole suit to grow in until confirmation time. Both the outside and inside cloth from the funeral carriage had been used. No one needed to know what it had been used for before, but people soon got to know.

The wise woman, Stine, and a couple of other equally wise women, who did not live on their wisdom, said that the clothes would bring sickness and disease into the household. "One cannot dress oneself in cloth from a funeral carriage without riding to the grave." The wooden-shoemaker's Johanne cried when she heard this talk. And it so happened that the tailor became more and more ill from that day on, until it seemed apparent who was going to suffer that fate. And it proved to be so.

On the first Sunday after Trinity, tailor Ölse died, leaving Maren alone to keep things together. She did, keeping faith in herself and in our Lord.

The following year Rasmus was confirmed. He was then ready to go to the city as an apprentice to a master tailor — not, after all, one with ten assistants at the table, but with one; little Rasmus might be counted as a half. He was happy, and he looked delighted indeed, but Johanne wept; she was fonder of him than she had realized. The tailor's wife remained in the old house and carried on the business.

It was at that time that the new King's Highway was opened, and the old one, by the willow tree and the tailor's, became a field path, with duckweed growing over the water left in the ditch there; the milepost tumbled over, for it had nothing to stand for, but the tree kept itself strong and beautiful, the wind whistling among its branches and leaves.

The swallows flew away, and the starlings flew away, but they came again in the spring. And when they came back the fourth time, Rasmus, too, came back to his home. He had served his apprenticeship, and was a handsome but slim youth. Now he would buckle up his knapsack and see foreign countries; that was what he longed for. But his mother clung to him; home was the best place! All the other children were scattered about; he was the youngest, and the house would be his. He could get plenty of work if he would go about the neighborhood — be a traveling tailor, and sew for a fortnight at this farm and a fortnight at that. That would be traveling, too. And Rasmus followed his mother's advice.

So again he slept beneath the roof of his birthplace. Again he sat under the old willow tree and heard it whistle. He was indeed good-looking, and he could whistle like a bird and sing new and old songs.

He was well liked at the big farms, especially at Klaus Hansen's, the second richest farmer in the parish. Else, the daughter, was like the loveliest flower to look at, and she was always laughing. There were people who were unkind enough to say that she laughed simply to show her pretty teeth. She was happy indeed, and always in the humor for playing tricks; everything suited her.

She was fond of Rasmus, and he was fond of her, but neither of them said a word about it. So he went about being gloomy; he had more of his father's disposition than his mother's. He was in a good humor only when Else was present; then they both laughed, joked, and played tricks; but although there was many a good opportunity, he did not say a single word about his love. "What good will it do?" was his thought. "Her parents look for a profitable marriage for her, and that I cannot give her. The wisest thing for me to do would be to leave." But he could not leave. It was as if Else had a string fastened to him; he was like a trained bird with her; he sang and whistled for her pleasure and at her will.

Johanne, the shoemaker's daughter, was a servant girl at the farm, employed for common work. She drove the milk cart in the meadow, where she and the other girls milked the cows; yes, and she even had to cart manure when it was necessary. She never came into the sitting room and didn't see much of Rasmus or Else, but she heard that the two were as good as engaged.

"Now Rasmus will be well off," she said. "I cannot begrudge him that." And her eyes became quite wet. But there was really nothing to cry about.

There was a market in the town. Klaus Hansen drove there, and Rasmus went along; he sat beside Else, both going there and coming home. He was numb from love, but he didn't say a word about it.

"He ought to say something to me about the matter," thought the girl, and there she was right. "If he won't talk, I'll have to frighten him into it."

And soon there was talk at the farm that the richest farmer in the parish had proposed to Else; and so he had, but no one knew what answer she had given.

Thoughts buzzed around in Rasmus' head.

One evening Else put a gold ring on her finger and then asked Rasmus what that signified.

"Betrothal," he said.

"And with whom do you think?" she asked.

"With the rich farmer?" he said.

"There, you have hit it," she said, nodding, and then slipped away.

But he slipped away, too; he went home to his mother's house like a bewildered man and packed his knapsack. He wanted to go out into the wide world; even his mother's tears couldn't stop him.

He cut himself a stick from the old willow and whistled as if he were in a good humor; he was on his way to see the beauty of the whole world.

"This is a great grief to me," said the mother. "But I suppose it is wisest and best for you to go away, so I shall have to put up with it. Have faith in yourself and in our Lord; then I shall have you back again merry and happy."

He walked along the new highway, and there he saw Johanne come driving with a load of rubbish; she had not noticed him, and he did not wish to be seen by her, so he sat down behind the hedge; there he was hidden—and Johanne drove by.

Out into the world he went; no one knew where. His mother thought, "He will surely come home again before a year passes. Now he will see new things and have new things to think about, but then he will fall back into the old folds; they cannot be ironed out with any iron. He has a little too much of his father's disposition; I would rather he had mine, poor child! But he will surely come home again; he cannot forget either me or the house."

The mother would wait a year and a day. Else waited only a month and then she secretly went to the wise woman, Stine Madsdatter, who, besides knowing something about "doctoring," could tell fortunes in cards and coffee and knew more than her Lord's Prayer. She, of course, knew where Rasmus was; she read it in the coffee grounds. He was in a foreign town, but she couldn't read the name of it. In this town there were soldiers and beautiful ladies. He was thinking of either becoming a soldier or marrying one of the young ladies.

This Else could not bear to hear. She would willingly give her savings to buy him back, but no one must know that it was she.

And old Stine promised that he would come back; she knew of a charm, a dangerous charm for him; it would work; it was the ultimate remedy. She would set the pot boiling for him, and then, wherever in all the world he was, he would have to come home where the pot was boiling and his beloved was waiting for him. Months might pass before he came, but come he must if he was still alive. Without peace or rest night and day, he would be forced to return, over sea and mountain, whether the weather were mild or rough, and even if his feet were ever so tired. He would come home; he had to come home.

The moon was in the first quarter; it had to be for the charm to work, said old Stine. It was stormy weather, and the old willow tree creaked. Stine cut a twig from it and tied it in a knot. That would surely help to draw Rasmus home to his mother's house. Moss and houseleek were taken from the roof and put in the pot, which was set upon the fire. Else had to tear a leaf out of the psalmbook; she tore out the last leaf by chance, that on which the list of errata appeared. "That will do just as well," said Stine, and threw it into the pot.

Many sorts of things went into the stew, which had to boil and boil steadily until Rasmus came home. The black cock in old Stine's room had to lose its red comb, which went into the pot. Else's heavy gold ring went in with it, and that she would never get again, Stine told her beforehand. She was so wise, Stine. Many things that we are unable to name went into the pot, which stood constantly over the flame or on glowing embers or hot ashes. Only she and Else knew about it.

Whenever the moon was new or the moon was on the wane, Else would come to her and ask, "Can't you see him coming?"

"Much do I know," said Stine, "and much do I see, but the length of the way before him I cannot see. Now he is over the first mountains; now he is on the sea in bad weather. The road is long, through large forests; he has blisters on his feet, and he has fever in his bones, but he must go on."

"No, no!" said Else. "I feel so sorry for him."

"He cannot be stopped now, for if we stop him, he will drop dead in the road!"

A year and a day had gone. The moon shone round and big, and the wind whistled in the old tree. A rainbow appeared across the sky in the bright moonlight.

"That is a sign to prove what I say," said Stine. "Now Rasmus is coming."
But still he did not come.

"The waiting time is long," said Stine.

"Now I am tired of this," said Else. She seldom visited Stine now and brought her no more gifts. Her mind became easier, and one fine morning they all knew in the parish that Else had said "yes" to the rich farmer. She went over to look at the house and grounds, the cattle, and the household belongings. All was in good order, and there was no reason to wait with the wedding.

It was celebrated with a great party lasting three days. There was dancing to the clarinet and violins. No one in the parish was forgotten in the invitations. Mother Ölse was there, too, and when the party came to an end, and the hosts had thanked the guests, and the trumpets had blown, she went home with the leavings from the feast.

She had fastened the door only with a peg; it had been taken out, the door stood open, and in the room sat Rasmus. He had returned home — come that very hour. Lord God, how he looked! He was only skin and bone; he was pale and yellow.

"Rasmus!" said his mother. "Is it you I see? How badly you look! But I am so happy in my heart to have you back."

And she gave him the good food she had brought home from the party, a piece of the roast and of the wedding cake.

He had lately, he said, often thought of his mother, his home, and the old willow tree; it was strange how often in his dreams he had seen the tree and the little barefooted Johanne. He did not mention Else at all. He was ill and had to go to bed.

But we do not believe that the pot was the cause of this, or that it had exercised any power over him. Only old Stine and Else believed that, but they did not talk about it.

Rasmus lay with a fever — an infectious one. For that reason no one came to the tailor's house, except Johanne, the shoemaker's daughter. She cried when she saw how miserable Rasmus was.

The doctor wrote a prescription for him to have filled at the pharmacy. He would not take the medicine. "What good will it do?" he said.

"You will get well again then," said his mother. "Have faith in yourself and in our Lord! If I could only see you get flesh on your body again, hear you whistle and sing; for that I would willingly lay down my life."

And Rasmus was cured of his illness, but his mother contracted it. Our Lord summoned her, and not him.

It was lonely in the house; he became poorer and poorer. "He is worn out," they said in the parish. "Poor Rasmus." He had led a wild life on his travels; that, and not the black pot that had boiled, had sucked out his marrow and given him pain in his body. His hair became thin and gray. He was too lazy to work. "What good will it do?" he said. He would rather visit the tavern than the church.

One autumn evening he was staggering through rain and wind along the muddy road from the tavern to his house, his mother had long since gone and been laid in her grave. The swallows and starlings were also gone, faithful as they were. Johanne, the shoemaker's daughter, was not gone; she overtook him on the road and then followed him a little way.

"Pull yourself together, Rasmus."

"What good will it do?" he said.

"That is an awful saying that you have," said she. "Remember your mother's words, 'Have faith in yourself and in our Lord.' You do not, Rasmus, but you must, and you shall. Never say, 'What good will it do?' for then you pull up the root of all your doings."

She followed him to the door of his house, and there she left him. He did not stay inside; he wandered out under the old willow tree and sat on a stone from the overturned milepost.

The wind whistled in the tree's branches; it was like a song; it was like talk. Rasmus answered it; he spoke aloud, but no one heard him except the tree and the whistling wind.

"I am getting so cold. It is time to go to bed. Sleep, sleep!"

And he walked away, not toward the house, but over to the ditch, where he tottered and fell. Rain poured down, and the wind was icy cold, but he didn't feel this. When the sun rose, and the crows flew over the bulrushes, he awoke, deathly ill. Had he laid his head where he put his feet, he would never have arisen; the green duckweed would have been his burial sheet.

Later in the day Johanne came to the tailor's house. She helped him; she managed to get him to the hospital.

"We have known each other since we were little," she said. "Your mother gave me both ale and food; for that I can never repay her. You will regain your health; you will be a man with a will to live!"

And Our Lord willed that he should live. But he had his ups and downs, both in health and mind.

The swallows and the starlings returned, and flew away, and returned again. Rasmus became older than his years. He sat alone in his house, which deteriorated more and more. He was poor, poorer now than Johanne.

"You have no faith," she said, "and if we do not believe in God, what have we? You should go to Communion," she said; "you haven't been since your confirmation."

"What good will it do?" he said.

"If you say that and believe it, then let it be; the Master does not want an unwilling guest at His table. But think of your mother and your childhood. Once you were a good, pious boy. Let me read a psalm to you."

"What good will it do?" he said.

"It always comforts me," she answered.

"Johanne, you have surely become one of the saints." And he looked at her with dull, weary eyes.

And Johanne read the psalm, but not from a book, for she had none; she knew it by heart.

"Those were beautiful words," he said, "but I could not follow you altogether. My head feels so heavy."

Rasmus had become an old man. But Else, if we may mention her, was no longer young, either; Rasmus never mentioned her. She was a grandmother. Her granddaughter was an impudent little girl.

The little one was playing with the other children in the village. Rasmus came along, supporting himself on his stick. He stopped, watched the children play, and smiled to them; old times were in his thoughts. Else's granddaughter pointed at him. "Poor Rasmus!" she shouted. The other little girls followed her example. "Poor Rasmus!" they shouted, and pursued the old man with shrieks. It was a gray, gloomy day, and many others followed. But after gray and gloomy days there comes a sun shiny day.

It was a beautiful Whitsunday morning. The church was decorated with green birch branches; there was a scent of the woods within it, and the sun shone on the church pews. The large altar candles were lighted, and Communion was being held. Johanne was among the kneeling, but Rasmus was not among them. That very morning the Lord had called him.

In God are grace and mercy.

Many years have since passed. The tailor's house still stands there, but no one lives in it. It might fall the first stormy night. The ditch is overgrown with bulrush and buck bean. The wind whistles in the old tree; it is as if one were hearing a song; the wind sings it; the tree tells it. If you do not understand it, ask old Johanne in the poorhouse.

She still lives there, she sings her psalm, the one she read for Rasmus. She thinks of him, prays to our Lord for him — she, the faithful soul. She can tell of bygone times, of memories that whistle in the old willow-tree.

GODFATHER'S PICTURE BOOK

GODFATHER could tell stories, so many of them and such long ones, and he could cut out paper figures and draw pictures. When it was nearly Christmas he would bring out a scrapbook with clean white pages, and on these he pasted pictures cut out of books and newspapers; and if there weren't enough for the story he was going to tell, he drew them himself. When I was a little boy I got several of these picture books, but the prettiest of them all was the one from "that memorable year when gas replaced the old oil lamps in Copenhagen" — and that was the inscription written on the first page.

"We must take great care of this book," said Father and Mother, "and only bring it out on important occasions."

But Godfather had written on the cover:

If you should tear the book, that's not a great wrong;
Other little friends have done worse for ever so long.

Best of all were the times when Godfather himself showed the book, read the verses and other writings in it, and told many things besides; then the story would become a very real one.

On the first page was a picture from "The Flying Post," showing Copenhagen with its Round Tower and Our Lady's Church. On its left was pasted an old lantern, on which was written, "Train oil," and on the right was a chandelier, with "Gas" written on it.

"See, that's the title page," said Godfather. "That's the beginning of the story you're going to hear. It could also be given as an entire play, if one could perform it. *Train Oil and Gas; or, The Life and Times of Copenhagen.* That's a very good title! At the bottom of the page is still another little picture; it's quite hard to understand, so I'll explain it to you. That is a hell horse. He shouldn't have come until the end of the book, but he has run on ahead to say that neither the beginning, nor the middle, nor the end is any good; he could have done it much better—if he could have done it at all. The hell horse, you see, stands hitched all day in the newspaper, and walks on the columns, they say. But in the evening he slips out, stations himself outside the poet's door, and neighs, so that the man inside will instantly die; but he won't die if there's any real life in him. The hell horse is usually a poor creature who can't understand himself and can't earn a living, and he gets his air and food by going around and neighing. I am certain that he doesn't like Godfather's picture book, but in spite of that, it may be worth at least the paper it's written on.

"Now that's the first page of the book; that's the title page.

"It was the very last evening on which the oil lamps were to be lighted; the town had gas, and it was so bright that the old street lamps seemed quite lost in it.

"I was in the street myself that evening," said Godfather. "The people were walking about, looking at the old and the new lighting. There were a great many people and twice as many legs as heads. The watchmen stood around sadly, for they didn't know how soon they would be dismissed, like the oil lamps. They could remember so far back, but dared not think forward. They had so many memories of quiet evenings and dark nights. I leaned up against a lamppost," continued Godfather, "and there was a great spluttering in the oil and the wick. I could hear what the lamp said, and you shall hear it, too.

" 'We've done the best we could,' said the lamp. 'We were good enough for our time, and have lighted up joy and sorrow; we have lived through many wonderful things; you might say we have been the night eyes of Copenhagen. Now let new lights take our place and take over our duties; but how many years they'll shine, and what they will light up, remain to be seen! Indeed, they shine a little stronger than we old fellows, but that's nothing; when you're molded like a gas chandelier, and have the connections they have, the one pours into the other. They have pipes going in all directions and can get strength from both inside the town and outside it. But each one of us oil lamps shines because of what he has in himself, and not because of any family connections. We and our ancestors have lighted Copenhagen from olden times, from immeasurably long ago. But since this is now the last evening that we'll stand and shine in the second row, so to speak, in the street here along with you, you shining comrades, we won't sulk or be envious. No, far from it; we'll be happy and good-natured. We are the old sentinels, being relieved by new guards in better uniforms than ours. We'll tell you what our family, way back to great-great-great-grandmother lantern, has seen and experienced—the whole history of Copenhagen. May you and your successors, right down to the last gas chandelier, experience and be able to relate such wonderful things as we can, when you get your discharge someday. And you'll get it! You may be sure of that! People are certain to find a better light than gas. I've heard a student say that there's a possibility they may someday burn sea water!' When the lamp said these words, the wick spluttered, as if it had water in it already."

Godfather had listened closely, thought it over, and decided it was an excellent idea of the old lantern, on this evening of the change from oil to gas, to tell and display the whole history of Copenhagen.

"You mustn't let a good idea slip," said Godfather. "I took it at once, went home, and made this picture book for you. It goes even farther back in time than the lamps could go. Here's the book, and here's the story!

COPENHAGEN'S LIFE AND TIMES

"It begins in darkness, on a coal-black page—that's the Dark Ages.

"Now let's turn the page," said Godfather. "Do you see the picture? Only the wild sea and the swelling northeast wind, driving heavy ice floes before it. There's no one out sailing on them, only great stone blocks, which rolled down onto the ice from the mountains of Norway. The north wind blows the ice away; he wants to show the German mountains what rocks are found up in the North. The ice floes are already down in the sound, off the coast of Zealand, where Copenhagen now stands; but there was no Copenhagen there then. There were great sandbanks under the water, and the ice floes with the big boulders struck against one of these. Then the whole ice field stuck so fast that the northeast wind couldn't move it again, and so he became as furious as could be and pronounced a curse on the sandbank, the 'Thieves' ground,' as he called it. He swore that if ever it should rise above the surface of the sea, thieves and robbers would live there, and the gallows and wheel be raised on it.

"But while he cursed and swore this way, the sun came out, and those bright and gentle spirits, the children of light, swayed and swung in its beams; they danced over the ice floes until they melted, and the great boulders sank to the sandy bottom of the sea.

" 'Sun scum!' said the northeast wind. 'Is that friendship and kinship? I'll remember and take revenge for that. Now I pronounce a curse!'

" 'We pronounce a blessing!' sang the children of light. 'The sandbank will rise, and we shall guard it. Truth, goodness, and beauty shall dwell there!'

" 'Stuff and nonsense!' said the northeast wind.

"You see, the lantern knew nothing of all this and therefore couldn't tell about it," said Godfather. "But I know it, and it's very important to the life and times of Copenhagen.

"Now we'll turn the page," said Godfather. "Years have passed, and the sandbank has lifted itself; a sea gull has settled on the biggest rock, which has jutted out of water. You can see it in the picture. Years and years have passed.

"The sea cast up dead fish onto the shore. Tough lyme grass sprang up, withered, rotted, and fertilized the soil; many different kinds of grasses and plants followed, until the bank became a green island. There the vikings landed, for there was level ground for fighting and good anchorage beside the island off the coast of Zealand.

"I think the first oil lamp was lit to cook fish over, and there were plenty of fishes here. The herring swam through the sound in great shoals; it was hard to force a boat through them. They glittered in the water as if there were lightning down there, and shone in the depths like the northern lights. The sound had a wealth of fishes; therefore houses were built on the coast of Zealand, with walls of oak and roofs of bark—there were trees enough for that purpose. Ships anchored in the harbor, oil lamps hanging from swaying ropes, and the northeast wind blew and sang, 'O-out!' If a lantern glimmered on the island it was a thieves' lantern, for smugglers and thieves plied their trade on Thieves' Island.

" 'I believe that all the evil I wished for is coming,' said the northeast wind. 'Soon the tree will come, from which I can shake the fruit.'

"And here is the tree," said Godfather. "Do you see the gallows on Thieves' Island? Robbers and murderers hang there in iron chains, exactly as they hung in those days. The wind blew until it rattled the long skeletons, but the moon shone down on them as serenely as it now shines on a country dance. The sun also shone down pleasantly, crumbling away the dangling skeletons, and from the sunbeams the children of light sang, 'We know it! We know it! Here it shall be beautiful in the days to come; here it shall be good and splendid!'

" 'Chicken prattle!' said the northeast wind.

"Now we'll turn the page," said Godfather.

"The bells were ringing in the town of Roskilde, where Bishop Absalon lived. He could both read his Bible and wield his sword; he had power and will. He wished to protect from assault the busy fishermen at the harbor, whose town had grown until it was now a market town. He sprinkled the unhallowed ground with holy water; thus, Thieves' Island received the mark of honor. Masons and carpenters set to work on it; at the Bishop's command, a building grew up, and the sunbeams kissed the red walls as they rose. There stood the house of Axel:[1]

> The castle, with its towers, so stately and high,
> Had balconies and stairs up to the sky
> Booo! Whooo!
> The northeast wind huffed and puffed,
> But the castle stood unyielding, unruffed.

"And outside it lay 'The Haven,' the merchants' harbor:

> Mermaids' bower amid seas of sheen,
> Built beside groves of green.

"The foreigners came there and bought the wealth of fish, and built shops and houses with bladders for windowpanes, as glass was too expensive. Warehouses followed, with gables and windlasses. See the old fellows sitting there in the shops—they dare not marry; they trade in ginger and pepper, the *pebersvende.*[2]

"The northeast wind whistled through the streets and lanes, sending the dust flying and tearing off a thatched roof. Cows and pigs wandered about in the street ditch.

---

[1]The Bishop was also known as Axel.

[2]Pepper sellers, whose employers did not allow them to marry. Old bachelors are referred to as *pebersvende.*

" 'I shall tame and subdue them!' said the northeast wind. 'I'll whistle around the houses and around Axel's house! I can't fail! They call it Gallows' Castle on Thieves' Island.' "

Then Godfather showed a picture of it, which he himself had drawn. On the wall were rows of stakes, and on every stake was the head of a captured pirate showing its teeth.

"That really happened," said Godfather. "And it's worth hearing and worth knowing about.

"Bishop Absalon was in his bath, and through the thin walls he heard the arrival of a ship of freebooters. He instantly sprang out of the bath and into his ship, blew his horn, and his crew assembled. The arrows shot into the backs of the robbers as they rowed desperately to escape. The arrows pierced into their hands, and there was no time to pull them out. Bishop Absalon caught everyone and cut their heads off, and every head was set up on the outer wall of the castle. The northeast wind blew with puffed-out cheeks—with bad weather in his jaw, as the sailors say.

" 'I'll stretch myself,' said the wind. 'Here I'll lie down and look the whole matter over.'

"It rested for hours, then blew for days. Years went past.

"The watchman appeared on the castle tower; he looked to the east, the west, the north, and the south. You can see it there in the picture," said Godfather, pointing it out. "You can see him there, but I'll tell you what *he* saw.

"There is open water from the wall of Stejleborg right out to Kjöge Bay, and a broad channel over to the coast of Zealand. In front of Serritslev and Solberg Meadows, with their large villages, the new town, with its gabled timber houses, is growing up more and more. There are entire streets for shoemakers and tailors, for grocers and beer sellers; there is a market place and there is a guildhall, and near the shore, where there was once an island, stands the splendid Church of St. Nicolaus. It has an immensely high tower and spire; how it is reflected in the clear water! Near this is Our Lady's Church, where Masses are sung, where incense gives out its fragrance and wax candles burn. The 'merchants' haven' is now the Bishop's town; the Bishop of Roskilde rules and reigns there.

"Bishop Erlandsen sits in Axel's house. There is good cooking in the kitchen; ale and claret are served to the sound of fiddles and kettledrums. Burning candles and lamps make the castle shine as if it were a lantern for the whole country and kingdom. The northeast wind whistles around the tower and walls, but they stand firmly. The northeast wind swoops around the western fortification of the town—only an old wooden fence—but it holds up well. Christopher I, King of Denmark, stands outside it; the rebels have beaten him at Skelskör, so he seeks shelter in the Bishop's town.

"The wind whistles, and says, like the Bishop, 'Keep out! Keep out! The gate is shut to you!'

"It is a time of trouble, dismal days, when every man is his own master. The Holstein banner waves from the castle tower. There is want and woe, for it is the night of anguish. War and the black death stalk the land in the pitch-dark night—but then comes Valdemar Atterdag. Now the Bishop's town is the King's town. It has gabled houses and narrow streets, watchmen and a town hall, and a permanent gallows by the west point. No man from out of town can be hanged on it; you must be a citizen to be allowed to dangle there, to get so high as to see Kjöge and the hens of Kjöge.

" 'That's a lovely gallows,' says the northeast wind. 'The beautiful is growing!' And it whistles and whoops.

"And from Germany blew trouble and want.

"The Hanseatic merchants came," continued Godfather, "from warehouse and counter, the rich traders of Rostock, Lübeck, and Bremen. They wanted to seize more than the golden goose from Valdemar's Tower; they had more power in the town of the Danish King than the Danish King himself. They came in armed ships, and no one was prepared. And King Eric had no desire to fight with his German kinsfolk; they were too many and too strong. So King Eric and all his courtiers escaped through the west port to the town of Sorö, to the quiet lake and green forests, to the song of love and the clang of goblets.

"But there was one left behind in Copenhagen, a kingly heart and a kingly mind. Do you see this picture here, this young woman, so fine and tender, with sea-blue eyes and yellow hair? It is the Queen of Denmark, Philippa, the English princess. She stayed in the distracted city, where the townspeople swarmed in panic in the narrow lanes and streets with steep stairs, sheds, and shops of lath and plaster. With the courage of a man, she summoned townspeople and peasants, to inspire and encourage them. They fitted out the ships and garrisoned the blockhouses; they fired with their carbines; there were fire and smoke and lightness of spirit — our Lord will never forsake Denmark! The sun shone into all hearts, and in all eyes was the bright gladness of victory. Blessed be Philippa! Blessed she was in hut and in house; and blessed she was in the King's castle, where she nursed the wounded and the sick. I have clipped a wreath and laid it around this picture," said Godfather. "Blessed be Queen Philippa!"

"Now we spring forward for years," said Godfather, "and Copenhagen springs with us. King Christian I has been to Rome to receive the Pope's blessing and has been greeted with honor and homage on the long journey. Here at home he is building a hall of red brick; there shall be learning there, displaying itself in Latin. The poor man's children, from plow and workshop, can also come there, to live upon alms, to attain the long black gown, and sing before the doors of citizens.

"Near the hall of learning, where everything is in Latin, is a little house where Danish rules, in language and in customs. There is beer soup for early breakfast, and dinner is at ten o'clock in the morning. The sun shines through small panes onto cupboards and bookcases; on the shelves are written treasures — Master Mikkel's *Rosary* and *Godly Comedies,* Henrik Harpestreng's *Leech-book,* and *Denmark's Rhyming Chronicle* by Brother Niels of Sorö. 'Every Danish man should know these,' says the master of the house, and he is the one to make them known. He is the Dutchman, Gotfred van Gehmen, Denmark's first printer, who practices the divine black art of printing.

"And the books enter the castle of the King and the houses of the citizens. Proverbs and songs are given immortality. Things that men dare not say either in sorrow or in joy are sung by the Bird of Folklore, allegorically and yet clearly. For it flies free and wide through the common man's room and the knightly castle; it sits and twitters like a falcon on the hand of the noble lady; it steals in like a tiny mouse and squeaks in the dungeon of the enslaved peasant.

" 'Merely words—all of it!' says the sharp northeast wind.

" 'It's the spring!' say the sunbeams. 'See how the green buds are peeping out!'

"Now we'll turn more pages in our picture book," said Godfather.

"How radiant Copenhagen is! There are tournaments and sports and splendid processions! Look at the gallant knights in armor and the noble ladies in silk and gold! King Hans gives his daughter, Elizabeth, to the Elector of Brandenburg. How young she is, and how happy she is! She is treading on velvet; there is a whole future in her thoughts—a future of domestic happiness. Close beside her is her royal brother, Prince Christian, with the melancholy eyes and the hot, passionate blood. He is beloved by the commoners, for he knows their burdens; in his thoughts he has the poor man's future. God alone decides our fate!

"Now we'll turn another leaf in the picture book," said Godfather. "The wind blows sharply and sings of the sharp sword and this difficult time of trouble.

"It is an icy-cold day in mid-April. Why is the crowd gathering outside the castle and before the old customhouse, where the King's ship lies with its sails and banners? People are crowded in the windows and on the roofs. There are sorrow and trouble, expectation and anxiety. They look toward the castle, now so still and empty, but where formerly there were torch dances in the gilded halls; they look at the balcony from which King Christian so often gazed out over the 'court bridge' and down the narrow court-bridge street to his dovelet, the little Dutch girl he brought from the town of Bergen. The shutters are bolted. As the crowd gazes toward the castle, the gate is opened and the drawbridge is let down. There comes King Christian with his faithful wife, Elizabeth; she will not forsake her royal lord, now when he is so hard pressed.

"There is fire in his blood and fire in his thoughts; he has wished to break with the olden times, to strike off the peasants' yoke, to do good to the commoners, to clip the wings of the 'greedy hawks,' but they have been too much for him. He leaves his country and his kingdom, to win allies and friends for himself abroad. His wife and loyal men go with him. Every eye is moist in this hour of parting.

"Voices are blended in the song of time, against him and for him, a three-part choir.

"Listen to the words of the nobles; they are written and printed: 'Woe to you, Christian the Wicked! The blood that poured out in the market place of Stockholm cries aloud and curses you!'

"And the monks' cry echoes the same refrain: 'Be you cast off by God and by us! You have called hither the Lutheran doctrine; you have given it church and pulpit and bid the tongue of the Devil speak out! Woe to you, Christian the Wicked!'

"But the peasants and commoners weep: 'Christian beloved of the people! No longer may the peasant be sold like cattle or exchanged for a hunting hound! That law shall bear you witness!' But the words of the poor man are only chaff before the wind.

"Now the ship sails past the castle, and the commoners line the ramparts, so that they may once more see the royal galley sail.

" 'The time is long; the time is hard. Trust neither in friends nor in kinsmen!'

"Uncle Frederick in the Castle of Kiel would like to be King of Denmark. King Frederick is before Copenhagen. See the picture here—'The Faithful Copenhagen.' Coal-black clouds are around it—in picture after picture; just look at each of them! It is all a resounding picture; it resounds still in song and story—those heavy, hard, and bitter times during the long procession of years.

"How did it go with that wandering bird, King Christian? The birds have sung about it, and they fly over distant lands and seas.

"Early in the spring the stork came from the south, across the land of Germany; it had seen what I will tell you now.

" 'I saw the fugitive King Christian crossing a heather-grown moor; he met a wretched cart drawn by only one horse. A woman sat in it, his sister, the Countess of Brandenburg. Faithful to the Lutheran religion, she had been exiled by her husband. And so on that dark heath the exiled children of a king met. The time is hard; the time is long. Trust neither friend nor kinsman!'

"The swallow came from Sönderborg Castle with a sad song, 'King Christian is betrayed! He sits in the dungeon tower, deep as a well; his heavy steps wear tracks in the stone floor, and his fingers leave their marks in the hard marble.'

Oh, what sorrow ever found such vent
As that in the furrows of the stone?

"The fish eagle has come from the tossing sea, which is open and free. A ship flies over it, bearing the brave Sören Norby from Fyn. Fortune is with him—but fortune is as changeable as wind and weather.

"In Jutland and Fyn the crows and ravens scream, 'We seek spoil! It is grand! Caw, caw! Here lie the bodies of horses and of men, too!' It is a time of trouble; it is during the Count of Oldenburg's war. The peasant raises his club and the townsman his knife, and loudly they shout, 'We shall slay the wolves and leave no cub of them alive!' Clouds of smoke roll up from the burning towns.

"King Christian is a prisoner in Sönderborg Castle; he cannot escape or see the bitter distress of Copenhagen. On the North Common stands Christian III, where his father stood before him. Despair is in the city, and plague and famine.

"A ragged, emaciated woman sits reclined against the church wall. She is a corpse; two living children lie on her lap and can suck only blood from the dead breast.

"Courage has collapsed; resistance collapses. Oh, you faithful Copenhagen!

"Fanfares are blown, hear the drums and trumpets! In rich garments of silk and velvet, with nodding plumes, the noble lords come on horses adorned with gold, riding to Old Market Square. Is there a customary festivity or tournament? Commoners and peasants in holiday attire flock in that direction. What is there to see? Is there a bonfire to burn popish images? Or is the hangman standing there, as he stood at the death fire of Slaghoek? The King, ruler of all the land, is a Lutheran, and this shall now be proclaimed with solemnity.

"Noble ladies and highborn maidens, with high collars and caps of pearls, sit behind the open windows and see all the splendor. Beneath a canopy near the King's throne, the councilors of state sit in antique dress on an outspread carpet. The King is silent, but his will, the will of the council of state, is proclaimed in the Danish tongue. Commoners and peasants are sternly rebuked for the opposition they have shown to the nobility. The commoner is humbled, and the peasant becomes a slave. Now condemning words are uttered against the bishops of the land. Their power is gone, and all the property of the church and cloisters is transferred to the King and the nobles.

"Pride and hatred are there, and pomp and misery, too.

> The poor bird comes limping, drooping,
> Comes stooping.
> The rich bird comes huffing,
> Comes puffing.

"The time of change brings heavy clouds, but sunshine, too; it then shines in the halls of learning and in the student's home. And names shine from it on down to our own days. There is Hans Tousen, the son of a poor smith of Fyn:

> This was the little lad who came from Birkende town;
> His name flew over Denmark; widely spread his renown.
> A Danish Martin Luther, he drew the Gospel sword,
> And gained a mighty victory for truth and for the Lord.

"There is also the immortal name of Petrus Palladius; that is the Latin, but in Danish it is Peter Plade, Bishop of Roskilde, also the son of a poor smith of Jutland. And among noblemen shines the name of Hans Friis, Chancellor of the kingdom. He would seat the students at his own table and see to their wants and those of the schoolboys as well. But one man above all others is greeted with cheers and song.

> So long as there's a student to be found
> Near Axel's Haven, at work or play,
> Will King Christian's name loudly resound
> And with hurrahs be greeted every day!

"Yes, there were sunbeams between the heavy clouds in that time of change.

"Now we turn the page.

"What is it that whistles and sings in the Great Belt under the coast of Samsö? A mermaid, with sea-green hair, rises from the sea; she reveals the future to the peasant. A prince shall be born who shall become a great and powerful king.

"He was born in the field, beneath the blossoming whitethorn. His name now lives in song and story, in the knightly halls and castles everywhere. The stock exchange came forth with tower and spire; Rosenborg Castle rose up and gazed far out over the ramparts; the students got their own house. And close by, where it still points to heaven, stood 'the Round Tower,' facing toward the island of Hveen, where Uranienborg once stood. Its golden domes glittered in the moonlight, and the mermaids sang of the man who lived there, whom kings and sages visited, the master sage of noble blood — Tycho Brahe. He raised the name of Denmark so high that it was known with the stars of heaven in all the cultured lands of the earth. And Denmark turned him away.

"In his sorrow he sang for comfort:

> Is not heaven everywhere
> What more do I require?

"His song lives in the hearts of the people, like the mermaid's song about Christian IV.

"Now comes a page that you must look at carefully," said Godfather.

"There is picture after picture here, just as there is verse after verse in the old ballads. It is a song, so happy in its beginning, so sorrowful at its close.

"A king's child is dancing in the castle of the King. How lovely she is to look at! She is sitting on the lap of Christian IV — his beloved daughter, Eleanore. She grows in all the virtues and graces of a woman. The foremost among the nobles, Corfits Ulfeldt, is her betrothed. She is still only a child and is beaten by her stern governess; she complains of this to her sweetheart, and rightly, too. How clever and cultured and learned she is! She can speak Latin and Greek, sing in Italian to her lute, and talk about the Pope and Martin Luther.

"Now King Christian lies in the vault in Roskilde Cathedral, and Eleanore's brother is King. In the palace at Copenhagen there are pomp and show; there are beauty and wit — and foremost is the Queen herself, Sophie Amalie of Lyneborg. Who can guide her horse as cleverly as she? Who dances with such grace? Who can talk with such wisdom and wit as the Queen of Denmark?

" 'Eleanore Christine Ulfeldt!' These are the words of the French Ambassador. 'She surpasses all in beauty and wit!'

"Up from the polished floor of the palace ballroom has grown the burdock of envy; it has clung there, worked itself in, and twisted around — contempt and scorn. 'That illegitimate creature! Her carriage shall stop at the bridge of the castle! Where the Queen drives, the commoner shall walk!' There is a storm of gossip, of lies and slander.

"Then Ulfeldt takes his wife by the hand in the still of the night. He has the keys to the town gates; he opens one of them, and horses wait outside. They ride to the shore and sail to Sweden.

"Now let's turn the page, just as fortune turned itself for those two.

"It is autumn. The days are short and the nights are long; it is gray and damp. The cold wind rises in its strength, and it whistles through the leaves of the trees on the ramparts. The leaves drop into Peter Oxe's courtyard, empty and forsaken of its owners. The wind sweeps over Christianshavn, around the mansion of Kai Lykke, which now is a penitentiary. He himself has been driven from home and honor; his escutcheon is smashed and his effigy hung on the highest gallows. Thus is he punished for his thoughtless, frivolous words about the powerful Queen of Denmark. The wind pipes loudly as it rushes over the open space where the mansion of the Lord High Steward once stood. Only one stone of it is now left, 'And that I drove down here as a boulder on the floating ice,' shrieks the wind. 'That stone stranded where since has grown Thieves' Island, under my curse, and so it became a part of the mansion of Lord Ulfeldt, where his lady sang to the sounding lute, and read Greek and Latin, and bore herself proudly. Now only the stone is here with its inscription:

> The traitor Corfits Ulfeldt
> In eternal scorn, shame, and disgrace.

" 'But where is the stately lady now? Whoo-ee-ooo!' blows the wind with a piercing shriek.

"For many years she has been shut up in the Blue Tower, behind the palace, where the sea water beats against the slimy walls. There is more smoke than warmth in the cell; its tiny window is high up under the ceiling. In what discomfort and misery sits the adored child of Christian IV, the daintiest of maids and matrons! Memory hangs curtains and tapestries on the smoke-blackened walls of her prison. She recalls the lovely days of her childhood, her father's gentle, beaming face; she recalls her splendid wedding, her days of pride, but also her days of misery in Holland, England, and Bornholm.

> Nothing seems too hard for wedded love to bear,
> And loyalty is not cause for shame or care.

"But he was with her in those days; now she is alone, alone forever. She does not know his grave; no one knows it.

> Faithfulness to her husband was her only crime.

"For long and many years she sat there, while life went on outside. Life never pauses, but we will for a moment here, and think of her and the words of the song.

> I keep my promise to my husband still,
> In want and dire need, and always will.

"Now do you see this picture here?" said Godfather. "It's winter, and the frost has thrown a bridge of ice between Laaland and Fyn, a bridge for Carl Gustav, who pushes on unchecked. There are plundering and burning, fear and want, throughout the whole land.

"Now the Swedes are encamped before Copenhagen. It is bitterly cold and the snow is blinding, but, true to their king and themselves, men and women stand ready to fight. Every tradesman, shopman, student, and schoolmaster is on the ramparts, ready to guard and defend, with no fear of the red-hot cannon balls. King Frederick has sworn he will die in his nest. There he rides to and fro, and the Queen is with him, and courage, patriotism, and discipline are there. Let the Swede don his white shroud and crawl forward in the white snow and try to storm the walls! Beams and stones are hurled down on him; even women come with steaming caldrons and pour boiling pitch and tar onto the storming enemy.

"That night King and peasant are one united power. Then there is relief, and there is victory. Church bells ring, and songs of thanksgiving resound. Commoners, on this spot you won your knightly spurs!

"What comes next? Look at this picture. Bishop Svane's wife drives in a closed carriage, which only the high and mighty nobility dare do. The proud young men stop the carriage; the bishop's wife must walk to the bishop's house.

"Is that the whole story? Something much greater is stopped next—the power of pride.

"Burgomaster Hans Nansen and Bishop Svane clasp hands to work in the name of the Lord. Their wise and honest talk is heard in the church and the house of the commoner. One handclasp of fellowship, and the harbor is blocked, the gates are locked, and the alarm bell rings.

"Power is granted to the King alone, who remains in his nest in the hour of peril; he governs, and rules over great and small. It is the time of absolute monarchy.

"Now let's turn the page, and time with it.

" 'Halloo, halloo, halloo!' The plow stands idle, and the heather grows wild, but the hunting is good. 'Halloo, halloo!' Listen to the sounding horn and the baying hounds! See the huntsmen, and look at the young and gay King himself, Christian V! There is merrymaking in palace and in town. In the halls are waxlights, in the courtyards torches, and in the streets of the town are new lamps. Everything is so new! Favors and gifts go to the barons and counts of the new nobility, brought in from Germany. Nothing is accepted now except titles and rank and the German language.

"But then there sounds a voice that is truly Danish, the voice of the weaver's son, who is now a bishop; it is the voice of Kingo, singing his beautiful psalms.

"There is another commoner's son, this time the son of a vintner, whose thoughts shine forth in law and justice. His book of laws has become gold-ground for the King's name, and will stand for ages to come. That commoner's son, the greatest man in the land, receives a coat of arms—and enemies as well, so that the sword of the executioner is raised over the head of Griffenfeld.

"But mercy is granted, with life imprisonment, and he is banished to a rocky islet off the coast of Trondhjem,

Munkholm—Denmark's St. Helena

"But the dance continues merrily in the palace hall; there are splendor and pomp there, and courtiers and ladies dance to lively music.

"Now these are the times of Frederick IV!

"See the proud ships with their flags of victory! See the tossing sea! It can tell of great deeds for the glory of Denmark. We remember the victorious Sehested and Gyldenlöve! We remember Hvitfeldt, who blew up his ship to save the Danish fleet, and flew to Heaven with Dannebrog.[1] We think of the struggles of those ages, and of the hero who sprang to the defense of Denmark from the mountains of Norway—Peder Tordenskjold. Across the surging sea his name thundres from country to country.

[1]The flag of Denmark.

Lightning flashed through the powder dust;
A thunderbolt roared through the whispering age.
A tailor's boy jumped down from the tailor's table;
From Norway's coast he sailed a little sloop.
And over Northern seas there flew again
The viking spirit, youthful, and clad in steel.

"Then a fresh breeze blew from the coast of Greenland, bringing a gentle fragrance, as if from the land of Bethlehem; it brought tidings of the Gospel light kindled by Hans Egede and his wife.

"So this half page has a golden ground; but the other half, which means sorrow, is ashen gray with black specks, as from fire and disease and pestilence.

"The plague is raging in Copenhagen. The streets are empty. The doors are barred, and where crosses are chalked on them the plague is inside, but where the cross is black all within are dead.

"The bodies are carried away by night, with no tolling bell; the half dead in the streets are taken with them. Funeral wagons rumble, piled with corpses. But from the taverns sound the horrid songs and wild shrieks of the drunkards. They try to forget their bitter distress in drink; they want to forget, and end—end! Yes, everything comes to an end. The page ends here, with the second time of distress and trial for Copenhagen.

"King Frederick IV is still alive. The course of the years has turned his hair gray. From the window of his palace he looks out on the stormy weather of late winter.

"In a little house near the Westgate a boy is playing with his ball; it bounces up into the loft. The child takes a candle and goes up to seek it, but he sets fire to the little house—to the whole street. The fire leaps into the air so that the clouds themselves reflect it! See how the flames grow higher! There is food for the fire—hay and straw, bacon and tar, piles of firewood for winter—and it all burns. There is weeping, shrieking; there is great panic. The old King rides through the tumult, commanding and encouraging. There is blowing up with gunpowder, and the tearing down of houses. Now the fire has swept into the north quarter, and the churches are burning, St. Peter's and Our Lady's. Listen to the bells playing their last tune, 'Turn from Us Thy Wrath, O Lord God of Mercy!'

"Only the 'Round Tower' and the castle are left standing, with smoking ruins about them. King Frederick is kind to the people; he is a friend to the homeless; he comforts and feeds them and is with them constantly. Blessed be Frederick IV!

"Now look at this page!

"See that gilded carriage with footmen around it and armed riders before and behind it, coming from the castle, where an iron chain is stretched to keep the people from coming too near! Every common man must cross the square with bare head; and therefore few are seen there; they avoid the place. There comes one now, with downcast eyes, and with hat in hand, and he is the one man of that time whom we can name with pride:

His voice like a cleansing storm wind rang.
To sunshine in the days which yet were to come!
Then smuggled-in tunes like grasshoppers sprang
In haste to return to where they were from.

"Witty and humorous—that is Ludvig Holberg. The Danish stage, the castle of his greatness, has been closed as if it were the dwelling place of shame. All merriment is banished; dance, song, and music are forbidden and gone. For the dark side of religion is now in power.

" 'The Danish prince!' his mother used to call him. Now come his days of sunshine, with the song of birds, with gladness and true Danish gaiety. Frederick V is King, and the chain is taken from the square beside the castle; the Danish theater is reopened; there are laughter and pleasure and good cheer. And the peasants again hold their summer festivals, for it is a time of joy after the time of fast and oppression. The beautiful lives again, blossoming and bearing fruit in sound, color, and creative art. Listen to Grétry's music! Watch Londemann's acting! And Denmark's Queen loves all that is Danish. God in His heaven bless you, beautiful and gentle Louise of England! The sunbeams sing in spirited chorus about the queens of Denmark—Philippa, Elizabeth, Louise!

"The earthly shells have long been buried, but the souls live, and the names live. England again sends a royal bride, Matilde, so young and so soon forsaken! In days to come poets will sing of your youthful heart and your hours of trial! And song has an indescribable power through all times and all peoples. See the burning of the castle of King Christian! They try to save the best they can find. Look at the men from the dockyard dragging away a basket of silverware and precious things—a great treasure! But suddenly through an open door, where the flames are brightest, they see a bronze bust of King Christian IV. Then they cast aside the treasure they are rescuing; his image means so much more to them that it must be saved, regardless of how heavy it may be to carry. They know him from the song of Ewald and the beautiful melody of Hartmann.

"Indeed, there is power in words and song, and someday it shall resound as strongly for the poor Queen Matilde.

"Now let's go further in our picture book.

"On Ulfeldt's Place stood the stone of shame, and where in the world is there one like it? By the Westgate a column was raised, and how many in the world are there like it?

"The sunbeams kissed the boulder foundations of the Column of Freedom. All church bells rang and the flags waved, and the people cheered for Crown Prince Frederick. The names of Bernstorff, Reventlow, Colbjörnsen were held in the hearts and were on the lips of old and young. With bright eyes and grateful hearts they read the blessed inscription on the column:

" 'The King has decreed that serfdom shall cease, the agrarian laws be set in order and enforced, so that the free peasant may become brave and enlightened, diligent and good, a worthy and happy citizen!'

"What a sunny day! Summer is in town!

"The spirits of light sang, 'The good is growing! The beautiful is growing! Soon the stone on Ulfeldt's Place shall fall, but the Column of Freedom shall stand in the sunlight, blessed by God, King and people.'

> We have an ancient highway;
> It goes to the ends of the earth.

"There in the open sea—open for friend and foe—was the foe! The mighty English fleet sailed up; a great power came against a little one. The battle was hard, but the people were valiant.

> Each stood firm, untiring, held his place,
> Stood and fought until death's embrace.

"They won the admiration of the enemy and inspired the poets of Denmark. The day of that battle is still commemorated with unfurled banners—Denmark's glorious Second of April, the Maundy Thursday battle at Copenhagen Harbor.

"Years passed. A fleet was seen in Öresund. Was it bound for Russia or for Denmark? No one knew, not even those on board the ships.

"There is a legend in the hearts of the people which tells that on that morning in Öresund, when the sealed orders were opened and the instructions to destroy the Danish fleet were read, a young captain stepped forward, a son of Britain, noble in word and deed. 'I swore,' he said, 'that I would fight for England's flag to my death, in open and honorable battle, but not overpower the weak!' And with that he jumped overboard!

> The fleet sailed toward Copenhagen just the same;
> But far from the place where the battle was to be
> Lay he, the captain—and unknown is his name—
> An ice-cold corpse, in the dark-blue sea.
> Shoreward he drifted, until Swedish men,
> Fishing beneath the stars with their nets,
> Found him, bore him to shore, and then
> Cast dice to win his epaulets!

"The enemy made for Copenhagen. The town was soon in flames. We lost our fleet, but not our courage and faith in God; He casteth down but He raiseth again. Our wounds healed, as those of the warriors in Valhalla. The history of Copenhagen is rich in consolation.

> Our faith, from the beginning of time to the end,
> Is that Our Lord is Denmark's friend;
> If we hold firmly, He will hold, too,
> And tomorrow the sun will shine on you.

"Soon the sun did shine on the rebuilt city, on the rich corn-fields, and on the skill and art of our people. It was a blessed summer day of peace, when poetry raised her Fata Morgana, so rich in color, through the words of Oehlenschläger.

"And a great discovery was made in science. It was a discovery far greater than the gold horn of ancient days, for a bridge of gold was found:

> A bridge for thought to flash like lightning
> At all times into other lands and nations.

"Hans Christian Örsted wrote his name on that bridge. And look! Beside the church by the castle a building was raised to which the poorest man and woman gladly gave their pennies.

"You will remember that in the first part of our picture book," said God-father, "the old stone blocks rolled down from the mountains of Norway and were carried here on the ice. They are raised up again from the sandy depths at the bidding of Thorvaldsen, in marble beauty, magnificent to look at!

"Remember all that I have shown you and all that I have told you! That sandbank in the sea raised itself up to become a breakwater in the harbor; it bore Axel's house, and the bishop's mansion, and the King's castle, and now it bears the temple of the beautiful. The words of the curse have vanished, but all that the children of sunlight sang in their gladness about the coming ages has been fulfilled. Many storms have passed; they will come again and pass again. The true and the good and the beautiful have the voctory.

"And that finishes the picture book, but not the history of Copen-hagen—far from it! Who knows what you may live to see! It has often looked black, and storms have raged, but the sunshine has never been blown away—it remains. And stronger yet than the brightest sunshine is God! Our Lord reigns over more than Copenhagen."

That is what Godfather said as he gave me the book. His eyes were shining; he was so certain of it all. And I took the book so gladly and proudly and carefully, just the way I carried my little sister for the first time.

And Godfather said, "You're quite welcome to show your picture book to people, and you may also tell them that I made it, pasted it, and drew the whole thing. But it's of great importance that they know at once where I got the idea for it. You know where, so tell them! The idea came from the old oil lamps, which, on the last evening they burned, showed the new gaslights, like a Fata Morgana, everything that had been seen from the time the first lamp was lit at the harbor until that evening when Copenhagen was lighted with both oil and gas.

"You may show the book to anybody you like; that is, to people with kindly eyes and friendly minds; but if a hell horse should come, then close God-father's picture book."

A GREAT GRIEF

THIS story really consists of two parts. The first part might be left out, but it gives us a few particulars, and these are useful.

We were staying in the country at a gentleman's seat, where it happened that the master was absent for a few days. In the meantime, there arrived from the next town a lady; she had a pug dog with her, and came, she said, to dispose of shares in her tan-yard. She had her papers with her, and we advised her to put them in an envelope, and to write thereon the address of the proprietor of the estate, "General War-Commissary Knight," &c.

She listened to us attentively, seized the pen, paused, and begged us to repeat the direction slowly. We complied, and she wrote; but in the midst of the "General War—" she struck fast, sighed deeply, and said, "I am only a woman!" Her Puggie had seated itself on the ground while she wrote, and growled; for the dog had come with her for amusement and for the sake of its health; and then the bare floor ought not to be offered to a visitor. His outward appearance was characterized by a snub nose and a very fat back.

"He doesn't bite," said the lady; "he has no teeth. He is like one of the family, faithful and grumpy; but the latter is my grandchildren's fault, for they have teased him; they play at wedding, and want to give him the part of the bridesmaid, and that's too much for him, poor old fellow."

And she delivered her papers, and took Puggie upon her arm. And this is the first part of the story which might have been left out.

PUGGIE DIED!! That's the second part.

It was about a week afterwards we arrived in the town, and put up at the inn. Our windows looked into the tan-yard, which was divided into two parts by a partition of planks; in one half were many skins and hides, raw and tanned. Here was all the apparatus necessary to carry on a tannery, and it belonged to the widow. Puggie had died in the morning, and was to be buried in this part of the yard; the grandchildren of the widow (that is, of the tanner's widow, for Puggie had never been married) filled up the grave, and it was a beautiful grave—it must have been quite pleasant to lie there.

The grave was bordered with pieces of flower-pots and strewn over with sand; quite at the top they had stuck up half a beer bottle, with the neck upwards, and that was not at all allegorical.

The children danced round the grave, and the eldest of the boys among them, a practical youngster of seven years, made the proposition that there should be an exhibition of Puggie's burial-place for all who lived in the lane; the price of admission was to be a trouser button, for every boy would be sure to have one, and each might also give one for a little girl. This proposal was adopted by acclamation.

And all the children out of the lane—yes, even out of the little lane at the back—flocked to the place, and each gave a button. Many were noticed to go about on that afternoon with only one suspender; but then they had seen Puggie's grave, and the sight was worth much more.

But in front of the tan-yard, close to the entrance, stood a little girl clothed in rags, very pretty to look at, with curly hair, and eyes so blue and clear that it was a pleasure to look into them. The child said not a word, nor did she cry; but each time the little door was opened she gave a long, long look into the yard. She had not a button—that she knew right well, and therefore she remained standing sorrowfully outside, till all the others had seen the grave and had gone away; then she sat down, held her little brown hands before her eyes, and burst into tears; this girl alone had not seen Puggie's grave. It was a grief as great to her as any grown person can experience.

We saw this from above; and looked at from above, how many a grief of our own and of others can make us smile! That is the story, and whoever does not understand it may go and purchase a share in the tan-yard from the window.

THE JUMPER

THE Flea, the Grasshopper, and the Skipjack* once wanted to see which of them could jump highest; and they invited the whole world, and whoever else would come, to see the grand sight. And there the three famous jumpers were met together in the room.

"Yes, I'll give my daughter to him who jumps highest," said the King, "for it would be mean to let these people jump for nothing."

The Flea stepped out first. He had very pretty manners, and bowed in all directions, for he had young ladies' blood in his veins, and was accustomed to consort only with human beings; and that was of great consequence.

Then came the Grasshopper: he was certainly much heavier, but he had a good figure, and wore the green uniform that was born with him. This person, moreover, maintained that he belonged to a very old family in the land of Egypt, and that he was highly esteemed there. He had just come from the field, he said, and had been put into a card house three stories high, and all made of picture cards with the figures turned inwards. There were doors and windows in the house, cut in the body of the Queen of Hearts.

"I sing so," he said, "that sixteen native crickets who have chirped from their youth up, and have never yet had a card house of their own, would become thinner than they are with envy if they were to hear me."

Both of them, the Flea and the Grasshopper, took care to announce who they were, and that they considered themselves entitled to marry a Princess.

The Skipjack said nothing, but it was said of him that he thought all the more; and directly the Yard Dog had smelt at him he was ready to assert that the Skipjack was of good family, and formed from the breastbone of an undoubted goose. The old councillor, who had received three medals for holding his tongue, declared that the Skipjack possessed the gift of prophecy; one could tell by his bones whether there would be a severe winter or a mild one; and that's more than one can always tell from the breastbone of the man who writes the almanac.

"I shall not say anything more," said the old King. "I only go on quietly, and always think the best."

Now they were to take their jump. The Flea sprang so high that no one could see him; and then they asserted that he had not jumped at all. That was very mean. The Grasshopper only sprang half as high, but he sprang straight into the King's face, and the King declared that was horribly rude. The Skipjack stood a long time considering; at last people thought that he could not jump at all.

"I only hope he's not become unwell," said the Yard Dog, and then he smelt at him again.

"Tap!" he sprang with a little crooked jump just into the lap of the Princess, who sat on a low golden stool.

Then the King said, "The highest leap was taken by him who jumped up to my daughter; for therein lies the point; but it requires head to achieve that, and the Skipjack has shown that he has a head."

*A children's toy, made from the breastbone of a goose, wax and a stick, which can be made to jump.

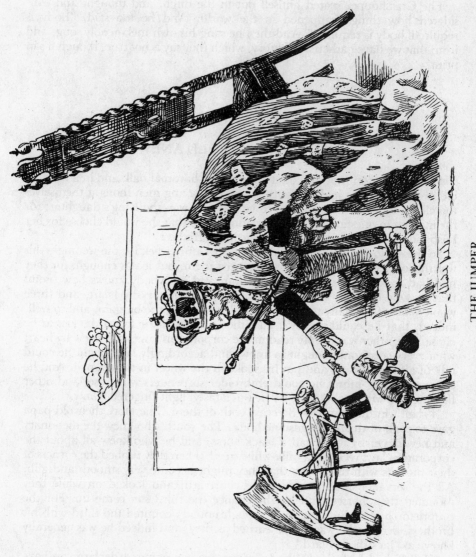

THE JUMPER

And so he had the Princess.

"I jumped highest, after all," said the Flea. "But it's all the same. Let her have the goose-bone with its lump of wax and bit of stick. I jumped to the highest; but in this world a body is required if one wishes to be seen."

And the Flea went into foreign military service, where it is said he was killed.

The Grasshopper seated himself out in the ditch, and thought and considered how things happened in the world. And he too said, "Body is required! body is required!" And then he sang his own melancholy song, and from that we have gathered this story, which they say is not true, though it's in print.

JACK THE DULLARD

AN OLD STORY TOLD ANEW

FAR in the interior of the country lay an old baronial hall, and in it lived an old proprietor, who had two sons, which two young men thought themselves too clever by half. They wanted to go out and woo the King's daughter; for the maiden in question had publicly announced that she would choose for her husband that youth who could arrange his words best.

So these two geniuses prepared themselves a full week for the wooing—this was the longest time that could be granted them; but it was enough, for they had had much preparatory information, and everybody knows how useful that is. One of them knew the whole Latin dictionary by heart, and three whole years of the daily paper of the little town into the bargain, and so well, indeed, that he could repeat it all either backwards or forwards, just as he chose. The other was deeply read in the corporation laws, and knew by heart what every corporation ought to know; and accordingly he thought he could talk of affairs of state, and put his spoke in the wheel in the council. And he knew one thing more: he could embroider suspenders with roses and other flowers, and with arabesques, for he was a tasty, light-fingered fellow.

"I shall win the Princess!" So cried both of them. Therefore their old papa gave to each of them a handsome horse. The youth who knew the dictionary and newspaper by heart had a black horse, and he who knew all about the corporation laws received a milk-white steed. Then they rubbed the corners of their mouths with fish-oil, so that they might become very smooth and glib. All the servants stood below in the courtyard, and looked on while they mounted their horses; and just by chance the third son came up. For the proprietor had really three sons, though nobody counted the third with his brothers, because he was not so learned as they, and indeed he was generally known as "Jack the Dullard."

"Hallo!" said Jack the Dullard, "where are you going? I declare you have put on your Sunday clothes!"

"We're going to the King's court, as suitors to the King's daughter. Don't you know the announcement that has been made all through the country?" And they told him all about it.

"My word! I'll be in it too!" cried Jack the Dullard; and his two brothers burst out laughing at him, and rode away.

"Father, dear," said Jack, "I must have a horse too. I do feel so desperately inclined to marry! If she accepts me, she accepts me; and if she won't have me, I'll have her; but she *shall* be mine!"

"Don't talk nonsense," replied the old gentleman. "You shall have no horse from me. You don't know how to speak—you can't arrange your words. Your brothers are very different fellows from you."

"Well," quoth Jack the Dullard, "If I can't have a horse, I'll take the Billy-goat, who belongs to me, and he can carry me very well!"

And so said, so done. He mounted the Billy-goat, pressed his heels into its sides, and galloped down the high street like a hurricane.

"Hei, houp! that was a ride! Here I come!" shouted Jack the Dullard, and he sang till his voice echoed far and wide.

But his brothers rode slowly on in advance of him. They spoke not a word, for they were thinking about the fine extempore speeches they would have to bring out, and these had to be cleverly prepared beforehand.

"Hallo!" shouted Jack the Dullard. "Here am I! Look what I have found on the high road." And he showed them what it was, and it was a dead crow.

"Dullard!" exclaimed the brothers, "what are you going to do with that?"

"With the crow? why, I am going to give it to the Princess."

"Yes, do so," said they; and they laughed, and rode on.

"Hallo, here I am again! Just see what I have found now: you don't find that on the high road every day!"

And the brothers turned round to see what he could have found now.

"Dullard!" they cried, "that is only an old wooden shoe, and the upper part is missing into the bargain; are you going to give that also to the Princess?"

"Most certainly I shall," replied Jack the Dullard; and again the brothers laughed and rode on, and thus they got far in advance of him; but——

"Hallo—hop rara!" and there was Jack the Dullard again. "It is getting better and better," he cried. "Hurrah! it is quite famous."

"Why, what have you found this time?" inquired the brothers.

"Oh," said Jack the Dullard, "I can hardly tell you. How glad the Princess will be!"

"Bah!" said the brothers; "that is nothing but clay out of the ditch."

"Yes, certainly it is," said Jack the Dullard; "and clay of the finest sort. See, it is so wet, it runs through one's fingers." And he filled his pocket with the clay.

But his brothers galloped on till the sparks flew, and consequently they arrived a full hour earlier at the town gate than could Jack. Now at the gate each suitor was provided with a number, and all were placed in rows immediately on their arrival, six in each row, and so closely packed together that they could not move their arms; and that was a prudent arrangement, for they would certainly have come to blows, had they been able, merely because one of them stood before the other.

All the inhabitants of the country round about stood in great crowds around the castle, almost under the very windows, to see the Princess receive the suitors; and as each stepped into the hall, his power of speech seemed to desert him, like the light of a candle that is blown out. Then the Princess would say, 'He is of no use! Away with him out of the hall!"

At last the turn came for that brother who knew the dictionary by heart; but he did not know it now; he had absolutely forgotten it altogether; and the boards seemed to re-echo with his footsteps, and the ceiling of the hall was made of looking-glass, so that he saw himself standing on his head; and at the window stood three clerks and a head clerk, and every one of them was writing down every single word that was uttered, so that it might be printed in the newspapers, and sold for a penny at the steet corners. It was a terrible ordeal, and they had, moreover, made such a fire in the stove, that the room seemed quite red hot.

"It is dreadfully hot here!" observed the first brother.

"Yes," replied the Princess, "my father is going to roast young pullets to-day."

"Baa!" there he stood like a baa-lamb. He had not been prepared for a speech of this kind, and had not a word to say, though he intended to say something witty. "Baa!"

"He is of no use!" said the Princess. "Away with him!"

And he was obliged to go accordingly. And now the second brother came in.

"It is terribly warm here!" he observed.

"Yes, we're roasting pullets to-day," replied the Princess.

"What — what were you — were you pleased to ob —— " stammered he — and all the clerks wrote down, "pleased to ob —— "

"He is of no use!" said the Princess. "Away with him!"

Now came the turn of Jack the Dullard. He rode into the hall on his goat.

"Well, it's most abominably hot here."

"Yes, because I'm roasting young pullets," replied the Princess.

"Ah, that's lucky!" exclaimed Jack the Dullard, "for I suppose you'll let me roast my crow at the same time?"

"With the greatest pleasure," said the Princess. "But have you anything you can roast it in? for I have neither pot nor pan."

"Certainly I have!" said Jack. "Here's a cooking utensil with a tin handle."

And he brought out the old wooden shoe, and put the crow into it.

"Well, that *is* a famous dish!' said the Princess. "But what shall we do for sauce?"

"Oh, I have that in my pocket," said Jack; "I have so much of it that I can afford to throw some away;" and he poured some of the clay out of his pocket.

"I like that!" said the Princess. "You can give an answer, and you have something to say for yourself, and so you shall be my husband. But are you aware that every word we speak is being taken down, and will be published in the paper to-morrow? Look yonder, and you will see in every window three clerks and a head clerk; and the old head clerk is the worst of all, for he can't understand anything."

But she only said this to frighten Jack the Dullard; and the clerks gave a great crow of delight, and each one spurted a blot out of his pen on to the floor.

"Oh, those are the gentlemen, are they?" said Jack; "then I will give the best I have to the head clerk." And he turned out his pockets, and flung the wet clay full in the head clerk's face.

"That was very cleverly done," observed the Princess. "I could not have done that; but I shall learn in time."

And accordingly Jack the Dullard was made a king, and received a crown and a wife, and sat upon a throne. And this report we have wet from the press of the head clerk and the corporation of printers — but *they* are not to be depended upon in the least.

JACK THE DULLARD

OLE THE TOWER-KEEPER

"IN the world it's always going up and down; and now I can't go up any higher!" So said Ole the tower-keeper. "Most people have to try both the ups and the downs; and, rightly considered, we all get to be watchmen at last, and look down upon life from a height."

Such was the speech of Ole, my friend, the old tower-keeper, a strange, talkative old fellow, who seemed to speak out everything that came into his head, and who for all that had many a serious thought deep in his heart. Yes, he was the child of respectable people, and there were even some who said that he was the son of a privy councillor, or that he might have been. He had studied, too, and had been assistant teacher and deputy clerk; but of what service was all that to him? In those days he lived in the clerk's house, and was to have everything in the house—to be at free quarters, as the saying is; but he was still, so to speak, a fine young gentleman. He wanted to have his boots cleaned with patent blacking, and the clerk could only afford ordinary grease; and upon that point they split. One spoke of stinginess, the other of vanity, and the blacking became the black cause of enmity between them, and at last they parted.

This is what he demanded of the world in general, namely, patent blacking, and he got nothing but grease. Accordingly, he at last drew back from all men, and became a hermit; but the church tower is the only place in a great city where hermitage, office and bread can be found together. So he betook himself up thither, and smoked his pipe as he made his solitary rounds. He looked upward and downward, and had his own thoughts, and told in his own way of what he read in books and in himself. I often lent him books—good books; and you may know by the company he keeps. He loved neither the English governess novels nor the French ones, which he called a mixture of empty wind and raisin-stalks: he wanted biographies, and descriptions of the wonders of the world. I visited him at least once a year, generally directly after New Year's day, and then he always spoke of this and that which the change of the year had put into his head.

I will tell the story of three of these visits, and will reproduce his own words whenever I can remember them.

FIRST VISIT

Among the books which I had lately lent Ole, was one which had greatly rejoiced and occupied him. It was a geological book, containing an account of the boulders.

"Yes, they're rare old fellows, those boulders!" he said; "and to think that we should pass them without noticing them! And over the street pavement, the paving stones, those fragments of the oldest remains of antiquity, one walks without ever thinking about them. I have done the very thing myself. But now I look respectfully at every paving-stone. Many thanks for the book! It has filled me with thought, and has made me long to read more on the subject. The romance of the earth is, after all, the most wonderful of all romances. It's a pity one can't read the first volume of it, because it is written in a language that we don't understand. One must read in the different strata, in the pebble-stones, for each separate period. Yes, it is a romance, a very wonderful romance, and we all have our place in it. We grope and ferret about, and yet remain where we are; but the ball keeps turning, without emptying the ocean over us; the clod on which we move about, holds, and does not let us through. And then it's a story that has been acting for thousands upon thousands of years and is still going on. My best thanks for the book about the boulders. Those are fellows indeed! They could tell us something worth hearing , if they only knew how to talk. It's really a pleasure now and then to become a mere nothing, especially when a man is as highly placed as I am. And then to think that we all, even with patent lacquer, are nothing more than insects of a moment on that ant-hill the earth, though we may be insects with stars and garters, places and offices! One feels quite a novice beside these venerable million-year-old boulders. On last New Year's eve I was reading the book, and had lost myself in it so completely, that I forgot my usual New Year's diversion, namely, the wild hunt to Amack. Ah, you don't know what that is!

"The journey of the witches on broomsticks is well enough known—that journey is taken on St. John's eve, to the Brocken; but we have a wild journey, also, which is national and modern, and that is the journey to Amack on the night of the New Year. All indifferent poets and poetesses, musicians, newspaper writers, and artistic notabilities,—I mean those who are no good,—ride in the New Year's night through the air to Amack. They sit backwards on their painting brushes or quill pens, for steel pens won't bear them—they're too stiff. As I told you, I see that every New Year's night, and could mention the majority of the riders by name, but I should not like to draw their enmity upon myself, for they don't like people to talk about their ride to Amack on quill pens. I've a kind of niece, who is a fishwife, and who, as she tells me, supplies three respectable newspapers with the terms of abuse and vituperation they use, and she has herself been at Amack as an invited guest; but she was carried out thither, for she does not own a quill pen, nor can she ride. She has told me all about it. Half of what she said is not true, but the other half gives us information enough. When she was out there, the festivities began with a song; each of the guests had written his own song, and each one sang his own song, for he thought that the best, and it was all one, all the same melody. Then those came marching up, in little bands, who are only busy with their mouths. There were ringing bells that rang alternately; and then came the little drummers that beat their tattoo in the family circle; and acquaintance was made with those who write without putting their names, which here means as much as using grease instead of patent blacking; and then there was the beadle with his boy, and the boy was worst off, for in general he gets no notice taken of him; then, too, there was the good street-sweeper with his cart, who turns over the dust-bin, and calls it 'good, very good, remarkably good.' And in the midst of the pleasure that was afforded by the mere meeting of these folks, there shot up out of the great dirt-heap at Amack a stem, a tree, an immense flower, a great mushroom, a perfect roof, which formed a sort of warehouse for the worthy company, for in it hung everything they had given to the world during the Old Year. Out of the tree poured sparks like flames of fire; these were the ideas and thoughts, borrowed from others, which they had used, and which now got free and rushed away like so many fireworks. They played at 'the stick burns,' and the young poets played at 'heart-burns,' and the witlings played off their jests, and the jests rolled away with a thundering sound, as if empty pots were being shattered against doors. 'It was very amusing!' my niece said; in fact, she said many things that were very malicious but very amusing, but I won't mention them, for a man must be good-natured, and not a carping critic. But you will easily perceive that when a man once knows the rights of the journey to Amack, as I know them, it's quite natural that on the New Year's night one should look out to see the wild chase go by. If in the New Year I miss certain persons who used to be there, I am sure to notice others who are new arrivals; but this year I omitted taking my look at the guests. I bowled away on the boulders, rolled back through millions of years, and saw the stones break loose high up in the north, saw them drifting about on icebergs, long before Noah's ark was constructed, saw them sink down to the bottom of the sea, and re-appear with a sand-bank, with that one that peered forth from the flood and said, 'This shall be Zealand!' I saw them become the dwelling-place of birds that are unknown to us, and then become the seat of wild chiefs of whom we know nothing, until with their axes they cut their Runic signs into a few of these stones, which then came into the calendar of time. But as for me, I had gone quite beyond all lapse of time, and had become a cipher and a nothing. Then three or four beautiful falling stars came down, which cleared the air, and gave my thoughts another direction. You know what a falling star is, do you not? The learned men are not at all clear about it. I have my own ideas about shooting stars, as the common people in many parts call them, and my idea is this: How often are silent thanksgivings offered up for one who has done a good and noble action! The thanks are often speechless, but they are not lost for all that. I think these thanks are caught up, and the sunbeams bring the silent, hidden thankfulness over the head of the benefactor; and if it be a whole people that has been expressing its gratitude through a long lapse of time, the thankfulness appears as a nosegay of flowers, and at length falls in the form of a shooting star over the good man's grave. I am always very much pleased when I see a shooting star, especially in the New Year's night, and then find out for whom the gift of gratitude was intended. Lately a gleaming star fell in the southwest, as a tribute of thanksgiving to many—many! 'For whom was that star intended?' thought I. It fell, no doubt, on the hill by the Bay of Plensberg, where the Danebrog waves over the graves of Schleppegrell, Läslöes, and their comrades. One star also fell in the midst of the land, fell upon Söro, a flower on the grave of Holberg, the thanks of the year from a great many—thanks for his charming plays!

"It is a great and pleasant thought to know that a shooting star falls upon our graves. On mine certainly none will fall—no sunbeam brings thanks to me, for here there is nothing worthy of thanks. I shall not get the patent lacquer," said Ole, "for my fate on earth is only grease, after all."

SECOND VISIT

It was New Year's day, and I went up on the tower. Ole spoke of the toasts that were drunk on the transition from the Old Year into the New—from one grave into the other, as he said. And he told me a story about the glasses, and this story had a very deep meaning. It was this:

"When on the New Year's night the clock strikes twelve, the people at the table rise up with full glasses in their hands, and drain these glasses, and drink success to the New Year. They begin the year with the glass in their hands; that is a good beginning for drunkards. They begin the New Year by going to bed, and that's a good beginning for drones. Sleep is sure to play a great part in the New Year, and the glass likewise. Do you know what dwells in the glass?" asked Ole. "I will tell you. There dwell in the glass, first, health, and then pleasure, then the most complete sensual delight; and misfortune and the bitterest woe dwell in the glass also. Now, suppose we count the glasses — of course I count the different degrees in the glasses for different people.

"You see, the first glass, that's the glass of health, and in that the herb of health is found growing. Put it up on the beam in the ceiling, and at the end of the year you may be sitting in the arbor of health.

"If you take the second glass — from this a little bird soars upward, twittering in guileless cheerfulness, so that a man may listen to his song, and perhaps join in 'Fair is life! no downcast looks! Take courage, and march onward!'

"Out of the third glass rises a little winged urchin, who cannot certainly be called an angel child, for there is goblin blood in his veins, and he has the spirit of a goblin — not wishing to hurt or harm you, indeed, but very ready to play off tricks upon you. He'll sit at your ear and whisper merry thoughts to you; he'll creep into your heart and warm you, so that you grow very merry, and become a wit, so far as the wits of the others can judge.

"In the fourth glass is neither herb, bird, nor urchin. In that glass is the pause drawn by reason, and one may never go beyond that sign.

"Take the fifth glass, and you will weep at yourself, you will feel such a deep emotion; or it will affect you in a different way. Out of the glass there will spring with a bang Prince Carnival, nine times and extravagantly merry. He'll draw you away with him; you'll forget your dignity, if you have any, and you'll forget more than you should or ought to forget. All is dance, song and sound: the masks will carry you away with them, and the daughters of vanity, clad in silk and satin, will come with loose hair and alluring charms; but tear yourself away if you can!

"The sixth glass! Yes, in that glass sits a demon, in the form of a little, well-dressed, attractive and very fascinating man, who thoroughly understands you, agrees with you in everything, and becomes quite a second self to you. He has a lantern with him, to give you light as he accompanies you home. There is an old legend about a saint who was allowed to choose one of the seven deadly sins, and who accordingly chose drunkenness, which appeared to him the least, but which led him to commit all the other six. The man's blood is mingled with that of the demon. It is the sixth glass, and with that the germ of all evil shoots up within us; and each one grows up with a strength like that of the grains of mustard-seed, and shoots up into a tree, and spreads over the whole world: and most people have no choice but to go into the oven, to be re-cast in a new form.

"That's the history of the glasses," said the tower-keeper Ole, "and it can be told with lacquer or only with grease; but I give it you with both!"

THIRD VISIT

On this occasion I chose the general "moving-day" for my visit to Ole, for on that day it is anything but agreeable down in the streets in the town; for they are full of sweepings, shreds, and remnants of all sorts, to say nothing of the cast-off rubbish in which one has to wade about. But this time I happened to see two children playing in this wilderness of sweepings. They were playing at "going to bed," for the occasion seemed especially favorable for this sport. They crept under the straw, and drew an old bit of ragged curtain over them-selves by way of coverlet. "It was splendid!" they said; but it was a little too strong for me, and besides, I was obliged to mount up on my visit to Ole.

"It's moving-day to-day," he said; "streets and houses are like a dust-bin — a large dust-bin; but I'm content with a cartload. I may get something good out of that, and I really did get something good out of it once. Shortly after Christmas I was going up the street; it was rough weather, wet and dirty — the right kind of weather to catch cold in. The dustman was there with his cart, which was full, and looked like a sample of streets on moving-day. At the back of the cart stood a fir tree, quite green still, and with tinsel on its twigs; it had been used on Christmas eve, and now it was thrown out into the street, and the dustman had stood it up at the back of his cart. It was droll to look at, or you may say it was mournful — all depends on what you think of when you see it; and I thought about it, and thought this and that of many things that were in the cart: or I might have done so, and that comes to the same thing. There was an old lady's glove, too: I wonder what that was thinking of? Shall I tell you? The glove was lying there, pointing with its little finger at the tree. 'I'm sorry for the tree,' it thought; 'and I was also at the feast, where the chandeliers glittered. My life was, so to speak, a ball night — a pressure of the hand, and I burst! My memory keeps dwelling upon that, and I have really nothing else to live for!' This is what the glove thought, or what it might have thought. 'That's a stupid affair with yonder fir tree,' said the potsherds. You see, potsherds think everything is stupid. 'When one is in the dust-cart,' they said, 'one ought not to give one's self airs and wear tinsel. I know that I have been useful in the world — far more useful than such a green stick.' This was a view that might be taken, and I don't think it quite a peculiar one; but for all that, the fir tree looked very well: it was like a little poetry in the dust-heap; and truly there is dust enough in the streets on moving-day. The way is dif-ficult and troublesome then, and I feel obliged to run away out of the con-fusion; or, if I am on the tower, I stay there and look down, and it is amusing enough.

"There are the good people below, playing at 'changing houses.' They toil and tug away with their goods and chattels, and the household goblin sits in an old tub and moves with them. All the little griefs of the lodging and the family, and the real cares and sorrows, move with them out of the old dwelling into the new; and what gain is there for them or for us in the whole affair? Yes, there was written long ago the good old maxim: 'Think on the great moving-day of death!' That is a serious thought. I hope it is not disagreeable to you that I should have touched upon it? Death is the most cer-tain messenger, after all, in spite of his various occupations. Yes, Death is the omnibus conductor, and he is the passport writer, and he countersigns our

OLE THE TOWER-KEEPER

service-book, and he is director of the savings bank of life. Do you understand me? All the deeds of our life, the great and the little alike, we put into this savings bank; and when Death calls with his omnibus, and we have to step in, and drive with him into the land of eternity, then on the frontier he gives us our service-book as a pass. As a provision for the journey, he takes this or that good deed we have done, and lets it accompany us; and this may be very pleasant or very terrific. Nobody has ever escaped the omnibus journey. There is certainly a talk about *one* who was not allowed to go—they call him the Wandering Jew: he has to ride behind the omnibus. If he had been allowed to get in, he would have escaped the clutches of the poets.

"Just cast your mind's eye into that great omnibus. The society is mixed, for king and beggar, genius and idiot, sit side by side. They must go without their property and money; they have only the service-book and the gift out of the savings bank with them. But which of our deeds is selected and given to us? Perhaps quite a little one, one that we have forgotten, but which has been recorded—small as a pea, but the pea can send out a blooming shoot. The poor bumpkin who sat on a low stool in the corner, and was jeered at and flouted, will perhaps have his worn-out stool given him as a provision; and the stool may become a litter in the land of eternity, and rise up then as a throne, gleaming like gold and blooming as an arbor. He who always lounged about, and drank the spiced draught of pleasure, that he might forget the wild things he had done here, will have his barrel given to him on the journey, and will have to drink from it as they go on; and the drink is bright and clear, so that the thoughts remain pure, and all good and noble feelings are awakened, and he sees and feels what in life he could not or would not see; and then he has within him the punishment, the *gnawing worm,* which will not die through time incalculable. If on the glasses there stood written *'oblivion,'* on the barrel *'remembrance'* is inscribed.

"When I read a good book, an historical work, I always think at last of the poetry of what I am reading, and of the omnibus of death, and wonder which of the hero's deeds Death took out of the savings bank for him, and what provisions he got on the journey into eternity. There was once a French king—I have forgotten his name, for the names of good people are sometimes forgotten, even by me, but it will come back some day;—there was a king who, during a famine, became the benefactor of his people; and the people raised up to his memory a monument of snow, with the inscription, 'Quicker than this melts didst thou bring help!' I fancy that Death, looking back upon the monument, gave him a single snow-flake as provision, a snow-flake that never melts, and this flake floated over his royal head, like a white butterfly, into the land of eternity. Thus, too, there was Louis XI. I have remembered *his* name, for one remembers what is bad—a trait of him often comes into my thoughts, and I wish one could say the story is not true. He had his lord high constable executed, and he could execute him, right or wrong; but he had the innocent children of the constable, one seven and the other eight years old, placed under the scaffold so that the warm blood of their father spurted over them, and then he had them sent to the Bastille, and shut up in iron cages, where not even a coverlet was given them to protect them from the cold. And King Louis sent the executioner to them every week, and had a tooth pulled out of the head of each, that they might not be too comfortable; and the elder of the boys said, 'My mother would die of grief if she knew that my younger brother had to suffer so cruelly; therefore pull out two of my teeth, and spare him.' The tears came into the hangman's eyes, but the king's will was stronger than the tears; and every week two little teeth were brought to him on a silver plate; he had demanded them, and he had them. I fancy that Death took these two teeth out of the savings bank of life, and gave them to Louis XI, to carry with him on the great journey into the land of immortality; they fly before him like two flames of fire; they shine and burn, and they bite him, the innocent children's teeth.

"Yes, that's a serious journey, the omnibus ride on the great moving-day! And when is it to be undertaken? That's just the serious part of it. Any day, any hour, any minute, the omnibus may draw up. Which of our deeds will Death take out of the savings bank, and give to us as provision? Let us think of the moving-day that is not marked in the calendar."

THE DROP OF WATER

OF course you know what is meant by a magnifying glass—one of those round spectacle-glasses that make everything look a hundred times bigger than it is? When any one takes one of these and holds it to his eye, and looks at a drop of water from the pond yonder, he sees above a thousand wonderful creatures that are otherwise never discerned in the water. But there they are, and it is no delusion. It almost looks like a great plateful of spiders jumping about in a crowd. And how fierce they are! They tear off each other's legs and arms and bodies, before and behind; and yet they are merry and joyful in their way.

Now, there once was an old man whom all the people called Kribble-Krabble, for that was his name. He always wanted the best of everything, and when he could not manage it otherwise, he did it by magic.

There he sat one day, and held his magnifying-glass to his eye, and looked at a drop of water that had been taken out of a puddle by the ditch. But what a kribbling and krabbling was there! All the thousands of little creatures hopped and sprang and tugged at one another, and ate each other up.

"That is horrible!" said old Kribble-Krabble. "Can one not persuade them to live in peace and quietness, so that each one may mind his own business?"

And he thought it over and over, but it would not do, and so he had recourse to magic.

"I must give them color, that they may be seen more plainly," said he; and he poured something like a little drop of red wine into the drop of water, but it was witches' blood from the lobes of the ear, the finest kind, at ninepence a drop. And now the wonderful little creatures were pink all over. It looked like a whole town of naked wild men.

"What have you there?" asked another old magician, who had no name—and that was the best thing about him.

"Yes, if you can guess what it is," said Kribble-Krabble, "I'll make you a present of it."

But it is not so easy to find out if one does not know.

And the magician who had no name looked through the magnifying-glass.

It looked really like a great town reflected there, in which all the people were running about without clothes. It was terrible! But it was still more terrible to see how one beat and pushed the other, and bit and hacked, and tugged and mauled him. Those at the top were being pulled down, and those at the bottom were struggling upwards.

"Look! look! his leg is longer than mine! Bah! Away with it! There is one who has a little bruise. It hurts him, but it shall hurt him still more."

And they hacked away at him, and they pulled at him, and ate him up, because of the little bruise. And there was one sitting as still as any little maiden, and wishing only for peace and quietness. But now she had to come out, and they tugged at her, and pulled her about, and ate her up.

"That's funny!" said the magician.

"Yes; but what do you think it is?" said Kribble-Krabble. "Can you find that out?"

"Why, one can see that easily enough," said the other. "That's Paris, or some other great city, for they're all alike. It's a great city!"

"It's a drop of puddle water!" said Kribble-Krabble.

TWO MAIDENS

HAVE you ever seen a maiden? I mean what our pavers call a maiden, a thing with which they ram down the paving-stones in the roads. A maiden of this kind is made altogether of wood, broad below, and girt round with iron rings. At the top she is narrow, and has a stick passed across through her waist, and this stick forms the arms of the maiden.

In the shed stood two Maidens of this kind. They had their place among shovels, hand-carts, wheelbarrows, and measuring-tapes; and to all this company the news had come that the Maidens were no longer to be called "maidens," but "hand-rammers," which word was the newest and the only correct designation among the pavers for the thing we all know from the old times by the name of "the maiden."

Now, there are among us human creatures certain individuals who are knows as "emancipated women," as, for instance, principals of institutions, dancers who stand professionally on one leg, milliners, and sick-nurses; and with this class of emancipated women the two Maidens in the shed associated themselves. They were "maidens" among the paver folk, and determined not to give up this honorable appellation, and let themselves be miscalled "rammers."

"Maiden is a human name, but hand-rammer is a thing, and we won't be called things—that's insulting us."

"My lover would be ready to give up his engagement," said the youngest, who was betrothed to a paver's hammer; and the hammer is the thing which drives great piles into the earth, like a machine, and therefore does on a large scale what ten maidens effect in a similar way. "He wants to marry me as a maiden, but whether he would have me were I a hand-rammer is a question, so I won't have my name changed."

"And I," said the elder one, "would rather have both my arms broken off."

But the Wheelbarrow was of a different opinion; and the Wheelbarrow was looked upon as of some consequence, for he considered himself a quarter of a coach, because he went about upon one wheel.

"I must submit to your notice," he said, "that the name 'maiden' is common enough, and not nearly so refined as 'hand-rammer,' or 'stamper,' which latter has also been proposed, and through which you would be introduced into the category of seals; and only think of the great stamp of state, which impresses the royal seal that gives effect to the laws! No, in your case I would surrender my maiden name."

"No, certainly not!" exclaimed the elder. "I am too old for that."

"I presume you have never heard of what is called 'European necessity?' " observed the honest Measuring Tape. "One must be able to adapt one's self to time and circumstances, and if there is a law that the 'maiden' is to be called 'hand-rammer,' why, she must be called 'hand-rammer,' and no pouting will avail, for everything has its measure."

"No; if there must be a change," said the younger, "I should prefer to be called 'Missy,' for that reminds one a little of maidens."

"But I would rather be chopped to chips," said the elder.

At last they all went to work. The Maidens rode—that is, they were put in a wheelbarrow, and that was a distinction; but still they were called "hand-rammers."

"Mai——!" they said, as they were bumped upon the pavement. "Mai—!" and they were very nearly pronouncing the whole word "maiden;" but they broke off short, and swallowed the last syllable; for after mature deliberation they considered it beneath their dignity to protest. But they always called each other "maiden," and praised the good old days in which everything had been called by its right name, and those who were maidens were called maidens. And they remained as they were; for the hammer really broke off his engagement with the younger one, for nothing would suit him but he must have a maiden for his bride.

THE BISHOP OF BÖRGLUM AND HIS WARRIORS

OUR scene is laid in Northern Jutland, in the so-called "wild moor." We hear what is called the "Wester-wow-wow"—the peculiar roar of the North Sea as it breaks against the western coast of Jutland. It rolls and thunders with a sound that penetrates for miles into the land; and we are quite near the roaring. Before us rises a great mound of sand—a mountain we have long seen, and towards which we are wending our way, driving slowly along through the deep sand. On this mountain of sand is a lofty old building—the convent of Börglum. In one of its wings (the larger one) there is still a church. And at this convent we now arrive in the late evening hour; but the weather is clear in the bright June night around us, and the eye can range far, far over field and moor to the Bay of Aalborg, over heath and meadow, and far across the deep blue sea.

Now we are there, and roll past between barns and other farm buildings; and at the left of the gate we turn aside to the Old Castle Farm, where the lime trees stand in lines along the walls, and, sheltered from the wind and weather, grow so luxuriantly that their twigs and leaves almost conceal the windows.

We mount the winding staircase of stone, and march through the long passages under the heavy roof-beams. The wind moans very strangely here, both within and without. It is hardly known how, but the people say—yes, people say a great many things when they are frightened or want to frighten others—they say that the old dead choir-men glide silently past us into the church, where mass is sung. They can be heard in the rushing of the storm, and their singing brings up strange thoughts in the hearers—thoughts of the old times into which we are carried back.

On the coast a ship is stranded; and the bishop's warriors are there, and spare not those whom the sea has spared. The sea washes away the blood that has flowed from the cloven skulls. The stranded goods belong to the bishop, and there is a store of goods here. The sea casts up tubs and barrels filled with costly wine for the convent cellar, and in the convent is already good store of beer and mead. There is plenty in the kitchen—dead game and poultry, hams and sausages; and fat fish swim in the ponds without.

The Bishop of Börglum is a mighty lord. He has great possessions, but still he longs for more—everything must bow before the mighty Olaf Glob. His rich cousin at Thyland is dead, and his widow is to have the rich inheritance. But how comes it that one relation is always harder towards another than even strangers would be? The widow's husband had possessed all Thyland, with the exception of the church property. Her son was not at home. In his boyhood he had already started on a journey, for his desire was to see foreign lands and strange people. For years there had been no news of him. Perhaps he had been long laid in the grave, and would never come back to his home, to rule where his mother then ruled.

"What has a woman to do with rule?" said the bishop.

He summoned the widow before a law court; but what did he gain thereby? The widow had never been disobedient to the law, and was strong in her just rights.

Bishop Olaf of Börglum, what dost thou purpose? What writest thou on yonder smooth parchment, sealing it with thy seal, and intrusting it to the horsemen and servants, who ride away, far away, to the city of the Pope?

It is the time of falling leaves and of stranded ships, and soon icy winter will come.

Twice had icy winter returned before the bishop welcomed the horsemen and servants back to their home. They came from Rome with a papal decree—a ban, or bull, against the widow who had dared to offend the pious bishop. "Cursed be she and all that belongs to her. Let her be expelled from the congregation and the Church. Let no man stretch forth a helping hand to her, and let friends and relations avoid her as a plague and a pestilence!"

"What will not bend must break," said the Bishop of Börglum.

And all forsake the widow; but she holds fast to her God. He is her helper and defender.

One servant only—an old maid—remained faithful to her; and with the old servant, the widow herself followed the plough; and the crop grew, although the land had been cursed by the Pope and by the bishop.

"Thou child of perdition, I will yet carry out my purpose!" cried the Bishop of Börglum. "Now will I lay the hand of the Pope upon thee, to summon thee before the tribunal that shall condemn thee!"

Then did the widow yoke the last two oxen that remained to her to a wagon, and mounted up on the wagon, with her old servant, and travelled away across the heath out of the Danish land. As a stranger she came into a foreign country, where a strange tongue was spoken and where new customs prevailed. Farther and farther she journeyed, to where green hills rise into mountains, and the vine clothes their sides. Strange merchants drive by her, and they look anxiously after their wagons laden with merchandise. They fear an attack from the armed followers of the robber-knights. The two poor women, in their humble vehicle drawn by two black oxen, travel fearlessly through the dangerous sunken road and through the darksome forest. And now they were in Franconia. And there met them a stalwart knight, with a train of twelve armed followers. He paused, gazed at the strange vehicle, and questioned the women as to the goal of their journey and the place whence they came. Then one of them mentioned Thyland in Denmark, and spoke of her sorrows, of her woes, which were soon to cease, for so Divine Providence had willed it. For the stranger knight is the widow's son! He seized her hand, he embraced her, and the mother wept. For years she had not been able to weep, but had only bitten her lips till the blood started.

It is the time of falling leaves and of stranded ships, and soon will icy winter come.

The sea rolled wine-tubs to the shore for the bishop's cellar. In the kitchen the deer roasted on the spit before the fire. At Börglum it was warm and cheerful in the heated rooms, while cold winter raged without, when a piece of news was brought to the bishop. "Jens Glob, of Thyland, has come back, and his mother with him." Jens Glob laid a complaint against the bishop, and summoned him before the temporal and the spiritual court.

"That will avail him little," said the bishop. "Best leave off thy efforts, knight Jens."

Again it is the time of falling leaves and stranded ships. Icy winter comes again, and the "white bees" are swarming, and sting the traveller's face till they melt.

"Keen weather to-day!" say the people, as they step in.

Jens Glob stands so deeply wrapped in thought, that he singes the skirt of his wide garment.

"Thou Börglum bishop," he exclaims, "I shall subdue thee after all! Under the shield of the Pope, the law cannot reach thee; but Jens Glob shall reach thee!"

Then he writes a letter to his brother-in-law, Olaf Hase, in Sallingland, and prays that knight to meet him on Christmas eve, at mass, in the church at Widberg. The bishop himself is to read the mass, and consequently will journey from Börglum to Thyland; and this is known to Jens Glob.

Moorland and meadow are covered with ice and snow. The marsh will bear horse and rider, the bishop with his priests and armed men. They ride the shortest way, through the waving reeds, where the wind moans sadly.

Blow thy brazen trumpet, thou trumpeter clad in fox-skin! it sounds merrily in the clear air. So they ride on over heath and moorland — over what is the garden of Fata Morgana in the hot summer, though now icy, like all the country—towards the church of Widberg.

The wind is blowing his trumpet too—blowing it harder and harder. He blows up a storm—a terrible storm—that increases more and more. Towards the church they ride, as fast as they may through the storm. The church stands firm, but the storm careers on over field and moorland, over land and sea.

Börglum's bishop reaches the church; but Olaf Hase will scarce do so, however hard he may ride. He journeys with his warriors on the farther side of the bay, in order that he may help Jens Glob, now that the bishop is to be summoned before the judgment seat of the Highest.

The church is the judgment hall; the altar is the council table. The lights burn clear in the heavy brass candelabra. The storm reads out the accusation and the sentence, roaming in the air over moor and heath, and over the rolling waters. No ferry-boat can sail over the bay in such weather as this.

Olaf Hase makes halt at Ottesworde. There he dismisses his warriors, presents them with their horses and harness, and gives them leave to ride home and greet his wife. He intends to risk his life alone in the roaring waters; but they are to bear witness for him that it is not his fault if Jens Glob stands without reinforcement in the church at Widberg. The faithful warriors will not leave him, but follow him out into the deep waters. Ten of them are carried away; but Olaf Hase and two of the youngest men reach the farther side. They have still four miles to ride.

It is past midnight. It is Christmas. The wind has abated. The church is lighted up; the gleaming radiance shines through the window-frames, and pours out over meadow and heath. The mass has long been finished, silence reigns in the church, and the wax is heard dropping from the candles to the stone pavement. And now Olaf Hase arrives.

In the forecourt Jens Glob greets him kindly, and says,

"I have just made an agreement with the bishop."

"Sayest thou so?" replied Olaf Hase. "Then neither thou nor the bishop shall quit this church alive."

And the sword leaps from the scabbard, and Olaf Hase deals a blow that makes the panel of the church door, which Jens Glob hastily closes between them, fly in fragments.

"Hold, brother! First hear what the agreement was that I made. I have slain the bishop and his warriors and priests. They will have no word more to say in the matter, nor will I speak again of all the wrong that my mother has endured."

The long wicks of the altar lights glimmer red; but there is a redder gleam upon the pavement, where the bishop lies with cloven skull, and his dead warriors around him, in the quiet of the holy Christmas night.

And four days afterwards the bells toll for a funeral in the convent of Börglum. The murdered bishop and the slain warriors and priests are displayed under a black canopy, surrounded by candelabra decked with crape. There lies the dead man, in the black cloak wrought with silver; the crozier in the powerless hand that was once so mighty. The incense rises in clouds, and the monks chant the funeral hymn. It sounds like a wail—it sounds like a sentence of wrath and condemnation, that must be heard far over the land, carried by the wind—sung by the wind—the wail that sometimes is silent, but never dies; for ever again it rises in song, singing even into our own time this legend of the Bishop of Börglum and his hard nephew. It is heard

THE BISHOP OF BÖRGLUM AND HIS WARRIORS

in the dark night by the frightened husbandman, driving by in the heavy sandy road past the convent of Börglum. It is heard by the sleepless listener in the thickly-walled rooms at Börglum. And not only to the ear of superstition is the sighing and the tread of hurrying feet audible in the long echoing passages leading to the convent door that has long been locked. The door still seems to open, and the lights seem to flame in the brazen candlesticks; the fragrance of incense arises; the church gleams in its ancient splendor; and the monks sing and say the mass over the slain bishop, who lies there in the black silver-embroidered mantle, with the crozier in his powerless hand; and on his pale proud forehead gleams the red wound like fire, and there burn the worldly mind and the wicked thoughts.

Sink down into his grave—into oblivion—ye terrible shapes of the times of old!

Hark to the raging of the angry wind, sounding above the rolling sea! A storm approaches without, calling aloud for human lives. The sea has not put on a new mind with the new time. This night it is a horrible pit to devour up lives, and to-morrow, perhaps, it may be a glassy mirror—even as in the old time that we have buried. Sleep sweetly, if thou canst sleep!

Now it is morning.

The new time flings sunshine into the room. The wind still keeps up mightily. A wreck is announced—as in the old time.

During the night, down yonder by Lökken, the little fishing village with the red-tiled roofs—we can see it up here from the window—a ship has come ashore. It has struck, and is fast embedded in the sand; but the rocket apparatus has thrown a rope on board, and formed a bridge from the wreck to the mainland; and all on board are saved, and reach the land, and are wrapped in warm blankets; and to-day they are invited to the farm at the convent of Börglum. In comfortable rooms they encounter hospitality and friendly faces. They are addressed in the language of their country, and the piano sounds for them with melodies of their native land; and before these have died away, the chord has been struck, the wire of thought that reaches to the land of the sufferers announces that they are rescued. Then their anxieties are dispelled; and at even they join in the dance at the feast given in the great hall at Börglum. Waltzes and Styrian dances are given, and Danish popular songs, and melodies of foreign lands in these modern times.

Blessed be thou, new time! Speak thou of summer and of purer gales! Send thy sunbeams gleaming into our hearts and thoughts! On thy glowing canvas let them be painted—the dark legends of the rough hard times that are past!

THE BELL-DEEP

"Ding-dong! ding-dong!" It sounds up from the "bell-deep" in the Odense-Au. Every child in the old town of Odense, on the island of Fünen, knows the Au, which washes the gardens round about the town, and flows on under the wooden bridges from the dam to the water-mill. In the Au grow the yellow water-lilies and brown feathery reeds; the dark velvety flag grows there, high and thick; old and decayed willows, slanting and tottering, hang far out over the stream beside the monk's meadow and by the bleaching ground; but opposite there are gardens upon gardens, each different from the rest, some with pretty flowers and bowers like little dolls' pleasure grounds, often displaying cabbage and other kitchen plants; and here and there the gardens cannot be seen at all, for the great elder trees that spread themselves out by the bank, and hang far out over the streaming waters, which are deeper here and there than an oar can fathom. Opposite the old nunnery is the deepest place, which is called the "bell-deep," and there dwells the old water spirit, the "Au-mann." This spirit sleeps through the day while the sun shines down upon the water; but in starry and moonlit nights he shows himself. He is very old. Grandmother says that she has heard her own grandmother tell of him; he is said to lead a solitary life, and to have nobody with whom he can converse save the great old church Bell. Once the Bell hung in the church tower; but now there is no trace left of the tower or of the church, which was called St. Alban's.

"Ding-dong! ding-dong!" sounded the Bell, when the tower still stood there; and one evening, while the sun was setting, and the Bell was swinging away bravely, it broke loose and came flying down through the air, the brilliant metal shining in the ruddy beam.

"Ding-dong! ding-dong! Now I'll retire to rest!" sang the Bell, and flew down into the Odense-Au, where it is deepest; and that is why the place is called the "bell-deep."

But the Bell got neither rest nor sleep. Down in the Au-mann's haunt it sounds and rings, so that the tones sometimes pierce upward through the waters; and many people maintain that its strains forebode the death of some one; but that is not true, for the Bell is only talking with the Au-mann, who is now no longer alone.

And what is the Bell telling? It is old, very old, as we have already observed; it was there long before grandmother's grandmother was born; and yet it is but a child in comparison with the Au-mann, who is quite an old quiet personage, an oddity, with his hose of eel-skin, and his scaly jacket with the yellow lilies for buttons, and a wreath of reed in his hair and seaweed in his beard; but he looks very pretty for all that.

What the Bell tells? To repeat it all would require years and days; for year by year it is telling the old stories, sometimes short ones, sometimes long ones, according to its whim; it tells of old times, of the dark hard times, thus:

"In the church of St. Alban, the monk had mounted up into the tower. He was young and handsome, but thoughtful exceedingly. He looked through the loophole out upon the Odense-Au, when the bed of the water was yet broad, and the monks' meadow was still a lake. He looked out over it, and over the rampart, and over the nuns' hill opposite, where the convent lay, and the light gleamed forth from the nun's cell. He had known the nun right well, and he thought of her, and his heart beat quicker as he thought. Ding-dong! ding-dong!"

Yes, this was the story the Bell told.

"Into the tower came also the dapper man-servant of the bishop; and when I, the Bell, who am made of metal, rang hard and loud, and swung to and fro, I might have beaten out his brains. He sat down close under me, and played with two little sticks as if they had been a stringed instrument; and he sang to it. 'Now I may sing it out aloud, though at other times I may not whisper it. I may sing of everything that is kept concealed behind lock and bars. Yonder it is cold and wet. The rats are eating her up alive! Nobody knows of it! Nobody hears of it! Not even now, for the bell is ringing and singing its loud Ding-dong! ding-dong!'

"There was a King in those days. They called him Canute. He bowed himself before bishop and monk; but when he offended the free peasants with heavy taxes and hard words, they seized their weapons and put him to flight like a wild beast. He sought shelter in the church, and shut gate and door behind him. The violent band surrounded the church; I heard tell of it. The crows, ravens and magpies started up in terror at the yelling and shouting that sounded around. They flew into the tower and out again, they looked down upon the throng below, and they also looked into the windows of the church, and screamed out aloud what they saw there. King Canute knelt before the altar in prayer; his brothers Eric and Benedict stood by him as a guard with drawn swords; but the King's servant, the treacherous Blake, betrayed his master. The throng in front of the church knew where they could hit the King, and one of them flung a stone through a pane of glass, and the King lay there dead! The cries and screams of the savage horde and of the birds sounded through the air, and I joined in it also; for I sang 'Ding-dong! ding-dong!'

"The church bell hangs high, and looks far around, and sees the birds around it, and understands their language. The wind roars in upon it through windows and loopholes; and the wind knows everything, for he gets it from the air, which encircles all things, and the church bell understands his tongue, and rings it out into the world, 'Ding-dong! ding-dong!'

"But it was too much for me to hear and to know; I was not able any longer to ring it out. I became so tired, so heavy, that the beam broke, and I flew out into the gleaming Au, where the water is deepest, and where the Au-mann lives, solitary and alone; and year by year I tell him what I have heard and what I know. Ding-dong! ding-dong!"

Thus it sounds complainingly out of the bell-deep in the Odense-Au. That is what grandmother told us.

But the schoolmaster says that there was not any bell that rung down there, for that it could not do so; and that no Au-mann dwelt yonder, for there was no Au-mann at all! And when all the other church bells are sounding sweetly, he says that it is not really the bells that are sounding, but that it is the air itself which sends forth the notes; and grandmother said to us that the Bell itself said it was the air who told it to him, consequently they are agreed on that point, and this much is sure.

"Be cautious, cautious, and take good heed to thyself," they both say.

The air knows everything. It is aroound us, it is in us, it talks of our thoughts and of our deeds, and it speaks longer of them than does the Bell down in the depths of the Odense-Au where the Au-mann dwells. It rings it out in the vault of heaven, far, far out, forever and ever, till the heaven bells sound "Ding-dong! ding-dong!"

THE PHOENIX BIRD

IN the Garden of Paradise, beneath the Tree of Knowledge, bloomed a rose bush. Here, in the first rose, a bird was born. His flight was like the flashing of light, his plumage was beauteous, and his song ravishing. But when Eve plucked the fruit of the tree of knowledge of good and evil, when she and Adam were driven from Paradise, there fell from the flaming sword of the cherub a spark into the nest of the bird, which blazed up forthwith. The bird perished in the flames; but from the red egg in the nest there fluttered aloft a new one—the one solitary Phoenix bird. The fable tells that he dwells in Arabia, and that every hundred years, he burns himself to death in his nest; but each time a new Phoenix, the only one in the world, rises up from the red egg.

The bird flutters round us, swift as light, beauteous in color, charming in song. When a mother sits by her infant's cradle, he stands on the pillow, and, with his wings, forms a glory around the infant's head. He flies through the chamber of content, and brings sunshine into it, and the violets on the humble table smell doubly sweet.

But the Phoenix is not the bird of Arabia alone. He wings his way in the glimmer of the Northern Lights over the plains of Lapland, and hops among the yellow flowers in the short Greenland summer. Beneath the copper mountains of Fablun, and England's coal mines, he flies, in the shape of a dusty moth, over the hymnbook that rests on the knees of the pious miner. On a lotus leaf he floats down the sacred waters of the Ganges, and the eye of the Hindoo maid gleams bright when she beholds him.

The Phoenix bird, dost thou not know him? The Bird of Paradise, the holy swan of song! On the car of Thespis he sat in the guise of a chattering raven, and flapped his black wings, smeared with the lees of wine; over the sounding harp of Iceland swept the swan's red beak; on Shakspeare's shoulder he sat in the guise of Odin's raven, and whispered in the poet's ear "Immortality!" and at the minstrels' feast he fluttered through the halls of the Wartburg.

The Phoenix bird, dost thou not know him? He sang to thee the Marseillaise, and thou kissedst the pen that fell from his wing; he came in the radiance of Paradise, and perchance thou didst turn away from him towards the sparrow who sat with tinsel on his wings.

The Bird of Paradise—renewed each century—born in flame, ending in flame! Thy picture, in a golden frame, hangs in the halls of the rich, but thou thyself often fliest around, lonely and disregarded, a myth—"The Phoenix of Arabia."

In Paradise, when thou wert born in the first rose, beneath the Tree of Knowledge, thou receivedst a kiss, and thy right name was given thee—thy name, Poetry.

THE SWAN'S NEST

BETWEEN the Baltic and the North Sea there lies an old swan's nest, wherein swans are born and have been born that shall never die.

In olden times a flock of swans flew over the Alps to the green plains around Milan, where it was delightful to dwell. This flight of swans men called the Lombards.

Another flock, with shining plumage and honest eyes, soared southward to Byzantium; the swans established themselves there close by the Emperor's throne, and spread their wings over him as shields to protect him. They received the name of Varangians.

On the coast of France there sounded a cry of fear, for the blood-stained swans that came from the North with fire under their wings; and the people prayed, "Heaven deliver us from the wild Northmen."

On the fresh sward of England stood the Danish swan by the open sea-shore, with the crown of three kingdoms on his head; and he stretched out his golden sceptre over the land. The heathens on the Pomerian coast bent the knee, and the Danish swans came with the banner of the Cross and with the drawn sword.

"That was in the very old times," you say.

In later days two mighty swans have been seen to fly from the nest. A light shone far through the air, far over the lands of the earth; the swan, with the strong beating of his wings, scattered the twilight mists, and the starry sky was seen, and it was as if it came nearer to the earth. That was the swan Tycho Brahe.

"Yes, then," you say; "but in our own days?"

We have seen swan after swan soar by in glorious flight. One let his pinions glide over the strings of the golden harp, and it resounded through the North. Norway's mountains seemed to rise higher in the sunlight of former days; there was a rustling among the pine trees and the birches; the gods of the North, the heroes, and the noble women, showed themselves in the dark forest depths.

We have seen a swan beat with his wings upon the marble crag, so that it burst, and the forms of beauty imprisoned in the stone stepped out to the sunny day, and men in the lands round about lifted up their heads to behold these mighty forms.

We have seen a third swan spinning the thread of thought that is fastened from country to country round the world, so that the word may fly with light-ning speed from land to land.

And our Lord loves the old swan's nest between the Baltic and the North Sea. And when the mighty birds come soaring through the air to destroy it, even the callow young stand round in a circle on the margin of the nest, and though their breasts may be struck so that their blood flows, they bear it, and strike with their wings and their claws.

Centuries will pass by, swans will fly forth from the nest, men will see them and hear them in the world, before it shall be said in spirit and in truth, "This is the last swan—the last song from the swan's nest."

THE PSYCHE

IN the fresh morning dawn, in the rosy air gleams a great Star, the brightest Star of the morning. His rays tremble on the white wall, as if he wished to write down on it what he can tell, what he has seen there and elsewhere during thousands of years in our rolling world. Let us hear one of his stories.

"A short time ago"—the Star's "short time ago" is called among men "centuries ago"—"my rays followed a young artist. It was in the city of the Popes, in the world-city, Rome. Much has been changed there in the course of time, but the changes have not come so quickly as the change from youth to old age. Then already the palace of the Caesars was a ruin, as it is now; fig trees and laurels grew among the fallen marble columns, and in the desolate bathing-halls, where the gilding still clings to the wall; the Coliseum was a gigantic ruin; the church bells sounded, the incense sent up its fragrant cloud, and through the streets marched processions with flaming tapers and glowing canopies. Holy Church was there, and art was held as a high and holy thing. In Rome lived the greatest painter in the world, Raphael; there also dwelt the first of sculptors, Michael Angelo. Even the Pope paid homage to these two, and honored them with a visit. Art was recognized and honored, and was rewarded also. But, for all that, everything great and splendid was not seen and known.

"In a narrow lane stood an old house. Once it had been a temple; a young sculptor now dwelt there. He was young and quite unknown. He certainly had friends, young artists, like himself, young in spirit, young in hopes and thoughts; they told him he was rich in talent, and an artist, but that he was foolish for having no faith in his own power; for he always broke what he had fashioned out of clay, and never completed anything; and a work must be completed if it is to be seen and to bring money.

" 'You are a dreamer,' they went on to say to him, 'and that's your misfortune. But the reason of this is, that you have never lived, you have never tasted life, you have never enjoyed it in great wholesome draughts, as it ought to be enjoyed. In youth one must mingle one's own personality with life, that they may become one. Look at the great master Raphael, whom the Pope honors and the world admires. He's no despiser of wine and bread.'

" 'And he even appreciates the baker's daughter, the pretty Fornarina,' added Angelo, one of the merriest of the young friends.

"Yes, they said a good many things of the kind, according to their age and their reason. They wanted to draw the young artist out with them into the merry wild life, the mad life as it might also be called; and at certain times he felt an inclination for it. He had warm blood, a strong imagination, and could take part in the merry chat, and laugh aloud with the rest; but what they called 'Raphael's merry life' disappeared before him like a vapor when he saw the divine radiance that beamed forth from the pictures of the great master; and when he stood in the Vatican, before the forms of beauty which the masters had hewn out of marble thousands of years since, his breast swelled, and he felt within himself something high, something holy, something elevating, great and good, and he wished that he could produce similar forms from the blocks of marble. He wished to make a picture of that which was within him, stirring upward from his heart to the realms of the Infinite; but how, and in what form? The soft clay was fashioned under his fingers into forms of beauty, but the next day he broke what he had fashioned, according to his wont.

"One day he walked past one of those rich palaces of which Rome has many to show. He stopped before the great open portal, and beheld a garden surrounded by cloistered walks. The garden bloomed with a goodly show of the fairest roses. Great white lilies with green juicy leaves shot upward from the marble basin in which the clear water was splashing; and a form glided past, the daughter of the princely house, graceful, delicate, and wonderfully fair. Such a form of female loveliness he had never before beheld—yet stay: he had seen it, painted by Raphael, painted as a Psyche, in one of the Roman palaces. Yes, there it had been painted; but here it passed by him in living reality.

"The remembrance lived in his thoughts, in his heart. He went home to his humble room, and modelled a Psyche of clay. It was the rich young Roman girl, the noble maiden; and for the first time he looked at his work with satisfaction. It had a meaning for him, for it was *she*. And the friends who saw his work shouted aloud for joy; they declared that this work was a manifestation of his artistic power, of which they had long been aware, and that now the world should be made aware of it too.

"The clay figure was lifelike and beautiful, but it had not the whiteness or the durability of marble. So they declared that the Psyche must henceforth live in marble. He already possessed a costly block of that stone. It had been lying for years, the property of his parents, in the courtyard. Fragments of glass, climbing weeds, and remains of artichokes had gathered about it and sullied its purity; but under the surface the block was as white as the mountain snow; and from this block the Psyche was to arise."

Now, it happened one morning—the bright Star tells nothing about this, but we know it occcurred—that a noble Roman company came into the narrow lane. The carriage stopped at the top of the lane, and the company proceeded on foot towards the house, to inspect the young sculptor's work, for they had heard him spoken of by chance. And who were these distinguished guests? Poor young man! or fortunate young man he might be called. The noble young lady stood in the room and smiled radiantly when her father said to her, "It is your living image." That smile could not be copied, any more than the look could be reproduced, the wonderful look which she cast upon the young artist. It was a fiery look, that seemed at once to elevate and to crush him.

"The Psyche must be executed in marble," said the wealthy patrician. And those were words of life for the dead clay and the heavy block of marble, and words of life likewise for the deeply-moved artist. "When the work is finished I will purchase it," continued the rich noble.

A new era seemed to have arisen in the poor studio. Life and cheerfulness gleamed there, and busy industry plied its work. The beaming Morning Star beheld how the work progressed. The clay itself seemed inspired since she had been there, and moulded itself, in heightened beauty, to a likeness of the well-known features.

"Now I know what life is," cried the artist rejoicingly; "it is Love! It is the lofty abandonment of self for the dawning of the beautiful in the soul! What my friends call life and enjoyment is a passing shadow; it is like bubbles among seething dregs, not the pure heavenly wine that consecrates us to life."

The marble block was reared in its place. The chisel struck great fragments from it; the measurements were taken, points and lines were made, the mechanical part was executed, till gradually the stone assumed a human female form, a shape of beauty, and became converted into the Psyche, fair and glorious — a divine being in human shape. The heavy stone appeared as a gliding, dancing, airy Psyche, with the heavenly innocent smile — the smile that had mirrored itself in the soul of the young artist.

The Star of the roseate dawn beheld and understood what was stirring within the young man, and could read the meaning of the changing color of his cheek, of the light that flashed from his eye, as he stood busily working, reproducing what had been put into his soul from above.

"Thou art a master like those masters among the ancient Greeks," exclaimed his delighted friends; "soon shall the whole world admire thy Psyche."

"My Psyche!" he repeated. "Yes, mine. She msut be mine. I, too, am an artist, like those great men who are gone. Providence has granted me the boon, and has made me the equal of that lady of noble birth."

And he knelt down and breathed a prayer of thankfulnesss to Heaven, and then he forgot Heaven for her sake — for the sake of her picture in stone — for her Psyche which stood there as if formed of snow, blushing in the morning dawn.

He was to see her in reality, the living, graceful Psyche, whose words sounded like music in his ears. He could now carry the news into the rich palace that the marble Psyche was finished. He betook himself thither, strode through the open courtyard where the waters ran splashing from the dolphin's jaws into the marble basins, where the snowy lilies and the fresh roses bloomed in abundance. He stepped into the great lofty hall, whose walls and ceilings shone with gilding and bright colors and heraldic devices. Gayly-dressed serving-men, adorned with trappings like sleigh horses, walked to and fro, and some reclined at their ease upon the carved oak seats, as if they were the masters of the house. He told them what had brought him to the palace, and was conducted up the shining marble staircase, covered with soft carpets and adorned with many a statue. Then he went on through richly-furnished chambers, over mosaic floors, amid gorgeous pictures. All this pomp and luxury seemed to weary him; but soon he felt relieved, for the princely old master of the house received him most graciously, almost heartily; and when he took his leave he was requested to step into the Signora's apartment, for she, too, wished to see him. The servants led him through more luxurious halls and chambers into her room, where she appeared the chief and leading ornament.

She spoke to him. No hymn of supplication, no holy chant, could melt his soul like the sound of her voice. He took her hand and lifted it to his lips. No rose was softer, but a fire thrilled through him from this rose — a feeling of power came upon him, and words poured from his tongue — he knew not what he said. Does the crater of the volcano know that the glowing lava is pouring from it? He confessed what he felt for her. She stood before him astonished, offended, proud, with contempt in her face, an expression of disgust, as if she had suddenly touched a cold unclean reptile. Her cheeks reddened, her lips grew white, and her eyes flashed fire, though they were dark as the blackness of night.

"Madman!" she cried, "away! begone!"

And she turned her back upon him. Her beautiful face wore an expression like that of the stony countenance with the snaky locks.

Like a stricken, fainting man, he tottered down the staircase and out into the street. Like a man walking in his sleep, he found his way back to his dwelling. Then he woke up to madness and agony, and seized his hammer, swung it high in the air, and rushed forward to shatter the beautiful marble image. But, in his pain, he had not noticed that his friend Angelo stood beside him; and Angelo held back his arm with a strong grasp, crying,

"Are you mad? What are you about?"

They struggled together. Angelo was the stronger; and, with a deep sigh of exhaustion, the young artist threw himself into a chair.

"What has happened?" asked Angelo. "Command yourself. Speak!"

But what could he say? How could he explain? And as Angelo could make no sense of his friend's incoherent words, he forbore to question him further, and merely said,

"Your blood grows thick from your eternal dreaming. Be a man, as all others are, and don't go on living in ideals, for that is what drives men crazy. A jovial feast will make you sleep quietly and happily. Believe me, the time will come when you will be old, and your sinews will shrink, and then, on some fine sunshiny day, when everything is laughing and rejoicing, you will lie there a faded plant, that will grow no more. I do not live in dreams, but in reality. Come with me. Be a man!"

And he drew the artist away with him. At this moment he was able to do so, for a fire ran in the blood of the young sculptor; a change had taken place in his soul; he felt a longing to tear from the old, the accustomed — to forget, if possible, his own individuality; and therefore it was that he followed Angelo.

In an out-of-the-way suburb of Rome lay a tavern much visited by artists. It was built on the ruins of some ancient baths. The great yellow citrons hung down among the dark shining leaves, and covered a part of the old reddish-yellow walls. The tavern consisted of a vaulted chamber, almost like a cavern, in the ruins. A lamp burned there before the picture of the Madonna. A great fire gleamed on the hearth, and roasting and boiling was going on there; without, under the citron trees and laurels, stood a few covered tables.

The two artists were received by their friends with shouts of welcome. Little was eaten, but much was drunk, and the spirits of the company rose. Songs were sung and ditties were played on the guitar; presently the Salterello sounded, and the merry dance began. Two young Roman girls, who sat as models to the artists, took part in the dance and in the festivity. Two charming Bacchantes were they; certainly not Psyches — not delicate, beautiful roses, but fresh, hearty, glowing carnations.

How hot it was on that day! Even after sundown it was hot. There was fire in the blood, fire in every glance, fire everywhere. The air gleamed with gold and roses, and life seemed like gold and roses.

"At last you have joined us, for once," said his friends. "Now let yourself be carried by the waves within and around you."

"Never yet have I felt so well, so merry!" cried the young artist. "You are right—you are all of you right. I was a fool—a dreamer. Man belongs to reality, and not to fancy."

With songs and with sounding guitars the young people returned that evening from the tavern, through the narrow streets; the two glowing carnations, daughters of the Campagna, went with them.

In Angelo's room, among a litter of colored sketches (studies) and glowing pictures, the voices sounded mellower, but not less merrily. On the ground lay many a sketch that resembled the daughters of the Campagna, in their fresh, hearty comeliness, but the two originals were far handsomer than their portraits. All the burners of the six-armed lamp flared and flamed; and the human flamed up from within, and appeared in the glare as if it were divine.

"Apollo! Jupiter! I feel myself raised to our heaven—to your glory! I feel as if the blossom of life were unfolding itself in my veins at this moment!"

Yes, the blossom unfolded itself, and then burst and fell, and an evil vapor arose from it, blinding the sight, leading astray the fancy; the firework of the senses went out, and it became dark.

He was again in his own room. There he sat down on his bed and collected his thoughts.

"Fie on thee!" these were the words that sounded out of his mouth from the depths of his heart. "Wretched man, go, begone!" And a deep painful sigh burst from his bosom.

"Away! begone!" These, her words, the words of the living Psyche, echoed through his heart, escaped from his lips. He buried his head in the pillows, his thoughts grew confused, and he fell asleep.

In the morning dawn he started up, and collected his thoughts anew. What had happened? Had all the past been a dream? The visit to her, the feast at the tavern, the evening with the purple carnations of the Campagna? No, it was all real—a reality he had never before experienced.

In the purple air gleamed the bright Star, and its beams fell upon him and upon the marble Psyche. He trembled as he looked at that picture of immortality, and his glance seemed impure to him. He threw the cloth over the statue, and then touched it once more to unveil the form—but he was not able to look again at his own work.

Gloomy, quiet, absorbed in his own thoughts, he sat there through the long day; he heard nothing of what was going on around him, and no man guessed what was passing in this human soul.

And days and weeks went by, but the nights passed more slowly than the days. The flashing Star beheld him one morning as he rose, pale and trembling with fever, from his sad couch; then he stepped towards the statue, threw back the covering, took one long, sorrowful gaze at his work, and then, almost sinking beneath the burden, he dragged the statue out into the garden. In that place was an old dry well, now nothing but a hole. Into this he cast the Psyche, threw earth in above her, and covered up the spot with twigs and nettles.

"Away! begone!" Such was the short epitaph he spoke.

The Star beheld all this from the pink morning sky, and its beam trembled upon two great tears upon the pale feverish cheeks of the young man; and soon it was said that he was sick unto death, and he lay stretched upon a bed of pain.

The convent Brother Ignatius visited him as a physician and a friend, and brought him words of comfort, of religion, and spoke to him of the peace and happiness of the church, of the sinfulness of man, of rest and mercy to be found in heaven.

And the words fell like warm sunbeams upon a teeming soil. The soil smoked and sent up clouds of mist, fantastic pictures, pictures in which there was reality; and from these floating islands he looked across at human life. He found it vanity and delusion — and vanity and delusion it had been to him. They told him that art was a sorcerer, betraying us to vanity and to earthly lusts; that we are false to ourselves, unfaithful to our friends, unfaithful towards Heaven; and that the serpent was always repeating within us, "Eat, and thou shalt become as God."

And it appeared to him as if now, for the first time, he knew himself, and had found the way that leads to truth and to peace. In the church was the light and the brightness of God — in the monk's cell he should find the rest through which the tree of human life might grow on into eternity.

Brother Ignatius strengthened his longings, and the determination became firm within him. A child of the world became a servant of the church — the young artist renounced the world, and retired into the cloister.

The brothers came forward affectionately to welcome him, and his inauguration was as a Sunday feast. Heaven seemed to him to dwell in the sunshine of the church, and to beam upon him from the holy pictures and from the cross. And when, in the evening, at the sunset hour, he stood in his little cell, and, opening the window, looked out upon old Rome, upon the desolated temples, and the great dead Coliseum — when he saw all this in its spring garb, when the acacias bloomed, and the ivy was fresh, and roses burst forth everywhere, and the citron and orange were in the height of their beauty, and the palm trees waved their branches — then he felt a deeper emotion than had ever yet thrilled through him. The quiet open Campagna spread itself forth towards the blue snow-covered mountains, which seemed to be painted in the air; all the outlines melting into each other, breathing peace and beauty, floating, dreaming — and all appearing like a dream!

Yes, this world was a dream, and the dream lasts for hours, and may return for hours; but convent life is a life of years — long years, and many years.

From within comes much that renders men sinful and impure. He fully realized the truth of this. What flames arose up in him at times! What a source of evil, of that which we would not, welled up continually! He mortified his body, but the evil came from within.

One day, after the lapse of many years, he met Angelo, who recognized him.

"Man!" exclaimed Angelo. "Yes, it is thou! Art thou happy now? Thou hast sinned against God, and cast away His boon from thee — hast neglected thy mission in this world! Read the parable of the intrusted talent! The MASTER, who spoke that parable, spoke the truth! What hast thou gained? What hast thou found? Dost thou not fashion for thyself a religion and a dreamy life after thine own idea, as almost all do? Suppose all this is a dream, a fair delusion!"

"Get thee away from me, Satan!" said the monk; and he quitted Angelo.

"There is a devil, a personal devil! This day I have seen him!" said the monk to himself. "Once I extended a finger to him, and he took my whole hand. But now," he sighed, "the evil is within me, and it is in yonder man; but it does not bow him down; he goes abroad with head erect, and enjoys his comfort; and I grasped at comfort in the consolations of religion. If it were nothing but a consolation? Supposing everything here were, like the world I have quitted, only a beautiful fancy, a delusion like the beauty of the evening clouds, like the misty blue of the distant hills!—when you approach them, they are very different! O eternity! Thou actest like the great calm ocean, that beckons us, and fills us with expectation—and when we embark upon thee, we sink, disappear, and cease to be. Delusion! away with it! begone!"

And tearless, but sunk in bitter reflection, he sat upon his hard couch, and then knelt down—before whom? Before the stone cross fastened to the wall? No, it was only habit that made him take this position.

The more deeply he looked into his own heart, the blacker did the darkness seem. "Nothing within, nothing without—this life squandered and cast away!" And this thought rolled and grew like a snowball, until it seemed to crush him.

"I can confide my griefs to none. I may speak to none of the gnawing worm within. My secret is my prisoner; if I let the captive escape, I shall be his!"

And the godlike power that dwelt within him suffered and strove.

"O Lord, my Lord!" he cried, in his despair, "be merciful and grant me faith. I threw away the gift thou hadst vouchsafed to me, I left my mission unfulfilled. I lacked strength, and strength thou didst not give me. Immortality—the Psyche in my breast—away with it!—it shall be buried like that Psyche, the best gleam of my life; never will it arise out of its grave!"

The Star glowed in the roseate air, the Star that shall surely be extinguished and pass away while the soul still lives on; its trembling beam fell upon the white wall, but it wrote nothing there upon being made perfect in God, nothing of the hope of mercy, of the reliance on the divine love that thrills through the heart of the believer.

"The Psyche within can never die. Shall it live in consciousness? Can the incomprehensible happen? Yes, yes. My being is incomprehensible. Thou art unfathomable, O Lord. Thy whole world is incomprehensible— a wonderwork of power, of glory and of love."

His eyes gleamed, and then closed in death. The tolling of the church bell was the last sound that echoed above him, above the dead man; and they buried him, covering him with earth that had been brought from Jerusalem, and in which was mingled the dust of many of the pious dead.

When years had gone by his skeleton was dug up, as the skeletons of the monks who had died before him had been; it was clad in a brown frock, a rosary was put into the bony hand, and the form was placed among the ranks of other skeletons in the cloisters of the convent. And the sun shone without, while within the censers were waved and the Mass was celebrated.

And years rolled by.

The bones fell asunder and became mingled with others. Skulls were piled up till they formed an outer wall around the church; and there lay also his head in the burning sun, for many dead were there, and no one knew their names, and his name was forgotten also. And see, something was moving in the sunshine, in the sightless cavernous eyes! What might that be? A sparkling lizard moved about in the skull, gliding in and out through the sightless holes. The lizard now represented all the life left in that head, in which once great thoughts, bright dreams, the love of art and of the glorious, had arisen, whence hot tears had rolled down, where hope and immortality had had their being. The lizard sprang away and disappeared, and the skull itself crumbled to pieces and became dust among dust.

Centuries passed away. The bright Star gleamed unaltered, radiant and large, as it had gleamed for thousands of years, and the air glowed red with tints fresh as roses, crimson like blood.

There, where once had stood the narrow lane containing the ruins of the temple, a nunnery was now built. A grave was being dug in the convent garden for a young nun who had died, and was to be laid in the earth this morning. The spade struck against a hard substance; it was a stone, that shone dazzling white. A block of marble soon appeared, a rounded shoulder was laid bare; and now the spade was plied with a more careful hand, and presently a female head was seen, and butterflies' wings. Out of the grave in which the young nun was to be laid they lifted, in the rosy morning, a wonderful statue of a Psyche carved in white marble.

"How beautiful, how perfect it is!" cried the spectators. "A relic of the best period of art."

And who could the sculptor have been? No one knew; no one remembered him, except the bright star that had gleamed for thousands of years. The star had seen the course of that life on earth, and knew of the man's trials, of his weakness—in fact, that he had been but human. The man's life had passed away, his dust had been scattered abroad as dust is destined to be; but the result of his noblest striving, the glorious work that gave token of the divine element within him—the Psyche that never dies, that lives beyond posterity—the brightness even of this earthly Psyche remained here after him, and was seen and acknowledged and appreciated.

The bright Morning Star in the roseate air threw its glancing ray downward upon the Psyche, and upon the radiant countenances of the admiring spectators, who here beheld the image of the soul portrayed in marble.

What is earthly will pass away and be forgotten, and the Star in the vast firmament knows it. What is heavenly will shine brightly through posterity; and when the ages of posterity are past, the Psyche—the soul—will still live on!

"THE WILL-O'-THE-WISP IS IN THE TOWN," SAYS THE MOOR WOMAN

THERE was a man who once knew many stories, but they had slipped away from him—so he said. The Story that used to visit him of its own accord no longer came and knocked at his door. And why did it come no longer? It is true enough that for days and years the man had not thought of it, had not expected it to come and knock; and if he had expected it, it would certainly not have come; for without there was war, and within was the care and sorrow that war brings with it.

**"THE WILL-O'-THE-WISP IS IN TOWN,"
SAYS THE MOOR-WOMAN**

The stork and the swallows came back from their long journey, for they thought of no danger; and, behold, when they arrived, the nest was burnt, the habitations of men were burnt, the hedges were all in disorder, and everything seemed gone, and the enemy's horses were stamping in the old graves. Those were hard, gloomy times, but they came to an end.

And now they were past and gone—so people said; yet no Story came and knocked at the door, or gave any tidings of its presence.

"I suppose it must be dead, or gone away with many other things," said the man.

But the story never dies. And more than a whole year went by, and he longed—oh, so very much!—for the Story.

"I wonder if the Story will ever come back again and knock?"

And he remembered it so well in all the various forms in which it had come to him, sometimes young and charming, like spring itself, sometimes as a beautiful maiden, with a wreath of thyme in her hair, and a beechen branch in her hand, and with eyes that gleamed like deep woodland lakes in the bright sunshine.

Sometimes it had come to him in the guise of a peddler, and had opened its box and let silver ribbon come fluttering out, with verses and inscriptions of old remembrances.

But it was most charming of all when it came as an old grandmother, with silvery hair, and such large, sensible eyes. She knew so well how to tell about the oldest times, long before the princesses spun with the golden spindles, and the dragons lay outside the castles, guarding them. She told with such an air of truth, that black spots danced before the eyes of all who heard her, and the floor became black with human blood; terrible to see and to hear, and yet so entertaining, because such a long time had passed since it all happened.

"Will it ever knock at my door again?" said the man, and he gazed at the door, so that black spots came before his eyes and upon the floor; he did not know if it was blood, or mourning crape from the dark heavy days.

And as he sat thus, the thought came upon him whether the Story might not have hidden itself, like the princess in the old tale. And he would now go in search of it; if he found it, it would beam in new splendor, lovelier than ever.

"Who knows? Perhaps it has hidden itself in the straw that balances on the margin of the well. Carefully, carefully! Perhaps it lies hidden in a certain flower—that flower in one of the great books on the book-shelf."

And the man went and opened one of the newest books, to gain information on this point; but there was no flower to be found. There he read about Holger Danske; and the man read that the tale had been invented and put together by a monk in France, that it was a romance, "translated into Danish and printed in that language;" that Holger Danske had never really lived, and consequently could never come again, as we have sung, and have been so glad to believe. And William Tell was treated just like Holger Danske. These were all only myths—nothing on which we could depend; and yet it is all written in a very learned book.

"Well, I shall believe what I believe!" said the man. "There grows no plantain where no foot has trod."

And he closed the book and put it back in its place, and went to the fresh flowers at the window. Perhaps the Story might have hidden itself in the red tulips, with the golden yellow edges, or in the fresh rose, or in the beaming camellia. The sunshine lay among the flowers, but no Story.

The flowers which had been here in the dark troublous time had been much more beautiful; but they had been cut off, one after another, to be woven into wreaths and placed in coffins, and the flag had waved over them! Perhaps the Story had been buried with the flowers; but then the flowers would have known of it, and the coffin would have heard it, and every little blade of grass that shot forth would have told of it. The Story never dies.

Perhaps it has been here once, and has knocked; but who had eyes or ears for it in those times? People looked darkly, gloomily, and almost angrily at the sunshine of spring, at the twittering birds, and all the cheerful green; the tongue could not even bear the old merry, popular songs, and they were laid in the coffin with so much that our heart held dear. The Story may have knocked without obtaining a hearing; there was none to bid it welcome, and so it may have gone away.

"I will go forth and seek it. Out in the country! out in the wood! and on the open sea beach!"

Out in the country lies an old manor house, with red walls, pointed gables, and a red flag that floats on the tower. The nightingale sings among the finely-fringed beech-leaves, looking at the blooming apple trees of the garden, and thinking that they bear roses. Here the bees are mightily busy in the summer-time, and hover round their queen with their humming song. The autumn has much to tell of the wild chase, of the leaves of the trees, and of the races of men that are passing away together. The wild swans sing at Christmas-time on the open water, while in the old hall the guests by the fireside gladly listen to songs and to old legends.

Down into the old part of the garden, where the great avenue of wild chestnut trees lures the wanderer to tread its shades, went the man who was in search of the Story; for here the wind had once murmured something to him of "Waldemar Daa and his Daughters." The Dryad in the tree, who was the Story-mother herself, had here told him the "Dream of the Old Oak Tree." Here, in the time of the ancestral mother, had stood clipped hedges, but now only ferns and stinging nettles grew there, hiding the scattered fragments of old sculptured figures; the moss is growing in their eyes, but they can see as well as ever, which was more than the man could do who was in search of the Story, for he could not find that. Where could it be?

The crows flew past him by hundreds across the old trees, and screamed, "Krah! da! — Krah! da!"

And he went out of the garden and over the grass-plot of the yard, into the alder grove; there stood a little six-sided house, with a poultry-yard and a duck-yard. In the middle of the room sat the old woman who had the management of the whole, and who knew accurately about every egg that was laid, and about every chicken that could creep out of an egg. But she was not the Story of which the man was in search; that she could attest with a Christian certificate of baptism and of vaccination that lay in her drawer.

Without, not far from the house, is a hill covered with red-thorn and broom. Here lies an old grave-stone, which was brought here many years ago from the churchyard of the provincial town, a remembrance of one of the most honored councillors of the place; his wife and his five daughters, all with folded hands and stiff ruffs, stand round him. One could look at them so long, that it had an effect upon the thoughts, and these reacted upon the stones, as if they were telling of old times; at least it had been so with the man who was in search of the Story.

As he came nearer, he noticed a living butterfly sitting on the forehead of the sculptured councillor. The butterfly flapped its wings, and flew a little bit farther, and then returned fatigued to sit upon the grave-stone, as if to point out what grew there. Four-leaved shamrocks grew there; there were seven specimens close to each other. When fortune comes, it comes in a heap. He plucked the shamrocks and put them in his pocket.

"Fortune is as good as red gold, but a new charming story would be better still," thought the man; but he could not find it here.

And the sun went down, round and large; the meadow was covered with vapor. The moor-woman was at her brewing.

It was evening. He stood alone in his room, and looked out upon the sea, over the meadow, over moor and coast. The moon shone bright, a mist was over the meadow, making it look like a great lake; and, indeed, it was once so, as the legend tells—and in the moonlight the eye realizes these myths.

Then the man thought of what he had been reading in the town, that William Tell and Holger Danske never really lived, but yet live in popular story, like the lake yonder, a living evidence for such myths. Yes, Holger Danske will return again!

As he stood thus and thought, something beat quite strongly against the window. Was it a bird, a bat or an owl? Those are not let in, even when they knock. The window flew open of itself, and an old woman looked in at the man.

"What's your pleasure?" said he. "Who are you? You're looking in at the first floor window. Are you standing on a ladder?"

"You have a four-leaved shamrock in your pocket," she replied. "Indeed, you have seven, and one of them is a six-leaved one."

"Who are you?" asked the man again.

"The Moor-woman," she replied. "The Moor-woman who brews. I was at it. The bung was in the cask, but one of the little moor-imps pulled it out in his mischief, and flung it up into the yard, where it beat against the window; and now the beer's running out of the cask, and that won't do good to anybody."

"Pray tell me some more!" said the man.

"Yes, wait a little," answered the Moor-woman. "I've something else to do just now." And she was gone.

The man was going to shut the window, when the woman already stood before him again.

"Now it's done," she said; "but I shall have half the beer to brew over again to-morrow, if the weather is suitable. Well, what have you to ask me? I've come back, for I always keep my word, and you have seven four-leaved shamrocks in your pocket, and one of them is a six-leaved one. That inspires respect, for that's an order that grows beside the sandy way; but that every one does not find. What have you to ask me? Don't stand there like a ridiculous oaf, for I must go back again directly to my bung and my cask."

And the man asked about the Story, and inquired if the Moor-woman had met it in her journeyings.

"By the big brewing-vat!" exclaimed the woman, "haven't you got stories enough? I really believe that most people have enough of them. Here are other things to take notice of, other things to examine. Even the children have gone beyond that. Give the little boy a cigar, and the little girl a new crinoline; they like that much better. To listen to stories! No, indeed, there are more important things to be done here, and other things to notice!"

"What do you mean by that?" asked the man, "and what do you know of the world? You don't see anything but frogs and Will-o'-the-Wisps!"

"Yes, beware of the Will-o'-the Wisps," said the Moor-woman, "for they're out—they're let loose—that's what we must talk about! Come to me in the moor, where my presence is necessary, and I will tell you all about it; but you must make haste, and come while your seven four-leaved shamrocks, for which one has six leaves, are still fresh, and the moon stands high!"

And the Moor-woman was gone.

It struck twelve in the town, and before the last stroke had died away, the man was out in the yard, out in the garden, and stood in the meadow. The mist had vanished, and the Moor-woman stopped her brewing.

"You've been a long time coming!" said the Moor-woman. "Witches get forward faster than men, and I'm glad that I belong to the witch folk!"

"What have you to say to me now?" asked the man. "Is it anything about the Story?"

"Can you never get beyond asking about that?" retorted the woman.

"Can you tell me anything about the poetry of the future?" resumed the man.

"Don't get on your stilts," said the crone, "and I'll answer you. You think of nothing but poetry, and only ask about that Story, as if she were the lady of the whole troop. She's the oldest of us all, but she takes precedence of the youngest. I know her well. I've been young, too, and she's no chicken now. I was once quite a pretty elf-maiden, and have danced in my time with the others in the moonlight, and have heard the nightingale, and have gone into the forest and met the Story-maiden, who was always to be found out there, running about. Sometimes she took up her night's lodging in a half-blown tulip, or in a field flower; sometimes she would slip into the church, and wrap herself in the mourning crape that hung down from the candles on the altar."

"You are capitally well-informed," said the man.

"I ought at least to know as much as you," answered the Moor-woman. "Stories and poetry—yes, they're like two yards of the same piece of stuff; they can go and lie down where they like, and one can brew all their prattle, and have it all the better and cheaper. You shall have it from me for nothing. I have a whole cupboard-full of poetry in bottles. It makes essences; and that's the best of it—bitter and sweet herbs. I have everything that people want of poetry, in bottles, so that I can put a little on my handkerchief, on holidays, to smell."

"Why, these are wonderful things that you're telling!" said the man. "You have poetry in bottles?"

"More than you can require," said the woman. "I suppose you know the history of 'the Girl who Trod on the Loaf, so that she might not soil her shoes'? That has been written, and printed too."

"I told that story myself," said the man.

"Yes, then you must know it; and you must know also that the girl sank into the earth directly, to the Moor-woman, just as Old Bogey's grandmother was paying her morning visit to inspect the brewery. She saw the girl gliding down, and asked to have her as a remembrance of her visit, and got her too; while I received a present that's of no use to me—a travelling druggist's shop—a whole cupboard-full of poetry in bottles. Grandmother told me where the cupboard was to be placed, and there it's standing still. Just look! You've your seven four-leaved shamrocks in your pocket, one of which is a six-leaved one, and so you will be able to see it."

And really in the midst of the moor lay something like a great knotted block of alder, and that was the old grandmother's cupboard. The Moor-woman said that this was always open to her and to every one in the land, if they only knew where the cupboard stood. It could be opened either at the front or at the back, and at every side and corner— a perfect work of art, and yet only an old alder stump in appearance. The poets of all lands, and especially those of our own country, had been arranged here; the spirit of them had been extracted, refined, criticised and renovated, and then stored up in bottles. With what may be called great aptitude, if it was not genius, the grandmother had taken as it were the flavor of this and of that poet, and had added a little devilry, and then corked up the bottles for use during all future times.

"Pray let me see," said the man.

"Yes, but there are more important things to hear," replied the Moor-woman.

"But now we are at the cupboard!" said the man. And he looked in. "Here are bottles of all sizes. What is in this one? and what in that one yonder?"

"Here is what they call may-balm," replied the woman. "I have not tried it myself. But I have not yet told you the 'more important' thing you were to hear. THE WILL-O'-THE-WISP'S IN THE TOWN! That's of much more consequence than poetry and stories. I ought, indeed, to hold my tongue; but there must be a necessity—a fate—a something that sticks in my throat, and that wants to come out. Take care, you mortals!"

"I don't understand a word of all this!" cried the man.

"Be kind enough to seat yourself on that cupboard," she retorted, "but take care you don't fall through and break the bottles—you know what's inside of them. I must tell of the great event. It occurred no longer ago than the day before yesterday. It did not happen earlier. It has now three hundred and sixty-three days to run about. I suppose you know how many days there are in a year?"

And this is what the Moor-woman told:

"There was a great commotion yesterday out here in the marsh! There was a christening feast! A little Will-o'-the-Wisp was born here—in fact, twelve of them were born all together; and they have permission, if they choose to use it, to go abroad among men, and to move about and command among them, just as if they were born mortals. That was a great event in the marsh, and accordingly all the Will-o'-the-Wisps, male and female, went dancing like little lights across the moor. There are some of them of the dog species, but those are not worth mentioning. I sat there on the cupboard, and had all the twelve little new-born Will-o'-the Wisps upon my lap. They shone like glow-worms; they already began to hop, and increased in size every moment, so that before a quarter of an hour had elapsed, each of them looked just as large as his father or his uncle. Now, it's an old-established regulation and favor, that when the moon stands just as it did yesterday, and the wind blows just as it blew then, it is allowed and accorded to all Will-o'-the-Wisps—that is, to all those who are born at that minute of time—to become mortals, and individually to exert their power for the space of one year.

"The Will-o'-the-Wisp may run about in the country and through the world, if it is not afraid of falling into the sea, or of being blown out by a heavy storm. It can enter into a person and speak for him, and make all the movements it pleases. The Will-o'-the-Wisp may take whatever form he likes, of man or woman, and can act in their spirit and in their disguise in such a way that he can effect whatever he wishes to do. But he must manage, in the course of the year, to lead three hundred and sixty-five people into a bad way, and in a grand style, too. To lead them away from the right and the truth; and then he reaches the highest point. Such a Will-o'-the Wisp can attain to the honor of being a runner before the devil's state coach; and then he'll wear clothes of fiery yellow, and breathe forth flames out of his throat. That's enough to make a simple Will-o'-the-Wisp smack his lips. But there's some danger in this, and a great deal of work for a Will-o'-the-Wisp who aspires to play so distinguished a part. If the eyes of the man are opened to what he is, and if the man can then blow him away, it's all over with him, and he must come back into the marsh; or if, before the year is up, the Will-o'-the-Wisp is seized with a longing to see his family, and so returns to it and gives the matter up, it is over with him likewise, and he can no longer burn clear, and soon becomes extinguished, and cannot be lit up again; and when the year has elapsed, and he has not led three hundred and sixty-five people away from the truth and from all that is grand and noble, he is condemned to be imprisoned in decayed wood, and to lie glimmering there, without being able to move; and that's the most terrible punishment that can be inflicted on a lively Will-o'-the-Wisp.

"Now, all this I know, and all this I told to the twelve little Will-o'-the-Wisps whom I had on my lap, and who seemed quite crazy with joy.

"I told them that the safest and most convenient course was to give up the honor, and do nothing at all; but the little flames would not agree to this, and already fancied themselves clad in fiery yellow clothes, breathing flames from their throats.

" 'Stay with us,' said some of the older ones.

" 'Carry on your sport with mortals,' said the others.

" 'The mortals are drying up our meadows; they've taken to draining. What will our successors do?'

" 'We want to flame; we will flame—flame!' cried the new-born Will-o'-the-Wisps.

"And thus the affair was settled.

"And now a ball was given, a minute long; it could not well be shorter. The little elf-maidens whirled round three times with the rest, that they might not appear proud, but they preferred dancing with one another.

"And now the sponsors' gifts were presented, and presents were thrown them. These presents flew like pebbles across the sea-water. Each of the elf-maidens gave a little piece of her veil.

" 'Take that,' they said, 'and then you'll know the higher dance, the most difficult turns and twists—that is to say, if you should find them necessary.

You'll know the proper deportment, and then you can show yourself in the very pick of society.'

"The night raven taught each of the young Will-o'-the Wisps to say, 'Goo—goo—good,' and to say it in the right place; and that's a great gift which brings its own reward.

"The owl and the stork——but they said it was not worth mentioning, and so we won't mention it.

"King Waldemar's wild chase was just then rushing over the moor, and when the great lords heard of the festivities that were going on, they sent a couple of handsome dogs, which hunt on the spoor of the wind, as a present; and these might carry two or three of the Will-o'-the Wisps. A couple of old Alpas, spirits who occupy themselves with Alp-pressing, were also at the feast; and from these the young Will-o'-the Wisps learned the art of slipping through every key-hole, as if the door stood open before them. These Alpas offered to carry the youngsters to the town, with which they were well acquainted. They usually rode through the atmosphere on their own back hair, which is fastened into a knot, for they love a hard seat; but now they sat sideways on the wild hunting dogs, took the young Will-o'-the-Wisps in their laps, who wanted to go into the town to mislead and entice mortals, and, whisk! away they were. Now, this is what happened last night. To-day the Will-o'-the Wisps are in the town, and have taken the matter in hand—but where and how? Ah, can you tell me that? Still, I've a lightning conductor in my great toe, and that will always tell me something."

"Why, this is a complete story," exclaimed the man.

"Yes, but it is only the beginning," replied the woman. "Can you tell me how the Will-o'-the-Wisps deport themselves, and how they behave? and in what shapes they have aforetime appeared and led people into crooked paths?"

"I believe," replied the man, "that one could tell quite a romance about the Will-o'-the-Wisps, in twelve parts; or, better still, one might make quite a popular play of them."

"You might write that," said the woman, "but it's best let alone."

"Yes, that's better and more agreeable," the man replied, "for then we shall escape from the newspapers, and not be tied up by them, which is just as uncomfortable as for a Will-o'-the-Wisp to lie in decaying wood, to have to gleam, and not to be able to stir."

"I don't care about it either way," cried the woman. "Let the rest write, those who can, and those who cannot likewise. I'll grant you an old bung from my cask that will open the cupboard where poetry's kept in bottles, and you may take from that whatever may be wanting. But you, my good man, seem to have blotted your hands sufficiently with ink, and to have come to that age of satiety that you need not be running about every year for stories, especially as there are much more important things to be done. You must have understood what is going on?"

"The Will-o'-the-Wisp is in town," said the man. "I've heard it, and I have understood it. But what do you think I ought to do? I should be thrashed if I were to go to the people and say, 'Look, yonder goes a Will-o'-the-Wisp in his best clothes!'"

"They also go in undress," replied the woman. "The Will-o'-the Wisp can assume all kinds of forms, and appear in every place. He goes into the church,

"THE WILL-O'-THE-WISP IS IN TOWN,"
SAYS THE MOOR-WOMAN

but not for the sake of the service; and perhaps he may enter into one or other of the priests. He speaks in the Parliament, not for the benefit of the country, but only for himself. He's an artist with the color-pot as well as in the theatre; but when he gets all the power into his own hands, then the pot's empty! I chatter and chatter, but it must come out, what's sticking in my throat, to the disadvantage of my own family. But I must now be the woman that will save a good many people. It is not done with my good will, or for the sake of a medal. I do the most insane things I possibly can, and then I tell a poet about it, and thus the whole town gets to know of it directly."

"The town will not take that to heart," observed the man; "that will not disturb a single person; for they will all think I'm only telling them a story if I say, 'The Will-o'-the-Wisp is in the town, says the Moor-woman. Take care of yourselves!' "

THE WINDMILL

A WINDMILL stood upon the hill, proud to look at, and it was proud too.

"I am not proud at all," it said, "but I am very much enlightened without and within. I have sun and moon for my outward use, and for inward use too; and into the bargain I have stearine candles, train oil and lamps, and tallow candles. I may well say that I'm enlightened. I'm a thinking being, and so well constructed that it's quite delightful. I have a good windpipe in my chest, and I have four wings that are placed outside my head, just beneath my hat. The birds have only two wings, and are obliged to carry them on their backs. I am a Dutchman by birth, that may be seen by my figure—a flying Dutchman. They are considererd supernatural beings, I know, and yet I am quite natural. I have a gallery round my chest, and house-room beneath it; that's where my thoughts dwell. My strongest thought, who rules and reigns, is called by others 'The Man in the Mill.' He knows what he wants, and is lord over the meal and the bran; but he has his companion, too, and she calls herself 'Mother.' She is the very heart of me. She does not run about stupidly and awkwardly, for she knows what she wants, she knows what she can do, she's as soft as a zephyr and as strong as a storm; she knows how to begin a thing carefully, and to have her own way. She is my soft temper, and the father is my hard one. They are two, and yet one; they each call the other 'My half.' These two have some little boys, young thoughts, that can grow. The little ones keep everything in order. When, lately, in my wisdom , I let the father and the boys examine my throat and the hole in my chest, to see what was going on there,—for something in me was out of order, and it's well to examine one's self,—the little ones made a tremendous noise. The youngest jumped up into my hat, and shouted so there that it tickled me. The little thoughts may grow—I know that very well; and out in the world thoughts come too, and not only of my kind, for as far as I can see, I cannot discern anything like myself; but the wingless houses, whose throats make no noise, have thoughts too, and these come to my thoughts, and make love to them, as it is called. It's wonderful enough—yes, there are many wonderful things. Something has come over me, or into me,—something has changed in the mill-work. It seems as if the one half, the father, had altered, and had received a better temper and a more affectionate helpmate—so young and good, and yet the same, only more gentle and good through the course of time. What was bitter has passed away, and the whole is much more comfortable.

"The days go on, and the days come nearer and nearer to clearness and to joy; and then a day will come when it will be over with me; but not over altogether. I must be pulled down that I may be built up again; I shall cease, but yet shall live on. To become quite a different being, and yet remain the same! That's difficult for me to understand, however enlightened I may be with sun, moon, stearine, train oil, and tallow. My old wood-work and my old brick-work will rise again from the dust!

"I will hope that I may keep my old thoughts, the father in the mill, and the mother, great ones and little ones—the family; for I call them all, great and little, the company of thoughts, because I must, and cannot refrain from it.

"And I must also remain 'myself,' with my throat in my chest, my wings on my head, the gallery round my body; else I should not know myself, nor could the others know me, and say, 'There's the mill on the hill, proud to look at, and yet not proud at all.'"

That is what the mill said. Indeed, it said much more, but that is the most important part.

And the days came, and the days went, and yesterday was the last day.

Then the mill caught fire. The flames rose up high, and beat out and in, and bit at the beams and planks, and ate them up. The mill fell, and nothing remained of it but a heap of ashes. The smoke drove across the scene of the conflagration, and the wind carried it away.

Whatever had been alive in the mill remained, and what had been gained by it has nothing to do with this story.

The miller's family—one soul, many thoughts, and yet only one—built a new, a splendid mill, which answered its purpose. It was quite like the old one, and people said, "Why, yonder is the mill on the hill, proud to look at!" But this mill was better arranged, more according to the time than the last, so that progress might be made. The old beams had become worm-eaten and spongy—they lay in dust and ashes. The body of the mill did not rise out of the dust as they had believed it would do. They had taken it literally, and all things are not to be taken literally.

IN THE NURSERY

FATHER, and mother, and brothers, and sisters, were gone to the play; only little Anna and her grandpapa were left at home.

"We'll have a play too," he said, "and it may begin immediately."

"But we have no theatre," cried little Anna, "and we have no one to act for us; my old doll cannot, for she is a fright, and my new one cannot, for she must not rumple her new clothes."

"One can always get actors if one makes use of what one has," observed grandpapa.

"Now we'll go into the theatre. Here we will put up a book, there another, and there a third, in a sloping row. Now three on the other side; so, now we have the side scenes. The old box that lies yonder may be the back stairs; and we'll lay the flooring on top of it. The stage represents a room, as every one may see. Now we want the actors. Let us see what we can find in the plaything-box. First the personages, and then we will get the play ready. One after the other; that will be capital! Here's a pipe-head, and yonder an odd glove; they will do very well for father and daughter."

"But those are only two characters," said little Anna. "Here's my brother's old waistcoat — could not that play in our piece, too?"

"It's big enough, certainly," replied grandpapa. "It shall be the lover. There's nothing in the pockets, and that's very interesting, for that's half of an unfortunate attachment. And here we have the nut-cracker's boots, with spurs to them. Row, dow, dow! how they can stamp and strut! They shall represent the unwelcome wooer, whom the lady does not like. What kind of a play while you have now? Shall it be a tragedy, or a domestic drama?"

"A domestic drama, please," said little Anna, "for the others are so fond of that. Do you know one?"

"I know a hundred," said grandpapa. "Those that are most in favor are from the French, but they are not good for little girls. In the meantime, we may take one of the prettiest, for inside they're all very much alike. Now I shake the pen! Cock-a-lorum! So now, here's the play, brin-bran-span new! Now listen to the play-bill."

And grandpapa took a newspaper, and read as if he were reading from it:

THE PIPE-HEAD AND THE GOOD HEAD
A Family Drama in One Act.
CHARACTERS.

MR. PIPE-HEAD, *a father.*	MR. WAISTCOAT, *a lover.*
MISS GLOVE, *a daughter.*	MR. DE BOOTS, *a suitor.*

"And now we're going to begin. The curtain rises. We have no curtain, so it has risen already. All the characters are there, and so we have them at hand. Now I speak as Papa Pipe-head! He's angry to-day. One can see that he's a colored meerschaum.

" 'Snik, snak, snurre, bassellurre! I'm master of this house! I'm the father of my daughter! Will you hear what I have to say? Mr. de Boots is a person in whom one may see one's face; his upper part is of morocco, and he has spurs into the bargain. Snikke, snakke, snak! He shall have my daughter!' "

"Now listen to what the Waistcoat says, little Anna," said grandpapa. "Now the Waistcoat's speaking. The Waistcoat has a laydown collar, and is very modest; but he knows his own value, and has quite a right to say what he says:

" 'I haven't a spot on me! Goodness of material ought to be appreciated. I am of real silk, and have strings to me.'

" ' — On the wedding day, but no longer; you don't keep your color in the wash.' This is Mr. Pipe-head who is speaking. 'Mr. de Boots is water-tight, of strong leather, and yet very delicate; he can creak, and clank with his spurs, and has an Italian physiognomy — ' "

"But they ought to speak in verses," said Anna, "for I've heard that's the most charming way of all."

"They can do that too," replied grandpapa; "and if the public demands it, they will talk in that way. Just look at little Miss Glove, how she's pointing her fingers!

" 'Could I but have my love,
Who then so happy as Glove!
Ah!
If I from him must part,
I'm sure 'twill break my heart!'
'Bah!'

The last word was spoken by Mr. Pipe-head; and now it's Mr. Waistcoat's turn:

" 'O Glove, my own dear,
Though it cost thee a tear,
Thou must be mine,
For Holger Danske has sworn it!"

"Mr. de Boots, hearing this, kicks up, jingles his spurs, and knocks down three of the side-scenes."

"That's exceedingly charming!" cried little Anna.

"Silence! silence!" said grandpapa. "Silent approbation will show that you are the educated public in the stalls. Now Miss Glove sings her great song with startling effects:

" 'I can't see, heigho!
And therefore I'll crow!
Kikkeriki, in the lofty hall!'

"Now comes the exciting part, little Anna. This is the most important in all the play. Mr. Waistcoat undoes himself, and addresses his speech to you, that you may applaud; but leave it alone, — that's considered more genteel.

" 'I am driven to extremities! Take care of yourself! Now comes the plot! You are the Pipe-head, and I am the good head — snap! there you go!"

"Do you notice this, little Anna?" asked grandpapa. "That's a most charming comedy. Mr. Waistcoat seized the old Pipe-head and put him in his pocket; there he lies, and the Waistcoat says:

" 'You are in my pocket; you can't come out till you promise to unite me to your daughter Glove on the left. I hold out my right hand.' "

"That's awfully pretty," said little Anna.

"And now the old Pipe-head replies:

" 'Though I'm all ear,
Very stupid I appear:
Where's my humor? Gone, I fear,
And I feel my hollow stick's not here,
Ah! never, my dear,
Did I feel so queer.

> Oh! pray let me out,
> And like a lamb led to slaughter
> I'll betroth you, no doubt,
> To my daughter.' "

"Is the play over already?" asked little Anna.

"By no means," replied grandpapa. "It's only all over with Mr. de Boots. Now the lovers kneel down, and one of them sings:

> " 'Father!'

and the other,

> " 'Come, do as you ought to do, —
> Bless your son and daughter.'

And they receive his blessing, and celebrate their wedding, and all the pieces of furniture sing in chorus,

> " 'Klink! clanks!
> A thousand thanks;
> And now the play is over!'

"And now we'll applaud," said grandpapa. "We'll call them all out, and the pieces of furniture too, for they are of mahogany."

"And is not our play just as good as those which the others have in the real theatre?"

"Our play is much better," said grandpapa. "It is shorter, the performers are natural, and it has passed away the interval before tea-time."

THE GOLDEN TREASURE

THE drummer's wife went into the church. She saw the new altar with the painted pictures and the carved angels. Those upon the canvas and in the glory over the altar were just as beautiful as the carved ones; and they were painted and gilt into the bargain. Their hair gleamed golden in the sunshine, lovely to behold; but the real sunshine was more beautiful still. It shone redder, clearer through the dark trees, when the sun went down. It was lovely thus to look at the sunshine of heaven. And she looked at the red sun, and she thought about it so deeply, and thought of the little one whom the stork was to bring, and the wife of the drummer was very cheerful, and looked and looked, and wished that the child might have a gleam of sunshine given to it, so that it might at least become like one of the shining angels over the altar.

And when she really had the little child in her arms, and held it up to its father, then it was like one of the angels in the church to behold, with hair like gold — the gleam of the setting sun was upon it.

"My golden treasure, my riches, my sunshine!" said the mother; and she kissed the shining locks, and it sounded like music and song in the room of the drummer; and there was joy, and life, and movement. The drummer beat a roll — a roll of joy. And the Drum said — the Fire-drum, that was beaten when there was a fire in the town:

"Red hair! the little fellow has red hair! Believe the drum, and not what your mother says! Rub-a dub, rub-a dub!"

And the town repeated what the Fire-drum had said.

The boy was taken to church, the boy was christened. There was nothing much to be said about his name; he was called Peter. The whole town, and the Drum too, called him Peter the drummer's boy with the red hair; but his mother kissed his red hair, and called him her golden treasure.

In the hollow way in the clayey bank, many had scratched their names as a remembrance.

"Celebrity is always something!" said the drummer; and so he scratched his own name there, and his little son's name likewise.

And the swallows came. They had, on their long journey, seen more durable characters engraven on rocks, and on the walls of the temples in Hindostan, mighty deeds of great kings, immortal names, so old that no one now could read or speak them. Remarkable celebrity!

In the clayey bank the martens built their nest. They bored holes in the deep declivity, and the splashing rain and the thin mist came and crumbled and washed the names away, and the drummer's name also, and that of his little son.

"Peter's name will last a full year and a half longer!" said the father.

"Fool!" thought the Fire-drum; but it only said, "Dub, dub, dub, rub-a-dub!"

He was a boy full of life and gladness, this drummer's son with the red hair. He had a lovely voice. He could sing, and he sang like a bird in the woodland. There was melody, and yet no melody.

"He must become a chorister boy," said his mother. "He shall sing in the church, and stand among the beautiful gilded angels who are like him!"

"Fiery cat!" said some of the witty ones of the town.

The Drum heard that from the neighbors' wives.

"Don't go home, Peter," cried the street boys. "If you sleep in the garret, there'll be a fire in the house, and the fire-drum will have to be beaten."

"Look out for the drumsticks," replied Peter; and, small as he was, he ran up boldly, and gave the foremost such a punch in the body with his fist, that the fellow lost his legs and tumbled over, and the others took their legs off with themselves very rapidly.

The town musician was very genteel and fine. He was the son of the royal plate-washer. He was very fond of Peter, and would sometimes take him to his home; and he gave him a violin, and taught him to play it. It seemed as if the whole art lay in the boy's fingers; and he wanted to be more than a drummer — he wanted to become musician to the town.

"I'll be a soldier," said Peter; for he was still quite a little lad, and it seemed to him the finest thing in the world to carry a gun, and to be able to march one, two — one, two, and to wear a uniform and a sword.

"Ah, you learn to long for the drum-skin, drum, dum, dum!" said the Drum.

"Yes, if he could only march his way up to be a general!" observed his father; "but before he can do that, there must be war."

"Heaven forbid!" said his mother.

"We have nothing to lose," remarked the father.

"Yes, we have my boy," she retorted.

"But suppose he came back a general!" said the father.

"Without arms and legs!" cried the mother. "No, I would rather keep my golden treasure with me."

"Drum, dum, dum!" The Fire-drum and all the other drums were beating, for war had come. The soldiers all set out, and the son of the drummer followed them. "Red-head. Golden treasure!"

The mother wept; the father in fancy saw him "famous;" the town musician was of opinion that he ought not to go to war, but should stay at home and learn music.

"Red-head," said the soldiers, and little Peter laughed; but when one of them sometimes said to another, "Foxey," he would bite his teeth together and look another way—into the wide world. He did not care for the nickname.

The boy was active, pleasant of speech, and good-humored; that is the best canteen, said his old comrades.

And many a night he had to sleep under the open sky, wet through with the driving rain or the falling mist; but his good humor never forsook him. The drum-sticks sounded, "Rub-a-dub, all up, all up!" Yes, he was certainly born to be a drummer.

The day of battle dawned. The sun had not yet risen, but the morning was come. The air was cold, the battle was hot; there was mist in the air, but still more gunpowder-smoke. The bullets and shells flew over the soldiers' heads, and into their heads—into their bodies and limbs; but still they pressed forward. Here or there one or other of them would sink on his knees, with bleeding temples and a face as white as chalk. The little drummer still kept his healthy color; he had suffered no damage; he looked cheerfully at the dog of the regiment, which was jumping along as merrily as if the whole thing had been got up for his amusement, and as if the bullets were only flying about that he might have a game of play with them.

"March! Forward! March!" This was the word of command for the drum. The word had not yet been given to fall back, though they might have done so, and perhaps there would have been much sense in it; and now at last the word "Retire" was given; but our little drummer beat "Forward! march!" for he had understood the command thus, and the soldiers obeyed the sound of the drum. That was a good roll, and proved the summons to victory for the men, who had already begun to give way.

Life and limb were lost in the battle. Bombshells tore away the flesh in red strips; bombshells lit up into a terrible glow the strawheaps to which the wounded had dragged themselves, to lie untended for many hours, perhaps for all the hours they had to live.

It's no use thinking of it; and yet one cannot help thinking of it, even far away in the peaceful town. The drummer and his wife also thought of it, for Peter was at the war.

"Now, I'm tired of these complaints," said the Fire-drum.

Again the day of battle dawned; the sun had not yet risen, but it was morning. The drummer and his wife were asleep. They had been talking about their son, as, indeed, they did almost every night, for he was out yonder in God's hand. And the father dreamt that the war was over, that the soldiers had returned home, and that Peter wore a silver cross on his breast. But the mother dreamt that she had gone into the church, and had seen the painted pictures and the carved angels with the gilded hair, and her own dear boy, the golden treasure of her heart, who was standing among the angels in white robes, singing so sweetly, as surely only the angels can sing; and that he had soared up with them into the sunshine, and nodded so kindly at his mother.

"My golden treasure!" she cried out; and she awoke. "Now the good God has him to Himself!" She folded her hands, and hid her face in the cotton curtains of the bed, and wept. "Where does he rest now? among the many in the big grave that they have dug for the dead? Perhaps he's in the water in the marsh! Nobody knows his grave; no holy words have been read over it!" And the Lord's Prayer went inaudibly over her lips; she bowed her head, and was so weary that she went to sleep.

And the days went by, in life as in dreams!

It was evening. Over the battle-field a rainbow spread, which touched the forest and the deep marsh.

It has been said, and is preserved in popular belief, that where the rainbow touches the earth a treasure lies buried, a golden treasure; and here there was one. No one but his mother thought of the little drummer, and therefore she dreamt of him.

And the days went by, in life as in dreams!

Not a hair of his head had been hurt, not a golden hair.

"Drum-ma-rum! drum-ma-rum! there he is!" the Drum might have said, and his mother might have sung, if she had seen or dreamt it.

With hurrah and song, adorned with green wreaths of victory, they came home, as the war was at an end, and peace had been signed. The dog of the regiment sprang on in front with large bounds, and made the way three times as long for himself as it really was.

And days and weeks went by, and Peter came into his parents' room. He was as brown as a wild man, and his eyes were bright, and his face beamed like sunshine. And his mother held him in her arms; she kissed his lips, his forehead, and his red hair. She had her boy back again; he had not a silver cross on his breast, as his father had dreamt, but he had sound limbs, a thing the mother had not dreamt. And what a rejoicing was there! They laughed and they wept; and Peter embraced the old Fire-drum.

"There stands the old skeleton still!" he said.

And the father beat a roll upon it.

"One would think that a great fire had broken out here," said the Fire-drum. "Bright day! fire in the heart! golden treasure! skrat! skr-r-at! skr-r-r-at!"

And what then? What then! — Ask the town musician.

"Peter's far outgrowing the drum," he said. "Peter will be greater than I."

And yet he was the son of a royal plate-washer; but all that he had learned in half a lifetime, Peter learned in half a year.

There was something so merry about him, something so truly kindhearted. His eyes gleamed, and his hair gleamed too — there was no denying that!

"He ought to have his hair dyed," said the neighbor's wife. "That answered capitally with the policeman's daughter, and she got a husband."

"But her hair turned as green as duckweed, and was always having to be colored up."

"She knows how to manage for herself," said the neighbors, "and so can Peter. He comes to the most genteel houses, even to the burgomaster's where he gives Miss Charlotte piano-forte lessons."

He *could* play! He could play, fresh out of his heart, the most charming pieces, that had never been put upon music-paper. He played in the bright nights, and in the dark nights, too. The neighbors declared it was unbearable, and the Fire-drum was of the same opinion.

He played until his thoughts soared up, and burst forth in great plans for the future:

"To be famous!"

And burgomaster's Charlotte sat at the piano. Her delicate fingers danced over the keys, and made them ring into Peter's heart. It seemed too much for him to bear; and this happened not once, but many times; and at last one day he seized the delicate fingers and the white hand, and kissed it, and looked into her great brown eyes. Heaven knows what he said; but we may be allowed to guess at it. Charlotte blushed to guess at it. She reddened from brow to neck, and answered not a single word; and then strangers came into the room, and one of them was the state councillor's son. He had a lofty white forehead, and carried it so high that it seemed to go back into his neck. And Peter sat by her a long time, and she looked at him with gentle eyes.

At home that evening he spoke of travel in the wide world, and of the golden treasure that lay hidden for him in his violin.

"To be famous!"

"Tum-me-lum, tum-me-lum, tum-me-lum!" said the Fire-drum. "Peter has gone clear out of his wits. I think there must be a fire in the house."

Next day the mother went to market.

"Shall I tell you news, Peter?" she asked when she came home. "A capital piece of news. Burgomaster's Charlotte has engaged herself to the state councillor's son; the betrothal took place yesterday evening."

"No!" cried Peter, and he sprang up from his chair. But his mother persisted in saying "Yes." She had heard it from the baker's wife, whose husband had it from the burgomaster's own mouth.

And Peter became as pale as death, and sat down again.

"Good Heaven! what's the matter with you?" asked his mother.

"Nothing, nothing; only leave me to myself," he answered but the tears were running down his cheeks.

"My sweet child, my golden treasure!" cried the mother, and she wept; but the Fire-drum sang, not out loud, but inwardly,

"Charlotte's gone! Charlotte's gone! and now the song is done."

But the song was not done; there were many more verses in it, long verses, the most beautiful verses, the golden treasures of a life.

"She behaves like a mad woman," said the neighbor's wife. "All the world is to see the letters she gets from her golden treasure, and to read the words that are written in the papers about his violin playing. And he sends her money too, and that's very useful to her since she has been a widow."

"He plays before emperors and kings," said the town musician. "I never had that fortune, but he's my pupil, and he does not forget his old master."

And his mother said,

"His father dreamt that Peter came home from the war with a silver cross. He did not gain one in the war, but it is still more difficult to gain one in this way. Now he has the cross of honor. If his father had only lived to see it!"

"He's grown famous!" said the Fire-drum, and all his native town said the same thing, for the drummer's son, Peter with the red hair — Peter whom they had known as a little boy, running about in wooden shoes, and then as a drummer, playing for the dancers — was become famous!

"He played at our house before he played in the presence of kings," said the burgomaster's wife. "At that time he was quite smitten with Charlotte. He was always of an aspiring turn. At that time he was saucy and an enthusiast. My husband laughed when he heard of the foolish affair, and now our Charlotte is a state councillor's wife."

A golden treasure had been hidden in the heart and soul of the poor child, who had beaten the roll as a drummer — a roll of victory for those who had been ready to retreat. There was a golden treasure in his bosom, the power of sound; it burst forth on his violin as if the instrument had been a complete organ, and as if all the elves of a midsummer night were dancing across the strings. In its sounds were heard the piping of the thrush and the full clear note of the human voice; therefore the sound brought rapture to every heart, and carried his name triumphant through the land. That was a great firebrand — the firebrand of inspiration.

"And then he looks so splendid!" said the young ladies and the old ladies too; and the oldest of all procured an album for famous locks of hair, wholly and solely that she might beg a lcok of his rich splendid hair, that treasure, that golden treasure.

And the son came into the poor room of the drummer, elegant as a prince, happier than a king. His eyes were as clear and his face was as radiant as sunshine; and he held his mother in his arms, and she kissed his mouth, and wept as blissfully as any one can weep for joy; and he nodded at every old piece of furniture in the room, at the cupboard with the tea-cups, and at the flower-vase. He nodded at the sleeping-bench, where he had slept as a little boy; but the old Fire-drum he brought out, and dragged it into the middle of the room, and said to it and to his mother:

"My father would have beaten a famous roll this evening. Now I must do it!"

And he beat a thundering roll-call on the instrument, and the Drum felt so highly honored that the parchment burst with exultation.

"He has a splendid touch!" said the Drum. "I've a remembrance of him now that will last. I expect that the same thing will happen to his mother, from pure joy over her golden treasure."

And this is the story of the Golden Treasure.

THE STORM SHAKES THE SHIELD

IN the old days, when grandpapa was quite a little boy, and ran about in little red breeches and a red coat, and a feather in his cap—for that's the costume the little boys wore in his time when they were dressed in their best—many things were very different from what they are now. There was often a good deal of show in the streets—show that we don't see nowadays, because it has been abolished as too old-fashioned. Still, it is very interesting to hear grandfather tell about it.

It must really have been a gorgeous sight to behold, in those days, when the shoemaker brought over the shield, when the court-house was changed. The silken flag waved to and fro, on the shield itself a double eagle was displayed, and a big boot; the youngest lads carried the "welcome," and the chest of the workmen's guild, and their shirt-sleeves were adorned with red and white ribbons; the elder ones carried drawn swords, each with a lemon stuck on its point. There was a full band of music, and the most splendid of all the instruments was the "bird," as grandfather called the big stick with the crescent on the top, and all manner of dingle-dangles hanging to it—a perfect Turkish clatter of music. The stick was lifted high in the air, and swung up and down till it jingled again, and quite dazzled one's eyes when the sun shone on all its glory of gold, and silver, and brass.

In front of the procession ran the Harlequin, dressed in clothes made of all kinds of colored patches artfully sewn together, with a black face, and bells on his head like a sledge horse. He beat the people with his bat, which made a great clattering without hurting them, and the people would crowd together and fall back, only to advance again the next moment. Little boys and girls fell over their own toes into the gutter, old women dispensed digs with their elbows, and looked sour, and took snuff. One laughed, another chatted; the people thronged the windows and door-steps, and even all the roofs. The sun shone; and although they had a little rain too, that was good for the farmer; and when they got wetted thoroughly, they only thought what a blessing it was for the country.

And what stories grandpapa could tell! As a little boy he had seen all these fine doings in their greatest pomp. The oldest of the policemen used to make a speech from the platform on which the shield was hung up, and the speech was in verse, as if it had been made by a poet, as, indeed it had; for three people had concocted it together, and they had first drunk a good bowl of punch, so that the speech might turn out well.

And the people gave a cheer for the speech, but they shouted much louder for the Harlequin, when he appeared in front of the platform, and made a grimace at them.

The fools played the fool most admirably, and drank mead out of spirit-glasses, which they then flung among the crowd, by whom they were caught up. Grandfather was the possessor of one of these glasses, which had been given him by a working mason, who had managed to catch it. Such a scene was really very pleasant; and the shield on the new court-house was hung with flowers and green wreaths.

"One never forgets a feast like that, however old one may grow," said grandfather. Nor did he forget it, though he saw many other grand spectacles in his time, and could tell about them too; but it was most pleasant of all to hear him tell about the shield that was brought in the town from the old to the new court-house.

Once, when he was a little boy, grandpapa had gone with his parents to see this festivity. He had never yet been in the metropolis of the country. There were so many people in the streets, that he thought that the shield was being carried. There were many shields to be seen; a hundred rooms might have been filled with pictures, if they had been hung up inside and outside. At the tailor's were pictures of all kinds of clothing, to show that he could stitch up people from the coarsest to the finest; at the tobacco manufacturer's were pictures of the most charming little boys, smoking cigars, just as they do in reality; there were signs with painted butter, and herring, clerical collars, and coffins, and inscriptions and announcements into the bargain. A person could walk up and down for a whole day through the streets, and tire himself out with looking at the pictures; and then he would know all about what people lived in the houses, for they had hung out their shields or signs; and, as grandfather said, it was a very instructive thing, in a great town, to know at once who the inhabitants were.

And this is what happened with these shields, when grandpapa came to the town. He told it me himself, and he hadn't "a rogue on his back," as mother used to tell me he had when he wanted to make me believe something outrageous, for now he looked quite trustworthy.

The first night after he came to the town had been signalized by the most terrible gale ever recorded in the newspapers — a gale such as none of the inhabitants had ever before experienced. The air was dark with flying tiles; old wood-work crashed and fell; and a wheelbarrow ran up the streets all alone, only to get out of the way. There was a groaning in the air, and a howling and a shrieking, and altogether it was a terrible storm. The water in the canal rose over the banks, for it did not know where to run. The storm swept over the town, carrying plenty of chimneys with it, and more than one proud weathercock on a church tower had to bow, and has never got over it from that time.

There was a kind of sentry-house, where dwelt the venerable old superintendent of the fire brigade, who always arrived with the last engine. The storm would not leave this little sentry-house alone, but must needs tear it from its fastenings, and roll it down the street; and, wonderfully enough, it stopped opposite to the door of the dirty journeyman plasterer, who had saved three lives at the last fire, but the sentry-house thought nothing of that.

The barber's shield, the great brazen dish, was carried away, and hurled straight into the embrasure of the councillor of justice; and the whole neighborhood said this looked almost like malice, inasmuch as they, and nearly all the friends of the councillor's wife, used to call that lady "the Razor'" for she was so sharp that she knew more about other people's business than they knew about it themselves.

A shield with a dried salt fish painted on it flew exactly in front of the door of a house where dwelt a man who wrote a newspaper. That was a very poor joke perpetrated by the gale, which seemed to have forgotten that a man who writes in a paper is not the kind of person to understand any liberty taken with him; for he is a king in his own newspaper, and likewise in his own opinion.

The weathercock flew to the opposite house, where he perched, looking the picture of malice — so the neighbors said.

The cooper's tub stuck itself up under the head of "ladies' costumes."

The eating-house keeper's bill of fare, which had hung at his door in a heavy frame, was posted by the storm over the entrance to the theatre, where nobody went. "It was a ridiculous list — horse-radish, soup, and stuffed cabbage." And now people came in plenty.

The fox's skin, the honorable sign of the furrier, was found fastened to the bell-pull of a young man who always went to early lecture, and looked like a furled umbrella. He said he was striving after truth, and was considered by his aunt "a model and an example."

The inscription "Institution for Superior Education" was found near the billiard club, which place of resort was further adorned with the words, "Children brought up by hand." Now, this was not at all witty; but, you see, the storm had done it, and no one has any control over that.

It was a terrible night, and in the morning — only think! — nearly all the shields had changed places. In some places the inscriptions were so malicious, that grandfather would not speak of them at all; but I saw that he was chuckling secretly, and there may have been some inaccuracy in his description, after all.

The poor people in the town, and still more the strangers, were continually making mistakes in the people they wanted to see; nor was this to be avoided, when they went according to the shields that were hung up. Thus, for instance, some who wanted to go to a very grave assembly of elderly men, where important affairs were to be discussed, found themselves in a noisy boys' school, where all the company were leaping over the chairs and tables.

There were also people who made a mistake between the church and the theatre, and that was terrible indeed!

Such a storm we have never witnessed in our day; for that only happened in grandpapa's time, when he was quite a little boy. Perhaps we shall never experience a storm of the kind, but our grandchildren may; and we can only hope and pray that all may stay at home while the storm is moving the shields.

THE BIRD OF POPULAR SONG

IT is winter-time. The earth wears a snowy garment, and looks like marble hewn out of the rock; the air is bright and clear; the wind is sharp as a well-tempered sword, and the trees stand like branches of white coral or blooming almond twigs, and here it is keen as on the lofty Alps.

The night is splendid in the gleam of the Northern Lights, and in the glitter of innumerable twinkling stars.

But we sit in the warm room, by the hot stove, and talk about the old times. And we listen to this story:

By the open sea was a giant's grave; and on the grave-mound sat at midnight the spirit of the buried hero, who had been a king. The golden circlet gleamed on his brow, his hair fluttered in the wind, and he was clad in steel

THE STORM SHAKES THE SHIELD

and iron. He bent his head mournfully, and sighed in deep sorrow, as an unquiet spirit might sigh.

And a ship came sailing by. Presently the sailors lowered the anchor and landed. Among them was a singer, and he approached the royal spirit, and said,

"Why mournest thou, and wherefore dost thou suffer thus?"

And the dead man answered,

"No one has sung the deeds of my life; they are dead and forgotten. Song doth not carry them forth over the lands, nor into the hearts of men; therefore I have no rest and no peace."

And he spoke of his works, and of his warlike deeds, which his contemporaries had known, but which had not been sung, because there was no singer among his companions.

Then the old bard struck the strings of his harp, and sang of the youthful courage of the hero, of the strength of the man, and of the greatness of his good deeds. Then the face of the dead one gleamed like the margin of the cloud in the moonlight. Gladly and of good courage, the form arose in splendor and in majesty, and vanished like the glancing of the northern light. Nought was to be seen but the green turfy mound, with the stones on which no Runic record has been graven; but at the last sound of the harp there soared over the hill, as though he had fluttered from the harp, a little bird, a charming singing-bird, with the ringing voice of the thrush, with the moving pathos of the human heart, with a voice that told of home, like the voice that is heard by the bird of passage. The singing-bird soared away, over mountain and valley, over field and wood—he was the Bird of Popular Song, who never dies.

We hear his song—we hear it now in the room while the white bees are swarming without, and the storm clutches the windows. The bird sings not alone the requiem of heroes; he sings also sweet gentle songs of love, so many and so warm, of Northern fidelity and truth. He has stories in words and in tones; he has proverbs and snatches of proverbs; songs which, like Runes laid under a dead man's tongue, force him to speak; and thus Popular Song tells of the land of his birth.

In the old heathen days, in the times of the Vikings, the popular speech was enshrined in the harp of the bard.

In the days of knightly castles, when the strongest fist held the scales of justice, when only might was right, and a peasant and a dog were of equal importance, where did the Bird of Song find shelter and protection? Neither violence nor stupidity gave him a thought.

But in the gabled window of the knightly castle, the lady of the castle sat with the parchment roll before her, and wrote down the old recollections in song and legend, while near her stood the old woman from the wood, and the travelling peddler who went wandering through the country. As these told their tales, there fluttered around them, with twittering and song, the Bird of Popular Song, who never dies so long as the earth has a hill upon which his foot may rest.

And now he looks in upon us and sings. Without are the night and the snow-storm. He lays the Runes beneath our tongues, and we know the land of our home. Heaven speaks to us in our native tongue, in the voice of the Bird of Popular Song. The old remembrances awake, the faded colors glow with a fresh lustre, and story and song pour us a blessed draught which lifts up our minds and our thoughts, so that the evening becomes as a Christmas festival.

The snow-flakes chase each other, the ice cracks, the storm rules without, for he has the might, he is lord — but not the LORD OF ALL.

It is winter time. The wind is sharp as a two-edged sword, the snow-flakes chase each other; it seems as though it had been snowing for days and weeks, and the snow lies like a great mountain over the whole town, like a heavy dream of the winter night. Everything on the earth is hidden away, only the golden cross of the church, the symbol of faith, arises over the snow grave, and gleams in the blue air and in the bright sunshine.

And over the buried town fly the birds of heaven, the small and the great; they twitter and they sing as best they may, each bird with his beak.

First comes the band of sparrows: they pipe at every trifle in the streets and lanes, in the nests and the houses; they have stories to tell about the front buildings and the back buildings.

"We know the buried town," they say; "everything living in it is piep! piep! piep!"

The black ravens and crows flew on over the white snow.

"Grub, grub!" they cried. "There's something to be got down there; something to swallow, and that's most important. That's the opinion of most of them down there, and the opinion is goo — goo — good!"

The wild swans come flying on whirring pinions, and sing of the noble and the great, that will still sprout in the hearts of men, down in the town which is resting beneath its snowy veil.

No death is there — life reigns yonder; we hear it on the notes that swell onward like the tones of the church organ, which seize us like sounds from the elf-hill, like the songs of Ossian, like the rushing swoop of the wandering spirits' wings. What harmony! That harmony speaks to our hearts, and lifts up our souls! It is the Bird of Popular Song whom we hear.

And at this moment the warm breath of heaven blows down from the sky. There are gaps in the snowy mountains, the sun shines into the clefts; spring is coming, the birds are returning, and new races are coming with the same home sounds in their hearts.

Hear the story of the year: "The night of the snow-storm, the heavy dream of the winter night, all shall be dissolved, all shall rise again in the beauteous notes of the Bird of Popular Song, who never dies!"

THE TOAD

THE well was deep, and therefore the rope had to be a long one; it was heavy work turning the handle when any one had to raise a bucketful of water over the edge of the well. Though the water was clear, the sun never looked down far enough into the well to mirror itself in the waters; but as far as its beams could reach, green things grew forth between the stones in the sides of the well.

Down below dwelt a family of the Toad race. They had, in fact, come head-over-heels down the well, in the person of the old Mother-Toad, who was still alive. The green Frogs, who had been established there a long time, and swam about in the water, called them "well-guests." But the new-comers seemed determined to stay where they were, for they found it very agreeable living "in a dry place," as they called the wet stones.

The Mother-Frog had once been a traveller. She happened to be in the water-bucket when it was drawn up, but the light became too strong for her, and she got a pain in her eyes. Fortunately she scrambled out of the bucket; but she fell into the water with a terrible flop, and had to lie sick for three days with pains in her back. She certainly had not much to tell of the things up above, but she knew this, and all the Frogs knew it, that the well was not all the world. The Mother-Toad might have told this and that, if she had chosen, but she never answered when they asked her anything, and so they left off asking.

"She's thick, and fat, and ugly," said the young green Frogs; "and her children will be just as ugly as she is."

"That may be," retorted the mother-Toad, "but one of them has a jewel in his head, or else I have the jewel."

The young frogs listened and stared; and as these words did not please them, they made grimaces and dived down under the water. But the little Toads kicked up their hind legs from mere pride, for each of them thought that he must have the jewel; and then they sat and held their heads quite still. But at length they asked what it was that made them so proud, and what kind of a thing a jewel might be.

"Oh, it is such a splendid and precious thing, that I cannot describe it," said the Mother-Toad. "It's something which one carries about for one's own pleasure, and that makes other people angry. But don't ask me any questions, for I shan't answer you."

"Well, I haven't got the jewel," said the smallest of the Toads; she was as ugly as a toad can be. "Why should I have such a precious thing? And if it makes others angry, it can't give me any pleasure. No, I only wish I could get to the edge of the well, and look out; it must be beautiful up there."

"You'd better stay where you are," said the old Mother-Toad, "for you know everything here, and you can tell what you have. Take care of the bucket, for it will crush you to death; and even if you get into it safely, you may fall out. And it's not every one who falls so cleverly as I did, and gets away with whole legs and whole bones."

"Quack!" said the little Toad; and that's just as if one of us were to say, "Aha!"

She had an immense desire to get to the edge of the well, and to look over; she felt such a longing for the green, up there; and the next morning, when it chanced that the bucket was being drawn up, filled with water, and stopped for a moment just in front of the stone on which the Toad sat, the little creature's heart moved within it, and our Toad jumped into the filled bucket, which presently was drawn to the top, and emptied out.

"Ugh, you beast!" said the farm laborer who emptied the bucket, when he saw the toad. "You're the ugliest thing I've seen for one while." And he made a kick with his wooden shoe at the toad, which just escaped being crushed by managing to scramble into the nettles which grew high by the well's brink. Here she saw stem by stem, but she looked up also; the sun shone through the leaves, which were quite transparent; and she felt as a person would feel who steps suddenly into a great forest, where the sun looks in between the branches and leaves.

"It's much nicer here than down in the well! I should like to stay here my whole life long!" said the little Toad. So she lay there for an hour, yes, for two hours. "I wonder what is to be found up here? As I have come so far, I must try to go still farther." And so she crawled on as fast as she could crawl, and got out upon the highway, where the sun shone upon her, and the dust powdered her all over as she marched across the way.

"I've got to a dry place now, and no mistake," said the Toad. "It's almost too much of a good thing here; it tickles one so."

She came to the ditch; and forget-me-nots were growing there, and meadow-sweet; and a very little way off was a hedge of whitethorn, and elder bushes grew there, too, and bindweed with white flowers. Gay colors were to be seen here, and a butterfly, too, was flitting by. The Toad thought it was a flower which had broken loose that it might look about better in the world, which was quite a natural thing to do.

"If one could only make such a journey as that!" said the Toad. "Croak! how capital that would be."

Eight days and eight nights she stayed by the well, and experienced no want of provisions. On the ninth day she thought, "Forward! onward!" But what could she find more charming and beautiful? Perhaps a little toad or a few green frogs. During the last night there had been a sound borne on the breeze, as if there were cousins in the neighborhood.

"It's a glorious thing to live! glorious to get out of the well, and to lie among the stinging-nettles, and to crawl along the dusty road. But onward, onward! that we may find frogs or a little toad. We can't do without that; nature alone is not enough for one." And so she went forward on her journey.

She came out into the open field, to a great pond, round about which grew reeds; and she walked into it.

"It will be too damp for you here," said the Frogs; "but you are very welcome! Are you a he or a she? But it doesn't matter; you are equally welcome."

And she was invited to the concert in the evening — the family concert; great enthusiasm and thin voices; we know the sort of thing. No refreshments were given, only there was plenty to drink, for the whole pond was free.

"Now I shall resume my journey," said the little Toad; for she always felt a longing for something better.

She saw the stars shining, so large and so bright, and she saw the moon gleaming; and then she saw the sun rise, and mount higher and higher.

"Perhaps after all, I am still in a well, only in a larger well. I must get higher yet; I feel a great restlessness and longing." And when the moon became round and full, the poor creature thought, "I wonder if that is the bucket which will be let down, and into which I must step to get higher up? Or is the sun the great bucket? How great it is! how bright it is! It can take up all. I must look out, that I may not miss the opportunity. Oh, how it seems to shine in my head! I don't think the jewel can shine brighter. But I haven't the jewel; not that I cry about that — no, I must go higher up, into splendor and joy! I feel so confident, and yet I am afraid. It's a difficult step to take, and yet it must be taken. Onward, therefore, straight onward!"

She took a few steps, such as a crawling animal may take, and soon found herself on a road beside which people dwelt; but there were flower gardens as well as kitchen gardens. And she sat down to rest by a kitchen garden.

"What a number of different creatures there are that I never knew! and how beautiful and great the world is! But one must look round in it, and not stay in one spot." And then she hopped into the kitchen garden. "How green it is here! how beautiful it is here!"

"I know that," said the Caterpillar, on the leaf; "my leaf is the largest here. It hides half the world from me, but I don't care for the world."

"Cluck, cluck!" And some fowls came. They tripped about in the cabbage garden. The Fowl who marched at the head of them had a long sight, and she spied the Caterpillar on the green leaf, and pecked at it, so that the Caterpillar fell on the ground, where it twisted and writhed.

The Fowl looked at it first with one eye and then with the other, for she did not know what the end of this writhing would be.

"It doesn't do that with a good will," thought the Fowl, and lifted up her head to peck at the Caterpillar.

The Toad was so horrified at this, that she came crawling straight up towards the Fowl.

"Aha, it has allies," quoth the Fowl. "Just look at the crawling thing!" And then the Fowl turned away. "I don't care for the little green morsel; it would only tickle my throat." The other fowls took the same view of it, and they all turned away together.

"I writhed myself free," said the Caterpillar. "What a good thing it is when one has presence of mind! But the hardest thing remains to be done, and that is to get on my leaf again. Where is it?"

And the little Toad came up and expressed her sympathy. She was glad that in her ugliness she had frightened the fowls.

"What do you mean by that?" cried the Caterpillar. "I wriggled myself free from the Fowl. You are very disagreeable to look at. Cannot I be left in peace on my own property? Now I smell cabbage; now I am near my leaf. Nothing is so beautiful as property. But I must go higher up."

"Yes, higher up," said the little Toad; "higher-up! She feels just as I do; but she's not in a good humor to-day. That's because of the fright. We all want to go higher up." And she looked up as high as ever she could.

The stork sat in his nest on the roof of the farm-house. He clapped with his beak, and the Mother-stork clapped with hers.

"How high up they live!" thought the Toad. "If one could only get as high as that!"

In the farm-house lived two young students; the one was a poet and the other a scientific searcher into the secrets of nature. The one sang and wrote joyously of everything that God had created, and how it was mirrored in his heart. He sang it out clearly, sweetly, richly, in well-sounding verses; while the other investigated created matter itself, and even cut it open where need was. He looked upon God's creation as a great sum in arithmetic—subtracted, multiplied, and tried to know it within and without, and to talk with understanding concerning it; and that was a very sensible thing; and he spoke joyously and cleverly of it. They were good, joyful men, those two,

"There sits a good specimen of a toad," said the naturalist. "I must have that fellow in a bottle of spirits."

"You have two of them already," replied the poet. "Let the thing sit there and enjoy its life."

"But it's so wonderfully ugly," persisted the first.

"Yes, if we could find the jewel in its head," said the poet, "I too should be for cutting it open.'

"A jewel!" cried the naturalist. "You seem to know a great deal about natural history."

"But is there not something beautiful in the popular belief that just as the toad is the ugliest of animals, it should often carry the most precious jewel in its head? Is it not just the same thing with men? What a jewel that was that Aesop had, and still more, Socrates!"

The Toad did not hear any more, nor did she understand half of what she had heard. The two friends walked on, and thus she escaped the fate of being bottled up in spirits.

"Those two also were speaking of the jewel," said the Toad to herself. "What a good thing that I have not got it! I might have been in a very disagreeable position."

Now there was a clapping on the roof of the farm-house. Father-Stork was making a speech to his family, and his family was glancing down at the two young men in the kitchen garden.

"Man is the most conceited creature!" said the Stork. "Listen how their jaws are wagging; and for all that they can't clap properly. They boast of their gifts of eloquence and their language! Yes, a fine language truly! Why, it changes in every day's journey we make. One of them doesn't understand another. Now, we can speak our language over the whole earth — up in the North and in Egypt. And then men are not able to fly, moreover. They rush along by means of an invention they call 'railway;' but they often break their necks over it. It makes my beak turn cold when I think of it. The world could get on without men. We could do without them very well, so long as we only keep frogs and earth-worms."

"That was a powerful speech," thought the little Toad. "What a great man that is yonder! and how high he sits! Higher than ever I saw any one sit yet; and how he can swim!" she cried, as the Stork soared away through the air with outspread pinions.

And the Mother-Stork began talking in the nest, and told about Egypt and the waters of the Nile, and the incomparable mud that was to be found in that strange land; and all this sounded new and very charming to the little Toad.

"I must go to Egypt!" said she. "If the Stork or one of his young ones would only take me! I would oblige him in return. Yes, I shall get to Egypt, for I feel so happy! All the longing and all the pleasure that I feel is much better than having a jewel in one's head."

And it was just she who had the jewel. That jewel was the continual striving and desire to go upward — ever upward. It gleamed in her head, gleamed in joy, beamed brightly in her longing.

Then, suddenly, up came the Stork. He had seen the Toad in the grass, and stooped down and seized the little creature anything but gently. The Stork's beak pinched her, and the wind whistled; it was not exactly agreeable, but she was going upward — upward towards Egypt — and she knew it; and that was why her eyes gleamed, and a spark seemed to fly out of them.

"Quunk!—ah!"

The body was dead—the Toad was killed! But the spark that had shot forth from her eyes; what became of that?

The sunbeam took it up; the sunbeam carried the jewel from the head of the toad. Whither?

Ask not the naturalist; rather ask the poet. He will tell it thee under the guise of a fairy tale; and the Caterpillar on the cabbage, and the Stork family belong to the story. Think! the Caterpillar is changed, and turns into a beautiful butterfly; the Stork family flies over mountains and seas, to the distant Africa, and yet finds the shortest way home to the same country—to the same roof. Nay, that is almost too improbable; and yet it is true. You may ask the naturalist, he will confess it is so; and you know it yourself, for you have seen it.

But the jewel in the head of the toad?

Seek it in the sun; see it there if you can.

The brightness is too dazzling there. We have not yet such eyes as can see into the glories which God has created, but we shall receive them by-and-by; and that will be the most beautiful story of all, and we shall all have our share in it.

THE PORTER'S SON

THE General lived in the grand first floor, and the porter lived in the cellar. There was a great distance between the two families—the whole of the ground floor, and the difference in rank; but they lived in the same house, and both had a view of the street, and of the courtyard. In the courtyard was a grass-plot, on which grew a blooming acacia tree (when it was in bloom), and under this tree sat occasionally the finely-dressed nurse, with the still more finely-dressed child of the General—little Emily. Before them danced about barefoot the little son of the porter, with his great brown eyes and dark hair; and the little girl smiled at him, and stretched out her hands towards him; and when the General saw that from the window, he would nod his head and cry, "Charming!" The General's lady (who was so young that she might very well have been her husband's daughter from an early marriage) never came to the window that looked upon the courtyard. She had given orders, though, that the boy might play his antics to amuse her child, but must never touch it. The nurse punctually obeyed the gracious lady's orders.

The sun shone in upon the people in the grand first floor, and upon the people in the cellar; the acacia tree was covered with blossoms, and they fell off, and next year new ones came. The tree bloomed, and the porter's little son bloomed too, and looked like a fresh tulip.

The General's little daughter became delicate and pale, like the leaf of the acacia blossom. She seldom came down to the tree now, for she took the air in a carriage. She drove out with her mamma, and then she would always nod at the porter's George; yes, she used even to kiss her hand to him, till her mamma said she was too old to do that now.

One morning George was sent up to carry the General the letters and newspapers that had been delivered at the porter's room in the morning. As he was running up stairs, just as he passed the door of the sand-box, he heard a faint piping. He thought it was some young chicken that had strayed there, and was raising cries of distress; but it was the General's little daughter, decked out in lace and finery.

"Don't tell papa and mamma," she whimpered; "they would be angry."

"What's the matter, little missie?" asked George.

"It's all on fire!" she answered. "It's burning with a bright flame!"

George hurried up stairs to the General's apartments; he opened the door of the nursery. The window curtain was almost entirely burnt, and the wooden curtain-pole was one mass of flame. George sprang upon a chair he brought in haste, and pulled down the burning articles; he then alarmed the people. But for him, the house would have been burned down.

The General and his lady cross-questioned little Emily.

"I only took just one lucifer-match," she said, "and it was burning directly, and the curtain was burning too. I spat at it, to put it out; I spat at it as much as ever I could, but I could not put it out; so I ran away and hid myself, for papa and mamma would be angry."

"I spat!" cried the General's lady; "what an expression! Did you ever hear your papa and mamma talk about spitting? You must have got that from down stairs!"

And George had a penny given him. But this penny did not go to the baker's shop, but into the savings-box; and soon there were so many pennies in the savings-box that he could buy a paint-box and color the drawings he made, and he had a great number of drawings. They seemed to shoot out of his pencil and out of his fingers' ends. His first colored pictures he presented to Emily.

"Charming!" said the General, and even the General's lady acknowledged that it was easy to see what the boy had meant to draw. "He has genius." Those were the words that were carried down into the cellar.

The General and his gracious lady were grand people. They had two coats of arms on their carriage, a coat of arms for each of them, and the gracious lady had had this coat of arms embroidered on both sides of every bit of linen she had, and even on her nightcap and her dressing-bag. One of the coats of arms, the one that belonged to her, was a very dear one; it had been bought for hard cash by her father, for he had not been born with it, nor had she; she had come into the world too early, seven years before the coat of arms, and most people remembered this circumstance, but the family did not remember it. A man might well have a bee in his bonnet, when he had such a coat of arms to carry as that, let alone having to carry two; and the General's wife had a bee in hers when she drove to the court ball, as stiff and as proud as you please.

The General was old and gray, but he had a good seat on horseback, and he knew it, and he rode out every day, with a groom behind him at a proper distance. When he came to a party, he looked somehow as if he were riding into the room upon his high horse; and he had orders, too, such a number that no one would have believed it; but that was not his fault. As a young man he had taken part in the great autumn reviews which were held in those days. He had an anecdote that he told about those days, the only one he knew. A subaltern under his orders had cut off one of the princes, and taken him prisoner, and the Prince had been obliged to ride through the town with a little band of captured soldiers, himself a prisoner behind the General. This was an ever-memorable event, and was always told over and over again every year by the General, who, moreover, always repeated the remarkable words he had used when he returned his sword to the Prince; those words were, "Only my subaltern could have taken your Highness prisoner; I could never have done it!" And the Prince had replied, "You are incomparable." In a real war the General had never taken part. When war came into the country, he had gone on a diplomatic career to foreign courts. He spoke the French language so fluently that he had almost forgotten his own; he could dance well, he could ride well, and orders grew on his coat in an astounding way. The sentries presented arms to him, one of the most beautiful girls presented arms to him, and became the General's lady, and in time they had a pretty, charming child, that seemed as if it had dropped from heaven, it was so pretty; and the porter's son danced before it in the courtyard, as soon as it could understand it, and gave her all his colored pictures, and little Emily looked at them, and was pleased, and tore them to pieces. She was pretty and delicate indeed.

"My little Roseleaf!" cried the General's lady, "thou art born to wed a prince."

The prince was already at the door, but they knew nothing of it; people don't see far beyond the threshold.

"The day before yesterday our boy divided his bread and butter with her!" said the porter's wife. "There was neither cheese nor meat upon it, but she liked it as well as if it had been roast beef. There would have been a fine noise if the General and his wife had seen the feast, but they did not see it."

George had divided his bread and butter with little Emily, and he would have divided his heart with her, if it would have pleased her. He was a good boy, brisk and clever, and he went to the night school in the Academy now, to learn to draw properly. Little Emily was getting on with her education too, for she spoke French with her "bonne," and had a dancing master.

"George will be confirmed at Easter," said the porter's wife; for George had got so far as this.

"It would be the best thing, now, to make an apprentice of him," said his father. "It must be to some good calling—and then he would be out of the house."

"He would have to sleep out of the house," said George's mother. "It is not easy to find a master who has room for him at night, and we shall have to provide him with clothes too. The little bit of eating that he wants can be managed for him, for he's quite happy with a few boiled potatoes; and he gets taught for nothing. Let the boy go his own way. You will say that he will be our joy some day, and the Professor says so too."

The confirmation suit was ready. The mother had worked it herself; but the tailor who did repairs had cut them out, and a capital cutter-out he was.

"If he had had a better position, and been able to keep a workshop and journeymen," the porter's wife said, "he might have been a court tailor."

The clothes were ready, and the candidate for confirmation was ready. On his confirmation day, George received a great pinchbeck watch from his godfather, the old iron monger's shopman, the richest of his godfathers. The watch was an old and tried servant. It always went too fast, but that is better than to be lagging behind. That was a costly present. And from the General's apartment there arrived a hymn-book bound in morocco, sent by the little lady to whom George had given pictures. At the beginning of the book his name was written, and her name, as "his gracious patroness." These words had been written at the dictation of the General's lady, and the General had read the inscription, and pronounced it "Charming!"

"That is really a great attention from a family of such position," said the porter's wife; and George was sent up stairs to show himself in his confirmation clothes, with the hymn-book in his hand.

The General's lady was sitting very much wrapped up, and had the bad headache she always had when time hung heavy upon her hands. She looked at George very pleasantly, and wished him all prosperity, and that he might never have her headache. The General was walking about in his dressing-gown. He had a cap with a long tassel on his head, and Russian boots with red tops on his feet. He walked three times up and down the room, absorbed in his own thoughts and recollections, and then stopped and said:

"So little George is a confirmed Christian now. Be a good man, and honor those in authority over you. Some day, when you are an old man, you can say that the General gave you this precept."

That was a longer speech than the General was accustomed to make, and then he went back to his ruminations, and looked very aristocratic. But of all that George heard and saw up there, little Miss Emily remained most clear in his thoughts. How graceful she was, how gentle, and fluttering, and pretty she looked. If she were to be drawn, it ought to be on a soap-bubble. About her dress, about her yellow curled hair, there was a fragrance as of a fresh-blown rose; and to think that he had once divided his bread and butter with her, and that she had eaten it with enormous appetite, and nodded to him at every second mouthful! Did she remember anything about it? Yes, certainly, for she had given him the beautiful hymn-book in remembrance of this; and when the first new moon in the first new year after this event came round, he took a piece of bread, a penny, and his hymn-book, and went out into the open air, and opened the book to see what psalm he should turn up. It was a psalm of praise and thanksgiving. Then he opened the book again to see what would turn up for little Emily. He took great pains not to open the book in the place where the funeral hymns were, and yet he got one that referred to the grave and death. But then he thought this was not a thing in which one must believe; for all that he was startled when soon afterwards the pretty little girl had to lie in bed, and the doctor's carriage stopped at the gate every day.

"They will not keep her with them," said the porter's wife. "The good God knows whom He will summon to Himself."

But they kept her after all; and George drew pictures and sent them to her. He drew the Czar's palace; the old Kremlin at Moscow, just as it stood, with towers and cupolas; and these cupolas looked like gigantic green and gold cucumbers, at least in George's drawing. Little Emily was highly pleased, and consequently, when a week had elapsed, George sent her a few more pictures, all with buildings in them; for, you see, she could imagine all sorts of things inside the windows and doors.

He drew a Chinese house, with bells hanging from every one of sixteen stories. He drew two Grecian temples with slender marble pillars, and with steps all round them. He drew a Norwegian church. It was easy to see that this church had been built entirely of wood, hewn out and wonderfully put together; every story looked as if it had rockers, like a cradle. But the most beautiful of all was the castle, drawn on one of the leaves, and which he called "Emily's Castle." This was the kind of place in which she must live. That is what George had thought, and consequently he had put into this building whatever he thought most beautiful in all the others. It had carved woodwork, like the Norwegian church; marble pillars, like the Grecian temple; bells in every story; and was crowned with cupolas, green and gilded, like those of the Kremlin of the Czar. It was a real child's castle, and under every window was written what the hall or the room inside was intended to be; for instance: "Here Emily sleeps;" "Here Emily dances;" "Here Emily plays at receiving visitors." It was a real pleasure to look at the castle, and right well was the castle looked at accordingly.

"Charming!" said the General.

But the old Count—for there was an old Count there, who was still grander than the General, and had a castle of his own—said nothing at all; he heard that it had been designed and drawn by the porter's little son. Not that he was so very little, either, for he had already been confirmed. The old Count looked at the pictures, and had his own thoughts as he did so.

One day, when it was very gloomy, gray, wet weather, the brightest of days dawned for George; for the Professor at the Academy called him into his room.

"Listen to me, my friend," said the Professor; "I want to speak to you. The Lord has been good to you in giving you abilities, and He has also been good in placing you among kind people. The old Count at the corner yonder has been speaking to me about you. I have also seen your sketches; but we will not say any more about those, for there is a good deal to correct in them. But from this time forward you may come twice a-week to my drawing-class, and then you will soon learn how to do them better. I think there's more of the architect than of the painter in you. You will have time to think that over; but go across to the old Count this very day, and thank God for having sent you such a friend."

It was a great house—the house of the old Count at the corner. Round the windows elephants and dromedaries were carved, all from the old times; but the old Count loved the new time best, and what it brought, whether it came from the first floor, or from the cellar, or from the attic.

"I think," said the porter's wife, "the grander people are, the fewer airs do they give themselves. How kind and straightforward the old count is! and he talks exactly like you and me. Now, the General and his lady can't do that. And George was fairly wild with delight yesterday at the good reception he met with at the Count's, and so am I to-day, after speaking to the great man. Wasn't it a good thing that we didn't bind George apprentice to a handicraftsman? for he has abilities of his own."

"But they must be helped on by others," said the father.

"That help he has got now," rejoined the mother; "for the Count spoke out quite clearly and distinctly."

"But I fancy it began with the General," said the father, "and we must thank them too."

"Let us do so with all my heart," cried the mother, "though I fancy we have not much to thank them for. I will thank the good God; and I will thank Him, too, for letting little Emily get well."

Emily was getting on bravely, and George got on bravely too. In the course of the year he won the little silver prize medal of the Academy, and afterwards he gained the great one too.

"It would have been better, after all, if he had been apprenticed to a handicraftsman," said the porter's wife, weeping; "for then we could have kept him with us. What is he to do in Rome? I shall never get a sight of him again, not even if he comes back; but that he won't do, the dear boy."

"It is fortune and fame for him," said the father.

"Yes, thank you, my friend," said the mother; "you are saying what you do not mean. You are just as sorrowful as I am."

And it was all true about the sorrow and the journey. But everybody said it was a great piece of good fortune for the young fellow. And he had to take leave, and of the General too. The General's lady did not show herself, for she had her bad headache. On this occasion the General told his only anecdote, about what he had said to the Prince, and how the Prince had said to him, "You are incomparable." And he held out a languid hand to George.

Emily gave George her hand too, and looked almost sorry; and George was the most sorry of all.

Time goes by when one has something to do; and it goes by, too, when one has nothing to do. The time is equally long, but not equally useful. It was useful to George, and did not seem long at all, except when he happened to be thinking of his home. How might the good folks be getting on, up stairs and down stairs? Yes, there was writing about that, and many things can be put into a letter—bright sunshine and dark, heavy days. Both of these were in the letter which brought the news that his father was dead, and that his mother was alone now. She wrote that Emily had come down to see her, and had been to her like an angel of comfort; and concerning herself, she added that she had been allowed to keep her situation as porteress.

The General's lady kept a diary, and in this diary was recorded every ball she attended and every visit she received. The diary was illustrated by the insertion of the visiting cards of the diplomatic circle and of the most noble families; and the General's lady was proud of it. The diary kept growing through a long time, and amid many severe headaches, and through a long course of half-nights, that is to say, of court balls. Emily had now been to a court ball for the first time. Her mother had worn a bright red dress, with black lace, in the Spanish style; the daughter had been attired in white, fair and delicate; green silk ribons fluttered like flag-leaves among her yellow locks, and on her head she wore a wreath of water-lillies. Her eyes were so blue and clear, her mouth was so delicate and red, she looked like a little water spirit, as beautiful as such a spirit can be imagined. The Princes danced with her, one after another of course; and the General's lady had not a headache for a week afterwards.

But the first ball was not the last, and Emily could not stand it; it was a good thing, therefore, that summer brought with it rest, and exercise in the open air. The family had been invited by the old Count to visit him at him castle. That was a castle with a garden which was worth seeing. Part of this garden was laid out quite in the style of the old days, with stiff green hedges; you walked as if between green walls with peep-holes in them. Box trees and yew trees stood there trimmed into the form of stars and pyramids, and water sprang from fountains in large grottoes lined with shells. All around stood figures of the most beautiful stone — that could be seen in their clothes as well as in their faces; every flower-bed had a different shape, and represented a fish, or a coat of arms, or a monogram. That was the French part of the garden; and from this part the visitor came into what appeared like the green, fresh forest, where the trees might grow as they chose, and accordingly they were great and glorious. The grass was green, and beautiful to walk on, and it was regularly cut, and rolled, and swept, and tended. That was the English part of the garden.

"Old time and new time," said the Count, "here they run well into one another. In two years the building itself will put on a proper appearance, there will be a complete metamorphosis in beauty and improvement. I shall show you the drawings, and I shall show you the architect, for he is to dine here to-day."

"Charming!" said the General.

" 'Tis like Paradise here," said the General's lady, "and yonder you have a knight's castle!"

"That's my poultry-house," observed the Count. "The pigeons live in the tower, the turkeys in the first floor, but old Elsie rules in the ground floor. She has apartments on all sides of her. The sitting hens have their own room, and the hens with chickens have theirs; and the ducks have their own particular door leading to the water."

"Charming!" repeated the General.

And all sailed forth to see these wonderful things. Old Elsie stood in the room on the ground floor, and by her side stood Architect George. He and Emily now met for the first time after several years, and they met in the poultry-house.

Yes, there he stood, and was handsome enough to be looked at. His face was frank and energetic; he had black shining hair, and a smile about his mouth, which said, "I have a brownie that sits in my ear, and knows every one of you, inside and out." Old Elsie had pulled off her wooden shoes, and stood there in her stockings, to do honor to the noble guests. The hens clucked, and the cocks crowed, and the ducks waddled to and fro, and said, "Quack, quack!" But the fair, pale girl, the friend of his childhood, the daughter of the General, stood there with a rosy blush on her usually pale cheeks, and her eyes opened wide, and her mouth seemed to speak without uttering a word, and the greeting he received from her was the most beautiful greeting a young man can desire from a young lady, if they are not related, or have not danced many times together, and she and the architect had never danced together.

The Count shook hands with him, and introduced him.

"He is not altogether a stranger, our young friend George."

The General's lady bowed to him, and the General's daughter was very nearly giving him her hand; but she did not give it to him.

"Our little Master George!" said the General. "Old friends! Charming!"

"You have become quite an Italian," said the General's lady, "and I presume you speak the language like a native?"

"My wife sings the language, but she does not speak it," observed the General.

At dinner, George sat at the right hand of Emily, whom the General had taken down, while the Count led in the General's lady.

Mr. George talked and told of his travels; and he could talk well, and was the life and soul of the table, though the old Count could have been it too. Emily sat silent, but she listened, and her eyes gleamed, but she said nothing.

In the verandah, among the flowers, she and George stood together; the rose-bushes concealed them. And George was speaking again, for he took the lead now.

"Many thanks for the kind consideration you showed my old mother," he said. "I know that you went down to her on the night when my father died, and you stayed with her till his eyes were closed. My heartiest thanks!"

He took Emily's hand and kissed it—he might do so on such an occasion. She blushed deeply, but pressed his hand, and looked at him with her dear blue eyes.

"Your mother was a dear soul!" she said. "How fond she was of her son! And she let me read all your letters, so that I almost believe I know you. How kind you were to me when I was a litle girl! You used to give me pictures."

"Which you tore in two," said George.

"No, I have still your drawing of the castle."

"I must build the castle in reality now," said George; and he became quite warm at his own words.

The General and the General's lady talked to each other in their room about the porter's son—how he knew how to behave, and to express himself with the greatest propriety.

"He might be a tutor," said the General.

"Intellect!" said the General's lady; but she did not say anything more.

During the beautiful summer-time Mr. George several times visited the Count at his castle; and he was missed when he did not come.

"How much the good God has given you that he has not given to us poor mortals," said Emily to him. "Are you sure you are very grateful for it?"

It flattered George that the lovely young girl should look up to him, and he thought then that Emily had unusually good abilities. And the General felt more and more convinced that George was no cellar-child.

"His mother was a very good woman," he observed. "It is only right I should do her that justice now she is in her grave."

The summer passed away, and the winter came; again there was talk about Mr. George. He was highly respected, and was received in the first circles. The General had met him at a court ball.

And now there was a ball to be given in the General's house for Emily, and could Mr. George be invited to it?

"He whom the King invites can be invited by the General also," said the General, and drew himself up till he stood quite an inch higher than before.

Mr. George was invited, and he came; princes and counts came, and they danced, one better than the other. But Emily could only dance one dance—the first; for she made a false step—nothing of consequence; but her foot hurt her, so that she had to be careful, and leave off dancing, and look at the others. So she sat and looked on, and the architect stood by her side.

"I suppose you are giving her the whole history of St. Peter's," said the General, as he passed by; and smiled, like the personification of patronage.

With the same patronizing smile he received Mr. George a few days afterwards. The young man came, no doubt, to return thanks for the invitation to the ball. What else could it be? But indeed there was something else, something very astonishing and startling. He spoke words of sheer lunacy, so that the General could hardly believe his own ears. It was "the height of rhodomontade," an offer, quite an inconceivable offer — Mr. George came to ask the hand of Emily in marriage!

"Man!" cried the General, and his brain seemed to be boiling. "I don't understand you at all. What is it you say? What is it you want? I don't know you. Sir! Man! What possesses you to break into my house? And am I to stand here and listen to you?" He stepped backwards into his bed-room, locked the door behind him, and left Mr. George standing alone. George stood still for a few minutes, and then turned round and left the room. Emily was standing in the corridor.

"My father has answered?" she said, and her voice trembled.

George pressed her hand.

"He has escaped me," he replied; "but a better time will come."

There were tears in Emily's eyes, but in the young man's eyes shone courage and confidence; and the sun shone through the window, and cast his beams on the pair, and gave them his blessing.

The General sat in his room, bursting hot. Yes, he was still boiling, until he boiled over in the exclamation, "Lunacy! porter! madness!"

Not an hour was over before the General's lady knew it out of the General's own mouth. She called Emily, and remained alone with her.

"You poor child," she said; "to insult you so! to insult us so! There are tears in your eyes, too, but they become you well. You look beautiful in tears. You look as I looked on my wedding-day. Weep on, my sweet Emily."

"Yes, that I must," said Emily, "if you and my father do not say 'yes.' "

"Child!" screamed the General's lady; "you are ill! You are talking wildly, and I shall have a most terrible headache! Oh, what a misfortune is coming upon our house! Don't make your mother die, Emily, or you will have no mother."

And the eyes of the General's lady were wet, for she could not bear to think of her own death.

In the newspapers there was an announcement. "Mr. George has been elected Professor of the Fifth Class, number Eight."

"It's a pity that his parents are dead and cannot read it," said the new porter people, who now lived in the cellar under the General's apartments. They knew that the Professor had been born and grown up within their four walls.

"Now he'll get a salary," said the man.

"Yes, that's not much for a poor child," said the woman.

"Eighteen dollars a year," said the man. "Why, it's a good deal of money."

"No, I mean the honor of it," replied the wife. "Do you think he cares for the money? Those few dollars he can earn a hundred times over, and most likely he'll get a rich wife into the bargain. If we had children of our own, husband, our child should be an architect and a professor too."

George was spoken well of in the cellar, and he was spoken well of in the first floor. The old Count took upon himself to do that.

The pictures he had drawn in his childhood gave occasion for it. But how did the conversation come to turn on these pictures? Why, they had been talking of Russia and of Moscow, and thus mention was made of the Kremlin, which little George had once drawn for Miss Emily. He had drawn many pictures, but the Count especially remembered one, "Emily's Castle," where she was to sleep, and to dance, and to play at receiving guests.

"The Professor was a true man," said the Count, "and would be a privy councillor before he died, it was not at all unlikely; and he might build a real castle for the young lady before that time came: why not?"

"That was a strange jest," remarked the General's lady, when the Count had gone away. The General shook his head thoughtfully, and went out for a ride, with his groom behind him at a proper distance, and he sat more stiffly than ever on his high horse.

It was Emily's birthday. Flowers, books, letters, and visiting cards came pouring in. The General's lady kissed her on the mouth, and the General kissed her on the forehead; they were affectionate parents, and they and Emily had to receive grand visitors, two of the Princes. They talked of balls and theatres, of diplomatic missions, of the government of empires and nations; and then they spoke of talent, native talent; and so the discourse turned upon the young architect.

"He is building up an immortality for himself," said one, "and he will certainly build his way into one of our first families."

"One of our first families!" repeated the General and afterwards the General's lady; "what is meant by one of our first families?"

"I know for whom it was intended," said the General's lady, "but I shall not say it. I don't think it. Heaven disposes, but I shall be astonished."

"I am astonished also!" said the General. "I haven't an idea in my head!" And he fell into a reverie, waiting for ideas.

There is a power, a nameless power, in the possession of favor from above, the favor of Providence, and this favor little George had. But we are forgetting the birthday.

Emily's room was fragrant with flowers, sent by male and female friends; on the table lay beautiful presents for greeting and remembrance, but none could come from George—none could come from him; but it was not necessary, for the whole house was full of remembrances of him. Even out of the ash-bin the blossom of memory peeped forth, for Emily had sat whimpering there on the day when the window-curtain caught fire, and George arrived in the character of fire engine. A glance out of the window, and the acacia tree reminded of the days of childhood. Flowers and leaves had fallen, but there stood the tree covered with hoar frost, looking like a single huge branch of coral, and the moon shone clear and large among the twigs, unchanged in its changings, as it was when George divided his bread and butter with little Emily.

Out of a box the girl took the drawings of the Czar's palace and of her own castle—remembrances of George. The drawings were looked at, and many thoughts came. She remembered the day when, unobserved by her father and mother, she had gone down to the porter's wife who lay dying. Once again she seemed to sit beside her, holding the dying woman's hand in hers, hearing the dying woman's last words: "Blessing George!" The mother was thinking of her son, and now Emily gave her own interpretation to those words. Yes, George was certainly with her on her birthday.

It happened that the next day was another birthday in that house, the General's birthday. He had been born the day after his daughter, but before her of course—many years before her. Many presents arrived, and among them came a saddle of exquisite workmanship, a comfortable and costly saddle—one of the Princes had just such another. Now, from whom might this saddle come? The General was delighted. There was a little note with the saddle. Now if the words on the note had been "many thanks for yesterday's reception," we might easily have guessed from whom it came. But the words were "From somebody whom the General does not know."

"Whom in the world do I not know?" exclaimed the General. "I know everybody;" and his thoughts wandered all through society, for he knew everybody there. "That saddle comes from my wife!" he said at last. "She is teasing me—charming!"

But she was not teasing him; those times were past.

Again there was a feast, but it was not in the General's house, it was a fancy ball at the Prince's, and masks were allowed too.

The General went as Rubens, in a Spanish costume, with a little ruff round his neck, a sword by his side, and a stately manner. The General's lady was Madame Rubens, in black velvet made high round the neck, exceedingly warm, and with a mill-stone round her neck in the shape of a great ruff—accurately dressed after a Dutch picture in the possession of the General, in which the hands were especially admired. They were just like the hands of the General's lady.

Emily was Psyche. In white crape and lace she was like a floating swan. She did not want wings at all. She only wore them as emblematic of Psyche.

Brightness, splendor, light and flowers, wealth and taste appeared at the ball; there was so much to see, that the beautiful hands of Madame Rubens made no sensation at all.

A black domino, with an acacia blossom in his cap, danced with Psyche.

"Who is that?" asked the General's lady.

"His Royal Highness," replied the General. "I am quite sure of it. I knew him directly by the pressure of his hand."

The General's lady doubted it.

General Rubens had no doubts about it. He went up to the black domino and wrote the royal letters in the mask's hand. These were denied, but the mask gave him a hint.

The words that came with the saddle: "One whom you do not know, General."

"But I do know you," said the General. "It was you who sent me the saddle."

The domino raised his hand, and disappeared among the other guests.

"Who is that black domino with whom you were dancing, Emily?" asked the General's lady.

"I did not ask his name," she replied, "because you knew it. It is the Professor. Your *protégé* is here, Count!" she continued, turning to that nobleman, who stood close by. "A black domino with acacia blossoms in his cap."

"Very likely, my dear lady," replied the Count. "But one of the Princes wears just the same costume."

"I knew the pressure of the hand," said the General. "The saddle came from the Prince. I am so certain of it that I could invite that domino to dinner."

"Do so. If it be the Prince he will certainly come," replied the Count.

"And if it is the other he will not come," said the General, and approached the black domino, who was just speaking with the King. The General gave a very respectful invitation "that they might make each other's acquaintance," and he smiled in his certainty concerning the person he was inviting. He spoke loud and distinctly.

The domino raised his mask, and it was George. "Do you repeat your invitation, General?" he asked.

The General certainly seemed to grow an inch taller, assumed a more stately demeanor, and took two steps backward and one step forward, as if he were dancing a minuet, and then came as much gravity and expression into the face of the General as the General could contrive to infuse into it; but he replied,

"I never retract my words! You are invited, Professor!" and he bowed with a glance at the King, who must have heard the whole dialogue.

Now, there was a company to dinner at the General's, but only the old Count and his *protégé* were invited.

"I have my foot under his table," thought George. "That's laying the foundation stone."

And the foundation stone was really laid, with great ceremony, at the house of the General and of the General's lady.

The man had come, and had spoken quite like a person in good society, and had made himself very agreeable, so that the General had often to repeat his "Charming!" The General talked of this dinner, talked of it even to a court lady; and this lady, one of the most intellectual persons about the court, asked to be invited to meet the Professor the next time he should come. So he had to be invited again; and he was invited, and came, and was charming again; he could even play chess.

"He's not out of the cellar," said the General; "he's quite a distinguished person. There are many distinguished persons of that kind, and it's no fault of his."

The Professor, who was received in the King's palace, might very well be received by the General; but that he could ever belong to the house was out of the question, only the whole town was talking of it.

He grew and grew. The dew of favor fell from above, so no one was surprised after all that he should become a Privy Councillor, and Emily a Privy Councillor's lady.

"Life is either a tragedy or a comedy," said the General. "In tragedies they die, in comedies they marry one another."

In this case they married. And they had three clever boys—but not all at once.

The sweet children rode on their hobby-horses through all the rooms when they came to see the grandparents. And the General also rode on his stick; he rode behind them in the character of groom to the little Privy Councillors.

And the General's lady sat on her sofa and smiled at them, even when she had her severest headache.

So far did George get, and much further; else it had not been worth while to tell the story of THE PORTER'S SON.

THE SNOWDROP

IT was winter-time; the air was cold, the wind was sharp, but within the closed doors it was warm and comfortable, and within the closed door lay the flower; it lay in the bulb under the snow-covered earth.

One day rain fell. The drops penetrated through the snowy covering down into the earth, and touched the flower-bulb, and talked of the bright world above. Soon the Sunbeam pierced its way through the snow to the root, and within the root there was a stirring.

"Come in," said the flower.

"I cannot," said the Sunbeam. "I am not strong enough to unlock the door! When the summer comes I shall be strong!"

"When will it be summer?" asked the Flower, and she repeated this question each time a new sunbeam made its way down to her. But the summer was yet far distant. The snow still lay upon the ground, and there was a coat of ice on the water every night.

"What a long time it takes! what a long time it takes!" said the Flower. "I feel a stirring and striving within me; I must stretch myself, I must unlock the door, I must get out, and must nod a good morning to the summer, and what a happy time that will be!"

And the Flower stirred and stretched itself within the thin rind which the water had softened from without, and the snow and the earth had warmed, and the Sunbeam had knocked at; and it shot forth under the snow with a greenish-white blossom on a green stalk, with narrow thick leaves, which seemed to want to protect it. The snow was cold, but was pierced by the Sunbeam, therefore it was easy to get through it, and now the Sunbeam came with greater strength than before.

"Welcome, welcome!" sang and sounded every ray, and the Flower lifted itself up over the snow into the brighter world. The Sunbeams caressed and kissed it, so that it opened altogether, white as snow, and ornamented with green stripes. It bent its head in joy and humility.

"Beautiful Flower!" said the Sunbeams, "how graceful and delicate you are! You are the first, you are the only one! You are our love! You are the bell that rings out for summer, beautiful summer, over country and town. All the snow will melt; the cold winds will be driven away; we shall rule; all will become green, and then you will have companions, syringas, laburnums, and roses; but you are the first, so graceful, so delicate!"

That was a great pleasure. It seemed as if the air were singing and sounding, as if rays of light were piercing through the leaves and the stalks of the Flower. There it stood, so delicate and so easily broken, and yet so strong in its young beauty; it stood there in its white dress with the green stripes, and made a summer. But there was a long time yet to the summer-time. Clouds hid the sun, and bleak winds were blowing.

"You have come too early," said Wind and Weather. "We have still the power, and you shall feel it, and give it up to us. You should have stayed quietly at home and not have run out to make a display of yourself. Your time is not come yet!"

It was a cutting cold! The days which now come brought not a single sunbeam. It was weather that might break such a little Flower in two with cold. But the Flower had more strength than she herself knew of. She was strong in joy and in faith in the summer, which would be sure to come, which had been announced by her deep longing and confirmed by the warm sunlight; and so she remained standing in confidence in the snow in her white garment, bending her head even while the snow-flakes fell thick and heavy, and the icy winds swept over her.

"You'll break!" they said, "and fade, and fade! What did you want out here? Why did you let yourself be tempted? The Sunbeam only made game of you. Now you have what you deserve, you summer gauk."*

"Summer gauk!" she repeated in the cold morning hour.

"O summer gauk!" cried some children rejoicingly; "yonder stands one—how beautiful, how beautiful! The first one, the only one!"

These words did the Flower so much good, they seemed to her like warm sunbeams. In her joy the Flower did not even feel when it was broken off. It lay in a child's hand, and was kissed by a child's mouth, and carried into a warm room, and looked on by gentle eyes, and put into water. How strengthening, how invigorating! The Flower thought she had suddenly come upon the summer.

The daughter of the house, a beautiful little girl, was confirmed, and she had a friend who was confirmed, too. He was studying for an examination for an appointment. "He shall be my summer gauk," she said; and she took the delicate Flower and laid it in a piece of scented paper, on which verses were written, beginning with summer gauk and ending with summer gauk. "My friend, be a winter gauk." She had twitted him with the summer. Yes, all this was in the verses, and the paper was folded up like a letter, and the Flower was folded in the letter, too. It was dark around her, dark as in those days when she lay hidden in the bulb. The Flower went forth on her journey, and lay in the post-bag, and was pressed and crushed, which was not at all pleasant; but that soon came to an end.

The journey was over; the letter was opened, and read by the dear friend. How pleased he was! He kissed the letter, and it was laid, with its enclosure of verses, in a box, in which there were many beautiful verses, but all of them without flowers; she was the first, the only one, as the Sunbeams had called her; and it was a pleasant thing to think of that.

She had time enough, moreover, to think about it; she thought of it while the summer passed away, and the long winter went by, and the summer came again, before she appeared once more. But now the young man was not

---

*The Danish name for the snowdrop signifies "summer gauk" or "summer fool;" "gauk" also means "cuckoo." The German gauch and the English gauk, as seen in Gutz-gauch, the cuckoo, and Gawthorpe, have the same origin. "A notorious gull and geck."—SHAKSPEARE.

pleased at all. He took hold of the letter very roughly, and threw the verses away, so that the Flower fell on the ground. Flat and faded she certainly was, but why should she be thrown on the ground? Still, it was better to be here than in the fire, where the verses and the paper were being burnt to ashes. What had happened? What happens so often:—the Flower had made a gauk of him, that was a jest; the girl had made a fool of him, that was no jest, she had, during the summer, chosen another friend.

Next morning the sun shone in upon the little flattened Snowdrop, that looked as if it had been painted upon the floor. The servant girl, who was sweeping out the room, picked it up, and laid it in one of the books which were upon the table, in the belief that it must have fallen out while the room was being arranged. Again the flower lay among verses—printed verses—and they are better than written ones—at least, more money has been spent upon them.

And after this years went by. The book stood upon the book-shelf,. and then it was taken up and somebody read out of it. It was a good book; verses and songs by the old Danish poet, Ambrosius Stub, which are well worth reading. The man who was now reading the book turned over a page.

"Why, there's a flower!" he said; "a snowdrop, a summer gauk, a poet gauk! That flower must have been put in there with a meaning! Poor Ambrosius Stub! he was a summer fool too, a poet fool; he came too early, before his time, and therefore he had to taste the sharp winds, and wander about as a guest from one noble landed proprietor to another, like a flower in a glass of water, a flower in rhymed verses! Summer fool, winter fool, fun and folly—but the first, the only, the fresh young Danish poet of those days. Yes, thou shalt remain as a token in the book, thou little snowdrop: thou hast been put there with a meaning."

And so the Snowdrop was put back into the book, and felt equally honored and pleased to know that it was a token in the glorious book of songs, and that he who was the first to sing and to write had been also a snowdrop, had been a summer gauk, and had been looked upon in the winter-time as a fool. The Flower understood this, in her way, as we interpret everything in our way.

That is the story of the Snowdrop.

OUR AUNT

You ought to have known our aunt; she was charming! That is to say, she was not charming at all as the word is usually understood; but she was good and kind, amusing in her way, and was just as any one ought to be whom people are to talk about and to laugh at. She might have been put into a play, and wholly and solely on account of the fact that she only lived for the theatre and for what was done there. She was an honorable matron; but Agent Fabs, whom she used to call "Flabs," declared that our aunt was stage-struck.

"The theatre is my school," said she, "the source of my knowledge. From thence I have resuscitated Biblical history. Now, 'Moses' and 'Joseph in Egypt'—there are operas for you! I get my universal history from the theatre, my geography, and my knowledge of men. Out of the French pieces I get to know life in Paris—slippery, but exceedingly interesting. How I have cried over "La Famille Roquebourg'—that the man must drink himself to death, so that she may marry the young fellow! Yes, how many tears I have wept in the fifty years I have subscribed to the theatre!"

Our aunt knew every acting play, every bit of scenery, every character, every one who appeared or had appeared. She seemed really only to live during the nine months the theatre was open. Summertime without a summer theatre seemed to be only a time that made her old; while, on the other hand, a theatrical evening that lasted till midnight was a lengthening of her life. She did not say, as other people do, "Now we shall have spring, the stork is here," or, "They've advertised the first strawberries in the papers." She, on the contrary, used to announce the coming of autumn, with "Have you heard they're selling boxes for the theatre? now the performances will begin."

She used to value a lodging entirely according to its proximity to the theatre. It was a real sorrow to her when she had to leave the little lane behind the playhouse, and move into the great street that lay a little farther off, and live there in a house where she had no opposite neighbors.

"At home," said she, "my windows must be my opera-box. One cannot sit and look into one's self till one's tired; one must see people. But now I live just as if I'd go into the country. If I want to see human beings, I must go into my kitchen, and sit down on the sink, for there only I have opposite neighbors. No; when I lived in my dear little lane, I could look straight down into the ironmonger's shop, and had only three hundred paces to the theatre; and now I've three thousand paces to go, military measurement."

Our aunt was sometimes ill, but however unwell she might feel, she never missed the play. The doctor prescribed one day that she should put her feet in a bran bath, and she followed his advice; but she drove to the theatre all the same, and sat with her feet in bran there. If she had died there, she would have been very glad. Thorwaldsen died in the theatre, and she called that a happy death.

She could not imagine but that in heaven there must be a theatre too. It had not, indeed, been promised us, but we might very well imagine it. The many distinguished actors and actresses who had passed away must surely have a field for their talent.

Our aunt had an electric wire from the theatre to her room. A telegram used to be dispatched to her at coffee-time, and it used to consist of the words, "Herr Sivertsen is at the machinery;" for it was he who gave the signal for drawing the curtain up and down and for changing the scenes.

From him she used to receive a short and concise description of every piece. His opinion of Shakspeare's "Tempest," was, "Mad nonsense! There's so much to put up, and the first scene begins with 'Water to the front of the wings.' " That is to say, the water had to come forward so far. But when, on the other hand, the same interior scene remained through five acts, he used to pronounce it a sensible, well-written play, a resting play, which performed itself, without putting up scenes.

In earlier times, by which name our aunt used to designate thirty years ago, she and the before-mentioned Herr Sivertsen had been younger. At that time he had already been connected with the machinery, and was, as she said, her benefactor. It used to be the custom in those days that in the evening performances in the only theatre the town possessed, spectators were admitted to the part called the "flies," over the stage, and every machinist had one or two places to give away. Often the flies were quite full of good company; it was said that generals' wives and privy councillors' wives had been up there. It was quite interesting to look down behind the scenes, and to see how the people walked to and fro on the stage when the curtain was down.

Our aunt had been there several times, as well when there was a tragedy as when there was a ballet; for the pieces in which there were the greatest number of characters on the stage were the most interesting to see from the flies. One sat pretty much in the dark up there, and most people took their supper up with them. Once three apples and a great piece of bread and butter and sausage fell down right into the dungeon of Ugolino, where that unhappy man was to be starved to death; and there was great laughter among the audience. The sausage was one of the weightiest reasons why the worthy management refused in future to have any spectators up in the flies.

"But I was there seven-and-thirty times," said our aunt, "and I shall always remember Mr. Sivertsen for that."

On the very last evening when the flies were still open to the public, the "Judgment of Solomon" was performed, as our aunt remembered very well. She had, through the influence of her benefactor, Herr Sivertsen, procured a free admission for the Agent Fabs, although he did not deserve it in the least, for he was always cutting his jokes about the theatre and teasing our aunt; but she had procured him a free admission to the flies, for all that. He wanted to look at this player-stuff from the other side.

"Those were his own words, and they were just like him," said our aunt.

He looked down from above on the "Judgment of Solomon," and fell asleep over it. One would have thought that he had come from a dinner where many toasts had been given. He went to sleep, and was locked in. And there he sat through the dark night in the flies, and when he woke, he told a story, but our aunt would not believe it.

"The 'Judgment of Solomon' was over," he said, "and all the people had gone away, up stairs and down stairs; but now the real play began, the after-piece, which was the best of all," said the agent. "Then life came into the affair. It was not the 'Judgment of Solomon' that was performed; no, a real court of judgment was held upon the stage." And Agent Fabs had the impudence to try and make our aunt believe all this. That was the thanks she got for having got him a place in the flies.

What did the agent say? Why, it was curious enough to hear, but there was malice and satire in it.

"It looked dark enough up there," said the agent; "but then the magic business began — a great performance, 'The Judgment in the Theatre.' The box-keepers were at their posts, and every spectator had to show his ghostly pass-book, that it might be decided if he was to be admitted with hands loose or bound, and with or without a muzzle. Grand people who came too late, when the performance had begun, and young people, who could not always watch the time, were tied up outside, and had list slippers put on their feet, with which they were allowed to go in before the beginning of the next act, and they had muzzles too. And then the 'Judgment on the Stage' began."

"All malice, and not a bit of truth in it," said our aunt.

The painter, who wanted to get to Paradise, had to go up a staircase which he had himself painted, but which no man could mount. That was to expiate his sins against perspective. All the plants and buildings, which the property-man had placed, with infinite pains, in countries to which they did not belong, the poor fellow was obliged to put in their right places before cock-crow, if he wanted to get into Paradise. Let Herr Fabs see how he would get in himself; but what he said of the performers, tragedians and comedians, singers and dancers, that was the most rascally of all. Mr. Fabs, indeed!—Flabs! He did not deserve to be admitted at all, and our aunt would not soil her lips with what he said. And he said, did Flabs, that the whole was written down, and it should be printed when he was dead and buried, but not before, for he would not risk having his arms and legs broken.

Once our aunt had been in fear and trembling in her temple of happiness, the theatre. It was on a winter day, one of those days in which one has a couple of hours of daylight, with a gray sky. It was terribly cold and snowy, but aunt must go to the theatre. A little opera and a great ballet were performed, and a prologue and an epilogue into the bargain; and that would last till late at night. Our aunt must needs go; so she borrowed a pair of fur boots of her lodger—boots with fur inside and out, and which reached far up her legs.

She got to the theatre, and to her box; the boots were warm, and she kept them on. Suddenly there was a cry of "Fire!" Smoke was coming from one of the side scenes, and streamed down from the flies, and there was a terrible panic. The people came rushing out, and our aunt was the last in the box, "on the second tier, left-hand side, for from there the scenery looks best," she used to say. "The scenes are always arranged that they look best from the King's side." Aunt wanted to come out, but the people before her, in their fright and heedlessness, slammed the door of the box; and there sat our aunt, and couldn't get out, and couldn't get in; that is to say, she couldn't get into the next box, for the partition was too high for her. She called out, and no one heard her; she looked down into the tier of boxes below her, and it was empty, and low, and looked quite near, and aunt in her terror felt quite young and light. She thought of jumping down, and had got one leg over the partition, the other resting on the bench. There she sat astride, as if on horseback, well wrapped up in her flowered cloak, with one leg hanging out—a leg in a tremendous fur boot. That was a sight to behold; and when it was beheld, our aunt was heard too, and was saved from burning, for the theatre was not burned down.

That was the most memorable evening of her life, and she was glad that she could not see herself, for she would have died with confusion.

Her benefactor in the machinery department, Herr Sivertsen, visited her every Sunday, but it was a long time from Sunday to Sunday. In the latter time, therefore, she used to have in a little child "for the scraps;" that is to say, to eat up the remains of the dinner. It was a child employed in the ballet, one that certainly wanted feeding. The little one used to appear, sometimes as an elf, sometimes as a page; the most difficult part she had to play was the lion's hind leg in the "Magic Flute;" but as she grew larger she could represent the fore-feet of the lion. She certainly only got half a guilder for that, whereas the hind legs were paid for with a whole guilder; but then she had to walk bent, and to do without fresh air. "That was all very interesting to hear," said our aunt.

She deserved to live as long as the theatre stood, but she could not last so long; and she did not die in the theatre, but respectably in her bed. Her last words were, moreover, not without meaning. She asked,

"What will the play be to-morrow?"

At her death she left about five hundred dollars. We presume this from the interest, which came to twenty dollars. This our aunt had destined as a legacy for a worthy old spinster who had no friends; it was to be devoted to a yearly subscription for a place in the second tier, on the left side, for the Saturday evening, "for on that evening two pieces were always given," it said in the will; and the only condition laid upon the person who enjoyed the legacy was, that she should think, every Saturday evening, of our aunt, who was lying in her grave.

This was our aunt's religion.

THE DRYAD

WE are travelling to Paris to the Exhibition.

Now we are there. That was a journey, a flight without magic. We flew on the wings of steam over the sea and across the land.

Yes, our time is the time of fairy tales.

We are in the midst of Paris, in a great hotel. Blooming flowers ornament the staircases, and soft carpets the floors.

Our room is a very cosy one, and through the open balcony door we have a view of a great square. Spring lives down there; it has come to Paris, and arrived at the same time with us. It has come in the shape of a glorious young chestnut tree, with delicate leaves newly opened. How the tree gleams, dressed in its spring garb, before all the other trees in the place! One of these latter had been struck out of the list of living trees. It lies on the ground with roots exposed. On the place where it stood, the young chestnut tree is to be planted, and to flourish.

It still stands towering aloft on the heavy wagon which has brought it this morning a distance of several miles to Paris. For years it had stood there, in the protection of a mighty oak tree, under which the old venerable clergyman had often sat, with children listening to his stories.

The young chestnut tree had also listened to the stories; for the Dryad who lived in it was a child also. She remembered the time when the tree was so little that it only projected a short way above the grass and ferns around. These were as tall as they would ever be; but the tree grew every year, and enjoyed the air and the sunshine, and drank the dew and the rain. Several times it was also, as it must be, well shaken by the wind and the rain; for that is a part of education.

The Dryad rejoiced in her life, and rejoiced in the sunshine, and the singing of the birds; but she was most rejoiced at human voices; she understood the language of men as well as she understood that of animals.

Butterflies, cockchafers, dragon-flies, everything that could fly came to pay a visit. They could all talk. They told of the village, of the vineyard, of the forest, of the old castle with its parks and canals and ponds. Down in the water dwelt also living beings, which, in their way, could fly under the water from one place to another—beings with knowledge and delineation. They said nothing at all; they were so clever!

And the swallow, who had dived, told about the pretty little goldfish, of the thick turbot, the fat brill, and the old carp. The swallow could describe all that very well, but, "Self is the man," she said. "One ought to see these things one's self." But how was the Dryad ever to see such beings? She was obliged to be satisfied with being able to look over the beautiful country and see the busy industry of men.

It was glorious; but most glorious of all when the old clergyman sat under the oak tree and talked of France, and of the great deeds of her sons and daughters, whose names will be mentioned with admiration through all time.

Then the Dryad heard of the shepherd girl, Joan of Arc, and of Charlotte Corday; she heard about Henry the Fourth, and Napoleon the First; she heard names whose echo sounds in the hearts of the people.

The village children listened attentively, and the Dryad no less attentively; she became a school-child with the rest. In the clouds that went sailing by she saw, picture by picture, everything that she heard talked about. The cloudy sky was her picture-book.

She felt so happy in beautiful France, the fruitful land of genius, with the crater of freedom. But in her heart the sting remained that the bird, that every animal that could fly, was much better off than she. Even the fly could look about more in the world, far beyond the Dryad's horizon.

France was so great and so glorious, but she could only look across a little piece of it. The land stretched out, world-wide, with vineyards, forests and great cities. Of all these Paris was the most splendid and the mightiest. The birds could get there; but she, never!

Among the village children was a little ragged, poor girl, but a pretty one to look at. She was always laughing or singing and twining red flowers in her black hair.

"Don't go to Paris!" the old clergyman warned her. "Poor child! if you go there, it will be your ruin."

But she went for all that.

The Dryad often thought of her; for she had the same wish, and felt the same longing for the great city.

The Dryad's tree was bearing its first chestnut blossoms; the birds were twitterng round them in the most beautiful sunshine. Then a stately carriage came rolling along that way, and in it sat a grand lady driving the spirited, light-footed horses. On the back seat a little smart groom balanced himself. The Dryad knew the lady, and the old clergyman knew her also. He shook his head gravely when he saw her, and said:

"So you went there after all, and it was your ruin, poor Mary!"

"That one poor?" thought the Dryad. "No; she wears a dress fit for a countess" (she had become one in the city of magic changes). "Oh, if I were only there, amid all the splendor and pomp! They shine up into the very clouds at night; when I look up, I can tell in what direction the town lies."

Towards that direction the Dryad looked every evening. She saw in the dark night the gleaming cloud on the horizon; in the clear moonlight nights she missed the sailing clouds, which showed her pictures of the city and pictures from history.

The child grasps at the picture-books, the Dryad grasped at the cloud-world, her thought-book. A sudden, cloudless sky was for her a blank leaf; and for several days she had only had such leaves before her.

It was in the warm summer-time: not a breeze moved through the glowing hot days. Every leaf, every flower, lay as if it were torpid, and the people seemed torpid, too.

Then the clouds arose and covered the region round about where the gleaming mist announced "Here lies Paris."

The clouds piled themselves up like a chain of mountains, hurried on through the air, and spread themselves abroad over the whole landscape, as far as the Dryad's eye could reach.

Like enormous blue-black blocks of rock, the clouds lay piled over one another. Gleams of lightning shot forth from them.

"These also are the servants of the Lord God," the old clergyman had said. And there came a bluish dazzling flash of lightning, a lighting up as if of the sun itself, which could burst blocks of rock asunder. The lightning struck and split to the roots the old venerable oak. The crown fell asunder. It seemed as if the tree were stretching forth its arms to clasp the messengers of the light.

No bronze cannon can sound over the land at the birth of a royal child as the thunder sounded at the death of the old oak. The rain streamed down; a refreshing wind was blowing; the storm had gone by, and there was quite a holiday glow on all things. The old clergyman spoke a few words for honorable remembrance, and a painter made a drawing, as a lasting record of the tree.

"Everything passes away," said the Dryad, "passes away like a cloud, and never comes back!"

The old clergyman, too, did not come back. The green roof of his school was gone, and his teaching-chair had vanished. The children did not come; but autumn came, and winter came, and then spring also. In all this change of seasons the Dryad looked toward the region where, at night, Paris gleamed with its bright mist far on the horizon.

Forth from the town rushed engine after engine, train after train, whistling and screaming at all hours in the day. In the evening, towards midnight, at daybreak, and all the day through, came the trains. Out of each one, and into each one, streamed people from the country of every king. A new wonder of the world had summoned them to Paris.

In what form did this wonder exhibit itself?

"A splendid blossom of art and industry," said one, "has unfolded itself in the Champ de Mars, a gigantic sunflower, from whose petals one can learn geography and statistics, and can become as wise as a lord mayor, and raise one's self to the level of art and poetry, and study the greatness and power of the various lands."

"A fairy tale flower," said another, "a many-colored lotus-plant, which spreads out its green leaves like a velvet carpet over the sand. The opening spring has brought it forth, the summer will see it in all its splendor, the autumn winds will sweep it away, so that not a leaf, not a fragment of its root shall remain."

In front of the Military School extends in time of peace the arena of war — a field without a blade of grass, a piece of sandy steppe, as if cut out of the Desert of Africa, where Fata Morgana displays her wondrous airy castles and hanging gardens. In the Champ de Mars, however, these were to be seen more splendid, more wonderful than in the East, for human art had converted the airy deceptive scenes into reality.

"The Aladdin's Palace of the present has been built," it was said. "Day by day, hour by hour, it unfolds more of its wonderful splendor."

The endless halls shine in marble and many colors. "Master Bloodless" here moves his limbs of steel and iron in the great circular hall of machinery. Works of art in metal, in stone, in Gobelins tapestry, announce the vitality of mind that is stirring in every land. Halls of paintings, splendor of flowers, everything that mind and skill can create in the workshop of the artisan, has been placed here for show. Even the memorials of ancient days, out of old graves and turf-moors, have appeared at this general meeting.

The overpowering great variegated whole must be divided into small portions, and pressed together like a plaything, if it is to be understood and described.

Like a great table on Christmas Eve, the Champ de Mars carried a wonder-castle of industry and art, and around this knickknacks from all countries had been ranged, knickknacks on a grand scale, for every nation found some remembrance of home.

Here stood the royal palace of Egypt, there the caravanserai of the desert land. The Bedouin had quitted his sunny country, and hastened by on his camel. Here stood the Russian stables, with the fiery glorious horses of the steppe. Here stood the simple straw-thatched dwelling of the Danish peasant, with the Dannebrog flag, next to Gustavus Vasa's wooden house from Dalarne, with its wonderful carvings. American huts, English cottages, French pavilions, kiosks, theatres, churches, all strewn around, and between them the fresh green turf, the clear springing water, blooming bushes, rare trees, hothouses, in which one might fancy one's self transported into the tropical forest; whole gardens brought from Damascus, and blooming under one roof. What colors, what fragrance!

Artificial grottoes surrounded bodies of fresh or salt water, and gave a glimpse into the empire of the fishes; the visitor seemed to wander at the bottom of the sea, among fishes and polypi.

"All this," they said, "the Champ de Mars offers;" and around the great richly-spread table the crowd of human beings moves like a busy swarm of ants, on foot or in little carriages, for not all feet are equal to such a fatiguing journey.

Hither they swarm from morning till late in the evening. Steamer after steamer, crowded with people, glides down the Seine. The number of carriages is continually on the increase. The swarm of people on foot and on horseback grows more and more dense. Carriages and omnibuses are crowded, stuffed and embroidered with people. All these tributary streams flow in one direction — towards the Exhibition. On every entrance the flag of France is displayed; around the world's bazaar wave the flags of all nations. There is a humming and a murmuring from the hall of the machines; from the towers the melody of the chimes is heard; with the tones of the organs in the churches mingle the hoarse nasal songs from the cafés of the East. It is a kingdom of Babel, a wonder of the world!

In very truth it was. That's what all the reports said, and who did not hear them? The Dryad knew everything that is told here of the new wonder in the city of cities.

"Fly away, ye birds! fly away to see, and then come back and tell me," said the Dryad.

The wish became an intense desire—became the one thought of a life. Then, in the quiet silent night, while the full moon was shining, the Dryad saw a spark fly out of the moon's disc, and fall like a shooting star. And before the tree, whose leaves waved to and fro as if they were stirred by a tempest, stood a noble, mighty, and grand figure. In tones that were at once rich and strong, like the trumpet of the Last Judgment bidding farewell to life and summoning to the great account, it said:

"Thou shalt go to the city of magic; thou shalt take root there, and enjoy the mighty rushing breezes, the air and the sunshine there. But the time of thy life shall then be shortened; the line of years that awaited thee here amid the free nature shall shrink to but a small tale. Poor Dryad! It shall be thy destruction. Thy yearning and longing will increase, thy desire will grow more stormy, the tree itself will be as a prison to thee, thou wilt quit thy cell and give up thy nature to fly out and mingle among men. Then the years that would have belonged to thee will be contracted to half the span of the ephemeral fly, that lives but a day: one night, and thy life-taper shall be blown out—the leaves of the tree will wither and be blown away, to become green never again!"

Thus the words sounded. And the light vanished away, but not the longing of the Dryad. She trembled in the wild fever of expectation.

"I shall go there!" she cried, rejoicingly. "Life is beginning and swells like a cloud; nobody knows whither it is hastening."

When the gray dawn arose and the moon turned pale and the clouds were tinted red, the wished-for hour struck. The words of promise were fulfilled.

People appeared with spades and poles; they dug round the roots of the tree, deeper and deeper, and beneath it. A wagon was brought out, drawn by many horses, and the tree was lifted up, with its roots and the lumps of earth that adhered to them; matting was placed around the roots, as though the tree had its feet in a warm bag. And now the tree was lifted on the wagon and secured with chains. The journey began—the journey to Paris. There the tree was to grow as an ornament to the city of French glory.

The twigs and the leaves of the chestnut tree trembled in the first moments of its being moved; and the Dryad trembled in the pleasurable feeling of expectation.

"Away! away!" it sounded in every beat of her pulse. "Away! away!" sounded in words that flew trembling along. The Dryad forgot to bid farewell to the regions of home; she thought not of the waving grass and of the innocent daisies, which had looked up to her as to a great lady, a young Princess playing at being a shepherdess out in the open air.

The chestnut tree stood upon the wagon, and nodded his branches; whether this meant "farewell" or "forward," the Dryad knew not; she dreamed only of the marvellous new things, that seemed yet so familiar, and that were to unfold themselves before her. No child's heart rejoicing in innocence—no heart whose blood danced with passion—had set out on the journey to Paris more full of expectation than she.

Her "farewell" sounded in the words "Away! away!"

The wheels turned; the distant approached; the present vanished. The region was changed, even as the clouds change. New vineyards, forests, villages, villas appeared—came nearer—vanished!

The chestnut tree moved forward, and the Dryad went with it. Steam-engine after steam-engine rushed past, sending up into the air vapory clouds, that formed figures which told of Paris, whence they came, and whither the Dryad was going.

Everything around knew it, and must know whither she was bound. It seemed to her as if every tree she passed stretched out its leaves towards her, with the prayer—"Take me with you! take me with you!" for every tree enclosed a longing Dryad.

What changes during this flight! Houses seemed to be rising out of the earth—more and more—thicker and thicker. The chimneys rose like flower-pots ranged side by side, or in rows one above the other, on the roofs. Great inscriptions in letters a yard long, and figures in various colors, covering the walls from cornice to basement, came brightly out.

"Where does Paris begin, and when shall I be there?" asked the Dryad.

The crowd of people grew; the tumult and the bustle increased; carriage followed upon carriage; people on foot and people on horseback were mingled together; all around were shops on shops, music and song, crying and talking.

The Dryad, in her tree, was now in the midst of Paris. The great heavy wagon all at once stopped on a little square planted with trees. The high houses around had all of them balconies to the windows, from which the inhabitants looked down upon the young fresh chestnut tree, which was coming to be planted here as a substitute for the dead tree that lay stretched on the ground.

The passers-by stood still and smiled in admiration of its pure vernal freshness. The older trees, whose buds were still closed, whispered with their waving branches, "Welcome! welcome!" The fountain, throwing its jet of water high up in the air, to let it fall again in the wide stone basin, told the wind to sprinkle the new-comer with pearly drops, as if it wished to give him a refreshing draught to welcome him.

The Dryad felt how her tree was being lifted from the wagon to be placed in the spot where it was to stand. The roots were covered with earth, and fresh turf was laid on top. Blooming shrubs and flowers in pots were ranged around; and thus a little garden arose in the square.

The tree that had been killed by the fumes of gas, the steam of kitchens, and the bad air of the city, was put upon the wagon and driven away. The passers-by looked on. Children and old men sat upon the bench, and looked at the green tree. And we who are telling this story stood upon a balcony, and looked down upon the green spring sight that had been brought in from the fresh country air, and said, what the old clergyman would have said, "Poor Dryad!"

"I am happy! I am happy!" the Dryad cried, rejoicing; "and yet I cannot realize, cannot describe what I feel. Everything is as I fancied it, and yet as I did not fancy it."

The houses stood there, so lofty, so close! The sunlight shone on only one of the walls, and that one was stuck over with bills and placards, before which the people stood still; and this made a crowd.

Carriages rushed past, carriages rolled past; light ones and heavy ones mingled together. Omnibuses, those over-crowded moving houses, came rattling by; horsemen galloped among them; even carts and wagons asserted their rights.

The Dryad asked herself if these high-grown houses, which stood so close around her, would not remove and take other shapes, like the clouds in the sky, and draw aside, so that she might cast a glance into Paris, and over it. Notre Dame must show itself, the Vendôme Column, and the wondrous building which had called and was still calling so many strangers to the city.

But the houses did not stir from their places. It was yet day when the lamps were lit. The gas-jets gleamed from the shops, and shone even into the branches of the trees, so that it was like sunlight in summer. The stars above made their appearance, the same to which the Dryad had looked up in her home. She thought she felt a clear pure stream of air which went forth from them. She felt herself lifted up and strengthened, and felt an increased power of seeing through every leaf and through every fibre of the root. Amid all the noise and the turmoil, the colors and the lights, she knew herself watched by mild eyes.

From the side streets sounded the merry notes of fiddles and wind instruments. Up! to the dance, to the dance! to jollity and pleasure! that was their invitation. Such music it was, that horses, carriages, trees, and houses would have danced, if they had known how. The charm of intoxicating delight filled the bosom of the Dryad.

"How glorious, how splendid it is!" she cried, rejoicingly. "Now I am in Paris!"

The next day that dawned, the next night that fell, offered the same spectacle, similar bustle, similar life; changing, indeed, yet always the same; and thus it went on through the sequence of days.

"Now I know every tree, every flower on the square here! I know every house, every balcony, every shop in this narrow cut-off corner, where I am denied the sight of this great mighty city. Where are the arches of triumph, the Boulevards, the wondrous building of the world? I see nothing of all this. As if shut up in a cage, I stand among the high houses, which I now know by heart, with their inscriptions, signs, and placards; all the painted confectionery, that is no longer to my taste. Where are all the things of which I heard, for which I longed, and for whose sake I wanted to come hither? What have I seized, found, won? I feel the same longing I felt before; I feel that there is a life I should wish to grasp and to experience. I must go out into the ranks of living men, and mingle among them. I must fly about like a bird. I must see and feel, and become human altogether. I must enjoy the one half-day, instead of vegetating for years in every-day sameness and weariness, in which I become ill, and at last sink and disappear like the dew on the meadows. I will gleam like the cloud, gleam in the sunshine of life, look out over the whole like the cloud, and pass away like it, no one knoweth whither."

Thus sighed the Dryad; and she prayed:

"Take from me the years that were destined for me, and give me but half of the life of the ephemeral fly! Deliver me from my prison! Give me human life, human happiness, only a short span, only the one night, if it cannot be otherwise; and then punish me for my wish to live, my longing for life! Strike me out of thy list. Let my shell, the fresh young tree, wither, or be hewn down, and burnt to ashes, and scattered to all the winds!"

A rustling went through the leaves of the tree; there was a trembling in each of the leaves; it seemed as if fire streamed through it. A gust of wind shook its green crown, and from the midst of that crown a female figure came forth. In the same moment she was sitting beneath the brightly-illuminated leafy branches, young and beautiful to behold, like poor Mary, to whom the clergyman had said, "The great city will be thy destruction."

The Dryad sat at the foot of the tree — at her house door, which she had locked, and whose key had thrown away. So young! so fair! The stars saw her, and blinked at her. The gas-lamps saw her, and gleamed and beckoned to her. How delicate she was, and yet how blooming! — a child, and yet a grown maiden! Her dress was fine as silk, green as the freshly-opened leaves on the crown of the tree; in her nut-brown hair clung a half-opened chestnut blossom. She looked like the Goddess of Spring.

For one short minute she sat motionless; then she sprang up, and, light as a gazelle, she hurried away. She ran and sprang like the reflection from the mirror that, carried by the sunshine, is cast, now here, now there. Could any one have followed her with his eyes, he would have seen how marvellously her dress and her form changed, according to the nature of the house or the place whose light happened to shine upon her.

She reached the Boulevards. Here a sea of light streamed forth from the gas-flames of the lamps, the shops and the cafés. Here stood in a row young and slender trees, each of which concealed its Dryad, and gave shade from the artificial sunlight. The whole vast pavement was one great festive hall, where covered tables stood laden with refreshments of all kinds, from champagne and Chartreuse down to coffee and beer. Here was an exhibition of flowers, statues, books, and colored stuffs.

From the crowd close by the lofty houses she looked forth over the terrific stream beyond the rows of trees. Yonder heaved a stream of rolling carriages, cabriolets, coaches, omnibuses, cabs, and among them riding gentlemen and marching troops. To cross to the opposite shore was an undertaking fraught with danger to life and limb. Now lanterns shed their radiance abroad; now the gas had the upper hand; suddenly a rocket rises! Whence? Whither?

Here are sounds of soft Italian melodies; yonder, Spanish songs are sung, accompanied by the rattle of the castanets; but strongest of all, and predominating over the rest, the street-organ tunes of the moment, the exciting "Can-Can" music, which Orpheus never knew, and which was never heard by the "Belle Hélenè." Even the barrow was tempted to hop upon one of its wheels.

The Dryad danced, floated, flew, changing her color every moment, like a humming-bird in the sunshine; each house, with the world belonging to it, gave her its own reflections.

As the glowing lotus-flower, torn from its stem, is carried away by the stream, so the Dryad drifted along. Whenever she paused, she was another being, so that none was able to follow her, to recognize her, or to look more closely at her.

Like cloud-pictures, all things flew by her. She looked into a thousand faces, but not one was familiar to her; she saw not a single form from home. Two bright eyes had remained in her memory. She thought of Mary, poor Mary, the ragged merry child, who wore the red flowers in her black hair.

Mary was now here, in the world-city, rich and magnificent as in that day when she drove past the house of the old clergyman, and past the tree of the Dryad, the old oak.

Here she was certainly living, in the deafening tumult. Perhaps she had just stepped out of one of the gorgeous carriages in waiting. Handsome equipages, with coachmen in gold braid, and footmen in silken hose, drove up. The people who alighted from them were all richly-dressed ladies. They went through the opened gate, and ascended the broad staircase that led to a building resting on marble pillars. Was this building, perhaps, the wonder of the world? There Mary would certainly be found.

"Sancta Maria!" resounded from the interior. Incense floated through the lofty painted and gilded aisles, where a solemn twilight reigned.

It was the Church of the Madeleine.

Clad in black garments of the most costly stuffs, fashioned according to the latest mode, the rich feminine world of Paris glided across the shining pavement. The crests of the proprietors were engraved on silver shields on the velvet-bound prayer-books, and embroidered in the corners of perfumed handkerchiefs bordered with Brussels lace. A few of the ladies were kneeling in silent prayer before the altars; others resorted to the confessionals.

Anxiety and fear took possession of the Dryad; she felt as if she had entered a place where she had no right to be. Here was the abode of silence, the hall of secrets. Everything was said in whispers, every word was a mystery.

The Dryad saw herself enveloped in lace and silk, like the women of wealth and of high birth around her. Had, perhaps, every one of them a longing in her breast, like the Dryad?

A deep, painful sigh was heard. Did it escape from some confessional in a distant corner, or from the bosom of the Dryad? She drew the veil closer around her; she breathed incense, and not the fresh air. Here was not the abiding-place of her longing.

Away! away—a hastening without rest. The ephemeral fly knows not repose, for her existence is flight.

She was out again among the gas candelabra, by a magnificent fountain.

"All its streaming waters are not able to wash out the innocent blood that was spilt here."

Such were the words spoken. Strangers stood around, carrying on a lively conversation, such as no one would have dared to carry on in the gorgeous hall of secrets whence the Dryad came.

A heavy stone slab was turned and then lifted. She did not understand why. She saw an opening that led into the depths below. The strangers stepped down, leaving the starlit air and the cheerful life of the upper world behind them.

"I am afraid," said one of the women who stood around, to her husband, "I cannot venture to go down, nor do I care for the wonders down yonder. You had better stay here with me."

"Indeed, and travel home," said the man, "and quit Paris without having seen the most wonderful thing of all—the real wonder of the present period, created by the power and resolution of one man!"

"I will not go down for all that," was the reply.

"The wonder of the present time," it had been called. The Dryad had heard and had understood it. The goal of her ardent longing had thus been reached, and here was the entrance to it. Down into the depths below Paris? She had not thought of such a thing; but now she heard it said, and saw the strangers descending, and went after them.

The staircase was of cast iron, spiral, broad and easy. Below there burned a lamp, and farther down, another. They stood in a labyrinth of endless halls and arched passages, all communicating with each other. All the streets and lanes of Paris were to be seen here again, as in a dim reflection. The names were painted up; and every house above had its number down here also, and struck its roots under the macadamized quays of a broad canal, in which the muddy water flowed onward. Over it the fresh streaming water was carried on arches; and quite at the top hung the tangled net of gas-pipes and telegraph-wires.

In the distance lamps gleamed, like a reflection from the world-city above. Every now and then a dull rumbling was heard. This came from the heavy wagons rolling over the entrance bridges.

Whither had the Dryad come?

You have, no doubt, heard of the CATACOMBS? Now they are vanishing points in that new underground world—that wonder of the present day—the sewers of Paris. The Dryad was there, and not in the world's Exhibition in the Champ de Mars.

She heard exclamations of wonder and admiration.

"From here go forth health and life for thousands upon thousands up yonder! Our time is the time of progress, with its manifold blessings."

Such was the opinion and the speech of men; but not of those creatures who had been born here, and who built and dwelt here—of the rats, namely, who were squeaking to one another in the clefts of a crumbling wall, quite plainly, and in a way the Dryad understood well.

A big old Father-Rat, with his tail bitten off, was relieving his feelings in loud squeaks; and his family gave their tribute of concurrence to every word he said:

"I am disgusted with this man-mewing," he cried—"with these outbursts of ignorance. A fine magnificence, truly! all made up of gas and petroleum! I can't eat such stuff as that. Everything here is so fine and bright now, that one's ashamed of one's self, without exactly knowing why. Ah, if we only lived in the days of tallow candles! and it does not lie so very far behind us. That was a romantic time, as one may say."

"What are you talking of there?" asked the Dryad. "I have never seen you before. What is it you are talking about?"

"Of the glorious days that are gone," said the Rat—"of the happy time of our great-grandfathers and great-grandmothers. Then it was a great thing to get down here. That was a rat's nest quite different from Paris. Mother Plague used to live here then; she killed people, but never rats. Robbers and smugglers could breathe freely here. Here was the meeting-place of the most interesting personages, whom one now only gets to see in the theatres where they act melodrama, up above. The time of romance is gone even in our rat's nest; and here also fresh air and petroleum have broken in."

Thus squeaked the Rat; he squeaked in honor of the old time, when Mother Plague was still alive.

A carriage stopped, a kind of open omnibus, drawn by swift horses. The company mounted and drove away along the Boulevard de Sebastopol, that is to say, the underground boulevard, over which the well-known crowded street of that name extended.

The carriage disappeared in the twilight; the Dryad disappeared, lifted to the cheerful freshness above. Here, and not below in the vaulted passages, filled with heavy air, the wonder work must be found which she was to seek in her short lifetime. It must gleam brighter than all the gas-flames, stronger than the moon that was just gliding past.

Yes, certainly, she saw it yonder in the distance, it gleamed before her, and twinkled and glittered like the evening star in the sky.

She saw a glittering portal open, that led to a little garden, where all was brightness and dance music. Colored lamps surrounded little lakes, in which were water-plants of colored metal, from whose flowers jets of water spurted up. Beautiful weeping willows, real products of spring, hung their fresh branches over these lakes like a fresh, green, transparent, and yet screening veil. In the bushes burnt an open fire, throwing a red twilight over the quiet huts of branches, into which the sounds of music penetrated — an ear tickling, intoxicating music, that sent the blood coursing through the veins.

Beautiful girls in festive attire, with pleasant smiles on their lips, and the light spirit of youth in their hearts — "Marys," with roses in their hair, but without carriage and postilion — flitted to and fro in the wild dance.

Where were the heads, where the feet? As if stung by tarantulas, they sprang, laughed, rejoiced, as if in their ecstacies they were going to embrace all the world.

The Dryad felt herself torn with them into the whirl of the dance. Round her delicate foot clung the silken boot, chestnut brown in color, like the ribbon that floated from her hair down upon her bare shoulders. The green silk dress waved in large folds, but did not entirely hide the pretty foot and ankle.

Had she come to the enchanted Garden of Armida? What was the name of the place?

The name glittered in gas-jets over the entrance. It was "Mabille."

The soaring upwards of rockets, the splashing of fountains, and the popping of champagne corks accompanied the wild bacchantic dance. Over the whole glided the moon through the air, clear, but with a somewhat crooked face.

A wild joviality seemed to rush through the Dryad, as though she were intoxicated with opium. Her eyes spoke, her lips spoke, but the sound of violins and of flutes drowned the sound of her voice. Her partner whispered words to her which she did not understand, nor do we understand them. He stretched out his arms to draw her to him, but he embraced only the empty air.

The Dryad had been carried away, like a rose-leaf on the wind. Before her she saw a flame in the air, a flashing light high up on a tower. The beacon light shone from the goal of her longing, shone from the red lighthouse tower of the Fata Morgana of the Champ de Mars. Thither she was carried by the wind. She circled round the tower; the workmen thought it was a butterfly that had come too early, and that now sank down dying.

The moon shone bright, gas-lamps spread light around, through the halls, over the all-world's buildings scattered about, over the rose-hills and the rocks produced by human ingenuity, from which waterfalls, driven by the power of "Master Bloodless," fell down. The caverns of the sea, the depths of the lakes, the kingdom of the fishes were opened here. Men walked as in the depths of the deep pond, and held converse with the sea, in the diving-bell of glass. The water pressed against the strong glass walls above and on every side. The polypi, eel-like living creatures, had fastened themselves to the bottom, and stretched out arms, fathoms long, for prey. A big turbot was making himself broad in front, quietly enough, but not without casting some suspicious glances aside. A crab clambered over him, looking like a gigantic spider, while the shrimps wandered about in restless haste, like the butterflies and moths of the sea.

In the fresh water grew water-lilies, nymphæa, and reeds; the gold-fishes stood up below in rank and file, all turning their heads one way, that the streaming water might flow into their mouths. Fat carps stared at the glass wall with stupid eyes. They knew that they were here to be exhibited, and that they had made the somewhat toilsome journey hither in tubs filled with water; and they thought with dismay of the land-sickness from which they had suffered so cruelly on the railway.

They had come to see the Exhibition, and now contemplated it from their fresh or salt-water position. They looked attentively at the crowds of people who passed by them early and late. All the nations in the world, they thought, had made an exhibition of their inhabitants, for the edification of the soles and haddocks, pike and carp, that they might give their opinions upon the different kinds.

"Those are scaly animals!" said a little slimy Whiting. "They put on different scales two or three times a day, and they emit sounds which they call speaking. We don't put on scales, and we make ourselves understood in an easier way, simply by twitching the corners of our mouths and staring with our eyes. We have a great many advantages over mankind."

"But they have learned swimming of us," remarked a well-educated Codling. "You must know I come from the great sea outside. In the hot time of the year the people yonder go into the water; first they take off their scales, and then they swim. They have learnt from the frogs to kick out with their hind legs, and row with their fore paws. But they cannot hold out long. They want to be like us, but they cannot come up to us. Poor people!"

And the fishes stared. They thought that the whole swarm of people whom they had seen in the bright daylight were still moving around them; they were certain they still saw the same forms that had first caught their attention.

A pretty Barbel, with spotted skin, and an enviably round back, declared that the "human fry" were still there.

"I can see a well set-up human figure quite well," said the Barbel. "She was called 'contumacious lady,' or something of that kind. She had a mouth and staring eyes, like ours, and a great balloon at the back of her head, and something like a shut-up umbrella in front; there were a lot of dangling bits of seaweed hanging about her. She ought to take all the rubbish off, and go as we do; then she would look something like a respectable barbel, so far as it is possible for a person to look like one!"

"What's become of that one whom they drew away with the hook? He sat on a wheel-chair, and had paper, and pen, and ink, and wrote down everything. They called him a 'writer.' "

"They're going about with him still," said a hoary old maid of a Carp, who carried her misfortune about with her, so that she was quite hoarse. In her youth she had once swallowed a hook, and still swam patiently about with it in her gullet. "A writer? That means, as we fishes describe it, a kind of cuttle or ink-fish among men."

Thus the fishes gossipped in their own way; but in the artificial water-grotto the laborers were busy; who were obliged to take advantage of the hours of night to get their work done by daybreak. They accompanied with blows of their hammers and with songs the parting words of the vanishing Dryad.

"So, at any rate, I have seen you, you pretty gold-fishes," she said. "Yes, I know you;" and she waved her hand to them. "I have known about you a long time in my home; the swallow told me about you. How beautiful you are! how delicate and shining! I should like to kiss every one of you. You others, also. I know you all; but you do not know me."

The fishes stared out into the twilight. They did not understand a word of it.

The Dryad was there no longer. She had been a long time in the open air, where the different countries—the country of black bread, the codfish coast, the kingdom of Russia leather, and the banks of eau-de-Cologne, and the gardens of rose oil—exhaled their perfumes from the world-wonder flower.

When, after a night at a ball, we drive home half asleep and half awake, the melodies still sound plainly in our ears; we hear them, and could sing them all from memory. When the eye of the murdered man closes, the picture of what it saw last clings to it for a time like a photographic picture.

So it was likewise here. The bustling life of day had not yet disappeared in the quiet night. The Dryad had seen it; she knew, thus it will be repeated to-morrow.

The Dryad stood among the fragrant roses, and thought she knew them, and had seen them in her own home. She also saw red pomegranate flowers, like those that little Mary had worn in her dark hair.

Remembrances from the home of her childhood flashed through her thoughts; her eyes eagerly drank in the prospect around, and feverish restlessness chased her through the wonder-filled halls.

A weariness that increased continually took possession of her. She felt a longing to rest on the soft Oriental carpets within, or to lean against the weeping willow without by the clear water. But for the ephemeral fly there was no rest. In a few moments the day had completed its circle.

Her thoughts trembled, her limbs trembled, she sank down on the grass by the bubbling water.

"Thou wilt ever spring living from the earth," she said mournfully. "Moisten my tongue—bring me a refreshing draught."

"I am no living water," was the answer. "I only spring upward when the machine wills it."

"Give me something of thy freshness, thou green grass," implored the Dryad; "give me one of thy fragrant flowers."

"We must die if we are torn from our stalks," replied the Flowers and the Grass.

"Give me a kiss, thou fresh stream of air—only a single life-kiss."

"Soon the sun will kiss the clouds red," answered the Wind; "then thou wilt be among the dead—blown away, as all the splendor here will be blown away before the year shall have ended. Then I can play again with the light loose sand on the place here, and whirl the dust over the land and through the air. All is dust!"

The Dryad felt a terror like a woman who has cut asunder her pulse-artery in the bath, but is filled again with the love of life, even while she is bleeding to death. She raised herself, tottered forward a few steps, and sank down again at the entrance to a little church. The gate stood open, lights were burning upon the altar, and the organ sounded.

What music! Such notes the Dryad had never yet heard; and yet it seemed to her as if she recognized a number of well-known voices among them. They came deep from the heart of all creation. She thought she heard the stories of the old clergyman, of great deeds, and of the celebrated names, and of the gifts that the creatures of God must bestow upon posterity, if they would live on in the world.

The tones of the organ swelled, and in their song there sounded these words:

"Thy wishing and thy longing have torn thee, with thy roots, from the place which God appointed for thee. That was thy destruction, thou poor Dryad!"

The notes became soft and gentle, and seemed to die away in a wail.

In the sky the clouds showed themselves with a ruddy gleam. The Wind sighed:

"Pass away, ye dead! now the sun is going to rise!"

The first ray fell on the Dryad. Her form was irradiated in changing colors, like the soap-bubble when it is bursting and becomes a drop of water; like a tear that falls and passes away like a vapor.

Poor Dryad! Only a dew-drop, only a tear, poured upon the earth, and vanished away!

THE THISTLE'S EXPERIENCES

BELONGING to the lordly manor-house was beautiful, well-kept garden, with rare trees and flowers; the guests of the proprietor declared their admiration of it; the people of the neighborhood, from town and country, came on Sundays and holidays, and asked permission to see the garden; indeed, whole schools used to pay visits to it.

Outside the garden, by the palings at the road-side, stood a great mighty Thistle, which spread out in many directions from the root, so that it might have been called a thistle bush. Nobody looked at it, except the old Ass which drew the milk-maid's cart. This Ass used to stretch out his neck towards the

Thistle, and say, "You are beautiful; I should like to eat you!" But his halter was not long enough to let him reach it and eat it.

There was great company at the manor-house—some very noble people from the capital; young pretty girls, and among them a young lady who came from a long distance. She had come from Scotland, and was of high birth, and was rich in land and in gold—a bride worth winning, said more than one of the young gentlemen; and their lady mothers said the same thing.

The young people amused themselves on the lawn, and played at ball; they wandered among the flowers, and each of the young girls broke off a flower, and fastened it in a young gentleman's buttonhole. But the young Scotch lady looked round, for a long time, in an undecided way. None of the flowers seemed to suit her taste. Then her eye glanced across the paling—outside stood the great thistle bush, with the reddish-blue, sturdy flowers; she saw them, she smiled, and asked the son of the house to pluck one for her.

"It is the flower of Scotland," she said. "It blooms in the scutcheon of my country. Give me yonder flower."

And he brought the fairest blossom, and pricked his fingers as completely as if it had grown on the sharpest rose bush.

She placed the thistle-flower in the buttonhole of the young man, and he felt himself highly honored. Each of the other young gentlemen would willingly have given his own beautiful flower to have worn this one, presented by the fair hand of the Scottish maiden. And if the son of the house felt himself honored, what were the feelings of the Thistle bush? It seemed to him as if dew and sunshine were streaming through him.

"I am something more than I knew of," said the Thistle to itself. "I suppose my right place is really inside the palings, and not outside. One is often strangely placed in this world; but now I have at least managed to get one of my people within the pale, and indeed into a buttonhole!"

The Thistle told this event to every blossom that unfolded itself; and not many days had gone by before the Thistle heard, not from men, not from the twittering of the birds, but from the air itself, which stores up the sounds, and carries them far around—out of the most retired walks of the garden, and out of the rooms of the house, in which doors and windows stood open, that the young gentleman who had received the thistle-flower from the hand of the fair Scottish maiden had also now received the heart and hand of the lady in question. They were a handsome pair—it was a good match.

"That match I made up!" said the Thistle; and he thought of the flower he had given for the buttonhole. Every flower that opened heard of this occurrence.

"I shall certainly be transplanted into the garden," thought the Thistle, "and perhaps put into a pot, which crowds one in. That is said to be the greatest of all honors."

And the Thistle pictured this to himself in such a lively manner, that at last he said, with full conviction, "I am to be transplanted into a pot."

Then he promised every little thistle flower which unfolded itself that it also should be put into a pot, and perhaps into a buttonhole, the highest honor that could be attained. But not one of them was put into a pot, much less into a buttonhole. They drank in the sunlight and the air; lived on the sunlight by day, and on the dew by night; bloomed—were visited by bees and hornets, who looked after the honey, the dowry of the flower, and they took the honey, and left the flower where it was.

"The thievish rabble!" said the Thistle. "If I could only stab every one of them! But I cannot."

The flowers hung their heads and faded; but after a time new ones came.

"You come in good time," said the Thistle. "I am expecting every moment to get across the fence."

A few innocent daisies, and a long thin dandelion, stood and listened in deep admiration, and believed everything they heard.

The old Ass of the milk-cart stood at the edge of the field-road, and glanced across at the blooming thistle bush; but his halter was too short, and he could not reach it.

And the Thistle thought so long of the thistle of Scotland, to whose family he said he belonged, that he fancied at last that he had come from Scotland, and that his parents had been put into the national escutcheon. That was a great thought; but, you see, a great thistle has a right to a great thought.

"One is often of so grand a family, that one may not know it," said the Nettle, who grew close by. He had a kind of idea that he might be made into cambric if he were rightly treated.

And the summer went by, and the autumn went by. The leaves fell from the trees, and the few flowers left had deeper colors and less scent. The gardener's boy sang in the garden, across the palings:

> "Up the hill, down the dale we wend,
>   That is life, from beginning to end."

The young fir trees in the forest began to long for Christmas, but it was a long time to Christmas yet.

"Here I am standing yet!" said the Thistle. "It is as if nobody thought of me, and yet I managed the match. They were betrothed, and they have had their wedding; it is now a week ago. I won't take a single step—because I can't."

A few more weeks went by. The Thistle stood there with his last single flower large and full. This flower had shot up from near the roots; the wind blew cold over it, and the colors vanished, and the flower grew in size, and looked like a silvered sunflower.

One day the young pair, now man and wife, came into the garden. They went along by the paling, and the young wife looked across it.

"There's the great thistle still growing," she said. "It has no flowers now."

"Oh, yes, the ghost of the last one is there still," said he. And he pointed to the silvery remains of the flower, which looked like a flower themselves.

"It is pretty, certainly," she said. "Such an one must be carved on the frame of our picture."

And the young man had to climb across the palings again, and to break off the calyx of the thistle. It pricked his fingers, but then he had called it a ghost. And this thistle-calyx came into the garden, and into the house, and into the drawing-room. There stood a picture—"The Young Couple." A thistle-flower was painted in the buttonhole of the bridegroom. They spoke about this, and also about the thistle-flower they brought, the last thistle-flower, now gleaming like silver, whose picture was carved on the frame.

And the breeze carried what was spoken away, far away.

"What one can experience!" said the Thistle Bush. "My firstborn was put into a buttonhole, and my youngest has been put in a frame. Where shall I go?"

And the Ass stood by the road-side, and looked across at the Thistle.

"Come to me, my nibble darling!" said he. "I can't get across to you."

But the Thistle did not answer. He became more and more thought-ful—kept on thinking and thinking till near Christmas, and then a flower of thought came forth.

"If the children are only good, the parents do not mind standing outside the garden pale."

"That's an honorable thought," said the Sunbeam. "You shall also have a good place."

"In a pot or in a frame?" asked the Thistle.

"In a story," replied the Sunbeam.

POULTRY MEG'S FAMILY

POULTRY MEG was the only person who lived in the new stately dwelling that had been built for the fowls and ducks belonging to the manor house. It stood there where once the old knightly building had stood with its tower, its pointed gables, its moat, and its drawbridge. Close by it was a wilderness of trees and thicket; here the garden had been, and had stretched out to a great lake, which was now moorland. Crows and choughs flew screaming over the old trees, and there were crowds of birds; they did not seem to get fewer when any one shot among them, but seemed rather to increase. One heard the screaming into the poultry-house, where Poultry Meg sat with the ducklings running to and fro over her wooden shoes. She knew every fowl and every duck from the moment it crept out of the shell; and she was fond of her fowls and her ducks, and proud of the stately house that had been built for them. Her own little room in the house was clean and neat, for that was the wish of the gracious lady to whom the house belonged. She often came in the company of grand noble guests, to whom she showed "the hens' and ducks' barracks," as she called the little house.

Here were a clothes cupboard, and an arm-chair, and even a chest of drawers; and on these drawers a polished metal plate had been placed, whereon was engraved the word "Grubbe," and this was the name of the noble family that had lived in the house of old. The brass plate had been found when they were digging the foundation; and the clerk has said it had no value except in being an old relic. The clerk knew all about the place, and about the old times, for he had his knowledge from books, and many a memorandum had been written and put in his table-drawer. But the oldest of the crows perhaps knew more than he, and screamed it out in her own language; but that was the crow's language, and the clerk did not understand that, clever as he was.

After the hot summer days the mist sometimes hung over the moorland as if a whole lake were behind the old trees, among which the crows and the daws were fluttering; and thus it had looked when the good Knight Grubbe had lived here — when the old manor house stood with its thick red walls. The dog-chain used to reach in those days quite over the gateway; through the tower one went into a paved passage which led to the rooms; the windows were narrow, and the panes were small, even in the great hall where the dancing used to be; but in the time of the last Grubbe, there had been no dancing in the hall within the memory of man, although an old drum still lay there that had served as part of the music. Here stood a quaintly carved cupboard, in which rare flower-roots were kept, for my Lady Grubbe was fond of plants and cultivated trees and shrubs. Her husband preferred riding out to shoot wolves and boars; and his little daughter Marie always went with him part of the way. When she was only five years old, she would sit proudly on her horse, and look saucily round with her great black eyes. It was a great amusement to her to hit out among the hunting-dogs with her whip; but her father would rather have seen her hit among the peasant boys, who came running up to stare at their lord.

The peasant in the clay hut close by the knightly house had a son named Sören, of the same age as the gracious little lady. The boy could climb well, and had always to bring her down the bird's nests. The birds screamed as loud as they could, and one of the greatest of them hacked him with its beak over the eye so that the blood ran down, and it was at first thought the eye had been destroyed; but it had not been injured after all. Marie Grubbe used to call him her Sören, and that was a great favor, and was an advantage to Sören's father — poor Jon, who had one day committed a fault, and was to be punished by riding on the wooden horse. This same horse stood in the courtyard, and had four poles for legs, and a single narrow plant for a back; on this Jon had to ride astride, and some heavy bricks were fastened to his feet into the bargain, that he might not sit too comfortably. He made horrible grimaces, and Sören wept and implored little Marie to interfere. She immediately ordered that Sören's father should be taken down, and when they did not obey her, she stamped on the floor, and pulled at her father's sleeve till it was torn to pieces. She would have her way, and she got her way, and Sören's father was taken down.

Lady Grubbe, who now came up, parted her little daughter's hair from the child's brow, and looked at her affectionately; but Marie did not understand why.

She wanted to go to the hounds, and not to her mother, who went down into the garden, to the lake where the water-lily bloomed, and the heads of bulrushes nodded amid the reeds; and she looked at all this beauty and freshness. "How pleasant!" she said. In the garden stood at that time a rare tree, which she herself had planted. It was called the blood-beech — a kind of negro growing among the other trees, so dark brown were the leaves. This tree required much sunshine, for in continual shade it would become bright green like the other trees, and thus lose its distinctive character. In the lofty chestnut trees were many birds' nests, and also in the thickets and in the grassy meadows. It seemed as though the birds knew that they were protected here, and that no one must fire a gun at them.

Little Marie came here with Sören. He knew how to climb, as we have already said, and eggs and fluffy-feathered young birds were brought down. The birds, great and small, flew about in terror and tribulation; the peewit from the fields, and the crows and daws from the high trees, screamed and screamed; it was just such din as the family will raise to the present day.

"What are you doing, you children?" cried the gentle lady; "that is sinful!"

Sören stood abashed, and even the little gracious lady looked down a little; but then he said, quite short and pretty,

"My father lets me do it!"

"Craw—craw! away—away from here!" cried the great black birds, and they flew away; but on the following day they came back, for they were at home here.

The quiet gentle lady did not remain long at home here on earth, for the good God called her away; and, indeed, her home was rather with Him than in the knightly house; and the church bells tolled solemnly when her corpse was carried to the church, and the eyes of the poor people were wet with tears, for she had been good to them.

When she was gone, no one attended to her plantations, and the garden ran to waste. Grubbe the knight was a hard man, they said; but his daughter, young as she was, knew how to manage him. He used to laugh and let her have her way. She was now twelve years old, and strongly built. She looked the people through and through with her black eyes, rode her horse as bravely as a man, and could fire off her gun like a practiced hunter.

One day there were great visitors in the neighborhood, the grandest visitors who could come. The young King, and his half-brother and comrade, the Lord Ulric Frederick Gyldenlöwe. They wanted to hunt the wild boar, and to pass a few days at the castle of Grubbe.

Gyldenlöwe sat at table next to Marie Grubbe, and he took her by the hand and gave her a kiss, as if she had been a relation; but she gave him a box on the ear, and told him she could not bear him, at which there was great laughter, as if that had been a very amusing thing.

And perhaps it was very amusing, for, five years afterwards, when Marie had fulfilled her seventeenth year, a messenger arrived with a letter, in which Lord Gyldenlöwe proposed for the hand of the noble young lady. There was a thing for you!

"He is the grandest and most gallant gentleman in the whole country," said Grubbe the knight; "that is not a thing to despise."

"I don't care so very much about him," said Marie Grubbe; but she did not despise the grandest man of all the country, who sat by the king's side.

Silver plate, and fine linen and woollen, went off to Copenhagen in a ship, while the bride made the journey by land in ten days. But the outfit met with contrary winds, or with no winds at all, for four months passed before it arrived; and when it came, my Lady Gyldenlöwe was gone.

"I'd rather lie on coarse sacking than lie in his silken beds," she declared. "I'd rather walk barefoot than drive with him in a coach!"

Late one evening in November two women came riding into the town of

Aarhuus. They were the gracious Lady Gyldenlöwe (Marie Grubbe) and her maid. They came from the town of Weile, whither they had come in a ship from Copenhagen. They stopped at Lord Grubbe's stone mansion in Aarhuus. Grubbe was not well pleased with this visit. Marie was accosted in hard words; but she had a bedroom given her, and got her beer soup of a morning; but the evil part of her father's nature was aroused against her, and she was not used to that. She was not of a gentle temper, and we often answer as we are addressed. She answered openly, and spoke with bitterness and hatred of her husband, with whom she declared she would not live; she was too honorable for that.

A year went by, but it did not go by pleasantly. There were evil words between the father and the daughter, and that ought never to be. Bad words bear bad fruit. What could be the end of such a state of things?

"We two cannot live under the same roof," said the father one day. "Go away from here to our old manor house; but you had better bite your tongue off than spread any lies among the people."

And so the two parted. She went with her maid to the old castle where she had been born, and near which the gentle, pious lady, her mother, was lying in the church vault. An old cowherd lived in the courtyard, and was the only other inhabitant of the place. In the rooms heavy black cobwebs hung down, covered with dust; in the garden everything grew just as it would; hops and climbing plants ran like a net between the trees and bushes, and the hemlock and nettle grew larger and stronger. The blood-beech had been outgrown by other trees, and now stood in the shade; and its leaves were green like those of the common trees, and its glory had departed. Crows and choughs, in great close masses, flew past over the tall chestnut trees, and chattered and screamed as if they had something very important to tell one another — as if they were saying, "Now she's come back again, the little girl who had their eggs and their young ones stolen from them; and as for the thief who had got them down, he had to climb up a leafless tree, for he sat on a tall ship's mast, and was beaten with a rope's end if he did not behave himself."

The clerk told all this in our own times; he had collected it and looked it up in books and memoranda. It was to be found, with many other writings, locked up in his table-drawer.

"Upward and downward is the course of the world," said he. "It is strange to hear."

And we will hear how it went with Marie Grubbe. We need not for that forget Poultry Meg, who is sitting in her capital hen-house, in our own time. Marie Grubbe sat down in her times, but not with the same spirit that old Poultry Meg showed.

The winter passed away, and the spring and the summer passed away, and the autumn came again, with the damp, cold sea-fog. It was a lonely, desolate life in the old manor house. Marie Grubbe took her gun in her hand and went out to the heath, and shot hares and foxes, and whatever birds she could hit. More than once she met the noble Sir Palle Dyre, of Nörrebäk, who was also wandering about with his gun and his dogs. He was tall and strong, and boasted of this when they talked together. He could have measured himself against the deceased Mr. Brockenhuus, of Egeskov, of whom the people still talked. Palle Dyre had, after the example of Brockenhuus, caused an iron chain with a hunting-horn to be hung in his gateway; and when he came riding home, he used to seize the chain, and lift himself and his horse from the ground, and blow the horn.

"Come yourself, and see me do that, Dame Marie," he said. 'One can breathe fresh and free at Nörrebäk.

When she went to his castle is not known, but on the altar candlestick in the church of Nörrebäk it was inscribed that they were the gift of Palle Dyre and Marie Grubbe, of Nörrebäk Castle.

A great stout man was Palle Dyre. He drank like a sponge. He was like a tub that could never get full; he snored like a whole sty of pigs, and he looked red and bloated.

"He is treacherous and malicious," said Dame Pally Dyre, Grubbe's daughter. Soon she was weary of her life with him, but that did not make it better.

One day the table was spread, and the dishes grew cold. Palle Dyre was out hunting foxes, and the gracious lady was nowhere to be found. Towards midnight Palle Dyre came home, but Dame Dyre came neither at midnight, nor next morning. She had turned her back upon Nörrebäk, and had ridden away without saying good-bye.

It was gray, wet weather; the wind grew cold, and a flight of black screaming birds flew over her head. They were not so homeless as she.

First she journeyed southward, quite down into the German land. A couple of golden rings with costly stones were turned into money; and then she turned to the east, and then she turned again and went towards the west. She had no food before her eyes, and murmured against everything, even against the good God himself, so wretched was her soul. Soon her body became wretched too, and she was scarcely able to move a foot. The peewit flew up as she stumbled over the mound of earth where it had built its nest. The bird cried, as it always cried, "You thief! you thief!" She had never stolen her neighbor's goods; but as a little girl she had caused eggs and young birds to be taken from the trees, and she thought of that now.

From where she lay she could see the sand-dunes. By the seashore lived fishermen; but she could not get so far, she was so ill. The great white sea-mews flew over her head, and screamed as the crows and daws screamed at home in the garden of the manor house. The birds flew quite close to her, and at last it seemed to her as if they became black as crows, and then all was night before her eyes.

When she opened her eyes again, she was being lifted and carried. A great strong man had taken her up in his arms, and she was looking straight into his bearded face. He had a scar over one eye, which seemed to divide the eyebrow into two parts. Weak as she was, he carried her to the ship, where he got a rating for it from the captain.

The next day the ship sailed away. Madame Grubbe had not been put ashore, so she sailed away with it. But she will return, will she not? Yes, but where, and when?

The clerk could tell about this too, and it was not a story which he patched together himself. He had the whole strange history out of an old authentic book, which we ourselves can take out and read. The Danish historian, Ludwig Holberg, who has written so many useful books and merry comedies, from which we can get such a good idea of his times and their people, tells in his letters of Marie Grubbe, where and how he met her. It is well worth hearing; but for all that, we don't at all forget Poultry Meg, who is sitting cheerful and comfortable in the charming fowl-house.

The ship sailed away with Marie Grubbe. That's where we left off.

Long years went by.

The plague was raging at Copenhagen; it was in the year 1711. The Queen of Denmark went away to her German home, the King quitted the capital, and everybody who could do so hurried away. The students, even those who had board and lodging gratis, left the city. One of these students, the last who had remained in the free college, at last went away too. It was two o'clock in the morning. He was carrying his knapsack, which was better stacked with books and writings than with clothes. A damp mist hung over the town; not a person was to be seen in the streets; the street-doors around were marked with crosses, as a sign that the plague was within, or that all the inmates were dead. A great wagon rattled past him; the coachman brandished his whip, and the horses flew by at a gallop. The wagon was filled with corpses. The young student kept his hand before his face, and smelt at some strong spirits that he had with him on a sponge in a little brass scent-case. Out of a small tavern in one of the streets there were sounds of singing and of unhallowed laughter, from people who drank the night through to forget that the plague was at their doors, and that they might be put into the wagon as the others had been. The student turned his steps towards the canal at the castle bridge, where a couple of small ships were lying; one of these was weighing anchor, to get away from the plague-stricken city.

"If God spares our lives and grants us a fair wind, we are going to Grönmud, near Falster," said the captain; and he asked the name of the student who wished to go with him.

"Ludwig Holberg," answered the student; and the name sounded like any other. But now there sounds in it one of the proudest names of Denmark; then it was the name of a young, unknown student.

The ship glided past the castle. It was not yet bright day when it was in the open sea. A light wind filled the sails, and the young student sat down with his face turned towards the fresh wind, and went to sleep, which was not exactly the most prudent thing he could have done.

Already on the third day the ship lay by the island of Falster.

"Do you know any one here with whom I could lodge cheaply?" Holberg asked the captain.

"I should think you would do well to go to the ferry-woman in Borrehaus," answered the captain. "If you want to be very civil to her, her name is Mother Sören Sörensen Müller. But it may happen that she may fly into a fury if you are too polite to her. The man is in custody for a crime, and that's why she manages the ferry-boat herself — she has fists of her own."

The student took his knapsack and betook himself to the ferry-house. The house door was not locked — it opened, and he went into a room with a brick floor, where a bench, with a great coverlet of leather, formed the chief article of furniture. A white hen, who had a brood of chickens, was fastened to the bench, and had overturned the pipkin of water, so that the wet ran across the floor. There were no people either here or in the adjoining room; only a cradle stood there, in which was a child. The ferry-boat came back with only one person in it. Whether that person was a man or a woman was not an easy matter to determine. The person in question was wrapped in a great cloak, and wore a kind of hood. Presently the boat lay to.

It was a woman who got out of it and came into the room. She looked very stately when she straightened her back; two proud eyes looked forth from beneath her black eyebrows. It was Mother Sören, the ferry-wife. The crows and daws might have called out another name for her, which we know better.

She looked morose, and did not seem to care to talk; but this much was settled, that the student should board in her house for an indefinite time, while things looked so bad in Copenhagen.

This or that honest citizen would often come to the ferry-house from the neighboring little town. There came Frank the cutler, and Sivert the exciseman. They drank a mug of beer in the ferry-house, and used to converse with the student, for he was a clever young man, who knew his "Practica," as they called it; he could read Greek and Latin, and was well up in learned subjects.

"The less one knows, the less it presses upon one," said Mother Sören.

"You have to work hard," said Holberg one day, when she was dipping clothes in the strong soapy water, and was obliged herself to split the logs for the fire.

"That's my affair," she replied.

"Have you been obliged to toil in this way from your childhood?"

"You can read that from my hands," she replied, and held out her hands, that were small indeed, but hard and strong, with bitten nails. "You are learned, and can read."

At Christmas-time it began to snow heavily. The cold came on, the wind blue sharp, as if there were vitriol in it to wash the people's faces. Mother Sören did not let that disturb her; she threw her cloak around her, and drew her hood over her head. Early in the afternoon—it was already dark in the house—she laid wood and turf on the hearth, and then she sat down to darn her stockings, for there was no one to do it for her. Towards evening she spoke more words to the student than it was customary with her to use; she spoke of her husband.

"He killed a sailor of Dragör by mischance, and for that he has to work for three years in irons. He's only a common sailor, and therefore the law must take its course."

"The law is there for people of high rank, too," said Holberg.

"Do you think so?" said Mother Sören; then she looked into the fire for a while; but after a time she began to speak again. "Have you heard of Kai Lykke, who caused a church to be pulled down, and when the clergyman, Master Martin, thundered from the pulpit about it, he had him put in irons, and sat in judgment upon him, and condemned him to death? Yes, and the clergyman was obliged to bow his head to the stroke. And yet Kai Lykke went scot-free."

"He had a right to do as he did in those times," said Holberg; "but now we have left those times behind us."

"You may get a fool to believe that," cried Mother Sören; and she got up and went into the room where the child lay. She lifted up the child, and laid it down more comfortably. Then she arranged the bed-place of the student. He had the green coverlet, for he felt the cold more than she, though he was born in Norway.

On New Year's morning it was a bright sunshiny day. The frost had been so strong, and was still so strong, that the fallen snow had become a hard mass, and one could walk upon it. The bells of the little town were tolling for church. Student Holberg wrapped himself up in his woollen cloak, and wanted to go to the town.

Over the ferry-house the crows and daws were flying with loud cries; one could hardly hear the church bells for their screaming. Mother Sören stood in front of the house, filling a brass pot with snow, which she was going to put on the fire to get drinking water. She looked up to the crowd of birds, and thought her own thoughts.

Student Holberg went to church. On his way there and on his return he passed by the house of tax-collector Sivert, by the town-gate. Here he was invited to take a mug of brown beer with treacle and sugar. The discourse fell upon Mother Sören, but the tax collector did not know much about her, and, indeed, few knew much about her. She did not belong to the island of Falster, he said; she had a little property of her own at one time. Her husband was a common sailor, a fellow of a very hot temper, and had killed a sailor of Dragör; and he beat his wife, and yet she defended him.

"I should not endure such treatment," said the tax-collector's wife. "I am come of more respectable people. My father was stocking-weaver to the Court."

"And consequently you have married a governmental official," said Holberg, and made a bow to her and to the collector.

It was on Twelfth Night, the evening of the festival of the Three Kings, Mother Sören lit up for Holberg a three-king candle, that is, a tallow candle with three wicks, which she had herself prepared.

"A light for each man," said Holberg.

"For each man?" repeated the woman, looking sharply at him.

"For each of the wise men from the East," said Holberg.

"You mean it that way," said she, and then she was silent for a long time. But on this evening he learned more about her than he had yet known.

"You speak very affectionately of your husband," observed Holberg, "and yet the people say that he ill-uses you every day."

"That's no one's business but mine," she replied. "The blows might have done me good when I was a child; now, I suppose, I get them for my sins. But I know what good he has done me," and she rose up. "When I lay sick upon the desolate heath, and no one would have pity on me, and no one would have anything to do with me, except the crows and daws, which came to peck me to bits, he carried me in his arms, and had to bear hard words because of the burden he brought on board ship. It's not in my nature to be sick, and so I got well. Every man has his own way, and Sören has his; but the horse must not be judged by the halter. Taking one thing with another, I have lived more agreeably with him than with the man whom they called the most noble and gallant of the King's subjects. I have had the Stadtholder Gyldenlöwe, the King's half-brother, for my husband; and afterwards I took Palle Dyre. One is as good as another, each in his own way, and I in mine. That was a long gossip, but now you know all about me."

And with those words she left the room.

It was Marie Grubbe! so strangely had fate played with her. She did not live to see many anniversaries of the festival of the Three Kings; Holberg has recorded that she died in June, 1716; but he has not written down, for he did not know, that a number of great black birds circled over the ferry-house, when Mother Sören, as she was called, was lying there a corpse. They did not scream, as if they knew that at a burial silence should be observed. So soon as she lay in the earth, the birds disappeared; but on the same evening in Jutland, at the old manor house, an enormous number of crows and choughs were seen; they all cried as loud as they could, as if they had some announcement to make. Perhaps they talked of him who, as a little boy, had taken away their eggs and their young; of the peasant's son, who had to wear an iron garter, and of the noble young lady, who ended by being a ferryman's wife.

"Brave! brave!" they cried.

And the whole family cried, "Brave! brave!" when the old house was pulled down.

"They are still crying, and yet there's nothing to cry about," said the clerk, when he told the story. "The family is extinct, the house has been pulled down, and where it stood is now the stately poultry-house, with gilded weathercocks, and the old Poultry Meg. She rejoices greatly in her beautiful dwelling. If she had not come here," the old clerk added, "she would have had to go into the work-house."

The pigeons cooed over her, the turkey-cocks gobbled, and the ducks quacked.

"Nobody knew her," they said; "she belongs to no family. It's pure charity that she is here at all. She has neither a drake father nor a hen mother, and has no descendants."

She came of a great family, for all that; but she did not know it, and the old clerk did not know it, though he had so much written down; but one of the old crows knew about it, and told about it. She had heard from her own mother and grandmother about Poultry Meg's mother and grandmother. And we know the grandmother too. We saw her ride, as child, over the bridge, looking proudly around her, as if the whole world belonged to her, and all the birds' nests in it; and we saw her on the heath, by the sand-dunes; and, last of all, in the ferry-house. The granddaughter, the last of her race, had come back to the old home, where the old castle had stood, where the black wild birds were screaming; but she sat among the tame birds, and these knew her and were fond of her. Poultry Meg had nothing left to wish for; she looked forward with pleasure to her death, and she was old enough to die.

"Grave, grave!" cried the crows.

And Poultry Meg has a good grave, which nobody knew except the old crow, if the old crow is not dead already.

And now we know the story of the old manor house, of its old proprietors, and of all Poultry Meg's family.

WHAT ONE CAN INVENT

THERE was once a young man who was studying to be a poet. He wanted to become one by Easter, and to marry, and to live by poetry. To write poems, he knew, only consists in being able to invent something; but he could not invent anything. He had been born too late—everything had been taken up before he came into the world, and everything had been written and told about.

"Happy people who were born a thousand years ago!" said he. "It was an easy matter for them to become immortal. Happy even was he who was born a hundred years ago, for then there was still something about which a poem could be written. Now the world is written out, and what can I write poetry about?"

Then he studied till he became ill and wretched, the wretched man! No doctor could help him, but perhaps the wise woman could. She lived in the little house by the wayside, where the gate is that she opened for those who rode and drove. But she could do more than unlock the gate. She was wiser than the doctor who drives in his own carriage and pays tax for his rank.

"I must go to her," said the young man.

The house in which she dwelt was small and neat, but dreary to behold, for there were no flowers near it—no trees. By the door stood a bee-hive, which was very useful. There was also a little potato-field, very useful, and an earth bank, with sloe bushes upon it, which had done blossoming, and now bore fruit, sloes, that draw one's mouth together if one tastes them before the frost has touched them.

"That's a true picture of our poetryless time, that I see before me now," thought the young man; and that was at least a thought, a grain of gold that he found by the door of the wise woman.

"Write that down!" said she. "Even crumbs are bread. I know why you come hither. You cannot invent anything, and yet you want to be a poet by Easter."

"Everything has been written down," said he. "Our time is not the old time."

"No," said the woman. "In the old time wise women were burnt, and poets went about with empty stomachs, and very much out at elbows. The present time is good, it is the best of times; but you have not the right way of looking at it. Your ear is not sharpened to hear, and I fancy you do not say the Lord's Prayer in the evening. There is plenty here to write poems about, and to tell of, for any one who knows the way. You can read it in the fruits of the earth, you can draw it from the flowing and the standing water; but you must understand how—you must understand how to catch a sunbeam. Now just you try my spectacles on, and put my ear-trumpet to your ear, and then pray to God, and leave off thinking of yourself."

The last was a very difficult thing to do—more than a wise woman ought to ask.

He received the spectacles and the ear-trumpet, and was posted in the middle of the potato-field. She put a great potato into his hand. Sounds came from within it; there came a song with words, the history of the potato, an every-day story in ten parts, an interesting story. And ten lines were enough to tell it in.

And what did the potato sing?

She sang of herself and of her family, of the arrival of the potato in Europe, of the misrepresentation to which she had been exposed before she was acknowledged, as she is now, to be a greater treasure than a lump of gold.

"We were distributed, by the King's command, from the council-houses through the various towns, and proclamation was made of our great value; but no one believed in it, or even understood how to plant us. One man dug a hole in the earth and threw in his whole bushel of potatoes; another put one potato here and another there in the ground, and expected that each was to come up a perfect tree, from which he might shake down potatoes. And they certainly grew, and produced flowers and green watery fruit, but it all withered away. Nobody thought of what was in the ground—the blessing—the potato. Yes, we have endured and suffered, that is to say, our forefathers have; they and we, it is all one."

What a story it was!

"Well, and that will do," said the woman. "Now look at the sloe bush."

"We have also some near relations in the home of the potatoes, but higher towards the north than they grew," said the Sloes. "There were Northmen, from Norway, who steered westward through mist and storm to an unknown land, where, behind ice and snow, they found plants and green meadows, and bushes with blue-black grapes—sloe bushes. The grapes were ripened by the frost just as we are. And they called the land 'wine-land,' that is, 'Groenland,' or 'Sloeland.' "

"That is quite a romantic story," said the young man.

"Yes, certainly. But now come with me," said the wise woman, and she led him to the bee-hive.

He looked into it. What life and labor! There were bees standing in all the passages, waving their wings, so that a wholesome draught of air might blow through the great manufactory; that was their business. Then there came in bees from without, who had been born with little baskets on their feet; they brought flower-dust, which was poured out, sorted, and manufactured into honey and wax. They flew in and out. The queen-bee wanted to fly out, but then all the other bees must have gone with her. It was not yet the time for that, but still she wanted to fly out; so the others bit off her majesty's wings, and she had to stay where she was.

"Now get upon the earth bank," said the wise woman. "Come and look out over the highway, where you can see the people."

"What a crowd it is!" said the young man. "One story after another. It whirls and whirls! It's quite a confusion before my eyes. I shall go out at the back."

"No, go straight forward," said the woman. "Go straight into the crowd of people; look at them in the right way. Have an ear to hear and the right heart to feel, and you will soon invent something. But, before you go away, you must give me my spectacles and my ear-trumpet again."

And so saying, she took both from him.

"Now I do not see the smallest thing," said the young man, "and now I don't hear anything more."

"Why, then, you can't be a poet by Easter," said the wise woman.

"But, by what time can I be one?" asked he.

"Neither by Easter nor by Whitsuntide! You will not learn how to invent anything."

"What must I do to earn my bread by poetry?"

"You can do that before Shrove Tuesday. Hunt the poets! Kill their writings and thus you will kill them. Don't be put out of countenance. Strike at them boldly, and you'll have carnival cake, on which you can support yourself and your wife too."

"What one can invent!" cried the young man. And so he hit out boldly at every second poet, because he could not be a poet himself.

We have it from the wise woman. She knows WHAT ONE CAN INVENT.

THE THORNY ROAD OF HONOR

AN old story yet lives of the "Thorny Road of Honor," of a marksman, who indeed attained to rank and office, but only after a lifelong and weary strife against difficulties. Who has not, in reading this story, thought of his own strife, and of his own numerous "difficulties?" The story is very closely akin to reality; but still it has its harmonious explanation here on earth, while reality often points beyond the confines of life to the regions of eternity. The history of the world is like a magic lantern that displays to us, in light pictures upon the dark ground of the present, how the benefactors of mankind, the martyrs of genius, wandered along the thorny road of honor.

From all periods, and from every country, these shining pictures display themselves to us. Each only appears for a few moments, but each represents a whole life, sometimes a whole age, with its conflicts and victories. Let us contemplate here and there one of the company of martyrs — the company which will receive new members until the world itself shall pass away.

We look down upon a crowded amphitheatre. Out of the "Clouds" of Aristophanes, satire and humor are pouring down in streams upon the audience; on the stage Socrates, the most remarkable man in Athens, he who had been the shield and defence of the people against the thirty tyrants, is held up mentally and bodily to ridicule — Socrates, who saved Alcibiades and Xenophon in the turmoil of battle, and whose genius soared far above the gods of the ancients. He himself is present; he has risen from the spectator's bench, and has stepped forward, that the laughing Athenians may well appreciate the likeness between himself and the caricature on the stage. There he stands before them, towering high above them all.

Thou juicy, green, poisonous hemlock, throw thy shadow over Athens — not thou, olive tree of fame!

Seven cities contended for the honor of giving birth to Homer — that is to say, they contended after his death! Let us look at him as he was in his lifetime. He wanders on foot through the cities, and recites his verses for a livelihood; the thought for the morrow turns his hair gray! He, the great seer, is blind, and painfully pursues his way — the sharp thorn tears the mantle of the king of poets. His song yet lives, and through that alone live all the heroes and gods of antiquity.

One picture after another springs up from the east, from the west, far removed from each other in time and place, and yet each one forming a portion of the thorny road of honor, on which the thistle indeed displays a flower, but only to adorn the grave.

The camels pass along under the palm trees; they are richly laden with indigo and other treasures of value, sent by the ruler of the land to him whose songs are the delight of the people, the fame of the country. He whom envy and falsehood have driven into exile has been found, and the caravan approaches the little town in which he has taken refuge. A poor corpse is carried out of the town gate, and the funeral procession causes the caravan to halt. The dead man is he whom they have been sent to seek — Firdusi — who has wandered the thorny road of honor even to the end.

The African, with blunt features, thick lips, and woolly hair, sits on the marble steps of the palace in the capital of Portugal, and begs. He is the submissive slave of Camoens, and but for him, and for the copper coins thrown to him by the passers-by, his master, the poet of the "Lusiad," would die of hunger. Now, a costly monument marks the grave of Camoens.

There is a new picture.

Behind the iron grating a man appears, pale as death, with long unkempt beard.

"I have made a discovery," he says, "the greatest that has been made for centuries; and they have kept me locked up here for more than twenty years!"

Who is the man?

"A madman," replies the keeper of the madhouse. "What whimsical ideas these lunatics have! He imagines that one can propel things by means of steam."

It is Solomon de Cares, the discoverer of the power of steam, whose theory, expressed in dark words, is not understood by Richelieu; and he dies in the madhouse.

Here stands Columbus, whom the street boys used once to follow and jeer, because he wanted to discover a new world; and he has discovered it. Shouts of joy greet him from the breasts of all, and the clash of bells sounds to celebrate his triumphant return; but the clash of the bells of envy soon drowns the others. The discoverer of a world — he who lifted the American gold land from the sea, and gave it to his king — he is rewarded with iron chains. He wishes that these chains may be placed in his coffin, for they witness to the world of the way in which a man's contemporaries reward good service.

One picture after another comes crowding on; the thorny path of honor and of fame is over-filled.

Here in dark night sits the man who measured the mountains in the moon; he who forced his way out into the endless space, among stars and planets; he, the mighty man who understood the spirit of nature, and felt the earth moving beneath his feet — Galileo. Blind and deaf he sits — an old man thrust through with the spear of suffering, and amid the torments of neglect, scarcely able to lift his foot — that foot with which, in the anguish of his soul, when men denied the truth, he stamped upon the ground, with the exclamation, "Yet it moves!"

Here stands a woman of childlike mind, yet full of faith and inspiration. She carries the banner in front of the combating army, and brings victory and salvation to her fatherland. The sound of shouting arises, and the pile flames up. They are burning the witch, Joan of Arc. Yes, and a future century jeers at the White Lily. Voltaire, the satyr of human intellect, writes "La Pucelle."

At the Thing or Assembly at Viborg, the Danish nobles burn the laws of the king. They flame up high, illuminating the period and the lawgiver, and throw a glory into the dark prison tower, where an old man is growing gray and bent. With his finger he marks out a groove in the stone table. It is the popular king who sits there, once the ruler of three kingdoms, the friend of the citizen and the peasant. It is Christian the Second. Enemies wrote his history. Let us remember his improvements of seven and twenty years, if we cannot forget his crime.

A ship sails away, quitting the Danish shores. A man leans against the mast, casting a last glance towards the Island Hueen. It is Tycho Brahe. He raised the name of Denmark to the stars, and was rewarded with injury, loss and sorrow. He is going to a strange country.

"The vault of heaven is above me everywhere," he says, "and what do I want more?"

And away sails the famous Dane, the astronomer, to live honored and free in a strange land.

"Ay, free, if only from the unbearable sufferings of the body!" comes in a sigh through time, and strikes upon our ear. What a picture! Griffenfeldt, a Danish Prometheus, bound to the rocky island of Munkholm.

We are in America, on the margin of one of the largest rivers; an innumerable crowd has gathered, for it is said that a ship is to sail against the wind and weather, bidding defiance to the elements. The man who thinks he can solve the problem is named Robert Fulton. The ship begins its passage, but suddenly it stops. The crowd begins to laugh and whistle and hiss—the very father of the man whistles with the rest.

"Conceit! Foolery!" is the cry. "It has happened just as he deserved. Put the crack-brain under lock and key!"

Then suddenly a little nail breaks, which had stopped the machine for a few moments; and now the wheels turn again, the floats break the force of the waters, and the ship continues its course; and the beam of the steam engine shortens the distance between far lands from hours into minutes.

O human race, canst thou grasp the happiness of such a minute of consciousness, this penetration of the soul by its mission, the moment in which all dejection, and every wound—even those caused by one's own fault—is changed into health and strength and clearness—when discord is converted to harmony—the minute in which men seem to recognize the manifestation of the heavenly grace in one man, and feel how this one imparts it to all?

Thus the thorny path of honor shows itself as a glory, surrounding the earth with its beams. Thrice happy he who is chosen to be a wanderer there, and, without merit of his own, to be placed between the builder of the bridge and the earth—between Providence and the human race.

On mighty wings the spirit of history floats through the ages, and shows—giving courage and comfort, and awakening gentle thoughts—on the dark nightly background, but in gleaming pictures, the thorny path of honor, which does not, like a fairy tale, end in brilliancy and joy here on earth, but stretches out beyond all time, even into eternity!

IN A THOUSAND YEARS

YES, in a thousand years people will fly on the wings of steam through the air, over the ocean! The young inhabitants of America will become visitors of old Europe. They will come over to see the monuments and the great cities, which will then be in ruins, just as we in our time make pilgrimages to the tottering splendors of Southern Asia. In a thousand years they will come!

The Thames, the Danube, and the Rhine still roll their course, Mont Blanc stands firm with its snow-capped summit, and the Northern Lights gleam over the land of the North; but generation after generation has become dust, whole rows of the mighty of the moment are forgotten, like those who already slumber under the hill on which the rich trader, whose ground it is, has built a bench, on which he can sit and look out across his waving corn fields.

"To Europe!" cry the young sons of America; "to the land of our ancestors, the glorious land of monuments and fancy—to Europe!"

The ship of the air comes. It is crowded with passengers, for the transit is quicker than by sea. The electro-magnetic wire under the ocean has already telegraphed the number of the aërial caravan. Europe is in sight. It is the coast of Ireland that they see, but the passengers are still asleep; they will not be called till they are exactly over England. There they will first step on European shore, in the land of Shakespeare, as the educated call it; in the land of politics, the land of machines, as it is called by others.

Here they stay a whole day. That is all the time the busy race can devote to the whole of England and Scotland. Then the journey is continued through the tunnel under the English Channel, to France, the land of Charlemagne and Napoleon. Moliere is named, the learned men talk of the classic school of remote antiquity. There is rejoicing and shouting for the names of heroes, poets, and men of science, whom our time does not know, but who will be born after our time in Paris, the centre of Europe, and elsewhere.

The air steamboat flies over the country whence Columbus went forth, where Cortez was born, and where Calderon sang dramas in sounding verse. Beautiful black-eyed women live still in the blooming valleys, and the oldest songs speak of the Cid and the Alhambra.

Then through the air, over the sea, to Italy, where once lay old, everlasting Rome. It has vanished! The Campagna lies desert. A single ruined wall is shown as the remains of St. Peter's, but there is a doubt if this ruin be genuine.

Next to Greece, to sleep a night in the grand hotel at the top of Mount Olympus, to say that they have been there; and the journey is continued to the Bosphorus, to rest there a few hours, and see the place where Byzantium lay; and where the legend tells that the harem stood in the time of the Turks, poor fishermen are now spreading their nets.

Over the remains of mighty cities on the broad Danube, cities which we in our time know not, the travellers pass; but here and there, on the rich sites of those that time shall bring forth, the caravan sometimes descends, and departs thence again.

Down below lies Germany, that was once covered with a close net of railway and canals, the region where Luther spoke, where Goethe sang, and

Mozart once held the sceptre of harmony. Great names shine there, in science and in art, names that are unknown to us. One day devoted to seeing Germany, and one for the North, the country of Oersted and Linnæus, and for Norway, the land of the old heroes and the young Normans. Iceland is visited on the journey home. The geysers burn no more, Hecla is an extinct volcano, but the rocky island is still fixed in the midst of the foaming sea, a continual monument of legend and poetry.

"There is really a great deal to be seen in Europe," says the young American, "and we have seen it in a week, according to the directions of the great traveller" (and here he mentions the name of one of his contemporaries) "in his celebrated work, 'How to See All Europe in a Week.' "

BY THE ALMSHOUSE WINDOW

NEAR the grass-covered rampart which encircles Copenhagen lies a great red house. Balsams and other flowers greet us from the long rows of windows in the house, whose interior is sufficiently poverty-stricken; and poor and old are the people who inhabit it. The building is the Warton Almshouse.

Look! at the window there leans an old maid. She plucks the withered leaf from the balsam, and looks at the grass-covered rampart, on which many children are playing. What is the old maid thinking of? A whole life drama is unfolding itself before her inward gaze.

"The poor little children, how happy they are—how merrily they play and romp together! What red cheeks and what angels' eyes! but they have no shoes nor stockings. They dance on the green rampart, just on the place where, according to the old story, the ground always sank in, and where a sportive, frolicsome child had been lured by means of flowers, toys and sweetmeats into an open grave ready dug for it, and which was afterwards closed over the child; and from that moment, the old story says, the ground gave way no longer, the mound remained firm and fast, and was quickly covered with the green turf. The little people who now play on that spot know nothing of the old tale, else would they fancy they heard a child crying deep below the earth, and the dewdrops on each blade of grass would be to them tears of woe. Nor do they know anything of the Danish King who here, in the face of the coming foe, took an oath before all his trembling courtiers that he would hold out with the citizens of his capital, and die here in his nest; they know nothing of the men who have fought here, or of the women who from here have drenched with boiling water the enemy, clad in white, and 'biding in the snow to surprise the city.

"No! the poor little ones are playing with light, childish spirits. Play on, play on, thou little maiden! Soon the years will come—yes, those glorious years. The priestly hands have been laid on the candidates for confirmation; hand in hand they walk on the green rampart. Thou hast a white frock on; it has cost thy mother much labor, and yet it is only cut down for thee out of an old larger dress! You will also wear a red shawl; and what if it hang too far down? People will only see how large, how very large it is. You are thinking of your dress, and of the Giver of all good—so glorious is it to wander on the green rampart!

"And the years roll by; they have no lack of dark days, but you have your cheerful young spirit, and you have gained a friend—you know not how. You met, oh, how often! You walk together on the rampart in the fresh spring, on the high days and holidays, when all the world come out to walk upon the ramparts, and all the bells of the church steeples seem to be singing a song of praise for the coming spring.

"Scarcely have the violets come forth, but there on the rampart, just opposite the beautiful Castle of Rosenberg, there is a tree bright with the first green buds. Every year this tree sends forth fresh green shoots. Alas! It is not so with the human heart! Dark mists, more in number than those that cover the northern skies, cloud the human heart. Poor child! thy friend's bridal chamber is a black coffin, and thou becomest an old maid. From the almshouse window, behind the balsams, thou shalt look on the merry children at play, and shalt see thine own history renewed."

And that is the life drama that passes before the old maid while she looks out upon the rampart, the green, sunny rampart, where the children, with their red cheeks and bare shoeless feet, are rejoicing merrily, like the other free little birds.

MOVING DAY

You surely remember Ole, the tower watchman. I have told you about two visits I paid him, and now I'll tell you of a third, although it won't be the last one.

I have gone up to see him generally on New Year's Day, but this time it was Moving Day, when everything down in the city streets is very unpleasant, for they are littered with heaps of rubbish and crockery and all kinds of sweepings, not to mention musty old straw that you have to trample about in. Well, there I was, and in the middle of this rubbish from attic and dustbin I saw a couple of children playing going to bed; they thought it looked so inviting there for that game. Yes, they snuggled down in the straw and drew a ragged old scrap of a curtain over them for a quilt. "That was wonderful!" they said. It was too much for me, so I hurried off to see Ole.

"It's Moving Day," he said. "Streets and alleys are dustbins, dustbins in the grand style; but one cartload is enough for me. I can always find something to pick out of it, and I did that, soon after Christmas. I was walking down the street, a damp, raw, and dirty street, and just the right kind of weather for catching cold. The rubbish man had drawn up his cart there; it was loaded and looked like a sample of Copenhagen streets on Moving Day. In the back of the cart was a fir tree still quite green and with tinsel still hanging on its twigs. It had been the centerpiece of a Christmas display, but now it was thrown out into the street and the rubbish man had stuck it up behind on his pile; a sight to laugh at or weep at—yes, you might even go so far as that—it all depends on your turn of mind. And I thought about it, and so did some of the odds and ends in the cart. At least they may have thought, which is just about the same. Here was a worn lady's glove; what was it thinking about? Shall I tell you? It lay there pointing its little finger straight at the fir tree. 'That fir tree touches me,' it thought. 'I have been to a party, too, among the lighted chandeliers. My life was just a night at a ball. A squeeze of the hand, and I burst; that's all I remember, so now I have nothing more to live for.' That's the way the glove thought, or it may have thought like that. 'That's a tasteless thing for that fir tree to do!' said the potsherds. But you see, broken crockery finds everything tasteless. 'When you come to the rubbish cart,' they said, 'it's time to give up your fine airs and your tinsel. As for ourselves, we've been of some use in the world — far more use than an old green stick like that!' You see, that was another point of view on the same subject, and many people have it. But still the fir tree looked pretty well, and it was a bit of poetry on the rubbish heap; there are many like that to be found in the streets on Moving Day. But the streets down there were crowded and tiresome, and I longed to get back up to my tower and stay there; so here I sit and look down on them from above, and that's very amusing.

"Down below the good people are changing houses; they work hard packing up and then go off with their movables, and the house goblin sits on the tail of the cart and moves with them. Household quarrels, family arguments, sorrows, and cares move from the old to the new houses, and so what do they and we get out of it all? Yes, that was told us already long ago, in the good old verse in the newpaper columns:

Remember Death's great Moving Day!

"It is a serious thought, but I hope it is not disagreeable to you to hear about it. Death is the most faithful administrator after all, in spite of his many petty duties. Have you ever thought about them?

"Death is a bus conductor; he is a passport writer; he signs his name to our references; and he is the director of life's great savings bank. Do you understand that? All our earthly deeds, great and small, are deposited in that savings bank. Then, when Death comes with his Moving Day bus, and we have to get in to be driven to eternity, he give us our references on the frontier as a passport. For our expense money on the journey he draws from the savings bank one of our deeds, whichever of them most distinctly characterizes our conduct; this may be very pleasant to us, or it may be very horrible!

"Nobody has ever escaped that omnibus journey. They tell stories, indeed, of one man who was not allowed to enter — they call him the Wandering Jew; he still has to run along behind it. If he had managed to get in, he would have escaped the treatment he received from the poets.

"Let's take an imaginary look into that big Moving Day omnibus. What a mixed group! Side by side sit kings and beggars, the genius and the idiot. On they must go, without goods or wealth, with only their references and their expense money from life's savings bank. But of each man's deeds, which one has been found and given to him? Perhaps only a very small one, no bigger than a pea, yet a great blooming vine may grow from it.

"The poor beggar, who sat on a low stool in the corner, and received blows and hard words, perhaps is given the battered stool to take, as a token and as expense money. That stool will become the cart to bear him into eternity, and there it will grow into a throne, gleaming with gold and blooming like an arbor.

"He who was always drinking from the bubbling cup of pleasure, and thus forgetting all the wrong things he had done here, receives a wooden keg as his lot. On the journey he has to drink from it; and that pure and cleansing drink will clear his thoughts and awaken his better and nobler nature, so that he sees and feels what before he could not or would not see. Thus be bears within him his own punishment, the gnawing worm that never dies. If on his wineglass was inscribed *Forgetfulness*, the inscription on the keg is *Memory*.

"Whenever I read a good historical book, I cannot help picturing to myself the person of whom I am reading at the final moment of all, when he begins to enter Death's omnibus. I cannot help wondering which of his deeds Death has given him from the savings bank, and what sort of expense money he will take with him to eternity.

"Once upon a time there was a French king—his name I have forgotten, for the names of good people can sometimes be forgotten by you and me, but it will surely come to light again, because in the time of famine this king became the savior of his people. In his honor they raised a monument of snow, with the inscription, 'More quickly than this melts did you help us!' I think, remembering that monument, that Death must have given him one single snowflake that would never melt but flew like a white butterfly above his royal head, on into the land of eternity.

"Then there was Louis XI—yes, I remember his name; one always remembers what is wicked—a sample of his doings often comes to mind; I wish I could say the story is untrue.

"He had his lord high chancelor beheaded, and that he had a right to do, justly or unjustly, but on the same scaffold he set up the chancelor's innocent children, the one eight and the other seven, so that they would be spattered with their father's warm blood. Then they were taken to the Bastille and set in an iron cage, without even a blanket to cover them. Every eighth day the King sent the executioner to them, to pull a tooth from each of them, so that they might suffer even more. The elder said, 'My mother would die of sorrow if she knew how my little brother suffered. Pray, pull out two of my teeth, and spare him! There were tears in the hangman's eyes when he heard this, but the King's will was stronger than the tears. Every eighth day a silver dish, with two children's teeth on it, was brought to the King; as he had demanded them, so he had them. And I think it was two teeth that Death drew out of life's savings bank for Louis XI to take with him on his journey to the great land of eternity. They flew before him like two fireflies; they glowed and burned and stung him, the teeth of those innocent children. "Yes, a serious drive it is, that bus drive on the great Moving Day. And when does our turn come?"

"That's why it's so very serious; any day, any hour, any minute the bus may come for us. Which of our deeds will Death draw from the savings bank and give us for the journey? Yes, think that over! That Moving Day will not be found on the calendar!"

A STRING OF PEARLS

THE railroad in Denmark still extends only from Copenhagen to Korsör;* it is a string of pearls. Europe has a wealth of these pearls; its most costly are named Paris, London, Vienna, Naples. And yet many a man will point out as his favorite pearl not one of these great cities but rather some little country

---

*This was in 1856.

town that is still the home of homes to him, the home of those dearest to him. Yes, often it is not a town at all, but a single homestead, a little house, hidden among green hedges, a place hardly visible as the train speeds by.

How many pearls are there on the line from Copenhagen to Korsör? We will consider just six, which most people must notice; old memories and poetry itself give a luster to these pearls, so that they shine in our thoughts.

Near the hill where stands the palace of Frederick VI, the home of Oehlen-schläger's* childhood, one of these pearls glistens, sheltered by Söndermarken's woody ground. It used to be called "The Cottage of Philemon and Baucis." Here lived Rahbek† and his wife, Camma; here, under their hospitable roof, assembled many of the generation's finest intellects from busy Copenhagen; it was the festival home of the intellectual. Now, don't say, "Ah, what a change!" No, it is still the home of the intellect, a conservatory for sick plants, for buds which do not have the strength to unfold their true beauty of color and form or show the blossoming and fruit-bearing which is hidden within them. The insane asylum, surrounded by human love, is truly a spot of holiness, a hospital for the sick plants that shall someday be transplanted to bloom in the paradise of God. The weakest minds are assembled now here, where once the strongest and keenest met to exchange thoughts and ideas, but still the flame of generosity mounts heavenward from "The Cottage of Philemon and Baucis."

Ancient Roskilde, the burial town of kings, by Hroar's Spring, now lies before us. The slender towers of the church lift up above the low town and mirror themselvs in Issefiord. Only one grave shall we seek here; it is not that of the mighty Queen Margrethe; no, within the white-walled churchyard which we speed close by is the grave, and over it lays a small, plain stone. The master of the organ, the reviver of the old Danish romances, rests here. We recall, "The clear waves rolled" and "There dwelt a king in Leire." Roskilde, burial place of kings—in your pearl we see the insignificant gravestone whereon is cut a lyre and the name Weyse.‡

Now we reach Sigersted, near the town of Ringsted. The bed of the river is low here; yellow corn waves over the spot where Hagbarth's boat lay at anchor, not far from Signe's maiden bower. Who does not know the legend of Hagbarth, who was hanged on the oak tree while the bower of Signe burst into flames? Who can forget that legend of immortal love?§

---

*Adam Gottlob Oehlenschläger (1779-1850), famous Danish poet and dramatist.

†Kund Lyne Rahbek (1760-1830), Etatsraad and professor.

‡Christoph Ernst Friedrich Weyse (1775-1842), noted Danish composer and organist.

§"Near Ringsted lies Sigersted, so called from King Sigur, who dwelt there. His daughter Signe loved a warrior named Hagbarth. Once when she was hunting a stag and followed it over Vrangstrup River, her horse fell under her; but Hagbarth leaped into the water and saved her life, carrying her to an island that may be seen in the river to this day. Afterward Hagbarth came to Signe in the disguise of a damsel, but was betrayed to King Sigur by Gunvar, the maiden's nurse. When all was discovered, and Hagbarth was seized by the king's men, the lovers determined to die together. Hagbarth was led away to be hanged on a hill, but, to convince himself of Signe's fidelity, he begged that his cloak be suspended on the gallows before he himself was hanged, saying that he wished to see how he would look. Meanwhile his lady love had flung all her treasures into a deep hole, still called Signe's Well—whence comes the saying that Sigersted holds more gold and silver than it knows. Then she shut herself up in her bower and watched the gallows where Hagbarth was to be hanged. When she saw his cloak suspended she imagined him dead, so set fire to her bower, and Hagborth, seeing it in flames, was confident of her love and cheerfully met his death. He was buried in Hage Hill. But the false nurse had no joy from her treachery, for she was afterward flung into a well, still known as Maiden Well." — THIELE, *Danmarks Folkesagn*, Vol. II.

"Beautiful Sorö, encircled by woods!" Your quiet old cloistered town peeps out through its mossy trees; the keen eyes of youth from the academy can look across the lake toward the world's highway and hear the roar of the locomotive's dragon as it speeds through the woods. Sorö, pearl of poetry, you are guarding the dust of Holberg!* Your palace of learning stands beside the deep woodland lake like a great white swan, and near by, like the bright starflower of the woods, there gleams a tiny cottage, whence pious hymns echo throughout the land; words are spoken within, and the peasant listens and learns of Denmark's bygone days. As the song of the bird is to the greenwood, so is Ingemann† to Sorö.

On to the town of Slagelse! What is mirrored here in this pearl's luster? Gone forever is the cloister of Antoorskov; vanished are the rich halls of the castle, even the last remaining wing; yet one relic of olden times still lingers here, the wooden cross on the hill. It has been repaired again and again, for it marks the spot where, legend tells us, Saint Anders‡ holy priest of Slagelse, awoke, after having been brought there from Jerusalem in a single night.

Korsör, birthplace of Baggesen,§ master of words and wit! The ruined old ramparts of the fallen fortress are now the last visible witness of your childhood home; their lengthening sunset shadows point to the spot where stood the house in which you were born. From these hills you looked toward Sprogö and sang in undying verse.

> Nowhere have roses so red a hue
> And nowhere are feathers so light and so blue,
> Nowhere the thorns so daintily grown,
> As those to childhood innocence known.

Humorous, charming singer! We shall weave for thee a garland of woodbine and fling it into the lake, so that the current may bear it to the coast of Kielerfiord, where your ashes rest. The tide shall bring you a greeting from the new generation, a greeting from your birthplace Korsör—where I drop my string of pearls.

"That quite right! A string of pearls does stretch from Copenhagen to Korsör," said Grandmother when she heard this read aloud. "It's a string of pearls for me now, as it was more than forty years ago. We had no railroad then; we spent days on a trip that can now be made in as many hours. That was in 1815, and I was twenty-one; that is a charming age! Although to be up in the sixties, that is also a wonderful age! In my young days it was a much rarer event than it is now to come to Copenhagen, which we considered the town of all towns! My parents hadn't visited it for twenty years, but at last they were going, and I was going with them. We had talked about that journey for

---

*Ludvig Holberg, a popular Danish author of prose and poetry, born in Bergen, Norway, 1684, died 1754.

†Bernhard Severin Ingemann (1789-1862), lector at the Academy of Sorö, poet and novelist.

‡Saint Anders was a pilgrim to the Holy Land in the early thirteenth century. When his companions were about to sail for home from Joppa with a fair wind, he refused to leave before hearing Mass, hence was left alone. As he was gazing after the ship, a horseman came up to him and asked him to ride with him. He mounted the horse, but fell asleep in the stranger's arms, and when he awoke he was lying on a hill outside Slagelse; his companions did not reach Denmark until long afterward.

§ Jens Baggesen (1764-1826), Danish poet.

years before, and now it was actually coming true; it seemed as though a new life were beginning for me, and really in a way a new life did begin for me.

"There was such a bustle of sewing and packing; and when at last we were ready to start, such a crowd of friends came to bid us farewell! It was a long journey we had ahead of us. Shortly before noon we drove out of Odense in my parents' Holstein carriage, and our friends waved to us from the windows all the way down the street, till we passed through St. Jörgen's Gate. The weather was beautiful; the birds sang, and everything was joyful; we forgot what a long and tiresome road it was to Nyborg. We reached it toward evening; but the little sailing vessel had to wait for the mail, which didn't arrive until night. Then we got on board, and as far as we could see the wide, smooth waters lay before us. We lay down and went to sleep in our clothes. When I awoke and came on deck next morning, I could see nothing at all; a heavy fog covered everything. When I heard the cocks crowing, I knew it must be sunrise; bells were ringing, but I didn't know where; then the mist lifted, and we found we were still lying very close to Nyborg. Later in the day a wind came up, but it was against us; we tacked back and forth, and at last were lucky enough to reach Korsör by a little past eleven that night, having spent twenty-two hours to go sixteen miles!

"It was good to get ashore, but it was dark; the lamps were weak, and it all seemed very strange to me, who had never been in any other town but Odense.

" 'Look!' said my father. 'Baggesen was born there! And Birckner* lived in that house!' When I heard that, somehow the dark old town with its narrow little streets seemed to grow larger and brighter. And we were so glad to feel solid earth under our feet! There was no sleep for me that night, for I was so excited over all that I had seen and heard since I had left home the day before.

"Next morning we had to leave early; there was a terrible road ahead of us, with great bumps and holes as far as Slagelse, and not much better from there on, and we wanted to get to the Crab Inn early, so that on the same day we could reach Sorö and visit the Möllers' Emil, as we called him then; yes, he was your grandfather, my late husband, the dean. He was a student at Sorö then, and had just passed his second examination.

"That afternoon we reached the Crab Inn, which was a gallant place at that time, the very best inn on the whole trip, with the prettiest country around it. Yes, but you must all admit that it still is. Madame Plambek was an industrious hostess, and everything in her house was as smoothly scoured as a larding board. On the wall they had, framed under glass, Baggesen's letter to her; it was indeed worth seeing, and I greatly enjoyed looking at it. Then he went to Sorö and found Emil there. You can imagine how glad we were to see him, and he to see us. He was so thoughtful and charming; he took us to see the church, and the graves of Absalon† and Holberg; he inspected the old monkish inscriptions with us, and sailed with us across the lake to Parnasset. It was the most wonderful evening I remember! I was thinking that to become a poet one had only to come to Sorö and meditate among those lovely,

---

*Michael Gottlieb Birckner (1756-1798).

†Absalon (1128-1201), Danish bishop, statesman, and warrior; founder of the city of Copenhagen.

peaceful scenes. By moonlight we followed the 'Philosopher's Walk,' as it's called, the wonderful and lonely little path beside the lake that joins the highway near the Crab Inn. Emil stayed for supper with us, and my father and my mother declared he had grown so sensible and looked so well. It was almost Whitsuntide, and he promised that in a few days he would be in Copenhagen to join us and his family. Ah, those few hours in Sorö and at the Crab Inn I count among the choicest pearls of my life!

"Next morning we again started very early, for we had a long trip to Roskilde, where we wanted to see the church and Father wanted to visit an old school friend that evening. We spent that night in Roskilde and reached Copenhagen by noon the next day. So we had spent about three days on a journey that can now be made in three hours—Korsör to Copenhagen. The pearls on that way have not grown more costly—that could never be—but the string is new and wonderful.

"I stayed with my parents in Copenhagen for three weeks. Emil was with us for eighteen whole days, and when we returned to Fünen he went with us as far as Korsör. There, before we parted, we were betrothed. So it is no wonder I should call the road from Copenhagen to Korsör a string of pearls.

"Afterward, when Emil received his post at Assens, we were married. We often talked about that journey to Copenhagen, and intended doing it again, but then your mother came along, and after her came her brothers and sisters, and with all of them there was much to do and take care of! Then your grandfather was promoted and made a dean; yes, everything was happiness and joy, but we never got to Copenhagen again. No, I have never been there since, though we often thought and talked about it. Now I'm much too old to travel by rail, but still I'm right glad there is a railway; it's a real blessing, because it brings you young ones to me more quickly!

"Nowadays Odense is hardly farther from Copenhagen than in my youth it was from Nyborg; you can speed to Italy in the time it took us to reach Copenhagen! Yes, that is certainly something! It doesn't matter that I just sit here always; let the others travel, so long as they sometimes travel to me.

"And you needn't laugh at me, you young people, for sitting so still here, day after day! I have really a wonderful journey ahead of me; I shall soon have to travel at a speed far greater than the railway's. For when our Lord calls me I shall go to join your grandfather; and when you have completed your work on this dear earth, you too will join us; and then, if we talk over the days of our mortal life, believe me, dear children, I shall say then as I do now, 'From Copenhagen to Korsör is a perfect string of pearls!' "

THE NEW CENTURY'S GODDESS

THE new century's Goddess—whom our great-grandchildren or perhaps a still later generation will know, but we shall not—when and how does she reveal herself? What does she look like? What is the theme of her song? Whose heartstrings will she touch? To what heights will she lift her century?

Why so many questions, in a busy day like ours, when poetry is very nearly superfluous, when it is agreed that the many "immortal" productions of today's poets will, in the future, perhaps exist only in the form of charcoal tracings on a prison wall, seen and read only by a few curiosity seekers?

Poesy is required to serve in the ranks—at least to accept the challenge in party wars, whether it be blood or ink that flows.

But this is only one-sided talk, many will say; poesy has not been entirely forgotten in our time.

No, there are still people who, when they are not busy, are conscious of a desire for poetry, and no sooner do they feel that spiritual rumbling in their respective nobler parts than they promptly go to a bookstore and buy four shillings' worth of poetry of the most approved styles. Others take much pleasure from whatever they can get at a bargain; they are contented with reading the scrap that is on the grocer's wrapping paper; it is much cheaper, and in our busy time we must take notice of that. There is demand for whatever is supplied, and that is enough! The poetry of the future, as well as the poetry of music, is reckoned with the Don Quixotiana; to speak of it is much like speaking of a voyage of discovery to Uranus.

Time is too short and precious for the mere plays of fantasy, and, to speak seriously for once, what is *poetry?* These resonant outpourings of feeling and thought, they are only the offspring of nervous vibrations. Enthusiasm, joy, pain, all the movements of the organism, the wise tell us, are but nerve vibrations. Each of us is but a string instrument.

But who touches the strings? Who causes them to vibrate into sound? The Spirit, the unseen Heavenly Spirit, who echoes in them *His* emotion, *His* feelings; and these are understood by other string instruments, which respond in melting harmonies or clashing dissonances. So it was, and so it will be, in mankind's mighty onward march in the consciousness of freedom.

Each century, each thousand years, one might even say, has its chief expression in its poetry. Born in the passing era, it comes forth and reigns in the new, succeeding era.

Thus she is already born, this Goddess of the New Century, amid the roar of today's machinery. We send her our greetings! May she hear this, or sometime read it, perhaps among the charcoal tracings we just mentioned.

The rocker of her cradle extended from the farthest point reached by the foot of man on polar voyages, as far as the living eye can gaze into the jet depth of the polar sky. We could never hear the rocking for the clatter of engines, the screams of locomotives, the thunder of quarry blasts, and the bursting of the Spirit's old bonds.

She is born in the vast factory of the present, where steam sets in action its power, and where Master Bloodless and his crew toil night and day.

She bears the womanly heart of love, the vestal's flame, and the furnace of passion. Hers is the lightning ray of intellect, in all its endless, shifting, prismatic hues of the ages. Fantasy's vast, swan-feathered tunic is her strength and pride; science wove it; the "elemental forces" gave it power of wing.

On her father's side, she is a child of the people, sound in sense and heart, with an earnest eye, and with humor on her lips. Her mother is the highborn, academy-trained emigrant's daughter, with gilded rococo reminiscences. The Goddess of the New Century has in her the blood and soul of both.

Upon her cradle were laid splendid birthday gifts. Plentiful as bonbons, the occult riddles of nature, with their solutions, are strewn there. The diver's bell gives mystic souvenirs from the deep. The map of the heavens, that high-hung Pacific Ocean with its countless isles, each a world in itself, is embroidered on the cradle cloth. The sun paints her pictures; photography has given her toys to play with.

The nurse has sung to her of Eivind Skalde-spiller and Firdausi, of the minnesingers, and what Heine, bold as a boy, sang from his poetic soul. Much, far too much, has the nurse told her; she knows the *Edda,* the old great-grandmothers' frightful tales, where horrors sweep the air with bloody wings. The whole of the Oriental *Thousand and One Nights* she heard in the quarter part of an hour.

The Goddess of the New Century is still a child, but she has sprung forth from her cradle and is governed by will, though she still doesn't know what she wants.

She is still at play in her vast nursery packed with treasures of art and the rococo. Greek tragedy and Roman comedy are carved there in marble. The folk songs of the nations cover the walls like withered vines; a kiss from her, and they blossom forth with freshness and sweet vapor. The mighty tones and thoughts of Beethoven, Mozart, Glück, and the other great masters surround her with eternal chords. On her bookshelves are many laid to rest who in their day were immortal; and there is yet room for many who in their day were immortal; and there is yet room for many another whose name we hear clicking from the telegraph of immortality but who dies with the telegram.

She has read an awful lot, far too much, for is she not born in our time? And all too much must again be forgotten; but the Goddess will know how to forget.

She doesn't think of her song, which will flourish in thousands of years to come, beside the legends of Moses and Bidpai's golden fable about the craft and luck of the fox. She doesn't think of her mission or of her melodious future; she is still playing, while the struggles of nations shake the air and sound figures of pen and cannon rush to and fro—runes of mystic reading.

She wears a Garibaldi hat, and when she reads her Shakespeare she stops for a moment to think: he can still be played when I am grown! Calderón rests in the tomb of his works, beneath the tablet of his glory. The Goddess is cosmopolitan, for she has bound together Holberg with Molière, Plautus, and Aristophanes; but most she reads her Molière.

She is free from the turbulence that drives the goats of the Alps, but still her soul yearns for the salt of life, as the goats pant for the mountain salt. There is calm in her heart as in the ancient Hebrew songs the voice of the nomad drifts over green pastures beneath starry skies; and yet in song her heart swells mightier than the heart of the inspired warrior from the Thessalonian mountains in the old days of Greece.

How goes it with her Christendom? She has learned the ins and outs of philosophy; the elements broke one of her milk teeth, but a new one grew. While yet in the cradle she ate of the fruit of knowledge and grew wise, so that Immortality flashed forth before her as mankind's happiest thought.

When begins the New Age of Poesy? When will the Goddess be known? When will she be heard?

On a wonderful spring morning she will come on the locomotive dragon, thundering over bridges and through dark tunnels; or on the back of the puffing dolphin across the calm but surging sea; or high in the air, carried by Montgolfier's bird, *Roc,* descending in the land where first her God-given voice shall greet the race of man. When? Will she come from the new-found land of Columbus, the land of freedom, where the native is hunted and the African is a beast of burden, the land from where we heard *The Song of Hiawatha?* Or from the antipodes, that golden nugget in the southern sea, the land of opposites, where our nighttime is their daytime, and where the black swans sing in mossy forests? Or maybe from the land where Memnon's pillar rings but we never understand the song of the Sphinx in the desert. From the isle of the coalpit, where, since the age of the great Elizabeth, Shakespeare has reigned? Or from Tycho Brahe's home, where he wasn't wanted; or from California's fairyland, where the redwood holds high its crown as king of the earth's forests?

When shall the star be lit, the star on the brow of the Goddess, the flower on whose petals is inscribed the century's ideal of beauty in form, color, and fragrance?

"What is the Goddess' new platform?" inquires the skillful politician of the day. "What does she stand for?"

Better ask what she does not stand for!

She will not appear as a ghost of bygone times! She will not fashion her dramas from the discarded architecture with the dazzling colors of lyric drapery! Her flight forth from among us will be as from the car of Thespis to the marble arena. She will not shatter normal human speech to fragments, to be clinked together for an artifical music box with tones from troubadour tournaments. Nor will she separate patrician Verse and plain plebeian Prose—twins are they in voice, quality, and power! Nor will she carve from the saga blocks of Iceland the ancient gods, for they are dead; no sympathy or fellowship awaits them in our day! Nor will she command her generation to occupy their thoughts with the fabric of a French novel; nor will she dull them with the chloroform of everyday history! She will bring the elixir of life; her song, whether in verse or prose, will be brief, clear, and rich. The nations' heartbeats are but letters in the endless alphabet of mankind's growth; she grasps each letter with equal lovingness, and ranges all in words, and weaves her words into rhythms for her Age's hymn.

And when shall the hour come?

It will be long to us who are still here; brief to those who have flown ahead.

The Chinese Wall will soon fall. The railways of Europe open old Asia's tightly sealed culture archives, and the opposing streams of human culture meet, mayhap with a thunderous crash. The oldsters of our days will tremble at that sound and hear in it a judgment, the fall of ancient gods, forgetting that times and peoples must pass from the earth, and only a tiny image, sealed in a word casket, remain of each, floating like a lotus flower on the stream of eternity, and telling us that all were flesh of our flesh, dressed in different attire. The Jewish image shines radiant from the Bible; the Greek from the *Iliad* and the *Odyssey;* and ours? Ask it of the coming Goddess, at judgment time, when the new heaven is lifted to light and sight at the judgment day.

All the power of steam and all the pressure of modern times were levers! Master Bloodless and his busy crew, who seem the all-powerful rulers of our day, are but its servants, black slaves to adorn the festive hall, open its treasures, set its tables, for the great feast day when the Goddess, a child of innocence, a maid of inspiration, a matron of calm wisdom, shall lift on high the wonderful Lamp of Poetry, that rich, full human heart flaming with the fire of God.

Greetings, you Goddess of Poetry's coming age! May our salutation be heard as is heard the worm's hymn of thanksgiving—the worm that is cut to pieces beneath the plow, while a new springtime is dawning and the plowman draws his furrow among us worms, crushing us, that your blessings may be bestowed upon the coming generation.

Greetings, you Goddess of the New Century!

WHAT THE MOON SAW

INTRODUCTION

IT is a strange thing, when I feel most fervently and most deeply, my hands and my tongue seem alike tied, so that I cannot rightly describe or accurately portray the thoughts that are rising within me; and yet I am a painter; my eye tells me as much as that, and all my friends who have seen my sketches and fancies say the same.

I am a poor lad, and live in one of the narrowest of lanes; but I do not want for light, as my room is high up in the house, with an extensive prospect over the neighbouring roofs. During the first few days I went to live in the town, I felt low-spirited and solitary enough. Instead of the forest and the green hills of former days, I had here only a forest of chimney-pots to look out upon. And then I had not a single friend; not one familiar face greeted me.

So one evening I sat at the window, in a desponding mood; and presently I opened the casement and looked out. Oh, how my heart leaped up with joy! Here was a well-known face at last—a round, friendly countenance, the face of a good friend I had known at home. In, fact, it was the MOON that looked in upon me. He was quite unchanged, the dear old Moon, and had the same face exactly that he used to show when he peered down upon me through the willow trees on the moor. I kissed my hand to him over and over again, as he shone far into my little room; and he, for his part, promised me that every evening, when he came abroad, he would look in upon me for a few moments. This promise he has faithfully kept. It is a pity that he can only stay such a short time when he comes. Whenever he appears, he tells me of one thing or another that he has seen on the previous night, or on that same evening. "Just paint the scenes I describe to you"—this is what he said to me—"and you will have a very pretty picture-book." I have followed his injunction for many evenings. I could make up a new "Thousand and One Nights," in my own way, out of these pictures, but the number might be too great, after all. The pictures I have here given have not been chosen at random, but follow in their proper order, just as they were described to me. Some great gifted painter, or some poet or musician, may make something more of them if he likes; what I have given here are only hasty sketches, hurriedly put upon the paper, with some of my own thoughts, interspersed; for the Moon did not come to me every evening—a cloud sometimes hid his face from me.

WHAT THE MOON SAW

FIRST EVENING

"Last night"—I am quoting the Moon's own words—"last night I was gliding through the cloudless Indian sky. My face was mirrored in the waters of the Ganges, and my beams strove to pierce through the thick intertwining boughs of the bananas, arching beneath me like the tortoise's shell. Forth from the thicket tripped a Hindoo maid, light as a gazelle, beautiful as Eve. Airy and etherial as a vision, and yet sharply defined amid the surrounding shadows, stood this daughter of Hindostan: I could read on her delicate brow the thought that had brought her hither. The thorny creeping plants tore her sandals, but for all that she came rapidly forward. The deer that had come down to the river to quench her thirst, sprang by with a startled bound, for in her hand the maiden bore a lighted lamp. I could see the blood in her delicate finger tips, as she spread them for a screen before the dancing flame. She came down to the stream, and set the lamp upon the water, and let it float away. The flame flickered to and fro, and seemed ready to expire; but still the lamp burned on, and the girl's black sparkling eyes, half veiled behind their long silken lashes, followed it with a gaze of earnest intensity. She knew that if the lamp continued to burn so long as she could keep it in sight, her betrothed was still alive; but if the lamp was suddenly extinguished, he was dead. And the lamp burned bravely on, and she fell on her knees, and prayed. Near her in the grass lay a speckled snake, but she heeded it not—she thought only of Bramah and of her betrothed. 'He lives!' she shouted joyfully, 'he lives!' And from the mountains the echo came back upon her, 'he lives!' "

SECOND EVENING

"Yesterday," said the Moon to me, "I looked down upon a small courtyard surrounded on all sides by houses. In the courtyard sat a clucking hen with eleven chickens; and a pretty little girl was running and jumping around them. The hen was frightened, and screamed, and spread out her wings over the little brood. Then the girl's father came out and scolded her; and I glided away and thought no more of the matter.

"But this evening, only a few minutes ago, I looked down into the same courtyard. Everything was quiet. But presently the little girl came forth again, crept quietly to the hen-house, pushed back the bolt, and slipped into the apartment of the hen and chickens. They cried out loudly, and came fluttering down from their perches, and ran about in dismay, and the little girl ran after them. I saw it quite plainly, for I looked through a hole in the henhouse wall. I was angry with the wilful child, and felt glad when her father came out and scolded her more violently than yesterday, holding her roughly by the arm; she held down her head, and her blue eyes were full of large tears. 'What are you about here?' he asked. She wept and said, 'I wanted to kiss the hen and beg her pardon for frightening her yesterday; but I was afraid to tell you.'

"And the father kissed the innocent child's forehead, and I kissed her on the mouth and eyes."

THIRD EVENING

"In the narrow street round the corner yonder— it is so narrow that my beams can only glide for a minute along the walls of the house, but in that minute I see enough to learn what the world is made of —in that narrow street I saw a woman. Sixteen years ago that woman was a child, playing in the garden of the old parsonage, in the country. The hedges of rose-bush were old, and the flowers were faded. They straggled wild over the paths, and the ragged branches grew up among the boughs of the apple trees; here and there were a few roses still in bloom—not so fair as the queen of flowers generally appears, but still they had colour and scent too. The clergyman's little daughter appeared to me a far lovelier rose, as she sat on her stool under the straggling hedge, hugging and caressing her doll with the battered pasteboard cheeks.

"Ten years afterwards I saw her again. I beheld her in a splendid ball-room: she was the beautiful bride of a rich merchant. I rejoiced at her happiness, and sought her on calm quiet evenings—ah, nobody thinks of my clear eye and my silent glance! Alas! my rose ran wild, like the rose bushes in the garden of the parsonage. There are tragedies in every-day life, and to-night I saw the last act of one.

"She was lying in bed in a house in that narrow street: she was sick unto death, and the cruel landlord came up, and tore away the thin coverlet, her only protection against the cold. 'Get up!' said he; 'your face is enough to frighten one. Get up and dress yourself, give me money, or I'll turn you out into the street! Quick—get up!' She answered, 'Alas! death is gnawing at my heart. Let me rest.' But he forced her to get up and bathe her face, and put a wreath of roses in her hair; and he placed her in a chair at the window, with a candle burning beside her, and went away.

"I looked at her, and she was sitting motionless, with her hands in her lap. The wind caught the open window and shut it with a crash, so that a pane came clattering down in fragments; but still she never moved. The curtain caught fire, and the flames played about her face; and I saw that she was dead. There at the open window sat the dead woman, preaching a sermon against *sin*—my poor faded rose out of the parsonage garden!"

FOURTH EVENING

"This evening I saw a German play acted," said the Moon. "It was in a little town. A stable had been turned into a theatre; that is to say, the stable had been left standing, and had been turned into private boxes, and all the timber work had been covered with coloured paper. A little iron chandelier hung beneath the ceiling, and that it might be made to disappear into the ceiling, as it does in great theatres, when the *ting-ting* of the prompter's bell is heard, a great inverted tub has been placed just above it."

" '*Ting-ting!*' and the little iron chandelier suddenly rose at least half a yard and disappeared in the tub; and that was the sign that the play was going to begin. A young nobleman and his lady, who happened to be passing through the little town, were present at the performance, and consequently the house was crowded. But under the chandelier was a vacant space like a little crater: not a single soul sat there, for the tallow was dropping, drip, drip! I saw everything, for it was so warm in there that every loophole had been opened. The male and female servants stood outside, peeping through the chinks, although a real policeman was inside, threatening them with a stick. Close by the orchestra could be seen the noble young couple in two old arm-chairs, which were usually occupied by his worship the mayor and his lady; but these latter were to-day obliged to content themselves with wooden forms, just as if they had been ordinary citizens; and the lady observed quietly to herself, 'One sees, now, that there is rank above rank;' and this incident gave an air of extra festivity to the whole proceedings. The chandelier gave little leaps, the crowd got their knuckles rapped, and I, the Moon, was present at the performance from beginning to end."

FIFTH EVENING

"Yesterday," began the Moon, "I looked down upon the turmoil of Paris. My eye penetrated into an apartment of the Louvre. An old grandmother, poorly clad—she belonged to the working class—was following one of the under-servants into the great empty throne-room, for this was the apartment she wanted to see—that she was resolved to see; it had cost her many a little sacrifice, and many a coaxing word, to penetrate thus far. She folded her thin hands, and looked round with an air of reverence, as if she had been in a church.

" 'Here it was!' she said, 'here!' and she approached the throne, from which hung the rich velvet fringed with gold lace. 'There,' she exclaimed, 'there!' and she knelt and kissed the purple carpet. I think she was actually weeping.

" 'But it was not *this very* velvet!' observed the footman, and a smile played about his mouth. 'True, but it was this very place,' replied the woman, 'and it must have looked just like this.' 'It looked so, and yet it did not,' observed the man: 'the windows were beaten in, and the doors were off their hinges, and there was blood upon the floor.' 'But for all that you can say, my grandson died upon the throne of France. Died!' mournfully repeated the old woman. I do not think another word was spoken, and they soon quitted the hall. The evening twilight faded and my light shone doubly vivid upon the rich velvet that covered the throne of France.

"Now who do you think this poor woman was? Listen, I will tell you a story.

"It happened, in the Revolution of July, on the evening of the most brilliantly victorious day, when every house was a fortress, every window a breastwork. The people stormed the Tuileries. Even women and children were to be found among the combatants. They penetrated into the apartments and halls of the palace. A poor half-grown boy in a ragged blouse fought among the older insurgents. Mortally wounded with several bayonet thrusts, he sank down. This happened in the throne-room. They laid the bleeding youth upon the throne of France, wrapped the velvet around his wounds, and his blood streamed forth upon the imperial purple. There was a picture! The splendid hall, the fighting groups! A torn flag upon the ground, the tricolor was waving above the bayonets, and on the throne lay the poor lad with the pale glorified countenance, his eyes turned towards the sky, his limbs writhing in the death agony, his breast bare, and his poor tattered clothing half hidden by the rich velvet embroidered with silver lilies. At the boy's cradle a prophecy had been spoken: 'He will die on the throne of France!' The mother's heart dreamt of a second Napoleon.

"My beams have kissed the wreath of *immortelles* on his grave, and this night they kissed the forehead of the old grandame, while in a dream the picture floated before her which thou mayest draw — the poor boy on the throne of France."

SIXTH EVENING

"I've been in Upsala," said the Moon: "I looked down upon the great plain covered with coarse grass, and upon the barren fields. I mirrored my face in the Tyris river, while the steamboat drove the fish into the rushes. Beneath me floated the waves, throwing long shadows on the so-called graves of Odin, Thor, and Friga. In the scanty turf that covers the hill-side names have been cut.* There is no monument here, no memorial on which the traveller can have his name carved, no rocky wall on whose surface he can get it painted; so visitors have the turf cut away for that purpose. The naked earth peers through in the form of great letters and names; these form a network over the whole hill. Here is an immortality, which lasts till the fresh turf grows!

"Up on the hill stood a man, a poet. He emptied the mead horn with the broad silver rim, and murmured a name. He begged the winds not to betray him, but I heard the name. I knew it. A count's coronet sparkles above it, and therefore he did not speak it out. I smiled, for I knew that a poet's crown adorns his own name. The nobility of Eleanora d'Este is attached to the name of Tasso. And I also know where the Rose of Beauty blooms!"

Thus spake the Moon, and a cloud came between us. May no cloud separate the poet from the rose!

SEVENTH EVENING

"Along the margin of the shore stretches a forest of firs and beeches, and fresh and fragrant is this wood; hundreds of nightingales visit it every spring. Close beside it is the sea, the ever-changing sea, and between the two is placed the broad high-road. One carriage after another rolls over it; but I did not follow them, for my eye loves best to rest upon one point. A Hun's Grave† lies there, and the sloe and blackthorn grow luxuriantly among the stones. Here is true poetry in nature.

"And how do you think men appreciate this poetry? I will tell you what I heard there last evening and during the night.

"First, two rich landed proprietors came driving by. 'Those are glorious trees!' said the first. 'Certainly; there are ten loads of firewood in each,' observed the other: 'it will be a hard winter, and last year we got fourteen dollars a load' — and they were gone. 'The road here is wretched,' observed another man who drove past. 'That's the fault of those horrible trees,' replied his

---

*Travellers on the Continent have frequent opportunities of seeing how universally this custom prevails among travellers. In some places on the Rhine, pots of paint and brushes are offered by the natives to the traveller desirous of "immortalizing" himself.

†Large mounds similar to the "barrows" found in Britain, are thus designated in Germany and the North.

neighbour; 'there is no free current of air; the wind can only come from the sea' — and they were gone. The stage coach went rattling past. All the passengers were asleep at this beautiful spot. The postillion blew his horn, but he only thought, 'I can play capitally. It sounds well here. I wonder if those in there like it?' — and the stage coach vanished. Then two young fellows came gallopping up on horseback. There's youth and spirit in the blood here! thought I; and, indeed, they looked with a smile at the moss-grown hill and thick forest. 'I should not dislike a walk here with the miller's Christine,' said one — and they flew past.

"The flowers scented the air; every breath of air was hushed; it seemed as if the sea were a part of the sky that stretched above the deep valley. A carriage rolled by. Six people were sitting in it. Four of them were asleep; the fifth was thinking of his new summer coat, which would suit him admirably; the sixth turned to the coachman and asked him if there were anything remarkable connected with yonder heap of stones. 'No,' replied the coachman, 'it's only a heap of stones; but the trees are remarkable.' 'How so?' 'Why I'll tell you how they are very remarkable. You see, in winter, when the snow lies very deep, and has hidden the whole road so that nothing is to be seen, those trees serve me for a landmark. I steer by them, so as not to drive into the sea; and you see that is why the trees are remarkable.'

"Now came a painter. He spoke not a word, but his eyes sparkled. He began to whistle. At this the nightingales sang louder than ever. 'Hold your tongues!' he cried testily; and he made accurate notes of all the colours and transitions — blue, and lilac, and dark brown. 'That will make a beautiful picture,' he said. He took it in just as a mirror takes in a view; and as he worked he whistled a march of Rossini. And last of all came a poor girl. She laid aside the burden she carried, and sat down to rest upon the Hun's Grave. Her pale handsome face was bent in a listening attitude towards the forest. Her eyes brightened, she gazed earnestly at the sea and the sky, her hands were folded, and I think she prayed, 'Our Father.' She herself could not understand the feeling that swept through her, but I know that this minute, and the beautiful natural scene, will live within her memory for years, far more vividly and more truly than the painter could portray it with his colours on paper. My rays followed her till the morning dawn kissed her brow."

EIGHTH EVENING

Heavy clouds obscured the sky, and the Moon did not make his appearance at all. I stood in my little room, more lonely than ever, and looked up at the sky where he ought to have shown himself. My thoughts flew far away, up to my great friend, who every evening told me such pretty tales, and showed me pictures. Yes, he has had an experience indeed. He glided over the waters of the Deluge, and smiled on Noah's ark just as he lately glanced down upon me, and brought comfort and promise of a new world that was to spring forth from the old. When the Children of Israel sat weeping by the waters of Babylon, he glanced mournfully upon the willows where hung the silent harps. When Romeo climbed the balcony, and the promise of true love fluttered like a cherub toward heaven, the round Moon hung, half hidden among the dark cypresses, in the lucid air. He saw the captive giant at St. Helena, looking from the lonely rock across the wide ocean, while great thoughts swept through his soul. Ah! what tales the Moon can tell. Human life is like a story to him. To-night I shall not see thee again, old friend. To-night I can draw no picture of the memories of thy visit. And, as I looked dreamily towards the clouds, the sky became bright. There was a glancing light, and a beam from the Moon fell upon me. It vanished again, and dark clouds flew past: but still it was a greeting, a friendly good-night offered to me by the Moon.

NINTH EVENING

The air was clear again. Several evenings had passed, and the Moon was in the first quarter. Again he gave me an outline for a sketch. Listen to what he told me.

"I have followed the polar bird and the swimming whale to the eastern coast of Greenland. Gaunt ice-covered rocks and dark clouds hung over a valley, where dwarf willows and barberry bushes stood clothed in green. The blooming lychnis exhaled sweet odours. My light was faint, my face pale as the water lily that, torn from its stem, has been drifting for weeks with the tide. The crown-shaped Northern Light burned fiercely in the sky. Its ring was broad, and from its circumference the rays shot like whirling shafts of fire across the whole sky, flashing in changing radiance from green to red. The inhabitants of that icy region were assembling for dance and festivity; but, ac-customed to this glorious spectacle, they scarcely deigned to glance at it. 'Let us leave the soul of the dead to their ball-play with the heads of the walruses,' they thought in their superstition, and they turned their whole attention to the song and dance. In the midst of the circle, and divested of his furry cloak, stood a Greenlander, with a small pipe, and he played and sang a song about catching the seal, and the chorus around chimed in with, *'Eia, Eia, Ah.'* And in their white furs they danced about in the circle, till you might fancy it was a polar bear's ball.

"And now a Court of Judgment was opened. Those Greenlanders who had quarrelled stepped forward, and the offended person chanted forth the faults of his adversary in an extempore song, turning them sharply into ridicule, to the sound of the pipe and the measure of the dance. The defendant replied with satire as keen, while the audience laughed, and gave their verdict. The rocks heaved, the glaciers melted, and great masses of ice and snow came crashing down, shivering to fragments as they fall; it was a glorious Greenland summer night. A hundred paces away, under the open tent of hides, lay a sick man. Life still flowed through his warm blood, but still he was to die—he himself felt it, and all who stood round him knew it also; therefore his wife was already sewing round him the shroud of furs, that she might not af-terwards be obliged to touch the dead body. And she asked, 'Wilt thou be buried on the rock, in the firm snow? I will deck the spot with thy *kayak,* and thy arrows, and the *angekokk* shall dance over it. Or wouldst thou rather be buried in the sea?' 'In the sea,' he whispered, and nodded with a mournful smile. 'Yes, it is a pleasant summer tent, the sea,' observed the wife. 'Thousands of seals sport there, the walrus shall lie at thy feet, and the hunt will be safe and merry!' And the yelling children tore the outspread hide from the window-hole, that the dead man might be carried to the ocean, the billowy ocean, that had given him food in life, and that now, in death, was to afford him a place of rest. For his monument, he had the floating, ever-changing icebergs, whereon the seal sleeps, while the storm bird flies round their gleaming summits!"

TENTH EVENING

"I knew an old maid, " said the Moon. "Every winter she wore a wrapper of yellow satin, and it always remained new, and was the only fashion she followed. In summer she always wore the same straw hat, and I verily believe the very same gray-blue dress.

"She never went out, except across the street to an old female friend; and in later years she did not even take this walk, for the old friend was dead. In her solitude my old maid was always busy at the window, which was adorned in summer with pretty flowers, and in winter with cress, grown upon felt. During the last months I saw her no more at the window, but she was still alive. I knew that, for I had not yet seen her begin the 'long journey,' of which she often spoke with her friend. 'Yes, yes,' she was in the habit of saying, 'when I come to die I shall take a longer journey than I have made my whole life long. Our family vault is six miles from here. I shall be carried there, and shall sleep there among my family and relatives.' Last night a van stopped at the house. A coffin was carried out, and then I knew that she was dead. They placed straw round the coffin, and the van drove away. There slept the quiet old lady, who had not gone out of her house once for the last year. The van rolled out through the town-gate as briskly as if it were going for a pleasant excursion. On the high-road the pace was quicker yet. The coachman looked nervously round every now and then — I fancy he half expected to see her sitting on the coffin, in her yellow satin wrapper. And because he was startled, he foolishly lashed his horses, while he held the reins so tightly that the poor beasts were in a foam: they were young and fiery. A hare jumped across the road and startled them, and they fairly ran away. The old sober maiden, who had for years and years moved quietly round and round in a dull circle, was now, in death, rattled over stock and stone on the public highway. The coffin in its covering of straw tumbled out of the van, and was left on the high-road, while horses, coachman, and carriage flew past in wild career. The lark rose up carolling from the field, twittering her morning lay over the coffin, and presently perched upon it, picking with her beak at the straw covering, as though she would tear it up. The lark rose up again, singing gaily, and I withdrew behind the red morning clouds."

ELEVENTH EVENING

"I will give you a picture of Pompeii," said the Moon. "I was in the suburb in the Street of Tombs, as they call it, where the fair monuments stand, in the spot where, ages ago, the merry youths, their temples bound with rosy wreaths, danced with the fair sisters of Laïs. Now, the stillness of death reigned around. German mercenaries, in the Neapolitan service, kept guard, played cards, and diced; and a troop of strangers from beyond the mountains came into the town, accompanied by a sentry. They wanted to see the city that had risen from the grave illumined by my beams; and I showed them the wheel-ruts in the streets paved with broad lava slabs; I showed them the names on the doors, and the signs that hung there yet: they saw in the little courtyard the basins of the fountains, ornamented with shells; but no jet of water gushed upwards, no songs sounded forth from the richly-painted chambers, where the bronze dog kept the door.

WHAT THE MOON SAW

"It was the City of the Dead; only Vesuvius thundered forth his everlasting hymn, each separate verse of which is called by men an eruption. We went to the temple of Venus, built of snow-white marble, with its high altar in front of the broad steps, and the weeping willows sprouting freshly forth among the pillars. The air was transparent and blue, and black Vesuvius formed the background, with fire ever shooting forth from it, like the stem of the pine tree. Above it stretched the smoky cloud in the silence of the night, like the crown of the pine, but in a blood-red illumination. Among the company was a lady singer, a real and great singer. I have witnessed the homage paid to her in the greatest cities of Europe. When they came to the tragic theatre, they all sat down on the amphitheatre steps, and thus a small part of the house was occupied by an audience, as it had been many centuries ago. The stage still stood unchanged, with its walled side-scenes, and the two arches in the background, through which the beholders saw the same scene that had been exhibited in the old times—a scene painted by nature herself, namely, the mountains between Sorento and Amalfi. The singer gaily mounted the ancient stage, and sang. The place inspired her, and she reminded me of a wild Arab horse, that rushes headlong on with snorting nostrils and flying mane—her song was so light and yet so firm. Anon I thought of the mourning mother beneath the cross at Golgotha, so deep was the expression of pain. And, just as it had done thousands of years ago, the sound of applause and delight now filled the theatre. 'Happy, gifted creature!' all the hearers exclaimed. Five minutes more, and the stage was empty, the company had vanished, and not a sound more was heard—all were gone. But the ruins stood unchanged, as they will stand when centuries shall have gone by, and when none shall know of the momentary applause and of the triumph of the fair songstress; when all will be forgotten and gone, and even for me this hour will be but a dream of the past."

TWELFTH EVENING

"I looked through the windows of an editor's house," said the Moon. "It was somewhere in Germany. I saw handsome furniture, many books, and a chaos of newspapers. Several young men were present: the editor himself stood at his desk, and two little books, both by young authors, were to be noticed. 'This one has been sent to me,' said he. 'I have not read it yet; what think *you* of the contents?' 'Oh,' said the person addressed—he was a poet himself—'it is good enough; a little broad, certainly; but, you see, the author is still young. The verses might be better, to be sure; the thoughts are sound, though there is certainly a good deal of common-place among them. But what will you have? You can't be always getting something new. That he'll turn out anything great I don't believe, but you may safely praise him. He is well read, a remarkable Oriental scholar, and has a good judgment. It was he who wrote that nice review of my 'Reflections on Domestic Life.' We must be lenient towards the young man."

" 'But he is a complete hack!' objected another of the gentlemen. 'Nothing worse in poetry than mediocrity, and he certainly does not go beyond this.'

" 'Poor fellow,' observed a third, 'and his aunt is so happy about him. It was she, Mr. Editor, who got together so many subscribers for your last translation.'

" 'Ah, the good woman! Well, I have noticed the book briefly. Undoubted talent—a welcome offering—a flower in the garden of poetry—prettily brought out—and so on. But this other book—I suppose the author expects me to purchase it? I hear it is praised. He has genius, certainly: don't you think so?'

" 'Yes, all the world declares as much,' replied the poet, 'but it has turned out rather wildly. The punctuation of the book, in particular, is very eccentric.'

" 'It will be good for him if we pull him to pieces, and anger him a little, otherwise he will get too good an opinion of himself.'

" 'But that would be unfair,' objected the fourth. 'Let us not carp at little faults, but rejoice over the real and abundant good that we find here: he surpasses all the rest.'

" 'Not so. If he is a true genius, he can bear the sharp voice of censure. There are people enough to praise him. Don't let us quite turn his head.'

" 'Decided talent,' wrote the editor, 'with the usual carelessness. that he can write incorrect verses may be seen in page 25, where there are two false quantities. We recommend him to study the ancients, etc.'

"I went away," continued the Moon, "and looked through the windows in the aunt's house. There sat the be-praised poet, the *tame* one; all the guests paid homage to him, and he was happy.

"I sought the other poet out, the *wild* one; him also I found in a great assembly at his patron's, where the tame poet's book was being discussed.

" 'I shall read yours also,' said Mæcenas; 'but to speak honestly—you know I never hide my opinion from you—I don't expect much from it, for you are much too wild, too fantastic. But it must be allowed that, as a man, you are highly respectable.'

"A young girl sat in a corner; and she read in a book these words:

" 'In the dust lies genius and glory,
But ev'ry-day talent will *pay*.
It's only the old, old story,
But the piece is repeated each day.' "

THIRTEENTH EVENING

The Moon said, "Beside the woodland path there are two small farmhouses. The doors are low, and some of the windows are placed quite high, and others close to the ground; and whitethorn and barberry bushes grow around them. The roof of each house is overgrown with moss and with yellow flowers and houseleek. Cabbage and potatoes are the only plants cultivated in the gardens, but out of the hedge there grows a willow tree, and under this willow tree sat a little girl, and she sat with her eyes fixed upon the old oak tree between the two huts.

"It was an old withered stem. It had been sawn off at the top, and a stork had built his nest upon it; and he stood in this nest clapping with his beak. A little boy came and stood by the girl's side: they were brother and sister.

" 'What are you looking at?' he asked.

" 'I'm watching the stork,' she replied: 'our neighbors told me that he would bring us a little brother or sister to-day; let us watch to see it come!'

" 'The stork brings no such things,' the boy declared, 'you may be sure of that. Our neighbor told me the same thing, but she laughed when she said it, and so I asked her if she could say 'On my honor,' and she could not; and I know by that the story about the storks is not true, and that they only tell it to us children for fun.'

" 'But where do babies come from, then?' asked the girl.

" 'Why, an angel from heaven brings them under his cloak, but no man can see him; and that's why we never know when he brings them.'

"At that moment there was a rustling in the branches of the willow tree, and the children folded their hands and looked at one another: it was certainly the angel coming with the baby. They took each other's hand, and at that moment the door of one of the houses opened, and the neighbour appeared.

" 'Come in, you two,' she said. 'See what the stork has brought. It is a little brother.'

"And the children nodded gravely at one another, for they had felt quite sure already that the baby was come."

FOURTEENTH EVENING

"I was gliding over the Lüneburg Heath," the Moon said. "A lonely hut stood by the wayside, a few scanty bushes grew near it, and a nightingale who had lost his way sang sweetly. He died in the coldness of the night: it was his farewell song that I heard.

"The morning dawn came glimmering red. I saw a caravan of emigrant peasant families who were bound to Hamburgh, there to take ship for America, where fancied prosperity would bloom for them. The mothers carried their little children at their backs, the elder ones tottered by their sides, and a poor starved horse tugged at a cart that bore their scanty effects. The cold wind whistled, and therefore the little girl nestled closer to the mother, who, looking up at my decreasing disc, thought of the bitter want at home, and spoke of the heavy taxes they had not been able to raise. The whole caravan thought of the same thing; therefore, the rising dawn seemed to them a message from the sun, of fortune that was to gleam brightly upon them. They heard the dying nightingale sing; it was no false prophet, but a harbinger of fortune. The wind whistled, therefore they did not understand that the nightingale sung, 'Fare away over the sea! Thou hast paid the long passage with all that was thine, and poor and helpless shalt thou enter Canaan. Thou must sell thyself, thy wife, and thy children. But your griefs shall not last long. Behind the broad fragrant leaves lurks the goddess of Death, and her welcome kiss shall breathe fever into thy blood. Fare away, fare away, over the heaving billows.' And the caravan listened well pleased to the song of the nightingale, which seemed to promise good fortune. Day broke through the light clouds; country people went across the heath to church; the black-gowned women with their white head-dresses looked like ghosts that had stepped forth from the church pictures. All around lay a wide dead plain, covered with faded brown heath, and black charred spaces between the white sand hills. The women carried hymn books, and walked into the church. Oh, pray, pray for those who are wandering to find graves beyond the foaming billows."

FIFTEENTH EVENING

"I know a Pulcinella,"* the Moon told me. "The public applaud vociferously directly they see him. Every one of his movements is comic, and is sure to throw the house into convulsions of laughter; and yet there is no art in it all—it is complete nature. When he was yet a little boy, playing about with other boys, he was already Punch. Nature had intended him for it, and had provided him with a hump on his back, and another on his breast; but his inward man, his mind, on the contrary, was richly furnished. No one could surpass him in depth of feeling or in readiness of intellect. The theatre was his ideal world. If he had possessed a slender well-shaped figure, he might have been the first tragedian on any stage; the heroic, the great, filled his soul; and yet he had to become a Pulcinella. His very sorrow and melancholy did but increase the comic dryness of his sharply-cut features, and increased the laughter of the audience, who showered plaudits on their favourite. The lovely Columbine was indeed kind and cordial to him; but she preferred to marry the Harlequin. It would have been too ridiculous if beauty and ugliness had in reality paired together.

"When Pulcinella was in very bad spirits, she was the only one who could force a hearty burst of laughter, or even a smile from him: first she would be melancholy with him, then quieter, and at last quite cheerful and happy. 'I know very well what is the matter with you,' she said; 'yes, you're in love!' And he could not help laughing. 'I and Love," he cried, "that would have an absurd look. How the public would shout!' 'Certainly, you are in love,' she continued; and added with a comic pathos, 'and I am the person you are in love with.' You see, such a thing may be said when it is quite out of the question—and, indeed, Pulcinella burst out laughing, and gave a leap into the air, and his melancholy was forgotten.

"And yet she had only spoken the truth. He *did* love her, love her adoringly, as he loved what was great and lofty in art. At her wedding he was the merriest among the guests, but in the stillness of night he wept: if the public had seen his distorted face then, they would have applauded rapturously.

"And a few days ago, Columbine died. On the day of the funeral, Harlequin was not required to show himself on the boards, for he was a disconsolate widower. The director had to give a very merry piece, that the public might not too painfully miss the pretty Columbine and the agile Harlequin. Therefore Pulcinella had to be more boisterous and extravagant than ever; and he danced and capered, with despair in his heart; and the audience yelled, and shouted '*bravo, bravissimo!*' Pulcinella was actually called before the curtain. He was pronounced inimitable.

"But last night the hideous little fellow went out of the town, quite alone, to the deserted churchyard. The wreath of flowers on Columbine's grave was already faded, and he sat down there. It was a study for a painter. As he sat with his chin on his hands, his eyes turned up towards me, he looked like a grotesque monument—a Punch on a grave—peculiar and whimsical! If the people could have seen their favourite, they would have cried as usual, '*Bravo, Pulcinella; bravo, bravissimo!*' "

*The comic or grotesque character of the Italian ballet, from which the English "Punch" takes his origin.

SIXTEENTH EVENING

Hear what the Moon told me. "I have seen the cadet who had just been made an officer put on his handsome uniform for the first time; I have seen the young bride in her wedding dress, and the princess girl-wife happy in her gorgeous robes; but never have I seen a felicity equal to that of a little girl of four years old, whom I watched this evening. She had received a new blue dress, and a new pink hat, the splendid attire had just been put on, and all were calling for a candle, for my rays, shining in through the windows of the room, were not bright enough for the occasion, and further illumination was required. There stood the little maid, stiff and upright as a doll, her arms stretched painfully straight out away from the dress, and her fingers apart; and oh, what happiness beamed from her eyes, and from her whole countenance! 'To-morrow you shall go out in your new clothes,' said her mother; and the little one looked up at her hat, and down at her frock, and smiled brightly. 'Mother,' she cried, 'what will the little dogs think, when they see me in these splendid new things?' "

SEVENTEENTH EVENING

"I have spoken to you of Pompeii," said the Moon; "that corpse of a city, exposed in the view of living towns: I know another sight still more strange, and this is not the corpse, but the spectre of a city. Whenever the jetty fountains splash into the marble basins, they seem to me to be telling the story of the floating city. Yes, the spouting water may tell of her, the waves of the sea may sing of her fame! On the surface of the ocean a mist often rests, and that is her widow's veil. The bridegroom of the sea is dead, his palace and his city are his mausoleum! Dost thou know this city? She has never heard the rolling of wheels or the hoof-tread of horses in her streets, through which the fish swim, while the black gondola glides spectrally over the green water. I will show you the place," continued the Moon, "the largest square in it, and you will fancy yourself transported into the city of a fairy tale. The grass grows rank among the broad flagstones, and in the morning twilight thousands of tame pigeons flutter around the solitary lofty tower. On three sides you find yourself surrounded by cloistered walks. In these the silent Turk sits smoking his long pipe, the handsome Greek leans against the pillar and gazes at the upraised trophies and lofty masts, memorials of power that is gone. The flags hang down like mourning scarves. A girl rests there: she has put down her heavy pails filled with water, the yoke with which she has carried them rests on one of her shoulders, and she leans against the mast of victory. That is not a fairy palace you see before you yonder, but a church: the gilded domes and shining orbs flash back my beams; the glorious bronze horses up yonder have made journeys, like the bronze horse in the fairy tale: they have come hither, and gone hence, and have returned again. Do you notice the variegated splendour of the walls and windows? It looks as if Genius had followed the caprices of a child, in the adornment of these singular temples. Do you see the winged lion on the pillar? The gold glitters still, but his wings are tied—the lion is dead, for the king of the sea is dead; the great halls stand desolate, and where gorgeous paintings hung of yore, the naked wall now peers through. The *lazzarone* sleeps under the arcade, whose pavement in old times

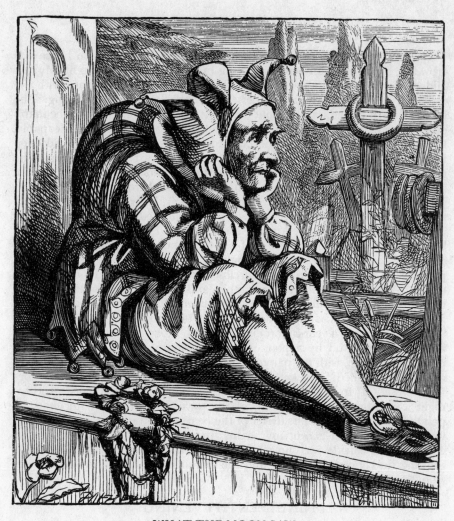

WHAT THE MOON SAW

was to be trodden only by the feet of high nobility. From the deep wells, and perhaps from the prisons by the Bridge of Sighs, rise the accents of woe, as at the time when the tambourine was heard in the gay gondolas, and the golden ring was cast from the *Bucentaur* to Adria, the queen of the seas. Adria! shroud thyself in mists; let the veil of thy widowhood shroud thy form, and clothe in the weeds of woe the mausoleum of thy bridegroom—the marble, spectral Venice."

EIGHTEENTH EVENING

"I looked down upon a great theatre," said the Moon. "The house was crowded, for a new actor was to make his first appearance that night. My rays glided over a little window in the wall, and I saw a painted face with the forehead pressed against the panes. It was the hero of the evening. The knighly beard curled crisply about the chin; but there were tears in the man's eyes, for he had been hissed off, and indeed with reason. The poor Incapable! But Incapables cannot be admitted into the empire of Art. He had deep feeling, and loved his art enthusiastically, but the art loved not him. The prompter's bell sounded; *'the hero enters with a determined air,'* so ran the stage direction in his part, and he had to appear before an audience who turned him into ridicule. When the piece was over, I saw a form wrapped in a mantle, creeping down the steps: it was the vanquished knight of the evening. The scene-shifters whispered to one another, and I followed the poor fellow home to his room. To hang one's self is to die a mean death, and poison is not always at hand, I know; but he thought of both. I saw how he looked at his pale face in the glass, with eyes half closed, to see if he should look well as a corpse. A man may be very unhappy, and yet exceedingly affected. He thought of death, of suicide; I believe he pitied himself, for he wept bitterly, and when a man has had his cry out he doesn't kill himself.

"Since that time a year had rolled by. Again a play was to be acted, but in a little theatre, and by a poor strolling company. Again I saw the well-remembered face, with the painted cheeks and the crisp beard. He looked up at me and smiled; and yet he had been hissed off only a minute before—hissed off from a wretched theatre, by a miserable audience. And to-night a shabby hearse rolled out of the town-gate. It was a suicide—our painted, despised hero. The driver of the hearse was the only person present, for no one followed except my beams. In a corner of the churchyard the corpse of the suicide was shovelled into the earth, and nettles will soon be growing rankly over his grave, and the sexton will throw thorns and weeds from the other graves upon it."

NINETEENTH EVENING

"I come from Rome," said the Moon. "In the midst of the city, upon one of the seven hills, lie the ruins of the imperial palace. The wild fig tree grows in the clefts of the wall, and covers the nakedness thereof with its broad grey-green leaves; trampling among heaps of rubbish, the ass treads upon green laurels, and rejoices over the rank thistles. From this spot, whence the eagles of Rome once flew abroad, whence they 'came, saw, and conquered,' our door leads into a little mean house, built of clay between two pillars; the wild vine hangs like a mourning garland over the crooked window. An old woman and her little granddaughter live there: they rule now in the palace of the Cæsars, and show to strangers the remains of its past glories. Of the splendid throne-hall only a naked wall yet stands, and a black cypress throws its dark shadow on the spot where the throne once stood. The dust lies several feet deep on the broken pavement; and the little maiden, now the daughter of the imperial palace, often sits there on her stool when the evening bells ring. The keyhole of the door close by she calls her turret window; through this she can see half Rome, as far as the mighty cupola of St. Peter's.

"On this evening, as usual, stillness reigned around; and in the full beam of my light came the little granddaughter. On her head she carried an earthen pitcher of antique shape filled with water. Her feet were bare, her short frock and her white sleeves were torn. I kissed her pretty round shoulders, her dark eyes, and black shining hair. She mounted the stairs; they were steep, having been made up of rough blocks of broken marble and the capital of a fallen pillar. The coloured lizards slipped away, startled, from before her feet, but she was not frightened at them. Already she lifted her hand to pull the door-bell — a hare's foot fastened to a string formed the bell-handle of the imperial palace. She paused for a moment — of what might she be thinking? Perhaps of the beautiful Christ-child, dressed in gold and silver, which was down below in the chapel, where the silver candlesticks gleamed so bright, and where her little friends sung the hymns in which she also could join? I know not. Presently she moved again — she stumbled: the earthen vessel fell from her head, and broke on the marble steps. She burst into tears. The beautiful daughter of the imperial palace wept over the worthless broken pitcher; with her bare feet she stood there weeping; and dared not pull the string, the bell-rope of the imperial palace!"

TWENTIETH EVENING

It was more than a fortnight since the Moon had shone. Now he stood once more, round and bright, above the clouds, moving slowly onward. Hear what the Moon told me.

"From a town in Fezzan I followed a caravan. On the margin of the sandy desert, in a salt plain, that shone like a frozen lake, and was only covered in spots with light drifting sand, a halt was made. The eldest of the company — the water gourd hung at his girdle, and on his head was a little bag of unleavened bread — drew a square in the sand with his staff, and wrote in it a few words out of the Koran, and then the whole caravan passed over the consecrated spot. A young merchant, a child of the East, as I could tell by his eye and his figure, rode pensively forward on his white snorting steed. Was he thinking, perchance, of his fair young wife? It was only two days ago that the camel, adorned with furs and with costly shawls, had carried her, the beauteous bride, round the walls of the city, while drums and cymbals had sounded, the women sang, and festive shots, of which the bridegroom fired the greatest number, resounded round the camel; and now he was journeying with the caravan across the desert.

"For many nights I followed the train. I saw them rest by the wellside among the stunted palms; they thrust the knife into the breast of the camel that had fallen, and roasted its flesh by the fire. My beams cooled the glowing sands, and showed them the black rocks, dead islands in the immense ocean of sand. No hostile tribes met them in their pathless route, no storms arose, no columns of sand whirled destruction over the journeying caravan. At home the beautiful wife prayed for her husband and her father. 'Are they dead?' she asked of my golden crescent; 'Are they dead?' she cried to my full disc. Now the desert lies behind them. This evening they sit beneath the lofty palm trees, where the crane flutters round them with its long wings, and the pelican watches them from the branches of the mimosa. The luxuriant herbage is trampled down, crushed by the feet of elephants. A troop of negroes are returning from a market in the interior of the land: the women, with copper buttons in their black hair, and decked out in clothes dyed with indigo, drive the heavily-laden oxen, on whose backs slumber the naked black children. A negro leads a young lion which he has brought, by a string. They approach the caravan; the young merchant sits pensive and motionless, thinking of his beautiful wife, dreaming, in the land of the blacks, of his white lily beyond the desert. He raises his head, and—" But at this moment a cloud passed before the Moon, and then another. I heard nothing more from him this evening.

TWENTY-FIRST EVENING

"I saw a little girl weeping," said the Moon; "she was weeping over the depravity of the world. She had received a most beautiful doll as a present. Oh, that was a glorious doll, so fair and delicate! She did not seem created for the sorrows of this world. But the brothers of the little girl, those great naughty boys, had set the doll high up in the branches of a tree and had run away.

"The little girl could not reach up to the doll, and could not help her down, and that is why she was crying. The doll must certainly have been crying too, for she stretched out her arms among the green branches, and looked quite mournful. Yes, these are the troubles of life of which the little girl had often heard tell. Alas, poor doll! it began to grow dark already; and suppose night were to come on completely! Was she to be left sitting on the bough all night long? No, the little maid could not make up her mind to that. 'I'll stay with you,' she said, although she felt anything but happy in her mind. She could almost fancy she distinctly saw little gnomes, with their high-crowned hats, sitting in the bushes; and further back in the long walk, tall spectres appeared to be dancing. They came nearer and nearer, and stretched out their hands towards the tree on which the doll sat; they laughed scornfully, and pointed at her with their fingers. Oh, how frightened the little maid was! 'But if one has not done anything wrong,' she thought, 'nothing evil can harm one. I wonder if I have done anything wrong?' And she considered. 'Oh, yes! I laughed at the poor duck with the red rag on her leg; she limped along so funnily, I could not help laughing; but it's a sin to laugh at animals.' And she looked up at the doll. 'Did you laugh at the duck too?' she asked; and it seemed as if the doll shook her head."

TWENTY-SECOND EVENING

"I looked down upon Tyrol," said the Moon, "and my beams caused the dark pines to throw long shadows upon the rocks. I looked at the pictures of

St. Christopher carrying the Infant Jesus that are painted there upon the walls of the houses, colossal figures reaching from the ground to the roof. St. Florian was represented pouring water on the burning house, and the Lord hung bleeding on the great cross by the wayside. To the present generation these are old pictures, but I saw when they were put up, and marked how one followed the other. On the brow of the mountain yonder is perched, like a swallow's nest, a lonely convent of nuns. Two of the sisters stood up in the tower tolling the bell; they were both young, and therefore their glances flew over the mountain out into the world. A travelling coach passed by below, the postillion wound his horn, and the poor nuns looked after the carriage for a moment with a mournful glance, and a tear gleamed in the eyes of the younger one. And the horn sounded faint and more faintly, and the convent bell drowned its expiring echoes."

TWENTY-THIRD EVENING

Hear what the Moon told me. "Some years ago, here in Copenhagen, I looked through the window of a mean little room. The father and mother slept, but the little son was not asleep. I saw the flowered cotton curtains of the bed move, and the child peep forth. At first I thought he was looking at the great clock, which was gaily painted in red and green. At the top sat a cuckoo, below hung the heavy leaden weights, and the pendulum with the polished disc of metal went to and fro, and said 'tick, tick.' But no, he was not looking at the clock, but at his mother's spinning wheel, that stood just underneath it. That was the boy's favourite piece of furniture, but he dared not touch it, for if he meddled with it he got a rap on the knuckles. For hours together, when his mother was spinning, he would sit quietly by her side, watching the murmuring spindle and the revolving wheel, and as he sat he thought of many things. Oh, if he might only turn the wheel himself! Father and mother were asleep; he looked at them, and looked at the spinning wheel, and presently a little naked foot peered out of the bed, and then a second foot, and then two little white legs. There he stood. He looked round once more, to see if father and mother were still asleep — yes, they slept; and now he crept *softly, softly,* in his short little nightgown, to the spinning wheel, and began to spin. The thread flew from the wheel, and the wheel whirled faster and faster. I kissed his fair hair and his blue eyes, it was such a pretty picture.

"At that moment the mother awoke. The curtain shook, she looked forth, and fancied she saw a gnome or some other kind of little spectre. 'In Heaven's name!' she cried, and aroused her husband in a frightened way. He opened his eyes, rubbed them with his hands, and looked at the brisk little lad. 'Why, that is Bertel,' said he. And my eye quitted the poor room, for I have so much to see. At the same moment I looked at the halls of the Vatican, where the marble gods are enthroned. I shone upon the group of the Laocoon; the stone seemed to sigh. I pressed a silent kiss on the lips of the Muses, and they seemed to stir and move. But my rays lingered longest about the Nile group with the colossal god. Leaning against the Sphinx, he lies there thoughtful and meditative, as if he were thinking on the rolling centuries; and little love-gods sport with him and with the crocodiles. In the horn of plenty sat with folded arms a little tiny love-god, contemplating the great solemn river-god, a true picture of the boy at the spinning wheel — the features were exactly the same. Charming and life-like stood the little marble form, and yet the wheel of the year has turned more than a thousand times since the time when it sprang forth from the stone. Just as often as the boy in the little room turned the spinning wheel had the great wheel murmured, before the age could again call forth marble gods equal to those he afterwards formed.

"Years have passed since all this happened," the Moon went on to say. "Yesterday I looked upon a bay on the eastern coast of Denmark. Glorious woods are there, and high trees, an old knightly castle with red walls, swans floating in the ponds, and in the background appears, among orchards, a little town with a church. Many boats, the crews all furnished with torches, glided over the silent expanse—but these fires had not been kindled for catching fish, for everything had a festive look. Music sounded, a song was sung, and in one of the boats the man stood erect to whom homage was paid by the rest, a tall sturdy man, wrapped in a cloak. He had blue eyes and long white hair. I knew him, and thought of the Vatican, and of the group of the Nile, and the old marble gods. I thought of the simple little room where little Bertel sat in his night-shirt by the spinning wheel. The wheel of time has turned, and new gods have come forth from the stone. From the boats there arose a shout: 'Hurrah, hurrah for Bertel Thorwaldsen!' "

TWENTY-FOURTH EVENING

"I will now give you a picture from Frankfort," said the Moon. "I especially noticed one building there. It was not the house in which Goethe was born, nor the old Council House, through whose grated windows peered the horns of the oxen that were roasted and given to the people when the emperors were crowned. No, it was a private house, plain in appearance, and painted green. It stood near the old Jews' Street. It was Rothschild's house.

"I looked through the open door. The staircase was brilliantly lighted: servants carrying wax candles in massive silver candlesticks stood there, and bowed low before an old woman, who was being brought downstairs in a litter. The proprietor of the house stood bare-headed, and respectfully imprinted a kiss on the hand of the old woman. She was his mother. She nodded in a friendly manner to him and to the servants, and they carried her into the dark narrow street, into a little house, that was her dwelling. Here her children had been born, from hence the fortune of the family had arisen. If she deserted the despised street and the little house, fortune would also desert her children. That was her firm belief."

The Moon told me no more; his visit this evening was far too short. But I thought of the old woman in the narrow despised street. It would have cost her but a word, and a brilliant house would have arisen for her on the banks of the Thames—a word, and a villa would have been prepared in the Bay of Naples.

"If I deserted the lowly house, where the fortunes of my sons first began to bloom, fortune would desert them!" It was a superstition, but a superstition of such a class, that he who knows the story and has seen this picture, need have only two words placed under the picture to make him understand it; and these two words are: "A mother."

TWENTY-FIFTH EVENING

"It was yesterday, in the morning twilight"—these are the words the Moon told me—"in the great city no chimney was yet smoking—and it was just at the chimneys that I was looking. Suddenly a little head emerged from one of them, and then half a body, the arms resting on the rim of the chimney-pot. 'Ya-hip! ya-hip!' cried a voice. It was the little chimney-sweeper, who had for the first time in his life crept through a chimney, and stuck out his head at the top. 'Ya-hip! ya-hip' Yes, certainly that was a very different thing to creeping about in the dark narrow chimneys! the air blew so fresh, and he could look over the whole city towards the green wood. The sun was just rising. It shone round and great, just in his face, that beamed with triumph, though it was very prettily blacked with soot.

" 'The whole town can see me now,' he exclaimed, 'and the moon can see me now, and the sun too. Ya-hip! ya-hip!' And he flourished his broom in triumph."

TWENTY-SIXTH EVENING

"Last night I looked down upon a town in China," said the Moon. "My beams irradiated the naked walls that form the streets there. Now and then, certainly, a door is seen; but it is locked, for what does the Chinaman care about the outer world? Close wooden shutters covered the windows behind the walls of the houses; but through the windows of the temple a faint light glimmered. I looked in, and saw the quaint decorations within. From the floor to the ceiling pictures are painted, in the most glaring colours, and richly gilt—pictures representing the deeds of the gods here on earth. In each niche statues are placed, but they are almost entirely hidden by the coloured drapery and the banners that hang down. Before each idol (and they are all made of tin) stood a little altar of holy water, with flowers and burning wax lights on it. Above all the rest stood Fo, the chief deity, clad in a garment of yellow silk, for yellow is here the sacred colour. At the foot of the altar sat a living being, a young priest. He appeared to be praying, but in the midst of his prayer he seemed to fall into deep thought, and this must have been wrong, for his cheeks glowed and he held down his head. Poor Soui-Hong! Was he, perhaps, dreaming of working in the little flower garden behind the high street wall? And did that occupation seem more agreeable to him than watching the wax lights in the temple? Or did he wish to sit at the rich feast, wiping his mouth with silver paper between each course? Or was his sin so great that, if he dared utter it, the Celestial Empire would punish it with death? Had his thoughts ventured to fly with the ships of the barbarians, to their homes in far distant England? No, his thoughts did not fly so far, and yet they were sinful, sinful as thoughts born of young hearts, sinful here in the temple, in the presence of Fo and the other holy gods.

"I know whither his thoughts had strayed. At the farther end of the city, on the flat roof paved with porcelain, on which stood the handsome vases covered with painted flowers, sat the beauteous Pu, of the little roguish eyes, of the full lips, and of the tiny feet. The tight shoe pained her, but her heart pained her still more. She lifted her graceful round arm, and her satin dress rustled. Before her stood a glass bowl containing four gold-fish. She stirred the bowl carefully with a slender lacquered stick, very slowly, for she, too, was lost in thought. Was she thinking, perchance, how the fishes were richly clothed in gold, how they lived calmly and peacefully in their crystal world, how they were regularly fed, and yet how much happier they might be if they were free? Yes, that she could well understand, the beautiful Pu. Her thoughts wandered away from her home, wandered to the temple, but not for the sake of holy things. Poor Pu! Poor Soui-hong!

"Their earthly thoughts met, but my cold beam lay between the two, like the sword of the cherub."

TWENTY-SEVENTH EVENING

"The air was calm," said the Moon; "the water was transparent as the purest ether through which I was gliding, and deep below the surface I could see the strange plants that stretched up their long arms towards me like the gigantic trees of the forest. The fishes swam to and fro above their tops. High in the air a flight of wild swans were winging their way, one of which sank lower and lower, with wearied pinions, his eyes following the airy caravan, that melted farther and farther into the distance. With outspread wings he sank slowly, as a soap bubble sinks in the still air, till he touched the water. At length his head lay back between his wings, and silently he lay there, like a white lotus flower upon the quiet lake. And a gentle wind arose, and crisped the quiet surface, which gleamed like the clouds that poured along in great broad waves; and the swan raised his head, and the glowing water splashed like blue fire over his breast and back. The morning dawn illuminated the red clouds, the swan rose strengthened, and flew towards the rising sun, towards the bluish coast whither the caravan had gone; but he flew alone, with a longing in his breast. Lonely he flew over the blue swelling billows."

TWENTY-EIGHTH EVENING

"I will give you another picture of Sweden," said the Moon. "Among dark pine woods, near the melancholy banks of the Stoxen, lies the old convent church of Wreta. My rays glided through the grating into the roomy vaults, where kings sleep tranquilly in great stone coffins. On the wall, above the grave of each, is placed the emblem of earthly grandeur, a kingly crown; but it is made only of wood, painted and gilt, and is hung on a wooden peg driven into the wall. The worms have gnawed the gilded wood, the spider has spun her web from the crown down to the sand, like a mourning banner, frail and transient as the grief of mortals. How quietly they sleep! I can remember them quite plainly. I still see the bold smile on their lips, that so strongly and plainly expressed joy or grief. When the steamboat winds along like a magic snail over the lakes, a stranger often comes to the church, and visits the burial vault; he asks the names of the kings, and they have a dead and forgotten sound. He glances with a smile at the worm-eaten crowns, and if he happens to be a pious, thoughtful man, something of melancholy mingles with the smile. Slumber on, ye dead ones! The Moon thinks of you, the Moon at night sends down his rays into your silent kingdom, over which hangs the crown of pine wood."

TWENTY-NINTH EVENING

"Close by the high-road," said the Moon, "is an inn, and opposite to it is a great waggon-shed, whose straw roof was just being re-thatched. I looked down between the bare rafters and through the open loft into the comfortless space below. The turkey-cock slept on the beam, and the saddle rested in the empty crib. In the middle of the shed stood a travelling carriage; the proprietor was inside, fast asleep, while the horses were being watered. The coachman stretched himself, though I am very sure that he had been most comfortably asleep half the last stage. The door of the servants' room stood open, and the bed looked as if it had been turned over and over; the candle stood on the floor, and had burnt deep down into the socket. The wind blew cold through the shed: it was nearer to the dawn than to midnight. In the wooden frame on the ground slept a wandering family of musicians. The father and mother seemed to be dreaming of the burning liquor that remained in the bottle. The little pale daughter was dreaming too, for her eyes were wet with tears. The harp stood at their heads, and the dog lay stretched at their feet."

THIRTIETH EVENING

"It was in a little provincial town," the Moon said; "it certainly happened last year, but that has nothing to do with the matter. I saw it quite plainly. To-day I read about it in the papers, but there it was not half so clearly expressed. In the taproom of the little inn sat the bear leader, eating his supper; the bear was tied up outside, behind the wood pile—poor Bruin, who did nobody any harm, though he looked grim enough. Up in the garret three little children were playing by the light of my beams; the eldest was perhaps six years old, the youngest certainly not more than two. 'Tramp, tramp' —somebody was coming upstairs: who might it be? The door was thrust open—it was Bruin, the great, shaggy Bruin! He had got tired of waiting down in the courtyard, and had found his way to the stairs. I saw it all," said the Moon. "The children were very much frightened at first at the great shaggy animal; each of them crept into a corner, but he found them all out, and smelt at them, but did them no harm. 'This must be a great dog,' they said, and began to stroke him. He lay down upon the ground, the youngest boy clambered on his back, and bending down a little head of golden curls, played at hiding in the beast's shaggy skin. Presently the eldest boy took his drum, and beat upon it till it rattled again; the bear rose upon his hind legs, and began to dance. It was a charming sight to behold. Each boy now took his gun, and the bear was obliged to have one too, and he held it up quite properly. Here was a capital playmate they had found; and they began marching—one, two; one, two.

"Suddenly some one came to the door, which opened, and the mother of the children appeared. You should have seen her in her dumb terror, with her face as white as chalk, her mouth half open, and her eyes fixed in a horrified stare. But the youngest boy nodded to her in great glee, and called out in his infantile prattle, 'We're playing at soldiers.' And then the bear leader came running up."

THIRTY-FIRST EVENING

The wind blew stormy and cold, the clouds flew hurriedly past; only for a moment now and then did the Moon become visible. He said, "I looked down from the silent sky upon the driving clouds, and saw the great shadows chasing each other across the earth. I looked upon a prison. A closed carriage stood before it; a prisoner was to be carried away. My rays pierced through the grated window towards the wall; the prisoner was scratching a few lines upon it, as a parting token; but he did not write words, but a melody, the outpouring of his heart. The door was opened, and he was led forth, and fixed his eyes upon my round disc. Clouds passed between us, as if he were not to see his face, nor I his. He stepped into the carriage, the door was closed, the whip cracked, and the horses gallopped off into the thick forest, whither my rays were not able to follow him; but as I glanced through the grated window, my rays glided over the notes, his last farewell engraved on the prison wall — where words fail, sounds can often speak. My rays could only light up isolated notes, so the greater part of what was written there will ever remain dark to me. Was it the death-hymn he wrote there? Were these the glad notes of joy? Did he drive away to meet death, or hasten to the embraces of his beloved? The rays of the Moon do not read all that is written by mortals."

THIRTY-SECOND EVENING

"I love the children," said the Moon, "especially the quite little ones — they are so droll. Sometimes I peep into the room, between the curtain and the window frame, when they are not thinking of me. It gives me pleasure to see them dressing and undressing. First, the little round naked shoulder comes creeping out of the frock, then the arm; or I see how the stocking is drawn off, and a plump little white leg makes its appearance, and a white little foot that is fit to be kissed, and I kiss it too.

"But about what I was going to tell you. This evening I looked through a window, before which no curtain was drawn, for nobody lives opposite. I saw a whole troop of little ones, all of one family, and among them was a little sister. She is only four years old, but can say her prayers as well as any of the rest. The mother sits by her bed every evening, and hears her say her prayers; and then she has a kiss, and the mother sits by the bed till the little one has gone to sleep, which generally happens as soon as ever she can close her eyes.

"This evening the two elder children were a little boisterous. One of them hopped about on one leg in his long white nightgown, and the other stood on a chair surrounded by the clothes of all the children, and declared he was acting Grecian statues. The third and fourth laid the clean linen carefully in the box, for that is a thing that has to be done; and the mother sat by the bed of the youngest, and announced to all the rest that they were to be quiet, for little sister was going to say her prayers.

"I looked in, over the lamp, into the little maiden's bed, where she lay under the neat white coverlet, her hands folded demurely and her little face quite grave and serious. She was praying the Lord's prayer aloud. But her mother interrupted her in the middle of her prayer. 'How is it,' she asked, 'that when you have prayed for daily bread, you always add something I can-

WHAT THE MOON SAW

not understand? You must tell me what that is.' The little one lay silent, and looked at her mother in embarrassment. 'What is it you say after *our daily bread?*' 'Dear mother, don't be angry: I only said, *and plenty of butter on it.*' "

LUCKY PEER

I

In the most fashionable street in the city stood a fine old house; the wall around it had bits of glass worked into it, so that when the sun or the moon shone it looked as if it were covered with diamonds. That was a sign of wealth, and there was great wealth inside. It was said that the merchant was a man rich enough to put two barrels of gold into his best parlor and could even put a barrel of gold pieces, as a savings bank against the future, outside the door of the room where his little son was born.

When the baby arrived in the rich house, there was great joy from the cellar up to the garret; and up there, there was still greater joy an hour or two later. The warehouseman and his wife lived in the garret, and there, too, at the same time, a little son arrived, given by our Lord, brought by the stork, and exhibited by the mother. And there, too, was a barrel outside the door, quite accidentally; but it was not a barrel of gold—it was a barrel of sweepings.

The rich merchant was a very kind, fine man. His wife, delicate and always dressed in clothes of high quality, was pious and, besides, was kind and good to the poor. Everybody rejoiced with these two people on now having a little son who would grow up and be rich and happy, like his father. When the little boy was baptized he was called Felix, which in Latin means "lucky," and this he was, and his parents were even more so.

The warehouseman, a fellow who was really good to the core, and his wife, an honest and industrious woman, were well liked by all who knew them. How lucky they were to have their little boy; he was called Peer.

The boy on the first floor and the boy in the garret each received the same amount of kisses from his parents and just as much sunshine from our Lord; but still they were placed a little differently—one downstairs, and one up. Peer sat the highest, way up in the garret, and he had his own mother for a nurse; little Felix had a stranger for his nurse, but she was good and honest—that was written in her service book. The rich child had a pretty baby carriage, which was pushed about by his elegantly dressed nurse; the child from the garret was carried in the arms of his own mother, both when she was in her Sunday clothes and when she had her everyday things on, and he was just as happy.

Both children soon began to observe things; they were growing, and both could show with their hands how tall they were, and say single words in their mother tongue. They were equally handsome, petted, and equally fond of sweets. As they grew up, they both got an equal amount of pleasure out of the merchant's horses and carriages. Felix was allowed to sit by the coachman, along with his nurse, and look at the horses; he would fancy himself driving.

Peer was allowed to sit at the garret window and look down into the yard when the master and mistress went out to drive; and when they had left, he would place two chairs, one in front of the other, up there in the room, and so he would drive himself; he was the real coachman—that was a little more than fancying himself to be the coachman.

They got along splendidly, these two; yet it was not until they were two years old that they spoke to each other. Felix was always elegantly dressed in silk and velvet, with bare knees, after the English style. "The poor child will freeze!" said the family in the garret. Peer had trousers that came down to his ankles, but one day his clothes were torn right across his knees, so that he got as much of a draft and was just as much undressed as the merchant's delicate little boy. Felix came along with his mother and was about to go out through the gate when Peer came along with his and wanted to go in.

"Give little Peer your hand," said the merchant's wife. "You two should talk to each other."

And one said, "Peer!" and the other said, "Felix!" Yes, and that was all they said at that time.

The rich lady coddled her boy, but there was one who coddled Peer just as much, and that was his grandmother. She was weak-sighted, and yet she saw much more in little Peer than his father or mother could see; yes, more than any person could.

"The sweet child," she said, "is surely going to get on in the world. He was born with a gold apple in his hand; I can see it even with my poor sight. Why, there is the shining apple!" And she kissed the child's little hand. His parents could see nothing, and neither could Peer; but as he grew to have more understanding, he liked to believe it.

"That is such a story, such a fairy tale, that Grandmother tells!" said the parents.

Yes, Grandmother could tell stories, and Peer was never tired of hearing always the same ones. She taught him a psalm and the Lord's Prayer as well, and he could say it, not as gabble but as words that meant something; she explained every single sentence in it to him. He gave particular thought to what Grandmother said about the words, "Give us this day our daily bread"; he was to understand that it was necessary for one to get wheat bread, for another to get black bread; one must have a great house when he had many people in his employ; another, in small circumstances, could live quite as happily in a little room in the garret. "So each person has what he calls 'daily bread.'"

Peer, of course, had his good daily bread—and the most delightful days, too, but they were not to last forever. The sad years of war began; the young men were to go away, and the older men as well. Peer's father was among those who were called in; and soon afterward it was heard that he had been one of the first to fall in battle against the superior enemy.

There was bitter grief in the little room in the garret. The mother cried; the grandmother and little Peer cried; and every time one of the neighbors came up to see them, they talked about "Papa," and then they cried all together. The widow, meanwhile, was given permission to stay in her garret flat, rent-free, during the first year, and afterward she was to pay only a small rent. The grandmother stayed with the mother, who supported herself by washing for several "single, elegant gentlemen," as she called them. Peer had neither sorrow nor want. He had plenty of food and drink, and Grandmother told him stories, such strange and wonderful ones about the wide world, that he asked her, one day, if the two of them might not go to foreign lands some Sunday and return home as prince and princess, wearing gold crowns.

"I am too old for that," said Grandmother, "and you must first learn a good many things and become big and strong; but you must always be a good and affectionate child—as you are now."

Peer rode around the room on hobbyhorses; he had two such horses. But the merchant's son had a real live horse; it was so small that it might well have been called a baby horse, which, in fact, Peer called it, and it never could become any bigger. Felix rode it in the yard; yes, and he even rode it outside the gate, when his father and a riding master from the king's stable were with him. For the first half-hour, Peer had not liked his horses and hadn't ridden them, for they were not real; and then he had asked his mother why he could not have a real horse like little Felix had, and his mother had said, "Felix lives down on the first floor, close by the stables, but you live high up under the roof. One cannot have horses up in the garret except like those you have. You should ride on them."

And so now Peer rode—first to the chest of drawers, the great mountain with its many treasures; both Peer's Sunday clothes and his mother's were there, and there were the shining silver dollars that she laid aside for rent; then he rode to the stove, which he called the black bear; it slept all summer long, but when winter came it had to be useful, to warm the room and cook the meals.

Peer had a godfather who usually came there every Sunday during the winter and got a good warm meal. Things had gone wrong for him, said the mother and the grandmother. He had begun as a coachman. He had been drinking and had fallen sleep at his post, and that neither a soldier nor a coachman should do. He then had become a cabman and driven a cab, or sometimes a carriage, and often for very elegant people. But now he drove a garbage wagon and went from door to door, swinging his rattle, "snurre-rurre-ud!" and from all the houses came the servant girls and housewives with their buckets full, and turned these into the wagon; rubbish and junk, ashes and sweepings, were all thrown in.

One day Peer came down from the garret after his mother had gone to town. He stood at the open gate, and there outside was Godfather with his wagon. "Would you like to take a drive?" he asked. Yes, Peer was willing to indeed, but only as far as the corner. His eyes shone as he sat on the seat with Godfather and was allowed to hold the whip. Peer drove with real live horses, drove right to the corner. Then his mother came along; she looked rather dubious, for it was not nice to see her own little son riding on a garbage wagon. She told him to get down at once. Still, she thanked Godfather; but at home she forbade Peer to drive with him again.

One day he again went down to the gate. There was no Godfather there to tempt him with a drive, but there were other temptations. Three or four small street urchins were down in the gutter, poking about to see what they could find that had been lost or had hidden itself there. Frequently they had found a button or a copper coin, but frequently, too, they had cut themselves on a broken bottle, or pricked themselves with a pin, which just now was the case. Peer simply had to join them, and when he got down among the gutter stones he found a silver coin.

Another day he was again down digging with the other boys; they only got dirty fingers; he found a gold ring, and then, with sparkling eyes, showed off his lucky find; whereupon the others threw dirt at him and called him Lucky Peer. They wouldn't permit him to be with them any more when they poked in the gutter.

Back of the merchant's yard there was some low ground that was to be filled up for building lots; gravel and ashes were carted and dumped out there, great heaps of it. Godfather helped deliver it in his wagon, but Peer was not allowed to drive with him. The street urchins dug in the heaps, dug with a stick and with their bare hands; they always found one thing or another that seemed worth picking up.

Then little Peer came along. They saw him and cried, "Get away from here, Lucky Peer!" And when, despite this, he came closer, they threw lumps of dirt at him. One of these struck against his wooden shoe and crumbled to pieces. Something shining rolled out, and Peter picked it up; it was a little heart made of amber. He ran home with it. The other boys did not notice that even when they threw dirt at him he was a child of luck.

The silver coin he had found was put away in his savings bank. The ring and the amber heart were shown to the merchant's wife downstairs, because the mother wanted to know if they were lost articles that should be returned to the police.

How the eyes of the merchant's wife shone on seeing the ring! It was her own engagement ring, one that she had lost three years before! That's how long it had lain in the gutter. Peer was well rewarded, and the money rattled in his little box. The amber heart was a cheap thing, the lady said; Peer might just as well keep that. At night the amber heart lay on the bureau, and the grandmother lay in bed.

"My, what is it that burns so!" she said. "It looks as if a small candle is lighted there." She got up to see, and it was the little heart of amber—yes, Grandmother, with her weak sight, frequently saw more than anyone else could see. She had her own thoughts about it. The next morning she took a narrow, strong ribbon, drew it through the opening at the top of the heart, and put it around her little grandson's neck.

"You must never take it off, except to put a new ribbon into it, and you must not show it to the other boys, either, for then they would take it from you, and you would get a stomach-ache!" That was the only painful sickness little Peer had known so far. There was a strange power, too, in that heart. Grandmother showed him that when she rubbed it with her hand, and a little straw was put next to it, the straw seemed to be alive and was drawn to the heart of amber and would not let go.

II

The merchant's son had a private tutor who taught him his lessons and who took walks with him, too. Peer was also to have an education, so he went to public school with a great number of other boys. They played together, and that was much more fun than going along with a tutor. Peer would not have changed places with him.

He was a lucky Peer, but Godfather was also a lucky peer, although his name was not Peer. He won a prize in the lottery, of two hundred dollars, on a ticket he shared with eleven others. He immediately bought some better clothes, and he looked very well in them. Luck never comes alone; it always has company, and so it did this time. Godfather gave up the garbage wagon and joined the theater.

"What's that!" said Grandmother. "Is he going into the theater? As what?"

As a machinist. That was an advancement. He became quite another person; and he enjoyed the plays very much, although he always saw them from the top or from the side. Most wonderful was the ballet, but that gave him the hardest work, and there was always danger of fire. They danced both in heaven and on earth. That was something for little Peer to see; and one evening when there was to be a dress rehearsal of a new ballet, in which everyone was dressed and made up as on the opening night when people pay to see all the magnificence, he had permission to bring Peer with him and put him in a place where he could see the whole show.

It was a Biblical ballet — *Samson.* The Philistines danced about him, and he turned the whole house down over them and himself; but there were both fire engines and firemen on hand in case of any accident.

Peer had never seen a stage play, not to mention a ballet. He put on his Sunday clothes and went with Godfather to the theater. It was just like a great drying loft, with many curtains and screens, big openings in the floor, lamps, and lights. There were so many tricky nooks and corners everywhere, from which people appeared, just as in a great church with its gallery pews. Peer was seated down where the floor slanted steeply and was told to stay there until it was all finished and he was sent for. He had three sandwiches in his pocket, so that he need not starve.

Soon it grew lighter and lighter; then up in front, just as if straight out of the earth, there came a number of musicians with both flutes and violins. In the seats next to Peer sat people dressed in street clothes; but there also appeared knights with gold helmets, beautiful maidens in gauze and flowers, even angels all in white, with wings on their backs. They seated themselves upstairs and downstairs, on the floor and in the balcony seats, to watch what was going on. They were all members of the ballet, but Peer did not know that. He thought they belonged in the fairy tales his grandmother had told him about. There then appeared a woman, and she was the most beautiful of all, with a gold helmet and spear; she seemed to be above all the others, and sat between an angel and a troll. Ah, how much there was to see! And yet the ballet had not even begun.

Suddenly everything became quiet. A man dressed in black moved a little fairy wand over all the musicians, and then they began to play; the music made a whistling sound through the theater, and the whole wall in front began to rise. One looked into a flower garden, where the sun shone and all the people danced and leaped. Such a wonderful sight Peer had never imagined. There were soldiers marching, and there was war, and there was a banquet, and there were the mighty Samson and his lover. But she was as wicked as she was beautiful; she betrayed him. The Philistines plucked his eyes out; he was forced to grind in the mill and to be mocked and insulted in the great banquet hall; but then he took hold of the heavy stone pillars that held up the roof and shook them and the whole house; it fell, and there burst forth wonderful flames of red and green fire.

Peer could have sat there his whole life long and looked on, even if the sandwiches were all eaten — and they *were* all eaten.

Now here was something to tell about, when he got home. It was impossible to get him to go to bed. He stood on one leg and laid the other on the table—that was what Samson's lover and all the other ladies had done. He made a treadmill out of Grandmother's chair and upset two chairs and a pillow over himself to show how the banquet hall had come down. He showed this—yes, and he even presented it with the music that belonged to it; there was no talking in the ballet. He sang high and low, with words and without words, and it was quite incoherent. It was like a whole opera. The most noticeable thing of all, meanwhile, was his beautiful, bell-clear voice, but no one spoke of that.

Peer previously had wanted to be a grocer's boy, to be in charge of prunes and powdered sugar. Now he found there was something much more wonderful, and that was to get into the Samson story and dance in the ballet. A great many poor children had taken that road, said the grandmother, and had become fine and honored people; yet no little girl of her family would ever be permitted to do so; but a boy—well, he stood more firmly. Peer had not seen a single one of the little girls fall down before the whole house fell, and then they all fell together, he said.

III

Peer wanted to, and felt he must, be a ballet dancer.

"He gives me no rest!" said his mother. At last, his grandmother promised to take him to the ballet master, who was a fine gentleman and had his own house, like the merchant. Would Peer ever be that rich? Nothing is impossible for our Lord. Peer had been born with a gold apple; luck had been laid in his hands—perhaps it was also in his legs.

Peer went to the ballet master and knew him at once; it was Samson himself. His eyes had not suffered at all at the hands of the Philistines. That was only acting in the play, he was told. And Samson looked kindly and pleasantly at him, and told him to stand up straight, look right at him, and show him his ankle. Peer showed him his whole foot and leg, too.

"So he got a place in the ballet," said Grandmother.

This was easily arranged with the ballet master, but before that, his mother and grandmother had spoken with several understanding people—first with the merchant's wife, who thought it a good career for a handsome, honest boy like Peer, but without any future. Then they had spoken with Miss Frandsen; she knew all about the ballet, and at one time, in Grandmother's younger days, she had been the most beautiful danseuse at the theater; she had danced goddesses and princesses, had been cheered and applauded wherever she had gone; but then she had grown older—we all do—and so no longer had she been given principal parts; she'd had to dance behind the younger ones; and when finally her dancing days had come to an end, she had become a wardrobe woman and dressed the others as goddesses and princesses.

"So it goes!" said Miss Frandsen. "The theater road is a delightful one to travel, but it is full of thorns. Jealousy grows there! Jealousy!"

That was a word Peer did not understand at all; but he came to understand it in time.

"No force or power can keep him from the ballet," said his mother.

"A pious Christian child, that he is," said Grandmother.

"And well brought up," said Miss Frandsen. "Well formed and moral! That I was in my heyday."

And so Peer went to the dancing school and got some summer clothes and thin-soled dancing shoes to make himself lighter. All the older girl dancers kissed him and said that he was a boy good enough to eat.

He had to stand up, stick his legs out, and hold on to a post so as not to fall, while he leaned to kick, first with his right leg, then with his left. It was not nearly so difficult for him as it was for most of the others. The ballet master patted him and said that he would soon be in the ballet; he was to play the child of a king who was carried on shields and wore a gold crown. This was practiced at the dancing school and rehearsed at the theater itself.

The mother and grandmother had to see little Peer in all his glory, and when they saw this, they both cried, although it was such a happy occasion. Peer, in all his pomp and glory, did not see them at all; but he did see the merchant's family, who sat in the loge nearest the stage. Little Felix was with them, in his best clothes. He wore buttoned gloves, just like a grown-up gentleman. He looked at Peer, and Peer looked at him; Peer was a king's child with a crown of gold. This evening brought the two children into closer relationship with one another.

A few days later, when they met each other at home in the yard, Felix went up to Peer and told him he had seen him when he was a prince. He knew very well that he was not a prince any longer, but then he had worn a prince's clothes and a gold crown. "I shall wear them again on Sunday," said Peer.

Felix did not see him Sunday, but he thought about it the whole evening. He would have liked very much to have been in Peer's place; he had not heard Miss Frandsen's warning that the road of the theater was a thorny one and that jealousy grew along it; nor did Peer know this yet, but he would very soon learn it.

His young companions, the dancing children, were not all so good as they ought to be, although they often played angels and had wings on them. There was a little girl, Malle Knallerup, who always—when she was dressed as a page, and Peer was a page—stepped maliciously on the side of his foot, so as to dirty his stockings. There was a wicked boy who always was sticking pins in his back; and one day he ate Peer's sandwiches—by mistake; but that was impossible, for Peer had meat balls on his sandwiches, and the other boy had only bread without butter; he could not have made a mistake.

It would be impossible to recite all the annoyances that Peer endured in two years, and the worst was yet to come.

There was a ballet performed called *The Vampire*. In it the smallest dancing children were dressed as bats, wore gray, knitted tights that fitted snugly to their bodies; black gauze wings were stretched from their shoulders. They were to run on tiptoe, as if they were light enough to fly, and then they were to whirl around on the floor. Peer could do this especially well; but his trousers and jacket, all of one piece, were old and worn and could not stand the strain. So just as he whirled around before the eyes of all the people, there was a rip right down his back, straight from his neck down to where the legs are fastened in, and all of his short, white shirt could be seen. All the people laughed. Peer felt it and knew what had happened; he whirled and whirled, but it grew worse and worse. People laughed louder and louder; the other vampires laughed with them, and whirled into him, and all the more dreadfully when the people clapped and shouted, "Bravo!"

"That is for the ripped vampire!" said the dancing children. And from then on they always called him Rippy.

Peer cried. Miss Frandsen comforted him. "It is only jealousy," she said; and now Peer knew what jealousy was.

Besides the dancing school, they had a regular school at the theater where the children were taught arithmetic and writing, history and geography — yes, and they even had a teacher in religion, for it is not enough to know how to dance; there is something more important in the world than wearing out dancing shoes. Here, too, Peer was quick, the very quickest of all, and got plenty of good marks; but his fellow students still called him Rippy. They were only teasing him; but at last he could not stand it any longer, and he swung and hit one of the boys, so that he was black and blue under the left eye and had to have grease paint on it in the evening when he appeared in the ballet. Peer got a scolding from the dancing master, and a worse one from the sweeping woman, for it was her son he had "given a sweeping."

IV

A good many thoughts went through little Peer's head. And one Sunday, when he was dressed in his best clothes, he went out without saying a word about it to his mother or his grandmother, not even to Miss Frandsen, who always gave him good advice; he went straight to the orchestra conductor; he thought this man was the most important one there was outside the ballet. Cheerfully he stepped in and said, "I am at the dancing school, but there is much jealousy there, and so I would rather be a player or a singer, if you would help me, please."

"Have you a voice?" asked the conductor, and looked quite pleasantly at him. "Seems to me I know you. Where have I seen you before? Wasn't it you who was ripped down the back?" And now he laughed. But Peer grew red; he was surely no longer Lucky Peer, as his grandmother had called him. He looked down at his feet and wished he were far away.

"Sing me a song!" said the conductor. "Come now, cheer up, my boy!" and he tapped him under the chin, and Peer looked up into his kind eyes and sang a song, "Mercy for Me," which he had heard at the theater, in the opera *Robert le Diable*.

"That is a difficult song, but you did it pretty well," said the conductor. "You have an excellent voice — as long as it doesn't rip in the back!" and he laughed and called his wife. She also had to hear Peer sing, and she nodded her head and said something in a foreign tongue. Just at that moment the singing master of the theater came in; it was really to him Peer should have gone if he wanted to be a singer; now the singing master came to him, quite accidentally, as it were; he also heard him sing "Mercy for Me," but he did not laugh, and he did not look so kindly at him as the conductor and his wife; still it was decided that Peer should have singing lessons.

"Now he is on the right track," said Miss Frandsen. "One gets much farther with a voice than with legs. If I had had a voice, I would have been a great songstress and would perhaps have been a baroness by now."

"Or a bookbinder's wife," said Mother. "Had you become rich, you surely would have taken the bookbinder."

We do not understand that hint, but Miss Frandsen did.

Peer had to sing for her and sing for the merchant's family, when they heard of his new career. He was called in one evening when they had company downstairs, and he sang several songs, among them "Mercy for Me." All the company clapped their hands, and Felix did, too; he had heard him sing before; in the stable Peer had sung the entire ballet of *Samson,* and that was the most delightful of all.

"One cannot sing a ballet," said the lady.

"Yes, Peer can," said Felix, and so they asked him to do it. He sang, and he talked; he drummed and he hummed; it was child's play, but fragments of well-known melodies came forth which really illustrated what the ballet was about. All the company found it very entertaining; they laughed and praised it, one louder than another. The merchant's wife gave Peer a huge piece of cake and a silver dollar.

How lucky the boy felt, until he discovered a gentleman who stood somewhat in the background, and who looked sternly at him. There was something harsh and severe in the man's black eyes; he did not laugh; he did not speak a single friendly word; this gentleman was the singing master from the theater.

Next forenoon, Peer went to him, and he stood there quite as severe-looking as before.

"What was the matter with you yesterday!" he said. "Could you not understand that they were making a fool of you? Never do that again, and don't you go running about and singing at doors, either inside or outside. Now you can go. I won't give you any singing lesson today."

When Peer left, he was dreadfully downcast; he had fallen out of the master's good graces. On the contrary, the master was really more satisfied with him than ever before. In all the absurdity which he had seen him perform, there was really some meaning, something quite unusual. The boy had an ear for music, and a voice as clear as a bell and of great compass; if it continued like that, then the little fellow's fortune was made.

Now began the singing lessons. Peer was industrious and Peer was clever. How much there was to learn, how much to know! The mother toiled and slaved to make an honest living, so that her son might be well dressed and neat and not look too shabby among the people to whom he now was invited. He was always singing and jubilant; they had no need at all of a canary bird, the mother said. Every Sunday he had to sing a psalm with his grandmother. It was delightful to hear his fresh voice lift itself up with hers. "It is much more beautiful than to hear him sing wildly!" That's what she called his singing when, like a little bird, his voice jubilantly gave forth with tones that seemed to come of themselves and make such music as they pleased. What tones there were in his little throat, what wonderful sounds in his little breast! Indeed, he could imitate a whole orchestra. There were both flute and bassoon in his voice, and there were violin and bugle. He sang as the birds sing; but man's voice is much more charming, even a little man's, when he can sing like Peer.

But in the winter, just as he was to go to the pastor to be prepared for confirmation, he caught cold; the little bird in his breast said, pip! The voice was ripped like the vampire's back-piece.

"It is no great misfortune, after all," thought Mother and Grandmother. "Now he doesn't go singing, tra-la, so he can think more seriously about his religion."

His voice was changing, the singing master said. Peer must not sing at all now. How long would it be? A year, perhaps two; perhaps the voice would never come again. That was a great grief.

"Think only of your confirmation now," said Mother and Grandmother. "Practice your music," said the singing master, "but keep your mouth shut."

He thought of his religion, and he studied his music; it sang and resounded within him. He wrote entire melodies down in notes, songs without words. Finally he wrote the words, too.

"You are a poet, too, little Peer," said the merchant's wife, to whom he carried his text and music. The merchant received a piece of music dedicated to him, a piece without words. Felix got one, too; and, yea, Miss Frandsen also did, and that went into her scrapbook, in which were verses and music by two who were once young lieutenants but now were old majors on half pay; the book had been given by "a friend," who had bound it himself.

And Peer was confirmed at Easter. Felix presented him with a silver watch. It was the first watch Peer had owned; he felt that this made him a man, for now he did not have to ask others what time it was. Felix came up to the garret, congratulated him, and handed him the watch; he himself was not to be confirmed until the autumn. They took each other by the hand, these two children of the house, both the same age, born the same day and in the same house. And Felix ate a piece of the cake that had been baked in the garret for the occasion of the confirmation.

"It is a happy day with solemn thoughts," said Grandmother.

"Yes, very solemn!" said Mother. "If only Father had lived to see Peer today!"

The following Sunday all three of them went to Communion. When they came home from church they found a message from the singing master, asking Peer to come to see him; and Peer went. Some good news awaited him, and yet it was serious, too. While he must give up singing for a year, and his voice must lie fallow like a field, as a peasant might say, during that time he was to further his education, not in the capital, where every evening he would be running to the theater, from which he could not keep away, but he was to go one hundred and twenty miles from home, to board with a schoolmaster who boarded a couple of other young men. There he was to learn language and science, which someday would be useful to him. The charge for a year's course was three hundred dollars, and that was paid by a "benefactor who does not wish his name to be known."

"It is the merchant," said Mother and Grandmother.

The day of departure came. A good many tears were shed, and kisses and blessings given; and then Peer rode the hundred and twenty miles on the railway, out into the wide world. It was Whitsuntide. The sun shone, and the woods were fresh and green; the train went rushing through them; new fields and villages were continually coming into view; country manors peeped out; the cattle stood in the pastures; Now they passed a station, then another, and market town after market town. At each stopping place there was a crowd of people, welcoming or saying good-bye; there was noisy talking, outside and in the carriages. Where Peer sat there was a lot of entertainment and chattering by a widow dressed in black. She talked about his grave, his coffin, and his corpse—meaning her child's. It had been such a poor little thing that there could have been no happiness for it had it lived. It had been a great relief for her and the little lamb when it had fallen asleep.

"I spared no expense on flowers on that occasion!" she said; "and you must remember that it died at a very expensive time, when the flowers had to be cut from potted plants! Every Sunday I went to my grave and laid a wreath on it with great white silk bows; the silk bows were immediately stolen by some little girls and used for dancing bows; they were so tempting! One Sunday I went there, and I knew that my grave was on the left of the main path, but when I got there, there was my grave on the right. 'How is this?' says I to the gravedigger. 'Isn't my grave on the left?'

" 'No, it isn't any longer!' the gravedigger answered. 'Madam's grave lies there all right, but the mound has been moved over to the right; that place belongs to another man's grave.'

" 'But I want my corpse in my grave,' says I, 'and I have a perfect right to say so. Shall I go and decorate a false mound, when my corpse lies without any sign on the other side? Indeed I won't!'

" 'Then Madam must talk to the dean.'

"He is such a good man, that dean! He gave me permission to have my corpse on the right. It would cost five dollars. I gave that with a kiss of my hand and walked back to my old grave. 'Can I now be very sure that it is my own coffin and my corpse that is moved?'

" 'That Madam can!' And so I gave each of the men a coin for the moving. But now, since it had cost so much, I thought I should spend something to make it beautiful, and so I ordered a monument with an inscription. But — will you believe it — when I got it, there was a gilded butterfly painted at the top. 'Why, that means Frivolity,' said I. 'I won't have that on my grave.'

" 'It is not Frivolity, Madam; it is Immortality.'

" 'I never heard that,' said I. Now, have any of you here in the carriage ever heard of a butterfly as a sign for anything but Frivolity? I kept quiet. I don't like long conversations. I composed myself, and put the monument away in my pantry. There it stood till my lodger came home. He is a student and has so many, many books. He assured me that it really stood for Immortality, and so the monument was placed on the grave."

And during all the chatter, Peer arrived at the station of the town where he was to live, and become just as wise as the student, and have just as many books.

V

Herr Gabriel, the honorable man of learning with whom Peer was to live as a boarding scholar, was at the railway station, to call for him. Herr Gabriel was a man as thin as a skeleton, with great, shiny eyes that stuck out so very far that one was almost afraid that when he sneezed they would pop out of his head entirely. He was accompanied by three of his own little boys; one of them stumbled over his own legs, and the other two stepped all over Peer's feet in their eagerness to get a close view of him. Two larger boys were with them, the older about fourteen years, fair-skinned, freckled, and full of pimples.

"Young Madsen, who will be a student in about three years, if he studies! Primus, son of a dean." That was the younger, who looked like a head of wheat. "Both are boarders, studying with me," said Herr Gabriel. "Our small stuff," he called his own boys.

"Trine, bring the newcomer's trunk on your wheelbarrow. The table is set for you at home."

"Stuffed turkey!" said the other two young gentlemen boarders.

"Stuffed turkey!" said the "small stuff"; and again one of them fell over his own legs.

"Caesar, look after your feet!" exclaimed Herr Gabriel.

And they walked into town and then out of it. There stood a great half-tumbled-down timber house, with a jasmine-covered summerhouse, facing the road. Here Madam Gabriel waited with more "small stuff," two little girls.

"The new pupil," said Herr Gabriel.

"A most hearty welcome!" said Madam Gabriel, a youthful, well-fed woman, red and white, with spit curls and a lot of pomade on her hair.

"Good heavens, how grown-up you are!" she said to Peer. "Why, you are a fully developed gentleman already. I thought that you were like Primus or young Madsen. Angel Gabriel, it's a good thing the inner door is nailed. You know what I think."

"Nonsense!" said Herr Gabriel. And they stepped into the room. There was a novel on the table, lying open, and a sandwich open on it. One might have thought that it had been placed there as a bookmark — it lay across the open page.

"Now I must be the housewife!" And with all five of her children, and the two boarders, she showed Peer through the kitchen, and the hallway, and into a little room, the windows of which looked out on the garden; that was to be his study and bedroom; it was next to Madam Gabriel's room, where she slept with all the five children; the connecting door, for decency's sake, and to prevent gossip "which spares nobody," had been nailed up by Herr Gabriel that very day, at Madam's express request.

"Here you can live just as if you were at your parents'. We have a theater, too, in the town. The pharmacist is the director of a private company, and we have traveling players. But now you are going to have your turkey." And so she showed Peer into the dining room, where the wash was drying on a line.

"That doesn't do any harm," she said. "It is only cleanliness, and that you are surely accustomed to."

So Peer sat down to eat the roast turkey, while the children of the house, but not the two boarders, who had withdrawn, gave a dramatic show for the entertainment of themselves and the stranger. There had lately been a traveling company of actors in town, which had played Schiller's *The Robbers*. The two oldest boys had been immensely taken with it. And they now performed the whole play at home — all the parts, notwithstanding that they remembered only these words: "Dreams come from the stomach." But they were spoken by all the characters in different tones of voice. There stood Amelia, with heavenly eyes and a dreamy look. "Dreams come from the stomach!" she said, and covered her face with both her hands. Carl Moor came forward with a heroic stride and manly voice, "Dreams come from the stomach," and at that the whole flock of children, boys and girls, rushed in; they were all robbers, and murdered one another, crying out, "Dreams come from the stomach."

That was Schiller's *The Robbers*. This performance and stuffed turkey were Peer's first introduction into Herr Gabriel's house. He then went to his little chamber, where through the window, into which the sun shone warmly, he could see the garden. He sat down and looked out. Herr Gabriel was walking there, absorbed in reading a book. He came closer and looked in; his eyes seemed fixed upon Peer, who bowed respectfully. Herr Gabriel opened his mouth as wide as he would, stuck out his tongue, and let it wag from one side to the other right in the face of the astonished Peer, who could not understand why he was treated in such a manner. Whereupon Herr Gabriel left, but then turned back to the window and again stuck his tongue out of his mouth.

Why did he do that? He was not thinking of Peer, or that the panes of glass were transparent from the outside; he saw only the reflection of himself in them, and he wanted to look at his tongue, as he had a stomach-ache, but Peer did not know all this.

Early in the evening Herr Gabriel went into his room, and Peer sat in his. Much later in the evening he heard quarreling—female quarreling—in Madam Gabriel's bedroom.

"I am going up to Gabriel and tell him what rascals you are!"

"We will also go to Gabriel and tell him what Madam is!"

"I shall have a fit!" she cried.

"Who wants to see a woman in a fit! Four skillings!"

Then Madam's voice sank deeper, but was distinctly heard. "What will the young man in there think of our house when he hears all this vulgarity!" At that the quarrel subsided, but then again rose louder and louder.

"Period! Finis," cried Madam. "Go and make the punch; it's better to agree than to quarrel!"

And then it was still. The door opened, and the girls left, and then Madam knocked on the door to Peer's room.

"Young man, now you have some idea of what it is to be a housewife. You should thank heaven that you don't have to bother with girls. I want to have peace, so I give them punch. I would gladly give you a glass—one sleeps so well after it—but no one dares go through the hallway door after ten o'clock; my Gabriel will not permit it. But you shall have some punch, nevertheless. There is a big hole in the door, stopped up with putty; I will push the putty out and put a funnel through the hole; you hold your waterglass under it, and I shall pour you some punch. Keep it a secret, even from my Gabriel. You must not worry him with household affairs."

And so Peer got his punch, and there was peace in Madam Gabriel's room, peace and quiet in the whole house. Peer went to bed, thought of his mother and grandmother, said his evening prayer, and fell asleep. What one dreams the first night one sleeps in a strange house has special significance, Grandmother had said. Peer dreamed that he took the amber heart, which he still constantly wore, laid it in a flowerpot, and it grew into a great tree, up through the ceiling and the roof; it bore thousands of hearts of silver and gold, so heavy that the flowerpot broke, and it was no longer an amber heart—it had become mold, earth to earth—gone, gone forever! Then Peer awoke; he still had the amber heart, and it was warm, warm against his own warm heart.

VI

Early in the morning the first study hours began at Herr Gabriel's. They studied French. At lunch the only ones present were the boarders, the children, and Madam. She drank her second cup of coffee here; her first she always took in bed. "It is so healthy when one is liable to spasms." She asked Peer what he had studied that day.

"French," he answered.

"It is an expensive language!" she said. "It is the language of diplomats and one used by distinguished people. I did not study it in my childhood, but when one is married to a learned man one gains from his knowledge, as one gains from his mother's milk. Thus, I have all the necessary words. I am quite sure I would know how to express myself in whatever company I happened to be."

Madam had acquired a foreign name by her marriage with a learned man. She had been baptized Mette after a rich aunt, whose heir she was to have been. She had got the name, but not the inheritance. Herr Gabriel rebaptized Mette as Meta, the Latin word for measure. At the time of her wedding, all her clothes, woolen and linen, were marked with the letters M. G., Meta Gabriel; but young Madsen, who was a witty boy, interpreted the letters M. G. to be a mark meaning "most good," and he added a big question mark in ink, on the tablecloths, the towels, and the sheets.

"Don't you like Madam?" asked Peer, when young Madsen made him privately acquainted with this joke. "She is so kind, and Herr Gabriel is so learned."

"She is a bag of lies!" said young Madsen; "and Herr Gabriel is a scoundrel. If I were only a corporal, and he a recruit, oh, how I would discipline him!" And a bloodthirsty expression came to young Madsen's face; his lips grew narrower than usual, and his whole face seemed one great freckle.

There were terrible words to hear, and they gave Peer a shock; yet young Madsen had the clearest right to think that way. It was a cruel thing on the part of parents and teachers that a fellow had to waste his best time, delightful youth, on learning grammar, names, and dates, which nobody cares anything about, instead of enjoying his liberty relaxing, and wandering about with a gun over his shoulder like a good hunter. "No, one has to be shut in and sit on a bench and look sleepily at a book; Herr Gabriel wants that. And then one is called lazy and gets the mark 'passable'; yes, one's parents get letters about it; that's why Herr Gabriel is a scoundrel."

"He gives lickings, too," added little Primus, who agreed with young Madsen. This was not very pleasant for Peer to hear. But Peer got no lickings; he was too grown-up, as Madam had said. He was not called lazy, either, for that he was not. He had his lessons alone. He was soon well ahead of Madsen and Primus.

"He has ability!" said Herr Gabriel.

"And one can see that he has been to dancing school!" said Madam.

"We must have him in our dramatic club," said the pharmacist, who lived more for the town's private theater than for his pharmacy. Malicious people applied to him the old stale joke that he must have been bitten by a mad actor, for he was completely insane about the theater.

"The young student was born for a lover," said the pharmacist. "In a couple of years he could be Romeo; and I believe that if he were well made up, and we put a little mustache on him, he could very well appear this winter."

The pharmacist's daughter—"great dramatic talent," said the father; "true beauty," said the mother—was to be Juliet; Madam Gabriel had to be the nurse, and the pharmacist, who was both director and stage manager, would take the role of the apothecary, which was small but of great importance. Everything depended on Herr Gabriel's permission for Peer to play Romeo. This had to be worked through Madam Gabriel; one had to know how to win her over—and this the pharmacist knew.

"You were born to be the nurse," he said, and thought that he was flattering her exceedingly. "That is actually the most important part in the play," he continued. "It is the comedy role; without it, the play would be too sad to sit through. No one but you, Madam Gabriel, has the quickness and life that should sparkle here."

All very true, she agreed, but her husband would surely never permit the young student to contribute whatever time would be required to play the part of Romeo. She promised, however, to "pump" him, as she called it. The pharmacist immediately began to study his part, and especially to think about his make-up. He wanted to look almost like a skeleton, a poor, miserable fellow, and yet a clever man—a rather difficult problem. But Madam Gabriel had a much harder one in "pumping" her husband to give his permission. He could not, he said, answer for it to Peer's guardians, who paid for his schooling and board, if he permitted the young man to play in tragedy. We cannot conceal the fact, however, that Peer had the greatest desire to do it. "But it won't work," he said.

"It's working," said Madam; "only let me keep on pumping." She would have given him punch, but Herr Gabriel did not like to drink it. Married people are often different; this is said without any offense to Madam.

"One glass and no more," she thought. "It elevates the mind and makes one happy, and that's what we ought to be—it is our Lord's will with us."

Peer was to be Romeo; that was pumped through by Madam. The rehearsals were held at the pharmacist's. They had chocolate and "genii'—that is to say, small biscuits. These were sold at the bakery, twelve for a penny, and they were so exceedingly small, and there were so many, that it was considered witty to call them genii.

"It is an easy matter to make fun," said Herr Gabriel, although he himself often gave nicknames to one thing and another. He called the pharmacist's house "Noah's ark, with its clean and unclean beasts," and that was only because of the affection which was shown by that family toward their pet animals. The young lady had her own cat, Graciosa, which was pretty and soft-skinned; it would lie in the window, in her lap, on her sewing work, or run over the table spread for dinner. The wife had a poultry yard, a duck yard, a parrot, and canary birds—and Polly could outcry them all together. Two dogs, Flick and Flock, walked about in the living room; they were by no means perfume bottles, and they lay on the sofa and on the family bed.

The rehearsal began, and it was only interrupted a moment by the dogs slobbering over Madam Gabriel's new gown, but that was out of pure friendship and it did not spot it. The cat also caused a slight disturbance; it insisted on giving its paw to Juliet and sitting on her head and wagging its tail. Juliet's tender speeches were divided equally between cat and Romeo. Every word that Peer had to say was exactly what he wished to say to the pharmacist's daughter. How lovely and charming she was, a child of nature, who, as Madam Gabriel expressed it, was perfect for the role. Peer began to fall in love with her.

There surely was instinct or something even higher in the cat. It perched on Peer's shoulders as if to symbolize the sympathy between Romeo and Juliet. With each successive rehearsal Peer's fervor became stronger, more apparent; the cat became more confidential, the parrot and the canary birds noisier; Flick and Flock ran in and out.

The evening of the performance came, and Peer was a perfect Romeo; he kissed Juliet right on her mouth.

"Perfectly natural!" said Madam Gabriel.

"Disgraceful!" said the Councilor, Herr Svendsen, the richest citizen and fattest man in the town. The perspiration poured from him; it was warm in the house, and warm within him as well. Peer found no favor in his eyes. "Such a puppy!" he said; "a puppy so long that one could break him in half and make two puppies of him."

Great applause—and one enemy! That was having good luck. Yes, Peer was a Lucky Peer. Tired and overcome by the exertions of the evening and the flattery shown him, he went home to his little room. It was past midnight; Madam Gabriel knocked on the wall.

"Romeo! I have some punch for you!"

And the funnel was put through the hole in the door, and Peer Romeo held his glass under.

"Good night, Madam Gabriel."

But Peer could not sleep. Everything he had said, and particularly what Juliet had said, buzzed through his head, and when he finally fell asleep he dreamed of a wedding—a wedding with Miss Frandsen! What strange things one can dream!

VII

"Now get that play-acting out of your head," said Herr Gabriel the next morning, "and let's get busy with some science."

Peer had come near to thinking like young Madsen, that a fellow was wasting his delightful youth, being shut in and sitting with a book in his hand. But when he sat with his book, there shone from it so many noble and good thoughts that Peer found himself quite absorbed in it. He learned of the world's great men and their achievements; so many had been the children of poor people: Themistocles, the hero, son of a potter; Shakespeare, a poor weaver's boy, who as a young man held horses outside the door of the theater, where later he was the mightiest man in poetic art of all countries and all time. He learned of the singing contest at Wartburg, where the poets competed to see who would produce the most beautiful poem—a contest like the old trial of the Grecian poets at the great public feasts. Herr Gabriel talked of these with especial delight. Sophocles in his old age had written one of his best tragedies and won the award over all the others. In this honor and fortune his heart broke with joy. Oh, how blessed to die in the midst of one's joy of victory! What could be more fortunate! Thoughts and dreams filled out little friend, but he had no one to whom he could tell them. They would not be understood by young Madsen or by Primus—nor by Madam Gabriel, either; she was either in a very good humor, or was the sorrowing mother, in which case she was dissolved in tears.

Her two little girls looked with astonishment at her. Neither they nor Peer could discover why she was so overwhelmed with sorrow and grief.

"The poor children!" she said. "A mother is always thinking of their future. The boys can take care of themselves. Caesar falls, but he gets up again; the two older ones splash in the water tub; they ought to be in the navy, and would surely marry well. But my two little girls! What will their future be? They will reach the age when the heart feels, and then I am sure that whoever each of them falls in love with will not be at all after Gabriel's liking; he will choose someone they'll despise, and that will make them so unhappy. As a mother, I have to think about these things, and that is my sorrow and grief. You poor children! You will be so unhappy!" she wept.

The little girls looked at her. Peer looked at her and felt rather sad; he could think of nothing to say, so he returned to his little room, sat down at the old piano, and tones and fantasies came forth as they streamed through his heart.

In the early morning he went to his studies with a clear mind and performed his duties, for someone was paying for his schooling. He was a conscientious, right-minded fellow. In his diary he recorded each day what he had read and studied, and how late he had sat up playing the piano—always mutely, so that he wouldn't awaken Madam Gabriel. It never said in his diary, except on Sunday, the day of rest, "Thought of Juliet," "Was at the pharmacist's," "Wrote a letter to Mother and Grandmother." Peer was still Romeo and a good son.

"Very industrious!" said Herr Gabriel. "Follow that example, young Madsen! Or you'll fail!"

"Scoundrel!" said young Madsen to himself.

Primus, the Dean's son, suffered from sleeping sickness. "It is a disease," said the Dean's wife; he was not to be treated with severity.

The deanery was only eight miles away; wealth and comfort were there.

"That man will die a bishop," said Madam Gabriel. "He has good connections at the court, and the Deaness is a lady of noble birth. She knows all about heraldry—that means coats of arms."

It was Whitsuntide. A year had passed since Peer came to Herr Gabriel's house. He had gained much knowledge, but his voice had not come back; would it ever come?

The Gabriel household was invited to the Dean's to a great dinner and a ball later in the evening. A good many guests came from the town and from the manor houses about. The pharmacist's family was invited; Romeo would see his Juliet, perhaps dance the first dance with her.

The deanery was a well-kept place, whitewashed, and without any manure heaps in the yard, and it had a dovecot painted green, around which twined an ivy vine. The Deaness was a tall, corpulent woman; "Athene, Glaucopis," Herr Gabriel called her; "the blue-eyed," not "the ox-eyed," as Juno was called, thought Peer. There was a certain distinguished kindness about her, and an effort to have an invalid look; she probably had sleeping sickness just like Primus. She was in a light-blue silk dress and wore great curls; the one on the right side was fastened with a large medallion portrait of her great-grandmother, a general's wife, and the one on the left with an equally large bunch of grapes made of white porcelain.

The Dean had a ruddy, plump face, with shining white teeth, well suited to biting into a roast fillet. His conversation always consisted of anecdotes. He could converse with everybody, but no one ever succeeded in carrying on a conversation with him.

The Councilor, too, was there, and among the strangers from the manors was Felix, the merchant's son; he had been confirmed and was now a most elegant young gentleman, both in clothes and manners; he was a millionaire, they said. Madam Gabriel did not have courage enough to speak to him.

Peer was overjoyed at seeing Felix, who came to him in a very genial manner and said that he had brought greetings from his parents, who read all the letters Peer wrote home to his mother and grandmother.

The dancing began. The pharmacist's daughter was to dance the first dance with the Councilor; that was a promise she had made at home to her mother and to the Councilor. The second dance had been promised to Peer; but Felix came and took her with a good-natured nod.

"Permit me to have this one dance; the young lady will give her permission only if you say so."

Peer kept a polite face; he said nothing, and Felix danced with the pharmacist's daughter, the most beautiful girl at the ball. He also danced the next dance with her.

"You will grant me the supper dance?" asked Peer, with a pale face.

"Yes, the supper dance," she answered with her most charming smile.

"You surely will not take my partner from me?" said Felix, who stood close by. "That's not being very friendly. We two old friends from town! You say that you are so glad to see me. Then you must allow me the pleasure of taking the lady to supper!" And he put his arm around Peer and laid his forehead jestingly against him. "Granted, isn't it? Granted!"

"No!" said Peer, his eyes sparkling with anger.

Felix gaily raised his arms and set his elbows akimbo, as if he were trying to look like a frog ready to leap. "You are perfectly right, young man! I would say the same if the supper dance were promised me, sir!" He drew back with a graceful bow to the young lady.

But shortly after, when Peer stood in a corner and adjusted his necktie, Felix returned, put his arm around his neck, and with the most coaxing look, said, "Be bighearted! My mother and your mother and old grandmother will all say that it is just like you. I am leaving tomorrow, and I will be terribly bored if I do not take the young lady to supper. My own friend, my only friend!"

Peer, as his only friend, could not resist that; he personally led Felix to the young beauty.

It was bright morning of the next day when the guests drove away from the Dean's. The Gabriel household was in one carriage, and the whole family went to sleep, except Peer and Madam.

She talked about the young merchant, the rich man's son, who was really Peer's friend; she had heard him say, "*Skaal,* my friend! To Mother and Grandmother!" There was something so "uninhibited, gallant in him," she said; "one saw at once that he is the son of rich people, or a count's child. That, the rest of us can't acquire. One must bow to that!"

Peer said nothing. He was depressed all day. At night, when bedtime had come and he lay in bed, sleep was chased away, and he said to himself, "One has to bow; one has to please!" That's what he had done; he had obeyed the rich young fellow; "because one is born poor, he is placed under obligation and subjection to these richly born people. Are they then better than we? And why were they created better than we?"

There was something vicious rearing up in him, something that his grandmother would be grieved at. He thought of her. "Poor Grandmother! You have also known what poverty is. Why has God permitted that?" And he felt anger in his heart, and yet at the same time he was conscious of having sinned in thoughts and words against the good God. He was grieved to think he had lost his child's mind; and his faith returned, as wholesome and rich as before. Happy Peer!

A week later a letter came from Grandmother. She wrote in the only way she could, mixing up big letters and small letters, but all her heart's love was in everything, big and small, that concerned Peer:

My own sweet, blessed boy:
I am thinking of you; I am longing for you, and so is your mother. She is getting along well; she takes washing. And the merchant's Felix came up to see us yesterday, with a greeting from you. You had both been at the Dean's ball, and you had been such a gentleman; but that you will always be, and make your old grandmother and your hard-working mother happy. She has something to tell you about Miss Frandsen.

And then followed a postscript from Peer's mother:

Miss Frandsen is going to be married, the old thing. The bookbinder, Herr Hof, has been appointed court bookbinder, in accordance with his petition. He has a great new sign, "Court Bookbinder Hof." And she will become Madam Hof. It is an old love that does not rust, my sweet boy.

YOUR MOTHER

Second Postscript: Grandmother has knitted you six pairs of woolen socks; you will get them at the first opportunity. I am also sending you a pork pie, your favorite dish. I know that you never get pork at Herr Gabriel's, since his wife is so afraid of what I have difficulty in spelling—"trichines." You must not believe in these, but just go ahead and eat.

YOUR OWN MOTHER

Peer read the letter, and it made him happy. Felix was so good; what a great injustice he had done him! They had separated at the Dean's without saying good-by to each other.

"Felix is better than I," said Peer.

VIII

In a quiet life, one day slips into the next, and month quickly follows month. Peer was already in the second year of his stay at Herr Gabriel's, who with great earnestness and determination, though Madam called it obstinacy, insisted that he should not again go on the stage.

Peer received from the singing master, who monthly paid the stipend for his instruction and support, a serious reminder not to think of the stage as long as he was placed there. And he obeyed; but his thoughts frequently traveled to the theater at the capital—they carried him, as if by magic, onto the stage there, where he was to have appeared as a great singer. Now his voice was gone, and it did not return, which often deeply grieved him. Who could comfort him? Neither Herr Gabriel nor Madam, but our Lord surely could. Consolation comes to us in many ways. Peer found it in sleep; he was indeed a Lucky Peer.

One night he dreamed that it was Whitsunday, and he was out in the beautiful green forest, where the sun shone through the branches and where all the ground was covered with anemones and primrose. Then the cuckoo began, "Cuckoo!" "How many years shall I live?" asked Peer, for one always asks the cuckoo that, the first time in the year one hears it cuckoo; and the cuckoo answered, "Cuckoo!" but no more; it was silent.

"Shall I live only one more year?" asked Peer. "That is really too little. Be so good as to cuckoo again!" Then the bird began again, "Cuckoo! Cuckoo!" Yes, and it went on without stopping, and Peer cuckooed with it, as realistically as if he, too, were a cuckoo; but his notes were stronger and clearer. All the songbirds joined in the warbling. Peer sang their songs, but far more beautifully. He had all the clear voice of his childhood, and rejoiced in song; he was so happy at heart. And then he awoke, but with the assurance that the "soundboard" was still in him, that his voice still lived and, some bright Whitsun morning, would burst forth in all its freshness; and so he slept, happy in this assurance.

But in none of the following days, weeks, or months did he have any feeling of his voice returning.

Every bit of news he could get of the theater at the capital was a true feast for his soul; it was spiritual bread to him. Crumbs are also bread, and he received crumbs thankfully—the smallest bits of news.

There was a flax dealer's family living near the Gabriels'. The mother, a highly respectable housewife, lively and laughing, but without any acquaintance or knowledge of the theater, had been at the capital for the first time and was delighted with everything there, even with the people, who had laughed at all she had said, she assured—and that was very likely.

"Were you at the theater also?" asked Peer.

"That I was," replied the flax dealer's wife. "How I steamed! You should have seen me sit and steam in that heat!"

"But what did you see? What play?"

"I will tell you that," she said. "I shall give you the whole play. I was there twice. The first evening it was a talking play. Out came the princess—'Ahbe, dahbe! Abe, dabe!'—how she could talk! Next came a man—'Ahbe, dahbe! Abe, dabe!' And then down fell Madam. Now they began again. The prince—'Ahbe, dahbe! Abe, dabe!' Then down fell Madam. She fell down five times that evening. The second time I was there, it was all singing—'Ahbe, dahbe! Abe, dabe!' And then down fell Madam again. It so happened that a countrywoman was sitting next to me; she had never been in the theater, and thought the show was all over; but I, who now knew all about it, said that when I was there last, Madam fell down five times. The singing evening she only did it three times. Yes, there you have both the plays, as true to life as I saw them."

Was it tragedy she had seen, since she said that Madam always fell down? Then it dawned on Peer what she meant. The great theater curtain that fell between the acts had a large female figure painted on it, a Muse with the comic and the tragic masks. This was the Madam who fell down. That had been the real comedy; what they had said and sung had been only "Ahbe, dahbe! Abe, dabe!' to the flax dealer's wife; but it had been a great pleasure, and so it had been to Peer, too, and not less to Madam Gabriel, who had heard this recital of the plays. She had sat with an expression of astonishment and a consciousness of mental superiority, for the pharmacist had said that she, as the nurse, had "carried" Shakespeare's *Romeo and Juliet.* "Down fell the Madam," as explained by Peer, afterward became a witty byword in the house every time a child, a cup, or one or another piece of furniture fell on the floor in the house.

"That is the way proverbs and familiar sayings are created," said Herr Gabriel, who carried everything into the sphere of learning.

New Year's Eve, at the stroke of twelve, the Gabriels and their boarders stood, each with a glass of punch, the only one Herr Gabriel drank the whole year, because punch is bad for a weak stomach. They drank a toast, *"Skaal,"* to the new year, and counted the strokes of the clock, "One, two——" to the twelfth stroke. "Down fell the Madam!" they said.

The new year rolled up and rolled along. By Whitsuntide, Peer had been two years in the house.

IX

Two years were gone, but the voice had not returned. How would the future be for our young friend?

He could always be a teacher in a school, opined Herr Gabriel; there was a livelihood in that, though nothing to be married on; however, that hadn't entered Peer's mind, no matter how large a place in his heart the pharmacist's daughter had.

"Be a teacher!" said Madam Gabriel; "a schoolmaster! Then you'll be the most boring individual on earth, just like my Gabriel. No, you were born for the theater. Be the greatest actor in the world; that is something more than being a teacher."

An actor! Yes, that was the goal.

He mentioned this in a letter to the singing master; he told of his longing and his hope. He longed most eagerly for the great city, where his mother and grandmother lived; he had not seen them for two long years. The distance was only one hundred and twenty miles; by fast train, he could be there in six hours. Why had they not seen one another? That is easily explained. On his departure, Peer had given his promise to stay where he was being sent and not to think of a visit. His mother was busy enough with her washing and ironing; yet she had often thought of making the great journey, even if it would cost a good deal of money, but this never materialized. Grandmother had a horror of railways; to travel by rail was to tempt the Lord. Nothing could induce her to travel by steam; she was an old woman, and she was not going to travel until she traveled up to our Lord.

That she said in May, but in June the old woman would travel, and all alone, the one hundred and twenty long miles, to the strange town, to strange people, and all to get to Peer. It would be a big occasion, yet the most dismal one that could occur to Mother and Grandmother.

The cuckoo had said "Cuckoo!" without end when Peer had asked it the second time, "How many years shall I live?" His health and spirits were good, and the future looked bright. He had received a delightful letter from his fatherly friend, the singing master. Peer was to go home, and they would see what could be done for him—what course he should take now that his voice was still gone.

"Appear as Romeo!" said Madam Gabriel. "Now you are old enough for the lover's part and have some flesh on your bones. You don't need to use make-up."

"Be Romeo!" said the pharmacist and the pharmacist's daughter.

Many thoughts went through his head and heart. But "Nobody knows what tomorrow will bring."

He sat down in the garden that stretched out to the meadow. It was evening, and there was moonlight. His cheeks burned; his blood was on fire; the air brought a delightful coolness. Over the moor hung a mist that rose and sank and made him think of the dance of the elfin maidens. Then into his mind came the old ballad about Knight Olaf, who rode out to ask the guests to his wedding, but was stopped by the elfin maidens, who drew him into their dance and play and thereby caused his death. It was a piece of folklore, an old poem. The moonlight and the mist over the moor formed pictures of it this evening.

Peer was soon in a state of half dreaming, looking out upon it all. The bushes seemed to have shapes of both humans and beasts; they stood motionless, while the mist rose like a great waving veil. Peer had seen something like this in a ballet at the theater, when elfin maidens were represented whirling and waving with veils of gauze; but here it was far more charming and more wonderful. A stage as large as this, no theater could have; none had so clear an air, so shining a moonlight.

Right in front in the mist, there distinctly appeared a female shape; the one became three, and the three became many; hand in hand they danced; they were floating girls. The air bore them along to the hedge where Peer stood. They nodded to him; they spoke; it was like the sound of silver bells. They danced into the garden about him; they enclosed him in their circle. Without thought, he danced with them, but not their dance. He whirled about, as in the unforgettable vampire dance, but he didn't think of that; he really didn't think at all; he was completely overwhelmed by all the magnificent beauty he saw about him.

The moor was a sea, so deep and dark blue, with water lilies that were bright with all conceivable colors. Dancing over the waves, they carried him upon their veil to the opposite shore, where the old viking burial mound had thown aside its grassy turf and risen into a castle of clouds, but the clouds were of marble. Flowering trees of gold and costly stones twined about the mighty blocks of marble; each flower was a brilliantly colored bird that sang with a human voice. It was like a choir of thousands and thousands of happy children. Was it heaven, or was it Elfin Hill?

The castle walls moved; they glided toward each other. They closed about him. He was inside, and the world of man was outside. He then felt anguish, a strange fear, as never before. There was no exit to be found, but from the floor way up to the roof, and from all the walls, there smiled at him lovely young girls; they were so lifelike to look at, and yet he thought: Are they but paintings? He wanted to speak to them, but his tongue found no words; his speech was completely gone; not a sound came from his lips. Then he threw himself upon the earth, more miserable than he had ever been.

One of the elfin maidens approached him; surely she meant well, for she had taken the shape he would most like to see; she looked like the pharmacist's daughter; he was almost ready to believe that it was she, but soon he saw that she was hollow in back and had only a beautiful front—open in the back, with nothing at all inside.

"One hour here is a hundred years outside," she said. "You have already been here a whole hour. Everyone you know and love outside these walls is dead. Stay with us! Yes, stay you must, or the walls will squeeze you until the blood flows from your brow!"

And the walls trembled, and the air became like that of a glowing bake oven. He found his voice.

"O Lord, O Lord, have You forsaken me?" he cried from the depths of his soul.

Then Grandmother stood beside him. She took him in her arms; she kissed his brows; she kissed his mouth.

"My own sweet little one!" she said. "Our Lord will not forsake you; he forsakes none of us, not even the greatest sinner. God be praised and honored for all eternity!"

And she brought forth her psalmbook, the same one from which she and Peer had sung on many a Sunday. How her voice rang! How full were her tones! All the elfin maidens laid their heads down for a well-needed rest. Peer sang with Grandmother, as before he had sung every Sunday; how strong and powerful, yet how soft, his voice was all at once! The walls of the castle moved; they became clouds and mist. Grandmother walked with him out of the hill into the tall grass, where the glowworms gleamed and the moon shone. But his feet were so tired now he could not move them; he sank down on the turf; it was the softest bed; there he rested well and awoke to the sound of a psalm.

Grandmother sat beside him, sat by his bed in the little chamber in Herr Gabriel's house. The fever was over; health and life had returned. He had been deathly ill. They had found him in a faint on that evening down in the garden; a violent fever had followed. The doctor had thought that he would not get up from it, but would die, and they had written to his mother about it. She and Grandmother had wanted to, and felt they must, go to him; both had not been able to leave, and so the old grandmother had gone, and gone by the railway.

"That I would only do for Peer," she said. "I did it in God's name; otherwise I would have had to believe that I flew with the evil ones on a broomstick on Midsummer Eve!"

X

The journey home was made with a glad and light heart. Grandmother deeply thanked our Lord that Peer was to outlive her. She had delightful traveling companions in the railway carriage—the pharmacist and his daughter; they talked about Peer, and loved Peer as if they were of the same family. He was to become a great actor, said the pharmacist. His voice had now returned, too, and there was a fortune in such a throat as his.

What a pleasure it was to the grandmother to hear such words! She lived on them; she believed them thoroughly. And then they arrived at the station in the capital, where the mother met her.

"God be praised for the railway!" said Grandmother, "and be praised, too, that I quite forgot I was on it! I owe that to these splendid people." And she pressed the hands of the pharmacist and his daughter. "The railway is a blessed discovery when one is through with it! One is in God's hands!"

And then she talked of her sweet boy, who was out of all danger, and who lived with well-to-do people, who kept two servant girls and a manservant. Peer was like a son in the house, and on the same footing with two children of distinguished families, one of whom was a dean's son. The grandmother had lodged at the post inn; it was terribly expensive, but then she had been invited to Madam Gabriel's; there she had stayed five days, and they were simply wonderful people, particularly the wife; she had urged her to drink punch, splendidly made but strong.

With God's help, Peer would be strong enough to come home to the capital in a month.

"He must have become very elegant and spoiled," said the mother.

"He will not feel at home here in the garret. I am very happy that the singing master has invited him to stay with him. And yet," cried the mother, "it is awfully sad that one should be so poor that one's child cannot live in his own home!"

"Don't say those words to Peer!" said Grandmother. "You don't understand him as I do."

"But he must have food and drink, no matter how fine he has grown, and he shall not go hungry so long as I can move my hands. Madam Hof has told me that he can eat his dinner twice a week with her, now that she is well off. She has known both prosperity and hard times. She has told me herself that one evening, in the box at the theater where the old danseuses have a place, she felt sick. The whole day long she had only had water and a caraway-seed bun, and she was ill from hunger, and very faint. 'Water! water!' cried the others. 'No! Some food!' she begged. 'Food!' She needed something nourishing, and had not the least need of water. Now she has her own larder and a well-spread table."

Peer was still one hundred and twenty miles away, but happy in the thought that he would soon be in the city, and at the theater, with all his dear old friends, whom now he would know how to value. Happiness sang and resounded within him and all about him; there was sunshine everywhere, in this happy time of youth, the time of hope and expectation. Every day he grew stronger; his good spirits and his color returned. But Madam Gabriel became very moved as the time for departure drew near.

"You are on your way to greatness; and there will be many temptations, for you are handsome—that you have become in our house. You are natural, just as I, and that will help when temptations come. One must not be too sensitive or unruly—sensitive like Queen Dagmar, who on Sunday laced her silk sleeves and then had pangs of conscience over such a minor thing; it should take more than that to affect one. I would never have grieved as Lucretia did. What did she stab herself for? She was pure and honest; she knew that, and everybody in the town knew that. What could she do about the misfortune which I won't talk about but which you at your age understand perfectly well? So she gave out a shriek and took the dagger! That wasn't necessary at all. I would not have done it, and neither would you; we are both natural people; one should be natural at all times, and that you will continue to be in your artistic career. How happy I shall be to read about you in the papers! Perhaps sometime you will come to our little town and appear as Romeo, but I shall not be the nurse then. I shall sit in the parquet and enjoy myself."

Madam had a lot of washing and ironing done the week he went away; so Peer could go home with a clean wardrobe, as he had had on his arrival there. She drew a new, strong ribbon through his amber heart; that was the only thing she wanted as a "remembrance souvenir," but she did not get it.

From Herr Gabriel he received a French lexicon, the one he had used during his school hours, and it had marginal notes in Herr Gabriel's own hand. Madam Gabriel gave him roses and quaking grass. The roses would wither, but the grass would keep all winter if it wasn't put into the water but was kept in a dry place. And she wrote a quotation from Goethe on a kind of album leaf: *Umgang mit Frauen ist das Element guter Sitten.* She gave a translation of it: "Companionship with women is the foundation of good manners. Goethe."

"He was a great man!" she said. "If he had only not written *Faust,* for I don't understand it. Gabriel says so, too."

Young Madsen presented Peer with a not badly done drawing he had made of Herr Gabriel hanging from the gallows, with a birch rod in his hand, and the inscription, "A great actor's first conductor on the road of science." Primus, the Dean's son, gave him a pair of slippers, which the Deaness herself had made, but so large that Primus could not fill them for a year or two yet. Upon the soles was written in ink, "A reminder of a sorrowing friend. Primus."

Herr Gabriel's entire household accompanied Peer to the train.

"It shall not be said that you left us *sans adieu!*" said Madam, and she kissed him at the railway station.

"I am not bashful!" she said. "When one does not do a thing secretly, one can do anything!"

The signal whistle blew — young Madsen and Primus shouted hurrahs; the "small stuff" joined in with them; Madam dried her eyes and waved with her pocket handkerchief; Herr Gabriel said only the word, *"Vale!"*

The villages and stations flew by. Were the people in them as happy as Peer? He thought of that, praised his good fortune, and thought of the invisible golden apple that Grandmother had seen lying in his hand when he was a child. He thought of his lucky find in the gutter and, above all, of his new-found voice and of the knowledge he had now acquired. He had become altogether another person. He sang inwardly with happiness; it took great self-control for him to keep from singing aloud in the car.

Now the towers of the city appeared, and the buildings began to show themselves. The train reached the station. There stood Mother and Grandmother, and someone with them, Madam Hof, well bound, Court Bookbinder Hof's wife, born Frandsen. Neither in want nor in prosperity did she forget her friends. She had to kiss him as his mother and his grandmother did.

"Hof could not come with me," she said; "he is home at work, binding a set of collected works for the King's private library. You have your good luck, and I have mine. I have my Hof and my own fireside corner with a rocking chair. Twice a week you are to eat with us. You will see my life at home; it is a complete ballet!"

Mother and Grandmother hardly had an opportunity to talk to Peer, but they looked at him and their eyes shone with delight. Then he had to take a cab to get to his new home at the singing master's. They laughed and they cried.

"What a wonderful man he is!" said Grandmother.

"He still has such a kind face, just as when he went away," said Mother; "and that he will keep in the theater."

The cab stopped at the singing master's door, but the master was out; his old servant opened the door and showed Peer up to his room, where there were portraits of composers on the walls and a white plaster bust stood gleaming on the stove. The old man, a little dull, but trustworthiness itself, showed him the drawers in the bureau and hooks for him to hang his clothes on, and said he was very willing to shine his boots. Then the singing master arrived and welcomed Peer with a hearty handshake.

"This is the apartment!" he said. "Make yourself at home. You may use my piano in the living room. Tomorrow we will hear how your voice is. This is our castle warden, our housekeeper." And he nodded to the old servant. "All is in order. Carl Maria von Weber, on the stove there, has been whitened in honor of your coming; he was terribly dirty. But it isn't Weber that's up there, after all; it is Mozart. Where did he come from?"

"It is the old Weber," said the servant; "I carried him myself to the plasterer, and I brought him home again this morning."

"But this a bust of Mozart, and not a bust of Weber."

"Pardon me, sir," said the servant; "it is the old Weber, who has been cleaned. The master does not recognize him now that he has been whitened." The plasterer could verify that.

But at the plasterer's he got the answer that Weber had been broken to pieces, and so he had given him Mozart instead; it was all the same on a stove.

The first day Peer was not to sing or play, but when our young friend came into the parlor, where the piano stood, and the opera *Joseph* lay open upon it, he sang "My Fourteenth Spring," and sang with a voice that was as clear as a bell. There was something so sincere about it, so innocent, and yet so strong and full. The singing master's eyes were wet with tears.

"That's the way it should be," he said, "and it will be even better. Now we shall close the piano. You need to rest."

"But I have promised my mother and grandmother to visit them tonight." And he hurried away. The setting sun shone over the home of his childhood; the bits of glass in the wall sparkled; it was like a diamond castle. Mother and Grandmother were waiting for him in the garret, a good many steps up, but he flew up, three stairs at a time, reached the door, and was received with kisses and embraces.

It was clean and tidy there in the little room. There stood the stove, the old bear, and the chest of drawers with the hidden treasure from his hobby-horse days; on the walls hung the three familiar pictures, the King's portrait, a picture of our Lord, and Father's silhouette, cut out of black paper. It was an excellent side view of him, said Mother, but it would have been more like him if the paper had been white and red, for that he was. A wonderful man! And Peer was the very picture of him.

There was much to talk about, much to tell. They were to have a head-cheese, and Madam Hof had promised to visit them later in the evening.

"But how is it that those two old people, Hof and Miss Frandsen, ever thought of getting married?" asked Peer.

"It has been in their thoughts these many years," said Mother. "You know, of course, that he was married. Well, he did it, they say, to irritate Miss Frandsen, who looked down on him when she was in her high and mighty state. His wife was wealthy, but she was very old, but lively, and on crutches! She could not die; he was waiting for it. It would not have surprised me if, like the man in the story, he had every Sunday put the old lady out in the open air, so that our Lord could see her and remember to send for her."

"Miss Frandsen sat quietly by and waited," said Grandmother. "I never believed she would attain this. But last year Madam Hof died, and so Frandsen came to be the wife in the house."

At that moment in came Madam Hof.

"We were talking about you," said Grandmother; "we were talking about your patience and reward."

"Yes," said Madam Hof. "It did not come in my youth, but one is always young enough, when one's health is good, says my Hof. He has the most charming flashes of wit. We were old, fine works, he says, both in one volume, and with a gilt top. I am so happy with my Hof and my corner by the fireside. A porcelain stove! There a fire is started in the evening, and it keeps warm all the next day. It is such a joy. It is as in the ballet of Circe's island. Do you remember me as Circe?"

"Yes, you were charming!" said Grandmother. "But how a person can change!" That was not at all said impolitely, and was not so taken. Then came the headcheese and the tea.

The next morning Peer paid a visit to the merchant's. The lady met him, pressed his hand, and asked him to take a seat by her. During their conversation he expressed his great gratitude; he knew that the merchant was his secret benefactor. The lady did not know it. "But it is like my husband," she said. "It is not worth talking about."

The merchant was almost angry when Peer mentioned this. "You are on the wrong track altogether," he said, as he closed the conversation and walked away.

Felix was a student and was to have a diplomatic career.

"My husband calls it madness," said the lady. "I have no opinion. Providence takes care of such things."

Felix did not show himself, for he was taking a lesson at his fencing master's.

At home Peer told how he had thanked the merchant, but that he would not receive his thanks.

"Who told you that he was, what you call him, your benefactor?" asked the singing master.

"My mother and my grandmother did," answered Peer.

"Well, then it must be he."

"You know about it?" said Peer.

"I know, but you will not find out from me. And from now on, we shall sing an hour here at home every morning."

XI

Once a week there was quartet music. Ears, soul, and thought were filled with the grand musical poems of Beethoven and Mozart. It had been a long time since Peer had heard good and well-played music. It was as if a kiss of fire traveled down his spine and shot through all his nerves. His eyes filled with tears. Every musical evening here at home was a festive evening to him, which made a deeper impression upon him than any opera at the theater, where something always disturbs one or imperfections are revealed. Sometimes the words do not come out right; they are so smoothed down in the singing that they are as intelligible to a Chinese as to a Greenlander; and sometimes the effect is weakened by faults in dramatic expression, and by a full voice sinking in places to the power of a music box or drawling out false tones. Lack of truthfulness in stage settings and costumes also is to be observed. All this was absent from the quartet. The music poems rose in all their grandeur; costly hangings decorated the walls in the concert room; here he was in the world of music, which its masters had created.

One evening, Beethoven's "Pastoral" Symphony was given by a great orchestra in the big public music hall. It was the andante movement, "the scene by the brook," that particularly, and with a strange power, stirred and excited our young friend. It carried him into the living, fresh woods; the lark and the nightingale rejoiced, and the cuckoo sang there. What beauty of nature; what a wellspring of refreshment there was! From this hour he knew within himself that it was the picturesque music, in which nature was reflected and the emotions of human hearts were set forth, that struck deepest into his soul. Beethoven and Haydn became his favorite composers.

He often spoke with the singing master about this, and with each conversation the two became closer friends. How rich in knowledge this man was, as inexhaustible as Mimir's* well. Peer listened to him; just as eagerly as he had to Grandmother's fairy tales and stories as a little boy, he now listened to those of the world of music, and came to know what the forest and the sea told, what sounds in the old giant mounds, what every bird sings with its bill, and what the flower silently exhales in fragrance.

The hour devoted to his singing lesson every morning was an hour of true delight for master and pupil; every little song was sung with freshness, expression, and simplicity; most charmingly did he sing the Schubert series of *Travel Songs*. Both the melodies and the words were heard to their full advantage; they blended together; they exalted and illumined one another, as is fitting. Peer was undeniably a dramatic singer. His ability showed progress each month, each week, day by day.

Our young friend grew in a wholesome, happy way, knowing no want or sorrow. His was a rich and wonderful life, with a future full of blessings before him. His trust in mankind was never deceived; he had a child's soul and a man's endurance, and everywhere he was received with gentle eyes and a kind welcome. Day by day the relations between him and the singing master grew more heartfelt and confidential; the two were like an elder and a younger brother, and the younger had all the fervor and warmth of a young heart, which was understood and returned in full measure by the elder.

The singing master's personality was characterized by a southern ardor, and one saw at once that this man could hate vehemently or love passionately, and, fortunately, this last governed in him. He was, moreover, so situated by a fortune his father had left him that he did not need to work, unless it interested and pleased him to do so. Secretly he did a great deal of good in a sensible way, but didn't want people to thank him or to talk about it.

"If I have done anything," he said, "it was because I could and should have done it. It was my duty."

*In Scandinavian mythology, a giant who, drinking the waters from the well at the foot of the world ash, knows past and future.

His old servant, "our warden," as he called him in jest, talked only with half a voice when he gave expression to his opinion about the master of the house. "I know what he has given away and done during years and days, and yet I don't know the half! The King ought to give him a star to wear on his breast. But he would not wear it; he would be furious, if I know him, should he be honored for his kind deeds. He is happy, more so than the rest of us, in whatever faith he has. He is just like a man out of the Bible."

And to that the old fellow gave additional emphasis, as if Peer could have some doubt.

He felt and understood well that the singing master was a true Christian in good deeds, an example for everyone; yet the man never went to church, and when Peer one day mentioned that the following Sunday he was going with his mother and his grandmother to our "Lord's table" and asked if the singing master ever did the same, the answer was, "No!" It seemed as if he wanted to say something more, as if, indeed, he had something to confide to Peer, but nothing was said.

One evening he read aloud from the newspaper about the beneficence of a couple of men, and that led him to speak of good deeds and their reward.

"When one does not think of it, it is sure to come. The reward for good deeds is like dates that are spoken of in the Talmud; they ripen late and then are sweet."

"Talmud?" asked Peer. "What sort of book is that?"

"A book," was the answer, "from which more than one seed of thought has been implanted in Christianity."

"Who wrote that book?"

"Wise men in the earliest times, wise men in various nations and religions. Here wisdom is preserved in a few words, as in Solomon's Proverbs. What kernels of truth! One reads here that men round about the whole earth, in all the centuries, have always been the same. 'Your friend has a friend, and your friend's friend has a friend; be discreet in what you say!' is found here. It is a piece of wisdom for all times. 'No one can jump over his own shadow!' is here, too, and, 'Wear shoes when you walk over thorns!' You ought to read this book. You will find in it the proof of culture more clearly than you will find it in the layers of the earth. For me, as a Jew, it is, moreover, an inheritance from my fathers."

"Jew?" said Peer. "Are you a Jew?"

"Did you not know that? How strange that we should not have spoken of it before today!"

Mother and Grandmother knew nothing about it, either; they had never thought anything about it, but always had known that the singing master was an honorable, wonderful man. It was through God's guidance that Peer had met him on his way; next to our Lord he owed him all his good fortune.

And now the mother divulged a secret that she had carried faithfully a few days only and that, under the pledge of secrecy, had been told her by the merchant's wife. The singing master must never know that this was revealed; it was he who had paid for Peer's support and education at Herr Gabriel's. From the evening when, at the merchant's house, he had heard Peer sing the ballet *Samson,* he alone had been his real friend and benefactor, but in secret.

XII

Madam Hof was expecting Peer at her house, and now he arrived there.

"Now you will meet my Hof," she said, "and you will meet my fireside corner. I never dreamed of this when I danced in *Circe* and *The Rose Elf in Provence*. Indeed, there are not many now who think of that ballet and of little Frandsen. *Sic transit gloria* in the moon! — that's what my Hof, who is a witty fellow, calls it in Latin, and he uses that phrase when I talk about my time of glory. He likes to poke fun at me, but he does it with a good heart."

The "fireside corner" was an inviting room with a low ceiling, a carpet on the floor, and portraits suitable for a bookbinder to have. There were pictures of Gutenberg, and of Franklin, of Shakespeare, Cervantes, Molière, and the two blind poets, Homer and Ossian. Lowest down hung one, enclosed in glass and a broad frame, of a danseuse, cut out of paper, with great gold spangles on a dress of gauze, the right leg lifted toward heaven, and with a verse written beneath:

> Who captures all hearts by her dancing?
> Who wears her wreath of art entrancing?
> Miss Emilie Frandsen!

It was written by Hof, who wrote charming verse, especially comic verse. He had clipped the picture out himself and pasted and sewed it before he had married his first wife. For many years it had lain in a drawer; now it was displayed here in the poet picture gallery — "my fireside corner," as Madam Hof called her little room. Here Peer and Hof were introduced to each other.

"Isn't he a wonderful man?" she said to Peer. "To me he is just the most wonderful."

"Yes, on Sunday, when I am well bound in my new clothes," said Herr Hof.

"You are wonderful without any binding," she said, and then she tipped her head down as if she realized that she had spoken a little too childishly for one of her age.

"Old love does not rust," said Herr Hof. "An old house on fire burns down to the ground."

"It is as with the phoenix bird," said Madam Hof; "one rises up young again. Here is my paradise. I don't care to be any other place — except for an hour or so at your mother's and grandmother's."

"And at your sister's," said Herr Hof.

"No, Angel Hof; that is no longer a paradise. I must tell you, Peer, they live in small circumstances, and amid big complications. One doesn't know what he dares say in that house. One dare mention the word 'darky,' for the eldest daughter is engaged to one who has some Negro blood in him. One doesn't dare say 'hunchback,' for that one of the children is. One doesn't dare talk about 'deficit' — my brother-in-law has been involved in such a mishap. One doesn't even dare say that he has been driving in the wood; wood has an ugly sound, for Wood was the name of the fellow who broke his engagement with the youngest daughter. I don't like to go out and sit and keep my mouth shut. If I don't dare talk, I want to be in my own house and sit in my fireside corner. Were it not too sinful, as they say, I would gladly ask our Lord to let us live as long as my fireside corner holds out, for here one grows better. Here is my paradise, and this my Hof has given me."

"She has a gold mill in her mouth," he said.

"And you have gold grains in your heart," she said.

> Grind, grind what the bag will hold.
> Emilie is as pure as gold!

he said, as she tickled him under the chin,

"He wrote that verse at this very moment! It's good enough to be printed!"

"Yes, and handsomely bound!" he said.

That's how these two old folks amused each other.

A year passed before Peer began to study a role at the theater. He chose *Joseph,* but he exchanged it for the role of George Brown in the opera *The White Lady.* He quickly learned the words and music, and from Walter Scott's novel, which had furnished the material for the opera, he obtained a clear, full picture of the young, spirited officer who visits his native hills and comes to his ancestral castle without knowing it; an old song awakens recollections of his childhood; luck is with him, and he wins a castle and a wife.

What he read became like something he himself had lived — a chapter of his own life's story. The richly melodious music was entirely in keeping. A long, long time passed before the first rehearsals began. The singing master did not think that there was any hurry for him to make his appearance, but finally the day to start arrived. He was not merely a singer; he was an actor, and his whole personality was thrown into the role. The chorus and the orchestra applauded him loudly at the outset, and the opening night was looked forward to with the greatest expectation.

"One can be a great actor in a dressing gown at home," said a good-natured companion, "can be very great by daylight, but only so-so before the footlights in a packed house. Time will tell."

Peer had no fear, but had a burning desire for the eventful evening. The singing master, on the contrary, was extremely nervous. Peer's mother had not the courage to go to the theater; she would be ill with fear for her dear boy. Grandmother was sick and must stay at home, the doctor had said; but the faithful friend, Madam Hof, promised to bring news the very same evening of how it all went. She should and would be at the theater, even if she were dying.

How long that evening was! How the three or four hours stretched into eternity! Grandmother sang a psalm and prayed with Mother to the good God for their little Peer, that he might this evening also be Lucky Peer. The hands of the clock moved slowly.

"Now Peer is beginning," they said. "Now he is in the middle. Now he has finished." The mother and grandmother looked at each other, but they didn't say another word.

In the streets there was the rumbling of carriages; people were driving home from the theater. The two women looked down from the window; the people who were passing talked in loud voices; they had come from the theater; what they knew would bring either gladness or sadness up into the garret of the merchant's house.

At last someone came up the stairs. Madam Hof burst in, followed by her husband. She flung herself about the neck of the mother and grandmother, but didn't say a word. She wept and sobbed.

"Lord God!" said Mother and Grandmother. "How did everything go for Peer?"

"Let me weep!" said Madam Hof, who was so moved, so overcome. "I cannot bear it. Ah, you dear people, you cannot bear it, either!" and her tears streamed down.

"Have they hissed him off?" cried Mother.

"No, not that!" said Madam Hof. "They have — oh, that I should live to see it!"

Then both Mother and Grandmother wept.

"Be calm, Emilie," said Herr Hof. "Peer has conquered! He has triumphed! They clapped so much that the house nearly tumbled down! I can still feel it in my hands. It was one storm of applause from the first row to the gallery. The entire royal family clapped, too. Really, it was what one may call a red-letter day in the annals of the theater. It was more than talent — it was genius."

"Yes, genius!" said Madam Hof; "those are my words. God bless you, Hof, because you said them for me! You good people, never would I have believed that one could both sing and act like that, though I have lived through a theater's whole history." She cried again; Mother and Grandmother laughed, while tears still ran down their cheeks.

"Now sleep well on that," said Herr Hof. "Come along, Emilie. Good night, good night!"

They left the garret room and two happy people there. These two were not alone long. The door opened, and Peer, who hadn't promised to come before the next forenoon, stood in the room. He well knew how the old people had followed him in their thoughts, how ignorant, too, they still must be of his success, and when driving by the house with the singing master, he had stopped outside; with the light still burning up in the garret, he had felt he must go to them.

"Splendid, glorious, superb! All went well!" he exclaimed jubilantly, and kissed his mother and his grandmother. The singing master nodded with a beaming face and pressed their hands.

"And now he must go home and have some rest," he said. And the late visit was over.

"Our Father in heaven, how gracious and good You are!" said these two poor women. They talked far into the night about Peer. Everywhere in the great city people talked about him — the young, handsome, wonderful singer. Lucky Peer had gone that far.

XIII

With great fanfare, the morning paper told of the debut as something out of the ordinary, the drama critic reserving his privilege of expressing his opinion in a following issue. The merchant invited Peer and the singing master to a grand dinner. It was an observance — a testimony of his and his wife's interest in the young man, who had been born in the house, in the same year and on the very same day as their own son.

The merchant made a beautiful speech and proposed a toast to the singing master, the man who had found and polished this "precious stone," a name one of the prominent papers had called Peer. Felix sat by his side and was the soul of gaiety and affection. After dinner he brought out his own cigars; they were better than the merchant's. "He can afford to get them," said the latter; "he has a rich father." Peer did not smoke—a great fault, but one which could be remedied easily enough.

"We must be friends," said Felix. "You have become the lion of the town! All the young ladies, and the old ones, too, for that matter, you have taken by storm. You are lucky with everything. I envy you, especially in that you can go in and out over there at the theater, among all the little girls."

To Peer that did not seem anything very worthy of envy.

He received a letter from Madam Gabriel. She was in a state of ecstasy over the splendid accounts in the papers of his debut and over what he would become as an artist. She and the girls had drunk a toast to him with punch. Herr Gabriel also had a share in his honor, and was quite sure that he, beyond most others, could pronounce foreign words correctly. The pharmacist ran about town and reminded everyone that it was at their little theater they had first seen and admired his talent, which now for the first time was recognized in the capital. "The pharmacist's daughter would surely be irritated," added Madam, "now that he could propose to baronesses and countesses." The pharmacist's daughter had been in too much of a hurry and given in too soon, for a month earlier she had become betrothed to the fat Councilor. The banns had been published, and they were to be married on the twentieth of the month.

It was just the twentieth of the month when Peer received this letter. He felt as if he had been pierced through the heart. At that moment it became clear to him that, during all the vacillation of his soul, she had been his steadfast thought. He cared more for her than anyone else in the world. Tears came into his eyes; he crumpled the letter in his hand. It was the first great grief of heart he had known since he had heard, with Mother and Grandmother, that his father had fallen in the war. He thought that all happiness was gone, that his future would be empty and sorrowful. The sunlight no longer beamed from his youthful face; the sunshine was put out in his heart.

"He doesn't look well," said Mother and Grandmother. "It is the hard work at that theater."

They could both see that he was not the same as before, and the singing master saw it, too.

"What is the matter?" he said. "May I not know what troubles you?"

At that his cheeks turned red, his tears flowed afresh, and he told him about his sorrow, his loss.

"I loved her so deeply!" he said. "Only now, when it is too late, is it really clear to me!"

"Poor, grieved friend! I understand you so well. Weep freely, and as soon as you can, hold onto the thought that whatever happens in the world happens for the best. I, too, have known and felt what you now are feeling. I, like you, once loved a girl; she was intelligent, pretty, and fascinating; she was to be my wife. I could offer her good circumstances, and she cared for me; but one condition had to be met before the marriage; her parents required it, and she required it; I must become a Christian!"

"And that you would not?"

"I could not. One cannot, with an honest conscience, jump from one religion to another without sinning either against the one he takes leave of or the one he steps into."

"Have you no faith?" said Peer.

"I have the God of my fathers. He is a light for my feet and my understanding."

They sat in silence for a while. Then the hands of the singing master touched the keys, and he played an old folk song. Neither of them sang the words; perhaps each was deep in his own thoughts.

Madam Gabriel's letter was not read again. She never dreamed what sorrow it had brought.

A few days later a letter arrived from Herr Gabriel; he also wished to offer his congratulations and "a commission," which perhaps was the real reason for the letter. He asked Peer to buy a little porcelain figure, namely, Amor and Hymen, Love and Marriage. "It is all sold out here in town," he wrote, "but can easily be bought in the capital. The money is enclosed with this. Send the thing as quickly as possible; it is a wedding present for the Councilor, at whose marriage I was with my wife." Moreover, Peer was told: "Young Madsen never will become a student; he has left the house and has painted the walls with embarrassing remarks against the family. A bad subject, that young Madsen. *Sunt pueri pueri, pueri puerilia tractant!* i.e., 'Boys are boys, and boys do boyish things.' I translate it since you are not a Latin scholar." And with that Herr Gabriel's letter closed.

XIV

Frequently, when Peer sat at the piano, there sounded tones in it that stirred within his breast and head. The tones rose into melodies, which now and then carried words along with them; they could not be separated from the melodies. Thus several little poems that were rhythmic and full of feeling came into being. They were sung in a subdued voice. It was as if they, shy and afraid of being heard, were gliding along in loneliness.

> Everything passes, like the wind that blows;
> There is nothing lasting here.
> From your cheek will fade the rose,
> As well as smile and tear.
>
> Why be burdened with pain and grief?
> Away with your trouble and sorrow,
> For everything goes, fades like the leaf;
> Time and man pass with the morrow.
>
> All vanishes, everything goes,
> Your youth, your hope, and your friend.
> Everything passes, like the wind that blows.
> Never to return, only to end!

"Where did you get that song and melody?" asked the singing master, who by chance saw the words and music written down.

"It came of itself, that and all these. They will never fly farther into the world."

"A downcast spirit sets out flowers, too," said the singing master, "but a downcast spirit dares not give advice. Now we must set sail and steer toward your next debut. What do you say to Hamlet, the melancholy young Prince of Denmark?"

"I know Shakespeare's tragedy," said Peer, "but not yet Thomas' opera."

"The opera should be called *Ophelia,*" said the singing master. In the tragedy, Shakespeare has made the Queen tell us of Ophelia's death, and this has become the high light in the musical rendering. One sees before his eyes, and feels in the tones, what before we could learn only from the narrative of the Queen.

> There is a willow grows aslant a brook,
> That shows his hoar leaves in the glassy stream;
> There with fantastic garlands did she come
> Of crow-flowers, nettles, daisies, and long purples
> That liberal shepherds give a grosser name,
> But our cold maids do dead men's fingers call them:
> There, on the pendent boughs her coronet weeds
> Clambering to hang, an envious sliver broke;
> When down her weedy trophies and herself
> Fell in the weeping brook. Her clothes spread wide,
> And, mermaid-like, awhile they bore her up:
> Which time she chanted snatches of old tunes,
> As one incapable of her own distress . . .

The opera brings all this before our eyes. We see Ophelia; she comes out playing, dancing, singing the old ballad about the mermaid who entices men down beneath the river, and while she sings and plucks the flowers the same tones are heard from the depths of the stream; they sound in the voices of the chorus alluringly from the deep water; she listens; she laughs; she draws near the brink; she holds onto the overhanging willow and stoops to pluck the white water lilies; gently she glides out onto them and, singing, reclines on their broad leaves; she swings with them and is carried by the stream out into the deep, where, like the broken flower, she sinks in the moonlight, with the mermaid's melody welling forth about her.

In this great scene it is as if Hamlet, his mother, his uncle, and the dead, avenging king were created only to make the frame for this exquisite picture. We do not get Shakespeare's *Hamlet,* just as in the opera *Faust* we do not get Goethe's *Faust.* The speculative is no material for music. It is the love element in both these tragedies that elevates them to musical poems.

The opera of *Hamlet* was presented on the stage. The actress who had Ophelia's part was admirable, and the death scene was very effective, while Hamlet himself received sympathetic greatness on this evening, a fullness of character that grew with each scene in which he appeared. Furthermore, people were astonished at the extent of the singer's voice, at the freshness shown in the high as well as in the deep tones, and that he, with an equal brilliancy of power, could sing Hamlet and George Brown.

In most of the Italian operas the singing parts are each like a canvas on which the gifted singer or songstress puts his or her soul and genius, and with the varied, wavy colors creates the form the poem requires. How much more glorious they must be able to reveal themselves when the music is composed and carried out through thought centered upon the character; and this Gounod and Thomas have understood.

That evening at the theater, the character of Hamlet was given flesh and blood, and he raised himself into the position of the leading personage in the opera. Unforgettable was the night scene on the ramparts, where Hamlet, for the first time, sees his father's ghost—the scene in the castle, before the stage that has been erected, where he flings out the words that are drops of poison—the terrible meeting with his mother, where the father's ghost stands with a vengeful attitude before the son—and finally, what power in his voice, what tones, at Ophelia's death! She was the sympathetic lotus flower upon the deep, dark sea; its waves rolled with a mighty force into the soul of the spectators. That evening Hamlet became the leading figure. The triumph was complete. "From whom did that boy get it?" said the merchant's rich wife, as she thought of Peer's parents and his grandmother up in the garret. The father had been a warehouseman, good and honorable, and had fallen as a soldier on the field of honor—the mother, a washerwoman—but that does not give the son culture; he had grown up in a charity school—and how much knowledge could a provincial schoolmaster give him in a period of two years?

"It is genius!" said the merchant. "Genius—that is born of God's grace."

"Most certainly!" said his wife. And she folded her hands as she talked to Peer. "Do you really feel humble in your heart at what you have received? Heaven has been inconceivably gracious to you! Everything is given you. You do not know how gripping your Hamlet is! You simply cannot imagine it! I have heard that many great poets do not themselves know the glory of what they have given; the philosophers must reveal it to them. Where did you get your conception of Hamlet?"

"I have thought about the character, have read a great deal of what has been written about Shakespeare's work, and then on the stage I have tried to put life into the person and his surroundings. I give my share, and our Lord gives the rest."

"Our Lord!" she said with a half-reproving look. "Do not use that name in such a manner! He gave you ability, but you surely do not believe that He has anything to do with the theater and opera!"

"Yes, most certainly!" said Peer courageously. "He has a pulpit there, too, and most people listen more there than in church!"

She shook her head. "God is with us in everything good and beautiful, but let us be careful not to take His name in vain. It is a gift of grace for one to be a great artist, but it is still better to be a good Christian." Felix, she felt, would never have compared the theater and the church before her, and she was glad.

"Now you have fallen out with Mamma!" said Felix, laughing.

"That was so far from my thoughts!"

"Don't trouble yourself about it. You will get into her good graces again next Sunday when you go to church. Stand outside her pew, and look up to the right, for there, in the balcony pew, is a little face which is worth looking at—the widow baroness' charming daughter. This is a well-meant bit of advice, and I'll give you some more. You cannot live where you are now. Move into a larger apartment—with a decent stairway!—or, if you won't leave the singing master, then let him live in better style. He has means enough, and you have a pretty good income. You must give a party, too, an evening supper. I could give it myself, and will do so, but you can invite a few of the little dancing girls. You're a lucky fellow! But I believe, heaven help me, that you don't yet understand how to be a young man!"

Peer did understand it exactly, in his own way. With his full, warm, young heart, he was in love with art; she was his bride; she returned his love and lifted him into gladness and sunshine. The depression that had crushed him evaporated soon; gentle eyes looked upon him, and everyone met him in a friendly and cordial manner. The amber heart, which he still wore constantly on his breast, where Grandmother once had hung it, was certainly a talisman; yes, so he thought, for he was not quite free from superstition—a childlike faith, one may call it. Every nature that has genius in it has something of this, and looks to and believes in its star. Grandmother had shown him the power that lay in the heart, how it could draw things to itself. His dream had shown him a tree growing out of his amber heart, bursting through ceiling and roof, and bearing thousands of hearts of silver and gold; that surely meant that in the heart, in his own warm heart, lay the power of his art, whereby he had won and still would win the thousands upon thousands of hearts.

Between him and Felix there was undoubtedly a kind of sympathy, different as they were from each other. Peer assumed that the difference between them lay in that Felix, as the rich man's son, had grown up amid temptations and desires and could afford to taste them.

He had, on the contrary, been more fortunately placed as a poor man's son.

Both of these two children of the house had since gained prominence. Felix would soon be a gentleman in waiting to the royal court, and that is the first step toward becoming a chamberlain; then one has a gold key behind.* Peer, always lucky, already had the gold key of genius in his hand, though it was invisible—the key that opens all the treasures of the earth, and all hearts, too.

XV

It was still wintertime. The sleigh bells jingled, and the clouds carried snowflakes in them, but wherever a sunbeam burst through them, it announced that spring was near. In the young heart there was a fragrance and a song that flowed out in picturesque tones and found expression in words:

> The snow is still upon the earth;
> O'er the lake, skaters race in mirth.
> The trees are frost-rimmed, full of crows;
> But tomorrow perhaps the winter goes.
> The sun breaks through the sky of gray;
> Spring is in town; it's like a summer day.
> The willow's woolen gloves fall from the tree.

*When dressed for court, a chamberlain wears a gold key hanging by a ribbon on the back of his coat.

Strike up, musicians, for a merry spree!
Sing, little birds! All voices blend!
For now the winter has come to an end!

Oh, to be kissed by the warming sun!
Come, pluck violets and primrose — what fun!
It's as if the forest its breath were holding,
While in the night each leaf is unfolding.
The cuckoos sing; you know their song.
Hear them sing that your life will be long.
The world is young, so be young with the young!
With thankful heart and merry tongue,
Sing of spring! All voices blend!
For never does youth come to an end!

Never does youth come to an end!
Life on earth is a magic blend
Of sunshine and storm, joy and pain.
Within our hearts a world was lain;
It vanishes not like a shooting star,
For man is the image of God afar.

God and nature remain ever young.
Teach us, O Spring, the song you've long sung.
Every little bird sings; all voices blend —
For never does youth come to an end!

"That is a complete musical painting," said the singing master, "and well adapted for chorus and orchestra. It is the best yet of your emotional compositions. You certainly must learn thorough bass, although it is not your destiny to be a composer."

Young music friends soon introduced the song at a great concert, where it attracted attention but aroused no expectations. Our young friend's career was open before him. His greatness and importance lay not only in the sympathetic tones of his voice, but in his remarkable dramatic talent as well; this he had shown as George Brown and as Hamlet. He very much preferred the regular opera to the light opera. It was contrary to his sound, natural sense to go from song to talk and back to song.

"It is," he said, "as if one were going from marble steps onto wooden steps, sometimes even onto mere henroosts, and then back onto marble. The whole poem should live and breathe in its passage through tones."

The music of the future, as the new movement in opera is called, and for which Wagner, in particular, is a banner-bearer, had a defender and admirer in our young friend. He found here characters so clearly drawn, passages so full of thought, and the entire action characterized by forward movement, without any standstill or frequent recurrence of melodies. "It is most unnatural to include those long arias."

"Yes," said the singing master. "But how they, in the works of most of the great masters, stand out as a most important part of the whole! That is as it should and must be. If the lyric has a home in any place, it is in the opera."

And he mentioned in *Don Giovanni*, Don Ottavio's aria, "Tears, cease your flowing." "How much it is like a beautiful lake in the woods, by whose bank one rests and enjoys the music that streams through it! I bow to the ingenuity that lies in this new musical movement, but I do not dance with you before that golden calf. Either it is not your heart's real opinion that you express, or else it is not quite clear to you."

"I will appear in one of Wagner's operas," said our young friend. "If I cannot express my meaning in words, I will do so by my singing and acting!"

The choice made was Lohengrin, the young mysterious knight who, in the boat drawn by the swan, glides over the river Scheldt to fight for Elsa of Brabant. Who had ever sung and acted so well the first song of the meeting, the love song in the bridal chamber, and the song of farewell when the Holy Grail's white dove hovers about the young knight who came, conquered, and vanished? This evening was, if possible, another step forward in the artistic greatness and significance of our young friend; and to the singing master it was a step forward in the recognition of the music of the future.

"Under certain conditions," he said.

XVI

At the great yearly exhibition of paintings, Peer and Felix met one day, before the portrait of a pretty young lady, the daughter of the widow baroness, as the mother was generally called; the latter's salon was the rendezvous for the world of distinction and for everyone of importance in art and science. The young baroness was in her sixteenth year, an innocent, beautiful child. The picture was a good likeness and done with artistic skill.

"Step into the hall near by," said Felix. "There stands the young beauty herself with her mother."

They stood engrossed in viewing a painting of characterization. It represented a field where two young married people were riding on the same horse, holding onto one another. The chief figure, however, was a young monk who was looking at the two happy travelers. There was a sorrowful, dreamy look on the young man's face; one could read his thoughts in it, the story of his life — an aim missed, great happiness lost! Happiness in human love he had not won.

The elder baroness saw Felix, who respectfully greeted her and the beautiful daughter. Peer showed the same customary politeness. The widow baroness knew him immediately from having seen him on the stage, and after speaking to Felix she said some friendly, obliging words to Peer as she pressed his hand.

"I and my daughter belong to your admirers."

How perfectly beautiful the young girl was at this moment! She looked with her gentle, clear eyes almost gratefully at him.

"I see in my house," said the widow baroness, "so many of the most distinguished artists. We common people stand in need of a spiritual airing. You will be heartily welcome. Our young diplomat," she pointed to Felix, "will bring you along the first time, and afterward I hope that you will find the way yourself."

She smiled at him. The young girl reached out her hand naturally and cordially, as if they had long known each other.

Late in the autumn, on a cold, sleety evening, the two young men went to the Baroness' home, the two born in the rich merchant's house. It was weather for driving and not walking, for the rich man's son and the first singer on the stage. Nevertheless, they walked, well wrapped up, with galoshes on their feet and Bedouin caps on their heads.

It was like entering a complete fairyland to come from the raw air into this home that displayed such luxury and good taste. In the vestibule, before the carpeted stairs, there was a great display of flowers among bushes and fan palms. A little fountain splashed water into a basin, which was surrounded by tall callas.

The great salon was magnificently lighted, and a large part of the company had already gathered. It soon became very crowded. People stepped on silk trains and laces, amid the humming, sonorous mosaic of conversation, which, on the whole, was the least worth while of all the splendor there.

Had Peer been a vain fellow, which he was not, he could have imagined that it was a party for him, so cordial was the reception he received from the lady of the house and the beaming daughter. Young and elderly ladies, yes, and gentlemen, too, paid him many compliments.

There was music. A young author read a well-written poem. There was singing, and tactfulness was shown in that no one urged our young and honored singer to make the affair complete. The lady of the house was a most attentive hostess, brilliant and genial, in that elegant salon.

That was his introduction into the great world, and our young friend was soon also one of the select group in the choice family circle. The singing master shook his head and laughed.

"How young you are, dear friend," he said, "that it can please you to be with these people! In a way they are good enough, but they look down on us plain citizens. For some of them it is only a matter of vanity, an amusement, and for others a sort of sign of exclusive culture, when they receive into their circle artists and the lions of the day. These belong in the salon much as the flowers in a vase; they decorate and then they are thrown away."

"How harsh and unreasonable!" said Peer. "You do not know these people; you do not want to know them!"

"No," answered the singing master. "I don't feel at home among them, nor do you, either. That they all remember and know. They pat you and look at you just as they pat and look at a race horse that is expected to win a wager. You belong to another race than they. They will let you go when you are no longer in the fashion. Don't you understand that? You are not proud enough. You are vain, and you show that by seeking these people's company."

"How very differently you would talk and judge," said Peer, "if you knew the widow baroness and a few of my friends there."

"I shall not come to know them," said the singing master.

"When is the engagement to be announced?" asked Felix one day. "Is it the mother or the daughter?" And he laughed. "Don't take the daughter, for then you'll have all the young nobility against you, and I, too, shall be your enemy, and the deadliest one!"

"What do you mean?" asked Peer.

"You are indeed the favorite. You can go in and out at all hours. With the mother, you'd get money and belong to a good family."

"Stop your joking," said Peer. "There is nothing amusing to me in what you say."

"It is not supposed to be amusing," said Felix. "It is a most serious matter, for you surely wouldn't let her grace sit and weep and be a double widow!"

"Leave the Baroness out of this conversation," said Peer. "Make fun over me if you want to, but over me alone, and I will answer you!"

"No one will believe that it is a love match on your side," continued Felix. "She is a little outside of the line of beauty. True, one does not live on intellect alone!"

"I thought you had more refinement and good sense," said Peer, "than to talk so disrespectfully of a lady you should esteem and whose house you visit, and I can't bear to listen to you any longer!"

"What are you going to do about it?" asked Felix. "Do you want to fight?"

"I know that you have learned that, and I have not, but I can learn!" And he left Felix.

A couple of days later the two children of the house meet again, the son from the first floor and the son from the garret. Felix talked to Peer as if no break had come between them. He answered courteously, but curtly, too.

"What is the matter now!" said Felix. "We two were a little irritable recently, but one must have his little joke, which doesn't necessarily mean one is flippant. I don't like to bear a grudge, so let us forgive and forget."

"Can you forgive yourself the manner in which you spoke of a lady to whom we both owe great respect?"

"I spoke very frankly!" said Felix. "In high society one can also talk with a razor edge, but no one takes that very seriously; it is the salt for the tasteless, everyday fish dinner, as the poet calls it. We are all just a little spiteful. You can also let a drop fall, my friend, a little drop of innocence that smarts!"

Soon they were seen arm in arm again. Felix well knew that more than one pretty young lady who otherwise would have passed him by without looking at him now noticed him because he was walking with the "idol of the stage." The footlights always cast a glamour over the theater's hero and lover, and it still shines about him when he shows himself on the street, in daylight, though it is more or less extinguished then. Most of the artists of the stage are like swans; one should see them in their element, not on the paving stones or the public promenade. There are exceptions, however, and to these belonged our young friend. His personality off the stage never disturbed the conception one had of him as George Brown, or Hamlet, or Lohengrin. To many a young heart these poetical and musical figures were the artist himself and rose to the exaltation of their ideal. He knew that this was the case and found a sort of pleasure in it. He was happy in his art and with the talents he possessed; still a shadow would come over the happy young face, and then from the piano would sound the melody to the words:

> All vanishes, everything goes,
> Your youth, your hope, and your friend.
> Everything passes, like the wind that blows,
> Never to return, only to end!

"How mournful!" said the widow baroness. "You have good fortune in full measure. I know no one who is as fortunate as you."

"Call no one fortunate before he is in his grave, the wise Solon said," he replied, and smiled through his seriousness. "It would be wrong, a sin, if I were not thankful and happy in my heart. I am that. I am thankful for what is entrusted to me, but I myself set a different value on this than others do. It is a beautiful piece of fireworks that soars forth and then goes out! So it is with the stage actor's work. The everlasting shining stars may be forgotten for the meteors of a moment, but when these are extinguished, there is no lasting trace of them other than what may be found in old records. A new generation does not know and cannot picture to itself those who delighted their grand-fathers from the stage; the youth of today perhaps applauds the luster of brass as fervently and loudly as the old folks once did the luster of pure gold. Far more fortunately placed than the performing artist are the poet, the sculptor, the painter, and the composer. They often experience trying conditions in the struggle of life and miss the merited appreciation, while those who exhibit their works live in luxury and in arrogance born of idolatry.

"Let the mob stand and admire the bright-colored cloud and forget the sun; the cloud vanishes, but the sun shines and beams for new generations."

He sat at the piano and improvised with a richness of thought and a power such as he never before had shown.

"Wonderfully beautiful!" broke in the widow baroness. "It was as if I heard the story of a whole lifetime. You gave your heart's song in the music."

"I thought of the *Thousand and One Nights,*" said the young girl, "of the lamp of fortune, of Aladdin!" And she looked at him with innocent, tearful eyes.

"Aladdin!" he repeated.

That evening was the turning point in his life. A new chapter surely began.

What happened to him during this fast-moving year? His fresh color left his cheeks, though his eyes shone far more clearly than before. He passed sleepless nights, but not in wild orgies, in revels and drinking, as so many great artists. He became less talkative, but more cheerful.

"What is it that fills you so?" said his friend, the singing master. "You do not confide everything to me!"

"I think of how fortunate I am!" he replied. "I think of the poor boy! I think of — Aladdin!"

XVII

Measured by the expectations of a poor-born child, Peer now led a prosperous, pleasant life. He was so well off that, as Felix once had said, he could give a big party for his friends. He thought of it, and thought of his two earliest friends, his mother and his grandmother. For them and himself he provided a festival.

It was wonderful spring weather, and the two old people were going to drive with him out of town and see a little country place that the singing master had recently bought. As he was seating himself in the carriage, a woman came along humbly clad, about thirty years old; she had a note recommending her, signed by Madam Hof.

"Don't you know me?" she said. "Little Curlyhead, they used to call me. The curls are gone; there is so much that is gone; but there are still good people left. We two have appeared together in the ballet. You have become

better off than I. You have become a great man. I am now separated from
two husbands and no longer at the theater."

The note requested a sewing machine for her.

"In what ballet have we two performed together?" asked Peer.

"In the *Tyrant of Padua*," she replied. "We were both pages, in blue velvet
and berets. Don't you remember little Malle Knallerup? I walked right
behind you in the procession."

"And stepped on the side of my foot!" said Peer, laughing.

"Did I?" she said. "Then I took too long a step. But you have gone far
ahead of me. You have understood how to use your head instead of your
legs." And she looked coquettishly at him with her melancholy face, quite
sure she had paid him a witty compliment. Peer was a generous fellow. She
should have the sewing machine, he promised. Little Malle had indeed been
one of those who in particular had driven him out of the ballet into a more
fortunate career.

He was soon outside the merchant's house, and he then ascended the stairs
to his mother's and his grandmother's. They were in their best clothes, and by
chance they had a visit from Madam Hof, who was at once invited to drive
with them; whereupon she had quite a struggle with herself, which ended in
her sending a note to Herr Hof to inform him that she had accepted the invitation.

"Such fine greetings Peer gets!" she said.

"How stylishly we are driving!" said Mother.

"And in such a beautiful, comfortable carriage," said Grandmother.

Near the town, close to the royal park, stood a cozy little house, surrounded
by vines and roses, hazels and fruit trees. Here the carriage stopped. This was
the country house. They were received by an old woman well acquainted with
Mother and Grandmother; she had often helped them with their washing and
ironing.

The garden was inspected, and the house was inspected. There was one
particularly charming thing—a little glasshouse with beautiful flowers in it. It
was connected with the sitting room; the sliding door between could be
pushed right into the wall.

"That is just like a coulisse on the stage," said Madam Hof. "It moves by
hand. And one can sit here just as in a bird cage, with chickweed all about. It
is called a winter garden."

The bedroom was equally delightful in its way. There were long, heavy
curtains at the windows, soft carpets, and two armchairs so comfortable that
Mother and Grandmother must try them.

"One would get very lazy sitting in them," said Mother.

"One loses his weight," said Madam Hof. "Indeed, here you two music
people can rest comfortably after your theatrical labors. I have also known
what they are! Yes, believe me, I can still dream of doing high kicks, and Hof
does high kicks by my side! Is it not charming—'two souls and one thought'!"

"The air is fresher here, and there is more room, than in the two small
rooms up in the garret," said Peer with beaming eyes.

"That there is," said Mother. "Still, home is nice, too. There you were
born, my sweet boy, and there I lived with your father."

"It is better here," said Grandmother. "Here you have a whole mansion. I
do not begrudge you and that noble man, the singing master, this home of
peace."

"Then I do not begrudge you this, Grandmother, and you, my dear blessed mother! You two shall always live here, and not, as in town, walk up so many steps and be in such narrow and small quarters. You shall have a servant to help you and shall see me as often as in town. Are you happy about it? Are you content with it?"

"What is all this the boy stands here and says!" said Mother.

"The house, the garden—it's all yours, Mother, and yours, Grandmother! To be able to give you all this is what I have striven for. My friend the singing master has faithfully helped me with getting it ready."

"What is all this you are saying, child!" exclaimed the mother. "You want to give us a gentleman's mansion! You sweet boy! Yes, you would do it if you could!"

"I am serious," he said. "The house is yours and Grandmother's." He kissed them both, and they burst into tears. Madam Hof shed just as many. "It is the happiest moment of my life!" exclaimed Peer, as he embraced all three of them.

And now they had to see everything all over again, since it was their own. They now had that beautiful little glasshouse in which to put their five or six pot plants from the garret roof. Instead of a little cupboard, they had here a great roomy pantry, and the kitchen was a complete, warm little chamber. The chimney had an oven and cooking stove; it looked like a great, shining flatiron, said Mother.

"Now you have a fireside corner just like I have!" said Madam Hof. "This is magnificent! You have attained all that people can attain on this earth, and you, too, my own, popular friend!"

"Not all!" said Peer.

"The little wife will come along!" said Madam Hof. "I have her already for you! I feel sure I know who she is! But I shall keep my mouth shut. You wonderful man! Isn't all this like a ballet!" She laughed with tears in her eyes, and so did Mother and Grandmother.

XVIII

To write the text and music for an opera, and be the interpreter of his own work on the stage, was a great and happy aim. Our young friend had a talent in common with Wagner, in that he could construct the dramatic poem himself; but did he, like Wagner, have the fullness of musical emotion to create a musical work of any significance?

Courage and doubt alternated in him. He could not dismiss this persistent thought of his. For years and days it had shone in his mind as a picture of fancy; now it was a possibility, his life's goal. Many free fancies were welcomed at the piano as birds of passage from that Land of Perhaps. The little ballads and the characteristic spring song gave promise of the still undiscovered land of tone. The widow baroness saw in them the sign of promise, as Columbus saw it in the fresh green weed that the currents of the sea bore toward him before he saw the land itself on the horizon.

Land was there! The child of fortune should reach it. A word thrown out was the seed of thought. She, the young, pretty, innocent girl, had spoken the word—Aladdin. Our young friend was a child of fortune like Aladdin; it shone within him.

With understanding and delight he read and reread the beautiful Oriental story. Soon it took dramatic form; scene after scene grew into words and music, and the more it grew, the richer the music thoughts became. At the close of the work it was as if the well of tone were now for the first time pierced, and all the abundant fresh water streamed forth. He then recomposed his work, and in stronger form, after months, arose the opera *Aladdin*.

No one knew of this work; no one had heard as much as a single bar of it, not even the most sympathetic of all his friends, the singing master. No one at the theater, when in the evening the young singer entranced his public with his voice and his masterful acting, had any idea that the young man who seemed so to live and breathe in his role lived far more intensely—yes, and for hours afterward lost himself in a mighty work of music that poured from his own soul.

The singing master had not heard a bar of the opera *Aladdin* before it was put on his table for examination, complete in notes and text. What judgment would be passed? Assuredly a strong and just one. The young composer passed from highest hope to the thought that the whole thing was only a selfdelusion.

Two days passed by, and not a word was exchanged about this important matter. Finally, the singing master stood before him with the score in his hands, which he now knew. There was a peculiar seriousness spread over his face that did not indicate his thoughts.

"I had not expected this," he said. "I had not believed if of you. Indeed, I do not yet have a clear judgment, so I dare not express it. Here and there there are faults in the instrumentation, faults that can easily be corrected. There are single things, bold and novel, that one must hear under proper conditions. As there is in Wagner a certain influence of Carl Maria von Weber, so there is noticeable in you a breath of Haydn. That which is new in what you have given is still rather remote to me, and you yourself are too near for me to be the right judge. I would rather not judge. I will embrace you!" he burst out, beaming with happiness. "How have you been able to do this!" And he embraced him in his arms. "Happy man!"

A rumor soon spread through the city, via the newspapers and gossip, about the new opera by the popular singer.

"He's a poor tailor who cannot put together a child's coat out of the scraps left over on his board," said one and another.

"Write the text, compose it, and sing it himself!" was also said. "That is a three-storied genius. But he really was born still higher—in a garret!"

"There are two at it, he and the singing master," they said. "Now they'll begin to beat the signal drum of the partnership of mutual admiration!"

The opera was given out for study. Those who took part would not give any opinion. "It shall not be said that it is judged from the theater," they remarked; and almost everyone put on a serious face that did not show any expectation.

"There are a good many horns in the piece," said a young trumpeter. "If only he doesn't run a horn into himself!"

"It has genius; it is brilliant, full of melody and character!" That was also said.

"Tomorrow at this time," said Peer, "the scaffold will be raised. The judgment is, perhaps, already passed."

"Some say that it is a a masterpiece," said the singing master, "others, that it is a mere patchwork."

"And where lies the truth?"

"Truth!" said the singing master. "Yes, tell me where. Look at that star up there. Tell me exactly where its place is. Shut one eye. Do you see it? Now look at it with the other only. The star has shifted its place. When each eye in the same person sees so differently, how differently must the great multitude see!"

"Happen what may," said our young friend, "I must know my place in the world, understand what I can and must create, or give up."

The evening came, the evening of decision. A popular artist was to be exalted to a higher place or humiliated in his gigantic, vain effort. Success or failure! The matter concerned the whole city. People stood all night in the street before the ticket office, to obtain seats. The house was crammed full. The ladies came with great bouquets; would they be carried home again or thrown at the victor's feet?

The widow baroness and the young, beautiful daughter sat in a box above the orchestra. There was a stir in the audience, a murmuring, a movement, which stopped at once as the leader of the orchestra took his place and the overture began.

Who does not remember Hanselt's piece, *"Si l'oiseau j' étais,"* which is like a twittering of birds? This was somewhat similar; there were jubilant, playing children, happy child voices mingling; the cuckoo cuckooed with them; the thrush sang. It was the play and jubilation of the innocent child mind—the mind of Aladdin. Then a thunderstorm rolled in; Noureddin displayed his power; a flash of deadly lightning split the mountain. Gentle, beckoning tones followed; a sound came from the enchanted grotto, where the lamp shone in the petrified cavern, while the wings of mighty spirits brooded over it. Now, in the tones of a French horn, sounded a psalm, which was as gentle and soft as if it were coming from the mouth of a child; a single horn was heard, and then another; more and more were blended in the same tones and rose in fullness and power, as if they were the trumpets of the judgment day. The lamp was in Aladdin's hand, and then there swelled forth a sea of melody and grandeur such as only the ruler of spirits and the masters of music can create.

The curtain rolled up in a storm of applause that sounded like a fanfare under the conductor's baton. A grown-up, handsome boy was playing; he was so big and yet so innocent; it was Aladdin, who leaped about among the other boys. Grandmother would at once have said, "That is Peer as he played and jumped about between the stove and the chest of drawers at home in the garret. He is not a year older in his soul!"

With what faith and sincerity he sang the prayer Noureddin bade him offer before he stepped down into the rocky cavern to obtain the lamp! Was it the pure, religious melody or the innocence with which he sang that enchanted all the listeners? The applause would not cease.

It would have been a profane thing to have repeated the song. It was demanded, but it was not given. The curtain fell; the first act was over.

Every critic was speechless; people were overcome with gladness and, in their appreciation, were certain of enjoying the rest of the evening.

A few chords sounded from the orchestra, and the curtain rose. The strains of music, as in Gluck's *Armida* and Mozart's *Magic Flute,* arrested the attention of everyone as the scene was disclosed, the scene in which Aladdin stood in the wonderful garden. Soft, subdued music sounded from flowers and stones, from springs and deep caverns, different melodies blending in one great harmony. An air of spirits was heard in the chorus; it was now far off, now near, swelling in might and then dying away. Arising from this harmony, and supported by it, was the song monologue of Aladdin — what one indeed calls a great aria, but so entirely in keeping with character and situation that it was a necessary dramatic part of the whole. The resonant, sympathetic voice, the intense music of the heart, subdued all listeners and seized them with a rapture that could not rise higher when he reached for the lamp of fortune that was embraced by the song of the spirits.

Bouquets rained down from all sides; a carpet of living flowers was spread out before his feet.

What a moment of life for the young artist — the highest, the greatest! A mightier one could never again be granted him, he felt. A wreath of laurel touched his breast and fell down in front of him.

He had seen from whose hand it had come. He saw the young girl in the box nearest the stage, the young baroness, rising like a spirit of beauty, loudly rejoicing over his triumph.

A fire rushed through him; his heart swelled as never before; he bowed, took the wreath, pressed it against his heart, and at the same moment fell backward. Fainted? Dead? What was it? The curtain fell.

"Dead!" resounded through the house. Dead in the moment of triumph, like Sophocles at the Olympian games, like Thorvaldsen in the theater during Beethoven's symphony. An artery in his heart had burst, and as by a flash of lightning his days here were ended, ended without pain, ended in an earthly triumph, in the fulfillment of his mission on earth. Lucky Peer! More fortunate than millions!

THE COURT CARDS

OH, so many dainty things can be cut out of pasteboard and pasted together! In this fashion there was cut and pasted a castle so large that it took up a whole table top, and it was painted so that it seemed to be built out of red brick. It had a shining copper roof; it had towers and a drawbridge; the water in the canals looked like plate glass, which is just what it was; and in the topmost tower there stood a watchman cut out of wood. He had a trumpet, but he didn't blow it.

All this belonged to a little boy named William. He raised and then lowered the drawbridge himself, and made his tin soldiers march over it. He opened the castle gate to peep into the spacious reception hall, where all the face cards from a pack — Hearts, Diamonds, Clubs and Spades — hung in frames upon the wall, like portraits in a real reception hall. The Kings each held a scepter and a crown. The Queens wore flowing veils over their shoulders, and in their hands each held a flower or a fan. The Knaves had halberds and nodding plumes.

One evening the little boy peered through the open gates of the castle to have a look at the Court Cards in the reception hall. It seemed to him that the

Kings saluted him with their scepters, the Queen of Spades waved the golden tulip she held, the Queen of Hearts raised her fan, and all four Queens graciously took notice of him. As he came a little closer to get a better view, his head struck against the castle and shook it. Then the four Knaves, of Hearts, Diamonds, Clubs, and Spades, lifted their halberds to warn him not to try to press his way through.

The little boy understood, and gave them a friendly nod. He nodded again, and then he said: "Say something," but the Court Cards said not a word. However, when he nodded a third time to the Knave of Hearts, the Knave jumped out of his card and placed himself in the middle of the floor.

"What's your name?" he asked the youngster. "You have bright eyes and good teeth, but you don't wash your hands often enough." This was not a very polite way to talk.

"My name is William," said the youngster. "This castle is mine, and you are the Knave of Hearts."

"I'm my King's and my Queen's Knave, not yours," said the Knave of Hearts. "I can get off of the card and out of the frame too. So can my gracious King and Queen, even more easily than I. We can march right out into the wide world, but that's such a tiresome journey, and we have grown weary of it. It's more convenient, and more pleasant for us to be sitting in the cards, just being ourselves."

"Were all of you really human beings once?" asked the youngster.

"Human beings?" the Knave of Hearts said. "Yes, but we were not as good as we should have been. Now please light a little wax candle for me. I'd like a red one best, for red is the color of my King and Queen. Then I shall tell our whole story to the lord of the castle—I believe you said you were the lord of the castle, didn't you? But don't interrupt me. If I speak, there must not be the slightest interruption.

"Do you see my King—the King of Hearts? Of these four Kings, he is the oldest, the first-born. He was born with a golden crown and a golden apple, and he began to rule immediately. His Queen was born wth a golden fan. She still has it. They had a wonderful time, even in childhood. They did not have to go to school. They could amuse themselves all day long, building up castles and knocking them down, setting up tin soldiers, and playing with dolls. If they asked for a slice of bread and butter, their bread was buttered on both sides and nicely sprinkled with brown sugar too. This was in the good old days which were called the golden age, but they tired of it all, and so did I. Yes, those were the good old days!— and then the King of Diamonds took over the government."

The Knave didn't say any more. The little boy waited to hear something else, but not a syllable was spoken, so after a while he asked, "What then?"

The Knave of Hearts made him no answer. He stood erect and silent, with his eyes fixed on the burning wax candle. The youngster nodded, and nodded again, but he got no response. He then turned to the Knave of Diamonds, and when he had nodded to him three times the Knave leaped from the card to the center of the floor. He said only two words: "Wax candle!"

Understanding what he wanted, little William at once lighted a red candle and placed it before him. The Knave of Diamonds presented arms with his halberd, and said:

"Then the King of Diamonds came to the throne—a King with a pane of glass in his chest. The Queen also had a pane of glass in her chest, so people could look right inside them, though in all other respects they were shaped as normal human beings. They were so pleasant that a monument was raised in their honor. It stood without falling for seven whole years, but it was built to stand forever." The Knave of Diamonds presented arms and stared at the red wax candle.

Immediately, without any nod of encouragement from little William, the Knave of Clubs stepped down, as serious as the stork that strides with such dignity across the meadow. Like a bird, the black three-leafed clover in the corner of the card flew past the Knave and back again, to fit itself where it had fitted before. Without waiting for his wax candle—as the other knaves had done—the Knave of Clubs said:

"Not everyone gets his bread buttered on both sides and powdered with sugar. My King and Queen had none of that. They were compelled to go to school and learn what they had not learned before. They too had panes of glass in their chests, but nobody looked through the glass except to see if something was wrong with their works inside, and if possible to find out some reason for scolding them. I know it. I have served my King and Queen all my life long. I know all about them, and I obey all their orders. They commanded me to say nothing more tonight, so I keep silence and present arms."

But William lighted a candle for this Knave too—a candle, white as snow. Quickly—even more quickly than the candle was lighted—the Knave of Spades appeared in the center of the hall. He hurried along, yet he limped as if he had a lame leg. It creaked and cracked as if it had once been broken. Yes, he had met with many ups and downs in his life. Now he spoke:

"Yes, you have each got a candle, and I shall get one too. I know that. But if we Knaves are honored so highly, our Kings and Queens should have triple honors. And it is right that my King and Queen should have *four* candles each. Their story and trials are so sad and unhappy that they have good reason to dress in mourning and to wear a grave-digger's spade on their coat of arms. Poor Knave that I am, in one game of cards I have been nicknamed 'Black Peter.' Yes! but I have a name that isn't even fit to mention." So he whispered, "In another game I am nicknamed 'Dirty Mads'—I who was once first cavalier to the King of Spades. Now I am last! The history of my royal master and mistress I will not tell, for they do not wish me to do so. The little lord of the castle may imagine their story for himself if he will, but it is a most melancholy one. They have sunk pretty low, and their fate is not apt to change for the better until we all go riding on the red horse, higher than there are clouds."

And little William proceeded to light three candles apiece for the Kings, and three for the Queens. But for the King and Queen of Spades, he lighted four candles apiece, and the whole reception hall became as dazzlingly bright as the wealthiest emperor's palace. The four Kings and Queens made each other serene bows and gracious curtsies. The Queen of Hearts fluttered her golden fan, and the Queen of Spades twirled her golden tulip in a wheel of fire. The royal couples came down from their cards and frames to move in a graceful minuet across the floor. They were dancing in and out among the candle flames, and the Knaves were dancing too.

Suddenly the entire reception hall was ablaze. The fire roared up through the windows and the walls, and everything was a curtain of flames that crackled and hissed. The whole castle was wrapped in fire and smoke. William was frightened. He ran shouting to his father and mother, "Fire, fire! My castle's on fire!" It sparkled and blazed, but from the flames it sang:

"Now we are riding the red horse, higher than the clouds. this is the way it behooves Kings and Queens to go. And this is the way it behooves their Knaves to follow."

Yes! That was the end of William's Castle, and of the Court Cards. William is still alive, and he washes his hands. It was not his fault that the castle burned.